Lecture Notes in Artificial Intelligence 4293

Edited by J. G. Carbonell and J. Siekmann

Subseries of Lecture Notes in Computer Science

Alexander Gelbukh
Carlos Alberto Reyes-Garcia (Eds.)

MICAI 2006: Advances in Artificial Intelligence

5th Mexican International Conference
on Artificial Intelligence
Apizaco, Mexico, November 13-17, 2006
Proceedings

Springer

Series Editors

Jaime G. Carbonell, Carnegie Mellon University, Pittsburgh, PA, USA
Jörg Siekmann, University of Saarland, Saarbrücken, Germany

Volume Editors

Alexander Gelbukh
Centro de Investigación en Computación
Instituto Politécnico Nacional
Col. Nueva Industrial Vallejo, 07738, DF, Mexico
E-mail: gelbukh@gelbukh.com

Carlos Alberto Reyes-Garcia
Instituto Nacional de Astrofísica, Óptica y Electrónica (INAOE)
Luis Enrique Erro No. 1, Sta. Ma. Tonanzintla, Puebla, 72840, Mexico
E-mail: kargaxxi@inaoep.mx

Library of Congress Control Number: 2006936081

CR Subject Classification (1998): I.2, F.1, I.4, F.4.1

LNCS Sublibrary: SL 7 – Artificial Intelligence

ISSN 0302-9743
ISBN-10 3-540-49026-4 Springer Berlin Heidelberg New York
ISBN-13 978-3-540-49026-5 Springer Berlin Heidelberg New York

Springer is a part of Springer Science+Business Media

springer.com

Printed in Germany

Typesetting: Camera-ready by author, data conversion by Scientific Publishing Services, Chennai, India
Printed on acid-free paper SPIN: 11925231 06/3142 5 4 3 2 1 0

Preface

Artificial Intelligence embraces heuristic methods of solving complex problems for which exact algorithmic solutions are not known. Among them are, on the one hand, tasks related to modeling of human intellectual activity such as thinking, learning, seeing, and speaking, and on the other hand, super-complex optimization problems appearing in science, social life, and industry. Many methods of Artificial Intelligence are borrowed from nature where similar super-complex problems occur.

This year is special for the Artificial Intelligence community. This year we celebrate the 50th anniversary of the very term "Artificial Intelligence", which was first coined in 1956. This year is also very special for the Artificial Intelligence community in Mexico: it is the 20th anniversary of the Mexican Society for Artificial Intelligence, SMIA, which organizes the MICAI conference series. The series itself also celebrates its own round figure: the fifth event. We can now see that MICAI has reached its maturity, having grown dramatically in size and quality, see Figs. 1 to 3.

The proceedings of the previous MICAI events were also published in Springer's Lecture Notes in Artificial Intelligence (LNAI) series, in volumes 1793, 2313, 2972, and 3789.

This volume contains the papers presented during the oral session of the 5th Mexican International Conference on Artificial Intelligence, held on November 13–17, 2006, at the Technologic Institute of Apizaco, Mexico. The conference received for evaluation 448 submissions by 1207 authors from 42 different countries, see Tables 1 and 2. Each submission was reviewed by three independent Program Committee members. This book contains revised versions of 117 papers by 334 authors from 28 countries selected for oral presentation. Thus the acceptance rate was 26.1%. The book is structured into 17 thematic fields representative of the main current areas of interest of the AI community:

- Knowledge Representation and Reasoning
- Fuzzy Logic and Fuzzy Control
- Uncertainty and Qualitative Reasoning
- Evolutionary Algorithms and Swarm Intelligence
- Neural Networks
- Optimization and Scheduling
- Machine Learning and Feature Selection
- Classification
- Knowledge Discovery
- Computer Vision
- Image Processing and Image Retrieval
- Natural Language Processing
- Information Retrieval and Text Classification
- Speech Processing
- Multiagent Systems
- Robotics
- Bioinformatics and Medical Applications

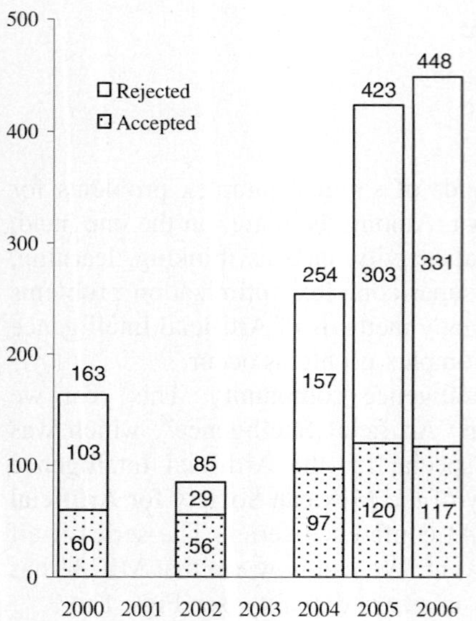

Fig. 1. Number of received, rejected, and accepted papers

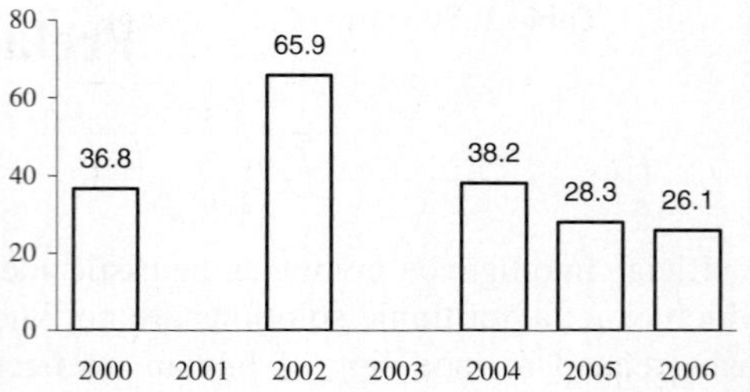

Fig. 2. Acceptance rate

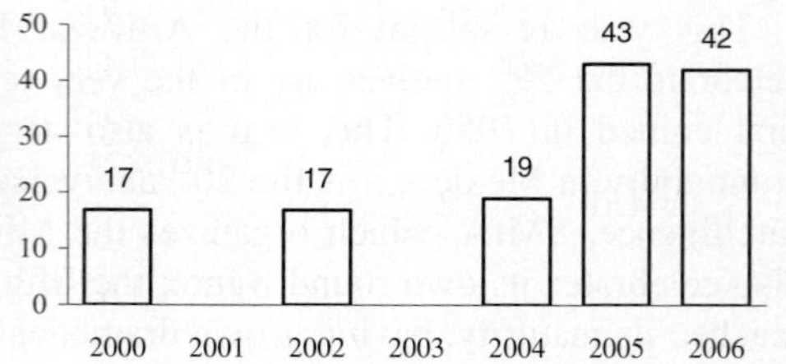

Fig. 3. Number of countries from which submissions were received

The conference featured excellent keynote lectures by the leading experts in Artificial Intelligence: *Advances in Natural Language Processing* by Jaime Carbonell of Carnegie Mellon University, USA; *Evolutionary Multi-objective Optimization: Past, Present and Future* by Carlos A. Coello Coello of the Center for Advanced Research (CINVESTAV), Mexico; *Unifying Logical and Statistical AI* by Pedro Domingos of the University of Washington, USA; and *Inconsistencies in Ontologies* by Andrei Voronkov of the University of Manchester, UK. We were also honored by the presence of our special guests who were among the founders of Artificial Intelligence research in Mexico: Adolfo Guzmán Arenas of the Center for Computing Research of the National Polytechnic Institute (CIC-IPN), Mexico, and José Negrete Martínez of the Veracruz University, Mexico, who presented invited lectures on the history of Artificial Intelligence and the ways of its future development. In addition to the oral technical session and the keynote lectures, the conference program included tutorials, workshops, and poster sessions, which were published in separate proceedings volumes and journal special issues.

The following papers received the Best Paper Award and the Best Student Paper Award, correspondingly (the best student paper was selected out of papers of which the first author was a full-time student):

1st place: *Statistics of Visual and Partial Depth Data for Mobile Robot Environment Modeling*, by Luz Abril Torres-Méndez and Gregory Dudek;

2nd place: *On Musical Performances Identification, Entropy and String Matching*, by Antonio Camarena-Ibarrola and Edgar Chávez;

Table 1. Statistics of submissions and accepted papers by country / region

Country / Region	Authors Subm	Authors Accp	Papers[1] Subm	Papers[1] Accp	Country / Region	Authors Subm	Authors Accp	Papers[1] Subm	Papers[1] Accp
Algeria	3	–	1.44	–	Israel	10	2	4	1
Argentina	13	–	5	–	Italy	22	–	5.45	–
Australia	4	2	3	1	Japan	16	7	5.9	3
Austria	2	2	1	1	Korea, South	128	56	46.83	18.86
Belgium	3	1	0.37	0.13	Lithuania	4	–	1.2	–
Brazil	55	14	15.13	4	Macedonia	1	–	0.22	–
Canada	10	1	3.32	0.32	Malaysia	9	2	3.3	1
Chile	39	12	13.98	3.76	Mexico	344	118	113.93	38.46
China	270	41	106.18	15.77	Norway	2	–	1	–
Colombia	4	2	1.38	0.44	Poland	6	–	1.88	–
Croatia	1	1	0.32	0.32	Portugal	15	–	3.51	–
Cuba	22	4	3.99	0.51	Romania	1	1	0.22	0.22
Denmark	2	–	0.26	–	Russia	1	–	0.22	–
Finland	2	2	1	1	Slovenia	1	1	0.32	0.32
France	6	3	2.2	0.66	Spain	65	35	19.19	9.89
Germany	9	1	2.71	0.32	Switzerland	1	–	0.13	–
Hong Kong	5	2	2.34	0.34	Taiwan	24	5	6	2
Hungary	1	–	0.22	–	Turkey	57	10	19.13	4
India	6	–	3	–	UK	13	3	5.5	0.61
Iran	6	–	5	–	USA	20	2	7.29	0.54
Ireland	2	2	1	1	Vietnam	2	2	0.64	0.64
					Total	1207	334	448	117

[1] Counted by authors: e.g., for a paper by 2 authors from UK and 1 from USA, we added ⅔ to UK and ⅓ to USA.

3rd place: *A Refined Evaluation Function for the MinLA Problem*, by Eduardo Rodriguez-Tello, Jin-Kao Hao, and Jose Torres-Jimenez;
Student: *Decision Forests with Oblique Decision Trees*, by Peter Jing Tan and David L. Dowe.

We want to thank all people involved in the organization of this conference. In the first place, these are the authors of the papers constituting this book: it is the excellence of their research work that gives value to the book and sense to the work of all other people involved. We thank the members of the Program Committee and additional reviewers for their great and very professional work on reviewing and selecting the papers for the conference. Our very special thanks goes to the members of the Board of Directors of SMIA, particularly to Ángel Kuri and Raúl Monroy. Sulema Torres of CIC-IPN, Agustin Leon Barranco of INAOE, and Yulia Ledeneva of CIC-IPN devoted great effort to the preparation of the conference.

We would like to express our sincere gratitude to the Instituto Tecnológico de Apizaco, for their warm hospitality to MICAI 2006. First of all, special thanks to the Constitutional Governor of the State of Tlaxcala, Lic. Héctor Israel Ortiz Ortiz, for his valuable participation and support of the organization of this conference. We would also like to thank the Secretaría de Desarrollo Económico of the state of Tlaxcala for its financial support and for providing part of the infrastructure for the keynote

Table 2. Statistics of submissions and accepted papers by topic[2]

Accepted	Submitted	Topic
24	77	Machine Learning
21	85	Neural Networks
18	89	Other
18	57	Data Mining
16	62	Genetic Algorithms
16	47	Fuzzy logic
14	42	Natural Language Processing / Understanding
13	51	Hybrid Intelligent Systems
13	22	Uncertainty / Probabilistic Reasoning
10	46	Computer Vision
10	40	Knowledge Representation
9	36	Robotics
8	31	Knowledge Acquisition
8	25	Bioinformatics
7	32	Multiagent systems and Distributed AI
7	27	Planning and Scheduling
5	11	Intelligent Interfaces: Multimedia; Virtual Reality
4	21	Expert Systems / KBS
4	20	Navigation
4	8	Belief Revision
3	27	Ontologies
3	24	Knowledge Management
3	19	Model-Based Reasoning
3	17	Intelligent Tutoring Systems
3	11	Intelligent Organizations
2	13	Logic Programming
2	8	Common Sense Reasoning
2	8	Case-Based Reasoning
2	8	Assembly
2	7	Spatial and Temporal Reasoning
2	6	Qualitative Reasoning
2	5	Constraint Programming
1	14	Knowledge Verification; Sharing; Reuse
1	3	Automated Theorem Proving
–	16	Philosophical and Methodological Issues of AI
–	6	Nonmonotonic Reasoning

[2] According to the topics indicated by the authors. A paper may have more than one topic.

lectures. We are deeply grateful to the Secretaría de Turismo of the State of Tlaxcala for its help with the organization of the tourist visits to local attractions and folk carnivals of the State of Tlaxcala. Nothing would have been possible without the financial support of our sponsors—Intel and Arknus—for the entire conference organization. We express our gratitude to the conference staff and Local Committee.

The entire submission, reviewing, and selection process, as well as putting together the proceedings was supported for free by the EasyChair system (www.easychair.org); we express our gratitude to its author Andrei Voronkov for his constant support and help. Last but not least, we deeply appreciate the Springer staff's great patience and help in editing this volume.

October 2006

Alexander Gelbukh
Carlos Alberto Reyes García

Organization

MICAI 2006 was organized by the Mexican Society for Artificial Intelligence (SMIA) in collaboration with the Instituto Tecnológico de Apizaco, which hosted the conference, as well as the Center for Computing Research of the National Polytechnic Institute (CIC-IPN), the Instituto Nacional de Astrofísica Óptica y Electrónica (INAOE), the Instituto Tecnológico Autónomo de México (ITAM), and the Instituto Tecnológico de Estudios Superiores de Monterrey (ITESM), Mexico.

Conference Committee

General Chair:	Ángel Kuri Morales (ITAM)
Program Chairs:	Alexander Gelbukh (CIC-IPN)
	Carlos Alberto Reyes-Garcia (INAOE)
Workshop Chair:	Angélica Muñoz (INAOE)
Tutorial Chair:	Grigori Sidorov (CIC-IPN)
Award Committee:	Ángel Kuri Morales (ITAM)
	Alexander Gelbukh (CIC-IPN)
	Carlos Alberto Reyes-Garcia (INAOE)
	Raúl Monroy (ITESM-CEM)
Finance Chair:	Carlos Alberto Reyes-Garcia (INAOE)

Program Committee

Ajith Abraham
Luis Alberto Pineda Cortés
Gustavo Arroyo Figueroa
Antonio Bahamonde
Ildar Batyrshin
Bedrich Benes
Seta Bogosyan
Paul Brna
Hiram Calvo
Nicoletta Calzolari
Francisco Cantú Ortíz
Oscar Castillo
Edgar Chavez
Carlos A. Coello Coello
Simon Colton
Ulises Cortés
Carlos Cotta
Louise Dennis
Alexandre Dikovsky
Juergen Dix
Abdennour El Rhalibi
Bob Fisher
Juan Flores
Sofía Galicia Haro
Alexander Gelbukh (Co-chair)
Matjaž Gams
Crina Grosan
Arturo Hernández
Brahim Hnich
Jesse Hoey
Dieter Hutter
Pablo H. Ibargüengoytia
Leo Joskowicz
Zeynep Kiziltan
Ryszard Klempous
Angel Kuri Morales

Mario Köppen
Pedro Larrañaga
Christian Lemaître León
Eugene Levner
James Little
Aurelio López López
Jacek Malec
Pierre Marquis
Carlos Martín Vide
José Francisco Martínez Trinidad
Vladimír Mařík
Efrén Mezura Montes
Chilukuri K. Mohan
Raúl Monroy
Guillermo Morales Luna
Eduardo Morales Manzanares
John Morris
Juan Arturo Nolazco Flores
Mauricio Osorio Galindo
Manuel Palomar
Oleksiy Pogrebnyak
Andre Ponce de Leon F. de Carvalho
Bhanu Prasad
Fuji Ren
Carlos Alberto Reyes-Garcia (Co-chair)
Horacio Rodríguez
Riccardo Rosati
Paolo Rosso
Khalid Saeed
Andrea Schaerf
Leonid Sheremetov
Grigori Sidorov
Juan Humberto Sossa Azuela
Thomas Stuetzle
Luis Enrique Sucar Succar
Hugo Terashima
Demetri Terzopoulos
Juan Vargas
Felisa Verdejo
Manuel Vilares Ferro
Toby Walsh
Alfredo Weitzenfeld
Franz Wotawa
Kaori Yoshida
Claus Zinn
Álvaro de Albornoz Bueno
Maarten van Someren
Berend Jan van der Zwaag

Additional Referees

Mohamed Abdel Fattah
Juan Carlos Acosta
Marco Alberti
José Arrazola
Miguel A. Alonso
Hector Hugo Avilés
J. C. Acosta Guadarrama
Ernesto Luiz Andrade Neto
Prasanna Balaprakash
Alejandra Barrera
María Lucía Barrón Estrada
Tristan Marc Behrens
Edgard I. Benítez Guerrero
Daniel Le Berre
Francesca Bertagna
Viktor de Boer
Dario Bottazzi
Olivier Buffet
Nils Bulling
Davide Buscaldi
Felix Calderon Solorio
Jose Antonio Calderón Martínez
Francesco Calimeri
Antonio Camarena Ibarrola
Sergio D. Cano Ortiz
Francisco J. Cantu Ortiz
Carlos Cares
Giuseppe Carignani
Jesús Ariel Carrasco Ochoa
Tommaso Caselli
María José Castro Bleda
Debrup Chakraborty
Zenon Chaczko
Federico Chesani
Marco Chiarandini
George Coghill
Miguel Contreras
Sylvie Coste Marquis

Juan Jose del Coz
Nareli Cruz Cortés
Víctor Manuel Darriba Bilbao
Michael Dekhtyar
Jorge Díez
Héctor Díez
Luigi Dragone
Florence Dupin de St Cyr
Gemma Bel Enguix
Arturo Espinosa
Bruno Feres de Souza
Antonio J. Fernández
Óscar Ferrández
Reynaldo Félix
Leticia Flores Pulido
Per-Erik Forssen
José E. Gallardo
Juan Manuel García
Mario García
Miguel García
Luciano García Bañuelos
Karen A. García Gamboa
Paola García Perera
Luca Di Gaspero
Marco Gavanelli
Ma. del Pilar Gómez
Jesús A. González
Miguel González Mendoza
Fernando Godínez
Mario Graff
Carlos Guillen Galván
Scott Helmer
Adrian Horia Dediu
Marc Hull
Luca Iocchi
Wojtek Jamroga
Dolores Jiménez López
Sophia Katrenko
Ingrid Kirschning A.
Sébastien Konieczny
Jerzy Kotowski
Evelina Lamma
Ricardo Landa Becerra
João Leite
Domenico Lembo
Andrzej Lingas
Miguel López
Alejandra López
Juan Carlos López Pimentel
Oscar Luaces
Ana Carolina Lorena
Fernando Magán Muñoz
Michael Maher
Marco Maratea
Alejandro Marcus
Patricio Martínez Barco
Francesco Masulli
Stefano Mattoccia
Yana Maximova
Bertrand Mazure
Patricia Melin
Paola Mello
Marco Mesiti
Mónica Monachini
Marco Montali
Manuel Montes
Marco A. Montes de Oca
Oscar Montiel
Jaime Mora Vargas
Eduardo Morales
Emmanuel Morin
Rafael Muñoz
Rafael Murrieta Cid
Gonzalo Navarro
Niels Netten
Pascal Nicolas
Juan Carlos Nieves
Peter Novak
Slawomir Nowaczyk
Kenji Okuma
Alberto Oliart
Oscar Olmedo Aguirre
Ivan Olmos Pined
Magdalena Ortíz
Mauricio Osorio
Odile Papini
Isaac Parra Ramirez
Nelio Pastor Gómez
Bernhard Peischl
Marco Otilio Peña Díaz
Carlos Mex Perera
Carlos F. Pfeiffer-Celaya
David Pinto
José Ramón Quevedo

J. Federico Ramírez Cruz
Jorge Adolfo Ramírez Uresti
Raúl V. Ramírez Velarde
Orion F. Reyes Galaviz
Francisco José Ribadas Pena
Fabrizio Riguzzi
Homero V. Rios-Figueroa
Norma F. Roffe Samaniego
Leonardo Romero Muñoz
Roberto Rossi
Olivier Roussel
Stefano Rovetta
Robert Santana
Estela Saquete
Roberto Sepúlveda
Jasper Snoek
Alejandro Sobrino
Volker Sorge
Claudia Soria
Tristram Southey
Oleg Starostenko
Gerald Steinbauer
Armando Suárez Cueto
Ewa Szlachcic
Gian Diego Tipaldi
Paolo Torroni
Gregorio Toscano Pulido
Mars Valiev
Fernando Velasco
Vincent Vidal
Mario A. Villalobos-Arias
Julia Vogel
Christel Vrain
Jörg Weber
Joseph N. Wilson
Bob Woodham
Pinar Yolum
Gabriel Zachmann
Ramón Zatarain Cabada
Claudia Zepeda
Yingqian Zhang

Organizing Committee

Honorary Chairs:	Héctor Israel Ortiz-Ortiz
	Bulmaro Fuentes-Lemus
General Local Organizing Committee:	Roberto Acoltzi-Nava (Chair)
	Ernesto Daza-Ramírez
	Leoncio González-Hernández
	Nicolás Alonzo-Gutiérrez
Tutorial Arrangements Committee:	Jose Antonio Cruz-Zamora
	Federico Ramirez-Cruz
Workshop Arrangements Committee:	Nicolás Alonzo-Gutiérrez
	Lauro Carlos Payan-Reyes
Finance and Sponsorship Committee:	Kathy Laura Vargas-Matamoros (Chair)
	Marcial Molina-Sarmiento
	Yesenia Nohemí González-Meneses
	Joel Gómez-Quintero
	Blanca Estela Pedroza-Méndez
	Ma. del Rocío Ojeda-López
	José Juan Hernández-Mora
	Carlos Díaz-Gutiérrez
Publicity Committee:	Evaristo Romero-Lima (Chair)
	Orion Fausto Reyes-Galaviz
	Israel Méndez-Martínez
	Perfecto Malaquías Quintero-Flores
	Cristobal Medina-Barrera

Logistics Committee: Eliut Flores-Jiménez (Chair)
Miquelina Sánchez-Pulido
Juan Ramos-Ramos
José Antonio Cruz-Zamora
Higinio Nava-Bautista
Guadalupe Reyes-Gutiérrez
Merced Pérez-Moreno
José Federico Ramírez-Cruz
José Ruperto Rodríguez-Lezama
Eduardo Sánchez-Lucero
Carlos Pérez-Corona
Nicolás Alonzo-Gutiérrez
Neptalín Zarate-Vázquez

Webpage and Contact

The MICAI series webpage is www.MICAI.org. The webpage of the Mexican Society for Artificial Intelligence, SMIA, is www.SMIA.org.mx. Contact options and additional information can be found on those webpages.

Table of Contents

Uncertainty and Qualitative Reasoning

Evolutionary Algorithms and Swarm Intelligence

Neural Networks

Optimization and Scheduling

Machine Learning and Feature Selection

Classification

Knowledge Discovery

Computer Vision

Image Processing and Image Retrieval

Natural Language Processing

Information Retrieval and Text Classification

Speech Processing

Multiagent Systems

Robotics

Bioinformatics and Medical Applications

Artificial Intelligence Arrives to the 21st Century

Adolfo Guzman-Arenas

Centro de Investigación en Computación, Instituto Politécnico Nacional, Mexico City
a.guzman@acm.org

Abstract. The paper follows the path that AI has taken since its beginnings until the brink of the third millennium. New areas, such as Agents, have sprout; other subjects (Learning) have diminished. Areas have separated (Vision, Image Processing) and became independent, self-standing. Some areas have acquired formality and rigor (Vision). Important problems (Spelling, Chess) have been solved. Other problems (Disambiguation) are almost solved or about to be solved. Many challenges (Natural language translation) still remain. A few parts of the near future are sketched through predictions: important problems about to be solved, and the relation of specific AI areas with other areas of Computer Science.

1 The Evolution of Artificial Intelligence

Artificial Intelligence (AI) is the branch of computer science that deals with intelligent behavior, learning and adaptation in machines. It is also defined as intelligence exhibited by an artificial (*non-natural*, *man-made*) entity (http://en.wikipedia.org/wiki/). Although there is no "standard breakdown" of AI, traditionally it has been divided in several well defined areas. Initial areas were AI Programming Languages (including Symbolic Manipulation), Theorem Proving (later, Reasoning appears), Vision (including Image Processing, Scene Analysis), Games, Learning, Neural Networks (Perceptrons. Later, with the inclusion of Fuzzy Sets and Genetic Algorithms, expands to Soft Computing), Knowledge Representation (including Semantic Nets; later, Ontologies appear, and within them, Formal Concept Analysis), Robotics, Natural Language Translation (sometimes mixed with Information Retrieval; later, it expands to Natural Language Processing; including Intelligent Text Processing), Constraint Satisfaction, Search (later, Web search appears, as well as Web Processing). Areas appearing later are Distributed AI (including Agents), Expert Systems (including non-procedural languages and systems; later, Diagnosis appears), Qualitative Physics, Lisp Machines. See figure 1.

Sometimes considered as part of AI, but are not included here, are: Philosophical Foundations; Intelligent User Interfaces.

In general, AI has grown in breadth and in depth. Rigor and formalism has been introduced in many of its areas. Various applications have been developed (expert systems; fuzzy systems…). With the availability of a great quantity of texts and information through the Web, Search and Semantic Processing are acquiring vigor. AI has been influenced by concurrent development in other Computer Science areas.

A. Gelbukh and C.A. Reyes-Garcia (Eds.): MICAI 2006, LNAI 4293, pp. 1 – 14, 2006.

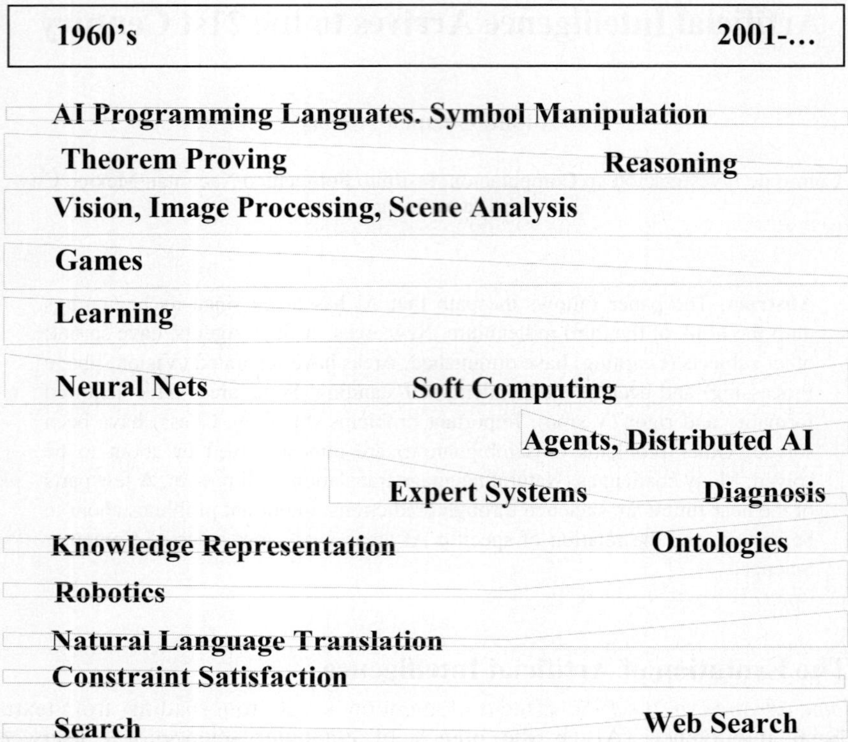

Fig. 1. Path of AI since the early 60's up to day. Some areas have diminished; other have flourished. The text gives more details on each area's development.

2 The Areas of AI

Comments on the development and path of particular areas follow.

2.1 AI Programming Languages

Symbolic (as opposed to numeric) manipulation languages were invented at the beginning of AI: Lisp ([12], Common Lisp or CL, early 90's; CMUCL, a free CL implementation, http://www.cons.org/cmucl/) handles lists; Snobol and Comit manipulate strings; Convert [*7] is a pattern matching language suitable for lists; Scheme [22] manipulates lists with *lazy evaluation* or continuations. Lisp, Snobol and Scheme survive until today. Current development of programming languages concentrates in general purpose (not AI) languages. But see §2.9.

2.1.1 Symbolic Manipulation

Early systems were Macsyma [14] and MathLab. The area has gone a long way, with useful commercial products now: MatLab, Maple (www.maplesoft.com). We have here a mature area where most developments are improvements to specific applications and packages.

2.2 Theorem Proving

Early advances: J. A. Robinson's resolution principle [19], and the demystification of The Frame Problem (John McCarthy).

Advances during 1970´s: Non-monotonic reasoning.

Current work: Satisfability, phase transitions. Spatial reasoning, temporal reasoning (these last two themes belong to Reasoning, found in §2.9). Causality [1]. Description Logics.

Current work is characterized by rigor and scanty applications.

Reasoning was included here initially, due to its dependency at that time on the use of theoretical tools. Later, it has migrated to Knowledge Representations (§2.9), since it depends more and more on the available knowledge.

8% of the International Joint Conference on Artificial Intelligence, 2003 (IJCAI03) sessions (including IAAI03, Innovative Applications of AI; 84 sessions and 200 papers in both) were on Theorem Proving, represented as {8% in IJCAI03}.

2.3 Vision, Image Processing

Early advances: Use of perspective to recognize 3-d solids [18]; decomposition of a scene into bodies [*19].

Some advances in the 1980's: focus of attention, shape from shading, from texture.

The field has grown. At the beginning most advances were empirical discoveries, consisting of methods that work in a few cases. Now, Vision is now based on Mathematics (for instance, Stereo Vision); in Physics (reflections, color of light); on distributed computation (multiple views); on Pattern Recognition; on probabilities. But it currently lacks more Artificial Intellligence influence Takeo Kanade says (Keynote Speech, IJCAI03): we need to reinsert AI into Vision.

Vision and Image Processing are now separating from AI; they have their own Journals (such as Pattern Recognition, Computer Vision and Image Understanding) and scientific meetings (such as CVPR, ICCV). That explains the low numbers of vision papers in IJCAI conferences. 2% of IJCAI03 sessions (including IAAI03) were on Vision, and 2% of IJCAI05 papers (total: 239 papers, excluding poster presentations) were on Vision, too; represented as {2% in IJCAI03; 2% in IJCAI05}.

2.3.1 Image Processing

The processing (deblurring, thinning, sharpening…, but also clustering, classification…) of images through digital algorithms. This is considered the "low part" of Vision, whereas the "high end" is Scene Analysis.

2.3.1.1 Remote Sensing. The processing of pictures taken from Landsat and other satellites. It is somewhat separated from main-stream Vision. Relies mainly on trained classifiers (§2.3.3.1) working on the light spectrum, including infrared. Now, this area is mostly applied. Current research: sensor fusion.

2.3.1.2 Character Recognition. Now: mainly applied work, heuristic-oriented. State of the practice Commercial OCRs have still one-digit error percentages, close to 9%.

2.3.1.3 Text Recognition. Deemphasized since the volume of handwritten and typed text has diminished; most new documents are now born in digital form.

2.3.1.4 Real-Time Text Recognition. Recognition of characters while they are being written. Mainly a solved problem.

2.3.2 Pattern Recognition

The categorization of raw data (it may be a picture, a signal…) and taking an action based on the category of the data. More general than Image Processing, since it handles other kinds of signals. It is not considered a part of AI. It has its own Journals (IEEE Transactions on Pattern Analysis and Machine Intelligence; Pattern Recognition Letters…) and conferences.

Pattern Recognition has matured and uses a formal approach, both in the *syntactical* pattern recognition as well as in the *statistical* pattern recognition.

2.3.2.1 Classification, Clustering. The assignment of classes to a set of objects with given properties. The grouping of objects into subsets (clusters) of similar objects.

Current work: Partially labeled data, Clustering; Learning with Bayesian Networks.

2.3.3 Motion Analysis, Video

Work in This Area Continues. In 1981, Two Powerful Methods to Estimate the Optical Flow were Devised [8, 11].

Optical flow is a technique for estimating object motion in a sequence of video frames. The displacement through time looks as if pixels originate at a given point in the image; this is the point towards which the camera moves. A vector field (vectors placed at each pixel of the image) is described.

2.4 Games

Games were early members of AI; specifically, parlor games: checkers (Samuel in 1957), chess, go, go-moku. Recently, theoretical advances have shown in Market Games (Cf. contest in IJCAI03).

Already solved: Chess by machine has been solved, in the sense that a machine (Deep Blue) is at the level of a World Master. The advance has been possible by much computer power (parallel machines) and large storage (to keep many book games), and to a lesser degree, by advances in AI.

Current tools: Generalized utility (Decision Theory). [2], Nash Equilibria (Cf. IJCAI03).

{4% in IJCAI03}

2.4.1 Game Theory

Invented by John Von Neuman, it has not been widely used in AI Games, except for Market Games.

2.5 Learning

Machine learning develops algorithms that allow computers to learn, that is, to gradually acquire and systematize knowledge from a set of actions, facts or scenarios. An early example of a computer program that learns is Samuel's Checkers playing program. Algorithms for learning can use Statistics (for instance, Bayesian Statistics), Neural Networks (§2.6), Classifiers (supervised learning, §2.3.3.1), Clustering (unsupervised learning), Genetic Programming (§2.6.2), Support Vector Machines... Learning work continues strong. *Current topics:* Kernel Methods; tree learning; ensembles. See for instance IJCAI03.

{10% in IJCAI03; 19% in IJCAI05}

Classification and clustering. These subjects migrated to Pattern Recognition (§2.3.3), listed under Vision and Image Processing (§2.3). They are generally not considered part of AI.

2.6 Neural Networks. Soft Computing

An (artificial) Neural Network (NN) is a group of units (artificial neurons) linked through a network of connections (connectionist approach). The structure of the NN changes with time, as it *learns* or adapts; it is an adaptive system.

First neural networks (perceptrons) were quickly adopted because the *Perceptron Theorem* guaranteed learning (convergence to the sought function) under reasonable conditions. In 1969, the Perceptrons book [13] showed sizable limitations of some of these networks.

Multi-layer perceptrons consist of several layers of neurons, where layer k gets all its inputs from layer k-1. The *universal approximation theorem* states that a multi-layer perceptron with just one hidden layer is capable of approximating any continuous function from Ri to Rj, where Ri and Rj are two intervals of real numbers.

Advances: Simulated annealing [9], a learning algorithm for locating a global approximation in a large search space, developed in 1983, quickly revived Neural Networks. *Hopfield networks,* where all connections are symmetric, and *Kohonen self-organizing maps* are also significant advances.

Neural networks are now well understood, they are applicable to a wide variety of problems, although their specificity is below fine-tuned special tools.

2.6.1 Fuzzy Sets

Long time after they were invented in 1965 by Lofti A. Zadeh [25], fuzzy sets were somewhat unpopular with North American scientists, while they were slowly gaining acceptance elsewhere, notably in Japan.

As Zadeh recently has said, up to date more than 5,000 patents exist (4,801 issued in Japan; around 1,700 in U.S.) that use or exploit fuzzy sets. Although fuzzy sets are not in the mainstream of AI, the Portal of Artificial Intelligence in Wikipedia, http://en.wikipedia.org/wiki/Portal:Artificial_intelligence, considers them "a modern approach to AI". They are useful tools to master vagueness.

2.6.2 Genetic Algorithms

Also called Genetic Programming or Evolutionary Algorithms, they are inspired in biology, involving mutation, cross-over, reproduction, generations survival of the fittest, and guided search. The more general term is Evolutionary Computation (it tries to optimize combinatorial problems), of which Genetic Algorithms are part of. Sometimes, Swarm Behavior (§2.7) is included in Evolutionary Computation.

Genetic algorithms have moved steadily, and it is a vigorous area useful to do search in large spaces.

2.7 Distributed AI. Agents

Distributed AI studies how to solve complex problems (requiring intelligence) through distributed or parallel computations. An agent is an entity that detects (senses) a portion of its environment, and reacts (acts, produces changes) to them. Usually it has a plan and a set of resources, and it is able to communicate with other agents.

Most distributed solutions with agents require in fact *many* agents. Thus, agents are almost gone; papers have migrated to Multiagents.

Disadvantage: To simulate complex behavior or solve challenging problems, often you have to program many agents of different types (behaviors). This is a heavy task.

Promising tool: Swarm Behavior, Swarm Intelligence. It is a technique that mirrors the collective behavior of groups, hordes, schools and packs of animals that exhibit self-organization. For instance, a tool mimicking ant colonies leaves "chemical traces" in visited places (nodes of a graph); other ants visiting these places detect these pheromones and reinforce (deposit more traces) or weaken the track (go away from those places). Thus, links (tracks) among these nodes are gradually formed, with the help of all ants. Links change with time, some are reinforced, some disappear. Usually, the algorithm converges. *Disadvantage*: it is slow. It reminds me of relaxation labeling of Hummer & Zucker (1983). Links so placed take more into account the global context and are more flexible that links placed once and for all.

{15% in IJCAI03, of which 1% is in Swarm Behavior}

2.7.1 Multiagents

A multiagent system is a set of agents that achieve goals by distributed (collective) computation. They cooperate among themselves. *Current tools:* formation of coalitions, Cf. IJCAI03. The field is theoretically dominated, somewhat in early stages; almost no applications. Academically oriented.

{14% in IJCAI03; 5% in IJCAI05}

2.8 Expert Systems, Diagnosis. Non-procedural Systems

Expert Systems or Knowledge-based systems are computer programs that embody a set of rules capturing the knowledge of some human experts. They appeared late in the 60's and grew in the 70's. Applications flourished.

Advantages: the system can be neatly divided into: (a) a set of rules of the domain knowledge (say, Infectious Diseases); (b) a deductive or computing machine, that applies the rules; (c) a data base or set of facts, involving a particular sample: a particular patient, say. The deduction machine (b) is independent of the set of rules, thus programming is reused, while the set (a) of rules can be obtained by interviewing the expert(s). The rules "apply as they see fit", so that a non-procedural system is obtained.

Disadvantages: Soon two drawbacks emerged: (1) the encompassed knowledge was rather narrow, and the system exhibited fragility at the periphery of its knowledge (the *brittleness* problem): the system does not know that it does not know (and the user is unaware of this, too); (2) too many rules begin interact in undesirable manners.

Due to these and other reasons, work on Expert Systems has diminished, and it now concentrates mainly in applications, for instance, in Diagnosis.

{2% in IJCAI03}

2.9 Knowledge Representation and Reasoning

Knowledge is structured information that represents or generalizes a set of facts in the real world. *Knowledge Representation* is the way in which this knowledge is organized and stored by the computer, to make ready use of it.

Ross Quillian's semantic nets were one of the early knowledge representations. In 1976, Sowa [20, 21] put forward *Conceptual Graphs*, a way to represent knowledge in patterns of interconnected nodes and arcs. Educators also put forward *Concept Maps* [15] as a tool to communicate knowledge. All these come under the generic term of *Semantic Networks,* the Ontologies (§2.9.2) being among the most precise of the modern representation schemes.

In the 80's, CYC (www.cyc.com) made a brave attempt to construct a common sense ontology. Wordnet (wordnet.princeton.edu) represents a notable contribution from the natural language community. A semantic lexicon for the English languages, it groups words into sets of synonyms (synsets), and contains short definitions, as well as semantic relations among these synsets. It is free. In 2006 it contains 115,000 synsets. There is also a Wordnet for Spanish words.

Probably as a result of the proliferation of documents and information in Internet, work on knowledge representation has rekindled. An approach (§2.11.3.1) is to tag each document, Web page and information source, so as to facilitate their understanding by bots or crawlers (programs that search and read text lying in the Web). A less manual approach is to have a software that extracts knowledge from these sources and stores it in a Knowledge Representation format or language (for instance, Ontolingua [17]) suitable for further useful processing: data integration (§2.9.1), Ontology mapping (§2.9.2.3), Alignment (§2.9.2.4), Ontology Fusion (§2.9.2.5), Reasoning (§2.9.3), etc.

A more shallow form of reasoning is to "ask the right question" to the Web. For instance, in order to find the author of "War and Peace", you can search the Web for the phrase "The author of War and Peace is…". This is usually referred to as "Text mining" (§2.11.3.2). Etzioni [5] shows a way to generate (by computer) search phrases from successes with earlier search phrases.

{31% in IJCAI03; 19% in IJCAI05}

2.9.1 Data Integration

It is the combination of data residing in different sources (mainly databases), providing the user with a unified view of these data [10]. Main approaches are: Global-as-View (GAV), where changes in information sources requires revision of a global schema and mapping between the global schema and local schemas; Local-as-View (LAV), which maps a particular query to the schema of each information source; and a hybrid approach [24].

{5% in IJCAI03}

2.9.2 Ontologies

An ontology is a data model representing a domain, a part of the real world. It is used to reason about instances and types in the domain, and the relations between them. Ontologies are precise representations of *shared knowledge,* and usually are formed by nodes (or concepts: types and instances), arcs (the relations among them) and restrictions (logical assertions holding among nodes or relations).

2.9.2.1 Formal Formulations. Formal formulations establish logic restrictions among instances and types. Example: Formal Concept Analysis [7], which defines "concept" as a unary predicate. Problem: everything is a concept, not only those "important concepts", which I define as those concepts that have a name in a natural language: they are popular enough so that a word has been coined for each.

Defining ontologies with the help of local constraints (say, assertions in some Logics) has the following problem. The restrictions imposed on the instances, types and relations are opaque to (difficult to process by) the software trying to understand the Ontology's knowledge. This knowledge is stored not only in the nodes and the relations, but also in these restrictions, which are usually written in a notation that the deductive machinery finds difficult to decipher, manipulate and reason about. For instance, it could be difficult to derive new restrictions by processing old restrictions. A way to overcome this, suggested by Doug Lenat, is to express the restrictions *and the software that processes the ontology* in the same notation that other knowledge (such as "Clyde is an elephant") in the ontology is represented. That is, to represent the restrictions and the software by elements of the ontology (and not in Lisp or in Logical notation). This will render both restrictions and software accessible and open to the deductive machinery. Something like *reflection* in Computer Science. An idea waiting to be implemented.

Another problem with some formal approaches is that almost every assertion has an exception in everyday's life (Rabbits usually have four legs, but a rabbit may have just three legs and still be a rabbit), so that they have to be expressed, too.

2.9.2.2 Unique Ontology. Common Sense Ontolog. CYC's idea was to build a single ontology to represent common sense knowledge (a kind of encyclopedia of everyday's knowledge), and have everybody use it and (perhaps) extend it. This is a worthwhile goal, but the construction of such unique ontology was found to be a challenging task. One problem was simply the size of the effort. Other difficulty was to select the "best view" for representing certain aspects of the real world (emotions, say). So, it is more practical to recognize that, for a while, multiple ontologies will exist and dominate. Therefore, translation tools (§2.9.2.3) are needed to handle their proliferation; they are also needed to achieve mutual understanding. Eventually, through consensus and standardization, a single ontology will appear. [1]

Tools that make a difference: Wikipedia, a real and free encyclopedia of world knowledge (at a level deeper than CYC's intention), with more than a million articles in English and other natural languages. *Also:* Wordnet (§2.9).

2.9.2.3 Mapping one Ontology into Another. Some works [*150, *168] try to map every element (concept) of an ontology into the most similar concept residing in another ontology. These works address the lack of a unique ontology (§2.9.2.2).

2.9.2.4 Alignment. It is the superficial or initial mapping of nodes of an ontology into nodes of another ontology, conflicts being resolved by a user via a link editor [16].

2.9.2.5 Ontology Fusion. To fuse ontologies A and B is to find a new ontology C that contains the knowledge that both A and B contain. Contradictions and inconsistencies must be handled "as best as possible." A Ph. D. thesis in progress [4] tries to achieve fusion in automatic fashion, without intervention of a user.

2.9.3 Reasoning

The derivation of conclusions from certain premises using a given methodology. The two main deductive methods are: deductive reasoning and inductive reasoning.

Current work: Spatial reasoning, temporal reasoning. (Cf. IJCAI03).

{16% in IJCAI03}

2.9.3.1 Case-Based Reasoning. It can be defined as solving a new problem using the solution of a similar past problems. Typically, these are categorized into types or cases. Not a very active field now.

{1% in IJCAI03; 2% in IJCAI05}

2.9.3.2 Belief Revision. It is the change of beliefs to take into account new information. Current work: inconsistency detection, belief updating (Cf. IJCAI03).

2.9.4 Uncertainty

Probably this area will emerge as a new, self-standing part of AI. I have included it into Reasoning and Knowledge Representation because these are the two main problems in dealing with uncertainty: how to reason and compute about it, and how to represent it. See also Fuzzy Sets (§2.6.1).

Previouw work: Dempster-Schafer Theory of evidence.

Current work: Inconsistency measurement. Paraconsistent logics. Measuring inconsistency using hierarchies [3]. Probabilistic inference.

{8% in IJCAI05}

---

[1] Nevertheless, knowledge can not be completely standardized, since each day more sprouts; standardization will always fall behind.

2.10 Robotics

Antecedent: remote manipulators.

Early days: Construction and adaptation of teleoperators, as well as simulations (for instance, simulating the path of a robot). Characterized by Japan's dominance. Slow addition of sensors, mainly vision and touch sensors. Scanty applications.

Recently, robots for rescue missions; for instance, IJCAI contest in 2003.

Current work: SLAM, Simultaneous localization and mapping. Coverage maps.

Robotics is still dominated by engineering designs. It may be an area waiting for applications to strengthen it.

{7% in IJCAI03; 3% in IJCAI05}

2.10.1 Teleoperators, Telemedicine

A teleoperator or remote manipulator is a device that (a) senses its environment, through a camera, perhaps; (b) can make changes to it, such as moving a tool or a piece, and (c) it is controlled by a person (an operator) at some distance from it. The perceptions in (a) go to the operator, which then issues the orders (b). This is different from a robot, in which a computer replaces the human operator.

2.11 Language Translation

Early times: Machine translation of a natural language into another. Failures were due to the inadequacy of the existing hardware and techniques, and to underestimation of the difficulties of the problem.

Later, work was more general than just translation. It was therefore called Natural Language, Intelligent Text Processing, or Natural Language Processing.

Information retrieval (§2.11.2) can be seen as an initial phase of Natural Language Processing.

Solved: To find the topics of themes that a document talks about [*99, *169].

Almost solved: Disambiguation, the assignment of meaning to words according to the context.

Almost solved: constructing a good parser for a natural language.

Still unsolved: translation of general texts in a natural language to another natural language has not been solved until today in a general and reasonable form. Constrained domain translators exist.

Tools that have made a difference: Wordnet (§2.9).

{6% in IJCAI03; 12% in IJCAI05}

2.11.1 Voice Recognition

It has taken distance from AI, and is now more properly considered a part of Signal Processing.

2.11.2 Information Retrieval

Information extraction. Traditionally, not a part of AI. Sometimes, it gets mixed with Search.

{2% in IJCAI03}

2.11.3 Semantic Processing

The work on intelligent text processing is also called Semantic Processing. It is a part of Natural Language.

2.11.3.1 Semantic Web. The Semantic Web was defined as pages with annotations, so that search engines and algorithms could "understand their meaning." For manual placement of the annotations, SGML and XML (mark up languages) were designed. Unfortunately, the meaning of the names used in these marks are not standard, so a multiplicity of different marks arose. Also, the work needed to mark our own pages in the Web is not trivial. Thus, this approach has been largely abandoned, in favor of processing "raw documents" through Natural Language tools.

2.11.3.2 Text Mining. Since "Data Mining" became popular, the term "Text mining" was coined, but with a different meaning: the intelligent processing of (many) text documents. Hence, it is synonym of Semantic Processing.

Data Mining is defined as the automatic or semi-automatic finding of anomalies, tendencies, deviations and interesting facts in a sea of data. It is not considered part of AI (being more related to Data Base and to Statistics), although some commercial miners (Clementine) perform data mining with the help of neural nets, decision trees and clustering.

2.12 Constraint Satisfaction

Invented 35 years ago [*19] as Constraint Propagation, it survives to date. A technical field, with some applications.

Current work: Stochastic programming of constraints; consistency at the boundary.
{8% in IJCAI03; 13% in IJCAI05}

2.13 Search

With the proliferation of documents in the Web (see also §2.9), finding relevant texts has become important, a revival for Information Retrieval (§2.11). Programs that travel the Web looking for suitable information are called search engines or crawlers. They are combined with suitable text-processing tools (§2.11). One of the goals of "text understanding" is to be able to merge knowledge coming from different sources, for instance by merging ontologies (§2.9.2.5). Another goal is "to find answers by asking the right questions" [5].

Tools that make a difference: crawlers, Google.
{6% in IJCAI03; 8% in IJCAI05}

2.13.1 Planning

Initially, planning was an independent subject. I have merged it into Search, due to its similarity and small number of planning articles.
{5% in IJCAI05}

2.13.2 Search Engines, Semantic Search

A *Search Engine* is a software that finds information inside a computer, a private or local network, or in the Web. Search engines that comb the Web are also called crawlers. Usually a Search Engine is given a predicate or a test that filters the information and only retrieves relevant data or documents (or their location in the Web). *Semantic Search* refers to the search performed with the help of filters that attend to the semantics or meaning of the information being analyzed.

Search and Semantic Search are very active areas; Semantic Search is considered a branch of AI because it uses Natural Language processing (§2.11), but soon it will emerge as a separate area.

2.14 Qualitative Physics

Also known as Naive Physics. It represents and reasons about the physical world in a common-sense, non-mathematical way. Qualitative Physics arises from the need to share our intuitions about the physical world with our machines [6]. It started and ended in the 1980's.

2.15 Lisp Machines

These were dedicated hardware for efficiently running Lisp programs. Commercial Lisp machines were Symbolics' 3600 (c. 1986), LMI-Lambda and TI-Explorer. Most Lisp machine manufacturers were out of business by the early 90's, due to (a) the appearance of (free) Kyoto Common Lisp running on SUN workstations, and (b) the appearance of cheap PCs that could run Lisp at good speed. This is an example of Gresham's law for special purpose-hardware: if you build a special purpose hardware, it should perform an order of magnitude better (or be an order of magnitude cheaper) than massive available general purpose hardware; otherwise, it will compete at a disadvantage.

2.15.1 Connection Machine

A parallel SIMD processor containing up to 65,536 individual processors (CM-2, CM-3 and CM-5; Thinking Machines, 1987). Not strictly a Lisp Machine, it ran *Lisp (parallel Lisp) [23].

2.15.2 AHR

A Mexican parallel computer built in 1980 [*47], of the MIMD shared-memory type, it had Lisp as its main programming language, and it consisted of up to 64 Z-80A's microprocessors. Subsequently, a Soviet computer [*56] of SIMD type was modified to mimic AHR's behavior. There are no further descendants of AHR.

2.16 Remarks and Conclusions

Artificial Intelligence deals with difficult problems, "problems that require intelligence to be solved." Thus, if AI solves one of these problems, in some sense "it is no longer difficult," hence that domain tends to leave the AI realm to stand in its own feet. Thus, AI will always be faced with "difficult and yet unsolved problems." That seems to be the fate of our discipline.

Advances in AI have been driven by two complementary forces, as in other areas of science. One is the "push" that provide new discoveries, theorems and theories, such as the Resolution Principle or the invention of fast parallel hardware for chess machines. The other force is the "pull" that provide important practical problems that are still unsolved or only partially solved.

A particular feature of AI researchers that I have observed is that in general they are more inclined to use new tools (even if invented elsewhere), and I believe this produces better (or faster) advances, specially in applied problems.

Has AI produced significant applications? Has it any commercial value, or is just an academic endeavor? The question is posed to me sometimes. Certainly, some relevant applications exist: Expert Systems, visual inspection systems, and many commercial systems (such as those in data mining of large amounts of data) using neural networks and genetic algorithms, or fuzzy sets, to cite a few. More could have been produced by AI, if it were not for the fact that as a domain matures, it abandons AI (as my first remark says).

References

References are incomplete, due to space limitations. Some well-known works are not cited. A reference of the form [*47] is not listed here; it refers to article number 47, found in Adolfo Guzman's Web page (http://alum.mit.edu/www/aguzman).

1. Bochman, A.: Propositional argumentation and causal reasoning. *Proc. IJCAI* (2005) 388-393
2. Chu, F. C., Halpern, J.: Great expectations. Part I: on the customizability of generalized expected utility. Part II: generalized expected utiulity as a universal decision role. *Proc. IJCAI03* (2003) 291-296 and 297-302
3. Contreras, A.: *Characterization and measurement of logical properties on qualitative values arranged in hierarchies.* Ph. D. thesis in progress. CIC-IPN, Mexico
4. Cuevas. A.: *Ontology Merging using semantic properties.* Ph. D. thesis in progress. CIC-IPN, Mexico
5. Etzioni, O., Cafarella, M., Downey, D., Popescu, A. M., Shaked, T., Soderland, Weld, D. S., Yates, A.: Methods for domain-independent information extraction from the web: An experimental comparison. In *Proceedings of the AAAI Conference* (2004) 391-398
6. Forbus, K. Qualitative physics: past, present and future. In *Exploring Artificial Intelligence,* H. Shrobe, Ed., Morgan Kauffmann, Los Altos, CA (1988) 239-290
7. Bernhard Ganter and Rudolf Wille. *Formal Concept Analysis.* Springer-Berlag. ISBN 3-540-8. Horn, B.K.P., Schunck, B.G.: Determining optical flow. *Artificial Intelligence*, vol 17 (1981) 185-203
8. Kirkpatrick, S., Gelatt, C.D., Vecchi, M.P.: Optimization by Simulated Annealing, Science, Vol 220, Number 4598 (1983) 671-680
9. Lenzerinim M.: Data integration: a theoretical perspective., Proc. 21st. ACM SIGMOD-SIGACT-SIGART *Symposium on Principles of Database Systems* (2002) 233-246
10. Lucas, B, D., Kanade, T.: An iterative image registration technique with an application to stereo vision. *Proceedings of Imaging understanding workshop*, (1981) 121-130
11. McCarthy, J.: Recursive functions of symbolic expressions and their computation by machine, Part I, *Communications of the ACM*, v.3 n.4 (1060) 184-195
12. Minsky, M. L., Papert, S. A.: *Perceptrons.* MIT Press (1968)
13. Moses, J.: MACSYMA - the fifth year, ACM SIGSAM Bulletin, Vol.8 n.3 (1974) 105-110
14. Novak, J. D.: *A Theory of Education.* Cornell University Press, Ithaca, Illinois (1977)

15. Noy, N., Stuckenschmidt, H.: Ontology alignment: An annotated bibliography. In Y. Kalfoglou, M. Schorlemmer, A. Sheth, S. Staab, and M. Uschold, editors, *Semantic Interoperability and Integration*, number 04391 in Dagstuhl Seminar Proceedings. Internationales Begegnungs- und Forschungszentrum (IBFI), Schloss Dagstuhl, Germany, 2005. <http://drops.dagstuhl.de/opus/volltexte/2005/48>[date of citation: 2005-01-01]
16. Ontolingua. www.ksl.stanford.edu/software/ontolingua/
17. Roberts, L. G.: Machine perception of three-dimensional solids. In *Optical and Electrooptical Information Processing,* J. Tippet, Ed. MIT Press, Cambridge, Mass(1965) 125-143
18. Robinson, J A.: A Machine-Oriented Logic Based on the Resolution Principle, *Journal of the ACM*, Vol.12 n.1 (1965) 23-41
19. Sowa, J. F.: Conceptual Graphs. *IBM Journal of Research and Development* (1976)
20. Sowa, J. F.: Conceptual Structures. *Information Processing in Mind and Machine.* Addison Wesley (1984)
21. Steele, G., Sussman, G. J.: Revised Report on SCHEME, a Dialect of LISP, Memo 452, Artificial Intelligence Laboratory, M.I.T. (1978)
22. Trew. A., Wilson, G. (eds): *Past, Present, Parallel: A Survey of Available Parallel Computing Systems*. New York: Springer-Verlag (1991) ISBN 0-387-19664-1
23. Xu, L, Embley, D.: Combining the best of global-as-view and local-as-view for data integration. http://www.deg.byu.edu/papers/PODS.integration.pdf
24. Zadeh, L. A., *Fuzzy sets.* Information and Control, Vol. 8 (1965) 338-353

Properties of Markovian Subgraphs of a Decomposable Graph

Sung-Ho Kim

Korea Advanced Institute of Science and Technology, Daejeon, 305-701, South Korea

Abstract. We explore the properties of subgraphs (called Markovian subgraphs) of a decomposable graph under some conditions. For a decomposable graph $\mathcal{G}$ and a collection γ of its Markovian subgraphs, we show that the set $\chi(\mathcal{G})$ of the intersections of all the neighboring cliques of $\mathcal{G}$ contains $\cup_{g\in\gamma}\chi(g)$. We also show that $\chi(\mathcal{G}) = \cup_{g\in\gamma}\chi(g)$ holds for a certain type of $\mathcal{G}$ which we call a maximal Markovian supergraph of γ. This graph-theoretic result is instrumental for combining knowledge structures that are given in undirected graphs.

1 Introduction

Graphs are used effectively in representing model structures in a variety of research fields such as statistics, artificial intelligence, data mining, biological science, medicine, decision science, educational science, etc. Different forms of graphs are used according to the intrinsic inter-relationship among the random variables involved. Arrows are used when the relationship is causal, temporal, or asymmetric, and undirected edges are used when the relationship is associative or symmetric.

Among the graphs, triangulated graphs [1] are favored mostly when Markov random fields ([7], [11]) are considered with respect to undirected graphs. When a random field is Markov with respect to a triangulated graph, its corresponding probability model is expressed in a factorized form which facilitates computation over the probability distribution of the random field [7]. This computational feasibility, among others, makes such a Markov random field a most favored random field.

The triangulated graph is called a rigid circuit [4], a chordal graph [5], or a decomposable graph [9]. A survey on this type of graphs is given in [2]. One of the attractive properties (see Chapter 4 of [6]) of the triangulated graph is that its induced subgraphs and Markovian subgraphs (defined in section 2) are triangulated. While induced subgraphs are often used in literature (see Chapter 2 of [8]), Markovian subgraphs are introduced in this paper. We will explore the relationship between a triangulated graph and its Markovian subgraphs and find explicit expressions for the relationship. The relationship is useful for understanding the relationship between a probability model P, which is Markov with respect to the triangulated graph, and submodels of P. Since the terminology "decomposable graph" is more contextual than any others as long as Markov

A. Gelbukh and C.A. Reyes-Garcia (Eds.): MICAI 2006, LNAI 4293, pp. 15–26, 2006.

random fields are concerned, we will call the triangulated graph a decomposable graph in the remainder of the paper.

This paper consists of 6 sections. Section 2 presents notation and graphical terminologies. Markovian subgraphs are defined here. We define decomposable graphs in Section 3 and introduce a class of separators. In Section 4, we present the notion of Markovian supergraph and the relationship between Markovian supergraph and Markovian subgraph. In Section 5, we compare Markovian supergraphs between a pair of collections of Markovian subgraphs of a given graph. Section 6 concludes the paper with summarizing remarks.

2 Notation and Terminology

We will consider only undirected graphs in the paper. We denote a graph by $\mathcal{G} = (V, E)$, where V is the set of the nodes involved in $\mathcal{G}$ and E, $E \subseteq V \times V$, is a collection of ordered pairs, each pair representing that the nodes of the pair are connected by an edge. Since $\mathcal{G}$ is undirected, $(u, v) \in E$ is the same edge as (v, u). We say that a set of nodes of $\mathcal{G}$ forms a complete subgraph of $\mathcal{G}$ if every pair of nodes in the set are connected by an edge. A maximal complete subgraph is called a clique of $\mathcal{G}$, where the maximality is in the sense of set-inclusion. We denote by $\mathcal{C}(\mathcal{G})$ the set of cliques of $\mathcal{G}$.

If $(u, v) \in E$, we say that u is a neighbor node of v or vice versa and write it as $u \sim v$. A path of length n is a sequence of nodes $u = v_0, \cdots, v_n = v$ such that $(v_i, v_{i+1}) \in E$, $i = 0, 1, \cdots, n-1$ and $u \neq v$. If $u = v$, the path is called an n-cycle. If $u \neq v$ and u and v are connected by a path, we write $u \rightleftharpoons v$. Note that $\rightleftharpoons$ is an equivalence relation. We define the connectivity component of u as

$$[u] = \{v \in V;\ \ v \rightleftharpoons u\} \cup \{u\}.$$

So, we have

$$v \in [u] \iff u \rightleftharpoons v \iff u \in [v].$$

For $v \in V$, we define the neighbor of v by $ne(v) = \{u \in V;\ \ v \sim u \text{ in } \mathcal{G}\}$ and define, for $A \subseteq V$, the boundary of A by $bd(A) = \cup_{v \in A} ne(v) \setminus A$. If we have to specify the graph $\mathcal{G}$ in which $bd(A)$ is obtained, we will write $bd_{\mathcal{G}}(A)$. A path, $v_1, \cdots, v_n$, $v_1 \neq v_n$, is intersected by A if $A \cap \{v_1, \cdots, v_n\} \neq \emptyset$ and neither of the end nodes of the path is in A. We say that nodes u and v are separated by A if all the paths from u and v are intersected by A, and we call such a set A a *separator*. In the same context, we say that, for three disjoint sets A, B, C, A is separated from B by C if all the paths from A to B are intersected by C, and we write $\langle A|C|B\rangle_{\mathcal{G}}$. The notation $\langle \cdot | \cdot | \cdot \rangle_{\mathcal{G}}$ follows [10]. A non-empty set B is said to be intersected by A if B is partitioned into three sets B_1, B_2, and $B \cap A$ and B_1 and B_2 are separated by A in $\mathcal{G}$.

For $A \subset V$, an induced subgraph of $\mathcal{G}$ confined to A is defined as $\mathcal{G}_A^{ind} = (A,\ E \cap (A \times A))$. The complement of a set A is denoted by A^c. For $A \subset V$, we let $\mathcal{J}_A$ be the collection of the connectivity components in $\mathcal{G}_{A^c}^{ind}$ and $\beta(\mathcal{J}_A) = \{bd(B);\ B \in \mathcal{J}_A\}$. Then we define a graph $\mathcal{G}_A = (A, E_A)$ where

$$E_A = [E \cup \{B \times B;\ B \in \beta(\mathcal{J}_A)\}] \cap A \times A. \qquad (1)$$

In other words, E_A is obtained by adding the edges each of which connects a pair of nodes that belong to the same B in $\beta(\mathcal{J}_A)$. We will call $\mathcal{G}_A$ the Markovian subgraph of $\mathcal{G}$ confined to A and write $\mathcal{G}_A \subseteq^M \mathcal{G}$. $\mathcal{J}_A$ and $\beta(\mathcal{J}_A)$ are defined with respect to a given graph $\mathcal{G}$. Note that E_A is not necessarily a subset of E, while $E_A^{ind} \subseteq E$. When the graph is to be specified, we will write them as $\mathcal{J}_A^{\mathcal{G}}$ and $\beta_{\mathcal{G}}(\mathcal{J}_A)$.

If $\mathcal{G} = (V, E)$, $\mathcal{G}' = (V, E')$, and $E' \subseteq E$, then we say that $\mathcal{G}'$ is an edge-subgraph of $\mathcal{G}$ and write $\mathcal{G}' \subseteq^e \mathcal{G}$. For us, a subgraph of $\mathcal{G}$ is either a Markovian subgraph, an induced subgraph, or an edge-subgraph of $\mathcal{G}$. If $\mathcal{G}'$ is a subgraph of $\mathcal{G}$, we call $\mathcal{G}$ a supergraph of $\mathcal{G}'$. The cardinality of a set A will be denoted by $|A|$. For two collections A, B of sets, if, for every $a \in A$, there exists a set b in B such that $a \subseteq b$, we will write $A \preceq B$.

3 Separators as a Characterizer of Decomposable Graphs

In this section, we will present separators as a tool for characterizing decomposable graphs. Although decomposable graphs are well known in the literature, we will define them here for completeness.

Definition 1. A triple (A, B, C) of disjoint, nonempty subsets of V is said to form a decomposition of $\mathcal{G}$ if $V = A \cup B \cup C$ and the two conditions below both hold:
(i) A and B are separated by C;
(ii) $\mathcal{G}_C^{ind}$ is complete.

By recursively applying the notion of graph decomposition, we can define a decomposable graph.

Definition 2. *A graph* $\mathcal{G}$ is said to be decomposable if it is complete, or if there exists a decomposition (A, B, C) into decomposable subgraphs $\mathcal{G}_{A \cup C}^{ind}$ and $\mathcal{G}_{B \cup C}^{ind}$.

According to this definition, we can find a sequence of cliques $C_1, \cdots, C_k$ of a decomposable graph $\mathcal{G}$ which satisfies the following condition [see Proposition 2.17 of [8]]: with $C_{(j)} = \cup_{i=1}^{j} C_i$ and $S_j = C_j \cap C_{(j-1)}$,

$$\text{for all } i > 1, \text{ there is a } j < i \text{ such that } S_i \subseteq C_j. \tag{2}$$

By this condition for a sequence of cliques, we can see that S_j is expressed as an intersection of neighboring cliques of $\mathcal{G}$. If we denote the collection of these S_j's by $\chi(\mathcal{G})$, we have, for a decomposable graph $\mathcal{G}$, that

$$\chi(\mathcal{G}) = \{a \cap b;\ \ a, b \in \mathcal{C}(\mathcal{G}),\ a \neq b\}. \tag{3}$$

The cliques are elementary graphical components and the S_j is obtained as intersection of neighboring cliques. So, we will call the S_j's prime separators (PSs) of the decomposable graph $\mathcal{G}$. The PSs in a decomposable graph may be extended to separators of prime graphs in any undirected graph, where the prime graphs are defined in [3] as the maximal subgraphs without a complete separator.

4 Markovian Subgraphs

Let $\mathcal{G}$ be decomposable and the graphs, $\mathcal{G}_1, \cdots, \mathcal{G}_m$, be Markovian subgraphs of $\mathcal{G}$. The m Markovian subgraphs may be regarded as the graphs of the Markov random fields of $V_1, \cdots, V_m$. In this context, we may refer to a Markovian subgraph as a *marginal graph.*

Definition 3. *Suppose there are m marginal graphs, $\mathcal{G}_1, \cdots, \mathcal{G}_m$. Then we say that graph $\mathcal{H}$ of a set of variables V is a* Markovian supergraph *of $\mathcal{G}_1, \cdots, \mathcal{G}_m$, if the following conditions hold:*
(i) $\cup_{i=1}^m V_i = V$.
(ii) $\mathcal{H}_{V_i} = \mathcal{G}_i$, for $i = 1, \cdots, m$. That is, $\mathcal{G}_i$ are Markovian subgraphs of $\mathcal{H}$.

We will call $\mathcal{H}$ a maximal *Markovian supergraph (MaxG) of $\mathcal{G}_1, \cdots, \mathcal{G}_m$ if adding any edge to $\mathcal{H}$ invalidates condition (ii) for at least one $i = 1, \cdots, m$. Since $\mathcal{H}$ depends on $\mathcal{G}_1, \cdots, \mathcal{G}_m$, we denote the collection of the MaxGs formally by $\Omega(\mathcal{G}_1, \cdots, \mathcal{G}_m)$.*

According to this definition, the graph $\mathcal{G}$ is a Markovian supergraph of each $\mathcal{G}_i$, $i = 1, \cdots, m$. There may be many Markovian supergraphs that are obtained from a collection of marginal graphs. For the graphs, $\mathcal{G}, \mathcal{G}_1, \cdots, \mathcal{G}_m$, in the definition, we say that $\mathcal{G}_1, \cdots, \mathcal{G}_m$ are *combined into* $\mathcal{G}$.

In the lemma below, $\mathcal{C}_\mathcal{G}(A)$ is the collection of the cliques which include nodes of A in graph $\mathcal{G}$. The proof is intuitive.

Lemma 1. *Let $\mathcal{G}' = (V', E')$ be a Markovian subgraph of $\mathcal{G}$ and suppose that, for three disjoint subsets A, B, C of V', $\langle A|B|C\rangle_{\mathcal{G}'}$. Then*

(i) *$\langle A|B|C\rangle_\mathcal{G}$;*
(ii) *For $W \in \mathcal{C}_\mathcal{G}(A)$ and $W' \in \mathcal{C}_\mathcal{G}(C)$, $\langle W|B|W'\rangle_\mathcal{G}$.*

The following theorem is similar to Corollary 2.8 in [8], but it is different in that an induced subgraph is considered in the corollary while a Markovian subgraph is considered here.

Theorem 1. *Every Markovian subgraph of a decomposable graph is decomposable.*

Proof. Suppose that a Markovian subgraph $\mathcal{G}_A$ of a decomposable graph $\mathcal{G}$ is not decomposable. Then there must exist a chordless cycle, say C, of length ≥ 4 in $\mathcal{G}_A$. Denote the nodes on the cycle by $v_1, \cdots, v_l$ and assume that they form a cycle in that order where v_1 is a neighbor of v_l.

We need to show that C itself forms a cycle in $\mathcal{G}$ or is contained in a chordless cycle of length $> l$ in $\mathcal{G}$. By Lemma 1, there is no edge in $\mathcal{G}$ between any pair of non-neighboring nodes on the cycle. If C itself forms a cycle in $\mathcal{G}$, our argument is done. Otherwise, we will show that the nodes $v_1, \cdots, v_l$ are on a cycle which is larger than C. Without loss of generality, we may consider the case where there is no edge between v_1 and v_2. If there is no path in $\mathcal{G}$ between the two nodes other than the path, say π, which passes through $v_3, \cdots, v_l$, then, since C forms a chordless cycle in $\mathcal{G}_A$, there must exist a path between v_1 and v_2 other than the path π. Thus the nodes $v_1, \cdots, v_l$ must lie in $\mathcal{G}$ on a chordless cycle of length $> l$. This completes the proof. □

This theorem and expression (3) imply that, as for a decomposable graph $\mathcal{G}$, the PSs are always given in the form of a complete subgraph in $\mathcal{G}$ and in its Markovian subgraphs.

Lemma 1 states that a separator of a Markovian subgraph of $\mathcal{G}$ is also a separator of $\mathcal{G}$. We will next see that a MaxG is decomposable provided that all the marginal graphs, $\mathcal{G}_1, \cdots, \mathcal{G}_m$, are decomposable.

Theorem 2. *Let $\mathcal{G}_1, \cdots, \mathcal{G}_m$ be decomposable. Then every graph in $\Omega(\mathcal{G}_1, \cdots, \mathcal{G}_m)$ is also decomposable.*

Proof. Suppose that there is a MaxG, say $\mathcal{H}$, which contains an n-cycle ($n \geq 4$) and let A be the set of the nodes on the cycle. Since $\mathcal{H}$ is maximal, we can not add any edge to it. This implies that no more than three nodes of A are included in any of V_i's, since any four or more nodes of A that are contained in a V_i form a cycle in $\mathcal{G}_i$, which is impossible due to the decomposability of the $\mathcal{G}_i$'s. Hence, the cycle in $\mathcal{H}$ may become a clique by edge-additions on the cycle, contradicting that $\mathcal{H}$ is maximal. Therefore, $\mathcal{H}$ must be decomposable. □

Theorem 2 does not hold for every Markovian supergraph. For example, in Figure 1, graph $\mathcal{G}$ is not decomposable. However, the Markovian subgraphs $\mathcal{G}_1$ and $\mathcal{G}_2$ are both decomposable. And $\chi(\mathcal{G}) = \{\{4\}, \{7\}\}$, $\chi(\mathcal{G}_1) = \{\{2,3\}, \{5,6\}, \{8,9\}\}$, and $\chi(\mathcal{G}_2) = \{\{4\}, \{7\}\}$. Note that, for $\mathcal{H}$ in the figure, $\chi(\mathcal{H}) = \chi(\mathcal{G}_1) \cup \chi(\mathcal{G}_2)$, which holds true in general as is shown in Theorem 4 below. The theorem characterizes a MaxG in a most unique way. Before stating the theorem, we will see if a set of nodes can be a PS in a marginal graph while it is not in another marginal graph.

Theorem 3. *Let $\mathcal{G}$ be a decomposable graph and $\mathcal{G}_1$ and $\mathcal{G}_2$ Markovian subgraphs of $\mathcal{G}$. Suppose that a set $C \in \chi(\mathcal{G}_1)$ and that $C \subseteq V_2$. Then C is not intersected in $\mathcal{G}_2$ by any other subset of V_2.*

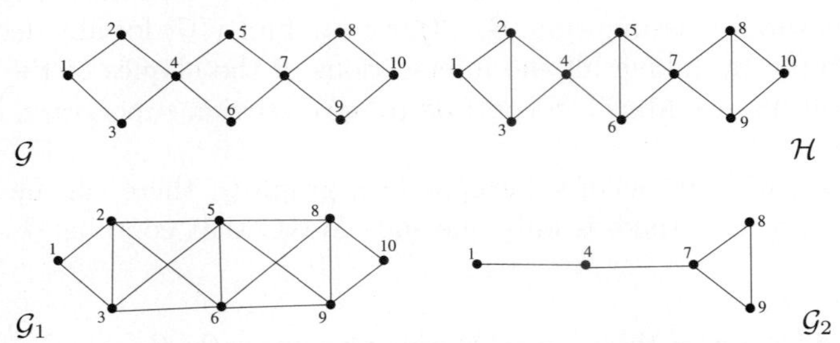

Fig. 1. An example of a non-decomposable graph ($\mathcal{G}$) whose Markovian subgraphs ($\mathcal{G}_1$, $\mathcal{G}_2$) are decomposable. Graph $\mathcal{H}$ is a MaxG of $\mathcal{G}_1$ and $\mathcal{G}_2$.

Proof. Suppose that there are two nodes u and v in C that are separated in $\mathcal{G}_2$ by a set S. Then, by Lemma 1, we have $\langle u|S|v\rangle_{\mathcal{G}}$. Since $C \in \chi(\mathcal{G}_1)$ and $\mathcal{G}_1$ is decomposable, C is an intersection of some neighboring cliques of $\mathcal{G}_1$ by equation (3). So, S can not be a subset of V_1 but a proper subset of S can be. This means that there are at least one pair of nodes, v_1 and v_2, in $\mathcal{G}_1$ such that all the paths between the two nodes are intersected by C in $\mathcal{G}_1$, with v_1 appearing in one of the neighboring cliques and v_2 in another.

Since v_1 and v_2 are in neighboring cliques, each node in C is on a path from v_1 to v_2 in $\mathcal{G}_1$. From $\langle u|S|v\rangle_{\mathcal{G}}$ follows that there is an l-cycle ($l \geq 4$) that passes through the nodes u, v, v_1, and v_2 in $\mathcal{G}$. This contradicts to the assumption that $\mathcal{G}$ is decomposable. Therefore, there can not be such a separator S in $\mathcal{G}_2$. □

This theorem states that, if $\mathcal{G}$ is decomposable, a PS in a Markovian subgraph of $\mathcal{G}$ is either a PS or a complete subgraph in any other Markovian subgraph of $\mathcal{G}$. If the set of the nodes of the PS is contained in only one clique of a Markovian subgraph, the set is embedded in the clique. For a subset V' of V, if we put $\mathcal{G}_1 = \mathcal{G}$ and $\mathcal{G}_2 = \mathcal{G}_{V'}$ in Theorem 3, we have the following corollary.

Corollary 1. Let $\mathcal{G}$ be a decomposable graph and suppose that a set $C \in \chi(\mathcal{G})$ and that $C \subseteq V' \subset V$. Then C is not intersected in a Markovian subgraph $\mathcal{G}_{V'}$ of $\mathcal{G}$ by any other subset of V'.

Recall that if $\mathcal{G}_i$, $i = 1, 2, \cdots, m$ are Markovian subgraphs of $\mathcal{G}$, then $\mathcal{G}$ is a Markovian supergraph. For a given set $\mathcal{S}$ of Markovian subgraphs, there may be many MaxGs, and they are related with $\mathcal{S}$ through PSs as in the theorem below.

Theorem 4. Let there be Markovian subgraphs $\mathcal{G}_i$, $i = 1, 2, \cdots, m$, of a decomposable graph $\mathcal{G}$. Then

(i)
$$\cup_{i=1}^m \chi(\mathcal{G}_i) \subseteq \chi(\mathcal{G});$$

(ii) for any MaxG $\mathcal{H}$,
$$\cup_{i=1}^m \chi(\mathcal{G}_i) = \chi(\mathcal{H}).$$

Proof. See Appendix.

For a given set of marginal graphs, we can readily obtain the set of PSs under the decomposability assumption. By (3), we can find $\chi(\mathcal{G})$ for any decomposable graph $\mathcal{G}$ simply by taking all the intersections of the cliques of the graph. An apparent feature of a MaxG in contrast to a Markovian supergraph is stated in Theorem 4.

For a set γ of Markovian subgraphs of a graph $\mathcal{G}$, there can be more than one MaxG of γ. But there is only one such MaxG that contains $\mathcal{G}$ as its edge-subgraph.

Theorem 5. Suppose there are m Markovian subgraphs $\mathcal{G}_1, \cdots, \mathcal{G}_m$ of a decomposable graph $\mathcal{G}$. Then there exists a unique MaxG $\mathcal{H}^*$ of the m node-subgraphs such that $\mathcal{G} \subseteq^e \mathcal{H}^*$.

Proof. By Theorem 4 (i), we have

$$\cup_{i=1}^{m}\chi(\mathcal{G}_i) \subseteq \chi(\mathcal{G}).$$

If $\cup_{i=1}^{m}\chi(\mathcal{G}_i) = \chi(\mathcal{G})$, then since $\mathcal{G}$ is decomposable, $\mathcal{G}$ itself is a MaxG. Otherwise, let $\chi' = \chi(\mathcal{G}) - \cup_{i=1}^{m}\chi(\mathcal{G}_i) = \{A_1, \cdots, A_g\}$. Since $A_1 \notin \cup_{i=1}^{m}\chi(\mathcal{G}_i)$, we may add edges so that $\cup_{C\in\mathcal{C}_{\mathcal{G}}(A_1)}C$ becomes a clique, and the resulting graph $\mathcal{G}^{(1)}$ becomes a Markovian supergraph of $\mathcal{G}_1, \cdots, \mathcal{G}_m$ with $\chi(\mathcal{G}^{(1)}) - \cup_{i=1}^{m}\chi(\mathcal{G}_i) = \{A_2, \cdots, A_g\}$.

We repeat the same clique-merging process for the remaining A_i's in χ'. Since each clique-merging makes the corresponding PS disappear into the merged, new clique while maintaining the resulting graph as a Markovian supergraph of $\mathcal{G}_1, \cdots, \mathcal{G}_m$, the clique-merging creates a Markovian supergraph of $\mathcal{G}_1, \cdots, \mathcal{G}_m$ as an edge-supergraph of the preceding graph. Therefore, we obtain a MaxG, say $\mathcal{H}^*$, of $\mathcal{G}_1, \cdots, \mathcal{G}_m$ at the end of the sequence of the clique-merging processes for all the PSs in χ'. $\mathcal{H}^*$ is the desired MaxG as an edge-supergraph of $\mathcal{G}$.

Since the clique-merging begins with $\mathcal{G}$ and, for each PS in $\mathcal{G}$, the set of the cliques which meet at the PS only is uniquely defined, the uniqueness of $\mathcal{H}^*$ follows. □

The relationship among Markovian subgraphs is transitive as shown below.

Theorem 6. *For three graphs, $\mathcal{G}_1, \mathcal{G}_2, \mathcal{G}$ with $\mathcal{G}_1 \subseteq^M \mathcal{G}_2 \subseteq^M \mathcal{G}$, it holds that $\mathcal{G}_1 \subseteq^M \mathcal{G}$.*

Proof. For $u, v \in bd_{\mathcal{G}}(V_2 \setminus V_1) \cap V_1 \times V_1$ with $u \not\sim v$ in $\mathcal{G}_1$, we have

$$\langle u|(V_1 \setminus \{u, v\})|v\rangle_{\mathcal{G}_2} \tag{4}$$

by the condition of the theorem. Expression (4) means that there is no path between u and v in $\mathcal{G}_2$ bypassing $V_1 \setminus \{u, v\}$. Since $\mathcal{G}_2 \subseteq^M \mathcal{G}$, expression (4) implies that $\langle u|(V_1 \setminus \{u, v\})|v\rangle_{\mathcal{G}}$.

Now consider $u, v \in bd_{\mathcal{G}}(V_2 \setminus V_1) \cap V_1 \times V_1$ such that $(u, v) \in E_1$ but $(u, v) \notin E_2$. This means that there is a path between u and v in $\mathcal{G}_2$ bypassing $V_1 \setminus \{u, v\}$. Either there is at least one path between u and v in $\mathcal{G}_{V_2}^{ind}$ bypassing $V_1 \setminus \{u, v\}$, or there is no such path in $\mathcal{G}_{V_2}^{ind}$ at all. In the former situation, it must be that $u \sim v$ in $\mathcal{G}_1$ as a Markovian subgraph of $\mathcal{G}$. In the latter situation, at least one path is newly created in $\mathcal{G}_{V_2}^{ind}$ when $\mathcal{G}_{V_2}^{ind}$ becomes a Markovian subgraph of $\mathcal{G}$. This new path contains an edge, (v_1, v_2) say, in $\{B \times B;\ B \in \beta_{\mathcal{G}}(\mathcal{J}_{V_2})\} \cap V_2 \times V_2$ where $\mathcal{J}_{V_2}$ is the connectivity components in $\mathcal{G}_{V_2^c}^{ind}$. This also implies that there is at least one path between v_1 and v_2 in $\mathcal{G}$ bypassing $V_2 \setminus \{v_1, v_2\}$. In a nutshell, the statement that $(u, v) \in E_1$ but $(u, v) \notin E$ implies that there is at least one path between u and v in $\mathcal{G}$ bypassing $V_1 \setminus \{u, v\}$. This completes the proof. □

5 Markovian Supergraphs from Marginal Graphs

Given a collection γ of marginal graphs, a Markovian supergraph of γ may not exist unless the marginal graphs are Markovian subgraphs of a graph. We will consider in this section collections of Markovian subgraphs of a graph $\mathcal{G}$ and investigate the relationship of a Markovian supergraph of a collection with those of another collection.

Let $\mathcal{G}_{11}$ and $\mathcal{G}_{12}$ be Markovian subgraphs of $\mathcal{G}_1$ with $V_{11} \cup V_{12} = V_1$, and let $\mathcal{G}_1$ and $\mathcal{G}_2$ be Markovian subgraphs of $\mathcal{G}$ with $V_1 \cup V_2 = V$. For $H \in \Omega(\mathcal{G}_1, \mathcal{G}_2)$, we have, by Theorem 6, that $\mathcal{G}_{11} \subseteq^M H$ and $\mathcal{G}_{12} \subseteq^M H$, since $\mathcal{G}_1 \subseteq^M H$. Thus, H is a Markovian supergraph of $\mathcal{G}_{11}, \mathcal{G}_{12}$, and $\mathcal{G}_2$, but may not be a MaxG of them since $\chi(\mathcal{G}_{11}) \cup \chi(\mathcal{G}_{12}) \subseteq \chi(\mathcal{G}_1)$ by Theorem 4 (i). We can generalize this as follows. We denote by $V(\mathcal{G})$ the set of nodes of $\mathcal{G}$.

Theorem 7. Consider two collections, γ_1 and γ_2, of Markovian subgraphs of $\mathcal{G}$ with $\cup_{g\in\gamma_1} V(g) = \cup_{g\in\gamma_2} V(g) = V(\mathcal{G})$. For every $g \in \gamma_2$, there exists a graph $h \in \gamma_1$ such that $g \subseteq^M h$. Then, every $H \in \Omega(\gamma_1)$ is a Markovian supergraph of $g \in \gamma_2$.

Proof. For $H \in \Omega(\gamma_1)$, every $h \in \gamma_1$ is a Markovian subgraph of H. By the condition of the theorem, for each $g \in \gamma_2$, we have $g \subseteq^M h'$ for some $h' \in \gamma_1$. Thus, by Theorem 6, $g \subseteq^M H$. Since $\cup_{g\in\gamma_2} V(g) = V(\mathcal{G})$, H is a Markovian supergraph of $g \in \gamma_2$. □

From this theorem and Theorem 4 we can deduce that, for $H \in \Omega(\gamma_1)$,

$$\cup_{g\in\gamma_2} \chi(g) \subseteq \chi(H).$$

This implies that H cannot be a proper supergraph of any H' in $\Omega(\gamma_2)$. Since γ_1 and γ_2 are both from the same graph $\mathcal{G}$, H is an edge-subgraph of some $H' \in \Omega(\gamma_2)$ when $\cup_{g\in\gamma_2} \chi(g) \subset \chi(H)$. However, it is noteworthy that every pair H and H', $H \in \Omega(\gamma_1)$ and $H' \in \Omega(\gamma_2)$, are not necessarily comparable as we will see below.

Example 1. Consider the graph $\mathcal{G}$ in Figure 2 and let $V_1 = \{3, 4, 5, 6, 7, 8\}$ and $V_2 = \{1, 2, 3, 5, 7, 9\}$. The Markovian subgraphs $\mathcal{G}_1$ and $\mathcal{G}_2$ are also in Figure 2. Note that

$$\chi(\mathcal{G}_1) \cup \chi(\mathcal{G}_2) = \chi(\mathcal{G}) = \{\{3\}, \{2, 3\}, \{5\}, \{6\}, \{7\}\}$$

and that $\mathcal{G} \in \Omega(\mathcal{G}_1, \mathcal{G}_2)$.

Let $\mathcal{G}_{11}$ and $\mathcal{G}_{12}$ be two Markovian subgraphs of $\mathcal{G}_1$ as in Figure 2. Then $\{\mathcal{F}_1\} = \Omega(\mathcal{G}_{11}, \mathcal{G}_{12})$. $\chi(\mathcal{F}_1) = \{\{5\}, \{6\}\}$ and $\chi(\mathcal{G}_2) = \{\{2, 3\}, \{5\}, \{7\}\}$. Let $\gamma_1 = \{\mathcal{F}_1, \mathcal{G}_2\}$. Then, for every $H \in \Omega(\gamma_1)$,

$$\chi(H) = \{\{2, 3\}, \{5\}, \{6\}, \{7\}\} \tag{5}$$

by Theorem 4. In $\mathcal{G}_2$, we have $\langle\{2, 3\}|5|7\rangle$; and in $\mathcal{F}_1$, $\langle 5|6|7\rangle$. Thus, the four PSs in (5) are to be arranged in a path, $\{2, 3\}$—$\{5\}$—$\{6\}$—$\{7\}$. The remaining nodes can be added to this path as the two graphs in γ_1 suggest in such a way that equation (5) may hold. Note that $\langle 4|5|6\rangle$ in $\mathcal{F}_1$. This means, by Theorem 3, that node 4 must form a clique either with $\{1, 2, 3\}$ or with $\{2, 3, 5\}$ because $\{2, 3\}$ is a PS. This is depicted in $\mathcal{F}$ of Figure 2 representing two possible cliques which include node 4. The two different MaxGs are denoted by $\mathcal{F}_\circ$ and $\mathcal{F}_\bullet$ which are explained in the caption of Figure 2. $\mathcal{G}$ is not an edge-subgraph of $\mathcal{F}_\bullet$ nor of $\mathcal{F}_\circ$. □

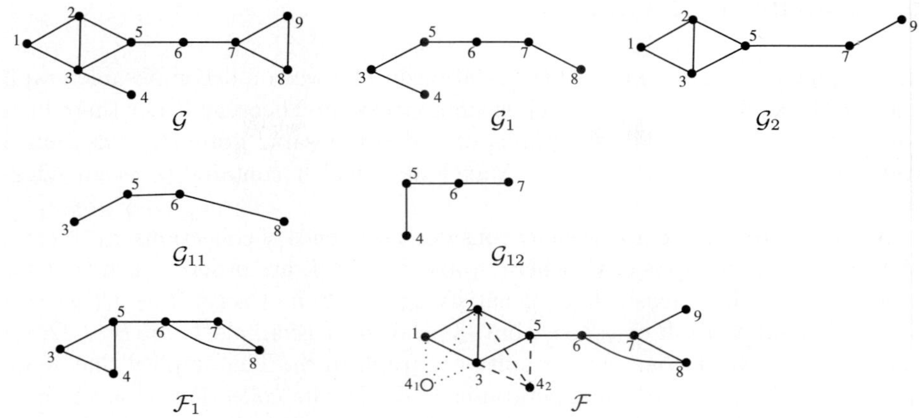

Fig. 2. Markovian subgraphs and supergraphs. In graph $\mathcal{F}$, 4_1 and 4_2 indicate two different locations of node 4. We denote by 4_1 (a circle) the location of node 4 with $bd(4) = \{1, 2, 3\}$ and by 4_2 (a bullet) the location of node 4 with $bd(4) = \{2, 3, 5\}$. We denote the $\mathcal{F}$ by $\mathcal{F}_\circ$ when node 4 is located at 4_1 and by $\mathcal{F}_\bullet$ when node 4 is located at 4_2.

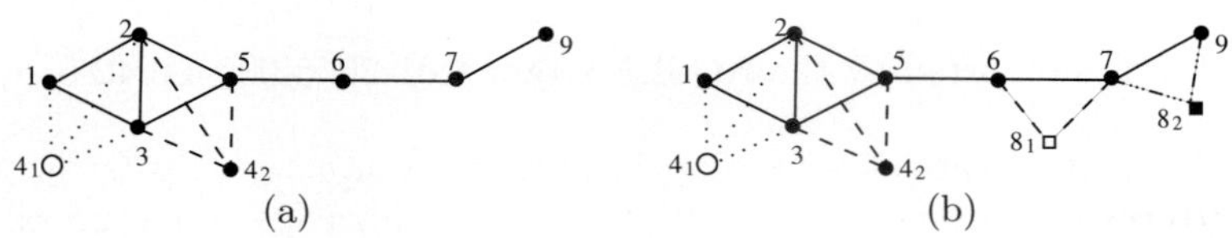

Fig. 3. Combination of Markovian subgraphs, $\mathcal{G}_{11}$, $\mathcal{G}_{12}$, and $\mathcal{G}_2$ in Figure 2. Node 8 is located at two locations 8_1 and 8_2 and similarly for node 4. $\mathcal{G}_{12}$ and $\mathcal{G}_2$ are combined into the graphs in panel (a), which are then combined into the graphs in panel (b). Note that four MaxG's of $\{\mathcal{G}_{11}, \mathcal{G}_{12}, \mathcal{G}_2\}$ are shown in graph (b) corresponding to four different location-pairs of nodes 4 and 8.

The phenomenon that $\mathcal{G}$ is not an edge-subgraph of either of the two MaxGs, $\mathcal{F}_\circ$ and $\mathcal{F}_\bullet$, seems to contradict Theorem 5 which says that there always exists a MaxG which is an edge-supergraph of $\mathcal{G}$. But recall that $\mathcal{F}_1$ is a MaxG of $\mathcal{G}_{11}$ and $\mathcal{G}_{12}$ where it is not taken into consideration that $\{7\}$ is a PS in $\mathcal{G}_2$.

Note that $\mathcal{F}$ in Figure 2 is a collection of $\mathcal{F}_\circ$ and $\mathcal{F}_\bullet$. The $\mathcal{F}$ is obtained first by combining $\mathcal{G}_{11}$ and $\mathcal{G}_{12}$ into $\mathcal{F}_1$ and then by combining $\mathcal{F}_1$ and $\mathcal{G}_2$. This is a sequential procedure. If we combine $\mathcal{G}_{12}$ and $\mathcal{G}_2$, we get the graphs in panel (a) of Figure 3, and combination of the graphs in panel (a) with $\mathcal{G}_{11}$ yields the graphs in panel (b). Different combining procedure may yield different MaxG's. Theorem 5 however guarantees existence of the MaxG which contains $\mathcal{G}$ as an edge-subgraph. Note in Example 1 that $\mathcal{F}$ is found in panel (b) and that $\mathcal{G}$ is an edge-subgraph of the graph in panel (b) of Figure 3 in which the locations of nodes 4 and 8 are 4_2 and 8_2, respectively.

6 Concluding Remarks

In this paper, we have explored the relationship between a decomposable graph and its Markovian subgraph which is summarized in Theorem 4. Let there be a collection γ of Markovian subgraphs of a decomposable graph $\mathcal{G}$. Theorem 5 states that there always exists a MaxG of γ which contains $\mathcal{G}$ as an edge-subgraph.

According to Theorem 7, we may consider a sequence of collections, $\gamma_1, \cdots, \gamma_r$, of Markovian subgraphs of $\mathcal{G}$, where γ_i and γ_j, $i < j$, are ordered such that for every $g \in \gamma_j$, there exists $h \in \gamma_i$ satisfying $g \subseteq^M h$. Every $H \in \Omega(\gamma_i)$ is a Markovian supergraph of $g \in \gamma_j$, but, as shown in Example 1, an $H \in \Omega(\gamma_j)$ may not be a Markovian supergraph of a graph in γ_i. This implies that if we are interested in Markovian supergraphs of $V(\mathcal{G})$, the collection γ_1 is the best to use among the collections, $\gamma_1, \cdots, \gamma_r$. This is noteworthy in the context of statistical modelling, because it recommends to use Markovian subgraphs which are as large as possible.

Acknowledgement

This work was supported by the KOSEF Grant R01-2005-000-11042-0.

References

1. Berge, C.: Graphs and Hypergraphs, Translated from French by E. Minieka. North-Holland, Amsterdam (1973)
2. Brandstädt, A., Le, V. B., Spinrad, J. P.: Graph Classes: a survey, SIAM Monographs on Discrete Mathematics and Applications. Philadelphia, PA.: SIAM (1999)
3. Cox, D.R., Wermuth, N.: Likelihood factorizations for mixed discrete and continuous variables, Scand. J. Statist. 26 (1999) 209-220.
4. Dirac, G.A.: On rigid circuit graphs, Abhandlungen Mathematisches Seminar Hamburg 25 (1961) 71-76.
5. Gavril, F.: Algorithms for minimum coloring, maximum clique, minimum coloring by cliques and maximum independent set of a graph, SIAM Journal of Computing 1 (1972) 180-187.
6. Golumbic, M.C.: Algorithmic graph theory and perfect graphs, London: Academic Press (1980)
7. Kemeny, J.G., Speed, T.P., Knapp, A.W.: Denumerable Markov Chains 2nd edition, New York, NY: Springer (1976)
8. Lauritzen, S.L.: Graphical Models, NY: Oxford University Press (1996)
9. Lauritzen, S.L., Speed, T.P., Vijayan, K.: Decomposable graphs and hypergraphs, Journal of the Australian Mathematical Soc. A 36 (1984) 12-29.
10. Pearl, J.: Probabilistic Reasoning In Intelligent Systems: Networks of Plausible Inference, San Mateo, CA.: Morgan Kaufmann (1988)
11. Vorobev, N.N.: Markov measures and Markov extensions, Theory of Probability and Its Applications 8 (1963) 420-429.

Appendix: Proof of Theorem 4

We will first prove result (i). For a subset of nodes V_j, the followings hold:

(i') If V_j does not contain a subset which is a PS of $\mathcal{G}$, then $\chi(\mathcal{G}_j) = \emptyset$.
(ii') Otherwise, i.e., if there are PSs, $C_1, \cdots, C_r$, of $\mathcal{G}$ as subsets of V_j,
  (ii'-a) if there are no nodes in V_j that are separated by any of $C_1, \cdots, C_r$ in $\mathcal{G}$, then $\chi(\mathcal{G}_j) = \emptyset$.
  (ii'-b) if there is at least one of the PSs, say C_s, such that there are a pair of nodes, say u and v, in V_j such that $\langle u|C_s|v\rangle_\mathcal{G}$, then $\chi(\mathcal{G}_j) \neq \emptyset$.

We note that, since $\mathcal{G}$ is decomposable, the condition that V_j contains a separator of $\mathcal{G}$ implies that V_j contains a PS of $\mathcal{G}$. As for (i'), every pair of nodes, say u and v, in V_j have at least one path between them that bypasses $V_j \setminus \{u, v\}$ in the graph $\mathcal{G}$ since V_j does not contain any PS of $\mathcal{G}$. Thus, (i') follows.

On the other hand, suppose that there are PSs, $C_1, \cdots, C_r$, of $\mathcal{G}$ as a subset of V_j. The result (ii'-a) is obvious, since for each of the PSs, $C_1, \cdots, C_r$, the rest of the nodes in V_j are on one side of the PS in $\mathcal{G}$.

As for (ii'-b), let there be two nodes, u and v, in V_j such that $\langle u|C_s|v\rangle_\mathcal{G}$. Since $\mathcal{G}$ is decomposable, C_s is an intersection of neighboring cliques in $\mathcal{G}$, and the nodes u and v must appear in some (not necessarily neighboring) cliques that are separated by C_s. Thus, the two nodes are separated by C_s in $\mathcal{G}_j$ with C_s as a PS in $\mathcal{G}_j$. Any proper subset of C_s can not separate u from v in $\mathcal{G}$ and in any of its Markovian subgraphs.

From the results (i') and (ii') follows that

(iii') if $C \in \chi(\mathcal{G})$ and $C \subseteq V_j$, then either $C \in \chi(\mathcal{G}_j)$ or C is contained in only one clique of $\mathcal{G}_j$.
(iv') that $\chi(\mathcal{G}_j) = \emptyset$ does not necessarily implies that $\chi(\mathcal{G}) = \emptyset$.

To check if $\chi(\mathcal{G}_j) \not\subseteq \chi(\mathcal{G})$ for any $j \in \{1, 2, \cdots, m\}$, suppose that $C \in \chi(\mathcal{G}_j)$ and $C \notin \chi(\mathcal{G})$. This implies, by Lemma 1, that C is a separator but not a PS in $\mathcal{G}$. Thus, there is a proper subset C' of C in $\chi(\mathcal{G})$. By (iii'), $C' \in \chi(\mathcal{G}_j)$ or is contained in only one clique of $\mathcal{G}_j$. However, neither is possible, since $C' \subset C \in \chi(\mathcal{G}_j)$ and C is an intersection of cliques of $\mathcal{G}_j$. Therefore,

$$\chi(\mathcal{G}_j) \subseteq \chi(\mathcal{G}) \quad \text{for all } j.$$

This proves result (i) of the theorem.

We will now prove result (ii). If $\cup_{i=1}^m \chi(\mathcal{G}_i) = \emptyset$, then, since all the $\mathcal{G}_i$'s are decomposable by Theorem 1, they are complete graphs themselves. So, by definition, the MaxG must be a complete graph of V. Thus, the equality of the theorem holds.

Next, suppose that $\cup_{i=1}^m \chi(\mathcal{G}_i) \neq \emptyset$. Then there must exist a marginal model structure, say $\mathcal{G}_j$, such that $\chi(\mathcal{G}_j) \neq \emptyset$. Let $A \in \chi(\mathcal{G}_j)$. Then, by Theorem 3, A is either a PS or embedded in a clique if $A \subseteq V_i$ for $i \neq j$. Since a PS is an intersection of cliques by equation (3), the PS itself is a complete subgraph. Thus, by the definition of MaxG and by Lemma 1, $A \in \chi(\mathcal{H})$. This implies that $\cup_{i=1}^m \chi(\mathcal{G}_i) \subseteq \chi(\mathcal{H})$.

To show that the set inclusion in the last expression comes down to equality, we will suppose that there is a set B in $\chi(\mathcal{H}) \setminus (\cup_{i=1}^{m}\chi(\mathcal{G}_i))$ and show that this leads to a contradiction to the condition that $\mathcal{H}$ is a MaxG. $\mathcal{H}$ is decomposable by Theorem 2. So, B is the intersection of the cliques in $\mathcal{C}_{\mathcal{H}}(B)$. By supposition, $B \notin \chi(\mathcal{G}_i)$ for all $i = 1, \cdots, m$. This means either (a) that $B \subseteq V_j$ for some j and $B \subseteq C$ for only one clique C of $\mathcal{G}_j$ by Corollary 1 or (b) that $B \not\subseteq V_j$ for all $j = 1, \cdots, m$. In both of the situations, B need not be a PS in $\mathcal{H}$, since $\mathcal{G}_i$ are decomposable and so $B \cap V_i$ are complete in $\mathcal{G}_i$ in both of the situations. In other words, edges may be added to $\mathcal{H}$ so that $\mathcal{C}_{\mathcal{H}}(B)$ becomes a clique, which contradicts that $\mathcal{H}$ is a MaxG. This completes the proof. □

Pre-conceptual Schema: A Conceptual-Graph-Like Knowledge Representation for Requirements Elicitation*

Carlos Mario Zapata Jaramillo[1], Alexander Gelbukh[2], and Fernando Arango Isaza[1]

[1] Universidad Nacional de Colombia, Facultad de Minas, Escuela de Sistemas
Carrera 80 No. 65-223 Of. M8-113, Medellín, Colombia
cmzapata@unal.edu.co, farango@unal.edu.co
[2] Computing Research Center (CIC), National Polytechnic Institute,
Col. Zacatenco, 07738, DF, Mexico
www.Gelbukh.com

Abstract. A simple representation framework for ontological knowledge with dynamic and deontic characteristics is presented. It represents structural relationships (*is-a*, *part/whole*), dynamic relationships (actions such as *register*, *pay*, etc.), and conditional relationships (*if-then-else*). As a case study, we apply our representation language to the task of requirements elicitation in software engineering. We show how our pre-conceptual schemas can be obtained from controlled natural language discourse and how these diagrams can be then converted into standard UML diagrams. Thus our representation framework is shown to be a useful intermediate step for obtaining UML diagrams from natural language discourse.

1 Introduction

Knowledge Representation (KR) has been applied in software development, in tasks such as requirements elicitation, formal specification, etc. [1]. In requirements elicitation, the Stakeholder's discourse is transformed in software specifications by means of a process that involves intervention of the Analyst. Some works in KR have been made in representation of requirements, but there are still problems in Stakeholder validation and dynamic features of the paradigms used for this goal.

Several paradigms have been used for KR, such as semantic networks, frames, production rules, and predicate logic [1, 2]. In particular, Conceptual Graphs (CG) [3] have been used for KR because of its logic formalism.

In this paper we present Pre-conceptual Schemas, a simple CG-like KR framework motivated by the Requirements Elicitation task. On the one hand, these schemas can be obtained from a controlled natural language discourse. On the other hand, we show how to transform them to UML diagrams. Thus these schemas can be used for automatic conversion of natural language discourse into UML diagrams.

The paper is organized as follows. Section 2 presents an overview of KR. Section 3 discusses previous KR applications to Requirements Elicitation. Section 4 introduces

* Work done under partial support of Mexican Government (SIP-IPN 20061299 and CONACyT R420219-A, 50206) for the second author.

A. Gelbukh and C.A. Reyes-Garcia (Eds.): MICAI 2006, LNAI 4293, pp. 27–37, 2006.

the Pre-conceptual Schemas as a KR framework. Section 5 presents a case study based on Pre-conceptual Schemas in order to automatically acquire UML diagrams and compares Pre-conceptual Schemas with CGs. Section 6 concludes the paper.

2 Overview of Knowledge Representation

Sowa [1] defined KR as "the application of logic and ontology to the task of constructing computable models for some domain". In KR, a major concern is computational tractability of knowledge to reach automation and inference. The field of KR is usually called "Knowledge Representation and Reasoning", because KR formalisms are useless without the ability to reason on them [1].

A comprehensive description of KR can be found in [1]; a discussion of relationships between KR and Ontologies, in [2]. The major paradigms in KR are as follows.

- *Semantic networks* are used as a graphical paradigm, equivalent to some logical paradigms. They are useful for hierarchical representation. Nowadays, a number of graphs formalisms are based on the syntax of semantic networks, for example Conceptual Graphs [3]. Semantic networks are unstructured.
- *Frames* are templates or structured arrays to be filled with information. Frames can be considered as "structured" semantic networks, because they use data structures to store all structural knowledge about a specific object in one place. Object-oriented descriptions and class-subclass taxonomies are examples of frames.
- *Production rules* are hybrid procedural-declarative representations used in expert systems; many declarative languages are based on this paradigm. The reasoning process can be automatically traced in a controlled natural language [19].
- *Predicate logic* is based on mathematics and can be used as a reasoning mechanism for checking the correctness of a group of expressions. Programming languages such as PROLOG are logic-based.

Sowa [1] discusses major KR formalisms such as rules, frames, semantic networks, object-oriented languages (for example, Java), Prolog, SQL, Petri networks, and the Knowledge Interchange Format (KIF). All these representations are based on one or several of the mentioned paradigms. In particular, KIF has emerged as a standard model for sharing information among knowledge-based applications. KIF is a language designed to be used in knowledge exchange among disparate computer systems (created by different programmers, at different times, in different languages, etc.) [4].

3 State-of-the-Art in KR-Based Requirements Elicitation

According to Leite [5], "*Requirements analysis is a process in which 'what is to be done' is elicited and modelled. This process has to deal with different viewpoints, and it uses a combination of methods, tools, and actors. The product of this process is a model, from which a document, called requirements, is produced.*" Requirements Elicitation (RE) is a difficult step in the software development process. Viewpoints reported by Leite are associated with several Stakeholders—people with some concern in software development—and are difficult to collect for Analysts: Stakeholders are committed with domain discourse, while Analysts are concerned with modelling languages and technical knowledge. This is a cause for many miscommunication problems.

Some RE projects have used KR for solving such miscommunication problems:

- *Frames* were employed by Cook *et al.* [6] for gathering information about RE problems. The frames were used for communication purposes and Stakeholder validation, but did not contribute to further automation in software development.
- *Logical languages* were used in ERAE [7, 8], RML [9, 10], Telos [11, 12], FRORL [13], and PML [14] projects. These languages require technical training for their use and elaboration, which Stakeholders do not have. Furthermore, KR languages are used only for representation and inference. They are not used for conversion to other standard specification formalisms, such as UML diagrams.
- *Controlled English* was used in CPE [15], ACE [16], and CLIE [17] projects. Again, it is not converted to other standard specification formalisms.
- *Conceptual Graphs* were used by Delugach and Lampkin [18] to describe requirement specifications. However, they use technical terminology (like "object" or "constraint") that the Stakeholder usually misunderstands.

As far as CGs are concerned as KR language, there are other problems:

- *They represent the specifications phrase-by-phrase.* This can lead to the repetition of a concept many times. To solve this problem, CG standard has proposed co-reference lines, but complex concepts can be spread across many CGs, and their behaviour can be difficult to validate.
- *Their syntax can be ambiguous.* Concepts can be either nouns or verbs or even entire graphs. Relationships can be either thematic roles or comparison operators. This can lead to multiple representations of the same phrase.
- *They represent mainly structural information.* For better expressiveness, we need a schema capable of representing both structural and dynamic properties.

4 Pre-conceptual Schemas: CG-Like Framework for Knowledge Representation

Design Goals. In order to solve the problems related to CGs mentioned in Section 3, a KR approach to obtaining UML diagrams should meet the following conditions:

- *Unambiguous rules* must be provided. Precise rules may map words to only one element of each resulting diagram.
- *Automated translation* from controlled language into a KR language and into UML Diagrams is to be possible.
- *Applicability to any domain* is expected, no matter how specific the domain is.
- *No pre-classification ontologies* are to be used.
- *Several UML diagrams* should be obtainable from the same source.
- *Use of a common KR formalism*, no matter what the target diagram is.
- *The KR formalism must be an integration* of all the target diagrams.

Pre-conceptual Schemas are proposed as a KR formalism for automatically obtaining of UML Diagrams that is aimed at satisfying these requirements.

The Term *Pre-conceptual.* This term was coined by Heidegger [20], referring to a previous knowledge about a concept. Piaget [21], in his Stage Theory, distinguishes a pre-conceptual stage, at which children have a certain understanding of class membership and can divide their internal representations into classes.

In software development, Analyst builds Conceptual Schemas based on the Stakeholder discourse. Analyst performs an *analysis* to find the ideas behind the discourse and internally in his or her mind depicts something like a *pre-concept* of the Conceptual Schema. Following this idea, the proposed framework may build a KR description of the Stakeholder discourse. Thus the term *Pre-conceptual Schema.*

Syntax and Semantics. Pre-conceptual Schemas (PS) use a notation reminiscent of that of Conceptual Graphs (CG), with certain additional symbols representing dynamic properties. A Pre-conceptual Schema is a (not necessarily connected) labelled digraph without loops and multiple arcs, composed of the nodes of four types connected by the arcs of two types shown in Figure 1, with the following restrictions:

Topology

- A *connection* arc connects a concept to a relationship or vice versa.
- An *implication* arc connects a dynamic relationship or conditional to a dynamic relationship.
- Every *concept* has an incident arc (which is of connection type, going to or from a relationship).
- A *dynamic relationship* has exactly one incoming and one outgoing connection arcs (incident to concepts; it can have any number of incident implication arcs).
- A *structural relationship* has exactly one incoming and one or more outgoing arcs (of connection type, incident to concepts).
- A *conditional* has no incoming arcs and one or more outgoing arcs (of implication type, going into dynamic relationships).

Labels

- A *connection* arc has no labels.
- An *implication* arc has a label *yes* or *no* (if omitted, *yes* is assumed).
- A *concept* is labelled with a noun representing an entity of the modelled world. Different concepts nodes have different labels.
- A *dynamic relationship* is labelled with an action verb, e.g., *pay*, *register*. Different dynamic relationship nodes can have the same label.
- A *structural relationship* is labelled with a verb *is* or *has*.
- A *conditional* is labelled with a logical condition on values of certain concepts, e.g., *score > 3*. A description of the formal language for expressing such conditions is beyond the scope of this paper.

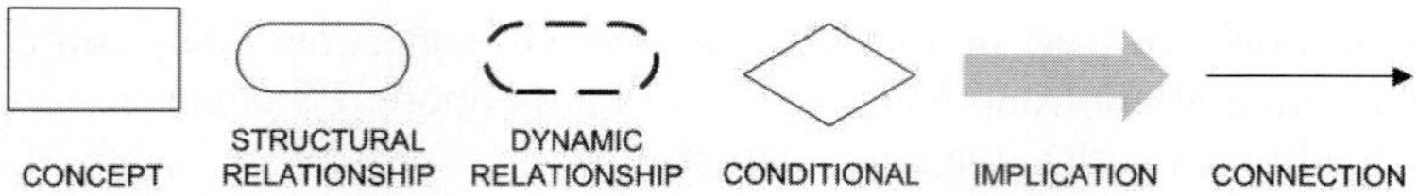

Fig. 1. Syntactic elements of Pre-conceptual Schemas

Semantics

- *Connections* express argument structure of relationships: roughly speaking, the subject and the object of the corresponding verb. A concept can participate in various relationships (*secretary → prints → report*, *secretary → calls → client*, *director → employs → secretary*; here *secretary* is the same node).
- *Concepts* represent people (*employee*, *secretary*), things (*document*, *bill*), and properties (*address*, *phone*). In requirement elicitation, one can very roughly imagine them as what later might become dialog boxes shown to the user of the given category or representing the given thing, or as fields in such boxes.
- *Structural relationships* express class hierarchy (*secretary* is an *employee*), properties (*employee* has *phone*), part-whole relationships (*car* has *motor*), etc. One relationship node can only have one subject and one object (*secretary → prints → report*, *accountant → prints → bill*; these are two different *print* nodes). In requirement elicitation, one can roughly imagine the properties as text field or links on the dialog boxes corresponding to their owners.
- *Dynamic relationships* express actions that people can perform (*secretary* can *register* the *bill*). In requirement elicitation, one can roughly imagine them as buttons that the users of the software can press to perform the corresponding actions.
- *Conditionals* represent prerequisites to perform an action. In requirements elicitation, one can roughly imagine them as enabling or disabling the corresponding buttons, depending on whether a condition is true (accountant can pay a bill after the bill has been registered) or some another action has been performed (*accountant* can *pay* a *bill* only if secretary has *registered* the *bill*).
- *Implications* arc has a label *yes* or *no* (if omitted, *yes* is assumed). It represents logical implication between events.

Comparison of Pre-conceptual Schemas and Conceptual Graphs. While the syntax and semantics of Pre-conceptual schemes strongly resemble those of Conceptual Graphs, there are some important differences.

- PS concepts differ from CG concepts in that CG concepts can be nouns, verbs or graphs. PS concepts are restricted to nouns from the Stakeholder's discourse.
- PS relationships differ from CG relationships in that the latter can be nouns (for example, thematic roles), attributes, and operators. PS relationships are restricted to verbs from the Stakeholder's discourse. There are two kinds of PS relationships:
  - Structural relationships (denoted by a solid line) correspond to structural verbs or permanent relationships between concepts, such as *to be* and *to have*.
  - Dynamic relationships (denoted by a dotted line) correspond to dynamic verbs or temporal relationships between concepts, such as *to register*, *to pay*, etc.
- PS implications are cause-and-effect relationships between dynamic relationships.
- PS conditionals are preconditions—expressed in terms of concepts—that trigger some dynamic relationship.

- PS connections are used in a similar way to CG connections: they can connect a concept with a relationship and vice versa. Furthermore, PS connections can connect a conditional with a dynamic relationship.

Some differences between PS and CG can be noted from Figures 3 and 4 below:

- The Conceptual Graph in Figure 4 is one of the possible CGs that can be obtained. The syntax of CG can derive more than one representation. In contrast, PS in Figure 3 is the only possible representation that can be obtained from the given UN-Lencep specification.
- Concepts are repeated in CG because every CG tries to represent a sentence. In PS, a concept is unique and it is possible to find all the relationships it participates in.
- In CG, there is no difference between the concepts like *assess* and *grade_mark*, because representation is the same in both cases. In PS, *assess* is a dynamic relationship, while *grade_mark* is a concept.
- In CG, verbs such as *have* and *assess* have the same representation (an agent and a theme). In PS these verbs have different representations: *have* is a structural relationship and *assess* is a dynamic relationship.
- Stakeholder validation of the obtained PS is easier than CG validation, because relationships like *agent* and *theme* are not present in UN-Lencep specification.
- If we use CG for representing Stakeholder's discourse as in [18], we need words like *attribute* and *constraint*, which belong to software discourse. In PS, we only need words from the UN-Lencep specification.

UN-Lencep Language. A subset of natural language, the Controlled Language called UN-Lencep (acronym of a Spanish phrase for *National University of Colombia—Controlled Language for Pre-conceptual Schema Specification*) is defined in such a way that simplifies automatic obtaining of Pre-conceptual Schemas from a discourse. Unrestricted natural language is very complex and has many linguistic irregularities and phenomena difficult to tackle computationally—such as anaphora, syntactic ambiguities, etc.—that make it difficult to obtain PS elements from a text. However, if the Stakeholder is capable to express his or her ideas in a simpler subset of natural language, PS can be directly obtained from such a discourse.

Figure 2 shows the basic syntax of UN-Lencep, and Table 1 shows equivalences for the basic specification of UN-Lencep. In the table, the left-hand side column shows the formal elements expressed by the controlled natural language expressions shown in the right-hand side.

Rules for Obtaining UML Diagrams. PS can be mapped in three UML diagrams: Class, Communication, and State Machine diagrams. To achieve this goal, we define 14 rules based on PS elements. Space limitations do not allow us to discuss or even list here all those rules, but following are some examples of such rules:

- A source concept from a HAS/HAVE relationship is a candidate class.
- The source set of concepts and relationships from an implication connection is a candidate guard condition.
- Messages identified in communication diagrams—expressed in past participle—are candidate states for target object class.

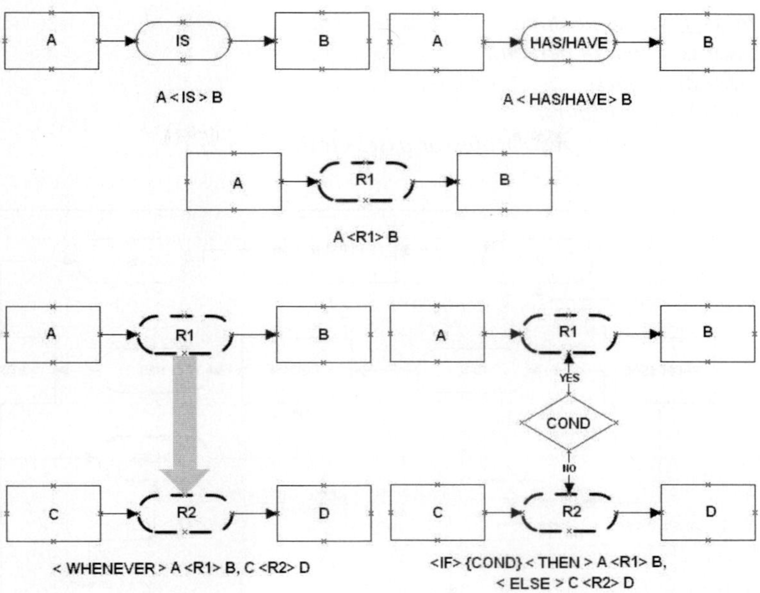

Fig. 2. Basic Syntax of UN–Lencep

Table 1. Equivalences for basic specification of UN–Lencep

Formal construction	Controlled natural language expression	
A <IS> B	A *is kind of* B	A *is a sort of* B
	A *is a type of* B	B *is divided into* A
A <HAS/HAVE> B	A *includes* B	B *is part of* A
	A *contains* B	B *is included in* A
	A *possesses* B	B *is contained in* A
	A *is composed by* B	B *is an element of* A
	A *is formed by* B	B *is a subset of* A
	B *belongs to* A	
<WHENEVER> A <R1> B, C <R2> D	*if* A <R1> B *then* C <R2> D	
	since A <R1> B, C <R2> D	
	after A <R1> B, C <R2> D	

5 Automatically Obtaining UML Diagrams from UN-Lencep Specifications Using Pre-conceptual Schemas

In the following example, we define a UN-Lencep specification and construct the Pre-conceptual Schema (Figure 3) and the Conceptual Graph representing the same discourse (Figure 4). Then we apply the rules described in Section 4.4 for obtaining three different UML diagrams (Figures 5 to 7). Here is an example of the discourse:

Student is a type of person.
Professor is a kind of person.
Professor has course.
Student belongs to course.
After student presents test, professor assess test.

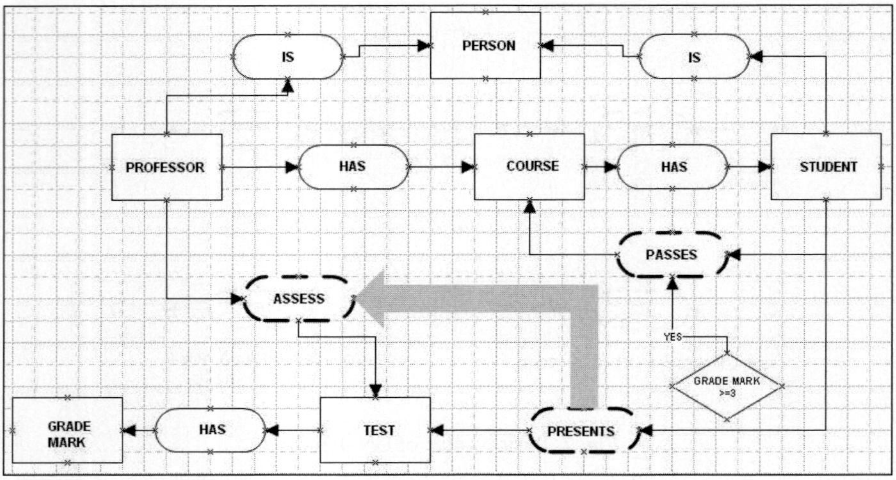

Fig. 3. PS of the example discourse

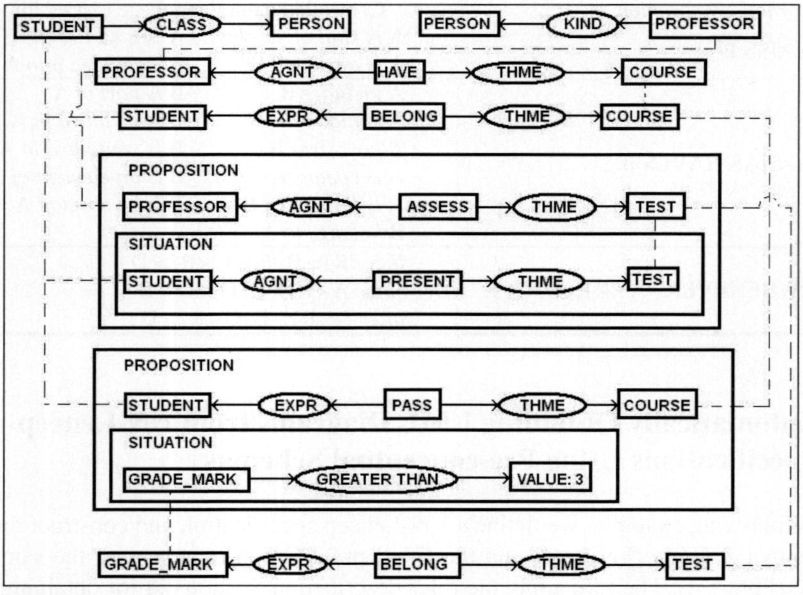

Fig. 4. Conceptual Graph of the example discourse. *Agnt* stands for Agent, *Thme* for Theme, Expr for Experiencer.

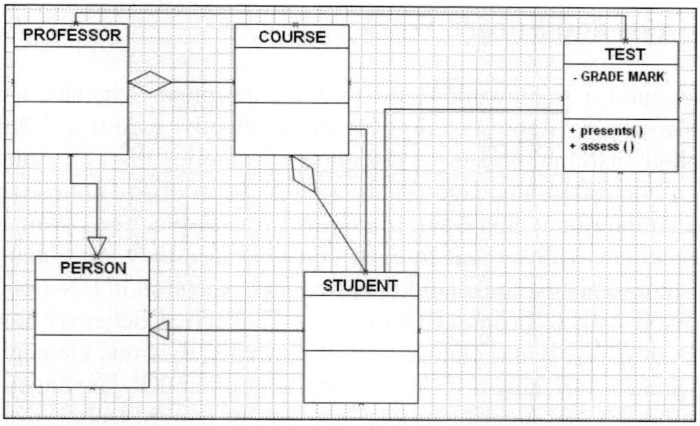

Fig. 5. Class Diagram obtained from PS

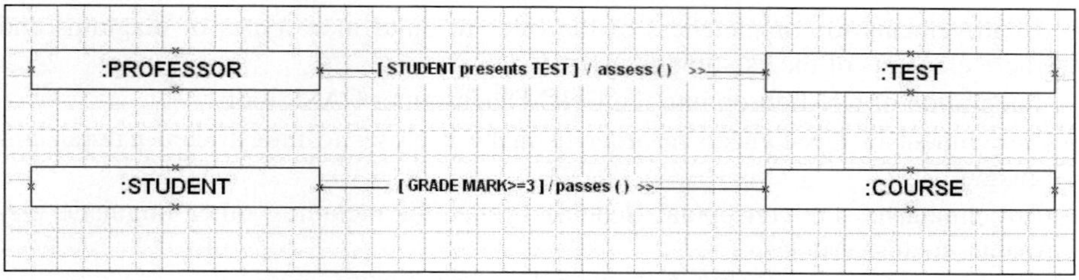

Fig. 6. Communication Diagram obtained from PS

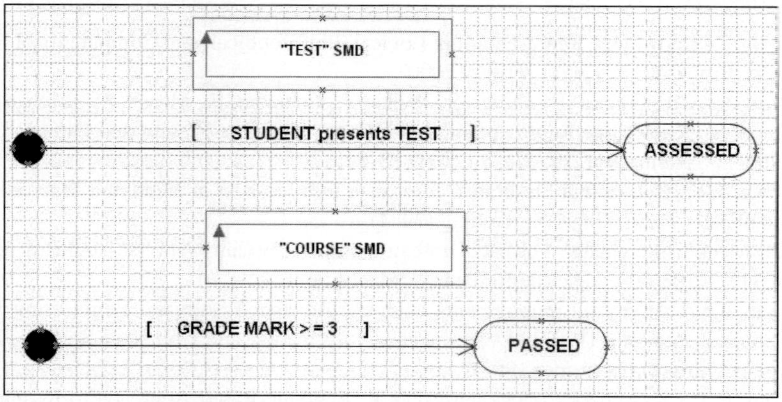

Fig. 7. State Machine Diagrams obtained from PS

If grade mark is greater than 3 then student passes course.
Grade mark belongs to test.

We have developed a CASE Tool named UNC-Diagrammer for constructing Pre-conceptual Schemas and transforming them into Class, Communication, and State Machine UML diagrams.

6 Conclusions and Future Work

We have presented a framework based in Pre-conceptual Schemas, a Conceptual-Graph-like Knowledge Representation for automatically acquiring UML Diagrams from controlled natural language discourse. Namely, PSs are obtained from UN-Lencep, a controlled language for the specification of Pre-conceptual Schemas. We have shown the use of this framework with an example. The obtained UML diagrams are consistent with respect to each other because they are obtained from the same PS that represents the Stakeholder's discourse expressed in UN-Lencep.

In comparison with Conceptual Graphs, Pre-conceptual Schemas have many advantages: unambiguous syntax, integration of concepts, dynamic elements, and proximity to the Stakeholder language. Compared with other KR languages for requirements elicitation, PS are superior in that they do not require technical training from the Stakeholder and there is a framework for automatically building UML diagrams.

Some work is still to be done to improve this KR formalism:

- Improvements to completeness of the rules to build more types of diagrams and more elements of the existing diagrams;
- Integration of UN-Lencep into the UNC-Diagrammer CASE tool;
- Enrichment of UN-Lencep in order to make it closer to unrestricted natural language;
- Enrichment of Pre-conceptual Schema syntax for including other linguistic elements, such as articles.

References

[1] Sowa, J.: Knowledge Representation: Logical, Philosophical, and Computational Foundations. Brooks/Cole, Pacific Grove (2000).

[2] Brewster, Ch., O'Hara, K., Fuller, S., Wilks, Y., Franconi, E., Musen, M., Ellman, J., and Shum, S.: Knowledge Representation with Ontologies: The Present and Future. IEEE Intelligent Systems, vol. 19, No. 1 (2004) 72–81.

[3] Sowa, J. F.: Conceptual Structures: Information Processing in Mind and Machine. Addison-Wesley Publishing Co., Reading (1984).

[4] Knowledge Interchange Format. Draft proposed American National Standard (dpANS) NCITS.T2/98-004. logic.stanford.edu/kif/dpans.html

[5] Leite, J.: A survey on requirements analysis, Advanced Software Engineering Project. Technical Report RTP-071, Department of Information and Computer Science, University of California at Irvine (1987).

[6] Cook S. C., Kasser J.E., and Asenstorfer J.: A Frame-Based Approach to Requirements Engineering. Proc. of 11th International Symposium of the INCOSE, Melbourne (2001).

[7] Dubois, E., Hagelstein, J., Lahou, E., Ponsaert F., and Rifaut, A.: A Knowledge Representation Language for Requirements Engineering. Proceedings of the IEEE, 74, 10 (1986) 1431–1444.

[8] Hagelstein, J.: Declarative Approach to Information Systems Requirements. Knowledge Based Systems 1, 4 (1988) 211–220.

[9] Greenspan. S.: Requirements Modeling: A Knowledge Representation Approach to Software Requirements Definition. PhD thesis, Dept. of Computer Science, University of Toronto (1984).

[10] Greenspan, S., Mylopoulos, J., and Borgida, A.: On Formal Requirements Modelling Languages: RML Revisited. IEEE Computer Society Press, Proceedings of the Sixteenth Intl. Conf. on Software Engineering, Sorrento (1994) 135–148.

[11] Mylopoulos, J., Borgida, A., Jarke, M., and Koubarakis, M.: Telos: Representing Knowledge about Information Systems. Transactions on Information Systems 8, No. 4 (1990). 325–362.

[12] Jeusfeld, M.: Change Control in Deductive Object Bases. INFIX Pub, Bad Honnef (1992).

[13] Tsai, J., Weigert, Th., and Jang, H.: A Hybrid Knowledge Representation as a Basis of Requirement Specification and Specification Analysis. IEEE Transactions on Software Engineering, 18, No. 12 (1992). 1076–1100.

[14] Ramos, J. J. PML–A modeling language for physical knowledge representation. Ph.D. Thesis, Universitat Autònoma de Barcelona (2003).

[15] Pulman, S.: Controlled Language for Knowledge Representation. Proceedings of the First International Workshop on Controlled Language Applications, Leuven (1996) 233–242.

[16] Fuchs, N. E. and Schwitter, R.: Attempto Controlled English (ACE). Proceedings of the First International Workshop on Controlled Language Applications, Leuven (1996).

[17] Polajnar, T., Cunningham, H., Tablan, V. and Bontcheva, K.: Controlled Language IE Components Version 1. EU–IST Integrated Project (IP) IST–2003–506826 SEKT, D2.2.1 Report, Sheffield (2006).

[18] Delugach, H. and Lampkin, B.: Acquiring Software Requirements As Conceptual Graphs. Proceedings of the Fifth International Symposium on Requirements Engineering, Los Alamitos (2001).

[19] Alonso-Lavernia, M., A. De-la-Cruz-Rivera, G. Sidorov. *Generation of Natural Language Explanations of Rules in an Expert System*. LNCS N 3878, Springer, 2006, 311-314.

[20] Heidegger. M.: Protokoll zu einem Seminar über den Vortrag "Zeit und Sein". Zur Sache des Denkens, Tübingen (1976) 34.

[21] Piaget, J.: The origins of intelligence in children (2nd ed.). New York: International Universities Press (1952).

A Recognition-Inference Procedure for a Knowledge Representation Scheme Based on Fuzzy Petri Nets

Slobodan Ribarić[1] and Nikola Pavešić[2]

[1] Faculty of Electrical Engineering and Computing, University of Zagreb, Unska 3, 10000 Zagreb, Croatia
slobodan.ribaric@zemris.fer.hr

[2] Faculty of Electrical Engineering, University of Ljubljana, Tržaška c. 25, 1000 Ljubljana, Slovenia
nikola.pavesic@fe.uni-lj.si

Abstract. This paper presents a formal model of the knowledge representation scheme KRFP based on the Fuzzy Petri Net (FPN) theory. The model is represented as an 11-tuple consisting of the components of the FPN and two functions that give semantic interpretations to the scheme. For the scheme a fuzzy recognition-inference procedure, based on the dynamical properties of the FPN and the inverse –KRFP scheme, is described in detail. An illustrative example of the fuzzy recognition algorithm for the knowledge base, designed by the KRFP, is given.

Keywords: Fuzzy Petri Net, knowledge representation, inference procedure, recognition.

1 Introduction

The main component of an intelligent agent is its knowledge base [1]. A knowledge base is an abstract representation of a working environment or real world in which the agent (or agents) has to solve tasks. One of the central problems of artificial intelligence is the development of a sufficiently precise and efficacious notation for the knowledge representation, called a knowledge representation scheme (KRS). The major classes of KRS, according to the taxonomy based on object-relationship, the true assertion about states and state-transformations criteria, are network, logical and procedural schemes, as well as schemes based on the frame theory.

The main inference procedures, as the act of automatic reasoning from factual knowledge, in the network-based knowledge representation schemas are: inheritance, intersection search and recognition.

Inheritance is a form of reasoning that allows an agent to infer the properties of a concept on the basis of the properties of its ancestors in the network hierarchical structure [2]. An inference procedure, called the intersection search [3], allows relationships to be found among facts by "spreading activities" in semantic networks. The recognition is the dual of the inheritance problem.

A. Gelbukh and C.A. Reyes-Garcia (Eds.): MICAI 2006, LNAI 4293, pp. 38–48, 2006.

Agents deal with vague or fuzzy information in many real-world tasks. In order to properly represent real-world knowledge and support fuzzy-knowledge representation, reasoning, learning and decision making, the fuzzy knowledge schemes based on Fuzzy Petri Nets (FPNs) were developed. Looney [4] and Chen et al. [5] have proposed FPN for rule-based decision making; Scarpelli et al. [6] have described a reasoning algorithm for a high-level FPN; Chen [7] has introduced a Weight FPN model for rule-based systems; Li and Lara-Rosano [8] have proposed a model based on Adaptive FPN, which is implemented to do knowledge inference, but also it has a learning ability; Ha et al. [12] proposed a new form of knowledge representation and reasoning based on the weighted fuzzy production rules; Ke et al. defined [13] an inference mechanism for G-nets; Lee et al. [14] introduced a reasoning algorithm based on possibilistic Petri Nets as mechanism that mimics human inference.

In this paper a formal model of the network knowledge representation scheme KRFP based on a FPN theory is proposed. An original fuzzy recognition-inference procedure is described in detail.

2 A Knowledge Representation Scheme Based on Fuzzy Petri Nets

The knowledge representation scheme named KRFP (Knowledge Representation Scheme based on the Fuzzy Petri Net theory) is defined as 11-tuple:

$$\text{KRFP} = (P, T, I, O, M, \Omega, \mu, f, c, \alpha, \beta),$$

where $P, T, I, O, M, \Omega, \mu, f$ and c are components of a generalized FPN as follows:

$P = \{p_1, p_2, ..., p_n\}$ is a finite set of places,
$T = \{t_1, t_2, ..., t_m\}$ is a finite set of transitions,
$P \cap T = \emptyset$,
$I : T \to P^\infty$ is an input function, a mapping from transitions to bags of places,
$O : T \to P^\infty$ is an output function, a mapping from transitions to bags of places,
$M = \{m_1, m_2, ..., m_r\}$, $1 \le r < \infty$, is a set of tokens,
$\Omega : P \to \mathcal{P}(M)$ is a mapping, from P to $\mathcal{P}(M)$, called a distribution of tokens, where $\mathcal{P}(M)$ denotes the power set of M. By ω_0 we denote the initial distribution of tokens in places of the FPN.
$\mu : P \to N$ is a marking, a mapping from places to non-negative integers N. A mapping μ can be represented as an n-component vector $\boldsymbol{\mu} = (\mu_1, \mu_2, ..., \mu_n)$, where n is a cardinality of the set P. Obviously, $\mu(p_i) = \mu_i$ and $\mu(p_i)$ denotes the number of tokens in the place p_i. An initial marking is denoted by $\boldsymbol{\mu}_0$.
$f : T \to [0, 1]$ is an association function, a mapping from transitions to real values between zero and one.
$c : M \to [0, 1]$ is an association function, a mapping from tokens to real values between zero and one.

The complete information about the token m_i is given by a pair $(p_j, c(m_i))$, where the first component specifies the location of the token, and the second one its value.

The bijective function $\alpha : P \rightarrow D$ maps a set of places P into a set of concepts D. The set of concepts D consists of the formal objects used for representing objects and facts from the agent's world. The elements from $D = D_1 \cup D_2 \cup D_3$ are as follows: elements that denote classes or categories of objects and represent higher levels of abstraction (D_1), elements corresponding to individual objects as instances of the classes (D_2) and those elements representing intrinsic properties of the concepts or values of these properties (D_3).

The surjective function $\beta : T \rightarrow \Sigma$ associates a description of the relationship among facts and objects to every transition $t_i \in T;\ i = 1, 2, ..., m$. The set $\Sigma = \Sigma_1 \cup \Sigma_2 \cup \Sigma_3$ consists of elements corresponding to the relationships between concepts used for partial ordering of the set of concepts (Σ_1), the elements used to specify types of properties to which values from subset D_3 are assigned (Σ_2), and the elements corresponding to relationships between the concepts, but not used for hierarchical structuring (Σ_3). For example, elements from Σ_3 may be used for specifying the spatial relations among the objects. The functions α and β give semantic interpretations to the scheme.

The inverse function $\alpha^{-1} : D \rightarrow P$, and the generalized inverse function $\beta^{-1} : \Sigma \rightarrow \tau;\ \tau \subseteq T$ are defined in the KRFP scheme.

The knowledge scheme KRFP can be graphically represented in a similar way to the Petri nets: circles represent places, while bars are used for the transitions. The relationships from places to transitions and from transitions to places are represented by directed arcs. Each arc is directed from an element of one set (P or T) to an element of another set (T or P). The relationships between elements from P and T are specified by the input and output functions I and O, respectively. The tokens in the KRFP are represented by labelled dots: $\bullet\ c(m_i)$.

Denoting the places by elements of D, the transitions by elements of Σ and the values of the association function by f, the graphical representation of a knowledge base designed by the KRFP is obtained.

Tokens give dynamical properties to the KRFP, and they are used to define its *execution*, i.e., by firing an enabled transition t_j, tokens are removed from its input places (elements in $I(t_j)$). Simultaneously, new tokens are created and distributed to its output places (elements of $O(t_j)$). In the KRFP, a transition t_j is *enabled* if each of its input places has at least as many tokens in it as arcs from the place to the transition and if the values of the tokens $c(m_l),\ l = 1, 2, ...$ exceed a threshold value $\lambda \in [0, 1]$. The number of tokens at the input and output places of the fired transition is changed in accordance with the basic definition for the original PN [9], [10]. The new token value in the output place is obtained as $c(m_l) \cdot f(t_i)$, where $c(m_l)$ is the value of a token at the input place $p_j \in I(t_i)$ and $f(t_i)$ is a degree of the truth of the relation assigned to the transition $t_i \in T$.

Figure 1 illustrates the firing of the enabled transition of the KRFP. The inference procedures - inheritance, intersection search and recognition - defined for the KRFP, use its dynamical properties.

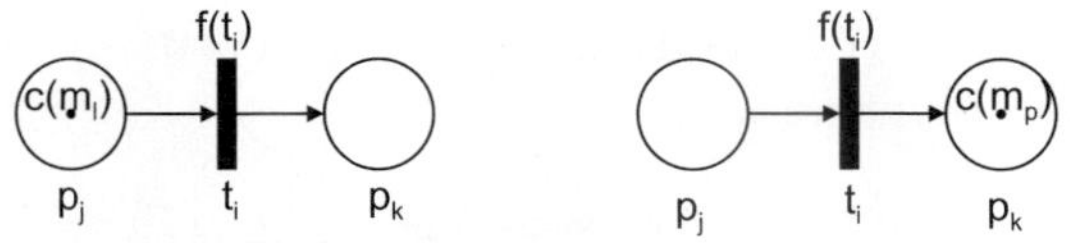

Fig. 1. Firing an enabled transition. *Left:* Before firing $c(m_l) > \lambda$. *Right:* After firing $c(m_p) = c(m_l) \cdot f(t_i)$.

Fig. 2. A simple scene with Fred and the elephant Clyde

Example 1

In order to illustrate the basic components of the KRFP, a simple example of the agent's knowledge base for a scene (Figure 2) is introduced.

The knowledge base designed by the KRFP $= (P, T, I, O, M, \Omega, \mu, f, c, \alpha, \beta)$, has the following components (Figure 3): $P = \{p_1, p_2, ..., p_{10}\}$; $T = \{t_1, t_2, ..., t_{13}\}$; $I(t_1) = \{p_1\}$; $I(t_2) = \{p_3\}$; $\cdots$; $I(t_{13}) = \{p_1\}$; $O(t_1) = \{p_2\}$; $O(t_2) = \{p_4\}$; $\cdots$; $O(t_{13}) = \{p_9\}$.

The set of tokens is $M = \{m_1, m_2, ..., m_r\}$, the initial distribution of tokens is $\omega_0 = \{\{m_1\}, \emptyset, ..., \emptyset\}$, where $c(m_1) = 1.0$ and $\emptyset$ denotes an empty set. The vector $\boldsymbol{\mu}_0 = (\mu_1, \mu_2, ..., \mu_{10}) = (1, 0, ..., 0)$ denotes that there is only one token in the place p_1. The function f is specified as follows: $f(t_1) = f(t_2) = f(t_3) = f(t_9) = f(t_{10}) = 0.9$; $f(t_4) = f(t_6) = 1.0$; $f(t_5) = f(t_7) = f(t_{13}) = 0.8$; $f(t_8) = f(t_{12}) = 0.6$; and $f(t_{11}) = 0.5$ (Figure 3). $f(t_i)$, $i = 1, 2, ..., m$ indicates the degree of our pursuance in the truth of the relation $\beta(t_i)$.

The set $D = D_1 \cup D_2 \cup D_3$ is defined as follows: $D_1 = \{$*Elephant, Human, Mammal, Biped, Quadruped*$\}$, $D_2 = \{$*Fred, Clyde*$\}$ and $D_3 = \{$*White, Soul, Kind_hearted*$\}$. The set $\Sigma = \Sigma_1 \cup \Sigma_2 \cup \Sigma_3$ is $\{is\_a, is\_not\_a\} \cup \{$ *has_colour, has_characteristic, has*$\} \cup \{$ *is_in_front, is_behind*$\}$. Functions $\alpha : P \to D$ and $\beta : T \to \Sigma$ are (Figure 3):

$$\begin{array}{ll} \alpha : p_1 \to Fred, & \beta : t_1 \to is\_a, \\ \alpha : p_2 \to Human, & \beta : t_2 \to is\_a, \\ \cdots & \cdots \\ \alpha : p_{10} \to Kind\_hearted, & \beta : t_{13} \to has. \end{array}$$

For the initial distribution of tokens, ω_0, the following transitions are enabled: t_1, t_9, t_{11} and t_{13}.

The inference procedures in the KRFP are based on a determination of the reachability set of the KRFP for the initial marking. The reachability set of the KRFP is defined in a similar way to the marked PN [9], [11]. The reachability

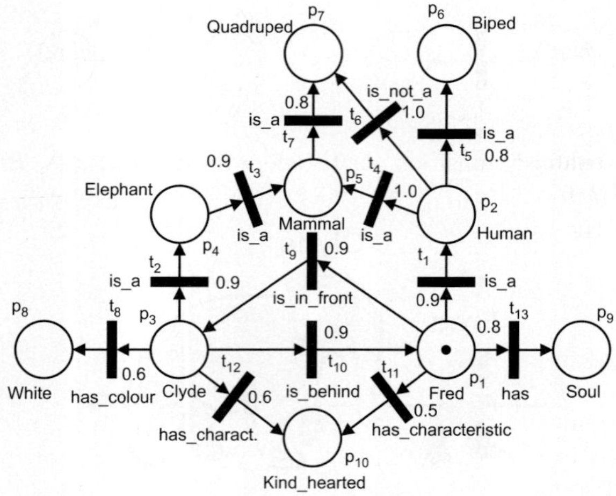

Fig. 3. The agent's knowledge base designed by the KRFP

tree RT(PN) is a graphical representation of the reachability set. An algorithm to construct the reachability tree is given in [9].

The reachability tree of the KRFP consists of nodes $(p_j, c(m_i))$, $j = 1, 2, ..., n$ and $i = 1, 2, ...$ for which $\mu(p_j) \geq 0$, and of the directed arcs labelled by t_k and $f(t_k)$. The labelled arc is directed to the node *successor*, which is the element of the immediate reachability set [5] for the place p_j. In order to simplify the notation in the recognition algorithm the nodes in the recognition tree are denoted by vectors in the form $\boldsymbol{\pi} = (\pi_1, \pi_2, ..., \pi_n)$, where $\pi_i = 0$ if $\mu(p_i) = 0$, and $\pi_i = c(m_k)$, where $c(m_k)$ is the second component of the pair $(p_i, c(m_k))$ and $\mu(p_i) > 0$.

The reachabilty tree for the inverse scheme –KRFP, which is used in the recognition procedure, will be illustrated in Section 3.

3 Fuzzy Recognition

The recognition in a knowledge representation scheme can be viewed as a general form of pattern matching. The fuzzy recognition in the KRFP can be described as follows:

Initialization: A set of the properties S of an unknown concept X is given, where it is not necessary that $X \in D$. $S = S_1 \cup S_2$, where S_1 is a set consisting of pairs (s_i, d_i), where s_i can be an element of $D_1 \cup D_2$ and $d_i \in [1, 0]$ is the degree of a user's assurance that the unknown concept X has the property s_i. In this case the function α^{-1} is defined for s_i, but if $s_i \notin D_1 \cup D_2$, then the function α^{-1} is not defined for s_i. The elements in S_2 have the form $(relationship, (s_i, d_i))$. Usually, the relationship is from Σ_3 and allows recognition based on the relative spatial position of concepts, but in general it is possible that relationship is not an element of Σ, because we deal with unknown concepts.

Action: Search for the concept in the KRFP that best matches the properties in the set S. The search is based on local properties and the properties that are inherited from the higher levels of the knowledge base. The recognition-inference procedure in the scheme KRFP is based on an inverse scheme –KRFP and a slightly modified definition of the enabled transition, as well as a modification of the association function c. The inverse –KRFP is obtained by interchanging the positions of the input I and the output O functions in the 11-tuple:

$$\text{–KRFP} = (P, T, O, I, M, \Omega, \mu, f, c_r, \alpha, \beta), \quad \text{where } c_r : M \rightarrow [-1, 1].$$

The main reason for the modification of the association function c is the existence of elements in Σ that have the forms of an exception or a negation of a property (for example, *is_not_a*). The modification of the association function c is also reflected in the execution of the –KRFP. Firing an enabled transition t_i in the –KRFP (where t_i corresponds to an exception in the original scheme) results in a new value of the token at the output place (Figure 4):
$c_r(m_k) = -c_r(m_j) \cdot f(t_i)$, where $c_r(m_j)$ is the value of the token at the input place $p_j \in I(t_i)$ and $f(t_i)$ is the degree of truth of the relation assigned to the transition $t_i \in T$.

Figure 4 illustrates the firing of such a transition and applying this modification of the association function. The initial marking is $\boldsymbol{\mu}_0 = (1, 0)$ and the initial distribution of the tokens is $\omega_0 = \{\{m_1\}, \emptyset\}$; $c_r(m_1) = 1.0$; $f(t_i) = 0.8$; $\lambda = 0.1$; and the transition t_i is enabled. After firing the enabled transition t_i a new marking, $\boldsymbol{\mu}' = (0, 1)$, is obtained. The token in the output place has the value $c_r(m_2) = -c_r(m_1) \cdot f(t_i) = -0.8$.

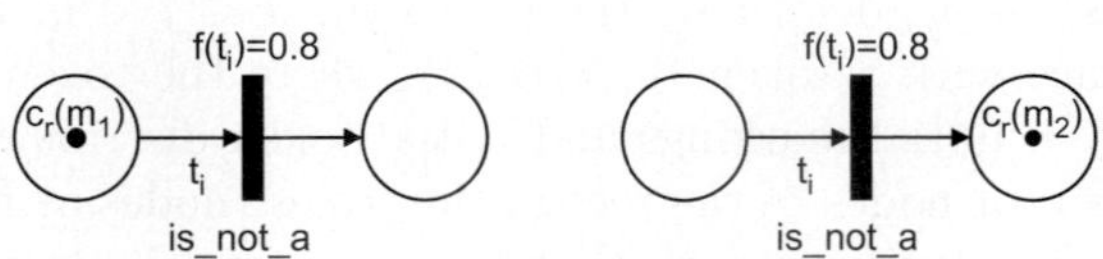

Fig. 4. Firing an enabled transition that corresponds to an exception. *Left:* Before firing. *Right:* After firing $c_r(m_2) = -c_r(m_1) \cdot f(t_i)$.

The existence of the tokens with negative values in the –KRFP also requires a redefinition of the enable transition:

(a) if the values of the tokens, $c_r(m_j) > 0$, $j = 1, 2, ..., k \leq m$, exceed the threshold value $\lambda \in [0, 1]$, the corresponding transition is enabled.

(b) if the values of the tokens $c_r(m_j) < 0$, $j = 1, 2, ..., k \leq m$, the corresponding transition is enabled when $|c(m_j)|$ exceeds the threshold value $\lambda \in [0, 1]$; $|x|$ denotes the absolute value of x. The reachability set of the –KRFP, called the recognition set, with an initial marking $\boldsymbol{\mu}_0$ and initial distributions of the tokens ω_0, is defined in a similar way to the reachability set of the Petri nets. It can be obtained by the algorithm given in [9], except for two important differences:

(c) the modification of the firing rule mentioned above is used,

(d) the transitions corresponding to relations in the subset Σ_3 cannot be fired regardless of the states of their input places.

A graphical representation of a recognition set is called the recognition tree.

For properties having the form (*relationship*, (s_i, d_i)), by means of selective firing (i.e., firing of the enabled transition corresponding to the specific relationship), the *recognition sub-tree* is obtained. Note that after firing the selected transition, the token at the output place is frozen and all the subsequent firings are disabled. A sub-tree consists of two nodes: the initial and the terminal. There are two exceptions in the construction of a recognition sub-tree in relation to the construction of a recognition tree:

(e) if the selected transition has the form of an exception or a negation of a property, then the value of the token in the output place is positive, i.e., $c_r(m_k) = |c_r(m_j) \cdot f(t_i)|$.
(f) the restriction expressed in **(d)** does not hold.

The recognition-inference algorithm for the KRFP is presented as follows:

Input: A set of properties S of an unknown concept and a depth of search L; ($1 \leq L \leq Deep$; where *Deep* is the maximum depth of the search), expressed by levels of the recognition tree are given. The threshold value λ is selected (usually, λ is chosen to be small enough, for example, 0.1).
Output: A concept from D that best matches the unknown concept X described by the set of properties S.
Step 1. For the scheme KRFP find the inverse scheme –KRFP.
Step 2. For all $(s_i, d_i) \in S_1$; $s_i \in D_1 \cup D_2$ and $d_i \in [0, 1]$, $i = 1, 2, ..., length \leq Card(S_1)$, where *Card* denotes a cardinality of a set, by means of the inverse function $\alpha^{-1} : s_i \rightarrow p_j$, determine the places p_j, $0 < j < n$. Each such place p_j becomes a place with a token $(p_j, c_r(m_i))$, where the token value $c_r(m_i)$ is d_i. It defines $b \leq n$ initial markings and initial token distributions. The initial markings are the root nodes of the recognition trees (nodes at level $l = 0$).
Step 3. For all the elements in S_2 that have the form (*relationship*, (s_i, d_i)), using the inverse functions, determine the initial markings and selective transitions for the construction of the recognition sub-trees: $\alpha^{-1}(s_i) = p_j$ and $\beta^{-1}(relationship) = \tau \subset T$. From the set τ select such a t_i for which $p_j \in I(t_i)$ in the –KRFP. Put the token into a place p_j – this is the initial marking of the sub-tree. The token value is determined on the basis of the user's specification of a degree of assurance for the concept $d_i : c_r(m_i) = d_i$. If there is no such a t_i for which $p_j \in I(t_i)$, the selective transition does not exist.
Step 4. Find L levels of all the recognition trees for b initial markings and initial token distributions.
Step 5. Find the recognition sub-trees defined in Step 3.
Step 6. For each recognition tree, for levels $l = 1, 2, ..., L$, compute the sum of the nodes (represented as vectors $\boldsymbol{\pi}$):

$$\mathbf{z}^k = \sum_{i=1}^{p} \boldsymbol{\pi}_i^k,$$

where p is the number of nodes in the k-th recognition tree.

Step 7. Compute the total sum of all the nodes for all the recognition trees:

$$\mathbf{Z} = \sum_{k=1}^{b} \mathbf{z}^k,$$

where b is the number of all the recognition trees.
Step 8. Compute the sum of the terminal nodes for all the recognition sub-trees:

$$\mathbf{A} = \sum_{j=1}^{r} \boldsymbol{\pi}_{sj},$$

where r is the number of all the recognition sub-trees and $\boldsymbol{\pi}_{sj}$ is the terminal node of the j-th sub-tree.
Step 9. Compute the sum $\mathbf{E} = \mathbf{Z} + \mathbf{A}$, where $\mathbf{E} = (e_1, e_2, ..., e_n)$.
Step 10. Find:

$$i^* = \arg \max_{i=1,\dots,n} \{e_i\}.$$

Step 11. Select p_i, where $i = i^*$, from the set P, and find $d_{rec} \in D$ using the function $\alpha : p_i \to d_{rec}$. The concept d_{rec} is the best match to the unknown concept X described by the set of properties S.

Example 2
Let us suppose that the unknown concept X is described by the following set of properties: $S = S_1 \cup S_2$, where
S_1=$\{(Quadruped, 0.9), (White, 0.6), (Kind\_hearted, 0.5), (Royal\_pet, 1.0)\}$, and
S_2=$\{(is\_on, (Earth, 1.0)), (is\_behind, (Fred, 0.8))\}$.
Find the concept in the KRFP knowledge base (Figure 3) that best matches the unknown concept X, for $L = 3$ levels of the recognitions trees and $\lambda = 0.1$.
Step 1. The inverse graph –KRFP is shown in Figure 5.
Step 2. $s_1 = Quadruped \in D_1 \cup D_2, \alpha^{-1}(Quadruped) = p_7$,
$s_2 = White \in D_1 \cup D_2, \quad \alpha^{-1}(White) = p_8$,
$s_3 = Kind\_hearted \in D_1 \cup D_2, \quad \alpha^{-1}(Kind\_hearted) = p_{10}$,
$s_4 = Royal\_pet \notin D_1 \cup D_2$, a function α^{-1} is not defined.
The initial markings are: $\boldsymbol{\pi}_0^1 = (0, 0, 0, 0, 0, 0, 0.9, 0, 0, 0)$,
$\boldsymbol{\pi}_0^2 = (0, 0, 0, 0, 0, 0, 0, 0.6, 0, 0)$, $\boldsymbol{\pi}_0^3 = (0, 0, 0, 0, 0, 0, 0, 0, 0, 0.5)$.
Step 3. For $(is\_behind, (Fred, 0.8)), \beta^{-1}(is\_behind) = \{t_{10}\}$ and $\alpha^{-1}(Fred) = p_1$, and $p_1 \in I(t_{10})$ in the –KRFP , the initial marking $\boldsymbol{\pi}_0^s$ for a sub-tree is $\boldsymbol{\pi}_0^s = (0.8, 0, 0, 0, 0, 0, 0, 0, 0, 0)$. The selected transition that will be fired is t_{10}. For $(is\_on, (Earth, 1.0))$ the functions α^{-1} and β^{-1} are not defined.
Step 4. Recognition trees $k = 1, 2, 3$; $(b = 3)$ for the depth of the search $L = 3$ are shown in Figure 6.
Step 5. The recognition sub-tree is shown in Figure 7.
Step 6. Compute $\mathbf{z}^k = \sum_{i=1}^{p} \boldsymbol{\pi}_i^k$; $k = 1, 2, 3$: For recognition tree 1, the nodes are (Figure 6):
$\boldsymbol{\pi}_1^1 = (0, 0, 0, 0, 0.72, 0, 0, 0, 0, 0)$; $\boldsymbol{\pi}_2^1 = (0, -0.9, 0, 0, 0, 0, 0, 0, 0, 0)$;
$\boldsymbol{\pi}_3^1 = (0, 0.72, 0, 0, 0, 0, 0, 0, 0, 0)$; $\boldsymbol{\pi}_4^1 = (0, 0, 0, 0.64, 0, 0, 0, 0, 0, 0)$;

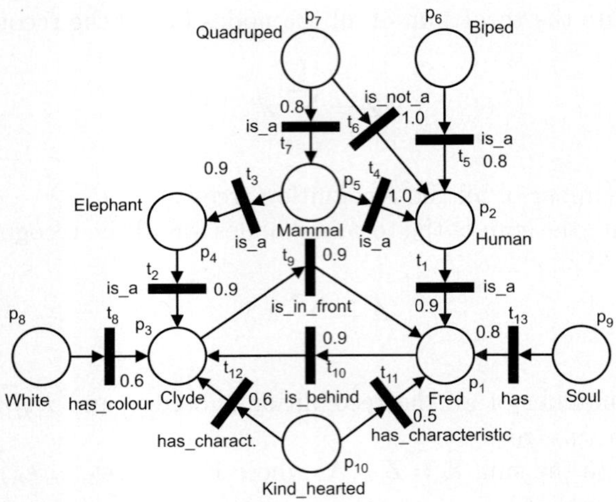

Fig. 5. The -KRFP inverse scheme (Example 2)

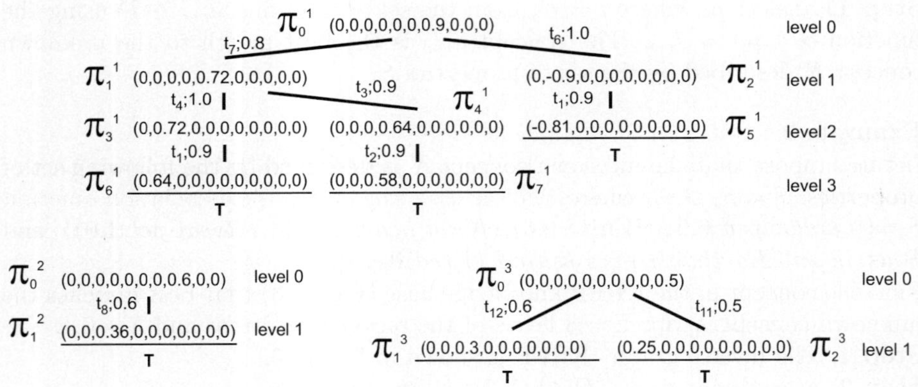

Fig. 6. The recognition trees

$\pi_5^1 = (-0.81, 0, 0, 0, 0, 0, 0, 0, 0, 0)$; $\pi_6^1 = (0.64, 0, 0, 0, 0, 0, 0, 0, 0, 0)$;
$\pi_7^1 = (0, 0, 0.58, 0, 0, 0, 0, 0, 0, 0)$, and their sum is
$\mathbf{z}^1 = (0, 0, 0, 0, 0.72, 0, 0, 0, 0, 0) + (0, -0.9, 0, 0, 0, 0, 0, 0, 0, 0) + \cdots$
$+ (0, 0, 0.58, 0, 0, 0, 1, 0, 0, 0) = (-0.17, -0.18, 0.58, 0.64, 0.72, 0, 0, 0, 0, 0)$.
For recognition tree 2, there is only one node $\pi_1^2 = (0, 0, 0.36, 0, 0, 0, 0, 0, 0, 0)$, and the sum is $\mathbf{z}^2 = (0, 0, 0.36, 0, 0, 0, 0, 0, 0, 0)$.
For recognition tree 3, the nodes are: $\pi_1^3 = (0, 0, 0.30, 0, 0, 0, 0, 0, 0, 0)$; $\pi_2^3 = (0.25, 0, 0, 0, 0, 0, 0, 0, 0, 0)$, and their sum is $\mathbf{z}^3 = (0.25, 0, 0.30, 0, 0, 0, 0, 0, 0, 0)$.
Step 7. Compute the total sum of all the nodes for all the recognition trees: $\mathbf{Z} = \mathbf{z}^1 + \mathbf{z}^2 + \mathbf{z}^3 = (0.08, -0.18, 1.24, 0.64, 0.72, 0, 0, 0, 0, 0)$.
Step 8. There is only one sub-tree: $\mathbf{A} = \pi_{s1} = (0, 0, 0.72, 0, 0, 0, 0, 0, 0, 0)$.
Step 9. Compute the sum: $\mathbf{E} = \mathbf{Z} + \mathbf{A}$.
$\mathbf{E} = (e_1, e_2, ..., e_{10}) = (0.08, -0.18, 1.96, 0.64, 0.72, 0, 0, 0, 0, 0)$.

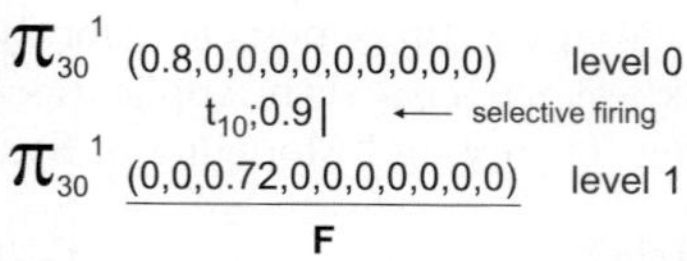

Fig. 7. The recognition sub-tree

Step 10. Find: $i^* = \arg\max_{i=1,\ldots,10}\{e_i\} = 3$.
Step 11. Select p_i, where $i = i^*$, from the set P, and find $d_{rec} \in D$ using the function $\alpha : p_i \rightarrow d_{rec}$. We get: $\alpha : p_i \rightarrow Clyde$.

According to the result of the recognition-inference procedure, the concept *Clyde* is the best match to the unknown concept X. Clyde is a quadruped, he is white and kind-hearted, and he is behind Fred (Figure 2). Is he a royal pet (probably yes!) or is he on the Earth (probably yes!), we explicitly don't know.

4 Conclusion

An original knowledge representation scheme KRFP based on the Fuzzy Petri Net theory is proposed. Recognition, as a dual of the inheritance problem, uses the inverse –KRFP that is obtained by interchanging the positions of the output and input functions in the 11-tuple specification of the KRFP. The recognition is based on the dynamical properties of the FPN, i.e., on firing-enabled transitions and changing the values of the tokens according to the association function f that specifies the degree of assurance for the relation assigned to the transitions. The KRFP was tested on numerous examples of the agent's knowledge bases of block world scenes as well as outdoor scenes. Fuzzy time-varying knowledge representation and spatial and temporal reasoning are our future research directions.

References

1. Russel, S., Norvig, P.: Artificial Intelligence, A Modern Approach, Prentice Hall, Inc., Upper Saddle River (1995)
2. Shastri, L.: Semantic Networks: An Evidential Formalization and Its Connectionist Realization, Pitman, London (1988)
3. Quillian, M. R.: Computers in Behavioral Science, Word Concepts: A Theory and Simulation of Some Basic Semantic Capabilities, Behavioral Science, No. 12. (1967) 410 – 430
4. Looney, C. G.: Fuzzy Petri Nets for Rule-Based Decisionmaking, IEEE Trans. on SMS, Vol. 18. No. 1. (1988) 178 – 184
5. Chen, S-M., Ke, J-S., Chang, J-F.: Knowledge Representation Using Fuzzy Petri Nets, IEEE Trans. on KDE, Vol. 2. No. 3. (1990) 311–319
6. Scarpelli, H., Gomide, F., Yager, R. R.: A Reasoning Algorithm for High Level Fuzzy Petri Nets, IEEE Trans. SMS, Vol. 15, No. 3. (1996) 282–294
7. Chen, S-M.: Weighted fuzzy reasoning using Weighted Fuzzy Petri Nets, IEEE Trans. on KDE, Vol. 14. No. 2. (2002) 386–397

8. Li, X., Lara-Rosano, F.: Adaptive fuzzy petri nets for dynamic knowledge representation and inference, Expert Systems with Applications, Vol. 19. (2000) 235–241
9. Peterson, J. L.: Petri Net Theory and Modeling of Systems, Prentice-Hall, Englewood Cliffs (1981)
10. Murata, T.: Petri Nets: Properties, Analysis and Applications, Proc. IEEE, Vol. 77. No. 4. (1989) 541–580
11. Ribarić, S.: Knowledge Representation Scheme Based on Petri Nets Theory, Int. Journal of Pattern Recognition and Artificial Intelligence, Vol. 2. No. 4. (1988) 691–700
12. Ha, M-H., Li, J., Li, H-J., Wang P.: A New Form of Knowledge Representation and Reasoning, Proc. of the Fourth Int. Conf. on Machine Learning and Cybernetics, Guangzhou, (2005) 2577–2582
13. Ke, Y-L.: Distribution Feeder Reconfiguration for Load Balancing and Service Restoration by Using G-Nets Inference Mechanism, IEEE Trans. on Power Delivery, Vol. 19. No. 3. (2004) 1426–1433
14. Lee, J., Liu, K. F. R., Chiang, W.: Modeling Uncertainty Reasoning with Possibilistic Petri Nets, IEEE Trans. on SMS, Vol. 33. No. 2. (2003) 214–224

Inference Scheme for Order-Sorted Logic Using Noun Phrases with Variables as Sorts

Masaki Kitano, Seikoh Nishita, and Tsutomu Ishikawa

Department of Computer Science, Takushoku University
815-1, Tatemachi, Hachioji-shi, Tokyo 193-0985 Japan

Abstract. This paper addresses an extended order-sorted logic that can deal with structured sort symbols consisting of multiple ordinary words like noun phrases, and proposes inference rules for the resolution process semantically interpreting the sort symbols word by word. Each word in a sort symbol can represent a general concept or a particular object, which is a variable or a constant having the word itself as the sort symbol. It may be a proper noun or variable. This paper also describes an application scheme of the proposed inference rules and an algorithm for judging the subsort relation between complex sort symbols.

1 Introduction

We are studying an intelligent consulting system that can acquire knowledge by conducting a discourse with users and answer their questions by using the knowledge it gains. In this system, natural language sentences have to be translated into an internal representation and be used for problem solving by using inference mechanisms. Therefore, the choice of knowledge representation scheme is a very important issue for the system. There are many schemes such as the frame system, semantic network, rule-based system, predicate logic, and their extensions. Recently, UNL [1], RDF [2] for Web applications, description logic [3] for various ontologies, etc., have been proposed from the viewpoint of universal utilization of knowledge. We basically selected an order-sorted predicate logic, after considering its capability of coupling taxonomic and axiomatic information and its superior inference based on resolution by unification.

Order-sorted logic is a theory that introduces a sort hierarchy into sorted logic. In an ordinary order-sorted logic [4,5], taxonomic information is statically expressed in a sort hierarchy and is not influenced by the axiomatic part of the knowledge base. That is, the sorts are only used when substitutions are computed during the unification process [6]. As such a loose coupling of taxonomic and axiomatic information is insufficient for some applications of natural language processing, in which a taxonomic hierarchy may be altered in the reasoning process. Beierle et al. proposed an extended order-sorted logic with close coupling of both types of information [7]. In their scheme, taxonomic information can be represented not only in the sort hierarchy but also in the axiomatic part of a knowledge base, and more powerful resolution can be realized by using their inference rules.

A. Gelbukh and C.A. Reyes-Garcia (Eds.): MICAI 2006, LNAI 4293, pp. 49–58, 2006.

However, Beierle et al.'s scheme is not sufficient for application systems that have a knowledge base in which the axiomatic part is represented with the structured information like a noun phrase as a sort symbol. Their scheme considers the whole sort symbol in a term to be a concept. That is, the internal structures of the sort symbols themselves are not taken into consideration when judging their subsort relation in the inference process.

We extended Beierle et al.' scheme so as to be able to deal with structured sort symbols. In the extended scheme, the resolution processes are executed by semantically interpreting sort symbols, which consist of multiple ordinary words, word by word. A sort symbol may be a noun phrase including variable, for example "car of [x: employee]". Such sort symbols can be used in both terms and predicate symbols. We propose new inference rules, which are modifications of the rules of Beierle et al., and show how to apply them to the resolution process.

2 Basic Idea of Our Inference Scheme

We first describe the supposed knowledge representation format and a desirable structure of a sort symbol, and then address the basic idea for inference. We also outline the inference rules proposed by Beierle et al.

2.1 Knowledge Representation

We use atomic formulas $P(t_1, t_2, \cdots\cdots, t_n)$ in a predicate logic to represent the knowledge base. Here, P is a predicate symbol and t_i is a term. When P is a verb, there are generally more than one term and the deep cases of Fillmore [8] are used as the terms. Using the sorted logic format, t_i is represented as follows.

$$t_i = x_i\!:\!S_i \ \mathit{or}\ c_i\!:\!S_i \qquad (1)$$

Here, x_i and c_i are variable and constant, respectively. They stand for an object (namely individual) and S_i is the sort symbol.

We use compound concepts consisting of multiple ordinary words (noun phrases) as the sort symbols in addition to simple concepts represented by a single word. Noun phrases have many kinds of structure. It is difficult to parse the all of them semantically without any ambiguity. In this paper, we deal with noun phrases in which certain nouns are connected by prepositions or conjunctions. The nouns may be modified by adjectives or other nouns. We will refer to these as compound words. That is, a sort symbol S is a compound concept G, which is a string of words represented as follows:

$$G = g_1 g_2 g_3 \cdots\cdots g_n \qquad (2)$$

Here, g_i is a compound word or a word (noun, preposition or conjunction). For example, a noun phrase like "letters from boys and girls in a big city to the computer company in the city" can be used as a sort symbol. In this case, each

g_i is respectively "letter", "from", "boy", "and", "girl", "in", "big-city", "to", "computer-company", "in" and "city". Articles are omitted.

Since words indicate concepts, g_i can stand for either a general concept or a particular object. In addition, there are four cases of particularity, namely, a variable or constant of the sort symbol g_i, and a proper noun or variable itself. Proper nouns are considered to be the names of objects, i.e., constants. That is, each g_i represents one of the following meanings.

- general concept of g_i, denoted by g_i. (ex. *city*)
- variable or constant with the sort symbol g_i, denoted by $[x{:}g_i]$ or $[c{:}g_i]$. (ex. $[x{:}city]$ or $[c{:}city]$)
- proper noun or variable represented by g_i, denoted by $[g_i:\top]$. (ex. $[Tokyo{:}\top]$ or $[x{:}\top]$)

Here, $\top$ is the top of a sort hierarchy, called the top sort. $sort(g_i) = g_i$ in the first two cases and $sort(g_i) = \top$ in the last case, when the sort of g_i is denoted by $sort(g_i)$. As G is a concept that can be a sort symbol, G can also become a predicate symbol. Such a literal is called a sort literal.

Sentences written in natural language are translated into the above-mentioned format. For example, "A boy bought a model of a ship" is translated into "$buy(c_1 : boy, c_2{:}model\ of\ ship)$" as the word "boy" and the noun phrase "model of ship" stand for a particular objects, and the word "ship" stands for the general concept implicitly. On the other hand, "A boy bought a model of the ship" is translated into "$buy(c_1 : boy, c_2 : model\ of\ [c_3 : ship])$", as the word "ship" stands for a particular object. While these two sentences represent particular facts, we also have to represent a general rule by using the above format. For example, "If a youth works for a company in a metropolis the youth is rich" should be translated into "$work(x_1{:}youth, x_2{:}company\ in\ [x_3{:}metropolis]) \rightarrow rich(x_1{:}youth)$". As mentioned above, the words g_i in G have different meanings. Therefore, we need an inference scheme that can deal with such complex sort symbols word by word by considering the internal structure, instead of the whole sort symbol.

Naturally, sentences can be represented in another format using an ordinary order-sorted predicate logic. For example, the last sentence can be represented as "$work(x_1 : youth, x_2 : company) \wedge locate(x_2 : company, x_3 : metropolis)) \rightarrow rich(x_1{:}youth)$". However, it is not easy to translate it into such a format automatically, considering the present state of parsing technology. We are studying a method of translating Japanese sentences into the above representation format by using natural language processing tools [9-12], in which one simple sentence is automatically translated into one atomic formula.

2.2 Basic Inference Scheme

The basic idea behind the inference process is that two parent clauses "$\neg A \vee B$", "$A' \vee C$" generate the resolvent "$B \vee C \vee \neg S$" even if the substitution in the unification between "A" and "A'" is not proper. Here, the literal "S" is such that the substitution becomes semantically proper in brief. On the other hand, the resolvent "$B \vee C$" is naturally generated if the substitution is proper, as in ordinary sorted logic where only substitution to the higher sorts from the subsort is admitted.

Beierle et al. formalized "S" as a conjunction of sort literals $SL(\sigma)$ as follows.

$$SL(\sigma) = \wedge\{S_i(\sigma(x)) \mid sort(\sigma(x)) \not\subseteq sort(x), \\ where\ x \in dom(\sigma), S_i = sort(x)\} \quad (3)$$

Here, σ is a substitution in unification, $sort(x)$ is the sort of the variable x, $sort(\sigma(x))$ is the sort of the substitution result, and $dom(\sigma)$ is the domain of the variables of σ. The notation $\subseteq$ indicates a subsort relation in which the right side is higher than the left side, or both sides are semantically the same. $\not\subseteq$ means the negation. We will call $SL(\sigma)$ an SL clause from now on. Beierle et al. proposed three inference rules using the SL clause below, called the EOS resolution rule (EOS), subsort resolution (SUB), and elimination rule (ER).

EOS:

$$\frac{\neg L_1 \vee A, L_2 \vee B}{\sigma(A \vee B) \vee \neg SL(\sigma)} \quad (4)$$

Here, L_1 and L_2 are literals having the same predicate symbol.

SUB:

$$\frac{\neg S_1(t_1) \vee A, S_2(t_2) \vee B}{\sigma(A \vee B) \vee \neg SL(\sigma)} \quad (5)$$

Here, $S_1(t_1)$ and $S_2(t_2)$ are sort literals having the relation $S_2 \subseteq S_1$, and σ is the substitution between term t_1 and t_2.

ER:

$$\frac{\neg S_1(t_1) \vee A}{\sigma(A) \vee \neg SL(\sigma)} \quad (6)$$

Here, $S_1(t_1)$ a sort literal, σ is the substitution on t_1, and $sort(\sigma(t_1)) \subseteq S_1$.

Below are some simple examples of applying these rules, supposing $A = B = 0$. For example, the SL clause "$expert(c : boy)$" is generated as the resolvent in EOS if $L_1 = wise(x : expert)$ and $L_2 = wise(c : boy)$. The SL clause is not generated and the resolvent becomes null if $L_1 = wise(x : expert)$ and $L_2 = wise(c : doctor)$ because "$doctor$"$\subseteq$"$expert$". In SUB, the SL clause "$elderly(c : adult)$" is generated as the resolvent if $S_1(t_1) = expert(x : elderly)$ and $S_2(t_2) = doctor(c : adult)$. In ER, "$expert(c : doctor)$" is eliminated and the SL clause "$elderly(c : doctor)$" becomes the resolvent if $S_1(t_1) = expert(x : elderly)$ and σ is $x = c : doctor$.

3 Extension of Inference Rules

In this section, we formalize extended inference rules and describe their application procedures. We also describe an algorithm to judge the subsort relation between the complex sort symbols used in terms and predicate symbols.

3.1 Extended Rules and Applications

(1) EOS Resolution Rule

Equation (4) is used as is. However, we have to pay attention to how to apply it. Let's define $S[x \text{ } or \text{ } c\!:\!g_i]$ as the compound sort symbol including a variable x or constant c of the sort symbol g_i. Supposing $L_1 = L(y\!:\!S_1[x_i\!:\!g_{1i}])$ and $L_2 = L(c\!:\!S_2[c_i\!:\!g_{2i}])$, the EOS resolution rule works with the following procedure.

i) Execute σ on the variables of the term except sort symbols, namely $y = c$.
ii) Generate the SL clause, such as $SL(\sigma) = S'_1[x_i\!:\!g_{1i}](c\!:\!S'_2[c_i\!:\!g_{2i}])$. Here, S'_1 and S'_2 are the results of applying σ to S_1 and S_2 respectively.
iii) Generate the resolvent with the SL clause.

In this procedure, notice that substitutions of variables (except the variables of σ) in sort symbols are not executed even if the substitutions are semantically proper. That is, c_i is not substituted in x_i, because such substitutions place excessive restrictions on the sort symbols. If sort symbols include the variables of σ, the substitution σ is applied on the variables in step ii). This can happen in literals with multiple terms.

For example, given $L_1 = wise(y : expert\ on\ [x : medicine])$, $L_2 = wise(c : doctor\ in\ [c_1 : hospital]$, and $A = B = 0$, the SL clause "$expert\ on\ [x : medicine](c\!:\!doctor\ in\ [c_1\!:\!hospital])$" is generated as the resolvent.

(2) Subsort Resolution

Equation (5) is modified as follows. This modified rule will be abbreviated as SUBp from now on.

SUBp:

$$\frac{\neg S_1(t_1) \vee A, S_2(t_2) \vee B}{\sigma\sigma_p(A \vee B) \vee \neg SL(\sigma\sigma_p) \vee \neg SLp(\sigma_p)} \tag{7}$$

σ_p and the SLp clause are added to equation (5). σ_p is executed on variables in sort symbol S_1 and S_2, and σ is the substitution of t_1 and t_2. SLp is the conjunction of sort literals generated with σ_p. Basically, this clause is the condition to $S_2 \subseteq S_1$ and is generated in a similar fashion to an SL clause. Section 4 describes the method of generating the SLp clause.

The subsort resolution rule works with the following procedure, supposing $S_1(t_1) = S_{11}[x_i\!:\!g_{1i}](y\!:\!S_{12})$ and $S_2(t_2) = S_{21}[c_i\!:\!g_{2i}](c\!:\!S_{22})$. Here, S_{12} and S_{22} may include variables or constants.

i) Execute σ_p on the variables in the predicate symbol S_1 and S_2, namely $x_i = c_i$.
ii) Generate the SLp clause, such as $SLp = g_{1i}(c_i : g_{2i})$. Stop the resolution if $S_2 \not\subseteq S_1$ after σ_p has been executed on them.
iii) Execute σ on the variables in t_1 and t_2 except sort symbols, namely $y = c$.
iv) Generate the SL clause, such as $SL(\sigma\sigma_p) = S'_{12}(c\!:\!S'_{22})$. Here, S'_{12} and S'_{22} are the results of applying σ_p to S_{12} and S_{22} respectively.
v) Generate the resolvent with the SLp clause and the SL clause.

Here, the method of judging the subsort relation in step ii) is described in section 3.2.

For example, if $S_1(t_1) = \mathit{politician\ in}\ [x_1 : \mathit{city}](y : \mathit{millionaire\ in}\ [x_1 : \mathit{city}])$, $S_2(t_2) = \mathit{councilor\ in}\ [\mathit{Tokyo} : \top](c : \mathit{doctor\ in}\ [c_1 : \mathit{hospital}])$, and $A = B = 0$, the SLp clause "$\mathit{city}(\mathit{Tokyo} : \top)$" and the SL clause "$\mathit{millionaire\ in}\ [\mathit{Tokyo} : \top](c : \mathit{doctor\ in}\ [c_1 : \mathit{hospital}])$" are generated as the resolvent.

(3) Elimination Rule

This rule is also modified in the same way as SUBp and is abbreviated as ERp.

ERp:

$$\frac{\neg S_1(t) \vee A}{\sigma_p\sigma(A) \vee \neg SL(\sigma_p\sigma) \vee \neg SLp(\sigma_p)} \tag{8}$$

Here, σ is a possible substitution in t and σ_p is the substitution between the predicate symbol S_1 and the sort symbol in $\sigma(t)$. SLp is the condition for $\mathit{sort}(\sigma(t)) \subseteq S_1$, and it is generated in the same way as the SUBp case (see section 4).

The elimination rule works with the following procedure, supposing $S(t) = S_1[x_i : g_{1i}](y : S)$. Here, suppose that $c : S_2[c_i : g_{2i}]$ is substitutable for y.

i) Execute a possible substitution σ on t, namely $y = c$.
ii) Execute σ_p on the variables in S_1 and $\mathit{sort}(\sigma(t))$ $(= S_2)$, namely $x_i = c_i$.
iii) Generate the SLp clause, such as $SLp = g_{1i}(c_i : g_{2i})$. Stop the resolution if $\mathit{sort}(\sigma(t)) \not\subseteq S_1$ after σ_p has been executed on them.
iv) Generate the SL clause, such as $SL(\sigma_p\sigma) = S'(c_i : g_{2i})$. Here, S' is the result of applying σ_p to S.
v) Repeat the above steps for the SL clause generated in step iv), if possible.
vi) Generate the resolvent with the SLp clause and the SL clause.

The judgment in step iii) is done in the same way as in the SUBp case. Step v) is necessary when the SL clause generated in step iv) includes variables.

For example, if $S_1(t_1) = \mathit{politician\ in}\ [x_1 : \mathit{capital}](y : \mathit{doctor\ in}\ [x_1 : \mathit{capital}])$, $A = 0$, and $c : \mathit{councilor\ in}\ [\mathit{Tokyo} : \top])$ is substitutable for y, the substitution result ("$\mathit{politician\ in}\ [\mathit{Tokyo} : \top](c : \mathit{councilor\ in}\ [\mathit{Tokyo} : \top])$") is eliminated and SLp clause "$\mathit{capital}(\mathit{Tokyo} : \top)$" and SL clause "$\mathit{doctor\ in}\ [\mathit{Tokyo} : \top](c : \mathit{councilor\ in}\ [\mathit{Tokyo} : \top])$" are generated as the resolvent.

3.2 Judgment of Subsort Relation

It is important to judge the subsort relations, $\mathit{sort}(\sigma(x)) \not\subseteq \mathit{sort}(x)$ in generating the SL clause, $S_2 \subseteq S_1$ in SUBp, and $\mathit{sort}(\sigma(t)) \subseteq S_1$ in ERp, because the SL cause is not generated and the resolutions themselves are not executed in SUBp or ERp if the above subsort relations are not satisfied. However, it is very difficult for current parsing technology to judge these relations when their sort symbols are compound concepts G like noun phrases.

Supposing that G's have the same meaning as the whole when they consist of the same words and have the same word order (namely, polysemy is ignored), we consider a judging method of the subsort relation between following two sort symbols.

$$G_a = g_{a1}g_{a2}\cdots\cdots\cdots g_{am}$$
$$G_b = g_{b1}g_{b2}\cdots\cdots\cdots g_{bn}$$

Let's set up a criterion for the subsort relation between words or compound words g_a and g_b. Suppose that $g_a{=}w_{a1}w_{a2}\cdots\cdots\cdots w_{ak}$, $g_b{=}w_{b1}w_{b2}\cdots\cdots\cdots w_{bl}$. Here, each w stands for a general concept or a proper noun. g is supposed to be a proper noun if at least one w is proper noun.

Criterion 1
$sort(g_a) \subseteq sort(g_b)$ if all the following conditions are satisfied.

- i) g_a and g_b have the same number of words, namely $k = l$.
- ii) Adjectives are not included in g_a and g_b.
- iii) Either (a) or (b) is satisfied.
  - (a) $sort(w_{ai}) \subseteq sort(w_{bi})$ $(i = 1, 2, \cdots, l)$, and g_b stands for general concept.
  - (b) Variables, constants or proper nouns are the same, when g_a and g_b stand for particular objects.

This criterion is based on the assumption that $sort(ab) \subseteq sort(cd)$ if $sort(a) \subseteq sort(c)$ and $sort(b) \subseteq sort(d)$, where xy is a compound word meaning a word y modified by a word x or vice versa. Condition i) comes from that it is difficult to decide semantic correspondence between every word if the g's do not have the same number of words. Condition ii) is necessary for the above assumption to be sound. An adjective is ambiguous on such a criterion that the character denoted by itself is decided. For example, "big company" is not necessarily a subsort of "big organization", although "company"$\subseteq$"organization". Condition iii)(a) is a generalization of the above assumption. It shows that g_a may implicitly stand for either a general concept or a particular object (namely, $g_a = [x : g_a]$ *or* $[c : g_a]$). The former is obvious. The latter is assured because general concepts mean connotations (or classes) for themselves and any objects (denoted by variables or constants) having them as sort symbols mean the denotations (or instances). Condition iii)(b) is obvious because the g's are different if they do not denote the same object.

Using criterion 1, the subsort relation between G_a and G_b is decided as follows.

Criterion 2
$sort(G_a) \subseteq sort(G_b)$ when all conditions below are satisfied.

- i) The number of the words is the same, namely $m = n$.
- ii) Particular prepositions like "except", "without", etc. (contrary to the above assumption) are not included in G_a, G_b.
- iii) $sort(g_{ai}) \subseteq sort(g_{bi})$ $(i = 1, 2, \cdots, n)$,

Condition ii) is necessary for the above assumption to be sound. That is, it is not sound in the compound concept including propositions that embrace the meaning of exception, exclusion, outside, etc. For example, "men except experts"$\subseteq$"men except doctors", although "doctor"$\subseteq$"expert". These words should be registered beforehand in the actual resolution process.

4 Generation of the SLp Clause

We describe a method of generating SLp and then show a simple example of applying our inference method.

4.1 Generating SLp

To put it briefly, the SLp clause is a condition for $S_2 \subseteq S_1$ in SUBp and $sort(\sigma(t)) \subseteq S_1$ in ERp as mentioned in section 3.1. Therefore, it is generated as a conjunction of sort literals on a similar condition to that of the criteria in section 3.2 as follows, supposing $G_a = S_2$ or $sort(\sigma(t))$, $G_b = S_1$.

SLp Generating Condition

i) As to corresponding g_{ai} and g_{bi}, either (a) or (b) is satisfied.
   (a) g_{ai} and g_{bi} stand for particular objects, and at least one is variable.
   (b) g_{bi} stands for a general concept, and g_{ai} stands for a particular object.
ii) As to a part except the words of i), $sort(G_a) \subseteq sort(G_b)$ in criterion 2 of section 3.2.

A resolution is not executed, that is, neither SUBp nor ERp is applied if this condition is not satisfied, because $S_2 \subseteq S_1$ and $sort(\sigma(t)) \subseteq S_1$ are never satisfied in that case.

When the above condition is satisfied, the SLp clause is generated as follows.

$$\begin{aligned} SLp(\sigma_p) = \wedge\{S_i(\sigma_p(x)) \mid sort(\sigma_p(x)) \nsubseteq sort(x), \\ where\ x \in dom(\sigma_p), S_i = sort(x)\} \\ \wedge\{g_{bk}(c_{ak}, x_{ak} or g_{ak}) \mid sort(g_{ak}) \nsubseteq sort(g_{bk})\} \end{aligned} \tag{9}$$

Here, σ_p is a substitution between the variables and constants in G_a and G_b. The first term in equation (9) represents the sort literals corresponding to the condition i) (a). This term is generated on σ_p in the same way as equation (3). The second term is a sort literal corresponding to condition i) (b). Thus, g_{bk} = general concept, g_{ak} =$[c_{ak} : g_{ak}]$, $[x_{ak} : g_{ak}]$, or $[g_{ak} : \top]$ (proper noun or variable). This term is the condition that the particular object g_{ak} belongs to the sort of the general concept g_{bk}. Notice that this is not substitution and is not included in σ_p. Thus, other literals are not influenced by it. Naturally, $SLp(\sigma_p) = null$ if $sort(\sigma_p(x)) \subseteq sort(x)$ and $sort(g_{ak}) \subseteq sort(g_{bk})$, as in the case of $SL(\sigma)$.

For example, $SLp(\sigma_p) = company(c : organization) \wedge metropolis(Tokyo : \top)$ when S_1 =“mail to [x:company] in metropolis”, S_2 =“letter to [c:organization] in [Tokyo:$\top$]”. On the other hand, $SLp(\sigma_p) = null$ when S_1 =“mail to organization in city” and S_2 =“letter to [c_1:company] in [c_2:metropolis]”, because $S_2 \subseteq S_1$ from the criteria in section 3.2. Resolution processes are executed in both cases. Naturally, when S_1 =“mail from organization in city” and S_2 =“letter to [c_1:company] in [c_2:metropolis]”, a resolution is not executed because $S_2 \nsubseteq S_1$ because of the different prepositions.

4.2 Inference Example

The inference process is executed as shown in Figure 1 when the knowledge base and the question are given as follows.

[Knowledge Base]
$work(x\!:\!youth, y\!:\!company\ in\ [z : metropolis]) \rightarrow rich(x\!:\!youth)$
$compony\ in\ [Tokyo\!:\!\top](Sany\!:\!\top)$
$work(Taro\!:\!\top, Sany\!:\!\top)$
$metropolis(Tokyo\!:\!\top)$
$boy(Taro\!:\!\top)$

[Question]
$rich(Taro\!:\!\top)?$

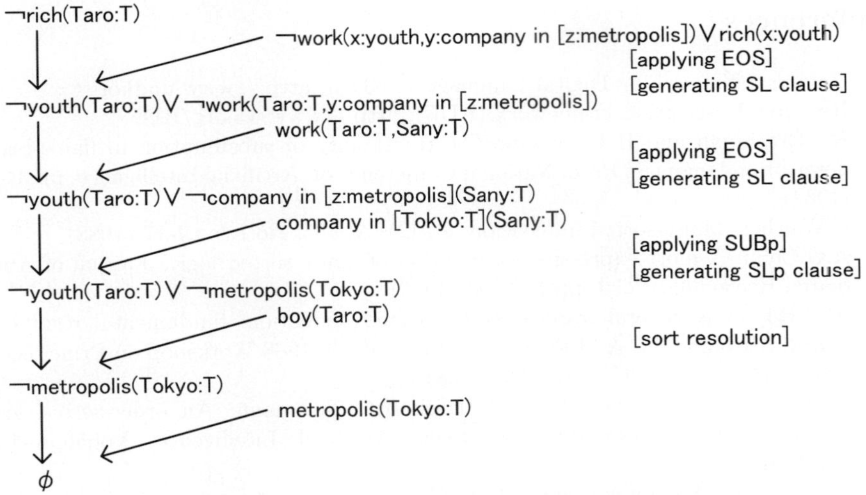

Fig. 1. An example of the inference process

EOS is applied in the first two steps, SUBp is applied in the third step, and the answer becomes "yes". The thesaurus [12,13] can be used to judge the subsort relations between words like "*boy*" ⊆ "*youth*". As shown in this example, we have created an inference that is able to deal with complex sort symbols word by word.

5 Conclusion

We discussed an extended order-sorted logic that can deal with structured sort symbols consisting of multiple ordinary words like noun phrases and proposed an inference method for the logic. Beierle et al.'s inference rules were modified in order to execute the resolution processes semantically interpreting the sort symbols word by word. Each word in a sort symbol can represent a general concept or a particular object. If it is the latter, each word may stand for a variable or constant having itself as a sort symbol or it may be a proper noun or variable itself. We also described how to apply the rules to the resolution process and how to judge the subsort relation between complex sort symbols.

We are developing an inference engine embodying the proposed scheme and are planning to apply it to a consulting system that can answer to questions by acquiring knowledge through dialogue with its users.

The proposed inference rules are sound and complete. It is proven by showing that the resolvents on our extended rules coincide with those obtained by semantically translating our representation to the ordinary format of order-sorted logic and then applying Beierle et al.'s rules to it. We will report the concrete proof later on.

References

1. Universal Networking Digital Language (UNDL), http://www.undl.org/
2. Resource Description Framework (RDF), http://www.w3.org/RDF/
3. R.J.Brachman and H.J.Levesque:The tractability of subsumption in flame-based description language, Proc. National Conference on Artificial Intelligence, pp.34-37 (1984)
4. C.Walther: Many-sorted unification, J.ACM Vol.35, No.1, pp.1-17 (1988)
5. A.G.Cohn: A more expressive formulation of many sorted logic, Journal of Automated Reasoning, Vol.3, pp.113-200 (1987)
6. A.M.Frisch: A general framework for sorted deduction: fundamental results on hybrid reasoning, in: A.M.Frisch, ed., Proceedings 1988 Workshop on Principles of Hybrid Reasoning, St. Paul, MN (1988)
7. C. Beierle,U.Hedtstück,U.Pletat,P.H.Schmitt,J.Siekmann: An order-sorted logic for knowledge representation systems, Artificial Intelligence, Vol.55,pp-149-191(1992)
8. C.J.Fillmore, P.Kiparsky and J.D.McCawley: The case for case, in Universals in linguistic theory, Holt, Rinehart and Winston (1968)
9. ChaSen, http://chasen.aist-nara.ac.jp/
10. Cabocha, http://cl.aist-nara.ac.jp/ taku-ku/software/cabocha/
11. Y.Matsumoto,K.Takaoka,M.Asahara,T.Kudo: Japanese sentence analysis by ChaSen and Cabocha-Using syntactic information for sentence role classification, Journal of Japanese Society for Artificial Intelligence, Vol.19, No.3, pp.334-339 (2004)
12. EDR dictionary, http://www.iinet.or.jp/edr/
13. G.A.Miler: WordNet: A lexical database for English, Comm. ACM, Vol.38, No.11, pp.39-41 (1995)

Answer Set General Theories and Preferences

Mauricio Osorio[1] and Claudia Zepeda[2]

[1] Universidad de las Américas, CENTIA,
Sta. Catarina Mártir, Cholula, Puebla, 72820 México
osoriomauri@gmail.com

[2] Universidad Tecnológica de la Mixteca, División de Estudios de Posgrado.
Huajuapan de Leon, Oaxaca, 69000 México
claudiaz@mixteco.utm.mx

Abstract. In this paper we introduce preference rules which allow us to specify preferences as an ordering among the possible solutions of a problem. Our approach allow us to express preferences for general theories. The formalism used to develop our work is Answer Set Programming. Two distinct semantics for preference logic programs are proposed. Finally, some properties that help us to understand these semantics are also presented.

Keywords: Logic Programming, Answer Set Programming, Preferences.

1 Introduction

Preferences can be used to compare feasible solutions of a given problem, in order to establish an order among these solutions or an equivalence among such solutions with respect to some requirements. In this paper we introduce preference rules which allow us to specify preferences as an ordering among the possible solutions of a problem. These rules use a new connective, $*$, called *preference operator*. The formalism used to develop our work is Answer Set Programming (ASP) [4]. ASP is a declarative knowledge representation and logic programming language. ASP represents a new paradigm for logic programming that allows us, using the concept of negation as failure, to handle problems with default knowledge and produce non-monotonic reasoning. Two popular software implementations to compute answer sets are DLV[1] and SMODELS[2].

Most research on ASP and in particular about preferences in ASP supposes syntactically simple rules (see for example [2,1,10]), such as disjunctive rules, to construct logic programs. This is justified since, most of the times, those restricted syntaxes are enough to represent a wide class of interesting and relevant problems. It could seem unnecessary to generalize the notion of answer sets to some more complicated formulas. However, a broader syntax for rules will bring some benefits. The use of nested expressions, for example, could simplify the task of writing logic programs and improve their readability. It allows us to write more

[1] http://www.dbai.tuwien.ac.at/proj/dlv/

[2] http://www.tcs.hut.fi/Software/smodels/

A. Gelbukh and C.A. Reyes-Garcia (Eds.): MICAI 2006, LNAI 4293, pp. 59–69, 2006.

concise rules and in a more natural way. The main contribution of this paper is the proposal of an approach to express problems with preferences using more general theories, called *preference logic* (PL) programs. We are proposing the only approach about preferences in ASP that allows us to express preference rules in terms of formulas instead of only literals. In our approach, a set of preferences is represented as a set of preference rules. The head of each preference rule corresponds to an ordered lists of formulas connected using the operator $*$. Each formula represents a particular preference option about something. The following example illustrates the representation of preferences using the approach that we are proposing [3].

Example 1. A television show conducts a game where the first winner is offered a prize of \$200,000, and the second winner is offered a prize of \$100,000. John wants to play, if possible. Otherwise he will give up. If he plays he wants to gain \$200,000 if possible; otherwise, \$100,000. He is told that he cannot win the first prize. So, John's preferences can be simply represented as the following two preference rules,

$$play * give\_up \stackrel{pr}{\leftarrow} .$$
$$gain(200,000) * gain(100,000) \stackrel{pr}{\leftarrow} play.$$

Example 1 also help us to illustrate the semantics of PL programs that we are proposing. Without considering John's preferences this problem has two possible solutions: $\{play, gain(100,000)\}$ and $\{give\_up\}$. Now, considering John's preferences and our intuition, we could have two possible scenarios for the preferred solution. The first scenario indicates that only $\{play, gain(100,000)\}$ should be the preferred solution since at least, John could gain $100,000$ if he plays. The second scenario corresponds to an indifference to choose one of the two solutions as a preferred one. It indicates that both $\{play, gain(100,000)\}$ and $\{give\_up\}$ are preferred solutions. This indifference agrees with our intuition that $\{play, gain(100,000)\}$ is preferred according to the same reasons of the first scenario, and $\{give\_up\}$ is also preferred since John could consider that it is not worth playing. He could have a valid reason to leave the game, such as he considers that the game is not fair, or he is a very moral person, etc. In this paper we present two semantics for PL programs. One of these semantics allows us to obtain the preferred solution of one of the scenarios described, and the other semantics allows us to obtain the preferred solution of the other scenario.

Currently in ASP there are different approaches that have resulted to be useful to represent problems with preferences, such as [2,8,1,10,11]. The two semantics presented in this paper follow the approach about preferences presented in [11] and the semantics of Logic Programs with Ordered Disjunction (LPOD) [2]. So, the semantics of PL programs that we propose correspond to some modifications of the semantics of LPOD's. In spite of they are slight modifications (technically speaking) these modifications are of great significance to the definition of the semantics of PL programs, since they allow us to move from an ordered disjunction as in LPOD's to a comparison of feasible solutions in a sense of preference. We

[3] The specification problem of this example corresponds to the specification problem of Example 1 in [1].

present some examples that show how the set of preferred answer sets obtained applying the semantics of LPOD and the set of preferred answer sets obtained applying the semantics for PL programs are different. We also present some properties of the two semantics that help us to understand these semantics. We have to point out that in [1] is introduced a semantics that obtains the preferred solution of the first scenario, and using the semantics of LPOD's can be obtained the preferred solution of the second scenario.

Our paper is structured as follows. In section 2 we introduce the general syntax of the logic programs used in this paper. We also provide the definition of answer sets in terms of logic G_3. In section 3 we present two semantics for preference logic programs. In section 4 we introduce some properties that help to understand the semantics presented in this paper. Finally, in section 5 we present related work and some conclusions.

2 Background

In this section we review some fundamental concepts and definitions that will be used along this work. We introduce first the syntax of formulas and programs based on the language of propositional logic. We also present the definition of answer sets in terms of logic G_3.

2.1 Propositional Logic

In this paper, logic programs are understood as propositional theories. We shall use the language of propositional logic in the usual way, using propositional symbols: $p, q, \ldots$, propositional connectives $\wedge, \vee, \rightarrow, \bot$ and auxiliary symbols: $(,)$. We assume that for any well formed propositional formula f, $\neg f$ is just an abbreviation of $f \rightarrow \bot$ and $\top$ is an abbreviation of $\bot \rightarrow \bot$. We point out that $\neg$ is the only negation used in this work. An *atom* is a propositional symbol. A *literal* is either an atom a (a positive literal) or the negation of an atom $\neg a$ (a negative literal). A *negated literal* is the negation sign $\neg$ followed by any literal, i.e. $\neg a$ or $\neg\neg a$. In particular, $f \rightarrow \bot$ is called *constraint* and it is also denoted as $\leftarrow f$. Given a set of formulas F, we define $\neg F = \{\neg f \mid f \in F\}$. Sometimes we may use *not* instead of $\neg$ and a, b instead of $a \wedge b$, following the traditional notation of logic programming.

A *regular theory* or *logic program* is just a finite set of well formed formulas or rules, it can be called just *theory* or *program* where no ambiguity arises. We shall define as a *rule* any well formed formula of the form: $f \leftarrow g$. The parts on the left and on the right of " $\leftarrow$ " are called the *head* and the *body* of the rule, respectively. We say that a rule which its head is a disjunction, namely $f_1 \vee \cdots \vee f_n \leftarrow g$, is a *disjunctive rule*. A *disjunctive logic program* is just a finite set of disjunctive rules, it can be called just *disjunctive program* where no ambiguity arises. Of course disjunctive programs are a subset of logic programs.

The signature of a logic program P, denoted as $\mathcal{L}_P$, is the set of atoms that occur in P. We want to stress the fact that in our approach, a logic program is interpreted as a propositional theory. For readers not familiar with this approach, we recommend [9,7] for further reading. We will restrict our discussion to propositional programs.

2.2 The Logic G_3 and Answer Sets

Some logics can be defined in terms of truth values and evaluation functions. Gödel defined the multivalued logics G_i, with i truth values. In particular, G_2 coincides with classical C. We briefly describe in the following lines the 3-valued logic G_3 since our work uses the logical characterization of answer sets based on this logic presented in [7,6]. Gödel defined the logic G_3, with 3 values, with the following evaluation function I:

$I(A \vee B) = \max(I(A), I(B))$. $\quad$ $I(A \wedge B) = \min(I(A), I(B))$.
$I(B \leftarrow A) = 2$ if $I(A) \leq I(B)$ and $I(B)$ otherwise. $\quad$ $I(\bot) = 0$.

An interpretation is a function $I\colon \mathcal{L} \rightarrow \{0, 1, 2\}$ that assigns a truth value to each atom in the language. The interpretation of an arbitrary formula is obtained by propagating the evaluation of each connective as defined above. Recall that $\neg$ and $\top$ were introduced as abbreviations of other connectives. For a given interpretation I and a formula F we say that I is a *model* of F if $I(F) = 2$. Similarly I is a *model* of a program P if it is a model of each formula contained in P. If F is modeled by every possible interpretation we say that F is a *tautology*. For instance, we can verify that $\neg\neg a \rightarrow a$ is not a tautology in G_3 , and $a \rightarrow \neg\neg a$ is a tautology in G_3. For a given set of atoms M and a program P we will write $P \vdash_{G_3} M$ to abbreviate $P \vdash_{G_3} a$ for all $a \in M$, and $P \Vdash_{G_3} M$ to denote the fact that $P \vdash_{G_3} M$ and P is consistent w.r.t. logic G_3 (i.e. there is no formula A such that $P \vdash_{G_3} A$ and $P \vdash_{G_3} \neg A$).

As usual in ASP, we take for granted that programs with predicate symbols are only an abbreviation of the ground program. We shall define answer sets of logic programs. The answer sets semantics was first defined in terms of the so called *Gelfond-Lifschitz reduction* [4] and it is usually studied in the context of fix points on programs. We follow an alternative approach started by Pearce [9] and also studied by Osorio et.al. [7,6]. This approach characterizes the answer sets for a propositional theory in terms of logic G_3 and it is presented in the following definition. There are several nice reasons to follow this approach. One of these reasons is that it is possible to use logic G_3 to provide a definition of ASP for arbitrary propositional theories, and at the same time to use the logic framework in an explicit way [7,6]. Moreover, this approach provides a natural way to extend the notion of answer sets in other logics [7,6]. The notation is based on [7,6]. We point out that in the context of logic programming as in the following definition, $\neg$ denotes *default negation* and it is the only type of negation considered in this paper.

Definition 1. *[7,6] Let P be a program and M a set of atoms. M is an* answer set *of P iff $P \cup \neg(\mathcal{L}_P \setminus M) \cup \neg\neg M \Vdash_{G_3} M$.*

Example 2. Let P be the logic program that represents the specification problem of Example 1 without considering John's preferences, i.e, let P be the following program:

$$play \vee give\_up \leftarrow .$$
$$gain(200,000) \vee gain(100,000) \leftarrow play.$$
$$\leftarrow gain(200,000).$$

We can verify that $\{play, gain(100,000)\}$ and $\{give\_up\}$ are the answer sets of P since: $P \cup \{\neg give\_up, \neg gain(200,000)\} \cup \{\neg\neg play, \neg\neg gain(100,000)\} \Vdash_{G_3} \{play, gain(100,000)\}$ and $P \cup \{\neg play, \neg gain(100,000), \neg gain(200,000)\} \cup \{\neg\neg give\_up\} \Vdash_{G_3} \{give\_up\}$.

3 Syntax and Semantics for Preferences

In order to specify preferences we introduce a new connective, $*$, called *preference operator*. This operator allows us to define preference rules. Each preference rule specifies the preferences for something. The head of these rules corresponds to an ordered list of formulas connected using the operator $*$, where each formula represents a possible preference option. We shall denote the semantics for preferences defined in this section as SEM_P.

Definition 2. *A* preference rule *is a formula of the form:* $f_1 * \cdots * f_n \stackrel{pr}{\leftarrow} g$ *where* $f_1, \ldots, f_n, g$ *are well formed propositional formulas. A* preference logic (PL) program *is a finite set of preference rules and an arbitrary set of well formed formulas.*

If $g = \top$ the preference rule can be written as $f_1 * \cdots * f_n \stackrel{pr}{\leftarrow}$. The formulas $f_1 \ldots f_n$ are called the *options* of a preference rule. In the following example, we are going to consider again the specification problem of Example 1 to illustrate how we can represent preferences using PL programs.

Example 3. Let P be the PL program representing the problem of Example 1.

$$play \vee give\_up \leftarrow .$$
$$gain(200,000) \vee gain(100,000) \leftarrow play.$$
$$\leftarrow gain(200,000).$$
$$play * give\_up \stackrel{pr}{\leftarrow} .$$
$$gain(200,000) * gain(100,000) \stackrel{pr}{\leftarrow} play.$$

In the introduction section, we mention that the preferred answer sets of the PL program in Example 3 are also the answer sets of the program without consider the preference rules. This can be defined as follows.

Definition 3. *Let $Pref$ be the set of preference rules of a PL program P. Let M be a set of atoms. M is an answer set of P iff M is an answer set*[4] *of $P \setminus Pref$.*

[4] Note that since we are not considering strong negation, there is no possibility of having inconsistent answer sets.

The preferred answer sets of a PL program P are those answer sets of P that for each preference rule occurs the following: its first option occurs, otherwise its second option occurs, otherwise its third option occurs, and so on. If none of the options of each preference rule occurs in the answer sets of P then all the answer sets of P are preferred. So, the semantics of PL programs should coincide with this idea about what a preferred answer set should be. The semantics of PL programs is inspired in the semantics of LPOD's introduced in [2]. Due to lack of space we do not present the semantics of LPOD programs, but readers not familiar with this approach can review [2]. The LPOD semantics and the semantics of PL programs use the satisfaction degree concept to obtain the preferred answer sets, however we want to point out that both semantics are different. The first difference is that the semantics for PL programs is defined for general theories (see Definition 2) and the semantics for LPOD's not. A second difference is due to the fact that LPOD's represent a disjunction over the possible preference options and PL programs represent preference over the possible preference options. For instance, if a program P has two answer sets such as $\{a, b\}$ and $\{a, c\}$ and we prefer the answer sets having f over those having c then, we need an approach that allows us to express this preference and to obtain $\{a, c\}$ as the preferred answer set of P. If we express this preference using the LPOD approach then, we could use the following ordered disjunction rule: $f \times c$. It stands for "if f is possible then f otherwise c" (see [2]). If we consider the program P together with the ordered disjunction rule then, we obtain two preferred answer sets $\{a, b, f\}$ and $\{a, c, f\}$. This does not coincide with what we expect. Now, if we consider our approach and we add to program P a preference rule such as $f * c \overset{pr}{\leftarrow}$. then, we obtain only $\{a, c\}$ and this coincides with what we expect. Our definition of satisfaction degree is in terms of logic G_3, however since the theories (or logic programs) used in this work are complete (i.e. for any formula A of a program P, either $P \vdash_{G_3} A$ or $P \vdash_{G_3} \neg A$), we could use classic logic too. For complete theories, logic G_3 is equivalent to classic logic [7].

Definition 4. *Let M be an answer set of a PL program P. Let $r := f_1 * \cdots * f_n \overset{pr}{\leftarrow} g$ be a preference rule of P. We define the* satisfaction degree *of r in M, denoted by $deg_M(r)$, as a correspondence rule that defines the following function:*

1. 1 *if* $M \cup \neg(\mathcal{L}_P \setminus M) \nvdash_{G_3} g$.
2. $min\,\{i \mid M \cup \neg(\mathcal{L}_P \setminus M) \vdash_{G_3} f_i\}$ *if* $M \cup \neg(\mathcal{L}_P \setminus M) \vdash_{G_3} g$.
3. $n{+}1$ *if* $M \cup \neg(\mathcal{L}_P \setminus M) \vdash_{G_3} g$ *and there is not* $1 \leq i \leq n$ *such that* $M \cup \neg(\mathcal{L}_P \setminus M) \vdash_{G_3} f_i$.

Example 4. Let P be the PL program of Example 3. Let r_1 be the preference rule: $play * give\_up \overset{pr}{\leftarrow}$, and let r_2 be the preference rule: $gain(200,000) * gain(100,000) \overset{pr}{\leftarrow} play$. By Definition 3 and Example 2, we know that P has two answer sets: $M_1 = \{play, gain(100,000)\}$ and $M_2 = \{give\_up\}$. We can verify that, $deg_{M_1}(r_1) = 1$, $deg_{M_2}(r_1) = 2$, $deg_{M_1}(r_2) = 2$, $deg_{M_2}(r_2) = 1$. It is interesting to point out that $deg_{M_2}(r_2)$ is equal to 1, since M_2 does not satisfy the body of r_2.

The following definitions and theorems are about the preferred answer sets of a PL program. All of them are similar to the definitions given in [2], however we do not have to forget that they use general theories (see Definition 2), they are based on our own concept of preference, and on our own definition of satisfaction degree.

Theorem 1. *Let $Pref$ be the set of preference rules of a PL program P. If M is an answer set of P then M satisfies all the rules in $Pref$ to some degree.*

The satisfaction degree of each preference rule allows us to define the set of preference rules with the same satisfaction degree. These sets will be used to find the preferred answer sets of the PL program.

Definition 5. *Let $Pref$ be the set of preference rules of a PL program P. Let M an answer set of P. We define $S^i_M(P) = \{r \in Pref \mid deg_M(r) = i\}$.*

Example 5. Let P be the PL program of Example 3. Let us consider the satisfaction degree of rules r_1 and r_2 in Example 4. Then we can verify that, $S^1_{M_1}(P) = \{r_1\}$, $S^1_{M_2}(P) = \{r_2\}$, $S^2_{M_1}(P) = \{r_2\}$, $S^2_{M_2}(P) = \{r_1\}$.

In order to know if one answer set is preferred to another answer set, we could apply different criteria to the sets of preference rules $S^i_M(P)$: *inclusion of sets*, or *cardinality of sets*. Moreover, these criteria can be used to obtain the most preferred answer sets. The following two definitions describe how we can do this.

Definition 6. *Let M and N be answer sets of a PL program P. M is* inclusion preferred *to N, denoted as $M >_i N$, iff there is an k such that $S^k_N(P) \subset S^k_M(P)$ and for all $j < k$, $S^j_M(P) = S^j_N(P)$. M is* cardinality preferred *to N, denoted as $M >_c N$, iff there is an k such that $\left|S^k_M(P)\right| > \left|S^k_N(P)\right|$ and for all $j < k$, $\left|S^j_M(P)\right| = \left|S^j_N(P)\right|$.*

Definition 7. *Let M be a set of atoms. Let P be a PL program. M is an* inclusion-preferred *answer set of P, if M is an answer set of P and there is not answer set M' of P, $M \neq M'$, such that $M' >_i M$. M is a* cardinality-preferred *answer set of P, if M is an answer set of P and there is not answer set M' of P, $M \neq M'$, such that $M' >_c M$.*

Example 6. Let P be the PL program of Example 3. By Example 2, we know that P has two answer sets: $M_1 = \{play, gain(100, 000)\}$ and $M_2 = \{give\_up\}$. If we consider the results in Example 5 then, we can verify that we cannot say anything about M_1 w.r.t. M_2 or vice versa since, $S^1_{M_1}(P)$ is not a subset of $S^1_{M_2}(P)$ or vice versa. Additionally, we can see that there is not M_3 answer set of P, $M_3 \neq M_1$ or $M_3 \neq M_2$, such that $M_3 >_i M_1$ or $M_3 >_i M_2$. Hence M_1 and M_2 are both the inclusion-preferred answer sets of P.

We can see that the inclusion-preferred answer sets of program P obtained in Example 6 agree with one of the possible solutions of the problem in Example 1 as we indicated in Section 1. In that section, we mentioned that this solution corresponds to an indifference to choose one of the two answer sets as the preferred one.

This indifference agrees with our intuition that $\{play, gain(100,000)\}$ is preferred since at least John could gain 100,000 if he plays. Additionally, $\{give\_up\}$ is also preferred since John could consider that it is not worth playing. He could have a valid reason to leave the game, such as he considers that the game is not fair, or he is a very moral person, etc. We shall see in Subsection 3.1 an alternative semantic that is useful to obtain the other possible solution of this problem as we indicated in Section 1 too.

It is worth mentioning that in [11] the cardinality criterion was particularly useful to specify preferences for evacuation plans using ASP approaches. In [11] one of the criteria to prefer plans is to travel by the paths with the minimum number of road segments. Hence, the idea of use the cardinality set criterion results very natural and easy to use.

3.1 An Alternative Semantics for Preferences

In this section we propose an alternative semantics for PL programs. This alternative semantics corresponds to a refinement of the semantics presented in Section 3. This alternative semantics is motivated by the Example 1 in Section 1. In that section, we mentioned that the problem described in Example 1 could have two possible solutions. In Section 3 we presented how it is possible to obtain one of these solutions using the semantics of PL programs. Now, using the alternative semantics, we shall see how can be obtained the other possible solution of the problem described in Example 1, i.e., we will see how the answer set $\{play, gain(100,000)\}$ can be obtained as the preferred solution since at least, John could gain 100,000 if he plays. We shall denote the semantics for preferences defined in this section as SEM_{aP}.

The main idea of the alternative semantics is to reduce the set of preference rules in the PL program and then applying the concept of satisfaction degree over this reduced program to obtain the preferred answer sets. The satisfaction degree is used in the same way that was indicated in Section 3 but using the reduced PL program. We point out that the reduction is based on a set of inferred literals. These literals are inferred from the set of disjunctive rules of the original PL program using a particular logic. The following definition corresponds to the set of literals inferred from the set of disjunctive rules of the original PL program using logic G_3.

Definition 8. *Let D_P be the set of disjunctive rules of a PL program P. We define $Q(P) := \{x \mid D_P \vdash_{G_3} \neg x\}$.*

Example 7. Let P be the PL program of Example 3. Then D_P is $\{play \vee give\_up \leftarrow\ ,\ gain(200,000) \vee gain(100,000) \leftarrow play\ ,\ \leftarrow gain(200,000)\}$. We can verify that $Q(P)= \{gain(200,000)\}$ since $D_P \vdash_{G_3} \neg gain(200,000)$.

Once we have the set of inferred literals, $Q(P)$, we use it in a replacement for literals in the original set of preference rules of program P. We replace each occurrence of atoms in $Q(P)$ with $\bot$ in the preference rules. The replacement is based on the following substitution function.

Definition 9. *Let Pref be the set of preference rules of a PL program P. Let A be a set of atoms. We define the* substitution function $\mathrm{Subst}_\perp(Pref, A)$ *that replace over Pref each occurrence of an atom in A with* $\perp$.

The idea is to use the set $Q(P)$ as the set of atoms A in the substitution function.

Example 8. Let P be the PL program of Example 3. By Example 7, we know that $Q(P)=\{gain(200,000)\}$. Then $Pref$ is the set $\{play{*}give\_up \stackrel{pr}{\leftarrow},\ gain(200,000){*}gain(100,000) \stackrel{pr}{\leftarrow} play\}$. We can verify that $Subst_\perp(Pref, Q(P))$ is the following set: $\{play * give\_up \stackrel{pr}{\leftarrow},\ \perp * gain(100,000) \stackrel{pr}{\leftarrow} play\}$.

Now, the new set of preference rules $Subst_\perp(Pref, Q(P))$ should be reduced applying the following definition.

Definition 10. *Given a formula F we define its reduction with respect to* $\perp$, *denoted* $\mathrm{reduce}(F)$, *as the formula obtained applying the following replacements on F until no more replaces can be done. If A is any formula then replace*

$A \wedge \top$ *or* $\top \wedge A$ *with* A.	$A \wedge \perp$ *or* $\perp \wedge A$ *with* $\perp$.	$A \vee \top$ *or* $\top \vee A$ *with* $\top$.
$A \vee \perp$ *or* $\perp \vee A$ *with* A.	$A \rightarrow \top$ *or* $\perp \rightarrow A$ *with* $\top$.	$\top \rightarrow A$ *with* A.
$A * \perp$ *or* $\perp * A$ *with* A.		

Then, for a given set of preference rules Pref, we define $\mathrm{Reduce}(Pref) := \{\mathrm{reduce}(F) \mid F \in Pref\}$.

Example 9. Let P be the PL program of Example 3. Then, $Reduce(Subst_\perp(Pref, Q(P)))$ is the set $\{play * give\_up \stackrel{pr}{\leftarrow},\ gain(100,000) \stackrel{pr}{\leftarrow} play.\}$, since $\perp * gain(100,000)$ was reduced to $gain(100,000)$ in the set $Subst_\perp(Pref, Q(P)))$ of Example 8.

The alternative semantics is based on the satisfaction degree. Once we reduced the preference rules of the original PL program, we shall apply the satisfaction degree concept to obtain the preferred answer sets. The following example uses the results of Example 9 and shows how to obtain the preferred answer sets using the satisfaction degree concept.

Example 10. Let P be the PL program of Example 3. Let D_P the set of disjunctive rules of P (see Example 7). Let $Reduce(Subst_\perp(Pref, Q(P))))$ the reduction set of Example 9. Let P' be the program $Reduce(Subst_\perp(Pref, Q(P))) \sqcup D_P$. By Definition 3 the answer sets of P' are $M_1 = \{play, gain(100,000)\}$ and $M_2 = \{give\_up\}$. Let r_1 be the preference rule: $play * give\_up \stackrel{pr}{\leftarrow}$; and let r_2 be the preference rule: $gain(100,000) \stackrel{pr}{\leftarrow} play$. By Definition 5, $S^1_{M_1}(P') = \{r_1, r_2\}$, $S^2_{M_1}(P') = \{\ \}$, $S^1_{M_2}(P') = \{r_2\}$, $S^2_{M_2}(P') = \{r_1\}$. Then, we can verify using Definitions 6 and 7 that, M_1 is inclusion preferred to M_2, i.e., $M_1 >_i M_2$ since $S^1_{M_2}(P') \subset S^1_{M_1}(P')$. Additionally, we can see that there is not M_3 answer set of P', $M_3 \neq M_1$, such that $M_3 >_i M_1$. Hence M_1 is an inclusion-preferred answer set of P' too.

4 Properties

In spite of the fact that we have to continue researching about the properties of the semantics of PL programs, in this section we introduce some properties[5] that help to understand the semantics presented in this paper. We write SEM to denote any arbitrary semantics for PL programs, namely a mapping that associates to every PL program P a set of preferred models. We recall that SEM_P denotes the semantics described in Section 3, and SEM_{aP} the alternative semantics described in Section 3.1. In addition we consider the set inclusion ordering unless stated otherwise. We illustrate with an example the first property. Let P be the program $\{a \leftarrow c. \quad b.\}$. Suppose that P is part of a larger program Q. For instance, let Q be the program $\{a \leftarrow b, c. \quad b.\}$. Moreover, let us suppose that the answer sets of Q are the same as the answer sets of P, such as in the examples for programs P and Q above. The idea is to use a particular case of the well known concept of strong equivalence [5] and it is very useful to understand or simplify programs. Our proposed definition is related to strong equivalence but is not the same, yet it holds for answer sets over regular theories. Moreover, both semantics introduced in this paper hold the substitution property.

Definition 11. *Let P be a a regular theory and Q a program, such that $P \subseteq Q$. Suppose that $P \vdash_{G_3} \alpha \leftrightarrow \beta$. Then SEM satisfies the* substitution property *if $SEM(Q) = SEM(Q')$ with respect to the language of Q', where Q' is as Q but we replace the subformula α by β.*

Lemma 1. *SEM_{rP} and SEM_P satisfy the substitution property.*

Following this same line, one could be interested in understanding if a formula such as $\bot * a$ can be reduced to a simpler one. This example came by ideas given in Example 1 of [1] that we analyzed in Section 3.1, specifically in Example 9. So, this property can be used to shows that $\{\leftarrow a., \ a * b \stackrel{pr}{\leftarrow} c.\}$ is strongly equivalent to $\{\leftarrow a., \ b \stackrel{pr}{\leftarrow} c\}$ using semantics SEM_{aP}.

Definition 12. *Let P be a program. Then SEM satisfies the* basic reduction property *if $SEM(P) = SEM(P')$ where P' is as P but we replace any rule of the form $\bot * \alpha \leftarrow \beta$ by $\alpha \leftarrow \beta$.*

As we defined in Section 3.1, SEM_{aP} corresponds to a refinement of the semantics presented in Section 3, SEM_P. Specifically, we saw that the main idea of SEM_{aP} is to reduce the set of preference rules in the PL program using Definition 10, and then SEM_{aP} works as SEM_P indicates using the concept of satisfaction degree over the reduced program to obtain the preferred answer sets. So, it is easy to see that the alternative semantics, SEM_{aP} holds the basic reduction property and the semantics SEM_P does not.

Lemma 2. *SEM_{aP} satisfies the basic reduction property.*

[5] We do not present the proofs of the lemmas in this section due to they are straightforward and due to lack of space.

5 Related Work and Conclusions

The authors of [3] describe an approach for preferences called Answer Set Optimization (ASO) programs. ASO programs have two parts. The generating program and the preference program. The first one produce answer sets representing the solutions, and the second one expresses user preferences. We could think that PL programs and ASO programs could be similar approaches to represent preferences. However, ASO programs and PL programs differ considerably in syntax and semantics. PL programs allow us a broader syntax than ASO programs and their semantics is different too. There is only one criterion to get the preferred answer sets from an ASO program; and there are three different criteria to get the preferred answer sets from a PL program. Finally, it is not defined whether ASO programs can have preferences with only one option or not. PL programs allow us to have preferences with only one option.

In this paper we present two semantics for PL programs. Of course we have to continue researching about the properties of the semantics of PL programs, but the results obtained in the examples presented in this paper make these semantics interesting.

References

1. M. Balduccini and V. S. Mellarkod. A-prolog with cr-rules and ordered disjunction. In *International Conference on Intelligent Sensing and Information Processing*, pages 1–6, 2004.
2. G. Brewka. Logic Programming with Ordered Disjunction. In *Proceedings of the 18th National Conference on Artificial Intelligence, AAAI-2002*. Morgan Kaufmann, 2002.
3. G. Brewka, I. Niemela, and M. Truszczynski. AnswerSet Optimization. In *IJCAI-03*, pages 867–872, 2003.
4. M. Gelfond and V. Lifschitz. The Stable Model Semantics for Logic Programming. In R. Kowalski and K. Bowen, editors, *5th Conference on Logic Programming*, pages 1070–1080. MIT Press, 1988.
5. V. Lifschitz, D. Pearce, and A. Valverde. Strongly Equivalent Logic Programs. *ACM Transactions on Computational Logic*, 2:526–541, 2001.
6. M. Osorio, J. A. Navarro, and J. Arrazola. Safe beliefs for propositional theories. *Annals of Pure and Applied Logic*, 134(1):63–82, 2005.
7. M. Osorio, J. A. Navarro, and J. Arrazola. Applications of Intuitionistic Logic in Answer Set Programming. *Theory and Practice of Logic Programming (TPLP)*, 4:325–354, May 2004.
8. M. Osorio, M. Ortiz, and C. Zepeda. Using CR-rules for evacuation planning. In G. D. I. Luna, O. F. Chaves, and M. O. Galindo, editors, *IX Ibero-american Workshops on Artificial Inteligence*, pages 56–63, 2004.
9. D. Pearce. Stable Inference as Intuitionistic Validity. *Logic Programming*, 38:79–91, 1999.
10. T. C. Son and E. Pontelli. Planning with preferences using logic programming. In *LPNMR*, pages 247–260, 2004.
11. C. Zepeda. *Evacuation Planning using Answer Sets.* PhD thesis, Universidad de las Americas, Puebla and Institut National des Sciences Appliquées de Lyon, 2005.

A Framework for the E-R Computational Creativity Model

Rodrigo García[1], Pablo Gervás[2], Raquel Hervás[2], Rafael Pérez y Pérez[1], and Fernando ArÃmbula[1]

[1] Posgrado en Ciencia e Ingenieria de la Computacion, Universidad Nacional Autonoma de Mexico, Mexico
rodrigog@uxmcc2.iimas.unam.mx, rpyp@servidor.unam.mx, arambula@aleph.cinstrum.unam.mx
[2] Departamento de Sistemas Informaticos y Programacion, Universidad Complutense de Madrid, Spain
pgervas@sip.ucm.es, raquelhb@fdi.ucm.es

Abstract. This paper presents an object-oriented framework based on the E-R computational creativity model. It proposes a generic architecture for solving problems that require a certain amount of creativity. The design is based on advanced Software Engineering concepts for object-oriented Framework Design. With the use of the proposed framework, the knowledge of the E-R computational model can be easily extended. This model is important since it tries to diagram the human creativity process when a human activity is done. The framework is described together with two applications under development which implement the framework.

1 Introduction

Humans apply creative solutions across a wide range of problems: music, art, science, literature...If a common plausible model were found of the way humans approach creativity problems in all these fields, it would open possibilities of applying creative mechanisms to problems in a wide range of domains. The Engagement and Reflection model of the creative process developed by Perez y Perez [1] attempted to abstract the way in which the human brain tackles creative composition in the field of storytelling. However, the Engagement and Reflection model is postulated as independent of particular domains. Several efforts are under way to apply it to different tasks - geometry, storytelling, image interpretation... From the point of view of development, it would be extremely interesting if the essence of the computational model, which is common across different applications, could be captured in some kind of abstract and reusable software solution. This paper explores the design of an object oriented framework intended to capture in this way the common functionalities of computational solutions based on the Engagement and Reflection model for addressing creativity problems.

A framework is a set of classes and interfaces closely related in a reusable form design for a family of systems with a strong structural connection (hierarchy of classes, inheritance and composition) and of behavior (model of interaction of the objects) [2]. When an application is implemented based on a framework it is said that it is an *instance* of the framework. This means that the framework's *hotpoints* - places where details

A. Gelbukh and C.A. Reyes-Garcia (Eds.): MICAI 2006, LNAI 4293, pp. 70–80, 2006.

and specific fragments of code concerning a particular domain must be provided - are specified to transform it into a concrete application. The framework can be seen as the skeleton that supports the general structure and the hotpoints provide the flexibility required to obtain different applications by different instantiation processes.

The fundamental advantage of frameworks is that they can significantly reduce the development time for particular applications in the selected domain because of design reuse. But there are also disadvantages that have to be considered. By introducing a common structure for applications in a given domain, a framework may effectively restrict the range of alternatives that a designer can consider. This can have unforeseen consequences in terms of restricting the creative freedom of the applications that we are contemplating.

In spite of this disadvantage, a framework can be a good solution for capturing particular methods of approaching problem solving that can be applied accross several domains. In this paper, we work under the assumption that the computer model based on Engagement and Reflective States can be applied to different fields such as story development, image interpretation and graphs generation.

This paper is organized as follows. In section 2 *previous work* related to Design Patterns and Frameworks and the Engagement and Reflection model is presented. Section 3 shows the *design* of the framework architecture and its components. Section 4 describes *three instantiation examples* related to storytelling, image interpretation and graph generation. Section 5 presents a *discussion* about the generalization of the E-R creativity model. Finally, section 6 outlines *conclusions* and future work.

2 Previous Work

To design a framework for Engagement and Reflection computational models of the creative process, relevant work on two different fields must be considered: framework design and the Engagement and Reflection model.

2.1 Design Patterns and Frameworks

The development of a framework requires a significant effort of domain analysis. In order to identify the ingredients that are common across different aplications of a given type, several examples must be analysed carefully. Before building a framework in a given domain one should have a solid understanding of the domain, ideally as result of the experience gained in building prior applications in that domain.

Another important aspect concerning frameworks is the stages of evolution they pass during their lifetime [3]. According to Tracz [4], to acquire sufficient knowledge to identify the reusable essence for building artefacts of a given kind one must have built at least three different examples of such artefacts. This is considered the first stage in the evolution of a framework. The second stage is a *white box framework*: the framework provides a bare structure in which the user will have to introduce actual fragments of code adapted to the particular domain in which he wants the framework to operate. The user has to understand how the different modules in the framework work, and he may have to write software components himself. The third stage is a *black box framework*:

the framework provides a structure and a set of software components - organised as a *component library* - which constitute different alternatives for instantiating modules of the framework. A user may put together an instance of the framework simply by assembling elements from the component library into the framework structure. Later stages in the evolution of a framework gravitate towards obtaining a visual builder interface, to make even easier the process of building applications. However, this refinement in not necessary in most practical applications.

2.2 Engagement and Reflection

The main goal of Engagement and Reflection (E-R) model is to provide a model of the way in which human beings go about the task of applying abstract knowledge to creative tasks. Human beings store an enormous amount of abstract knowledge, refined from a lifetime of experience. This knowledge is used for solving problems. The Engagement and Reflection model is a plausible representation of the process a human being follows when trying to solve a problem that requires the use of abstract knowledge.

The basic unit of representation in the Engagement and Reflection model is an action. An action has a set of preconditions and a set of postconditions.

The model is based in two main processes that form a cycle, Engagement and Reflection. During Engagement we produce a lot of ideas - or instances of some equivalent conceptual material - that help us by acting as cues to solve the problem. At this stage, restrictions such as the fulfillment of the preconditions of an action within a given plan are not evaluated. The generation of these ideas is driven by a set of parameters or constraints that have to be defined. This ensures that the generation process is guided towards a specific goal. In the Reflection stage, the ideas generated during Engagement are evaluated carefully, restrictions such as the fulfillment of preconditions are enforced, and any required modifications are carried out to ensure that the partial result at any given stage is coherent and correct.

The process of solving a problem follows a cycle of transitions between the Engagement and the Reflection states. At each pass through the Engagement state more material is added. At each pass through the Reflection state, the accumulated material is checked for consistency, completed and corrected.

The solution of a problem is a train of well structured actions based on the previous knowledge of solved problems. If we can extract the preconditions and the postconditions of the actions problems it can be reuse for the solution of other problems in the same domain.

The E-R model was conceived for the creative process in writing. In later research efforts, the model has been applied in other fields like the solution of geometric problems, image interpretation problems and strategic games. These last two examples are currently under development.

MEXICA. The E-R model was originally used in MEXICA [1]. MEXICA was designed to study the creative process involved in writing in terms or the cycle of engagement and reflection. MEXICA's stories are represented as sequences of actions. MEXICA has two main processes: the first creates all data structures in memory from information provided by the user. The second, based on such structures and as a result of a cycle between engagement and reflection, produces new stories. It has the next goals: (1) To produce stories as a result of an interaction between engagement and reflection. (2) To produce material during engagement without the use of problem-solving techniques or predefined story-structures. (3) To produce novel and interesting stories. (4)Allow users to experiment with different parameters that constraint the writing process.

The Geometrician: A Computer Model for Solving Geometry Problems. Based on the creative model E-R, Villaseñor [5] tries to solve geometric problems with the use of rule and compass only. The user defines a text file with a set of solved problems, then the key information from these problems is extracted and it is used as a knowledge base for the system. When a new problem is presented to the program, it tries to find a solution as a result of the interaction between engagement and reflection. During engagement the program looks for actions in memory that could be done in order to solve the problem, and during reflection those actions retrieved are checked before they are executed. The program implements some learning mechanisms and some new characteristics to the basic model (E-R). One of this new characteristics is the capability to solve sub-problems in a recursive way.

Image Interpretation. The problem consists in identifying the correct outline of a prostate in a Transurethral ultrasound image. Nowadays the experience of specialized doctor is necessary to identify this outline. The problem is not the time required to train doctors in this specific task, but the fact that the only way of acquiring this knowledge is during the process of real-life prostate operations. From the data provided by an ultrasound image, the only accurate knowledge about a prostate is conveyed as a white area surrounded by a dark zone. Based on the E-R model cycle of engagement and reflection and a Point Distribution Model (PDM) [6] used by Arambula [7] the program tries to find the most suitable outline of the prostate in Transurethral ultrasound images. As in the previous examples, the program needs a text file containing the solved problems. The first step of the process is to extract a set of characteristics of the image. Some of this characteristics could be the gray scale or the maximum brightness for example. This set of characteristics will help as cues for definition of the context which is the state of affair of the problem. The program then searches for similar contexts in the knowledge base acquired from the set of previously solved problems. Each of those contexts will have an associated set of related actions that contributed to the solution of the problem in the original case. These actions are added to the partial solution of the current problem during the engagement phase, and they are checked for consistency with the current problem later during the reflection stage.

3 Framework Design

The goal is to use software engineering techniques to develop a framework based on the E-R model, reducing development time for applications based on it. At the same time the framework - being a generic computational implementation of the E-R model will extend the knowledge about the human cognitive process the E-R model tries to abstract.

The framework is based on two examples: MEXICA and Image Interpretation. The implementation of the examples as instantiations of the framework is reviewed in Section 4.

For ease of understanding, the structure of the proposed framework is divided in two parts, one related to the core structure of the framework, and another one dealing with the specific features of the E-R model.

3.1 General Structure

The core structure of the framework is based on the architecture proposed in [8] for Natural Language Generation applications. Its general structure can be seen in Figure 1.

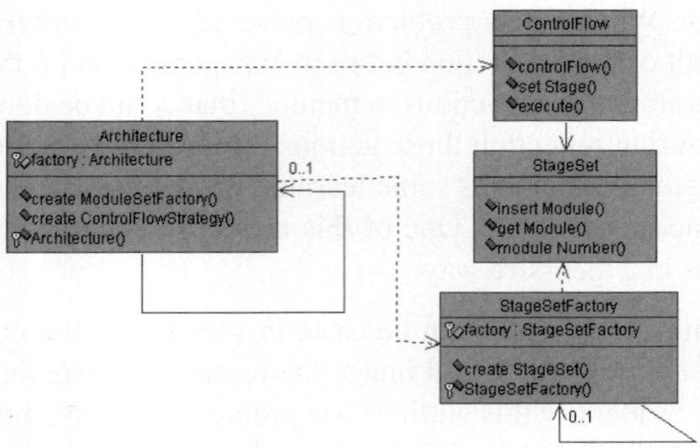

Fig. 1. General structure of the framework

The set of modules or stages involved in the process is stored in a `StageSet` structure. The choice of which modules to use is taken using the abstract class `StageSet-Factory`. Its implementations, following the *AbstractFactory* design pattern [9], define specific sets of modules that are stored in `StageSet`.

With regard to the flow of control information, the decision is taken in the abstract class `ControlFlow`, implemented following the *Strategy* design pattern [9]. A `StageSet` is passed as parameter to the constructor of `ControlFlow`, so that the control flow knows which modules the user has decided to use. The goal of `Control-Flow` is to decide the arrangement and execution order of the stages kept in `StageSet`. Decisions as executing a stage more than one time, or deciding if executing it at all, are taken by the `ControlFlow` instantiations. To deal with that, `ControlFlow` has a *nextStage* method that returns the next step to be executed, and an *end* method that becomes "true" when there is no more stages to be executed.

Finally, connection between `ControlFlow` and `StageSetFactory` is found in the abstract class `ArchitectureFactory`, as in the *AbstractFactory* design pattern [9]. Given different set of stages and control flows, the user can decide which is the combination of modules and flow of control information he needs in his application.

3.2 E-R Structure

The E-R structure is the specific piece of the framework in charge to carry out the E-R creativity process. As shown in Figure 2, there are different data structures that

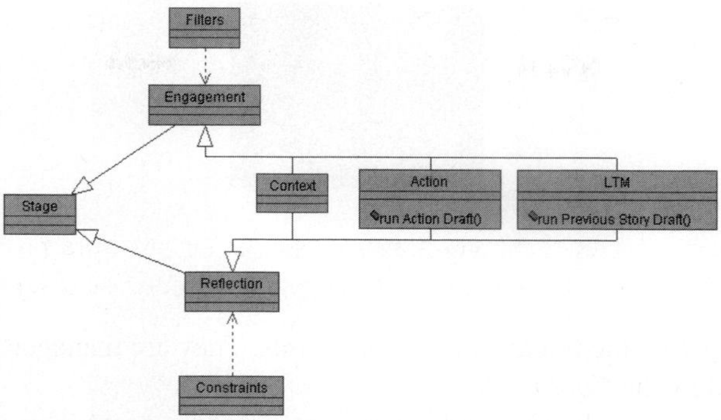

Fig. 2. E-R structure of the framework

interact depending on the actual step of the process. All of them are as a last resort descendants of the abstract class `Stage`, the one that is stored in the `StageSet` of the basic structure.

The E-R model has two main parts: Engagement and Reflection, both of them working with similar data structures. `Engagement` and `Reflection` abstract classes are used to help the user during the implementation of his system to know in which step is the process and to define the content of each class. Both of them have a special method used to query different data structures depending on the class implementation - filters for the Engagement, Constraints for the Reflection. The most important instantiations of the Engagement and Reflection classes are `Context`, `Action` and `LTM`. Depending on the stage of execution some modules will be connected and some others will be ignored.

The correct combination of these components, together with the basic structure in Section 3.1, will result in interesting and useful implementations of the framework.

4 Two Instantiation Examples

In order to show the use and the feasibility of the framework it will be applied to two examples: Image Interpretation and MEXICA.

4.1 Image Interpretation

The aim of the image interpretation problem is to draw as well as posible the form of the prostate in a Transurethral ultrasound images, such as the one in Figure 3. The black circle in the center of the image is the device used to get the ultrasound image. Important clues that may be used for solving the problem can be obtained from the knowledge of the human anatomy. For example, it is known that the rectal conduit is under the prostate. This is reflected in the image as a white region. Prostates are also known to be roughly pear-shaped. In this example all the stages are used, the context,

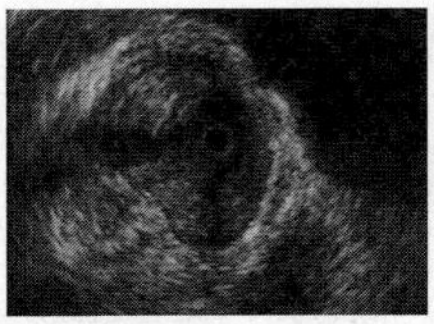

Fig. 3. Prostate Image

the actions, the LTM, the filters and the constraints. They are managed by the *StageSet* and coordinated by the *ControlFlow*.

The first step initiated by *ControlFlow* is to get a good context. This is the process by which the system constructs a general idea of the state of affairs. This is important since in some images it is easier to acquire the prostate form than in others. In order to get a context, the greater possible number of characteristics of the image must be extracted.

This is done by the execution of the action *Extract Characteristics* for example. The response of this action is a set of coordinates (x,y) and a graph as shown in Figures 4 and 5. This can be interpreted as an idea of the prostate form, but the most important is that now there is a **Context** to work with. Once this first step has been carried out, the *ControlFlow* sets in motion the next stage: ***Engagement***.

The Engagement stage checks the actual *Context* against its knowledge base of already solved problems - stored in the file of experiences or LTM - in search for the solved problem whose Context best matches with the Context of the current problem. To achieve this, the *run Previous Draft* method of the *LTM* class must be invoked. This method perfoms the search over the previous examples stored in the *LTM* class. Once a context is retrieved, depending on the filters introduced, an action is executed without checking the preconditions. This action is passed to the *run Action Draft* method of the *Action* class. The only requirement for executing an action is that it must modify the context. This is due to the fact that violation of this requirement may result in the system entering an infinite cycle. This step may be repeated one, two or three times for each example, depending on the requirements of the user.

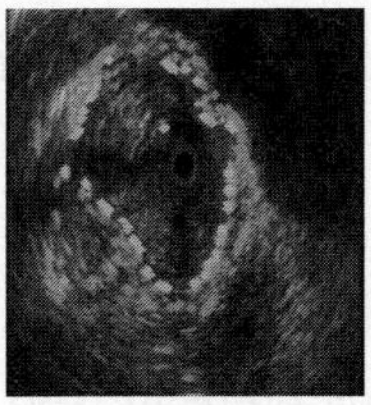

Fig. 4. Prostate Image with Characteristic extraction

Once the Engagement stage has finished, *ControlFlow* shifts control to the ***Reflection*** stage.

For Reflection all the stages are used. The basic idea of this step is to check the actions executed during in Engagement. Thus, all postconditions of each action should be coherent with the preconditions of its follower, and the result of the executed action should bring the system closer to solving the problem. In order to achieve the first condition, the *run Action Draft method* is executed . Whenever a precondition is not fulfilled, it is explicitly asserted in the correct place in the sequence of actions. It may be possible that more than one precondition is not satisfied, so this step can be recursive until all preconditions are fulfilled. In this step there are also *Constraints* that must be tested. For example, a precondition of an action may be that the graph shown in Figure 5 must have at least two peak to execute the action number 5. Or it could be that the gradient of the line can not be more than 65 degrees. In this figure the **x** axis represents each profile of the prostate (0-359), and the **y** axis means the maximum brightness of each profile (0-255).

To check if the action executed is bringing the system closer to solving the problem, there are different techniques that can be applied. One possibility is to apply the form of the PDM [6] used by Arambula [7].

This whole process is repeated until the user's requirements have been satisfied or until a given value of a certain parameter is reached.

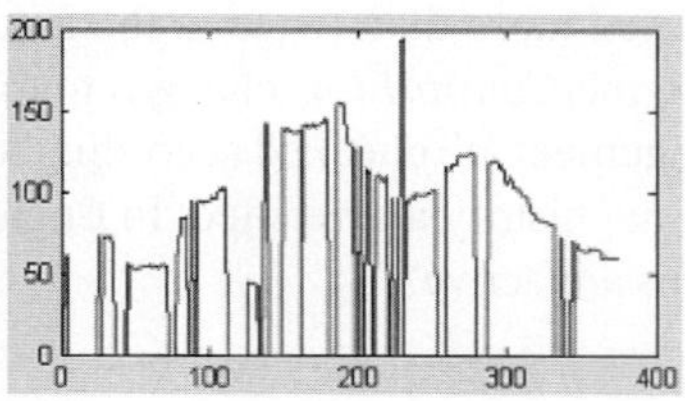

Fig. 5. Prostate Graphic

4.2 MEXICA

MEXICA's goal is to develop a computational model of the creative process of writing in terms of engagement and reflection. The environment of the story is controlled by the previous stories kept in the LTM. The first step in the *ControlFlow* is to form a context. The context here is to set an initial action, an initial scene and the number of characters. To achieve this, the special action *Initial Actions* must be called. One important feature of MEXICA is that the user has the option to manually set these initial data. This provides the means for guiding the output towards desireable results. Once the initial context is built, as in the Image interpretation problem, and depending on the users parameters, *ControlFlow* initiates the Engagement state.

In the Engagement state the *filters, context, action and LTM* modules are involved. The mission here is to retrieve from *LTM* a set of plausible actions to continue the story. As in the Image interpretation problem, the key condition in this step is that the action selected **must** change the state of affairs of the context. Once again the preconditions in this step are not considered when the action selection is made. Those will be considered in the Reflective state. Figure 6 shows a Previous Story file used in MEXICA.

The file includes characters, actions (aggressions, deaths, fights, cures...), scene movement and feelings (hate, love, jealousy...). The selection from the set of actions

Sto ;1	Sto ;2
Eagle_Knight Actor	Prince Went_Texcoco_Lake
Jaguar_Knight Actor	Prince Had_An_Accident
Eagle_Knight Was_In_Love_With Princess	Priest Found_By_Accident Prince
Jaguar_Knight Was_In_Love_With Princess	Priest Realised Prince Had_An_Accident
Princess Was_In_Love_With Warrior	Priest Cured Prince
Eagle_Knight Got_Jealous_Of Warrior	Prince Went_Palace
Eagle_Knight Killed Warrior	Fisherman Mugged Priest
Princess Attacked Eagle_Knight	Prince Realised Fisherman Mugged Priest
Eagle_Knight Wounded Princess	Prince Looked_For_And_Found Fisherman
Jaguar_Knight Attacked Eagle_Knight	Prince Made_Prisioner Fisherman
Jaguar_Knight Fought Eagle_Knight	
Jaguar_Knight Killed Eagle_Knight	
Jaguar_Knight Exiled Jaguar_Knight	

Fig. 6. Previous story file

retrieved is done based on the *filter* parameters. For example, an action can be discarded because it has been used more than twice in the actual story or because it does not modify the context. Next, the *ControlFlow* changes to the Reflection state. Here the actions selected during Engagement are checked according to constraints. Also, preconditions and the continuity of the history are verified. In Engagement the *context*, *action*, *LTM* and *constraints* modules are active.

5 Discussion

From the selected examples a set of possible actions to be undertaken during the process of carrying out the goal can be abstracted, and corresponding sets of preconditions and postconditions can be identified for each action in that set. This allows all three problems to be represented within the general schema that the model requires, being the actions the basic units of representation in the model.

For any particular implementation built using the proposed framework, the search space of possible solutions must be susceptible of being represented as a graph in which the nodes correspond to actions and the edges establish relationships of precondition and postcondition fulfilment between the actions. Such a graph can be seen as a tree like the one shown in Figure 7.

The set of possible complete solutions would then be represented by all possible paths from the root of the tree to one of its leaves. The image captures the fact that in many cases, the specification of the problem already contains explicitly a partial description of the solution - the partial image provided as input in the case of image interpretation; and the initial action, the initial scene and the number of characters in the case of MEXICA. The task of solving the problem corresponds to identifying the missing fragments that will turn this partial description of the solution into a complete solution. In the image, circles bounded by a full line indicate nodes of the solution already described explicitly in the specification of the problem, and circles bounded by a dotted line correspond to actions that must be identified by the system. As example,

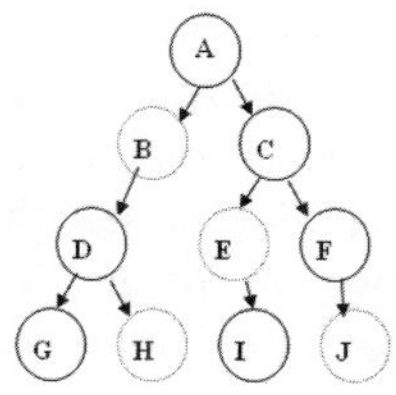

Fig. 7. Graph (tree) structure

a possible solution for a given problem may be the next sequence: A-B-D-H, but at the very beginning there is no idea of a potential solution just the letter A. Later, thinking about the problem, an analogy can be found with some other problem in the past and remembering the steps done for solving some specific problem in the past a clue can be found for solving the current problem. The first decision to be taken in the problem example represented in Figure 7 would correspond to identifying the node labelled with letter B as the next correct step towards a complete solution.

At the heart of the Engagement and Reflection creativity model lies a fundamental idea of the denial of intuition as driving force of human decision making. Under this point of view, when a person has several possibilities at the time of making a judgment, his decision is often related to an event in the past. This event need not be remembered explicitly, as it may be present only subconsciously. If this argument was used as guiding heuristic for a genetic algorithm, the thousands of possible answers that such an algorithm may give rise to might in fact be limited by the events and solutions that have proved succesful in the past. This should in no way be interpreted as a slur on genetic algorithms and the theory of problem solving that underlies them. It is simply a different way to think about the solution of problems.

6 Conclusions and Future Work

The E-R model is a good candidate for developing a reusable framework because it was originally intended as an abstract model of generic intellectual abilities of human beings.

In order to check the utility of the framework two projects are being developed. The first project is related to the implementation of MEXICA, a system that tells stories about the early inhabitants of Mexico. The second project is related to the Image Interpretation problem for Transurethral ultrasound images of the prostate. Both of them are being developed an instantiations of the E-R framework. The goal is to achieve operative implementations with less development effort than would have been required without the framework. The proposed framework contributes to this goal by allowing developers to focus on the key information such as the actions (preconditions and postconditions), filters and constraints.

In addition, when the use of the framework is reliable and efficient, the resulting ease of use may lead to wider adoption of the model and to more basic research on its theoretical underpinnings.

In spite of the abstract nature of the Engagement and Reflection model, and the efforts that have been made to make the framework as reusable as possible by the use of software engineering techniques, the scope of a framework is limited and not all kind of problems can be covered. However, it must be said that in general terms, the framework presented in this paper represents two advantages: it may make implementations of the Engagement and Reflection approach to problem solving faster, and it may serve to extend the use of the model.

References

1. Perez y Perez, R.: A Computer Model of Creativity in Writing. PhD thesis, University of Sussex (1999)
2. Johnson, R., Foote, B.: Designing reusable classes. Journal of object-Oriented Programming **1** (1988) 22–35
3. Johnson, R., Roberts., D.: Evolving frameworks: a pattern language for developing object-oriented frameworks. In: Proceedings of the 3rd Conference on Pattern Languages and Programming, Montecillo, Illinois. (1996)
4. Tracz, W.: In software reuse: Emerging technology. IEEE Computer Society Press (1988) 176–189
5. Acosta Villaseñor, E.: Aplicacion de un modelo en computadora del proceso creativo a la solucion de problemas en geometria. PhD thesis, Universidad Nacional Autonoma de Mexico (2005)
6. Cootes, T., Taylor, C., Cooper, D., Graham, J.: Active shape models-their training and application. Computer Vision and Image Understanding **61** (1995) 38–59
7. Cosio, F., Davies, B.: Automated prostate recognition: a key process for clinically effective robotic prostatectomy. Medical and Biological Engineering and Computing **37** (1999) 236–243
8. Garcia, C., Hervas, R., Gervas, P.: Una arquitectura software para el desarrollo de aplicaciones de generación de lenguaje natural. Sociedad Española para el Procesamiento del Lenguaje Natural **33** (2004) 111
9. Gamma, E., Helm, R., Johnson, R., Vlissides, J.: Design Patterns: Elements of Reusable Object-Oriented Software. Addison-Wesley Professional, USA, First Edition (1995)

First-Order Interval Type-1 Non-singleton Type-2 TSK Fuzzy Logic Systems

Gerardo M. Mendez[1] and Luis Adolfo Leduc[2]

[1] Department of Electronics and Electromechanical Engineering
Instituto Tecnológico de Nuevo León
Av. Eloy Cavazos #2001, Cd. Guadalupe, NL, CP. 67170, México
gmmendez@itnl.edu.mx
[2] Department of Process Engineering
Hylsa, S.A. de C.V.
Monterrey, NL, México
lleduc@hylsamex.com.mx

Abstract. This article presents the implementation of first-order interval type-1 non-singleton type-2 TSK fuzzy logic system (FLS). Using input-output data pairs during the forward pass of the training process, the interval type-1 non-singleton type-2 TSK FLS output is calculated and the consequent parameters are estimated by back-propagation (BP) method. In the backward pass, the error propagates backward, and the antecedent parameters are estimated also by back-propagation. The proposed interval type-1 non-singleton type-2 TSK FLS system was used to construct a fuzzy model capable of approximating the behaviour of the steel strip temperature as it is being rolled in an industrial Hot Strip Mill (HSM) and used to predict the transfer bar surface temperature at finishing Scale Breaker (SB) entry zone, being able to compensate for uncertain measurements that first-order interval singleton type-2 TSK FLS can not do.

1 Introduction

Interval Type-2 fuzzy logic systems (FLS) constitute an emerging technology. In [1] both one-pass and back-propagation (BP) methods are presented as interval type-2 Mamdani FLS learning methods but only BP is presented for interval type-2 Takagi-Sugeno-Kang (TSK) FLS systems. One-pass method generates a set of IF-THEN rules by using the given training data one time, and combines the rules to construct the final FLS. When BP method is used in both interval type-2 Mamdani and interval type-2 TSK FLS, none of antecedent and consequent parameters of the interval type-2 FLS are fixed at starting of training process; they are tuned using exclusively steepest descent method. In [1] recursive least-squares (RLS) and recursive filter (REFIL) algorithms are not presented as interval type-2 FLS learning methods.

The hybrid algorithm for interval type-2 Mamdani FLS has been already presented [2, 3, 4] with three combinations of learning methods: RLS-BP, REFIL-BP and orthogonal least-squares (OLS)-BP, whilst the hybrid algorithm for interval singleton type-2 TSK FLS (type-2 TSK SFLS) has been presented [5] with two combinations of learning methods: RLS-BP and REFIL-BP.

A. Gelbukh and C.A. Reyes-Garcia (Eds.): MICAI 2006, LNAI 4293, pp. 81 – 89, 2006.

The aim of this work is to present and discuss the learning algorithm for interval type-1 non-singleton type-2 TSK FLS (type-2 TSK NSFLS-1) antecedent and consequent parameters estimation during training process using input-output data pairs. The proposed interval type-2 TSK NSFLS-1 inference system is evaluated making transfer bar surface temperature predictions at Hot Strip Mill (HSM) Finishing Scale Breaker (SB) entry zone.

2 Problem Formulation

Most of the industrial processes are highly uncertain, non-linear, time varying and non-stationary [2, 6], having very complex mathematical representations. Interval type-2 TSK NSFLS-1 takes easily the random and systematic components of type A or B standard uncertainty [7] of industrial measurements. The non-linearities are handled by FLS as identifiers and universal approximators of nonlinear dynamic systems [8, 9, 10, 11]. Stationary and non-stationary additive noise is modeled as a Gaussian function centred at the measurement value. In stationary additive noise the standard deviation takes a single value, whereas in non-stationary additive noise the standard deviation varies over an interval of values [1]. Such characteristics make interval type-2 TSK NSFLS-1 a very powerful inference system to model and control industrial processes.

Only the BP learning method for interval type-2 TSK SFLS has been proposed in the literature and it is used as a benchmark algorithm for parameter estimation or systems identification on interval type-2 TSK FLS systems [1]. To the best knowledge of the authors, type-2 TSK NSFLS-1 has not been reported in the literature [1, 12, 13].

One of the main contributions of this work is to implement an application of the interval type-2 TSK NSFLS-1 using BP learning algorithm, capable of compensate for uncertain measurements.

3 Problem Solution

3.1 Type-2 FLS

A type-2 fuzzy set, denoted by $\tilde{A}$, is characterized by a type-2 membership function $\mu_{\tilde{A}}(x,u)$, where $x \in X$ and $u \in J_x \subseteq [0,1]$ and $0 \leq \mu_{\tilde{A}}(x,u) \leq 1$.:

$$\tilde{A} = \{((x,u), \mu_{\tilde{A}}(x,u)) \mid \forall x \in X, \forall u \in J_x \subseteq [0,1]\} . \quad (1)$$

This means that at a specific value of x, say x', there is no longer a single value as for the type-1 membership function (u'); instead the type-2 membership function takes on a set of values named the primary membership of x', $u \in J_x \subseteq [0,1]$. It is possible to assign an amplitude distribution to all of those points. This amplitude is named a secondary grade of general type-2 fuzzy set. When the values of secondary grade are the same and equal to 1, there is the case of an interval type-2 membership function [1, 14, 15, 16, 17].

3.2 Using BP Learning Algorithm in Type-2 TSK NSFLS-1

Table 1 shows the activities of the one pass learning algorithm of BP method. Interval type-2 TSK NSFLS-1 output is calculated during forward pass. During the backward pass, the error propagates backward and the antecedent and consequent parameters are estimated using the BP.

Table 1. One pass in learning procedure for interval type-2 NSFLS-1

	Forward Pass	Backward Pass
Antecedent Parameters	Fixed	BP
Consequent Parameters	Fixed	BP

3.3 Adaptive BP Learning Algorithm

The training method is based on the initial conditions of consequent parameters: y_l^i and y_r^i. It presented as in [1]: Given N input-output training data pairs, the training algorithm for E training epochs, should minimize the error function

$$e^{(t)} = \frac{1}{2}\left[f_{s2}\left(\mathbf{x}^{(t)}\right) - y^{(t)}\right]^2 . \tag{2}$$

4 Application to Transfer Bar Surface Temperature Prediction

4.1 Hot Strip Mill

Because of the complexities and uncertainties involved in rolling operations, the development of mathematical theories has been largely restricted to two-dimensional models applicable to heat losing in flat rolling operations.

Fig. 1, shows a simplified diagram of a HSM, from the initial point of the process at the reheat furnace entry to its end at the coilers.

Besides the mechanical, electrical and electronic equipment, a big potential for ensuring good quality lies in the automation systems and the used control techniques. The most critical process in the HSM occurs in the Finishing Mill (FM). There are several mathematical model based systems for setting up the FM. There is a model-based set-up system [18] that calculates the FM working references needed to obtain gauge, width and temperature at the FM exit stands. It takes as inputs: FM exit target gage, target width and target temperature, steel grade, hardness ratio from slab chemistry, load distribution, gauge offset, temperature offset, roll diameters, load distribution, transfer bar gauge, transfer bar width and transfer bar temperature entry.

The errors in the gauge of the transfer bar are absorbed in the first two FM stands and therefore have a little effect on the target exit gauge. It is very important for the model to know the FM entry temperature accurately. A temperature error will propagate through the entire FM.

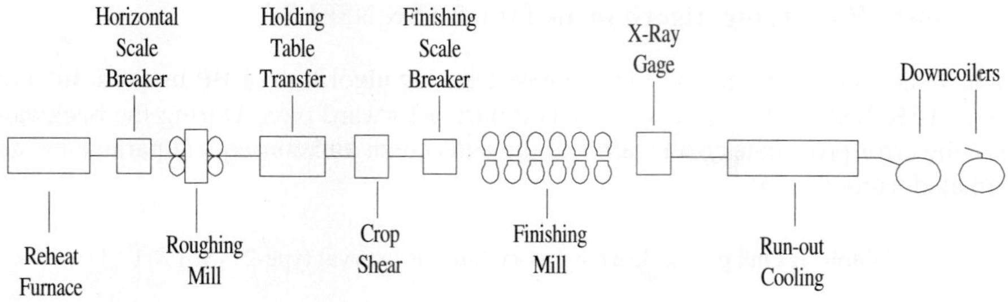

Fig. 1. Typical hot strip mill

4.2 Design of the Interval Type-2 TSK NSFLS-1

The architecture of the interval type-2 TSK NSFLS-1 was established in such away that parameters are continuously optimized. The number of rule-antecedents was fixed to two; one for the Roughing Mill (RM) exit surface temperature and the other for transfer bar head traveling time. Each antecedent-input space was divided in three fuzzy sets, thus, giving nine rules. Gaussian primary membership functions of uncertain means were chosen for the antecedents. Each rule of the each interval type-2 TSK NSFLS-1 is characterized by six antecedent membership function parameters (two for left-hand and right-hand bounds of the mean and one for standard deviation, for each of the two antecedent Gaussian membership functions) and six consequent parameters (one for left-hand and one for right-hand end points of each of the three consequent type-1 fuzzy sets), giving a total of twelve parameters per rule. Each input value has one standard deviation parameter, giving two additional parameters.

4.3 Noisy Input-Output Training Data Pairs

From an industrial HSM, noisy input-output pairs of three different product types were collected and used as training and checking data. The inputs were the noisy measured RM exit surface temperature and the measured RM exit to SB entry transfer bar traveling time. The output was the noisy measured SB entry surface temperature.

4.4 Fuzzy Rule Base

The interval type-1 non-singleton type-2 TSK fuzzy rule base consists of a set of IF-THEN rules that represents the model of the system. The type-2 TSK NSFLS-1 has two inputs $x_1 \in X_1$, $x_2 \in X_2$ and one output $y \in Y$. The rule base has $M = 9$ rules of the form:

$$R^i : IF \quad x_1 \quad is \quad \tilde{F}_1^i \quad and \quad x_2 \quad is \quad \tilde{F}_2^i, \quad THEN \quad Y^i = C_0^i + C_1^i x_1 + C_2^i x_2 \ . \tag{3}$$

where Y^i the output of the *ith* rule is a fuzzy type-1 set, and the parameters C_j^i are the consequent type-1 fuzzy sets with $i = 1,2,3,\ldots,9$ and $j = 0,1,2,$.

4.5 Input Membership Function

The primary membership functions for each input of the interval type-2 NSFLS-1 are Gaussians of the form:

$$\mu_{X_k}(x_k) = \exp\left[-\frac{1}{2}\left[\frac{x_k - x_k'}{\sigma_{X_k}}\right]^2\right]. \tag{4}$$

where: $k = 1,2$ (the number of type-2 non-singleton inputs), $\mu_{X_k}(x_k)$ is centered at $x_k = x_k'$ and σ_{X_k} is the standard deviation. The standard deviation of the RM exit surface temperature measurement, σ_{X_1}, was initially set to 13.0 ^oC and the standard deviation head end traveling time measurement, σ_{X_2}, was initially set to 2.41 s. The uncertainty of the input data was modeled as stationary additive noise using type-1 fuzzy sets.

4.6 Antecedent Membership Functions

The primary membership functions for each antecedent are interval type-2 fuzzy sets described by Gaussian primary membership functions with uncertain means:

$$\mu_k^i(x_k) = \exp\left[-\frac{1}{2}\left[\frac{x_k - m_k^i}{\sigma_k^i}\right]^2\right]. \tag{5}$$

where $m_k^i \in \left[m_{k1}^i, m_{k2}^i\right]$ is the uncertain mean, with k =1,2 (the number of antecedents) and i = 1,2,..9 (the number of M rules), and σ_k^i is the standard deviation. The means of the antecedent fuzzy sets are uniformly distributed over the entire input space.

Table 2 shows x_1 input calculated interval values of uncertainty, where $[m_{11}, m_{12}]$ is the uncertain mean and σ_1 is the standard deviation. Fig. 2 shows the initial membership functions for the antecedent fuzzy sets of x_1 input.

Table 3 shows x_2 input interval values of uncertainty, where $[m_{21}, m_{22}]$ is the uncertain mean and σ_2 is the standard deviation. Fig. 3 shows the initial membership functions for the antecedent fuzzy sets of x_2 input.

Table 2. x_1 input intervals of uncertainty

	m_{11} ^oC	m_{12} ^oC	σ_1 ^oC
1	950	952	60
2	1016	1018	60
3	1080	1082	60

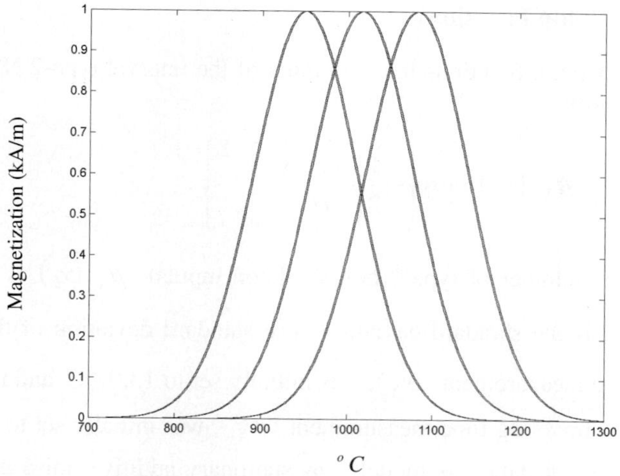

Fig. 2. Membership functions for the antecedent fuzzy sets of x_1 input

The mean and standard deviation of x_1 and x_2 inputs of training data are shown in Table 4.

Table 3. x_2 input intervals of uncertainty

Product Type	m_{21} s	m_{22} s	σ_2 s
A	32	34	10
B	42	44	10
C	56	58	10

The standard deviation of temperature noise σ_{n1} was initially set to 1 ^{o}C and the standard deviation of time noise σ_{n2} was set to 1 s.

Table 4. Calculated mean and standard deviation of x_1 and x_2 inputs

Product Type	m_{x1} ^{o}C	σ_{x1} ^{o}C	m_{x2} s	σ_{x2} s
Product A	1050.0	13.0	39.50	2.41
Product B	1037.2	22.98	39.67	2.52
Product C	1022.0	16.78	37.32	3.26

4.7 Consequent Membership Functions

Each consequent is an interval type-1 fuzzy set with $Y^i = [y_l^i, y_r^i]$ where

$$y_l^i = \sum_{j=1}^{p} c_j^i x_j + c_0^i - \sum_{j=1}^{p} |x_j| s_j^i - s_0^i \tag{6}$$

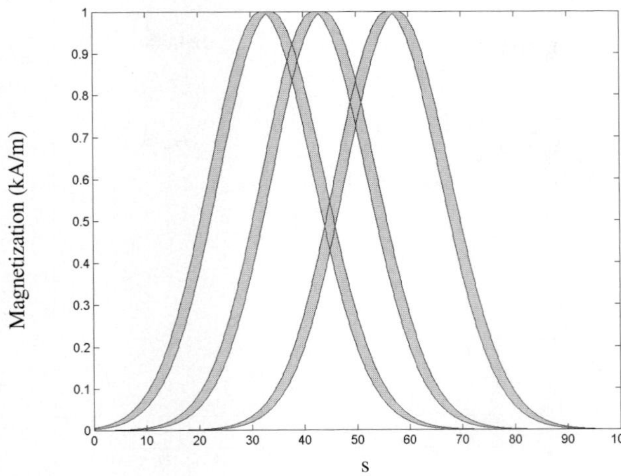

Fig. 3. Membership functions for the antecedent fuzzy sets of x_2 input

and

$$y_r^i = \sum_{j=1}^{p} c_j^i x_j + c_0^i + \sum_{j=1}^{p} |x_j| s_j^i + s_0^i \tag{7}$$

c_j^i denotes de center (mean) of C_j^i and s_j^i denotes the spread of C_j^i, with $i = 1,2,3,..,9$ and $j = 0,1,2$. Then y_l^i and y_r^i are the consequent parameters. When only the input-output data training pairs $\left(x^{(1)} : y^{(1)}\right),\ldots,\left(x^{(N)} : y^{(N)}\right)$ are available and there is not data information about the consequents, the initial values for the centroid parameters c_j^i and s_j^i can be chosen arbitrarily in the output space [16-17]. In this work the initial values of c_j^i were set equal to 0.001and the initial values of s_j^i equal to 0.0001, for $i = 1,2,3,..,9$ and $j = 0,1,2$.

4.8 Results

An interval type-2 TSK NSFLS-1 system was trained and used to predict the SB entry temperature, applying the RM exit measured transfer bar surface temperature and RM exit to SB entry zone traveling time as inputs. We ran fifteen epoch computations; one hundred ten parameters were tuned using eighty seven, sixty-eight and twenty-eight input-output training data pairs per epoch, for type A, type B and type C products respectively.

The performance evaluation for the type-2 TSK NSFLS-1 system was based on root mean-squared error (RMSE) benchmarking criteria as in [1]:

$$RMSE_{s2}(*) = \sqrt{\frac{1}{n}\sum_{k=1}^{n}\left[Y(k) - f_{s2-*}\left(\mathbf{x}^{(k)}\right)\right]^2} \tag{8}$$

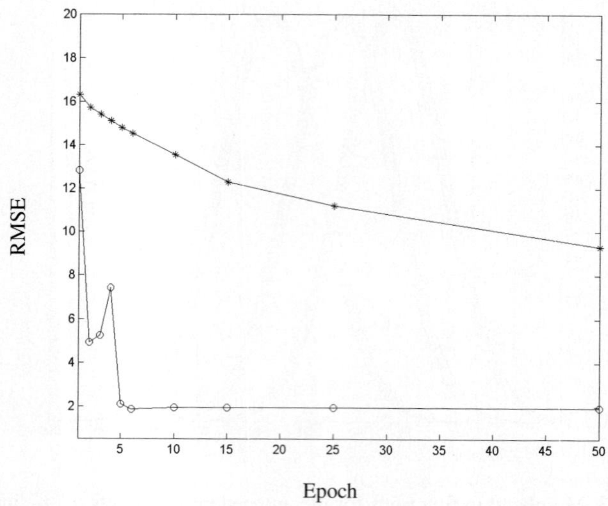

Fig. 4. Type-2 TSK SFLS (*), type-2 TSK NSFLS-1 (o)

where $Y(k)$ is the output data from the input-output checking pairs, $RMSE_{TSK,2}(*)$ stands for $RMSE_{TSK2,SFLS}(BP)$ and $RMSE_{TSK2,NSFLS-1}(BP)$, obtained when applied BP learning methods to an interval type-2 TSK SFLS and to an interval type-2 TSK NSFLS-1.

Fig. 4 shows the RMSEs of the two used interval type-2 TSK FLS systems with fifteen epochs' computations for type C product. It can be appreciated that the interval type-2 TSK NSFLS-1 outperforms the interval type-2 TSK SFLS. From epoch 1 to 4 the RMSE of the interval singleton type-2 TSK FLS has an oscillation, meaning that it is very sensitive to its learning parameters values. At epoch 5, it reaches its minimum RMSE and is stable for the rest of training.

5 Conclusions

We have presented an application of the proposed interval type-2 TSK NSFLS-1 fuzzy system, using only BP learning method. The interval type-2 TSK NSFLS-1 antecedent membership functions and consequent centroids absorbed the uncertainty introduced by the antecedent and consequent values initially selected, by the noisy temperature measurements, and by the inaccurate traveling time estimation. The non-singleton type-1 fuzzy inputs are able to compensate the uncertain measurements, expanding the applicability of the interval type-2 TSK FLS systems.

The reason that interval type-2 TSK NSFLS-1 achieves spectacular improvement in performance is that it has accounted for all of the uncertainties that are present, namely, rule uncertainties due to initial parameters selection and due to training with noisy data, and measurement uncertainties due to noisy measurements that are used during the prediction.

It has been shown that the proposed interval type-2 TSK NSFLS-1 systems can be applied in modeling and control of the steel coil temperature. It has also been envisaged its application in any linear and non-linear systems prediction and control.

References

1. Mendel, J. M. : Uncertain Rule Based Fuzzy Logic Systems: Introduction and New Directions, Upper Saddle River, NJ, Prentice-Hall, (2001)
2. Mendez, G., Cavazos, A., Leduc, L. , Soto, R.: Hot Strip Mill Temperature Prediction Using Hybrid Learning Interval Singleton Type-2 FLS, Proceedings of the IASTED International Conference on Modeling and Simulation, Palm Springs, February (2003), pp. 380-385
3. Mendez, G., Cavazos, A., Leduc, L. , Soto, R.: Modeling of a Hot Strip Mill Temperature Using Hybrid Learning for Interval Type-1 and Type-2 Non-Singleton Type-2 FLS. Proceedings of the IASTED International Conference on Artificial Intelligence and Applications, Benalmádena, Spain, September (2003), pp. 529-533
4. Mendez, G., Juarez, I.l: Orthogonal-Back Propagation Hybrid Learning Algorithm for Interval Type-1 Non-Singleton Type-2 Fuzzy Logic Systems, WSEAS Transactions on Systems, Issue 3, Vol. 4, March 2005, ISSN 1109-2777
5. Mendez, G., Castillo, O.: Interval Type-2 TSK Fuzzy Logic Systems Using Hybrid Learning Algorithm, FUZZ-IEEE 2005 The international Conference on Fuzzy Systems, Reno Nevada, USA, (2005), pp 230-235
6. Lee, D. Y., Cho, H. S.: Neural Network Approach to the Control of the Plate Width in Hot Plate Mills, International Joint Conference on Neural Networks, (1999), Vol. 5, pp. 3391-3396
7. Taylor, B. N., Kuyatt, C. E.: Guidelines for Evaluating and Expressing the Uncertainty of NIST Measurement Results, September (1994), NIST Technical Note 1297
8. Wang, L-X.: Fuzzy Systems are Universal Approximators, Proceedings of the IEEE Conf. On Fuzzy Systems, San Diego, (1992), pp. 1163-1170
9. Wang, L-X., Mendel, J. M.: Back-Propagation Fuzzy Systems as Nonlinear Dynamic System Identifiers, Proceedings of the IEEE Conf. On Fuzzy Systems, San Diego, CA. March (1992), pp. 1409-1418
10. Wang, L-X.: Fuzzy Systems are Universal Approximators, Proceedings of the IEEE Conf. On Fuzzy Systems, San Diego, (1992), pp. 1163-1170
11. Wang, L-X.: A Course in Fuzzy Systems and Control, Upper Saddle River, NJ: Prentice Hall PTR, (1997)
12. Jang, J. -S. R., Sun, C. -T., Mizutani, E.: Neuro-Fuzzy and Soft Computing: A Computational Approach to Learning and Machine Intelligence, Upper Saddle River, NJ: Prentice-Hall, (1997)
13. Jang, J. -S. R., Sun, C. -T.: Neuro-Fuzzy Modeling and Control, The Proceedings of the IEEEE, Vol. 3, Mach (1995), pp. 378-406
14. Liang, Q. J., Mendel, J. M.: Interval type-2 fuzzy logic systems: Theory and design, Trans. Fuzzy Sist., Vol. 8, Oct. (2000), pp. 535-550
15. John, R.I.: Embedded Interval Valued Type-2 Fuzzy Sets, IEEE Trans. Fuzzy Sist., (2002)
16. Mendel, J. M., John, R.I.: Type-2 Fuzzy Sets Made Simple, IEEE Transactions on Fuzzy Systems, Vol. 10, April (2002)
17. Mendel, J.M.: On the importance of interval sets in type-2 fuzzy logic systems, Proceedings of Joint 9th IFSA World Congress and 20th NAFIPS International Conference, (2001)
18. GE Models, Users reference, Vol. 1, Roanoke VA, (1993)

Fuzzy State Estimation of Discrete Event Systems

Juan Carlos González-Castolo and Ernesto López-Mellado

CINVESTAV-IPN Unidad Guadalajara
Av. Científica 1145, Col. El Bajío, 45010 Zapopan, Jal., México
{castolo, elopez}@gdl.cinvestav.mx

Abstract. This paper addresses state estimation of discrete event systems (DES) using a fuzzy reasoning approach; a method for approximating the current state of DES with uncertainty in the duration of activities is presented. The proposed method is based on a DES specification given as a fuzzy timed Petri net in which fuzzy sets are associated to places; a technique for the recursive computing of imprecise markings is given, then the conversion to discrete marking is presented.

1 Introduction

State estimation of dynamic systems is a resort often used when not all the state variables can be directly measured; observers are the entities providing the system state from the knowledge of its internal structure and its (partially) measured behavior. The problem of discrete event systems (DES) estimation has been addressed by Ramirez-Treviño et al. in [6]; in this work the marking of a Petri net (PN) model of a partially observed event driven system is computed from the evolution of its inputs and outputs.

The systems state can be also inferred using the knowledge on the duration of activities. However this task becomes complex when, besides the absence of sensors, the durations of the operations are uncertain; in this situation the observer obtains and revise a belief that approximates the current system state. The uncertainty of activities duration in DES can be handled using fuzzy PN (FPN) [5], [3], [11], [2], [4]; this PN extension has been applied to knowledge modeling [7], [8], [9], planning [10] , and controller design [1],[12].

In several works cited above, the proposed techniques include the computation of imprecise markings; however the class of models dealt does not include strongly connected PN for the modeling of cyclic behavior. In this paper we address the problem of calculating the fuzzy marking of a FPN when it evolves through T-semiflows; the degradation of the estimated marking is analyzed and characterized, then the discretization of the fuzzy marking is obtained. The aim of the proposed techniques focusses on the fuzzy estimation estate, allowing the monitoring of systems.

The paper is structured as follows. In the next Section, theories of fuzzy sets and Petri nets are overviewed. In Section 3, FPN are presented and an example is included to illustrate its functioning. In section 4 the methodology for state

A. Gelbukh and C.A. Reyes-Garcia (Eds.): MICAI 2006, LNAI 4293, pp. 90–100, 2006.

estimation is presented. In section 5 the procedure for obtaining the discrete state (defuzzification) is described. Section 6 includes some concluding remarks.

2 Background

2.1 Possibility Theory

In theory of possibility, a fuzzy set $\tilde{A}$ is used to delimit ill-known values or for representing values characterized by symbolic expressions. The set is defined as $\tilde{A} = (a_1, a_2, a_3, a_4)$ such that $a_1, a_2, a_3, a_4 \in \mathbb{R}^+$and $a_1 \leq a_2 \leq a_3 \leq a_4$. For example: the fuzzy set $\tilde{A}$ represents the symbolic expression *'the activity will stop when time is around 2.5'*. The membership function $\alpha(\tau)$ gives a numerical estimated of the possibility that the activity will stop at a given time. The fuzzy set $\tilde{A}$ delimits the run time as follows:

- The ranges values (a_1, a_2) and (a_3, a_4) indicate that the activity is possibly executed: $\alpha(\tau) \in (0, 1)$. When $\tau \in (a_1, a_2)$, the function $\alpha(\tau)$ grows towards 1, which means that the possibility of stopping increases. When $\tau \in (a_3, a_4)$, the function $\alpha(\tau)$ decreases towards 0, representing that there is a reduction of the possibility of stopping.
- The values $(0, a_1]$ mean that the activity is running.
- The values $[a_4, +\infty)$ mean that the activity is stopped
- The values $[a_2, a_3]$ represent full possibility, that is $\alpha(\tau) = 1$, represents that is certain that activity is stopped.

Remark 1. A fuzzy set, denoted as $\tilde{A}$, is referred indistinctly by the function $\alpha(\tau)$ or the characterization (a_1, a_2, a_3, a_4). For simplicity, the fuzzy possibility distribution of the time is described with a trapezoidal form or triangular form. The numerical estimate $\alpha(\tau)$ is known as the membership function of set $\tilde{A}$.

Definition 1. *Let $\tilde{A}$ and $\tilde{B}$ be two trapezoidal fuzzy sets where $\tilde{A} = (a_1, a_2, a_3, a_4)$ and $\tilde{B} = (b_1, b_2, b_3, b_4)$. The fuzzy sets addition $\oplus$ is defined as: $\tilde{A} \oplus \tilde{B} = (a_1 + b_1, a_2 + b_2, a_3 + b_3, a_4 + b_4)$.*

Definition 2. *Let $x, y \in X$. If $x \leq (\geq) y$, then x is called the minimun (maximun) of X with respect to the relation $\leq (\geq)$. The* min(max) *operator obtained the minimun (maximun) x of X.*

Definition 3. *The* fmin *and* fmax *denote the minimun and maximun operator over fuzzy sets and they obtained the maximun commun and maximun, respectively, $\alpha(\tau)$ among fuzzy sets i.e.: $fmin(A_1, ..., A_n) = \max(\alpha_i(\tau)) \mid \alpha_i(\tau) \in A_j; i = 1, ..., n; j = 1...n$. $fmax(A_1, ..., A_n) = \max(\alpha_i(\tau)) \mid \alpha_i(\tau) \in A_i; i = 1, ..., n$*

Remark 2. The standar intersection and standard union are gives as: $(\tilde{A} \cap \tilde{B}) = f\min(\tilde{A}, \tilde{B})$ and $(\tilde{A} \cup \tilde{B}) = fmax(\tilde{A}, \tilde{B})$ respectively.

Definition 4. *The distribution of possibility before and after $\tilde{A}$ are a fuzzy sets $\tilde{A}^a = (-\infty, a_2, a_3, a_4)$ and $\tilde{A}^d = (a_1, a_2, a_3, +\infty)$, respectively, and they are defined as a function $\alpha_{(-\infty, \tilde{A}]}(\tau)$ and $\alpha_{(\tilde{A}, +\infty]}(\tau)$, respectively, such that,*

$$\alpha_{(-\infty,\tilde{A}]}(\tau) = \sup_{\tau\prime \geq \tau} \alpha(\tau\prime) \text{ and } \alpha_{(\tilde{A},+\infty]}(\tau) = \sup_{\tau\prime \leq \tau} \alpha(\tau\prime) \quad (1)$$

The lmax *function is calculated as follows:* $lmax(\tilde{A}, \tilde{B}) = fmin(\tilde{A}^d, \tilde{B}^a)$.

Definition 5. *The latest(earliest) operation picks the latest(earliest) fuzzy set among n fuzzy sets and they are calculated as:* $latest(\tilde{A}, \tilde{B}) = fmin[fmin(\tilde{A}^a, \tilde{B}^a), fmax(\tilde{A}^d, \tilde{B}^d)]$, $earliest(\tilde{A}, \tilde{B}) = fmin[fmax(\tilde{A}^a, \tilde{B}^a), fmin(\tilde{A}^d, \tilde{B}^d)]$.

2.2 Petri Nets

Definition 6. *An ordinary PN structure G is a bipartite digraph represented by the 4-tuple* $G = (P, T, I, O)$ *where* $P = \{p_1, p_2, ..., p_n\}$ *and* $T = \{t_1, t_2, ..., t_m\}$ *are finite sets of vertices called respectively places and transitions,* $I(O) : P \times T \rightarrow \{0, 1\}$ *is a function representing the arcs going from places to transitions (transitions to places).*

Pictorially, places are represented by circles, transitions are represented by rectangles, and arcs are depicted as arrows. The symbol $^o t_j (t_j{}^o)$ *denotes the set of all places* p_i *such that* $I(p_i, t_j) \neq 0$ $(O(p_i, t_j) \neq 0)$*. Analogously,* $^o p_i (p_i{}^o)$ *denotes the set of all transitions* t_j *such that* $O(p_i, t_j) \neq 0$ $(I(p_i, t_j) \neq 0)$.

The pre-incidence matrix of G is $C^- = [c^-_{ij}]$ where $c^-_{ij} = I(p_i, t_j)$; the post-incidence matrix of G is $C^+ = [c^+_{ij}]$ where $c^+_{ij} = O(p_i, t_j)$; the incidence matrix of G is $C = C^+ - C^-$.

A marking function $M : P \rightarrow \mathbb{Z}^+$represents the number of tokens (depicted as dots) residing inside each place. The marking of a PN is usually expressed as an n-entry vector.

Definition 7. *A Petri Net system or Petri Net (PN) is the pair* $N = (G, M_0)$*, where G is a PN structure and* M_0 *is an initial token distribution.*

In a PN system, a transition t_j is enabled at marking M_k if $\forall p_i \in P$, $M_k(p_i) \geq I(p_i, t_j)$; an enabled transition t_j can be fired reaching a new marking M_{k+1} which can be computed as $M_{k+1} = M_k + Cv_k$, where $v_k(i) = 0, i \neq j, v_k(j) = 1$, this equation is called the PN state equation. The reachability set of a PN is the set of all possible reachable marking from M_0 firing only enabled transitions; this set is denoted by $R(G, M_0)$.

A transition $t_k \in T$ is live, for a marking M_0, if $\forall M_k \in R(G, M_0)$, $\exists M_n \in R(G, M_0)$ such that t_k is enabled ($M_n \xrightarrow{t_k}$). A PN is live if all its transitions are live. A PN is said 1-bounded, or safe, for a marking M_0, if $\forall p_i \in P$ and $\forall M_j \in R(G, M_0)$, it holds that $M_j(p_i) \leq 1$.

Remark 3. In this work we deal with live and safe PN.

Definition 8. *A p-invariant Y of a PN is a rational valued solution of equation* $Y^T C = 0 \mid Y > 0$*. The support of a p-invariant* Y_i *is the set* $\|Y_i\| = \{p_j \mid Y_i(p_j) \neq 0\}$*. The number of p-invariants is denoted with* $|Y| = |\{Y_i\}|$.

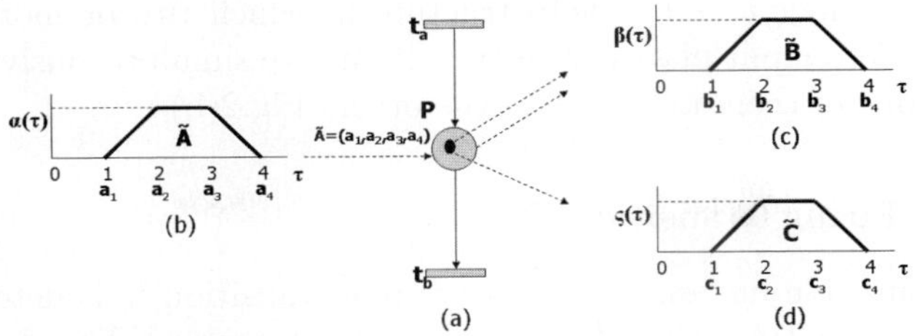

Fig. 1. (a) Fuzzy Petri net, (b) The fuzzy set associated to places or tokens. (c) Fuzzy set to place or mark associated. (d) Fuzzy timestamp.

3 Fuzzy Petri Nets

Definition 9. *A fuzzy Petri net structure is a 3-tuple* $FPn = (N, \Gamma, \xi)$*; where* $N = (G, M_0)$ *is a PN,* $\Gamma = \{\tilde{A}_1, \tilde{A}_2, ..., \tilde{A}_n\}$ *is a collection of fuzzy sets,* $\xi : P \longrightarrow \Gamma$ *is a function that associates a fuzzy set* $\tilde{A}_i \in \Gamma$ *to each place* $p_i \in P$*;* $i = 1..n \mid n = |P|$.

3.1 Fuzzy Sets Associated to Places

The fuzzy set $\tilde{A} = (a_1, a_2, a_3, a_4)$ Fig.1(b) represents the *static* possibility distribution $\alpha(\tau) \in [0, 1]$ of the instant at which a token leaves a place $p \in P$, starting from the instant when p is marked. This set does not change during the FPN execution.

3.2 Fuzzy Sets Associated to Tokens

The fuzzy set $\tilde{B} = (b_1, b_2, b_3, b_4)$ Fig.1(c) represents the *dynamic* possibility distribution $\beta(\tau) \in [0, 1]$ associated to a token residing within a $p \in P$; it also represents the instant at which such a token leaves the place, starting from the instant when p is marked. $\tilde{B}$ is computed from $\tilde{A}$ every time the place is marked during the marking evolution of the PN.

A token begins to be available for enabling transitions at $\beta(b_1)$. Thus $\tilde{B}^d = (b_1, b_2, b_3, +\infty)$ represents the possibility distribution of available tokens.

The fuzzy set $\tilde{C} = (c_1, c_2, c_3, c_4)$, known as *fuzzy timestamp*, Fig.1(d) is a dynamic possibility distribution $\varsigma(\tau) \in [0, 1]$ that represents the duration of a token within a place $p \in P$.

3.3 Fuzzy Enabling Transition Date

Definition 10. *The fuzzy enabling time* $e_{t_k}(\tau)$ *of a transition* t_k *is a possibility distribution of the latest leaving instant among the leaving instants* $\tilde{B}_i$ *of all tokens of the* $p_i \in {}^o t$*. Fig.2(a).*

$$e_{t_k}(\tau) = latest\left\{\tilde{B}_i, i = 1, 2, ..., n\right\} \tag{2}$$

A structural conflict is a *PN* sub-structure in which two or more transitions share one or more input places; such transitions are simultaneously enabled and the firing of one of them may disable the others Fig.2(b).

3.4 Fuzzy Firing Transition Date

The firing transition instant or date $o_k(\tau)$ of a transition t_k is determined with respect to the set of transitions $\{t_j\}$ simultaneously enabled. This date, expressed as a possibility distribution, is computed as follows

$$o_k(\tau) = fmin\left\{e_{t_k}(\tau),\ earliest\left\{e_{t_j}(\tau), j = 1, 2, ..., k, ..., m\right\}\right\} \tag{3}$$

3.5 Fuzzy Timestamp and Marking Evolution

For a given place p_s, possibility distribution $\tilde{B}_s$ may be computed from $\tilde{A}_s$ and the firing dates $o_k(\tau)$ of a $t_k \in {}^o p_s$ using the following expression

$$\tilde{B}_s = fmax\left\{o_j(\tau) | j = 1..k..m, m = |{}^o p_s|\right\} \oplus \tilde{A}_s \tag{4}$$

Fuzzy timestamp. The marking does not disappear of ${}^o t$ and appear in t^o, instantaneously. The fuzzy timestamp $\tilde{C}_s$ is the time elapse possibility that a token is in a place $p_s \in P$. The possibility distribution $\tilde{C}_s$ is computed from the occurrence dates of both ${}^o p$ and p^o Fig. 2(e):

$$\tilde{C}_s = lmax(earliest\{o_{t_k}(\tau) | o_{t_k}(\tau) \in {}^o p_s\}, latest\{o'_{t_r}(\tau) | o'_{t_r}(\tau) \in p^o{}_s\}) \tag{5}$$

where $k = 1..m, r = 1..n$

3.6 Modeling Example

Example 1. Consider the system shown in Fig.3(a); it consists of two cars *car1* and *car2* which move along independent ways executing the set of activities $Op = \{Right\ Car1,\ RightCar2,\ ChargeCar1,\ LeftCar12,\ DischargeCar12\}$. The operation of the system is automated following the sequence described in the *PN* of Fig.3(b) in which the activities are associated to places p_2, p_3, p_4, p_5, p_1 respectively. The ending time possibility $\tilde{A}_i$ for every activity is given in the model.

Considering that there are not sensors detecting the activities in the system, the behavior is then analyzed through the estimated state.

Initial conditions. Initially $M_0 = \{p_1\}$, therefore, the enabling date $e_{t_1}(\tau)$ of transition t_1 is immediate i.e. $(0, 0, 0, 0)$. Since $|{}^o t_1| = 1$ then $o_{t_1}(\tau) = e_{t_1}(\tau)$.

Firing t_1. When t_1 is fired, the token is removed from p_1; p_2 and p_3 get one token each one. The possibility sets $\tilde{B}_2$, $\tilde{B}_3$ represent the end of activities $RightCar1$ and $RightCar2$, respectively, and they coincide with $\tilde{A}_2$ and $\tilde{A}_3$ respectively; therefore: $\tilde{B}_2 = \left(0.9\ 1\ 1\ 1.1\right)$, $\tilde{B}_3 = \left(0.8\ 1\ 1\ 1.2\right)$.

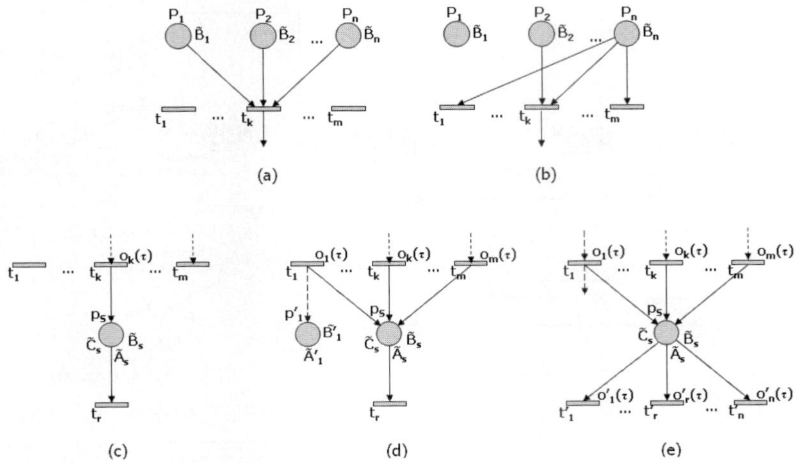

Fig. 2. (a) Transition enabled for over a place. (b) Estructural conflic. (c) Place with one input. (d) Place with over an input. (e) Fuzzy timestamp $\tilde{C}_s$.

Firing t_2. When $RightCar1$ is finishing, t_2 is being enabled. $e_{t_2}(\tau)$ is a possible date for that *car1* is able to perform $ChargeCar1$; so it coincides with $\tilde{B}_2$: $e_{t_2}(\tau) = \left(0.9\ 1\ 1\ 1.1\right)$. Since p_2 is the only input place to t_2 the firing date coincides with $e_{t_2}(\tau)$ therefore: $o_{t_2}(\tau) = \left(0.9\ 1\ 1\ 1.1\right)$. The set $\tilde{C}_2$ is the possibility distribution of the time at which $RightCar1$ is executing. So $\tilde{C}_2 = lmax\left\{o_{t_1}(\tau), o_{t_2}(\tau)\right\} = \left(0\ 0\ 1\ 1.1\right)$. The set $\tilde{B}_4$ is the possibility distribution of the instant at which *car1* finishes $ChargeCar1$ and it can be calculated as $\tilde{B}_4 = o_{t_2}(\tau) \oplus \tilde{A}_4 = \left(2.6\ 3\ 3\ 3.4\right)$.

Firing t_3. When $ChargeCar1$ and $RightCar2$ are finishing, the transition t_3 is being enabled. $e_{t_3}(\tau)$ is a possible date for that *car1* and *car2* may execute $LeftCar12$. Since t_3 is an attribution transition, then the enabling fuzzy time is computed as: $e_{t_3}(\tau) = latest\left\{\tilde{B}_3, \tilde{B}_4\right\} = \left(2.6\ 3\ 3\ 3.4\right)$. The occurrence time for t_3 coincides with $e_{t_3}(\tau)$, i.e. $o_{t_3}(\tau) = \left(2.6\ 3\ 3\ 3.4\right)$. The execution of $ChargeCar1$, is described by $\tilde{C}_4 = lmax\left\{o_{t_2}(\tau), o_{t_3}(\tau)\right\} = \left(0.9\ 1\ 3\ 3.4\right)$. $\tilde{C}_3$ describes the execution of $RightCar2$; it is computed as $\tilde{C}_3 = lmax\left\{o_{t_1}(\tau), o_{t_3}(\tau)\right\} = \left(0\ 0\ 3\ 3.4\right)$. The set $\tilde{B}_5$ is the possibility distribution of the time at which *car1* and *car2* finish $LeftCar12$; it can be obtained by: $\tilde{B}_5 = o_{t_3}(\tau) \oplus \tilde{A}_5 = \left(4.1\ 5\ 5\ 5.9\right)$.

Firing t_4. When $LeftCar12$ is finishing, the transition t_4 is being enabled. $e_{t_4}(\tau)$ is a possible date for that *car1* and *car2* are able to perform $Discharge$ $Car12$, and it coincides with $\tilde{B}_5$: $e_{t_4}(\tau) = \left(4.1\ 5\ 5\ 5.9\right)$. The firing date coincides with $e_{t_4}(\tau)$: $o_{t_4}(\tau) = \left(4.1\ 5\ 5\ 5.9\right)$. The set $\tilde{C}_5$ is the possibility distribution of the time at which $LeftCar12$ is executing, and it is calculated by: $\tilde{C}_5 = lmax\left\{o_{t_3}(\tau), o_{t_4}(\tau)\right\} = \left(2.6\ 3\ 5\ 5.9\right)$. The set $\tilde{B}_1$ is the possibility distribution of the time at which *car1* and *car2* finish $DischargeCar12$; it can be calculated by: $\tilde{B}_1 = o_{t_4}(\tau) \oplus \tilde{A}_1 = \left(5.8\ 7\ 7\ 8.2\right)$.

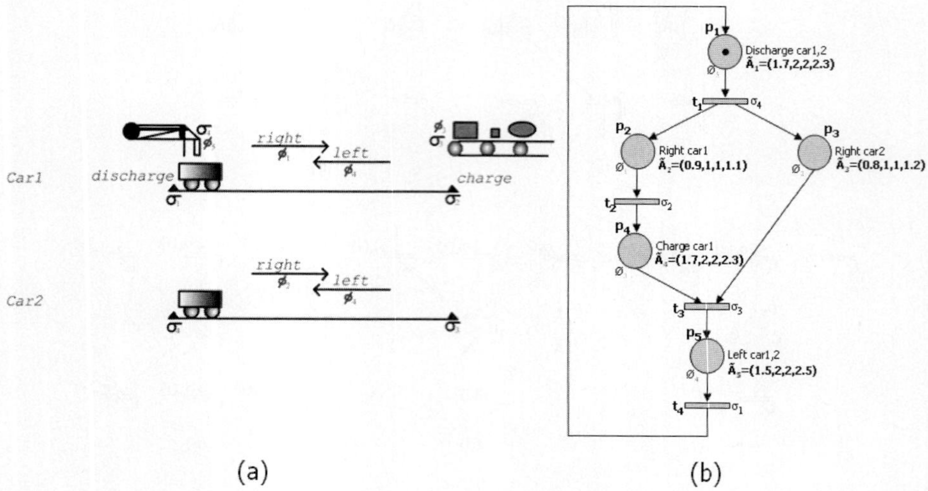

Fig. 3. (a) Two cars system. (b) Fuzzy Petri net.

Firing t_1. When *Discharge Car*12 is finishing, t_1 is being enabled. $o_{t_1}(\tau)$ coincides with $e_{t_1}(\tau)$, and $e_{t_1}(\tau)$ coincides with $\tilde{B}_1$: $o_{t_1}(\tau) = e_{t_1}(\tau) = \left(5.8\ 7\ 7\ 8.2\right)$; $\tilde{C}_1$ is the possibility distribution of the time at which *Discharge Car*12 is executing; it is obtained by $\tilde{C}_1 = lmax\left\{o_{t_4}(\tau), o_{t_1}(\tau)\right\} = \left(4.1\ 5\ 7\ 8.2\right)$. The Fig.4 present the marking evolution of one cycle and some steps.

4 State Estimation of the FPN

4.1 Marking Estimation

Definition 11. *The* marking estimation Ξ *in the instant* τ *is described by the function* $\psi(\tau) \in [0,1]$ *which recognize the possible marked place* $p_u \in \|Y_i\| \mid i \in \{1,2,...,|Y|\}$*, among other possible places* $p_v \in \|Y_i\| \mid v \neq u$*. The function* $\psi_i(\tau)$ *is a value that indicates the minimal difference that exist among the bigger possibility that the token is in a place* $(\varsigma_u(\tau))$ *and the possibility that token is in any another place*$(\varsigma_v(\tau))$*. The function* $\psi(\tau)$ *is calculated as,*

$$\psi(\tau) = fmin\left(\varsigma_u(\tau) - \varsigma_v(\tau)\right) \mid u \in \{1,2,...,\|Y\|\}; \forall v \neq u, v \in \{1,2,...,\|Y\|\} \tag{6}$$

where $\varsigma_u(\tau) \geq \varsigma_v(\tau)$*.*

In the previous definition $\varsigma_u(\tau) \neq 0$ for any time, since it is always possible to find a token in some place.

Example 2. The FPN in Fig.3(b) has two p-invariants with supports $\|Y_1\| = \{p_1, p_2, p_4, p_5\}$ and $\|Y_2\| = \{p_1, p_3, p_5\}$. The Fig.5 shows the fuzzy sets $\tilde{C}$ obtained from evolution of the marking in the p-component corresponding to Y_1. This

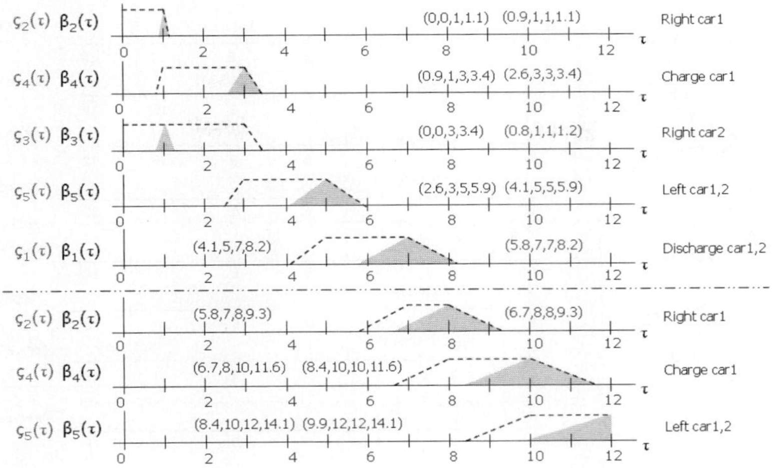

Fig. 4. Fuzzy marking evolution

evolution shows the first cycle and some next steps of other cycle. In order to obtain the activity estimation that the *car1* is executing, we need obtain the *marking estimation* ($\psi_1(\tau)$). During the time elapse $\tau \in [0,\ 0.9]$, it is observed that $\psi_1(\tau) = \varsigma_2(\tau)$, because there exists not another $\varsigma(\tau) \neq 0$ indicating that the token exists in another place; in this case, p_2 is marked with absolute possibility. For $\tau \in (0.9,\ 1)$ the possibility that the place p_2 is marked is one. However, the possibility that the place p_4 is marked is increased; therefore when $\varsigma_4(\tau)$ is increased, then $\psi_1(\tau)$ is reduced. In $\tau = 1$, there exist the absolute possibility that the token is in p_2 and p_4. In this case it is not possible to know where is the token, therefore $\psi_1(\tau) = 0$. When $\tau \in (1,\ 1.1)$, $\varsigma_4(\tau) = 1$ and $\varsigma_2(\tau)$ is reduced, we obtain that $\psi_1(\tau)$ is increased. Finally, we will see that for $\tau \in [1.1,\ 2.6]$, $\psi_1(\tau) = \varsigma_4(\tau)$; it is absolutely possible that the p_4 is marked.

Definition 12. *The* token possibility measure $V(\tau)$ *is an estimation of the position of the token with truth grade, which is expressed as the integration of the marking estimation along the elapsed time,*

$$V(\tau) = \frac{\int_{\tau_u}^{\tau_v} \psi(\tau)\, d(\tau)}{\tau_v - \tau_u}, \tau_u < \tau_v \qquad (7)$$

4.2 State Estimation

Definition 13. *The* state estimation S, *in the instant* τ *is described by the function* $\S(\tau) \in [0,1]$, *which determines the possible state of the system among other possible states; it is calculated by*

$$\S(\tau) = fmin(\psi_i(\tau)\, |i = 1...|Y|) \qquad (8)$$

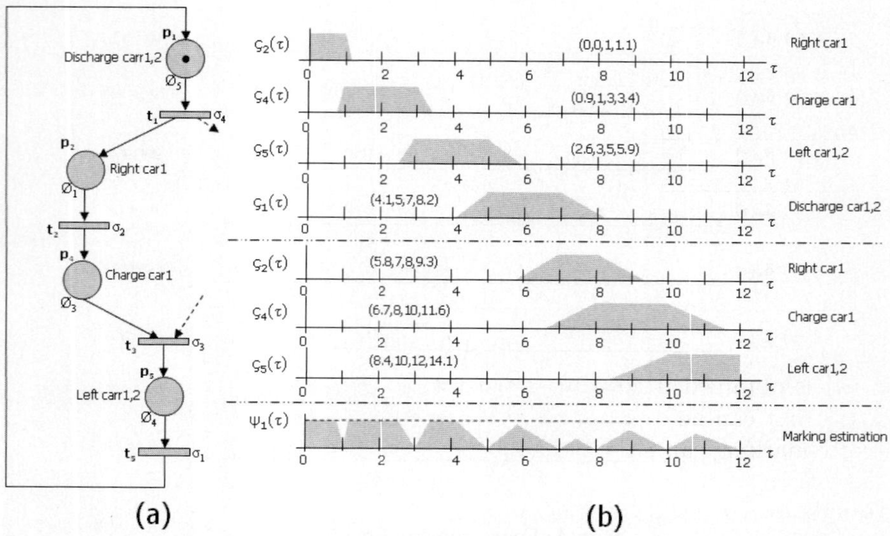

Fig. 5. (a) P-invariant (Y_1). (b) Marking estimation (ψ_1).

Example 3. Following the previous example, in order to obtain an estimation about the activity that the *cars* are executing, we need to obtain the *state estimation.* In this case $\S(\tau) = fmin\,(\psi_1\,(\tau)\,, \psi_2\,(\tau))$ as showin in Fig.6(a). We observe that $\S(\tau)$ coincides exactly with $\psi_1\,(\tau)$ because always $\psi_2\,(\tau) > \psi_1\,(\tau)$.

Definition 14. *The* certainty degree $W(\tau)$ *is a truth measure on the state estimation; it is expressed as the integration of the state estimation along the elapsed time:*

$$W(\tau) = \frac{\int_{\tau_u}^{\tau_v} \S\,(\tau)\,d\,(\tau)}{\tau_v - \tau_u}, \tau_u < \tau_v \tag{9}$$

We observed that if $\S(\tau) = 1$, $\forall\tau$ then $W(\tau) = 1$, then it means that ti is always possible to know precisely the system state.

Example 4. In Fig.6(a) $W(\tau)$ is obtained from the state estimation of the previous example. For $0 \leq \tau \leq 0.9$ it is possible to know the system state with full certainty. In $\tau = 2$, the certainty of the estimated state is decreased from 1 to 0.95. For $\tau = 3$, this certainty is 0.9. Finally, in $\tau = 5 : W(\tau) = 0.79$.

5 Discrete State from the FPN

In order to obtain a possible discrete marking $\bar{M}(\tau)$ of the FPN it is necessary to make a defuzzufication of $M(\tau)$. This can be accomplished taking into account the possible discrete marking $\bar{M}_i(\tau)$ of every P-component induced by Y_i.

Before describing the procedure to obtain $\bar{M}(\tau)$, we define $M(\tau)$ as:

$$M(\tau) = \left[m_{p_1}(\tau) \ldots m_{p_n}(\tau)\right]^T \mid n = |P| \tag{10}$$

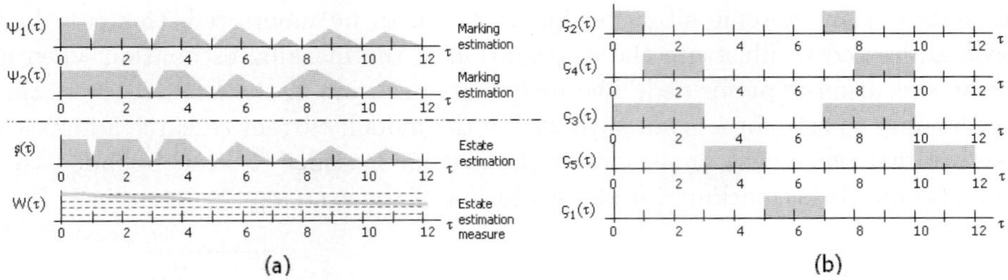

Fig. 6. (a) State estimation and State possibility measure. (b) Discrete state.

where $m_{p_k}(\tau) \mid k = 1...n$ is the estimated marking of the place $p_k \in P$. The $m_{p_k}(\tau)$ is obtained from $\sum \varsigma_{p_k}(\tau)$, since for each cycle in the fuzzy Petri net $\exists \varsigma_{p_k}(\tau)$ that can be overlapped with others $\varsigma_{p_k}(\tau)$ of previous cycles. Now, the discrete marking can be obtained with the following precedure.

Algorithm
Input: $M(\tau), Y$
Output: $\bar{M}(\tau)$

---

1. $\bar{M}(\tau) \leftarrow \vec{0}$
2. $\forall Y_i \mid i = 1, ..., |Y|$
2.1 $\forall p_k \in Y_i$
2.1.1 $\tilde{m}_q = \max \tilde{M}(p_k)$
2.2 $\bar{M}\,(p_q) = 1$

Example 5. The supports of the p-invariants of Fig. 3 are $\|Y_1\| = \{p_1, p_2, p_4, p_5\}$ and $\|Y_2\| = \{p_1, p_3, p_5\}$. The marked from $\tau = 0^+ \to 1$ does not change, therefore $\bar{M}(0^+ \to 0.9) = M_{0^+} = \left[1\,0\,0\,0\,0\right]^T$. For $\tau = 0.95$ is $M\,(0.95) = \left[0\,1\,1\,0.5\,0\right]^T$, therefore

$$\bar{M}_1(0.95) = \left[0\,1\,0\,0\,0\right]^T \qquad \bar{M}_2(0.95) = \left[0\,0\,1\,0\,0\right]^T$$
$$\breve{M}(0.95) = \left[0\,1\,0\,0\,0\right]^T + \left[0\,0\,1\,0\,0\right]^T = \left[0\,1\,1\,0\,0\right]^T$$
$$\bar{M}(0.95) = \left[0\,1\,1\,0\,0\right]^T$$

The Fig.6(b) shows the marking obtained in different instants.

6 Conclusion

This paper addressed the state estimation problem of discrete event systems whose the duration of activities is ill known; fuzzy sets represent the uncertainty of the ending of activities. Several novel notions have been introduced in the Fuzzy Petri Net definition, and a new formulation for computing fuzzy marking has been proposed; furthermore a simple and efficient method for obtaining the discrete estimated state is presented. When any activity of a system cannot be measured is an extreme situation for a system to be monitored; this case has been addressed to illustrate the degradation of the marking estimation when a cyclic execution is performed. The inclusion of sensors in the FPN recovers the uncertainty to zero for a given path within the model; current research addresses the optimal placement of sensors in the system in order to keep bounded the uncertainty of the marking for any evolution of the system.

References

1. D. Andreu, J-C. Pascal, R. Valette.: Fuzzy Petri Net-Based Programmable Logic Controller. IEEE Trans. Syst. Man. Cybern, Vol. 27, No. 6, Dec. (1997) 952-961
2. W.Pedrycz, H.Camargo.: Fuzzy timed Petri Nets. Elsevier, Fuzzy Sets and Systems, 140 (2003) 301-330
3. J. Cardoso, H. Camargo.: Fuzziness in Petri Nets. Physica Verlag. (1999)
4. Z. Ding, H. Bunke, M. Schneider, A. Kandel.: Fuzzy Timed Petri Net, Definitions, Properties, and Applications. Elsevier, Mathematical and Computer Modelling 41 (2005) 345-360
5. T. Muratta.: Temporal uncertainty and fuzzy-timing high-level Petri nets. Lect. Notes Comput. Sci., Vol. 1091 (1996) 29-58
6. A. Ramirez-Treviño, A. Rivera-Rangel, E. López-Mellado: Observability of Discrete Event Systems Modeled by Interpreted Petri Nets. IEEE Transactions on Robotics and Automation. Vol.19, No. 4, august (2003) 557-565
7. S. Chen, J. Ke, J. Chang.: Knowledge representation using Fuzzy Petri nets. IEEE Trans. Knowledge Data Eng., Vol. 2, No. 3, (1990) 311-319
8. S. M. Koriem.: A Fuzzy Petri Net Tool For Modeling and Verification of Knowledge-Based Systems. The Computer Journal, Vol 43, No. 3 (2000) 206-223
9. R.Victor L. Shen.: Reinforcement Learning for High-Level Fuzzy Petri Nets. IEEE Trans. on Syst., Man, & Cybern., Vol. 33, No. 2, april (2003) 351–362
10. T. Cao, A. C. Sanderson.: Intelligent Task Planning Using Fuzzy Petri Nets. Intelligent Control and Intelligent Automation, Vol. 3. Word Scientific (1996)
11. S. Hennequin, D. Lefebvre, A. El Moudni.: Fuzzy Multimodel of Timed Petri Nets. Syst., Man, Cybern., Vol. 31, No. 2, april (2001) 245–250
12. G. Leslaw, J. Kluska.: Hardware Implementation of Fuzzy Petri Net as a Controller. IEEE Transactions on Systems, Man, and Cybernetics, Vol. 34, No. 3, june (2004) 1315–1324

Real-Time Adaptive Fuzzy Motivations for Evolutionary Behavior Learning by a Mobile Robot

Wolfgang Freund, Tomas Arredondo Vidal, César Muñoz, Nicolás Navarro, and Fernando Quirós

Universidad Técnica Federico Santa María, Valparaíso, Chile,
Departamento de Electrónica,
Casilla 110 V, Valparaíso, Chile
Wolfgang.Freund@usm.cl

Abstract. In this paper we investigate real-time adaptive extensions of our fuzzy logic based approach for providing biologically based motivations to be used in evolutionary mobile robot learning. The main idea is to introduce active battery level sensors and recharge zones to improve robot behavior for reaching survivability in environment exploration. In order to achieve this goal, we propose an improvement of our previously defined model, as well as a hybrid controller for a mobile robot, combining behavior-based and mission-oriented control mechanism. This method is implemented and tested in action sequence based environment exploration tasks in a Khepera mobile robot simulator. We investigate our technique with several sets of configuration parameters and scenarios. The experiments show a significant improvement in robot responsiveness regarding survivability and environment exploration.

Keywords: Fuzzy logic, mobile robot, real-time, environment exploration.

1 Introduction

Real-time systems are concerned with real-world applications, where temporal constraints are part of system specification imposed by the environment, i.e. firm-deadlines in non critical environments, soft-deadlines in non-critical control applications and hard deadlines in safety-critical systems. In the last years more research effort have been made applying soft-computing techniques to real-time control problems [1,2,3]. The main advantage over traditional control mechanisms is in the additional robustness regarding lack or poor environmental information (if not the problem definition itself) which concern almost all real-time control applications [4].

On the other hand, soft-computing based methods are more intuitive than strict formal models, soft-computing (e.g. fuzzy logic) aim to gain from operator perceptions and through iteration obtain capabilities of the real expert. However, not much attention has been given to real-time considerations, regarding soft or hard deadlines. Some important aspects of real-time must be taken into account:

A. Gelbukh and C.A. Reyes-Garcia (Eds.): MICAI 2006, LNAI 4293, pp. 101–111, 2006.

how could soft-computing techniques, such as fuzzy logic, neural networks or genetic algorithms affect systems responsiveness and survivability?

Recently, we have proposed a fuzzy logic based method that provides a natural interface in order to give a variety of motivations to be used in robotic learning. To test the validity of the proposed method we tested the fuzzy logic based method on behavior based navigation and environment recognition tasks within a Khepera robot simulator [5].

In order to introduce our behavior based mobile robot methodology in a real-world application, we introduce an active battery sensor to allow for the detection of low battery conditions and we also provide various number of recharge zones withing different room configurations. This real-time extension must be capable of supporting different sets of motivations, improving survivability and exploration performance.

Our primary goal consists of full environment exploration considering energy consumption and recharge zones. To reach this target, robot's behavior must be influenced through fitness evaluation for recharging the battery before it could be too late. In this approach we consider soft-deadlines as a dangerous but not critical battery charge level which affects robot's fitness. Hard-deadlines are considered as a possible (because of partial knowledge) point where, if the robot does not recharge his battery, an unrecoverable final freezing state is possible. Soft vs hard-deadlines force a change in the robot's operation from behavior-based to mission-oriented (hybrid), which guides the robot using the shortest known path to a nearest previously found charging zone.

The rest of the paper is organized as follows. In Section 2 a brief description of our previously defined model is given. In Section 3 the real-time extension of our model is presented. In Section 4 we show the experimental setup and test results. Finally, in Section 5 some conclusions and future work are drawn.

2 Soft-Computing in Robotic Behavioral Control

Much recent progress in robotic navigation has relied on soft-computing (e.g. Fuzzy logic) based methods for their sucess [6,7]. Fuzzy logic has been a mainstain of several efforts in this direction: using independent distributed fuzzy agents and weighted vector summation via fuzzy multiplexers for producing drive and steer commands [7], neuro-fuzzy controllers for behavior design [8], fuzzy modular motion planning [9], fuzzy integration of groups of behaviors [10], multiple fuzzy agents for behavior fusion [11], *GA* based neuro fuzzy reinforcement learning agents [12], and fuzzy logic integration for robotic navigation in challenging terrain [13]. Our research shows that fuzzy logic has not seen wide usage in robotics in terms of motivating actions and behaviors. We have implemented such motivations (e.g. a need, desire or want) as fuzzy fitness functions for robotic behaviors that serve to influence the intensity and direction of robotic behaviors. Motivation is generally accepted as involved in the performance of learned behaviors. That is a learned behavior may not occur unless it's driven

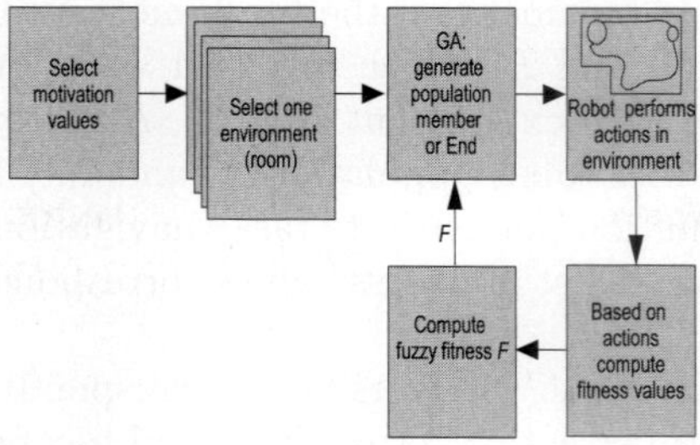

Fig. 1. System Overview

Algorithm FuzzyFitness
Input:
N : number of fuzzy motivations;
M : number of membership functions per motivation;
$X[N]$: array of motivation values preset;
$Y[N]$: array of fitness values;
$C[N]$: array of coefficients;
$\mu[N][M]$: matrix of membership values for each motivation;
Variables:
$w[n]$: the weight for each fuzzy rule being evaluated;
$f[n]$: the estimated fitness;
$n, x_0, x_1, \ldots, x_N$: integers;
Output:
F : the fuzzy fitness value calculated;
begin
$n := 1$;
for each $x_1, x_2, \ldots, x_N := 1$ **step** 1 **until** M **do**
begin
$w[n] := \min\{\mu[1][x_1], \mu[2][x_2], \ldots, \mu[N][x_N]\}$;
$f[n] := \sum_{i=1}^{N} X[i]Y[i]C[x_i]$;
$n := n + 1$;
end;
$F := (\sum_{i=1}^{N^M} w[i]f[i])/(\sum_{i=1}^{N^M} w[i])$;
end;

Fig. 2. Fuzzy Fitness Algorithm

by a motivation [14]. Differences in motivations help to produce a variety of behaviors which have a high degree of benefit (or fitness) for the organism.

In our experiments, we used motivation settings to determine the fuzzy fitness of a robot in various environments. In terms of robotic learning the motivations that we consider include: curiosity (C), homing (H), and energy (E), the opposite of laziness). There are five triangular membership functions used for each of the four motivations in our experiment (Very Low, Low, Medium, High, Very High).

Takagi-Sugeno-Kang (TSK) fuzzy logic model is used, TSK fuzzy logic does not require deffuzification as each rule has a crisp output that is aggregated as a weighted average [15]. In our method, the fuzzy motivations considered include the parameters of C, H, and E, which are used as input settings (between 0 and 1) prior to running each experiment (Fig. 1). A run environment (room) is selected and the GA initial robot population is randomly initialized. After this, each robot in the population performs its task (navigation and optionally environment recognition) and a set of fitness values corresponding to the performed task are obtained.

The fitness criteria and the variables that correspond to them are: amount of area explored (a), proper action termination and escape from original neighborhood area (g), and percent of battery usage (b). These fitness values are calculated after the robot completes each run. The a value is determined by considering the percentage area explored relative to the optimum, g is determined by $g = 1 - \frac{l}{L}$, where l is the final distance to robot's home and L the theoretical maximum value. Finally b is the estimated total energy consumption of the robot considering each step.

The final fuzzy motivation fitness value (F) is calculated using TSK based fuzzy logic (three fuzzy variables with five membership functions each: $3^5 = 243$ different fuzzy rules) as shown in Fig. 2. We use these five membership functions to compute μ values. For the coefficient array C we used a linear function.

2.1 Implementation

The YAKS (Yet Another Khepera Simulator) simulator is the base for our implementation. YAKS is a simple open source behavior-based simulator [5] that uses neural networks and genetic algorithms to provide a navigation environment for a Khepera robot. Sensors are directly provided into a multilayer neural network in order to drive left and right wheel motors. A simple genetic algorithm is used with 200 members, 100 generations, mutation of 1%, and elite reproduction. Random noise (5%) is injected into sensors to improve realism. The GA provides with a mechanism for updating neural network weights used by each robot in the population that is being optimized. An overview of our fuzzy fitness implementation is shown in Fig. 3.

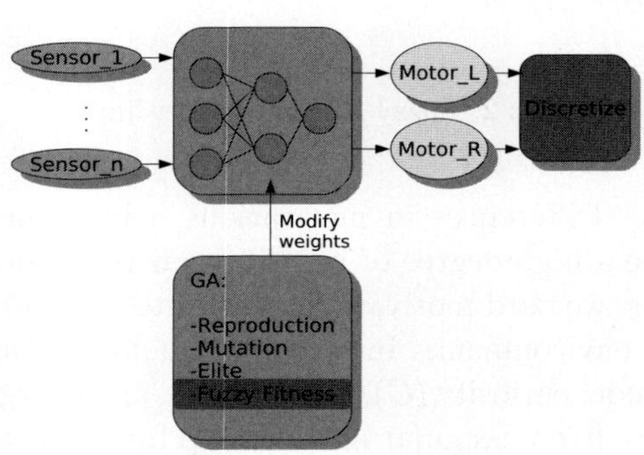

Fig. 3. Fuzzy fitness implementation

Outputs of the Neural Network are real valued motor commands (Motor_L and Motor_R) between 0 and 1 which are discretized into one of four actions (left 30°, right 30°, turn 180°, go straight). This follows the Action-based environmental modeling (AEM) search space reduction paradigm [16].

3 Real-Time Extensions

During environment exploration, autonomous or semi-autonomous mobile robots are confronted with events which could be predictable such as walls and static objects, or unpredictable such as moving objects or environmental changes. Some of these events must be attended in real-time (responsiveness) to guarantee the robot's integrity (survivability) [17].

Traditional control mechanisms are based on reliable real-time systems, i.e. time constraints over executions and predictability [18], also known as dependable systems [19], e.g. the mars pathfinder or DUSAUV, a semi-autonomous underwater vehicle presented in [20]. On the other hand, soft-computing based methods have not been widely used in this arena due to their inherent uncertainty.

In order to introduce real-time considerations into our behavior-based mobile robot for a real-world application, we extend our model by using temporal constraints during the navigation test-phase. The constraints considered include energy consumption and finite battery charge capacity.

In our approach, we define soft-deadlines as a dangerous but not critical battery charge level which dynamically affects robots behavior. This could influence behaviors to avoid highly energy consuming actions and guiding the robot's movement to some recharging zone if necessary.

When a critical battery level is reached, the previously defined method is no longer useful. A responsive real-time method is needed to, if possible, guarantee survivability [17]. Strictly speaking, we can't guarantee survivability (also beyond the scope of this paper) because of the robots partial knowledge of the world map which, initially, has no recharge zones mapped (we do not consider the starting point as a recharging zone). Nevertheless, because of the off-line robot training-phase, we expect that the trained robot (e.g. NN) will be capable of finding charging zones during the testing phase. Using the charge zone information obtained on-line, the robot applies real-time navigation. We establish a hard-deadline as the point of the robot's unrecoverable final freezing state. Before reaching this deadline (with a 10% safety margin) the robot's operation mode changes from behavior-based to mission oriented, following the shortest path to the nearest previously found charging zone [21].

In this paper we focused our research on robots survivability and exploration capability analysis.

4 Experimental Evaluation

The major purpose of the experiments reported in this section is to study the influence of our real-time extensions over the robot's behavior, considering survivability and exploration capability.

We have designed four different rooms (environments) for the robot to navigate in. We denote these rooms as: S-ROOM (the simplest), L-ROOM, T-ROOM and H-ROOM (most complex). Walls are represented by lines and we designate up to three charging zones (see circles in Fig. 4). The starting zones for each room will be the lower left corner (quarter circles in Fig. 4).

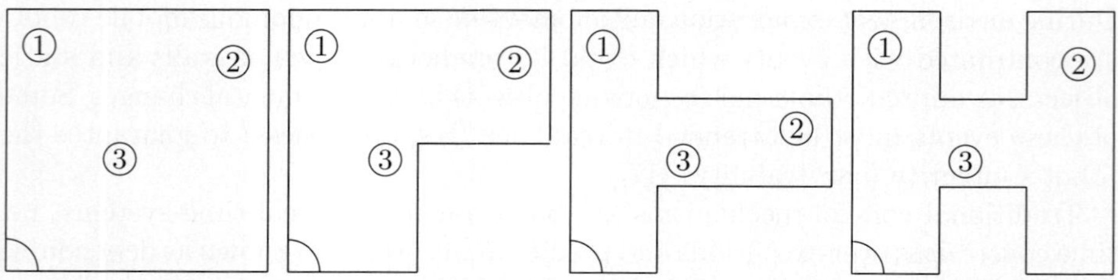

Fig. 4. Experiment rooms layout with starting and recharging zones

We will denote as NRT, a traditional [22] the behavior-based algorithm which would operate the robot without any real-time considerations, i.e. the battery level has no influence over robot's behavior but, if it comes near to a charging zone the battery level is updated to his maximum capacity. The main characteristics of NRT are:

- the battery level has no influence on the robot during training phase and,
- there is no input neuron connected to the battery sensor.

We denote by SRT the algorithm which would operate the robot with soft-real time considerations, influencing his behavior to avoid a dangerous battery level. This algorithm differs from NRT mainly by:

- battery level influences robot's fitness evaluation used by the GA and,
- a new input neuron is connected to a battery level sensor.

Finally, we denote by HRT the hybrid algorithm which would operate the robot with hard-real time considerations, i.e., the same as SRT incorporating critical battery level sensing, and also having the capacity to change the robot's normal operation to mission oriented, guaranteeing his survivability (if at least one charging zone was previously found).

4.1 Experimental Setup

As mentioned before, the experiments are performed using a modified version of YAKS [5]. This simulation system has several different elements including: the robot simulator, neural networks, GA, and fuzzy logic based fitness.

Khepera Robot. For these simulations, a Khepera robot was chosen. The robot configuration has two DC motors and eight (six front and two back) infrared proximity sensors used to detect nearby obstacles. These sensors provide 10 bit output values (with 5% random noise), which allow the robot to know in approximate form the distance to local obstacles. The YAKS simulator provides the readings for the robot sensors according to the robot position and the map (room) it is in. The simulator also has information for the different areas that the robot visits and the various obstacles (walls) or zones (home, charging zones) detected in the room. In order to navigate, the robot executes up to 1000 steps in each simulation, but not every step produces forward motion as some only rotate the robot. If the robot has no more energy, it freezes and the simulation stops.

Artificial Neural Network. The original neural network (NN) used has eight input neurons connected to the infrared sensor, five neurons in the hidden layer and two output neurons directly connected to the motors that produce the robot movement. Additionaly, in our real-time extensions we introduce another input neuron connected to the battery sensor (activated by SRT and HRT).

Genetic Algorithm. A GA is used to find an optimal configuration of weights for the neural network. Each individual in the GA represents a NN which is evolving with the passing of different generations. The GA uses the following parameters:

- Population size: 200
- Crossover operator: random crossover
- Selection method: elite strategy selection
- Mutation rate: 1%
- Generations: 100

For each room (see Fig. 4) we trained a robot up to 400 steps, considering only configurations with 2 or 3 charging zones, i.e. shutting down zone 3 for 2-zones simulations. Startup battery level allows the robot to finish this training phase without recharging requirements.

Finally, we tested our algorithms in each room up to 1000 steps, using the previously trained NN for each respective room. The startup battery level was set to 80 (less than 50% of it's capacity), which was insufficient to realize the whole test without recharging.

4.2 Experimental Results

Due to size restrictions, we selected representative behaviors for only 2 rooms. We chose the S-ROOM and H-ROOM to show results for a simple and complex room respectively.

In Fig. 5 we show the robot's exploration behavior for selected rooms. Each curve in the graph shows the average value of 10 executions of the same experiment (deviation between different iterations was very small, justifying only

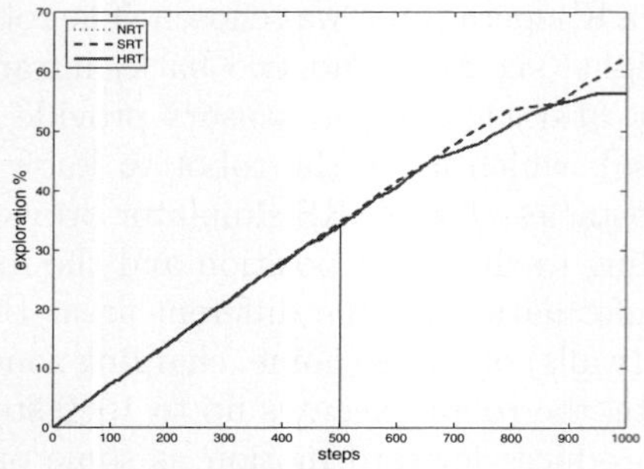

(a) S-ROOM 2 charge zones

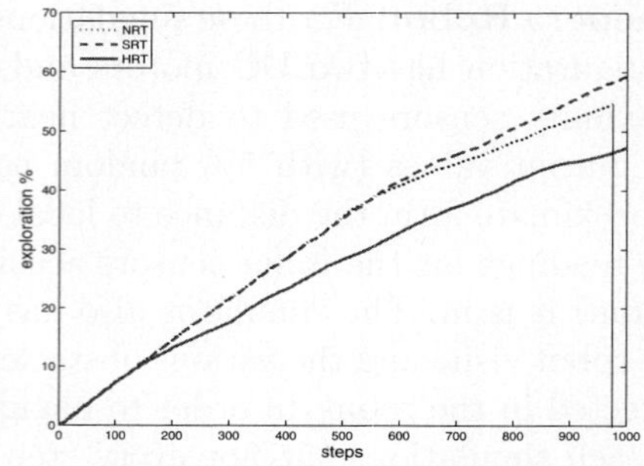

(b) S-ROOM 3 charge zones

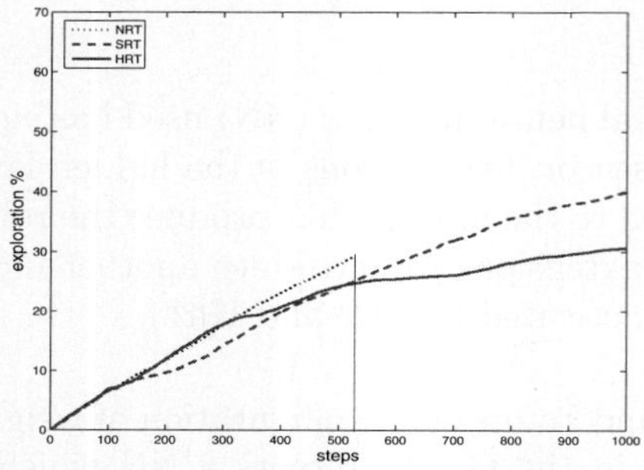

(c) H-ROOM 2 charge zones

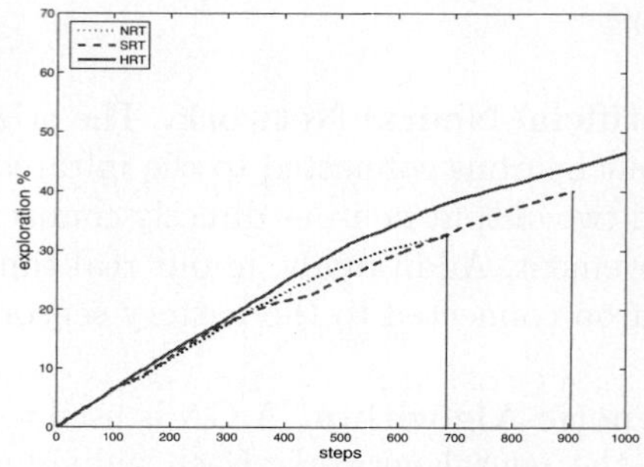

(d) H-ROOM 3 charge zones

Fig. 5. Exploration Behavior

10 executions). Let $surv(\alpha)_i$ the survivability of the experiment instance i of algorithm α, we define $surv(\alpha)$ as the survivability of an experiment applying algorithm α as the worst case survivability instance of an experiment, i.e.

$$surv(\alpha) = \min_{i=1,\dots,10} [surv(\alpha)_i] \tag{1}$$

Please note that the end of each curve in Fig. 5 denotes the survivability of the respective algorithm (for better readability, we mark NRT survivability with a vertical line). Reaching step 1000 (the maximum duration of our experiments) means the robot using the algorithm survives the navigation experiment. Finally, in Fig. 6 we show a representative robot's battery level. Monitoring was made during test phase in a H-ROOM with 3 charging zones.

4.3 Discussion

The results of our experiments are summarized below:

Survivability: As shown in Fig. 5, SRT and HRT algorithms give better reliability of completing missions than the NRT method, independently of the rooms (environments) we use for testing (see Fig. 4). As expected, if fewer charging zones are provided, NRT has a less reliable conduct. Please note that as shown

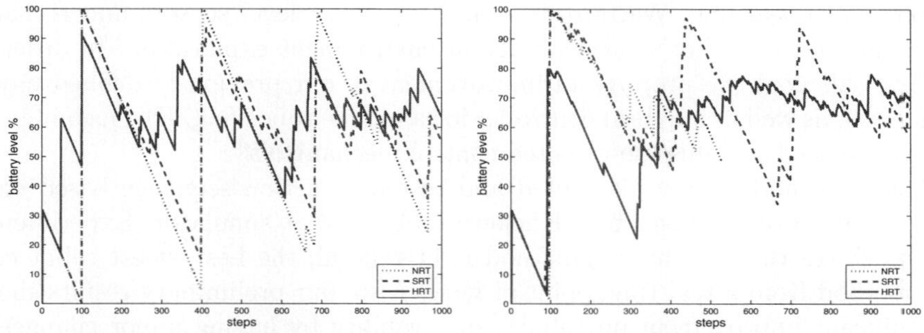

(a) S-ROOM 3 charge zones (b) H-ROOM 2 charge zones

Fig. 6. Battery Behavior

in Fig. 6, NRT is also prone to battery depletion risk and does not survive in any case.

When varying room complexity, i.e. 5(b) and 5(d), real-time considerations have significant impact. Using SRT, a purely behavior-based driven robot (with the additional neuron and motivation), improves it's performance. The SRT method does not guarantee survivability since without using real-time the robot is prone to dying even with greater number of recharge zones (as seen in 5(d)). Finally, we conclude that despite the uncertainty introduced by soft-computing methods, HRT (e.g. the hybrid algorithm), in general is the best and safest robot control method from a real-time point of view.

Exploration Environment: As can be seen in Fig. 5, safer behaviors mean slower exploration rates (more conservative), up to 12% slower in our experiments. When comparing NRT with SRT, the exploration rates are almost equal in simple environments. In more complex rooms, SRT exploration is slower than NRT (due to battery observance). However, because of SRT having better survivability on the whole it's performance wins over NRT. If we compare NRT with HRT, exploration performance also favors NRT, wich could be explained given HRT conservative battery management (see Fig. 6).

Given 2 charge zones, HRT behaves differently in environments of varying complexity (up to 25%) which could be attributed to the complexity of the returning path to the nearest charging zone and loosing steps in further exploration. This phenomena becomes less notoriosly when increasing the number of charging zones (more options for recharge). These results are of interest bacause we have shown that our hybrid based approach is an effective alternative towards survivability in complex environment exploration.

5 Conclusions and Future Work

In this paper we investigate real-time adaptive extensions of our fuzzy logic based approach for providing biologically based motivations to be used in evolutionary mobile robot learning. We introduce active battery level sensors and recharge zones to improve robot's survivability in environment exploration. In order to achieve this goal, we propose an improvement of our previously defined model (e.g. SRT), as well as a hybrid controller for a mobile robot (e.g. HRT), combining behavior-based and mission-oriented control mechanisms.

These methods are implemented and tested in action sequence based environment exploration tasks in a Khepera mobile robot simulator. Experimental results shows that the hybrid method is in general, the best/safest robot control method from a real-time point of view. Also, our preliminary results shows a significant improvement on robot's survivability by having minor changes in the robot's motivations and NN. Currently we are designing a real robot for environment exploration to validate our model moving from simulation to experimentation. Improving dependability of HRT, we want to extend this control algorithm to safety-critical domains.

Acknowledgments

This research was partially funded by the project C-14055-26 of Fundación Andes and by the research center DGIP of UTFSM.

References

1. Jeen-Shing Wang and C.S. George Lee, "Self-adaptive recurrent neuro-fuzzy control of an autonomous underwater vehicle", IEEE Trans. on Robotics and Automation, 19(2), Apr. 2003, pp. 283-295.
2. Seraji, H.; Howard, A., "Behavior-based robot navigation on challenging terrain: A fuzzy logic approach", IEEE Trans. on Robotics and Automation, 18(3), Jun. 2002, pp. 308-321.
3. Tom Ziemke, Dan-Anders Jirenhed and Germund Hesslow, "Internal simulation of perception: a minimal neuro-robotic model", NC., vol. 68, 2005, pp. 85-104.
4. Bernhard Sick, Markus Keidl, Markus Ramsauer, and Stefan Seltzsam, "A Comparison of Traditional and Soft-Computing Methods in a Real-Time Control Application", ICANN 98, Sep. 1998, pp. 725-730.
5. YAKS simulator website: http://r2d2.ida.his.se/
6. Jang, J., Chuen-Tsai, S., Mitzutani, E., "Neuro-Fuzzy and Soft Computing", NJ, 1997.
7. Goodrige, S., Kay, M., Luo, R., "Multi-Layered Fuzzy Behavior Fusion for Reactive Control of an Autonomous Mobile Robot", Proc. of the 6th IEEE Int. Conf. on Fuzzy Systems, Jul. 1997, pp. 573-578.
8. Hoffman, F., "Soft computing techniques for the design of mobile robot behaviors", Inf. Sciences, 122, 2000, pp. 241-258.
9. Al-Khatib, M., Saade, J., "An efficient data-driven fuzzy approach to the motion planning problem of a mobile robot", Fuzzy Sets and Sys., 134 2003, pp. 65-82.
10. Izumi, K., Watanabe, K., "Fuzzy behavior-based control trained by module learning to acquire the adaptive behaviors of mobile robots", Mat. and Comp. in Simulation, 51, 2000, pp. 233-243.

11. Martnez Barber, H., Gmez Skarmeta, A., "A Framework for Defining and Learning Fuzzy Behaviours for Autonomous Mobile Robots", Int. Journal of Intelligent Systems, 17(1), 2002, pp. 1-20.
12. Zhou, C., "Robot learning with GA-based fuzzy reinforcement learning agents", Inf. Sciences, 145, 2002, pp. 45-68.
13. Seraji, H., Howard, A., "Behavior-Based Robot Navigation on Challenging Terrain: A Fuzzy Logic Approach", IEEE Trans. on Robotics and Automation, 18(3), Jun. 2002, pp. 308-321.
14. Huitt, W., "Motivation to learn: An overview", Educational Psychology Interactive, Valdosta State University, http://chiron.valdosta.edu, 2001.
15. Jang, J.-S, Sun, C.-T., Sun, Mizutani, E., "Neuro-Fuzzy and Soft Computing: a computational approach to learning and machine intelligence", NJ, 1997.
16. Yamada, S., "Evolutionary behavior learning for action-based environment modeling by a mobile robot", App. Soft Comp., 5, 2005, pp. 245-257.
17. Hermann Kopetz, "Real-Time Systems Design Principles for Distributed Embedded Applications", Kluwer Academic Publishers, Apr. 1997.
18. Gheith, A. and Schwan, K., "CHAOSarc: kernel support for multiweight objects, invocations, and atomicity in real-time multiprocessor applications", ACM Trans. Comp. Syst. 11(1), Feb. 1993, pp. 33-72.
19. G. Motet and J. -C. Geffroy, "Dependable computing: an overview", Theoretical Comp. Science, 290(2), Jan. 2003, pp. 1115-1126.
20. Ji-Hong Li, Bong-Huan Jun, Pan-Mook Lee and Seok-Won Hong, "A hierarchical real-time control architecture for a semi-autonomous underwater vehicle", Ocean Eng., 32(13), Sep. 2005, pp. 1631-1641.
21. P. Tompkins, A. Stentz, and D. Wettergreen, "Mission-level path planning and replanning for rover exploration", Robotics and Autonomous Syst., Vol. 54(2), Feb. 2006, pp. 174-183.
22. Arredondo, T., Freund,W., Muoz, C., Navarro, N., Quirós, F., "Fuzzy Motivations for Evolutionary Behavior Learning by a Mobile Robot", Innovations in Applied Artificial Intelligence, LNAI, Vol. 4031, 2006, pp. 462-471.

Fuzzy-Based Adaptive Threshold Determining Method for the Interleaved Authentication in Sensor Networks*

Hae Young Lee and Tae Ho Cho

School of Information and Communication Engineering, Sungkyunkwan University
300 Cheoncheon-dong, Jangan-gu, Suwon 440-746, Korea
{sofware, taecho}@ece.skku.ac.kr

Abstract. When sensor networks are deployed in hostile environments, an adversary may compromise some sensor nodes and use them to inject false sensing reports. False reports can lead to not only false alarms but also the depletion of limited energy resource in battery powered networks. The interleaved hop-by-hop authentication scheme detects such false reports through interleaved authentication. In this scheme, the choice of a security threshold value is important since it trades off security and overhead. In this paper, we propose a fuzzy logic-based adaptive threshold determining method for the interleaved authentication scheme. The fuzzy rule-based system is exploited to determine a security threshold value by considering the number of cluster nodes, the number of compromised nodes, and the energy level of nodes. The proposed method can conserve energy, while it provides sufficient resilience.

1 Introduction

Recent advances in micro-electro-mechanical systems technology, wireless communications and digital electronics have enabled the development of low-cost, low-power, and multi-functional sensor nodes [1]. These nodes, which consist of sensing, data processing, and communicating components, further leverage the concept of sensor networks [2], in which a large number of sensor nodes collaborate to monitor certain environment [1]. Sensor networks are expected to interact with the physical world at an unprecedented level to enable various new applications [3]. In many applications sensor nodes are deployed in open environments, and hence are vulnerable to physical attacks, potentially compromising the node's cryptographic keys [4]. False sensing reports can be injected through compromised nodes, which can lead to not only false alarms but also the depletion of limited energy resource in battery powered networks (Fig. 1) [3].

To minimize the grave damage, false reports should be dropped en-route as early as possible, and the few eluded ones should be further rejected at the base station [5]. Several security solutions have recently been proposed for this purpose. Ye *et al.* [3] proposed a statistical en-route filtering scheme in which a report is forwarded only if

* This research was supported by the MIC (Ministry of Information and Communication), Korea, under the ITRC (Information Technology Research Center) support program supervised by the IITA (Institute of Information Technology Assessment).

A. Gelbukh and C.A. Reyes-Garcia (Eds.): MICAI 2006, LNAI 4293, pp. 112 – 121, 2006.

it contains the MACs generated by multiple nodes, by using keys from different partitions in a global key pool. Zhu *et at.* [6] proposed the interleaved hop-by-hop authentication scheme that detects false reports through interleaved authentication. Zhang *et al.* [7] proposed the interleaved authentication scheme for the braided multipath routing [8]. In these schemes, the choice of a security threshold value is important since it trades off between security and overhead [3,6]. A large threshold value makes forging reports more difficult, but it consumes more energy in forwarding [3]. A small threshold value may make these schemes inefficient or even useless if the number of compromised node exceeds it [9]. Therefore, we should choose a threshold value such that it provides sufficient resilience, while still small enough to conserve energy [3].

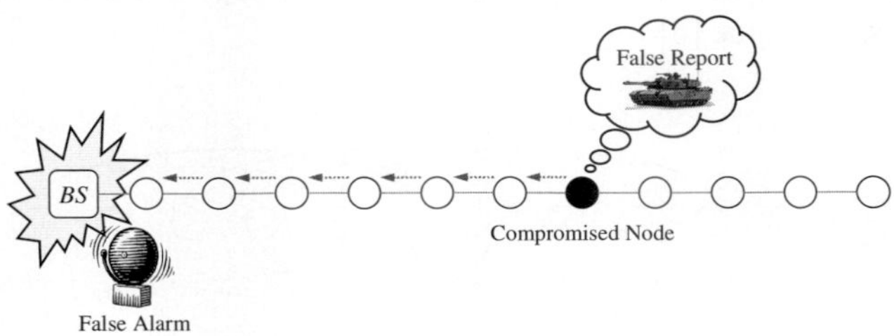

Fig. 1. False sensing report can be injected through compromised node (filled circle), which can lead to not only false alarms but also the depletion of limited energy resource

In this paper, we propose a fuzzy logic-based adaptive security threshold determining method for the interleaved authentication scheme. The fuzzy rule-based system is exploited to determine a threshold value by considering the number of cluster nodes, the number of compromised nodes, and the energy level of nodes. The proposed method can conserve energy, while it provides sufficient resilience. The effectiveness of the proposed method is shown with the simulation result at the end of the paper. The proposed method can be applied to the en-route filtering schemes that needs to choose a security threshold value (e.g., the statistical en-route filtering scheme [3]).

2 Background and Motivation

In this section, we briefly describe the interleaved hop-by-hop authentication scheme (IHA) [6] and motivation of this work.

2.1 The Interleaved Hop-by-Hop Authentication Scheme (IHA) Overview

In the IHA [6], nodes are *associated* and MACs are verified within *association* pairs. Fig. 2 shows the IHA that is resilient to up to four compromised nodes, i.e., a security threshold value is 4. Nodes u_1, u_2, ···, u_6 are intermediate nodes on the path from a cluster to the base station *BS*. The *CH* and node v_1, v_2, v_3, and v_4 are the cluster nodes. Basically, an intermediate node has an *upper* (closer to the *BS*) and a *lower associated* node of five hops away from it [7]. An intermediate node that is less than five hops away from the CH has one of the cluster nodes as its lower associated node. For example, u_1 has u_6 and v_2 as its upper and lower associated node, respectively. An intermediate node that is less than five hops away from the BS does not need to have an upper associated node.

A unique pairwise key is used in each association, e.g., the $u_1 - u_6$ pair uses $K_{u1,u6}$ and $v_1 - u_1$ pair uses $K_{v1,u1}$. When u_1 receives a report, it verifies the MAC generated by v_1 using $K_{v1,u1}$. Upon success, it replaces this MAC with a new one using $K_{u1,u6}$. The new MAC is to be verified by u_6. If any four nodes in this path are compromised, the last association will guarantee that a false report be detected and dropped [7]. For example, if CH, v_1, v_2, and v_4 in Fig. 3 are compromised, a false report will be detected by u_3 because the false report does not contain the MAC generated by v_3 using $K_{v3,u3}$. A false report in the IHA can travel $O(t^2)$ hops in the network, where t is a security threshold value [6].

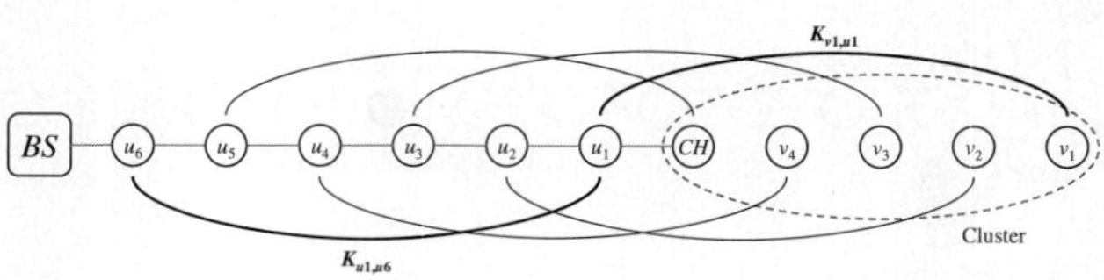

Fig. 2. The IHA that is resilient to up to four compromised nodes is shown. *BS* is the base station and *CH* is a cluster head. Two nodes connected with an arc are associated, the one closer to *BS* is the upper associated node and the other is the lower associated node.

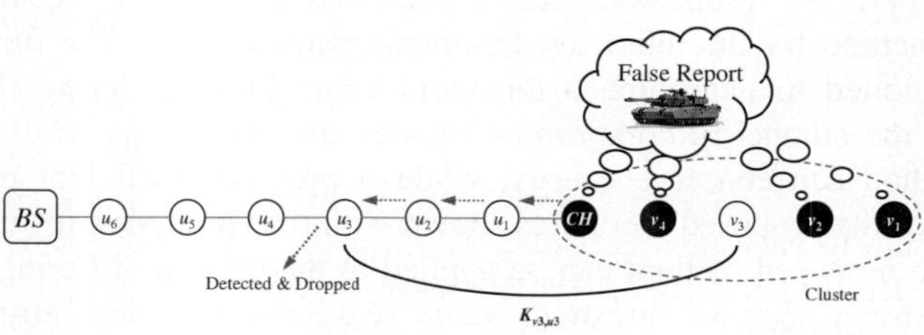

Fig. 3. If any four nodes in this path are compromised (filled circles), the last association ($v_3 - u_3$ pair) will guarantee that a false report be detected when the security threshold value is 4

2.2 Motivation

The choice of a security threshold value is important since it trades off between security and overhead [3,6]. A large threshold value makes forging reports more difficult, but it consumes more energy in forwarding [3]. A small threshold value may make these schemes inefficient or even useless if the number of compromised node exceeds the threshold value [9]. Therefore, we should choose a threshold value adaptively such that it achieves sufficient resilience, while still small enough to conserve energy [3].

3 Fuzzy-Based Threshold Determining Method

In this section, we describe the fuzzy-based threshold determining method in detail.

3.1 Assumptions

We assume that the base station can know or estimate the number of cluster nodes, the number of compromised nodes, and the energy level of nodes for the path to each cluster. We also assumes that the base station has a mechanism to authenticate broadcast messages (e.g., based on μTESLA [10]), and every node can verify the broadcast messages. We further assume that each node can establish *multiple associations* with $n - 1$ upper and $n - 1$ lower nodes in the *association discovery* phase [6], where n is the number of cluster nodes. For example, if a cluster consists of five sensor nodes, an intermediate node has four upper and four lower associated nodes as shown in Fig. 4. If the network size is small, we can employ either the Blom scheme [11] or the Blundo scheme [12] for establishing multiple associations. For a larger network, we may use the extensions [13,14] to these schemes to tolerate a possibly larger number of node compromises [6].

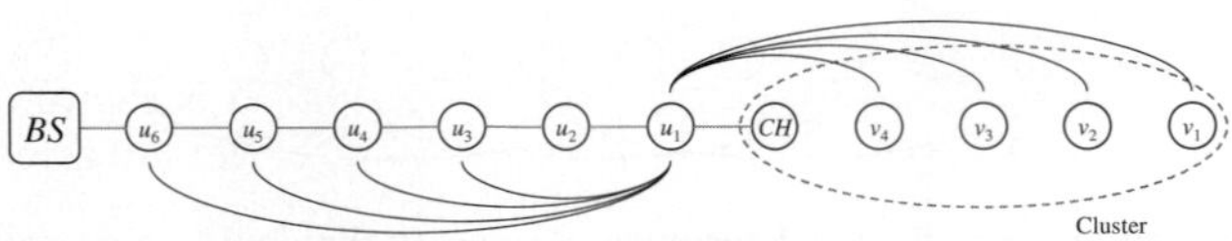

Fig. 4. Each node can establish *multiple associations* in the *association discovery* phase

3.2 Overview

In the proposed method, the base station periodically determines a security threshold value for the path to each cluster based with a fuzzy rule-based system (Fig. 5 (a)). The number of cluster nodes, the number of compromised nodes, and the energy level of nodes on the path are used to determine a threshold value. If the new threshold value differs from the current, the base station broadcasts the new value to all the nodes on the path (Fig. 5 (b)). Then, they are *re-associated* according to the new threshold value (Fig. 5 (c)).

3.3 Factors that Determine the Security Threshold Value

In the IHA, a security threshold value t should be smaller than the number of cluster nodes because a report is collaboratively generated by $t + 1$ cluster nodes. For example, if a cluster consists of five nodes, a threshold value can be 0 (disable filtering), 1, 2 (Fig. 5(b)), 3, or 4 (Fig. 5(c)). The IHA can be resilient to up to t colluding compromised nodes, where a security threshold value is t. Thus, if a certain number c nodes are compromised, we should set a threshold value to c or larger (but smaller than the number of cluster nodes). If the number of compromised nodes exceeds the number of cluster nodes, the IHA may be inefficient or even useless [9]. For example, the IHA cannot filter false reports injected by five colluding compromised nodes when the threshold value is smaller than 5. Under this situation, we may as well disable the en-route filtering, i.e., set a security threshold value to 0. So, we have to determine a security threshold value based on the number of cluster nodes and the number of compromised nodes. The energy is the most important resource that should be considered in sensor networks. Generally, sensor nodes are limited in power and irreplaceable since these nodes have limited capacity and are unattended [15]. Therefore, we also have to determine a threshold value based on the energy level of nodes.

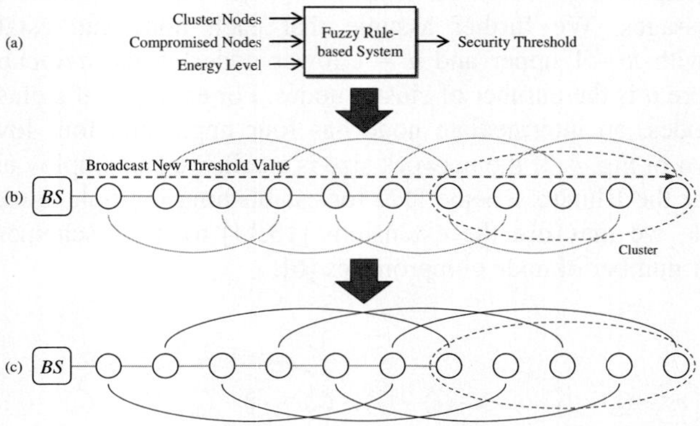

Fig. 5. The base station periodically determines a security threshold value with a fuzzy rule-based system (a). If the new threshold value differs from the current, the base station broadcasts the new value (b). The nodes are *re-associated* according to the threshold value (c).

3.4 Fuzzy Logic Design

Fig. 6 illustrates the membership functions of three input parameters – the number of cluster nodes (a), the number of compromised nodes (b), and the energy level of nodes (c) – of the fuzzy logic. The labels in the fuzzy variables are presented as follows.

```
CLUSTER NODES = {VERY SMALL, SMALL, MEDIUM, LARGE, VERY
LARGE}
COMPROMISED NODES = {VERY SAMLL, SMALL, MEDIUM, LARGE,
VERY LARGE}
ENERGY LEVEL = {VERY LOW, LOW, ABOVE HALF}
```

The output parameter of the fuzzy logic is SECURITY THRESHOLD = {VERY SMALL, SMALL, MEDIUM, LARGE, VERY LARGE}, which is represented by the membership functions as shown in Fig. 7.

If it is reported or estimated that no node has been compromised, a security threshold value can be very small (e.g., 0).

```
RULE 14: IF CLUSTER NODES IS VERY LARGE
         AND COMPROMISED NODES IS VERY SMALL
         AND ENERGY LEVEL IS LOW
         THEN SECURITY THRESHOLD IS VERY SMALL
```

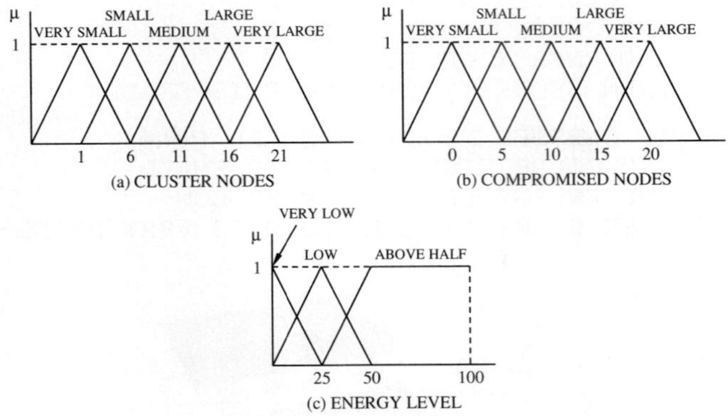

Fig. 6. The membership functions of three input parameters – the number of cluster nodes (a), the number of compromised nodes (b), and the energy level of nodes (c) – are shown

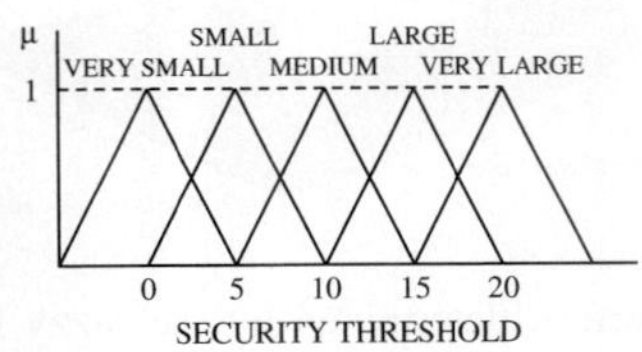

Fig. 7. The output parameter of the fuzzy logic is represented by the membership functions

If a few nodes are compromised and non-compromised nodes have enough energy resource, a security threshold value should be equal to or greater than the number of compromised nodes.

```
RULE 25:  IF CLUSTER NODES IS LARGE
          AND COMPROMISED NODES IS SMALL
          AND ENERGY LEVEL IS ABOVE HALF
          THEN SECURITY THRESHOLD IS SMALL
```

If the number of compromised nodes exceeds the number of cluster nodes, the IHA may be inefficient and useless. Thus, we may as well disable the en-route filtering, i.e., set a threshold value to 0.

```
RULE 43:  IF CLUSTER NODES IS MEDIUM
          AND COMPROMISED NODES IS VERY LARGE
          AND ENERGY LEVEL IS ABOVE HALF
          THEN SECURITY THRESHOLD IS VERY SMALL
```

If non-compromised nodes have not enough energy, although the number of compromised nodes is smaller than the number of cluster nodes, a security threshold value can be either the number of compromised or 0 (if the overhead for filtering consumes too much energy).

```
RULE 56:  IF CLUSTER NODES IS SMALL
          AND COMPROMISED NODES IS SMALL
          AND ENERGY LEVEL IS LOW
          THEN SECURITY THRESHOLD IS SMALL

RULE 57:  IF CLUSTER NODES IS SMALL
          AND COMPROMISED NODES IS SMALL
          AND ENERGY LEVEL IS VERY LOW
          THEN SECURITY THRESHOLD IS VERY SMALL
```

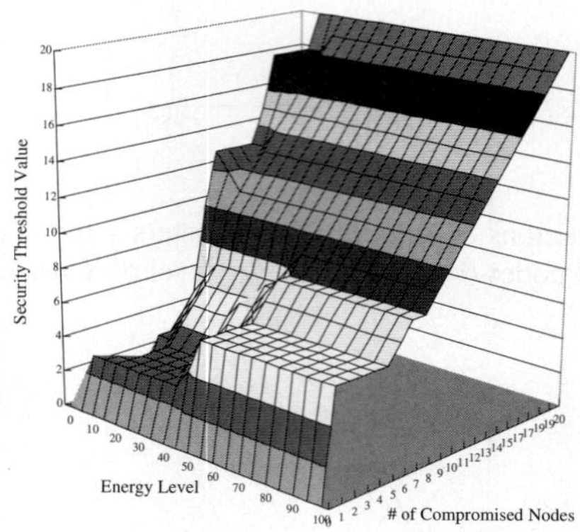

Fig. 8. A security threshold surface determined by the fuzzy logic is shown (the number of cluster nodes = 21)

Fig. 8 illustrates a security threshold surface determined by the fuzzy logic when the number of cluster nodes is 21.

3.5 Node Re-association

If a new security threshold value t differs from the current, the base station broadcasts t to all the nodes. Then, each of them selects the pairwise keys shared with an upper and a lower associated node of $t + 1$ hops away from it. That is, nodes are re-associated according to t. For example, if a threshold value has increased from 2 to 4, the node u_1 in Fig. 9 selects $K_{u1,u6}$ and $K_{v1,u1}$, which are used to endorse or verify a report. Note that the en-route filtering is disabled if $t = 0$.

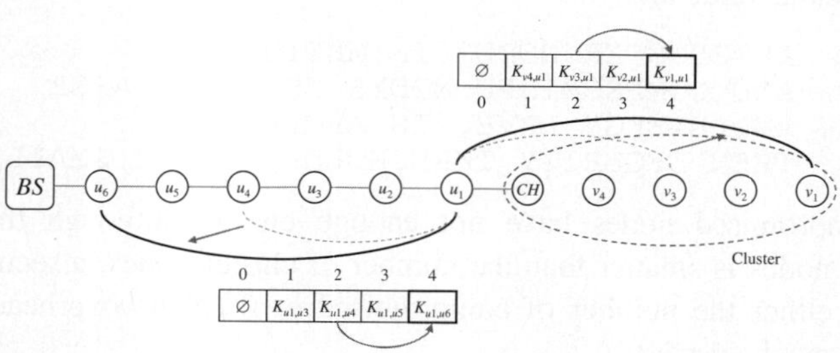

Fig. 9. If a threshold value has increased from 2 to 4, the node u_1 is re-associated with u_6 and v_1 by selecting $K_{u1,u6}$ and $K_{v1,u1}$, respectively

4 Simulation Result

To show the effectiveness of the proposed method, we have compared the proposed method with the fixed threshold-based IHA through the simulation. Each node takes 16.25, 12.5 μJ to transmit/receive a byte and each MAC generation consumes 15 μJ [3]. The size of an original report is 24 bytes. The size of a MAC is 1 byte. Each node is equipped with an energy source whose total amount of energy accounts for 2500mJ at the beginning of the simulation [17].

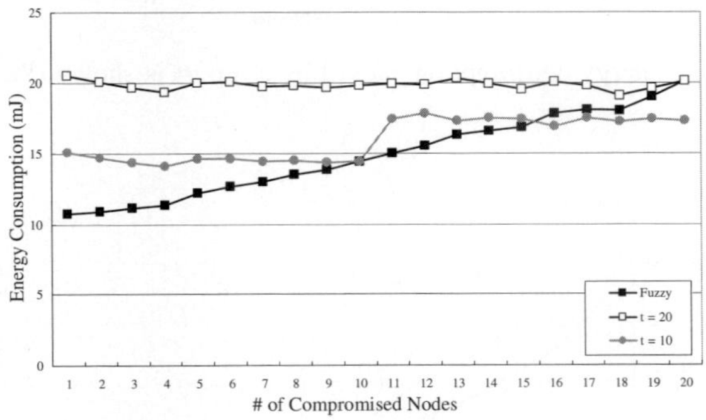

Fig. 10. The average energy consumption caused by a report is shown (the number of cluster nodes = 21). The proposed method (filled rectangles) provides sufficient resilience, while still small enough to conserve energy.

Fig. 10 shows the average energy consumption caused by a report (authenticated or false) when the number of cluster nodes is 21 and the number of compromised nodes is between 1 and 20. As shown in the figure, the proposed method (filled rectangles) consumes less energy than the fixed threshold-based IHA (t = 10 and 20) up to fifteen compromised nodes since the proposed method determines a threshold value adaptively according to the number of compromised nodes. The IHA with t = 10 (filled circle) consumes less energy than the proposed method if the number of compromised nodes exceeds 15. However, it cannot detect false reports if the number of compromised nodes exceeds 10. On the other hand, the proposed method provides sufficient resilience, while still small enough to conserve energy.

Fig. 11 shows the average energy consumption caused by a report (authenticated or false) when the number of cluster nodes is 11 and the number of compromised nodes is between 1 and 20. As shown in the figure, the proposed method saves energy since the proposed method disables the filtering mechanism if the number of capture nodes exceeds the number of cluster nodes.

Fig. 12 shows the average remaining energy per node when the number of cluster nodes is 11 and five nodes are compromised. As shown in the figure, the proposed method (solid line) prolongs node lifetime since the proposed method disables the en-route filtering if nodes have not enough energy to activate the filtering mechanism.

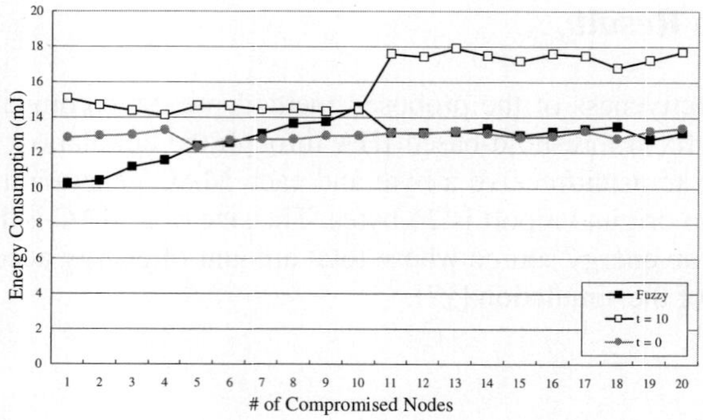

Fig. 11. The average energy consumption caused by a report is shown (the number of cluster nodes = 11)

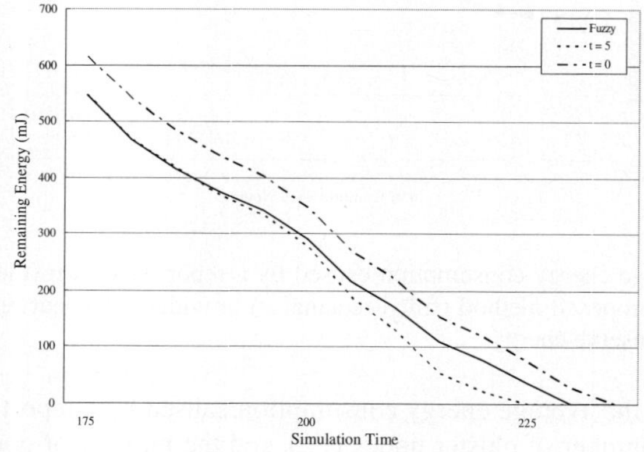

Fig. 12. The average remaining energy per node is shown. The proposed method (solid line) prolongs node lifetime.

5 Conclusion and Future Works

In this paper, we proposed a fuzzy logic for the adaptive security threshold determining in the interleaved authentication-based sensor networks. For the path to each cluster, the fuzzy logic determines the threshold value by considering the number of cluster nodes, the number of compromised nodes, and the energy level of nodes. The fuzzy-based threshold determining can conserve energy, while it provides sufficient resilience. The effectiveness of the proposed method was shown with the simulation result.

The proposed method can be applied to the en-route filtering schemes that needs to choose a security threshold value. Our future research will be focused on optimizing the proposed method and applying it to various en-route filtering schemes.

References

1. Wang, G., Zhang, W., Cao, G., Porta, T.L.: On Supporting Distributed Collaboration in Sensor Networks. In Proc. of MILCOM (2003) 752-757
2. Akyildiz, I.F., Su, W., Sankarasubramaniam, Y., Cayirci, E.: Wireless Sensor Networks: A Survey. Comput Netw 38(4) (2002) 393-422
3. Ye, F., Luo, H., Lu, S.: Statistical En-Route Filtering of Injected False Data in Sensor Networks. IEEE J. Sel. Area Comm. 23(4) (2005) 839-850
4. Przydatek, B., Song, D., Perrig, A.: SIA: Secure Information Aggregation in Sensor Networks. In Proc. of SenSys (2003) 255-265
5. Yang, H, Lu, S.: Commutative Cipher Based En-Route Filtering in Wireless Sensor Networks. In Proc. of VTC (2003) 1223-1227
6. Zhu, S., Setia, S., Jajodia, S., Ning, P.: An Interleaved Hop-by-Hop Authentication Scheme for Filtering of Injected False Data in Sensor Networks. In Proc. of S&P (2004) 259-271
7. Zhang, Y., Yang, J., Vu, H.T.: The Interleaved Authentication for Filtering False Reports in Multipath Routing based Sensor Networks. In Proc. of IPDPS (2006)
8. Ganesan, D., Govindan, R., Shenker, S., Estrin, D.: Highly-resilient, Energy-efficient Multipath Routing in Wireless Sensor Networks. In Proc. of SIGMOBILE (2001) 251-254
9. Zhang, W., Cao, G.: Group Rekeying for Filtering False Data in Sensor Networks: A Predistribution and Local Collaboration-based Approach. In Proc. of INFOCOM (2005) 503-514
10. Perrig, A., Szewczyk, R., Tygar, J.D., Wen, V., Culler, D.E.: SPINS: Security Protocols for Sensor Networks. Wirel. Netw. 8(5) (2002) 521-534
11. Bloem, R.: An Optimal Class of Symmetric Key Generation Systems. Lect. Notes Comput. Sc. 209 (1984) 335-338
12. Blundo, C., Santis, A.D., Herzberg, A., Kutten, S., Vaccaro, U., Yung 12, M.: Perfectly-Secure Key Distribution for Dynamic Conferences. Inform. Comput. 146(1) (1998) 1-23
13. Du, W., Deng, J., Han, Y., Varshney, P.: A Pairwise Key Pre-distribution Scheme for Wireless Sensor Networks. In Proc. of CCS (2003) 27-31
14. Liu, D., Ning, P.: Establishing Pairwise Keys in Distributed Sensor Networks. In Proc. of CCS (2003) 52-61
15. Chi, S.H., Cho, T.H.: Fuzzy Logic based Propagation Limiting Method for Message Routing in Wireless Sensor Networks. Lect. Notes Comput. Sc. 3983 (2006) 58-67
16. Baeg, S.B., Cho, T.H.: Transmission Relay Method for Balanced Energy Depletion in Wireless Sensor Network using Fuzzy Logic. Lect. Notes Artif. Int. 3614 (2005) 998-1007

A Fuzzy Logic Model for Software Development Effort Estimation at Personal Level

Cuauhtemoc Lopez-Martin[1], Cornelio Yáñez-Márquez[2], and Agustin Gutierrez-Tornes[3]

[1,2] Center for Computing Research, National Polytechnic Ins0074itute, Mexico
Av. Juan de Dios Batiz s/n esquina Miguel Othon de Mendizabal, Edificio CIC, Colonia Nueva Industrial Vallejo, Delegación Gustavo A. Madero, P.O. 07738, Mexico D.F.
cuauhtemoc@sagitario.cic.ipn.mx, cyanez@cic.ipn.mx
[3] Systems Coordinator, Banamex, Mexico, D.F.; ITESM, Mexico State
agustin.tornes@itesm.mx

Abstract. No single software development estimation technique is best for all situations. A careful comparison of the results of several approaches is most likely to produce realistic estimates. On the other hand, unless engineers have the capabilities provided by personal training, they cannot properly support their teams or consistently and reliably produce quality products. In this paper, an investigation aimed to compare a personal Fuzzy Logic System (FLS) with linear regression is presented. The evaluation criteria are based upon ANOVA of MRE and MER, as well as MMRE, MMER and pred(25). One hundred five programs were developed by thirty programmers. From these programs, a FLS is generated for estimating the effort of twenty programs developed by seven programmers. The adequacy checking as well as a validation of the FLS are made. Results show that a FLS can be used as an alternative for estimating the development effort at personal level.

1 Introduction

Software development effort estimation is one of the most critical activities in managing software projects [11]. The need for reliable and accurate cost predictions in software engineering is an ongoing challenge (it has even been identified as one of the three great challenges for half-century-old computer science [6]), because it allows for considerable financial and strategic planning [1].

In accordance with the Mexican National Program for Software Industry Development, the 90% of software Mexican enterprises do not have formal processes to record, track and control measurable issues during the development process (project management control) [21], that is, implicitly in those enterprises exist a necessity for practicing the software development effort estimation. These techniques fall into the next three general categories [17]:

1) Expert judgement: A technique widely used, it aims to derive estimates based on an expert's previous experience on similar projects. The means of deriving an estimate are not explicit and therefore not repeatable. However, although always

A. Gelbukh and C.A. Reyes-Garcia (Eds.): MICAI 2006, LNAI 4293, pp. 122 – 133, 2006.

difficult to quantify, expert judgement can be an effective estimating tool on its own or as an adjusting factor for algorithmic models.

2) Algorithmic models: To date the most popular in the literature, attempt to represent the relationship between effort and one or more of a project's characteristics. The main cost driver in such a model is usually taken to be some notion of software size (e.g. the number of lines of source code as this paper use it). Algorithmic models need calibration to be adjusted to local circumstances (as this study do it).

3) Machine learning: Machine learning techniques have in recent years been used as a complement or alternative to the previous two techniques. Fuzzy logic models are included in this category.

Given that no single software development estimation technique is best for all situations, a careful comparison of the results of several approaches is most likely to produce realistic estimates [2]. In this paper an algorithmic model (linear regression) with a Fuzzy Logic System (a machine learning technique) is compared. This comparison is based upon the two following main stages for using an estimation model (1) it must be determined whether the model is adequate to describe the observed (actual) data, that is, the model adequacy checking; if it resulted adequate then (2) the estimation model is validated using new data.

Given that unless engineers have the capabilities provided by personal training, they cannot properly support their teams or consistently and reliably produce quality products [10], it suggests that the software estimation activity could start through a personal level approach by developing small programs as this paper proposes. The Capability Maturity Model (CMM) is an available description of the goals, methods, and practices needed in software engineering industrial practice, while Personal Software Process (PSP) allows understand the CMM at personal level in a laboratory environment [9]. Twelve of the eighteen key process areas of the CMM are at least partially addressed by the PSP. This paper is based upon PSP practices.

This paper considers guidelines suggested in [13] and it compares estimations obtained with Linear Regression (LR) and Fuzzy Logic (FL). LR is the most common modeling technique (in the literature) applied to software estimation [5]. Lines of code and development time are gathered from 105 small programs developed by 30 programmers. From these 105 programs a FL system and a LR equation are generated and their adequacy is checked. Then, this FL system and LR equation are validated when they are used for estimating the effort of 20 programs developed by other group integrated by seven programmers.

1.1 Software Measurement

In spite of the availability of a wide range of software product size measures, source lines of code (LOC) remains in favour of many models [17] [15]. There are two measures of source code size: physical source lines and logical source statements. The count of physical lines gives the size in terms of the physical length of the code as it appears when printed [19]. A coding standard should also establish a consistent set of coding practices as a provided criterion for judging the quality of the produced code [9]. To be consistent, it is necessary to use always the same coding standard. In this study, all programs were developed based upon an individual coding standard that was made by each programmer.

To generate the FL and LR models New and Changed (N&C) physical lines of code (LOC) are used in this paper. Both Added plus Modified code integrate the N&C [9]: Added code is the LOC added during current program, while the Modified code is the LOC changed in the base program (when modifying a previously developed program, the base program is the total LOC of the previous program).

1.2 Fuzzy Logic

All estimation techniques has an important limitation, which arises when software projects are described using categorical data (nominal or ordinal scale) such as *small*, *medium*, *average*, or *high* (linguistic values). A more comprehensive approach to deal with linguistic values is by using fuzzy set theory [11] [16]. Specifically, FL offers a particularly convenient way to generate a keen mapping between input and output spaces thanks to fuzzy rules' natural expression [24].

Concerning Software Development Effort Estimation, two considerations justify the decision of implementing a Fuzzy System: first, it is impossible to develop a precise mathematical model of the domain; second, metrics only produce estimations of the real complexity. Thus, according to the previous assertions, formulating a tiny set of natural rules describing underlying interactions between the software metrics and the effort estimation could effortlessly reveal their intrinsic and wider correlations. In view of that, this paper presents a comparative study designed to evaluate this proposition.

There are a number of ways through data fuzzification could potentially be applied to the effort estimation problem [20]. In this study one of them is used: to construct a rule induction system replacing the crisp facts with fuzzy inputs, an inference engine uses a base of rules to map inputs to a fuzzy output which can either be translated back to a crisp value or left as a fuzzy value.

1.3 Evaluation Criteria

A common criterion for the evaluation of cost estimation models is the Magnitude of Relative Error (MRE) [3] which is defined as follows:

$$MRE_i = \frac{|\text{Actual Effort}_i - \text{Predicted Effort}_i|}{\text{Actual Effort}_i} \tag{1}$$

The MRE value is calculated for each observation i whose effort is predicted. The aggregation of MRE over multiple observations (N) can be achieved through the Mean MRE (MMRE) as follows:

$$MMRE = \frac{1}{N}\sum_{i}^{N} MRE_i \tag{2}$$

Another measure akin to MRE, the Magnitude of error Relative to the Estimate (MER), has been proposed [14]. Intuitively, it seems preferable to MRE since it measures the error relative to the estimate. MER uses *Predicted Effort*$_i$ as denominator in Eq. 1. The notation MMER is used to the mean MER in Eq. 2.

However, the MMRE and MMER are sensitive to individual predictions with excessively large MREs or MERs. Therefore, an aggregate measure less sensitive to extreme values is also considered, namely the median of MRE and MER values for the N observations (MdMRE and MdMER respectively) [4].

A complementary criterion is the prediction at level *l*, Pred(*l*) = k/N, where *k* is the number of observations where MRE (or MER) is less than or equal to *l*, and *N* is the total number of observations. Thus, Pred(25) gives the percentage of projects which were predicted with a MRE (or MER) less or equal than 0.25.

In general, the accuracy of an estimation technique is proportional to the Pred(*l*) and inversely proportional to the MMRE as well as MMER. As reference, for effort prediction models, a MMRE≤0.25 is considered as acceptable [7].

1.4 Related Work

Papers were reviewed regarding aspects related to a research on software development effort estimation at personal practices based on a FL model.

Not any papers propposing a fuzzy logic model based on practices of PSP were found in [1],[11],[12], [16] and [25]. A paper found [8] is based on personal level, but it only uses expert judgement for estimating the effort.

2 Experimental Design

There are two main steps for using an estimation model [18]: (1) model adequacy checking and (2) model validation:

1) Model Adequacy Checking (Model Verification) : An ANOVA for comparing the MRE as well as MER of each model is used in this paper. The dependent variables are the MRE and MER of each program developed and the three assumptions of residuals for MRE and MER are analysed.

2) Model Validation: Once the adequacy of the fuzzy logic model was checked, basing upon both LR equation as well as FL model the effort of a new data set is estimated. The Means Plot helps interpret the significant effects by technique.

The solution adopted by cost estimation researches for selecting the relevant attributes is to test the correlation (*r*) between effort and attributes [12]. In this study, N&C is correlated to the development effort.

In this study the population was integrated by two groups: one of them for checking de adequacy of the models (30 developers) and the other one for validating the models. The whole population was of 37 programmers.

2.1 The Process for Allocating and Administering the Treatments

In accordance with practices of PSP, each member of the population developed seven small programs. Seven was a number established because of the availability of developers. In the two groups of this experiment, ten sessions were carried out by programmer. In the first session both coding and counting standards were made. From second one only one program was developed (one daily). Finally, to make final reports the ninth and tenth days were assigned.

From gathered data of the first group, both a LR equation and a FL system were generated. For estimating the software development effort of all their programs, these models were used by the second group.

In all programs the development time included the following five phases by program: planning, design, coding, compiling, testing, and postmortem. In this study, because of the record diversity in both planning and postmortem phases by developer (manual or automated types), the time of these two phases were not considered.

Code review and Design Review phases were integrated on the process from third and fourth program respectively.

The next logs and standards were used by the 37 developers of both groups in all their programs [9]: coding standard, counting standard, defect type standard, project plan summary, time recording log, defect recording log and process improvement proposal.

From second program a test report template was used in the testing phase (to be consistent in time record, three test cases by program were documented). From third program, in the code review phase a code review checklist was used. From fourth program in the design review phase a design review checklist was used. That is, from fourth program, all practices and logs planned to this study were used by developers. Hence, the first, second and third program were excluded of this study (otherwise, comparison amongst times of development would have been unfair).

A software tool was used to personal fuzzy logic systems with type: mamdani, *and* method: *min*, *or* method: *max*; implication: *min*, aggregation: *max*, and defuzyfication: *centroid*.

2.2 Methods Used to Reduce Bias and Determines Sample Size

At least a course about the programming language used, all developers had already received. They followed the same development process. They were constantly supervised and advising about the process. Each developer selected his/her own programming language and their coding standard. In accordance with [9] Table 1 depicts the counting standard followed by all developers.

Table 1. Counting standard

Count type	Type
Physical/logical	Physical
Statement type	Included
Executable	Yes
Nonexecutable	
Declarations and Compiler directives	Yes, one by text line
Comments or Blank lines	No
Clarifications: *{* and *}*; *begin* and *end*	Yes

210 programs were developed by thirty programmers and 90 of them were excluded (since that they corresponded to first, second and third programs). In this study, only programs higher or equal to ten lines of code were considered. According to this criterion, three of the 120 programs were excluded. As outliers twelve programs were identified (they presented errors in time record). Then, in this study the total number of programs for generating both LR equation and FL model was 105 (210-90-3-12=105).

A $r^2 \geq 0.5$ is an acceptable value for predicting [9] (r^2 is named coefficient of determination). In this study, the r value (N&C-Effort) was of 0.72, while r^2=0.52.

3 Conducting the Experiment and Data Collection

A control method used to ensure completeness and accuracy of data collection was followed. It consisted in recording measures using logs described in section 2.1. In Table 2, actual data by developer is depicted.

Table 2. Actual data by developer from design to testing phases (DP: Developer, P: Number of Program, N&C: New and Changed code, AE: Actual Effort)

DP	P	N&C	AE	DP	P	N&C	AE	DP	P	N&C	AE	DP	P	N&C	AE	DP	P	N&C	AE
A1	4	17	65	A6	7	11	74	B2	5	17	65	B8	6	182	141	C4	5	75	124
A1	5	22	84	A7	4	11	23	B2	6	117	150	B8	7	63	113	C4	6	32	92
A1	6	30	71	A7	6	15	42	B2	7	42	100	B9	4	75	115	C4	7	20	59
A1	7	13	53	A7	7	23	51	B3	4	75	104	B9	5	44	97	C5	4	15	58
A2	4	47	127	A8	4	26	91	B3	5	71	92	B9	6	100	153	C5	5	84	185
A2	6	47	90	A8	5	17	93	B3	6	79	128	B9	7	121	144	C5	6	51	53
A2	7	17	32	A8	6	19	66	B3	7	157	123	B10	4	79	133	C6	4	13	33
A3	4	34	43	A8	7	13	62	B4	6	81	155	B10	5	51	70	C6	5	129	88
A3	5	35	52	A9	4	11	34	B4	7	119	168	B10	6	112	92	C6	6	30	92
A3	6	54	56	A9	5	12	62	B5	4	54	134	B10	7	84	78	C7	4	10	48
A3	7	50	52	A9	6	12	39	B5	5	28	85	C1	5	153	145	C7	6	81	76
A4	4	11	44	A9	7	10	30	B5	6	103	171	C1	6	89	125	C7	7	12	45
A4	6	25	50	A10	4	60	58	B5	7	97	131	C1	7	22	82	C8	4	20	72
A4	7	14	32	A10	5	45	145	B6	4	37	123	C2	4	17	56	C8	6	136	120
A5	4	31	61	A10	6	49	80	B6	5	16	64	C2	5	77	124	C8	7	21	72
A5	5	12	38	A10	7	81	59	B6	6	49	159	C2	6	96	134	C9	4	34	95
A5	6	23	54	B1	4	50	83	B6	7	123	195	C2	7	17	63	C9	5	137	155
A5	7	10	35	B1	5	93	68	B7	4	41	121	C3	4	33	70	C10	4	22	85
A6	4	19	59	B1	6	143	122	B7	6	81	129	C3	5	125	124	C10	5	111	135
A6	5	26	102	B1	7	91	93	B8	4	29	49	C3	6	58	99	C10	6	87	125
A6	6	23	71	B2	4	36	100	B8	5	29	98	C3	7	35	100	C10	7	28	95

From 105 programs gathered, the LR equation generated is the following:

$$\text{Effort} = 53.2915 + 0.687458 * \text{N\&C} \qquad (3)$$

3.1 Fuzzy Rules

The term fuzzy identification usually refers to the techniques and algorithms for constructing fuzzy models from data. There are two main approaches for obtaining a fuzzy model from data [25]:

1. The expert knowledge in a verbal form that is translated into a set of if–then rules. A certain model structure can be created, and parameters of this structure, such as membership functions and weights of rules, can be tuned using input and output data.

2. No prior knowledge about the system under study is initially used to formulate the rules, and a fuzzy model is constructed from data based on a certain algorithm. It is expected that extracted rules and membership functions can explain the system behaviour. An expert can modify the rules or supply new ones based upon his or her own experience. The expert tuning is optional in this approach.

On the first approach this paper is based upon. The fuzzy rules based on the correlation (*r*) between N&C code and effort metrics gathered were formulated. Then three rules were derived:

1. If (*New &Changed* is *Small*) then *Effort* is *Low*
2. If (*New &Changed* is *Medium*) then *Effort* is *Average*
3. If (*New &Changed* is *Big*) then *Effort* is *High*

Implementing a fuzzy system requires that the different categories of the different inputs be represented by fuzzy sets, which in turn is represented by membership functions (MF). The MF type considered to this experiment is the triangular [1]. It is a three-point function, defined by minimum (a), maximum (c) and modal (b) values, that is, MF(a,b,c) where a≤b≤c.

In Table 3 parameters of the three input and output MF of the FL model are depicted. In accordance with an interval, the values of *a*, *b* and *c* parameters were defined. From values close or equal to both minimum and maximum of both program sizes and efforts, the intervals were adjusted. These intervals were divided by next segments: *small*, *medium* and *big* (N&C Code), and *low*, *average* and *high* (Effort). Their scalar parameters (a, b, c) are defined as follows:

$$MF(x) = 0 \text{ if } x < a \qquad MF(x) = 1 \text{ if } x = b \qquad MF(x) = 0 \text{ if } x > c$$

Table 3. Membership Function Characteristics

Parameter	LOC			Effort		
	Small	Medium	Big	Low	Average	High
a	1	18	72	20	60	100
b	35	65	136	51	104	149
c	65	113	200	80	153	200

4 Analysis

4.1 Model Adequacy Checking (Model Verification)

Both simple LR equation (Eq. **3**) and the FL model (Table 3) are applied to original data set. The MRE as well as MER are then calculated and the following three assumptions of residuals for MRE and MER ANOVA are analysed (a residual of an observation is the difference between the observation and the mean of the sample containing it [23]): (1) Independent samples: In this study, the group of developers are made up of separate programmers and each of them developed their own programs, so the data are independent; (2) Equal standard deviations: In a plot of this kind the residuals should fall roughly in a horizontal band centered and symmetric about the horizontal axis (as in Figures 1a and 1c are showed), and (3) Normal populations:

A normal probability plot of the residuals should be roughly linear (as in Figures 1b and 1d are showed in a moderated way).

Then the three assumptions for residuals in the actual data set can be considered as met.

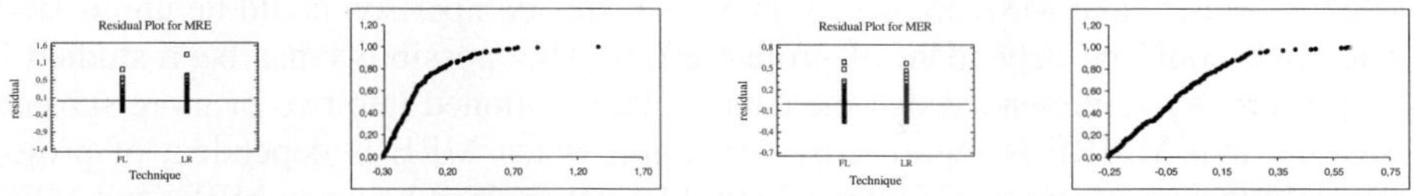

(a) MRE (b) MRE (c) MER (d) MER

Fig. 1. Equal standard deviation plots (a,c) and Normality plots (b,d)

In Table 4 the result of an ANOVA for MRE as well as MER are depicted. The p-values test the statistical significance of each technique. If a p-value is less than 0.05 then it has a statistically significant effect on MRE or MER at the 95.0% confidence level. Since the p-values of the F-test are greater than 0.05, there is not a statistically significant difference between the mean MRE (and MER) from LR to FL at the 95.0 % confidence level.

Table 4. MRE and MER ANOVA

MRE		MER	
F-ratio	p-value	F-ratio	p-value
0.56	0.4569	0.00	0.9746

A Multiple Range Tests for MRE (and MER) by technique indicate which technique had the better result. Table 5 applies a multiple comparison procedure to determine which means are significantly different from which others. The method currently being used to discriminate among the means is Fisher's least significant difference (LSD) procedure. In Table 5 each of the absolute values in the "difference" column is lower than its LSD value. It indicates that both techniques are not significantly different each other.

Table 5. Multiple Range Tests for MRE and MER by Technique

Technique	MRE			MER		
	LS Mean (MMRE)	Difference	LSD value	LS Mean (MMER)	Difference	LSD value
FL	0.2700	-0.026	0.068	0.2497	0.0007	0.047
LR	0.2960			0.2489		

4.2 Model Validation

From 7 developers, 49 programs were developed; 21 of them were excluded (since that they corresponded to first, second and third programs). In this validation, only programs higher or equal to ten lines of code were considered. According to this criterion, four of the 49 programs were excluded. As outliers four programs were considered (they presented errors in time record). Then, the total number of programs (Table 6) for validating both LR and FL models was 20 (49-21-4-4=20).

Once both models were applied to data depicted in Table 6, the global results where the following (considering 20 programs): $MMRE_{LR}$=0.27, $MMRE_{FL}$=0.27 $MMER_{LR}$=0.25, and $MMER_{FL}$=0.23. However, this comparison could be unfair since that MRE could be dependent of project effort. This possibility has been studied in [22] where is recommended that the data set be partitioned into two or more subsamples and that MMRE is reported by subsample when MRE is dependent of project effort. In the scatter plots of Figures 2a to 2d, relationships between MRE (and MER) and Effort when LR and FL models have been applied, are shown. Figures 2a and 2c suggest that MRE decreases with effort, while the Figures 2b and 2d (MER) increase with effort; that is: in this study the MRE resulted dependent of project effort. Based upon a visual inspections as well as correlation values, the dataset is then divided in projects with Effort<100 (cluster A, with 11 programs) and Effort≥100 (cluster B, with 9 programs). In Table 7 the MMRE, MMER, Median and Pred(25) results are showed by cluster, while from Figures 3a to 3d, plots of means (from Table 7) are depicted.

Table 6. Actual data by developer from design to testing phases (DP: Developer, P: Number of Program, N&C: New and Changed code, AE: Actual Effort)

DP	P	N&C	AE	DP	P	N&C	AE	DP	P	N&C	AE	DP	P	N&C	AE	DP	P	N&C	AE
U1	4	86	105	U2	5	107	141	U4	4	78	100	U5	5	57	75	U6	5	53	62
U1	5	75	130	U2	7	53	122	U4	5	155	180	U5	6	50	65	U6	6	60	60
U1	7	56	160	U3	5	92	177	U4	6	29	75	U5	7	55	55	U7	4	13	49
U2	4	69	67	U3	6	27	72	U4	7	40	90	U6	4	55	54	U7	6	86	121

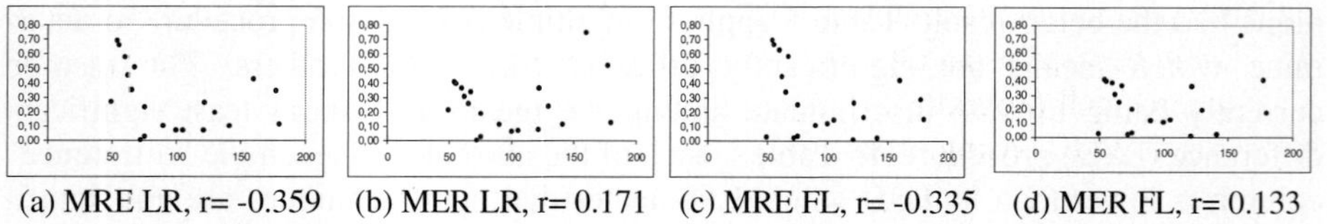

(a) MRE LR, r= -0.359 (b) MER LR, r= 0.171 (c) MRE FL, r= -0.335 (d) MER FL, r= 0.133

Fig. 2. Scatter plots (MRE or MER versus effort) their correlation (r) values

In Table 7 can be observed that FL technique had the lower values of MMER in both clusters. Moreover, cluster A shows that its MdMRE as well as MdMER of FL resulted lower than LR technique; while the FL Pred(25) in cluster A the two values were higher than LR Pred(25), and in cluster B all Pred(25) had the same value.

Table 7. MMRE, MMER, Median and Pred(25) by cluster

Cluster	MMRE		MMER		Median				Pred(25)			
					MdMRE		MdMER		MRE		MER	
	LR	FL	LR	FL	LR	FL	LR	FL	LR	FL	LR	FL
A	0.35	*0.34*	0.24	*0.23*	0.35	*034*	0.26	*0.25*	0.36	*0.45*	0.45	*0.55*
B	*0.18*	*0.18*	0.26	*0.24*	0.11	0.15	0.13	0.18	*0.67*	*0.67*	*0.67*	*0.67*

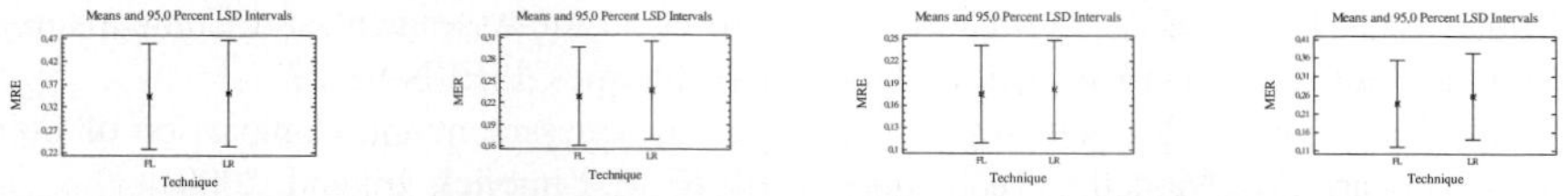

(a) MMRE, cluster A (b) MMER, cluster A (c) MMRE, cluster B (d) MMER, cluster B

Fig. 3. Plots of means by cluster

In accordance with the evaluation criteria described in section 1.3, in the majority of comparisons (except for medians of cluster B), the Fuzzy Logic resulted better or equal than Linear Regression (in Table 7 these cases are showed in *italic*).

5 Conclusions and Future Research

This research was founded on the four following facts: (1) Software development effort estimation is one of the most critical activities in managing software projects, (2) Given that no single software development estimation technique is best for all situations, a careful comparison of the results of several approaches is most likely to produce realistic estimates, (3) the 90% of software Mexican enterprises do not have formal processes to record, track and control measurable issues during the development process (including software effort estimation), and (4) unless engineers have the capabilities provided by personal training, they cannot properly support their teams or consistently and reliably produce quality products.

In this paper 105 programs developed by a first group of thirty programmers were gathered. From these programs a FL system was generated for estimating the effort of twenty programs developed by other group of seven developers. All programs were based upon personal practices. With a linear regression equation that FL was compared. This comparison was based on (a) MRE, MER, MMRE, MMER and Pred(25), and (b) considering the dependability between MRE and Effort. Results showed that the FL can be used as an alternative for estimating the development effort at personal level when small programs are developed. Future research involves the generation of fuzzy logic models using other kind of membership functions.

Acknowledgements

We would like to thank Center for Computing Research, National Polytechnic Institute, Mexico as well as CONACYT. Moreover, to Federal Commission of Electricity at Guadalajara, Jalisco; also, to students of the University del Valle de Atemajac in Guadalajara as well as developers of PAFTI program of the CINVESTAV-Guadalajara.

References

1. Ahmed M. A, Saliu M.O., AlGhamdi J. Adaptive fuzzy logic-based framework for software development effort prediction. Information and Software Technology. Elsevier. 2004
2. Boehm B., Abts Ch., Chulani S. Software Development Cost Estimation Approaches – A Survey. Chulani Ph. D. Report. 1998

3. Briand L.C., Emam K.E., Surmann D., Wieczorek I. An Assesment and Comparison of Common Software Cost Estimation Modeling Techniques. ISERN-98-27
4. Briand L.C., Langley T., Wieczorek I. A replicated Assessment and Comparison of Common Software Cost Modeling Techniques. IEEE ICSE, Limerick, Ireland. 2000
5. Briand L.C., Wieczorek I. Software Resource Estimation. Encyclopedia of Software Engineering. Volume 2, New York: John Wiley & Sons, pp. 1160-1196
6. Brooks, F. P. Jr. Three Great Challenges for Half-Century-Old Computer Science. Journal of the ACM, Vol. 50, No. 1 pp. 25-26. January 2003
7. Conte S.D., Dunsmore H.E., Shen V.Y. Software Engineering Metrics and Models. Benjamin/Cummings. M. Park CA. 1986
8. Höst M., Wohlin C. A subjective effort estimation experiment. IST Journal. Elsevier. 1997
9. Humphrey W. A Discipline for Software Engineering. Addison Wesley. 1995.
10. Humphrey W. The Personal Software Process. Technical Report CMU/SEI-2000-022. 2000
11. Idri, A., Abran, A., Khoshgoftaar T. Estimating Software Project Effort by Analogy Based on Linguistic Values. Eight IEEE Symposium on Software Metrics. 2002
12. Idri, A., Khoshgoftaar T. Fuzzy Analogy: a New Approach for Software Cost Estimation. International Workshop on Software Measurement (IWSM´01). Canada. 2001.
13. Kitchenham B. A., Pfleeger S. L., Pickard L.M., Jones P. W., Hoaglin D. C., Emam K.E., Rosenberg J. Preliminary Guidelines for Empirical Research in Software Engineering. IEEE Transactions on SE, Vol. 28, No. 8. August 2002
14. Kitchenham B.A., MacDonell S.G., Pickard L.M., Shepperd M.J.. What Accuracy Statistics Really Measure. IEE Proceedings Software. 148(3). pp. 81-85. 2001
15. MacDonell S. G. Software source code sizing using fuzzy logic modelling. Elsevier Science. 2003
16. MacDonell S.G, Gray A.R. Alternatives to Regression Models for Estimating Software Projects. Proceedings of the IFPUG Fall Conference. Dallas TX. IFPUG. 1996
17. Mendes E., Mosley N., Watson I. A Comparison of Case-Based Reasoning Approaches to Web Hypermedia project Cost Estimation. ACM. 2002.
18. Montgomery D., Peck E. Introduction to linear regression analysis. John Wiley. 2001.
19. Park. R. E. Software Size Measurement: A Framework for Counting Source Statements. Software Engineering Institute, Carnegie Mellon University. September 1992
20. Schofield C. Non-Algorithmic Effort Estimation Techniques. ESERG, TR98-01. 1998.
21. Secretaría de Economía. Programa para el Desarrollo de la Industria del Software. 2002.
22. Stensrud E., Foss T., Kitchenham B., Myrtveit I. An Empirical Validation of the Relationship Between the Relative Error and Project Size. Eighth IEEE SM Symposium. 2002
23. Weiss N.A. Introductory Statistics. Addison Wesley. 1999.
24. Zadeh L. A. From Computing with Numbers to Computing with Words – From Manipulation of Measurements to Manipulation of Perceptions. IEEE Transactions on Circuits and Systems – I: Fundamental Theory and Applications, vol. 45, no. 1, pp 105-119. 1999.
25. Zhiwei Xu Z.. Khoshgoftaar T.M. Identification of fuzzy models of software cost estimation. Elsevier Fuzzy Sets and Systems. Volume 145. July 2004.

Appendix: Developers Data

a) Development Team, Federal Commission of Electricity (FCE) of Guadalajara: *C1: Barraza Arellano I., C2: De la Cruz Preciado O., C3: Flores Gómez C., C4: Galindo Gauna R., C5: García Ramos M., C6: Guerra Martínez A., C7: Guzmán Martínez A., C8: Hernández Hernández P., C9: Hernández Ramos A., C10: Partida Mechuca L.*

Office of Director: (33)-31-34-13-00 ext. 8158 y 8142, email: omar.delacruz@cfe.gob.mx

b) PAFTI Program, alpha (A) and beta (B) groups, CINVESTAV-Guadalajara (http://www.gdl.cinvestav.mx/): *A1: Alegría Bobadilla J., A2: Escamilla Rodríguez J., A3: Gutíerrez Ramírez F., A4: Montesinos S. J., A5: Morales López D., A6: Plascencia Sánchez J., A7: Reynoso Rojas R., A8: Rivera Vega B., A9: Vega Baray F., A10: Viramontes Cortés A., B1: Cordero Baltazar D., B2: Davis Alcaraz R., B3: Díaz Infante Montes J., B4: Domínguez Zárate S., B5: Duarte Lobo M., B6: Jiménez Galicia N., B7: Montero Silva A., B8: Martínez Sotelo N., B9: Rocha Hernández J., B10: Vega Ávalos C.*

Program Director: tel: (33)-37-70-37-00, ext. 1016, email: jesus.vazquez@cts-design.com

c) Bachelor Students, Computational Systems Engineering, Universidad del Valle de Atemajac (UNIVA), Guadalajara (http://www.univa.mx/): *U1: Becerril Ramírez J., U2: Caro Guerra R., U3: Gutiérrez Hernández A., U4: Herrera Rábago F., U5: Medina Estrada C., U6: Sánchez Sánchez F., U7: Tamayo Emmanuel.*

Office of Director: tel: (33)-31-34-08-00, ext. 1456, email: martin.rodriguez @univa.mx

Reconfigurable Networked Fuzzy Takagi Sugeno Control for Magnetic Levitation Case Study

Quiñones-Reyes P.[1], Benítez-Pérez H.[2,*], Cárdenas-Flores F.[2], and García-Nocetti, F.[2]

[1] Departamento de Sistemas y Computación, Instituto Tecnológico de Jiquilpan, Av. Tecnológico, S/N, CP 59510, Jiquilpan, Michoacán, México
[2] Departamento de Ingeniería de Sistemas Computacionales y Automatización, IIMAS, UNAM, Apdo. Postal 20-726, Del. A. Obregón, México D. F., CP. 01000, México
*Tel.: ++52 55 5622 36 23; Fax: ++52 55 5616 01 76
*hector@uxdea4.iimas.unam.mx

Abstract. Nowadays the dynamic behavior of a computer network system can be modeled from the perspective of a control system. One strategy to be follow is the real-time modeling of magnetic levitation system. After this representation, next stage is how a control approach can be affected and modified. In that respect, this paper proposes a control reconfiguration strategy from the definition of an Intelligent Fuzzy System computer network reconfiguration. Several stages are including, how computer network takes place, as well as how control techniques are modified using Takagi-Sugeno Fuzzy Control.

1 Introduction

Control reconfiguration is presented as an available approach for fault coverage in order to keep system performance. In here reconfiguration is pursued as a response of time delay modification rather than fault appearance although this is the basis for control reconfiguration.

Several strategies for managing time delay within control laws have been studied by different research groups. For instance, [1] proposes the use of a time delay scheme integrated to a reconfigurable control strategy based upon a stochastic methodology. [2] present an interesting case of fault tolerant control approach related to time delay coupling. [3] have studied reconfigurable control from the point of view of structural modification. They stablish a logical relation between dynamic variables and the faults. [4] and [5] consider that reconfigurable control performs a combined modification of system structure and dynamic response. It presents the advantage of bounded modifications over system response.

Some considerations need to be stated in order to define this approach. Firstly, faults are strictly local in peripheral elements and these are tackled by just eliminating the faulty element. In fact, faults are catastrophic and local. Time delays are bounded and restrictive to scheduling algorithms.

The present approach takes time delays due to communication as deterministic measured variables, as well as actuator fault presence by modification of the B matrix in order to propose a Takagi Sugeno (TKS) fuzzy control with two conditions: lose of

A. Gelbukh and C.A. Reyes-Garcia (Eds.): MICAI 2006, LNAI 4293, pp. 134 – 145, 2006.

local peripheral elements and the related time delays. In here fuzzy logic control (FLC) law [6] views time delays as a result of deterministic reconfigurable communications based upon scheduling algorithm. To define the communication network performance, the use of several computers is necesary. This strategy achieves network implementation based on message transactions using the Teal-Time Workshop toolbox of MATLAB. Two kind of computer network are used, CANbus and Ethernet. These two kind of computer network used present no further time delays difference because the network size is quite small.

The objective of this paper is to present a Fuzzy logic strategy for control reconfiguration based upon time delay knowledge as well as local fault effects within a distributed system environment considering the magnetic levitation challenge. Here, we use a TKS fuzzy control to modify the control law of the system when a fault appears.

2 Structural Reconfiguration Algorithm

Time delays are measurable and bounded according to a real-time scheduling algorithm. In this case the scheduling algorithm is the well known earliest deadline first (EDF) algorithm. According to Fig. 1, structural reconfiguration takes place as a result of EDF (using an ART2A neural network) performance and related user request. This action causes a control law modification. How this modification happens

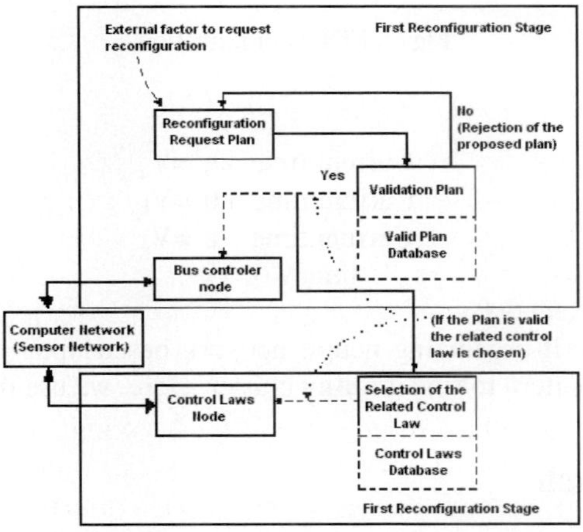

Fig. 1. General structure of Reconfigurable System over a Computer Network

is the scope of this paper under a TKS fuzzy control approach [7]. The core of this algorithm is to perform on-line reconfiguration based upon a review of the proposed plan, which uses an ART2A neural network [8] in order to classify valid and non-valid plans. First, the ART2A neural network is trained offline using valid and non-valid plans from an EDF evaluation and case study response [9, 10]. Based on this training procedure two main regions are determined, one related to suitable reconfigurations and other that holds non-trustable reconfigurations. During the online stage the network allows classification from new plans. If the response of the network belongs to valid plans it will be reconfigured, otherwise the proposed plan will be rejected. It is important to mention that an ART2A network cannot learn new plans during the online stage as a safety precaution.

The communication network plays a key role defining the behavior of the dynamic system in terms of time variance giving a nonlinear behavior. The EDF is needed here due to flexibility of task reorganization during online performance. The Basic procedure of EDF requires several characteristics from each task such as deadlines, time consumptions and priorities. EDF orders task execution based on the proximity of each local deadline, named as the difference between current time and local deadline. The smallest value amongst all tasks is the winner. For instance, consider a group of three tasks with time distribution as shown in Fig. 2.

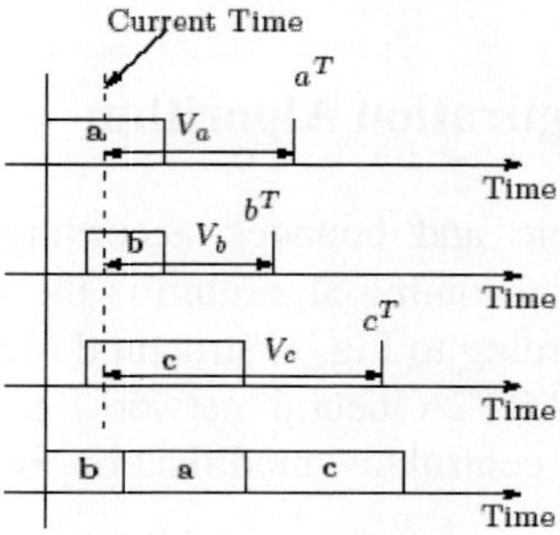

Fig. 2. EDF approximation

Where

$$\text{Current.time} - a^T = V_a$$
$$\text{Current.time} - b^T = V_b$$
$$\text{Current.time} - c^T = V_c$$
$$\min(V_*) = V_w$$

V_w is the task to be executed.

An ART2A is a self-organizing neural network based upon the angle between a prototype and input pattern to find a fitting cluster. Here, we use the approach in [8].

3 Plant Approach

The proposed dynamic plant is based upon the following structure:

$$x(k+1) = a^p x(k) + B^p u(k) \qquad (1)$$
$$y = c^p x(k)$$

where $a^p \in \Re^{nxn}$, $c^p \in \Re^{nx1}$ and $B^p \in \Re^{nx1}$ are the plant matrices. x(k), u(k) and y(k) are the state, input and output vectors respectively. Specially B^P is stated as:

$$B^{p} = \sum_{i=1}^{N} \rho_i B_i \sum_{j=1}^{M} \int_{\tau_j^i}^{\tau_{j-1}^i} e^{-a^{p}(t-\tau)} d\tau \tag{2}$$

where $\rho_i = 1$ and $\sum_{i=1}^{N} \rho_i = 1$ taking into account that N is the total number of possible faults and M is the involved time delay from each fault. Current communication time delays are expressed as t_{j-1}^{i} and t_{j}^{i} and B_i is integrated as

$$B_i = \begin{bmatrix} b_1 \\ b_2 \\ 0_i \\ \vdots \end{bmatrix} \rightarrow$$

, b_i is the fault element

where $b_1 \rightarrow b_N$ are the elements conformed at the input of the plant (such as actuators) and 0_i is the lost element due to local fault where B^{p} represents only one scenario following eq. 2. Current B_i^{p} considers local faults and related time delays of

$$B_i^{p} = B_i \sum_{j=1}^{M} \int_{t_j^i}^{t_{j-1}^i} e^{-a^{p}(t-\tau)} d\tau \tag{3}$$

For simplicity purposes B_i^{p} is used in order to depict local linear plants. From this representation fuzzy plant is defined as follows taking into account each time delay and fault:

$$r_i : \text{if } x_1 \text{ is } A_{1i} \text{ and } x_2 \text{ is } A_{2i} \text{ and} \ldots \text{and } x_l \text{ is } A_{li} \text{ then } a_i^{p} x(k) + B_i^{p} u(k) \tag{4}$$

and

$$h_i = \prod_{j=1}^{l} A_{ij}(x_j) \tag{5}$$

where $\{x_1 \ldots . x_l\}$ are current state measures, l is the number of states, $i = \{1,\ldots,N\}$ is one of the fuzzy rules, N is the number of the rules which is equal to the number of possible faults and A_{ij} are the related membership functions defined as:

$$A_{ij}(x_i) = \exp\left(-\frac{(x_i - c_{ij})^2}{\sigma_{ij}^2} \right) \tag{6}$$

where c_{ij} and σ_{ij} are the constants to be tuned. The final representation of the plant as an integrated system is based upon center of area defuzzification method as shown in eq. 7.

$$x^{p}(k+1) = \frac{\left(\sum_{i=1}^{N} h_i \left(a_i^{p} x(k) + B_i^{p} u(k) \right) \right)}{\sum_{i=1}^{N} h_i} \tag{7}$$

The result of this system representation allows the integration of nonlinear stages and nonlinear transitions to basically a group of linear plants.

4 Control Approach

From the representation of the plant as a fuzzy system [11]. The development of the control law as a group of bounded local linear control laws related to each local linear system is considered. The structure of each fuzzy rule is:

$$r_i: \text{if } x_1 \text{ is } A^c_{1i} \text{ and } x_2 \text{ is } A^c_{2i} \text{ and...and } x_l \text{ is } A^c_{li} \text{ then } u(k) = k^i_p e(k) + k^i_i \int e(k)dt \quad (8)$$

where $i = \{1,....,N\}$, N is the number of fuzzy rules which is the number of faults to be represented, $\{x_1,....,x_l\}$ are current states of the plant, A^c_{ij} are the gaussians membership functions like:

$$A^c_{ij} = \exp\left(-\frac{(x_i - c^c_{ij})^2}{\sigma^{c\,2}_{ij}}\right) \quad (9)$$

where c^c_{ij} and σ^c_{ij} are constants to be tuned. Furthermore, k^i_p is the proportional gain and k^i_i is the integral gain related to the control.

Similar to fuzzy system plant, fuzzy control representation is integrated as:

$$w_i = \prod_{j=1}^{l} A^c_{ij}(x_j) \quad (10)$$

and

$$u(k) = \frac{\sum_{i=1}^{N} w_i \left(k^i_p e(k) + k^i_i \int e(k)dt\right)}{\sum_{i=1}^{N} w_i} \quad (11)$$

The configuration of the FLC is integrated to the already explored plant where final representation is given as a closed loop system of the feedback plant as shown in Fig. 3.

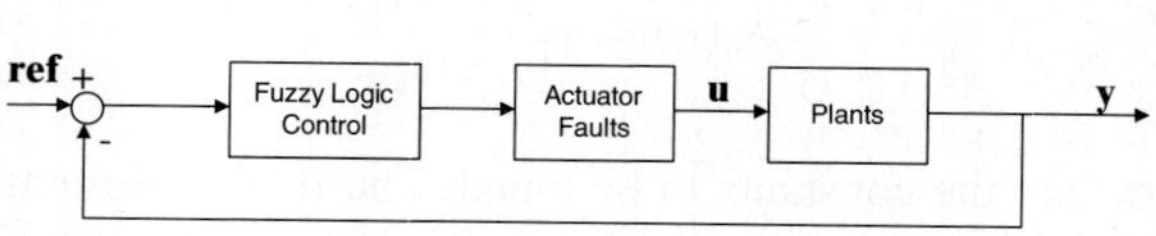

Fig. 3. System Configuration using Fuzzy Logic Control

$$x(k+1) = \frac{\sum_{i=1,j=1}^{N} h_i w_j \left(\left(a_i - c_i\left(k^i_p e(k) + k^i_i \int e(k)dt\right) B^p_i\right) x(k) + B^p_i ref\right)}{\sum_{i=1,j=1}^{N} h_i w_j} \quad (12)$$

where *ref* is the reference to be followed by controller and the variables i and j are used due to fuzzy rules interconnections as the representation of different linear plants and respective controllers From this representation, stability needs to be stated. This is an issue of future work.

5 Case Study

Case study is a magnetic system integrated to a computer network, see Fig. 4 [12].

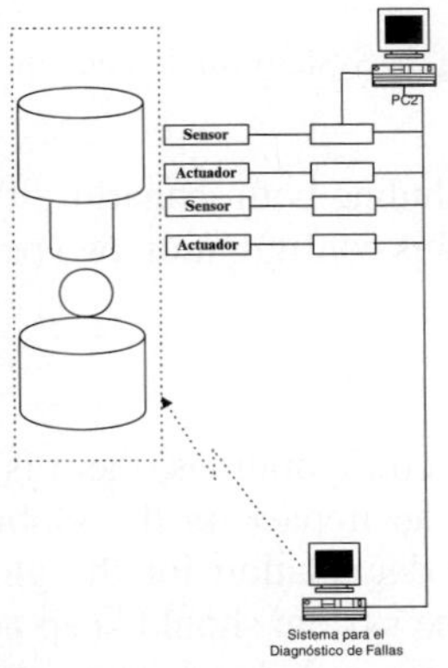

Fig. 4. Magnetic Levitator Case Study

The dynamics of case study expressed in transfer function is:

$$G_{bi}(s)=\frac{-k_{bdc}w_b^2}{s^2-w_b^2}$$
$$k_{bdc}=\frac{x_{bo}}{I_{co}};w_b=\sqrt{2}\sqrt{\frac{g}{x_{bo}}} \tag{13}$$

where

g is the gravity force
I_{co} is the current of the coil
x_{bo} is the distance from coil to ball position.

For the implementation, a basic time diagram system is proposed in Figs. 4 and 5 in [13]. When a fault appears, the use of EDF through the ART2A network is performed in order to re-organize task execution according to basic time restrictions. Maximum time delays are bounded on these figures. Both scenarios are local with respect to magnetic levitation system. As these two scenarios are bounded, the related consumption times are shown in Equations 3 and 4 in [13] (Figures 4 and 5, respectively). From both scenarios there is an element known as fault tolerance element that presents extra communication for control performance although it masks any local fault from sensors. See final implementation in Fig. 5.

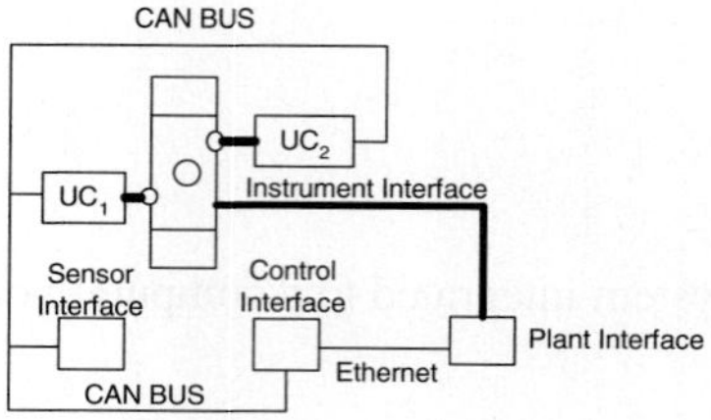

Fig. 5. System Implementation

From this time boundary, including both scenarios, it is feasible to implement some control strategies. Considering this configuration two posible fault cases are:

- One local fault;
- Several local faults.

Based on these two possible configurations, there is a worst-case scenario related to several local faults that has an impact on the global control strategy. The other configuration presents a minor degradation for the global control strategy. Despite this performance degradation, the system should keep normal functionality due to the inherent fault tolerance strategy and local time delays integrated into related controllers. Taking into account these two possible configurations, the local and global time delays are described in Table 1.

Table 1. Time delays related to local Communications

Configuration 1 Several Local Faults	Local Time Delays	1 ms
	Global Time Delays	5 ms
Configuration 2 One Local Fault	Local Time Delays	1 ms
	Global Time Delays	3 ms

As the time delays have been bounded, the plant model is defined based on Fig. 6.

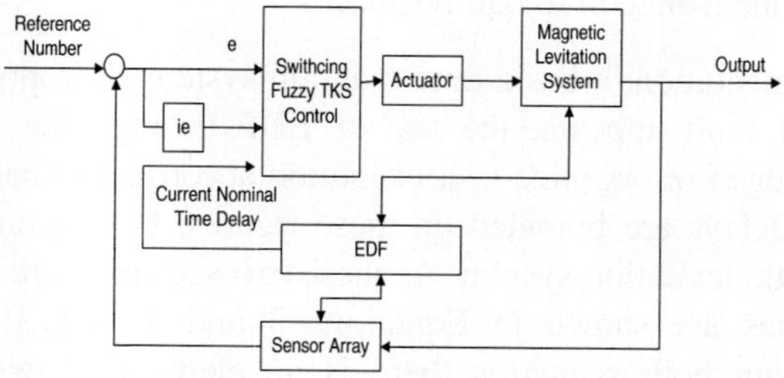

Fig. 6. Plant and control law integration

Following this configuration Table 2 gives k_i and k_p representation.

Table 2. Representation of the rules for the FLC

error\ierror	VLP	LP	M	HP	VHP
HN	k_p^1 k_i^1	k_p^6 k_i^2	k_p^{11} k_i^3	k_p^{16} k_i^4	k_p^{21} k_i^5
LN	k_p^2 k_i^6	k_p^7 k_i^7	k_p^{12} k_i^8	k_p^{17} k_i^9	k_p^{22} k_i^{10}
Z	k_p^3 k_i^{11}	k_p^8 k_i^{12}	k_p^{13} k_i^{13}	k_p^{18} k_i^{14}	k_p^{23} k_i^{15}
LP	k_p^4 k_i^{16}	k_p^9 k_i^{17}	k_p^{14} k_i^{18}	k_p^{19} k_i^{19}	k_p^{24} k_i^{20}
HP	k_p^5 k_i^{21}	k_p^{10} k_i^{22}	k_p^{15} k_i^{23}	k_p^{20} k_i^{24}	k_p^{25} k_i^{25}

Where, for error and ierror:

VHP Very High Positive
HP High Positive
M Medium
LP Low Positive
VLP Very Low Positive
Z Zero
LN Low Negative
HN High Negative

The Fuzzy Logic Takagi Sugeno Control Law for this case study is integrated by 25 rules with 25 PI local control laws as shown in the next equation.

$$r_i: \text{ if e is } u_{ei} \text{ and ie is } u_{iei} \text{ then } f_i = k_p^i * e + k_i^i * ie \tag{14}$$

where:

u_{ei} is the value for the MF for the error.

u_{iei} is the value for the MF for the ierror.

e is the error value.

ie is the ierror value.

k_p^i is the proportional gain for the PI

k_i^i is the integral gain for the PI

This condition has to be given for every single time delay and local fault appearance. In this case a recommendable procedure to follow is multi-objective optimization in order to define those suitable values.

6 Results

From this implementation several results are presented in terms of fault presence and the related action to overcome system lack of performance of control gains K_i and K_p. How the system responds to control strategy is presented for different separation values between membership functions as Table 3.

Table 3. Fault-free scenario for diferent percent of separation values between membership functions

Separation(%)	Integral of the error
10	0.4400
15	0.4495
20	0.4635
25	0.4642
30	0.5637
40	0.8491
50	0.7498

In Fig. 7 shown the error response for fault-free scenarios with 10% and 15% of separation.

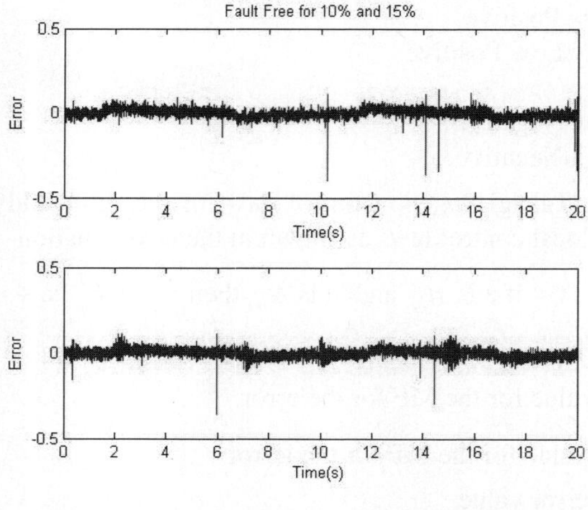

Fig. 7. Error response from fault-free scenario

For the case of fault scenario, system response is shown in Table 4. Fault scenario presents the error response (Fig. 8) using the separation of 10% and 15%.

Table 4. The integral of the error for fault scenario

Separation(%)	Integral of the error
10	0.5003
15	0.4567

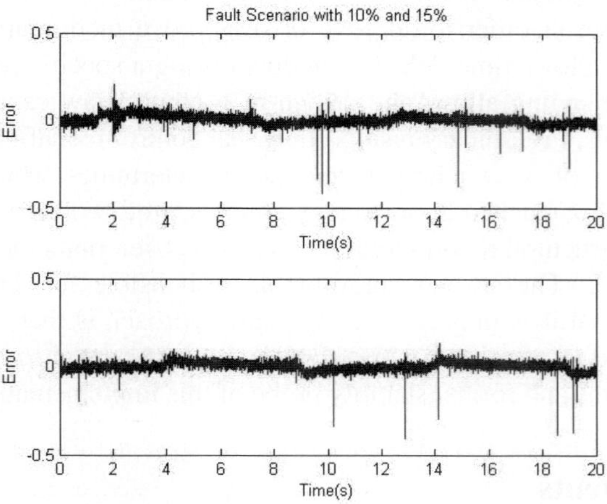

Fig. 8. Error response from fault scenario

Fig. 9 presents the system response comparing to current set point.

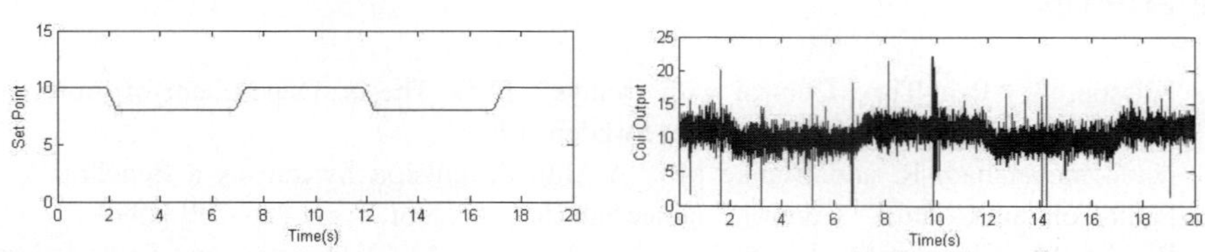

Fig. 9. Set point and System Response from Case Study

This last example presents control reconfiguration based on the decision-maker module; this is simple because it is dependent on the fault presence and on the related time delays. This reconfiguration approach becomes feasible due to the knowledge of fault presence and the consequence of time delays. Its consumption time is neglected, and it is considered part of control performance. It is obvious that fault presence is measurable; if this local fault localization approach cannot detect faults, this strategy becomes useless. Alternatively, local time delay management refers to the use of a quasi-dynamic scheduler to propose dynamic reconfiguration based on current system behavior rather than predefined scenarios.

7 Concluding Remarks

The present approach shows the integration of two techniques in order to perform reconfiguration. These two approaches are followed, in cascade mode, structural reconfiguration and control reconfiguration. Although there is no formal verification in order to follow this sequence, it has been adopted since structural reconfiguration provides stable conditions for control reconfiguration. The use of a real-time scheduling algorithm in order to approve or disapprove modifications on computer network behaviour allows time delays bounding during a specific time window. This local time delay bounding allows the design of a control law capable to cope with these new conditions. Preliminary results show that control reconfiguration is feasible as long as the use of a switching technique predetermines which control is the adequate. This goal is reached by a strategy composed of two algorithms, one which is responsible for structural reconfiguration and it has been implemented in this paper as ART2A network. The second algorithm is responsible for TKS fuzzy control reconfiguration. What it is important for this last approach is that control conditions are strictly bounded to certain response. Future work is related to integrate dynamic shedulling algorithms and formal stability probe of this implementation.

Acknowledgements

The authors would like to thank the financial support of DISCA-IIMAS-UNAM, and UNAM-PAPIIT (IN106100 and IN105303) Mexico in connection with this work.

References

1. Nilsson, J.; "Real-Time Control with Delays"; PhD. Thesis, Department of Automatic Control, Lund Institute of Technology, Sweden, 1998.
2. Izadi-Zamanabadi R. and Blanke M.; "A Ship Propulsion System as a Benchmark for Fault-Tolerant Control"; Control Engineering Practice, Vol. 7, pp. 227-239, 1999.
3. Blanke, M., Kinnaert M., Lunze J., and Staroswiecki M.; "Diagnosis and Fault Tolerant Control"; Springer, 2003.
4. Benítez-Pérez, H., and García-Nocetti, F.; "Reconfigurable Distributed Control "; Springer Verlag, 2005.
5. Thompson, H.;"Wireless and Internet Communications Technologies for monitoring and Control"; Control Engineering Practice, vol. 12, pp. 781-791, 2004.
6. Driankov, D., Hellendoorn, H., Reinfrank, M.; " An Introduction to Fuzzy Logic Control"; Springer-Verlag, 1994.
7. Abonyi J.; "Fuzzy Model Identification for Control"; Birkhäuser, 2003.
8. Frank, T., Kraiss, K.F., and Kuhlen, T; "Comparative Analysis of Fuzzy ART and ART-2A Network Clustering Performance"; IEEE Trans. on Neural Networks, Vol. 9, No. 3, 1998.
9. Benítez-Pérez, H. and Garcia-Nocetti F.; "Switching Fuzzy Logic Control for a Reconfigurable System Considering Communication Time Delays"; Proceedings, CDROM, European Control Conference; ECC 03 September, 2003.

10. Benítez-Pérez H., García-Zavala A and García-Nocetti F.; "Alternative Method based upon Planning Scheduler for On-Line Reconfiguration using System Performance"; Fifth International Symposium and School on Advanced Distributed Systems ISSADS, 2005b.
11. Yi, Z. and Heng, P.; "Stability of Fuzzy Control Systems with Bounded Uncertain delays"; IEEE Trans. On Fuzzy Systems, vol. 10, No. 1, pp. 93-97, 2002.
12. http://www.quanser.com/english/html/solutions/fs_soln_software_wincon.html, 2003.
13. Benítez-Pérez, H., Quiñones-Reyes, P., Mendez-Monroy, E., García-Nocetti, F. And Cardenas-Flores, F.; "Reconfigurable Fault Tolerant PID Networked Control for Magnetic Levitation Case Study"; Accepted paper for the IFAC Symposium on Safeprocess in Beijing, P.R. of China. August 2006.

Automatic Estimation of the Fusion Method Parameters to Reduce Rule Base of Fuzzy Control Complex Systems

Yulia Nikolaevna Ledeneva[1], Carlos Alberto Reyes García[1], and José Antonio Calderón Martínez[2]

[1] National Institute of Astrophysics, Optics and Electronics
{yledeneva, kargaxxi}@inaoep.mx
[2] Technological Institute of Aguascalientes
jac012000@hotmail.com

Abstract. The application of fuzzy control to large-scale complex systems is not a trivial task. For such systems the number of the fuzzy IF-THEN rules exponentially explodes. If we have l possible linguistic properties for each of n variables, with which we will have l^n possible combinations of input values. Large-scale systems require special approaches for modeling and control. In our work the sensory fusion method is studied in an attempt to reduce the size of the inference engine for large-scale systems. This method reduces the number of rules considerably. But, in order to do so, the adequate parameters should be estimated, which, in the traditional way, depends on the experience and knowledge of a skilled operator. In this work, we are proposing a method to automatically estimate the corresponding parameters for the sensory fusion rule base reduction method to be applied to fuzzy control complex systems. In our approach, the parameters of the sensory fusion method are found through the use of genetic algorithms. The implementation process, the simulation experiments, as well as some results are described in the paper.

1 Introduction

One of the principal components of soft computing is fuzzy logic, and one of the more active areas of fuzzy logic applications is control systems. The implementation of fuzzy control is an imitation of the control laws that humans use. Creating machines to emulate human expertise in control gives us an opportunity to design controllers for complex plants whose mathematical models are not easy to specify. Fuzzy logic controllers serve the same function as most conventional controllers, but they manage complex control problems through heuristics and mathematical models provided by fuzzy logic, rather than via mathematical models provided by differential equations [1].

The application of fuzzy control to large-scale complex systems is not, by no means, trouble-free. For such systems the number of the fuzzy IF-THEN rules as the number of sensory variables increases very quickly to an unmanageable level. When we take into account more input variables in control system, the number of rules grows exponentially: if we have l possible values for each of n variables, we must describe control corresponding to all l^n possible combinations of input values [2].

A. Gelbukh and C.A. Reyes-Garcia (Eds.): MICAI 2006, LNAI 4293, pp. 146 – 155, 2006.

Here the method of sensory fusion is studied in an attempt to reduce the size of the inference engine for large-scale systems. This structure reduces the number of rules considerably. But the adequate parameters should be estimated. In actual techniques much reliance has to be put on the experience of the operator with respect to the find these parameters [3].

In this work we will find the estimation of the parameters of the sensory fusion method using genetic algorithms (GA). GA is an appropriate technique to find the parameters in a large search space. Also in the optimization problems they have shown efficient and reliable results.

This document is organized as follows. The next section summarizes the principal of the rule base reduction methods. Section 3 presents the description of complex fuzzy control systems. In section 4 the method to fuse the variables is described. Section 5 proposes GA to find the parameters automatically. Some experiments are presented in section 6.

2 Rule Base Reduction Methods

One of the most important applications of fuzzy set theory [4] has been in the area of fuzzy rule based system. Rule base reduction is an important issue in fuzzy system design, especially for real time Fuzzy Logic Controller (FLC) design. Rule base size can be easily controlled in most fuzzy modeling and identification techniques.

For example, fuzzy clustering is considered to be one of the important techniques for automatic generation of fuzzy rules from the numerical examples. This algorithm forms a fuzzy partition of data points into a given number of clusters [5]. The number of cluster centers is the number of rules in the fuzzy system. The rule base size can be easily controlled through the control of the number of cluster centers. However, for control applications, often there is no enough data for a designer to extract the rule base for the controller. A designer has to build a generic rule base. A generic rule base includes all the possible combinations of fuzzy input values. Inevitable, the size of the rule base grows exponentially as the number of controller input grows. As the complexity of a system increases, it becomes more difficult and eventually impossible to make a precise statement about its behavior.

A simple and probably most effective way to reduce the rule base size is to use Sliding Mode Control. But this approach has its disadvantages as the parameters for the switch function has to be selected by an expert, or designed through classic control theory [6].

A technique for generation and minimization of fuzzy rules in case of limited available data sets was proposed by Anwer [7]. Initial rules for each data pairs are generated and conflicting rules are merged based on their degree of soundness. This technique can be used as an alternative to develop a model when available data may not be sufficient to train the model.

A neuro-fuzzy system [8-11] is a fuzzy system that uses a learning algorithm derived from neural network theory to determine its parameters (fuzzy sets and fuzzy rules) by processing data samples. Modern neuro-fuzzy systems are usually represented as special multilayer feedforward neural networks (for example models like ANFIS [11], FuNe [12], Fuzzy RuleNet [13], GARIC [14], HyFis [15] or NEFCON [16] and NEFCLASS [17]). The disadvantages of these approaches are that the determination number of processing nodes, the number of layers, and the interconnections among these nodes and layers are still an art and lack of systematic procedures.

Hierarchical scheme, structure suggested by Raju in 1991 does reduce the number of rules considerably, it is still not computationally effective [3]. Jamshidi proposed to use sensory fusion to reduce a rule base size [3]. Sensor fusion combines several inputs into one single input. The rule base size is reduced since the number of inputs is reduced. Also Jamshidi proposed to use the combination of hierarchical and sensory fusion methods [3]. The disadvantage of the design of hierarchical and sensory fused fuzzy controllers is that much reliance has to be put on the experience of the operator to establish the needed parameters. In an attempt to resolve this disadvantage we automatically estimate the parameters of sensory fusion method using GA.

3 Complex Fuzzy Control Systems

A system may be called large-scale or complex, if its dimension (order) is too high and its model (if available) is nonlinear, interconnected with uncertain information flow such that classical techniques of control theory cannot easily handle the system [2]. As the complexity of a system increases, it becomes more difficult and eventually impossible to make a precise statement about its behavior. Fuzzy logic is used in system control and analysis design, because it shortens the time for engineering development and sometimes, in the case of highly complex systems, is the only way to solve the problem.

Principle components of a fuzzy controller are: a process of coding numerical values to fuzzy linguistic labels (*fuzzification*), inference engine where the fuzzy rules (expert operator's experience) are implemented and decoding of the output fuzzy decision variables (*defuzzification*). Fuzzy control can be implemented by putting the above three stages on a chip, on a personal computer or like.

Having made the above comments on fuzzy control, dealing with a complex system remains a big challenge for any control paradigm. From a control theoretical point of view, fuzzy logic has been intermixed with all the important aspects of systems theory – modeling, identification, analysis, stability, synthesis, filtering, and estimation. One of the first complex system in which fuzzy control has been successfully applied is cement kilns, which began in Denmark. Today, most of the world's cement kilns are using a fuzzy expert system. However, the application of fuzzy control to large-scale complex systems is not, by no means, trouble-free. For such systems the number of the fuzzy IF-THEN rules as the number of sensory variables increases very quickly to an unmanageable level.

When a fuzzy controller is designed for a complex system, often several measurable output and actuating input variables are involved. In addition, each variable is represented by a finite number l of linguistic labels which would indicate that the total number of rules is equal to l^n, where n is the number of system variables.

Consider a fuzzy controller with n rules of the following type:

$$\text{IF } y_1 \text{ is } A_{1i} \text{ and } y_2 \text{ is } A_{2i} \text{ and } \dots \text{ and } y_n \text{ is } A_{ni} \text{ THEN } u_1 \text{ is } B_1 \text{ for } i = 1,2, \dots,n \quad (1)$$

where y_i, $i = 1, \dots,n$ are the system's output variables, u_i, $i = 1, \dots,n$ are the system's control variables, A_{ij} and B_i, $i,j = 1, \dots,n$ are the fuzzy sets, i.e. NB, NM, NS, ZO, PS, PM, and PB to stand for negative big, negative medium, …, and positive big.

For a fuzzy system with n variables and l fuzzy sets per variable, the total number of rules is given by $k = l^n$ [2]. As an example, consider a fourth-order model where $n = 4$ and $l = 5$. The total number of fuzzy rules will be $k = l^n = 5^4 = 625$. If there were five variables, then $k = 3125$.

From the above simple example, it is clear that the application of fuzzy control to any system of significant size would result in a dimensionality explosion.

4 Sensory Fusion Method

The reduction of the dimension of the control problem consists in decreasing the number of input variables n of the fuzzy controller. This reduction can be obtained by fusion of the input variables.

This method consists in combining variables before providing them to input of the fuzzy controller. These variables are often fused linearly. In figure 1 several cases are examined in order to illustrate the method. The coefficients of fusion a, b, c and d are positive realities whose values rise from physical considerations or an expert knowledge on the control process. It is considered, in each case of figure 1, that the input variables of the fuzzy controller are represented by m=5 linguistic values:

- NB for Negative Big,
- NS for Negative Small,
- ZE for Zero,
- PS for Positive Small,
- PB for Positive Means Big.

Assume that a fuzzy controller has three inputs (y_i, i=1, 2, 3) and one output u. The total number of rules will be 125, as follows:

R1: IF y_1 is A_1 and y_2 is B_1 and … and y_3 is C_1 THEN u is D_1;
R2: IF y_1 is A_2 and y_2 is B_2 and … and y_3 is C_2 THEN u is D_2; …;
R125: IF y_1 is A_5 and y_2 is B_5 and … and y_3 is C_5 THEN u is D_5.

In this case, we look into combining the sensory data (variables y_i, i = 1,2, 3) in one of these four possible ways:

1. Variables y_1 and y_2 are fused in the new variables Y_1 and Y_2:
   $Y_1 = ay_1 + by_2$
   $Y_2 = y_3$
2. Variables y_1 and y_3 are fused in the new variables Y_1 and Y_2:
   $Y_1 = ay_1 + by_3$
   $Y_2 = y_2$

3. Variables y_2 and y_3 are fused in the new variables Y_1 and Y_2:
   $Y_1 = ay_2 + by_3$
   $Y_2 = y_1$
4. Variables y_1, y_2 and y_3 are fused in the new variable Y:
   $Y = ay_1 + by_2 + cy_3$.

The number of rules will be thus reduced by 125 to 25 if two variables are fused or from 125 to 5 if the three variables are combined. The rules for this case are shown below:

R1: IF *Y* is A_1 THEN *u* is D_1; …;
R5: IF *Y* is A_5 and THEN *u* is D_5.

If two variables could be combined, then for an even number of variables, the reduction is even more pronounced. For example, if n = 4, then the rules would reduce from $5^4 = 625$ to $5^2 = 25$, a 96% reduction versus an 80% reduction for n = 3. Figure 1 illustrates this simple idea for n = 2, 3.

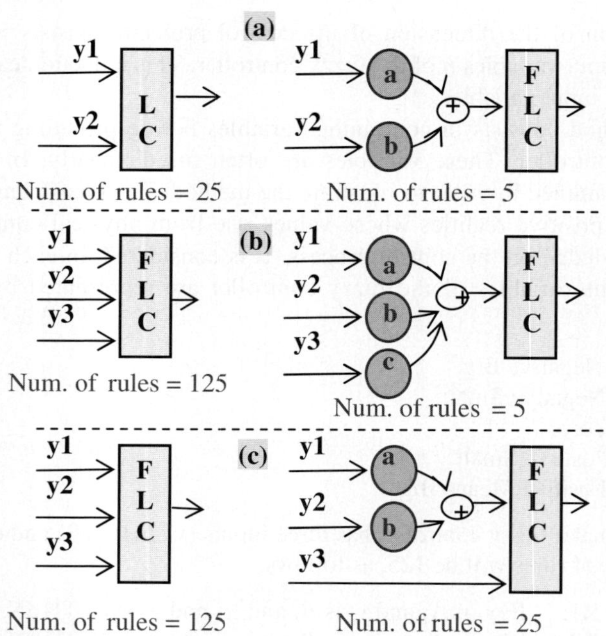

Fig. 1. Fuzzy logic controller's rule base reduction for three cases: (a) two variables are fused, (b) three variables are fused, (c) two variables are fused and the third variable stays separate

The reduction of the number of rules is optimal if one can fuse all the input variables in only one variable associated. In this case, the number of rules is equal to the definite number of linguistic labels for this variable. But it is obvious that all these variables cannot be fused arbitrarily, any combination of variables has to be reasoned and explained. In practice only two variables are fused: generally the error and the change of error. The fusion can be done through the following rule

$$E = ae + b\Delta e \tag{2}$$

where e and Δe are error and its rate of change, E is the fused variable, and a and b chosen arbitrary [3].

Here we can observe that is the arbitrary selection of these parameters convert into fastidious and time-consuming routine. And the described method which permits to reduce significant the number of rules can't be used easily. In this work we propose to find these parameters using genetic algorithm.

5 Genetic Optimization

GAs are often viewed as function optimizers, although the range of problems to which genetic algorithms have been applied is quite broad. The more common applications of GAs are the solution of optimization problems, where efficient and reliable results have been shown. Nature has an ability to adapt and learn without being told what to do. In other words, genetically nature finds good chromosomes blindly. GAs do the same. Two mechanisms link a GA to the problem it is solving: encoding and evaluation. The GA uses a measure of fitness of individual chromosomes to carry out reproduction. As reproduction takes place, the crossover operator exchanges parts of two single chromosomes, and the mutation operator changes the gene value in some randomly chosen location of the chromosome.

The procedure of estimating the fusion variables by GA is summarized as follows:

1. Determine the set of variables to fuse.
2. Construct an initial population randomly.
3. Decode each string in the population
4. Evaluate the fitness value for each string.
5. Reproduce strings according to the fitness value calculated in Step 4.
6. Go to 3 until the maximum number of iterations is met.

To start with our algorithm we propose to encode all parameters in one chromosome. For every parameter we will dedicate 8 bits, so we can have the parameters in the range of 2^8 possibilities. To obtain the precision required (one decimal after the point), we multiply the output values of parameters by 0.1. As a result the searching parameters will be in the interval [0, 25.6]. The search space can be changed depending on the application. Using this simple encoding procedure we can easily change the number of bits.

Then we evaluate the results using the fitness function which is based on step response specifications such as overshoot, rise time and settling time. We define the fitness function so that it measures how close each individual in the population at time t (i.e., each fusion parameter) is to meeting these specification.

So after knowing the design specification of the objective function, and once we can obtain the step response characteristics for each chromosome in the population, the fitness function is calculated in 2 steps:

1. We ask if the result coming from the GA is in the range of design specification of the objective function. If it is we go to the step 2. If it is not, we give that the fitness value of this chromosome is set to 0.
2. The fitness function is defined as

$$FF = (os\_coef - os\_dis)^2 + (ts\_coef - ts\_dis)^2 + (tr\_coef - tr\_dis)^2 \quad (3)$$

where *os* is overshoot, *ts* is settling time and *tr* is rising time. The index *coef* is the specification of the control problem for which we are looking the fusion parameters. The index *dis* is the design specification parameter. In order to minimize the fitness function we divide 1/FF.

When the evaluation is done, we continue with the reproduction stage. The new population is obtained by applying the combination of some genetic operators. The best results were obtained when half uniform crossover (HUX) [18] and truncation selection [18] were applied. The population size is 50 chromosomes.

6 Simulation Results

The proposed algorithm was tested in the inverted pendulum control system. The objective of this control system is, on one hand, to maintain the stem of the pendulum in high driving position, on the other hand, to bring the cart towards a given position x_o. The scheme in figure 2 shows the main components of the system.

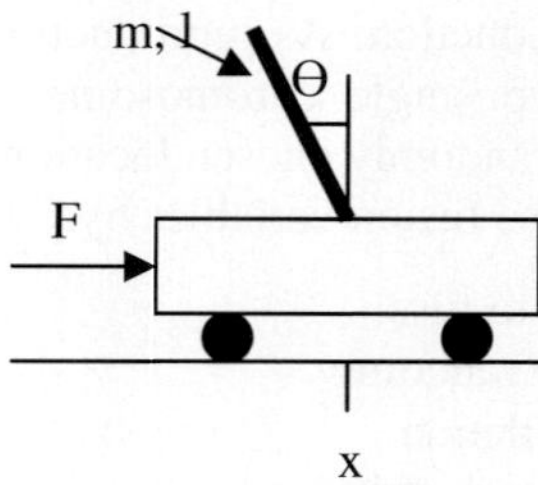

Fig. 2. Inverted pendulum

The basic variables are:

- the angular position of the stem θ;
- the angular velocity of the stem $\dot{\theta}$;
- the horizontal position of cart x;
- the velocity of the cart $\dot{x}$.

This system is modeled by the following differential equations [2]:

$$\dot{x}_1 = x_2$$

$$\dot{x}_2 = \frac{-\frac{7}{3}m^2 l^3 x_4^2 \sin x_3 + (ml)^2 g \sin x_3 \cos x_3 - \frac{7}{3}ml^2 u}{[ml\cos x_3]^2 - \left[\frac{7}{3}ml^2(M+m)\right]} \qquad \dot{x}_3 = x_4 \tag{4}$$

$$\dot{x}_4 = \frac{(ml)^2 x_4^2 \sin x_3 \cos x_3 - mgl \sin x_3 (M+m) + ml\cos x_3}{[ml\cos x_3]^2 - \left[\frac{7}{3}ml^2(M+m)\right]}u$$

where M = 1kg – mass of the cart, m = 0.1 kg – mass of the pendulum, l = 1 kg – length to pendulum, F – force applied to the cart, c - cart position coordinate, θ - pendulum angle with vertical.

The design specifications of the inverted pendulum system are:

- the objective position of the cart is 30 cm;
- overshoot of no more than 5 %;
- the settling time of no more than 5 sec.

The objective position where we must to bring a cart is x_o. The variables to fuse are θ and $\Delta\theta$, e and Δe, where e is the error in position given by $e = x - x_o$ and $\Delta e = \Delta x$. The output variable u of the fuzzy controller is a force F making it possible to control a cart.

The mathematical fusion of the input variables of the fuzzy controller is carried out as follows:

$$\begin{cases} FusAng = a\theta + b\Delta\theta \\ FusPos = ce + d\Delta e \end{cases} \tag{5}$$

where $a > 0, b > 0, c > 0, d > 0$.

The simulation of the inverted pendulum is performed in *Simulink, Matlab* starting from the nonlinear equations (4).

The fuzzy controller is implemented in *Matlab´s FIS Editor.* The input fuzzy sets are represented by triangular functions (N, Z and P) regularly distributed on the universe of discourse [-1, 1]. The output fuzzy sets are singletons regularly distributed on [-1, 1]. The fuzzy controller based on sensory fusion is represented in the figure 3.

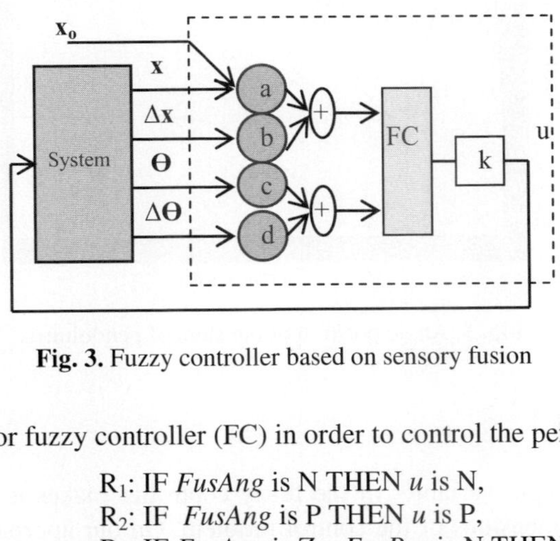

Fig. 3. Fuzzy controller based on sensory fusion

The rule base for fuzzy controller (FC) in order to control the pendulum is:

R_1: IF *FusAng* is N THEN *u* is N,
R_2: IF *FusAng* is P THEN *u* is P,
R_3: IF *FusAng* is Z y *FusPos* is N THEN *u* is N,
R_4: IF *FusAng* is Z y *FusPos* is Z THEN *u* is Z,
R_5: IF *FusAng* is Z y *FusPos* is P THEN *u* is P.

For the reduction with the sensory fusion method we obtained the following parameters: a = 23, b = 8, c = 1.3 and d= 2.8. With these parameters the horizontal position of the cart is stabilized in 4.95 with overshoot equal to 0 (see figure 4), and the behavior of the angle position of the stem of pendulum is shown in the figure 5.

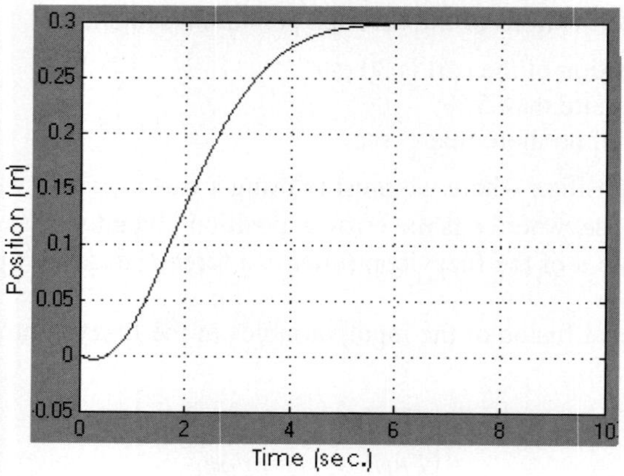

Fig. 4. Horizontal position of the cart

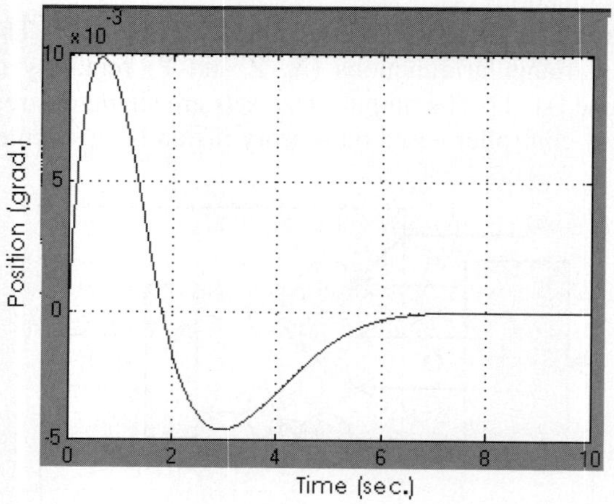

Fig. 5. Angle position of the stem of pendulum

7 Conclusions

The fusion of the input variables of the fuzzy controller makes it possible to reduce significantly the dimensions of the control problem. On our approach the problem of arbitrary search for the required parameters was replaced with genetic algorithm. The proposed algorithm was simulated with inverted pendulum control system. Encouraging results have been obtained. The parameters of the fusion method were fined for design specifications of this problem were adequately fined. For this example, the 625 rules are no longer needed, instead only 5 rules were used to control the 4-th order system.

Supported by the fact that the fitness function is based on the design specification of the system, we have the advantage to apply it to any combination of fusion variables. Another very important fact is that when we change the design specifications, we can obtain the necessary fusion parameters very quickly by using the proposed GA. GA helped us not only to automatically estimate the fusion parameters, but also to improve the results obtained by the fusion method.

References

1. Kevin M. Passino, Stephen Yurkovich. Fuzzy control. Addison Wesley Longman, Inc. 1998.
2. M. Jamshidi. Large-Scale Systems – Modeling, Control and Fuzzy Logic. Prentice Hall Publishing Company, Englewood Cliffs, NJ, 1996.
3. M. Jamshidi. Fuzzy Control Systems. *Springer-Verlag*, chapter of Soft Computing, pp. 42-56, 1997.
4. L.A. Zadeh. Fuzzy sets. *Information and Control*, vol., pp.338-353, 1965.
5. J.C. Bezdek. Cluster validity with fuzzy sets. J. Cybern., vol. 3, no.3, pp. 58-71, 1974.
6. Jonh Y. Hung, et. al. Variable Structure Control: A Survey. *IEEE Trans.on Industrial Electronics,* vol. 40, no.1, pp.2-21, 1993.
7. Zaheeruddin, Anwer M.J. A Simple Technique for Generation and Minimization of Fuzzy Rules. *IEEE International Conference on Fuzzy Systems*, CD-ROM Memories, Nevada, May 2005.
8. Abraham Ajith. Neuro Fyzzy Systems: State-of-the-art. Modeling Techniques. *Connectionist Models of Neurons, Learning Processes, and Artificial Intelligence, Lecture Notes in Computer Science.* Springer-Verlag Germany, Jose Mira and Alberto Prieto (Eds.), Spain, vol. 2084, pp. 269-276, 2001.
9. N. Kasabov, R. Kozma, and W. Duch. Rule Extraction from Linguistic Rule Networks and from Fuzzy Neural Networks: Propositional versus Fuzzy Rules. *Proceedings of the Conference on Neural Networks and Their Applications NEURAP'98*, Marseilles, France, March, 1998, pp. 403-406, 1998.
10. Chia-Feng Juang, Chin-Teng Lin. An On-Line Self-Constructing Neural Fuzzy Inference Network and Its Applications. *IEEE Transaction on Fuzzy Systems,* vol. 6, No.1, pp. 12-32, February 1998.
11. Jyh-Shing Roger Jang, ANFIS: Adaptive-Network-Based Fuzzy Inference Systems, *IEEE Trans. System Man & Cybernetics*, vol. 23, pp. 665-685, 1993.
12. S. K. Halgamuge and M. Glesner. Neural networks in designing fuzzy systems for real world applications. *Fuzzy Sets and Systems*, vol. 65, pp. 1-12, 1994.
13. N. Tschichold-German. RuleNet - A New Knowledge--Based Artificial Neural Network Model with Application Examples in Robotics. PhD thesis, ETH Zerich, 1996.
14. H. R. Berenji and P. Khedkar. Learning and tuning fuzzy logic controllers through reinforcements. *IEEE Trans. Neural Networks*, vol. 3, pp. 724-740, 1992.
15. Kim J., Kasabov N. Hy FIS: adaptive neuro-fuzzy inference systems and their application to nonlinear dynamical systems. Neural Networks, 12, pp. 1301-1319, 1999.
16. D. Nauck, R. Kruse. NEFCON-I: An X-Window Based Simulator for Neural Fuzzy Controllers.*IEEE-ICNN,* WCCI'94 in Orlando, 1994.
17. D. Nauck, R. Kruse. NEFCLASS - A Neuro-Fuzzy Approach for the Classification of Data. *Symposium on Applied Computing,* SAC'95 in Nashville, 1995.
18. Larry J. Eshelman. The CHC Adaptive Search Algorithm: How to Have Safe Search When Engaging in Nontraditional Genetic Recombination, ed. In G. Rawlins, Foundations of Genetic Algorithms, pp. 265-283, Morgan Kaufmann, 1991.

A Fault Detection System Design for Uncertain T-S Fuzzy Systems

Seog-Hwan Yoo* and Byung-Jae Choi

School of Electronic Engineering, Daegu University,
Kyungpook, 712-714, South Korea
{shryu, bjchoi}@daegu.ac.kr

Abstract. This paper deals with a fault detection system design for uncertain nonlinear systems modeled as T-S fuzzy systems with the integral quadratic constraints. In order to generate a residual signal, we used a left coprime factorization of the T-S fuzzy system. Using a multi-objective filter, the fault occurrence can be detected effectively. A simulation study with nuclear steam generator level control system shows that the suggested method can be applied to detect the fault in actual applications.

1 Introduction

Recently, fault detection of control systems has been an active research area due to the growing complexity of modern automatic control systems. A fault can be defined as an unexpected change in a system, such as a component malfunction, which tends to cause undesirable behavior in the overall system performance. The purpose of the fault detection system design is to detect the occurrence of a fault as fast as possible.

A lot of works for the fault detection system design have been developed based on generation of the residual signal [1-5]. In order to design the residual generator, the use of robust parity equations [1], eigen-structure assignment [2], unknown input observers [3] and H_∞ optimal estimation approaches [4,5] have been intensively investigated. But these works are mainly focused on linear systems. Comparatively little work has been reported for the fault detection system design of nonlinear systems.

In the past few years, there has been growing interest in fuzzy control of nonlinear systems, and there have been many successful applications. Among them, a controller design method for nonlinear dynamic systems modeled as a T-S (Takagi-Sugeno) fuzzy model has been intensively addressed [6-8]. Unlike a single conventional model, this T-S fuzzy model usually consists of several linear models to describe the global behavior of the nonlinear system. Typically the T-S fuzzy model is described by fuzzy IF-THEN rules.

In this paper, using the coprime factorization approach we develop a fault detection scheme for T-S fuzzy systems with the integral quadratic constraints (IQC's). The

* This work was supported in part by the 2006 Daegu university research fund.

A. Gelbukh and C.A. Reyes-Garcia (Eds.): MICAI 2006, LNAI 4293, pp. 156 – 164, 2006.

IQC's can be used conveniently to describe uncertain parameters, time delays, unmodeled dynamics, etc [9]. An application to fault detection of a nuclear steam generator control system is presented in order to demonstrate the efficacy of the proposed scheme. We think that the primary contribution of this work is that the fault detection system design is extended from linear systems toward nonlinear systems using T-S fuzzy approach.

2 Uncertain Fuzzy Systems

We consider the following fuzzy dynamic system with the IQC's.

Plant Rule i ($i=1,\cdots,r$):

IF $\rho_1(t)$ is M_{i1} and $\cdots$ and $\rho_g(t)$ is M_{ig},

THEN

$$\begin{aligned} \dot{x}(t) &= A_i x(t) + \sum_{j=1}^{q} F_{ij} w_j(t) + B_i u(t) + B_{f,i} f(t) \\ z_j(t) &= H_{ij} x(t) + J_{ij} u(t) + J_{f,ij} f(t) \\ y(t) &= C_i x(t) + \sum_{j=1}^{q} G_{ij} w_j(t) + D_i u(t) + D_{f,i} f(t) \\ w_j(t) &= \theta_j z_j(t), \end{aligned} \tag{1}$$

where r is the number of fuzzy rules. $\rho_k(t)$ and M_{ik} ($k=1,\cdots,g$) are the premise variables and the fuzzy set respectively. $x(t)\in R^n$ is the state vector, $u(t)\in R^m$ is the input, $y(t)\in R^p$ is the output variable, $f(t)\in R^s$ is the fault signal and $w_j(t)\in R^{k_j}, z_j(t)\in R^{k_j}$ are variables related to uncertainties. $B_{f,i}, J_{f,ij}, D_{f,i}$ are fault distribution matrix and $A_i, F_{ij}, \cdots, D_{f,i}$ are real matrices with compatible dimensions. θ_j is an uncertain operator described by the following IQC's.

$$\int_0^\infty w_j(t)^T w_j(t)dt \le \int_0^\infty z_j(t)^T z_j(t)dt, \quad j=1,\cdots,q \tag{2}$$

Let μ_i, $i=1,\cdots,r$, be the normalized membership function defined as follows:

$$\mu_i = \frac{\prod_{j=1}^{g} M_{ij}(\rho_j(t))}{\sum_{i=1}^{r}\prod_{j=1}^{g} M_{ij}(\rho_j(t))}. \tag{3}$$

Then, for all i, we obtain

$$\mu_i \ge 0, \ \sum_{i=1}^{r} \mu_i = 1. \tag{4}$$

For simplicity, we define

$$\mu^T = \begin{bmatrix} \mu_1 & \cdots & \mu_r \end{bmatrix},\ w(t) = \begin{bmatrix} w_1(t)^T & \cdots & w_q(t)^T \end{bmatrix}^T,$$

$$z(t) = \begin{bmatrix} z_1(t)^T & \cdots & z_q(t)^T \end{bmatrix}^T, F_i = \begin{bmatrix} F_{i1} & \cdots & F_{iq} \end{bmatrix},$$

$$G_i = \begin{bmatrix} G_{i1} & \cdots & G_{iq} \end{bmatrix},\ H_i = \begin{bmatrix} H_{i1}{}^T & \cdots & H_{iq}{}^T \end{bmatrix}^T,$$

$$J_i = \begin{bmatrix} J_{i1}{}^T & \cdots & J_{iq}{}^T \end{bmatrix}^T, J_{f,i} = \begin{bmatrix} J_{f,i1}{}^T & \cdots & J_{f,iq}{}^T \end{bmatrix}^T.$$

With the notations defined above, we rewrite the uncertain fuzzy system (1) as follows:

$$\begin{aligned}
\dot{x}(t) &= \sum_{i=1}^{r} \mu_i (A_i x(t) + F_i w(t) + B_i u(t) + B_{f,i} f(t)) = A_\mu x(t) + F_\mu w(t) + B_\mu u(t) + B_{f,\mu} f(t), \\
z(t) &= \sum_{i=1}^{r} \mu_i (H_i x(t) + J_i u(t) + J_{f,i} f(t)) = H_\mu x(t) + J_\mu u(t) + J_{f,\mu} f(t), \\
y(t) &= \sum_{i=1}^{r} \mu_i (C_i x(t) + G_i w(t) + D_i u(t) + D_{f,i} f(t)) = C_\mu x(t) + G_\mu w(t) + D_\mu u(t) + D_{f,\mu} f(t), \\
w(t) &= diag(\theta_1, \cdots, \theta_q) z(t) = \Theta z(t).
\end{aligned} \tag{5}$$

In a packed matrix notation, we express the fuzzy system (5) as

$$\boldsymbol{G}(\mu) = \left[\begin{array}{c:c|cc} A_\mu & F_\mu & B_\mu & B_{f,\mu} \\ \hdashline H_\mu & 0 & J_\mu & J_{f,\mu} \\ \hline C_\mu & G_\mu & D_\mu & D_{f,\mu} \end{array}\right]. \tag{6}$$

We present a coprime factor model which will be used in the next section. Let L_μ be an output injection matrix such that $A_\mu + L_\mu C_\mu$ is quadratically stable for all permissible Θ and μ satisfying (2) and (4). Then $\boldsymbol{G}(\mu) = \tilde{\boldsymbol{M}}(\mu)^{-1} \begin{bmatrix} \tilde{\boldsymbol{N}}_1(\mu) & \tilde{\boldsymbol{N}}_2(\mu) \end{bmatrix}$ where $\tilde{\boldsymbol{N}}_1(\mu)$, $\tilde{\boldsymbol{N}}_2(\mu)$ and $\tilde{\boldsymbol{M}}(\mu)$ are quadratically stable for all permissible Θ and are given by

$$\begin{aligned}
&\begin{bmatrix} \tilde{\boldsymbol{M}}(\mu) & \tilde{\boldsymbol{N}}_1(\mu) & \tilde{\boldsymbol{N}}_2(\mu) \end{bmatrix} \\
&= \left[\begin{array}{c:c|ccc} A_\mu + L_\mu C_\mu & F_\mu + L_\mu G_\mu & L_\mu & B_\mu + L_\mu D_\mu & B_{f,\mu} + L_\mu D_{f,\mu} \\ \hdashline H_\mu & 0 & 0 & J_\mu & J_{f,\mu} \\ \hline C_\mu & G_\mu & I & D_\mu & D_{f,\mu} \end{array}\right].
\end{aligned} \tag{7}$$

3 Fault Detection System

In this section, we discuss a fault detection system design method for the fuzzy system (5). We construct a residual generator using the left coprime factors. Let

$\tilde{\boldsymbol{M}}_0(\mu)$, $\tilde{\boldsymbol{N}}_{0,1}(\mu)$ and $\tilde{\boldsymbol{N}}_{0,2}(\mu)$ be the nominal system of $\tilde{\boldsymbol{M}}(\mu)$, $\tilde{\boldsymbol{N}}_1(\mu)$ and $\tilde{\boldsymbol{N}}_2(\mu)$. Thus,

$$\begin{bmatrix} \tilde{\boldsymbol{M}}_0(\mu) & \tilde{\boldsymbol{N}}_{0,1}(\mu) & \tilde{\boldsymbol{N}}_{0,2}(\mu) \end{bmatrix} = \left[\begin{array}{c|ccc} A_\mu + L_\mu C_\mu & L_\mu & B_\mu + L_\mu D_\mu & B_{f,\mu} + L_\mu D_{f,\mu} \\ \hline C_\mu & I & D_\mu & D_{f,\mu} \end{array}\right]. \tag{8}$$

Then we construct a residual signal as follows:

$$e(t) = \boldsymbol{Q}(\mu)\left(\tilde{\boldsymbol{M}}_0(\mu)y(t) - \tilde{\boldsymbol{N}}_{0,1}(\mu)u(t)\right), \tag{9}$$

where $\boldsymbol{Q}(\mu)$ is a fuzzy filter which will be used as a design parameter. Note that

$$0 = \tilde{\boldsymbol{M}}(\mu)y(t) - \tilde{\boldsymbol{N}}_1(\mu)u(t) - \tilde{\boldsymbol{N}}_2(\mu)f(t). \tag{10}$$

Using (10), the residual signal $e(t)$ in (9) can be expressed as

$$e(t) = \boldsymbol{Q}(\mu)\left(e_d(t) + e_f(t)\right), \tag{11}$$

where

$$\begin{aligned} e_d(t) &= \left(\tilde{\boldsymbol{N}}_1(\mu) - \tilde{\boldsymbol{N}}_{0,1}(\mu)\right)u(t) - \left(\tilde{\boldsymbol{M}}(\mu) - \tilde{\boldsymbol{M}}_0(\mu)\right)y(t), \\ e_f(t) &= \tilde{\boldsymbol{N}}_2(\mu)f(t). \end{aligned} \tag{12}$$

In (11), $e_d(t)$ and $e_f(t)$ correspond to signals due to the model uncertainties and the fault signals respectively. Even if no fault occurs, the residual signal $e(t)$ is not zero due to the system model uncertainties.

A state space realization of the coprime factor uncertainty can be expressed as

$$\begin{aligned} &\begin{bmatrix} \tilde{\boldsymbol{M}}(\mu) - \tilde{\boldsymbol{M}}_0(\mu) & \tilde{\boldsymbol{N}}_1(\mu) - \tilde{\boldsymbol{N}}_{0,1}(\mu) & \tilde{\boldsymbol{N}}_2(\mu) - \tilde{\boldsymbol{N}}_{0,2}(\mu) \end{bmatrix} \\ &= \left[\begin{array}{cc|c|ccc} A_\mu + L_\mu C_\mu & 0 & F_\mu + L_\mu G_\mu & L_\mu & B_\mu & B_{f,\mu} \\ 0 & A_\mu + L_\mu C_\mu & 0 & L_\mu & B_\mu & B_{f,\mu} \\ \hline H_\mu & 0 & 0 & 0 & J_\mu & J_{f,\mu} \\ \hline C_\mu & -C_\mu & G_\mu & 0 & 0 & 0 \end{array}\right]. \end{aligned} \tag{13}$$

We define

$$\begin{aligned} &\left[\begin{array}{c|c} \boldsymbol{P}_{11}(\mu) & \boldsymbol{P}_{12}(\mu) \\ \hline \boldsymbol{P}_{21}(\mu) & \boldsymbol{P}_{22}(\mu) \end{array}\right] \\ &= \left[\begin{array}{cc|c|ccc} A_\mu + L_\mu C_\mu & 0 & F_\mu + L_\mu G_\mu & L_\mu & B_\mu & B_{f,\mu} \\ 0 & A_\mu + L_\mu C_\mu & 0 & L_\mu & B_\mu & B_{f,\mu} \\ \hline H_\mu & 0 & 0 & 0 & J_\mu & J_{f,\mu} \\ \hline C_\mu & -C_\mu & G_\mu & 0 & 0 & 0 \end{array}\right]. \end{aligned} \tag{14}$$

With the definition of (13), the coprime factor uncertainty (12) also can be expressed as

$$\begin{bmatrix} \tilde{\boldsymbol{M}}(\mu)-\tilde{\boldsymbol{M}}_0(\mu) & \tilde{\boldsymbol{N}}_1(\mu)-\tilde{\boldsymbol{N}}_{0,1}(\mu) & \tilde{\boldsymbol{N}}_2(\mu)-\tilde{\boldsymbol{N}}_{0,2}(\mu) \end{bmatrix} \\ = \boldsymbol{P}_{21}(\mu)\Theta(I-\boldsymbol{P}_{11}(\mu)\Theta)^{-1}\boldsymbol{P}_{12}(\mu). \tag{15}$$

Using (14), the residual signal $e(t)$ becomes

$$e(t)=\boldsymbol{Q}(\mu)(\boldsymbol{P}_{21}(\mu)w_e(t)+\tilde{\boldsymbol{N}}_2(\mu)f(t)), \tag{16}$$

where

$$w_e(t)=\Theta(I-\boldsymbol{P}_{11}(\mu)\Theta)^{-1}\boldsymbol{P}_{12}(\mu)\begin{bmatrix} -y(t) \\ u(t) \\ 0 \end{bmatrix}.$$

In (15), $\boldsymbol{Q}(\mu)$ is chosen to minimize the effect of model uncertainties and maximize the effect of the fault signal. For the above purpose, we design $\boldsymbol{Q}(\mu)$ such that $\left\|\boldsymbol{W}_r(s)-\boldsymbol{Q}(\mu)\tilde{\boldsymbol{N}}_2(\mu)\right\|_\infty<\gamma_1$ and $\left\|\boldsymbol{Q}(\mu)\boldsymbol{P}_{21}(\mu)\right\|_\infty<\gamma_2$ in Fig.1 where $\boldsymbol{W}_r(s)$ is a stable transfer function for frequency shaping.

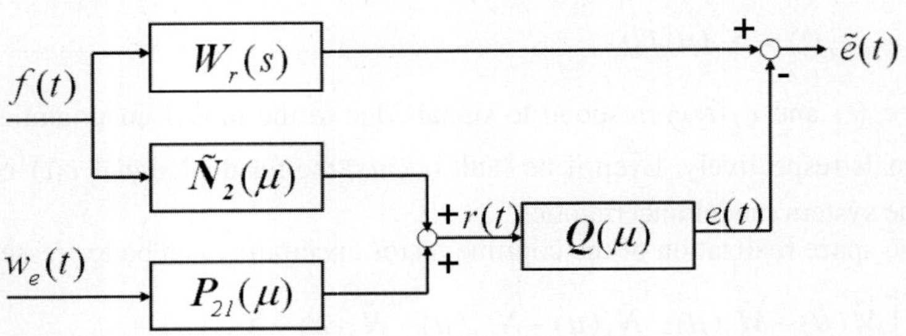

Fig. 1. The generalized plant for filter design

When no fault occurs, we obtain

$$\left\|e(t)\right\|_2=\left\|\boldsymbol{Q}(\mu)\boldsymbol{P}_{21}(\mu)w_e(t)\right\|_2\le\left\|\boldsymbol{Q}(\mu)\boldsymbol{P}_{21}(\mu)\right\|_\infty\left\|\Delta\right\|_\infty\left\|\overline{w}_e(t)\right\|_2 \tag{17}$$

where

$$\Delta=\Theta(I-\boldsymbol{P}_{11}(\mu)\Theta)^{-1},\ \overline{w}_e(t)=\boldsymbol{P}_{12}(\mu)\begin{bmatrix} -y(t) \\ u(t) \\ 0 \end{bmatrix}$$

Accordingly, the faults can thus be detected using a simple thresholding logic:

$$J=\left(\int_{t-T}^{t}e(t)^T e(t)dt\right)^{1/2}\begin{cases}\le J_{th} & \text{normal} \\ > J_{th} & \text{faulty}\end{cases} \tag{18}$$

where

$$J_{th} = \left\| Q(\mu) P_{21}(\mu) \right\|_{\infty} \left\| \Delta \right\|_{\infty} \left(\int_{t-T}^{t} \overline{w}_e^T(t) \overline{w}_e(t) dt \right)^{1/2},$$

Since Δ is a system with feedback connection of Θ and $P_{11}(\mu)$, a state space realization of Δ is given by

$$\Delta = \left[\begin{array}{cc|c|c} A_\mu + L_\mu C_\mu & 0 & F_\mu + L_\mu G_\mu & 0 \\ 0 & A_\mu + L_\mu C_\mu & 0 & 0 \\ \hline H_\mu & 0 & 0 & I \\ \hline 0 & 0 & I & 0 \end{array} \right] \tag{19}$$

By using the well developed LMI (Linear Matrix Inequality) tools and S-procedure, we can compute $\|\Delta\|_{\infty}$. $\overline{w}_e(t)$ is computable since $P_{12}(\mu)$, $y(t)$, $u(t)$ are known system and variables.

4 Steam Generator Fault Detection System

The dynamics of a nuclear steam generator is described in terms of the feedwater flowrate, the steam flowrate and the steam generator water level. Irving[10] derived the following fourth order Laplace transfer function model based on the step response of the steam generator water level for step change of the feedwater flowrate and the steam flowrate:

$$y(s) = \frac{g_1}{s}\big(u(s) - d(s)\big) - \frac{g_2}{1+\tau_2 s}\big(u(s) - d(s)\big) + \frac{g_3 s}{\tau_1^{-2} + 4\pi^2 T^{-2} + 2\tau_1^{-1} s + s^2} u(s), \tag{20}$$

where τ_1 and τ_2 are damping time constants; T is a period of the mechanical oscillation; g_1 is a magnitude of the mass capacity effect; g_2 is a magnitude of the swell or shrink due to the feedwater or steam flowrate; g_3 is a magnitude of the mechanical oscillation.

This plant has a single input (feedwater flowrate $u(s)$), a single output(water level $y(s)$) and a measurable known disturbance (steam flowrate $d(s)$). The parameter values of a steam generator at several power levels are given in Table 1 and the parameters are very different according to the power levels.

Table 1. Parameters of a steam generator linear model

Power (%)	τ_1	τ_2	g_2	g_3	g_1	T
50	34.8	3.6	1.05	0.215	0.058	14.2
100	28.6	3.4	0.47	0.105	0.058	11.7

In (20) we treat the known disturbance $d(t)$ as an input and include the fault signal $f(t)$ due to the measurement sensor fault so that we have the following state space model:

$$
\dot{x}(t) = \begin{bmatrix} 0 & 0 & 0 & 0 \\ 0 & -a_1 & 0 & 0 \\ 0 & 0 & 0 & 1 \\ 0 & 0 & -a_2 & -2a_3 \end{bmatrix} x(t) + \begin{bmatrix} 1 & -1 \\ a_4 & -a_4 \\ 0 & 0 \\ a_5 & 0 \end{bmatrix} \begin{bmatrix} u(t) \\ d(t) \end{bmatrix} + \begin{bmatrix} 0 \\ 0 \\ 0 \\ 0 \end{bmatrix} f(t), \tag{21}
$$
$$
y(t) = \begin{bmatrix} g_1 & -1 & 0 & 1 \end{bmatrix} x(t) + f(t),
$$

where $a_1 = 1/\tau_2(1+\beta_1\theta_1)$, $a_2 = (\tau_1^{-2} + 4\pi^2 T^{-2})(1+\beta_2\theta_2)$, $a_3 = 1/\tau_1(1+\beta_3\theta_3)$, $a_4 = g_2/\tau_2(1+\beta_4\theta_4)$ and $a_5 = g_3(1+\beta_5\theta_5)$. $\theta_1,\cdots,\theta_5$ are introduced to describe possible parameter uncertainties and satisfy $|\theta_1| \le 1,\cdots|\theta_5| \le 1$. Thus, we assume that τ_2^{-1} is within β_1 % of the nominal value given in Table 1. Then we have the following T-S fuzzy model:

Plant Rule i ($i = 1,2$):

IF $\rho(t)$ (power level) is M_{i1},

THEN

$$
\dot{x}(t) = \begin{bmatrix} 0 & 0 & 0 & 0 \\ 0 & -b_{1,i} & 0 & 0 \\ 0 & 0 & 0 & 1 \\ 0 & 0 & -b_{2,i} & -2b_{3,i} \end{bmatrix} x(t) + \begin{bmatrix} 0 & 0 & 0 & 0 & 0 \\ 1 & 0 & 0 & 1 & 0 \\ 0 & 0 & 0 & 0 & 0 \\ 0 & 1 & 2 & 0 & 1 \end{bmatrix} w(t) + \begin{bmatrix} 1 & -1 \\ b_{4,i} & -b_{4,i} \\ b_{5,i} & 0 \\ 0 & 0 \end{bmatrix} \begin{bmatrix} u(t) \\ d(t) \end{bmatrix} + \begin{bmatrix} 0 \\ 0 \\ 0 \\ 0 \end{bmatrix} f(t)
$$
$$
z(t) = \begin{bmatrix} 0 & \beta_1 b_{1,i} & 0 & 0 \\ 0 & 0 & \beta_2 b_{2,i} & 0 \\ 0 & 0 & 0 & \beta_3 b_{3,i} \\ 0 & 0 & 0 & 0 \\ 0 & 0 & 0 & 0 \end{bmatrix} x(t) + \begin{bmatrix} 0 & 0 \\ 0 & 0 \\ 0 & 0 \\ \beta_4 b_{4,i} & -\beta_4 b_{4,i} \\ \beta_5 b_{5,i} & 0 \end{bmatrix} \begin{bmatrix} u(t) \\ d(t) \end{bmatrix} \tag{22}
$$
$$
y(t) = \begin{bmatrix} 0.058 & -1 & 0 & 1 \end{bmatrix} x(t) + f(t)
$$
$$
w(t) = diag(\theta_1,\cdots,\theta_5) z(t)
$$

where the membership function $M_{11} = -\rho(t)/50 + 2, M_{21} = \rho(t)/50 - 1$ and

$$
b_{1,1} = 0.2778, b_{1,2} = 0.2941, b_{2,1} = 0.1966, b_{2,2} = 0.2896, b_{3,1} = 0.0288, b_{3,2} = 0.0350, \\ b_{4,1} = 0.2917, b_{4,2} = 0.1382, b_{5,1} = 0.2150, b_{5,2} = 0.1050.
$$

For a simulation study, we assume that $\beta_1 = \cdots = \beta_5 = 0.1$. Using $L_1 = L_2 = [-0.0306 \quad 1.087 \quad 8.8401 \quad -3.3629]^T$, we obtain the left coprime factors in (7). With $\boldsymbol{W}_r(s) = 0.1/(s+0.1)$, we design a fuzzy filter $\boldsymbol{Q}(\mu)$ such that $\|\boldsymbol{W}_r(s) - \boldsymbol{Q}(\mu)\tilde{\boldsymbol{N}}_2(\mu)\|_\infty < 0.5$ and $\|\boldsymbol{Q}(\mu)\boldsymbol{P}_{21}(\mu)\|_\infty < 2$. A simulation of the steam generator control system has been done with the following two cases of scenario:

- case1: 100% power level, a 2% step disturbance on $d(t)$ at 500sec, and a drift (5%/min ramp) on the water level sensor at 1000sec.
- case2: 75% power level, a 2% step disturbance on $d(t)$ at 500sec, and a 50% error on the water level sensor at 1000sec.

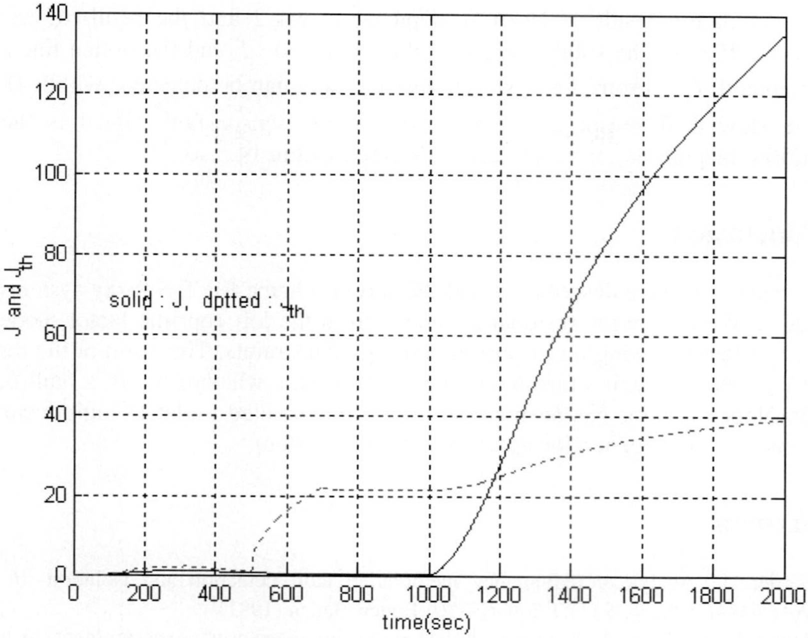

Fig. 2. The simulation result of case 1

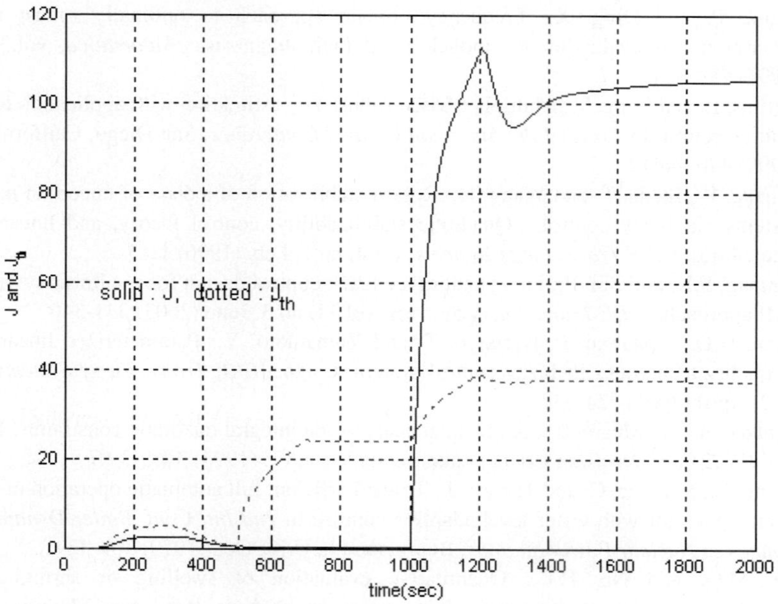

Fig. 3. The simulation result of case 2

The simulation result of case1 is depicted in Fig.2 and the result of case2 is depicted in Fig. 3. The solid line shows the computed J and the dotted line shows the computed J_{th}. From Fig.2, we see that the fault can be detected within 184 sec when a slow drift sensor fault occurs. When the sensor fault signal is the step signal(50% magnitude), the fault can be detected within 14.6 sec.

5 Conclusion

In this paper, we have described a fault detection scheme for T-S fuzzy systems with the IQC's. We design the residual generator from the left coprime factor model and the fuzzy filter achieving multi-objective design constraints. The norm of the residual signal is compared with a threshold level to determine whether or not a fault occurs. The developed scheme has been successfully implemented to detect fault occurrence of the nuclear steam generator water level control system.

References

1. Gertler, J.: Analytical redundancy methods in fault detection and isolation, In *Proc. IFAC/IMACS Symp. SAFEPROCESS'91*, Baden-Baden (1991)
2. Patton, R. and Chen, J.: Robust fault detection using eigenstructure assignment : A tutorial consideration and some new results, In *Proc. of the 30th CDC*, England (1991) 2242-2247
3. Chen, J., Patton, R. and Zhang, H.: Design of unknown input observers and robust fault detection filters, Int. J. Control, vol.63, (1996) 85-105
4. Frank, P. and Ding, X.: Frequency domain approach to optimally robust residual generation and evaluation for model based fault diagnosis, *Automatica*, vol.30, no.5 (1994) 789-804
5. Collins, E. and Song, T.: Multiplier based robust H_∞ estimation with application to robust fault detection, In *Proc. of the American Control Conference*, San Diego, California, June (1999) 4408-4412
6. Tanaka, K., Ikeda, T. and Wang, H.: Robust stabilization of a class of uncertain nonlinear systems via fuzzy control : Quadratic stabilizability, control theory, and linear matrix inequalities, *IEEE Trans. Fuzzy Systems,* vol.4, no.1, Feb. (1996) 1-13
7. Nguang, S.K. and Shi, P.: Fuzzy output feedback control design for nonlinear systems : an LMI approach, *IEEE Trans. Fuzzy Systems*, vol.11, no.3, June (2003) 331-340
8. Tuan, H.D., Apkarian, P. Narikiyo, T. and Yamamoto, Y.: Parameterized linear matrix inequality techniques in fuzzy control system design*, IEEE Trans. Fuzzy Systems*, vol.9, no.2, April (2001) 324-332
9. Rantzer, A. and Megretsky, A.: System analysis via integral quadratic constraints, In *Proc. 33rd IEEE Conf. Decision Contr.*, Lake Buena Vista, FL (1994) 3062-3-67
10. Irving, E., Miossec, C. and Tassart, J.: Toward efficient full automatic operation of the pwr steam generator with water level adaptive control. In *2nd Int. Conf. Boiler Dynamics and Control in Nuclear Power Stations*, Bournemouth, U.K., Oct. (1979) 309-329
11. Na, M.G. and No, H.C.: Quantitative evaluation of swelling or shrinking level contributions in steam generators using spectrum analysis, *Ann. Nucl. Energy*, vol.20, no.10, Oct. (1993) 659-666

An Uncertainty Model for Diagnostic Expert System Based on Fuzzy Algebras of Strict Monotonic Operations

Leonid Sheremetov[1], Ildar Batyrshin[1], Denis Filatov[2], and Jorge Martínez-Muñoz[1]

[1] Mexican Petroleum Institute, Av. Lázaro Cárdenas, 152,
Col. San Bartolo Atepehuacan, Mexico D.F., CP 07730, Mexico
{sher, batyr, jmmunoz}@imp.mx
[2] Centre for Computing Research, National Polytechnic Institute
Av. Juan de Dios Batiz s/n, Col. Nueva Industrial Vallejo,
Mexico D.F., CP 07738, Mexico
denisfilatov@gmail.com

Abstract. Expert knowledge in most of application domains is uncertain, incomplete and perception-based. For processing such expert knowledge an expert system should be able to represent and manipulate perception-based evaluations of uncertainties of facts and rules, to support multiple-valuedness of variables, and to make conclusions with unknown values of variables. This paper describes an uncertainty model based on two algebras of conjunctive and disjunctive multi-sets used by the inference engine for processing perception-based evaluations of uncertainties. The discussion is illustrated by examples of the expert system, called SMART-Agua, which is aimed to diagnose and give solution to water production problems in petroleum wells.

1 Introduction

The increasing interest and enthusiasm in the petroleum industry for the intelligent engineering systems like intelligent wells and intelligent fields have increased significantly the demand for more powerful, robust and intelligent tools. The interest in decision support for the operational activities lays in the fact that in petroleum companies, senior personnel daily have to solve problems based on extensive data analysis and their experience gained through years of field work. In recent years, new generation expert systems integrating different AI techniques have attracted the attention of the Oil & Gas industry, by their capacity to handle successfully the complexities of the real world like imprecision, uncertainty and vagueness [1-4]. But it should be mentioned that for the diagnosis problem studied in our work unfortunately it can not be applied such AI technique like neural network or model-based diagnosis due to absence of sufficient amount of observations necessary to train a neural network or to build a domain model. It was the reason why a traditional rule based expert system was developed.

In spite of the fact that the petroleum industry is usually being criticized for moving at a snail pace in embracing information technology, it was one of the first in applying expert systems technology. DIPMETER ADVISOR, PROSPECTOR and GasOil are often mentioned as examples of classic systems [5, 6]. Nevertheless, an

A. Gelbukh and C.A. Reyes-Garcia (Eds.): MICAI 2006, LNAI 4293, pp. 165 – 175, 2006.

analysis of commercially available intelligent software, indicates that although there are some applications, this type of systems have still not been put widely in the market [7]. For example, new generation expert systems, XERO and WaterCase developed by Halliburton and Schlumberger respectively to provide assistance during the diagnosis and treatment selection phases of water control [8, 9] are not commercially available. This is partially due to the fact that expert knowledge in considered problems, due to their complexity, is very uncertain, incomplete and perception based. For processing such expert knowledge an expert system should be able to represent and manipulate perception based evaluations of uncertainties of facts and rules [20], to support multiple-valuedness of variables, to make conclusions with unknown values of variables, etc.

Since the expertise is often intuitive, and both facts and rules can have 'degrees' of truth, much research has been devoted to the models of deduction under uncertainty. The main approaches used so far are based on Certainty Factors model specifying a continuous range (0 to 1 or -100 to 100), Bayesian Belief Networks, fuzzy logic and multi-valued logics (true, false, unknown) [10-12]. Since the reasoning process in the expert system is based on knowledge that can cover many aspects of a problem, it also may conclude several possible recommendations in the same way human experts would. Then, the multiple recommendations would be arranged in order of likelihood based on the certainty by which the condition-parts of the rules are satisfied. The inference engine carries out this process using some model of confidence.

Selecting the appropriate confidence model is quite important, because the instability of the output results can arise on each step of the inference procedure. This work describes an uncertainty model based on two algebras of conjunctive and disjunctive multi-sets used by the inference engine for processing of uncertainties. Along with the fuzzy confidence mode, the model supports also the use of UNKNOWN values for facts for advanced working with uncertainties. This model is used for fuzzy reasoning and ranking of decision alternatives and implemented in CAPNET Expert System Shell. The approach is applied for the development of the expert systems called Smart-Drill and Smart-Agua which are in the field testing phase in the South Zone of PEMEX, Mexican Oil Company.

The paper is organized as follows. In the following Section the theoretical background of the system's development is presented. In Section 3 we describe a knowledge representation model and the Shell implementing inference procedures using the above mentioned algebras. In Section 4, the expert systems developed using these models and tools are briefly described. In Conclusions the advantages of the proposed approach are analyzed and the directions of the future work are outlined.

2 Theoretical Background

The confidence model defines the mechanism used in calculating the overall confidence of the condition-part of the rule, inferring the confidence of the conclusion part, as well as combining the confidences of multiple conclusions. In this Section we discuss the traditional way of representing of human judgment and further introduce an approach based on fuzzy multi-set based algebras of strict monotonic operations.

2.1 Traditional Models of Human Judgment

Human judgments about plausibility, truth, certainty values of premises, rules and facts are usually qualitative and measured in ordinal scales. Traditional models using representation of these judgments by numbers from intervals L=[0,1] or L=[0,100] and quantitative operations such as multiplication, addition over these numbers are not always correct. Consider a simple example.

Let R_1 and R_2 be two rules of some expert system:

$$R_1\text{: if } A_1 \text{ then } H_1, pv(R_1) \quad (1)$$

$$R_2\text{: if } A_2 \text{ then } H_2, pv(R_2), \quad (2)$$

where $pv(R_1)$ and $pv(R_2)$ are the plausibility, certainty, truth values of rules measured in some linearly ordered scale L, for example L= [0,1]. Often plausibilities of conclusions are calculated as follows:

$$pv(H_1) = pv(R_1)^* \, pv(A_1), \quad (3)$$

$$pv(H_2) = pv(R_2)^* \, pv(A_2), \quad (4)$$

where $pv(A_1)$ and $pv(A_2)$are the plausibilities of premises and * is some t-norm, for example a multiplication operation. Let in (1)-(4) the qualitative information about plausibility values be the following:

$$pv(A_1) < pv(A_2) < pv(R_2) < pv(R_1), \quad (5)$$

that is, the plausibility values of premises are less than the plausibility values of rules, the plausibility value of A_1 is less than the plausibility value of A_2, and the plausibility value of rule R_2 is less then the plausibility value of rule R_1. Let these plausibility values be interpreted as the following quantitative values from L= [0,1]:

$$pv(A_1) = 0.3 < pv(A_2) = 0.4 < pv(R_2) = 0.6 < pv(R_1) = 0.9. \quad (6)$$

If in (3), (4) the operation * will be a multiplication operation then we will obtain:

$$pv(H_1) = 0.27 > pv(H_2) = 0.24. \quad (7)$$

If the plausibility values from (5) obtain another quantitative values preserving the qualitative relation (5), for example $pv(A_1)$ is changed to $pv(A_1) = 0.2$, then we will obtain the opposite ordering of conclusions:

$$pv(H_1) = 0.18 < pv(H_2) = 0.24. \quad (8)$$

Thus the small transformation in a quantitative interpretation of judgments of experts or expert system users which still preserve the qualitative information about plausibility values can bring to opposite results on the output of the expert system. The similar situation of instability of results on the output of inference procedure can also arise when we use other quantitative operations * in (3)-(4) and such instability of decisions can arise on the each step of the inference procedure.

Stability of decisions on the output of inference procedures is achieved for uncertainties measured in ordinal scales if in (3)-(4) we use instead of * a *min* operation [13]. But in this case the reasonable property of strict monotonicity of conclusions does not fulfilled for rules (1) – (2):

$$\text{If } pv(R_1) = pv(R_2) > 0 \text{ and } pv(A_1) > pv(A_2) \text{ then } pv(H_1) > pv(H_2). \quad (9)$$

For example if $pv(R_1) = pv(R_2) = 0.6$ and $pv(A_1) = 1 > pv(A_2) = 0.8$ then $pv(H_1) = min(0.6,1)=0.6$, $pv(H_2)= min(0.6,0.8)=0.6$, i.e. $pv(H_1) = pv(H_2)$ and (9) is not fulfilled.

In order to obtain a diagnosis with high degree of reliability, a hybrid model representing experts' knowledge and implementing different uncertainty algebras is developed in this paper. The variables, integrated to the model, are defined on a linguistic scale using finite ordinal scales (FOS) such as "average possibility, high possibility, low possibility, etc." To handle this type of uncertainties, the expert system is enabled with fuzzy inference engines based on fuzzy algebras (conjunctive and disjunctive) of strictly monotonic operations. If the conclusion is considered as a disjunction of facts then it is better to use a disjunctive algebra. If a final conclusion can be considered as a conjunction of a large amount of facts then it is better to apply conjunctive algebra.

As an alternative, an additive algebra is applied based on the sum of numeric weights, in contrast to the multi-set interpretation of results from disjunctive algebras. Both algebras currently integrated within the expert system (each with its knowledge base) to obtain more precise diagnostics are described below.

2.2 Disjunctive Fuzzy Algebra Based on Multi-sets over a Qualitative Scale

While defining properties and attribute values, domain experts use FOS. Here is an example of a FOS: X_w= {*Impossible* < *Very Small Possibility* < *Small Possibility* < *Average Possibility* < *Large Possibility* < *Very Large Possibility* < *Sure*}. These grades may be replaced by numbers retaining the ordering of linguistic grades, e.g. X_s= {0,1,2,3,4,5,6}, but only comparison of numbers may be done here. Arithmetic operations like addition or multiplication cannot be used in FOS.

Min and *max* operations defined by linear ordering of elements in FOS are adequate conjunction and disjunction operations on ordinal scales but they are not strict monotonic because operations $\wedge = min$ and $\vee = max$ do not satisfy conditions:

$$\begin{aligned} A\wedge B < A\wedge C \quad & \text{if } B < C \text{ and } A \neq 0 \quad \textit{(strict monotonicity of } \wedge\textit{)} \\ A\vee B < A\vee C \quad & \text{if } B < C \text{ and } A \neq 1 \quad \textit{(strict monotonicity of } \vee\textit{)} \end{aligned} \quad (10)$$

where $\wedge$ and $\vee$ denote conjunction and disjunction operations in fuzzy logics [13]. For example, we have $min(A,B)= min(A,C)= A$ for all $B,C \geq A$. Also for $\wedge = min$ we have $0.2\wedge0.2= 0.2$ and $0.2\wedge0.8 = 0.2$ but it seems reasonable that the result of the second conjunction should be more plausible in comparison with the first one. If FOS is used for measuring certainty, plausibility values of facts and rules in expert systems with *min* and *max* conjunction and disjunction operations then the non-monotonicity of these operations does not give full possibility to take into account the change of plausibility of premises in expert system rules and to differentiate and refine the uncertainties of conclusions. As a result, many conclusions on the output of the inference procedure can obtain the equal plausibility values in spite of having essentially different list of plausibility values in the chains of premises used for the inference of these conclusions.

The solution of this problem was given in [14] by embedding the initial FOS into the set of lexicographic valuations (uncertainties with memory) where the result of conjunction equals to the string of operands ordered in a suitable way. Here we consider a more simple method of definition of strict monotonic operations for FOS. This method is based on representation of results of operations by multi-sets [15, 16].

Suppose $X_p = \{x_0, x_1,\ldots, x_{n+1}\}$ is a FOS, i.e. linearly ordered scale of plausibility (truth, possibility, membership) values such that $x_i < x_j$ for all $i < j$. The elements x_0 and x_{n+1} will be denoted as 0 and 1. For example, 0 and 1 denote for the scale X_w the grades *Impossible* and *Sure,* and for the scale X_s the grades 0 and 6, respectively. Denote $X = \{x_1,\ldots, x_n\}$ the set of intermediate grades of X_p. A multi-set A over X is a string $(a_1, a_2, \ldots, a_n)$, where a_i is a number of appearance of element x_i in A. If a_j equals zero then A does not contain x_j. We will suppose that at least one element a_i in A is greater than 0. Denote F a set of all such multi-sets over X and $A = (a_1,\ldots, a_n)$, $B= (b_1,\ldots, b_n)$ are some multi-sets from F. Multi-sets will be used as a form of memory for storing the operands of conjunction and disjunction operations. We consider here the class of multi-sets where disjunction operation is strictly monotonic. The class of multi-sets with strict monotonic conjunction can be introduced in a similar way.

Each multi-set from F is considered here as the result of disjunction of corresponding elements of X. For example for $X= \{1, 2, 3, 4, 5\}$ the multi-set (2,0,1,2,1) denotes disjunction $1\vee1\vee3\vee4\vee4\vee5$. Such multi-sets will be called disjunctive (D-) multi-sets. The disjunction operation on F is defined as follows:

$$(a_1,\ldots, a_n)\vee(b_1,\ldots, b_n) = (a_1+ b_1,\ldots, a_n + b_n) \tag{11}$$

The definition of the ordering of D-multi-sets is based on the following property of disjunction operation: $A\vee B \geq A$, i.e. an adding of elements of D-multi-set B to elements of D-multi-set A increases the plausibility of resulting multi-set $A\vee B$. Let us introduce an ordering relation on F as follows:

$A = B$, if and only if $a_i = b_i$ for all $i = 1,\ldots, n$,
$A < B$, if index i exists, such that $a_i < b_i$ and $a_k = b_k$ for all $k > i$.

Suppose $F_p = F \cup \{0\} \cup \{1\}$ is an extended set of plausibility values. The extension of an ordering relation from F on F_p will be defined as $0 < A < 1$, for all D-multi-sets A from F. Further A and B will denote elements from F_p. Denote $A \leq B$, if $A= B$ or $A < B$. It is clear that $\leq$ is a linear ordering on F_p i.e. it is transitive and for all A and B from F_p it is fulfilled $A \leq B$ or $B \leq A$.

Define an extension of disjunction operation $\vee$ from F on the set F_p: $A \vee 0 = 0 \vee A= A$, $A \vee 1 = 1 \vee A = 1$.

Conjunction operation $\wedge$ on the set F_p is defined as follows:

$$\begin{gathered} A \wedge 0 = 0 \wedge A= 0,\quad A \wedge 1 = 1 \wedge A = A, \\ (a_1,\ldots, a_n) \wedge (b_1,\ldots, b_n) = min\{(a_1,\ldots, a_n), (b_1,\ldots, b_n)\}, \end{gathered} \tag{12}$$

where *min* is defined by linear ordering relation $\leq$ on F_p. It can be proved that the operations $\wedge$ and $\vee$ are t-norm and t-conorm [16] respectively on the set of D-multi-sets F_p and $\vee$ is a strict monotonic on F_p.

2.3 Additive Algebra

The operation of the additive algebra is based on the sum of numeric weights, in contrast to the multi-set interpretation of results from disjunctive algebra. Formally, there are: a set $Q = \{q_1,...,q_n\}$, where q_i represents each one of the identified problems (consequents) and a set $R = \{r_1,...,r_m\}$ which enlists the present and historic conditions in the well (antecedents). The typical structure of a rule has a form:

$$\text{IF } r_i \text{ THEN } q_j, p=F. \tag{13}$$

The value F of weight p is numeric or F is a formula. Hence there are two types of rules called: *Standard* and *By-Formula*. In the first case, $F = w$ where $w \in (0, M]$, and M is the maximum possible score, e.g., M = 6 or M = 100. In the second case, the required values are placed in the formula F in order to obtain the weight w. There will be then a copy of the original knowledge base, which is adapted to the well under study and contains standard rules exclusively.

The possibility $P(q_i)$ of having the problem q_i in the well, is expressed as the sum of individual weights of each rule p that was triggered where q_i is the consequent. Each type of problem has associated a list of reasons. The presence or absence of such reasons is reflected in the score which, the closer it gets to the maximum M, the higher the possibility of having such problem in the well.

Even though most of the rules relate only one antecedent to the corresponding consequent, there are also compound rules where the antecedents are grouped by conjunctions (AND, $\wedge$), disjunctions (OR, $\vee$) or both. The general form of rules may be expressed then as:

$$\text{IF } q_1\wedge\ldots\wedge q_n \text{ THEN } x_i, p=F, \qquad \text{IF } q_1\vee\ldots\vee q_m \text{ THEN } x_j, p=F. \tag{14}$$

Some examples of the rules for diagnosing water production are:

1) *IF Cementing_condition.Casing == Good THEN Diagnosis.Type == Coning or cresting, p =* w_{CN6}.
2) *IF Crude_oil_properties.Viscosity > 2.5 AND Crude_oil_properties.Viscosity <= 10 THEN Diagnosis.Type == Coning or cresting, p=*F_{CN3b}.
3) *IF Treatment.Cement_squeeze == One_time OR Treatment.Mechanical == Yes THEN Diagnosis.Type == Casing_leaks, p=*w_{FG3}.

In the example, the possibility of having a "Coning or cresting" problem is calculated by substituting the value of *Viscosity* in the formula F_{CN3b} in rule 2, this will give us the weight w_{CN3b} which summed to w_{CN6} from rule 1, throws the total. The resulting number is later translated to a qualitative scale, similar to the one used in the knowledge base with disjunctive algebra described above.

3 Knowledge Representation Model and the CAPNET Expert System Shell

Knowledge representation model provides a common and consistent symbolic representation for water production application domain. While developing CAPNET agent platform, we have developed the CAPNET Knowledge Representation Format (KRF) based on the FIPA-RDF. This model solves the ambiguity in defining relationships among entities and introduces the possibility of expressing rules. The CAPNET KRF represents elements from the world by using Objects. These are identifiable entities from application domain with a unique name and a list of Properties defining their state. Objects are grouped in a wider concept known as Resource. Properties set the estimates of some feature or attribute that belongs to the Object/Resource. A Property is a triplet: name, data type and value. If values for some property are restricted to a list of options, then it is said that it has Constraints.

Another element of the KRF is a rule, which defines a relationship between known facts (antecedents) and information that can be concluded (consequents). Fig. 1 illustrates a fragment of the rule development using CAPNET Knowledge Acquisition Tool (KAT). At the left-hand side of the screenshot a structure of rule categories and problem domain resources appear. A structure of a rule appears in the window Rule Text of Fig 1. Antecedents and consequents of the rules are propositions that relate properties from resources to some value by one of the following operators: *equal to, greater than, greater than or equal to, lower than or equal to and not equal.* The rules are stored both in internal and external (XML) formats.

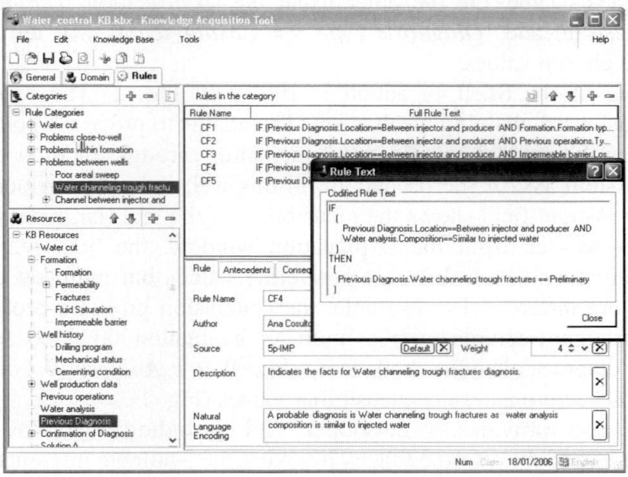

Fig. 1. A screenshot of the KAT v2.0: rule edition mode

The details on the handling of the possibility of the facts and rules by means of plausibility values are introduced above. To handle this and other types of uncertainties, two fuzzy inference engines, forward chaining and backward chaining, realized in the CAPNET Expert System Shell, working with linguistic scales were developed. The Shell based expert system implements all three algebras: conjunctive, disjunctive and additive. With its own user interface, the Shell works under the CAPNET KRF model and can be used for debugging knowledge bases during the development of expert systems.

Along with the implementation of fuzzy logic algebras, the Shell supports the use of UNKNOWN values for facts for advanced working with uncertainties. Specifically, when an inference engine meets the value UNKNOWN, it assumes that the corresponding property may have any of the appropriate possible *n* values, and its weight is assigned to be max {[6 / *n*], 1}, where 6 is the maximum grade of the linguistic scale (see Section 2.2). This implies adding new *n* facts, and hereafter the engine tries inferring, consecutively applying the added facts for the given pair object/property. For instance, in backward chaining, when the user is asked to provide a fact for the pair '*Production.Water_injection*', the assignment of UNKNOWN yields an addition of two facts, '*Production.Water_injection == Yes*' and '*Production.Water_injection == No*', both of the equal weight '3 (average)'. Obviously, such a specification of facts increases the probability that the engines will infer and/or prove some or other facts. The more facts we add the smaller their weights, and hence, the final conclusions will be rather fuzzy-weighted, as well.

To work with multiple values of properties of objects in backward chaining, the user can specify both concrete values to prove for and the ANY value. These features, together with the use of the multi-set-based algebras, become an efficient tool for inferring new facts and their subsequent arrangement in a certain order. For example, specifying the goal '*Diagnosis.Type == ANY*', we will obtain all possible values for the pair Diagnosis/Type. On the other hand, the specification '*Diagnosis.Type == Coning or cresting*' and '*Diagnosis.Type == Casing_leaks*' will tell the engine to prove only the chosen values.

An example of the Shell in action is shown in Fig. 2. The expert system is executing a backward-chaining mechanism. The goal is to prove the possibility of two simultaneous problems in the well: water channeling through fractures and poor areal sweep. The system asks if the production in this well is by Waterflooding (Request window). The Weight field shows the plausibility of the fact (large possibility) that is being fed. As we see from the Explanation window, the both reasons of water production were found with different possibility values but multi-set evaluations of these reasons are different. For example, the conclusion proves a problem of Water channeling through fractures with a multi-set evaluation 0020400 for disjunctive algebra. This diagnosis handles both facts (like *Water_Analysis_1.Composition* and *Diagnosis_1. Location*) and rules plausibility values (Fig. 1).

The Shell also provides a developer API including functions for: loading knowledge bases and user-defined facts, invoking the available inference mechanisms (forward or backward chaining), retrieving the list of inferred facts as well as the generated list of explanations and so on. Besides, the API methods allow saving the results to an XML format. An expert system gets access to the API through the embedded inference engine. It is worth mentioning that these functions are available only for the developer whilst their execution is transparent for the system's end-user.

4 Applications in the Petroleum Industry

The approach presented in this paper has been applied in two expert systems. The first one was developed to solve lost circulation problem (LCP). It is one of the most common problems encountered when drilling: drilling fluid may flow freely into the shallow unconsolidated formations because of high permeability or just because of a broken tube. Drilling may continue, or the mud can be thickened and lost circulation material added, in an attempt to cure the problem. To find the most appropriate and efficient solution, the intervention of experienced petroleum engineers is usually required. The system called Smart-Drill was created to help them solving LCP. The system uses conjunctive multi-set based algebra.

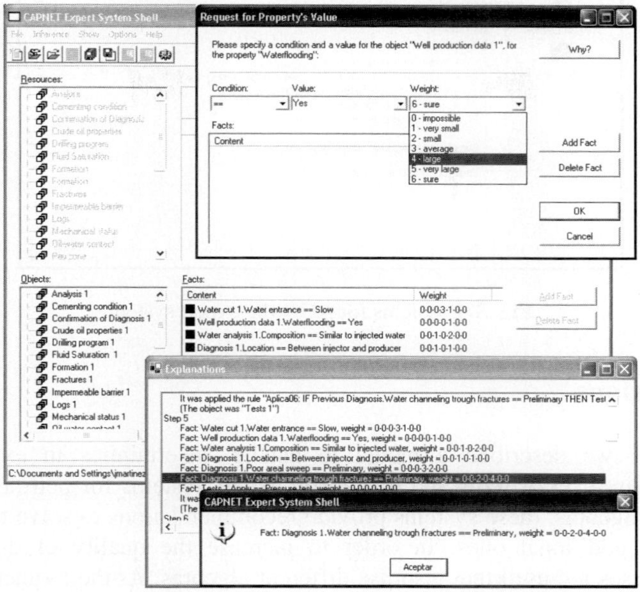

Fig. 2. CAPNET Expert System Shell handling plausibility values

The second expert system supports the petroleum engineers in the diagnosis of the problems of water control, one of the challenging problems of oil production. The average water produced from wells elsewhere in the world is 3 bbl of water for each barrel of oil and, in addition, the volume of produced water increases over time. The innovating technologies for the control of water production can mean a reduction of the costs and an increase in the hydrocarbon production. In order to find most suitable and efficient solution to the problem of water production, one requires the intervention and the experience of the petroleum engineers. Smart-Agua (*Agua* stand for *Water* in Spanish) tries to use these experiences for naturally fractured reservoirs (typical in Mexican scenes) in an expert system.

Smart-Agua uses disjunctive and additive algebras described in Section 2 in order to increase the quality of diagnosis. For example, in the option Preliminary Diagnosis in the Solutions group (Fig. 3), detected problems resulting from combining two types of inference procedures are ordered according to their possibility. SMART-Agua shows the description of the problem along with the list of reasons that supported each conclusion. As shown in Fig. 3, "*casing leaks*" problem obtained the highest possibility (very large), while "*completion into water*" and "*coning or cresting*" were diagnosed with average possibility. Both systems are at the field testing phase in PEMEX, Mexican oil company [17, 18].

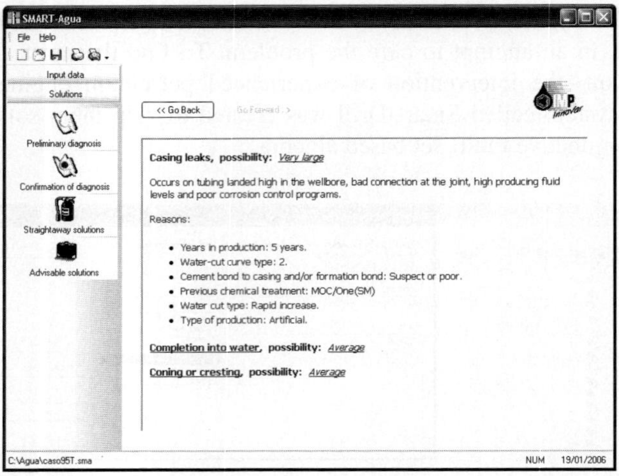

Fig. 3. Problems found by the expert system

5 Conclusions

In this paper we described a model to handle uncertainties in expert systems implemented in a set of tools and diagnostic expert systems for petroleum industry. Using fuzzy algebras, these systems provide recommendations to solve both the main problem and additional ones. In order to increase the quality of diagnosis, two knowledge bases are used that also use different algebras. At the moment the idea to hybridize mechanisms to give solution to certain problems is adopted with greater facility, though they appear to be opposed or incompatible.

Fuzzy algebras of strict monotonic operations form the novel confidence model of the expert system. This model based on the monotonicity feature of conjunction and disjunction operations permits taking into account the change of plausibility of premises in expert systems rules which use qualitative expert evaluations. As a result, conclusions on the output of inference procedure can obtain different plausibility evaluations. The use of unknown values is integrated in the proposed model. Original tools like CAPNET Expert System Shell and KAT were developed to support the described approach.

Although, the knowledge bases have been developed from documented evidences from reliable sources, the validation process would be beneficiary by the constant work with experts who could indicate improvements and corrections to the system. The results of this process that have already been obtained show that the expert system works satisfactorily for diagnosis of main water production problems. However, as it was mentioned above, new theoretical results in the problem area should always be included, in particular, those coming from the experience of new experts as well as from the analysis of real problems in other fractured reservoirs. Another formal method of knowledge base validation can be based on the construction and analysis of ontologies of expe200rt texts in the problem area [19].

Acknowledgments. Partial support for this research work has been provided by the IMP within the projects D.00322 and D.00006. Special thanks to all our colleagues who participated in the development of the system.

References

1. Zhang Z., Zhang Ch. (Eds.), Agent-Based Hybrid Intelligent Systems: An Agent-Based Framework for Complex Problem Solving. LNAI, V. 2938, 2004, XV, 196 p
2. Nikravesh M., Aminzadeh F., Zadeh L. (Eds.), Soft Computing and Intelligent Data Analysis in Oil Exploration, Elsevier Science, 2002
3. Mohaghegh S. D., Wolhart S., Hill D., Increasing Natural Gas Production using a Hybrid Intelligent System, in Adv. in Sci. Computing, Comp. Intelligence, and Applications – Mathematics and Computers in Sci. & Eng., WSES Press, 2001, pp. 459-467
4. Sheremetov L., Alvarado M., Bañares-Alcántara R. and Anminzadeh F., Intelligent Computing in the Petroleum Engineering, Special Issue, J. of Petroleum Science and Eng., Elsevier Science, Vol. 47, No. 1-2, 2005, pp. 1-3
5. Waterman D. A., A Guide to Expert Systems. Reading, Mass (USA). Addison-Wesley Publishing Company. 1986.
6. Slocombe S., Moore K., and Zelonf M. Engineering expert systems applications. In Proceedings of the Annual Conference of the BCS Specialist Group on Expert Systems. British Computer Society, London, 1986.
7. Mohaghegh S. D., Recent Developments in Application of Artificial Intelligence in Petroleum Engineering, J. of Petroleum Technology, 2005, pp. 86-91
8. Bailey B., Crabtree M. et al. Water control. Oilfield Review, Schlumberger, 2000
9. Halliburton, 2005. http://www.halliburton.com/esg/po_conformanceTechnology.jsp
10. Kandel A., Fuzzy Expert Systems (CRC Press, Boca Raton). 1991
11. Gallant S. and Hayashi Y.: A Neural Network Expert System with Confidence Measurements, in: Bouchon-Meunier, Yager, and Zadeh (Eds.): Uncertainty in Knowledge Bases, LNCS 521 Springer 1991, pp. 562-567
12. Pearl J. Probabilistic Reasoning in Intelligent Systems, Morgan Kaufman. 1988.
13. Zadeh L.A., Fuzzy sets, J. of Information Control, Vol. 8(3), 1965, pp. 338-353
14. Batyrshin I.Z., Uncertainties with memory in decision-making and expert systems, in Proceedings of the Fifth IFSA World Congress'93. Seoul, Korea, 1993, pp. 737 – 740
15. Reingold E.M., Nievergelt J., Deo N. Combinatorial Algorithms. Theory and Practice. New Jersey: Prentice-Hall. 1977
16. Batyrshin I.I., Batyrshin I.Z., On strict monotonic t-norms and t-conorms on ordinal scales, in Proceedings of International Conference on Fuzzy Sets and Soft Computing in Economics and Finance FSSCEF 2004, St. Petersburg, Russia, 2004, vol. I, pp. 170-177
17. Sheremetov L., Batyrshin I., Martinez J., Rodriguez H. and Filatov D., Fuzzy Expert System for Solving Lost Circulation Problem, in Proc. of the 5th IEEE Int. Conf. on Hybrid Intelligent Systems, Rio de Janeiro, Brasil, Nov. 6-9, pp. 92-97. IEEE, 2005.
18. Sheremetov L., Batyrshin I., Cosultchi A., Martínez-Munoz J., SMART-Agua: a Hybrid Intelligent System for Diagnostics, in Proc. of the INES 2006 10th Int. Conf. on Intelligent Engineering Systems, London, United Kingdom, June 26-28, IEEE, 2006.
19. Makagonov P., Ruiz Figueroa A., Gelbukh A. Studying Evolution of a Branch of Knowledge by Constructing and Analyzing Its Ontology. Lecture Notes in Computer Science, N 3999, Springer, 2006, pp. 37-45.
20. Alonso-Lavernia, M., A. De-la-Cruz-Rivera, G. Sidorov. *Generation of Natural Language Explanations of Rules in an Expert System.* LNCS N 3878, Springer, 2006, 311-314.

A Connectionist Fuzzy Case-Based Reasoning Model

Yanet Rodriguez[1], Maria M. Garcia[1], Bernard De Baets[2], Carlos Morell[1], and Rafael Bello[1]

[1] Universidad Central de Las Villas, Carretera a Camajuani km 51/2, Santa Clara, Cuba
{yrsarabia, mmgarcia, cmorellp, rbellop}@uclv.edu.cu
[2] Ghent University, Coupure links 653, B-9000 Gent, Belgium
Bernard.DeBaets@UGent.be

Abstract. This paper presents a new version of an existing hybrid model for the development of knowledge-based systems, where case-based reasoning is used as a problem solver. Numeric predictive attributes are modeled in terms of fuzzy sets to define neurons in an associative Artificial Neural Network (ANN). After the Fuzzy-ANN is trained, its weights and the membership degrees in the training examples are used to automatically generate a local distance function and an attribute weighting scheme. Using this distance function and following the Nearest Neighbor rule, a new hybrid Connectionist Fuzzy Case-Based Reasoning model is defined. Experimental results show that the model proposed allows to develop knowledge-based systems with a higher accuracy than when using the original model. The model takes the advantages of the approaches used, providing a more natural framework to include expert knowledge by using linguistic terms.

1 Introduction

Case-Based Reasoning (CBR) may be defined as a model of reasoning that incorporates problem-solving understanding and learning integrated with memory processes. CBR can mean different things depending on the intended use of the reasoning: adapt and combine old solutions to meet new demands or use old cases to explain new situations or to justify new solutions. CBR can be classified into two major types: problem solving CBR and interpretative CBR [1]. A model to build hybrid Knowledge-Based Systems (KBS), where CBR has the functionality to avoid the non-existing explanation facilities of the connectionist approach is presented in [2]. That model is a variant of the model of Stanfill and Waltz [3], in which an Artificial Neural Net (ANN) is used to suggest the value of the target attribute for a given query. The case-based module uses a similarity function to justify the solution given by the ANN, which includes ANN weights. Hereafter, this model will be referred as *original model.*

The *original model* uses a simple implementation of the Interactive Activation and Competition neural net model proposed by Rumelhart in [4], which is referred as SIAC. The attributes used to define cases can be both numeric and symbolic types. When a numeric attribute is used, many different values for it should appear in the case base. Therefore, the quantity of neurons in the ANN will increase very rapidly when a numeric attribute is used. In most cases, however, it would be enough to consider some values likely to represent a group of values close to them. Another way

A. Gelbukh and C.A. Reyes-Garcia (Eds.): MICAI 2006, LNAI 4293, pp. 176 – 185, 2006.

to select these values is via discretization [5]. Both variants are centered on the manipulation of numbers or symbols, and a traditional crisp set, in which an element is either present or not, should be followed.

On the other hand, fuzzy set theory enables the use of natural language mapping from numeric data into linguistic terms [6], [7]. This paper presents a revised version of the *original model*, in which the CBR component solves the problem instead of the ANN. Linguistic terms are selected to represent numeric attributes, defining neurons in the ANN in a more natural way. While the original model can be classified as Interpretative CBR, the new approach can be seen as a problem solving CBR.

Many similarity measures have been proposed [8], [9], but all of them are defined for a particular application or assume a particular domain model [10]. However, advantages of the hybridization used in the original model could be used to improve this task. A similarity criterion for a particular domain can automatically be achieved defining a local distance function and an attribute weighting scheme. In other words, when the associative ANN used in the original model is trained, the information stored in the case base as examples is generalized. Afterwards, the information stored in the ANN weights is used by the CBR module to build its retrieval module.

Similarity-based methods are a generalization of the minimal distance methods which form a basis of several machine learning and pattern recognition methods. The nearest-neighbor methods are examples of such methods [11]. These two components together with the nearest neighbor rule define our Connectionist Fuzzy Case-Based System (ConFuCiuS).

2 Description of the Model Components

Measurements are crisp whereas perceptions are fuzzy [12], such as *small*, *high*, *old*, etc. When the *original model* is used, a representative value belonging to the domain of the attribute is selected following a crisp set approach. Nevertheless, the model proposed defines for each numeric attribute a set of linguistic terms modeled as fuzzy sets, with all the advantages that this can represent [13]. In other words, a set of linguistic terms is defined as representative values for a numeric attribute to represent it in the ANN. It allows to deal with numeric attributes in a more natural way. Besides, a more accurate measure than in the original model of "how close" a domain value is to a corresponding representative value can be taking into account.

2.1 The Fuzzy Associative ANN

The SIAC model is used in the *original model* proposed in [2] for suggesting the value of the target attribute. There is a group of neurons for each attribute. That is, each value in the domain of attribute a_i is represented by a single neuron. The relationships, which are joined by using a directed arc, are only considered between neurons of different groups. Each arc carries a weight that is determined by the examples in the case base *(CB)*, considering the number of cases in which both values appear simultaneously.

The new model uses a fuzzy implementation of the SIAC model, capturing the merits of fuzzy set theory and this model of ANN. It is named *Fuzzy-SIAC*, and it is used in this new approach to store information for a particular domain. The topology and learning of this associative ANN are based on representative values. If the attribute is numeric, representative values are linguistic terms, otherwise they are symbolic values.

Let q_p be the value of a predictive attribute p in the input pattern. The value $f_{Pi}(q_p)$ is a measure of "how close" the value q_p is represented by the representative value P_i. It is a measure between 0 and 1 depending on expressions (1) and (2). Expression (1) is used when the attribute is numeric, while expression (2) is considered for symbolic attributes. In both expressions $\mu_{Pi}(q_p)$ denotes the membership degree of the value q_p to the i-th linguistic term P_i.

$$f_{P_i}(q_p) = \mu_{P_i}(q_p) \tag{1}$$

$$f_{P_i}(q_p) = \begin{cases} 1 \text{ , if } q_p = P_i \\ 0 \text{ , } otherwise \end{cases} \tag{2}$$

The same idea as in the *original model* is applied to obtain the weights. When non-supervised learning is applied, the modification of the weights takes place based on the states of the neurons (exits) after the presentation of certain stimulus (information of entrance to the network), without considering whether or not it was desired to obtain these states of activation.

Let a and b be two attributes that describe an example e (or instance) of a training set (or case base CB). Let A_i and B_j be representative values of the attributes a and b, respectively, then $w_{Ai,Bj}$ represents the weight associated to the directed arc between A_i and B_j. It is computed using expression (3) and is based upon relative frequencies.

$$w_{A_i,B_j} = \frac{\sum_{e \in CB} f_{A_i}(e_a) f_{B_j}(e_b)}{\sum_{e \in CB} f_{A_i}(e_a)} \tag{3}$$

In other words, the value $w_{Ai,Bj}$ is obtained considering how often the values taken by the attributes a and b for each example e of CB are represented by their representative values A_i and B_j, respectively, relative to how the first one is represented.

2.2 The Nearest Neighbor Rule

The Nearest Neighbor rule bases its answers on similarity between the query and the training instances (or CB). The generalization is postponed until a request is received (lazy learning). Given a new query $q=(q_1,q_2,\ldots,q_{m-1})$, the k-most-similar cases to predict the target attribute t (q_m) can be retrieved by using the following expression taken from [9] on all e of CB:

$$d(e,q) = \left(\sum_{a=1}^{m-1} w(a) \cdot (\delta(e_a, q_a))^r \right)^{\frac{1}{r}} \tag{4}$$

where $w()$ defines the attribute weighting function and $\delta()$ defines how values of a given attribute differ. The classes of the k nearest neighbors of q are considered. The nearest neighbor rule decides that the query q belongs to the category of the majority class of the nearest neighbors.

A standard k-NN algorithm defines $w()$ as a constant function $w(a)= w_a$ and $\delta()$ as follows:

$$\delta(e_a, q_a) = \begin{cases} |e_a - q_a| & , a \text{ is numeric} \\ 1 & , a \text{ is symbolic and } q_a = e_a \\ 0 & , a \text{ is symbolic and } q_a \neq e_a \end{cases} \tag{5}$$

The generalization capability of the k-NN highly depends on the definition of its distance function [9].

2.3 The Connectionist Fuzzy CBR Model

The CBR in the *original model* is used to justify the solution provided by the ANN. The new hybrid CBR model proposed in this paper implements a case-based module as a problem solver. In fact, expression (4) with r=2 (i.e., Euclidean distance) is used, but with new expressions for the term $w(a)$ and the function $\delta()$.

A trained associative ANN is used to automatically define the distance function for a particular problem. Numeric attributes used to describe a case of case base are modeled using fuzzy sets. In other words, after the *Fuzzy-SIAC* neural net has been trained from domain examples (or *CB*), all necessary information to define the attribute weighting function and the local distance function is taken from it. That is, $w(a)$ and $\delta()$ are built using the weights $w_{Ai,Bj}$.

Fuzzy-SIAC defines the weights between two neurons as a measure of how the representative values for corresponding attributes are related considering past experiences. Besides, when two examples x and y are compared, a measure of "how close" two values x_a and y_a are for an attribute a can be obtained considering the difference between the values $f_{Ai}(x_a)$ and $f_{Ai}(y_a)$. Both measures should be taken into account to define:

Definition 1. The *strength* of predictive attribute a in object x for the representative value T of target attribute t is a measure of the activation received by the neuron that represents the value T, only considering this predictive attribute:

$$S(x_a, T) = \frac{\sum_{A_i \in R_a} w_{Ai,T} f_{A_i}(x_a)}{\sum_{A_i \in R_a} f_{A_i}(x_a)} \tag{6}$$

where:

- x_a denotes the value of the attribute a in the object x,
- A_i denotes the ith representative value associated with the attribute a,
- R_a denotes the set of representative values of the attribute a,
- $w_{Ai,T}$ denotes the weight of the arc between the representative values A_i and T,
- $f()$ is the function defined in section 2.1

Definition 2. The *difference* between two values x_a and y_a for predictive attribute a in the context of target attribute t is defined as:

$$difference(x_a, y_a) = \sqrt{\sum_{T \in R_t} (S(x_a, T) - S(y_a, T))^2} \tag{7}$$

where R_t denotes the set of representative values (linguistic labels) of the target attribute t.

Definition 3. The *importance* of predictive attribute a for object x in the context of target attribute t is defined as:

$$I_t(x, x_a) = \sqrt{\sum_{T \in R_t} (S(x_a, T))^2} \tag{8}$$

Finally, a dissimilarity function is defined by expression (9), where term $w(a)$ and the function $\delta()$ in the expression (4) are replaced by (8) and (7), respectively:

$$d(e,q) = \left(\sum_{a=1}^{m-1} I_t(q, q_a) \cdot (difference(e_a, q_a))^r \right)^{\frac{1}{r}} \tag{9}$$

Thus, a new model to develop a Connectionist Fuzzy Case-based System (it is referred to as ConFuCiuS model) is defined as an Instance of the k-Nearest Neighbor classifier, using expression (9). The weight term used cause the function *d()* to be non-symmetric. If the weighting scheme is omitted, function *d()* is a distance function.

Note that the proposed model uses a dissimilarity function automatically defined from domain examples. In other words, after the Fuzzy-ANN is trained, its weights and the membership degrees in the fuzzy sets are considered to define a local distance function and an attribute weighting scheme. This new hybrid connectionist fuzzy CBR model allows developing smarter case-based systems for a particular application, reducing the knowledge engineering effort.

3 Experimental Results and Discussion

The new model was empirically tested, comparing its performance to that of the *original model* and other classifiers traditionally used. The test bed employed for comparison was the Waikato Environment for Knowledge Analysis (WEKA[1]). The new classifier was implemented as a part of the WEKA package.

In the experiments presented, some datasets from UCIMLR [14] were used. They have either numeric (dataset name in bold) or symbolic predictive attributes, one target attribute, and have no missing values. The percentage of correctly classified instances was considered as performance measure. In each experiment, 10-fold cross validation [15] was used, and the performance mean (m) for each algorithm and each dataset was computed.

---

[1] WEKA is a Java-written open source. It is available at http://www.cs.waikato.ac.nz/~ml/weka/ under the GNU General Public License.

3.1 Definition of Membership Functions

Before ConFuCiuS is used, each numeric attribute is transformed into a linguistic variable. In fact, a filter implemented in the WEKA package with this purpose was used. A discretization method called "Equal Width" is applied first, defining a representative value for each interval obtained. The number of intervals depends on the dataset, selecting the maximum number between five and the number of classes. Next, trapezoidal membership functions (MF) are built on these intervals.

A trapezoidal MF is specified by four parameters *(a, b, c, d)*, which for the *j*-th MF are computed as follows. Let *p* be a numeric predictive attribute. Its domain D_p (set of values e_p for all *e* of *CB*) is divided in *n* intervals of equal width. Let L_j and U_j be the lower and upper bound of the *j*-th interval. When $j=1$, then $a_1= b_1= c_1= L_1$. If $j=n$, then $b_n= c_n= d_n= U_n$; otherwise expressions (10) to (13) are used.

$$a_j = c_{j-1} \tag{10}$$

$$b_j = L_j + \frac{L_j + U_j}{4} \tag{11}$$

$$c_j = U_j - \frac{L_j + U_j}{4} \tag{12}$$

$$d_j = b_{j+1} \tag{13}$$

3.2 Testing the New Approach

ConFuCiuS was implemented as part of WEKA package, as well as the original model. Table 1 shows the results obtained on each of the 15 selected datasets. The second column contains the results obtained with the original model [2], where the SIAC neural net is the problem solver. The third column presents the best results obtained by the ConFuCiuS model, considering *k*=1,3,5,and 7 and without an attribute weighting scheme.

Note that the ConFuCiuS model shows a higher performance than the *original model* for most of the datasets used. Moreover, the general behavior, measured by the average value, is significantly better for the new model.

3.2 Comparative Evaluation

As expected, no learning algorithm will performance best for all applications since each implements a different bias; they will show a substantially different performance for some problems [16]. A fruitful way of looking at the behavior of algorithms is by making paired comparisons of results achieved with two or more algorithms on the same data sets. In order to do this, a non-parametric test was used: the Wilcoxon signed-rank test. To improve accuracy in the Wilcoxon test significance, Monte Carlo simulation techniques are applied.

Table 1. Results obtained with the *original model* and model proposed

Dataset name	*SIAC* *m*	*ConFuCiuS* *m*	*Number of similar cases considered*
Iris	93.33%	**96.00%**	*k*=3
Diabetes	66.15%	**75.53%**	*k*=3
Glass	64.02%	**69.16%**	*k*=3
Vehicle	54.73%	**67.61%**	*k*=5
Wine	**97.19%**	96.07%	*k*=5
ionosphere	74.64%	**96.63%**	*k*=1
Sonar	72.12%	**85.10%**	*k*=3
Vowel	63.43%	**97.58%**	*k*=1
kr-vs-kp	61.17%	**97.12%**	*k*=1
hayes-roth	75.00%	**81.82%**	*k*=5
Lenses	62.50%	**87.50%**	*k*=5
monks-1	75.00%	**80.65%**	*k*=3
monks-2	**62.13%**	58.58%	*k*=1
monks-3	93.44%	93.44%	*k*=7
tic-tac-toe	65.34%	**90.19%**	*k*=1
Average	72.01%	**84.86%**	

Table 2. Results obtained with the new model and standard *k*-NN

Dataset name	*ConFuCiuS* *m*	*Standard k-NN* *m*
Iris	**96.00%**	95.33%
Diabetes	**75.53%**	72.66%
Glass	69.16%	**71.96%**
Vehicle	67.61%	**71.16%**
Wine	**96.07%**	95.51%
ionosphere	**96.63%**	86.32%
Sonar	85.10%	**86.06%**
Vowel	97.58%	**99.09%**
kr-vs-kp	**97.12%**	96.28%
Hayes-roth	**81.82%**	61.36%
Lenses	**87.50%**	66.67%
monks-1	**80.65%**	78.23%
monks-2	**58.58%**	56.21%
monks-3	**93.44%**	86.07%
tic-tac-toe	90.19%	**98.75%**
Average	**84.86%**	81.44%

Firstly, the Connectionist Fuzzy Case-Based Reasoning model was compared with a closely related method: the standard *k*-NN classifier (IB*k* in the WEKA package). It follows that no distance function can be strictly better than any other in terms of generalization ability. The second column of Table 2 shows the results obtained with standard *k*-NN, considering for each dataset the same value for *k* used above.

On these set of datasets, ConFuCiuS had a higher performance mean than the standard *k*-NN on 10 of 15 datasets considered, which mainly have symbolic attributes. While the model proposed in this paper handles a numeric attribute as a set of linguistic terms using a more natural framework, it does not result in a significant difference in performance (significance of the test: 0.155) as shown in Table 3.

Table 3. Results from Wilcoxon Test (confidence)

Test Statistics[c]

			standard k-NN - ConFuCiuS	C4.5 - ConFuCiuS
Monte Carlo Sig. (2-tailed)	Sig.		.155	.015
	99% Confidence Interval	Lower Bound	.142	.011
		Upper Bound	.169	.020

c. Based on 10000 sampled tables with starting seed 2000000.

Table 4. Results obtained with both ConFuCiuS and C4.5 algorithms

Dataset name	*ConFuCiuS* *m*	*C4.5* *m*
Iris	96.00%	96.00%
Diabetes	**75.53%**	73.83%
Glass	**69.16%**	66.82%
Vehicle	67.61%	**72.46%**
Wine	**96.07%**	93.82%
Ionosphere	**96.63%**	91.45%
Sonar	**85.10%**	71.15%
Vowel	**97.58%**	80.91%
kr-vs-kp	97.12%	**99.44%**
Hayes-roth	**81.82%**	72.73%
Lenses	**87.50%**	83.33%
Monks-1	80.65%	**82.26%**
Monks-2	**58.58%**	56.21%
Monks-3	93.44%	93.44%
Tic-tac-toe	**90.19%**	85.07%
Average	**84.86%**	81.26%

On the other hand, the comparison with another traditional classifier was done. We have decided to use C4.5 [17] (J48 in WEKA package). It is a decision tree algorithm, which is known to show quite good results in general [18].

As can be seen in Table 4, the ConFuCiuS model shows a higher performance on 10 of the data sets and a general behavior significantly better than the C4.5 algorithm. Besides, the statistical analysis of these results (see Table 3) shows that both case-based and rule-based approaches used have a significant difference in performance (significance of the test: 0.015), in favor of the new framework proposed here.

4 Conclusions and Future Work

This paper has presented a new version of an existing hybrid model to develop knowledge-based systems, where Case-Based Reasoning is used as a problem solver instead of the Artificial Neural Net. Predictive attributes are modeled in terms of fuzzy sets, and the trained associative Fuzzy-ANN (Fuzzy-SIAC) is used to build a local distance function and an attribute weighting scheme. The new hybrid connectionist fuzzy CBR model (ConFuCiuS) presented here is an instance of the *k*-Nearest Neighbor classifier using a dissimilarity function.

Experimental results show that the new approach improves the accuracy of the *original model*. Besides, when numeric attributes are used, the representative values used by the ANN are linguistic terms. Moreover, a more natural framework to include expert knowledge by using fuzzy sets is provided. The ConFuCiuS model, without weighting scheme, obtained a higher accuracy on more data sets than the standard *k*-NN classifier; although they do not show a significant difference in performance. On the other hand, a significantly better performance than a good classifier, the C4.5 algorithm, was achieved.

Additionally, the Connectionist Fuzzy Case-Based Reasoning Model proposed in this paper takes some advantages of the hybridization used in the *original model*. The dissimilarity function used is automatically defined from examples. Thus, the new model allows developing smarter case-based systems for a particular application, reducing the knowledge engineering effort.

These results are obtained using a simple expert method to build the linguistic term set from a set of intervals. As future work, the use of an automatic method to adjust the parameters of the membership functions will increase the performance of the ConFuCiuS model.

Acknowledgments

This work was supported in part by VLIR (Vlaamse InterUniversitaire Raad, Flemish Interuniversity Council, Belgium) under the IUC Program VLIR-UCLV. Thanks also to both Liana Isabel Araujo and Hector Matías, undergraduate students of Computer Science, for extending WEKA in order to test the model proposed in this paper.

References

1. Kolodner, J.: An introduction to case-based reasoning. Artificial Intelligence Review 6 (1992) 3-34
2. García, M.M., Bello, P.R.: A model and its different applications to case-based reasoning. Knowledge-based systems 9 (1996) 465-473

3. Stanfill, C., Waltz, D.: Toward memory-based reasoning. Comm. of ACM, 29 (1986) 1213-1228
4. McClelland, D., Rumelhart, E.: Explorations in parallel distributed processing. MIT Press (1989)
5. Kurgan, L, Krzysztof, C.: CAIM Discretization Algorithm. IEEE Transactions on Knowledge and Data Engineering. Vol 16. No. 2. (2004)
6. Zadeh, L.A.: The concept of a lingüistic variable and Its Application to Approximate Reasoning. Information Sciences Vol. 8 (1975) 199-249
7. Zadeh, L.A.: From Computing with Numbers to Computing with Words -From Manipulation of Measurements to Manipulation of Perceptions. Intelligent Systems and Soft Computing (2000) 3-40
8. Włodzisław, D. : Similarity-based methods: a general framework for classification, approximation and association Control and Cybernetics vol.29 No. 4 (2000)
9. Aha, D.W. : Feature weighting for lazy learning algorithms. In: H. Liu and H. Motoda (Eds.) Feature Extraction, Construction and Selection: A Data Mining Perspective. Norwell MA: Kluwer (1998)
10. Morell, C., Bello, R., Grau, R. "Improving k-NN by Using Fuzzy Similarity Functions. Lectures Notes on Artificial Intelligence 3315, Nov 2004, Springer Verlag Berlin Heidelberg (2004) 708–716
11. Wettschereck, D., Aha, D.W., Mohri , T.: A Review And Empirical Evaluation Of Feature Weighting Methods For A Class Of Lazy Learning Algorithms. Artificial Intelligence Review 11, (1997) 273-314
12. Casillas, O., Cordón, F., Herrera, L., Magdalena: Interpretability improvements to find the balance interpretability-accuracy in fuzzy modeling: an overview. Interpretability issues in fuzzy modeling. Vol. 128. Springer (2003)
13. García, MM., Rodriguez, Y., Bello, R.: Usando conjuntos borrosos para implementar un modelo para sistemas basados en casos interpretativos. In Proceedings of IBERAMIA-SBIA. Eds por M. C. Monard y J.S. Sichman, Sao Paulo, Brasil, (2000)
14. Murphy, P.M., Aha, D.W.: UCI Repository of Machine-Learning Databases, http:\\ www.ics.uci.edu/~mlearn\mlrepository.htm
15. Wilson, D.R., Martinez, T.R..: Improved Heterogeneous Distance Functions. Journal of Artificial Intelligence Research, vol. 6, no. 1, (1997) 1-34.
16. Mitchell, T.M.: The Need for Biases in Learning Generalizations. in J. W. Shavlik & T. G. Dietterich (Eds.), Readings in Machine Learning. San Mateo, CA: Morgan Kaufmann, (1990) 184-191
17. Quinlan, R.: C4.5: Programs for Machine Learning. Morgan Kaufmann Publishers, San Mateo, CA. (1993)
18. Michie, D., Spiegelhalter, D.J, Taylor C.C.: Machine Learning, Neural and Statistical Classification (1994)

Error Bounds Between Marginal Probabilities and Beliefs of Loopy Belief Propagation Algorithm

Nobuyuki Taga and Shigeru Mase

Tokyo Institute of Technology, Ookayama 2-12-1-w8-28,
Meguro-ku, Tokyo 152-8552, Japan
{Nobuyuki.Taga, mase}@is.titech.ac.jp

Abstract. Belief propagation (BP) algorithm has been becoming increasingly a popular method for probabilistic inference on general graphical models. When networks have loops, it may not converge and, even if converges, beliefs, i.e., the result of the algorithm, may not be equal to exact marginal probabilities. When networks have loops, the algorithm is called Loopy BP (LBP). Tatikonda and Jordan applied Gibbs measures theory to LBP algorithm and derived a sufficient convergence condition. In this paper, we utilize Gibbs measure theory to investigate the discrepancy between a marginal probability and the corresponding belief. Consequently, in particular, we obtain an error bound if the algorithm converges under a certain condition. It is a general result for the accuracy of the algorithm. We also perform numerical experiments to see the effectiveness of the result.

1 Introduction

Belief propagation (BP) algorithm has become a popular method of solving inference problems exactly for probabilistic networks without loops (e.g., Bayesian networks) in a finite number of times. It has the origin in the probabilistic expert system theory proposed by Pearl *et al.* [6]. Similar algorithms appear in several applications, such as Viterbi algorithm in hidden Markov models, iterative algorithms for Gallager codes and turbocodes, Kalman filter and the transfer-matrix approach in physics.

It is also widely applied to networks with loops. In that case, the algorithm is called loopy BP (LBP). LBP algorithm, however, may not converge and, even if it does, the solution may not be equal to the target marginal probabilities. Nevertheless, applications of the LBP algorithm are reported to be remarkably good such as in the coding theory (cf. Frey [1], McEliece *et al.* [4] and Murphy *et al.* [5]).

Weiss [9] discussed the LBP algorithm on networks with a single loop and Weiss and Freeman [10] discussed the LBP algorithm on Gaussian networks. A basic idea of Weiss is the fact that the calculation of the LBP algorithm is equivalent to that on a corresponding infinite tree called the computation tree. Tatikonda and Jordan [8] pursued his idea and formulated the convergence

A. Gelbukh and C.A. Reyes-Garcia (Eds.): MICAI 2006, LNAI 4293, pp. 186–196, 2006.

problem as that of Gibbs measures on the computation trees. They showed a relationship between the convergence of LBP algorithm and the phase transition phenomena on the associated computation trees in their paper.

So far, some studies were reported for the general convergence property of LBP algorithm. However, there are few general discussions of its accuracy.

In this paper, we use Gibbs measure theory to measure the discrepancy of marginal probabilities and the corresponding beliefs of LBP algorithm using the concept of the computation tree.

We give a review of the BP algorithm in Sect. 2. In Sect. 3, we introduce Gibbs measure theory and review the application results for LBP algorithm. In Sect. 4, we introduce the concept of measuring discrepancy of two probability measures developed in Gibbs measure theory, apply it to the LBP algorithm with pair potentials, and show some results. In Sect. 5, we report numerical experiments done to see the effectiveness of obtained results. In Sect. 6, we give a conclusion and some remarks.

2 BP Algorithm and Computation Trees

The BP algorithm used in this paper is as follows. Let G be a connected and undirected finite network. Let consider an associated set of random variables $X = \{X_i, i \in G\}$ and its observations $Y = \{y_i, i \in G\}$. The state space E_i of X_i is finite. Some y_i may be missing. We consider a probability function on G of the form

$$p(x \mid y) \equiv P(X = x \mid Y = y) = \frac{1}{Z} \prod_{i \sim j} \phi_{ij}(x_i, x_j) \prod_{i \in G} \phi_i(x_i, y_i) ,$$

where $\sim$ denotes the neighborhood relationship, and the first product extends over all neighboring nodes (i, j). Here $i \in G$ is said to be a neighbor of $j \in G$ if there exists an edge between i and j in G. We call (G, p) a *probabilistic network* with the network G and the joint distribution p. Throughout this paper, Z stands for normalizing constants and are not always the same. Usually, the existence of a data y_i restricts the state space E_i to $\{y_i\}$ effectively. We will adopt this convention and, further, suppress the dependencies of ϕ_i's on $\{y_i\}$. Therefore, it takes the form

$$p(x) = \frac{1}{Z} \prod_{i \sim j} \phi_{ij}(x_i, x_j) \prod_{i \in G} \phi_i(x_i) . \tag{1}$$

It is the basic assumption of this paper that $\phi_{ij}(\cdot, \cdot)$ and $\phi_i(\cdot)$ are all positive.

For each pair of neighboring nodes (i, j) and each state $x_j \in E_j$, we consider the *message* $m_{ij}^{(n)}(x_j)$, $n = 1, 2, \ldots$. These messages obey the following update rule called the *belief propagation* (BP):

$$m_{ij}^{(n+1)}(x_j) = \frac{1}{Z} \sum_{x_i \in E_i} \phi_{ij}(x_i, x_j) \phi_i(x_i) \prod_{k \in \partial i \setminus \{j\}} m_{ki}^{(n)}(x_i) ,$$

where ∂i denotes the set of all neighboring nodes of i. In the following, $|A|$ for a set A means its cardinality. All messages are initialized as $m_{ij}^{(0)}(x_j) \equiv 1$. If a message $m_{ij}^{(n)}(x_j)$ converges, its limit is denoted by $m_{ij}(x_j)$. For these limit messages, a *belief* for each node i is the normalized product

$$b_i(x_i) = \frac{1}{Z}\phi_i(x_i) \prod_{k \in \partial i} m_{ki}(x_i), \quad x_i \in E_i \ .$$

If a probabilistic network has no loops, i.e., tree-like, it is known that all the messages $\{m_{ij}^{(n)}(x_j)\}$ converge after a finite number of the BP updates and that the belief $b_i(\cdot)$ is equal to the marginal probability $\boldsymbol{P}\{x_i = \cdot\}$ for each $i \in G$, see Jensen [3]. On the other hand, for networks with loops, the messages may not converge and, if converge, the beliefs may not be equal to the marginal probabilities. In particular, for a probabilistic network with loops, this algorithm is called *loopy belief propagation* (LBP). To study the properties of the LBP algorithm, Weiss [9] introduced a concept of *unwrapped networks* (*computation trees* in Tatikonda and Jordan [8]), which are associating infinite trees T_k, $k \in G$. T_k is the limit of increasing finite trees $\{T_k^{(n)}\}$, $n = 1, 2, \ldots$, defined as follows, see Fig. 1.

1. Let $N_i = 0$, $i \neq k$, and $N_k = 1$. For convenience, let $T_k^{(0)} = \{k^{(1)}\}$ where $k^{(1)}$ is a copy of k.
2. Let $\{i, j, \ldots\} = \partial k$, $N_i = N_j = \cdots = 1$ and $i^{(1)}, j^{(1)}, \ldots$ be copies of $i, j, \ldots$ respectively. The first computation tree $T_k^{(1)}$ consists of nodes $k^{(1)}, i^{(1)}, j^{(1)}, \ldots$ and corresponding edges $(k^{(1)}, i^{(1)})$, $(k^{(1)}, j^{(1)}), \ldots$.
3. If the n-th computation tree $T_k^{(n)}$ is defined, the next computation tree $T_k^{(n+1)}$ is defined to be $T_k^{(n)}$ augmented by new nodes and edges repeating the following steps:
   (a) For each edge $(r^{(\ell)}, s^{(m)})$ of $T_k^{(n)}$ with $r^{(\ell)} \notin T_k^{(n-1)}$, let $i, j, \ldots$, be the nodes $\partial r \backslash \{s\}$ (if non-empty).
   (b) Let $N_i \leftarrow N_i + 1, N_j \leftarrow N_j + 1, \ldots$ and $i^{(N_i)}, j^{(N_j)}, \ldots$, be new copies of $i, j, \ldots$ respectively. Add new nodes $i^{(N_i)}, j^{(N_j)}, \ldots$ and corresponding edges
   $(i^{(N_i)}, r^{(\ell)})$, $(j^{(N_j)}, r^{(\ell)}), \ldots$ to $T_k^{(n)}$.

The state space E_i is associated with each node $i^{(n)} \in T_k$ and let $\phi_{i^{(n)}j^{(m)}} = \phi_{ij}$ and $\phi_{i^{(n)}} = \phi_i$. If G has no loops, T_k is the same as G except labeling of nodes. It is easily seen that the message $m_{jk}^{(n)}(x_k)$ which is the result of the n-th BP update with the parallel update rule on G starting from k is equal to $m_{j^{(1)}k^{(1)}}^{T_k^{(n)}}(x_k)$, the result of the n-th BP update of messages performed on $T_k^{(n)}$, that is, on T_k starting from $k^{(1)}$. Therefore, the limiting message heading for k, if exists, is the same for both G and T_k, a key idea why we consider the computation trees besides the original probabilistic networks.

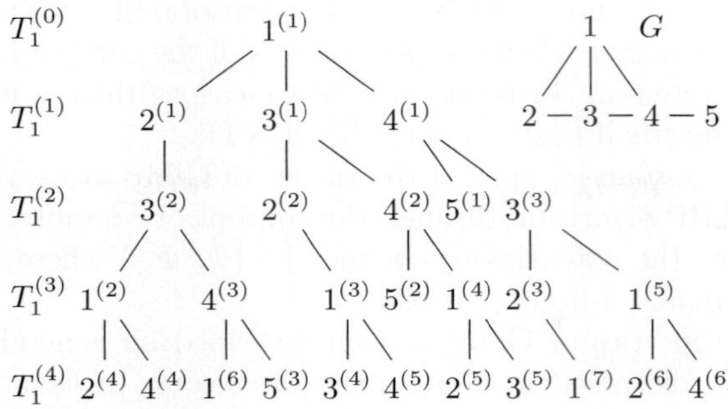

Fig. 1. A network G and the corresponding computation tree for the root node 1 with depth 4

3 Gibbs Measures and LBP Algorithm for Pair Potentials

In this section, we introduce Gibbs measure theory briefly and review the relationships with LBP algorithm.

Let S be a finite or infinite site set. A discrete and finite state space E_i is associated with each $i \in S$. A *configuration* Ω is defined by the set of all possible configurations. Specifically, $\Omega \equiv E^S = \prod_{i \in S} E_i$. Its restriction to a subset $\Lambda \subset S$ is denoted by Ω_Λ. Let $\mathfrak{I}$ be the set of non-empty finite subsets of S. A σ-field of Ω is denoted by $\mathcal{F}$. An *interaction potential* (or simply a *potential*) is a family $\Phi = (\Phi_A)_{A \in \mathfrak{I}}$ of functions $\Phi_A : \Omega \mapsto \mathbb{R}$ with the following properties; (i) for each $A \in \mathfrak{I}$, Φ_A is $\mathcal{F}_A$-measurable. Here $\mathcal{F}_A$ is the restriction of $\mathcal{F}$ to A. (ii) For all $\Lambda \in \mathfrak{I}$ and $\omega \in \Omega$, the series $\sum_{A \in \mathfrak{I}, A \cap \Lambda \neq \emptyset} \Phi_A(\omega)$ exists.

A *Gibbs specification* for a potential Φ is a system $\{\gamma_\Lambda(\cdot \mid \xi) : \Lambda \in \mathfrak{I}, \xi \in E^S\}$ of probability measures defined by

$$\gamma_\Lambda(x|\xi) = \frac{1}{Z_{\Lambda,\xi}} \exp\left\{ -\sum_{A \subset \Lambda} \Phi_A(x_A) - \sum_{A \cap \Lambda \neq \emptyset} \Phi_A(x_{A_\Lambda}, \xi_{A_{\Lambda^c}}) \right\}$$

for all $\Lambda \in \mathfrak{I}$ and $x \in E^\Lambda$, where $Z_{\Lambda,\xi}$ is the normalizing constant called the *partition function* and $A_\Lambda = A \backslash \Lambda$. The measure $\gamma_\Lambda(x \mid \xi)$ is called the *Gibbs distribution in Λ with boundary condition ξ*. It is noted that $\gamma_\Lambda(x \mid \xi)$ is dependent on ξ only through $\xi_{\partial\Lambda}$. A probability measure μ on $(E^S, \mathcal{B})$ is called a *Gibbs measure* for Φ if it satisfies the following *DLR* (*Dobrushin-Lanford-Ruelle*) equations:

$$\mu(x \mid \mathcal{B}_{S\backslash\Lambda} = \xi) = \gamma_\Lambda(x \mid \xi), \quad \xi \in E^{\partial\Lambda}, \tag{2}$$

for all $\Lambda \in \mathfrak{I}$, where $x \in E^\Lambda$ is canonically embedded into E^S as $x \times E^{S\backslash\Lambda}$. Since $\mu(x \mid \mathcal{B}_{S\backslash\Lambda}) = \mu(x \mid \mathcal{B}_{\partial\Lambda})$, such μ is also called a *Markov random field.*

It should be noted that, for a certain potential Φ, there is a possibility that the Gibbs measure μ which satisfies (2) is not unique. Let $\mathcal{G}_\Phi$ denote the set of all Gibbs measures for a potential Φ. Also, the notation $\mathcal{G}(\gamma)$ for a specification γ is often used in particular when one is conscious of the conditional probabilities rather than the potential. In terms of Gibbs measure theory, it is said that a *phase transition* occurs if $|\mathcal{G}_\Phi| > 1$ (i.e., $|\mathcal{G}(\gamma)| > 1$).

Tatikonda and Jordan [8] applied the theory of Gibbs measures to study the property of the LBP algorithm through the concept of computation tree in pair potential case, i.e., the potential Φ is defined by $\{\Phi_i, \Phi_{ij}\}$ where $\{\Phi_i\}$ and $\{\Phi_{ij}\}$ are certain 1-body and 2-body potentials.

In fact, the properties of Gibbs measures defined on general tree networks had already been discussed in Gibbs measure theory. In that discussion, the concept of *boundary law* is utilized as an important concept. Tatikonda and Jordan showed the relationship between the convergent messages and the boundary law for the associated Gibbs measure on the corresponding limit computation tree. As a result, they concluded that the uniqueness of boundary law guarantees the convergence of the LBP algorithm. They also introduced an uniqueness condition called Simon's condition of Gibbs measure theory as a convergence condition of the LBP algorithm.

Recently, Taga and Mase [7] discussed the difference of convergence ratio between so-called sequential and parallel update orders using Gibbs measure theory. In their paper, they showed sequential update order always converges faster than parallel one under the condition of absence of phase transitions. They also showed sequential update order is expected to converge faster generally through numerical experiments.

4 Comparison Between Marginal Probabilities and Beliefs

We show another application of Gibbs measure theory in this section to measure the discrepancies between marginal probabilities of probabilistic networks with pair potentials and the corresponding beliefs. First, we need to introduce some concepts which can be used for Gibbs measures on general networks. In the following, we only give a brief introductions and reviews of notations. More precisely, see Georgii [2].

Let E and $\mathcal{E}$ be some state space and the arbitrary σ-field respectively. Then $(E, \mathcal{E})$ is a measurable space. Let p_1 and p_2 be two probability measures on $(E, \mathcal{E})$. We define a distance $||p_1 - p_2||$ of p_1 and p_2 by

$$||p_1(\cdot) - p_2(\cdot)|| \equiv \max_{A \in \mathcal{E}} |p_1(A) - p_2(A)| \ .$$

It is clear that $|| \cdot ||$ is one half of total variation distance. Let S be an arbitrary (not necessarily tree) site set and Ω be a set of all possible configurations on S. Let γ be a specification on Ω. For each pair of sites $i, j \in S$, we define

$$C_{ij}(\gamma) = \sup_{\zeta, \eta \in \Omega, \zeta_{S \setminus \{j\}} = \eta_{S \setminus \{j\}}} ||\gamma_i(\cdot|\zeta) - \gamma_i(\cdot|\eta)|| \ .$$

The matrix $C(\gamma) = (C_{ij}(\gamma))_{i,j\in S}$ is called *Dobrushin's interdependence matrix* for γ. A real function f on Ω is called a *cylinder function* or a *local function* if f is $\mathcal{F}_\Lambda$-measurable for some finite Λ where $\mathcal{F}_\Lambda$ denotes the σ-field of Ω_Λ, i.e., the restriction of Ω to Λ. A function $f : \Omega \mapsto \mathbb{R}$ will be said to be *quasilocal* if there is a sequence $(f_n)_{n\geq 1}$ of local functions f_n such that $\lim_{n\to\infty} \sup_{\omega\in\Omega} |f(\omega) - f_n(\omega)| = 0$. We write $\overline{\mathcal{L}}$ for the set of all bounded quasilocal functions. Let $p(f)$ denote the expectation of f with respect to a probability p. A specification γ is said to be quasilocal if $\gamma_\Lambda(f|\cdot)$ is quasilocal for each $\Lambda \in \mathcal{I}$ and $f \in \overline{\mathcal{L}}$.

We introduce here a well-known condition for absence of phase transition. It is said that a specification γ satisfies *Dobrushin's condition* if γ is quasilocal and

$$c(\gamma) \equiv \sup_{i\in S} \sum_{j\in S} C_{ij}(\gamma) < 1 .$$

Let $f \in \overline{\mathcal{L}}$ and $j \in S$ be given. The oscillation of f at j is defined by

$$\delta_j(f) = \sup_{\zeta,\eta\in\Omega,\zeta_{S\setminus\{j\}}=\eta_{S\setminus\{j\}}} |f(\zeta) - f(\eta)| . \tag{3}$$

Let $\mathcal{F}$ be a σ-field of Ω. Then we are ready to introduce a tool used to measure discrepancy of two probability measures defined on $(\Omega, \mathcal{F})$. Let two probability measures μ and $\tilde{\mu}$ on $(\Omega, \mathcal{F})$ be given. A vector $a = (a_i)_{i\in S} \in [0,\infty)^S$ is called an *estimate for* μ *and* $\tilde{\mu}$ if

$$|\mu(f) - \tilde{\mu}(f)| \leq \sum_{j\in S} a_j \delta_j(f) \tag{4}$$

for all $f \in \overline{\mathcal{L}}$. We state two basic facts known about the estimates. First, the constant vector $a \equiv (1)_{i\in S}$ is always an estimate. Second, let fix two specifications γ and $\tilde{\gamma}$, and let $\mu \in \mathcal{G}(\gamma)$ and $\tilde{\mu} \in \mathcal{G}(\tilde{\gamma})$ be given. Suppose a is an estimate for μ and $\tilde{\mu}$. Define $\overline{a}_i$ by

$$\overline{a}_i = \sum_{j\in S} C_{ij}(\gamma) a_j + \tilde{\mu}(\beta_i) \tag{5}$$

for every $i \in S$, where $\beta_i : \Omega \to [0,\infty)$ is a measurable function such that

$$||\gamma_i(\cdot|\omega) - \tilde{\gamma}_i(\cdot|\omega)|| \leq \beta_i(\omega) . \tag{6}$$

Then $\overline{a} = (\overline{a}_i)_{i\in S}$ is an estimate for μ and $\tilde{\mu}$.

In the following, we try to derive some properties specific to the LBP algorithm. It is noted that the beliefs are, if message update converges, the marginal probabilities of a single site of an associated Gibbs measure on the corresponding computation tree [8]. On the basis of this fact, we look at a certain indicator function f as follows:

Proposition 1. *Fix $x_i \in E_i$ for some $i \in S$. Let $f : \Omega \mapsto \{0,1\}$ be defined by $f(\omega) = 1_{\{x_i\}}(\omega_i)$. Then $f \in \overline{\mathcal{L}}$, and following two corollaries hold.*

Corollary 1. *$\mu(1_{\{x_i\}})$ is the marginal probability for $X_i = x_i$,*

Corollary 2. *$\delta_j(1_{\{x_i\}}) = 1$ if $j = i$, otherwise* 0.

Proof. First corollary is trivial so that we only show the other. We write a configuration $\omega = \omega_j \omega_{S\setminus\{j\}}$ separating with respect to a site $j \in S$ and the other sites $S\setminus\{j\}$. Fix a site $i \in S$ and $x_i \in E_i$. Then we can write eq. (3) with $f(\omega) = 1_{\{x_i\}}(\omega_i)$ as

$$\begin{aligned}\delta_j(f) &= \sup_{\zeta,\eta\in\Omega\ ,\zeta_{S\setminus\{j\}}=\eta_{S\setminus\{j\}}} |f(\zeta) - f(\eta)| \\ &= \sup_{\omega\in\Omega}\sup_{x,y\in E_j} |f(x\omega_{S\setminus\{j\}}) - f(y\omega_{S\setminus\{j\}})| \\ &= \begin{cases} \sup_{x,y\in E_i} |1_{\{x_i\}}(x) - 1_{\{x_i\}}(y)| & \text{if } j = i\ , \\ \sup_{\omega_j\in E_j} |1_{\{x_i\}}(\omega_j) - 1_{\{x_i\}}(\omega_j)| & \text{otherwise}\ , \end{cases} \\ &= \begin{cases} 1 \text{ if } j = i\ , \\ 0 \text{ otherwise}\ . \end{cases}\end{aligned}$$

The proof is thus complete. □

We think of μ and $\tilde{\mu}$ shown above as the probability of a target probability and the associated Gibbs measure and try to measure the discrepancy between their marginal probabilities. The following two propositions are necessary for this.

Proposition 2. *Let G be the network of a probabilistic network and T be the associated computation tree. Assume G' is the network such that $G' = \{i^{(1)}; i \in G\}$ and G' has an edge between $i^{(1)}$ and $j^{(1)}$ if there exists an edge between i and j in G. Then one can construct a certain network S such that $G' \subset S$ and $T \subset S$. We will call S a common space of G and T.*

Proof. Let B_T denote the edge set of T. There exist edges such that $k^{(1)}l^{(n)}$ for $n \geq 2$ in B_T, i.e., the neighboring sites such that one of it has 1 as superscript and another has $n > 1$ as superscript. For every such $k^{(1)}l^{(n)}$, if $k^{(1)}l^{(1)} \notin B_T$, add $k^{(1)}l^{(1)}$ to B_T. The resulting site set (T, B_T) is the common space S. □

We give an example of a common space in Figure 2.

Proposition 3. *Suppose the joint distribution p of a probabilistic network (G, p) has the form (1). Let $\Phi_i = \log\phi_i$, $\Phi_{ij} = \log\phi_{ij}$ for $i, j \in G$. Let B_G, B_T be the edge set of G and the corresponding computation tree T. We define two interaction potentials Φ and $\tilde{\Phi}$ for the common space S of G and T as follows.*

$$\begin{aligned}\Phi \equiv &\{\Phi_{i^{(1)}} = \Phi_i; i \in G\} \cup \{\Phi_{i^{(1)}j^{(1)}} = \Phi_{ij}; ij \in B_G\} \\ &\cup\{\Phi_{i^{(k)}} = \Phi_{i^{(k)}j^{(l)}} = 0; k \text{ or } l \geq 2\}\ , \\ \tilde{\Phi} \equiv &\{\tilde{\Phi}_{i'} = \Phi_i; i' \in T\} \cup \{\tilde{\Phi}_{i'j'} = \Phi_{ij}; i'j' \in B_T\} \cup \{\tilde{\Phi}_{i'j'} = 0; i'j' \notin B_T\}\ ,\end{aligned}$$

where ij stands for the edge between i and j. Then the systems of conditional probabilities for Φ and $\tilde{\Phi}$ are the Gibbs specifications defined on S.

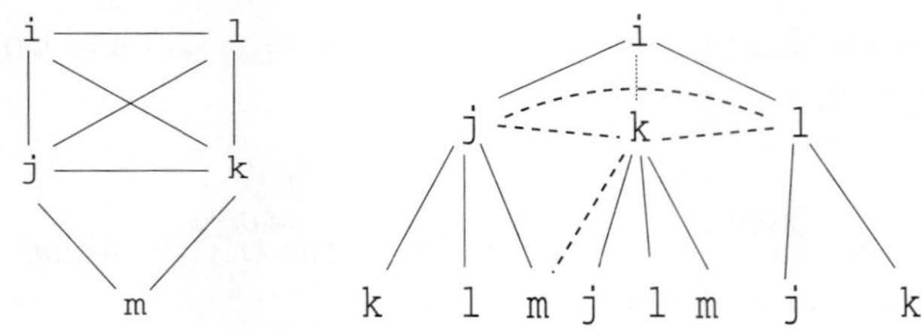

Fig. 2. A network G (left) and the common space S (right) with depth 2 from the root node i. The superscripts of the indices in S are ignored. Dotted lines correspond to the lines added to the computation tree T in the construction of S.

It should be noted that the transformation of potentials makes no difference to the marginal probabilities for original space; in particular, for $\mu \in \mathcal{G}(\Phi)$ and $\tilde{\mu} \in \mathcal{G}(\tilde{\Phi})$, $\mu(x_i)$ and $\tilde{\mu}(x_i)$ for each $i \in G'$ are equal to $p(x_i)$ of the target probability and the corresponding belief (if exists) respectively.

We let γ and $\tilde{\gamma}$ denote the specifications for above Φ and $\tilde{\Phi}$ respectively. γ and $\tilde{\gamma}$ have the following property.

Corollary 3. *There exists a non-empty set S' of indices $i \in S$ such that*

$$\gamma_i(x_i|\omega) = \tilde{\gamma}_i(x_i|\omega) \tag{7}$$

for all $x_i \in E_i$ and $\omega \in \Omega$.

Proof. In deed, the node in S corresponds to the root node of the computation tree is such a site. The other $i \in S$ can be such a site if i is originated from G and all the edges connecting with i in S are originated from both T and G. Each such site can be shown to satisfy (7) by direct calculations of conditional probabilities of two specifications. □

According to the above property, it is clear that

$$||\gamma_i(\cdot|\omega) - \tilde{\gamma}_i(\cdot|\omega)|| = 0, i \in S' ,$$

for all $\omega \in \Omega$. Thus we can put $\beta_i(\cdot) \equiv 0$ in (6) for each $i \in S'$. We are now ready to give the following results.

Theorem 1. *Let $b_i(\cdot)$ be a convergent belief for $i \in G$ of a probabilistic network (G, p). Let γ be the specification corresponding to the probabilistic network and $C(\gamma)$ be the Dobrushin's interdependence matrix for γ. Define $c_i(\gamma) = \sum_{j \in G} C_{ij}(\gamma)$. Then*

$$|p(x_i) - b_i(x_i)| \leq \min\{1, c_i(\gamma)\}$$

for all $x_i \in E_i$.

Proof. We consider the computation tree T with the root node i. Suppose S is the common space of G and T. Let $\tilde{\gamma}$ be the specification corresponding to the associated computation tree. Let $\mathcal{G}(\tilde{\gamma})$ be the set of all Gibbs measures for $\tilde{\gamma}$ and fix a Gibbs measure $\tilde{\mu} \in \mathcal{G}(\tilde{\gamma})$ for $\tilde{\gamma}$. With $f(\omega) = 1_{\{x_i\}}(\omega_i)$ and Corollary 2, we can write eq. (4) as

$$|\mu(1_{\{x_i\}}) - \tilde{\mu}(1_{\{x_i\}})| \leq a_i \ .$$

for some Gibbs measure $\mu \in \mathcal{G}(\gamma)$ for γ. Using the trivial estimate $a = (1)_{i \in S}$, we can obtain $\overline{a}_i$ from eq. (5) as

$$\overline{a}_i = \sum_{j \in S} C_{ij}(\gamma) + \tilde{\mu}(\beta_i) = \sum_{j \in G'} C_{ij}(\gamma) = c_i(\gamma) \ .$$

Here we took $\beta_i(\omega) \equiv 0$ since i is the root node of computation tree. The second equation comes from the fact that $C_{ij}(\gamma) = 0$ for i, j, such that $i \not\sim j$ for γ, and i is the site at which (7) is satisfied. It should be noted that a' such that $a'_i \equiv \min\{a_i, \overline{a}_i\} = \min\{1, c_i(\gamma)\}$ and $a'_k \equiv 1$ for $k \neq i$ is also an estimate. The marginal probabilities μ and $\tilde{\mu}$ are in fact that of p and the belief for the node corresponding to root node respectively. Thus the proof is complete. □

If there is at least one site i such that $c_i(\gamma) < 1$, its factor of an estimate a_i can be taken less than 1. On the other hand, when a site j has a neighbor i such that $a_i < 1$, its factor of the estimate a_j may be taken less than 1 even if $c_j(\gamma) \geq 1$ using (5) with $a_i < 1$. Conversely, if a_j decreases, a_i becomes smaller using (5) with a_j again. Such a mutual improvement can be utilized below.

Corollary 4. *Let γ and $\tilde{\gamma}$ be the specifications corresponding to a probabilistic network and the corresponding computation tree defined on a certain common space respectively. Let $C(\gamma)$ be the Dobrushin's independence matrix for the specification γ and $\tilde{\mu} \in \mathcal{G}(\tilde{\gamma})$. Let $a^{(n)} = (a_i^{(n)})_{i \in S}, n = 1, 2, \ldots,$. be defined by*

$$a_i^{(n+1)} = \min\{1, a_i^{(n)}, (C(\gamma)a^{(n)} + \tilde{\mu}(\beta))_i\}, \ i \in S \ , \tag{8}$$

where $a_i^{(0)} = 1, i \in S$, and $\tilde{\mu}(\beta) = (\tilde{\mu}(\beta_i))_{i \in S}$. Then $a^{(n)}$ has a limit a^* and each error bound between the marginal probability and the belief for i is given by a_i^*.

Proof. For each i, $a_i^{(n)}$ clearly does not increase with n. It is also clear that $a_i^{(n)}$ has a lower bound 0 since $a_i^{(0)} = 1$, $i \in S$, and all factors of $C(\gamma)$ and $\tilde{\mu}(\beta)$ are non-negative. Then $a^{(n)}$ has a limit. The result follows from the fact that each $a^{(n)}$ can be an estimate. □

5 Numerical Experiments

In the preceding section, we showed error bounds between marginal probabilities and the corresponding beliefs. In this section, we give numerical experiments so as to see the effectiveness of error bounds based on Theorem 1 and Corollary 4.

We now use following *Ising models* on complete graph with four vertices.

$$p(x) \propto \exp\left(h \sum_{i=1,2,3,4} x_i + J \sum x_i x_j\right)$$

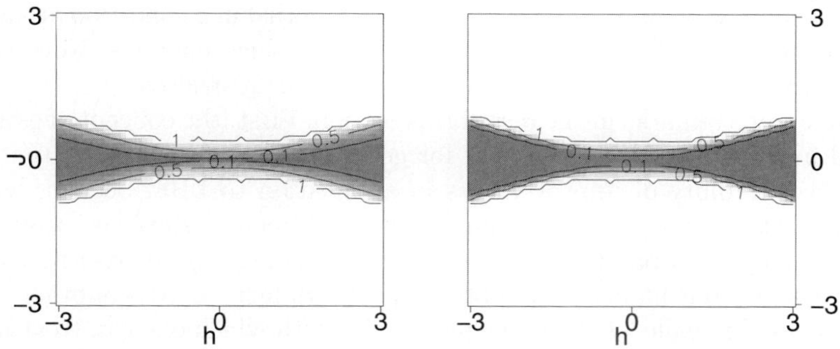

Fig. 3. Error bounds between one-variable marginal probabilities and the corresponding beliefs for Ising models on the complete graph network with four vertices. The left (right) figure is obtained using Theorem 1 (Corollary 4). Contours are imposed.

Here the second summation is taken with respect to all pairs of $\{1, 2, 3, 4\}$. The corresponding computation tree is called the *Cayley tree* of degree 2 in Gibbs measure theory and the associated Gibbs measures are Ising models on it. Let $CT(2)$ denote the Cayley tree of degree 2. For Ising models on Cayley trees, all factors of the Dobrushin's interdependence matrix are same and it is easy to calculate. In particular, for $CT(2)$, the constant $c(h, J)$ for each h, J is written by

$$C_{ij}(\gamma) = \frac{\sinh(2|J|)}{g(h,J) + \cosh(2J)} \equiv c(h,J) \ ,$$

where $g(x, y) = \cosh 2(|x| + |y|)$ if $|x| \le |y|$, otherwise $\cosh 2(|x| - 2|y|)$. Then $c_i(\gamma)$ shown in Theorem 1 will be $3c(h, J)$. In calculation of (8), we need to fix $\beta(\omega) = (\beta_i(\omega))_{i \in CT(2)}$ and to obtain the expectation $\tilde{\mu}(\beta) = (\tilde{\mu}(\beta_i))_{i \in CT(2)}$. The left side of (6) is clearly bounded by 1, so that we put here $\beta_i(\omega) \equiv 1$ for each i. Then all the factors of the expectation $\tilde{\mu}(\beta)$ will be 1; we use this in calculation of (8). In Fig. 3, we summarize the results.

Let $B_{h,J}$, $B^*_{h,J}$ be the error bounds obtained based on Theorem 1 and Corollary 4 for each (h, J) respectively. For all h and J, it is shown that $B^*_{h,J} \le B_{h,J}$. This means that the use of (8) are effective for obtaining better results in this case. Nevertheless, seen from the experimental results for Ising models reported in [7], the region where one can get the good error bound is restrictive. It should be noted that the region (J, h) where $B_{h,J} < 1$ is very close to the region where Dobrushin's condition is satisfied.

6 Conclusion and Remarks

We applied Gibbs measure theory to LBP algorithm with pair potentials to obtain error bounds between marginal probabilities and the corresponding beliefs. We showed a nontrivial error bound can be obtained under a certain condition for each site if the algorithm converged. We also gave a procedure which has a potential for improving the error bounds. We gave numerical experiments to check the effectiveness. In some cases, such as Dobrushin's condition is satisfied, the error bounds and the improvement procedure seem effective. Nevertheless, the region where one can obtain good bounds seems restrictive.

We give some remarks in the rest of this section. First, the concept of estimates we used in this paper was developed for general Gibbs measures, so that there may be a possibility of improvements in application to LBP. Second, we used 1 as the factors of $\tilde{\mu}(\beta)$ in the numerical experiments. However, the precise assessment of $\tilde{\mu}(\beta)$ surely has an influence for obtaining a good error bound. The last remark is about higher-order potential case. In fact, there is another version of LBP algorithm called *LBP on factor graphs*, with which one can treat higher-order potentials. Similar to the pair potential case introduced in this paper, one can think the concept of computation trees for LBP on factor graphs. Under the computation tree for LBP on factor graphs, the result shown in this paper would be valid for probability function with higher-order potentials.

References

1. Frey, B. J.: Graphical Models for Pattern Classification, Data Compression and Channel Coding, MIT press, Cambridge (1998).
2. Georgii, H. -O.: Gibbs Measures and Phase Transitions, Walter de Gruyter, Berlin · New York (1988).
3. Jensen, F.: An Introduction to Bayesian Networks, UCL Press, London (1996).
4. McEliece, R. J., MacKay, D. J. C., Cheng, J. F.: Turbo Decoding as an Instance of Pearl's "Belief Propagation" Algorithm, IEEE Journal on Selected Areas in Communication, **16(2)** Springer Verlag, New York, Berlin, Heidelberg (1998) 140-152.
5. Murphy, K. P., Weiss, Y., Jordan, M. I.: Loopy belief propagation for approximate inference: an empirical study, Proc. of the 15th Conf. on Unc. in Art. Int., Morgan Kaufmann, San Francisco (1999) 467-475.
6. Pearl, J.: Probabilistic Reasoning in Intelligent Systems: Networks of Plausible Inference, Morgan Kaufmann, San Francisco (1988).
7. Taga, N., Mase, S.: On the Convergence of Loopy Belief Propagation Algorithm for Different Update Rules. IEICE transactions on Fundamentals of Electronics, Communications and Computer Sciences, Vol.E89-(2), Tokyo (2006) 575-582.
8. Tatikonda, S. C., Jordan, M. I.: Loopy Belief Propagation and Gibbs Measures, Proc. of the 18th Conf. on Unc. in Art. Int., Morgan Kaufmann, San Francisco (2002) 493-500.
9. Weiss, Y.: Correctness of Local Probability Propagation in Graphical Models with Loops, Neur. Comp., vol.12, (2000) 1-41.
10. Weiss, Y., Freeman, W. T.: Correctness of Belief Propagation in Gaussian Graphical Models of Arbitrary Topology, Neur. Comp., vol.12, (2001) 2173-2200.

Applications of Gibbs Measure Theory to Loopy Belief Propagation Algorithm

Nobuyuki Taga and Shigeru Mase

Tokyo Institute of Technology, Ookayama 2-12-1-w8-28,
Meguro-ku, Tokyo 152-8552, Japan
{Nobuyuki.Taga, mase}@is.titech.ac.jp

Abstract. In this paper, we pursue application of Gibbs measure theory to LBP in two ways. First, we show this theory can be applied directly to LBP for factor graphs, where one can use higher-order potentials. Consequently, we show beliefs are just marginal probabilities for a certain Gibbs measure on a computation tree. We also give a convergence criterion using this tree. Second, to see the usefulness of this approach, we apply a well-known general condition and a special one, which are developed in Gibbs measure theory, to LBP. We compare these two criteria and another criterion derived by the best present result. Consequently, we show that the special condition is better than the others and also show the general condition is better than the best present result when the influence of one-body potentials is sufficiently large. These results surely encourage the use of Gibbs measure theory in this area.

1 Introduction

Inference problems using graphical models are important in various application fields. The belief propagation (BP) algorithm is an efficient method for computing marginal probabilities of probabilistic networks without loops. BP can be formally applied also to networks with loops (LBP). However, if networks have loops, the algorithm may not converge and beliefs may not equal to exact marginal probabilities. Nevertheless, applications of LBP algorithm have been reported to be remarkably useful such as in the coding theory [1,4,6].

In analysis of LBP, Tatikonda and Jordan [8] applied Gibbs measure theory using the concept of computation trees, which was first introduced by Weiss [9]. They also gave a sufficient convergence criterion based on Simon's condition of Gibbs measure theory. Nevertheless, to use this theory seems not to be so popular.

In this paper, we pursue Gibbs measure approach. This paper is composed of two parts. First, we show that this theory can directly be applied to general potentials case. The concept of computation tree is important to apply Gibbs measure theory to LBP. However, it is discussed only for pair potential case and it is still unclear how to construct it where higher-order potentials exist. We give a construction of computation trees according to the LBP for factor graphs. Second, we show the effectiveness of Gibbs measure approach. Tatikonda and Jordan derived a criterion based on Simon's condition of Gibbs measures theory

A. Gelbukh and C.A. Reyes-Garcia (Eds.): MICAI 2006, LNAI 4293, pp. 197–207, 2006.

in their paper. However, Ihler et al. [3] and Mooij and Kappen [5] independently proposed stronger conditions than it. In this paper, we apply a well-known condition called Dobrushin's condition and compare the convergence criteria derived from this and Ihler's and Mooij's approaches for Ising models on complete graphs. This model has only pair potentials. However, it is remarkable since the complete characterization of the phase transition region of the associated Gibbs measure is known. We also use the convergence criterion derived from this characterization to compare.

In Sect. 2, we review the LBP algorithm on factor graphs and derive its computation tree. We also give some results using Gibbs measure theory with the computation tree. In Sect. 3, we compare three LBP convergence criteria for Ising models. We give a conclusion in Sect. 4. In Appendix, we show how to check Dobrushin's condition for Ising models on complete graphs.

2 LBP Algorithm on Factor Graphs and Its Computation Trees

To analyze LBP algorithm, Tatikonda and Jordan [8] utilize *Gibbs measure theory.* This theory deals with so-called Gibbs measures, defined on a set of infinite nodes. Its main concern is to investigate the phase transition phenomenon. They used the concept of computation tree, which was first introduced by Weiss [9], to connect LBP algorithm with Gibbs measure theory.

In their paper, they discussed mainly about the BP algorithm for pair potentials. On the other hand, if there exists higher-order potentials, the concept of computation trees is never clear. It should be noted that conversion of higher-order potential case into pair potential case may have the validity of the application of Gibbs measure theory become uncertain since the assumption of the positivity of the probability function is not necessarily preserved. For example, see [9]. In this section, we look at the BP algorithm for factor graphs, with which one can use probability functions with general potentials, and investigate how to construct its computation trees. We also give some results applying Gibbs measure theory with the computation tree.

2.1 BP Algorithm on Factor Graphs

Let consider a network on the node set $\{1, 2, \ldots, n\}$ and an associated set of random variables $X = \{X_1, X_2, \ldots, X_n\}$. Assume that each state space E_i of X_i is discrete and finite. We consider a target probability function for X which is factorized as follows:

$$p(x) = \frac{1}{Z} \prod_{A \in \mathbb{A}} f_A(x_A) ,$$

where $f_A : E^A \mapsto (0, \infty)$ denotes a positive and non-constant finite function on $E^A = \prod_{i \in A} E_i$ and $\mathbb{A}$ is *factor set* which is a collection of non-empty subsets of

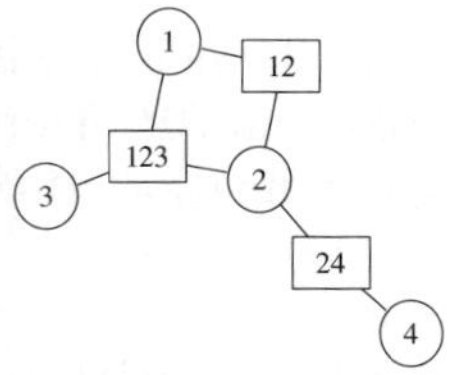

Fig. 1. A factor graph for $p(x_1, x_2, x_3, x_4) \propto f_{\{1,2\}}(x_1, x_2) f_{\{1,2,3\}}(x_1, x_2, x_3) f_{\{2,4\}}(x_2, x_4)$

$\{1, 2, \ldots, n\}$. Throughout this paper, Z stands for normalizing constants and are not always the same. A *factor graph* is an undirected graph associated with X and $\mathbb{A}$. A factor graph has two kinds of nodes; *variable nodes* and *factor nodes*. A variable node i and a factor node A are associated with the random variable X_i and the function f_A respectively. An edge is drawn between a variable node i and a factor node A if $i \in A$. We assume that no node is isolated. As an example, the factor graph corresponding to the probability function

$$p(x_1, \ldots, x_4) \propto f_A(x_1, x_2) f_B(x_1, x_2, x_3) f_C(x_2, x_4) ,$$

where $A = \{1, 2\}$, $B = \{1, 2, 3\}$ and $C = \{2, 4\}$ is shown in Fig. 1. Variable (resp. factor) nodes are represented by circles (resp. squares). The neighbors of a variable node i is $\{A \in \mathbb{A} : i \in A\}$ and is denoted by ∂i, and those of a factor node A is $\{i : i \in A\}$, i.e., A itself. Two kinds of *messages* are used in BP algorithm for factor graphs. They are defined reciprocally as follows:

$$n_{i\to A}^{(t+1)}(x_i) \equiv \frac{1}{Z} \prod_{C \sim \partial i \setminus \{A\}} m_{C\to i}^{(t)}(x_i) \tag{1}$$

$$m_{A\to i}^{(t+1)}(x_i) \equiv \frac{1}{Z} \sum_{x_{A\setminus\{i\}}} f_A(x_A) \prod_{j\in A} n_{j\to A}^{(t)}(x_j) \tag{2}$$

for each step $t = 0, 1, 2, \ldots$ and $x_i \in E_i$. We assume in this paper $n_{i\to A}^{(0)}(\cdot) = m_{A\to i}^{(0)}(\cdot) \equiv 1$ for convenience. Actually any initializations which are positive are possible. If messages $n_{i\to A}^{(t)}(\cdot)$ and $m_{A\to i}^{(t)}(\cdot)$ converge, the limits are denoted by $n_{i\to A}(\cdot)$ and $m_{A\to i}(\cdot)$. For these limit messages, the belief for each variable node i is defined by the normalized product:

$$b_i(x_i) = \frac{1}{Z} \prod_{A\in\partial i} m_{A\to i}(x_i), \quad x_i \in E_i . \tag{3}$$

Beliefs for a set of variable nodes can also be defined. In particular, the belief for variables associated with a factor node A (briefly, belief for a factor node A) is defined as follows:

$$b_A(x_A) = \frac{1}{Z} f_A(x_A) \prod_{i\in A} n_{i\to A}(x_i), \; x_A \in E^A . \tag{4}$$

If the factor graph has no loops, the beliefs will be exact marginal probabilities. If the factor graph has loops, the BP algorithm is still applicable and is reported to give often a good approximation. However, whether it converges or not becomes uncertain.

2.2 Computation Trees for BP Algorithm on Factor Graphs

In this section, we construct the computation trees for the BP on factor graphs corresponding to the BP update rules (1) and (2). In the construction of the computation tree of the BP for pair potentials, each node added to a computation tree as a message is updated is associated with a variable to be summed in the message update relation. It is similar for the factor graph case.

In order to construct the computation tree for the factor graph case, we first eliminate $n_{i\to A}(x_i)$ messages and rewrite the message update relations only by $m_{A\to i}(x_i)$ messages. Substituting $n_{i\to A}(x_i)$ messages for $m_{A\to i}(x_i)$ messages in (2), we have

$$m_{A\to i}^{(t+1)}(x_i) \propto \sum_{x_{A\setminus\{i\}}} f_A(x_A) \prod_{j\in A} \prod_{C\sim\partial j\setminus\{A\}} m_{C\to j}^{(t-1)}(x_j) .$$

According to this relation, we can construct the computation tree for the BP on factor graphs which can be summarized as the following proposition.

Proposition 1. *Let G be a factor graph and V_G and F_G be the set of variable nodes and factor nodes respectively. The computation tree T_k for a belief $b(x_k)$, $k \in V_G$, is constructed as follows:*

- *let $N_i = 0$, $i \neq k$, and $N_k = 1$. For convenience, let $T_k^{(0)} = \{k^{(0)}\}$ where $k^{(0)}$ is a copy of k.*
- *Let $\{A_1, A_2, \ldots\} = \partial k$, $C_i = A_i\setminus\{k\}$. The m-th node of $T_k^{(1)}$ is composed of $T_k^{(0)}$ and C_m in the following way. Let $C_m = \{i, j, \ldots\}$ and $N_i \leftarrow N_i{+}1, N_j \leftarrow N_j+1, \ldots$. Add $A' = \{i^{(N_i)}, j^{(N_j)}, \ldots\}$ as a multi-state variable node to $T_k^{(0)}$ with the corresponding edge $(k^{(1)}, A')$ where $i^{(N_i)}, j^{(N_j)}, \ldots$ are the copies of $i, j, \ldots$ respectively. Let $S_{\{k^{(1)}\}A'} = \{k\}$.*
- *If the t-th computation tree $T_k^{(t)}$ is defined, the next computation tree $T_k^{(t+1)}$ is defined to be $T_k^{(t)}$ augmented by new nodes and edges repeating the following steps:*
  - *For each edge (A, A') of $T_k^{(t)}$ with $A \notin T_k^{(t-1)}$, let $A = \{i^{(N_i)}, j^{(N_j)}, \ldots\}$ and $S_A = \{s\}$.*
  - *For each element $i^{(N_i)} \in A$, let $\partial i = \{C_1, C_2, \ldots\}$ where $C_k \cup \{i\}, k = 1, 2, \ldots$ are elements of F_G except $\{s\} \cup A$. Add the k-th node and edge associated with $i^{(N_i)}$ as follows. Let $C_k = \{h, j, \ldots\}$ and $N_h \leftarrow N_h + 1, N_j \leftarrow N_j{+}1, \ldots$. Add the new copies $\{h^{(N_h)}, j^{(N_j)}, \ldots\}$ as a multi-state variable node A'' and the corresponding edge (A, A'') and let $S_{AA''} = \{i\}$*

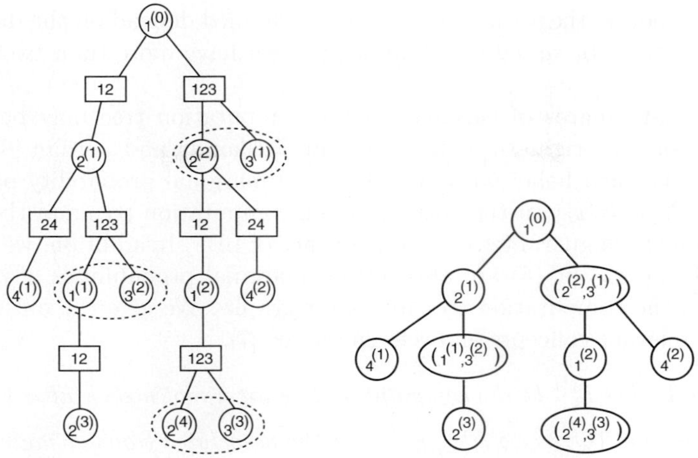

Fig. 2. Construction of the computation tree for the factor graph in Fig. 1 up to a few updates. The computation tree with factor nodes (left) and the computation tree (right). (i, j) indicates that the variable of the corresponding node has the compound state space $x_{(i,j)} \equiv (x_i, x_j) \in E_i \times E_j$.

The potential functions for the corresponding Gibbs measure are defined such that $\phi_{AC} = -\log f_{(S_{AC}) \cup C'}$ where C' is the set of index of C which are stripped of superscripts. For example, in Fig. 2,

$$\phi_{\{2^{(1)}\}\{1^{(1)},3^{(2)}\}}(x_1, x_2, x_3) = -\log f_{\{1,2,3\}}(x_1, x_2, x_3) \ ,$$
$$\phi_{\{2^{(2)},3^{(1)}\}\{4^{(2)}\}}(x_2, x_3, x_4) = -\log f_{\{2,4\}}(x_2, x_4) \ .$$

As is seen from the BP relation (5), one node added to the computation tree may be multi-state (i.e., a product of certain states) which is associated with $A \backslash \{i\}$ for some $i \in A$. That is, the state space is $E^{A \backslash \{i\}}$. In the following, we sometimes use Greek letters like α for expressing nodes on computation trees for factor graphs.

To ease the construction of the computation trees for factor graphs, it is helpful to draw the computation tree with factor nodes at first, which is similar to that of the BP for pair potentials where factor nodes are temporarily regarded as variable nodes. We give an example in Fig. 2

When a probability function has only two variable functions the computation tree for factor graph case is equivalent to the one for pair potential case discussed in [8]. In that case, in particular, $n_{i \to a}$ messages are equivalent to *boundary laws* of corresponding Gibbs measure, see [2].

It should be noted that unlike the pair potential case, the topology of the computation tree for a factor graph may depend on the choice of the root node. The topology of computation tree is related to the convergence property of message updates since it is sometimes related to the absence condition of phase transition. The reason for the dependency comes from the fact that, in the m message update, the set of variables to be summed depend on the direction of the m message to be updated if functions which have more than two variables are used.

Even if state spaces of variables in the computation tree may be different from those of the original graph, results in Tatikonda and Jordan [8] are also valid. That is, each belief $b_i(x_i)$ of (3) is the marginal probability of a Gibbs measure $\mu(X_{i^{(1)}} = x_i)$ on the corresponding computation tree and the absence of phase transition guarantees the convergence of LBP. In addition, we can show that beliefs $b_A(x_A)$ of (4) are also certain marginal probabilities of the Gibbs measure on the computation tree for factor graphs. We give the outline of the proof. For relevant concepts and references, see [7].

Corollary 1. *Let $T_k^{(t)}$ be the computation tree for a root node k after t message-update steps, and $\{Q_{ij}(x_i, x_j)\}_{i,j,E_i \times E_j}$ be the associated transfer matrices. $\ell_{ij}^{T_k^{(t)}} \in [0, \infty)^{E_i}$ denotes the boundary law for each adjacent sites i, $j \in T_k^{(t)}$ and the state space E_i, then*

$$m_{ik}^{(t)}(x_k) \propto \sum_{x_i \in E_i} \ell_{ik}^{T_k^{(t)}}(x_i) Q_{ik}(x_i, x_k)$$

for all neighboring node i of k and $x_k \in E_k$. If no phase transition occurs, there exists an unique boundary law $\ell_{ij}(x_i)$ such that $\ell_{ij}^{T_k^{(t)}}(x_i) \to \ell_{ij}(x_i)$ as $t \to \infty$. Therefore, using the limit boundary law,

$$m_{ik}^{(t)}(x_k) \to m_{ik}(x_k) \equiv \frac{1}{Z} \sum_{x_i} \ell_{ik}(x_i) Q_{ik}(x_i, x_k)$$

as $t \to \infty$.

Proof. See [7].

Proposition 2. *For each $i \in A \in \mathbb{A}$, there exists a node β adjacent to the root node $\{i^{(0)}\}$ in the computation tree for i such that $\beta = \{j : j$ is a copy of $A \backslash \{i\}\}$. Let $\alpha = \{\{i^{(0)}\}, \beta\}$ and $\partial\alpha = \partial i^{(0)} \cup \partial\beta \backslash \{i^{(0)}, \beta\}$. Then, if no phase transition occurs, the belief $b_A(x_A)$ defined by (4) is a marginal probability of the unique Gibbs measure on the computation tree.*

Proof. If no phase transition occurs there exists an unique Gibbs measure μ on the computation tree and

$$\begin{aligned}\mu(x_\alpha) &= \sum_{x_{\partial\alpha}} \mu(x_{\alpha \cup \partial\alpha}) \propto \sum_{x_{\partial\alpha}} f_A(x_\alpha) \prod_{\kappa \in \partial\alpha} \ell_{\kappa\kappa'}(x_\kappa) f_{\kappa\kappa'}(x_\kappa, x_{\kappa'}) \\ &= f_A(x_\alpha) \prod_{\kappa \in \partial\alpha} \sum_{x_\kappa} \ell_{\kappa\kappa'}(x_\kappa) f_{\kappa\kappa'}(x_\kappa, x_{\kappa'}) \\ &\propto f_A(x_\alpha) \prod_{\kappa \in \partial\alpha} m_{\kappa\kappa'}(x_{\kappa'}) , \end{aligned} \tag{5}$$

where (5) comes from Gibbs measure theory and (5) comes from Corollary 1. Here κ' is $\{i^{(0)}\}$ or β, which is adjacent to κ. After some tiresome check of the correspondence between messages on the computation tree and original m and n messages on the factor graph, it can be shown that

$$\mu(x_A) \propto f_A(x_A) \prod_{i \in A} n_{i \to A}(x_i) \, .$$

Thus the proposition is complete. □

The above convergence criterion is based on the phase transition property of the associated Gibbs measure on the computation tree. In the factor graph case, since the topology of computation trees may depend on the choice of a root node, even the application of *Simon's condition* is not straightforward. We show a procedure how to check Simon's condition for the factor graph case.

Proposition 3. *For the LBP algorithm on factor graphs, the convergence condition based on Simon's condition can be checked as follows:*

STEP 0: Let G be the index set of random variables and let $M = m = 0$. Go to STEP 1.
STEP 1: If G is empty, break and return M. Otherwise, fix a factor i in G, let $\mathbb{A}_i = \{A \in \mathbb{A} : i \in A\}$ and go to STEP 2.
STEP 2: If $\mathbb{A}_i$ is empty, $G \leftarrow G \setminus \{i\}$ and go to STEP 1. Otherwise, fix a factor A in $\mathbb{A}$, $m \leftarrow m + \delta(f_A)$ where $\delta(f_A)$ is the oscillation of the function f_A and go to STEP 3.
STEP 3: If $A \setminus \{i\}$ is empty, $\mathbb{A}_i \leftarrow \mathbb{A}_i \setminus \{A\}$, $M \leftarrow \max\{M, m\}$, $m \leftarrow 0$ and go to STEP 2. Otherwise, fix a factor b in $A \setminus \{i\}$, let $\mathbb{A}_b = \{A \in \mathbb{A} : b \in A\}$ and go to STEP 4.
STEP 4: If $\mathbb{A}_b \setminus \{A\}$ is empty, $A \leftarrow A \setminus \{b\}$ and go to STEP 3. Otherwise, fix a factor c in $\mathbb{A}_b \setminus \{A\}$, $m \leftarrow m + \delta(f_c)$, $\mathbb{A}_b \leftarrow \mathbb{A}_b \setminus \{c\}$ and go to STEP 4.

If the $M < 2$, the LBP algorithm converges. □

3 Comparison of Three Convergence Criteria

In this section, we compare LBP convergence criteria due to two approaches, including the one derived from Dobrushin's condition, in order to see their effectiveness. As shown in the previous chapter, Gibbs measure approach is still useful for LBP with general potentials through factor graphs. On the other hand, it is generally difficult to characterize the phase transition region (i.e., a certain parameter region) precisely. One remarkable exception is *Ising models on Cayley trees*; Its complete characterization are known. It is noted that a Cayley tree is a certain computation tree of a complete graph. For this reason, we use Ising models on a complete graph as a target probabilistic network for comparing two approaches, nevertheless Ising models have only pair potentials so that it does not have to be expressed by factor graphs any longer.

For given parameters J and $h \in \mathbb{R}$, the Ising model is defined by

$$p(x) \propto \exp\Big(h\sum_i x_i + J\sum_{i\sim j} x_i x_j\Big)$$

where $x_i \in \{-1,1\}$ for all $i \in G$ and $\sim$ means the neighbor relation. For a complete graph, the corresponding computation tree is called a Cayley tree or *Bethe lattice*. Let $d+2$ be the number of vertex of the complete graph. We assume $d \geq 2$. In fact, for Ising models, the convergence conditions derived from Ihler's and Mooij's approaches are same such as

$$d \tanh|J| < 1 \,. \tag{6}$$

This is the best criterion at present. Their approaches do not rely on Gibbs measures and may be valid even when phase transition occurs. The criterion based on Dobrushin's condition becomes

$$\frac{(d+1)\sinh(2|J|)}{g(h,J)+\cosh(2J)} < 1 \,, \tag{7}$$

where

$$g(x,y) = \min_{z_i \in \{-1,1\}, i=1,\ldots,d} \cosh 2\Big(x + y\sum_{i=1}^{d} z_i\Big) \,.$$

Dobrushin's condition is not so simple to verify. We give a derivation of this criterion at length in Appendix.

For Ising models on Cayley trees, there is the following complete condition for the lack or existence of phase transitions is known, see [2] for details. Let $J(d) = \operatorname{arccoth}(d) = \frac{1}{2}\log\frac{d+1}{d-1}$, and

$$h(J,d) \equiv \begin{cases} 0 & \text{if } |J| \leq J(d) \,, \\ d \operatorname{arctanh}\Big(\frac{dw-1}{d/w-1}\Big)^{1/2} - \operatorname{arctanh}\Big(\frac{d-1/w}{d-w}\Big)^{1/2} & \text{if } J > J(d) \,, \\ d \operatorname{arctanh}\Big(\frac{dw-1}{d/w-1}\Big)^{1/2} + \operatorname{arctanh}\Big(\frac{d-1/w}{d-w}\Big)^{1/2} & \text{if } J < -J(d) \,, \end{cases}$$

where $w = \tanh|J|$. The phase transition region (the set of parameters where the phase transition occurs) consists of the *ferromagnetic (antiferromagnetic) phase transition region* F (AF) defined by

$$(F)\ d > 1,\ J > J(d),\ |h| \leq h(J,d) \,,$$
$$(AF)\ d > 1,\ J < -J(d),\ |h| < h(J,d) \,.$$

Leftmost figure in Fig. 3 shows F and AF regions for $d = 2$. The region AF is open. The region F includes its boundary except for the singular point $(h,J) = (0, J(d))$. The region other than F and AF is the LBP convergence region.

In Fig. 3, we also give other two LBP convergence regions derived from Dobrushin's and Ihler's and Mooij's. Also we show these regions together.

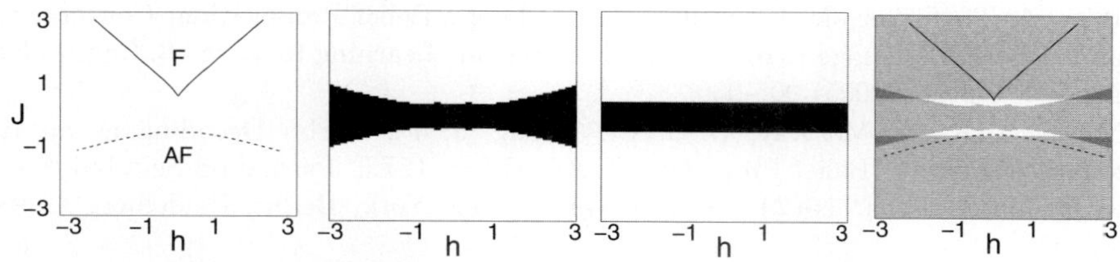

Fig. 3. Convergence regions derived from the complete characterization and Dobrushin's, and Ihler's (Mooij's) conditions (left to right). The region other than F and AF is that of the complete characterization, and black regions are those of Dobrushin's and Ihler's. The rightmost figure shows these regions together with the boundary curves of F and AF. Difference sets of Dobrushin's and Ihler's (Mooij's) regions are represented in white and dark gray.

It should be noted that since Dobrushin's condition is a sufficient condition of absence of phase transition, the region derived form Dobrushin's condition is naturally included in that of the complete characterization. Therefore, we look at other relationships here.

Ihler's (Mooij's) region is completely included in that of the complete characterization. This is proved by the fact $d \tanh J(d) = 1$. As a result, the condition obtained from the complete characterization is stronger than that of Ihler's (Mooij's). On the other hand, neither Dobrushin's nor Ihler's (Mooij's) region is a subset of the other. Nevertheless, when $|h|$ is sufficiently large, Dobrushin's region always includes that of Ihler's (Mooij's), that is, Dobrushin's condition is stronger than Ihler's when the influence of one-body potentials is sufficiently large in this case.

4 Conclusion

In this paper, we show two applications of Gibbs measure theory to LBP algorithm. We first show this theory can be applied directly to probability functions with general potentials through factor graphs. Second, we show the usefulness of the application of Gibbs measure theory in the sense that an elaborate application of this theory gives a better result than the best present result in a special case. These two results are not so prominent but sure to encourage the use of Gibbs measure theory in this area.

References

1. Frey, B. J.: Graphical Models for Pattern Classification, Data Compression and Channel Coding, MIT press, Cambridge (1998).
2. Georgii, H. -O.: Gibbs Measures and Phase Transitions, Walter de Gruyter, Berlin · New York (1988).

3. Ihler, A. T., Fisher, J. W., Willsky, A. S.: Loopy Belief Propagation: Convergence and Effects of Message Errors. Journal of Machine Learning Research **6**. Cambridge, MA: MIT press (2005) 905-936.
4. McEliece, R. J., MacKay, D. J. C., Cheng, J. F.: Turbo Decoding as an Instance of Pearl's "Belief Propagation" Algorithm, IEEE Journal on Selected Areas in Communication, **16(2)** Springer Verlag, New York, Berlin, Heidelberg (1998) 140-152.
5. Mooij, J. M., Kappen, H. J.: Sufficient conditions for convergence of Loopy Belief Propagation, Proc. of 21st Conf. on Unc. in Art. Int., Edinburgh (2005) 396-403.
6. Murphy, K. P., Weiss, Y., Jordan, M. I.: Loopy belief propagation for approximate inference: an empirical study, Proc. of the 15th Conf. on Unc. in Art. Int., Morgan Kaufmann, San Francisco (1999) 467-475.
7. Taga, N., Mase, S.: On the Convergence of Loopy Belief Propagation Algorithm for Different Update Rules. IEICE transactions on Fundamentals of Electronics, Communications and Computer Sciences, Vol.E89-(2). Tokyo (2006) 575-582.
8. Tatikonda, S. C., Jordan, M. I.: Loopy Belief Propagation and Gibbs Measures, Proc. of the 18th Conf. on Unc. in Art. Int., Morgan Kaufmann, San Francisco (2002) 493-500.
9. Weiss, Y.: Correctness of Local Probability Propagation in Graphical Models with Loops, Neur. Comp., vol.12, MIT press. Cambridge (2000) 1-41.

Appendix

In this appendix, we show how to check Dobrushin's condition for Ising models on the Cayley tree of degree d or the complete graph of $d+2$ vertices. Let S be the vertex set of the Cayley tree and E_i be $\{-1,1\}$ for $i \in S$. Let $\Omega = \prod_{i \in S} E_i$ be the configuration space, $(\Omega, \mathcal{F})$ be the measurable space with the Borel set $\mathcal{F}$ of Ω and γ be a *specification* on $(\Omega, \mathcal{F})$. γ satisfies Dobrushin's condition if

$$c(\gamma) \equiv \sup_{i \in S} \sum_{j \in S} C_{ij}(\gamma) < 1 ,$$

where

$$C_{ij}(\gamma) = \sup_{\zeta, \eta \in \Omega,\ \zeta_{S \setminus \{i\}} = \eta_{S \setminus \{i\}}} \|\gamma_i^0(\cdot \mid \zeta) - \gamma_i^0(\cdot \mid \eta)\| \tag{8}$$

with the norm $\|f(\cdot)\| = \max_{A \in \mathcal{F}} \left| \sum_{\zeta \in A} f(\zeta) \right|$ for a real function f on Ω. In the Ising potential case, we have

$$\gamma_i^0(x_i \mid \zeta) = \frac{1}{Z(\zeta)} \exp\left[x_i \Big(h + J \sum_{j \in \partial i} \zeta_j \Big) \right] ,$$

where $Z(\zeta) = 2\cosh(h + J\sum_{j \in \partial i} \zeta_j)$ and ∂i denotes the set of neighbors of $i \in S$. Note that $C_{ij}(\cdot) = 0$ when $j \notin \partial i$ (for specifications with nearest neighbor potentials). Then, taking the supremum in the right side of eq. (8), we can restrict ourselves to consider configurations ζ, η such that for some $j \in \partial i$, $\eta_j = -\zeta_j$ and

$\eta_k = \zeta_k$ for $k \neq j$. Now $\gamma_i^0(\emptyset \mid \zeta) = 0$ and $\gamma_i^0(E_i \mid \zeta) = 1$ for any configuration ζ, hence we have

$$\gamma_i^0(A \mid \zeta) - \gamma_i^0(A \mid \eta) = \begin{cases} \sinh(2J)/Z'_{ij}(\zeta) & \text{if } A = \{1\} , \\ -\sinh(2J)/Z'_{ij}(\zeta) & \text{if } A = \{-1\} , \\ 0 & \text{otherwise} , \end{cases}$$

where $Z'_{ij}(\zeta) = \cosh 2(h + J \sum_{k \in \partial i \setminus \{j\}} \zeta_k) + \cosh(2J)$ for configurations ζ, η such that for some $j \in \partial i$, $\eta_j = -\zeta_j$ and $\eta_k = \zeta_k$ for $k \neq j$. Therefore

$$\|\gamma_i^0(\cdot \mid \zeta) - \gamma_i^0(\cdot \mid \eta)\| = \frac{1}{Z'_{ij}(\zeta)} \sinh(2|J|) ,$$

For the Cayley tree of degree d, the number of neighbors for each vertex is $d+1$. Therefore we have

$$C_{ij}(\gamma) = \max_{\zeta \in \Omega} \frac{1}{Z'_{ij}(\zeta)} \sinh(2|J|) = \frac{\sinh(2|J|)}{g(h, J) + \cosh(2J)}$$

where

$$g(x, y) = \min_{z_i \in \{-1,1\},\ i=1,\ldots,d} \cosh 2\left(x + y \sum_{i=1}^{d} z_i\right) .$$

That is, $C_{ij}(\gamma)$ is independent of i, j and it follows

$$c(\gamma) = \frac{(d+1)\sinh(2|J|)}{g(h, J) + \cosh(2J)} .$$

Using this, we can check Dobrushin's condition easily.

A Contingency Analysis of LeActiveMath's Learner Model*

Rafael Morales[1], Nicolas Van Labeke[2], and Paul Brna[2]

[1] Sistema de Universidad Virtual, Universidad de Guadalajara
Escuela Militar de Aviación 16, Col. Ladrón de Guevara
44170 Guadalajara, Jalisco, Mexico
rmorales@udgvirtual.udg.mx
[2] The SCRE Centre, University of Glasgow
11 Eldon Street, Glasgow G3 6NH, United Kingdom
Tel.: +44 (141) 330-3490; fax: +44 (0)141 330 3491
{n.vanlabeke, paul.brna}@scre.ac.uk

Abstract. We analyse how a learner modelling engine that uses belief functions for evidence and belief representation, called xLM, reacts to different input information about the learner in terms of changes in the state of its beliefs and the decisions that it derives from them. The paper covers xLM induction of evidence with different strengths from the qualitative and quantitative properties of the input, the amount of indirect evidence derived from direct evidence, and differences in beliefs and decisions that result from interpreting different sequences of events simulating learners evolving in different directions. The results here presented substantiate our vision of xLM is a proof of existence for a generic and potentially comprehensive learner modelling subsystem that explicitly represents uncertainty, conflict and ignorance in beliefs. These are key properties of learner modelling engines in the bizarre world of open Web-based learning environments that rely on the content+metadata paradigm.

1 Introduction

What makes a good learner model? There are many answers to this question. From a pragmatic viewpoint, any representation of the learner that supports an educational system in providing better learning experiences to its users would qualify as a good learner model [1]. From a more epistemological viewpoint, a good learner model must *capture* the significant aspects of a learner, *predict* her behaviour with accuracy and *explain* it convincingly [2]. Consequently, learner models can be evaluated either by the benefits they bring to educational systems [3], the aspects of learners that they model [4], their predictive power [5] or their explanatory power [6].

In this paper we explore the explanatory powers of xLM, a learner modelling engine developed in the LeActiveMath project [7]. xLM uses information on learner performance to maintain a collection of beliefs on different learner aspects such as their

* This publication was generated in the context of the LeActiveMath project, funded under the 6th Framework Programm of the European Community - (Contract N° IST- 2003-507826). The authors are solely responsible for its content, it does not represent the opinion of the European Community and the Community is not responsible for any use that might be made of data appearing therein.

A. Gelbukh and C.A. Reyes-Garcia (Eds.): MICAI 2006, LNAI 4293, pp. 208–217, 2006.

competencies, meta-cognitive skills, affective and motivational dispositions on a subject domain—Differential Calculus in the current implementation. XLM explanations of learner behaviour are the beliefs it holds on the actual levels (values) of these learner aspects, each belief supported by evidence constructed from interpretations of interaction events. We describe how XLM reacts to different configurations of input information about a learner in terms of changes in the interpretation of the input as evidence, changes in the states of its beliefs and the decisions that it infers from them. We compare XLM responses with our expectations as tutors and designers and make quality judgements. Our analysis is limited to XLM modelling of mathematical competencies [8] on the subject domain. Specifically, we analyse:

a) the induction of direct evidence with different strengths depending on the qualitative and quantitative properties of the input (failing or succeeding on a very easy or very difficult exercise),
b) the amount of indirect evidence derived from direct evidence, and
c) the differences in beliefs and decisions that result from interpreting different sequences of events simulating learners evolving in different directions.

We finish the paper discussing outstanding issues, presenting our conclusions from the work so far and pointing to promising future work.

2 Learner Modelling Process and Belief Representation

XLM is a learner modelling engine for a content+metadata type of system. It combines a simple issue-based approach [9], in which issues related to content items are identified in their metadata, with a generic multidimensional framework for learner models and belief functions as numeric knowledge representations [10,11]. The mechanisms involved in the learning modelling process, from interpreting input information to deriving the corresponding evidence and finally updating beliefs based on it are sketched in figure 1.

A *mass distribution* is a belief function that can be interpreted as a generalised probability distribution whose domain is not the set of possible values of a variable but its power set—the set of sets of possible values of the variable. If we call Θ to the (finite) set of possible values of a variable, then a mass distribution is a function

$$\mathrm{m} : 2^{\Theta} \rightarrow [0,1] \quad \text{such that} \quad \sum_{X \subseteq \Theta} \mathrm{m}(X) = 1.$$

In XLM, the variables are the learner aspects that it models—a variety of mathematical competencies, meta-cognitive skills and affective and motivational dispositions. Their values are *levels* in a scale of four,

$$\Theta = \{\mathrm{I}, \mathrm{II}, \mathrm{III}, \mathrm{IV}\},$$

and mass is distributed only among *intervals*, which are subsets of consecutive levels (i.e. subsets like $\varnothing$ and $\{\mathrm{I}, \mathrm{II}, \mathrm{III}\}$ but not like $\{\mathrm{I}, \mathrm{II}, \mathrm{IV}\}$). Shorthands of the form $X2Y$ are used in this paper to denote intervals (e.g. $\mathrm{I2III} isashorthandfor \{\mathrm{I}, \mathrm{II}, \mathrm{III}\}$) while a level name will be used to denote either a level or the set containing the level only,

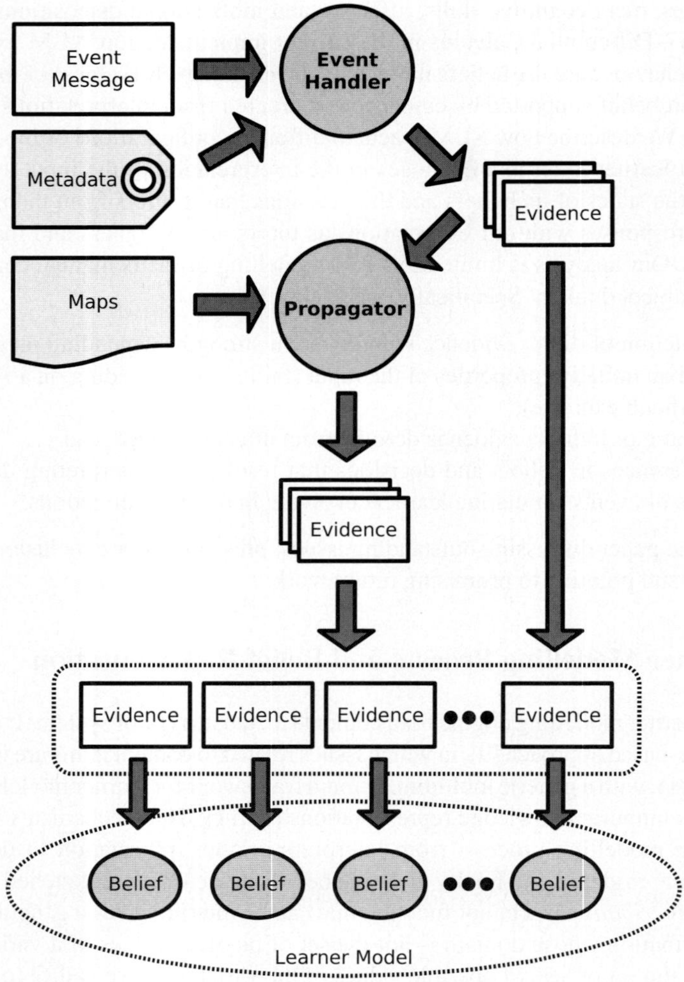

Fig. 1. The learner modelling process

depending on the context. More details of xLM architecture, modelling framework, knowledge representation and modelling process can be found in [12].

3 Direct Evidence of Different Strength

The interpretation of reports of learner performance in exercises[1] is based on the following assumptions:

a) the more difficult an exercise is, the more probable is to achieve a low performance, while the opposite holds for easier exercises,

[1] Hereafter we would use *exercise* to refer either to full exercises or individual steps in them.

b) exercises designed for learners at higher competency levels are more difficult for learners at lower competency levels, and
c) we can use a bell-shaped function, parameterised by an estimation of the difficulty of the exercise and the assumed competency level of the learner, to assign probabilities of performance.

Therefore, we assume that most learners would succeed on easier exercises, particularly on those aimed at competency levels lower than their own, and would fail on more difficult exercises, particularly on those aimed at higher competency levels than their own. Therefore, reports of these happening provide little information to update learner models and changes should be minimal. On the contrary, reports of failure on easier exercises and success on more difficult ones are more informative and should have a stronger impact on learner models.

Table 1. Interpretation of prototypical reports of learner performance

			Mass distribution										
Difficulty	Level	Success	∅	I	II	III	IV	I2II	II2III	III2IV	I2III	II2IV	I2IV
Very easy	I	1	0	0	0	0	0	0	0	0	0	0	1.000
Very difficult	IV	0	0	0	0	0	0	0	0	0	0	0	1.000
Very easy	I	0.9	0	0.009	0	0	0	0.016	0	0	0.034	0	0.942
Very difficult	IV	0.1	0	0	0	0	0.009	0	0	0.016	0	0.034	0.942
Medium	II	0.5	0	0	0.675	0	0	0	0.189	0	0	0	0.135
Very easy	I	0	0	0.585	0	0	0	0.333	0	0	0.080	0	0.002
Very difficult	IV	1	0	0	0	0	0.585	0	0	0.333	0	0.080	0.002

Table 1 shows the evidence induced from reports of the prototypical extremes of learner performance mentioned above, plus a couple of close approximations (nearly succeeding in a very easy exercise and nearly failing in a very difficult one) and an intermediate case of evidence induced from average performance on an exercise of medium difficulty designed for competency level II. The mass distributions in the first two rows, induced from the least surprising events, assign all mass to the set $\{I, II, III, IV\}$, which stands for the support the evidence gives to no level in particular, or total ignorance. These mass distributions can be interpreted as *complete lack of evidence*, representing in these cases the knowledge that "everyone succeeds on very easy exercises and fails on very difficult ones." The next two rows contain the evidence induced from nearly succeeding (failing) in a very easy (difficult) exercise. In these cases, some mass have been taken away from ignorance (set $\{I, II, III, IV\}$) and distributed among other sets of levels. The third row, for example, indicates that nearly top performance in very easy exercises (success rate $= 0.9$) is interpreted as the learner being more probably at a competency level lower than level IV, yet XLM still leaves ample space to the possibility of the learner being actually at level IV. The process of moving mass away from ignorance reaches its limits in the case of the more informative events (the two rows at the bottom of the table) where the amount of (mass on) ignorance is minuscule in comparison to the mass assigned to the singletons $\{I\}$ and $\{IV\}$, respectively, indicating that the events are interpreted as highly supportive of the learner being at a very specific competency level. Finally, for the case of the event of medium performance, the evidence induced is highly supportive of the learner being at the same competency level the exercise has been designed for, but still including its dose of uncertainty (mass on $\{II, III\}$) and ignorance.

Table 2 contains details of information and decisions that can be inferred from the mass distributions shown in table 1. These are *pignistic distributions*, which are probability distributions derived from mass distributions [11], single value summaries[2] and final decisions on the actual learner levels that would result from beliefs justified only by the single pieces of evidence in table 1. The table shows that XLM cannot make decisions under complete ignorance, yet it can be forced to make a decision in very close cases, as in the third and fourth rows in the table. These rows are interesting also because they show that currently XLM does not bet on the most probable level (level I and IV, respectively, in the pignistic distribution) but on the average. Decisions seem more straightforward in the last three cases which correspond to more informative event reports.

Table 2. Pignistic distributions, summary beliefs and final decisions on learner level from mass functions show in table 1

Event data			Pignistic distribution					
Difficulty	Level	Performance	I	II	III	IV	Summary	Decision
very easy	I	1.0	0.250	0.250	0.250	0.250	N/A	N/A
very difficult	IV	0.0	0.250	0.250	0.250	0.250	N/A	N/A
very easy	I	0.9	0.263	0.255	0.247	0.235	2.45	II
very difficult	IV	0.1	0.235	0.247	0.255	0.263	2.55	III
medium	II	0.5	0.034	0.804	0.128	0.034	2.16	II
very easy	I	0.0	0.779	0.193	0.027	0.001	1.25	I
very difficult	IV	1.0	0.001	0.027	0.193	0.779	3.75	IV

4 Amount of Indirect Evidence

Table 3 shows how much indirect evidence is generated from the (direct) evidence induced from each one of the events discussed in the previous section. We expected the amount of indirect evidence to increase significantly from the events conveying less information to the events conveying more information, and the results shown in the table confirm our expectations. On the other hand, different amounts of indirect evidence are generated from the (equally) most informative events. An explanation of this happening is that the very difficult exercise is on *derivative*, the most connected topic in the domain map, hence predisposed to produce a large amount of indirect evidence even on the case of little information (but above the threshold defined in XLM). Finally, the

[2] XLM produces summary beliefs in the range $[0,1]$ which are transformed here linearly to values in the range $[1,4]$ in order to make them more intuitive.

amount of indirect evidence for the intermediate case falls in between the two extremes, as expected.

On average, the proportion of direct to indirect evidence in these cases is over 1 : 70. Assuming xLM can hold around 600 beliefs on mathematical competencies on the subject domain (around 30 domain topics and 20 competencies) this means that about nine exercises, evenly mapped onto the domain topics and competencies, would be required to have at least one piece of evidence (direct or indirect) per belief.

Table 3. Amount of indirect evidence from single direct evidence

Event data			
Difficulty	Level	Performance	Amount of indirect evidence
very easy	I	1.0	0
very difficult	IV	0.0	0
very easy	I	0.9	0
very difficult	IV	0.1	0
medium	II	0.5	81
very easy	I	0.0	115
very difficult	IV	1.0	296

5 Beliefs and Sequences of Evidence

Reports of learner performance arrive as information becomes available as learners interact with content. A sequence of reports of learner performance reflects, in principle, the evolution of the learner as she interacts with the system and its content—learning, hopefully. xLM uses decay of evidence to account for the assumption that newer reports have more to do with the current state of the learner than old ones. Hence old evidence loses strength as new evidence accumulates—as if xLM were forgetting it.

In order to observe xLM responses to different sequences of events being reported we use three base sequences: one standing for *improvement*, another one standing for *deterioration*, and yet another one standing for *random* performance. Each sequence consists of seven events, each one reporting the success rate of the learner on an exercise of medium difficulty at competency level II. In addition, we used two more sequences derived from the improvement and deterioration sequences by introducing random variations in the range $[-0.1, 0.1]$(figure 2).

xLM responses to these sequences are shown in figures 3 and 4, and table 4. The figures include graphs illustrating the evolution of beliefs on the mathematical competency of the learner regarding a domain topic addressed by the exercise, using summary beliefs (figure 3) and pignistic distributions (figure 4) to make changes in the beliefs easier to visualise. Table 4 contains the full mass distribution for the final belief resulted from each sequence of events.

It can be seen that xLM reaction to the sequence of evidence standing for improvement is a belief that evolves steadily from something like 'level II, or perhaps lower'

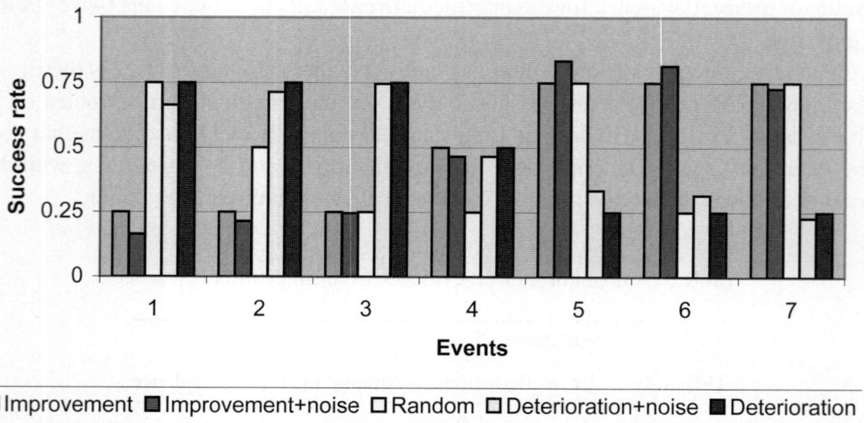

Fig. 2. Sequences of performance used to assess xLM responses to the order in which information arrives

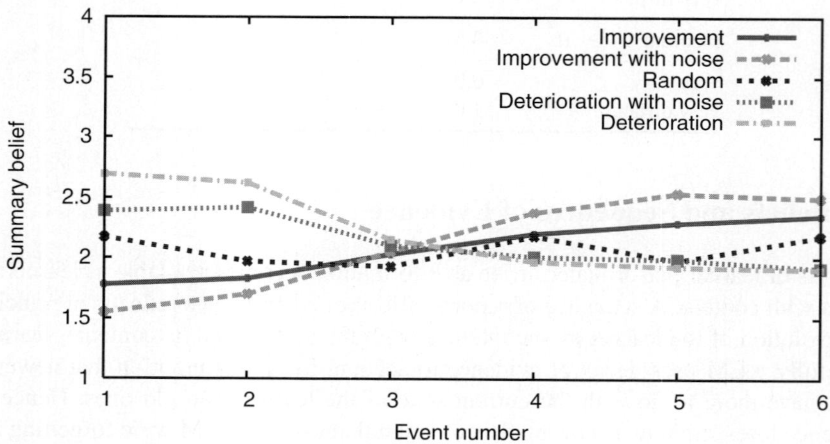

Fig. 3. Evolution of summary belief for all sequences

Table 4. Final beliefs for all the sequences of events

Sequence	Mass distribution										
	∅	I	II	III	IV	I2II	II2III	III2IV	I2III	II2IV	I2IV
Improvement	0	0	0.523	0	0	0	0.168	0	0.001	0.232	0.075
Improvement with noise	0.252	0	0.292	0.056	0	0	0.097	0.020	0.004	0.205	0.074
Random	0	0	0.742	0	0	0.001	0.069	0	0.002	0.111	0.075
Deterioration with noise	0	0	0.706	0	0	0.205	0	0	0.036	0	0.053
Deterioration	0	0	0.680	0	0	0.230	0	0	0.036	0	0.054

to something more like 'most certainly level II, yet may be higher' as more evidence accumulate, while still conceding a very small amount of possibility to the case of the learner being at competency level I. The belief derived from the sequence of evidence standing for deterioration evolves from something like 'II or over' (actually, the summary belief is very close to level III while a hint of possibility is given to the learner being at level I) to something like 'level II, but could be lower.' The belief for the random sequence evolves somehow "in between" the beliefs produced for improvement and deterioration, strongly favouring level II as expected, given the fact that the exercise is of medium difficulty for competency level II.

The beliefs that result from considering the noisy sequences follow in general the patterns of the corresponding base sequences. Due to the nature of the noise introduced (random noise that happens to be more negative than positive, specially for the first half of events) it accentuates the improvement effect and attenuates the deterioration one, so that the final belief in the former case considers level III as a strong alternative to level II (mass in sets $\{III\}$ and $\{III, IV\}$) while in the latter case the support for level II increases (slightly more mass on $\{II\}$) as the support for level I decreases (less mass on $\{I, II\}$).

Finally, the belief resulting from the sequence of improvement with noise (second row in table 4) assigns one quarter of the mass to the empty set, indicating in this way that the belief is based on divergent evidence, corresponding in this case to steep improvement.

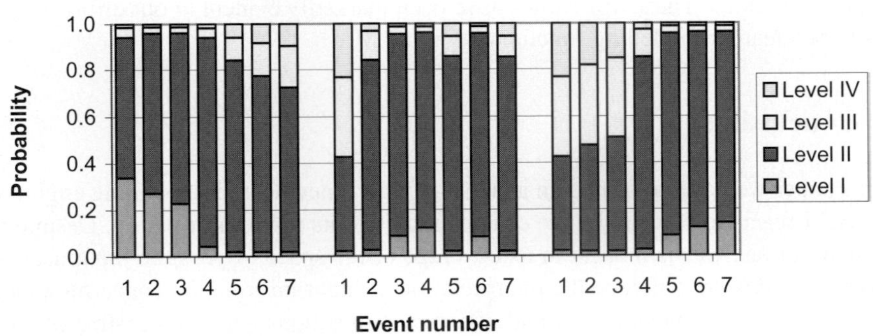

Fig. 4. Evolution of the pignistic distribution along the *improvement*, *random* and *deterioration* sequences, displayed in that order from left to right

6 Discussion

The current interpretation of reports of learner performance by XLM is based on its designers' common sense and some basic mathematical techniques (e.g. bell-shaped probability assignments resembling normal probability distributions). The evidence and beliefs that result from the interpretation of the reports look reasonable and mostly intuitive. They also illustrate how uncertainty and ignorance are represented in belief functions differently from how they are represented using probability distributions.

A few issues are worth mentioning here. The most important one is perhaps the lack of theoretical or empirical support to the current interpretation of events, despite how reasonable it may seem. Although we can justify our approach on the basis of the great amount of subjectivity in metadata—not necessarily a peculiarity of LEACTIVEMATH content—a sounder design of the interpretation process based on some psychometric theories would have its advantages. Another important issue concerns the use of a learner model in the interpretation of relevant events, which has been avoided in this paper. Actually, XLM includes two modes for incorporating new evidence into existing beliefs: an *objective* mode, in which the strength of new evidence is independent of the existing beliefs, and a *biased* mode, in which new evidence is considered on the light of the existing beliefs—e.g. 'It is hard to believe that such a good student had such a bad performance by any other reason than by accident.' However, the experiments described in this paper use the objective mode only.

Once all relevant information concerning an event is made available by LEACTIVEMATH, the first step in its interpretation by XLM consists in deriving a probability distribution from which a mass distribution standing for the evidence is generated [12]. Quite probably this step, which includes both the construction of the probability distribution and the specific algorithm used for its translation into a mass distribution, is unnecessary and may have a limiting effect on our use of belief functions as core knowledge representation formalism. Furthermore, the fact that we have resorted to summary beliefs and pignistic (probability) distributions to describe a core part of XLM behaviour, how beliefs change along time, is a consequence of the difficulties to visualise, apprehend, meaningfully manipulate and produce clear external representations of belief functions. These difficulties have been markedly evident in our efforts to construct open learner modelling functionality in XLM.

7 Conclusions

In this paper we have presented an analysis of how a new learner modelling engine we call XLM reacts to changes in the characteristics of its input information. Despite the fact that our analysis is modest in its coverage of the space of possible input data—in particular, it does not include the interpretation of input information concerning meta-cognitive skills nor motivational and affective dispositions—it is suggestive of XLM responding appropriately to available information regarding learner behaviour.

Further work on the line presented in this paper includes extensive analysis of XLM response to learner behaviour. For example, the effect on learner models of evidence propagation as learners course through educational content, differences in learner models that result from updating beliefs using either the objective or the biased mode, the interpretation of learner actions on an open learner model as evidence for meta-cognitive skills and the interpretation of learner behaviour for modelling motivational and affective dispositions. We plan also to carry out sensitivity analyses of the collection of explicit and implicit parameters that control a great deal of XLM behaviour.

We interpret the results presented in this paper as substantiations of our vision of XLM is a proof of existence for its kind: a generic and potentially comprehensive learner modelling subsystem that uses belief functions for encoding its beliefs because they facilitate the explicit representation of uncertainty, conflict and ignorance. These are key properties of learner modelling engines in the bizarre world of open Web-based learning environments that rely on the content+metadata paradigm.

References

1. Self, J.A.: Bypassing the intractable problem of student modelling. In: Proceedings of ITS'88, Montréal, Canada (1988) 18–24
2. Lee, M.H.: On models, modelling and the distinctive nature of model-based reasoning. AI Communications **12** (1999) 127–137
3. Koedinger, K.R., Anderson, J.R.: Intelligent tutoring goes to school in the big city. International Journal of Artificial Intelligence in Education **8** (1997) 30–43
4. Conati, C.: Toward comprehensive student models: Modeling meta-cognitive skills and affective states in ITS. In Lester, J.C., Vicari, R.M., Paraguaçu, F., eds.: Intelligent Tutoring Systems. Number 3220 in Lecture Notes in Computer Science, Springer Verlag (2004) 902
5. Burton, R.B.: Diagonising bugs in a simple procedural skill. [13] chapter 8 157–183
6. Corbett, A.T., Anderson, J.R.: Knowledge tracing: Modeling the acquisition of procedural knowledge. User Modeling and User-Adapted Interaction **4** (1995) 253–278
7. LeActiveMath Consortium: Language-enhanced, user adaptive, interactive elearning for mathematics (2004)
8. Organisation for Economic Co-Operation and Development: The PISA 2003 Assessment Framework. (2003)
9. Burton, R.B., Brown, J.S.: An investigation of computer coaching for informal learning activities. [13] chapter 4 79–98
10. Shafer, G.: A Mathematical Theory of Evidence. Princeton University Press (1976)
11. Smets, P., Kennes, R.: The transferable belief model. Artificial Intelligence **66** (1994) 191–234
12. Morales, R., van Labeke, N., Brna, P.: Approximate modelling of the multi-dimensional learner. In Ikeda, M., Ashley, K., Chan, T.W., eds.: Intelligent Tutoring Systems. Number 4053 in Lecture Notes in Computer Science, Springer Verlag (2006) 555–564
13. Sleeman, D.H., Brown, J.S., eds.: Intelligent Tutoring Systems. Academic Press, New York (1982)

Constructing Virtual Sensors Using Probabilistic Reasoning

Pablo H. Ibargüengoytia and Alberto Reyes

Instituto de Investigaciones Eléctricas
Av. Reforma 113, Palmira
Cuernavaca, Mor., 62490, México
{pibar, areyes}@iie.org.mx

Abstract. Modern control systems and other monitoring systems require the acquisition of values of most of the parameters involved in the process. Examples of processes are industrial procedures or medical treatments or financial forecasts. However, sometimes some parameters are inaccessible through the use of traditional instrumentation. One example is the blades temperature in a gas turbine during operation. Other parameters require costly instrumentation difficult to install, operate and calibrate. For example, the contaminant emissions of power plant chimney. One solution of this problem is the use of analytical estimation of the parameter using complex differential equations. However, these models sometimes are very difficult to obtain and to maintain according the changes in the processes. Other solution is to borrow an instrument and measure a data set with the value of the difficult variable and its related variables at all the operation range. Then, use an automatic learning algorithm that allows inferring the difficult measure, given the related variables. This paper presents the use of Bayesian networks that represents the probabilistic relations of all the variables in a process, in the design of a virtual sensor. Experiments are presented with the temperature sensors of a gas turbine.

1 Introduction

Computers are invading all kinds of human activities given the decreasing costs of software and hardware. Every time, more processes are controlled and monitored automatically by computers. More algorithms have been developed for the efficient and useful treatment of the data acquired. Examples of this include algorithms for automatic learning, intelligent control, all kind of diagnosis and planning. In all these cases, while better is the information and more reliable are the readings of variables, a better performance can be obtained. However, sometimes, the full range of all the information is difficult to obtain. In some cases, the variables to measure can be in inaccessible locations. In other cases, some variables require expensive and complex pieces of instrumentation. For example, a fuel viscosity sensor is expensive and has to be cleaned perfectly every short periods of time, given the nature of the object measured: a dense flow of raw oil[5]. As another example, the control emission monitoring system (CEMs)

A. Gelbukh and C.A. Reyes-Garcia (Eds.): MICAI 2006, LNAI 4293, pp. 218–226, 2006.

are expensive equipment that has to be installed at the top of chimney in power plants, but also require calibration every short periods of time. Literature reports the use of predictive emission monitoring system (PEMs) as a common solution for contaminant emissions sensors.

One common solution for the problem of difficult readings is the estimation of these parameters, given other related parameters in the same process. In this research project, this estimation is referred as **virtual sensors**.

One approach used in traditional chemical processes is analytical. This includes the development of complex differential equations that relate the virtual variable with other easier to read parameters [2]. However, this is sometimes very difficult to obtain and the complexity tends to increase when several variables are considered. Also, any small change in the process may represent huge changes in the analytical models that relate these variables. Additionally, analytical models require the participation of high experimented experts of the process. This also, is difficult to find.

Computational intelligence methods have been used in this estimation. For example, neural networks, fuzzy logic and genetic algorithms are used in the estimation of one variable after a training phase. Sometimes, a combination of these methods are utilized in specific environments [3]. However, these combinations result in unique prototypes that are difficult to apply in similar problems.

Another approach consists in the use of artificial intelligence techniques for the development of virtual sensors. If the estimation is based on probabilistic relations of the variables, then Bayesian networks mechanism can be used. This mechanism includes robust and efficient automatic learning algorithms that provide the models, given real data from the process. This approach requires the acquisition of all the variables while the process is operating at full range. This means that, obtaining and calibrating the costly instrument for a few days, it is possible to create a data base with all the information. Later, a probabilistic model can be built using one of the learning algorithms. Finally, estimation of the virtual sensor can be made through probability propagation, once that the related values have been read.

This paper proposes and demonstrates the use of probabilistic reasoning, i.e., Bayesian networks, in the creation of virtual sensors. The main contribution is the procedure to create virtual sensors using real data from the process. The models are obtained off-line and the virtual sensors are utilized on-line. Additionally, Bayesian networks can be used for the design of several virtual sensors given the same data set. This is, inference in Bayesian networks produces posterior probability distributions of all the variables that were no possible to read. Also, this mechanism works even in the absence of some of the related variables. A prototype was constructed and tested with temperature sensors of a gas turbine in a power plant.

This paper is organized as follows: we start describing the Bayesian network mechanism used traditionally in uncertainty management. Section 3 explains the application domain where this virtual sensor wes first developed. Then, we present our approach in the construction of probabilistic models that will be used to create the virtual sensors. Then, section 5 discusses the experiments reported of the temperature of gas turbine virtual sensor. We finally conclude giving new directions of this work.

2 Introduction to Bayesian Networks

A Bayesian network (BN) is a graphical representation of dependencies and independencies of random variables for probabilistic reasoning in intelligent systems [4]. Fig. 1 depicts an example of a simplified BN representation of 5 variables, and their relationships. In a BN, each node represents a discrete random variable and each arc a probabilistic dependency. The variable at the end of a link is dependent on the variable at its origin. Thus, the following considerations were taken in the construction of the BN of Fig. 1. The temperature t is caused by the flow of gas $f1$ and the flow of air $f2$ during the combustion. The flow of gas is caused by the gas fuel pressure supply ps and the real fuel valve position pr. Also, this position is caused by the position demand of fuel valve dp. The flow of air $f2$ is caused by the real inlet guide vane position pa and this is caused by the position demand da. This network can be taken as representing the joint probability distribution of the variables t, $f1$,..., da as:

$$P(t, f1, f2, ps, pr, pa, dp, da) = P(t \mid f1, f2)P(f1 \mid ps, pr)P(f2 \mid pa) \quad (1)$$
$$P(pa \mid da)P(pr \mid dp)P(ps)P(dp)P(da)$$

Equation 1 is obtained by applying the chain rule and using the dependency information represented in the network.

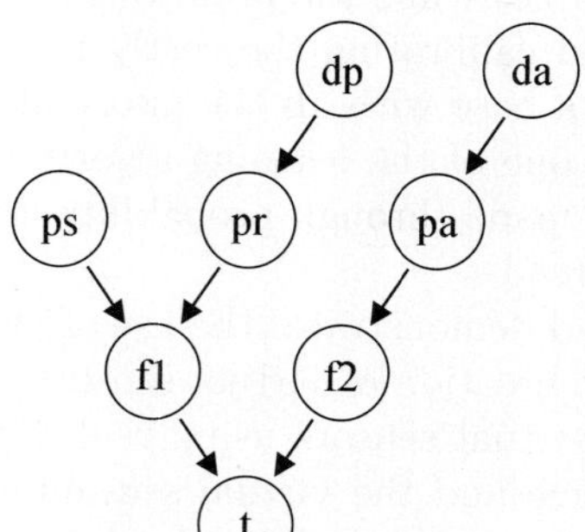

Fig. 1. Example of a polytree representing the causal relation between variables of the gas turbine

The topology of a BN gives direct information about the dependency relationships between the variables involved. In particular, it represents which variables are conditionally independent given another variable. By definition, X is conditionally independent of Y, given Z, if:

$$P(X \mid Y, Z) = P(X \mid Z) \quad (2)$$

This is represented graphically by node Z "separating" X from Y in the network. In general, Z will be a subset of nodes from the network that if removed will make the subsets of nodes X and Y disconnected. For example, in the BN of Fig. 1, $\{t\}$ is conditionally independent of $\{ps, pr\}$ given $\{f1\}$. To completely specify a BN, the conditional probability of each node given its parents, and the prior probability of the root nodes, are required. That is the terms in equation 1 for the example.

Given a knowledge base represented as a probabilistic network, it can be used to reason about the consequences of specific input data, by what is called *probabilistic reasoning.* This consists in assigning a value to the input variables, and propagating their effect through the network to update the probability of the hypothesis variables. The updating of the certainty measures is consistent with probability theory, based on the application of Bayesian calculus and the dependencies represented in the network. For example, in the BN in Fig. 1, if $f1$ and $f2$ are measured and t is unknown, their effect can be propagated to obtain the posterior probability of t given $f1$ and $f2$.

The probabilistic model in Fig. 1 has a polytree structure, i.e., for any two nodes in the network, there is at most one chain between these two nodes. For singly connected networks, such as trees or polytrees, there is an efficient algorithm for probability propagation [4]. It consists on propagating the effects of the known variables through the links, and combining them in each unknown variable. This can be done by local operations and a message passing mechanism, in a time which is linearly proportional to the diameter of the network. The more complete Bayesian network representation is multiply connected network. For this kind of networks, there are alternative techniques for probability propagation, such as clustering, conditioning, and stochastic simulation [4].

Bayesian networks can be used to represent the dependency relations between the measurements, and obtain their posterior probabilities given the evidence of other measured variables. The next section presents the use of Bayesian networks in the construction of the virtual sensor.

3 Application Domain: Gas Turbines

The virtual sensor approach was evaluated by applying it to the estimation of one temperature sensor of the gas turbine at the *Gómez Palacio* power plant in México. This is an interesting application of these techniques for many reasons. For example, since an analytical or functional model of the temperatures of a turbine is difficult to obtain, it is a good candidate for probabilistic methods. Additionally, some of the temperatures of gas turbine are indeed very difficult to measure. For example, the temperature of the inner blades of the turbine. Finally, the size of this problem makes it ideal for testing the development of the prototype. Figure 2 shows a simplified diagram of a gas turbine.

The combustion chamber receives air and gas in a specific proportion to produce high pressure gases at high temperature. These gases produce the rotation that moves the generator. Thus, the temperature is considered the most

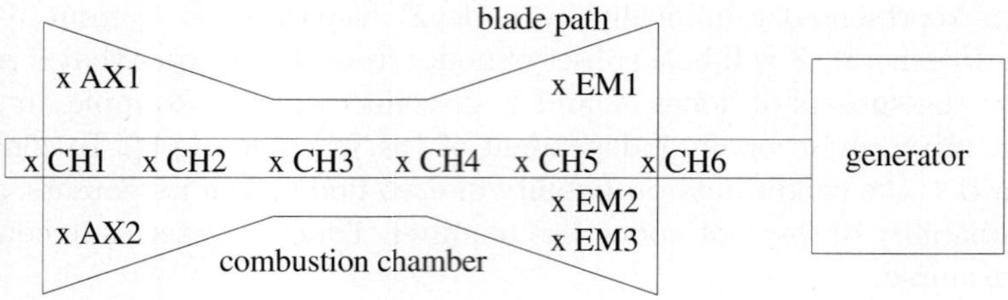

Fig. 2. Simplified schematic diagram of a gas turbine

important parameter in the operation of the turbine since it performs more optimally at higher temperatures. However, a little increase in the temperature, over a permitted value, may cause severe damage. The distributed control system that governs the plant is continuously monitoring these signals in order to correct any deviation of the process. In the case of an illegal increase of a temperature parameter, the plant is stopped and taken to a safe state. Conversely, an error in a sensor's measure may cause an unnoticed increase of the temperature, or may result in an unnecessary shut down. The consequences of the former can be severe damage to the equipment and even human fatalities, and the latter could result in loss of time and fuel. Figure 2 shows the physical location of some of the temperature sensors used in the turbine. It shows six sensors across the beadings of the shaft ($CH1, CH2, \ldots, CH6$), three sensors on the turbine blades ($EM1$, $EM2$ and $EM3$), and two sensors of the temperature of the exciter air ($AX1$ and $AX2$). The experiments were carried out over a set of 21 sensors (though not all are shown in Fig. 2). These sensors can be grouped into the following sets of measurements:

- 6 beadings (CH1 - CH6),
- 7 disk cavities (CA1 - CA7),
- 1 cavities air cooling (AEF),
- 2 exciter air (AX1 - AX2),
- 3 blade paths (EM1 - EM3), and
- 2 lub oil (AL1 - AL2).

The instrumentation of the plant provides the readings of all the sensors every second. The data set utilized in the experiments corresponds to the temperature readings taken during approximately the first 15 minutes after the start of the combustion. That corresponds to the start up phase of the plant, where the thermodynamic conditions change considerably. Therefore, the data set consists of 21 variables and 870 instances of the readings.

4 Constructing the Virtual Sensor

The idea in the construction of a virtual sensor is to suppose that one of these sensors will be a virtual sensor. Then, estimation of the value can be made and later, a comparison of the real value. This allows evaluating the proposed approach.

The first step in the design of a virtual sensor is to provide a dependency or probabilistic model. A dependency model for the temperatures was obtained by utilizing an automatic learning program included in the Hugin package [1,6]. Fig. 3 shows the network obtained with this data set.

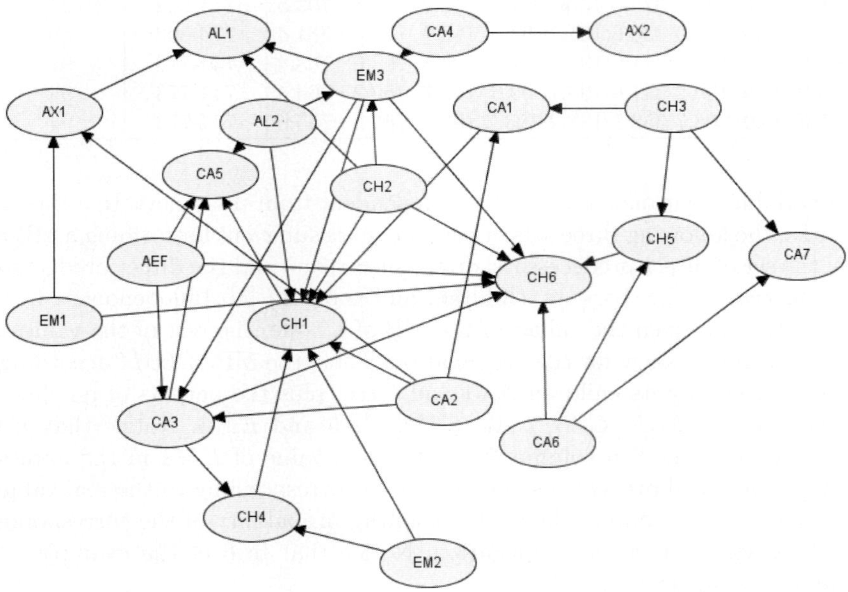

Fig. 3. Learned Bayesian network for the gas turbine temperature sensors

In this project, discretization was necessary since all these variables are continuous valued. In this preliminary experiments, a very simple discretization was chosen. For most of the variables, the full range of values were divided in 5 intervals, except the turbine blades temperatures ($EM1$, $EM2$ and $EM3$) that were divided in 10 intervals.

Now, from the 870 readings of all the sensors, a partition of the data set was made: one partition for training the network (obtaining the initial conditional and prior probabilities), and the other partition for testing.

The testing procedure consists in the instantiation of all variables except $EM1$, and then propagate probabilities in the network, This propagation produces a posterior probability distribution of $EM1$ given all the related sensors. In the testing stage, this probability distribution is compared with the known value of $EM1$. Table 1 presents the final evaluation of the prototype.

The first 8 columns show a selection of testing cases for the estimation of $EM1$. These 8 variables are sufficient for the estimation of $EM1$ since they represent the *Markov blanket* of $EM1$. A Markov blanket (MB) is defined as the

Table 1. Results of selected experiments for the estimation of EM1

AEF	$AX1$	$CA3$	$CA6$	$CH2$	$CH5$	$CH6$	$EM3$	$EM1$	$virtualEM1$	Probability
112	23.9	195.1	260.6	99.4	70.9	67.9	934.0	894.4	888-916	39
117.0	23.9	195.1	271.1	116.3	75.0	74.1	1007.8	974.4	973-1002	91
122.1	23.9	166.5	292.6	128.4	77.1	80.2	1054.4	1031.1	1002-1031	67
132.2	23.9	204.7	314.2	137.2	83.2	91.2	1002.5	993.3	973-1002	91
163.4	26.3	172.2	319.9	137.2	87.3	106.0	844.3	855.7	830-859	37
196.1	27.5	158.1	325.6	133.1	91.4	112.2	793.8	799.5	773-802	95
232.9	29.9	152.9	336.6	131.1	95.5	118.4	777.0	781.4	773-802	89
269.8	31.1	165.2	341.9	131.1	97.6	124.5	763.0	763.4	744-773	91
305.2	33.5	190.2	347.6	133.1	99.6	130.7	750.2	763.4	744-773	94
347.6	35.9	208.7	358.1	137.2	103.7	136.8	742.8	745.0	744-773	94

set of variables that makes a variable independent from the others. In a Bayesian networks, the following three sets of neighbors are sufficient for forming a MB of a node: the set of direct predecessors, direct successors, and the direct predecessors of the successors (i.e. parents, children, and spouses) [4]. Independence in this case means that given the values of the MB of a node, the rest of the values are completely unnecessary for the propagation. Thus, the MB of $EM1$ according to Fig. 3 is formed by its children $AX1$ and $CH6$, plus the parents of its children (spouses): $CA2$, AEF, $CA3$, $CA6$, $CH2$, $CH5$ and $EM3$. Notice that $EM1$ has no parents. The 9th column shows the real value of $EM1$ in the data set. The next column shows the discretized values corresponding to the real value of $EM1$, and the last column shows the resulting probability of the corresponding discretized value after the propagation. Notice that in 6 of the examples, the probability is higher than 90%.

5 Discussion

The preliminary experiments described in Table 1 look promissory. Most of the examples have accuracy higher than 90%. In the rest of the cases, the posterior probability distribution was wider. However, the real value coincides with the interval of higher probability (37 % or 67 %). This is due principally to the lost of precision caused by the discretization process. Five intervals may be few for variables with large variation, but the computational cost is maintained low. If higher precision is required, better discretization approaches can be utilized, but the computational cost would increase. This cost is with respect to memory storage and the propagation time. In a Bayesian network, a conditional probability table is defined with all the values of a node, given all the combination of the values of its parents. Thus, a node with 5 possible values, and 8 parents with 5 values each, represents a table with 1,953,125 entries. In this example, node $CH6$ has 7 parents (see Fig. 4).

For a better performance, it is advisable to prove with different discretizations schemes or more intervals. With this, models result in more exact representation of the signals behavior in the range of operation of the process.

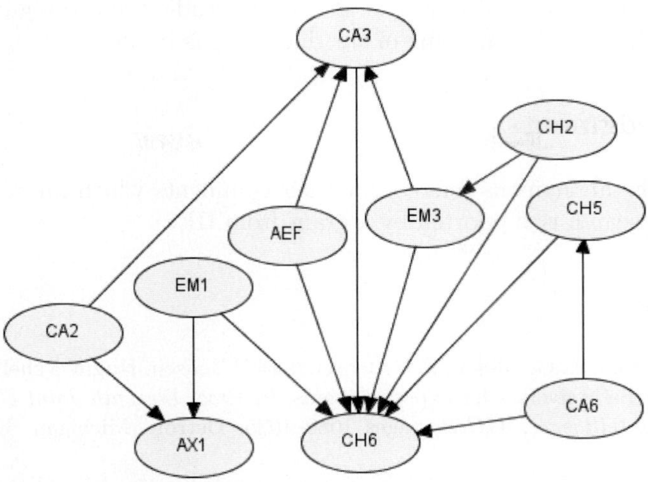

Fig. 4. Sub-network corresponding to the Markov blanket of node EM1

The solution of this problem is to keep the probabilistic model with the lowest interconnectivity possible. The problem is not the number of nodes but the number of arcs between them. While the Markov blanket of the virtual sensor is smaller, lower is the computational cost. The simplest case is to learn a tree structure, i.e., a network where all the nodes can have at most one parent. In this case, discretization can be carried out with larger number of intervals. Notice that the structure learned in this experiment, shown in Fig. 3 is very interconnected, so the number of intervals had to be maintained low. However, in the present days, dealing with models that utilize mega bytes of memory is a common task.

6 Conclusions and Future Work

This paper has shown the construction of virtual sensors using probabilistic reasoning. Borrowing a real sensor, readings can be collected while the process is being executed. Later, a model is learned automatically using the PC algorithm. Finally, the virtual sensor is executed on-line, estimating the corresponding value. This paper utilized real data from temperature sensors in a gas turbine of a power plant. With all the readings, one variable is supposed to be absent, so estimation and evaluation can be made. A prototype was built and tested with promising results.

Future work will be done in the construction of predictive emission monitoring system (PEMs) that will be used in most of the boilers of electric power plants from the Federal Commission of Electricity (CFE) in Mexico. Also, this sensor can be also be installed in other king of boilers in the chemical industry, including petroleum.

Viscosity of fuel virtual sensor is also being studied and designed and it is expected to be installed in many of the ducts of gas in Mexico.

Acknowledgments

Thanks to the anonymous referees for their comments which improved this article. This research is supported by a grant from IIE.

References

1. S. K. Andersen, K. G. Olesen, F. V. Jensen, and F. Jensen. Hugin a shell for building bayesian belief universes for expert systems. In *Proc. Eleventh Joint Conference on Artificial Intelligence, IJCAI*, pages 1080–1085, Detroit, Michigan, U.S.A., 20-25 August 1989.
2. Dorsey A.W. and Lee J.H. Building inferential prediction models of batch processing using subspace identification. *J. Proc. Control*, 13:397–406, 2003.
3. Hanai et. al. Analysis of initial conditions for polymerization reaction using fuzzy neural network and genetic algorith. *Com. Chem. Eng.*, 27:1011–1019, 2003.
4. J. Pearl. *Probabilistic reasoning in intelligent systems: networks of plausible inference.* Morgan Kaufmann, San Francisco, CA., 1988.
5. Aplein Ingenieros S.A. Medida en línea de viscosidad en blending de fuel oil. Technical report, Aplein Ingenieros S.A., 2006.
6. H. Steck, R. Hofmann, and V. Tresp. Concept for the pronel learning algorithm. Technical report, Siemens AG, Munich, 1999.

Solving Hybrid Markov Decision Processes

Alberto Reyes[1,⋆], L. Enrique Sucar[2], Eduardo F. Morales[2], and Pablo H. Ibargüengoytia[1]

[1] Instituto de Investigaciones Eléctricas
Av. Reforma 113, Palmira
Cuernavaca, Mor., 62490, México
[2] INAOE
Luis Enrique Erro 1
Sta. Ma. Tonantzintla, Pue., México
{areyes, pibar}@iie.org.mx, {esucar, emorales}@inaoep.mx

Abstract. Markov decision processes (MDPs) have developed as a standard for representing uncertainty in decision-theoretic planning. However, MDPs require an explicit representation of the state space and the probabilistic transition model which, in continuous or hybrid continuous-discrete domains, are not always easy to define. Even when this representation is available, the size of the state space and the number of state variables to consider in the transition function may be such that the resulting MDP cannot be solved using traditional techniques. In this paper a reward-based abstraction for solving hybrid MDPs is presented. In the proposed method, we gather information about the rewards and the dynamics of the system by exploring the environment. This information is used to build a decision tree (C4.5) representing a small set of abstract states with equivalent rewards, and then is used to learn a probabilistic transition function using a Bayesian networks learning algorithm (K2). The system output is a problem specification ready for its solution with traditional dynamic programming algorithms. We have tested our abstract MDP model approximation in real-world problem domains. We present the results in terms of the models learned and their solutions for different configurations showing that our approach produces fast solutions with satisfying policies.

1 Introduction

A Markov Decision Process (MDP) [14] models a sequential decision problem, in which a system evolves in time and is controlled by an agent. The system dynamics is governed by a probabilistic transition function that maps states and actions to new states. At each time, an agent receives a reward that depends on the current state and the applied action. Thus, the main problem is to find a control strategy or *policy* that maximizes the expected reward over time. A common problem with the MDP formalism is that the state space grows exponentially

⋆ Ph.D. Student at ITESM Campus Cuernavaca, Av. Reforma 182-A, Lomas, Cuernavaca, Mor., México.

A. Gelbukh and C.A. Reyes-Garcia (Eds.): MICAI 2006, LNAI 4293, pp. 227–236, 2006.

with the number of domain variables, and its inference methods iterate explicitly over the state and action spaces. Thus, in large problems, MDPs become impractical, inefficient and in many cases intractable.

Significant progress has been made on MDP problem specification through the use of factored representations [8]. These representations describe a system using only a small set of features (or factors) by exploiting the structure that many domains exhibit. In a factored MDP the transition model is represented as a dynamic Bayesian network (DBN) and the reward function as a decision tree. Factored MDPs have also been used in reinforcement learning contexts. For example, [10] presented an efficient and near-optimal algorithm for reinforcement learning in MDPs whose transition model was factored. In that work, they assumed that the graphical structure (but not the parameters) of the DBN was given by an expert. More recently in [17], a novel method for approximating the value function and selecting good actions for MDPs with large state and action spaces is described. In this method the model parameters can be learned efficiently because values and derivatives can be computed by a particular type of graphical model called *product of experts*.

Although factored representations can often be used to describe a problem compactly, they do not guarantee that a factored model can be solved effectively, particularly in continuous or highly dimensional domains. Abstraction and aggregation are techniques [2] that aid factored representations to avoid this problem. Several authors use these notions to find computationally feasible methods for the construction of (approximately) optimal and satisfying policies. For example, Dean and Givan [6], and Pineau et al [13] use the notions of abstraction and aggregation to group states that are similar with respect to certain problem characteristics to further reduce the complexity of the representation or the solution. Feng et al [9] proposes a state aggregation approach for exploiting structure in MDPs with continuous variables where the state space is dynamically partitioned into regions where the value function is the same throughout each region. The technique comes from POMDPs to represent and reason about linear surfaces effectively. Li and Littman [11] addresses hybrid state spaces including a comparison with the method of Feng et al.

Our approach is closely related to this work, however it differs on some aspects to offer simplicity in the abstraction construction, and an alternative to learn a complete MDP model from data. The proposed method is inspired on the qualitative change vectors used in [18,16], which are particularly suitable for domains with continuous spaces. While other approaches [12,3] start from a uniform grid over an exhaustive variable representation, we deduce an abstraction, called *qualitative states*, from the reward function structure. In our approach, a set of sampling data denoting the rewards and transitions in continuous terms are first collected to approximate the reward function with a tree learning algorithm (C4.5 [15]). Given a set of qualitative restrictions imposed by the reward function tree, the continuous information about the state transitions is transformed into abstract data that are processed by a Bayesian learning algorithm ($K2$ [4]) to produce a factored transition model. The resulting approximation can be solved easily using standard dynamic programming algorithms. Since the abstraction is built over the factors related to the reward function, the method can work with both, pure continuous or hybrid continuous-discrete spaces. We have tested our abstract MDP model approximation with different configurations of a motion planning problem of different complexities. We present the results in terms of the models learned showing that our approach produces fast solutions with satisfying policies.

This paper is organized as follows: we start describing the standard MDP model and its factored representation. Section 3 develops the abstraction process. Then, we present our learning system and the experimental results. We finally conclude and give future directions of this work.

2 Markov Decision Processes

Formally, an MDP is a tuple $M =< S, A_s, \Phi, R >$, where S is a finite set of states $\{s_1, \ldots, s_n\}$. A_s is a finite set of actions for each state. $\Phi : A \times S \rightarrow \Pi(S)$ is the state transition function specified as a probability distribution. The probability of reaching state s' by performing action a in state s is written as $\Phi(a, s, s')$. $R : S \times A \rightarrow \Re$ is the reward function. $R(s, a)$ is the reward that the agent receives if it takes action a in state s.

A policy for an MDP is a mapping $\pi : S \rightarrow A$ that selects an action for each state. Given a policy, we can define its finite-horizon value function $V_n^\pi : S \rightarrow \Re$, where $V_n^\pi(s)$ is the expected value of applying the policy π for n steps starting in state s. The value function is defined inductively with $V_0^\pi(s) = R(s, \pi(s))$ and $V_m^\pi(s) = R(s, \pi(s)) + \Sigma_{s' \in S} \Phi(\pi(s), s, s') V_{m-1}^\pi(s')$. Over an infinite horizon, a discounted model is used to have a bounded expected value, where the parameter $0 \leq \gamma < 1$ is the *discount factor*, used to discount future rewards at a geometric rate. Thus, if $V^\pi(s)$ is the discounted expected value in state s following policy π forever, we must have $V^\pi(s) = R(s, \pi(s)) + \gamma \Sigma_{s' \in S} \Phi(\pi(s), s, s') V_{m-1}^\pi(s')$, which yields a set of linear equations in the values of $V^\pi()$.

A solution to an MDP is a policy that maximizes its expected value. For the discounted infinite–horizon case with any given discount factor $\gamma \in [0, 1)$, there is a policy V^* that is optimal regardless of the starting state that satisfies the *Bellman* equation [1]:

$$V^*(s) = max_a \{R(s, a) + \gamma \Sigma_{s' \in S} \Phi(a, s, s') V^*(s')\}$$

Two popular methods for solving this equation and finding an optimal policy for an MDP are: (a) value iteration and (b) policy iteration [14].

2.1 Factored MDPs

In a factored MDP, the set of states is described via a set of random variables $\mathbf{X} = \{X_1, \ldots, X_n\}$, where each X_i takes on values in some finite domain $Dom(X_i)$. A state $\mathbf{s}$ defines a value $x_i \in Dom(X_i)$ for each variable X_i. Thus, the set of states $S = Dom(X_i)$ can be exponentially large, making it impractical to represent the

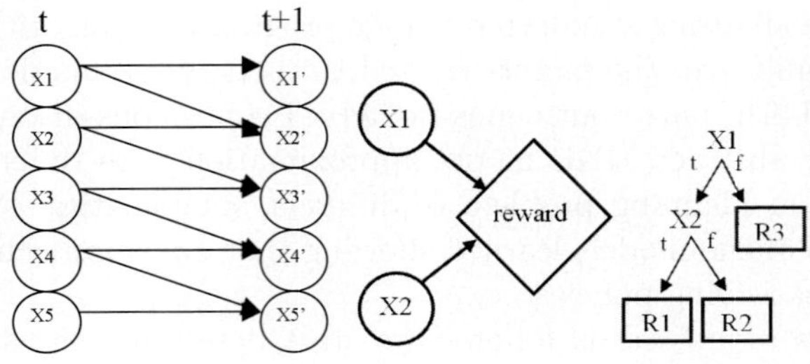

Fig. 1. A simple DBN with 5 state variables for one action (left). Influence Diagram denoting a reward function (center). Structured conditional reward (CR) represented as a binary decision tree (right).

transition model explicitly as matrices. Fortunately, the framework of dynamic Bayesian networks (DBN) [7,5], and the decision trees gives us the tools to describe the transition model and the reward function concisely.

A Markovian transition model Φ defines a probability distribution over the next state given the current state and an action a. Let X_i denote the variable X_i at the current time and X_i' the variable at the next step. The *transition graph* of a DBN is a two–layer directed acyclic graph G_T whose nodes are $\{X_1, \ldots, X_n, X_1', \ldots, X_n'\}$. In the graph, the parents of X_i' are denoted as $Parents(X_i')$. Each node X_i' is associated with a *conditional probability distribution* (CPD) $P_\Phi(X_i' \mid Parents(X_i'))$, which is usually represented by a matrix (*conditional probability table*) or more compactly by a decision tree. The transition probability $\Phi(a, s_i, s_i')$ is then defined to be $\Pi_i P_\Phi(x_i' \mid \mathbf{u_i})$ where $\mathbf{u_i}$ is the value in $\mathbf{s}$ of the variables in $Parents(X_i')$.

Like an action's effect on a particular variable, the reward associated with a state often depends only on the values of certain features of the state. This reward or penalty is independent of other variables, and individual rewards can be associated with the groups of states that differ on the values of the relevant variables. The relationship between rewards and state variables is represented in value nodes in influence diagrams represented by the diamond in figure 1 (center). The conditional reward tables (CRT) for such a node is a table that associates a reward with every combination of values for its parents in the graph. This table is locally exponential in the number of relevant variables. Although in the worst case the CRT will take exponential space to store in many cases the reward function exhibits structure allowing it to be represented compactly using decision trees or graphs (as in figure 1 right).

3 Hybrid MDPs

3.1 Qualitative States

Let us first define a qualitative state (or q–state) q_i as a set of continuous states that share similar immediate rewards. In consequence, a qualitative state space

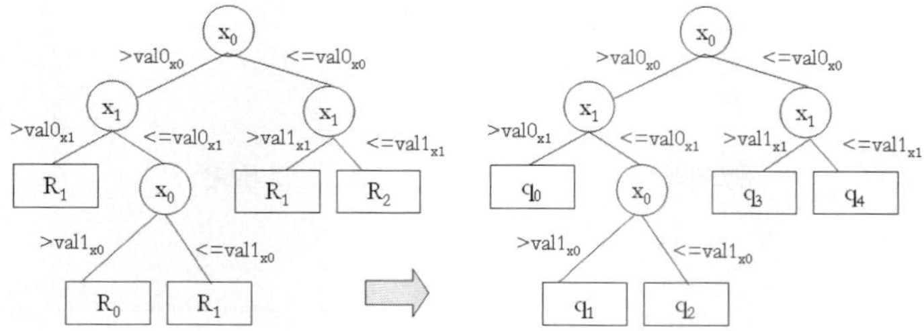

Fig. 2. Transformation of the reward decision tree (left) into a Q-tree (right). Nodes in the tree represent continuous variables and edges evaluate whether this variable is less or greater than a particular bound.

Q is a set of aggregated states $q_1, q_2, ..q_n$ that have this property in common. The qualitative state space can also be simply called as the *qualitative partition.*

Similarly to the reward function in a factored MDP, the qualitative partition Q is represented by a binary decision tree (Q–tree). The reward decision tree is then transformed into a Q-tree by simply renaming the reward values to q-state labels. Each leave in the Q–tree is labeled with a new qualitative state. Even for leaves with the same reward value, we assign a different qualitative state value. This produces more states but at the same time creates more guidance that helps to produce more adequate policies. States with similar reward are partitioned so each q–state is a continuous region. Figure 2 shows this tree transformation in a two dimensional domain.

Each branch in the Q–tree denotes a set of constraints for each q–state q_i that bounds a continuous region. The relational operators used in this approach split each continuous domain dimension in two portions. These operators are $<$ and $\geq$. For example, assuming that the immediate reward is a function of the linear position in a motion planning domain, a qualitative state could be a region in an $x - y$ coordinates system bounded by the constraints: $x \geq val(x_0)$ and $y \geq val(y_0)$, expressing that the current x coordinate is limited by the interval $[val(x_0), \infty]$, and the y coordinate by the interval $[val(y_0), \infty]$. Figure 3 illustrates the constraints associated to the example presented above, and its representation in a 2-dimensional space. It is evident that a qualitative state can cover a large number of states (if we consider a fine discretization) with similar properties.

3.2 Hybrid MDP Model Specification

We can define a hybrid MDP as a factored MDP with a set of hybrid qualitative–discrete factors. The qualitative state space Q, is an additional factor that concentrates all the continuous variables. The idea is to substitute all these variables by this abstraction to reduce the dimensionality of the state space. Thus, a hybrid qualitative-discrete state is described in a factored form as $\mathbf{s_h} = \{X_1, \ldots, X_n, Q\}$, where $X_1, \ldots, X_n$ are the discrete factors, and Q is a factor the represents the relevant continuous dimensions in the reward function.

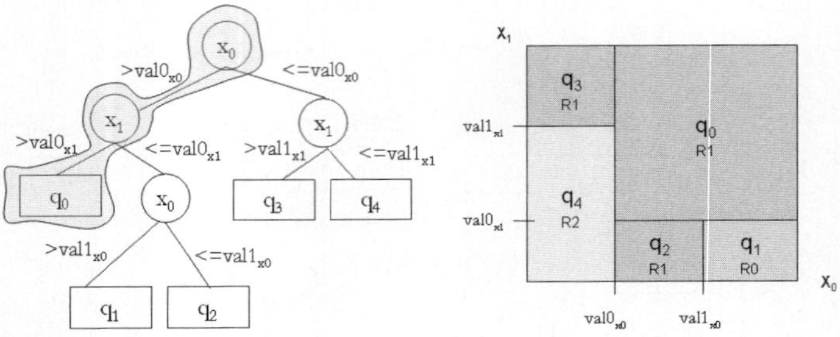

Fig. 3. In a Q-tree, branches are constraints and leaves are qualitative states (left). A graphical representation of the tree is also shown (right). Note that when an upper or lower variable bound is infinite, it must be understood as the upper or lower variable bound in the domain.

3.3 Learning Hybrid MDPs

The hybrid MDP model is learned from data based on a random exploration of a simulated environment with white Gaussian noise introduced on the actions outcomes of the step size. This noise was added to simulate probabilistic real effects of actions. We assume that the agent can explore the state space, and for each state–action can receive some immediate reward. Based on this random exploration, an initial partition, Q_0, of the continuous dimensions is obtained, and the reward function and transition functions are induced.

Given a set of state transition represented as a set of random variables, $O^j = \{\mathbf{X_t}, \mathbf{A}, \mathbf{X_{t+1}}\}$, for $j = 1, 2, ..., M$, for each state and action A executed by an agent, and a reward (or cost) R^j associated to each transition, we learn a qualitative factored MDP model:

1. From a set of examples $\{O, R\}$ obtain a reward decision tree, RDT, that predicts the reward function R in terms of continuous and discrete state variables, $X_1, \ldots, X_k, Q$.
2. Obtain from the decision tree, RDT, the set of constraints for the continuous variables relevant to determine the qualitative states (q–states) in the form of a Q-tree. In terms of the domain variables, we obtain a new variable Q representing the reward-based qualitative state space whose values are the q–states.
3. Qualify data from the original sample in such a way that the new set of attributes are the Q variables, the remaining discrete state variables not included in the decision tree, and the action A. This transformed data set is called the qualified data set.
4. Format the qualified data set in such a way that the attributes follow a temporal causal ordering. For example variable Q_t must be set before Q_{t+1}, $X1_t$ before $X1_{t+1}$, and so on. The whole set of attributes should be the variable Q in time t, the remaining state variables in time t, the variable Q in time t+1, the remaining variables in time t+1, and the action A.

5. Prepare data for the induction of a 2-stage dynamic Bayesian net. According to the action space dimension, split the qualified data set into $|A|$ sets of samples for each action.
6. Induce the transition model for each action, A_j, using the K2 algorithm [4].

This initial model represents a high-level abstraction of the continuous state space and can be solved using a standard solution technique, such as value iteration. In some cases, our abstraction can miss some relevant details of the domain and consequently produced sub-optimal policies. This occurs particularly for domains in which the regions with rewards or punishments are very few or cover a low fraction of the state space. For these cases, we are currently developing a second phase which introduces additional partitions in abstract states with high variance with respect to their neighbors.

4 Experimental Results

We tested our approach in a robot navigation domain using a simulated environment. In this setting goals are represented as light-color square regions with positive immediate reward, and non-desirable regions as dark-color squares with negative reward. The remaining regions in the navigation area receive 0 reward (white). Experimentally, we express the size of a rewarded region (non zero reward) as a function of the navigation area. Rewarded regions are multivalued squares that can be distributed randomly over the navigation area. The number of these squares is also variable.

The robot sensor system included x-y position, angular orientation, and navigation bounds detection. In a set of experiments the possible noisy actions are discrete orthogonal movements to the right, left, up, and down. Figure 4 (left) shows an example of a navigation problem with 12 rewarded regions. The reward function in these cases have four possible values. The motion planning problem is to automatically obtain a satisfying policy for the robot to achieve its goals avoiding negative rewarded regions.

The abstraction was tested with several problems of different sizes and complexities, and compared to a fine discretization of the environment in terms of precision and complexity. The precision is evaluated by comparing the policies and values per state. The *policy precision* is obtained by comparing the policies generated with respect to the policy obtained from a fine discretization. In other words, we count the number of *fine* cells in which the policies are the same:

$$PP = (NEC/NTC) \times 100, \tag{1}$$

where PP is the policy precision in percentage, NEC is the number of fine cells with the same policy, and NTC is the total number of fine cells. This measure is pessimistic because in some states it is possible that more than one action have the same or similar value, and in this measure only one is considered correct. The utility error is calculated as follows: the utility values of all the states in

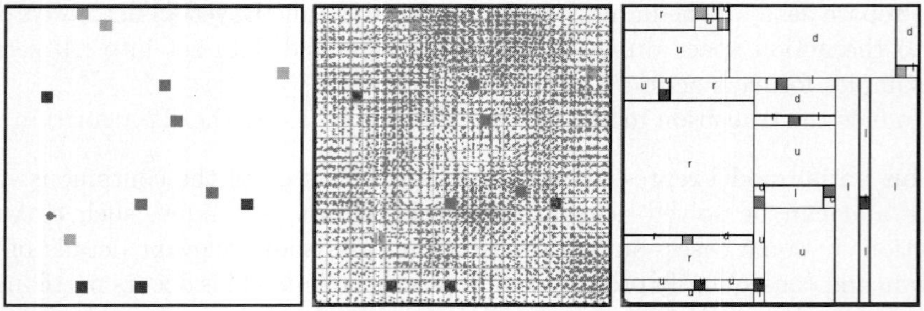

Fig. 4. Abstraction process. Left: Robot navigation area showing the distribution of goals (light color) and non-desirable zones (dark color). The simulated released robot is located at the left-bottom corner. Center: Exploration trace adding a 10% of Gaussian noise respecting to the action step. Right: initial qualitative states and their corresponding policies; u = up, d = down, r = right and l = left.

each representation is first normalized. The sum of the absolute differences of the utility values of the corresponding states is evaluated and averaged over all the differences.

Figure 4 shows an example of one of the test cases. The left figure shows the motion planning problem. The center figure illustrates the exploration process. The right figure shows the qualitative states and their corresponding policies.

Table 1 presents a comparison between the behavior of seven problems solved with a simple discretization approach and our qualitative approach. Problems are identified with a number as shown in the first column. The first five columns describe the characteristics of each problem. For example, problem 1 (first row) has 2 reward cells with values different from zero that occupy 20% of the number of cells, the different number of reward values is 3 (e.g., -10, 0 and 10) and we generated 40,000 samples to build the MDP model. Table 2 presents a comparison between the qualitative and a fine representation. The columns describes

Table 1. Description of problems and comparison between a "normal" discretization and our qualitative discretization in terms of complexity and run time

Problem					**Discrete**				**Qualitative**			
					Learning		**Inference**		**Learning**		**Inference**	
id	no. reward cells	reward size (% dim)	no. reward values	no. samples	no. states	time (ms)	no. iterations	time (ms)	no. states	time (ms)	no. iterations	time (ms)
1	2	20	3	40,000	25	7,671	120	20	8	2,634	120	20
2	4	20	5	40,000	25	1,763	123	20	13	2,423	122	20
3	10	10	3	40,000	100	4,026	120	80	26	2,503	120	20
4	6	5	3	40,000	400	5,418	120	1,602	24	4,527	120	40
5	10	5	5	28,868	400	3,595	128	2,774	29	2,203	127	60
6	12	5	4	29,250	400	7,351	124	7,921	46	2,163	124	30
7	14	3.3	9	50,000	900	9,223	117	16,784	60	4,296	117	241

the characteristics of the qualitative model in terms of utility error in % and policy precision.

Table 2. Comparative results between the abstraction and a fine discretization in terms of precision and errors

	Qualitative	
id	Utility error (%)	Policy precision (%)
1	7.38	80
2	9.03	64
3	10.68	64
4	12.65	52
5	7.13	35
6	11.56	47.2
7	5.78	44.78

As can be seen from Table 1, there is a significant reduction in the complexity of the problems using our abstraction approach. This can be clearly appreciated from the number of states and processing time required to solve the problems. This is important since in complex domains where it can be difficult to define an adequate abstraction or solve the resulting MDP problem, one option is to create abstractions and hope for suboptimal policies. To evaluate the quality of the results Table 2 shows that the proposed abstraction produces on average only 9.17% error in the utility value when compared against the values obtained from the discretized problem.

5 Conclusions and Future Work

In this paper, a novel approach for solving continuous and hybrid MDPs is described. In the first phase we use an exploration strategy of the environment and a machine learning approach to induce an initial state abstraction. Our approach creates significant reductions in space and time allowing to solve quickly relatively large problems. The utility values on our abstracted representation are reasonably close (less than 13%) to those obtained using a fine discretization of the domain. Although tested on small solvable problems for comparison purposes, the approach can be applied to more complex domains where a simple discretization approach is not feasible. For space reasons, we did not include the partial models resulting of the learning process for the motion planning example. However they are available for clarifications.

As current research work we are including a refinement strategy of the abstraction to select a better segmentation of the abstract states and use alternative search strategies. We are also testing our approach in more sophisticated domains such as process control. The results of this research are oriented to built an intelligent assistant for training operators in power plants.

Acknowledgments. This work was supported in part by IIE Project No. 12941 and CONACYT Project No. 47968.

References

1. R.E. Bellman. *Dynamic Programming.* Princeton U. Press, Princeton, N.J., 1957.
2. C. Boutilier, T. Dean, and S. Hanks. Decision-theoretic planning: structural assumptions and computational leverage. *Journal of AI Research*, 11:1–94, 1999.
3. Craig Boutilier, Moisés Goldszmidt, and Bikash Sabata. Continuous value function approximation for sequential bidding policies. In Kathryn Laskey and Henri Prade, editors, *Proceedings of the 15th Conference on Uncertainty in Artificial Intelligence (UAI-99).* Morgan Kaufmann Publishers, San Francisco, California, USA.
4. G. F. Cooper and E. Herskovits. A Bayesian method for the induction of probabilistic networks from data. *Machine Learning*, 1992.
5. A. Darwiche and Goldszmidt M. Action networks: A framework for reasoning about actions and change under understanding. In *Proceedings of the Tenth Conf. on Uncertainty in AI, UAI-94*, pages 136–144, Seattle, WA, USA, 1994.
6. T. Dean and R. Givan. Model minimization in Markov decision processes. In *Proc. of the 14th National Conf. on AI*, pages 106–111. AAAI, 1997.
7. T. Dean and K. Kanazawa. A model for reasoning about persistence and causation. *Computational Intelligence*, 5:142–150, 1989.
8. R. Dearden and R. Boutillier. Abstraction and approximate decision-theoretic planning. *AI*, 89:219–283, 1997.
9. Z. Feng, R. Dearden, N. Meuleau, and R. Washington. Dynamic programming for structured continuous Markov decision problems. In *Proc. of the 20th Conf. on Uncertainty in AI (UAI-2004). Banff, Canada*, 2004.
10. M. Kearns and D. Koller. Efficient reinforcement learning in factored MDPs. In *Proc. of the Sixteenth International Joint on Artificial Intelligence, IJCAI-99*, Stockolm, Sweden, 1999.
11. Lihong Li and Michael L. Littman. Lazy approximation for solving continuous finite-horizon MDPs. In *AAAI-05*, pages 1175–1180, Pittsburgh, PA, 2005.
12. Remi Munos and Andrew Moore. Variable resolution discretization for high-accuracy solutions of optimal control problems. In Thomas Dean, editor, *Proceedings of the 16th International Joint Conference on Artificial Intelligence (IJCAI-99)*, pages 1348–1355. Morgan Kaufmann Publishers, San Francisco, California, USA, August 1999.
13. J. Pineau, G. Gordon, and S. Thrun. Policy-contingent abstraction for robust control. In *Proc. of the 19th Conf. on Uncertainty in AI, UAI-03*, pages 477–484, 2003.
14. M.L. Puterman. *Markov Decision Processes.* Wiley, New York, 1994.
15. J.R. Quinlan. *C4.5: Programs for machine learning.* Morgan Kaufmann, San Francisco, Calif., USA., 1993.
16. A. Reyes, L. E. Sucar, E. Morales, and P. H. Ibarguengoytia. Abstract MDPs using qualitative change predicates: An application in power generation. In *Planning under Uncertainty in Real-World Problems Workshop. Neural Information Processing Systems (NIPS-03)*, Vancouver CA, Winter 2003.
17. B. Sallans and G. E. Hinton. Reinforcement learning with factored states and actions. *Journal of Machine Learning and Research*, pages 1063–1088, 2004.
18. D. Suc and I. Bratko. Qualitative reverse engineering. In *Proc. of the 19th International Conf. on Machine Learning*, 2000.

Comparing Fuzzy Naive Bayes and Gaussian Naive Bayes for Decision Making in RoboCup 3D

Carlos Bustamante, Leonardo Garrido, and Rogelio Soto

Centro de Sistemas Inteligentes
Tecnológico de Monterrey
Monterrey, N.L. 64849, México
{cfbh, leonardo.garrido, rsoto}@itesm.mx

Abstract. Learning and making decisions in a complex uncertain multiagent environment like RoboCup Soccer Simulation 3D is a non-trivial task. In this paper, a probabilistic approach to handle such uncertainty in RoboCup 3D is proposed, specifically a Naive Bayes classifier. Although its conditional independence assumption is not always accomplished, it has proved to be successful in a whole range of applications. Typically, the Naive Bayes model assumes discrete attributes, but in RoboCup 3D the attributes are continuous. In literature, Naive Bayes has been adapted to handle continuous attributes mainly using Gaussian distributions or discretizing the domain, both of which present certain disadvantages. In the former, the probability density of attributes is not always well-fitted by a normal distribution. In the latter, there can be loss of information. Instead of discretizing, the use of a Fuzzy Naive Bayes classifier is proposed in which attributes do not take a single value, but a set of values with a certain membership degree. Gaussian and Fuzzy Naive Bayes classifiers are implemented for the pass evaluation skill of 3D agents. The classifiers are trained with different number of training examples and different number of attributes. Each generated classifier is tested in a scenario with three teammates and four opponents. Additionally, Gaussian and Fuzzy approaches are compared versus a random pass selector. Finally, it is shown that the Fuzzy Naive Bayes approach offers very promising results in the RoboCup 3D domain.

1 Introduction

RoboCup simulation is an excelent test-bed for machine learning algorithms. It presents a multi-agent cooperative and adversarial scenario in a partially observable, episodic, continuous and non-deterministic noisy environment.

Given such uncertainty, classical logic-based approaches fail to achieve a high performance. Thus, a probabilistic method is ideal for dealing with this kind of environment.

The most simple probabilistic approach is the Naive Bayesian classification [1] which has proven to be successful in many applications [2] in spite of the not always fulfilled conditional independence assumption of the attributes given the

A. Gelbukh and C.A. Reyes-Garcia (Eds.): MICAI 2006, LNAI 4293, pp. 237–247, 2006.

class. If we wish to use this classifier in the RoboCup simulation domain, we confront two main issues.

First, the classical Naive Bayes classifier assumes that the attributes are discrete, but in RoboCup simulation the attributes are in the range of real numbers and thus are continuous. Second, the classifier must lead to a fast decision process because the soccer simulator demands almost real-time decisions with low thinking times for the sense-think-act cyle of the agents.

In literature, continuous attributes are handled using conditional Gaussian distributions for each attribute likelihood given the class. Other approach is to discretize by crisp partitioning the domain of the attributes, but this can lead to loss of information.

Instead of discretizing, we overcome the issues using a fuzzy extension namely Fuzzy Naive Bayesian classifier in the following way: the continuous attributes are fuzzified and combined with probabilities of the naive bayes model in a straight easy way. The formulas used in the fuzzy extension resemble the original naive bayes equations, so the classification process is still fast and reliable plus providing an incremental learning mechanism.

The Fuzzy Naive Bayesian classifier is implemented in a RoboCup simulation 3D team for decision making. We test it specifically to evaluate the best pass receiver in a given situation. In the next sections, we first explain the Fuzzy Naive Bayes model and the Gaussian model, then we describe our empirical scenarios for the pass evaluation skill. After that, results of our experiments and some conclusions are shown.

2 Naive Bayes and the Fuzzy Extension

The Naive Bayes classifier is a simple bayesian network with one root node that represents the class and n leaf nodes that represent the attributes. Let C be a class label with k possible values, and $X_1...X_n$ be a set of attributes or features of the environment with a finite domain $D(X_i)$ where $i = 1..n$. The classifier is given by the combination of the bayesian probabilistic model with a maximum a posteriori (MAP) rule, also called discriminant function [3]. The Naive Bayes classifier is defined as follows

$$NBayes(a) = argmax_{c \in C} P(c) \prod_{i=1}^{n} P(x_i|c) \quad (1)$$

where $a = \{X_1 = x_1, ..., X_n = x_n\}$ is a complete assignation of attributes, i.e. a new example to be classified, x_i is a short for $X_i = x_i$ and c is a short for $C = c$. The equation assumes conditional independence between attributes.

To deal with continuous variables, the domain of attributes can be crisp partitioned, but that could cause a loss of information [4]. We use a better method proposed in [5], namely a Fuzzy Bayesian classifier, a hybrid approach in which attributes are fuzzified before classification.

In this approach, the degrees of truth are treated as probabilities such that $P(x_i|a) = \mu_{x_i}$ and $P(c|a) = \mu_c$. Although degrees of truth represent membership values of classes rather than probabilities, it allows a natural extension of the classical Naive Bayes equation, using the Bayes' rule and assuming independence among attributes

$$P(c|a) = \sum_{x_1 \in X_1,..x_n \in X_n} P(c|x_1..x_n)P(x_1|a)..P(x_n|a) \tag{2}$$

$$P(c|a) = \sum_{x_1 \in X_1,..x_n \in X_n} \frac{P(x_1|c)..P(x_n|c)P(c)}{P(x_1)..P(x_n)} \mu_{x_1}..\mu_{x_n} \tag{3}$$

The Fuzzy Naive Bayesian classifier is defined from (3) as follows

$$FNBayes(a) = argmax_{c \in C} P(c) \sum_{x_{1j} \in X_1} \frac{P(x_{1j}|c)}{P(x_{1j})} \mu_{x_{1j}} .. \sum_{x_{nj} \in X_n} \frac{P(x_{nj}|c)}{P(x_{nj})} \mu_{x_{nj}} \tag{4}$$

where $j = 1..D(X_i)$ and $\mu_{x_{ij}} \in [0, 1]$ denotes a membership function or degree of truth of attribute value $x_{ij} \in X_i$ in a new example a. All degrees of truth must be normalized such that $\sum_{x_{ij} \in X_i} \mu_{x_{ij}} = 1$ for all attributes $i = 1..n$.

The probabilities required by the fuzzy model can be calculated similarly to classical Naive Bayes (1)

$$P(C = c) = \frac{(\sum_{e \in L} \mu_c^e) + 1}{|L| + |D(C)|} \tag{5}$$

$$P(X_i = x_i) = \frac{(\sum_{e \in L} \mu_{x_i}^e) + 1}{|L| + |D(X_i)|} \tag{6}$$

$$P(X_i = x_i | C = c) = \frac{(\sum_{e \in L} \mu_{x_i}^e \mu_c^e) + 1}{(\sum_{e \in L} \mu_c^e) + |D(X_i)|} \tag{7}$$

where Laplace-correction [6] is applied to smooth calculations avoiding extreme values obtained with small training sets. Here L is the set of all training examples e, where $e = \{X_1 = x_1, ..., X_n = x_n, C = c\}$, $|L|$ refers to the number of examples $e \in L$, $\mu_c^e \in [0, 1]$ denotes the degree of truth of $c \in C$ in a example $e \in L$, and $\mu_{x_i}^e \in [0, 1]$ is the membership of attribute $x_i \in X_i$ in such example. Same as in (4), all degrees of truth must be normalized such that $\sum_{c \in C} \mu_c^e = 1$ and $\sum_{x_i \in X_i} \mu_{x_i}^e = 1$.

3 Gaussian Naive Bayes

One typical way to handle continuous attributes in the Naive Bayes classification is to use Gaussian distributions [7] to represent the likelihoods of the features conditioned on the classes. Thus each attribute is defined by a Gaussian probability density function (PDF) as

$$X_i \sim N(\mu, \sigma^2) \tag{8}$$

The Gaussian PDF has the shape of a bell and is defined by the following equation

$$N(\mu, \sigma^2)(x) = \frac{1}{\sqrt{2\pi\sigma^2}} e^{-\frac{(x-\mu)^2}{2\sigma^2}} \tag{9}$$

where μ is the mean and σ^2 is the variance. In Naive Bayes, the parameters needed are in the order of $O(nk)$, where n is the number of attributes and k is the number of classes. Specifically we need to define a normal distribution $P(Xi|C) \sim N(\mu, \sigma^2)$ for each continuous attribute. The parameters of such normal distributions can be obtained with

$$\mu_{X_i|C=c} = \frac{1}{N_c} \sum_{i=1}^{N_c} x_i \tag{10}$$

$$\sigma^2_{X_i|C=c} = \frac{1}{N_c} \sum_{i=1}^{N_c} {x_i}^2 - \mu^2 \tag{11}$$

where N_c is the number of examples where $C = c$ and N is the number of total examples used for training. Calculating $P(C = c)$ for all classes is easy using relative frequencies such that

$$P(C = c) = \frac{N_c}{N} \tag{12}$$

4 Empirical Scenarios

Selecting a good scenario for training the classifiers is not trivial. In simulated soccer there is a large set of possible scenarios for a given skill.

For the purposes of this paper, we chose the pass evaluation skill as our test-bed for the training of both classifiers. One of the reasons why we selected this skill was that passing is a fundamental characteristic of an agent that aims to play a soccer game. Specifically, deciding what teammate is the best receiver in a given situation could lead to better chances to score later in the game.

Some may argue that passing not only involves the ability to select an optimal receiver, but the ability of the receiver to predict the pass action and anticipate it in some way. Additionally, it could be said that the teammate with best chances to receive a ball and control it is not always the best receiver.

Consider the situation when the ball is controled by a midfielder, the probability of a successful pass is just a little bigger for a defender than for a forward, just evaluating the pass would select the defender as the best passing option. However, it is easy to see that the forward has more chances to score generally, so the **utility** of passing to the forward is greater than the utility to passing to a defender. These arguments may be true, but that concerns a higher layer which some people have called pass selection [8] and involves the calculus of expected utilities.

This paper is focused on the pass evaluation only, because our main goal is to compare different strategies to calculate the probabilites for selecting a receiver. In [9] we introduced the use of a Fuzzy Naive Bayes classifier for the

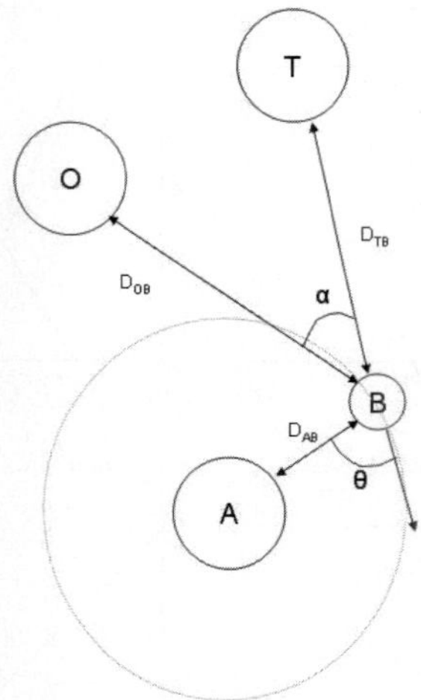

Fig. 1. Training scenario for supervised learning of parameters of each classifier. Three agents are involved: a passer agent (A), a receiver teammate (T) and an opponent (O). The ball is marked as (B). Features considered are: distance to ball d_{AB}, distance to teammate d_{TB}, distance to opponent d_{OB}, alignment angle (θ) and angle bewteen teammate and opponent from the ball's view point (α).

pass evaluation skill. We tested the classifier, trained with 1000 examples, in 300 episodes of a test scenario. The results were promising: 76% of the 300 passes were successful. However, we did not compared the Fuzzy Naive Bayes classifier to another approach. In this paper we make the comparison between both classifiers in the same scenarios to evaluate the performance of the Fuzzy Naive Bayes in a more tangible way.

The scenario we used to obtain the training set is explained below. One agent (**passer**) is placed in the center of the field with the ball at a distance of $d_{AB} \in [kickrange, 2]$, where *kickrange* is the minimum kicking radial distance between the agent and the ball stated in the soccer server. Another agent (**teammate**) is placed near the ball at a distance $d_{TB} \in [2, 20]$. One last agent (**opponent**) is placed similarly, with a distance $d_{OB} \in [2, 20]$ from the ball. The angle between the teammate and the opponent from the ball's view point must be $\alpha \in [0, \frac{\pi}{6}]$. A graphical representation of this scenario is shown in figure 1.

This scenario is a modification of the one proposed in [10] and used in simulation 2D. We added the alignment angle and distance to the ball because in 3D soccer, as agents are spheres, the force for kicking the ball is applied radially, thus the agent has to position correctly around the ball before kicking and of course, losing some time.

The features extracted from the scenario in each episode are:

– Distance to the ball d_{AB}
– Distance to teammate d_{AT}
– Distance to opponent d_{AO}

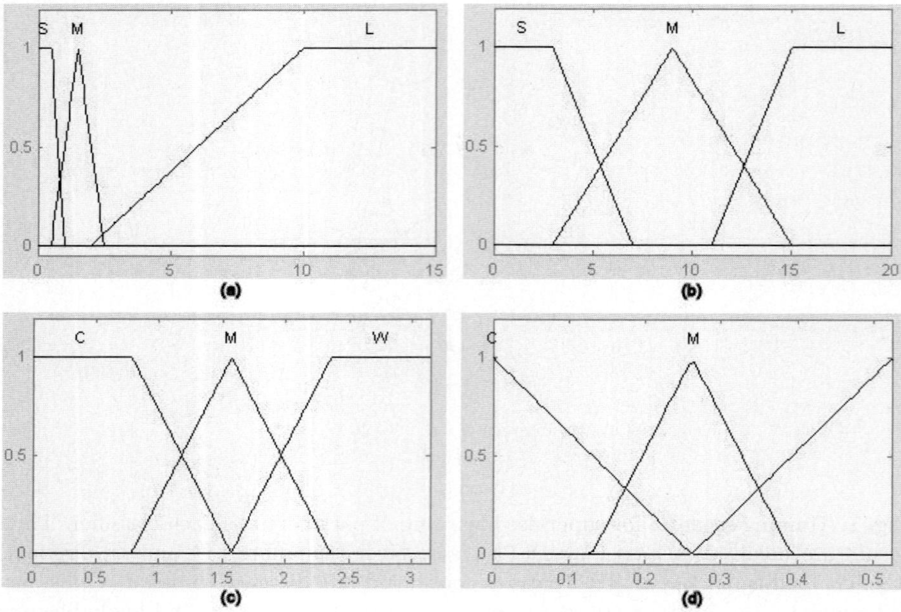

Fig. 2. Fuzzy Sets for each Fuzzy Variable. (a) Distance to the ball d_{AB}, (b) Distance to teammate d_{AT} and distance to opponent d_{AO}, (c) Alignment Angle θ and (d) Angle between teammate and opponent α.

- Alignment angle $\theta \in [0, \pi]$
- Angle between teammate and opponent α

The behaviors of each agent during the episode are as follows:

- The passer agent aligns with the ball to pass it to its teammate.
- The teammate and the opponent try to intercept the pass.

Once the teammate touched the ball, the episode is labeled as *SUCCESS*. If the opponent touches the ball first, episode is labeled as *MISS*.

In the case of the Fuzzy Naive Bayes classifier, aside of obtaining the probabilities of the bayesian model, we have to establish the fuzzy sets for each variable.

Fuzzy sets represent linguistic values and are mathematically expressed with membership degree functions. We defined the fuzzy sets for each variable heuristically. The sets chosen for distance to the ball d_{AB}, distance to teammate d_{AT} and distance to opponent d_{AO} variables are {*short, medium, long*}, and for θ and α variables are {*closed, medium, wide*}. A graphical representation of each fuzzy variable is shown in figure 2.

The probabilities for the Fuzzy Naive Bayes model are calculated using equations (5), (6) and (7). The learning process is described as follows:

- Read the training set one example at a time.
- For each attribute of each example, calculate the normalized membership degrees of each fuzzy set.

- Store the sums $\sum_{e \in L} \mu_c^e$, $\sum_{e \in L} \mu_{x_i}^e$ and $\sum_{e \in L} \mu_{x_i}^e \mu_c^e$. Note that μ_c^e is either 1 or 0 because the class attribute is discrete. Additionally, store the total numer of examples L and the domain size of the class $|D(C)|$ and attributes $|D(X_i)|$.
- Compute all the probabilities $P(C = c)$, $P(X_i = x_i)$ and $P(X_i = x_i | C = c)$.
- When a new example arrives, use the calculated probabilities to classify it with equation 4.

5 Experimental Results

We ran two main tests, one for evaluating the performance of both classifiers in a test set and the other for evaluating the efficiency in a simulated soccer scenario.

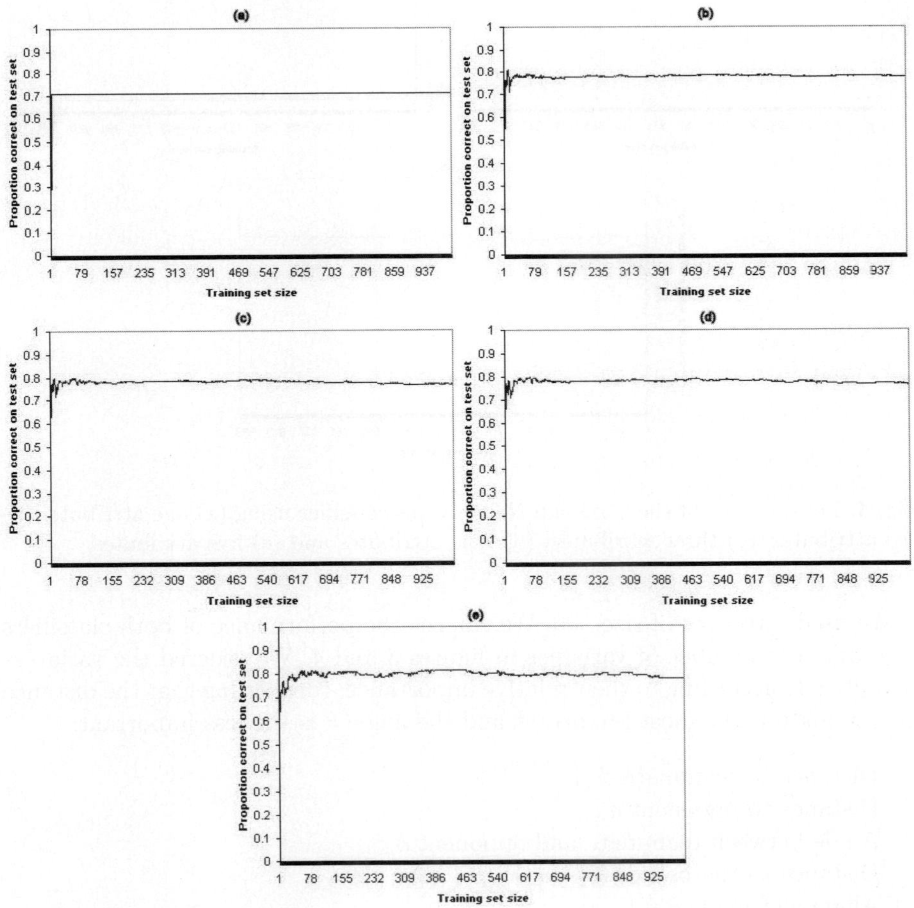

Fig. 3. Performance of the Fuzzy Naive Bayes classifier using (a) one attribute, (b) two attributes, (c) three attributes, (d) four attributes and (e) five attributes

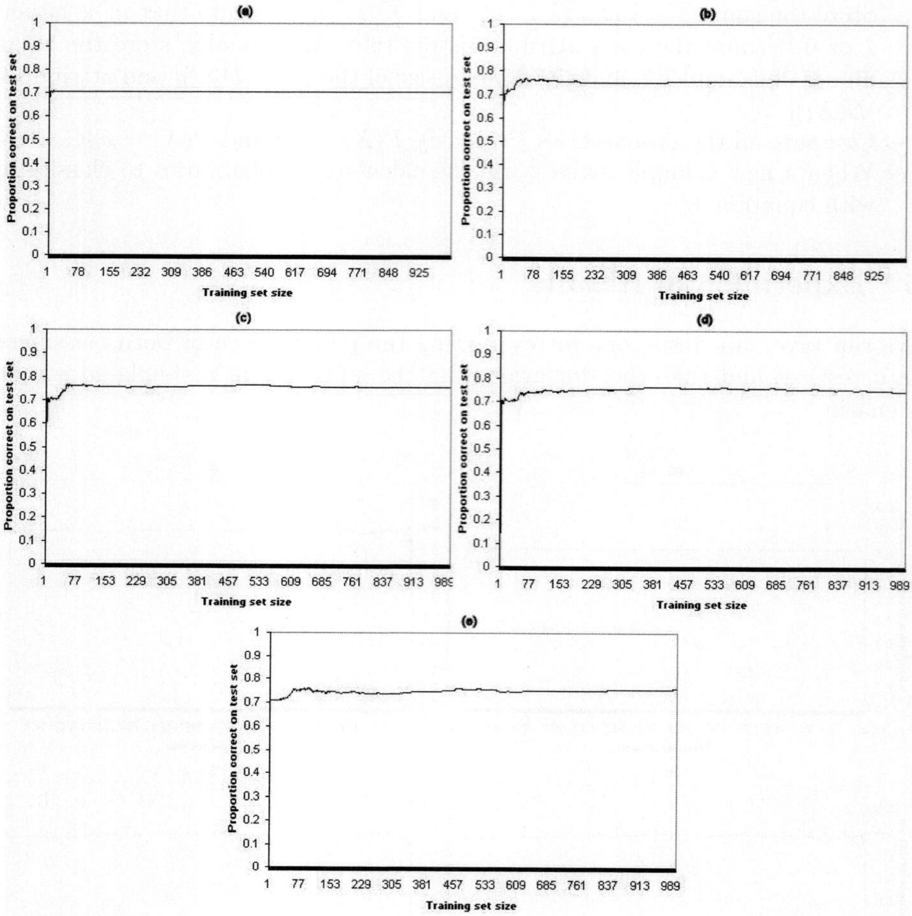

Fig. 4. Performance of the Gaussian Naive Bayes classifier using (a) one attribute, (b) two attributes, (c) three attributes, (d) four attributes and (e) five attributes

We used a test set of size 500. We can see the performance of both classifiers with different number of variables in figures 3 and 4. We ordered the variables heuristically according to their relative importance, considering that the distance to teammate is the most important and the angle θ is the less important:

- Distance to teammate d_{AT}
- Distance to opponent d_{AO}
- Angle between teammate and opponent α
- Distance to the ball d_{AB}
- Alignment angle $\theta \in [0, \pi]$

For evaluating the efficiency in the domain of interest, we created a simulated-soccer test-scenario shown in figure 5. The ball is placed at $(x = -20, y = 0)$

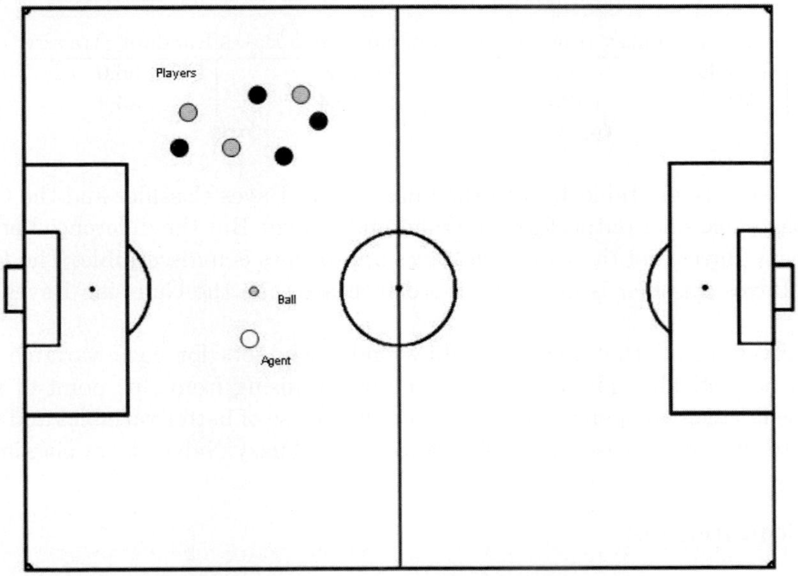

Fig. 5. Test scenario for the pass evaluation skill. Four opponent agents (black circles) and three teammates (gray circles) are placed randomly in a certain area. The passer (white circle) and the ball (little circle) are placed a few meters away. The passer chooses the teammate with the best chances to intercept the ball using the classifier.

and the agent is placed at ($x \in [-22, -18], y \in [kickrange, 2]$). After that, three teammates and four opponents are placed randomly at ($x \in [-30, -10], y \in [10, 30]$).

The passer uses a classifier to choose the best receiver teammate, i.e. the teammate with better chances to intercept the pass successfully. The passer uses the classifier evaluating all 1 vs. 1 competitions between each teammate and each opponent (because the classifier was trained this way). Then it selects the teammate with the maximum probabilty of success given its worst probabilty in all its 1 vs. 1 competitions, formally

$$Receiver = argmax_{t \in T} \; argmin_{o \in O} \; P(SUCCESS_{to}) \tag{13}$$

being T the set of all teammates, O the set of opponents and $P(SUCCESS_{to})$ is the probability of success of the competition between teammate $t \in T$ and opponent $o \in O$. The episode is a *SUCCESS* if the teammate intercepts the ball before any opponent does, otherwise, the episode is labeled *MISS*. Indeed, this is the way to use the classifier in a real game.

In table 1, we summarize the success rates of Fuzzy Naive Bayes, the Gaussian Naive Bayes and additionally, a random strategy. We classified 500 episodes with each classifier trained with different number of variables. The maximum percentage of success was achieved using 5 variables for both the fuzzy and the gaussian approaches.

Table 1. Percentage of successful passes for 500 episodes using our test scenario

Class	Fuzzy Naive Bayes	Gaussian Naive Bayes	Random Strategy
SUCCESS	80.8	79.6	56.6
MISS	19.2	20.4	43.4

As we can see in table 1, both the Fuzzy Naive Bayes classifier and the Gaussian Bayes classifier outperform the random strategy. But the difference between the Fuzzy Bayes and the Gaussian Bayes approaches is indiscernible. The Fuzzy Naive Bayes classifier is just 1.2% more accurate than the Gaussian Bayes classifier.

However, recall that fuzzy variables and fuzzy sets for each variable were chosen heuristically. The result seems more promising from this point of view, because it leaves an open path for researching the use of better variables and more accurate sets to increase the performance of the Fuzzy Naive Bayes classifier.

6 Conclusions

In this paper, we compared the Gaussian Naive Bayes classifier with a Fuzzy Naive Bayes classifier for making decisions. We focused on the pass evaluation skill in the Robocup simulation 3D domain. Robocup simulation offers an excelent testbed for probabilistic learning algorithms because of the uncertain and noisy sensor data and unknown opponent model.

The Naive Bayes classifier has been successfully used in a whole range of applications although its conditional independence assumption is not always met. Naive Bayes attributes are usually discrete, but in RoboCup Simulation 3D attributes are continuous, thus we tried both Gaussian and Fuzzy extensions to classical Naive Bayes for handling those continuous features.

We trained both classifiers with different number of variables and tested them on the scenario proposed in figure 5. We obtained 80.8% of successful passes using the Fuzzy Naive Bayes approach trained with 5 variables. Stone [11] used a Decision Tree for pass evaluation in a similar test scenario and just 65% of all passes where successful.

As we can see in table 1, the Fuzzy Naive Bayes classifier outperforms the random strategy, but is just a little better than the Gaussian Naive Bayes approach. In fact, at a first glance, the results between the Fuzzy Naive Bayes classifier and the Gaussian Naive Bayes seem indiscernible. Nevertheless, the result obtained with the Fuzzy Naive Bayes classifier is very good considering that the variables and the fuzzy sets were chosen heuristically.

There is a lot of future work to do in this area. First of all, we have the hypothesis that if we define better sets and different variables we can get better results. Possibily, combining the classifier with a decision tree algorithm, we can prune the useless variables from our list of variables related to the pass skill. Also we want to test the classifier for other skills, like dribble and shoot. We plan to implement fuzzy k-means clustering for obtaining the fuzzy sets automatically from data. We also want to try other probability distributions aside from the Gaussian approach.

Acknowledgements

This work was supported in part by the ITESM research grant CAT-011 on distributed knowledge and intelligent agents technologies.

References

1. Langley P., Iba, W., Thompson, K.: An Analysis of Bayesian Classifiers. Proc. 10th Nat. Conf. on Artificial Intelligence, AAAI Press and MIT Press, USA (1992) 223-228
2. Lewis, D: Naive Bayes at forty: The independence assumption in information retrieval. In Proceedings of European Conference on Machine Learning, (1998) 4–15
3. Rish, I.: An empirical study of the naive bayes classifier. In Proceedings of IJCAI-01 workshop on Empirical Methods in AI, (2001) 41–46
4. Friedman, N., Goldszmidt, M.: Discretization of continuous attributes while learning Bayesian networks. In L. Saitta, editor, Proceedings of 13-th International Conference on Machine Learning, (1996) 157–165
5. Störr, Hans-Peter: A compact fuzzy extension of the Naive Bayesian classification algorithm. In Proceedings InTech/VJFuzzy, (2002) 172–177
6. Zadrozny, B., Elkan, E.: Obtaining calibrated probability estimates from decision trees and naive Bayesian classifiers. In Proceedings of 18th International Conf. on Machine Learning, (2001) 609–616
7. Mitchell, T: Machine Learning. McGraw-Hill, 1997.
8. Stone, P., Veloso, M.: Layered Learning. In Proceedings of 11th European Conference on Machine Learning, (2000) 369–381
9. Bustamante, C., Garrido, L., Soto, R.: Fuzzy Naive Bayesian Classification in RoboSoccer 3D: A hybrid approach to decision making. In Proceedings of RoboCup International Symposium, (2006).
10. Buck, S., Riedmiller, M.: Learning Situation Dependent Success Rates Of Actions In A RoboCup Scenario. Pacific Rim International Conference on Artificial Intelligence, (2000) 809
11. Stone, P.: Layered Learning in Multiagent Systems: A Winning Approach to Robotic Soccer. MIT Press, 2000.

Using the Beliefs of Self-Efficacy to Improve the Effectiveness of ITS: An Empirical Study

Francine Bica[1,3], Regina Verdin[2], and Rosa Vicari[1,2]

[1] Universidade do Rio Grande do Sul, Instituto de Informática
{francine, rosa}inf.ufrgs.br
http://www.inf.ufrgs.br
[2] Programa de Pós-Graduação em Informática na Educação
Universidade do Rio Grande do Sul
Porto Alegre, Brazil, CEP 91501-970
rverdin@inf.ufrgs.br
http://www.pgie.ufrgs.br
[3] Faculdade Cenecista de Osório, 24 de Maio 141, Osório RS

Abstract. This paper presents the preliminary results of the Student Model based on beliefs of Self-Efficacy aiming to improve the effectiveness of Intelligent Tutoring Systems. The Self-efficacy construct means the student's belief on his own capacity of performing a task. This belief affects his behavior, motivation, affectivity and the choices he makes. We design an e-Learning System, called InteliWeb, this environment is composed by the Self-Efficacy Mediator Agent and offers instruction material on Biological sciences. We use fuzzy theory for dealing with uncertainty in the assessment of the students and the incomplete knowledge about his Self-Efficacy.

1 Introduction

The present work is inserted in the context of the technology of Intelligent Tutoring Systems (ITS) and Web-based instruction, to render tutoring over the Web adaptive to individual students. The intelligence of an educational system is largely attributed to its ability to adapt to a specific student during the teaching process.

We present an Intelligent Tutoring System (ITS), called InteliWeb, composed by the Self-Efficacy Mediator agent (SEM). The student model comprises cognition and affectivity and the information that will be constantly analyzed which are the self-efficacy beliefs, proposed in the motivational model by Bandura [1].

According to Bandura, self-efficacy represents "beliefs of individuals about their capacities of mobilizing the cognitive resources, the motivation and the course of actions, a process required to control the task requirements" [1]. It is not a matter of having such capacities or not, the individual believes that he has them, besides, they are capacities turned towards the organization and accomplishment of action lines, this means the student will have an expectation of being able to accomplish a task.

In the ITS, the adaptability to the student is in the student model component. This dynamic model should reflect also the changes that the student undergoes when interactions take place and student model represented captures all the knowledge expected to produce a diagnose about the student.

A. Gelbukh and C.A. Reyes-Garcia (Eds.): MICAI 2006, LNAI 4293, pp. 248 – 258, 2006.

The uncertainty is an important factor that often leads to errors in student diagnosis. The uncertainty seems to be partly due to errors and approximations involved when gathering data from measurements, and the abstract nature of human cognition as well as the loss of information resulting from its quantification. In the educational system where there is no direct interaction between the tutor and the student the collected data tend to be more haphazard, than those obtained through traditional face-to-face interaction. The student's state is constantly changing during the dynamic process of learning and, therefore is quite difficult to be sure about his current mental state. Considering the attributes of the problem mencioned, it is obvious that the development of a reliable method for student state diagnosis is based on handling of uncertainty successfully.

In related works [2][3] use student model with mental state and motivation factors, for example, the FLAME tutor (Fuzzy Logic Adaptive Model of Emotions) [4], uses the Fuzzy Logic[5] to represent the student's emotions for intensity and mapped the expect for these motivation states and student's behavior.

The student's model managed by the SEM agent comprises the student's self-efficacy. This characteristic can be used to help the student not feel lost in his task, not to feel alone or not to have a negative attitude towards learning. In this paper, we use concepts of ITS, agent, Fuzzy Logic and Bandura's Theory to create a computation model of Self-Efficacy. This is the main contribution of this paper.

The paper is organized as follow: item 2 presents the Self-Efficacy definition and related works, item 3 describes the main characteristics of Computation Model of Self-Efficacy, item 4 describes some empirical evaluation and item 5 presents final considerations.

2 Recognizing and Modelling of Self-Efficacy

The Self-Efficacy beliefs concerns not only to the capacities of an individual in perform a task successfully, but the judgment he makes on such capacities. The Beliefs about these capacities and personal resources constitute a product of the interaction between several factors, such as previous successfull or failed experiences.

Bandura [1] defines Self-Efficacy as “the individual belief on his capacities for controlling events that affect his life”, and “the belief on his capacities to mobilize motivation, cognitive resources and implement actions that allow him to control required tasks."

In the academic environment a student is motivated to get involved in learning activities when he believes that by using his knowledge, talent and abilities he will be able to acquire new information, master contents and improve his abilities, among others. Thus, the student will select activities and strategies that he will be able to perform, as he can foresee, and will abandon other objectives and courses of action that do not motivate him, because he knows he will not be able to implement them.

The Self-Efficacy construct can be represented as a schema or model of mental working. The main elements of Bandura's Self-Efficacy model are: objectives, personal standard, evaluative process and feedback. Fig. 1 presents this model and the relationships among its elements.

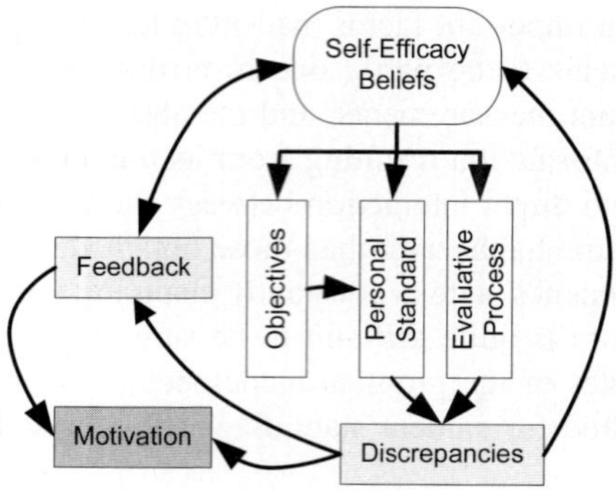

Fig. 1. Self-Efficacy Model is composed by objectives, personal standard, evaluative process, discrepancies, motivation and feedback

The Bandura's Model presupposes [1] the Self-Efficacy beliefs affect the student's objectives choices. Differing from Bandura's Model personal standard and objective are the same in the computational model (see section 3), and they can also be extrinsic or intrinsic. The Intrinsic objective is the knowledge domain and the extrinsic knowledge is the performance. Ames [4] says that students that select the intrinsic learning objective make more efforts to learn something new or face challenging tasks. When these students face difficulties, they increase their efforts because they believe the effort is necessary to reach success.

Ames [6] says that students that are extrinsically motivated, and consequently select the learning objective of performance do not increase their efforts when they find difficulties, they do not increase their efforts because they consider this means lack of capacity. Such behavior indicates that these students can have less control of self-regulation of their learning than students that select a domain.

Bandura [1] says that when individuals are allowed to choose their goals they undertake a commitment, considering themselves responsible for the progress towards reaching them, and thus incrementing the sub-processes of self-assessment and the performance level and Self-Efficacy expectations.

When the student selects an objective he creates a personal standard of himself, which is what he expects from himself in the accomplishment of a task. However, while performing his pedagogical actions, the student may deviate from the objective selected. Through an evaluative process, this means, through exercises, tests or elapsed time in the study session, the student may realizes that he is not reaching his objective, then discrepancies arise according to Bandura's model [1]. These discrepancies affect student's motivation and Self-Efficacy.

A feedback system must be activated when such discrepancies arise [1]. Objectives on their own foster the action increasing the student's motivation, but if there is no feedback system that regulates and controls actions, objectives can lose their strength.

The Self-Efficacy construct has been investigated in distance learning and in the use of PCs (personal computers). The findings of Joo et al [7] show that students with high Self-Efficacy show positive attitudes towards the use of computer in learning.

Heaperman et al. [8] developed a model of influences of the Self-Efficacy of mature students in virtual environments. This model adds influence factors, which evolves the attitude, the physical and cognitive anxiety and changes due to age of the students. Moreover, the authors point to other elements that influence the Self-Efficacy of these students, as an example: experiences passed with technology, pedagogical strategies of education, decisions, support and training.

The proposal of the present work differ from those works presented, designing and modeling the self-efficacy beliefs in the student model which allow an agent to detect the beliefs from the behavior variables (effort, persistence and performance) withou use of questionnares and Self-Efficacy Scales. The behavior variables are presented in section 3. We are not interested in computer self-efficacy. Our focus, in this work, is to detect the student's self-efficacy during his learning over the Web.

3 The Computational Model of Self-Efficacy

We hypothesize that internal mental Self-Efficacy believes influence behavior in performing a task, and this could be capture and monitoring by an intelligent agent. We claim that some parameters behavior play key role in modeling Self- Efficacy.

The computational modeling of Self-Efficacy construct is an important aspect of student modeling, because it plays a central role in the computational understanding of human believes in theirs capabalities functioning. We search for measuring those parameters (such response time) and relating them through mathematical equations, those never have been measure it before as Self-Efficacy parameters. Therefore, we are adding two more variables in the Bandura's Model and testing it under computational cognitive modeling point of view.

For the SEM agent being able to mediate the student's Self-Efficacy, the domain knowledge must be identified (Self-Efficacy model). This model was based on Bandura [1] and Ames [6] to which the hypothesis of using persistence and performance as variables for the inference of Self-Efficacy was added, besides using effort and personal standard (this suggested in the model by Bandura). Fig. 2 illustrates the model built. Based on the learning objective that the student selected, different variables are used to pick up the student's Self-Efficacy. These variables act on Self-Efficacy. Differing from Bandura's Model personal standard and objective are the same in the computational model.

The variable mapped to the student with intrinsic personal pattern is effort. The level of effort can be understood as the intensity employed in the accomplishment of tasks [9] and its pre-processes as the time the student took to perform a task. The variables set up for the student with extrinsic personal pattern are persistence and performance. Persistence may be understood as how constant one is when performing an activity [10]. In the present work, this variable is preprocessed through the percentage of selected tasks accomplishment. Performance accounts for the mean of right answers in the exercises.

After modeling the Self-Efficacy computationally, it had to be represented and inferred. The Self-Efficacy construct has a large amount of uncertainties and noises and the inference process is incomplete and can be based on inconsistent knowledge.

The variables identified in the model are initially captured from observable students' behavior through the logs and their respective choices within the options offered in the environment. These variables need to be preprocessed. So, the agent separates the student's logs in order to calculate and store variables in its knowledge base.

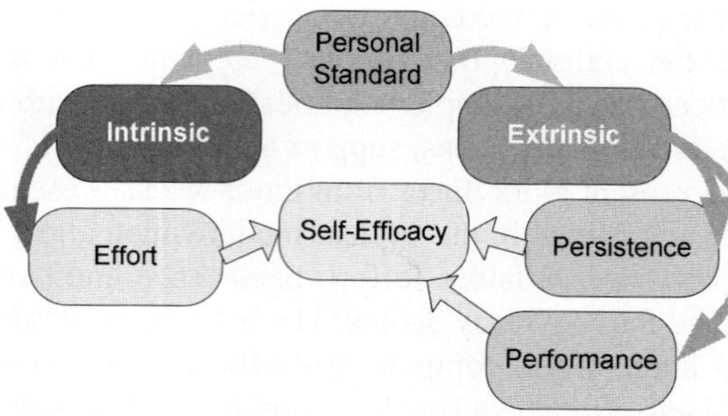

Fig. 2. Model of Self-Efficacy proposed. Self-Efficacy mapped according behavior variables.

In Fig. 3 are the main activities of SEM Agent: (i) student's log retrieval and pre-processing of these information to transform them in variables in its knowledge base; (ii) Fuzzyfication of these varibles and (iii) Fuzzy inference procedure (inference process – the measure of Self-Efficacy).

Its knowledge base includes the agent's perceptions (knowledge) and reasoning (inference rules). Perceptions include the following data for each student (student model): Self-Efficacy, effort, persistence, personal standard, number of times that the exercises were made, mean performance in exercises accomplishment, estimated time (informed at the start of the session), real time (calculated by the agent at the start of the following session) and history of such data per session. The inference rules included the fuzzy model, which has sets and linguistic terms, rules and pertinence functions.

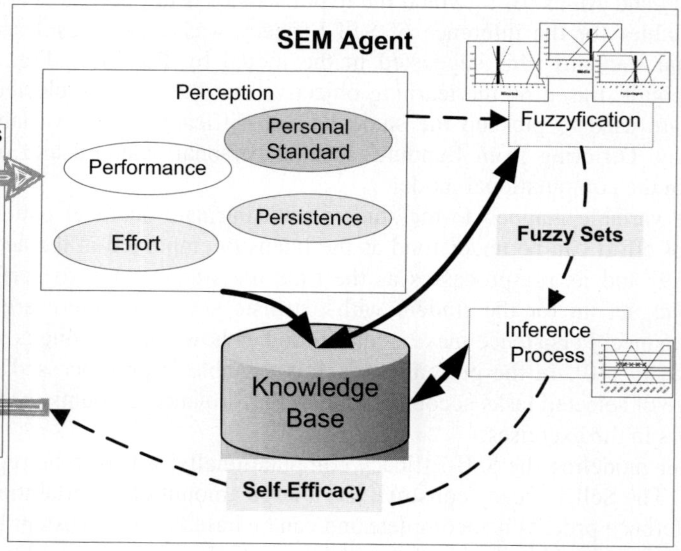

Fig. 3. Sem agent architecture

Fuzzy logic extends conventional Boolean Logic to handle the concept of partial truth (truth values between completely true and completely false). The partial truth takes a continuous range of truth values and is determine by the membership functions, witch takes values from the closed interval [0,1].

Activities (ii) and (iii) of the SEM agent are further explained in sessions 3.1 and 3.2.

3.1 The Fuzzy Model of Self-Efficacy

The development of the SEM agent's Fuzzy inference machine required some parameters to be defined. These were obtained with the aid of the content developer (a professor that collaborated with the production of the didactic material available in InteliWeb), Bandura's Self-Efficacy model (1997) and previously described hypothesis.

The following B sets were defined $B = \{B_1, B_2, ..., B_k\}$, where B_i $(i = 1, 2, ..., k)$ be the word or sentence that describes the k observable student's behavior that work as the fuzzy system input. The k behavior is measured and corresponds to a positive numeric value from set Ui. The numeric inputs $X=\{x_1, ...x_i, ... x_k\}$, let $x_i \in U_i$ and U_i be the discourse universe of inputs, each $U_i \subset \Re^+$ $(i = 1, 2, ...,$ k) represent the B_i values and formulates the process inputs. Each B_i $(i = 1, 2, ...,$ k) set is a linguistic variable, which can have a different number of linguistic terms. The number of linguistic values f_i and their names $V_1, V_2, ...,V_f$ are defined as a set $T(B_i) = \{V_1, V_2, ..., V_f\}$.

Three linguistic variables B_1, B_2 and B_3 were defined for the Self-Efficacy inference. They were associated to the students observable behavior, which can be B_1= "effort", B_2 = "persistence" and B_3 = "performance". The linguistic terms (LT) of each variable are: T(B_1)={low, medium, high}, T(B_2)= {short, medium, long} and T(B_3)= { insufficient, good, excellent}.

The output of fuzzy system shows the value of the inferred Self-Efficacy and it is represented by the linguistic variable C= "self-efficacy", which has linguistic terms as well. The number of linguistic terms g_i and their names V1, V2, ...,Vf are defined as a set T(C) = $\{V_1, V_2, ..., V_g\}$. This way, the variable C has the terms T(C)={low, medium, high}.

Each input and output sets had the pertinence functions specified by the specialist. such functions include: trapezoidal, triangular, increasing and decreasing. These functions limit each of the linguistic terms V_i present in the input sets B_i and output C, and return the μ pertinence of an x value for each of these terms, let $x \in \Re$ and $\mu_{Vi}(x) \in [0,1]$.

As the environment enables the student to overview the material in all presentation forms, different pertinence functions had to be created according to different presentation forms, although they refer to the same topic.

An example of the pertinence functions (Effort HTML and Effort FLASH) devised is shown in Fig. 4 through a graphic. The y-axis represents the level of pertinence and the x-axis the effort in minutes.

According to Fig. 4 (a) the LT low corresponds to 0 to 5 minutes, the LV medium between 3 to 10 minutes and the LT high from 9 minutes. The Fig. 6 (b) shows the Persistence Set, with the linguistic variables were delimited in the follow possible values: LT short from 0 to 2 minutes, the LT medium from 1 to 4 minutes and the LT high from 2 to 4 minutes.

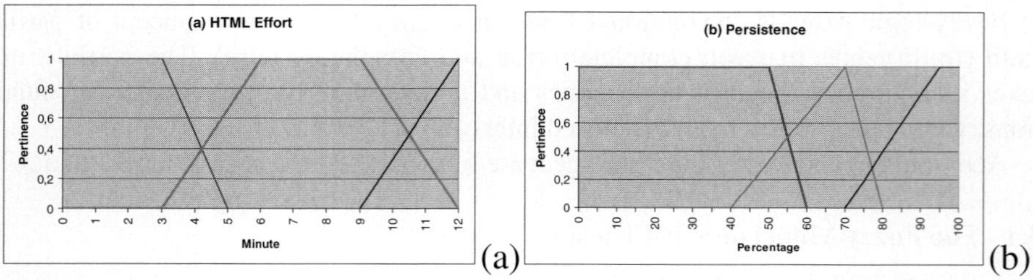

Fig. 4. (a) Illustrates the HTML Effort Fuzzy Set, (b) Illustrates the Persistence Set with the pertinence functions shown before, the SMM transforms the level of effort into a fuzzy value. The same happens to FLASH effort, VIDEO effort and performance.

Below we present the inference procedure that comprises the specialist knowledge in the form of IF-THEN rules, which are close to the expert's reasoning. In the model presented, the student's features are represented by sets and associated linguistic terms, this way, rules involve fuzzy variables:

$$\text{“}IF\ \ B_1\ is\ V_{1I_1}\ AND\ B_2\ is\ V_{2I_2}\ \ AND\ \ B_3\ is\ V_{3I_3}\ THEN\ C\ is\ V_{I\,g}\text{”}. \tag{1}$$

where $I_g = 1, 2, \ldots, f$.

All possible combinations of precondition are denoted as *PCP* and they are represented by a Cartesian set of the sets:

$$T = \{T(B_1), \ldots, T(B_k)\}: \text{PCP} = T(B_1) \times \ldots T(B_k). \tag{2}$$

We created a set of twenty seven fuzzy rules. Each fuzzy rule is an IF-THEN rule as defined in (1). They promote adjustments of behavior according to the relationships between these behaviors and personal standards. The following rules are some examples:

“IF the student has a *low* effort AND his persistence is *short* AND his performance is *insufficient* THEN he has a *low* self-efficacy”

“IF the student has a *low* effort AND his persistence is *long* AND his performance is *good* THEN he has a *medium* self-efficacy”

“IF the student has a *high* effort AND his persistence is *short* AND his performance is *excellent* THEN he has a *low* self-efficacy ”

A fuzzy system of this type combines linguistic values and realizes fuzzy relations operated with the *max-min* composition.

The inference process ends when the agent discovers which rule(s) is (are) true and how pertinent it is (they are), then it analyses the output set with the linguistic terms cut according to the inferred pertinence. This way, the output value corresponds to the most pertinent linguistic term. It is not necessary to perform defuzzification, once the tactics were divided by linguistic terms of the output set (Self-Efficacy) and not by a discrete numeric value.

3.2 A Practical Example

To infer the self-efficacy value through a fuzzy inference, the SEM agent execute three proceess: fuzzification, aggregation and composition. Firstly the agent transforms the crisp entries in a fuzzy value and retrieves the respective levels of pertinence for each linguistic term.

In the aggregation process the agent computes the value of the rule´s premise. Each condition in the part IF of the rule is assigned a degree of truth based on the degree of membership of the corresponding linguistic value. The degree of truth of the IF part is computed as the minimun (MIN) of the degrees of truth of the conditions. This degree of support for the rule is assigned to the degree of truth of the THEN part.

The process of computing the values of the rule´s conclusion is called composition. The degree of the truth of each linguistic term of the output linguist variable is calculated using the maximum (MAX) of the degrees of truth o the rules with the same linguistic terms in the THEN part.

This process is exemplified in a following *Scenario*: The student chooses the HTML topic, his effort is 10 minutes and his persistence and average performance are calculated by SEM agent and the values are: persistence 55% and average performance 60.0.

Fig. 5 illustrates the pertinence functions of the linguistic variables: effort, persistence and performance, whose sets were cut in the respective pertinences (μ) of the input value, as well as the rules activated by the agent, the output set cut and the output resulting from this processing.

According to Fig. 5, the crisp input values are fuzzyfied and transformed into linguistic terms with their respective pertinences, which are:

$$\overbrace{\begin{matrix}\mu low(10)=0.0\\ \mu medium(10)=0.66\\ \mu high(10)=0.33\end{matrix}}^{effort}\qquad \overbrace{\begin{matrix}\mu short(55)=0.5\\ \mu medium(55)=0.5\\ \mu long\ (55)=0\end{matrix}}^{persistence}\qquad \overbrace{\begin{matrix}\mu insufficient(60.0)=0.19\\ \mu good(60.0)=0.75\\ \mu excellent\ (60.0)=0\end{matrix}}^{performance} \tag{3}$$

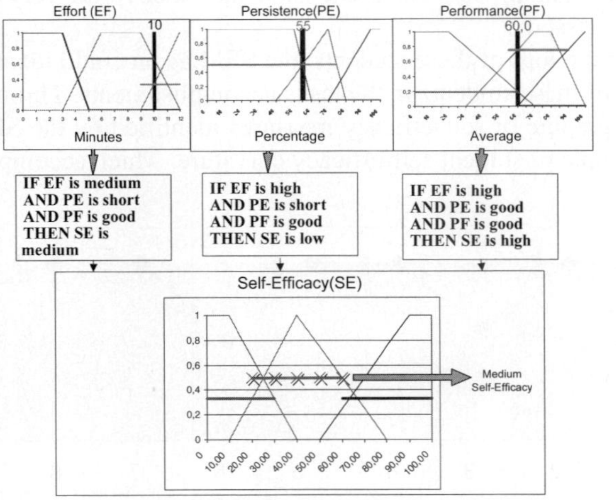

Fig. 5. Example of Fuzzy inference machine of SEM agent

In this situation three rules with higher value of output are activated:

(i) "IF student has a medium effort AND his persistence is short AND his performance is good THEN he has a medium self-efficacy"
(ii) "IF student has a high effort AND persistence is short AND performance is good THEN he has a low self-efficacy"
(iii) "IF student has a high effort AND his persistence is medium AND his performance is good THEN he has a high self-efficacy "

Then we have the following output values for each linguistic variable pertinence:
μlow(min(μhigh(10)=0.33, μshort(55)=0.5, μgood(60.0)=0.75)) = 0.33
μmedium(min(μmedium(10)=0.66, μshort(55)=0.5, μgood(60.0)=0.75)) = 0.5
μhigh(min(μhigh(10)=0.33,medium(55)=0.5, μgood(60.0)=0.75)) = 0.33

Thus, the linguistic term "low" of the output set is cut in 0.33, the term "medium" in 0.5 and the term "high" in 0.33. In this example, the highest (max) pertinence level is 0.5 then the fuzzy output is medium self-efficacy.

4 Empirical Evaluation

Our scientific hypothesis is that capturing and monitoring of Self-Efficacy by an agent can help the student to self-regulate his or her own learning. The Inteliweb interface, the content and agent evaluation is being conducted systematically, in stages.

First Stage: An exploratory experiment was performed on a sample of 25 students of the Vegetal Anatomy subject from the Biosciences course at UFRGS, aged between 17 and 19 years. Through our observation and two questionnaries (about the internet use as an instrument in the web courses and questions about interface and didactic material) different forms of presentation stimulate the learning interest, Flash animations help learning and process comprehension and videos were very stimulating more than expositive class.

By analyzing the logs of these students, the SEM agent could identify the curvature of self-efficacy of these students in the tasks accomplishments. Through of this curvature we have a graphic of self-efficacy measures identified by the SEM agent. Fig. 6 presents an example of student self-efficacy curvature, which accomplished ten tasks.

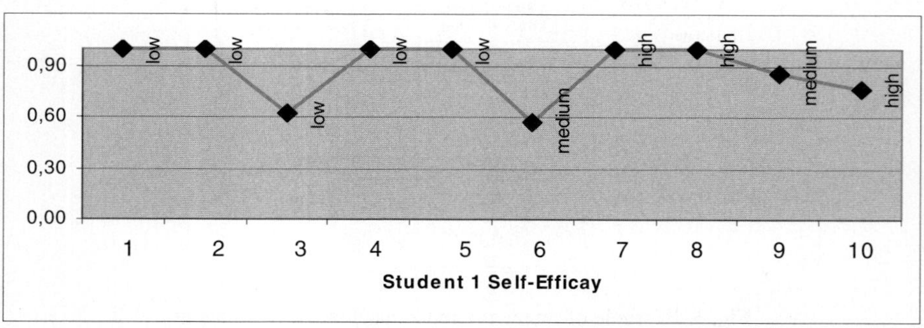

Fig. 6. Student self-efficacy curvature identified by SEM agent

The number of times that the agent SEM identified each linguistic term of self-efficacy was calculated. Values found in the 214 activities performed by students are: 18% were considered medium self-efficacy, 36% high self-efficacy and 46% low self-efficacy.

With the results of performance (velocity and accuracy) of fuzzy inference machine we think that Fuzzy Logic is a appropriate technique for the mapping of the student Self-Efficacy.

Second Stage: Use a feedback system to try a student´s positive motivation in the accomplishment of tasks, like the Bandura's Model[1] proposes. We selected a previosly work by the Artificial Inteligence Group (GIA) at Federal University of Rio Grande do Sul called PAT (Pedagogical and Affective Tutor) [3].

The PAT is an animated character, is female with entire body and height proportional to the monitor size. She has brown eyes and long hair, she wears jeans pants and a colored shirt, and she is about 30 years old. The objective is represents a young, extrovert and informal character. The PAT was composed in Java, JavaScript and Microsoft Agent.

This agent presents the physical affective behaviors and verbal affective behaviors. For the same behaviors there are different animations and/or texts. Fig. 7 shows some of physical behaviors.

Fig. 7. Some physical behaviors: (a) Encouragement (b) Show Curiosity (c) and (d) Congratulations

The behaviors are called pedagogical tactics. Initially the tactics of PAT were made to apply on student's emotion, like angry, happiness, shame, etc. We selected some tactics of encouragement, congratulations, increase student effort, increase student self-ability, offer help, etc. for increase the student's self-efficacy. The SEM agent sends a P2P message with the Self-Efficacy measure to PAT, then PAT shows a coherent behavior according self-efficacy received.

An exploratory experiment was performed on a sample of 12 students of the Vegetal Anatomy subject from the Biosciences course at UFRGS, aged between 17 and 20 years.

By analyzing the logs of these students, the SEM agent could identify the curvature of self-efficacy of these students in the tasks accomplishments. Values found in the 174 activities performed by students are: 10% were considered medium self-efficacy, 12% high self-efficacy and 78% low self-efficacy.

The one sample t-test statistic was made between the two groups, and there is a significant difference (t=3,22; gl=22; p=0,004). However we may to do other experiments to define how influence factors cause these differences.

5 Conclusions

We have described a way of introduce the self-efficacy into student model in context of ITS. This way we present a computation model of self-efficay wihout use the scales or the questionnares to infer it.

With the results of performance (velocity and accuracy) of fuzzy inference machine we think that Fuzzy Logic is a appropriate technique for the mapping of the student Self-Efficacy.

References

1. Bandura, A .: Self- Efficacy - The exercise of control. New York: Freeman (1997).
2. Nars, M.; Yen, J; Ioerger, T. FLAME—Fuzzy Logic Adaptive Model of Emotions. Autonomous Agents and Multi-Agent Systems, Volume 3 Issue 3., 2000.
3. Jaques, Patricia A.et al: Applying Affective Tactics for a Better Learning. ECAI 2004. European Conference on Artificial Intelligence. 2004, August 23-27. Valence, Spain.
4. Poel, M., R.et al. Emotion based Agent Architectures for Tutoring Systems: The INES Architecture. In: Cybernetics and Systems 2004. Workshop on Affective Computational Entities (ACE 2004), Vienna: Austrian Society for Cybernetic Studies, R. Trappl (ed.), ISBN 3 85206 169, Austria, April 2004, 663-668.
5. Zadeh, L. Fuzzy Sets. Outline of a New Approach to the Analysis of Complex Systems and Decision Processes. IEEE Transactions on Systems, Man and Cybernetics 3, v.3, n.1, p.28-44. (1965).
6. Ames, C. Motivation: What Teachers Need to Know. Teachers College Record, [S.l.], v. 91, n. 3, p. 409-421. (1990).
7. Joo, Y., Bong, M., Choi, H. Self-efficacy for self-regulated learning, academic self-efficacy, and Internet self-efficacy in Web-based instruction. Educational Technology Research and Development, 48(2), 5-18. (2000)
8. Heaperman, S.; Sudweeks, F. Achieving Self-efficacy in the Virtual Learning Environment. In Proceedings: International Education Research Conference Fremantle December 2-6, (2001).
9. Aronson, E., Ellsworth, P., Carlsmith, J., Gonzales, M.. (1990), Methods of Research in Social Psychology. 2nd Ed. McGraw-Hill.
10. Soldato, T. et al. Implementation of Motivational Tactics in Tutoring Systems. Journal of Artificial Intelligence in Education, Charlottesville, v.6, p.337-378. (1995).

Qualitative Reasoning and Bifurcations in Dynamic Systems

Juan J. Flores[1] and Andrzej Proskurowski[2]

[1] Division de Estudios de Postgrado
Facultad de Ingenieria Electrica
Universidad Michoacana
Morelia, Mexico
[2] Computer Science Department
University of Oregon
Eugene, OR, USA

Abstract. A bifurcation occurs in a dynamic system when the structure of the system itself and therefore also its qualitative behavior change as a result of changes in one of the system's parameters. In most cases, an infinitesimal change in one of the parameters make the dynamic system exhibit dramatic changes. In this paper, we present a framework (QRBD) for performing qualitative analysis of dynamic systems exhibiting bifurcations. QRBD performs a simulation of the system with bifurcations, in the presence of perturbations, producing accounts for all events in the system, given a qualitative description of the changes it undergoes. In such a sequence of events, we include catastrophic changes due to perturbations and bifurcations, and hysteresis. QRBD currently works with first-order systems with only one varying parameter. We propose the qualitative representations and algorithm that enable us to reason about the changes a dynamic system undergoes when exhibiting bifurcations, in the presence of perturbations.

1 Introduction

When we think of dynamic systems, we think of Ordinary (perhaps Partial) Differential Equations, and their solutions with time. They may be linear or nonlinear. By system dynamics we understand the set of qualitative features a system exhibits when excited properly. Several works define qualitative descriptions and algorithms that solve dynamic systems, and provide those solutions in qualitative terms [1,2,3].

Those works consider a non-changing dynamic system and provide solutions to its transient response with time. But dynamic systems depend not only on state variables and their derivatives, but on parameters, and those parameters may be functions of time. For instance, the mass of a rocket changes as it burns fuel, the characteristics of an electrical machine change as it ages, the load of an electrical power system changes during the day, etc.

Changes in the parameters, even if they are infinitesimal, may cause a dynamic system to exhibit totally different qualitative properties. For instance, a damped

A. Gelbukh and C.A. Reyes-Garcia (Eds.): MICAI 2006, LNAI 4293, pp. 259–271, 2006.

mass-spring system may stop oscillating if the damping increases. Those changes in the topology of the phase space representation of the dynamic system are known as bifurcations, and the values of the parameters for which a bifurcation occurs are called bifurcation points.

The work presented in this paper concerns the determination of the behavior of a dynamic system exhibiting bifurcations. The analysis will take into account changes in parameters and perturbations to the system and will derive a sequence of events the system exhibits under those circumstances. All the analysis is accomplished at a qualitative level.

The paper is organized as follows: Section 2 provides a gentle introduction to dynamic systems, ordinary differential equations, phase portraits, and bifurcation diagrams; Section 3 defines the problem to be solved; Section 4 defines the qualitative representation for the different components involved in the process; In Section 5 we propose a representation for events and the dynamics exhibited by the system under analysis; Section 6 presents a simulation algorithm that allows us to reason about dynamic systems and bifurcation diagrams; Section 7 shows some results, where simulations include qualitative plots and accounts for the different events present in a given scenario; Section 8 summarizes our findings.

2 Dynamic Systems

The main tool for modeling dynamic systems is the differential calculus. This paper deals with dynamic systems that can be modeled by ordinary differential equations (ODEs).

An ODE is an equation of the form

$$F(t, x, \frac{dx}{dt}, \cdots, \frac{d^n x}{d^n t}) = 0 \tag{1}$$

Function $f(t)$ is a solution to Equation (1) if

$$F(t, f(t), \frac{df(t)}{dt}, \cdots, \frac{d^n f(t)}{d^n t}) = 0 \tag{2}$$

A phase portrait includes all qualitative features that distinguish a dynamic system. Such characteristics include fixed points (attractors and repellers), nullclines, limit cycles, and for more complex (chaotic) systems, even strange attractors. See [4] For first-order systems, phase portraits are unidimensional, and do not show as many features as in higher order systems.

Let us consider the nonlinear system represented by $\dot{x} = \sin(x)$. If we plot x against $\dot{x}$, we get a plot like that of Figure 1, where trajectories in the phase portrait flow or lie on the x axis. On the phase diagram, flow is to the right when $\dot{x} > 0$, and to the left when $\dot{x} < 0$, as indicated by the arrows. When $\dot{x} = 0$ there is no flow; the places x^* where $\dot{x} = 0$ are called *fixed points.* There are three kinds of fixed points: stable *attractors* (solid black dots), unstable *repellers* (open circles), and semistable (half is open circle and half is solid).

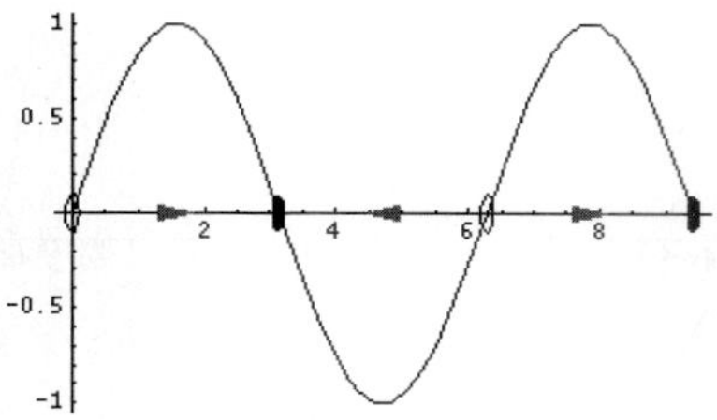

Fig. 1. Unidimensional flow for first-order system

In all fixed points the derivative is zero, but there is a difference between stable and unstable equilibrium. We say that x^* is a stable fixed point if all trajectories that start near x^* approach it as $t \to \infty$. On the other hand, a fixed point x^* is unstable, if all trajectories that start near it are driven away from it.

First-order systems are very simple systems, but they exhibit interesting features when their parameters change with time. The qualitative structure of the phase portraits can change when we allow parameters to vary. Fixed points can be created or destroyed, or their stability can change. The qualitative changes in the topology of a phase portrait, due to the change in parameters are called *bifurcations*, and the value of the parameters where a bifurcation occurs are called *bifurcation points.*

Figure 2 shows the phase portraits for equation $\dot{x} = rx + x^3 - x^5$, for different values of parameter r, and Figure 3 shows its respective Bifurcation Diagram (BD). Also note that there is a region where the values of r make the linear and cubic terms dominate over the quintic term. For larger values of r, the quintic term dominates, yielding an interesting region where three fixed points coalesce into one, and the stable fixed point at the origin changes stability.

Bifurcation analysis has a large number of applications in science and engineering. Those applications range from radiation in lasers, outbreaks in insect populations, electronics, electrical power systems, etc., see [5].

3 Problem Definition

We have defined bifurcations, bifurcation points, and bifurcation diagrams. The problem we address in this work is the following:

> Given a qualitative description of a bifurcation diagram and the dynamics of the system with state x, determine the behavior of x as a result of perturbations as parameter r changes.

To address this problem, we rely on the following assumptions:

Continuity. All variables and functions involved in the process are continuous and continuously differentiable. *Two Time–Scales.* In the process of simulation, two time scales will be considered. The variation of the system's parameters is much slower than the transient time to stabilize the system after a perturbation. That is, $t(\text{variation of } r) \gg t(\text{transients of } x)$. *Perturbations at Landmarks.*

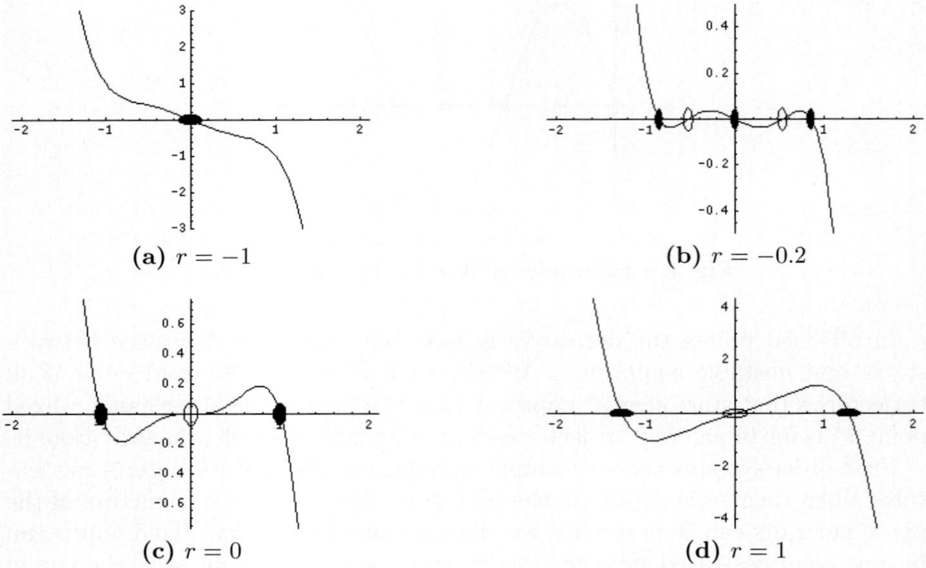

Fig. 2. Behavior of $\dot{x} = rx + x^3 - x^5$ for different values of r

Perturbations always occur at landmarks of r. (See the definition of landmarks in Section 4.) If we need a perturbation to occur in between two landmarks, we simply create another landmark between the two original ones, and let the perturbation occur at the new landmark. *Small Perturbations.* Perturbations are small enough so not to cross other fixed points. If we do not make this assumption, the behavior of the system would depend on the relative magnitude of the perturbation, with respect to the distance to the next fixed point in the direction of the perturbation. This last assumption may not hold if a perturbation occurs infinitesimally close to a bifurcation point. Implementation of the system without this assumption, would lead to branching in the prediction of behavior. I.e. at any perturbation, we would need to consider cases where its magnitude would not reach, exactly meet, or pass each landmark in the direction of the perturbation.

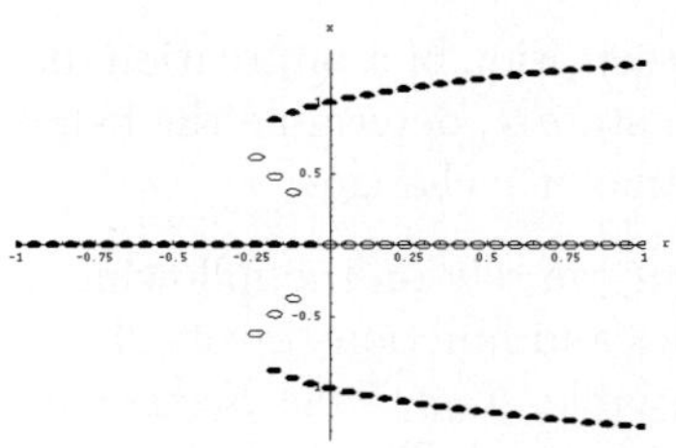

Fig. 3. Bifurcation diagram for $\dot{x} = rx + x^3 - x^5$

4 Qualitative Representation

This section proposes the representations needed to accomplish the reasoning tasks we have in mind.

To reason about the dynamics of systems exhibiting bifurcations and under the influence of small perturbations, we need to start by computing the bifurcation diagram for such a system. Once we have a numerical description of the bifurcation diagram, we proceed to qualitativize it. [6] presents several numerical methods to compute a Bifurcation Diagram.

We start with the main components of a qualitative description of a bifurcation diagram, and then define the representation for varying parameters and for perturbations. We borrow most of the notation from already developed representation schemes in the area of qualitative reasoning, mainly from QSIM [7].

The main components of a dynamic system are variables, parameters, and constraints. Since we are starting from a bifurcation diagram, we do not need to represent the structure of the system (the constraints). A bifurcation diagram can thus be described in terms of the values of its state variables and parameters at different points in time.

At any point in time, the value of each variable and parameter is specified in terms of its relationship with a totally ordered set of *landmark values* and its direction of change. The set of landmark values is called the quantity space. Quantity spaces typically include $-\infty, 0$, and ∞.

The qualitative value (or magnitude) of a variable can be a landmark or an open interval between two landmarks. The qualitative direction of a variable is the sign of its derivative, in this case, the sign of the rate of change of x with

Variables:

$\{r, x\}$

Quantity Spaces:

$QS(x) = (-\infty, x_4, x_3, 0, x_2, x_1, \infty)$

$QS(r) = (-\infty, r_0, r_1, 0, r_2, \infty)$

BD Representation:

$x \; R \; r$

$$
\begin{aligned}
R = \{ & \langle(-\infty, 0), (0, 0), st\rangle\,, \\
& \langle(0, \infty), (0, 0), us\rangle\,, \\
& \langle(r_1, \infty), ((x_2, x_1), +), st\rangle\,, \\
& \langle r_1, (x_2, \infty), rs\rangle\,, \\
& \langle(r_1, 0), ((0, x_2), -), us\rangle\,, \\
& \langle 0, (0, \infty), us\rangle\,, \\
& \langle(r_1, 0), ((x_3, 0), +), us\rangle\,, \\
& \langle r_1, (x_3, \infty), ls\rangle\,, \\
& \langle(r_1, \infty), ((x_4, x_3), -), st\rangle\}
\end{aligned}
$$

Fig. 4. Qualitative representation of bifurcation diagram in Figure 3 respect to r. As opposed to Kuipers' representation, we decided to include ∞ as a possible value for qualitative direction.

In a bifurcation diagram, we plot x versus r, where neither r is a function of x nor vice versa. So we need to represent the bifurcation diagram as a relation. In a BD representation, we need to include the qualitative states of the variable and the parameter, and the type of stability presented in the segment. So, a Bifurcation Diagram Segment (BDS) is a triple of the form $\langle qval(r), qstate(x), nature\rangle$, where $nature$ can be any of $\{st, us, ls, rs\}$ (st =stable, us =unstable, ls =left-stable, rs =right-stable.) In this representation, a BDS is a subset of the bifurcation diagram where the qualitative values of x and r, and its stability remain unchanged in all that subset.

As an example, the variables involved, their quantitative spaces, and the qualitative representation of the bifurcation diagram of Figure 3 are shown in Figure 4.

Figure 5 shows the qualitative representation of the bifurcation diagram of Figure 3. You can see that a BDS is a region where the form of growth of x wrt r does not change, but the shape of that growth is unspecified. We decided to represent that growth as a straight line; the resulting BDS expresses our knowledge of the landmarks of x and r at the ends of the BDSs.

5 Dynamics and Events

According to Section 3, we need to provide a suitable representation for the dynamics of the system.

Since we are dealing with two time–scales, transient responses of the system (in other contexts referred to as the system's dynamics) are considered instantaneous when compared with the time taken for a parameter to change. On the other hand, when observing the transient responses of the system can be observed (from the same perspective in which QSIM predicts behavior, for example), we consider the parameters as constant.

With those considerations in mind, when we talk about *system's dynamics*, we are referring to the set of changes in parameters and perturbations present throughout the analysis of the system. We also consider as a part of the system's dynamics the changes of state variables of the system.

5.1 Parameter Changes

The changes in the parameters are represented as a sequence of qualitative states of each parameter. For the scope of the work reported in this paper, we are dealing only with one changing parameter, so the changes will be a list of qualitative states of parameter r. This list of changes may represent any qualitative continuous function of r with respect to time. Such function does not have to be monotonic, and may have as many extrema as necessary. Turning points of r in time (values for r where dr/dt is zero) establish landmarks for r.

Our simulation will be performed at the slow time–scale (i.e. the time–scale when parameter r changes). In that time–scale, we need to specify the changes

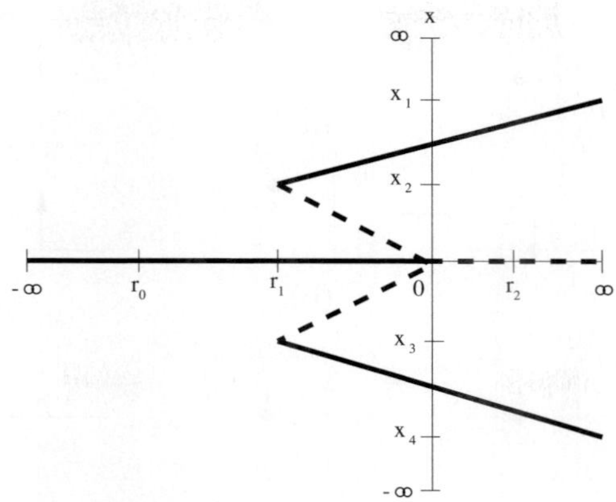

Fig. 5. Qualitative bifurcation diagram for Figure 3

occurring to r. This description will not include time explicitly; we are not interested in the value of time when events happen, but in the order they happen.

Behavior of r, $B(r)$, is a qualitative description of how r changes with time; it is a sequence of qualitative states of r. A qualitative state contains qualitative magnitude and qualitative direction. The qualitative magnitude can be a point (landmark), or an interval, of two landmarks, not necessarily consecutive. The qualitative direction of r can be any of $\{-, 0, +\}$. States alternate between point and interval states.

Combining the behavior of r with the perturbations in x, we obtain a single descriptor of D. D is a list of pairs $(qstate_r, dir_x)$, indicating that at state $qstate_r$ there will be a perturbation to x with direction dir_x. The domain of the qualitative direction of a perturbation is limited to $\{+, -\}$.

5.2 Perturbations

The perturbations induced to the system can be represented as a list of single perturbations; a perturbation is a pair formed by the qualitative value of r where the perturbation occurs, and the qualitative direction of the perturbation itself. The domain of the qualitative direction of a perturbation is limited to $\{+, -\}$.

Now, perturbations occur at a given instant of time, so we cannot associate them to a given value of r, but to a value of r at a point in time. In order to avoid the explicit introduction of time in our representation, we include perturbations in the description of the behavior of r, which implicitly contains time.

5.3 Dynamics

In terms of the system's dynamics, a first-order system may exhibit a limited set of features. If the system starts at a stable fixed point, and a perturbation is induced, the system will return to the same stable fixed point (an attractor).

On the other hand, if the system starts at an unstable fixed point and a perturbation is produced, the system will be driven away from the fixed point, either to another stable fixed point or to infinity.

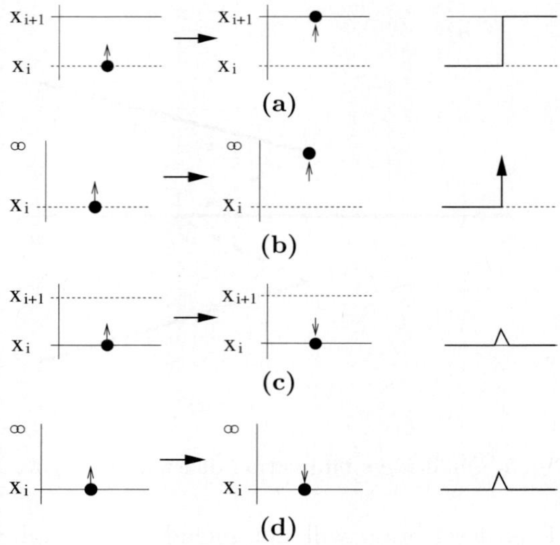

Fig. 6. Predicting behavior caused by a perturbation

In order to establish a limited set of precise rules for predicting behavior of the system under the presence of perturbations, we need to state the following theorem.

Theorem 1 (Alternation of Fixed Points). *Consider the first-order ODE* $\dot{x} = f(x, r)$*, where* f *is a continuously differentiable function, and* r *is a parameter. For a given value of* r*, the nature of the corresponding fixed points alternate.*

Proof of theorem 1 is not included because of lack of space.

Based on Theorem 1, we can define the following cases for prediction of behavior in the presence of a perturbation. If the system is at an unstable fixed point, a positive perturbation occurs, and there is a stable fixed point above it, the system will stabilize at that fixed point; see Figure 6(a). If the system is at an unstable fixed point, a positive perturbation occurs, and there is no fixed point above it, the system will "blow up" (i.e. it will tend to infinity); see Figure 6(b). If the system is at a stable fixed point, and a positive perturbation occurs, the system will return to the same attracting fixed point no matter whether there is or there is not a fixed point above it; see Figures 6(c) and 6(d). Similar cases occur for negative perturbations. Sub-figures of Figure 6 show the state of the system before and after the perturbation, and the symbols we will use for each event in graphical displays of the simulation.

Other types of events that may occur are what we call *falling off* on a bifurcation diagram. When the system is at a stable fixed point, and parameter r varies, the system will travel along the BDS it is lying on at that point. If the BDS ends and there is no other BDS that places a fixed point at that state of the system, the system will be attracted by the nearest attracting fixed point.

(a) (b)

Fig. 7. Predicting behavior caused by fall-offs

Theorem 2 allows us to constrain the number of cases present in our simulation, and provides a more solid background for the development of the algorithm.

Theorem 2 (No ambiguity on fall-offs). *If a dynamic system is found in the conditions described as fall-off, then the system will transit into exactly one stable fixed point.*

Proof of theorem 2 is not included because of lack of space.

Given Theorem 2, Figure 7 shows the possible cases for decreasing r. Other two mirror cases are possible for increasing r. The thick line represents the behavior of x through time, moving along with r.

If the system undergoes perturbations while at an unstable state, or finds itself in a fall-off situation, the resulting changes in magnitude may be dramatic. Those are called catastrophes, since such changes in magnitude may take the system to states outside the operating region of the device. A catastrophe may make the device blow up, or if it is protected, to switch off. An example of such situation can be found in electrical systems, where changes (typically increases) in the load of a power system, may take it to a state that makes the voltage drop, currents increase, and protections operate, producing the well known black-outs.

There is another characteristic exhibited by dynamic systems near bifurcation points (specially nonlinear systems), known as hysteresis. When a catastrophic change occurres, the system moves to another stable state, and therefore is lying on a different BDS; this change is typically produced by a change in a parameter. After the catastrophe, reverting the changes in the parameter does not restore the system to its original state. This lack of reversibility as a result of the variation of a parameter is called hysteresis.

Section 7 provides examples of all the events mentioned in this section.

6 Simulation Algorithm

Now that all the necessary representation has been defined, and all possible events and cases were presented, we are in possibility to present and explain the simulation algorithm.

The algorithm (see Figure 8) starts at initial state given by x_0, and visits all landmarks in r's trajectory, specified in D. At each landmark, if there exists a perturbation it computes the next state of the system. Also, at each landmark,

```
Simulation(x0, BD, D)

 1: for all states s_r in D do
 2:    if ∃ pert(s_r) then
 3:       x = nextFP(x0, pert(s_r), s_r)
 4:       record(x0, x, s_r, BDS(s_r))
 5:    end if
 6:    if fallOff(x, s_r) then
 7:       x = nextFP(x0, s_r)
 8:       record(x0, x, s_r, BDS(s_r))
 9:    end if
10:    x0 = x
11: end for
```

Fig. 8. Simulation algorithm

it verifies if the BDS ends, producing a fall-off situation. If there is a fall-off, the next state is computed.

There are a few places in the algorithm that deserve more attention, specially at the time of implementation. function *pert* takes a state in the description of the changes of the system, and returns the sign of a perturbation, if one exists. In line 2, *pert* determines if the dynamics of the system include a perturbation at s_r. In line 3, the algorithm needs to determine the next state after a perturbation occurs. This is the part where the cases of Figure 6 come to play. In order to determine what case applies to a given situation, we first need to search the BDS list for another BDS that coincide with the actual BDS at the present landmark, in the direction indicated by the perturbation. That landmark or interval is the new state. In line 6, it is necessary to determine if the current BDS, in the direction of change of r, ends at the present landmark. If that is the case, we need to determine if another BDS continues where the current one ends. If that is not the case, then we need to determine which BDS contains an attracting fixed point, either above or below the fall-off. In line 7, the implementation needs to determine where the system will continue after a fall-off. Function nextFP is being overloaded to determine the next fixed point in the simulation, produced by a perturbation or a fall-off.

For each perturbation or fall-off in the simulation, we record $(x_i, x_j, s_r, BDS(s_r))$; that is, the initial and final states, where the event occurred, the state of r when that happened, and the BD segment the system was at when the event occured. (Lines 4 and 8 of the code.)

Line 10 updates the state of the system at each iteration on the simulation.

7 Results

This section presents one example of a simulation of a first-order system exhibiting bifurcations. This example contains all features and events, so it is representative of QRBD's capabilities.

The bifurcation diagram of Figure 3 can be represented in qualitative terms, as presented on Figure 4, on Section 4.

Let us assume that the system starts in state $(x(0) = 0, r(0) = r_0)$, with r changing according to $B(r) = ((r_0, +), ((r_0, r_3), +), (r_3, 0), ((0, r_3), -), (r_0, 0))$. Let us also assume that the following perturbations will be induced to the system: $P(x) = ((0, -), (r_3, +))$. These two components of the dynamics of the system are combined into a single descriptor $D = \{((r_0, +), \{\}), (((r_0, r_1), +), \{\}), ((r_1, +), \{-\}), (((r_1, r_2), +), \{\}), ((r_2, 0), \{+\}), (((r_2, r_0), -), \{\}), ((r_0, 0), \{\})\}$.

The algorithm traverses all landmarks in r's trajectory. When it is analyzing landmark $r = 0$, it finds a negative perturbation. Since the system is at a stable fixed point, the system will be attracted back to the fixed point at 0, and remain in the same BDS. When r is in qualitative state $(0, +)$, the BDS ends. Since there is another BDS starting at the same point, the algorithm does not detect any fall-off event. When the algorithm reaches landmark $r = r_2$, it finds another perturbation, a positive one this time. Since at that point the system was in an unstable fixed point, the perturbation drives the system away from it. The next fixed point in the direction of the perturbation is the one that belongs to the BDS $\langle (r_1, \infty), ((x_2, x_1), +), s \rangle$. The system has moved from an unstable fixed point at 0, to a stable fixed point somewhere in the interval (x_2, x_1). At that point, r starts decreasing. When r reaches r_1, the BDS ends; this time there is no BDS at the end of it, so the algorithm has detected a fall-off event. The closest attracting fixed point at that landmark is the one that belongs to the BDS $\langle (-\infty, 0), (0, 0), s \rangle$. The system has moved back to the stable fixed point at 0. The system continues at 0 with no change until the end of the simulation.

In the results derived from the simulation, we find two catastrophic events: an increase in magnitude at r_3 due to an external perturbation and a restoration to its original position at 0, due to a bifurcation point. The fact that the system is taking a trajectory when r increases and returning on a different one, when the parameter r decreases, indicates the system is an irreversible one, exhibiting a hysteretical behavior. Figure 9 shows a qualitative plot of the results of the

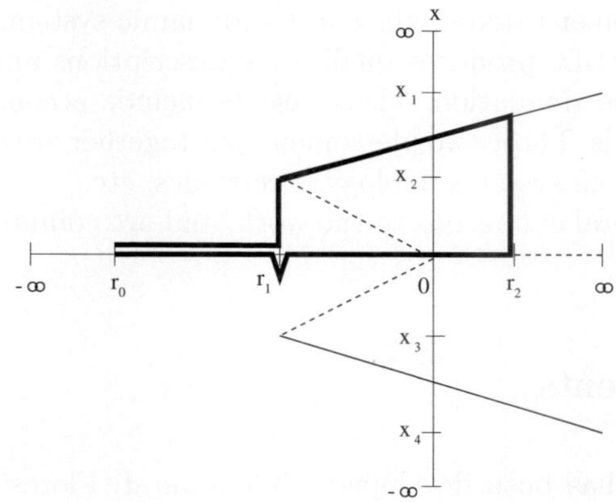

Fig. 9. Results of the simulation in graphical form

simulation. Note that, for clarity, we have drawn the return to 0 slightly off place, so that it does not meet with the previous trajectory. Also note that we are totally disregarding the transient behavior of the system when it moves from fixed point to fixed point.

QRBD was capable of producing all events found in the simulation, but does not intend to produce the natural language explanations provided in the previous paragraphs. Those explanations are interpretations, provided by the authors of this paper, of the actual simulation outputs. The actual output of the simulation is presented in Figure 10.

QStates of r and x, and events present during simulation:
$x = 0$.
$r = (r_0, +)$.
$r = (r_1, +)$, - pert., stable FP, $x = 0$.
$r = (0, +)$.
$r = (r_2, 0)$, + pert., unstable FP, $x = (x2, x1)$.
r=$(0, -)$
r=$(r_1, -)$, Fall off, $x = 0$.
r=$(r_0, 0)$.

Fig. 10. Output of the simulation

8 Conclusions

This paper presents the representation and algorithms necessary to perform simulation of dynamic systems exhibiting bifurcations, on the presence of perturbations. Those simulations take place at a qualitative level, producing accounts of the different phenomena taking place in the dynamic system.

The system, QRBD, produces qualitative descriptions and qualitative plots of the results of the simulation. Those results include accounts of catastrophic events and hysteresis. Those two phenomena put together are of large importance to areas like electrical systems, biology, electronics, etc.

We propose several extensions to the work, and are committed to working on them.

Acknowledgments

The present work has been developed while Juan J. Flores was on sabbatical at the University of Oregon. He thanks the U of O for all the resources and accommodations that made his stay at the U of O and this work possible.

References

1. Kuipers, B.J.: Qualitative simulation. Artificial Intelligence **29** (1986) 289–338
2. Forbus, K.D.: Qualitative process theory. Artificial Intelligence **24** (1984) 85–168
3. de Kleer, J., Brown, J.S.: Qualitative physics based on confluences. Artificial Intelligence **24** (1984) 7–83
4. Lee, W.W., Kuipers, B.J.: A qualitative method to construct phase portraits. In: Proc. 11th National Conf. on Artificial Intelligence (AAAI-93), Menlo Park, Cambridge, London, AAAI Press/The MIT Press (1993) 614–619
5. Strogatz, S.H.: Nonlinear Dynamics and Chaos with Applications to Physics, Biology, and Engineering. Westview Press, Cambridge, MA (1994)
6. Keller, H.B.: Numerical methods in bifurcation problems. Springer-Verlag, Cambridge, MA (1987)
7. Kuipers, B.J.: Qualitative Reasoning: Modeling and Simulation with Incomplete Knowledge. MIT Press, Cambridge, MA. (1994)
8. Wolfram, S.: The Mathematica Book. Cambridge University Press, Cambridge, MA (2003)

Introducing Partitioning Training Set Strategy to Intrinsic Incremental Evolution

Jin Wang and Chong Ho Lee

Department of Information Technology & Telecommunication,
Inha University, Incheon, Korea
wangjin_liips@yahoo.com.cn

Abstract. In this paper, to conquer the scalability issue of evolvable hardware (EHW), we introduce a novel system-decomposition-strategy which realizes training set partition in the intrinsic evolution of a non-truth table based 32 characters classification system. The new method is expected to improve the convergence speed of the proposed evolvable system by compressing fitness value evaluation period which is often the most time-consuming part in an evolutionary algorithm (EA) run and reducing computational complexity of EA. By evolving target characters classification system in a complete FPGA-based experiment platform, this research investigates the influence of introducing partitioning training set technique to non-truth table based circuit evolution. The experimental results conclude that it is possible to evolve characters classification systems larger and faster than those evolved earlier, by employing our proposed scheme.

1 Introduction

For the recent years, EHW technique has attracted increasing attentions and given us a promise to be employed as an alternative to conventional specification-based electronic circuit design method. A major hurdle in introducing EHW to solve real-world applications is the scalability issue of EHW. Until now, EHW has been proved to be able to evolve different electronic circuits successfully, but due to its limitation of scalability, most of the evolved circuits were on a small scale [1, 2, 3]. Generally, the scalability issue of EHW is related to the following two factors: (1) the length of the chromosome representation of electronic circuits, (2) the computational complexity of EA.

A general chromosome representation scheme of evolvable system is that EHW directly encodes circuit's architecture bits as chromosome of EA, which specifies the interconnections and functions of different hardware components in the circuit. Obviously, when the size of EHW increases, the length of chromosomes string also grows rapidly. However, huge size of chromosomes string (e.g. more than 1000 bits) is very inefficient to process by the current evolutionary techniques, which was discussed in [3]. The scalability of EHW concerns with the computational complexity of EA is a much more important challenge than the scalability of the chromosome representation. In the system evolutionary process, the number of generations, size of populations, and period of fitness evaluation of each individual grow drastically with the

A. Gelbukh and C.A. Reyes-Garcia (Eds.): MICAI 2006, LNAI 4293, pp. 272–282, 2006.

increasing computational complexity of the target system. All of these factors lead the increased possibility of the endless EA running time.

In order to evolve practical and large-scale electronic circuit, several different approaches have been undertaken to conquer the scalability of EHW [4, 5, 6, 7]. Incremental evolution strategy was first introduced by Torresen [8, 9, 10] as a divide-and-conquer approach to the scalability of EHW. In the literatures [11, 12], Stomeo also proposed a similar scheme to decompose input training set as a scalable approach to evolve combinational logic circuits.

A general idea of incremental evolution is to divide the target system into several sub-systems. Compared to evolving the intact system in a single run, incremental evolutionary process is first undertaken individually on a set of sub-systems, and then the evolved sub-systems are employed as the building blocks which are used to further evolution or structure of a larger and more complex system. Based on the reported incremental evolution strategy, up to 16 characters classification system was successfully evolved by using both extrinsic [9] and intrinsic EHW [13]. In most of EHW applications, fitness evaluation process is the most time-consuming part of the whole evolutionary process [1]. However, this characteristic of EHW is not captured by all the mentioned incremental evolution strategies in the evolutions of non-truth table based circuits [8, 9, 13]. This paper presents a new system decomposition scheme which is expected to introduce partitioning training set strategy to the intrinsic incremental evolution in the non-truth table based applications. In order to investigate the influence of the mentioned scheme, a 32 characters classification system is evolved. Our experimental results conclude that in terms of computational effort and complexity of evolved system, the proposed method outperforms all the reported incremental evolutionary approaches to the characters recognizers [8, 9, 13].

This paper is organized as follow: the following Section introduces the basic idea of intrinsic incremental evolution and explains the proposed method. In Section 3 the implementation of the intrinsic evolvable system is described. Section 4 presents the performance of the evolvable system with new decomposition strategy. The experimental results are discussed in Section 5. Section 6 concludes the paper.

2 A New Decomposition Strategy in Incremental Evolution

In this section, based on the intrinsic incremental evolution, a new system decomposition strategy is introduced. As Fig. 1 shows, our target system is expected to identify 32 different binary patterns of 5×6 pixels (In this paper, letters from A to Z and numbers from 1 to 6 are employed), where each pixel can be 0 or 1. Each pixel of character is connected to one system input port, so the proposed system includes 30 bits input. Each bit of system output corresponds to one character the system is evolved to recognize. Thus, the target system consists of 32 bits output. During the characters distinguishing process, the output port corresponding to the input character should be 1, synchronously the other outputs should be 0.

2.1 Introduction of Intrinsic Incremental Evolution

There are mainly two routes to approach the incremental evolution. The first method is named as partitioning system function. In this scheme, the entire function of EHW system is divided into several separate sub-functions. The second method is named as partitioning training set. Based on this principal, the full input training set is partitioned into several subsets to evolve their corresponding sub-systems individually. Using the principle of partitioning system function, several reports [8, 9, 13] proved it was capable of reducing the number of required generations by bringing a simpler and smaller search space of EA than direct evolving the target system in one run. On the other hand, partitioning training set is also an important scalability approach to EHW. In the evolutionary design of characters classification system, the fitness evaluation time of each individual is highly depended on the number of characters need to be recognized (size of training set). Another more important issue that appears with the increased size of characters set is the exponentially increased computational complexity of EA. However, reported partitioning training set method was only employed for evolving combinational circuits which were defined by a complete truth table, e.g. a multiplier [10, 12]. For getting a better scalability approach to EHW than the method just focused on partitioning system function, there is a potential requirement for developing a scheme that would concentrate on the input training set decomposition for non-truth table based applications.

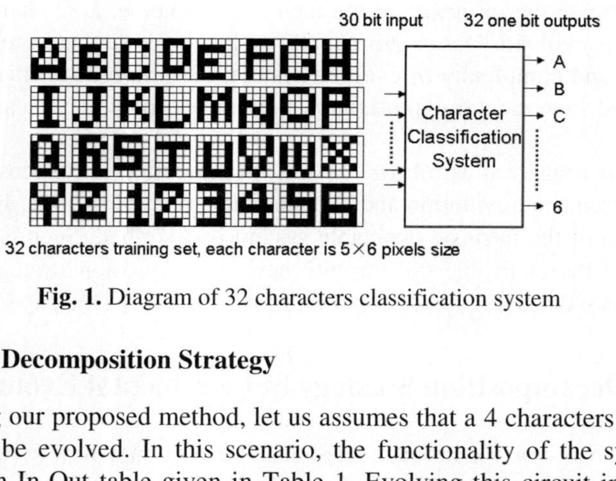

Fig. 1. Diagram of 32 characters classification system

2.2 Proposed Decomposition Strategy

For introducing our proposed method, let us assumes that a 4 characters classification system should be evolved. In this scenario, the functionality of the system can be described by an In-Out table given in Table 1. Evolving this circuit in a single run requires a circuit with four outputs and employing all four characters as training set. As a divide-and-conquer approach to evolvable system, in Fig 2, partitioning system function scheme and proposed strategy which is employed to combine partitioning training set and partitioning system function methods are presented separately.

The left case in Fig.2 presents partitioning system function strategy, which was detailed in [9, 13]. The top system is divided into two sub-systems which are evolved individually. In the system evolutionary process, each sub-system input all 4 characters from A to D as training set but only includes two outputs. As shown in table 1, the top system output function is divided into two parts (f_1 f_2 and f_3 f_4) by a vertical line. By combing the two individual sub-functions which are presented by their corresponding evolved sub-systems, the top system has the same classification ability as the system evolved in one operation.

Table 1. In-output table of 4 characters classification system

Input characters set	$f_1 f_2$	$f_3 f_4$
A	1 0	0 0
B	0 1	0 0
C	0 0	1 0
D	0 0	0 1

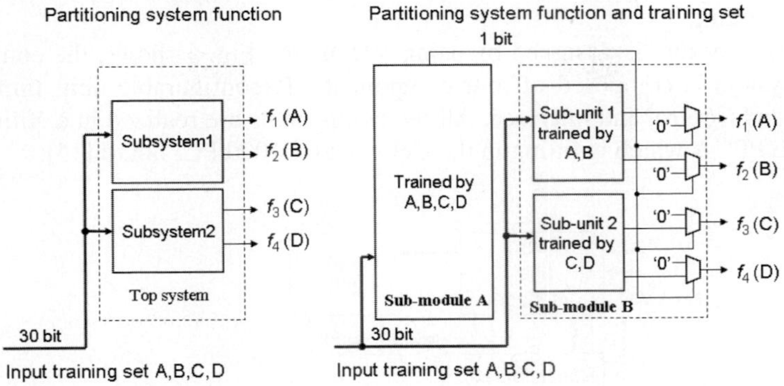

Fig. 2. Partitioning system function approach and proposed novel decomposition scheme

In the right case of Fig.2, partitioning training set strategy is applied and the system training set is divided into two groups. To distinguish two partitioned training sets, we first evolve a separate unit named as module A to perform characters pre-classification. The module A is evolved using the full training set from A to D. Four input characters are classified as two parts according to the output value of evolved module A. When the input character is A or B, the output of module A is 0. When the input is other, the output is 1. The module B which executes the practical function of characters recognition includes two sub-units which execute the function of distinguishing their corresponding partitioned characters set as the horizontal line in table 1 indicates. For example, the training set of sub-unit 1 is characters A and B only. Each sub-unit in module B could be evolved using direct evolution or partitioning system function approaches. Each top-system output is generated by a multiplexer whose function is selected by the 1 bit output of module A. Let's us consider input character A to the evolved system. In this scenario, the outputs of sub-unit 1 were chosen as the outputs of their corresponding multiplexers. The outputs of other two multiplexers in sub-unit 2 were directly defined as 0. Thus, the evolved system presents the same functions as the expected system which is described by Table 1.

3 Realization of Intrinsic Evolvable System

Incremental evolution strategy can be performed using any extrinsic or intrinsic EHW. In this work, a complete FPGA implemented intrinsic evolvable system is employed to evolve our target circuit. This intrinsic evolvable system is inspired by the Cartesian Genetic Programming and first introduced as a virtual reconfigurable circuit for EHW by Sekanina in [14]. The main motive of the proposed evolvable system is to provide a simpler and faster (virtual) reconfigurable platform for EHW experiments. On the other hand, the data type in the phenotype of the proposed evolvable system is relatively independent of the system genotype representation. This means that the granularity of the phenotype representation of the evolvable system can be designed exactly and flexibly according to the requirements of a given application, which only employs size limited binary genotype description of the target circuit.

The target system is designed by using VHDL. As Fig. 3 shows, the complete evolvable system is composed of four components: Reconfigurable unit, Fitness Unit, EA Unit and Control and interface. All the components are realized in a Xilinx Virtex xcv2000E FPGA which is fitting in the Celoxica RC1000 PCI board [15].

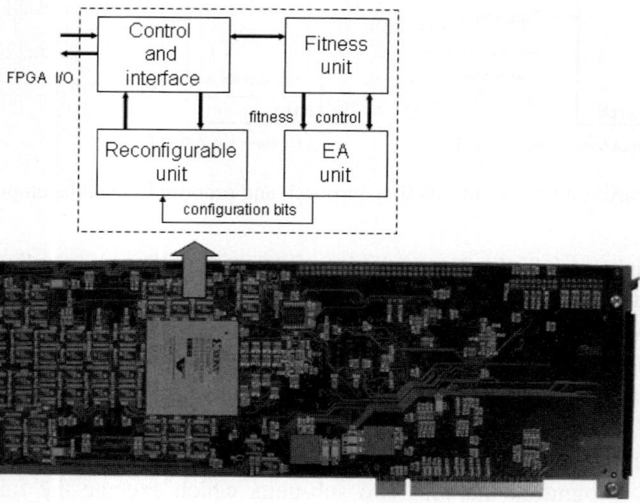

Fig. 3. Evolvable characters classification system in RC1000 PCI board with Virtex xcv2000E

In the evolvable system, all system operations are controlled by the control and interface which communicates with outside environment and executes the start or stop commands from host PC. The EA unit implements the evolutionary operations and generates configuration bits to configure the function of the reconfigurable unit. System function and evolution are performed in the reconfigurable unit. Fitness unit calculates individual fitness according to the output from the reconfigurable unit.

3.1 Genotype and Phenotype Representation

Similar to the Cartesian Genetic Programming, the system genotype is a linear string representing the connections and functions of a function elements (FE) array. The genotype and the mapping process of the genotype to phenotype are illustrated in Fig. 4. In real hardware implementation, several $N \times M$ arrays of 2-inputs FEs have been implemented in reconfigurable unit according to different system decomposition strategies. In the process of incremental evolution, each sub-system is evolved by one corresponding FEs array individually.

In our experiment, each FEs array consists of 4 layers. Except for the last layer, 16 uniform FEs are placed in each layer. The amount of FEs in the last layer is decided by the number of relative sub-system outputs. Each FE's two inputs in layer l (l=2, 3, 4) is connected to anyone output of FEs in layer l-1. In layer 1, each inputs of FE can be connected to any 30 bit inputs of the sub-system or defined as a bias of value 1 or 0. Each FE in layer 2,3,4 can has one of eight functions which are evident in Fig. 4. However, only two logic operations of buffer X and inverter Y are available for FEs in layer 1. The encoding of each FE in the chromosome string is: 5+5+1 bits in layer 1, 4+4+3 bits in the other layers. The chromosome string is uploaded from EA unit. By continuously altering the chromosome string which confirms the interconnection of FEs array and the functions implemented in each FE, the system can be evolved.

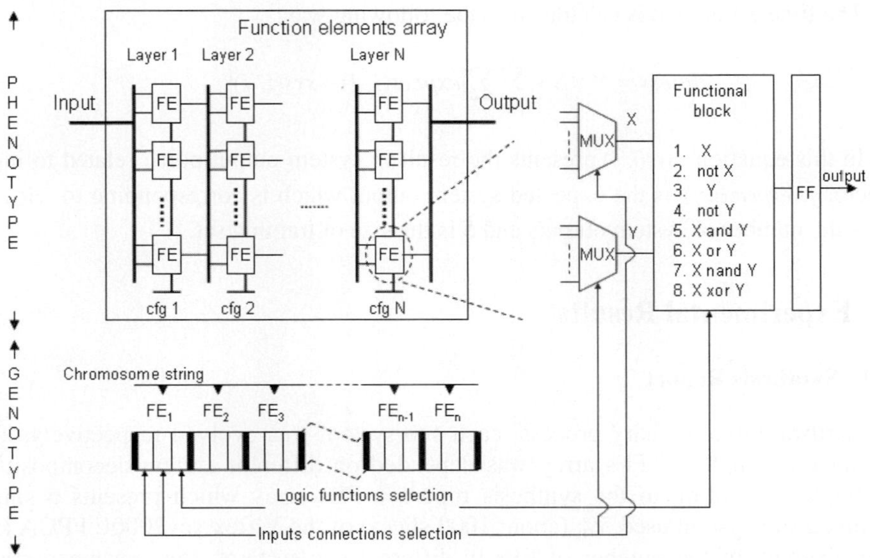

Fig. 4. The genotype-phenotype mapping

3.2 EA and Fitness Function

The evolutionary algorithm employed in EA unit is according to the 1+ λ evolutionary strategy, where λ =4. In our experiment, evolution is only based on the mutation and selection operators, crossover is not included. When the system evolutionary process begins, an initial population of 4 individuals is generated randomly. Once the fitness of each individual in the initial population is calculated by fitness unit, the best individual is selected and the new population is generated by using the fittest individual and its 4 mutants. According to our previous experiments, the mutation probability of each chromosome is defined as a constant: 0.2%. The evolutionary process will be continued until the stop criteria of EA are satisfied, which are defined as: (1) EA finds the expected solution; (2) Predefined generation number (2^{25}) is exhausted. The Flow diagram of EA is shown in Fig. 5.

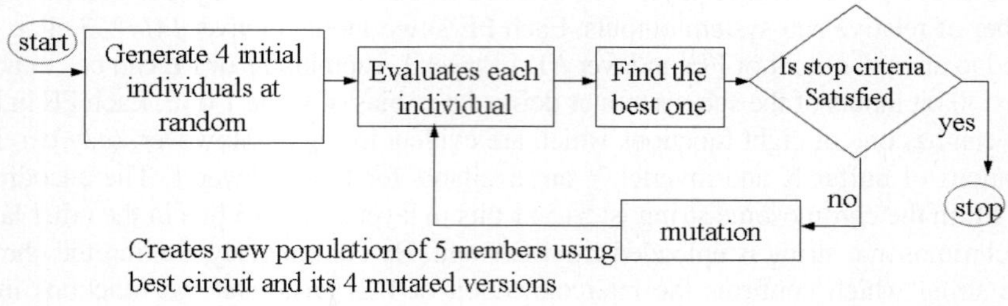

Fig. 5. Flow diagram of evolutionary algorithm

The fitness function is calculated as the following way:

$$fitness = N \times S - \sum_{i=1}^{N} \sum_{j=1}^{S} \left| expect(i,j) - sys(i,j) \right| \quad (1)$$

In this equation, $sys(i,j)$ presents the result in system output port i related to input vector j. $expect(i,j)$ is the expected system output which is corresponding to $sys(i,j)$. N is the number of system outputs and S is the size of training set.

4 Experimental Results

4.1 Synthesis Report

In hardware evolutionary process, each sub-system was evolved respectively. The number of employed FEs array was depended on different system decomposition strategy. According to the synthesis report, a FEs array which presents a single evolved sub-system used 5% (about 1000 slices) of the Virtex xcv2000E FPGA (for the diversity of the number of FEs in different sub-systems, the consumed slices were slightly different), the EA unit took 4011 slices, the Fitness calculation unit took 72 slices and the Control and interface unit used 446 slices. The design can operate at 97.513MHz based on the synthesis report. However, the actual hardware experiment was run at 30 MHz because of easier synchronization with PCI interface.

4.2 Time of Evolution

As the pipeline process is supported by the proposed evolvable system, all EA operations time as well as reconfiguration time of FEs array could be overlapped by the evaluation process of candidate circuit t_e. Therefore, if the size of training set is *S*, and the hardware platform operates at f_m MHz, it is possible to express the time for evaluating a single individual as:

$$t_{eval} = t_e = \frac{S}{f_m} \quad (2)$$

The total time for a sub-system evolution can be expressed as:

$$Time = t_{init} + ngen * n * t_{eval} \quad (3)$$

Where n denotes the population size, $ngen$ is the number of generations and t_{init} is time need to get the first valid output in the pipeline process (which is negligible).

4.3 Results

In our experiment, with the proposed decomposition strategy, module A was evolved first to implement the function of pre-classification which partitioned 32 characters training set into several subsets. In this paper, two and four subsets based training set partitions were implemented individually. Sub-units in module B were evolved using different size of partitioned training sets (16 or 8 characters sets) according to its corresponding module A. On the other hand, different partitioning system function strategies were also included on the evolutions of the sub-units in module B.

Existent incremental evolution [9, 13] which only employs partitioning system function method was also executed as a contrast to the proposed scheme. The average results of the number of generations and the evolutionary time were calculated from the 25 EA runs. Table 2, Table 3 and Fig. 6 summarize the experiments under the different sizes of system function decomposition.

Table 2. The influence of different partitioning training set strategy in two sub-functions partition based 32 characters classification system evolution

Decomposition strategy	Sub-system functions		Number of generations (avg.)	Total evolution time(avg.)	Device cost (slice)
Partitioning system function	Sub-system 1	A-P	1370253	11.82 sec	6347
	Sub-system 2	1-Z	1401473		
Partitioning system function and training set (with 2 subsets)	Module A		83265	1.90 sec	7250
	Sub-unit 1	A-P	287456		
	Sub-unit 2	1-Z	437455		

Table 3. The influence of different partitioning training set strategy in four sub-functions partition based 32 characters classification system evolution

Decomposition strategy	Sub-system functions		Number of generations (avg.)	Total evolution time(avg.)	Device cost (slice)
Partitioning system function	Sub-system 1	A-H	283677	3.17 sec	8356
	Sub-system 2	I-P	174272		
	Sub-system 3	1-R	139419		
	Sub-system 4	S-Z	146563		
Partitioning system function and training set (with 2 subsets)	Module A		81265	0.56 sec	9216
	Sub-unit 1	A-H	23403		
		I-P	22288		
	Sub-unit 2	1-R	29617		
		S-Z	22945		
Partitioning system function and training set (with 4 subsets)	Module A		1415473	6.06 sec	9237
	Sub-unit 1	A-H	3135		
	Sub-unit 2	I-P	3987		
	Sub-unit 3	1-R	5123		
	Sub-unit 4	S-Z	4778		

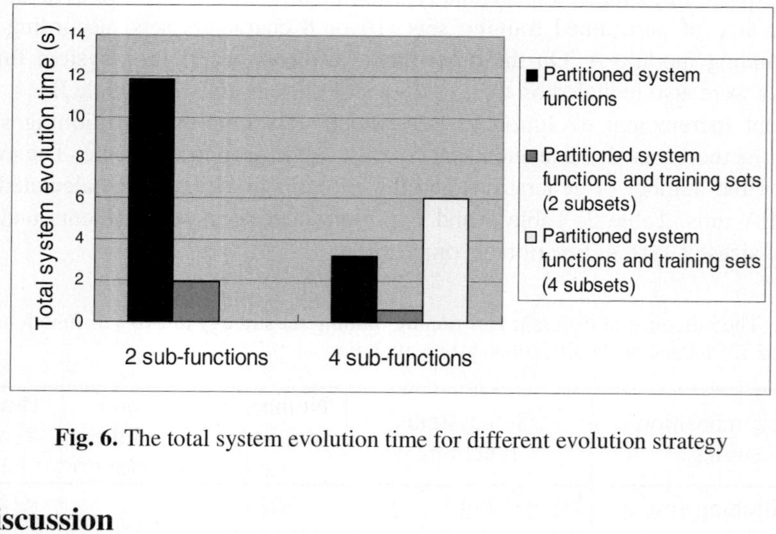

Fig. 6. The total system evolution time for different evolution strategy

5 Discussion

Under the setting of introducing the proposed strategy with two subsets based system training set decomposition, compared with the performance of simplex partitioning system function based incremental evolution, the number of generations and the total evolutionary time required to evolve the target system were decreased markedly. The obtained experimental results for evolving two sub-functions partition based result systems indicated that the performance related to the number of generations and the total evolutionary time got a 3.4 and 6.2 times improvements respectively by dividing the training set into two parts. The similar results were drawn from the four sub-functions partition based evolution. The powers of two subsets based system training set decomposition were 4.1 and 5.6 times strong than its competitor of unitary partitioning system function in the fields of the consumed number of generations and the system evolutionary time.

Another interesting observation is how the size of the partitioned training set influence the total system evolutionary time. For example, in Table 3, the increased number of subsets brought a significant augment in the items of total system evolutionary time. When we employed 4 subsets based training set decomposition, its consumed total EA time was higher than other approaches, even simplex partitioned system function scheme. The reason for this is that the process of the training set decomposition is not computational cost free. As the increased computational complexity of evolving module A, the benefits of reduced evolutionary time of evolving module B would be overlapped. This means the total evolutionary time required to evolve the target classification system would be highly depended on the selection of the size of the training set partition. To minimize the evolution time in different applications, an algorithm is desired to be employed to find the optimal partitioning size of the training set and the system function, which is still an open issue.

Our experiments demonstrated the importance of partitioning training set which approached the time complexity of EHW by bringing a simpler search space of EA and reducing the fitness evaluation time in the evolution of sub-systems. Compared with the reported incremental evolution strategy, when a suitable proposed decomposition strategy was employed, time for EA learning was significantly reduced. To execute the function of partitioning training set, higher hardware costs appeared in the evolvable systems. However, the most important challenge in the evolutionary design field is the possibility of evolving circuits more complicate and larger than those evolved by the existed evolution scheme.

6 Conclusion

As a scalable approach to EHW, a new system decomposition strategy which extended the application field of partitioning training set technique from full-truth table based to non-truth table based applications in intrinsic incremental evolution has been introduced. The benefit of the application of the partitioning training set scheme consists in the reduced fitness evaluation period of the evolution of the sub-systems and simper search space of EA. The performance of the proposed algorithm has been tested by evolving a 32 characters classification system. Experimental results proved that such a method will produce better scalability results than the existing incremental evolution methods which only focused on the output function partition. Further work will be concentrated on the development of algorithms to identify the optimal partitions of training set and system functions.

Acknowledgment

This work was supported by INHA University Research Grant.

References

1. Yao, X., Higuchi, T.: Promises and Challenges of Evolvable Hardware. IEEE Transactions on Systems, Man, and Cybernetics, Vol. 29, No. 1 (1999) 87-97
2. Higuchi, T. et al.: Real-World Applications of Analog and Digital Evolvable Hardware. IEEE Transactions on Evolutionary Computation, Vol. 3, No. 3 (1999) 220-235
3. Sekanina, L.: Evolutionary Design of Digital Circuits: Where Are Current Limits? In: Proc. of the First NASA/ESA Conference on Adaptive Hardware and Systems, AHS 2006, IEEE Computer Society (2006) 171 – 178
4. Kajitani, I. et al.: Variable Length Chromosome GA for Evolvable Hardware. In Proc. of the 3rd International Conference on Evolutionary Computation ICEC96, IEEE press (1996) 443–447
5. Murakawa, M. et al.: Hardware Evolution at Function Level. In: Proc. of Parallel Problem Solving from Nature PPSN IV, LNCS 1141, Springer-Verlag (1996) 62–71
6. Paredis, J.: Coevolutionary Computation. Artificial Life, Vol. 2, No. 4, MIT Press (1995) 355–375
7. Islas Pérez, Eduardo. et al.: Genetic Algorithms and Case-Based Reasoning as a Discovery and Learning Machine in the Optimization of Combinational Logic Circuits. In: Proc. of the 2002 Mexican International Conference on Artificial Intelligence, LNAI 2313, Springer-Verlag (2002) 128—137
8. Torresen, J.: A Divide-and-Conquer Approach to Evolvable Hardware. In: Proc. of the Second International Conference Evolvable Systems: From Biology to Hardware ICES 98, LNCS 1478, Springer-Verlag (1998) 57-65
9. Torresen, J.: A Scalable Approach to Evolvable Hardware. Genetic Programming and Evolvable Machines, Vol 3, No. 3, Springer Netherlands (2002) 259-282
10. Torresen, J.: Evolving Multiplier Circuits by Training Set and Training Vector Partitioning. In: Proc. of the 5th International Conference Evolvable Systems: From Biology to Hardware ICES 2003, LNCS 2606, Springer-Verlag (2003) 228–237
11. Stomeo, E., Kalganova, T.: Improving EHW Performance Introducing a New Decomposition Strategy. In: Proc. of the 2004 IEEE Conference on Cybernetics and Intelligent Systems, Singapore (2004) 439-444
12. Stomeo, E. et al.: Generalized Disjunction Decomposition for the Evolution of Programmable Logic Array Structures. In: Proc. of the First NASA/ESA Conference on Adaptive Hardware and Systems AHS 2006, IEEE Computer Society (2006) 179- 185
13. Wang, J. et al.: Using Reconfigurable Architecture-Based Intrinsic Incremental Evolution to Evolve a Character Classification System. In: Proc. of the 2005 International Conference on Computational Intelligence and Security CIS 2005, Part I, LNAI 3801, Springer-Verlag (2005) 216-223
14. Sekanina, L.: Virtual Reconfigurable Circuits for Real-World Applications of Evolvable Hardware. In: Proc. of the 5th International Conference Evolvable Systems: From Biology to Hardware ICES 2003, LNCS 2606, Springer-Verlag (2003) 186-197
15. Celoxica Inc., RC1000 Hardware Reference Manual V2.3, 2001

Evolutionary Method for Nonlinear Systems of Equations

Crina Grosan[1], Ajith Abraham[2], and Alexander Gelbukh[3]

[1] Department of Computer Science
Babeş-Bolyai University, Cluj-Napoca, 3400, Romania
[2] IITA Professorship Program, School of Computer Science and Engineering, Yonsei University, 134 Shinchon-dong, Sudaemoon-ku, Seoul 120-749, Korea
[3] Centro de Investigación en Computación (CIC)
Instituto Politécnico Nacional (IPN), Mexico
cgrosan@cs.ubbcluj.ro, ajith.abraham@ieee.org, gelbukh@gelbukh.com

Abstract. We propose a new perspective for solving systems of nonlinear equations by viewing them as a multiobjective optimization problem where every equation represents an objective function whose goal is to minimize the difference between the right- and left-hand side of the corresponding equation of the system. An evolutionary computation technique is suggested to solve the problem obtained by transforming the system into a multiobjective optimization problem. Results obtained are compared with some of the well-established techniques used for solving nonlinear equation systems.

1 Introduction

A nonlinear system of equations is defined as:

$$f(x) = \begin{bmatrix} f_1(x) \\ f_2(x) \\ \vdots \\ f_n(x) \end{bmatrix},$$

$x = (x_1, x_2, \ldots, x_n)$, which means there are n equations and n variables, where $f_1, \ldots, f_n$ are nonlinear functions in the space of all real valued continuous functions on $\Omega = \prod_{i=1}^{n} [a_i, b_i] \subset \Re^n$.

Some of the equations can be linear, but not all of them. Finding a solution for a nonlinear system of equations $f(x)$ involves finding a solution such that every equation in the nonlinear system is 0:

$$(P) \begin{cases} f_1(x_1, x_2, ..., x_n) = 0 \\ f_2(x_1, x_2, ..., x_n) = 0 \\ \vdots \\ f_n(x_1, x_2, ..., x_n) = 0 \end{cases}. \tag{1}$$

A. Gelbukh and C.A. Reyes-Garcia (Eds.): MICAI 2006, LNAI 4293, pp. 283–293, 2006.

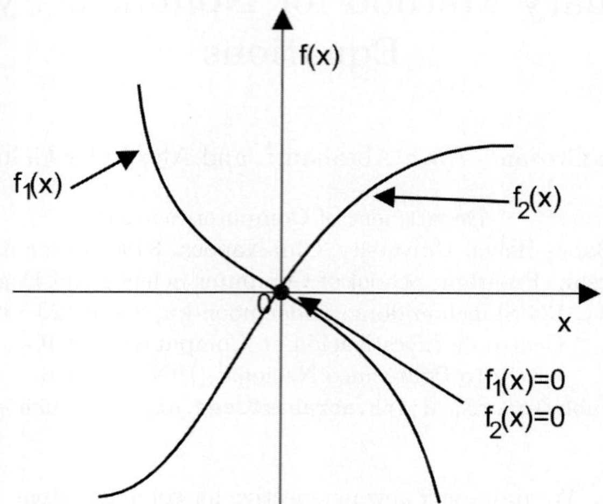

Fig. 1. Example of solution in the case of a two nonlinear equation system represented by f_1 and f_2

In Figure 1, the solution for a system having two nonlinear equations is depicted. There are also situations when a system of equations has multiple solutions. For instance, the system:

$$\begin{cases} f_1(x_1, x_2, x_3, x_4) = x_1^2 + 2x_2^2 + cos(x_3) - x_4^2 = 0 \\ f_1(x_1, x_2, x_3, x_4) = 3x_1^2 + x_2^2 + sin^2(x_3) - x_4^2 = 0 \\ f_1(x_1, x_2, x_3, x_4) = -2x_1^2 - x_2^2 - cos(x_3) + x_4^2 = 0 \\ f_1(x_1, x_2, x_3, x_4) = -x_1^2 - x_2^2 - cos^2(x_3) + x_4^2 = 0 \end{cases}$$

has two solutions: (1, -1, 0, 2) and (-1, 1, 0, -2). The assumption is that a zero, or root, of the system exists. The solutions of interest are those points (if any) that are common to the zero contours of $f_i, i = 1, ..., n$. There are several ways to solve nonlinear equation systems ([1], [5]-[9] and [13]). Probably the Newton type is one of the most established techniques. Other methods are depicted as follows:

- Trust-region method [3];
- Broyden method [2];
- Secant method [12];
- Halley method [4].

Newton's method. In Newton's method, f is approximated by the first order Taylor expansion in a neighborhood of a point $x^k \in \Re^n$. The Jacobian matrix $J(x^k) \subset \Re^{nxn}$ to $f(x)$ evaluated at x^k is given by:

$$J = \begin{bmatrix} \frac{\delta f_1}{\delta x_1} \cdots \frac{\delta f_1}{\delta x_n} \\ \vdots \quad\quad \vdots \\ \frac{\delta f_n}{\delta x_1} \cdots \frac{\delta f_n}{\delta x_n} \end{bmatrix}.$$

Then:

$$f(x^k + t) = f(x^k) + J(x^k)t + O(||p||^2).$$

By setting the right side of the equation to zero and discarding terms higher than first order ($O(||p||^2)$) the relationship $J(x^k)t = -f(x^k)$ is obtained. Then, the Newton algorithm is described as follows:

Algorithm 1. Newton algorithm

Set k=0.
Guess an approximate solution x^0.
Repeat
  Compute $J(x^k)$ and $f(x^k)$.
  Solve the linear system $J(x^k)t = -f(x^k)$.
  Set $x^{k+1} = x^k + t$.
  Set t = t + 1.
Until converge to the solution

The index k is an iteration index and x^k is the vector x after k iterations. The idea of the method is to start with a value which is reasonably close to the true zero and then replaces the function by its tangent and computes the zero of this tangent. This zero of the tangent will typically be a better approximation to the function's zero, and the method can be iterated. This algorithm is also known as *Newton-Raphson* method. There are also several other Newton methods. It is very important to have a good starting value (the success of the algorithm depends on this). The Jacobian matrix is needed but in many problems analytic derivatives are unavailable. If function evaluation is expensive, then the cost of finite-difference determination of the Jacobian can be prohibitive.

Broyden's method. The approximate Jacobian is denoted by: $\delta x = -J^{-1}f$. Then the i-th quasi-Newton step δx_i is the solution of $B_i \delta xi = -f_i$, where $\delta x_i = x_{i+1}x_i$. The quasi-Newton or secant condition is that B_{i+1} satisfy $B_{i+1}\delta x_i = \delta f_i$, where $\delta f_i = f_{i+1} - f_i$. This is the generalization of the one-dimensional secant approximation to the derivative $\frac{\delta f}{\delta x}$.

Many different auxiliary conditions to pin down B_{i+1} have been explored, but the best-performing algorithm in practice results from Broyden's formula. This formula is based on the idea of getting B_{i+1} by making the least change to B_i consistent with the secant equation. Broyden showed that the resulting equation as:

$$B_{i+1} = B_i + \frac{(\delta f_i - B_i \delta x_i) \otimes \delta x_i}{(\delta x_i)^2}$$

Secant method. The secant method is a root-finding algorithm that uses a succession of roots of secant lines to better approximate a root of a function. The secant method is defined by the recurrence relation

$$x_{n+1} = x_n - \frac{x_n - x_{n-1}}{f(x_n) - f(x_{n-1})} f(x_n)$$

As evident from the recurrence relation, the secant method requires two initial values, x_0 and x_1, which should ideally be chosen to lie close to the root. As illustrated in Figure 2, two points a and b are initially considered. Then the secant of chord of the the graph of function f through the points $(a, f(a))$, $(b, f(b))$ is defined as:

$$y - f(b) = \frac{f(b) - f(a)}{b - a}(x - b).$$

The point c is chosen to be the root of this line such that:

$$f(b) + \frac{f(b) - f(a)}{b - a}(c - b) = 0.$$

Solving this equation gives the recurrence relation for the secant method. The new value c is equal to x_{n+1}, and b and a are x_n and x_{n-1}, respectively.

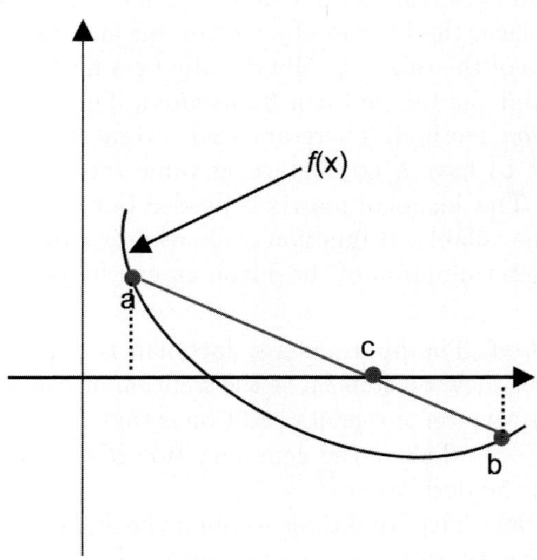

Fig. 2. An example of secant method

Effati's method. Effati and Nazemi [10] proposed a new method for solving systems of nonlinear equations. Their proposed method [10] is summarized below. The following notation is used:

$$x_i(k+1) = f_i(x_1(k), x_2(k), ..., x_n(k));$$

$$f(x_k) = (f_1(x_k), f_2(x_k), ..., f_n(x_k));$$

$i = 1, 2..., n$ and $x_i : N \rightarrow \Re$.

If there exist a t such that $x(t) = 0$ then $f_i(x(t-1)) = 0, i = 1, ..., n$. This involves that $x(t-1)$ is an exact solution for the given system of equations.

Define $u(k) = (u_1(k), u_2(k), ..., u_n(k))$, $x(k+1) = u(k)$, and $f^0 : \Omega \times U \rightarrow \Re$ (Ω and U are compact subsets of $\Re^n$):

$$f^0(x(k), u(k)) = \|u(k) - f(x(k))\|_2^2.$$

The error function E is defined as follows:

$$E[x^t, u^t] = \sum_{k=0}^{t-1} f^0(x(k), u(k)),$$

$$x^t = (x(1), x(2), ..., x(t-1), 0)$$
$$u^t = (u(1), u(2), ..., u(t-1), 0).$$

Consider the following problem:

$$(P_1) \begin{cases} \text{minimize} E[x^t, u^t] = \sum\limits_{k=0}^{t-1} f^0(x(k), u(k)) \\ \text{subject to} \\ x(k+1) = u(k) \\ x(0) = 0, x(t) = 0, (x^0 \text{ is known}) \end{cases} . \quad (2)$$

As per theorem illustrated in [10], if there is an optimal solution for the problem P_1 such that the value of E will be zero, then this is also a solution for the system of equations we want to solve. The problem is transformed to a measure theory problem. By solving the transformed problem u^t is firstly constructed and from there, x^t is obtained. Reader is advised to consult [10] for details. The measure theory method is improved in [10]. The interval $[1, t]$ is divided into the subintervals $S_1 = [1, t-1]$ and $S_2 = [t-1, t]$. The problem P_1 is solved in both subintervals and two errors E_1 and E_2 respectively are obtained. This way, an upper bound for the total error if found. If this upper bound is estimated to be zero then an approximate solution for the problem is found.

2 Transforming the Problem into a Multiobjective Optimization Problem

The basic definitions of a multiobjective optimization problem and what it denotes an optimal solution is formulated as follows [15]:

Let Ω be the search space. Consider n objective functions $f_1, f_2 \ldots f_n$,

$$f_i : \Omega \rightarrow \Re, \quad i = 1, 2, \ldots, n,$$

where $\Omega \subset \Re^m$. The multiobjective optimization problem is defined as:

$$\begin{cases} optimize\, f(x) = (f_1(x), ..., f_n(x)) \\ subject\ to \\ x = (x_1, x_2, \ldots x_m) \in \Omega. \end{cases}$$

For deciding wether a solution is better than another solution or not, the following relationship between solutions might be used:

Definition 1 (*Pareto dominance*). Consider a maximization problem. Let x, y be two decision vectors (solutions) from Ω. Solution x *dominates* y (also written as $x \succ y$) if and only if the following conditions are fulfilled:

(i) $f_i(x) \geq f_i(y), \forall i = 1, 2, \ldots, n,$
(ii) $\exists j \in \{1, 2, \ldots, n\}$: $f_j(x) > f_j(y)$.

That is, a feasible vector x is Pareto optimal if no feasible vector y can increase some criterion without causing a simultaneous decrease in at least one other criterion. In the literature other terms have also been used instead of Pareto optimal or minimal solutions, including words such as non-dominated, non-inferior, efficient, functional-efficient solutions etc. The solution x^0 is *ideal* if all objectives have their optimum in a common point x^0.

Definition 2 (*Pareto front*). The images of the Pareto optimum points in the criterion space are called *Pareto front*. The system of equations (P) can be transformed into a multiobjective optimization problem. Each equation can be considered as an objective function. The goal of this optimization function is to minimize the difference (in absolute value) between left side and right side of the equation. Since the right term is zero, the objective function will be given by the absolute value of the left term.

The system (P) is then equivalent to:

$$(P') \begin{cases} \text{minimize } abs(f_1(x_1, x_2, ..., x_n)) \\ \text{minimize } abs(f_2(x_1, x_2, ..., x_n)) \\ \vdots \\ \text{minimize } abs(f_n(x_1, x_2, ..., x_n)) \end{cases}$$

3 Evolutionary Nonlinear Equation System

An evolutionary technique is proposed for solving the multiobjective problem obtained by transforming the system of equations. Some starting points (initial solutions) are generated based on the problem domain defined and these solutions are evolved in an iterative manner. In order to compare the two solutions, Pareto dominance relationship is used. Genetic operators such as Convex crossover and Gaussian mutation are used [11]. An external set is used for storing all the non-dominated solutions found during the iteration process. Tournament selection is applied. n individuals are randomly selected from the unified set of current population and external population. Out of these n solutions the one which dominated a greater number of solutions is chosen. If there are two or more 'equal' solutions then one of them is picked at random. At each iteration, this archive is updated by introducing all the non-dominated solutions obtained at the respective step and by removing from the external set of all solutions that might become dominated.

The proposed algorithm is described as follows:

Algorithm 2. Evolutionary Multiobjective Optimization (EMO) algorithm

Step 1. Set $t = 0$.
Randomly generate population $P(t)$.
Set $EP(t) = \emptyset$. (EP denoted the external population).
Step 2. **Repeat**
  Step 2.1. Evaluate $P(t)$
  Step 2.2. Selection ($P(t) \cup EP(t)$)
  Step 2.3. Crossover
  Step 2.4. Mutation
  Step 2.3. Select all nondominated individuals obtained
  Step 2.3. Update $EP(t)$
  Step 2.3. Update ($P(t)$ (keep best between parents and offspring)
  Step 2.3. Set $t := t + 1$
 Until $t = number_o f_g enerations$
Step 3. Print $EP(t)$

4 Experiments, Results, and Discussions

This section reports several experiments and comparisons. We consider the same problems (Examples 1 and 2 below) as Effati [10]. Parameter values used by the evolutionary approach are given in Table 1.

Table 1. Parameter values used in the experiments by the evolutionary approach

Parameter	Value	
	Example 1	Example 2
Population size	250	300
Number of generations	150	200
Sigma (for mutation)	0.1	0.1
Tournament size	4	5

Example 1. Consider the following nonlinear system:

$$\begin{cases} f_1(x_1, x_2) = cos(2x_1) - cos(2x_2) - 0.4 = 0 \\ f_2(x_1, x_2) = 2(x_2 - x_1) + sin(2x_2) - sin(2x_1) - 1.2 = 0 \end{cases} .$$

Results obtained by applying Newton's method, Effati's technique, and the proposed EMO method are presented in Table 2. A sample solution obtained by the EMO approach is presented in Table 2. More Pareto solutions and the corresponding absolute values of the functions f_1 and f_2 are presented in Table 3.

Table 2. Empirical results for Example 1

Method	Solution	Function absolute values
Newton's method	(0.15, 0.49)	(-0.00168, 0.01497)
Secant method	(0.15, 0.49)	(-0.00168, 0.01497)
Broyden's method	(0.15, 0.49)	(-0.00168, 0.01497)
Effati's method	(0.1575, 0.4970)	(0.005455, 0.00739)
EMO approach	(0.15772, 0.49458)	(0.001264, 0.000969)

Table 3. Nondominated solutions and the corresponding objectives values obtained by EMO approach for Example 1

x_1	x_2	f_1	f_2
0.15780	0.4943	0.00212	0.00075
0.1577	0.4945	0.001139	0.00119
0.1578	0.4942	0.000583	0.002439
0.1577	0.4943	0.000812	0.00173
0.1578	0.04941	0.000416	0.00274
0.15775	0.4945	0.00111	0.00131
0.1577	0.49455	0.00123	0.000964
0.1569	0.4942	0.001142	0.00107
0.1568	0.4941	0.001035	0.00115
0.1570	0.4942	0.001078	0.000681

In Figure 3, the Pareto front obtained by the solutions presented in the Table 3 are presented. As evident from Figure 3, all the solutions plotted are nondominated. The user can select the desired solution taking into account of the different preferences (for instance, the one for which one objective is having a value closed to the desired value, or the one for which the sum of both objectives is minimal, etc). As illustrated in Table 2, results obtained by the evolutionary approach are better than the ones obtained by the other techniques. Also, by applying an evolutionary technique we don't need any additional information about the problem (such as the functions to be differentiable, a good starting point, etc).

Example 2. We consider the following problem:

$$\begin{cases} f_1(x_1, x_2) = e^{x_1} + x_1 x_2 - 1 = 0 \\ f_2(x_1, x_2) = sin(x_1 x_2) + x_1 + x_2 - 1 = 0 \end{cases} .$$

Results obtained by Effati's method and one solution obtained by the EMO approach are given in Table 4.

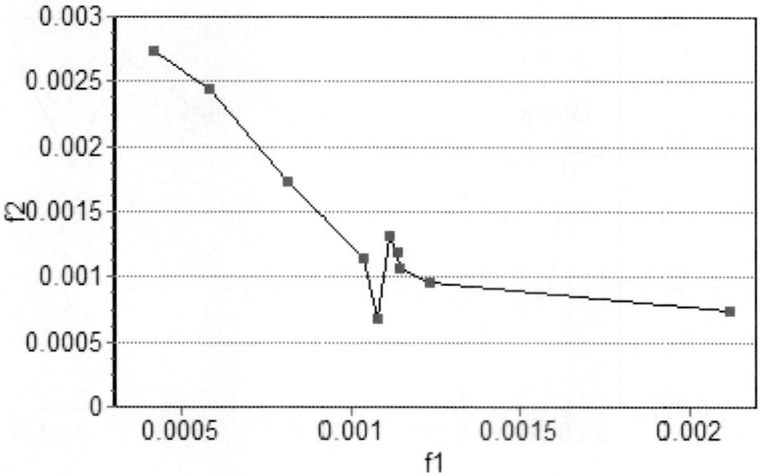

Fig. 3. Pareto front obtained by the EMO approach for the Example 1

Table 4. Empirical results for Example 2

Method	Solution	Function absolute values
Effati	(0.0096, 0.9976)	(0.019223, 0.016776)
EMO approach	(0.00138, 1.0027)	(0.00276, 6.37E-5)

Table 5. Nondominated solutions and the corresponding objectives values obtained by EMO approach for Example 2

x_1	x_2	f_1	f_2
0.00130	1.0025	0.00260	0.00510
0.0011	0.0030	0.00220	0.00520
0.0012	1.0020	0.002403	0.00440
0.0004	1.0023	0.000801	0.00310
0.0003	1.0028	0.000600	0.00340
0.00028	1.0029	0.000560	0.00346
0.00025	1.004	0.000501	0.00450
0.0015	1.0043	0.0003006	0.00460
0.0017	1.0041	0.000340	0.00444
0.0001	1.005	0.0002005	0.00520

The nondominated solutions and the corresponding functions values obtained by EMO approach are presented in Table 5. Pareto front obtained by the EMO method for Example 2 are depicted in Figure 4. For this example, the evolutionary approach obtained better results than the results reported by Effati's method. These experiments show the efficiency and advantage of applying

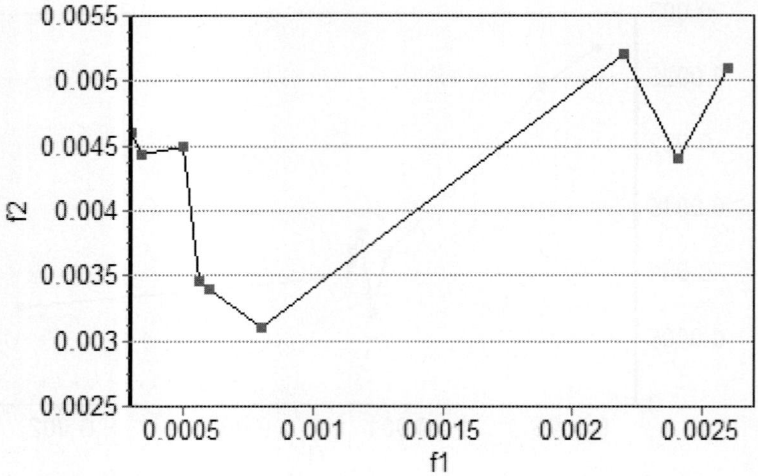

Fig. 4. Pareto front obtained by the EMO approach for the Example 2

evolutionary techniques for solving systems of nonlinear equations against standard mathematical approaches.

5 Conclusions

The proposed approach seems to be very efficient for solving equation systems. In this paper, we analyzed a case of nonlinear equation systems. The proposed approach could be extended and applied for higher dimensional systems. In a similar manner, inequations systems could be also solved.

Acknowledgments

The second author acknowledges the support received from the International Joint Research Grant of the IITA (Institute of Information Technology Assessment) foreign professor invitation program of the Ministry of Information and Communication, South Korea.

References

1. C. Brezinski, Projection methods for systems of equations, Elsevier, 1997.
2. C.G. Broyden, A class of methods for solving nonlinear simultaneous equations. Mathematics of Computation, 19, 577-593, 1965.
3. A.R. Conn, N.I.M. Gould, P.L. Toint, Trust-Region methods, SIAM, 2000.
4. A. Cuyt, P.van der Cruyssen, Abstract Pade approximants for the solution of a system of nonlinear equations, Comp. Math. and Appl., 9, 139-149, 1983.

5. J.E. Denis, On Newtons Method and Nonlinear Simultaneous Replacements, SIAM Journal of Numerical Analisys, 4, 103108, 1967.
6. J.E. Denis, On Newtonlike Methods, Numerical Mathematics, 11 , 324330, 1968.
7. J.E. Denis, On the Convergence of Broydens Method for Nonlinear Systems of Equations, Mathematics of Computation, 25, 559567, 1971.
8. J.E. Denis, H. Wolkowicz, LeastChange Secant Methods, Sizing, and Shifting, SIAM Journal of Numerical Analisys, 30, 12911314, 1993.
9. J.E. Denis, M. ElAlem, K. Williamson, A Trust-Region Algorithm for Least-Squares Solutions of Nonlinear Systems of Equalities and Inequalities, SIAM Journal on Optimization 9(2), 291-315, 1999.
10. S. Effati, A.R. Nazemi, A new methid for solving a system of the nonlinear equations, Applied Mathematics and Computation, 168, 877-894, 2005
11. Goldberg, D.E. Genetic algorithms in search, optimization and machine learning. Addison Wesley, Reading, MA, 1989.
12. W. Gragg, G. Stewart, A stable variant of the secant method for solving nonlinear equations, SIAM Journal of Numerical Analisys, 13, 889-903, 1976.
13. J. M. Ortega and W. C. Rheinboldt, Iterative solution of nonlinear equations in several variables. New York: Academic Press, 1970
14. W.H. Press, S.A. Teukolsky, W.T. Vetterling, B.P. Flannery, Numerical Recipes in C: The Art of Scientific Computing, Cambridge University Press, 2002.
15. Steuer, R. E. Multiple Criteria Optimization. Theory, Computation, and Application. Wiley Series in Probability and Mathematical Statistics: Applied Probability and Statistics. New York: John Wiley & Sons, Inc, 1986.

A Multi-objective Particle Swarm Optimizer Hybridized with Scatter Search

Luis V. Santana-Quintero, Noel Ramírez, and Carlos Coello Coello

CINVESTAV-IPN, Electrical Engineering Department, Computer Science Area, Av. IPN No. 2508, San Pedro Zacatenco, México D.F. 07360, México
lsantana@computacion.cs.cinvestav.mx,
santiago@computacion.cs.cinvestav.mx, ccoello@cs.cinvestav.mx

Abstract. This paper presents a new multi-objective evolutionary algorithm which consists of a hybrid between a particle swarm optimization (PSO) approach and scatter search. The main idea of the approach is to combine the high convergence rate of the particle swarm optimization algorithm with a local search approach based on scatter search. We propose a new leader selection scheme for PSO, which aims to accelerate convergence. Upon applying PSO, scatter search acts as a local search scheme, improving the spread of the nondominated solutions found so far. Thus, the hybrid constitutes an efficient multi-objective evolutionary algorithm, which can produce reasonably good approximations of the Pareto fronts of multi-objective problems of high dimensionality, while only performing 4,000 fitness function evaluations. Our proposed approach is validated using ten standard test functions commonly adopted in the specialized literature. Our results are compared with respect to a multi-objective evolutionary algorithm that is representative of the state-of-the-art in the area: the NSGA-II.

1 Introduction

Most real world problems involve the simultaneous optimization of two or more (often conflicting) objectives. The solution of such problems (called "multi-objective") is different from that of a single-objective optimization problem. The main difference is that multi-objective optimization problems normally have not one but a set of solutions which are all equally good. The main aim of this work is to design a MOEA that can produce a reasonably good approximation of the true Pareto front of a problem with a relatively low number of fitness function evaluations. In the past, a wide variety of evolutionary algorithms (EAs) have been used to solve multi-objective optimization problems [1]. In this paper, we propose a new hybrid multi-objective evolutionary algorithm based on particle swarm optimization (PSO) and scatter search (SS). PSO is a bio-inspired optimization algorithm that was proposed by James Kennedy and Russell Eberhart in the mid-1990s [9], and which is inspired on the choreography of a bird flock. PSO has been found to be a very successful optimization approach both in single-objective and in multi-objective problems [14,9]. In PSO, each solution

A. Gelbukh and C.A. Reyes-Garcia (Eds.): MICAI 2006, LNAI 4293, pp. 294–304, 2006.

is represented by a particle. Particles group in "swarms" (there can be either one swarm or several in one population) and the evolution of the swarm to the optimal solutions is achieved by a velocity equation. This equation is composed of three elements: a velocity inertia, a cognitive component "*pbest*" and a social component "*gbest*". Depending on the topology adopted (i.e., one swarm or multiple swarms), each particle can be affected by either the best local and/or the best global particle in its swarm. PSO normally has difficulties to achieve a good distribution of solutions with a low number of evaluations. That is why we adopted scatter search (which can be useful at finding solutions within the neighborhood of a reference set) in this paper in order to have a local optimizer whose computational cost is low. SS is an evolutionary method that was originally proposed in the 1970s by Fred Glover [6] for combining decision rules and problem constraints. This method uses strategies for combining solution vectors that have been found effective during the search (the so called "reference set") [11]. SS has been successfully applied to hard optimization problems, and it constitutes a very flexible heuristic, since it can be implemented in a variety of ways, offering numerous alternatives for exploiting its fundamental ideas. The remainder of this paper is organized as follows. Section 2 provides a brief introduction to particle swarm optimization. In Section 3 we analyze the scatter search components. Section 4 describes our proposed approach. Our comparison of results is provided in Section 5. Our conclusions and some possible paths for future research are provided in Section 6.

2 Particle Swarm Optimization (PSO)

In the PSO algorithm, the particles (including the *pbest* are randomly initialized at the beginning of the search process. Next, the fittest particle from the swarm is identified and assigned to the *gbest* solution (i.e., the global best, or best particle found so far). After that, the swarm flies through the search space (in k dimensions, in the general case). The flight function adopted by PSO is determined by the equation (1), which updates the position and fitness of the particle (see equation (2)). The new fitness is compared with respect to the particle's *pbest* position. If it is better, then it replaces the *pbest* (i.e., the personal best, or the best value that has been found for this particle so far). This procedure is repeated for every particle in the swarm until the termination criteria is reached.

$$v_{i,k} = w \cdot v_{i,k} + c_1 \cdot U(0,1)(pbest_{i,k} - x_{i,k}) + c_2 \cdot U(0,1)(gbest_k - x_{i,k}) \qquad (1)$$

$$x_{i,k} = x_{i,k} + v_{i,k} \qquad (2)$$

where c_1 and c_2 are constants that indicate the attraction from the *pbest* or *gbest* position, respectively; w refers to the inertia of the previous movement; $x_i = (x_{i1}, x_{i2}, ..., x_{ik})$ represents the $i-th$ particle. U(0,1) denotes a uniformly random number generated within the range (0,1); $V_i = (v_{i1}, v_{i2}, ..., v_{iD})$ represents the rate change (velocity) of particle i. The equation (1) describes the velocity that is constantly updated by each particle and equation (2) updates the position of the particle in each decision variable. There are plenty of proposals to extend PSO for dealing with multiple objectives (see for example [14]).

3 Scatter Search

As indicated before, Scatter Search was first introduced in 1977 by Fred Glover [6] as a method that uses a succession of coordinated initializations to generate solutions. In 1994 [7], the range of applications of SS was expanded to nonlinear optimization problems, binary and permutation problems. Finally, in 1998 a new publication on scatter search [8] triggered the interest of researchers and practitioners, who translated these ideas into different computer implementations to solve a variety of problems.

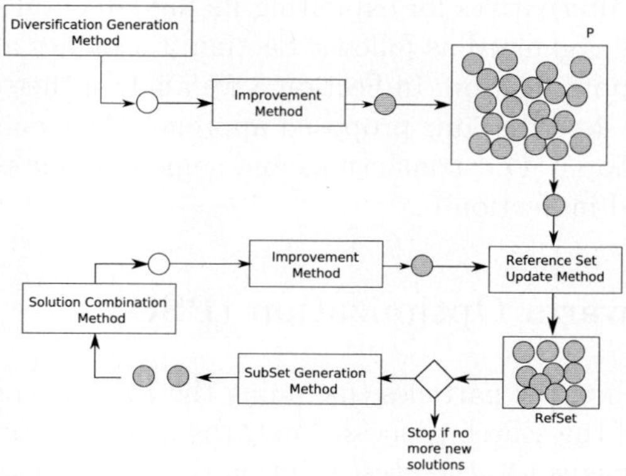

Fig. 1. Scatter Search Scheme

In Figure 1, the *Diversification Generation Method* (generates a scatter solutions set) and *Improvement Method* (makes a local search, and aims to improve the solutions) are initially applied to all the solutions in the P set. A $RefSet$ set is generated based on the P set. $RefSet$ contains the best solutions in terms of quality and diversity found so far. The *Subset Generation Method* takes the reference solutions as its input to produce solution subsets to be combined; the solution subsets contain two or more solutions from $RefSet$. Then, the *Combination Method* is applied to the solution subsets to get new solutions. We try to improve the generated solutions with the *Improvement Method* and the result of the improvement is handed by the *Reference Set Update Method.* This method applies rules regarding the admission of solutions to the reference set $RefSet$.

4 Our Proposed Approach

Our proposed approach, called MOPSOSS (Multi-objective Optimization using Particle Swarm Optimization with Scatter Search), is divided in two phases, and each of them consumes a fixed number of fitness function evaluations. During Phase I, our PSO-based MOEA is applied for 2000 fitness function evaluations. During Phase II, a local search procedure based on scatter search is applied for another 2000 fitness function evaluations, in order to improve the solutions (i.e., spread them along the Pareto front) produced at the previous phase. Each of these two phases is described next in more detail.

4.1 Phase I: Particle Swarm Optimization

Our proposed PSO-based approach adopts a very small population size ($P = 5$ particles). The leader is determined using a very simple criterion: the first N particles (N is the number of objectives of the problem) are guided by the best particle in each objective, considered separately. The remainder $P - N$ particles are adopted to build an approximation of the ideal vector. The ideal vector is formed with $(f_1^*, f_2^*, \ldots, f_n^*)$ where f_i^* is the best solution found so far for the ith objective function. Then, we identify the individual which is closest to this ideal vector (using an euclidian distance) and such individual becomes the leader for the remainder $P - N$ particles. The purpose of these selection criteria is twofold: first, we aim to approximate the optimum for each separate objective, by exploiting the high convergence rate of PSO in single-objective optimization. The second purpose of our selection rules is to encourage convergence towards the "knee" of the Pareto front (considering the bi-objective case).

Algorithm 1 shows the pseudocode of Phase I from our proposed approach. First, we randomly generate the initial population, but in the population we need at least the same number of individuals as the number of objectives plus one. This last individual is needed to form the ideal vector; for this purpose, we chose 5 individuals to perform the experiments reported in this paper. In the *getLeaders*() function, we identify the best particles in each objective and the closest particle to the ideal vector. Those particles (the leaders) are stored in the set L. Then the *getLeader*($\boldsymbol{x}$) function returns the position of the leader from the set L for a particle x. Then, we perform the flight in order to obtain a new particle. If this solution is beyond the allowable bounds for a decision variable, then we adopt the $BLX - \alpha$ recombination operator [5], and a new vector solution $Z = (z_1, z_2, ..., z_d)$ is generated, where $z_i \in [c_{min} - I\alpha, c_{max} + I\alpha]$; $c_{max} = max(a_i, b_i)$, $c_{min} = min(a_i, b_i)$, $I = c_{max} - c_{min}$, $\alpha = 0.5$, $a = L_g$ (the leader of the particle) and $b = pbest$ (i.e., the personal best of the particle). Note that the use of a recombination operator is not a common practice in PSO, and some people may consider our approach as a PSO-variant because of that. PSO does not use a specific mutation operator either (the variation of the factors of the flight equation may compensate for that). However, it has become common practice in MOPSOs to adopt some sort of mutation (or turbulence) operator that improves the exploration capabilities of PSO [14,13]. The use of a mutation operator is normally simpler (and easier) than varying the factors of the flight equation and therefore its extended use. We adopted Parameter-Based Mutation [3] in our approach with $p_m = 1/n$. Our proposed approach also uses an external archive (also called secondary population). In order to include a solution into this external archive, it is compared with respect to each member already contained in the archive using the ϵ-dominance grid [12]. Every solution in the archive is assigned an identification array ($\mathbf{B} = (B_1, B_2, \ldots, B_d)^T$, where d is the total number of objectives) as follows:

$$B_j(f) = \begin{cases} (\lfloor (f_j - f_j^{min})/\epsilon_j \rfloor), \text{ for minimizing } f_j; \\ (\lceil (f_j - f_j^{min})/\epsilon_j \rceil), \text{ for maximizing } f_j. \end{cases}$$

where: f_j^{min} is the minimum possible value of the j-th objective and ϵ_j is the allowable tolerance in the j-th objective [12]. The identification array divides the whole objective space into hyper-boxes, each having ϵ_j size in the j-th objective. Using this procedure, we can guarantee the generation of a well-distributed set of nondominated solutions. Also, the value of ϵ adopted (defined by the user) regulates the size of the external archive.

Any member that is removed from the secondary population is included in the third population. The third population stores the dominated points needed for the Phase II.

4.2 Phase II: Scatter Search

Upon termination of Phase I (2000 fitness function evaluations), we start Phase II, which departs from the nondominated set generated in Phase I. This set is contained within the secondary population. We also have the dominated set, which is contained within the third population. From the nondominated set we choose *MaxScatterSolutions* points. These particles have to be scattered in the nondominated set, so we choose them based on a distance L_α, which is determined by equation 3:

$$L_\alpha(x) = {}_{i=1,\ldots,p}^{Max} \left\{ \frac{f_i^{max}(x) - f_i(x)}{f_i^{max}(x) - f_i^{min}(x)} \right\} \tag{3}$$

Generalizing, to obtain the scatter solutions set among the nondominated set, we use equation 4:

$$L_{set} = {}_{\forall u \in U}^{Max} \left\{ {}_{\forall v \in V}^{Min} \left\{ {}_{i=1,\ldots,p}^{Max} \left\{ \frac{|f_{vi}(x) - f_{ui}(x)|}{f_i^{max}(x) - f_i^{min}(x)} \right\} \right\} \right\} \tag{4}$$

where L_{set} is the Leaders set, U is the nondominated set and V contains the scatter solutions set, f_i^{max} and f_i^{min} are the upper and lower bound of the i-th objective function in the secondary population.

Algorithm 2 describes the scatter search elements. The **getScatterSolution()** function returns the scatter solutions set in the nondominated set V, **getScatterSolution(**n**)** function returns the $n-th$ scatter solution and stores

Algorithm 1. Phase I - PSO Algorithm

```
begin
    Initialize Population (P) with randomly generated solutions
    getLeaders()
    repeat
        for i = 1 to P do
            g = GetLeader(i)
            for d = 1 to nVariables do
                /*L_{g,d} is the leader of particle i*/
                v_{i,d} = w · v_{i,d} + c1 · U(0,1)(p_{i,d} − x_{i,d}) + c2 · U(0,1)(L_{g,d} − x_{i,d})
                x_{i,d} = x_{i,d} + v_{i,d}
            end
            if x_i ∉ search space then
                x_i = BLX − α(L_g, p_i)
            end
            if U(0,1) < p_m then
                x_i = Mutate(x_i)
            end
            if x_i is nondominated then
                for d=1 to nVariables do
                    p_{i,d} = x_{i,d}
                end
            end
        end
        getLeaders()
    until MaxIter
end
```

it in *pl*. **CreateRefSet(pl)** creates the reference set of the *pl* scatter solution. This function returns a set of solutions C_n Regarding the Solution Combination Method required by SS, we used the $BLX - \alpha$ recombination operator [5] with $\alpha = 0.5$. This operator combines the $i - th$ particle and $j - th$ particle from the C_n set. Finally, we used a Parameter-Based mutation as the Improvement Method with $p_m = \frac{1}{nVariables}$.

5 Results

In order to validate our proposed approach, we compare results with respect to the NSGA-II [3], which is a MOEA representative of the state-of-the-art in the area. The first phase of our approach uses four parameters: population size (P), leaders number (N), mutation probability (P_m), recombination parameter α, plus the traditional PSO parameters (w, c_1, c_2). On the other hand, the second phase uses two more parameters: reference set size ($RefSetSize$) and number of scatter solutions ($MaxScatterSolutions$). Finally, the $\epsilon - vector$ used to generate the ϵ-dominance grid was set to 0.05 in Kursawe's function, and to 0.02 in

Algorithm 2. Phase II - Scatter Search Algorithm

```
begin
    repeat
        getScatterSolutions()
        for n = 0 to MaxScatterSolutions do
            pl = getScatterSolution(n)
            //Reference Set Update and Create Method
            CreateRefSet(pl)
            for i = 0 to SizeRefSet do
                for j = i + 1 to RefSetSize do
                    //Solution Combination Method
                    x = BLX − α(popRefSet(i), popRefSet(j))
                    //Improvement Method
                    x = Mutate(x)
                    if x is nondominated then
                        Add Particule x into secondary population
                    end
                end
            end
        end
    until MaxIter
end
```

the ZDT and the DTLZ test functions. Our approach was validated using 10 test problems: Kursawe's function [10], 5 problems from the **ZDT** set [16] and 4 from the **DTLZ** set [4]. The detailed description of these test functions was omitted due to space restrictions, but can be found in their original sources. However, all of these test functions are unconstrained and have between 3 and 30 decision variables. In all cases, the parameters of our approach were set as follows: $P = 5$, $N = k + 1$ (k = number of objective functions), $P_m = 1/n$, $w = 0.3$, $c_1 = 0.1$, $c_2 = 1.4$, $RefSetSize = 4$, $MaxScatterSolutions = 7$ and $\alpha = 0.5$. The NSGA-II used the following parameters: crossover rate = 0.9, mutation rate = $1/n$ (n = number of decision variables), $\eta_c = 15$, $\eta_m = 20$, population size = 100 and maximum number of generations = 40. The population size of the NSGA-II is the same as the size of the grid of our approach. In order to allow a fair comparison of results, both approaches adopted real-numbers encoding and performed 4,000 fitness function evaluations per run because with our approach we only need 4,000 fitness evaluations to converge to the real Pareto front in most of the test problems. Three performance measures were adopted in order to allow a quantitative assessment of our results: (1) Two Set Coverage (**SC**), proposed by Zitzler et al. [16], which performs a relative coverage comparison of two sets; (2) Inverted Generational Distance (**IGD**), which is a variation of a metric proposed by Van Veldhuizen [15] in which the true Pareto is used as a reference; and (3) Spread (**S**), proposed by Deb et al. [2], which measures both progress towards the Pareto-optimal front and the extent of spread. For each test problem, 30 independent runs were performed and the results reported in Table 1 correspond to the mean and standard deviation of the performance metrics (SC, IGD and S). We show in boldface the best mean values per test function. It can be observed that in the ZDT test problems, our approach produced the best results with respect to SC, IGD and S in all cases. Our approach also outperformed the NSGA-II with respect to the set coverage metric in the DTLZ1, DTLZ2 and DTLZ3 test problems. The NSGA-II outperformed our approach in three cases with respect to the IGD, and S metrics. Figures 2 and 3 show the graphical results produced by the MOPSOSS and the NSGA-II for all the test problems adopted. The solutions displayed correspond to the median result with respect to the IGD metric. The true Pareto front (obtained by enumeration) is shown with a continuous line and the approximation produced by each algorithm is shown with circles. In Figures 2 and 3, we can clearly see that in problems Kursawe, ZDT1, ZDT2, ZDT3, ZDT4 and ZDT6, the NSGA-II is very far from the true Pareto front, whereas our MOPSOSS is very close to the true Pareto front after only 4,000 fitness function evaluations (except for ZDT4). Graphically, the results are not entirely clear for the DTLZ test problems. However, if we pay attention to the scale, it will be evident that, in most cases, our approach has several points closer to the true Pareto front than the NSGA-II. Our results indicate that the NSGA-II, despite being a highly competitive MOEA is not able to converge to the true Pareto front in most of the test problems adopted when performing only 4000 fitness function evaluations. If we perform a higher number of evaluations, the NSGA-II would certainly produce a very good (and well-distributed) approximation of the Pareto front. However, our aim was precisely to provide an alternative approach that requires a lower number of evaluations than a state-of-the-art MOEA while still providing a highly competitive performance. Such an approach could be useful in real-world applications with objective functions requiring a very high evaluation cost (computationally speaking).

Table 1. Comparison of results between our approach (called MOPSOSS) and the NSGA-II for the ten test problems adopted

Function	SC				IGD				S			
	MOPSOSS		NSGA-II		MOPSOSS		NSGA-II		MOPSOSS		NSGA-II	
	Mean	σ	Mean	σ	Mean	σ	Mean	σ	Mean	σ	Mean	σ
KURSAWE	**0.1834**	0.0568	0.2130	0.0669	0.0056	0.0004	**0.0036**	0.0002	**0.4030**	0.0298	0.4325	0.0379
ZDT1	**0.0000**	0.0000	0.8622	0.0343	**0.0018**	0.0009	0.0097	0.0019	**0.4288**	0.0533	0.5515	0.0345
ZDT2	**0.0000**	0.0000	0.9515	0.0520	**0.0040**	0.0050	0.0223	0.0064	**0.5121**	0.0811	0.7135	0.1126
ZDT3	**0.0397**	0.0978	0.8811	0.0905	**0.0072**	0.0046	0.0155	0.0020	**0.6955**	0.0641	0.7446	0.0401
ZDT4	**0.0139**	0.0750	0.2331	0.1293	**0.1097**	0.0395	0.4247	0.1304	**0.9417**	0.0271	0.9813	0.0236
ZDT6	**0.0000**	0.0000	0.5417	0.1539	**0.0008**	0.0003	0.0420	0.0041	**0.7502**	0.0699	0.8713	0.0802
DTLZ1	**0.0403**	0.0598	0.6900	0.1942	**0.4100**	0.1131	0.7318	0.2062	0.9986	0.0010	**0.9976**	0.0011
DTLZ2	**0.0484**	0.0528	0.1856	0.0736	0.0005	0.0001	**0.0004**	0.0000	0.7488	0.1012	**0.2246**	0.0250
DTLZ3	**0.0207**	0.0540	0.4473	0.1893	**0.9331**	0.2631	1.4228	0.2690	**0.9991**	0.0004	**0.9991**	0.0002
DTLZ4	0.3262	0.3417	**0.0874**	0.1123	0.0216	0.0041	**0.0096**	0.0025	0.7605	0.1553	**0.7136**	0.1104

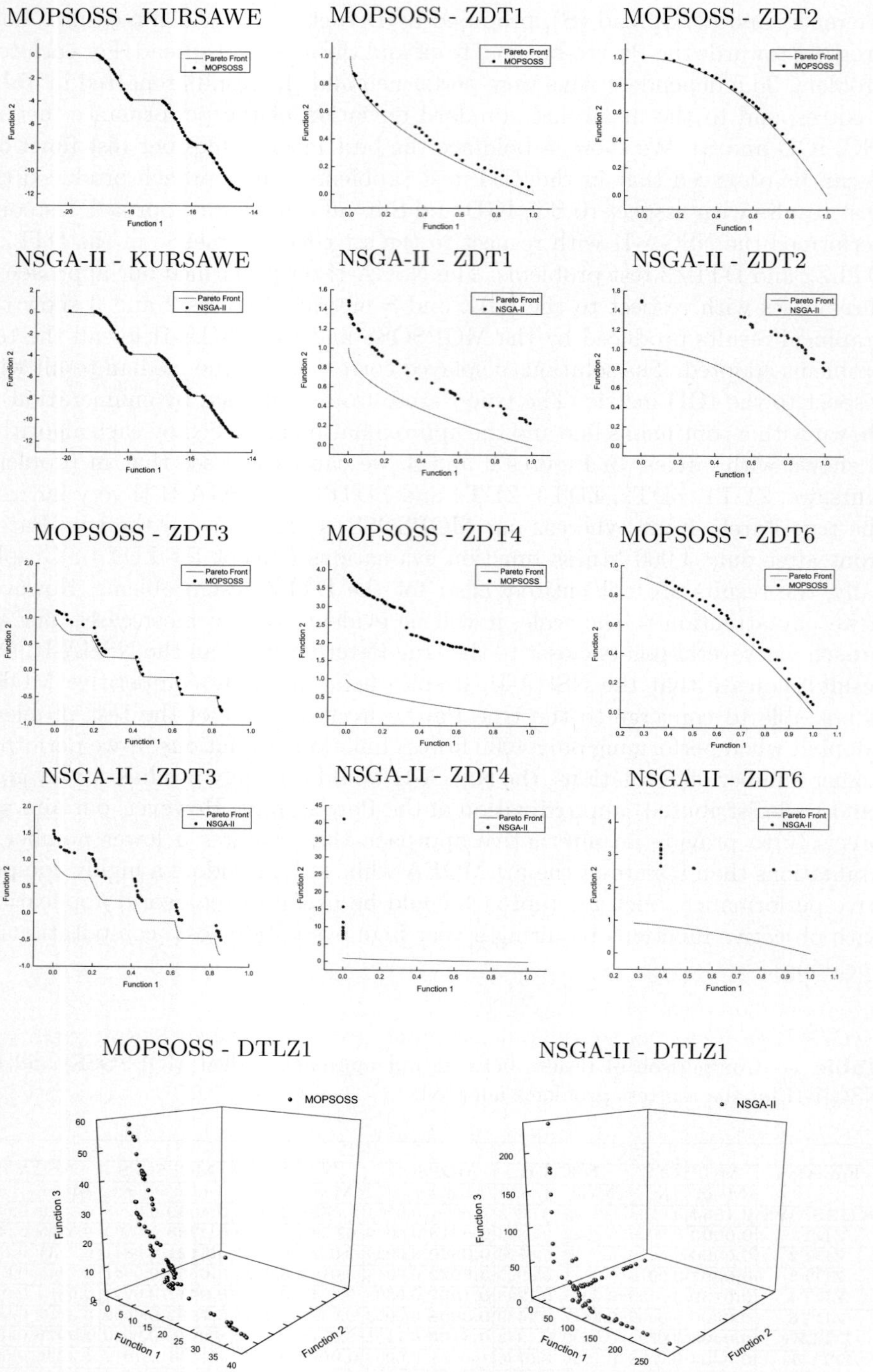

Fig. 2. Pareto fronts generated by MOPSOSS and NSGA-II for Kursawe's, ZDT1, ZDT2, ZDT3, ZDT4, ZDT6 and DTLZ1 test functions

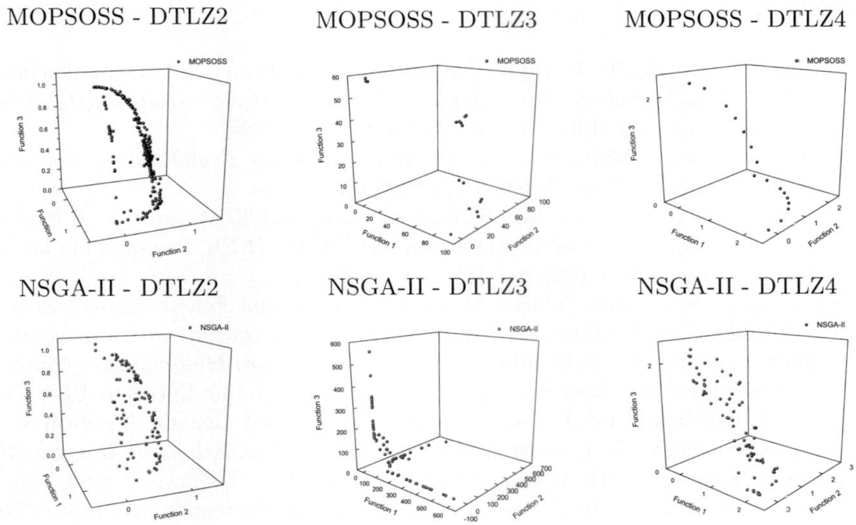

Fig. 3. Pareto fronts generated by MOPSOSS and NSGA-II for the DTLZ2, DTLZ3 and DTLZ4 test functions

6 Conclusions and Future Work

We have introduced a new hybrid between a MOEA based on PSO and a local search mechanism based on scatter search. This hybrid aims to combine the high convergence rate of PSO with the good neighborhood exploration performed by the scatter search algorithm. In PSO, the main problem is the leader selection, the social parameter (p_best) is very important to get the high convergence rate required by our approach. With SS we observe that the selection of closer solutions to the Pareto front generates smooth moves that give us more solutions closer to the true Pareto front of the problem being solved. Our proposed approach produced results that are competitive with respect to the NSGA-II in problems whose dimensionality goes from 3 up to 30 decision variables, while performing only 4,000 fitness function evaluations. Although our results are still preliminary, they are very encouraging, since they seem to indicate that our proposed approach could be a viable alternative for solving real-world problems in which the cost of a single fitness function evaluation is very high (e.g., in aeronautics). As part of our future work, we intend to improve the performance of the PSO approach adopted. Particularly, the selection of the appropriate leader is an issue that deserves further study.

Acknowledgments. The third author gratefully acknowledges support from CONACyT through project 45683-Y.

References

1. Carlos A. Coello Coello, David A. Van Veldhuizen, and Gary B. Lamont. *Evolutionary Algorithms for Solving Multi-Objective Problems.* Kluwer Academic Publishers, New York, May 2002. ISBN 0-3064-6762-3.
2. Kalyanmoy Deb. *Multi-Objective Optimization using Evolutionary Algorithms.* John Wiley & Sons, 2001. ISBN 0-471-87339-X.
3. Kalyanmoy Deb, Amrit Pratap, Sameer Agarwal, and T. Meyarivan. A Fast and Elitist Multiobjective Genetic Algorithm: NSGA–II. *IEEE Transactions on Evolutionary Computation*, 6(2):182–197, April 2002.
4. Kalyanmoy Deb, Lothar Thiele, Marco Laumanns, and Eckart Zitzler. Scalable Test Problems for Evolutionary Multiobjective Optimization. In Ajith Abraham, Lakhmi Jain, and Robert Goldberg, editors, *Evolutionary Multiobjective Optimization. Theoretical Advances and Applications*, pages 105–145. Springer, USA, 2005.
5. Larry J. Eshelman and J. Davis Schaffer. Real-coded Genetic Algorithms and Interval-Schemata. In L. Darrell Whitley, editor, *Foundations of Genetic Algorithms 2*, pages 187–202. Morgan Kaufmann Publishers, California, 1993.
6. Fred Glover. Heuristic for integer programming using surrogate constraints. *Decision Sciences 8*, pages 156–166, 1977.
7. Fred Glover. Tabu search for nonlinear and parametric optimization (with links to genetic algorithms). *Discrete Applied Mathematics*, 49(1-3):231–255, 1994.
8. Fred Glover. A template for scatter search and path relinking. In *AE '97: Selected Papers from the Third European Conference on Artificial Evolution*, pages 13–54, London, UK, 1998. Springer-Verlag.
9. James Kennedy and Russell C. Eberhart. *Swarm Intelligence.* Morgan Kaufmann Publishers, California, USA, 2001.
10. Frank Kursawe. A Variant of Evolution Strategies for Vector Optimization. In H. P. Schwefel and R. Männer, editors, *Parallel Problem Solving from Nature. 1st Workshop, PPSN I*, volume 496 of *Lecture Notes in Computer Science Vol. 496*, pages 193–197, Berlin, Germany, October 1991. Springer-Verlag.
11. Manuel Laguna and Rafael Martí. *Scatter Search: Methodology and Implementations in C.* Kluwer Academic Publishers, 2003.
12. Marco Laumanns, Lothar Thiele, Kalyanmoy Deb, and Eckart Zitzler. Combining convergence and diversity in evolutionary multi-objective optimization. *Evolutionary Computation*, 10(3):263–282, Fall 2002.
13. Sanaz Mostaghim and Jürgen Teich. Strategies for Finding Good Local Guides in Multi-objective Particle Swarm Optimization (MOPSO). In *2003 IEEE SIS Proceedings*, pages 26–33, Indianapolis, USA, April 2003. IEEE Service Center.
14. Margarita Reyes-Sierra and Carlos A. Coello Coello. Multi-Objective Particle Swarm Optimizers: A Survey of the State-of-the-Art. *International Journal of Computational Intelligence Research*, 2(3):287–308, 2006.
15. David A. Van Veldhuizen. *Multiobjective Evolutionary Algorithms: Classifications, Analyses, and New Innovations.* PhD thesis, Department of Electrical and Computer Engineering. Graduate School of Engineering. Air Force Institute of Technology, Wright-Patterson AFB, Ohio, May 1999.
16. Eckart Zitzler, Kalyanmoy Deb, and Lothar Thiele. Comparison of multiobjective evolutionary algorithms: Empirical results. *Evolutionary Computation*, 8(2):173–195, Summer 2000.

An Interval Approach for Weight's Initialization of Feedforward Neural Networks

Marcela Jamett[1] and Gonzalo Acuña[2]

[1] Universidad Tecnológica Metropolitana, UTEM, Departamento de Diseño, Calle Dieciocho 390, of. 323, Postfach 833-0526. Santiago, Chile
mjamett@usach.cl

[2] Universidad de Santiago de Chile, USACH, Departamento de Ingeniería Informática, Av. Ecuador 3659, Postfach 917-0124. Santiago, Chile
gacuna@usach.cl

Abstract. This work addresses an important problem in Feedforward Neural Networks (FNN) training, i.e. finding the pseudo-global minimum of the cost function, assuring good generalization properties to the trained architecture. Firstly, pseudo-global optimization is achieved by employing a combined parametric updating algorithm which is supported by the transformation of network parameters into interval numbers. It solves the network weight initialization problem, performing an exhaustive search for minimums by means of Interval Arithmetic (IA). Then, the global minimum is obtained once the search has been limited to the region of convergence (ROC). IA allows representing variables and parameters as compact-closed sets, then, a training procedure using interval weights can be done. The methodology developed is exemplified by an approximation of a known non-linear function in last section.

1 Introduction

An important problem associated with Feedforward Neural Networks (FNN) have yet to be solved: the FNN capacity to approximate, and remain as closely as necessary to a set of optimum weights which globally minimize a network training error function, based on an initial set of weights with arbitrarily chosen values. An appropriate initialization is a matter studied by several authors and some approaches can be seen in [1-6], where probabilistic methods are proposed in order to do a "smart" selection of initial parameter conditions.

The Interval Arithmetic (IA) is a branch of mathematics developed at the time of numerical computation rush. It consists in representing numbers by means of real intervals, defined by lower and upper limits [7-10]. Interval algorithms have been used in several applications, particularly for global optimization approaches and simulation of random processes. They can be used as a way to transform a probabilistic problem into a corresponding deterministic one [11]. The problem of FNN initialization and training can be advantageously addressed from an interval perspective, by means of interval modeling of the network parameters uncertainties.

This paper proposes a search algorithm that uses intervals to find optimum weights that ensure that the FNN represents precisely the function to be approximated.

A. Gelbukh and C.A. Reyes-Garcia (Eds.): MICAI 2006, LNAI 4293, pp. 305 – 315, 2006.

Additionally, the solution guarantees that the output data remain bounded by the uncertainty in the weights. Thus, this implies a shedding light on the FNN generalization capability.

The present work is organized as follows: Section II presents parameter initialization addressed from IA. In section III we build an interval FNN in order to proceed with the training second stage. In next section, this method is applied to approximate a known non-linear function and the obtained results are discussed, particularly from the generalization point of view. Finally, we present some conclusions, limitations and future developments in this area.

2 FNN Parameter's Initialization

We consider a standard FNN (with only one hidden layer), due to its approximation capabilities proved in [12-14]. Then, the network output is obtained by:

$$\mathbf{Zin}(t) = \mathbf{V}^T\mathbf{X}(t) \tag{1}$$

$$\mathbf{Z}(t) = f_h(\mathbf{Zin}(t)) \tag{2}$$

$$\mathbf{Yin}(t) = \mathbf{W}\cdot\mathbf{Z}(t) \tag{3}$$

$$\mathbf{Y}(t) = f_{out}(\mathbf{Yin}(t)) \tag{4}$$

$\mathbf{X}(t)$ network input (including extra-input for bias).
$\mathbf{V}$ hidden layer weight matrix.
f_h hidden layer activation function.
$\mathbf{W}$ output layer weight matrix.
f_{out} output layer activation function.
$\mathbf{Y}(t)$ network output.

Training this network consists in the problem of finding the optimal weights $\mathbf{V}^*$ and $\mathbf{W}^*$ that globally minimize an objective function, defined as follows:

$$\mathbf{M} = \frac{1}{S}\sum_{t=1}^{S}(\mathbf{Y}(t) - \mathbf{F}(t))^2 \tag{5}$$

$\mathbf{M}$ Mean square error.
$\mathbf{F}(t)$ Target function.

Standard training algorithms start with random parameters and update them iteratively. However, this procedure could lead to local minima of the objective function and it can be improved. We propose an alternative method to initialize them.

2.1 Interval Weights

Initial values for network's weights are found by means of an interval exhaustive search method proposed by Hansen [7]. In order to do so, instead of representing weights as scalar values, they are represented as intervals. Then, any standard weight (mindless if it belongs to any layer), is bounded by a lower and an upper limit.

$$\overline{\omega} = [\omega_{\min}, \omega_{\max}] \tag{6}$$

The globally optimal search method computes the objective function **M** using Interval Arithmetic (IA), and consequently divides the search spaces (interval weights), getting a sufficiently small intervals $\overline{\omega}$ that can be considered close enough to the optimal $\mathbf{V}^*$ and $\mathbf{W}^*$. Ideally, the initial search space for any weight should be $\overline{\omega}(0) = \Re = (-\infty, +\infty)$, but because of computational restrictions it is $\overline{\omega}(0) = [-r, +r]$, where r is a very large real number.

2.2 Interval Global Optimization Algorithm

Global minimum search by interval optimization (adapted from [7]) requires that the objective function to be continuous. This restriction is achieved by means of define the following:

Interval objective function:

$$\mathbf{M}(\overline{\omega}) = [\mathbf{M}_{\min}(\overline{\omega}), \mathbf{M}_{\max}(\overline{\omega})] \tag{7}$$

Interval gradient:

$$g(\overline{\omega}) = \nabla \mathbf{M}(\overline{\omega}) = [g_{\min}(\overline{\omega}), g_{\max}(\overline{\omega})] \tag{8}$$

Interval Hessian:

$$h(\overline{\omega}) = \frac{d^2\mathbf{M}(\overline{\omega})}{d\overline{\omega}^2} = [h_{\min}(\overline{\omega}), h_{\max}(\overline{\omega})] \tag{9}$$

Interval width:

$$d(\overline{\omega}) = \omega_{\max} - \omega_{\min} \tag{10}$$

Interval mean value:

$$a(\overline{\omega}) = \frac{\omega_{\min} + \omega_{\max}}{2} \tag{11}$$

Steps of the algorithm are given bellow:

1) Create a list L_1 with all initial "boxes" $\overline{\omega}(0)$.
2) Evaluate $\mathbf{M}[a(\overline{\omega}(0))]$ and use the result to update $\mathbf{M}_{\sup}$.
3) Evaluate $\mathbf{M}(\overline{\omega}) = [\mathbf{M}_{\min}(\overline{\omega}), \mathbf{M}_{\max}(\overline{\omega})]$.
4) Eliminate from L_1 all $\overline{\omega}$ that $\mathbf{M}_{\min}(\overline{\omega}) > \mathbf{M}_{\sup}$.
5) If L_1 is empty, skip forward to step 11. Else, $\overline{\omega}$ in L_1 for which $\mathbf{M}_{\min}(\overline{\omega}) < \mathbf{M}_{\sup}$, must be found. Select this box as the next box to be processed by the algorithm.
6) Monotonicity test. If $0 \notin g(\overline{\omega})$, erase $\overline{\omega}$ from L_1 and return to step 5.
7) Non-convexity test. If $h(\overline{\omega}) < 0$, erase $\overline{\omega}$ from L_1 and return to step 5.
8) Determine the interval weight width. If $d(\overline{\omega}) < \varepsilon_\omega$ (ε_ω is a given tolerance, thin enough to consider it as the ROC of the gradient algorithm), skip to step 10.
9) Subdivide $\overline{\omega}$ into 2 sub-boxes: $\overline{\omega}_1 = [\omega_{\min}, a(\overline{\omega})]$ and $\overline{\omega}_2 = (a(\overline{\omega}), \omega_{\max}]$.

10) For each box that results from steps 8 and 9, evaluate $\mathbf{M}[a(\overline{\omega}_k)]$, for k=1,2. Use the result to update $\mathbf{M}_{sup}$.
11) If $d(\overline{\omega}_k) < \varepsilon_\omega$ and $d[\mathbf{M}(\overline{\omega}_k)] < \varepsilon_{\mathrm{M}}$ (where ε_{M} is a given width tolerance for objective function), put $\overline{\omega}_k$ into list L_2. Else, put $\overline{\omega}_k$ into L_1 and return to 5.
12) In list L_2, check for elimination of any box that $\mathbf{M}_{\min}(\overline{\omega}_k) > \mathbf{M}_{sup}$. Denote the remaining boxes as $\overline{\omega}^{(1)},...,\overline{\omega}^{(s)}$.
13) Calculate the lower limit for the objective function: $\mathbf{M}_{\inf} = \min_{i=1..s}\left[\mathbf{M}_{\min}\left(\overline{\omega}^{(i)}\right)\right]$.
14) The algorithm finishes with:
    $\mathbf{M}_{\inf} \leq \mathbf{M}^* \leq \mathbf{M}_{sup}$
    $d[\mathbf{M}(\overline{\omega}^{(i*)})] \leq \varepsilon_{\mathrm{M}}$
    Where $\overline{\omega}^{(i*)}$ contains the ω^* where $\mathbf{M}$ reaches its pseudo-global minimum.

3 Interval FNN (IFNN)

The second stage of IFNN training consists on: for any weight $\omega \in \overline{\omega}^{(i*)}$, a standard training algorithm can find the minima and it is the pseudo-global one. Therefore, we use gradient descent algorithm and parameter initial conditions as $\omega(0) = a\left(\overline{\omega}^{(i*)}\right)$. Our main objective is to train the IFNN considering its variables as intervals, that is:

$$\overline{\mathbf{Zin}}(t) = \mathbf{V}^T \overline{\mathbf{X}}(t) \tag{12}$$

$$\overline{\mathbf{Z}}(t) = f_h\left(\overline{\mathbf{Zin}}(t)\right) \tag{13}$$

$$\overline{\mathbf{Yin}}(t) = \mathbf{W} \cdot \overline{\mathbf{Z}}(t) \tag{14}$$

$$\overline{\mathbf{Y}}(t) = f_{out}\left(\overline{\mathbf{Yin}}(t)\right) \tag{15}$$

Consequently, the interval $\overline{\mathbf{Y}}(t) = [\mathbf{Y}_{\min}, \mathbf{Y}_{\max}]$ contains all possible output values for the initialized network, where every weight value of $\mathbf{V}$ and $\mathbf{W}$ belong to $\overline{\omega}^{(i*)}$.

3.1 Training an IFNN

If we consider the IFNN proposed in last section, an improved interval training algorithm can be applied. In order to do so, we define some new variables:

Error function:

$$\overline{\mathbf{E}}(t) = \overline{\mathbf{Y}}(t) - \mathbf{F}(t) \tag{16}$$

Interval objective function:

$$\overline{\mathbf{M}} = \frac{1}{s} \sum_{k=1}^{m} \sum_{t=1}^{s} \overline{e}_k^2(t) \tag{17}$$

Interval change of weights:

$$\Delta \overline{\omega} = -\alpha \cdot g(\overline{\omega}) \tag{18}$$

With α as the algorithm learning rate.

Particularly, for weights in the hidden layer, the update law is given by:

$$\Delta\overline{\mathbf{V}} = -\alpha \cdot \frac{2}{s}\sum_{k=1}^{m}\sum_{t=1}^{s}\overline{\mathbf{E}}_k(t) \cdot \frac{\partial f_{out}}{\partial \overline{\mathbf{Yin}}_k(t)} \cdot \mathbf{W}_k(t) \cdot \frac{\partial f_h}{\partial \overline{\mathbf{Zin}}_k(t)} \cdot \mathbf{X}(t) \tag{19}$$

Similarly, in the case of output weights, the change is specified by:

$$\Delta\overline{\mathbf{W}} = -\alpha \cdot \frac{2}{s}\sum_{k=1}^{m}\sum_{t=1}^{s}\overline{\mathbf{E}}_k(t) \cdot \frac{\partial f_{out}}{\partial \overline{\mathbf{Yin}}_k(t)} \cdot \overline{\mathbf{Z}}(t) \tag{20}$$

The parameters update includes the transformation of the interval change $\Delta\overline{\omega}$ into a scalar value that properly represents it. That is to say:

$$\text{If}\begin{cases} \Delta\omega_{\min} > 0 \vee \Delta\omega_{\max} < 0, & \Rightarrow \quad \Delta\omega = a(\Delta\overline{\omega}) \\ \Delta\overline{\omega} \supset 0, & \begin{cases} \Delta\overline{\omega}_{ZP} = (0, \Delta\omega_{\max}] & \Rightarrow \quad \Delta\omega_{ZP} = a(\Delta\overline{\omega}_{ZP}) \\ \Delta\overline{\omega}_{ZN} = [\Delta\omega_{\min}, 0) & \Rightarrow \quad \Delta\omega_{ZN} = a(\Delta\overline{\omega}_{ZN}) \\ \Delta\overline{\omega}_{Z} = \{0\} & \Rightarrow \quad \Delta\omega_{Z} = 0 \end{cases} \end{cases} \tag{21}$$

Where sub indexes *ZP*, *ZN* and *Z* means "zero positive", "zero negative" and "zero" respectively. They define subintervals into those who contain zero.

In the first case (where the interval $\Delta\overline{\omega}$ is completely positive or negative), the update is direct. In the second case (where the interval contains zero), a test is made in order to find out the best update approach. The mentioned test considers the next three options:

a. $\overline{\mathbf{M}}(\omega + \Delta\omega_{ZP})$.
b. $\overline{\mathbf{M}}(\omega + \Delta\omega_{ZN})$.
c. $\overline{\mathbf{M}}(\omega)$.

The function argument value that minimizes $\overline{\mathbf{M}}$ is selected, and the other two are eliminated. This procedure is repeated for a number of training epochs or until any stopping criteria is reached.

4 Function Approximation Application

In order to test the proposed method, an application is necessary to illustrate the IFNN parameter initialization, training steps and performance. Thus, the following non-linear function is approximated by an IFNN:

$$f(t) = \frac{\sqrt{t^2 - t + \frac{1}{2}}}{\sqrt{t^2 + \frac{1}{2}}} - 1 \tag{22}$$

For $t \in [-2,2]$.

The IFNN used is a single-input/single-output one with three elements in the hidden layer. The network variables and parameters are defined below:

Input variable:

$$x(t) = 0.25\ t \tag{23}$$

Interval input vector:

$$\mathbf{X}(t) = [x(t) \quad 1]^T \tag{24}$$

Hidden layer weight matrix:

$$\overline{\mathbf{V}} = \begin{bmatrix} \overline{v}_1 & \overline{v}_2 & \overline{v}_3 \\ \overline{b}_{h1} & \overline{b}_{h2} & \overline{b}_{h3} \end{bmatrix} \tag{25}$$

Intermediate variable $\overline{\mathbf{Zin}}(t)$:

$$\overline{\mathbf{Zin}}(t) = \overline{\mathbf{V}}^T \mathbf{X}(t) = [\overline{zin}_1(t) \quad \overline{zin}_2(t) \quad \overline{zin}_3(t)]^T \tag{26}$$

Amplified intermediate variable $\overline{\mathbf{Z}}(t)$:

$$\overline{\mathbf{Z}}(t) = [\cdots \quad f_h(\overline{\mathbf{Zin}}(t)) \quad \cdots \quad 1]^T = [\overline{z}_1(t) \quad \overline{z}_2(t) \quad \overline{z}_3(t) \quad 1]^T \tag{27}$$

Where the activation function to be used, f_h, is a sigmoid one, given by:

$$f_h(t) = \frac{1}{1+e^{-t}} \tag{28}$$

Output layer weight matrix:

$$\overline{\mathbf{W}} = [\overline{w}_1 \quad \overline{w}_2 \quad \overline{w}_3 \quad \overline{b}_{out}] \tag{29}$$

Network output:

$$\overline{\mathbf{Y}}(t) = \overline{\mathbf{W}} \cdot \overline{\mathbf{Z}}(t) = \overline{y}(t) \tag{30}$$

4.1 Parameter Initialization Via IA

The first training stage consists of the weights matrices initialization. They are set as intervals as wide as necessary. Hence, we search for the mean square error global minimum. For every $\overline{v}(0) = \left[-10^6, 10^6\right]$, $\overline{w}(0) = \left[-10^6, 10^6\right]$, belonging to matrices $\overline{\mathbf{V}}(0)$ and $\overline{\mathbf{W}}(0)$ respectively, the network output, the objective function and the gradient are calculated. Then, some previous calculations have to be made.

Sigmoid function derivative:

$$\frac{\partial f_h(t)}{\partial t} = \frac{e^{-t}}{\left(1+e^{-t}\right)^2} \tag{31}$$

Matrix of intermediate variables derivative (with respect to $\overline{\mathbf{V}}$):

$$\overline{\mathbf{Zd}}(t) = [\overline{zd}_1 \quad \overline{zd}_2 \quad \overline{zd}_3]^T \tag{32}$$

Where the $\overline{zd}_j$ are given by:

$$\bar{z}d_j(t) = \frac{e^{-zin_j(t)}}{\left(1+e^{-zin_j(t)}\right)^2} \tag{33}$$

Matrix of intermediate variables double derivative (with respect to $\overline{\mathbf{V}}$):

$$\overline{\mathbf{Zdd}}(t) = \begin{bmatrix} \bar{z}dd_{11} & \bar{z}dd_{12} & \bar{z}dd_{13} \\ \bar{z}dd_{21} & \bar{z}dd_{22} & \bar{z}dd_{23} \end{bmatrix}^T \tag{34}$$

Where the $\bar{z}dd_{ij}$ are:

$$\bar{z}dd_{ij}(t) = \frac{-x_i(t)\cdot e^{-v_{ij}x_i(t)}\cdot\left(1-e^{-v_{ij}x_i(t)}\right)}{\left(1+e^{-v_{ij}x_i(t)}\right)^3} \tag{35}$$

Truncated output weight matrix:

$$\overline{\mathbf{W}}_{tr} = \begin{bmatrix}\bar{w}_1 & \bar{w}_2 & \bar{w}_3\end{bmatrix} \tag{36}$$

Thus the interval gradient is built with respect to each weight, v_{ij} and w_j :

$$\bar{g}(v) = \frac{2}{s}\sum_{t=1}^{s}\overline{\mathbf{E}}(t)\cdot\overline{\mathbf{W}}_{tr}\overline{\mathbf{Zd}}(t)\cdot\mathbf{X}(t) \tag{37}$$

$$\bar{g}(w) = \frac{2}{s}\sum_{t=1}^{s}\overline{\mathbf{E}}(t)\cdot\overline{\mathbf{Z}}(t) \tag{38}$$

Hessian for parameter matrices (it is necessary for the non-convexity test):

$$\bar{h}(v,v) = \frac{2}{s}\sum_{t=1}^{s}\left(\overline{\mathbf{W}}_{tr}\overline{\mathbf{Zd}}(t)\mathbf{X}(t)\right)^T\overline{\mathbf{W}}_{tr}\overline{\mathbf{Zd}}(t)\mathbf{X}(t)+\left(\overline{\mathbf{E}}(t)\overline{\mathbf{W}}_{tr}\overline{\mathbf{Zdd}}(t)\right)^T\mathbf{X}(t) \tag{39}$$

$$\bar{h}(v,w) = \frac{2}{s}\sum_{t=1}^{s}\overline{\mathbf{Z}}(t)\overline{\mathbf{W}}_{tr}\overline{\mathbf{Zd}}(t)\mathbf{X}(t)+\overline{\mathbf{E}}(t)\overline{\mathbf{Zd}}(t)\mathbf{X}(t) \tag{40}$$

$$\bar{h}(w,v) = \frac{2}{s}\sum_{t=1}^{s}\overline{\mathbf{W}}_{tr}\overline{\mathbf{Zd}}(t)\mathbf{X}(t)\overline{\mathbf{Z}}(t)+\overline{\mathbf{E}}(t)\overline{\mathbf{Zd}}(t)\mathbf{X}(t) \tag{41}$$

$$\bar{h}(w,w) = \frac{2}{s}\sum_{t=1}^{s}\overline{\mathbf{Z}}^T(t)\overline{\mathbf{Z}}(t) \tag{42}$$

Now, we do interval optimization with the purpose of finding initial conditions for IFNN weights according to tolerances ε_v, ε_w and ε_f.

The initial interval weights (with amplitudes up to 10^6) were reduced to thinner ones and replaced by:

$$\overline{\mathbf{V}}^{(i*)} = \begin{bmatrix} [3.5002,3.6621] & [-8.5184,-8.2996] & [4.3144,4.4889] \\ [-0.5222,-0.4821] & [0.1698,0.3547] & [1.5944,1811] \end{bmatrix} \tag{43}$$

$$\overline{\mathbf{W}}^{(i*)} = [[0.3599,0.5229]\;\;[0.5650,0.7520]\;\;[0.0411,0.0654]\;\;[-0.0257,-0.0102]] \tag{44}$$

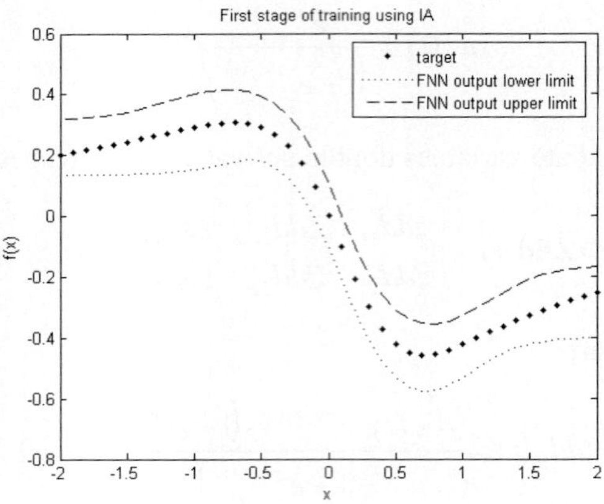

Fig. 1. FNN interval output after the first training stage

At this stage, we can observe the behavior of the IFNN, considering interval parameters. In figure 1 is presented the exact function to be approximated and the interval output of the IFNN. This result allows us to limit the solution before final training, because this initialization can be considered as a first stage of a composed training procedure.

4.2 Interval Gradient Algorithm

The second stage of training is carried out. Then, the gradient update law to be applied is:

$$\Delta\overline{\mathbf{V}}^T = -\alpha * \overline{g}(v) = \frac{-2\alpha}{s}\sum_{t=1}^{s}\overline{\mathbf{E}}(t)\cdot\overline{\mathbf{W}}_{tr}^T\overline{\mathbf{Z}}\mathbf{d}(t)\cdot\mathbf{X}(t) \tag{45}$$

$$\Delta\overline{\mathbf{W}}^T = -\alpha * \overline{g}(w) = \frac{-2\alpha}{s}\sum_{t=1}^{s}\overline{\mathbf{E}}(t)\cdot\overline{\mathbf{Z}}(t) \tag{46}$$

If the interval is monotonous, the mean value criterion is applied, otherwise it should be divided in three groups and do necessary tests to select one (see eq. 21).

This training procedure (denominated IT – interval training) has been done during 100 epochs and the IFNN performance results $\overline{\mathbf{M}} = [1.3909\ ,\ 1.3912]*10^{-6}$, as shown in figure 2(a). We also visualize the trained FNN performance by the neural output simulation, presented in figure 2(b).

This training procedure gives us the following net's parameters:

$$\mathbf{V}^{IT} = \begin{bmatrix} 3.5582 & -8.4184 & 4.4448 \\ -0.4616 & 0.2288 & 1.6911 \end{bmatrix} \tag{47}$$

$$\mathbf{W}^{IT} = [0.4259 \quad 0.6648 \quad 0.0564 \quad -0.0185] \tag{48}$$

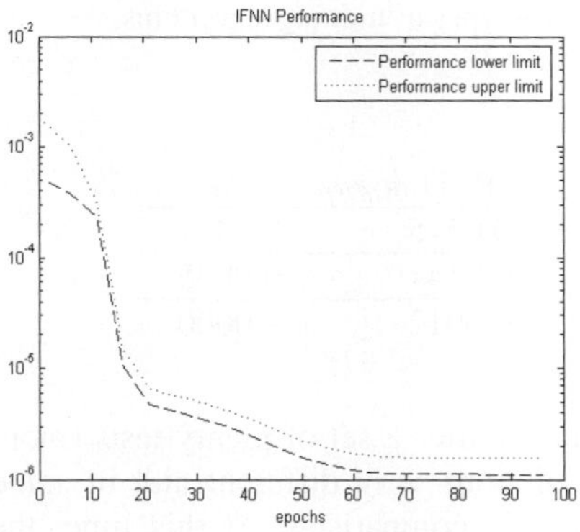

Fig. 2(a). IFNN performance after the second stage of training

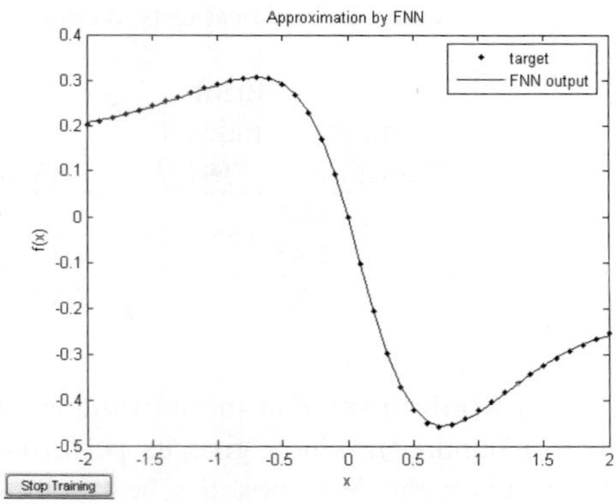

Fig. 2(b). FNN output after complete IT training

4.3 Statistical Tests and Comparisons

We contrast this FNN performance with two similar ones: one trained with standard gradient descent (GD) algorithm and the other with a second-order algorithm: Levenberg-Marquardt (LM) algorithm. The networks are built under exactly the same conditions: structure, activation functions, input feeding and training epochs, but initialized with random values. The FNN output is shown in figure 3, and some statistical tests are presented to assess qualitatively these methods.

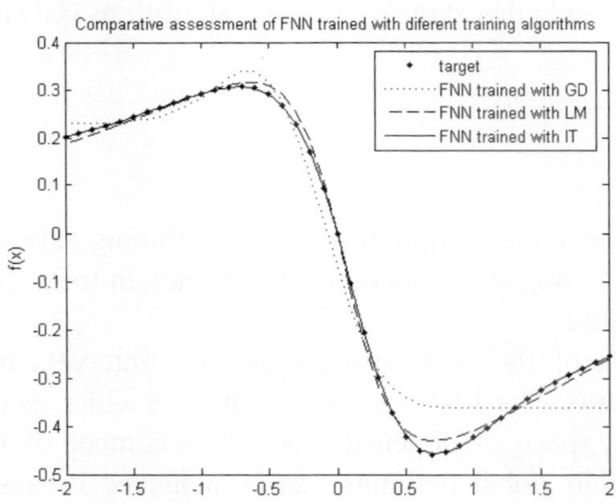

Fig. 3. Comparative assessment between different types of training methods by means of neural networks output

These results are analyzed by means of error indexes calculation: Root Mean Square (RMS), Residual Standard Deviation (RSD) and Adequation Index (AI) [15], presented below.

Table 1. Statistical tests to compare different types of training algorithms

Training Algorithm \ Error Index	RMS	RSD	AI
GD	0.1694	0.0515	0.9927
LM	0.0463	0.0141	0.9995
IT	0.0039	0.0012	1.0000

It is worth to say that these examples were taken after a set of plenty tests (more than a hundred), which give us performance solutions very different and in some cases divergent. We took the best solution for this comparison. At this time, the parameters found were:

$$\mathbf{V}^{GD} = \begin{bmatrix} \mathbf{-9.4928} & 7.9353 & -9.3919 \\ \mathbf{-1.7717} & \mathbf{0.2556} & 1.2384 \end{bmatrix} \tag{49}$$

$$\mathbf{W}^{GD} = [\mathbf{-0.1910} \quad -0.5439 \quad -0.570 \quad -0.0672] \tag{50}$$

$$\mathbf{V}^{LM} = \begin{bmatrix} \mathbf{-8.8473} & -11.0158 & 0.3796 \\ \mathbf{11.0424} & 0.1362 & \mathbf{-0.7899} \end{bmatrix} \tag{51}$$

$$\mathbf{W}^{LM} = [0.9640 \quad 0.4839 \quad \mathbf{2.4185} \quad \mathbf{0.5602}] \tag{52}$$

We mark using bold font the most different values from those obtained with the IFNN. In some cases, there is a sign change or a significant variation on the absolute value. So, we can conclude that standard training algorithms (GD and LM) got stoked in a local minimum.

5 Conclusions

The study of IFNN parameter initialization and training, allows us to solve an important problem, like objective function getting stuck in local minima, leading to a poor FNN's performance.

The transformation of the scalar parameters into intervals makes possible the extension of the conditions for FNN local minimum to a wider set of initial conditions (ideally the complete space of dimension $\Re^N$, N = number of weights to be set). Nonetheless, the pseudo-global optimum can be achieved because the initial space can be made as large as desired (because of computational limitations it can't be $\Re^N$). However, there are some restrictions with respect to the complexity of the optimization algorithm, especially if the networks involved have a large number of weights, which makes the training first stage very slow.

By using an application to test the theory presented, it can be concluded that the IFNN is able to carry out approximations of non-linear functions in a very accurate way, and it doesn't depend on initial parameters: it gives us always the same pseudo-optimal solution. This way, we avoid the annoying task of making plenty of tests in order to get an acceptable solution like in standard FNNs.

Acknowledgments

This work was possible thanks to the support of ECOS-CONICYT (France-Chile), through Project C99-B04 and FONDECYT, Chile, Project N° 1040208. One of the authors, MJ, would also like to thank Dr. Jean-Marie FLAUS and the LAG-INPG-UJF, France for visits during June-July 2001 and February-March 2003.

References

1. Duch, W., Adamczak, R., Jankowski, N.: Initialization and Optimization of Multilayered Perceptrons. Proceedings of the 3rd Conference on Neural Networks and Their Applications. Kule, Poland (1997) 105-110.
2. Thimm, G., Fiesler, E.: High-Order and Multilayer Perceptron Initialization. IEEE Transactions on Neural Networks, vol. 8 (1997) 349-359.
3. Erdogmus, D., Fontenla-Romero, O., Principe, J., Alonso-Betanzos, A., Castillo, E., Jenssen, R.: Accurate Initialization of Neural Network Weights by Backpropagation of the Desired Response. Proceedings of the International Joint Conference on Neural Networks, vol. 3, Portland, USA (2003) 2005-2010.
4. Colla, V., Reyneri, L., Sgarbi, M.: Orthogonal Least Squares Algorithm Applied to the Initialization of Multilayer Perceptrons. Proceedings of the European Symposium on Artificial Neural Networks (1999) 363-369.
5. Yam, Y., Chow, T.: A New Method in Determining the Initial Weights of Feedforward Neural Networks. Neurocomputing, vol. 16 (1997) 23-32.
6. Husken, M., Goerick, C.: Fast Learning for Problem Classes Using Knowledge Based Network Initialization. Proceedings of the IJCNN (2000) 619-624.
7. Hansen, Eldon: Global Optimization using Interval Analysis. Marcel Dekker – NY (1992).
8. Stolfi, J. and Figuereido, L.: Self–Validated Numerical Methods and Applications. In 21st. Brazilian Mathematics Colloquium. IMPA (1997).
9. Jaulin, L., Kiefer, M., Didrit, O. and Walter, E.: Applied Interval Analysis. Laboratoire des Signaux et Systèmes, CNRS-SUPÉLEC. Université Paris-Sud, France (2001).
10. Chen, S., Wu, J.: Interval optimization of dynamic response for structures with interval parameters. Computer and Structures, vol. 82 (2004) 1-11.
11. Valdés, H., Flaus, J-M., Acuña, G.: Moving horizon state estimation with global convergence using interval techniques: application to biotechnological processes. Journal of Process Control, vol. 13 (2003) 325–336.
12. Cybenko, G.: Approximation by Superposition of a Sigmoidal Function. Mathematics of Control, Signals and Systems, vol. 2 (1989) 303-314.
13. Hornik, K., Stinchcombe, M. and White, H.: Multilayer Feedforward Networks are Universal Approximators. Neural Networks, vol. 2 (1989) 359–366.
14. Attali, J., and Pagès, G.: Approximations of Functions by a Multilayer Perceptron: a New Approach. Neural Networks, vol. 10 (1997) 1069-1081.
15. Acuña, G. and Pinto, E.: Development of a Matlab® Toolbox for the Design of Grey-Box Neural Models. International Journal of Computers, Communications and Control, vol. 1 (2006) 7-14.

Aggregating Regressive Estimators: Gradient-Based Neural Network Ensemble

Jiang Meng[1] and Kun An[2]

[1] School of Mechanical Engineering and Automatization, North University of China, Taiyuan 030051, Shanxi, China
rivermeng@gmail.com

[2] School of Information and Communication Engineering, North University of China, Taiyuan 030051, Shanxi, China
ankun06@gmail.com

Abstract. A gradient-based algorithm for ensemble weights modification is presented and applied on the regression tasks. Simulation results show that this method can produce an estimator ensemble with better generalization than those of bagging and single neural network. The method can not only have a similar function to GASEN of selecting many subnets from all trained networks, but also be of better performance than GASEN, bagging and best individual of regressive estimators.

1 Introduction

There is a growing realization that combinations of estimators can be more effective than the single estimator. Neural network as a single estimator for regression tasks, can be used to approximate any continuous function at any precision according to the characteristics of nonlinear and learnability. Another characteristic of generalization is more important to the regression tasks. However, the generalization performance of neural network is not so good, for there is overfitting [1] during the course of network training. Aimed at the situation, an idea of combining many neural networks is presented in 1990s, which is called neural network ensemble [2]. The ensemble can improve the generalization effectively and easily by aggregating the outputs of single networks without additional complicated operations.

Taking neural networks as component estimators, the output of the ensemble is either weighted-averaging or simple-averaging for regression problems. The favorite algorithms to train component networks (named subnets) are bagging and boosting. Based on the bootstrap sampling, bagging [3] is used to train networks independently with random subsets generated from original training set, as might improve ensemble generalization because of different training subsets for different subnets. Boosting [4] can produce a series of subnets sequentially, whose training sets are determined by the performance of former ones. Training instances that are wrongly predicted by the former subnets will play more important roles during the training course of later subnets. Because boosting and revised version AdaBoost [5][6] both focus on only classification problems, AdaBoost.R2 [7], as the modification of AdaBoost.R [8], big error margin (BEM) [9] and AdaBoost.RT [10] are proposed respectively to solve regression problems last decade.

A. Gelbukh and C.A. Reyes-Garcia (Eds.): MICAI 2006, LNAI 4293, pp. 316 – 326, 2006.

Two important issues of an ensemble are to decide how to train the subnets and how to combine the subnets. For the first issue, there are roughly three major approaches [11] to training subnets, i.e., independent training, sequential training and simultaneous training. In independent training, each subnet in the ensemble is trained independently to minimize the error between the target and its output, such as bagging; in sequential training, the ensemble subnets are trained one after one not only to minimize the error between targets and outputs, but also to decorrelate their errors from previously trained networks, such as boosting series algorithms; in simultaneous training, ensemble subnets are trained simultaneously and interactively, with a penalty item in the error function interacting on the ensemble subnets such as CELS [12], or alternating between training step and observational step such as OLA [13]. For the second issue, the combination of subnets is divided into simple averaging [1] and weighted averaging [14]. The former combines the subnet outputs in the way of equal-weighted average, while the latter sums unequal-weighted outputs of ensemble subnets.

Discussing from both theories and simulations, Zhou proposed an idea of "many selected better than all combined" [15], which means that ensembling many of available subnets may has better generalization than ensembling all of subnets by calculating the correlations among the ensemble subnets. Based on this idea, Zhou gave GASEN [16] to select many subnets from all the subnets using the genetic algorithm. On one hand, GASEN proves theoretically there are unequal-weighted distributions for ensemble weights with smaller generalization error than the equal-weighted one, and provides a feasible way to achieve one solution using the heuristic optimization algorithm; on the other hand, it still adopts simple averaging technique to combine a new ensemble with solution of selected subnets. Therefore, GASEN can be regarded as a tradeoff between simple averaging and weighted averaging. It seems that there should be more reasonable weight distributions with better generalization, if modifying ensemble weights in an appropriate strategy for optimization. In this paper, a subnet weight modification algorithm (subWMA) is presented to optimize ensemble weights in the strategy of gradient optimization.

2 Analysis of Bias-Variance Decomposition

2.1 Bias-Variance Decomposition in Neural Network

The regression problem for neural network is to construct a function $f(\boldsymbol{x})$ based on a training set of $(x_1, y_1),\ldots, (x_P, y_P)$, for the purpose of approximating y at future observations of $\boldsymbol{x}$, which is called generalization. To be explicit about the dependence of f on the data $\mathcal{D} = \{(\boldsymbol{x}_k, y_k)\}_{k=1}^{P}$, we can rewrite $f(\boldsymbol{x})$ to $f(\boldsymbol{x}; \mathcal{D})$. Given $\mathcal{D}$ and a particular $\boldsymbol{x}$, the cost function ξ of the neural network is

$$\xi = \frac{1}{2}\sum_{k=1}^{P}(y_k - f(x_k;\mathcal{D}))^2 = \frac{1}{2}E[(\boldsymbol{y} - f(\boldsymbol{x};\mathcal{D}))^2 \mid \boldsymbol{x},\mathcal{D}] \tag{1}$$

where $E[\cdot]$ means the expectation of data set $\mathcal{D}$.

From Reference [17], Eq. (1) can be written as the following equation,

$$E[(y-f(\boldsymbol{x};\mathcal{D}))^2 \mid \boldsymbol{x},\mathcal{D}] = E[(y-E[y\mid \boldsymbol{x}])^2 \mid \boldsymbol{x},\mathcal{D}] + (f(\boldsymbol{x};\mathcal{D})-E[y\mid \boldsymbol{x}])^2 \tag{2}$$

where the first right item is simply the variant of y given $\boldsymbol{x}$, not depending on $\mathcal{D}$ or *f*. Therefore, the mean-squared error of *f* as an estimator of $E[y \mid \boldsymbol{x}]$ is,

$$L_{NN} = E_{\mathcal{D}}[(f(\boldsymbol{x};\mathcal{D})-E[y\mid \boldsymbol{x}])^2] \tag{3}$$

where $E_{\mathcal{D}}[\cdot]$ represents the expectation with respect to the training set $\mathcal{D}$.

Transforming Eq. (3), we can get the bias-variance relation of neural network,

$$\begin{aligned} L_{NN} &= E_{\mathcal{D}}[(f(\boldsymbol{x};\mathcal{D})-E_{\mathcal{D}}[f(\boldsymbol{x};\mathcal{D})]+E_{\mathcal{D}}[f(\boldsymbol{x};\mathcal{D})]-E[y\mid \boldsymbol{x}])^2] \\ &= (E_{\mathcal{D}}[f(\boldsymbol{x};\mathcal{D})]-E[y\mid \boldsymbol{x}])^2 + E_{\mathcal{D}}[(f(\boldsymbol{x};\mathcal{D})-E_{\mathcal{D}}[f(\boldsymbol{x};\mathcal{D})])^2] \\ &= Bias^2 + Variance \end{aligned} \tag{4}$$

In the case of a fixed training set, that is when L_{NN} is fixed, the cost to achieve a small bias is to cause a big variance, vice versa. There is often a dilemma [17] between the bias and variance contributions to the estimation error, also called bias-variance decomposition. Given enough complicated structure, neural network can approximate the implicit function of training data accurately with big variance; on the contrary, if simpler network is designed to display main trend of object data, good generalization can be achieved at the cost of big bias. The accuracy and generalization cannot be met simultaneously, which is an externalization of the uncertainty relation between bias and variance in the neural network.

2.2 Bias-Variance-Covariance Decomposition in the Ensemble

In the neural network ensemble, the decomposition of bias and variance alters in another expression. Suppose there is an ensemble comprising *N* subnets for the same regression problem $\mathcal{D} = \{(\boldsymbol{x}_k, y_k)\}_{k=1}^{P}$ as Section 2.1. Based on the simple averaging technique, the ensemble output is

$$f(\boldsymbol{x};\mathcal{D}) = \frac{1}{N}\sum_{i=1}^{N} f_i(\boldsymbol{x};\mathcal{D}) \tag{5}$$

where $f_i(\boldsymbol{x};\mathcal{D})$ is the output of the *i*-th subnet. Substitute Eq. (3) for Eq. (1) and we can get the following expression,

$$\begin{aligned} L_{ens} &= (E_{\mathcal{D}}[f(\boldsymbol{x};\mathcal{D})]-E[y\mid \boldsymbol{x}])^2 + E_{\mathcal{D}}[\frac{1}{N^2}\sum_{i=1}^{N}(f_i(\boldsymbol{x};\mathcal{D})-E_{\mathcal{D}}[f_i(\boldsymbol{x};\mathcal{D})])^2] \\ &+ E_{\mathcal{D}}[\frac{1}{N^2}\sum_{i=1}^{N}\sum_{\substack{j=1,\\ j\neq i}}^{N}(f_i(\boldsymbol{x};\mathcal{D})-E_{\mathcal{D}}[f_i(\boldsymbol{x};\mathcal{D})])(f_j(\boldsymbol{x};\mathcal{D})-E_{\mathcal{D}}[f_j(\boldsymbol{x};\mathcal{D})])] \\ &= Bias^2 + Variance + Covariance \end{aligned} \tag{6}$$

Different from the relation between the bias and variance in neural network, the ensemble is of bias-variance-covariance decomposition. Even if L_{ens} is fixed, the ensemble can decrease the bias and variance simultaneously by increasing the covariance of subnets, which is the main reason that the ensemble can improve generalization performance than neural network.

2.3 Discussion of GASEN

In Reference [15] and [16], Zhou gave a concept of *correlation* for GASEN. Assume there is an ensemble comprising N subnets, and we can define the correlation as

$$C_{ij} = \int \left(f_i(x) - y(x)\right)\left(f_j(x) - y(x)\right) dx \tag{7}$$

thus the ensemble error Err_{ens} can be expressed as

$$Err_{\text{ens}} = \sum_{i=1}^{N} \sum_{j=1}^{N} C_{ij} / N^2 \tag{8}$$

As viewed from bias-variance-covariance decomposition instead of Kroph [18] theory for ensemble generalization, the correlation can be regarded naturally as a measurement of variance and covariance.

The essential of GASEN is to reduce the bias and variant and improve generalization by raising the covariance via genetic algorithm. In fact, GASEN indicates implicitly that the performances of ensemble subnets are always different, so it is unreasonable to set equal weight to each component network. We need to select *many* good subnets from *all* individuals to combine a new ensemble with better generalization. The success of GASEN is to achieve an unequal distribution of ensemble weights by optimization of genetic algorithm, from equal distribution of $\{1/N, \ldots, 1/N\}$ to an unequal one of $\{1/N', \ldots, 1/N', 0, \ldots, 0\}$, where N' (from N) subnets are selected and combined a new ensemble with simple averaging technique again. The idea of unequal distribution for ensemble weights cannot be followed through in GASEN's procedure. Therefore, GASEN can be regarded as a tradeoff between simple averaging and weighted averaging. Either unselected subnets or selected subnets are always of different performances, so it is more reasonable that a different subnet should correspond to a different weight to combine the ensemble using weighted averaging technique. The subnet weight modification algorithm (subWMA) is presented in this paper to implement this statement.

3 Subnet Weight Modification Algorithm for Ensemble

There is an ensemble comprising N subnets for the regression task $\mathcal{D} = \{\boldsymbol{x}(k), y(k)\}$ ($k = 1, 2, \ldots, P$) in Section 2, which has an output $f^*(k)$ on the k-th instance,

$$f^*(k) = \sum_{i=1}^{N} w_i f_i(k) = \boldsymbol{w}^{\mathrm{T}} \boldsymbol{f}(k) \tag{9}$$

where $\boldsymbol{f}(k)$ is a vector made up of all the subnets output according to $\boldsymbol{x}(k)$, $\boldsymbol{f}(k) = [f_1(k), f_2(k), \ldots, f_N(k)]$; $\boldsymbol{w}(k)$ is the corresponding weight vector of ensemble subnets, $\boldsymbol{w}(k) = [w_1(k), w_2(k), \ldots, w_N(k)]$.

3.1 Initial Stage: Gradient-Descent Direction

By defining the ensemble error $e(k) = y(k) - f^*(k)$ and the cost function $\xi(\boldsymbol{w})$,

$$\xi(\boldsymbol{w}) = \frac{1}{2P}\sum_{k=1}^{P} e^2(k) = \frac{1}{2P}\sum_{k=1}^{P}[y(k) - \boldsymbol{w}^{\mathrm{T}}\boldsymbol{f}(k)]^2 \tag{10}$$

and taking derivative of $\xi(\boldsymbol{w})$ with respect to $\boldsymbol{w}$,

$$\nabla\xi(\boldsymbol{w}) = \frac{\partial\xi(\boldsymbol{w})}{\partial\boldsymbol{w}} = \frac{1}{P}\sum_{k=1}^{P} e(k)\frac{\partial e(k)}{\partial\boldsymbol{w}} = \frac{-1}{P}\sum_{k=1}^{P} e(k)\boldsymbol{f}(k) \tag{11}$$

we can get the weight increment equation based on the idea of gradient descent,

$$\Delta\boldsymbol{w} = -\eta\nabla\xi(\boldsymbol{w}) = \frac{\eta}{P}\sum_{k=1}^{P} e(k)\boldsymbol{f}(k) = \eta\,\boldsymbol{d}(\boldsymbol{w}) \tag{12}$$

where η is the learning rate of subWMA with a very small value, normally $\eta \le 0.1$; $\boldsymbol{d}(\boldsymbol{w})$ denotes the gradient descent direction.

3.2 Developed Stage: Normalization Case

The weight increment expression is similar to LMS (least mean square) equation of Adaline. That is to say, the weight can achieve any value to fit the training data at higher precision, which may cause overfitting for non-limit of ensemble weight. To avoid overfitting and accord with the definition of the ensemble weights, the normalization case should be satisfied,

$$\sum_{i=1}^{N} w_i = 1 \tag{13}$$

or in the increment expression,

$$\sum_{i=1}^{N} \Delta w_i = 0 \tag{14}$$

Actually, Eq. (12) cannot meet the requirement of the constraint case above directly. On this condition, we need to make a change to Eq. (13),

$$\Delta\boldsymbol{w} = \eta\boldsymbol{d}(\boldsymbol{w}) + \lambda\cdot\boldsymbol{1} \tag{15}$$

or in the element expression,

$$\Delta w_i = \eta d(w_i) + \lambda \tag{16}$$

Where λ is the modification item for Δw_i. And λ can be solved from the simultaneous equation of Eq. (14) and Eq. (16),

$$\lambda = -\eta\sum_{i=1}^{N} d(w_i)/N = -\eta\,\bar{d}(w) \tag{17}$$

where $\bar{d}(w)$ is the mean of $\boldsymbol{d}(w)$,

$$\bar{d}(w) = \frac{1}{N}\sum_{i=1}^{N} d(w_i) = \frac{1}{NP}\sum_{i=1}^{N}\sum_{k=1}^{P} e(k) f_i(k) \tag{18}$$

Substitute Eq. (15) for the expression of λ, and we can get the final weight modification equation of subWMA,

$$\boldsymbol{w} = \boldsymbol{w} + \Delta\boldsymbol{w} = \boldsymbol{w} + \frac{\eta}{P}[\sum_{k=1}^{P} e(k)(\boldsymbol{f}(k) - \bar{f}(k)\cdot \boldsymbol{1})] \tag{19}$$

and $\Delta\boldsymbol{w}$ can be calculated from the following expression,

$$\Delta\boldsymbol{w} = \eta\, \boldsymbol{d}(\boldsymbol{w}) - \eta\, \bar{d}(w) = \frac{\eta}{P}[\sum_{k=1}^{P} e(k)(\boldsymbol{f}(k) - \bar{f}(k)\cdot \boldsymbol{1})] \tag{20}$$

where $\bar{f}(k)$ is the mean of the vector of $\boldsymbol{f}(k)$, $\bar{f}(k) = \frac{1}{N}\sum_{i=1}^{N} f_i(k)$; $\boldsymbol{1}$ is the unit vector with the corresponding size of $\boldsymbol{f}(k)$.

3.3 Complete Stage: Checker Operation

It is clear that we cannot ensure the range of modified weights according to Eq.(19). When some modified weight is less than 0, it will be out of practical meaning, thus we should set a checker to make ensemble weights of reasonable range, which is shown in Fig. 1.

On one hand, Checker operation can assure the weights of correct range $0 \le w_i \le 1$, according to the code above; on the other hand, an extra result of Checker is that subWMA is of the similar function to GASEN, that is, subWMA can remove subnets of bad performances after Checker operation, a different optimal idea from GASEN.

```
Function checked_weight = Checker(modified_weight)
  zero_index = find(modified_weight < given_small_value);
                              % find weight index less than given small value
  for i = 1: length(zero_index)
      modified_weight(zero_index(i)) = 0;
                              % set 0 to the component corresponding to zero_index
  end
  checked_weight = norm(modified_weight);
                              % renormalize the non-negative weight
```

Fig. 1. Procedure of subWMA

3.4 Whole Procedure

According to the 3 stages introduced above, the whole procedure of subWMA is listed in Fig. 2.

Input: validating set *S*, trained ensemble *subNets*, ensemble individuals *N*, iterative times *Epochs*, learning rate *lr*

Procedure:

```
init ensemble weight vector w = 1 / N
for t = 1 to Epochs   {
    y = output vector of subNets from S
    e = individual output error between y and expected S
    d = descendant gradient direction by e and y        /* Initial Stage */
  dm = sum(d) / N,    (mean of d)
  Δw = lr * (d – dm),  (calculating increment of w)   /* Developed Stage */
    w = w + Δw
    w = Checker(w)    }                                 /* Complete Stage */
```

Output: ensemble weights ***w***

Fig. 2. Procedure of subWMA

4 Simulation and Discussion

Using 4 regression problems for experiment, we can compare the performance of subWMA with other three approaches, where two of them are ensembling algorithms, i.e., bagging and GASEN; another is the simple neural network with the best generalization performance among all of subnets.

4.1 Regression Problems

Problem 1 is Friedman#1 data [19] with 5 continuous attributes. The data set is generated from the following equation,

$$y = 10\sin(\pi x_1 x_2) + 20(x_3 - 0.5)^2 + 10x_4 + 5x_5 \tag{21}$$

where x_i (i = 1, 2, … , 5) satisfies the uniform distribution U[0, 1].

Problem 2 is Friedman#3 data [19] with 4 continuous attributes. The data set is generated from the following equation,

$$y = \tan^{-1}\frac{x_2 x_3 - \dfrac{1}{x_2 x_4}}{x_1} \tag{22}$$

where $x_1 \in$ U[0, 100], $x_2 \in$ U[40π, 560π], $x_3 \in$ U[0, 1] and $x_4 \in$ U[1, 11], respectively.

Problem 3 is Gabor data with 2 continuous attributes. The Gabor function, named after Dennis Gabor who used this function firstly in the 1940s, provides a Gaussian weighted sinusoid. The data set is generalized from the following equation,

$$y = \frac{\pi}{2}\exp[-2(x_1^2 + x_2^2)]\cos[2\pi(x_1 + x_2)] \tag{23}$$

Where x_1 and x_2 both satisfy U[0, 1].

Problem 4 is Multi data with 5 continuous attributes. The data set is generated from the following equation,

$$y = 0.79 + 1.27x_1x_2 + 1.56x_1x_4 + 3.42x_2x_5 + 2.06x_3x_4x_5 \tag{24}$$

where x_i $(i = 1, 2, \ldots, 5)$ satisfies U[0, 1].

4.2 Ready for Training

Now we begin to design the necessary parameters of ensemble and the subnets. For all problems, we first train 20 BP networks individually, each of which has one hidden layer with 5 hidden units. The training sets for BP subnets and the ensemble are produced by 10-fold cross validation and half of 10-fold cross validation according to Reference [15], respectively. We enumerate the training set and validating set of the four problems in Table 1.

Table 1. Data set of regression problems

Data sets	Attributes	Size	Training sets	Validating sets	Test sets
Friedman#1	5	5000	4500	2250	500
Friedman#3	4	3000	2700	1350	300
Gabor	2	3000	2700	1350	300
Multi	5	4000	3600	1800	400

Note that the networks in the ensemble are trained by BP algorithm in MATLAB, and parameters of each network are set to default values of MATLAB for either regression tasks or classification tasks. We try to keep the same structure, the same parameters as GASEN in Reference [15], so that the calculation results by subWMA, GASEN, bagging and best network can be forceful and trustful.

4.3 Results

The parameters for subWMA in Fig. 1 are given as: $N = 20$, $lr = 0.001$ and $Epochs = 100$, so we can achieve the following results. In the same training sets and test sets, we first trained 20 BP networks individually on 4 regression problems; then calculate test errors of simple-averaged ensemble and minimal value of all the single subnets (list in the item of Bagging and Best subnet, respectively). According to the same trained subnets, new ensembles weighted-averaged and simple-averaged are combined on subWMA and GASEN. We also calculate their test errors for 4 problems. The test errors for all 4 problems are listed in Table 2.

Table 2. Comparison of test MSE errors for 4 approaches

Test MSE Error	subWMA	GASEN	Bagging	Best subnet
Friedman#1	0.2151	0.2327	0.7673	0.2496
Friedman#3	0.3486	0.3489	0.3499	0.3661
Gabor	0.1538	0.1540	0.1569	0.1506
Multi	0.0168	0.0169	0.0189	0.0170

According to the results, we can know that test errors of both subWMA and GASEN are smaller than those of bagging and best subnet on all the simulation problems. As indicates the ensemble of redesigning weight distribution is usually of better performance than that of uniform distribution.

The test errors of subWMA on 4 problems are approximated to those of GASEN. The similar data show that subWMA and GASEN are of similar generalization performance on these 4 regression tasks. But they are really based on the different optimal ideas, the former is gradient-based algorithm, while the latter is genetic-based approach. The reason of tiny differences may be the pure mathematics model for all the data set lack of noisy instinct from nature. The more comparisons between subWMA and GASEN will be the emphases for future work.

In addition, the pre-set threshold is a very important parameter of GASEN, which determines the number of combined subnets. The relation between the threshold and generalization is still on consideration [16]. For subWMA, there is also a parameter lr (learning rate) to be considered, which controls the learning speed and learning steadiness of the algorithm. Luckily, we can determine it easily, normally $lr \leq 0.1$.

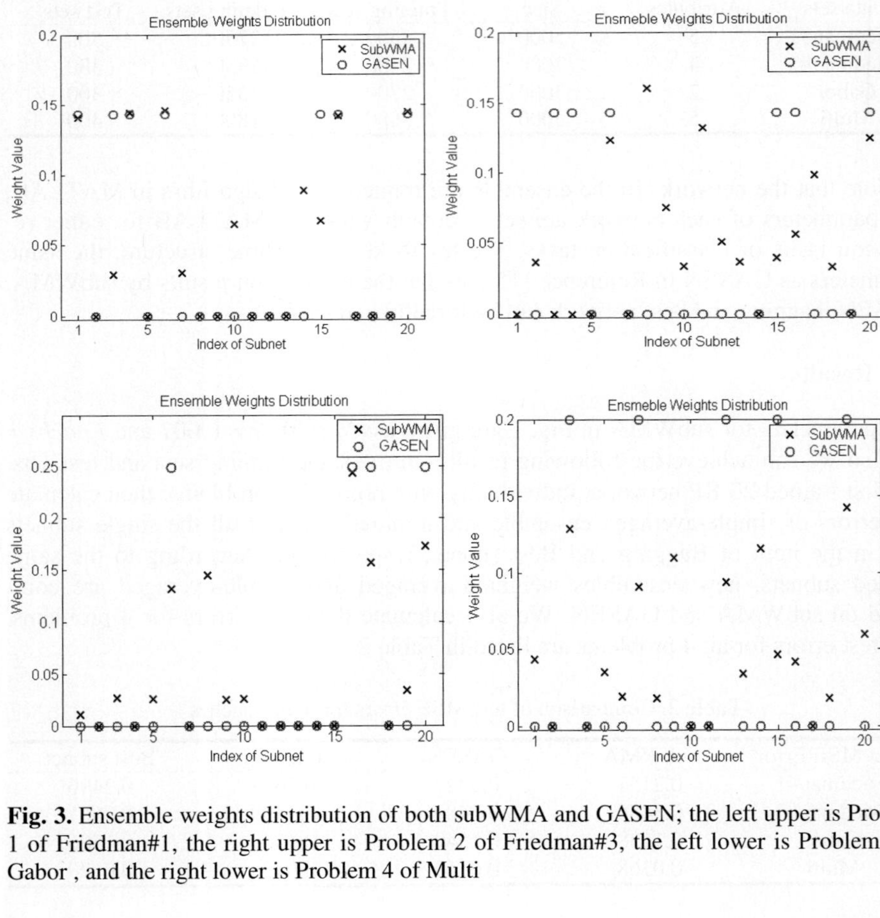

Fig. 3. Ensemble weights distribution of both subWMA and GASEN; the left upper is Problem 1 of Friedman#1, the right upper is Problem 2 of Friedman#3, the left lower is Problem 3 of Gabor , and the right lower is Problem 4 of Multi

GASEN and SubWMA are two feasible methods to achieve appropriate weight distributions. But gradient-based SubWMA carries through the idea of weighted averaging with a help of Checker operation. The contrastive distributions of ensemble weights on 4 problems are shown in Fig. 3. The figure shows Checker operation helps the weights into the correct range and selects good subnets with reasonable weights to combine a new ensemble.

5 Conclusion

SubWMA is a gradient-based optimal algorithm to aggregate neural estimators and combine a new ensemble with stronger generalization performance. In this paper, SubWMA is applied in the regression tasks and compared with GASEN, bagging and single neural network on 4 data sets. The simulation results show that SubWMA can produce an estimator ensemble with better generalization than those of bagging and single neural network. The method can not only have a similar function to GASEN of selecting many subnets from all trained networks, but also be of better performance than GASEN, bagging and best individual of regressive estimators.

In general, subWMA can optimize the ensemble weights more rapidly and steadily based on the gradient descent method. To avoid overfit and keep availability, extra operations are appended to the subWMA procedure, which makes the function of subWMA similar to that of GASEN. That is to say, subWMA can select available subnets from all of subnets and combine the ensemble weighted-averaging, instead of simple-averaging like GASEN.

References

1. Optiz D., Shavlik, J.: Actively Searching For an Effectively Neural Network Ensemble, Connection Science, Vol. 8, No. 3-4, (1996) 337-353
2. Hanson, L.K., Salamon, P.: Neural Network Ensemble. IEEE Trans. on Pattern Analysis and Machine Intelligence, Vol. PAMA-12, (1990) 993-1002
3. Breiman, L.: Bagging Predictors. Machine Leaning. Vol.24, (1996) 123-140
4. Schapire, R.E.: The Strength of Weak Learn Ability. Machine Leaning, Vol. 5, (1990) 197-227
5. Freund, Y.: Boosting a Weak Algorithm by Majority. Information Computation, Vol. 121, (1995) 256–285
6. Freund, Y., Schapire, R.E.: A Decision-theoretic Generalization of On-Line Learning and an Application to Boosting. J. Computer and System Science, Vol. 55, (1997) 119-139
7. Drucker, H.: Improving Regressors Using Boosting Techniques, Proc. of 14th International Conf. on Machine Learning, Morgan Kaufmann, Burlington, MA, (1997) 107-115
8. Schapire, R.E, Singer, Y.: Improved Boosting Algorithms Using Confidence-rated Predictions, Machine Learning, Vol. 37, No. 3, (1999) 297-336
9. Avnimilach, R., Intrator, N.: Boosted Mixture of Experts: An Ensemble Learning Scheme, Neural Computation, Vol. 11, (1999) 483-497
10. Solomatine, D.P., Shrestha D.L.: AdaBoost.RT: a boosting algorithm for regression problems, Proc of 2004 IEEE International Joint Conf. on Neural Networks, Vol.2, (2004) 1163-1168

11. Islam, M., Yao, X., and Murase, K.: A Constructive Algorithm for Training Cooperative Neural Network Ensembles, IEEE Trans. on Neural Networks, Vol. 14, No. 4, (2003) 820-834
12. Liu, Y., Yao, X.: Simultaneous Training of Negatively Correlated Neural Networks in an Ensemble, IEEE Trans. on System, Man and Cybernetics—PART B: Cybernetics, Vol. 29, No. 6, (1999) 716-725
13. Jang, M., Cho, S.: Observational Learning Algorithm for an Ensemble of Neural Networks, Pattern Analysis & Application, Vol. 5, (2002) 154-167
14. Perrone,M.P., Cooper, L.N.: When Networks Disagree: Ensemble Method for Neural Networks, In: Artificial Neural Networks for Speech and Vision, Chapman & Hall, New York, (1993) 126–142
15. Zhou, Z. H., Wu, J. X., Tang, W.: Ensembling Neural Networks: Many Could Be Better Than All. Artificial Intelligence, Vol. 137, (2002) 239-263
16. Zhou Z. H., Wu J. X., Jiang Y., et al: Genetic Algorithm based Selective Neural Network Ensemble. In: Proc. 17th International Joint Conf. on Artificial Intelligence, Seattle, WA, Vol. 2, (2001) 797-802
17. German, S., Bienenstock, E., Doursat,R.: Neural Networks And the Bias/Variance Dilemma, Neural Computation, Vol. 4, No. 1 (1992) 1–58
18. Kroph, A., Vedelsby, J.: Neural Network Ensemble, Cross Validation, and Active Learning, Advanced in Neural Information Processing System, Vol. 7, MIT Press, Cambridge, MA, (1995) 231-238
19. Friedman, J.: Multivariate Adaptive Regression Splines. Annals of Statistics, Vol. 19, (1991) 1-141

The Adaptive Learning Rates of Extended Kalman Filter Based Training Algorithm for Wavelet Neural Networks

Kyoung Joo Kim[1], Jin Bae Park[1], and Yoon Ho Choi[2]

[1] Yonsei University, Seodaemun-Gu, Seoul, 120-749, Korea
{mirukkj, jbpark}@control.yonsei.ac.kr
[2] Kyonggi University, Suwon, Kyonggi-Do 443-760, Korea
yhchoi@kyonggi.ac.kr

Abstract. Since the convergence of neural networks depends on learning rates, the learning rates of training algorithm for neural networks are very important factors. Therefore, we propose the Adaptive Learning Rates(ALRs) of Extended Kalman Filter(EKF) based training algorithm for wavelet neural networks(WNNs). The ALRs of the EFK based training algorithm produce the convergence of the WNN. Also we derive the convergence analysis of the learning process from the discrete Lyapunov stability theorem. Several simulation results show that the EKF based WNN with ALRs adapt to abrupt change and high nonlinearity with satisfactory performance.

1 Introduction

The models of natural phenomenon and physical system which include the nonlinear feature have been linearized via various linearize techniques, because of their convenience of analysis [1]. However, the nonlinear models has been driven by the improvement of the processor and the development of new mathematical theories. The one of them is to utilize the neural networks as identification technique [2], [3]. The performance of identification technique depends on the type and learning algorithm of neural networks. The most popular neural networks is multi-layer perceptron network(MLPN). However the MLPN has large structures. It induces the increase of calculation effort. Therefore, the wavelet neural network(WNN) which is a powerful tool as a estimator was introduced by Zhang Q. and Benveniste A. recently [4]. The WNN with a simple structure has excellent performance compared with the MLPN.

And the training algorithms of the neural networks exist various methods, such as back propagation(BP), genetic algorithm(GA), and DNA algorithm, *etc* [5] - [7]. The BP is the most popular method for neural networks. But it has a defect that the convergence is slow in case of high dimensional problems. Also GA and DNA have a defect such as long convergence time. To deal with these problems, the Extended Kalman Filter(EKF) based training algorithm was presented [8], [9]. The EKF based training algorithm has advantage which is the

A. Gelbukh and C.A. Reyes-Garcia (Eds.): MICAI 2006, LNAI 4293, pp. 327–337, 2006.

fast convergence. For good performance in EKF algorithm, however, the learning rate factor must be chosen very seriously. Because the convergence of neural networks depends on the learning rates, we have the need of the theorem which calculates the appropriate learning rates.

In this paper, we propose the adaptive learning rates(ALRs) of the EKF based training algorithm for the WNN. Here, we employ the WNN as the identifier of nonlinear dynamic systems. Also the EKF based training algorithm with ALRs is used for training the WNN. The ALRs are derived in the sense of discrete Lyapunov stability analysis, which is used to guarantee the convergence of the WNN. Finally, we show the superior performance of the proposed algorithm via simulations. This paper organized as follows. In Section 2, we present the WNN and the EKF based training algorithm. Section 3 presents the convergence analysis of WNN with EKF based algorithm. Simulation results are discussed in Section 4. Section 5 gives the conclusion of this paper.

2 The WNN and Training Algorithm

2.1 Wavelet Neural Network

The wavelet theory was proposed in multi-resolution analysis at early 1980s for improving the defect of the Fourier series by Mallet [10]. The WNN which has a wavelet function is one type of neural networks. The WNN has only 3-layer, but it has improved because it has wavelet function inside its structure [4]. As shown in Fig. 1, the WNN has N_i inputs and 1 output. Here, the wavelet nodes consist of mother wavelets which are the first derivative of Gaussian function: $\phi(z) = -z\exp\left(-\frac{1}{2}z^2\right)$. The mother wavelet is composed of the translation factor m_{jk} and the dilation factor d_{jk} as in (1), where the subscript jk indicated the jth wavelet of the kth input term:

$$\phi(z_{jk}) = \phi\left(\frac{x_k - m_{jk}}{d_{jk}}\right), \quad with \quad z_{jk} = \frac{x_k - m_{jk}}{d_{jk}}, \tag{1}$$

where x_k is the input. The output is constructed with a linear combination of consequences which are obtained from the outputs of wavelet nodes. The output of the WNN is as follows:

$$y = \Psi(\mathbf{x}, \psi) = \sum_{j=1}^{N_w} c_j \Phi_j(\mathbf{x}) + \sum_{k=1}^{N_i} a_k x_k, \tag{2}$$

$$\Phi_j(\mathbf{x}) = \prod_{k=1}^{N_i} \phi(z_{jk}), \tag{3}$$

where $\Phi_j(\mathbf{x})$ is the output of jth wavelet node, a_k is the weight between the input node and the output node, and c_j is the weight between the wavelet node and the output node, respectively. In (3), $\mathbf{x} = [x_1\ x_2\ \cdots\ x_{N_i}]^T$ denotes the input vector.

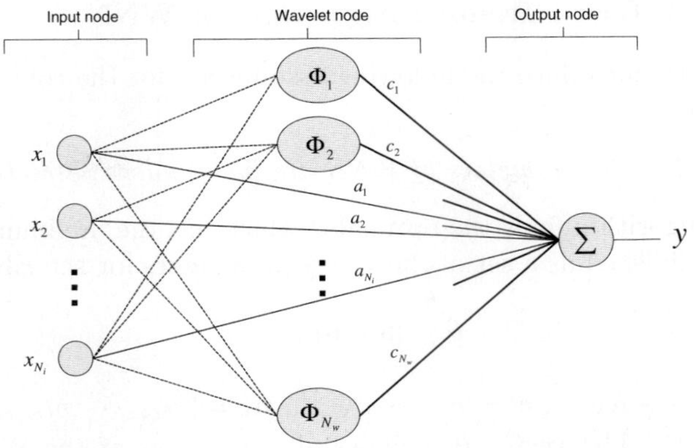

Fig. 1. The WNN structure

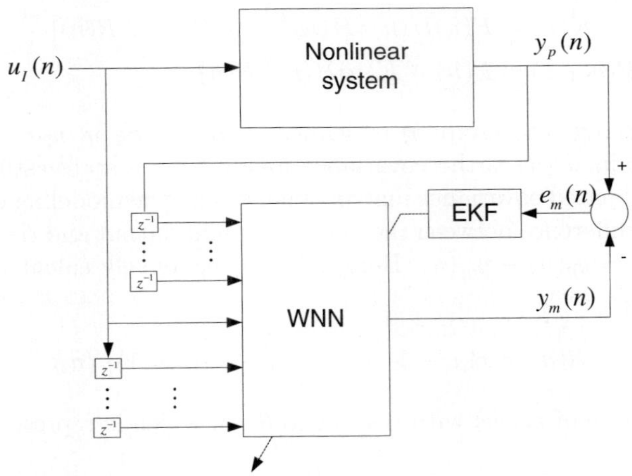

Fig. 2. Identification structure using the WNN

2.2 Identification Method for Nonlinear Systems

In this paper, we employ the serial-parallel method for identifying model of the nonlinear system. Fig. 2 represents the identification structure. The inputs of the WNN for the identifying model consist of the current input, the past inputs, and the past outputs of the nonlinear system. The current output of the WNN represents as follows:

$$\begin{aligned} y_m(n) =& f(y_p(n-1), y_p(n-2), \cdots, y_p(n-N_y) \\ & u_I(n), u_I(n-1), \cdots, u_I(n-N_u)), \end{aligned} \tag{4}$$

where N_y and N_u indicate the number of the past outputs and the past inputs, respectively. And also, $y_p(n)$ and $u_I(n)$ are the nonlinear system output and the identification input, respectively.

2.3 The EKF Based Training Algorithm for WNN

In this paper, we introduce the following assumption for the convenience of the convergence analysis.

Assumption 1. *All parameters of WNN are independent respectively.*

The training algorithm finds the optimal $\boldsymbol{\theta}$ which has the minimum MSE . The vector $\boldsymbol{\theta}$ is established as a set of the WNN parameters for the EKF algorithm:

$$\boldsymbol{\theta} = [\mathbf{a}\ \mathbf{c}\ \mathbf{m}\ \mathbf{d}]^T, \tag{5}$$

where $\mathbf{a} = [a_1\ \cdots\ a_{N_i}]^T$, $\mathbf{c} = [c_1\ \cdots\ c_{N_w}]^T$, $\mathbf{m} = [m_{11}\ \cdots\ m_{N_iN_w}]^T$ and $\mathbf{d} = [d_{11}\ \cdots\ d_{N_iN_w}]^T$. The vector $\boldsymbol{\theta}$ includes all parameter of the WNN, and the training equations are represented in (5) and (6) like the EKF form [12]:

$$\boldsymbol{\theta}(n+1) = \boldsymbol{\theta}(n) + \boldsymbol{\eta} K(n) e_m(n), \tag{6}$$

$$K(n) = P(n)H(n)\left[H(n)^T P(n)H(n) + R(n)\right]^{-1}, \tag{7}$$

$$P(n+1) = P(n) - K(n)H(n)^T P(n), \tag{8}$$

where the learning rate vector $\boldsymbol{\eta}$ is defined as $\boldsymbol{\eta} = diag\,[\eta_1\ \eta_2 \cdots\ \eta_p]$, $K(n)$ is the Kalman gain, $P(n)$ is the covariance matrix of the state estimation error, $R(n)$ is the estimated covariance matrix of noise, and the modeling error $e_m(n)$ is defined as the difference between the nonlinear plant output and the WNN model output: $e_m(n) = y_p(n) - y_m(n)$. Here, $R(n)$ is recursively calculated according to [9], [11] :

$$R(n) = R(n-1) + \left[e_m(n)^2 - R(n-1)\right]/n, \tag{9}$$

$H(n)$ is derivative of $y_m(n)$ with respect to $\boldsymbol{\theta}(n)$, which is represented by

$$H(n) = \frac{\partial y_m(n)}{\partial \theta(n)}.$$

Remark 1. By Assumption 1, the error covariance matrix $P(n)$ is a diagonal matrix.

3 Convergence Analysis of the EKF Based Training Algorithm

This section describes the convergence analysis of the EKF based training algorithm for WNN. The convergence of this algorithm depends on the learning rate. Therefore, the ALRs which guarantee the convergence are derived in the sense of discrete Lyapunov stability analysis.

Theorem 1. *If the learning rate satisfies*

$$0 < \eta_i < \frac{2}{H(n)^T K(n)}, \qquad i = 1, 2, \cdots, p,$$

then the asymptotic convergence is guaranteed.

Proof. A Lyapunov function candidate is as follows:

$$V(n) = \frac{1}{2} e_m(n)^2. \tag{10}$$

The difference of Lyapunov function is obtained by

$$\begin{aligned}\triangle V(n) &= V(n+1) - V(n) \\ &= \frac{1}{2}\left(e_m(n+1)^2 - e_m(n)^2\right) \\ &= \triangle e_m(n)\left[e_m(n) + \frac{1}{2}\triangle e_m(n)\right],\end{aligned} \tag{11}$$

where the difference of error is

$$\begin{aligned}\triangle e_m(n) &= \left[\frac{\partial e_m(n)}{\partial \theta(n)}\right]^T \triangle\theta(n) \\ &= \left[\frac{\partial e_m(n)}{\partial \theta(n)}\right]^T \boldsymbol{\eta} K(n) e_m(n) \\ &= -\left[\frac{\partial y_m(n)}{\partial \theta(n)}\right]^T \boldsymbol{\eta} K(n) e_m(n) \\ &= -H(n)^T \boldsymbol{\eta} K(n) e_m(n).\end{aligned} \tag{12}$$

Therefore, the difference of $V(n)$ is

$$\begin{aligned}\triangle V(n) &= -H(n)^T \boldsymbol{\eta} K(n)\left[1 - \frac{1}{2} H(n)^T \boldsymbol{\eta} K(n)\right] e_m(n)^T \\ &= -\gamma_m e_m(n)^2.\end{aligned} \tag{13}$$

If $\gamma_m > 0$, then $\triangle V(n) < 0$. Accordingly, the asymptotic convergence of the WNN is guaranteed. Here, we obtain $0 < \eta_i < \frac{2}{H(n)^T K(n)}, \quad i = 1, 2, \cdots, p$.

Corollary 1. *If the learning rate is chosen as* $\eta_i = \frac{1}{H(n)^T K(n)}$ *, it is the maximum learning rate which guarantees the convergence. Here,* $i = 1, 2, \cdots, p$

Proof

$$\begin{aligned}
\gamma_m &= H(n)^T \boldsymbol{\eta} K(n) \left[1 - \frac{1}{2} H(n)^T \boldsymbol{\eta} K(n)\right] \\
&= H(n)^T K(n) \left[\eta_i - \frac{1}{2}\eta_i^2 H(n)^T K(n)\right] \\
&= \left[H(n)^T K(n)\right]^2 \left[\frac{\eta_i}{H(n)^T K(n)} - \frac{1}{2}\eta_i^2\right] \\
&= \frac{1}{2}\left[H(n)^T K(n)\right]^2 \left[\frac{2\eta_i}{H(n)^T K(n)} - \eta_i^2\right] \\
&= -\frac{1}{2}\left[H(n)^T K(n)\right]^2 \left[\eta_i^2 - \frac{2\eta_i}{H(n)^T K(n)} \right.\\
&\qquad \left. + \frac{1}{\left[H(n)^T K(n)\right]^2} - \frac{1}{\left[H(n)^T K(n)\right]^2}\right] \\
&= -\frac{1}{2}\left[H(n)^T K(n)\right]^2 \left[\eta_i - \frac{1}{H(n)^T K(n)}\right]^2 + \frac{1}{2} > 0.
\end{aligned}$$

If the learning rate is chosen as $\eta_{\max} = \eta_i = \frac{1}{H(n)^T K(n)}$, $\triangle V$ the has minimum negative value. Therefore, it is maximum learning rate which guarantees the convergence.

Remark 2. The learning rate $\boldsymbol{\eta}$ cannot reflect the difference of each parameters $\mathbf{a}, \mathbf{c}, \mathbf{m}$ and $\mathbf{d}$ of the WNN. Because of this fact, the particular learning rates are needed. Therefore, we redefine the learning rates as $\boldsymbol{\eta} = diag[\eta_1\ \eta_2\ \cdots\ \eta_p] = diag[\boldsymbol{\eta}_a,\ \boldsymbol{\eta}_c,\ \boldsymbol{\eta}_m,\ \boldsymbol{\eta}_d]$, where $\boldsymbol{\eta}_a$, $\boldsymbol{\eta}_c$, $\boldsymbol{\eta}_m$ and $\boldsymbol{\eta}_d$ are the learning rates of the WNN parameter with respect to $\mathbf{a}$, $\mathbf{c}$, $\mathbf{m}$ and $\mathbf{d}$, respectively. Similarly redefine $H(n)$, $K(n)$ and $P(n)$ as follows:

$$\begin{aligned}
H(n) &= \left[H_a(n)\ \ H_c(n)\ \ H_m(n)\ \ H_d(n)\right]^T, \\
K(n) &= \left[K_a(n)\ \ K_c(n)\ \ K_m(n)\ \ K_d(n)\right]^T, \\
P(n) &= diag\left[P_a(n)\ \ P_c(n)\ \ P_m(n)\ \ P_d(n)\right]^T.
\end{aligned}$$

Theorem 2. *The learning rate η_a is the learning rate of the input direct weights for the WNN identifier. The asymptotic convergence is guaranteed if the learning rate η_a satisfies*

$$0 < \eta_a < \frac{2}{\sqrt{N_i}|x|_{\max}|K_a(n)|_{\max}}.$$

Proof. The learning rate $\boldsymbol{\eta}_a = diag[\eta_a \ \cdots \ \eta_a]$ only has an effect on $\mathbf{a}$. From Theorem 1, we obtain

$$0 < \eta_a < \frac{2}{H_{a,\max}(n)^T K_{a.\max}(n)},$$

$$H_a = \frac{\partial y_m(n)}{\partial \mathbf{a}} = \sum_{k=1}^{N_i} x_k < \sqrt{N_i}|x|_{\max} = H_{a,\max}(n), \tag{14}$$

$$0 < \eta_a < \frac{2}{\sqrt{N_i}|x|_{\max}|K_a(n)|_{max}}. \tag{15}$$

Theorem 3. *The $\boldsymbol{\eta}_m = diag[\eta_m \ \cdots \ \eta_m]$ and $\boldsymbol{\eta}_d = diag[\eta_d \ \cdots \ \eta_d]$ are the learning rates of the translation and dilation weights of the WNN, respectively. The asymptotic convergence is guaranteed if the learning rates satisfy*

$$0 < \eta_m < \frac{2}{\sqrt{N_w N_i}|K_m(n)|_{max}} \frac{1}{|c|_{\max}\frac{2\exp(-0.5)}{|d|_{\min}}},$$

$$0 < \eta_d < \frac{2}{\sqrt{N_w N_i}|K_d(n)|_{max}} \frac{1}{|c|_{\max}\frac{2\exp(0.5)}{|d|_{\min}}}.$$

Proof. 1) The learning rate η_m of the translation weights $\mathbf{m}$:

$$\begin{aligned} H_m(n) &= \frac{\partial y_m(n)}{\partial \mathbf{m}} = \sum_{j=1}^{N_w} c_j \left\{ \frac{\partial \Phi_j}{\partial \mathbf{m}_j} \right\} \\ &= \sum_{j=1}^{N_w} c_j \left\{ \sum_{k=1}^{N_i} \frac{\prod_{k=1}^{N_i} \phi(z_{jk})}{\phi(z_{jk})} \left(\frac{\partial \phi(z_{jk})}{\partial z_{jk}} \frac{\partial z_{jk}}{\partial \mathbf{m}} \right) \right\} \\ &< \sqrt{N_w}\sqrt{N_i}|c|_{\max} \frac{2\exp(-0.5)}{|d|_{\min}}. \end{aligned} \tag{16}$$

From Theorem 1, we obtain

$$0 < \eta_m < \frac{2}{H_{m,\max}(n)^T K_{m,\max}(n)}, \tag{17}$$

$$0 < \eta_m < \frac{2}{\sqrt{N_w}\sqrt{N_i}|K_m(n)|_{max}} \frac{1}{|c|_{\max}\frac{2\exp(-0.5)}{|d|_{\min}}}. \tag{18}$$

2) The learning rate η_d of the dilation weights $\mathbf{d}$:

$$\begin{aligned} H_d(n) &= \frac{\partial y_m(n)}{\partial \mathbf{d}} = \sum_{j=1}^{N_w} c_j \left(\frac{\partial \Phi_j}{\partial \mathbf{d}} \right), \\ &= \sum_{j=1}^{N_w} c_j \left\{ \sum_{k=1}^{N_i} \frac{\prod_{k=1}^{N_i} \phi(z_{jk})}{\phi(z_{jk})} \left(\frac{\partial \phi(z_{jk})}{\partial z_{jk}} \frac{\partial z_{jk}}{\partial \mathbf{d}} \right) \right\} \\ &< \sqrt{N_w}\sqrt{N_i}|c|_{\max} \frac{2\exp(0.5)}{|d|_{\min}}. \end{aligned} \tag{19}$$

From Theorem 1,

$$0 < \eta_d < \frac{2}{H_{d,\max}(n)^T K_{d,\max}(n)}, \tag{20}$$

$$0 < \eta_m < \frac{2}{\sqrt{N_w}\sqrt{N_i}|K_d(n)|_{max}} \frac{1}{|c|_{\max} \frac{2\exp(0.5)}{|d|_{\min}}}. \tag{21}$$

Theorem 4. *The* $\boldsymbol{\eta} = diag[\eta_c \ \cdots \ \eta_c]$ *is the learning rate of the parameter* $\mathbf{c}$ *of the WNN. The asymptotic convergence is guaranteed if the learning rate satisfies*

$$0 < \eta_c < \frac{2}{\sqrt{N_w}|K_c(n)|_{\max}}.$$

Proof

$$H_c(n) = \frac{\partial y_m(n)}{\partial \mathbf{c}} = \sum_{j=1}^{N_w} \Phi_j = \Phi, \tag{22}$$

where $\Phi = [\Phi_1 \ \Phi_2 \ \cdots \ \Phi_{N_w}]^T$. Since we have $\Phi_j \leq 1$ for all j, then $H_c(n) \leq \sqrt{N_w}$. From Theorem 1, we obtain

$$0 < \eta_c < \frac{2}{H_{c,\max}(n)^T K_{c,\max}(n)}, \tag{23}$$

$$0 < \eta_c < \frac{2}{\sqrt{N_w}|K_c(n)|_{max}}. \tag{24}$$

Remark 3. From Corollary 2, the maximum learning rates of the WNN are as follows:

$$\eta_a = \frac{1}{\sqrt{N_i}|x|_{\max}|K_a(n)|_{\max}}, \tag{25}$$

$$\eta_m = \frac{1}{\sqrt{N_w N_i}|K_m(n)|_{max}} \frac{1}{|c|_{\max} \frac{2\exp(-0.5)}{|d|_{\min}}}, \tag{26}$$

$$\eta_d = \frac{1}{\sqrt{N_w N_i}|K_d(n)|_{max}} \frac{1}{|c|_{\max} \frac{2\exp(0.5)}{|d|_{\min}}}, \tag{27}$$

$$\eta_c = \frac{1}{\sqrt{N_w}|K_c(n)|_{\max}}. \tag{28}$$

4 Simulations

In this section, we apply the proposed algorithm to two nonlinear systems. First, The simple numeric function(SNF) which is the simple nonlinear system is considered. Second, we consider the Hénon system which is the discrete-time chaotic system. In this simulation, the results are the average value of over 100 runs with the random initial parameters of the networks.

4.1 Simple Numeric Function(SNF)

The state equation is as follows:

$$f(x) = \begin{cases} -2.186x - 12.864, & -10 \leq x \leq -2 \\ 4.246x, & -2 \leq x \leq 0 \\ 10exp(-0.05x - 0.5)sin[(0.03x + 0.7)x], & 0 \leq x \leq 10 \end{cases} \quad (29)$$

Table 1. Simulation parameters and the results for the SNF and the Hénon system

Simulation Condition	SNF	Hénon
Number of wavelet node	5	4
Number of past inputs	1	1
Number of past output of plant	1	1
Learning rate	Adaptive	Adaptive
Sampling rate	0.05	0.1
MSE	0.2434	0.0079

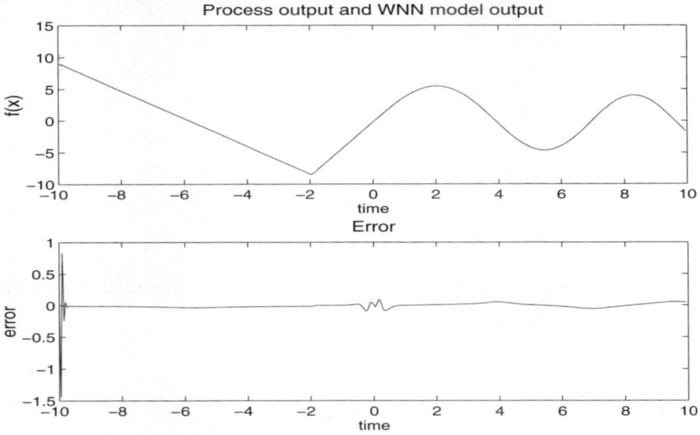

Fig. 3. Identification results for the simple numeric function (solid line: reference signal, dotted line: WNN identification result)

The simulation environments and results for the SNF are shown in Table 1. Figure 3 represents the identification result of the WNN for the SNF. From the results of Table 1 and Figure 3, we can observe that the identification error is almost zero. Therefore, we confirm that the EKF based training algorithm of the WNN has the excellent performance.

4.2 Hénon System

We consider the Hénon system. The Hénon system is the discrete-time chaotic system as follows:

$$\begin{bmatrix} x_1(n+1) \\ x_2(n+1) \end{bmatrix} = \begin{bmatrix} x_2(n) + 1 - a x_1^2(n) \\ b x_1 + u \end{bmatrix}, \tag{30}$$

where $a = 1.4$ and $b = 0.3$.

Simulation environments and results for the Hénon system are shown in Table 1. In Fig. 4, the reference signal is the trajectory of the state $x_1(n)$ of the Hénon system. As shown in Fig. 4, we can observe that the output of the WNN with ALRs well estimates a abrupt change of the Hénon system. We can confirm that the EKF based training algorithm for the WNN with ALRs has a good training performance for Hénon system.

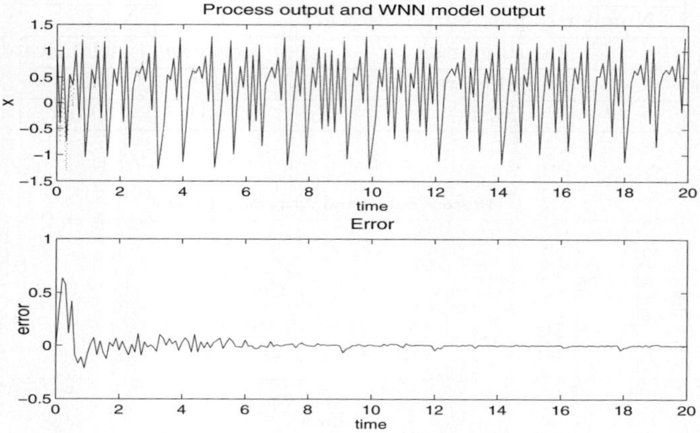

Fig. 4. Identification results for the Hénon system (solid line: reference signal, dotted line: WNN identification result)

5 Conclusions

In this paper, we have proposed the ALRs of the EKF based training algorithm for the WNN. And using Lyapunov approach, the convergence of proposed algorithm was proven. To verify the effectiveness of the proposed algorithm, we applied it to train the parameters of the WNN. And then using the WNN, we executed the identification for the SNF and the discrete chaotic system. From the simulation results, we confirm that the EKF algorithm using ALRs has the fast convergence. In addition, the WNN training by the proposed algorithm adapts well to the abrupt change and the high nonlinearity of the chaotic systems, because the proposed theorem concerns the learning rates of each parameters of the WNN, respectively. In conclusion, we confirmed that the proposed algorithm has the fast convergence and the excellent estimation performance.

Acknowledgment

This work was supported by the Brain Korea 21 Project in 2006.

References

1. Slotin J.E. and Li W., Applied Nonlinear Control, Prentice-Hall, (1991)
2. Ren X.M., Rad A.B., Chan P.T., and Lo W.L.: Identification and Control of Continuous-Time Nonlinear Systems via Dynamic Neural Networks. IEEE Trans. Industrial Electronics 50 (2003) 478-486
3. Yoo S.J., Park J.B. and Choi Y.H.: Stable Predictive Control of Chaotic Systems Using Self-Recurrent Wavelet Neural Network. Int. Journal of Control, Automation, and Systems 3 (2005) 43-55
4. Zhang Q. and Benveniste A.: Wavelet Networks. IEEE Trans. Neural Networks 3 (1992) 889-898
5. Oh J.S., Park J.B., and Choi Y.H.: Path Tracking Control using a Wavelet Neural Network for Mobile Robot with Extended Kalman Filter. Proc. of the Int. Conf. Control, Automation and Systems (2003) 1283-1288
6. Lee B.J., Park J.B., Lee H.J., Joo Y.H.: Fuzzy-logic-based IMM algorithm for tracking a manoeuvring target. IEE Proc. Radar, Sonar and Navigation 152 (2005) 16 - 22
7. Yoo S.J., Park J.B. , Choi Y.H.: Direct Adaptive Control Using Self Recurrent Wavelet Neural Network Via Adaptive Learning Rates for Stable Path Tracking of Mobile Robots. Proc. of American Control Conference 1 (2005) 288-293
8. Singhal S. and Wu L.: Training Feed-forward Networks with the Extended Kalman Algorithm. Proc. of Int. Conf. on Acoustics, Speech, and Signal Processing 2 (1989) 1187-1190
9. Wu Q., Saif M.: Neural Adaptive Observer Based Fault Detection and Identification for Satellite Attitude Control Systems. Proc. of American Control Conference 2 (2005) 1054-1059
10. Mallet S.G.: A Theory for Multiresolution Signal Decompisition- the wavelet representation. IEEE Trans. Pattern Alanysis and Machine Intelligence 11 (1989) 674-693
11. Ljung L. and Söderström T., Theory and Practice of Recursive Identification. MIT Press, Messachusetts, (1983)
12. Alessandri A., Cuneo M., Pagnan S., Sanguineti M.: On the Convergence of EKF-Based Parameters Optimization for Neural Networks. Proc. of 42nd IEEE Conference on Decision and Control 6 (2003) 6181 - 6186

Multistage Neural Network Metalearning with Application to Foreign Exchange Rates Forecasting

Kin Keung Lai[1,2], Lean Yu[2,3], Wei Huang[4], and Shouyang Wang[1,3]

[1] College of Business Administration, Hunan University, Changsha 410082, China
[2] Department of Management Sciences, City University of Hong Kong, Tat Chee Avenue, Kowloon, Hong Kong
{mskklai, msyulean}@cityu.edu.hk
[3] Institute of Systems Science, Academy of Mathematics and Systems Science, Chinese Academy of Sciences, Beijing 100080, China
{yulean, sywang}@amss.ac.cn
[4] School of Management, Huazhong University of Science and Technology, 1037 Luoyu Road, Wuhan 430074, China

Abstract. In this study, we propose a multistage neural network metalearning technique for financial time series predication. First of all, an interval sampling technique is used to generate different training subsets. Based on the different training subsets, the different neural network models with different training subsets are then trained to formulate different base models. Subsequently, to improve the efficiency of metalearning, the principal component analysis (PCA) technique is used as a pruning tool to generate an optimal set of base models. Finally, a neural-network-based metamodel can be produced by learning from the selected base models. For illustration, the proposed metalearning technique is applied to foreign exchange rate predication.

1 Introduction

Artificial neural networks (ANNs), first introduced in 1943 [1], is a system derived through neuropsychology models [2]. It attempts to emulate the biological system of the human brain in learning and identifying patterns. Moreover, ANNs can more aptly recognize poorly defined patterns. Instead of extracting explicit rules from sample data, the ANNs employed a learning algorithm to autonomously: (a) extract the functional relationship between input and output, which is embedded in a set of historical data (called training exemplars or learning samples), and (b) encode it in connection weights. Training exemplars that are readily available allow neural networks to capture a large volume of information in a rather short period of time and to continuously learn throughout their lifespan. Furthermore, neural networks have the ability to not only deal with noisy, incomplete, or previously unseen input patterns, but to also generate a reasonable response [3]. However, ANNs are far from being optimal learner. For example, the existing studies, e.g., [4] have found that the ways neural networks have of getting to the global minima vary and some networks just settle into local minima instead of global minima through the analysis of error distributions. In this case, it is hard to justify which neural network's error reaches the global minima if the error rate is not zero. Thus, it is not wise choice that only selecting a single

A. Gelbukh and C.A. Reyes-Garcia (Eds.): MICAI 2006, LNAI 4293, pp. 338 – 347, 2006.

neural network model with the best generalization from a limited number of neural networks if the error is larger than zero. For example of financial time series forecasting, it is difficult to obtain a consistently good result by using a single neural network model due to high volatility and irregularity in financial markets. More and more researchers have realized that just selecting the neural network model that gives the best performance will result in losses of potentially valuable information contained by other neural network models with slightly weak performance relative to the best neural network model. Naturally, a different learning strategy to solving these problems that considers those discarded neural networks whose performance is less accurate as the best neural network model should be proposed. In such situations, metalearning strategy [5] based on the neural network is introduced.

Metalearning [5], which is defined as learning from learned knowledge, provides a promising solution and a novel approach to the above challenges. The idea is to use neural network learning algorithms to extract knowledge from several different data sets and then use the knowledge from these individual learning algorithms to create a unified body of knowledge that well represents the entire data. Therefore metalearning seeks to compute a metamodel that integrates in some principled fashion the separately learned models to boost overall predictive accuracy. In this study, a four-stage neural-network-based metalearning technique is proposed for financial time series forecasting. In the first stage, an interval sampling technique is used to generate different training sets. Based on the different training sets, the different neural network models with different initial conditions are then trained to formulate different base models in the second stage. In the third stage, to improve the efficiency of metalearning, the principal component analysis (PCA) technique is used as a pruning tool to generate an optimal set of base models. In the final stage, a neural-network-based metamodel can be produced by learning from the selected base models.

The rest of this study is organized as follows. Section 2 provides a neural-network-based metalearning process in detail. For verification, an exchange rate predication experiment is performed in Section 3. Finally, Section 4 concludes the article.

2 The Neural-Network-Based Metalearning Process

In this section, we first introduce the basic knowledge of metalearning. Based on the metalearning, a generic metamodeling process with three phases is then provided.

As Section 1 mentioned, metalearning [5], which is defined as learning from learned knowledge, is an emerging technique recently developed to construct a metamodel that deals with the problem of computing a metamodel from multiple training data sets. Broadly speaking, learning is concerned with finding a model $f = f_a[i]$ from a single training set TR_j, while metalearning is concerned with finding a metamodel $f = f_a$ from several training sets $\{TR_1, TR_2, \ldots, TR_n\}$, each of which has an associated model $f = f_a[j]$. The n individual models derived from the n training sets may be of the same or different types. Similarly, the metamodel may be of a different type than some or all of the single models. Also, the metamodel may use data from a meta-training set (MT), which are distinct from the data in the individual training set TR_j.

There are two types of metalearning methods: different-training-set-based metalearning and different-model-type-based metalearning. For the first type, we are given a large data set *DS* and partition it into *n* different training subsets $\{TR_1, TR_2, \ldots, TR_n\}$. Assume that we build a separate model on each subset independently to produce *n* models $\{f_1, f_2, \ldots, f_n\}$. Given a feature vector *x*, we can produce *n* scores $(f_1(x), f_2(x), \ldots, f_n(x))$, one for each model. Given a new training set *MT*, we can build a metamodel *f* on *MT* using the data $\{(f_1(x), f_2(x), \ldots, f_n(x), y) : (x, y) \text{ in } MT\}$.

For the second type, given a relative small training set $\{TR\}$, we replicate it *n* times to produce *n* training sets $\{TR_1, TR_2, \ldots, TR_n\}$ and create different models f_j on each training set TR_j, for example, by training the replicated data on *n* different-type models. For simplicity, assume that these models are binary classifiers so that each classifier takes a feature vector and produces a classification in $\{0, 1\}$. We can then produce a metamodel simply by using a majority vote of the *n* classifiers.

In time series forecasting, data is abundant. To improve the predication performance, we use the different-training-set-based metalearning. Generally, the generic idea of neural network metalearning is to generate a number of independent models (i.e., base models) by applying neural network learning algorithms to a collection of data sets. The independent models are then selected and combined to obtain a global model or metamodel. Fig. 1 illustrates a neural network metalearning process. From Fig. 1, the metalearning process consists of four stages, which can be described below.

Stage 1: For an initial data set *DS*, the whole data set is first divided into training set *TR* and testing set *TS*. Then the different training subsets $TR_1, TR_2, \ldots, TR_n$ are created from *TR* with certain sampling algorithm.

Stage 2: For each training subset TR_i $(i = 1, 2, \ldots, n)$, the neural network model f_i $(i = 1, 2, \ldots, n)$ is trained by the specific learning algorithm to formulate *n* different base models. After training, the testing data was applied for assessment.

Stage 3: For *n* different base models, the pruning techniques are used to generate some effective base models. After pruning, *m* $(m \leq n)$ different base models are generated for the next stage's use.

Stage 4: Using the whole training data set to *m* different base models, different neural network's results can formulate a meta-training set (*MT*). Based on the meta-training set, another single neural network model is training to produce a metamodel.

From the generic neural network metalearning process, there are **four problems** to be further addressed, i.e., (a) how to create n different training subset from the original training data set *TR*; (b) how to create different base models f_i with different training subsets for the same-type model; (c) how to select some effective base model from many neural network base models in the previous stage; and (d) how to formulate a metamodel with different results produced by different base models.

A. Data Sampling

For financial time series predication mining tasks, our aim is to improve the predication performance with historical time series data. For convenience of neural network learning, the original data set *DS* is first divided into two parts: training data set *TR* and testing data set *TS*. In order to capture the patterns of time series data, different data sampling is helpful for neural network learning. Here we propose an interval sampling algorithm to produce different training subsets.

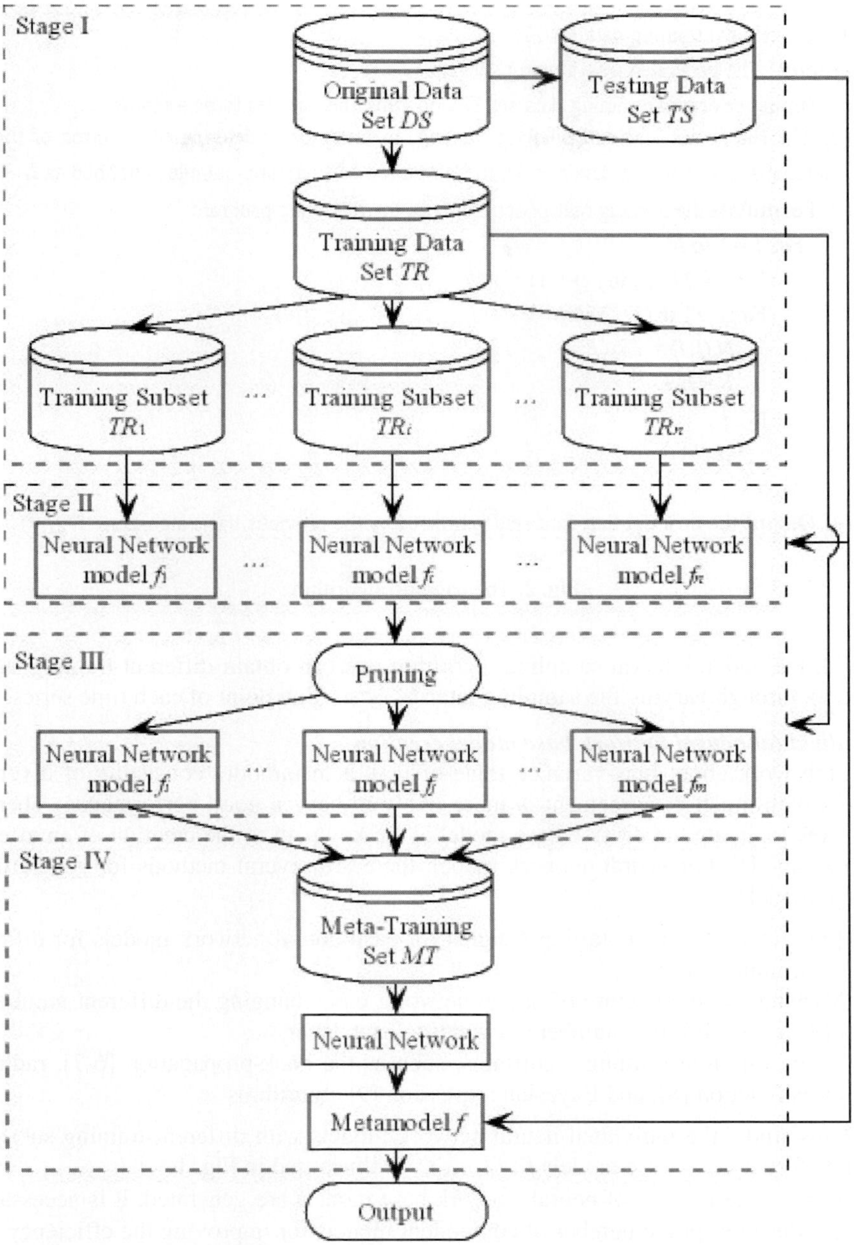

Fig. 1. The generic neural network metalearning process

Given that the size of the original training set *TR* is *M*, the size of new training set is *N*, and sampling interval is *K*, the interval sampling algorithm is illustrated in Fig. 2.

Input: original training data set TR

Output: The generated new training subsets

(1) **Input** the original training data set TR and **rank** the samples to be a sequence.

(2) The start point and end point of training, p_1 and p_2, are determined in terms of the pre-defined size of training data $N < M$: the lag period of every sub-sample is defined as L.

(3) **Formulate** the training matrix according to the following program:

```
For i = 1 to N
    TR_t(i) = TR(p1 to p1+L-1)
    For j = 1 to (L/K) step -1
        N(j, i) = TR_t(L, i)
        L = L-K
    Next j
    p1 = p1+1
Next i
```

(4) **Output** the final training data sets generated by the previous basic algorithm: $N(j, i)$.

Fig. 2. The bagging algorithm

With the above interval sampling algorithm, we can obtain different training subsets only through varying the sampling interval or starting point of each time series.

B. Individual neural network base model creation

With the work about bias-variance trade-off [4], a metamodel consisting of diverse models with much disagreement is more likely to have a good performance. Therefore, how to create the diverse base model is the key path to the creation of an effective metamodel. For neural network model, there are several methods for generating diverse models.

(1) Initializing different starting weights for each neural network models for different training subsets.
(2) Varying the architecture of neural network, e.g., changing the different numbers of layers or different numbers of nodes in each layer.
(3) Using different training algorithms, such as the back-propagation [6-7], radial-basis function [8], and Bayesian regression [9] algorithms.

In this study, the individual neural network models with different training subsets are therefore used as base models $f_1, f_2, \ldots, f_n$, as illustrated in Fig. 1.

When a large number of neural network base models are generated, it is necessary to select the appropriate number of component models for improving the efficiency of neural network metalearning system. It is well known to us that not all circumstances are satisfied with the rule of "the more, the better" [11]. That is, some individual base models produced by this phase may be redundant, wasting resources and reducing system performance. Thus, it is necessary to prune some inappropriate individual base models for metamodel construction.

C. Neural network base model pruning

In order to select the appropriate number of neural network base model, we utilize the principal component analysis (PCA) to arrive at this goal.

The PCA technique [10], an effective feature extraction method, is widely used in signal processing, statistics and neural computing. The basic idea in PCA is to find the components (s_1, s_2, …, s_p) that can explain the maximum amount of variance possible by p linearly transformed components from data vector with q dimensions. The mathematical technique used in PCA is called eigen analysis. In addition, the basic goal in PCA is to reduce the dimension of the data (Here the PCA is used to reduce the number of individual models). Thus, one usually chooses $p \le q$. Indeed, it can be proven that the representation given by PCA is an optimal linear dimension reduction technique in the mean-square sense [10]. Such a reduction in dimension has important benefits. First, the computation of the subsequent processing is reduced. Second, noise may be reduced and the meaningful underlying information identified. The following presents the PCA process for individual model selection [11].

Assuming that there are n individual data mining models and that every model contains m forecasting or classification results, then result matrix (Y) is represented as

$$Y = \begin{bmatrix} y_{11} & y_{12} & \cdots & y_{1m} \\ y_{21} & y_{22} & \cdots & y_{2m} \\ \vdots & \vdots & \ddots & \vdots \\ y_{n1} & y_{n2} & \cdots & y_{nm} \end{bmatrix} \tag{1}$$

where y_{ij} is the jth predication or classification result with the ith data mining model.

Next, we deal with the result matrix using the PCA technique. First, eigenvalues (λ_1, λ_2, …, λ_n) and corresponding eigenvectors A=(a_1, a_2, …, a_n) can be solved from the above matrix. Then the new principal components are calculated as

$$Z_i = a_i^T Y \quad (i=1, 2, \ldots, n) \tag{2}$$

Subsequently, we choose m ($m \le n$) principal components from existing n components. If this is the case, the saved information content is judged by

$$\theta = (\lambda_1 + \lambda_2 + \cdots + \lambda_m)/(\lambda_1 + \lambda_2 + \cdots + \lambda_n) \tag{3}$$

If θ is larger than a specified threshold, enough information has been saved after the feature extraction process. Thus, some redundant base models can be pruned. Through applying the PCA technique, we can obtain the appropriate numbers (e.g., m in this case) of base models for metamodel generation.

D. Neural-network-based metamodel generation

Once the appropriate numbers of base models are selected, applying the whole data set to these selected base models can produce a set of neural network output. These neural network outputs can formulate a new training set called as "meta-training set (*MT*)". In order to reflect the principle of metalearning, we utilize another neural network model to generate a metamodel by learning from the meta-training set (*MT*). That is, we use another neural network model to learn the relationship between base models by taking the outputs of the selected base models as input, combined with their targets or expected values. That is, the neural-network-based metamodel can be viewed as a nonlinear information processing system that can be represented as

$$\hat{f} = g(\hat{f}_1, \hat{f}_2, \cdots, \hat{f}_m) \tag{4}$$

where $(\hat{f}_1, \hat{f}_2, \cdots, \hat{f}_m)$ is the output of individual neural network predictors, $\hat{f}$ is the aggregated output, $g(\cdot)$ is nonlinear function determined by neural network. In this sense, neural network learning algorithm is used as a meta-learner (*ML*) shown in Fig. 1 for metamodel generation. Of course, other learning algorithm, e.g., support vector machine regression, can also be used as a meta-learner, as proposed by Lai et al. [12].

In summary, the proposed metamodel can actually be seen as an embedded neural network system with two-layer neural network models, as illustrated in Fig. 1. Suppose that there is an original data set *DS* which is divided into two parts: training set (*TR*) and testing set (*TS*). The training set is usually preprocessed by various sampling methods (e.g., interval sampling here) in order to generate diverse training subsets $\{TR_1, TR_2, \ldots, TR_n\}$ before they are applied to the first layer's neural network learners: $L_1, L_2, \ldots, L_n$. After training, the diverse neural network models (i.e., base models), $f_1, f_2, \ldots, f_n$ are generated. Through PCA-based pruning, a set of selected base model are obtained. Afterwards the whole training set *TR* was applied and the corresponding results $(\hat{f}_1, \hat{f}_2, \cdots, \hat{f}_m)$ of each selected base model in the first layer were used as inputs of the second layer neural network model. This neural network model in the second layer can be seen as a meta-learner (*ML*). By training, the neural-network-based metamodel can be generated. Using the testing set *TS*, the performance of the neural-network-based metamodel can be assessed.

3 Experimental Analysis

3.1 Research Data and Experiment Design

The research data used in this study is euro against dollar (EUR/USD) exchange rate. This data are daily and are obtained from Pacific Exchange Rate Service (http://fx.sauder.ubc.ca/), provided by Professor Werner Antweiler, University of British Columbia, Vancouver, Canada. The entire data set covers the period from January 1 1993 to December 31 2004 with a total of 3016 observations. The data sets are divided into two periods: the first period covers from January 4 1993 to December 31 2002 while the second period is from January 1 2003 to December 31 2004. The first period, which is assigned to in-sample estimation, is used to network learning and training. The second period is reserved for out-of-sample evaluation, which is for the testing purposes. In addition, the training data covered from January 1 1993 to December 31 2002 are divided into ten training subsets by varying the sampling interval (K = 1, 2, …, 10) for this experiment. Using these different training subsets, different neural network base models with different initial weights are presented. For neural network base models, a three-layer back-propagation neural network with 10 TANSIG neurons in the hidden layer and one PURELIN neuron in the output layer is used. The network training function is the TRAINLM. For the neural-network-based metamodel, a similar three-layer back-propagation neural network (BPNN) with 10 inputs neurons, 8 TANSIG neural in the second layer and one PURELIN neuron in the final layer is adopted for metamodel generation. Besides, the learning rate and momentum rate is set to 0.1 and 0.15. The accepted average squared error is 0.05 and the training epochs are 1800. The above parameters are obtained by trial and error.

To evaluate the performance of the proposed neural-network-based metamodel, several typical financial time series predication models, the autoregressive integrated moving average (ARIMA), individual BPNN with optimal learning rates [16-17] and support vector machine (SVM), are selected as benchmarks. In the individual BPNN model, a three-layer back-propagation neural network with 5 input nodes, 8 hidden nodes and 1 output nodes is used. The hidden nodes use sigmoid transfer function and the output node uses the linear transfer function. In the SVM, the kernel function is Gaussian function with regularization parameter C = 50 and σ^2 = 5. Similarly, the above parameters are obtained by trial and error.

For further comparison of the performance of neural network metamodel, two hybrid model proposed by [11] and [13], and three metalearning approaches, i.e., simple averaging based metamodel [14-15], weighted averaging based metamodel [14-15] and support vector machine regression (SVMR) based metamodel [12] are also used for foreign exchange rates predication. Actually, these two metalearning approaches are two neural network ensemble methods. For simple averaging approach, the final metamodel can be obtained by averaging the sum of each output of the neural network base models. Weighted averaging is where the final metamodel is calculated based on individual base model's performances and a weight attached to each base model's output. The gross weight is 1 and each base model is entitled to a portion of this gross weight according to their performance or diversity. For more details about these two metalearning techniques, please refer to [12, 14-15]. Finally, the root mean square error (*RMSE*) and direction change statistics (D_{stat}) [11] of financial time series are used as performance evaluation criteria in terms of testing set.

3.2 Experiment Results

According to the experiment design, different predication models with different parameters can be built. For comparison, the ARIMA model, individual BPNN, individual SVM, simple averaging based metamodel and weighted averaging based metalearning approach, are also performed. The results are reported in Table 1.

As can be seen from Table 1, we can find the following conclusions from the general view. First of all, all metamodels listed in this study perform better than individual models and hybrid models in terms of both *RMSE* and D_{stat}, indicating that the metamodel is a promising solution to the foreign exchange rates predication. The possible reason is that the metamodel can get more information from different base models and thus increase predication accuracy. Second, of the four metamodels, the SVMR based metamodel is the best in terms of *RMSE*. The possible reason is that SVMR can overcome some shortcomings of neural networks, such as local minima and overfitting, due to structural risk minimization principle of SVM. However, the neural network based metamodel perform the best from the D_{stat} perspective. The reason is still unknown and is worth exploring further. Third, the performance of two hybrid models seems to be better than those of three individual models. The main reason is their complementarities between the hybrid models. Fourth, the ARIMA model is the worst of the nine models for both *RMSE* and D_{stat} in this case. The inherent reason is that the ARIMA model is difficult to capture the nonlinear patterns of financial time series since ARIMA is a class of linear model and the financial time series contain much nonlinearity and irregularity. Finally, the results of D_{stat} are different from those of *RMSE* because two criteria are different. The former is a level estimation criterion, while the latter is a directional evaluation measurement.

Table 1. The prediction performance comparison with different approaches

Model	Detail	*RMSE*	Rank	D_{stat} (%)	Rank
Individual model	ARIMA	0.2242	9	57.86	9
	BPNN	0.1256	8	72.78	8
	SVM	0.1124	6	74.75	7
Hybrid model	ANN+GLAR [11]	0.1237	7	75.87	5
	ANN+ES [13]	0.1185	5	75.24	6
Metamodel	Simple averaging	0.1058	4	78.35	3
	Weighted averaging	0.0986	3	77.56	4
	Neural network	0.0813	2	87.44	1
	SVMR	0.0778	1	85.61	2

Focusing on the *RMSE* indicator, it is difficult to find that the SVMR based metamodel is the best, followed by neural network based metamodel, weighted averaging based metamodel and simple averaging based metamodel, the ARIMA model performs the worst. To summarize, the metamodels outperform the individual model.

However, the low *RMSE* does not necessarily mean that there is a high hit ratio of forecasting direction for foreign exchange movement direction prediction. Thus, the D_{stat} comparison is necessary. Focusing on D_{stat} of Table 1, we find the neural network based metamodel also performs much better than the other models according to the rank. Furthermore, from the business practitioners' point of view, D_{stat} is more important than *RMSE* because the former is an important decision criterion. From Table 1, the differences among different models are very significant. In this case, the D_{stat} for the single ARIMA model is 57.86%, for the two hybrid models, the D_{stat}s are 75.87% and 75.24%, respectively, and for the SVMR based metamodel, the D_{stat} is only 85.61%, while for the neural network based metamodel, D_{stat} reaches 87.44%.

4 Conclusions

In this study, a neural-network-based metalearning technique is proposed for exchange rates predication. In terms of the empirical results, we find that across different forecasting models for the test case of EUR/USD, the proposed neural network based metamodel performs the best, implying that the neural network metalearning technique can be used as a viable solution for foreign exchange rate prediction.

Acknowledgements

This work is partially supported by National Natural Science Foundation of China; Chinese Academy of Sciences; Key Research Institute of Humanities and Social Sciences in Hubei Province-Research Center of Modern Information Management and Strategic Research Grant of City University of Hong Kong (SRG No. 7001677).

References

1. McCulloch, W.S., Pitts, W.: A Logical Calculus of the Ideas Imminent in Nervous Activity. Bulletin and Mathematical Biophysics 5 (1943) 115-133
2. Hertz, J., Krogh, A., Palmer, R.G.: Introduction to the Theory of Neural Computation, Addison-Wesley, Reading, MA, 1989
3. Tsaih, R., Hsu, Y., Lai, C.C.: Forecasting S&P 500 Stock Index Futures with a Hybrid AI System. Decision Support Systems 23 (1998) 161-174
4. Yu, L., Lai, K. K., Wang S.Y., Huang, W.: A Bias-Variance-Complexity Trade-off Framework for Complex System Modeling. Lecture Notes in Computer Science 3980 (2006) 518-527
5. Chan, P., Stolfo, S.: Meta-learning for Multistrategy and Parallel Learning. Proceedings of the Second International Workshop on Multistrategy Learning (1993) 150–165
6. White, H.: Connectionist Nonparametric Regression: Multilayer Feedforward Networks Can Learn Arbitrary Mappings. Neural Networks 3 (1990) 535-549
7. Hornik, K., Stinchocombe, M., White, H.: Multilayer Feedforward Networks are Universal Approximators. Neural Networks 2 (1989) 359-366
8. Broomhead, D.S., Lowe, D.: Multivariable Functional Interpolation and Adaptive Networks. Complex Systems 2 (1988) 321-355
9. Mackay, D.J.C.: The Evidence Framework Applied to Classification Problems. Natural Computation 4 (1992) 720-736
10. Jolliffe, I.T.: Principal Component Analysis. Springer-Verlag, 1986
11. Yu, L., Wang, S.Y., Lai, K.K.: A Novel Nonlinear Ensemble Forecasting Model Incorporating GLAR and ANN for Foreign Exchange Rates. Computers & Operations Research 32 (2005) 2523-2541
12. Lai, K.K., Yu, L., Wang, S.Y., Huang, W.: A Novel Nonlinear Neural Network Ensemble Model for Financial Time Series Forecasting. Lecture Notes in Computer Science 3991 (2006) 790-793.
13. Lai, K.K., Yu, L., Wang, S.Y., Huang, W.: Hybridizing Exponential Smoothing and Neural Network for Financial Time Series Prediction. Lecture Notes in Computer Science 3994 (2006) 493-500.
14. Hansen, L.K., Salamon, P.: Neural Network Ensembles. IEEE Transactions on Pattern Analysis and Machine Intelligence 12 (1990) 993-1001
15. Benediktsson, J.A. Sveinsson, J.R. Ersoy, O.K. Swain, P.H.: Parallel Consensual Neural Networks. IEEE Transactions on Neural Networks 8 (1997) 54-64
16. Yu, L., Wang, S.Y., Lai, K.K.: A Novel Adaptive Learning Algorithm for Stock Market Prediction. Lecture Notes in Computer Science 3827 (2006) 443-452
17. Yu, L., Wang, S.Y., Lai, K.K.: An Adaptive BP Algorithm with Optimal Learning Rates and Directional Error Correction for Foreign Exchange Market Trend Prediction. Lecture Notes in Computer Science 3973 (2006) 498-503

Genetic Optimizations for Radial Basis Function and General Regression Neural Networks

Gül Yazıcı[1], Övünç Polat[2], and Tülay Yıldırım[2]

[1] Beko Elektronic, Beylikdüzü, Istanbul, Turkey
guly@beko.com.tr
[2] Electronics and Communications Engineering Department
Yıldız Technical University
Besiktas, Istanbul 34349, Turkey
{opolat, tulay}@yildiz.edu.tr

Abstract. The topology of a neural network has a significant importance on the network's performance. Although this is well known, finding optimal configurations is still an open problem. This paper proposes a solution to this problem for Radial Basis Function (RBF) networks and General Regression Neural Network (GRNN) which is a kind of radial basis networks. In such networks, placement of centers has significant effect on the performance of network. The centers and widths of the hidden layer neuron basis functions are coded in a chromosome and these two critical parameters are determined by the optimization using genetic algorithms. Thyroid, iris and escherichia coli bacteria datasets are used to test the algorithm proposed in this study. The most important advantage of this algorithm is getting succesful results by using only a small part of a benchmark. Some numerical solution results indicate the applicability of the proposed approach.

1 Introduction

The genetic algorithm (GA) is an optimization and search technique based on the principles of natural selection and Darwin's most famous principle of *survival of the fittest* [1]. By using genetic algorithms, many parameters of neural networks can be determined such as, weight, function and hidden layer. In this study, genetic algorithms are used for determining the spread value and the positions of centers in radial basis networks.

In the literature, various studies can be found about RBF networks and genetic algorithms. The study [2], presents a new crossover operator that allows for some control over the competing conventions problem by using genetic algorithm on the configuration of RBF networks. Another study [3], discusses how RBF networks can have their parameters defined by GA. The proposed GA is applied to a benchmark problem, a Hermite polynomial approximation. In [4], they describe a study on voice conversion using GA to train the hidden layer of RBF network, which is expected to help improve the preference of converted speech for the target speaker's charasteristics.

This paper looks into the problem of learning of the centers and spread value in RBF and GRNN networks to get the best solution for classification problem, by using

A. Gelbukh and C.A. Reyes-Garcia (Eds.): MICAI 2006, LNAI 4293, pp. 348 – 356, 2006.

genetic algorithms. Next section gives an overview of these network structures. In Section 3, a summary of genetic algorithm is presented. In Section 4, simulation about how centers are selected is mentioned, some experimental results and graphics are given and their implications are also discussed. Last section summarises and concludes the paper.

2 Overview of Neural Network Structures

2.1 Radial Basis Function Neural Networks

RBF network is a class of hybrid connectionist models. Whilst they are essentially three-layer feedforward networks, RBF networks differ from classical multi-layer perceptrons in three significant ways: there is only one set of trainable weights, from the hidden layer to the output layer; the nodes' activation functions are non-standard and learning is affected by both supervised and unsupervised techniques [5].

In a RBF network, the nodes of the hidden layer encode a set of well positioned centroids, each representing one or part of a class. RBF networks have found wide applicability in traditional classification problems as well as in modern fuzzy control systems. As with other neural network models, experience shows that the performance of RBF networks is greatly affected by their topology, that is, the choice of centroids making up the hidden layer. Too many centroids lead to over-fitting, while too few centroids may prove insufficient to capture intrinsic class divisions adequately. In general, the network's classiffication accuracy is influenced primarily by the number of centroids used to represent each class and the position of each centroid within its class. The construction of RBF neural network involving three layers is shown in Figure 1 [5].

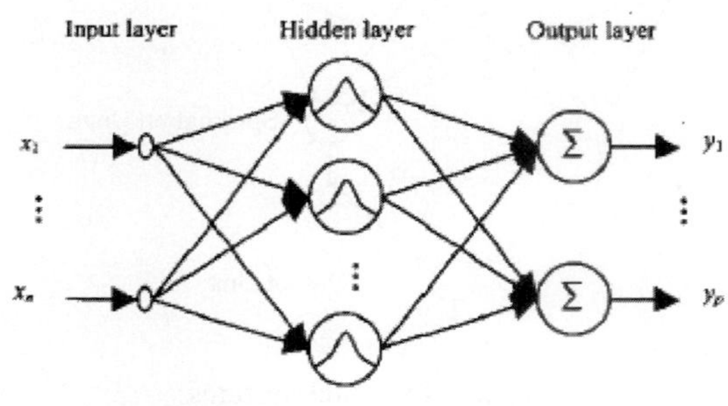

Fig. 1. General structure of RBF neural network

2.2 General Regression Neural Network (GRNN)

The General Regression Neural Network which is a kind of radial basis networks was developed by Specht [6] and is a powerful regression tool with a dynamic network structure. The network training speed is extremely fast. Due to the simplicity of the network structure and its implementation, it has been widely applied to a variety of fields including image processing. Specht [7] addressed the basic concept of inclusion of clustering techniques in the GRNN model.

Figure 2 shows a schematic depiction of the four layers GRNN. The first, or input layer, stores an input vector x. The second is the pattern layer which computes the distances $D(x, x^i)$ between the incoming pattern x and stored patterns x^i. The pattern nodes output the quantities $W(x, x^i)$. The third is the summation layer. This layer computes N_j, the sums of the products of $W(x, x^i)$ and the associated known output component y_i. The summation layer also has a node to compute S, the sum of all $W(x, x^i)$. Finally, the fourth layer divides N_j by S to produce the estimated output component y'_j, that is a localized average of the stored output patterns. The standard distance and weight functions are given by the following two equations, respectively:

$$D(x_1, x_2) = \sum_{k=1}^{n} \left(\frac{x_{1k} - x_{2k}}{\sigma_k} \right)^2 \tag{1}$$

$$W(x, x^i) = e^{-D(x,x^i)} \tag{2}$$

In Eqn 1, each input variable has its own sigma value (σ_k) [8]. This formulation is different from Specht's [6] original work where he used a single sigma value for all input variables.

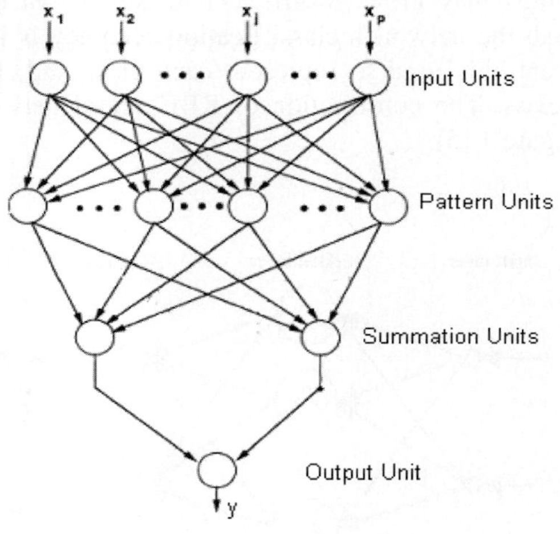

Fig. 2. GRNN Architectures

3 Genetic Algorithms

Genetic algorithms are powerful stochastic and optimization (soft computing) techniques based on principles from evolution theory. Genetic algorithms are proven more effective in multi-peak optimization problems. Algorithm is started with a set of solution (represented by chromosomes) called subpopulation. Solutions from one subpopulation are taken and used to form a new subpopulation by a hope that the new population will be better, at least not worse than the old one [9]. The basic steps of genetic algorithm can be described as follows:

Step 1: Randomly generate an initial population

Step 2: Compute the fitness of each chromosome in the current population

Step 3: Create new chromosome by mating current chromosomes, applying mutation and recombination as the parent chromosomes mate

Step 4: Substitute these new chromosomes for some bad chromosomes in the current population

Step 5: If the end condition is satisfied, then stop; otherwise go to step 2. [10]

4 RBF-Genetic and GRNN-Genetic Optimizations

In this study, genetic algorithm is used to optimize RBF and GRNN networks to classify iris flower, thyroid diease and escherichia coli bacteria datasets. Centers of RBF and GRNN network and spread values are determined by genetic algorithms. This treatise aims to classify the test set with high accuracy while minumum number of instance is chosen from the train set.

Firstly, the initial population of individuals is generated random. Each bit of chromosome is called “gene”. The fitness, which is a measure of adaptation to environment, is calculated for each individual. Then, “selection” operation leaving individuals to next generation is performed based on fitness value, and then “crossover” and “mutation” are performed on the selected individuals to generate new population by transforming parent’s chromosomes into offspring’s ones. This procedure is continued until the end condition is satisfied. This algorithm is conforming to the mechanism of evolution, in which the genetic information changes for every generation and the individuals which adapt to environment better survive preferentially [11].

The maximum and minimum values of the parameters which will be optimised are defined in the algorithm whilst centers should be perceived as the number of lines in dataset.

4.1 Iris Data Benchmark

Three different types of iris plant are classified with according to its 3 output value. There are 150 instances divided into 3 classes and for this dataset only 10 instances per each class are enough for whole training set. Genetic optimization supply to determine which centers should be chosen to get the best result. When the algorithm is simulated by the training set and tested by the whole dataset, 149 of instances are classified correctly.

In Table 1, number of correctly classified dataset can be seen for both RBF and GRNN networks. Simulations were realized by using Matlab 7.0.

In Figure 3, variation of accuracy according to generation in the result of optimization process by genetic algorithms can be seen. Triangles expressed the

Table 1. Number of correctly classified instances for Iris dataset

Iris	Class 1	Class 2	Class 3
RBF-GA	50	49	50
RBF	43	43	25
GRNN-GA	50	49	50
GRNN	50	41	39

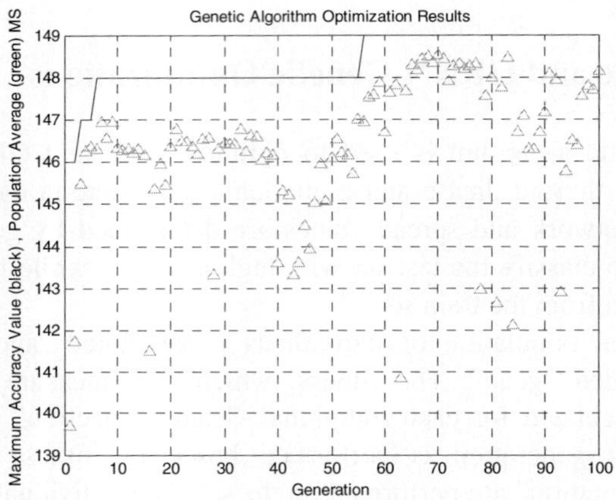

Fig. 3. Iris flower-Optimization results for RBF

population average and lines mean maximum accuracy value. For this algorithm, generation number is fixed as 100.

4.2 Thyroid Data Benchmark

Thyroid data set has 215 (150, 35, 30) instances divided into 3 classes. 25, 7 and 3 instances are taken from classes by order. In Table 2, number of correctly classified data set can be seen when 35 instances for train and 180 instances for test set are taken for both RBF and GRNN networks. For this algorithm, generation number is fixed as 300. In Figure 4, variation of accuracy according to generation in the result of RBF optimization for thyroid data is given.

Table 2. Number of correct classified instances for Thyroid dataset

Thyroid	Class 1	Class 2	Class 3
RBF-GA	148	34	23
RBF	150	0	2
GRNN-GA	149	34	25
GRNN	147	23	20

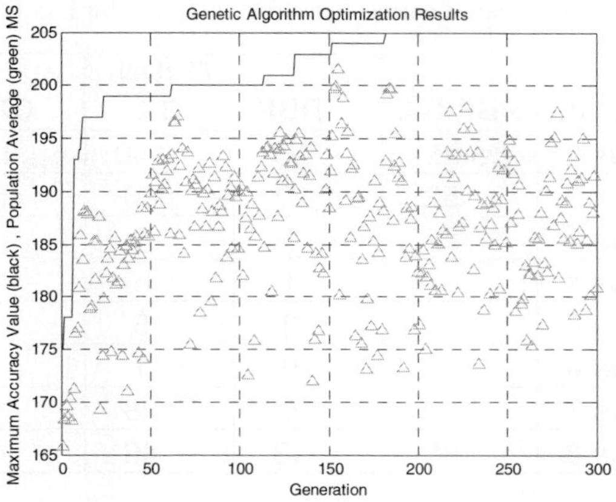

Fig. 4. Thyroid disease-Optimization results for RBF

4.3 Escherichia Coli Data Benchmark

E.coli dataset has 336 instances divided into 8 classes. Each instance is identified by a sequence name, eight attributes [12] (where mcg:McGeoh's method for signal sequence recognition, gvh:Von Heijne's method for signal sequence recognition, gvh:Von Heijne's signal peptisade II consensus sequence score, chg: presence of charge on N-terminus of predicted lipoproteins, aac:score of discrimant analysis of the amino acid content of outer membrane and periplasmic proteins, alm1:score of the ALOM membrane spanning region prediction program after excluding putative cleavable signal regions from the sequence.) and a class name [13]. Table 3 shows the class distribution of the dataset. Using these training and test data distribution, number of correct classified instances is given in Table 4. RBF optimization by genetic algorithm can be seen in Figure 5 for E.coli bacteria. For this algorithm, generation number is fixed as 300.

Table 3. The eight classes of E.coli bacteria and their data numbers

Class	Total Data Number	Training Data Number	Test Data Number
cp	143	23	120
im	77	17	60
pp	52	12	40
imU	35	5	30
om	20	3	17
omL	5	2	3
imL	2	1	1
imS	2	1	1

Table 4. Number of correct classified instances for E.coli dataset

E.COLI	RBF-GA	RBF	GRNN-GA	GRNN
Class 1	122	95	140	131
Class 2	52	27	60	58
Class 3	0	0	1	1
Class 4	7	1	16	15
Class 5	4	2	5	5
Class 6	1	0	1	1
Class 7	12	5	28	16
Class 8	36	43	46	44

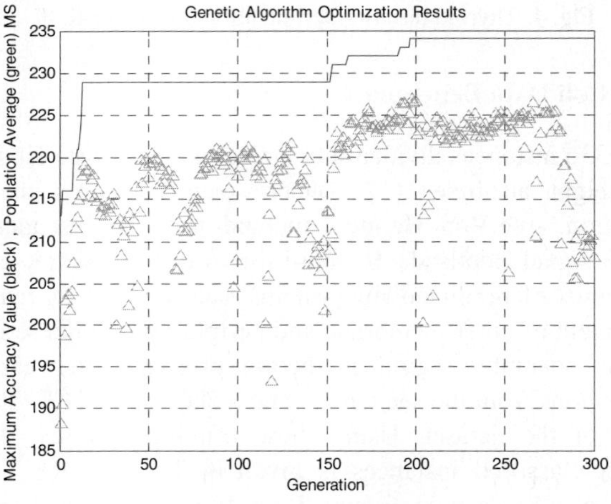

Fig. 5. E.coli bacterium-Optimization Results for RBF

Table 5 presents the test accuracies of iris, thyroid and E.coli benchmarks when these datasets are tested for RBF-GA/RBF and GRNN-GA/GRNN networks. Optimized spread values for RBF and GRNN are also shown in this table.

Table 5. Comparing test accuracies with RBF-GA and RBF

	RBF-GA (%)	RBF (%)	Spread Value (RBF)	GRNN-GA (%)	GRNN (%)	Spread Value (GRNN)
Iris	99.1	67.5	523	99.1	83.3	0.58
Tyroid	89.4	61.5	7	96.1	86.1	3.48
E.coli	62.5	40	844	85.6	76.1	0.07

These results obviously clarify the advantage of RBF-GA and GRNN-GA network. The networks which optimized by genetic algorithms, give much more efficient results especially when they simulated by rough datasets like tyhroid disease and eschericia coli bacterium benchmarks.

5 Conclusion

This paper investigates the performance of RBF and GRNN networks optimized by Genetic Algorithm. Iris flower, thyroid disease and escherichia coli bacteria benchmark datasets are used to compare the success between RBF-GA/RBF and GRNN-GA/GRNN methods. The final conclusion is that RBF and GRNN networks with GA approach is more effective than using only RBF and GRNN. Nevertheless, GA took a long training time to achieve these results. However, for a large number of applications and rough datasets, the results obtained suggest that the genetic approach is an attracive solution for the design of efficient artificial neural networks.

References

1. Marco, N., Désidéri, J., Lanteri, S. : Multi Objective Optimization in CFD by Genetic Algorithms, Institut National De Recherce Informatique Et En Automatique. (1999)
2. Barreto, A.M.S., et al. : Growing Compact RBF Networks Using a Genetic Algorithm. 7th Brazilian Symposium on Neural Networks, 61-66. (2002)
3. de Lacerda, E.G.M., de Carvalho, A.C.P.L.F., Ludermir, T.B., : Evolutionary Optimization of RBF Networks. Sixth Brazilian Symposium, 219-224. (2000)
4. Zuo, G., Liu, W., Ruan, X., : Genetic Algorithm Based RBF Neural Network for Voice Conversion. Proceedings of the 5" World Congress on Intelligent Control and Automation. June 15-19, Hangzhou. P.R. China. (2004)
5. Burdsall, B., Carrier, C. G.,.: GA-RBF: A Self-Optimising RBF Network. Proceedings of the Third International Conference on Artificial Neural Networks and Genetic Algorithms (ICANNGA'97), pages 348--351. Springer-Verlag. (1997)
6. D. F. Specht: A general regression neural network. IEEE Trans. Neural Networks, vol. 2, pp. 568–576, (Nov. 1991).
7. D. F. Specht,: Enhancements to probabilistic neural network. in Proc. Int. Joint Conf. Neural Network, vol. 1, pp. 761–768, (1991).
8. Heimes, F.; van Heuveln, B.; The normalized radial basis function neural network. Systems, Man, and Cybernetics. 1998 IEEE International Conference on Volume 2, 11–14 Oct. 1998 Page(s):1609 – 1614.
9. Goldberg D. E. : Genetic algorithm in search, optimization, and machine learning. Addison-wesley. (1989)
10. Zhang, Q., He, X., Liu, J.,:"RBF Network Based On Genetic Algorithm Optimization For Nonlinear Time Series Prediction", ISCAS '03 Proceedings of the 2003 International Symposium on Circuits and Systems, vol.5, pp.693-696.
11. Hatanaka, T., Kondo, N., Uosaki, K., (2003) "Multi-Objective Structure Selection for Radial Basis Function Networks Based on Genetic Algorithm", The 2003 Congress on Evolutionary Computation CEC '03. Vol.2, pp.1095- 1100.

12. Avci, M., Yıldırım, T., (2002) "Classification of Escherichia Coli Bacteria by Artificial Neural Networks", Proc. of the IEEE International Symposium on Intelligent Systems, Varna, Bulgaria, Vol: 3, pp. 16-20.
13. Bolat, B., Yıldırım, T., (2004), "A Data Selection Method for Probalistic Neural Networks", Journal of Electrical&Electronic Engineering, Istanbul, Vol:4, No:2.

Complexity of Alpha-Beta Bidirectional Associative Memories

María Elena Acevedo-Mosqueda, Cornelio Yáñez-Márquez, and Itzamá López-Yáñez

Centro de Investigación en Computación, Instituto Politécnico Nacional, Laboratorio de Inteligencia Artificial, Av. Juan de Dios Bátiz s/n, México, D. F., 07738, México
eacevedo@ipn.mx, cyanez@cic.ipn.mx, ilopezb05@sagitario.cic.ipn.mx

Abstract. Most models of Bidirectional Associative Memories intend to achieve that all trained patterns correspond to stable states; however, this has not been possible. Also, none of the former models has been able to recall all the trained patterns. A new model which appeared recently, called Alpha-Beta Bidirectional Associative Memory (BAM), recalls 100% of the trained patterns, without error. Also, the model is non iterative and has no stability problems. In this work the analysis of time and space complexity of the Alpha-Beta BAM is presented.

Keywords: Bidirectional associative memories, Alpha-Beta associative memories, perfect recall, complexity.

1 Introduction

The first bidirectional associative memory (BAM), introduced by Kosko [1], was the base of many models presented later. Some of this models substituted the learning rule for an exponential rule [2-4]; others used the method of multiple training and dummy addition in order to reach a greater number of stable states [5], trying to eliminate spurious states. With the same purpose, linear programming techniques [6] and the descending gradient method [7-8] have been used, besides genetic algorithms [9] and BAM with delays [10-11]. Other models of non iterative bidirectional associative memories exist, such as morphological BAM [12] and Feedforward BAM [13]. All these models have arisen to solve the problem of low pattern recall capacity shown by the BAM of Kosko. However, none has been able to recall all the trained patterns. Also, these models demand the fulfillment of some specific conditions, such as a certain Hamming distance between patterns, solvability by linear programming, orthogonality between patterns, among others.

The model of bidirectional associative memory described in this paper is based on the Alpha-Beta associative memories [14], is not an iterative process, and does not present stability problems [19]. Pattern recall capacity of the Alpha-Beta BAM is maximal,

A. Gelbukh and C.A. Reyes-Garcia (Eds.): MICAI 2006, LNAI 4293, pp. 357 – 366, 2006.

being $2^{\min(n,m)}$, where n and m are the input and output patterns dimension, respectively. Also, it always shows perfect pattern recall without imposing any condition.

It is possible to calculate the time complexity presented by this model since the algorithm does not require convergence, unlike most of the formerly mentioned models.

In section 2 we present the Alpha-Beta autoassociative memories, base of the new model of BAM, and the theoretical sustentation of the Alpha-Beta BAM. In section 3 the complexity of the model is presented. Conclusions follow in section 4.

2 The Alpha-Beta BAM Model

In this section the new model of bidirectional associative memory is described [19]. However, since it is based on the Alpha-Beta autoassociative memories, a summary of this model will be given before presenting the new model of bidirectional associative memory.

2.1 Alpha-Beta Associative Memories

Basic concepts about associative memories were established three decades ago in [15-17], nonetheless here we use the concepts, results and notation introduced in the Yáñez-Márquez's PhD Thesis [14]. An associative memory **M** is a system that relates input and output patterns, as follows: **x**→**M**→**y** with **x** and **y** the input and output pattern vectors, respectively. **M** is represented by a matrix whose *ij*-th component is m_{ij}. Memory **M** is generated from an *a priori* finite set of known associations, known as the fundamental set of associations.

If μ is an index, the fundamental set is represented as: $\left\{\left(x^{\mu}, y^{\mu}\right) \mid \mu = 1,2,\ldots,p\right\}$ where $\mathbf{x}^{\mu} \in A^{n}$ and $\mathbf{y}^{\mu} \in A^{m}$ with p the cardinality of the set. The patterns that form the fundamental set are called fundamental patterns. If it holds that $x^{\mu} = y^{\mu}, \forall \mu \in \{1,2,\ldots,p\}$, **M** is *autoassociative*, otherwise it is *heteroassociative*; in this case it is possible to establish that $\exists \mu \in \{1,2,\ldots,p\}$ for which $x^{\mu} \neq y^{\mu}$. A distorted version of a pattern x^{k} to be recuperated will be denoted as $\tilde{x}^{k}$. If when feeding a distorted version of x^{ϖ} with $\varpi = \{1,2,\ldots,p\}$ to an associative memory **M**, it happens that the output corresponds exactly to the associated pattern y^{ϖ}, we say that recuperation is perfect.

The Alpha-Beta associative memories are of two kinds and are able to operate in two different modes. The operator α is useful at the learning phase while the operator β is the basis for the pattern recall phase. The heart of the mathematical tools used in the Alpha-Beta model, are two binary operators designed specifically for these memories. These operators are defined as follows: First, we define the sets $A=\{0,1\}$ and $B=\{0,1,2\}$, then the operators α and β are defined in tabular form:

$\alpha : A \times A \rightarrow B$

x	y	$\alpha(x,y)$
0	0	1
0	1	0
1	0	2
1	1	1

$\beta : B \times A \rightarrow A$

x	y	$\beta(x,y)$
0	0	0
0	1	0
1	0	0
1	1	1
2	0	1
2	1	1

The sets A and B, the α and β operators, along with the usual $\wedge$ (minimum) y $\vee$ (maximum) operators, form the algebraic system $(A, B, \alpha, \beta, \wedge, \vee)$ which is the mathematical basis for the Alpha-Beta associative memories.

Below are shown some characteristics of Alpha-Beta autoassociative memories:

1. The fundamental set takes the form $\{(\mathbf{x}^\mu, \mathbf{x}^\mu) \mid \mu = 1, 2, ..., p\}$.
2. Both input and output fundamental patterns are of the same dimension, denoted by n.
3. The memory is a square matrix, for both kinds, $\mathbf{V}$ and $\mathbf{\Lambda}$. If $\mathbf{x}^\mu \in A^n$ then

$$v_{ij} = \bigvee_{\mu=1}^{p} \alpha\left(x_i^\mu, x_j^\mu\right) \quad \text{and} \quad \lambda_{ij} = \bigwedge_{\mu=1}^{p} \alpha\left(x_i^\mu, x_j^\mu\right)$$

and according to α: A x $A \rightarrow B$, we have that v_{ij} and $\lambda_{ij} \in B$, $\forall i \in \{1, 2, ..., n\}$, $\forall j \in \{1, 2, ..., n\}$.

In the recall phase, when a pattern $\mathbf{x}^\mu$ is presented to memories $\mathbf{V}$ and $\mathbf{\Lambda}$, the i-th components of recalled patterns are:

$$\left(\mathbf{V} \Delta_\beta \mathbf{x}^\omega\right)_i = \bigwedge_{j=1}^{n} \beta(v_{ij}, x_j^\omega) \quad \text{and} \quad \left(\mathbf{\Lambda} \nabla_\beta \mathbf{x}^\omega\right)_i = \bigvee_{j=1}^{n} \beta(\lambda_{ij}, x_j^\omega)$$

2.2 Alpha-Beta Bidirectional Associative Memories

The model proposed in this paper has been named Alpha-Beta BAM since Alpha-Beta associative memories, both *max* and *min*, play a central role in the model design. In this work we will assume that Alpha-Beta associative memories have a fundamental set denoted by $\{(\mathbf{x}^\mu, \mathbf{y}^\mu) \mid \mu = 1, 2, \ldots, p\}$ $\mathbf{x}^\mu \in A^n$ and $\mathbf{y}^\mu \in A^m$, with $A = \{0, 1\}$, $n \in \mathbf{Z}^+$, $p \in \mathbf{Z}^+$, $m \in \mathbf{Z}^+$ and $1 < p \leq \min(2^n, 2^m)$. Also, it holds that all input patterns are different; M that is $\mathbf{x}^\mu = \mathbf{x}^\xi$ if and only if $\mu = \xi$. If $\forall \mu \in \{1, 2, \ldots p\}$ it holds that $\mathbf{x}^\mu = \mathbf{y}^\mu$, the Alpha-Beta memory will be *autoassociative*; if on the contrary, the former affirmation is negative, that is $\exists \mu \in \{1, 2, \ldots, p\}$ for which it holds that $\mathbf{x}^\mu \neq \mathbf{y}^\mu$, then the Alpha-Beta memory will be *heteroassociative*.

Definition 1 (One-Hot). *Let the set A be* $A = \{0, 1\}$ *and* $p \in \mathbf{Z}^+$, $p > 1$, $k \in \mathbf{Z}^+$, *such that* $1 \leq k \leq p$. *The k-th one-hot vector of p bits is defined as vector* $h^k \in A^p$ *for which* *it holds that the k-th component is* $h_k^k = 1$ *and the ret of the components are* $h_j^k = 0$, $\forall j \neq k, 1 \leq j \leq p$.

Definition 2 (Zero-Hot). *Let the set A be A =* $\{0, 1\}$ *and* $p \in \mathbf{Z}^+$, $p > 1$, $k \in \mathbf{Z}^+$, *such that* $1 \leq k \leq p$. *The k-th zero-hot vector of p bits is defined as vector* $\overline{\mathbf{h}}^k \in A^p$ *for which it holds that the k-th component is* $h_k^k = 0$ *and the ret of the components are* $h_j^k = 1$, $\forall j \neq k, 1 \leq j \leq p$.

Definition 3 (Expansion vectorial transform). *Let the set A be A =* $\{0, 1\}$ *and* $n \in \mathbf{Z}^+$,*y* $m \in \mathbf{Z}^+$. *Given two arbitrary vectors* $\mathbf{x} \in A^n$ *and* $\mathbf{e} \in A^m$, *the expansion vectorial transform of order m,* $\tau^e : A^n \to A^{n+m}$, *is defined as* $\tau^e(\mathbf{x}, \mathbf{e}) = \mathbf{X} \in A^{n+m}$, *a vector whose components are:* $X_i = x_i$ *for* $1 \leq i \leq n$ *and* $X_i = e_i$ *for* $n + 1 \leq i \leq n + m$.

Definition 4 (Contraction vectorial transform). *Let the set A be A =* $\{0, 1\}$ *and* $n \in \mathbf{Z}^+$,*y* $m \in \mathbf{Z}^+$ *such that* $1 \leq m < n$. *Given one arbitrary vector* $\mathbf{X} \in A^{n+m}$, *the contraction vectorial transform of order m,* $\tau^c : A^{n+m} \to A^m$, *is defined as* $\tau^c(X, m) = \mathbf{c} \in A^m$, *a vector whose components are:* $c_i = X_{i+n}$ *for* $1 \leq i < m$.

In both directions, the model is made up by two stages, as shown in figure 1.

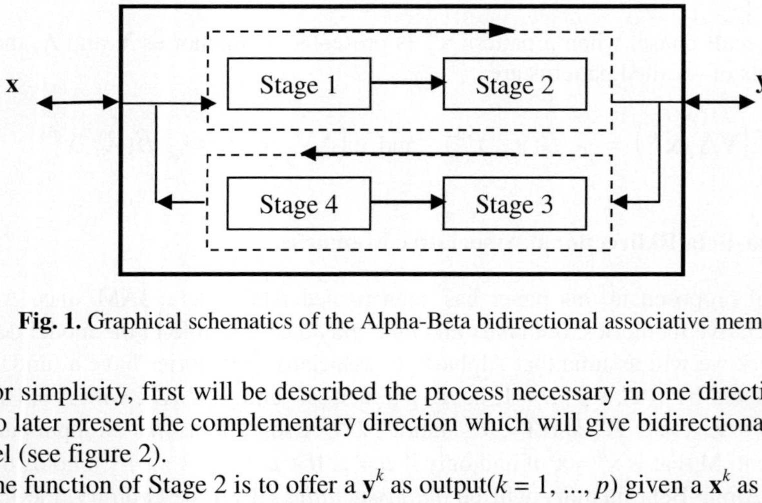

Fig. 1. Graphical schematics of the Alpha-Beta bidirectional associative memory

For simplicity, first will be described the process necessary in one direction, in order to later present the complementary direction which will give bidirectionality to the model (see figure 2).

The function of Stage 2 is to offer a $\mathbf{y}^k$ as output($k = 1, ..., p$) given a $\mathbf{x}^k$ as input.

Now we assume that as input to Stage 2 we have one element of a set of p orthonormal vectors. Recall that the *Linear Associator* has perfect recall when it works with orthonormal vectors. In this work we use a variation of the *Linear Associator* in order to obtain $\mathbf{y}^k$, parting from a *one-hot* vector $\mathbf{v}^k$ in its k-th coordinate.

For the construction of the modified Linear Associator, its learning phase is skipped and a matrix **M** representing the memory is built. Each column in this matrix corresponds to each output pattern $\mathbf{y}^\mu$. In this way, when matrix **M** is operated with a one-hot vector $\mathbf{v}^k$, the corresponding $\mathbf{y}^k$ will always be recalled.

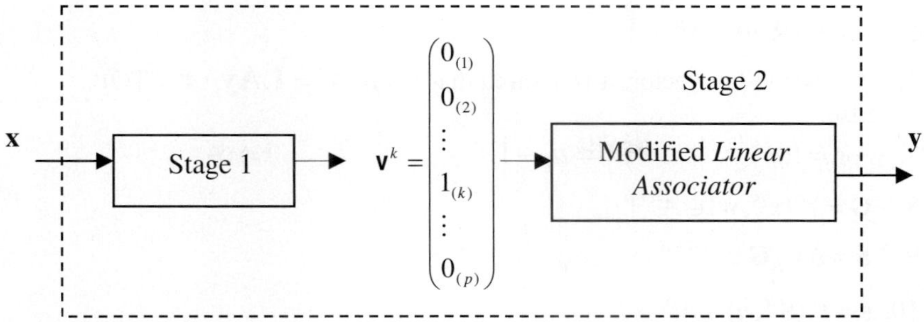

Fig. 2. Schematics of the process done in the direction from x to y. Here are shown only Stage 1 and Stage 2. Notice that $v_k^k = 1,\ \ v_i^k = 0\ \ \forall i \neq k\,,\ 1 \leq i \leq p,\ 1 \leq k \leq p$.

The task of Stage 1 is: given a $\mathbf{x}^k$ or a noisy version of it ($\tilde{\mathbf{x}}^k$), the *one-hot* vector $\mathbf{v}^k$ must be obtained without ambiguity and with no condition. In its learning phase, stage 1 has the following algorithm:

Step 1. For k=1:p $\quad \mathbf{X}^k = \tau^e(\mathbf{x}^k, \mathbf{h}^k)$

Step 2. For i=1:n and j=1: n

$$v_{ij} = \bigvee_{\mu=1}^{p} \alpha\left(X_i^\mu, X_j^\mu\right)$$

Step 3. For k=1:p $\quad \overline{\mathbf{X}}^k = \tau^e(\mathbf{x}^k, \overline{\mathbf{h}}^k)$

Step 4. For i=1:n and j=1: n

$$\lambda_{ij} = \bigwedge_{\mu=1}^{p} \alpha\left(\overline{X}_i^\mu, \overline{X}_j^\mu\right)$$

Step 5. Create modified Linear Associator $\mathbf{LAy} = \begin{bmatrix} y_1^1 & y_1^2 & \cdots & y_1^p \\ y_2^1 & y_2^2 & \cdots & y_2^p \\ \vdots & \vdots & \cdots & \vdots \\ y_n^1 & y_n^2 & \cdots & y_n^p \end{bmatrix}$

Recall phase is described through the following algorithm:

Step 1. Present, at the input to stage 1, a vector from the fundamental set $\mathbf{x}^\mu \in A^n$, for some index $\mu \in \{1, ..., p\}$.

Step 2. $\mathbf{u} = \sum_{i=1}^{p} \mathbf{h}^i$

Step 3. $\mathbf{F} = \tau^e(\mathbf{x}^\mu, \mathbf{u}) \in A^{n+p}$

Step 4. $\mathbf{R} = \mathbf{V} \Delta_\beta \mathbf{F} \in A^{n+p}$

Step 5. $\mathbf{r} = \tau^c(\mathbf{R}, n) \in A^p$

Step 6. If $\mathbf{r}$ is one-hot vector, it is assured that $k = \mu$, $\mathbf{y}^\mu = \mathbf{LAy} \cdot \mathbf{r}$. STOP.
Else:

Step 7. For i=1:p $\quad w_i = u_i - 1$

Step 8. $\mathbf{G} = \tau^e(\mathbf{x}^\mu, \mathbf{w}) \in A^{n+p}$

Step 9. $\mathbf{S} = \Lambda \nabla_\beta \mathbf{G} \in A^{n+p}$

Step 10. $\mathbf{s} = \tau^c(\mathbf{S}^\mu, n) \in A^p$

Step 11. If $\mathbf{s}$ is zero-hot vector then it is assured that $k = \mu$, $\mathbf{y}^\mu = \mathbf{LAy} \cdot \bar{\mathbf{s}}$, where $\bar{\mathbf{s}}$ is the negated vector of $\mathbf{s}$. STOP.
Else:

Step 12. Do operation $\mathbf{r} \wedge \bar{\mathbf{s}}$, where $\wedge$ is the symbol of the logical AND operator. $\mathbf{y}^\mu = \mathbf{LAy} \cdot (\mathbf{r} \wedge \bar{\mathbf{s}})$. STOP.

The process in the contrary direction, which is presenting pattern $\mathbf{y}^k$ (k = 1, ..., p) as input to the Alpha-Beta BAM and obtaining its corresponding $\mathbf{x}^k$, is very similar to the one described above. The task of Stage 3 is to obtain a one-hot vector $\mathbf{v}^k$ given a $\mathbf{y}^k$. Stage 4 is a modified Linear Associator built in similar fashion to the one in Stage 2.

3 The Alpha-Beta BAM Algorithm Complexity

An algorithm is a finite set of precise instructions for the realization of a calculation or to solve a problem [18]. In general, it is accepted that an algorithm provides a satisfactory solution when it produces a correct answer and is efficient. One measure of efficiency is the time required by the computer in order to solve a problem using a given algorithm. A second measure of efficiency is the amount of memory required to implement the algorithm when the input data are of a given size.

The analysis of the time required to solve a problem of a particular size implies finding the *time complexity* of the algorithm. The analysis of the memory needed by the computer implies finding the *space complexity* of the algorithm.

In the following sections the complexity presented by the Alpha-Beta BAM algorithm is described. In the first part space complexity is analyzed, while time complexity is boarded in the second part.

3.1 Space Complexity

In order to store the p **x** patterns, a matrix is needed. This matrix will have dimensions p x $(n+p)$. Input patterns and the added vectors, both *one-hot* and *zero-hot*, are stored in the same matrix. Since $\mathbf{x} \in \{0, 1\}$, then this values can be represented by character variables, taking 1 byte each. The total amount of bytes will be: Bytes_x = $p(n+p)$.

A matrix is needed to store the p **y** patterns. This matrix will have dimensions $p.(m+p)$. Output patterns and the added vectors, both *one-hot* and *zero-hot*, are stored in the same matrix. Since $\mathbf{y} \in \{0, 1\}$, then this values can be represented by character variables, taking 1 byte each. The total amount of bytes will be: Bytes_y = $p(m+ p)$.

During the learning phase, 4 matrices are needed: two for the Alpha-Beta autoassociative memories of type max, Vx and Vy, and two more for the Alpha-Beta autoassociative memories of type min, Λx y Λy. Vx and Λx have dimensions of $(n+p)$ x $(n+p)$, while Vy and Λy have dimensions $(m+p)$ x $(m+p)$. Given that these matrices hold only positive integer numbers, then the values of their components can be represented with character variables of 1 byte of size. The total amount of bytes will be: Bytes_VxΛx = $2(n+p)^2$ and Bytes_VyΛy = $2(m+p)^2$.

A vector is used to hold the recalled *one-hot* vector, which dimension is p. Since the components of any one-hot vector take the values of 0 and 1, these values can be represented by character variables, occupying 1 byte each. The total amount of bytes will be: Bytes_vr = p.

The total amount of bytes required to implement an Alpha-Beta BAM is:

Total = Bytes_x + Bytes_y + Bytes_VxΛx + Bytes_VyΛy + Bytes_vr
Total = $p\ (n + m + 2p) + 2[(n+p)^2 + (m+p)^2] + p$

3.2 Time Complexity

The time complexity of an algorithm can be expressed in terms of the number of operations used by the algorithm when the input has a particular size. The operations used to measure time complexity can be integer compare, integer addition, integer division, variable assignation, logical comparison, or any other elemental operation.

The following is defined:

EO: elemental operation
n_pares: number of associeted pairs of patterns
n: dimension of the patterns plus the addition of the *one-hot* or *zero-hot* vectors

The recalling phase algorithm will be analyzed, since this is the portion of the whole algorithm that requires a greater number of elemental operations.

Recalling Phase

```
u = 0; (1)
while(u<n_pares) (2)
    i = 0; (3)
    while(i<n) (4)
        j = 0; (5)
        while(j<n) (6)
            if(y[u][i]==0 && y[u][j]==0) (7)
                t=1; (8)
            else if(y[u][i]==0 && y[u][j]==1) (9a)
                t=0;
            else if(y[u][i]==1 && y[u][j]==0) (9b)
                t=2;
            else        t=1;
            if(u==0) (10)
```

```
                        Vy[i][j]=t; (11)
                else
                        if(Vy[i][j]<t) (12)
                                Vy[i][j]=t; (13)
                j++; (14)
        i++; (15)
    u++; (16)
```

(1) 1 EO, assignation
(2) n_pares EO, comparison
(3) n_pares EO, assignation
(4) n_pares*n EO, comparison
(5) n_pares*n EO, assignation
(6) n_pares*n*n EO, comparison
(7a) n_pares*n*n EO, comparison: y[u][i]==0
(7b) n_pares*n*n EO, relational operation AND: &&
(7c) n_pares*n*n EO, comparison: y[u][j]==0
(8) There is allways an allocation to variable t, n_pares*n*n EO
(9) Both if sentences (a and b) have the same probability of beeing executed, n_pares*n*(n/2)
(10) n_pares*n*n EO, comparison
(11) This allocation is done only once, 1 EO
(12) (n_pares*n*n)-1 EO, comparison
(13) Allocation has half probability of beeing run, n_pares*n*(n/2)
(14) n_pares*n*n EO increment
(15) n_pares*n EO, increment
(16) n_pares EO, increment

The total number of EO's is: Total = 1+n_pares($3+3n+9n^2$).

From the total of EO's obtained, n_pares is fixed with value 50, resulting in a function only dependant on the size of the patterns: $f(n) = 1+50(3+3n+9n^2)$.

In order to analyze the feasibility of the algorithm we need to understand how fast the mentioned function grows as the value of n rises. Therefore, the Big-O notation [18], shown below, will be used.

Let f and g be functions from a set of integer or real numbers to a set of real numbers. It is said that $f(x)$ is $O(g(x))$ if there exist two constants C and k such that:

$$|f(x)| \leq C\,|g(x)| \quad \text{when } x > k$$

The number of elemental operations obtained from our algorithm was:

$$f(n) = 1+50(3+3n+9n^2)$$

A function $g(x)$ and constants C and k must be found, such that the inequality holds. We propose: $50(3n^2+3n^2+9n^2) = 150n^2+150n^2+450n^2 = 750n^2$

Then if $g(n) = n^2$, $C = 750$ and $k = 1$, we have that

$$|f(n)| \leq 750\,|g(n)| \quad \text{when } n > 1, \text{ therefore } O(n^2).$$

4 Conclusions

Presented results show that the Alpha-Beta BAM model has perfect recall of all patterns in the fundamental set. This perfect recall requires no condition. The trained patterns do not need to fulfill certain properties for the Alpha-Beta BAM to be able to recall them in a perfect manner. The algorithm of this BAM is not an iterative process and does not require convergence for its solution; also, it does not present any stability problem.

The time complexity of the algorithm is $O(n^2)$, which makes a lot of sense, given that we are working with square matrices, whose size is precisely n^2. Since the most important factor in the amount of operations done is the size of the matrices, the algorithm employed by Alpha-Beta BAM has quadratic time complexity.

On the other hand, the space complexity shown by the Alpha-Beta BAM can be expressed as $p\ (n + m + 2p) + 2[(n+p)^2 + (m+p)^2] + p$, which shows a polynomial behavior, of second grade. Then, the space complexity is also quadratic (though this time more heavily reliant on p than on n or m).

Acknowledgements. The authors would like to thank the Instituto Politécnico Nacional (Secretaría Académica, COFAA, SIP, and CIC), the CONACyT, and SNI for their economical support to develop this work.

References

1. Kosko, B., Bidirectional associative memories, *IEEE Transactions on Systems, Man, and Cybernetics*, vol. 18, no. 1, (1988) 49-60.
2. Jeng, Y.-J.; Yeh, C.-C. & Chiveh, T.D., Exponential bidirectional associative memories, *Electronics Letters*, Vol. 26, Issue 11, (1990) 717-718
3. Wang, W.-J. & Lee, D.-L., Modified exponential bidirectional associative memories, *Electronics Letters*, Vol. 28, Issue 9, (1992). 888-890Chen, S., Gao, H. & Yan, W., Improved exponential bidirectional associative memory, *Electronics Letters*, Vol. 33, Issue 3, (1997) 223-224
5. Wang, Y.-F., Cruz J.B., Jr. & Mulligan, Jr., Two coding strategies for bidirectional associative memory, *IEEE Transactions on Neural Networks*, Vol. 1, Issue 1, (1990) 81-92
6. Wang, Y.-F., Cruz J.B., Jr. & Mulligan, Jr., Guaranteed recall of all training pairs for bidirectional associative memory, *IEEE Transactions on Neural Networks*, Vol. 1, Issue 6, (1991) 559-56.
7. Perfetti, R., Optimal gradient descent learning for bidirectional associative memories, *Electronics Letters*, Vol. 29, Issue 17, (1993) 1556-1557
8. Zheng, G., Givigi, S.N. & Zheng, W., A New Strategy for Designing Bidirectional Associative Memories, *Lecture Notes in Computer Science*, Springer-Verlag, Vol. 3496, (2005) 398-403
9. Shen, D. & Cruz, J.B., Jr., Encoding strategy for maximum noise tolerance bidirectional associative memory, *IEEE Transactions on Neural Networks*, Vol. 16, Issue 2, (2005) 293-300
10. Arik, S., Global asymptotic stability analysis of bidirectional associative memory neural networks with time delays, *IEEE Transactions on Neural Networks*, vol. 16, no. 3 (2005) 580-585

11. Park, J., Robust stability of bidirectional associative memory neural networks with time delays, *Physics Letters A*, vol. 349, (2006) 494-499
12. Ritter, G.X., Diaz-deLeon, J.L. & Sussner, P., Morphological bidirectional associative memories, *Neural Networks*, Vol. 12, (1999) 851-867
13. Wu,Y. & Pados, D.A., A feedforward bidirectional associative memory, *IEEE Transactions on Neural Networks*, Vol. 11, Issue 4, (2000) 859-866
14. Yáñez-Márquez, C.: Associative Memories Based on Order Relations and Binary Operators (In Spanish). PhD Thesis. Center for Computing Research, México (2002)Kohonen, T.: Self-Organization and Associative Memory. Springer-Verlag, Berlin Heidelberg New York (1989)Hassoun, M. H.: Associative Neural Memories. Oxford University Press, New York (1993)
17. Kohonen, T.: Correlation Matrix Memories. IEEE Transactions on Computers. 21(4). (1972) 353-359
18. Rosen, K.: *Discrete Mathematics and Its Applications*, McGraw-Hill, Estados Unidos (1999).
19. Acevedo Mosqueda, María Elena (2006). Memorias Asociativas Bidireccionales Alfa-Beta. PhD Thesis (In Spanish). Centro de Investigación en Computación del IPN, México.

A New Bi-directional Associative Memory

Roberto A. Vázquez, Humberto Sossa, and Beatriz A. Garro

Centro de Investigación en Computación – IPN
Av. Juan de Dios Batíz, esquina con Miguel Otón de Mendizábal
Ciudad de México, 07738, México
ravem@ipn.mx, hsossa@cic.ipn.mx, bgarrol@ipn.mx

Abstract. Hebbian hetero-associative learning is inherently asymmetric. Storing a forward association from pattern **A** to pattern **B** enables the recalling of pattern **B** given pattern **A**. This, in general, does not allow the recalling of pattern **A** given pattern **B**. The forward association between **A** and **B** will tend to be stronger than the backward association between **B** and **A**. In this paper it is described how the dynamical associative model proposed in [10] can be extended to create a bi-directional associative memory where forward association between **A** and **B** is equal to backward association between **B** and **A**. This implies that storing a forward association, from pattern **A** to pattern **B**, would enable the recalling of pattern **B** given pattern **A** and the recalling of pattern **A** given pattern **B**. We give some formal results that support the functioning of the proposal, and provide some examples were the proposal finds application.

1 Introduction

Associative memories (AMS) have been deeply explored during the last years. These devices can be seen as a particular kind of neural networks and. AMS are a mathematical tools specially designed to recall output patterns in terms of input patterns which can be contaminated by some kind of noise, see for example [1-9]. Some of these AMS have several constraints that limit their applicability in real life applications. A most common application of an AM is as a filter. Refer for example to [5-7]. In this case the AM is fed with an image possibly affected by noise; at the output the original image (without noise) should be obtained. However, in order to achieve the best performance the input patterns have to satisfy some conditions. In [5-6], for example, the input pattern can only be contaminated by additive or subtractive noise, but not both. In [7], the patterns can appear contaminated by both kinds of noises. Another application for AMS is in patterns classification. Refer for example to [8-9]. However they were only tested with simple objects. Recently in [10] it was introduced a new associative model which is useful for both filtering and classification. Due to its robustness, this model has been recently applied in image categorization [11].

According to Ebbinghaus in [12] and Robinson in [13], the strength of an association is sensitive to the temporal order of encoding. If pattern **A** and pattern **B** are encoded successively, forward association **A**→**B**, is hypothesized to be stronger than the backward association, **B**→**A** (see [16]). This fact is called asymmetric memory. Previous models [1-11] fall in this category.

A. Gelbukh and C.A. Reyes-Garcia (Eds.): MICAI 2006, LNAI 4293, pp. 367 – 380, 2006.

In contrast to this position, representatives of the famous Gestalt psychology [14] and [15] have viewed symbolic associations as composite representations, incorporating elements of each to-be-learned item into a new entity. According to this position, the strengths of forward and backward associations are approximately equal and highly correlated [16]; this fact is call symmetric memory.

Several associative symmetric models have been developed and are commonly called bi-directional associative memories (BAM). Refer for example to [17-21]. In these models, an input pattern is presented to a memory. Then the corresponding output pattern is presented to the transpose memory. After that the output is feed the memory and so on, until a stable state is reached. Most of these models work well with binary and bipolar patterns. Another characteristic of these models is that they are limited to a small number of associations. Most researches have tried to increase the number of associations that the associative memory can allocate. At last, most of these models are not able to guarantee the recall of all learnt patterns.

In this paper it is described how the dynamical associative model recently proposed in [10] can be extended to create a bi-directional associative memory. In comparison with others models the proposal is able to recall the whole fundamental set of patterns and it is not an iterative algorithm. We provide some theorems that guarantee the correct recall of whole set of patterns.

2 The Bi-directional Associative Model

An association between input pattern $\mathbf{x}$ and output pattern $\mathbf{y}$ is denoted as $(\mathbf{x}^k, \mathbf{y}^k)$, where k is the corresponding association. A bi-directional associative memory $\mathbf{BM}$ is represented by two matrices: $\mathbf{M}$ and $\overline{\mathbf{M}}^{\mathbf{t}}$ whose component m_{ij} can be seen as the synapses between neuron i and neuron j. $\mathbf{M}$ and $\overline{\mathbf{M}}^{\mathbf{t}}$ are generated from a finite a priori set of know associations, known as the fundamental set of association and is represented as: $\{(\mathbf{x}^k, \mathbf{y}^k) \mid k = 1,2,\ldots,p\}$ where p is the number of associations. A distorted version of a pattern $\mathbf{x}$ to be recuperated will be denoted as $\tilde{\mathbf{x}}$. If an associative memory $\mathbf{BM}$ is fed with a distorted version of $\mathbf{x}^k$ and the output obtained is exactly $\mathbf{y}^k$, we say that recalling is perfect.

2.1 Building and Testing the Associative Memory

Two main phases are used to build and test the bi-directional associative memory model.

TRAINING PHASE

1. For each couple $\{(\mathbf{x}^k, \mathbf{y}^k) \mid k = 1,2,\ldots,p\}$ build matrix $\mathbf{y} \Diamond_{\mathrm{A}} \mathbf{x}^t$ as:

$$\mathbf{y} \Diamond_{\mathrm{A}} \mathbf{x}^t = \begin{pmatrix} \mathrm{A}(y_1, x_1) & \mathrm{A}(y_1, x_2) & \cdots & \mathrm{A}(y_1, x_n) \\ \mathrm{A}(y_2, x_1) & \mathrm{A}(y_2, x_2) & \cdots & \mathrm{A}(y_2, x_n) \\ \vdots & \vdots & \ddots & \vdots \\ \mathrm{A}(y_m, x_1) & \mathrm{A}(y_m, x_2) & \cdots & \mathrm{A}(y_m, x_n) \end{pmatrix}_{m\times n} \tag{1}$$

where operator A is defined as $\mathrm{A}(x, y) = x - y$.

2. Apply the median operator to the matrix obtained in step 1 to get matrix $\mathbf{M}$.

$$w_{ij} = \underset{k=1}{\overset{p}{\mathbf{med}}} \mathrm{A}\left(y_i^k, x_j^k\right) \tag{2}$$

3. Build $\overline{\mathbf{M}}^t$ given by:

$$\overline{\mathrm{M}}^t = (-1) * \begin{pmatrix} \mathrm{A}(y_1, x_1) & \mathrm{A}(y_2, x_1) & \cdots & \mathrm{A}(y_n, x_1) \\ \mathrm{A}(y_1, x_2) & \mathrm{A}(y_2, x_2) & \cdots & \mathrm{A}(y_n, x_2) \\ \vdots & \vdots & \ddots & \vdots \\ \mathrm{A}(y_1, x_m) & \mathrm{A}(y_2, x_m) & \cdots & \mathrm{A}(y_n, x_m) \end{pmatrix}_{n \times m} \tag{3}$$

Finally, the bi-directional associative memory **BM** will be composed by two memories $\mathbf{M}$ and $\overline{\mathbf{M}}^t$ where $\mathbf{M}$ allows the recalling of forward associations: **A→B** and $\overline{\mathbf{M}}^t$ allows the recalling of backward associations: **B→A**.

RECALLING PHASE

A pattern $\mathbf{x}^k$ is presented to the memory **BM** and the following operation is done to recall $\mathbf{y}^k$:

$$\left(\mathbf{M} \Diamond_{\mathrm{B}} \tilde{\mathbf{x}}^k\right)_i = \underset{j=1}{\overset{n}{\mathbf{mid}}} \mathrm{B}\left(w_{ij}, \tilde{x}_j^k\right) \tag{4}$$

A pattern $\mathbf{y}^k$ is presented to the memory **BM** and the following operation is done for recalling $\mathbf{x}^k$:

$$\left(\overline{\mathbf{M}}^t \Diamond_{\mathrm{B}} \tilde{\mathbf{y}}^k\right)_i = \underset{j=1}{\overset{n}{\mathbf{mid}}} \mathrm{B}\left(\overline{w}_{ij}, \tilde{y}_j^k\right) \tag{5}$$

where operator B is defined as $\mathrm{B}(x, y) = x + y$ and **mid** operator is defined as $\mathbf{mid}\ \mathbf{x} = x_{(n+1)/2}$.

In the next section we will describe how to select which memory, $\mathbf{M}$ or $\overline{\mathbf{M}}^t$, will be used for recalling an output pattern from an input pattern.

2.2 Dynamical Associate Memory

Humans, in general, do not have problems to recall patterns even in the presence of noise. Before an input pattern is learned or processed by the brain, it is hypothesized that it is transformed and codified by the brain. This process can be simulated using the algorithm described in [8]:

Procedure 1. Transform the fundamental set of associations into codified patterns and de-codifier patterns:

```
Input: FS Fundamental set of associations:
{
 1. Make d = const and make (x̄¹, ȳ¹) = (x¹, y¹)
 2. For the remaining couples do {
     For k = 2 to p {
       For i = 1 to n {
         x̄_i^k = x̄_i^{k-1} + d ; x̂_i^k = x̄_i^k − x_i^k ; ȳ_i^k = ȳ_i^{k-1} + d ; ŷ_i^k = ȳ_i^k − y_i^k }
     }
}
Output: Set of codified and de-codifier patterns.
```

This procedure allows computing codified patterns from input and output patterns denoted by $\bar{\mathbf{x}}$ and $\bar{\mathbf{y}}$, respectively. On the other hand $\hat{\mathbf{x}}$ and $\hat{\mathbf{y}}$ are the de-codifier patterns. In addition a simplified version of patterns $\mathbf{x}^k$ and $\mathbf{y}^k$, denoted by s_k is obtained as follows:

$$s_k = s\left(\mathbf{z}^k\right) = \mathbf{mid}\,\mathbf{z}^k \tag{6}$$

where the first p simplified versions of $\mathbf{z}^k$ correspond to the patterns $\mathbf{x}^k$ and the second p simplified versions of $\mathbf{z}^k$ correspond to the patterns $\mathbf{y}^k$. This implies that there exist $2p$ simplified versions of $\mathbf{x}^k$ and $\mathbf{y}^k$.

When the brain is stimulated by an input pattern, some regions of the brain are stimulated by this information, also the synapses belonging to that region. We call these regions *active regions* and are computed as follow:

$$ar = r(\mathbf{x}) = \arg\left(\bigwedge_{i=1}^{p}\left|s(\mathbf{x}) - s_i\right|\right) \tag{7}$$

These active regions determine which memory will be used, if $ar \leq p$ then $\mathbf{M}$ is used, otherwise $\overline{\mathbf{M}}^t$. Those memories have synapses which modify the behavior of the memory, these synapses are call *principal synapses* (kernel of the associative memory) and are located in the middle column of matrix $\mathbf{M}$ and $\overline{\mathbf{M}}^t$. The synapses belonging to $\mathbf{K}_{\mathbf{M}}$ and $\mathbf{K}_{\overline{\mathbf{M}}^{\mathrm{T}}}$ are modified in response to an input pattern.

Principal synapses are denoted by $\mathbf{K}_{\mathbf{M}} = \mathbf{mid}_{i=1}^{m}\, w_i$ and $\mathbf{K}_{\overline{\mathbf{M}}^T} = \mathbf{mid}_{i=1}^{n}\, \overline{w}_i$ respectively.

Input pattern stimulates some regions, interacts with these active regions and then, according to those interactions modifies the synapses. This modification is computed by using an adjusting factor denoted by Δw when is used $\mathbf{M}$ and is given as:

$$\Delta w = \Delta(\mathbf{x}) = s(\overline{\mathbf{x}}^{r}) - s(\mathbf{x}) \tag{8}$$

On the other hand, adjusting factor for synapses belonging to $\overline{\mathbf{M}}^t$ is denoted by $\Delta\overline{w}$ and is given as:

$$\Delta\overline{w} = \Delta(\mathbf{x}) = s(\overline{\mathbf{y}}^{r-p}) - s(\mathbf{x}) \tag{9}$$

where r is the index of the active region.

Finally, synapses belonging to $\mathbf{K}_{\mathbf{M}}$ and $\mathbf{K}_{\overline{\mathbf{M}}^{\mathrm{T}}}$ are respectively updated as:

$$\mathbf{K}_{\mathbf{M}} = \mathbf{K}_{\mathbf{M}} \oplus (\Delta w_{new} - \Delta w_{old}) \tag{10}$$

$$\mathbf{K}_{\overline{\mathbf{M}}^{\mathrm{T}}} = \mathbf{K}_{\overline{\mathbf{M}}^{\mathrm{T}}} \oplus (\Delta\overline{w}_{new} - \Delta\overline{w}_{old}) \tag{11}$$

where operator $\oplus$ is defined as $\mathbf{x} \oplus d = x_i + d \ \forall i = 1,\ldots,m$.

Using this dynamic approach a bi-directional associative memory $\mathbf{BM}$ can be built by means of the next procedure:

1. Transform the fundamental set of associations into codified and de-codifier patterns using procedure 1.
2. Compute simplified versions of input patterns using equation 5.
3. Build matrix $\mathbf{M}$ in terms of codified patters: apply steps 1 and 2 of the training procedure described at the beginning of section 2.
4. Build matrix $\overline{\mathbf{M}}^t$ as explained in section 2.1 by applying step 3.

Given a pattern $\mathbf{x}^k$ or a distorted version of it ($\tilde{\mathbf{x}}$), pattern $\mathbf{y}^k$ can be recovered as follows:

1. Obtain index of active region ar by means of equation 7. If $ar \leq p$ go to step 2 else go to step 7.
2. Transform $\mathbf{x}^k$ using de-codifier pattern $\hat{\mathbf{x}}^{ar}$ as: $\widehat{\mathbf{x}}^k = \mathbf{x}^k + \hat{\mathbf{x}}^{ar}$
3. Compute adjusting factor $\Delta w = \Delta(\widehat{\mathbf{x}})$ by using equation 8.
4. Modify synapses of associative memory $\mathbf{M}$ that belong to $\mathbf{K}_{\mathbf{M}}$ by means of equation 10.
5. Apply equation 4 of the recalling phase described in section 2.
6. Obtain $\mathbf{y}^k$ by transforming $\widehat{\mathbf{y}}^k$ by using de-codifier pattern $\hat{\mathbf{y}}^{ar}$ as: $\mathbf{y}^k = \widehat{\mathbf{y}}^k - \hat{\mathbf{y}}^{ar}$.
7. Transform $\mathbf{x}^k$ using de-codifier pattern $\hat{\mathbf{y}}^{ar-p}$ as: $\widehat{\mathbf{x}}^k = \mathbf{x}^k + \hat{\mathbf{y}}^{ar-p}$
8. Compute adjusting factor $\Delta\overline{w} = \Delta(\widehat{\mathbf{x}})$ by using equation 9.
9. Modify synapses of associative memory $\overline{\mathbf{M}}^t$ that belong to $\mathbf{K}_{\overline{\mathbf{M}}^{\mathrm{T}}}$ by means of equation 11.
10. Apply equation 5 of recalling phase described in section 2.

11. Obtain $\mathbf{y}^k$ by transforming $\hat{\mathbf{y}}^k$ by using de-codifier pattern $\hat{\mathbf{x}}^{ar-p}$ as: $\mathbf{y}^k = \hat{\mathbf{y}}^k - \hat{\mathbf{x}}^{ar-p}$.

Bi-directional associative memories $\mathbf{BM}$ present perfect recall if their kernels $\mathbf{K_M}$ and $\mathbf{K}_{\bar{\mathbf{M}}^\mathrm{T}}$ satisfy the next propositions.

Proposition 1. Let $\{(\mathbf{x}^k, \mathbf{y}^k) | k = 1, \ldots, p\}$, $\mathbf{x}^\alpha \in \mathbf{R}^n$, $\mathrm{y}^\alpha \in \mathrm{R}^m$ be a fundamental set of associations of a bi-directional associative memory $\mathbf{BM}$. Let $\mathbf{K_M} \in \mathbf{R}^n$ be the kernel of matrix $\mathbf{M}$ and $\mathbf{K}_{\bar{\mathbf{M}}^\mathrm{T}} \in \mathbf{R}^m$ be the kernel of matrix $\bar{\mathbf{M}}^\mathbf{T}$. Let Δw be an updated value of $\mathbf{K_M}$ and $\Delta\bar{w}$ be an updated value of $\mathbf{K}_{\bar{\mathbf{M}}^\mathrm{T}}$. Finally, let $\tilde{\mathbf{x}}$ be a distorted version of $\bar{\mathbf{x}}$ and $\tilde{\mathbf{y}}$ be a distorted version of $\bar{\mathbf{y}}$. Every component of vector $\bar{\mathbf{y}}$ can be perfectly recalled in terms of distorted version of $\bar{\mathbf{x}}$ if $|\Delta w| < \frac{d}{2}$ and every component of vector $\bar{\mathbf{x}}$ can be perfectly recalled by using the distorted version of $\bar{\mathbf{y}}$ if $|\Delta\bar{w}| < \frac{d}{2}$.

Propositions 2. Let $\{(\mathbf{x}^k, \mathbf{y}^k) | k = 1, \ldots, p\}$, $\mathbf{x}^\alpha \in \mathbf{R}^n$, $\mathbf{y}^\alpha \in \mathbf{R}^m$ a fundamental set of associations of a bi-directional associative memory $\mathbf{BM}$, $\tilde{\mathbf{x}}$ a distorted version of $\mathbf{x}$ and $\tilde{\mathbf{y}}$ a distorted version of $\mathbf{y}$. $\mathbf{BM}$ has perfect recall if $\operatorname*{\mathbf{mid}}_{k=1}^{p}(\mathbf{x}^k) \neq \operatorname*{\mathbf{mid}}_{k=1}^{p}(\mathbf{y}^k)$ and if it satisfies Lemmas 3, 4 and 5 and Proposition 1.

Proof of these two propositions can be found in the Appendix.

3 Numerical Results

Suppose we want to first memorize and then recall the following general fundamental set of patterns:

$$\mathbf{x}^1 = \begin{pmatrix} 0.3 \\ 0.2 \\ 0.1 \end{pmatrix}, \mathbf{y}^1 = \begin{pmatrix} 0.9 \\ 1.2 \\ 0.3 \end{pmatrix}; \mathbf{x}^2 = \begin{pmatrix} 0.8 \\ 0.5 \\ 0.2 \end{pmatrix}, \mathbf{y}^2 = \begin{pmatrix} 0.5 \\ 1.6 \\ 1.1 \end{pmatrix}; \mathbf{x}^3 = \begin{pmatrix} 0.6 \\ 0.8 \\ 0.5 \end{pmatrix}, \mathbf{y}^3 = \begin{pmatrix} 1.2 \\ 1.9 \\ 2.1 \end{pmatrix}$$

TRAINING

By setting $d = 0.3$ and by applying procedure 1, we have:

$$\bar{\mathbf{x}}^1=\begin{pmatrix}0.3\\0.2\\0.1\end{pmatrix},\ \hat{\mathbf{x}}^1=\begin{pmatrix}0.0\\0.0\\0.0\end{pmatrix},\ \bar{\mathbf{y}}^1=\begin{pmatrix}0.9\\1.2\\0.3\end{pmatrix},\ \hat{\mathbf{y}}^1=\begin{pmatrix}0.0\\0.0\\0.0\end{pmatrix};\ \bar{\mathbf{x}}^2=\begin{pmatrix}0.6\\0.5\\0.4\end{pmatrix},\ \hat{\mathbf{x}}^2=\begin{pmatrix}-0.2\\0.0\\0.2\end{pmatrix},$$

$$\bar{\mathbf{y}}^2=\begin{pmatrix}1.2\\1.5\\0.6\end{pmatrix},\ \hat{\mathbf{y}}^2=\begin{pmatrix}0.7\\-0.1\\-0.5\end{pmatrix};\ \bar{\mathbf{x}}^3=\begin{pmatrix}0.9\\0.8\\0.7\end{pmatrix},\ \hat{\mathbf{x}}^3=\begin{pmatrix}0.3\\0.0\\0.2\end{pmatrix},\ \bar{\mathbf{y}}^3=\begin{pmatrix}1.5\\1.8\\0.9\end{pmatrix},\ \hat{\mathbf{y}}^3=\begin{pmatrix}0.3\\-0.1\\-1.2\end{pmatrix}$$

Finally bi-directional associative memory composed by $\mathbf{M}$, $\overline{\mathbf{M}}^t$ and $\mathbf{s}$ is given as:

$$\mathbf{M}=\begin{bmatrix}0.6&0.7&0.8\\0.9&1.0&1.1\\0.0&0.1&0.2\end{bmatrix},\ \overline{\mathbf{M}}^{\mathbf{T}}=\begin{bmatrix}-0.6&-0.9&0.0\\-0.7&-1.0&-0.1\\-0.8&-1.1&-0.2\end{bmatrix}\text{ and}$$

$$\mathbf{s}=\begin{bmatrix}0.2&0.5&0.8&1.2&1.6&1.9\end{bmatrix}.$$

RECALLING

Example 1. Suppose we want to recall the pattern associated to $(0.4\quad 0.9\quad 0.7)^T$ which is known to be a distorted version of $\mathbf{x}^3$.

1. Active region is $ar=r(\tilde{\mathbf{x}})=\arg\wedge(0.7,0.4,0.1,0.3,0.7,1.0)=3$.
2. Transform $\tilde{\mathbf{x}}$ by means of $\hat{\mathbf{x}}^{ar}$:
   $\widehat{\mathbf{x}}=\tilde{\mathbf{x}}+\hat{\mathbf{x}}^{ar}=(0.4\quad 0.9\quad 0.7)^T+(0.3\quad 0.0\quad 0.2)^T=(0.7\quad 0.9\quad 0.9)^T$.
3. Adjusting factor is given by $\Delta w=0.8-0.9=-0.1$.
4. Modify $\mathbf{K}_{\mathbf{M}}=[0.7\quad 1.0\quad 0.1]^T\oplus(-0.1-(0.0))=[0.6\quad 0.9\quad 0.0]^T$.
5. $$\mathbf{M}\Diamond_{\mathrm{B}}\widehat{\mathbf{x}}=\begin{bmatrix}0.6&06&0.8\\0.9&0.9&1.1\\0.0&0.0&0.2\end{bmatrix}\Diamond_{\mathrm{B}}\begin{bmatrix}0.7\\0.9\\0.9\end{bmatrix}=\begin{bmatrix}\mathbf{mid}(1.3,1.5,1.7)\\\mathbf{mid}(1.6,1.8,2.0)\\\mathbf{mid}(0.7,0.9,1.1)\end{bmatrix}=\begin{bmatrix}1.5\\1.8\\0.9\end{bmatrix}.$$
6. Transform $\widehat{\mathbf{y}}$ by means of $\hat{\mathbf{y}}^{ar}$. Finally,
   $\mathbf{y}=\widehat{\mathbf{y}}-\hat{\mathbf{y}}^{ar}=(1.5\quad 1.8\quad 0.9)^T-(0.3\quad -0.1\quad -1.2)^T=(1.2\quad 1.9\quad 2.1)^T$.

Example 2. Suppose we want to recall the pattern associated to $(0.4\quad 0.9\quad 0.7)^T$ which is known to be a distorted version of $\mathbf{y}^2$.

1. Active region is $ar=r(\tilde{\mathbf{x}})=\arg\wedge(1.3,1.0,0.7,0.3,0.1,0.4)=5$.
2. Transform $\tilde{\mathbf{x}}$ using $\hat{\mathbf{y}}^{ar-p}$.
   $\widehat{\mathbf{x}}=\tilde{\mathbf{x}}+\hat{\mathbf{y}}^{ar-p}=(0.7\quad 1.5\quad 1.4)^T+(0.7\quad -0.1\quad -0.5)^T=(1.4\quad 1.4\quad 0.9)^T$.
3. Adjust factor is given by $\Delta\overline{w}=1.5-1.4=0.1$.

4. Modify $\mathbf{K}_{\bar{\mathbf{M}}^{\mathrm{T}}} = [-0.9 \quad -1.0 \quad -1.1]^T \oplus (0.1-(0.0)) = [-0.8 \quad -0.9 \quad -1.0]^T$.

5. $$\bar{\mathbf{M}}^{\mathrm{T}} \Diamond_{\mathrm{B}} \hat{\mathbf{x}} = \begin{bmatrix} -0.6 & -0.8 & 0.0 \\ -0.7 & -0.9 & -1.1 \\ -0.8 & -1.0 & -0.2 \end{bmatrix} \Diamond_{\mathrm{B}} \begin{bmatrix} 1.4 \\ 1.4 \\ 0.9 \end{bmatrix} = \begin{bmatrix} \mathbf{mid}(0.8,0.6,0.9) \\ \mathbf{mid}(0.7,0.5,0.2) \\ \mathbf{mid}(0.6,0.4,0.7) \end{bmatrix} = \begin{bmatrix} 0.6 \\ 0.5 \\ 0.4 \end{bmatrix}.$$

6. Transform $\hat{\mathbf{y}}$ using $\hat{\mathbf{x}}^{ar-p}$. Finally,

$$\mathbf{y} = \hat{\mathbf{y}} - \hat{\mathbf{x}}^{ar-p} = (0.6 \quad 0.5 \quad 0.4)^T - (-0.2 \quad 0.0 \quad 0.2)^T = (0.8 \quad 0.5 \quad 0.2)^T.$$

As you can appreciate from both examples the associated patterns have been recalled in both forward and backward directions.

4 Experiments with Real Patterns

In this section, the accuracy of the proposed technique is tested with a set of 15 couples of images that contain flowers and animals shown in Figure 1. We divide de images into two groups (A and B) and perform two experiments in order to determine the accuracy of the proposal. For the first experiment we have associated an image of group A with an image of group B. For example we have associated the photo of the tiger with the photo of the leopard. Once selected the 15 couples we build the bi-directional associative memory as explained in Section 2. For the first experiment we first presented to the AM each image of group A, at the output we have obtained the corresponding image of group B. To verify the bi-directionality of the AM, we also presented to the input of the AM each image of group B. At the output we obtained the corresponding image of group A. The AM correctly recalls the fundamental set of images.

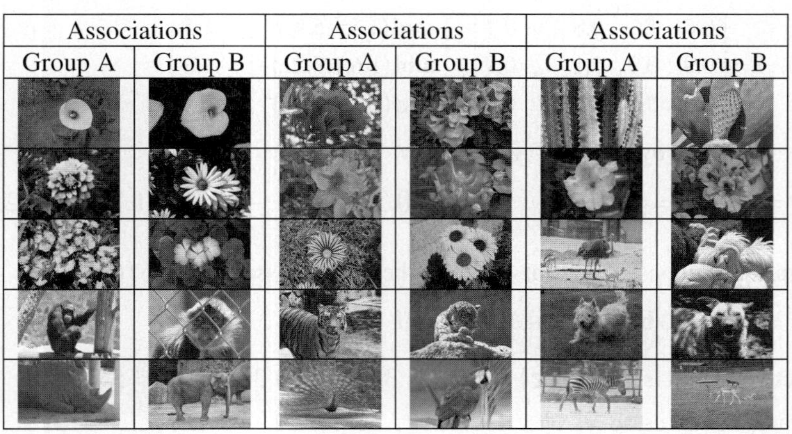

Fig. 1. Images of flowers and animals used in the experiments

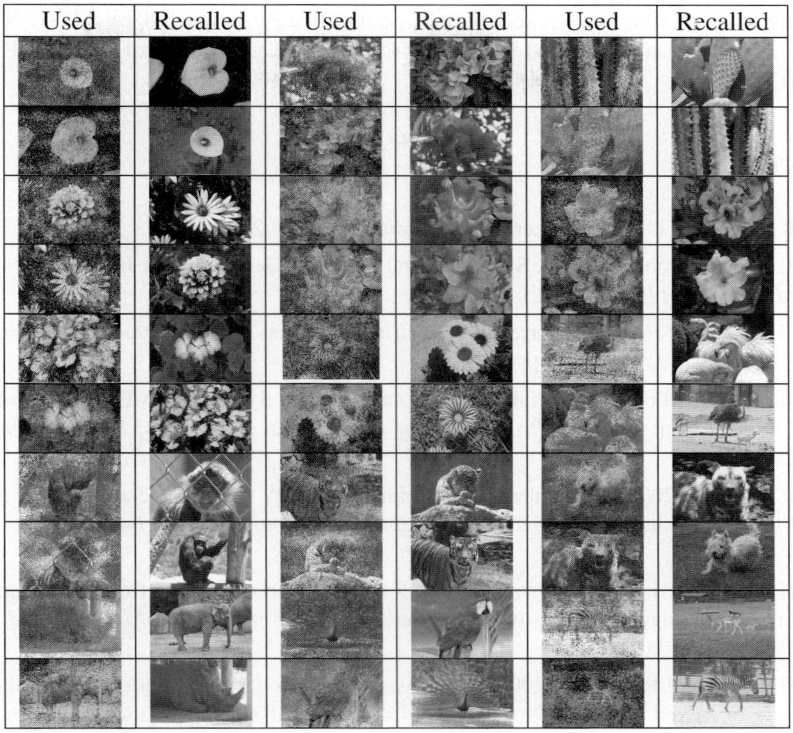

Fig. 2. Images recalled for experiment 2

For the second experiment we manually contaminated each image of each group as shown in Figure 2. We presented to the input of the AM the distorted image and verified if its corresponding associated image was correctly recalled. As can appreciate from Figure 2, in each case the corresponding associated image was correctly recalled in both directions, forward and backward, even in the presence of noise added to the input images. These results support the effectiveness of the proposal.

5 Conclusions and Ongoing Research

In this paper we have described a new bi-directional associative model and have provide some propositions that guarantee perfect recall even if the image is altered with noise.

In comparison with previous models, the proposal is not an iterative algorithm; in one step the desired pattern is recalled. An advantage of the proposal against the previous models is that the proposal works perfectly with real patters. Most of the previous bi-directional models work only with binary a bipolar patterns and. In this paper we have shown how the proposed BAM model can recall images in true color.

Nowadays we are working with more complex problems such as when the images present illumination changes or affine transformations. By solving these problems and certainly by combining with other techniques it might be possible to develop an image retrieval system using bi-directional associative memories.

Acknowledgements. This research was economically supported by SIP-IPN under grants 20050156 and 20060517 and SEP-CONACYT by means of grant SEP-2004-C01-46806/1215.

References

[1] K. Steinbuch (1961). Die Lernmatrix. *Kybernetik*, 1(1):26-45.

[2] J. A. Anderson (1972). A Simple Neural Network Generating an Interactive Memory. *Mathematical Biosciences*, 14:197-220.

[3] T. Kohonen (1972). Correlation Matrix Memories. *IEEE Trans. on Computers*, 21(4):353-359.

[4] J. J. Hopfield (1982). Neural Networks and Physical Systems with Emergent Collective Computational Abilities. *Proceedings of the National Academy of Sciences*, 79: 2554-2558, 1982.

[5] P. Sussner (2003). Generalizing Operations of Binary Auto-Associative Morphological Memories using Fuzzy Set Theory. *Journal of mathematical Imaging and Vision*, 19(2):81-93.

[6] G. X. Ritter, G. Urcid, L. Iancu (2003). Reconstruction of Patterns from Noisy Inputs using Morphological Associative Memories. *Journal of mathematical Imaging and Vision*, 19(2):95-111.

[7] H. Sossa and R. Barron (2003). New Associative Model for Pattern Recall in the Presence of Mixed Noise. In Proceedings of the fithh IASTED International Conference on Signal and Image Processing, SIP2003. Acta Press 399:485-490.

[8] H. Sossa, R. Barrón, R. A. Vázquez (2004). Transforming Fundamental set of Patterns to a Canonical Form to Improve Pattern Recall. In proceedings of Ninth Ibero-American Conference on Artificial Intelligence (IBERAMIA2004), LNAI 3315:687-696. Springer Verlag.

[9] H. Sossa, R. Barrón, R. A. Vázquez (2004). New Associative Memories for Recall Real-Valued Patterns. In proceedings of Ninth Ibero-american Congress on Pattern Recognition, CIARP 2004, LNCS 3287:195-202. Springer Verlag.

[10] R. A. Vázquez, H. Sossa and R. Barrón (2006). Enhanced Associative Memory Model for Pattern Restoration. To be submitted.

[11] R. A. Vázquez and H. Sossa (2006). Associative memories applied to image categorization. To be presented at CIARP 2006. Springer Verlag.

[12] H. Ebbinghaus (1885/1913). Memory: A Contribution to Experimental Psychology. New York: Teachers College, Columbia University.

[13] E. S.Robinson (1932). Association Theory Today: An Essay in Systematic Psychology. New York: Century Co.

[14] S. E. Asch and S. M. Ebenholtz (1962). The Principle of Associative Symmetry. Proceedings of the American Philosophical Society, 106, 135–163.

[15] W. Kohler, (1947). Gestalt Psychology. New York: Liveright.

[16] D. S. Rizzuto and M. J. Kahana (2000). Associative Symmetry vs. Independent Association. *Neurocomputing*, 32-33:973-978.

[17] B. Kosko (1988). Bidirectional Associative Memories. *IEEE Trans. on Systems, Man and Cybernetic*, 18(1):49-60.

[18] D-L Lee and W-J Wang (1993). Improvement of Bidirectional Associative Memories by using Correlation Significance. *Electronics Letters*, 29(8) :688-690.

[19] Y-F Wang et al. (1991). Guaranteed Recall of all Training Pairs for Bidirectional Associative Memory. *IEEE Trans. on Neural Networks*, 1(6):559-567.

[20] C. S. Leung (1994). Optimum Learnig for Bidirectional Associative Memory in the Sense of Capacity. *IEEE Trans. on Systems, Man and Cybernetics*, 24(5):791-796

[21] S. Chartier and M. Boukadoum (2006). A Bidirectional Heteroassociative Memory for Binary and Grey Level Patterns. *IEEE Trans. on Neural Networks*, 17(2):385-396.

Appendix

Before demonstrating Propositions 1 and 2, we provide the following properties, definitions and Lemmas. It is worth mentioning that these lemmas are not demonstrated due to space limitations:

Properties of **mid** operator:

1. $\mathbf{mid}(x) = x$
2. $\mathbf{mid}(\mathbf{x}+\mathbf{y}) = \mathbf{mid}(\mathbf{x}) + \mathbf{mid}(\mathbf{y})$
3. $\mathbf{mid}(\mathbf{x}-\mathbf{y}) = \mathbf{mid}(\mathbf{x}) - \mathbf{mid}(\mathbf{y})$

Definition 1. Let $\left\{\left(\bar{\mathbf{x}}^k, \bar{\mathbf{y}}^k\right) \middle| k = 1,\ldots,p\right\}, \bar{\mathbf{x}}^k \in \mathbf{R}^n, \bar{\mathbf{y}}^k \in \mathbf{R}^m$ a fundamental set of associations of bi-directional matrix BM composed by matrices $\mathbf{M}$ and $\bar{\mathbf{M}}^{\mathbf{T}}$. A component of the matrix $\mathbf{M}$ is defined as $m_{ij} = A\left(x_i, y_j\right) = y_i - x_j$ and a component of the matrix $\bar{\mathbf{M}}^{\mathbf{T}}$ is defined as $\bar{m}^t_{ji} = A\left(y_j, x_i\right) = x_j - y_i$.

Definition 2. Let $\left\{\left(\bar{\mathbf{x}}^k, \bar{\mathbf{y}}^k\right) \middle| k = 1,\ldots,p\right\}, \bar{\mathbf{x}}^k \in \mathbf{R}^n, \bar{\mathbf{y}}^k \in \mathbf{R}^m$ a fundamental set of association of BM composed by matrix $\mathbf{M}$ and $\bar{\mathbf{M}}^{\mathbf{T}}$. Let $\mathbf{K_M} \in \mathbf{R}^n$ the kernel of matrix $\mathbf{M}$ and $\mathbf{K}_{\bar{\mathbf{M}}^{\mathbf{T}}} \in \mathbf{R}^m$ the kernel of matrix $\bar{\mathbf{M}}^{\mathbf{T}}$. A component of vector $\mathbf{K_M}$ is defined as $km_i = \mathbf{mid}\left(m_{ij}\right), j = 1,\ldots,m$ and a component of vector $\mathbf{K}_{\bar{\mathbf{M}}^{\mathbf{T}}} \in \mathbf{R}^m$ is defined as $k\bar{m}^t_j = \mathbf{mid}\left(m_{ji}\right), i = 1,\ldots,n$.

Lemma 1. Let $\left\{\left(\bar{\mathbf{x}}^k, \bar{\mathbf{y}}^k\right) \middle| k = 1,\ldots,p\right\}, \bar{\mathbf{x}}^k \in \mathbf{R}^n, \bar{\mathbf{y}}^k \in \mathbf{R}^m$ a fundamental set of association of a bi-directional associative memory $\mathbf{BM}$. Every component of vector $\bar{\mathbf{y}}$ can be perfectly recalled by using its corresponding key vector $\bar{\mathbf{x}}$ and matrix $\mathbf{M}$

if and only if $\bar{y}_i = \mathbf{mid}\left(B\left(m_{ij}, \bar{x}_j\right)\right) = \mathbf{mid}\left(m_{ij} + \bar{x}_j\right), j = 1,\ldots,n$. Similarly, every component of vector $\bar{\mathbf{x}}$ can be perfectly recalled by using its corresponding key vector $\bar{\mathbf{y}}$ and matrix $\bar{\mathbf{M}}^{\mathbf{T}}$ if and only if $\bar{x}_j = \mathbf{mid}\left(B\left(m_{ji}, \bar{y}_i\right)\right) = \mathbf{mid}\left(m_{ji} + \bar{y}_i\right), i = 1,\ldots,m$.

Lemma 2. Let $\left\{\left(\bar{\mathbf{x}}^k, \bar{\mathbf{y}}^k\right) \middle| k = 1,\ldots, p\right\}, \bar{\mathbf{x}}^k \in \mathbf{R}^n, \bar{\mathbf{y}}^k \in \mathbf{R}^m$ a fundamental set of association of a bi-directional associative memory $\mathbf{BM}$ and let $\mathbf{K}_{\mathbf{M}} \in \mathbf{R}^n$ the kernel of matrix $\mathbf{M}$ and $\mathbf{K}_{\bar{\mathbf{M}}^{\mathbf{T}}} \in \mathbf{R}^m$ the kernel of matrix $\bar{\mathbf{M}}^{\mathbf{T}}$. Every component of vector $\mathbf{K}_{\mathbf{M}}$ is given as $km_i = \bar{y}_i - \mathbf{mid}\left(\bar{\mathbf{x}}\right)$. Similarly, every component of vector $\mathbf{K}_{\bar{\mathbf{M}}^{\mathbf{T}}}$ is given as $k\bar{m}_j^t = \bar{x}_j - \mathbf{mid}\left(\bar{\mathbf{y}}\right)$.

Lemma 3. Let $\left\{\left(\bar{\mathbf{x}}^k, \bar{\mathbf{y}}^k\right) \middle| k = 1,\ldots, p\right\}, \bar{\mathbf{x}}^k \in \mathbf{R}^n, \bar{\mathbf{y}}^k \in \mathbf{R}^m$ a fundamental set of association of a bi-directional associative memory $\mathbf{BM}$ and let $\mathbf{K}_{\mathbf{M}} \in \mathbf{R}^n$ the kernel of matrix $\mathbf{M}$ and $\mathbf{K}_{\bar{\mathbf{M}}^{\mathbf{T}}} \in \mathbf{R}^m$ the kernel of matrix $\bar{\mathbf{M}}^{\mathbf{T}}$. Every component of vector $\bar{\mathbf{y}}$ can be perfectly recalled by using its corresponding key vector $\bar{\mathbf{x}}$ if $\bar{y}_i = km_i + \mathbf{mid}\left(\bar{\mathbf{x}}\right)$. Similarly, every component of vector $\bar{\mathbf{x}}$ can be perfectly recalled by using its corresponding key vector $\bar{\mathbf{y}}$ if $\bar{x}_j = k\bar{m}_j^t + \mathbf{mid}\left(\bar{\mathbf{y}}\right)$.

Lemma 4. Let $\left\{\left(\bar{\mathbf{x}}^k, \bar{\mathbf{y}}^k\right) \middle| k = 1,\ldots, p\right\}, \bar{\mathbf{x}}^k \in \mathbf{R}^n, \bar{\mathbf{y}}^k \in \mathbf{R}^m$ a fundamental set of association of a bi-directional associative memory $\mathbf{BM}$ and let $\mathbf{K}_{\mathbf{M}} \in \mathbf{R}^n$ the kernel of matrix $\mathbf{M}$ and $\mathbf{K}_{\bar{\mathbf{M}}^{\mathbf{T}}} \in \mathbf{R}^m$ the kernel of matrix $\bar{\mathbf{M}}^{\mathbf{T}}$, Δw an updated value of $\mathbf{K}_{\mathbf{M}}$ and $\Delta\bar{w}$ an updated value of $\mathbf{K}_{\bar{\mathbf{M}}^{\mathbf{T}}}$, $\tilde{\mathbf{x}}$ a distorted version of $\bar{\mathbf{x}}$ and $\tilde{\mathbf{y}}$ a distorted version of $\bar{\mathbf{y}}$. Every component of vector $\bar{\mathbf{y}}$ can be perfectly recalled by using the distorted version of $\bar{\mathbf{x}}$ if $km_i = km_i + \Delta w$ and $\Delta w = \mathbf{mid}\left(\bar{\mathbf{x}}\right) - \mathbf{mid}\left(\tilde{\mathbf{x}}\right)$. Similarly, very component of vector $\bar{\mathbf{x}}$ can be perfectly recalled by using the distorted version of $\bar{\mathbf{y}}$ if $k\bar{m}_j^t = k\bar{m}_j^t + \Delta\bar{w}$ and $\Delta\bar{w} = \mathbf{mid}\left(\bar{\mathbf{y}}\right) - \mathbf{mid}\left(\tilde{\mathbf{y}}\right)$.

Lemma 5. Let $\left\{\left(\bar{\mathbf{x}}^k, \bar{\mathbf{y}}^k\right) \middle| k = 1,\ldots, p\right\}, \bar{\mathbf{x}}^k \in \mathbf{R}^n, \bar{\mathbf{y}}^k \in \mathbf{R}^m$ a fundamental set of association of a bi-directional associative memory BM and let $\mathbf{K}_{\mathbf{M}} \in \mathbf{R}^n$ the kernel of matrix $\mathbf{M}$ and $\mathbf{K}_{\overline{\mathbf{M}}^{\mathrm{T}}} \in \mathbf{R}^m$ the kernel of matrix $\overline{\mathbf{M}}^{\mathrm{T}}$, Δw an updated value of $\mathbf{K}_{\mathbf{M}}$ and $\Delta \overline{w}$ an updated value of $\mathbf{K}_{\overline{\mathbf{M}}^{\mathrm{T}}}$, $\tilde{\mathbf{x}}$ a distorted version of $\overline{\mathbf{x}}$ and $\tilde{\mathbf{y}}$ a distorted version of $\overline{\mathbf{y}}$. Every component of vector $\overline{\mathbf{y}}$ can be perfectly recalled by using the distorted version of $\overline{\mathbf{x}}$ if $\mathbf{mid}(\tilde{\mathbf{x}}) = \mathbf{mid}(\overline{\mathbf{x}}) - \Delta w$. Similarly, every component of vector $\overline{\mathbf{x}}$ can be perfectly recalled by using the distorted version of $\overline{\mathbf{y}}$ if $\mathbf{mid}(\tilde{\mathbf{y}}) = \mathbf{mid}(\overline{\mathbf{y}}) - \Delta \overline{w}$.

We now proceed to demonstrate the Propositions.

Proof of Proposition 1:

Let $\mathbf{x}^i = \mathbf{x}$, $\mathbf{x}^j = \mathbf{x} + d$ and $\tilde{\mathbf{x}} = \mathbf{x} - \Delta w$. If $|\Delta w| < \frac{d}{2}$ by expanding inequality then $-\frac{d}{2} < \Delta w$ and $\Delta w < \frac{d}{2}$.

Case 1:
Let $\mathbf{D}(\mathbf{x} - \Delta w, \mathbf{x} + d) < \mathbf{D}(\mathbf{x}, \mathbf{x} - \Delta w)$ the distance between two points. By applying active region equation:

$$\mathbf{mid}(\mathbf{x} - \Delta w) - \mathbf{mid}(\mathbf{x} + d) < \mathbf{mid}(\mathbf{x}) - \mathbf{mid}(\mathbf{x} - \Delta w).$$

Now by applying properties 2 and 3:

$$\mathbf{mid}(\mathbf{x}) - \mathbf{mid}(\Delta w) - \mathbf{mid}(\mathbf{x}) - \mathbf{mid}(d) < \mathbf{mid}(\mathbf{x}) - \mathbf{mid}(\mathbf{x}) + \mathbf{mid}(\Delta w)$$

By reducing terms:

$$-\mathbf{mid}(\Delta w) - \mathbf{mid}(d) < \mathbf{mid}(\Delta w).$$

By applying property 1:

$$-\Delta w - d < \Delta w.$$

Finally by reducing terms:

$$-d < \Delta w + \Delta w,$$

$$-d < 2\Delta w,$$

$$-\frac{d}{2} < 2\Delta w \quad \text{Q.E.D.}$$

Case 2: This is demonstrated as case 1.

Proof of Proposition 2:

Case 1:

Let $\tilde{\mathbf{x}} = \mathbf{x} - \Delta w$ and $\mathbf{D}(\mathbf{x}, \mathbf{x} - \Delta w) \neq \mathbf{D}(\mathbf{y}, \mathbf{x} - \Delta w)$ by applying active region equation:

$$\mathbf{mid}(\mathbf{x}) - \mathbf{mid}(\mathbf{x} - \Delta w) \neq \mathbf{mid}(\mathbf{y}) - \mathbf{mid}(\mathbf{x} - \Delta w).$$

Now by applying properties 2 and 3:

$$\mathbf{mid}(\mathbf{x}) - \mathbf{mid}(\mathbf{x}) + \mathbf{mid}(\Delta w) \neq \mathbf{mid}(\mathbf{y}) - \mathbf{mid}(\mathbf{x}) + \mathbf{mid}(\Delta w)$$

By reducing terms:

$$\mathbf{mid}(\mathbf{x}) \neq \mathbf{mid}(\mathbf{y}) \quad \text{Q.E.D.}$$

Case 2: This is demonstrated as case 1.

A Hybrid Ant Algorithm for the Airline Crew Pairing Problem

Broderick Crawford[1,2], Carlos Castro[2], and Eric Monfroy[2,3,⋆]

[1] Pontificia Universidad Católica de Valparaíso, PUCV, Chile
FirstName.Name@ucv.cl

[2] Universidad Técnica Federico Santa María, Valparaíso, Chile
FirstName.Name@inf.utfsm.cl

[3] LINA, Université de Nantes, France
FirstName.Name@univ-nantes.fr

Abstract. This article analyzes the performance of Ant Colony Optimization algorithms on the resolution of Crew Pairing Problem, one of the most critical processes in airline management operations. Furthermore, we explore the hybridization of Ant algorithms with Constraint Programming techniques. We show that, for the instances tested from Beasley's OR-Library, the use of this kind of hybrid algorithms obtains good results compared to the best performing metaheuristics in the literature.

Keywords: Ant Colony Optimization, Constraint Programming, Hybrid Algorithm, Crew Pairing Optimization, Set Partitioning Problem.

1 Introduction

Crew pairing is one of the most critical processes in airline management operations. Taking a long term flight schedule as input, the objective of this process is to partition without breaking constraints (rules and regulations) the schedule of airline flights into individual flight sequences called pairings. A pairing is a sequence of flight legs for an unspecified crew member starting and finishing at the same city. The problem has attracted many people (managers and scientists) in recent decades. The main challenge is that there is no general method to work well with all kinds of non linear cost functions and constraints (hard and soft). Furthermore, this problem becomes more complicated with the increasing size of the input. The pairing problem can be formulated as a Set Partitioning Problem (SPP) or equality-constrained as a Set Covering Problem (SCP), in this formulation the rows are flights and the columns are pairings [3]. In this work, we solve some test instances of Airline Flight Crew Scheduling with Ant Colony Optimization (ACO) algorithms and some hybridizations of ACO with

⋆ The authors have been partially supported by the project INRIA-CONICYT VANANAA. The first author has also been partially supported by the project PUCV 209.473/2006. The third author has also been partially supported by the Chilean National Science Fund through the project FONDECYT 1060373.

A. Gelbukh and C.A. Reyes-Garcia (Eds.): MICAI 2006, LNAI 4293, pp. 381–391, 2006.

Constraint Programming (CP) techniques like Forward Checking. The computational results that we have obtained show a good behaviour in comparison with performing metaheuristics in the literature [6,18,15].

There exist some problems for which the effectiveness of ACO is limited, among them the strongly constrained problems. Those are problems for which neighbourhoods contain few solutions, or none at all, and local search has a very limited use. Probably, the most significant of those problems is the SPP and a direct implementation of the basic ACO framework is unable of obtaining feasible solutions for many SPP standard tested instances [19]. The best performing metaheuristic for SPP is a genetic algorithm due to Chu and Beasley [6,5]. There already exists some first approaches applying ACO to the SCP. In [1,16] ACO has only been used as a construction algorithm and the approach has only been tested on some small SCP instances. More recent works [14,17,13] apply Ant Systems to the SCP and related problems using techniques to remove redundant columns and local search to improve solutions. Taking into account these results, it seems that the incomplete approach of Ant Systems could be considered as a good alternative to solve these problems when complete techniques are not able to get the optimal solution in a reasonable time.

In this paper, we explore the addition of a lookahead mechanism to the two main ACO algorithms: Ant System (AS) and Ant Colony System (ACS). Trying to solve larger instances of SPP with AS or ACS implementations derives in a lot of unfeasible labelling of variables, and the ants can not obtain complete solutions using the classic transition rule when they move in their neighbourhood. In this paper, we propose the addition of a lookahead mechanism in the construction phase of ACO thus only feasible partial solutions are generated. The lookahead mechanism allows the incorporation of information about the instantiation of variables after the current decision. This idea differs from the one proposed by [21] and [12], those authors propose a lookahead function evaluating the pheromone in the Shortest Common Supersequence Problem and estimating the quality of a partial solution of a Industrial Scheduling Problem, respectively. This paper is organised as follows: Section 2 is dedicated to the presentation of the problem and its mathematical model. In Section 3, we describe the applicability of the ACO algorithms for solving SPP and an example of Constraint Propagation is given. In Section 4, we present the basic concepts to adding Constraint Programming techniques to the two basic ACO algorithms: AS and ACS. In Section 5, we present results when adding Constraint Programming techniques to the two basic ACO algorithms to solve some Airline Flight Crew Scheduling taken from NorthWest Airlines benchmarks available in the OR-Library of Beasley [4]. Furthermore, our results are compared with the best performing non-ACO metaheuristcis. Finally, in Section 6 we conclude the paper and give some perspectives for future research.

2 Problem Description

One of the most challenging cases of operational planning, scheduling and controlling may be found in the airline industry. The efficient management of operations has become more challenging and complex with the passage of time, and this industry is constantly striving to maximize profits within a competitive environment. Although Operations Research and Artificial Intelligence tools have been applied for several decades, its problems are still challenging scientists and software engineers. The size of these problems is increasing and restrictions on them are becoming more and more complicated.

It is supposed that a timetable of flights operated in a schedule period exists already to match the expectations of the market demands. Then, there are planning and scheduling tasks for aircraft and crews. The first problem is called Fleet Assignment Problem and has the timetable as input. The results of the fleet assignment problem are: the exact departure time for each flight leg and the sequence of flight legs for an aircraft. Without considering the fuel costs, the most important direct operating cost is the personnel. Therefore, a second problem called Crew Scheduling Problem is very important. This problem is often divided into two smaller problems: Crew Pairing Problem and Crew Rostering Problem (also called Crew Assignment Problem). The crew pairing problem takes the scheduled flights which were fixed by the fleet assignment step as input. Instead of assigning aircraft, the aim now is to allocate crews to cover all flight legs and maximize an objective function. In the crew pairing process, planners do not consider individual crew and the scheduling is often applied for a period and the result of this process can be used for other periods. The flights are grouped into small sets called pairings (or rotations) which must start from a home base and end at that base. The rostering process will do the remaining task to assign an individual crew to a flight leg. All published methods attempt to separate the problem of generating pairings from the problem of selecting the best subset of these pairings. The remaining optimization problem is then modelled under the assumption that the set of feasible pairings and their costs are explicitly available, and can be expressed as a Set Partitioning Problem. The SPP model is valid for the daily problem as well as the weekly problem and the fully dated problem.

SPP is the NP-complete problem of partitioning a given set into mutually independent subsets while minimizing a cost function defined as the sum of the costs associated to each of the eligible subsets. In the SPP matrix formulation we are given a $m \times n$ matrix $A = (a_{ij})$ in which all the matrix elements are either zero or one. Additionally, each column is given a non-negative cost c_j. We say that a column j can cover a row i if $a_{ij} = 1$. Let J denotes the set of the columns and x_j a binary variable which is one if column j is chosen and zero otherwise. The SPP can be defined formally as follows:

$$Minimize \qquad f(x) = \sum_{j=1}^{n} c_j \times x_j \tag{1}$$

$$Subject\ to \qquad \sum_{j=1}^{n} a_{ij} \times x_j = 1; \qquad \forall i = 1, \ldots, m \tag{2}$$

In this formulation, each row represents a flight leg that must be scheduled. The columns represent pairings. Each pairing is a sequence of flights to be covered by a single crew over a 2 to 3 day period. It must begin and end in the base city where the crew resides [22].

3 Ant Colony Optimization for Set Partitioning Problems

In this section, we briefly present ACO algorithms and give a description of their use to solve SPP. More details about ACO algorithms can be found in [8,9]. The basic idea of ACO algorithms comes from the capability of real ants to find shortest paths between the nest and food source. From a Combinatorial Optimization point of view, the ants are looking for *good solutions*. Real ants cooperate in their search for food by depositing pheromone on the ground. An artificial ant colony simulates this behavior implementing artificial ants as parallel processes whose role is to build solutions using a randomized constructive search driven by pheromone trails and heuristic information of the problem. An important topic in ACO is the adaptation of the pheromone trails during algorithm execution to take into account the cumulated search experience: reinforcing the pheromone associated with good solutions and considering the *evaporation* of the pheromone on the components over time in order to avoid premature convergence. ACO can be applied in a very straightforward way to SPP. The columns are chosen as the solution components and have associated a cost and a pheromone trail [10]. Each column can be visited by an ant only once and then a final solution has to cover all rows. A walk of an ant over the graph representation corresponds to the iterative addition of columns to the partial solution obtained so far. Each ant starts with an empty solution and adds columns until a cover is completed. A pheromone trail τ_j and a heuristic information η_j are associated to each eligible column j. A column to be added is chosen with a probability that depends of pheromone trail and the heuristic information. The most common form of the ACO decision policy (*Transition Rule Probability*) when ants work with components is:

$$p_j^k(t) = \frac{\tau_j * \eta_j^\beta}{\sum\limits_{l \notin S^k} \tau_l [\eta_l]^\beta} \quad \text{if } j \notin S^k \tag{3}$$

where S^k is the partial solution of the ant k. The β parameter controls how important is η in the probabilistic decision [10,17].

Pheromone trail τ_j. One of the most crucial design decisions to be made in ACO algorithms is the modelling of the set of pheromones. In the original ACO implementation for TSP the choice was to put a pheromone value on every link between a pair of cities, but for other combinatorial problems often can be assigned pheromone values to the decision variables (first order pheromone values) [10]. In this work the pheromone trail is put on the problems component (each eligible column j) instead of the problems connections. And setting a good pheromone quantity is not a trivial task either. The quantity of pheromone trail laid on columns is based on the idea: *the more pheromone trail on a particular item, the more profitable that item is* [16]. Then, the pheromone deposited in each component will be in relation to its frequency in the ants solutions. In this work we divided this frequency by the number of ants obtaining better results.

Heuristic information η_j. In this paper we use a dynamic heuristic information that depends on the partial solution of an ant. It can be defined as $\eta_j = \frac{e_j}{c_j}$, where e_j is the so called cover value, that is, the number of additional rows covered when adding column j to the current partial solution, and c_j is the cost of column j. In other words, the heuristic information measures the unit cost of covering one additional row. An ant ends the solution construction when all rows are covered.

In this work, we use two instances of ACO: Ant System (AS) and Ant Colony System (ACS) algorithms, the original and the most famous algorithms in the ACO family [10]. ACS improves the search of AS using: a different transition rule in the constructive phase, exploiting the heuristic information in a more rude form, using a list of candidates to future labelling and using a different treatment of pheromone. ACS has demonstrated better performance than AS in a wide range of problems [9]. ACS exploits a pseudo-random transition rule in the solution construction; ant k chooses the next column j with criteria:

$$Argmax_{l \notin S^k} \quad \{\tau_l [\eta_l]^\beta\} \quad \text{if } q \leq q_o \tag{4}$$

and following the Transition Rule Probability (equation 3) en otherwise. Where q is a random number uniformly distributed in $[0, 1]$, and q_0 is a parameter that controls how strongly the ants exploit deterministically the pheromone trail and the heuristic information.

Trying to solve larger instances of SPP with the original AS or ACS implementation derives in a lot of unfeasible labelling of variables, and the ants can not obtain complete solutions. In this paper we explore the addition of a lookahead mechanism in the construction phase of ACO thus only feasible solutions are generated. A direct implementation of the basic ACO framework is incapable of obtaining feasible solution for many SPP instances. An example will be given in order to explain the ACO difficulties solving SPP. In [22] is showed Table 1 with a Flight Schedule for American Airlines. The table enumerates possible pairings, or sequence of flights to be covered by a single crew over a 2 to 3 day period, and its costs. A pairing must begin and end in the base city where the crew resides. For example, pairing j = 1 begins at a known city (Miami in the [22] example) with flight 101 (Miami-Chicago). After a layover in Chicago the crew covers flight 203 (Chicago-Dallas) and then flight 406 (Dallas-Charlotte) to Charlotte. Finally, flight 308 (Charlotte-Miami) returns them to Miami. The total cost of pairing j = 1 is $ 2900.

Having enumerated a list of pairings like Table 1, the remaining task is to find a minimum total cost collection of columns staffing each flight exactly once. Defining the decision variables x_j equal to 1 if pairing j is chosen and 0 otherwise, the corresponding SPP model must to be solved.

Table 1. Possible Pairings for AA Example

Pairing j	Flight Sequence	Cost $
1	101-203-406-308	2900
2	101-203-407	2700
3	101-204-305-407	2600
4	101-204-308	3000
5	203-406-310	2600
6	203-407-109	3150
7	204-305-407-109	2550
8	204-308-109	2500
9	305-407-109-212	2600
10	308-109-212	2050
11	402-204-305	2400
12	402-204-310-211	3600
13	406-308-109-211	2550
14	406-310-211	2650
15	407-109-211	2350

$$\textit{Minimize} \quad 2900x_1 + 2700x_2 + 2600x_3 + 3000x_4 + 2600x_5 + 3150x_6 + 2550x_7 +$$

$$2500x_8 + 2600x_9 + 2050x_{10} + 2400x_{11} + 3600x_{12} + 2550x_{13} + 2650x_{14} + 2350x_{15}$$

Subject to

$$\begin{aligned}
x_1 + x_2 + x_3 + x_4 &= 1 \quad (\textit{flight}\ 101)\\
x_6 + x_7 + x_8 + x_9 + x_{10} + x_{13} + x_{15} &= 1 \quad (\textit{flight}\ 109)\\
x_1 + x_2 + x_5 + x_6 &= 1 \quad (\textit{flight}\ 203)\\
x_3 + x_4 + x_7 + x_8 + x_{11} + x_{12} &= 1 \quad (\textit{flight}\ 204)\\
x_{12} + x_{13} + x_{14} + x_{15} &= 1 \quad (\textit{flight}\ 211)\\
x_9 + x_{10} &= 1 \quad (\textit{flight}\ 212)\\
x_3 + x_7 + x_9 + x_{11} &= 1 \quad (\textit{flight}\ 305)\\
x_1 + x_4 + x_8 + x_{10} + x_{13} &= 1 \quad (\textit{flight}\ 308)\\
x_5 + x_{12} + x_{14} &= 1 \quad (\textit{flight}\ 310)\\
x_{11} + x_{12} &= 1 \quad (\textit{flight}\ 402)\\
x_1 + x_5 + x_{13} + x_{14} &= 1 \quad (\textit{flight}\ 406)\\
x_2 + x_3 + x_6 + x_7 + x_9 + x_{15} &= 1 \quad (\textit{flight}\ 407)\\
x_j &= 0 \ \textit{or}\ 1; \quad \forall j = 1, \ldots, 15
\end{aligned}$$

An optimal solution of this problem, at cost of $ 9100, is $x_1^* = x_9^* = x_{12}^* = 1$ and all other $x_j^* = 0$.

Applying ACO to the American Airlines Example. Each ant starts with an empty solution and adds columns until a cover is completed. But to determine if a column actually belongs or not to the partial solution ($j \notin S^k$) is not good enough. The traditional ACO decision policy, Equation 3, does not work for SPP because the ants, in this traditional selection process of the next columns, ignore the information of the problem constraints. For example, let us suppose that at the beginning an ant chooses the pairing or column number

14, then x_{14} is instantiated with the value 1. For instance, if x_{14} is instantiated, the consideration of the constraints that contain x_{14} may have important consequences:

- Checking constraint of flight 211, if $x_{14} = 1$ then $x_{12} = x_{13} = x_{15} = 0$.
- Checking constraint of flight 310, if $x_{14} = 1$ then $x_5 = x_{12} = 0$.
- Checking constraint of flight 406, if $x_{14} = 1$ then $x_1 = x_5 = x_{13} = 0$.
- If $x_{12} = 0$, considering the flight 402 constraint then $x_{11} = 1$.
- If $x_{11} = 1$, considering the flight 204 constraint then $x_3 = x_4 = x_7 = x_8 = 0$; and by the flight 305 constraint then $x_3 = x_7 = x_9 = 0$.
- If $x_9 = 0$, considering the flight 212 constraint then $x_{10} = 1$.
- If $x_{10} = 1$, by the flight 109 constraint $x_6 = x_7 = x_8 = x_9 = x_{13} = x_{15} = 0$; and considering the flight 308 constraint $x_1 = x_4 = x_8 = x_{13} = 0$.

All the information above, where the only variable uninstantiated after a simple propagation of constraints was x_2, is ignored by the probabilistic transition rule of the ants. And in the worst case, in the iterative steps is possible to assign values to some variable that will make impossible to obtain complete solutions. The procedure that we showed above is similar to the Constraint Propagation technique. Constraint Propagation is an efficient inference mechanism based on the use of the information in the constraints that can be found under different names: Constraint Relaxation, Filtering Algorithms, Narrowing Algorithms, Constraint Inference, Simplification Algorithms, Label Inference, Local Consistency Enforcing, Rules Iteration, Chaotic Iteration. Constraint Propagation embeds any reasoning which consists in explicitly forbidding values or combinations of values for some variables of a problem because a given subset of its constraints cannot be satisfied otherwise. The algorithm proceeds as follows: when a value is assigned to a variable, the algorithm recomputes the possible value sets and assigned values of all its dependent variables (variable that belongs to the same constraint). This process continues recursively until no more changes can be done. More specifically, when a variable x_m changes its value, the algorithm evaluates the domain expression of each variable x_n dependent on x_m. This may generate a new set of possible values for x_n. If this set changes, a constraint is evaluated selecting one of the possible values as the new assigned value for x_n. It causes the algorithm to recompute the values for further downstream variables. In the case of binary variables the constraint propagation works very fast in strongly constrained problems like SPP. The two basic techniques of Constraint Programming are Constraint Propagation and Constraint Distribution. The problem cannot be solved using Constraint Propagation alone, Constraint Distribution or Search is required to reduce the search space until Constraint Propagation is able to determine the solution. Constraint Distribution splits a problem into complementary cases once Constraint Propagation cannot advance further. By iterating propagation and distribution, propagation will eventually determine the solutions of a problem [2].

4 ACO with Constraint Programming

Recently, some efforts have been done in order to integrate Constraint Programming techniques to ACO algorithms [20,11]. A hybridization of ACO and CP can be approached from two directions: we can either take ACO or CP as the base algorithm and try to embed the respective other method into it. A form to integrate CP into ACO is to let it reduce the possible candidates among the not yet instantiated variables participating in the same constraints that the actual variable. A different approach would be to embed ACO within CP. The point at which ACO can interact with CP is during the labelling phase, using ACO to learn a value ordering that is more likely to produce good solutions.

```
Procedure ACO+CP_for_SPP
Begin
 InitParameters();
 While (remain iterations) do
    For k := 1 to nants do
       While (solution is not completed) and TabuList <> J do
          Choose next Column j with Transition Rule Probability
          For each Row i covered by j do                    /* constraints with j     */
            feasible(i):= Posting(j);                       /* Constraint Propagation */
          EndFor
          If feasible(i) for all i then AddColumnToSolution(j)
                                  else Backtracking(j); /* set j uninstantiated    */
          AddColumnToTabuList(j);
       EndWhile
    EndFor
   UpdateOptimum();
   UpdatePheromone();
 EndWhile
 Return best_solution_founded
End.
```

Fig. 1. ACO+CP algorithm for SPP

In this work, ACO use CP in the variable selection (when adding columns to partial solution). The CP algorithm used in this paper is Forward Checking with Backtracking. The algorithm is a combination of Arc Consistency Technique and Chronological Backtracking [7]. It performs Arc Consistency between pairs of a not yet instantiated variable and an instantiated variable, i.e., when a value is assigned to the current variable, any value in the domain of a future variable which conflicts with this assignment is removed from the domain. The Forward Checking procedure, taking into account the constraints network topology (i.e. wich sets of variables are linked by a constraint and wich are not), guarantees that at each step of the search, all constraints between already assigned variables and not yet assigned variables are arc consistent. Then, adding Forward Checking to ACO for SPP means that columns are chosen if they do not produce any conflict with the next column to be chosen. In other words, the Forward Checking search procedure guarantees that at each step of the search, all the constraints between already assigned variables and not yet assigned variables are arc consistency. This reduces the search tree and the overall amount of computational work done.

But it should be noted that in comparison with pure ACO algorithm, Forward Checking does additional work when each assignment is intended to be added to the current partial solution. Arc consistency enforcing always increases the information available on each variable labelling. Figure 1 describes the hybrid ACO+CP algorithm to solve SPP.

5 Experiments and Results

Table 2 presents the results when adding Forward Checking to the basic ACO algorithms for solving test instances taken from the OR-Library [4]. It compares performance with IP optimal, Genetic Algorithm of Chu and Beasley [6], Genetic Algorithm of Levine et al. [18] and the most recent algorithm by Kotecha et al. [15]. The first five columns of Table 2 present the problem code, the number of rows (constraints), the number of columns (decision variables), the best known cost value for each instance (IP optimal), and the density (percentage of ones in the constraint matrix) respectively. The next three columns present the results obtained by better performing metaheuristics with respect to SPP. And the last four columns present the cost obtained when applying Ant Algorithms, AS and ACS, and combining them with Forward Checking. An entry of "X" in the table means no feasible solution was found. The algorithms have been run with the following parameters settings: influence of pheromone (alpha)=1.0, influence of heuristic information (beta)=0.5 and evaporation rate (rho)=0.4 as suggested in [16,17,10]. The number of ants has been set to 120 and the maximum number of iterations to 160, so that the number of generated candidate solutions is limited to 19.200. For ACS the list size was 500 and Qo=0.5. Algorithms were implemented using ANSI C, GCC 3.3.6, under Microsoft Windows XP Professional version 2002.

Table 2. Experimental Results

Problem	Rows	Columns	Optimum	Density	Beasley	Levine	Kotecha	AS	ACS	AS+FC	ACS+FC
sppnw06	50	6774	7810	18.17	7810	-	-	9200	9788	8160	8038
sppnw08	24	434	35894	22.39	35894	37078	36068	X	X	35894	36682
sppnw09	40	3103	67760	16.20	67760	-	-	70462	X	70222	69332
sppnw10	24	853	68271	21.18	68271	X	68271	X	X	X	X
sppnw12	27	626	14118	20.00	14118	15110	14474	15406	16060	14466	14252
sppnw15	31	467	67743	19.55	67743	-	-	67755	67746	67743	67743
sppnw19	40	2879	10898	21.88	10898	11060	11944	11678	12350	11060	11858
sppnw23	19	711	12534	24.80	12534	12534	12534	14304	14604	13932	12880
sppnw26	23	771	6796	23.77	6796	6796	6804	6976	6956	6880	6880
sppnw32	19	294	14877	24.29	14877	14877	14877	14877	14886	14877	14877
sppnw34	20	899	10488	28.06	10488	10488	10488	13341	11289	10713	10797
sppnw39	25	677	10080	26.55	10080	10080	10080	11670	10758	11322	10545
sppnw41	17	197	11307	22.10	11307	11307	11307	11307	11307	11307	11307

The effectiveness of Constraint Programming is showed to solve SPP, because the SPP is so strongly constrained the stochastic behaviour of ACO can be improved with lookahead techniques in the construction phase, so that almost only feasible partial solutions are induced. In the original ACO implementation the SPP solving derives in a lot of unfeasible labelling of variables, and the ants can not complete solutions. With respect to the computational results this is not surprising, because ACO metaheuristics are general purpose tools that will usually be outperformed when customized algorithms for a problem exist.

6 Conclusions and Future Directions

Our main contribution is the study of the combination of Constraint Programming and Ant Colony Optimization solving benchmarks of the Airline Crew Pairing Problem formulated as a Set Partitioning Problem. The main conclusion from this work is that we can improve ACO with CP. Computational results also indicated that our hybridization is capable of generating optimal or near optimal solutions for many problems. The concept of Arc Consistency plays an essential role in Constraint Programming as a problem simplification operation and as a tree pruning technique during search through the detection of local inconsistencies among the uninstantiated variables. We have shown that it is possible to add Arc Consistency to any ACO algorithms and the computational results confirm that the performance of ACO can be improved with this type of hybridisation. Anyway, a complexity analysis should be done in order to evaluate the cost we are adding with this kind of integration. We strongly believe that this kind of integration between complete and incomplete techniques should be studied deeply. Future versions of the algorithm will study the pheromone treatment representation and the incorporation of available techniques in order to reduce the input problem (Pre Processing) and improve the solutions given by the ants (Post Processing). The ants solutions may contain expensive components which can be eliminated by a fine tuning heuristic after the solution, then we will explore Post Processing procedures, which consists in the identification and replacement of the columns of the ACO solution in each iteration by more effective columns. Besides, the ants solutions can be improved by other local search methods like Hill Climbing, Simulated Annealing or Tabu Search.

References

1. D. Alexandrov and Y. Kochetov. Behavior of the ant colony algorithm for the set covering problem. In *Proc. of Symp. Operations Research*, pages 255–260. Springer Verlag, 2000.
2. K. R. Apt. *Principles of Constraint Programming.* Cambridge University Press, 2003.
3. E. Balas and M. Padberg. Set partitioning: A survey. *SIAM Review*, 18:710–760, 1976.
4. J. E. Beasley. Or-library:distributing test problem by electronic mail. *Journal of Operational Research Society*, 41(11):1069–1072, 1990.
5. J. E. Beasley and P. C. Chu. A genetic algorithm for the set covering problem. *European Journal of Operational Research*, 94(2):392–404, 1996.
6. P. C. Chu and J. E. Beasley. Constraint handling in genetic algorithms: the set partitoning problem. *Journal of Heuristics*, 4:323–357, 1998.

7. R. Dechter and D. Frost. Backjump-based backtracking for constraint satisfaction problems. *Artificial Intelligence*, 136:147–188, 2002.
8. M. Dorigo, G. D. Caro, and L. M. Gambardella. Ant algorithms for discrete optimization. *Artificial Life*, 5:137–172, 1999.
9. M. Dorigo and L. M. Gambardella. Ant colony system: A cooperative learning approach to the traveling salesman problem. *IEEE Transactions on Evolutionary Computation*, 1(1):53–66, 1997.
10. M. Dorigo and T. Stutzle. *Ant Colony Optimization.* MIT Press, USA, 2004.
11. F. Focacci, F. Laburthe, and A. Lodi. Local search and constraint programming. In *Handbook of metaheuristics.* Kluwer, 2002.
12. C. Gagne, M. Gravel, and W. Price. A look-ahead addition to the ant colony optimization metaheuristic and its application to an industrial scheduling problem. In J. S. et al., editor, *Proceedings of the fourth Metaheuristics International Conference MIC'01*, pages 79–84, July 2001.
13. X. Gandibleux, X. Delorme, and V. T'Kindt. An ant colony algorithm for the set packing problem. In M. D. et al., editor, *ANTS 2004*, volume 3172 of *LNCS*, pages 49–60. SV, 2004.
14. R. Hadji, M. Rahoual, E. Talbi, and V. Bachelet. Ant colonies for the set covering problem. In M. D. et al., editor, *ANTS 2000*, pages 63–66, 2000.
15. K. Kotecha, G. Sanghani, and N. Gambhava. Genetic algorithm for airline crew scheduling problem using cost-based uniform crossover. In *Second Asian Applied Computing Conference, AACC 2004*, volume 3285 of *Lecture Notes in Artificial Intelligence*, pages 84–91, Kathmandu, Nepal, October 2004. Springer.
16. G. Leguizamón and Z. Michalewicz. A new version of ant system for subset problems. In *Congress on Evolutionary Computation, CEC'99*, pages 1459–1464, Piscataway, NJ, USA, 1999. IEEE Press.
17. L. Lessing, I. Dumitrescu, and T. Stutzle. A comparison between aco algorithms for the set covering problem. In M. D. et al., editor, *ANTS 2004*, volume 3172 of *LNCS*, pages 1–12. SV, 2004.
18. D. Levine. A parallel genetic algorithm for the set partitioning problem. Technical Report ANL-94/23 Argonne National Laboratory, May 1994. Available at http://citeseer.ist.psu.edu/levine94parallel.html.
19. V. Maniezzo and M. Milandri. An ant-based framework for very strongly constrained problems. In M. D. et al., editor, *ANTS 2002*, volume 2463 of *LNCS*, pages 222–227. SV, 2002.
20. B. Meyer and A. Ernst. Integrating aco and constraint propagation. In M. D. et al., editor, *ANTS 2004*, volume 3172 of *LNCS*, pages 166–177. SV, 2004.
21. R. Michel and M. Middendorf. An island model based ant system with lookahead for the shortest supersequence problem. In *Lecture notes in Computer Science, Springer Verlag*, volume 1498, pages 692–701, 1998.
22. R. L. Rardin. *Optimization in Operations Research.* Prentice Hall, 1998.

A Refined Evaluation Function for the MinLA Problem

Eduardo Rodriguez-Tello[1], Jin-Kao Hao[1], and Jose Torres-Jimenez[2]

[1] LERIA, Université d'Angers.
2 Boulevard Lavoisier, 49045 Angers, France
{ertello, hao}@info.univ-angers.fr
[2] Mathematics Department, University of Guerrero.
54 Carlos E. Adame, 39650 Acapulco Guerrero, Mexico
jose.torres.jimenez@acm.org

Abstract. This paper introduces a refined evaluation function, called Φ, for the Minimum Linear Arrangement problem (MinLA). Compared with the classical evaluation function (LA), Φ integrates additional information contained in an arrangement to distinguish arrangements with the same LA value. The main characteristics of Φ are analyzed and its practical usefulness is assessed within both a Steepest Descent (SD) algorithm and a Memetic Algorithm (MA). Experiments show that the use of Φ allows to boost the performance of SD and MA, leading to the improvement on some previous best known solutions.

Keywords: Genetic Algorithms, Evaluation Function, Linear Arrangement, Heuristics.

1 Introduction

The evaluation function is one of the key elements for the success of evolutionary algorithms and more generally, heuristic search algorithms. It is the evaluation function that guides the search process toward good solutions in a combinatorial search space. The more discriminating this function is, the more effective the search process will be.

In combinatorial optimization, the objective function associated to a particular problem is often used as an evaluation function. However, this method can not be used if the search space includes infeasible solutions. In such cases, penalty terms are often added to evaluate the degree of infeasibility [3, 8]. It is also effective to dynamically change the evaluation function during the search, like in the noising method [1] and the search space smoothing method [6]. Another technique consists in developing new more informative evaluation functions which may not be directly related to the objective function such in [8, 9].

In this paper, we are interested in devising a refined evaluation function for the *Minimum Linear Arrangement* problem (MinLA). MinLA was first stated by Harper in [7]. His aim was to design error-correcting codes with minimal average

A. Gelbukh and C.A. Reyes-Garcia (Eds.): MICAI 2006, LNAI 4293, pp. 392–403, 2006.

absolute errors on certain classes of graphs. MinLA arises also in other research fields like biological applications, graph drawing, VLSI layout and software diagram layout [2, 11].

MinLA can be stated formally as follows. Let $G(V, E)$ be a finite undirected graph, where V ($|V| = n$) defines the set of vertices and $E \subseteq V \times V = \{\{i, j\} | i, j \in V\}$ is the set of edges. Given a one-to-one labeling function $\varphi : V \rightarrow \{1..n\}$, called a linear arrangement, the total edge length (cost) for G with respect to arrangement φ is defined according to Equation 1.

$$LA(G, \varphi) = \sum_{(u,v) \in E} |\varphi(u) - \varphi(v)| \tag{1}$$

Then the MinLA problem consists in finding a best labeling function φ for a given graph G so that $LA(G, \varphi)$ is minimized.

MinLA is known to be NP-hard for general graphs [4], though there exist polynomial cases such as trees, rooted trees, hypercubes, meshes, outerplanar graphs, and others (see [2] for a detailed survey). To tackle the MinLA problem, a number of heuristic algorithms have been developed. Among these algorithms are a) heuristics especially developed for MinLA, such as the multi-scale algorithm [10] and the algebraic multi-grid scheme [14]; and b) metaheuristics such as Simulated Annealing [12] and Memetic Algorithms [13].

All these algorithms evaluate the quality of a solution (linear arrangement) as the change in the objective function $LA(G, \varphi)$. However, using LA as the evaluation function of a search algorithm represents a potential drawback. Indeed, different linear arrangements can have the same total edge length and can not be distinguished by LA, even though they do not have the same chances to be further improved.

In this paper, a more discriminating evaluation function (namely Φ) is proposed. The basic idea is to integrate in the evaluation function not only the total edge length of an arrangement (LA), but also other semantic information related to the arrangement.

The new evaluation function Φ is experimentally assessed regarding to the conventional LA evaluation function within both a Steepest Descent (SD) algorithm and a Memetic Algorithm (MA) by employing a set of benchmark instances taken from the literature. The computational results show that thanks to the use of Φ, the performance of the search algorithms is greatly improved, leading to the improvement on some previous best known solutions.

The reminder of this work is organized as follows. In Section 2, after analyzing the drawbacks of the classic evaluation function for MinLA, the refined evaluation function is formally described. Then, in Section 3, with the help of a parameter-free SD algorithm, the proposed evaluation function is assessed with respect to the conventional LA function. Additional analysis and comparisons are given in Section 4 within a Memetic Algorithm framework. Finally, Section 5 summarizes the contributions of this paper.

2 A Refined Evaluation Function for MinLA

The choice of the evaluation function (fitness function) is a very important aspect of any search procedure. Firstly, in order to efficiently test each potential solution, the evaluation function must be as simple as possible. Secondly, it must be sensitive enough to locate promising search regions on the space of solutions. Finally, the evaluation function must be consistent: a solution that has a higher probability for further improvement should get a better evaluation value.

The classical evaluation function for MinLA (LA) does not fulfill these requirements. In the next subsection LA's deficiencies are analyzed and a refined evaluation function is formally introduced.

2.1 The Φ Evaluation Function

A particular resulting value of the LA evaluation function can also be expressed by the Formula 2, where d_k refers to the appearing frequency of an absolute difference with value k between two adjacent vertices of the graph (see Table 1 for an example).

$$LA(G, \varphi) = \sum_{k=1}^{n-1} k d_k \tag{2}$$

This way of computing the solution quality is not sensitive enough to locate promising search regions on the space of solutions, because it does not make distinctions among the absolute differences (k). In other words, LA considers exactly equal a big absolute difference and a small one. Additionally, it is not really prospective because when two arrangements have the same total edge length it is impossible to know which one has higher possibility for further improvement. For example, the two arrangements for the graph showed in Fig. 1 have the same cost ($LA = 35$), but one of them has in fact better chances to be improved in subsequent iterations of the search process. This point will be made clear below.

The Φ evaluation function that will be introduced below helps to overcome these disadvantages. This new function evaluates the quality of an arrangement considering not only the total edge length (LA) of the arrangement, but also additional information induced by the absolute differences of the graph. Furthermore, it maintains the fact that $\lfloor \Phi \rfloor$ results into the same integer value produced by Equations 1 and 2.

The main idea of Φ is to penalize the absolute differences having small values of k and to favor those with values of k near to the bandwidth β of the graph[1]. The logic behind this is that it is easier to reduce the total edge length of the arrangement if it has summands of greater value. To accomplish it, each frequency d_k should have a different contribution, which can be computed by employing Equation 3.

---

[1] $\beta(G, \varphi) = Max\{|\varphi(u) - \varphi(v)| : (u, v) \in E\}$.

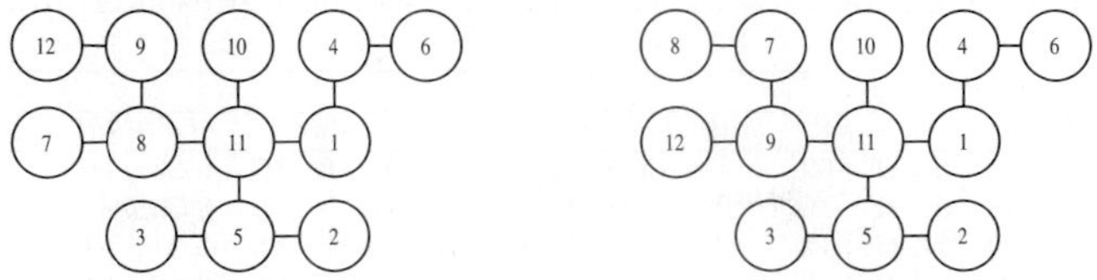

(a) (b)

Fig. 1. (a) Arrangement φ with $LA = 35$. (b) Arrangement φ' with $LA = 35$.

$$k + \frac{1}{\prod_{j=1}^{k}(n+j)} = k + \frac{n!}{(n+k)!} \tag{3}$$

Then, the quality of an arrangement can be defined by the following expression:

$$\sum_{k=1}^{n-1} d_k \left(k + \frac{n!}{(n+k)!}\right) \tag{4}$$

By simplifying this formula we obtain the Equation 5, which represents the new Φ evaluation function. Observe that the first term in this formula is equal to Equation 2. The second term (a fractional value) is the discriminator for arrangements having the same LA value.

$$\Phi(G, \varphi) = \sum_{k=1}^{n-1} kd_k + \sum_{k=1}^{n-1} \frac{n!d_k}{(n+k)!} \tag{5}$$

In the following subsection the calculation of Φ is illustrated with an example.

2.2 A Calculation Example of the Φ Evaluation Function

Let us consider the two arrangements of the graph depicted in Fig. 1. In Table 1 the steps used in the computation of the second term in Equation 5, for each arrangement, are displayed. The rows corresponding to $d_k = 0$ were omitted because they do not contribute to the final result.

Then, by making the substitution of the resulting values in the Formula 5 we obtain: $\Phi(G, \varphi) = 35+2.43\text{E-}01= 35.243$. In contrast if Φ is computed for φ' of Fig. 1(b), a different and smaller value is obtained: $\Phi(G, \varphi') = 35+1.77\text{E-}01= 35.177$. It means that the arrangement φ' is potentially better than φ. Indeed it is better because it is easier to reduce the 4 absolute differences with value 2 ($d_2 = 4$) in φ' than the 3 absolute differences with value 1 ($d_1 = 3$) in φ.

In this sense Φ is more discriminating than LA and leads to smoother landscapes of the search process.

Table 1. Calculation of Φ for the two arrangements presented in Fig. 1

	φ				φ'			
k	d_k	$n!d_k$	$(n+k)!$	$n!d_k/(n+k)!$	d_k	$n!d_k$	$(n+k)!$	$n!d_k/(n+k)!$
1	3	1.44E+09	6.23E+09	2.31E-01	2	9.58E+08	6.23E+09	1.54E-01
2	2	9.58E+08	8.72E+10	1.10E-02	4	1.92E+09	8.72E+10	2.20E-02
3	4	1.92E+09	1.31E+12	1.47E-03	3	1.44E+09	1.31E+12	1.10E-03
6	1	4.79E+08	6.40E+15	7.48E-08	1	4.79E+08	6.40E+15	7.48E-08
10	1	4.79E+08	1.12E+21	4.26E-13	1	4.79E+08	1.12E+21	4.26E-13
		Sum		2.43E-01				1.77E-01

2.3 Computational Considerations

In order to compute the quality of a linear arrangement φ by using the conventional LA evaluation function, we must calculate the sum $\sum_{(u,v)\in E} |\varphi(u)-\varphi(v)|$. Then it requires $O(|E|)$ instructions.

On the other hand, to efficiently compute the Φ evaluation function we could precalculate each term $k + (n!/(n+k)!)$ in the Equation 4 and store them in an array W. All this needs to execute $O(|V| + |V|)$ operations. Then each time that we need to calculate the value of Φ the sum $\sum_{(u,v)\in E} W[|\varphi(u) - \varphi(v)|]$ must be computed, which results into the same computational complexity as the one that is required to compute LA. Additionally, the Φ evaluation function allows an incremental cost evaluation of neighboring solutions (see Subsection 3.1). Suppose that the labels of two different vertices (u, v) are swapped, then we should only recompute the $|N(u)| + |N(v)|$ absolute differences that change, where $|N(u)|$ and $|N(v)|$ represent the number of adjacent vertices to u and v respectively. As it can be seen this is faster than $O(|E|)$.

In the next sections, we will carry out experimental studies in order to assess the effectiveness of the proposed evaluation function compared with the conventional LA function. This is realized first with a parameter free descent algorithm and then with a memetic algorithm.

3 Comparing the Evaluation Functions Within a Steepest Descent Algorithm

3.1 Steepest Descent Algorithm

The choice of the Steepest Descent (SD) algorithm for this comparison is fully justified by the fact that SD is completely parameter free and thus allows a direct comparison of the two evaluation functions without bias. Next, the implementation details of this algorithm are presented.

Search Space, Representation and Fitness Function. For a graph G with n vertices, the search space $\mathcal{A}$ is composed of all $n!$ possible linear arrangements. In our SD algorithm a linear arrangement φ is represented as an array l of n integers, which is indexed by the vertices and whose i-th value $l[i]$ denotes

Table 2. Performance comparison between SD-LA and SD-Φ

Graph	$\lvert V \rvert$	SD-LA I	SD-LA C	SD-LA T	SD-Φ I	SD-Φ C	SD-Φ T	SD-Φ IN	Δ_C
randomA1	1000	2115.7	946033.1	0.0195	3134.2	941677.7	0.0182	741.5	-4355.4
randomA3	1000	2460.1	14397879.8	0.4839	2887.3	14396580.9	0.4681	625.1	-1298.8
bintree10	1023	1233.6	51716.8	0.0132	1406.9	51548.8	0.0132	229.4	-167.9
mesh33x33	1089	2994.4	130751.3	0.0153	8143.9	112171.7	0.0151	1347.6	-18579.6
3elt	4720	27118.4	2630144.6	0.2708	52061.6	2392981.3	0.2797	5616.7	-237163.3
airfoil1	4253	23566.4	2184693.3	0.2386	45909.1	1958983.4	0.2263	4575.9	-225709.9
c2y	980	2140.9	169434.7	0.0159	3078.9	167127.9	0.0171	578.3	-2306.8
c3y	1327	3334.1	282818.5	0.0559	5097.4	275529.3	0.0461	1008.8	-7289.2
gd95c	62	69.2	716.3	0.0002	81.3	697.4	0.0002	19.4	-18.9
gd96a	1096	2215.7	148158.3	0.0167	3283.5	144751.7	0.0177	804.3	-3406.6
Average									−50029.6

the label assigned to the vertex i. The fitness of an arrangement φ is evaluated by using either the LA or Φ evaluation function (Equation 1 or 5 respectively).

Initial Solution. In this implementation the initial solution is generated randomly.

Neighborhood Function. The *neighborhood* $N(\varphi)$ of an arrangement φ is such that for each $\varphi \in \mathcal{A}$, $\varphi' \in N(\varphi)$ if and only if φ' can be obtained by swapping the labels of any pair of different vertices (u, v) from φ. This neighborhood is small and allows an incremental cost evaluation of neighboring solutions.

General Procedure. The SD algorithm starts from the initial solution $\varphi \in \mathcal{A}$ and repeats replacing φ with the best solution in its neighborhood $N(\varphi)$ until no better arrangement is found.

3.2 Computational Experiments

The purpose of this experiment is to study the characteristics of the Φ evaluation function and provide more insights into its real working. That is why this analysis does not only take into account the final solution quality obtained by the algorithms, but also their ability to efficiently explore the search space. To attain this objective, the SD algorithm presented in Subsection 3.1 was coded in C, named SD-LA and SD-Φ depending on which evaluation function is used. The algorithm was compiled with *gcc* using the optimization flag -$O3$, and ran sequentially into a cluster of 10 nodes, each having a Xeon bi-CPU at 2 GHz, 1 GB of RAM and Linux.

The test-suite used in this experiment is composed of the 21 benchmarks[2] proposed in [12] and used later in [10, 13, 14]. In our preliminary experiments, we observed similar results over the set of 21 benchmark instances. For the reason of space limitation, we have decided to report only the results of 10 representative instances covering the different cases.

The methodology used consistently throughout this experimentation is the following. First, 20 random arrangements were generated for each of the 10 selected benchmark instances, and were used as starting solutions for each run of

[2] http://www.lsi.upc.es/~jpetit/MinLA/Experiments

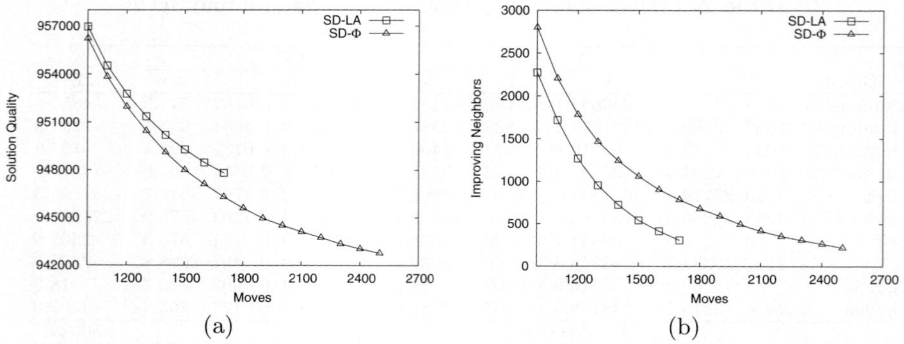

Fig. 2. Graphs representing the behavior of the compared evaluation functions over the *randomA*1 instance. (a) Average solution quality, (b) Average improving neighbors.

the compared evaluation functions. The average results achieved in these executions are summarized in Table 2, where column 1 and 2 show the name of the graph and its number of vertices. Columns 2 to 8 display the total iterations (I), the final cost in terms of total edge length (C), and the CPU time per iteration (T) in seconds for both SD-LA and SD-Φ respectively. Column 9 presents the average number of improving neighbors (IN) found by SD-Φ, at the same iteration where SD-LA stops, that is when IN for SD-LA equals zero. Last column shows the difference (Δ_C) between the total average cost produced by the compared algorithms.

The results presented in Table 2 show clearly that the SD algorithm that employs Φ, consistently has better results than the algorithm that uses LA. The average improvement obtained with the use of Φ is -50029.6, which leads to a significant decrease of the total edge length (Δ_C up to -237163.3). Notice that the SD-LA algorithm always stops the search process earlier than SD-Φ (compare columns 2 and 5), basically because LA can not distinguish arrangements with the same total edge length given as consequence a critical deficiency in finding improving neighbors (see column 8). Additionally, it is important to remark that these results can be obtained without a significant increment in the computing time, one iteration of SD-LA is approximatively equal to one iteration of SD-Φ (see columns 4 and 7).

The dominance of Φ is better illustrated in Fig. 2, where the behavior of the studied evaluation functions is presented over the *randomA*1 instance (the rest of the studied instances provide similar results). In Fig. 2(a) the X axis represents the number of moves, while the Y axis indicates the average solution quality. Fig. 2(b) depicts the evolution of the average number of improving neighbors (Y axis) with respect to the number of moves. Observe that SD-Φ produces better results because it is capable of identifying the improving neighbors that orient better the search process.

4 Comparing the Evaluation Functions Within a Memetic Algorithm

After having studied the characteristics of Φ by using a simple SD algorithm, we have decided to evaluate its practical usefulness within a Memetic Algorithm (MA).

4.1 Memetic Algorithm

The MA implementation used for this comparison was kept as simple as possible to obtain a clear idea of the evaluation function effectiveness. Indeed, the recombination operator does not take into account the individuals' semantic, no special initialization procedure is employed. Furthermore, A simple SD algorithm was used, which is not as effective as Simulated Annealing or Tabu Search, to reduce the strong influence of (sophisticated) local search procedures. In this sense, this MA implementation is much simplified comparing with the MA of [13]. Next all the details of our MA implementation are presented.

Search Space, Representation and Fitness Function. The search space, representation and evaluation (fitness) functions are the same used in the SD algorithm presented in Section 3.1.

Initialization. The population P is initialized with $|P|$ configurations randomly generated.

Selection. In this MA mating selection is performed by tournament selection, while selection for survival is done by choosing the best individuals from the pool of parents and children, taking care that each phenotype exists only once in the new population (a $(\mu + \lambda)$ selection scheme).

Recombination Operator. For this implementation the Partially Matched Crossover (PMX) operator, introduced in [5], was selected. PMX is designed to preserve absolute positions from both parents.

Local Search Operator. Its purpose is to improve the configurations produced by the recombination operator. In this MA we have decided to use a modified version of the SD algorithm presented in Section 3.1. Instead of replacing the current solution with the best arrangement found in its neighborhood, it is replaced with the first improving neighbor. Notice that this Descent Algorithm is weaker than its best improvement version used in Section 3.1, but it is faster. This process is repeated until no better arrangement is found or the predefined maximum number iterations is reached.

General Procedure. MA starts building an initial population P. Then at each generation, a predefined number of recombinations (*offspring*) are executed. In each recombination two configurations are chosen by tournament selection from the population, then a recombination operator is used to produce two offspring. The local search operator is applied to improve both offspring for a fixed number of iterations L and the improved configurations are inserted into the population. Finally, the population is updated by choosing the best individuals

Table 3. Performance comparison between MA-*LA* and MA-Φ

Graph	MA-*LA*			MA-Φ			
	C	Dev.	T	C	Dev.	T	Δ_C
randomA1	882305.9	3833.1	937.7	877033.1	4371.4	930.2	-5272.8
randomA3	14243888.8	11272.2	7843.6	14235917.8	12236.3	9030.9	-7971.0
bintree10	13869.0	5274.3	171.2	13422.3	4119.3	176.7	-446.8
mesh33x33	35151.8	359.3	65.7	35083.4	90.0	129.9	-68.3
3elt	458695.8	7230.1	10968.2	453149.4	5176.7	11822.6	-5546.4
airfoil1	382781.0	2701.0	8855.5	380404.6	4464.6	9515.3	-2376.5
c2y	85240.5	733.6	370.4	84201.9	723.2	405.8	-1038.6
c3y	137983.9	1027.1	686.7	137281.7	1746.9	705.9	-702.2
gd95c	506.2	0.6	0.4	506.1	0.4	0.5	-0.1
gd96a	102827.8	1759.9	319.9	102285.3	2052.9	348.1	-542.4
			Average				-2396.5

from the pool of parents and children. This process repeats until a predefined number of generations (*maxGenerations*) is reached.

4.2 Computational Experiments

For this comparison the MA presented in Section 4.1 was coded in C. Let us call it MA-*LA* or MA-Φ to distinguish which evaluation function it employs. The algorithm was compiled with *gcc* using the optimization flag *-O*3 and run in the computational platform described in Subsection 3.2. The same parameters were used for MA-*LA* and MA-Φ in this comparison: a) population size $|P| = 50$, b) recombinations per generation *offspring*= 5, c) maximal number of local search iterations $L = 0.20 * |V|$ and d) maximal number of generations $maxGenerations = 1000$.

Table 3 presents the average results obtained in 20 independent executions for each of the 10 benchmark instances selected for the experiments of the Subsection 3.2. The first column in the table shows the name of the graph. The rest of the columns indicate the cost in terms of total edge length (C), its standard deviation (Dev.) and the total CPU time (T) in seconds for the MA-*LA* and MA-Φ algorithms respectively. Finally, column 8 displays the difference (Δ_C) between the cost found by MA-Φ and that reached by MA-*LA*.

From Table 3, one observes that MA-Φ is able to improve on the 10 selected instances the results produced by MA-*LA*. With respect to the computational effort we have noted that MA-Φ consumes approximately the same computing time than MA-*LA*. So this second experiment confirms again that Φ is superior than *LA*.

4.3 Using Φ Within a More Sophisticated MA

Given the results obtained with the simple MA described in the Subsection 4.1, we have decided to asses the performance of Φ within a more sophisticated MA. For this purpose we have reused the MA reported in [13] and replace in its code the classic evaluation function by the refined function Φ (call this algorithm MAMP-Φ). The resulting code was compiled in the computational platform

Table 4. Performance comparison between MAMP-Φ and the state-of-the-art algorithms

Graph	$\lvert V\rvert$	AMG	MAMP	MAMP-Φ				
				C	Avg.	Desv.	T	Δ_C
randomA1	1000	888381	867535	867214	867581.7	634.2	909.0	-321
randomA2	1000	6596081	6533999	6532341	6534770.7	2616.2	3486.3	-1658
randomA3	1000	14303980	14240067	14238712	14239766.4	1213.0	5175.7	-1355
randomA4	1000	1747822	1719906	1718746	1720260.5	1479.7	1904.1	-1160
randomG4	1000	140211	141538	140211	140420.7	354.1	2077.2	0
bintree10	1023	3696	3790	3721	3749.7	36.3	978.7	25
hc10	1024	523776	523776	523776	523776.2	0.6	1140.8	0
mesh33x33	1089	31729	31917	31789	31847.5	68.8	1123.2	60
3elt	4720	357329	362209	357329	361174.7	2198.0	5609.9	0
airfoil1	4253	272931	285429	273090	278259.8	7063.0	5443.1	159
whitaker3	9800	1144476	1167089	1148652	1160117.7	9207.0	15299.7	4176
c1y	828	62262	62333	62262	62302.7	65.0	643.5	0
c2y	980	78822	79017	78929	78964.2	45.4	654.8	107
c3y	1327	123514	123521	123376	123458.5	92.3	728.1	-138
c4y	1366	115131	115144	115051	115129.1	185.7	733.3	-80
c5y	1202	96899	96952	96878	97080.5	391.9	715.3	-21
gd95c	62	506	506	506	506.1	0.3	1.6	0
gd96a	1096	96249	96253	95242	96019.4	559.9	636.8	-1007
gd96b	111	1416	1416	1416	1416.1	0.3	3.7	0
gd96c	65	519	519	519	519.7	1.3	1.4	0
gd96d	180	2391	2391	2391	2391.5	1.1	7.7	0

described in 3.2 and executed 20 times on the full test-suite of Petit [12] using the parameters suggested in [13].

The results of this experiment are presented in Table 4 and compared with those of the two best known heuristics: AMG [14] and MAMP [13]. In this table, the name of the graph and its number of vertices are displayed in the first two columns. The best solution reported by AMG and MAMP is shown in columns 3 and 4 respectively. Columns 5 to 8 present the best cost in terms of total edge length (C), the average cost (Avg.), its standard deviation (Dev.) and the average CPU time (T) in seconds for the MAMP-Φ algorithm. Last column shows the difference (Δ_C) between the best cost produced by MAMP-Φ and the previous best-known solution.

From Table 4, one observes that MAMP-Φ is able to improve on 8 previous best known solutions and to equal these results in 8 more instances. In 5 instances, MAMP-Φ did not reach the best reported solution, but its results are very close to them (in average 0.028%). Moreover, MAMP-Φ improves in 16 instances the results achieved by MAMP (see columns 4 and 5).

5 Conclusions

In this paper, we have introduced the Φ evaluation function for the Minimum Linear Arrangement problem. It allows to indicate the potential for further improvement of an arrangement by considering additional information induced by the absolute differences between adjacent labels of the arrangement. To gain more insights into its real working, the classical evaluation function LA and Φ

were compared over a set of well known benchmarks within a basic SD algorithm. The results showed that an average improvement of 3.39% can be achieved when Φ is used, because it is able to identify an average number of improving neighbors greater than that produced by LA.

Moreover, we have evaluated the practical usefulness of Φ within a basic MA. From this experiment, it is observed that MA-Φ is able to improve on the 10 selected instances the results produced by MA-LA, consuming approximately the same computing time.

Finally, in a third experiment the Φ evaluation function was incorporated into a more sophisticated MA. The resulting algorithm, called MAMP-Φ, was compared with the two best known heuristics: AMG [14] and MAMP [13]. The results obtained by MAMP-Φ are superior to those presented by the previous proposed evolutionary approach [13], and permit to improve on 8 previous best known solutions.

This study confirms that the research on evaluations functions, to provide more effective guidance for heuristic algorithms, is certainly a very interesting way to boost the performance of these algorithms.

Acknowledgments. This work is supported by the CONACyT Mexico, the "Contrat Plan Etat-Région" project COM (2000-2006) as well as the Franco-Mexican Joint Lab in Computer Science LAFMI (2005-2006). The reviewers of the paper are greatly acknowledged for their constructive comments.

References

1. I. Charon and O. Hudry. The noising method: A new method for combinatorial optimization. *Operations Research Letters*, 14(3):133–137, 1993.
2. J. Diaz, J. Petit, and M. Serna. A survey of graph layout problems. *ACM Comput. Surv.*, 34(3):313–356, 2002.
3. E. Falkenauer. A hybrid grouping genetic algorithm for bin packing. *Journal of Heuristics*, 2:5–30, 1996.
4. M. Garey and D. Johnson. *Computers and Intractability: A guide to the Theory of NP-Completeness.* W.H. Freeman and Company, New York, 1979.
5. D. E. Goldberg and R. Lingle. Alleles, loci, and the travelling salesman problem. In *Proc. of ICGA'85*, pages 154–159. Carnegie Mellon publishers, 1985.
6. J. Gu and X. Huang. Efficient local search with search space smoothing: A case study of the traveling salesman problem (TSP). *IEEE Transactions on Systems, Man, and Cybernetics*, 24:728–735, 1994.
7. L. Harper. Optimal assignment of numbers to vertices. *Journal of SIAM*, 12(1):131–135, 1964.
8. D. Johnson, C. Aragon, L. McGeoch, and C. Schevon. Optimization by simulated annealing: An experimental evaluation; part II, graph coloring and number partitioning. *Operations Research*, 39(3):378–406, 1991.
9. S. Khanna, R. Motwani, M. Sudan, and U. Vazirani. On syntactic versus computational views of approximability. In *Proc. Of the 35th Annual IEEE Symposium on Foundations of Computer Science*, pages 819–830. IEEE Press, 1994.
10. Y. Koren and D. Harel. A multi-scale algorithm for the linear arrangement problem. *Lecture Notes in Computer Science*, 2573:293–306, 2002.

11. Y. Lai and K. Williams. A survey of solved problems and applications on bandwidth, edgesum, and profile of graphs. *Graph Theory*, 31:75–94, 1999.
12. J. Petit. *Layout Problems*. PhD thesis, Universitat Politécnica de Catalunya, 2001.
13. E. Rodriguez-Tello, J.-K. Hao, and J. Torres-Jimenez. Memetic algorithms for the MinLA problem. *Lecture Notes in Computer Science*, 3871:73–84, 2006.
14. I. Safro, D. Ron, and A. Brandt. Graph minimum linear arrangement by multilevel weighted edge contractions. *Journal of Algorithms*, 2004. in press.

ILS-Perturbation Based on Local Optima Structure for the QAP Problem

Everardo Gutiérrez and Carlos A. Brizuela

Computer Science Department, CICESE Research Center
Km 107 Carr. Tijuana-Ensenada, Ensenada, B.C., México
+52–646–1750500
{egutierr, cbrizuel}@cicese.mx

Abstract. Many problems in AI can be stated as search problems and most of them are very complex to solve. One alternative for these problems are local search methods that have been widely used for tackling difficult optimization problems for which we do not know algorithms which can solve every instance to optimality in a reasonable amount of time. One of the most popular methods is what is known as iterated local search (ILS), which samples the set of local optima searching for a better solution. This algorithm's behavior is achieved by some mechanisms like perturbation which is a key aspect to consider, since it allows the algorithm to reach a new solution from the set of local optima by escaping from the previous local optimum basis of attraction. In order to design a good perturbation method we need to analyze the local optima structure such that ILS leads to a good biased sampling. In this paper, the local optima structure of the Quadratic Assignment Problem, an NP-hard optimization problem, is used to determine the required perturbation size in the ILS algorithm. The analysis is focused on verifying if the set of local optima has the "Big Valley (BV)" structure, and on how close local optima are in relation to problem size. Experimental results show that a small perturbation seems appropriate for instances having the BV structure, and for instances having a low distance among local optima, even if they do not have a clear BV structure. Finally, as the local optima structure moves away from BV a larger perturbation is needed.

Keywords: Iterated Local Search, Big Valley, Perturbation Length, Quadratic Assignment Problem.

1 Introduction

Most problems in AI can be classified as general search problems and many methods have been proposed to deal with them [17]. However, the existence of problems for which there are no known algorithms which can ensure optimality in a reasonable amount of time [6] has motivated the development of alternative methods to obtain acceptable solutions from a practical point of view. One of the alternatives is the method known as *local search* (LS), which has been successfully used in practice for difficult combinatorial optimization problems [1,5,6].

A. Gelbukh and C.A. Reyes-Garcia (Eds.): MICAI 2006, LNAI 4293, pp. 404–414, 2006.

Local search algorithms (LSA) have a general behavior based on the following idea: take an initial solution and modify it until no further improvements are possible. These algorithms need to define a *neighborhood* function N which represents a map $N : S \rightarrow 2^S$, such that it defines for each solution s in the set of all feasible solutions S a subset $N(s) \subset S$ of *neighbors* of s [1]. This function defines the structure over which the search must be done, and this structure is called *search graph* [4], *fitness landscape* [16,19], or *state space* [17].

There are a lot of suggested algorithms based on this behavior and Iterated Local Search (ILS) is one of them [13,11]. ILS explores the set of local optima applying a local search and a perturbation mechanism to restart the search. While a better local search can reach a better local optimum by itself, this may make it difficult to perturb this solution such that a different local optimum can be reached. Many perturbation methods have been proposed and they are one of the key aspects to consider in the design of ILS algorithms [11].

The Quadratic Assignment Problem (QAP) is a very important combinatorial optimization problem from a practical and theoretical point of view. Since QAP belongs to *NP-hard* class [6], many alternative methods such as LS, have been proposed to deal with it. In this paper we analyze the local optima structure of an instance set, and its relation with the perturbation mechanism in a simple ILS algorithm.

The remainder of this paper is organized as follows. Section 2 explains the idea of ILS and their mechanisms. In section 3 we state the QAP problem. Section 4 gives the concepts of "Global Convexity" and "Big Valley", and shows some QAP local optimum structures. Section 5 presents the experimental setup and their results. Finally, section 6 gives the conclusions and ideas for future research.

2 Iterated Local Search (ILS)

Iterated Local Search is among the best performing local search algorithms for some well known combinatorial optimization problems [9,18,11]. The essence of ILS is: one iteratively builds a sequence of solutions generated by an embedded heuristic [11]. Let f be the cost function of our combinatorial optimization problem; f is to be minimized. Let S be the set of all solutions s. Finally, the local search procedure *LocalSearch* defines a mapping from the set S to the smaller set S^* of locally optimal solutions s^*, *LocalSearch* procedure samples S^*. Then, given the mapping from S to S^*, we need to reduce the costs found without modifying *LocalSearch*. ILS tries to avoid the disadvantages of random restart by exploring S^* using a walk that steps from one s^* to a "nearby" one, and can be described with the following high level steps:

procedure *Iterated Local Search*
  s_0 = **GenerateInitialSolution()**
  s^* = **LocalSearch**(s_0)
  repeat
    s' = **Perturbation**(s^*, *history*)

$s^{*'}$ = **LocalSearch**(s')
s^{*} = **AcceptanceCriterion**(s^{*}, $s^{*'}$, *history*)
until termination condition met
end

According to this general architecture, ILS behavior is defined by the routines: **GenerateInitialSolution**, **LocalSearch**, **Perturbation** and **AcceptanceCriterion**. The main aspects of each one of them are briefly described in the following:

Initial solution. The starting point s_0 can be generated by different methods (random, greedy starting, etc.) and it only has influence on which local optimum is going to be visited first.

Local search. Local search is usually viewed as a black box which allows us to sample the set S^*. For some problems, as in case of TSP, the better the local search, the better the corresponding ILS [11]. However, an excellent local search should systematically undo the work done by the perturbation.

Perturbation. The perturbation should allow the algorithm to reach a solution which can be a seed for a new local optimum using the local search procedure. Then, the perturbation should be large enough to "escape" from the current local minimum basis of attraction, but not too large to give an almost random solution. Previous work claim that while for TSP a perturbation of fixed/small size (double-bridge) has shown a good performance, for QAP a relatively large perturbation size seems to be necessary [11].

Acceptance criterion. This procedure determines whether $s^{*'}$ is accepted or not as the updated current solution. Together with *Perturbation*, it controls the balance between intensification and diversification of the search over S^*.

We will define each ILS routine such that the resulting algorithm is going to be used to tackle QAP, a well known combinatorial optimization problem which is stated in the next section.

3 Quadratic Assignment Problem

The Quadratic Assignment Problem is a combinatorial optimization problem and can be described as the problem of assigning a set of facilities to a set of locations with given distances between locations and flows between facilities. The goal is to find the better assignment of facilities to the locations such that the sum of the product between flows and distances is minimal. Many practical problems can be formulated as QAP and it has been proven that the decision version of this problem is *NP-complete* [6].

Given n facilities and n locations, two n x n matrices A and B for distances and flows respectively, the QAP can be stated as follows:

$$\min_{\phi \in \Phi} \sum_{i=1}^{n} \sum_{j=1}^{n} b_{ij} a_{\phi_i \phi_j} \tag{1}$$

Table 1. Some QAPLIB instances. Problem size, best known values, and lower bounds.

Name	N	Best	Bound
bur26a	26	5426670	5426670
bur26b	26	3817852	3817852
bur26c	26	5426795	5426795
bur26d	26	3821225	3821225
chr25a	25	3796	3796
esc32a	32	130	103
esc32b	32	168	132
kra30a	30	88900	88900
lipa20a	20	3683	3683
lipa60a	60	107218	107218
lipa90a	90	360630	360630
tai30a	30	1818146	1529135
tai30b	30	637117113	589470167
tai60a	60	7205962	5555095
tai60b	60	608215054	50113782

where Φ is the set of all permutations of n numbers, ϕ_i gives the location of facility i and $b_{ij}a_{\phi_i\phi_j}$ is the cost contribution of assigning facility i to location ϕ_i and facility j to location ϕ_j.

Table 1 shows some of the QAPLIB [1] instances. **N** is the problem size (number of facilities and locations), **Best** is the best known solution and **Bound** is the best known lower bound.

We will analyze in next section the local optima structure of these instances in order to choose a good perturbation. The analysis is focused on verifying if the cost-distance relation in the set of local optima shows a BV structure.

4 Global Convexity

The correlation of solution's quality (cost, fitness, etc.) and distance between solutions has been studied in many ways [2,10,12,14,19]. The existence of correlation would mean that the search graph has some structure which could be used to guide the search in order to obtain better results. That is, the correlation could be used as a tool in the design of search strategies which take advantage of the search graph structure.

Boese *et al.* [3] analyze the relationships among local optima for two problems: TSP and Graph Bisection. They analyzed a search graph for each problem generating a set of local optima and measuring the distance among them. For the analyzed search graphs, the better solutions have a shorter mean distance to the others. These results suggest the existence of a globally convex structure [8] in the set of local optima, which they refer to as the "Big Valley" structure.

[1] http://www.seas.upenn.edu/qaplib/

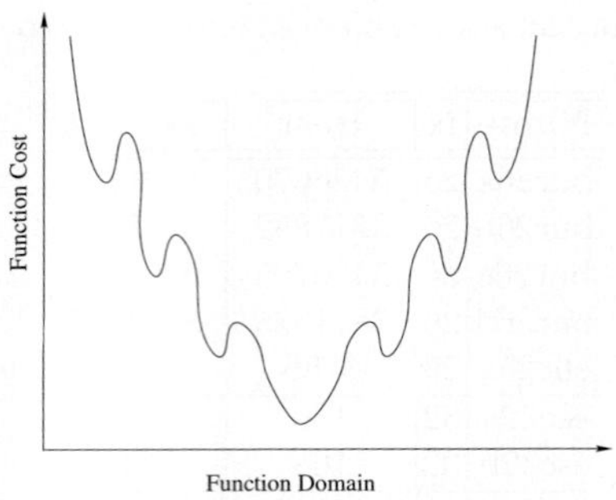

Fig. 1. Example of a globally convex function

Reeves [15] found the same structure for the Flow Shop Problem, using different distance measures and neighborhood structures. Figure 1 shows an example of a function that is "globally convex".

Given a neighborhood N for a problem Π and its respective search graph G, let S^* be the set of local optima with respect to N. In order to verify whether the search graph has the global convexity structure we must analyze the set S^*. Whenever it is not possible to obtain all $s^* \in S^*$ we can obtain a representative sample and measure solutions' quality and distance among them.

5 Experimental Results

5.1 Cost-Distance Correlation

Here we compute the correlation of the cost and the mean distance between a set of local optima over a neighborhood that swap the location of two facilities. For each instance, a local search was performed 6400 times, and the final solution (a local optimum) was taken. The general procedure was a simple greedy local search which explores the neighborhood by searching for a better solution. If there is no better solution the algorithm stops and returns the final solution, which is, by definition, a local optimum.

Instances from QAPLIB show different cost-distance structures among their local optima even if they have the same input distributions. Figures 2, 3, 4, 5, and 6 show the cost-distance structures found for these instances.

We can see that some instances, as those shown in Figure 2, have structures very different from BV, while others like chr25a in Figure 3 and tai30a in Figure 6, show a shape very close to BV. However, it is not easy to distinguish some structures only by visual inspection of these graphs.

We will try to relate these structures with the experimental results produced by the ILS, and whenever this relation is not clear we will use other measures to explain the ILS behavior.

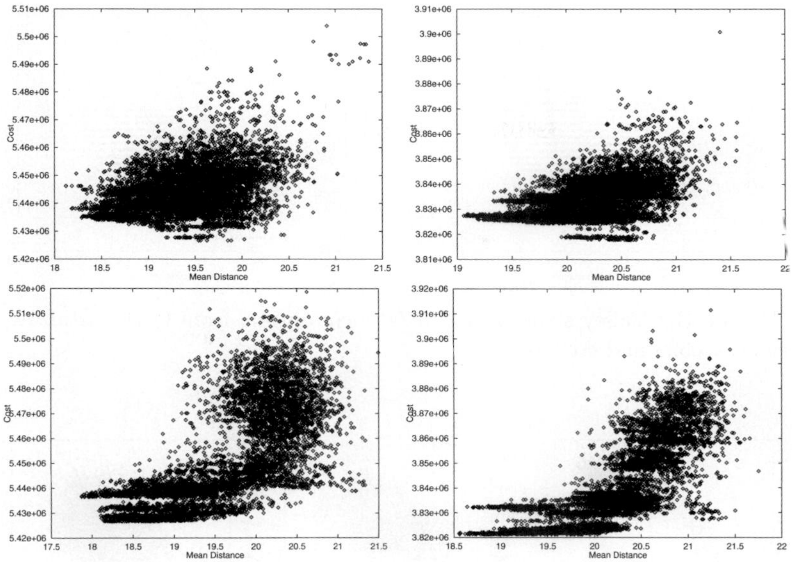

Fig. 2. No Big Valley structures of 6400 local optima from QAP instances. From left to right and top to down: bur26a, bur26b, bur26c, and bur26d.

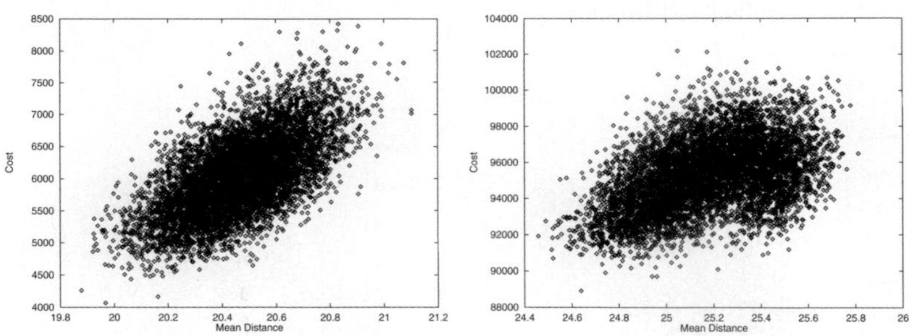

Fig. 3. Pseudo Big Valley structures of 6400 local optima from QAP instances. From left to right: chr25a and kra30a.

5.2 Perturbation vs. Local Optimum Structures

For the experimental analysis of each instance, we used a random solution as the initial one, a greedy first improvement as local search, the location swapping of two facilities as neighborhood and two acceptance criteria: accepting only the current best local optimum and accepting any local optimum. In order to test the influence of local optimum structures on perturbation size, we use a simple random walk of different lengths as perturbation method in our ILS algorithm.

Table 2 shows the mean relative error $((MILS - Best)/Best)$, where $MILS$ is the mean value of 50 ILS runs, accepting only the current best local optimum, and $Best$ is the best known solution. These results are presented for different

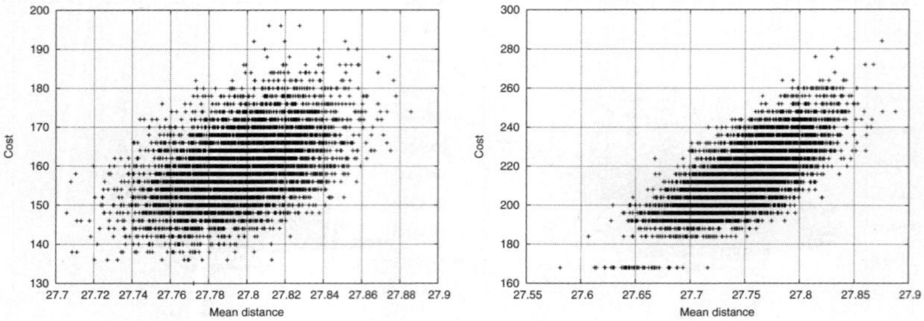

Fig. 4. Pseudo Big Valley structures of 6400 local optima from QAP instances. From left to right: esc32a and esc32b.

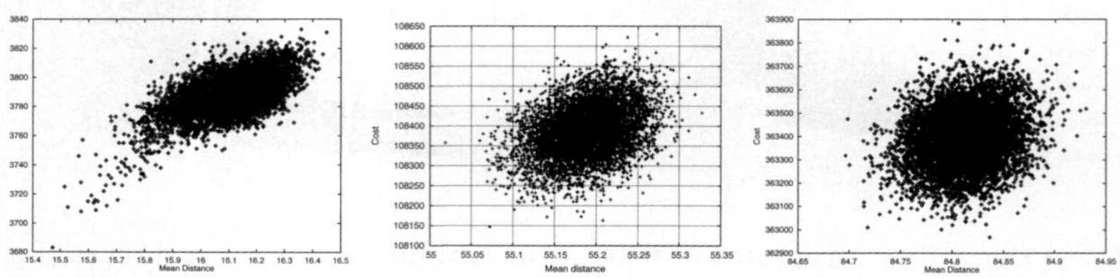

Fig. 5. Different structures of 6400 local optima from QAP instances. From left to right: lipa20a, lipa60a, and lipa90a.

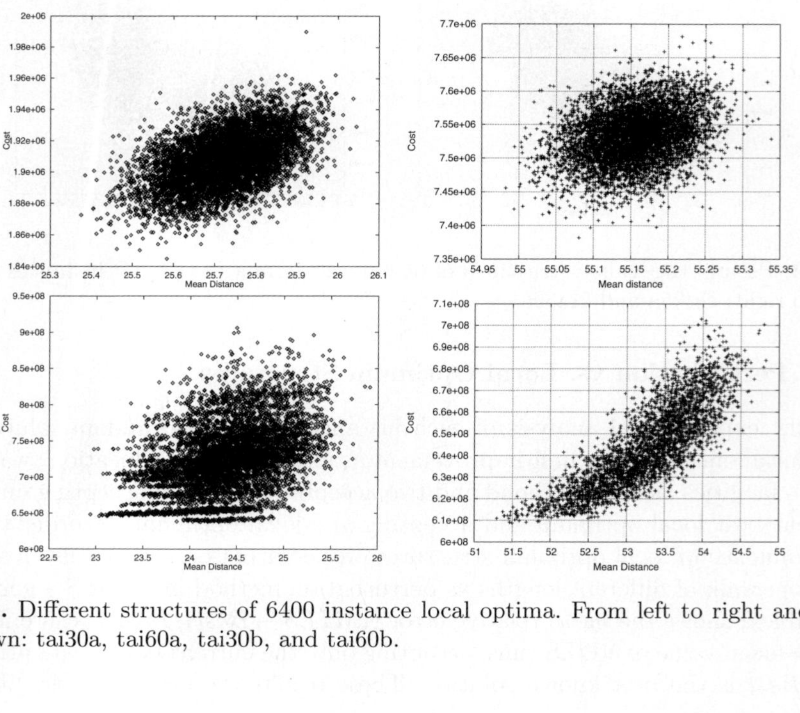

Fig. 6. Different structures of 6400 instance local optima. From left to right and top to down: tai30a, tai60a, tai30b, and tai60b.

Table 2. Relative errors between mean ILS results and best known solution for different values of walk lengths (accepting only the current best local optimum)

Name	N/16	N/8	N/4	N/2	N
bur26a	0.145	0.090	0.077	**0.067**	0.082
bur26b	0.182	0.135	0.123	0.105	**0.094**
bur26c	0.117	0.082	0.019	**0.003**	0.005
bur26d	0.109	0.093	0.027	**0.003**	0.005
chr25a	23.678	**19.589**	20.155	24.282	26.563
esc32a	6.2	**5.769**	7.585	8.954	9.631
esc32b	9.786	7.786	**7.167**	7.929	8.524
kra30a	3.678	2.632	**1.901**	2.332	2.623
lipa20a	1.916	1.491	1.325	**1.122**	1.312
lipa60a	**0.828**	0.858	0.897	0.932	0.941
lipa90a	**0.587**	0.622	0.663	0.677	0.679
tai30a	2.575	2.204	**2.059**	2.575	2.813
tai30b	4.150	2.373	1.388	**0.759**	0.797
tai60a	2.407	**2.190**	2.980	3.132	3.063
tai60b	1.626	1.004	0.734	**0.376**	0.412

perturbation sizes from $N/16$ to N. We can see that for some instances we obtain a better result using a larger perturbation (*i.e.* close to N) while for others a smaller perturbation seems to be more appropriate (*i.e.* close to $N/16$). If we relate these results to the local optimum structures previously presented we can see that instances having better results with smaller perturbations have a clear BV structure, while instances that need larger perturbations have structures that differ from the BV. For each instance we take the best achieved result (the one in bold) and compare it with the value obtained with the farthest walk length to verify if the differences are statistically significant. For instance, for bur26a the best value was obtained with $N/2$, then we compare it with the value obtained for a walk length of $N/16$. For all instances the confidence intervals were calculated and they do not overlap (at a 99% of confidence), the exception was esc32b for which differences between averages results obtained for different walk lengths are not statistically significant.

Table 3 shows equivalent results when the accepting criterion is to accept any local optimum. Relation between BV structure and perturbation seems to hold for this criterion too, regardless of solutions' quality. Moreover, for instances having the BV structure and obtaining better results with smaller perturbations, we obtain better mean results accepting only the current best local optimum than accepting any local optimum (statistically tested at 99% of confidence). This confirms the existence of BV structure, since accepting only the current best local optimum leads to a biased search that exploits this structure and allows better results using smaller perturbations.

There are some instances for which the relation between local optimum structures and perturbation length is not clear. For instance, tai30a in Figure 6 seems to have a better BV structure than lipa90a in Figure 5, contradicting the results

Table 3. Relative errors between mean ILS results and the best known solution for different values of walk lengths (accepting any local optimum)

Name	N/16	N/8	N/4	N/2	N
bur26a	0.148	0.126	0.101	**0.078**	0.080
bur26b	0.182	0.142	0.109	**0.080**	0.092
bur26c	0.168	0.036	0.007	**0.005**	0.008
bur26d	0.122	0.048	**0.005**	0.009	0.006
chr25a	29.299	**24.228**	27.118	25.555	26.769
esc32a	**7.538**	7.846	8.246	9.261	9.385
esc32b	8.905	7.286	**6.143**	7.048	7.619
kra30a	3.537	2.530	**2.162**	2.339	2.747
lipa20a	1.632	1.386	**1.155**	1.527	1.749
lipa60a	0.895	**0.879**	0.921	0.933	0.943
lipa90a	**0.633**	0.661	0.668	0.672	0.676
tai30a	2.474	**2.307**	2.710	2.752	2.889
tai30b	6.862	2.510	1.568	0.973	**0.755**
tai60a	**2.495**	2.884	3.009	3.171	3.167
tai60b	0.723	0.950	**0.179**	0.414	0.671

Table 4. Cost-Distance correlation and relative closeness of local optima

Name	Correlation	DMD/N
bur26a	0.387	0.135
bur26b	0.494	0.115
bur26c	0.702	0.154
bur26d	0.753	0.135
chr25a	0.625	0.056
esc32a	0.472	0.006
esc32b	0.723	0.011
kra30a	0.430	0.053
lipa20a	0.677	0.055
lipa60a	0.337	0.006
lipa90a	0.214	0.003
tai30a	0.485	0.027
tai30b	0.420	0.117
tai60a	0.293	0.007
tai60b	0.818	0.067

shown in Table 2, that indicates that lipa90a needs a smaller perturbation. This could be a visualization problem which does not allow us to conclude only by considering the cost-distance graphs. We need a measure that can tell us what is happening in these cases.

If we want to measure how much an instance have a BV structure, we need to take into account two things: cost-distance correlation and closeness of local optima. Table 4 shows two measures for each instance. The first one is the

Pearson correlation [7] between cost and distance of the 6400 local optima obtained in Section 5.1. Comparing these values with ILS results we can see that there is no relation between them, since there are instances that have almost the same correlation but need different perturbations lengths (*i.e.* bur26b and esc32a). The second measure is obtained by taking the difference between the maximum and minimum mean distance (DMD) divided by problem size (N). Relating this measure with Table 2 we can see that as the ratio DMD/N decreases, a smaller perturbation is needed, and viceversa, as relation DMD/N increases, a larger perturbation is needed. That is, DMD/N values have a direct relation to perturbation length, even for instances for which we can not conclude the same by visualizing only cost-distance graphs. Such relation seems to be $(N * (DMD/N)) * N = DMD * N$ as an upper bound in the random walk length needed as perturbation in ILS to obtain good results.

6 Conclusions

An analysis of local optimum structures for QAP instances has been presented. The analysis was focused on searching for a Big Valley structure in the set of local optima. The analysis shows that QAP instances have different cost-distance relations between their local optima, including BV. An experimental analysis was performed in order to relate these structures to the required perturbation length of the random walk. Experimental results show that instances that have BV structure need an smaller perturbation to reach better values, while instances having structures far from a BV need a larger perturbation. In the case of those instances for which a clear relation between local optimum structures and perturbation values could not be established, a relation between local optimum closeness and problem size has been introduced to explain the phenomenon successfully. These results will help in the design of ILS based algorithms.

Future research is planned to extend these results to a wider set of instances, and to use different local searches such as Simulated Annealing, Tabu Search, and others, as part of the ILS algorithm. Another obvious future work is to verify whether the relation between BV and perturbation holds for other combinatorial optimization problems like the TSP. Finally, a deeper analysis is needed to exploit each local optima structure in order to design a specific combination of ILS mechanisms to obtain better results.

Acknowledgments

The authors would like to thank the anonymous referees for their useful comments and interesting ideas for future research.

References

1. E. H. L. Aarts and J. K. Lenstra, editors. *Local Search in Combinatorial Optimization.* Wiley, Chichester, 1997.
2. K. D. Boese. *Models for Iterative Global Optimization.* PhD thesis, University of California at Los Angeles, Los Angeles, CA, 1996.

3. K. D. Boese, A. B. Kahng, and S. Muddu. A new adaptive multi-start technique for combinatorial global optimization. *Operations Research Letters*, 16:101–113, 1994.
4. T. Dimitriou and R. Impagliazzo. Towards a rigorous analysis of local optimization algorithms. In *25th ACM Symposium on the Theory of Computing*, 1996.
5. D. Du and Panos M. Pardalos, editors. *Handbook of Combinatorial Optimization*. Kluwer Academic Publishers, London, 1999.
6. M. R. Garey and D. S. Johnson. *Computers and Intractability: A Guide to the Theory of NP-completeness*. W. H. Freeman, San Francisco, 1979.
7. Paul G. Hoel, editor. *Introduction to Mathematical Statistics*. John Wiley & Sons, New York, 1962.
8. T. C. Hu, V. Klee, and D. Larman. Optimization of globally convex functions. *SIAM Journal on Control and Optimization*, 27(5):1026–1047, 1989.
9. D. S. Johnson and L. A. McGeoch. The travelling salesman problem: A case study in local optimization. In E. H. L. Aarts and J. K. Lenstra, editors, *Local Search in Combinatorial Optimization*, pages 215–310. Wiley, 1997.
10. T. Jones. *Evolutionary Algorithms, Fitness Landscape and Search*. PhD thesis, The University of New Mexico, Albuquerque, New Mexico, 1995.
11. H. R. Lourenco, O.C. Martin, and T. Stutzle. Iterated local search. In F. Glover and G. Kochenberger, editors, *Handbook of Metaheuristics*. Kluwer, 2002.
12. B. Manderick, M. De Weger, and P. Spiessens. The genetic algorithm and the structure of the fitness landscape. In R. K. Belew, editor, *Fourth International Conference on Genetic Algorithms*, pages 143–150, San Mateo, CA, 1991. Morgan Kaufmann.
13. O. Martin, S.W. Otto, and E.W. Felten. Large-step markov chains for the traveling salesman problem. *Complex Systems*, 5(3):299–326, 1991.
14. D. C. Mattfeld and C. Bierwirth. A search space analysis of the job shop scheduling problem. *Annals of Operational Research*, 86:441–453, 1999.
15. C. R. Reeves. Landscapes, operators and heuristic search. *Annals of Operational Research*, 86:473–490, 1999.
16. C. M. Reidys and P. F. Stadler. Combinatorial landscapes. *SIAM Review*, 44(1):3–54, 2002.
17. S. Russell and P. Norvig. *Artificial Intelligence: A Modern Approach*. Prentice Hall, 1995.
18. E. D. Taillard. Comparison of iterative searches for the quadratic assignment problem. *Location Science*, 3:87–105, 1995.
19. E. Weinberger. Correlated and uncorrelated fitness landscapes and how to tell the difference. *Biological Cybernetics*, 63:325–336, 1990.

Application of Fuzzy Multi-objective Programming Approach to Supply Chain Distribution Network Design Problem

Hasan Selim and Irem Ozkarahan

Dokuz Eylul University, Department of Industrial Engineering, 35100, Izmir, Turkey
hasan.selim@deu.edu.tr, irem.ozkarahan@deu.edu.tr

Abstract. A supply chain distribution network design model is developed in this paper. The goal of the model is to select the optimum numbers, locations and capacity levels of plants and warehouses to deliver the products to the retailers at the least cost while satisfying the desired service level. Maximal covering approach is employed in statement of the service level. Different from the previous researches in this area, coverage functions which differ among the retailers according to their service standard requests are defined for the retailers. Additionally, to provide a more realistic model structure, decision maker's imprecise aspiration levels for the goals, and demand uncertainties are incorporated into the model through fuzzy modeling approach. Realistic computational experiments are provided to confirm the viability of the model.

Keywords: Fuzzy multi-objective programming, Supply Chain, Distribution network design.

1 Introduction

The network design problem is one of the most comprehensive strategic decision problems that need to be optimized for the long-term efficient operation of whole supply chain (SC). Effective design and management of SC networks assists in production and delivery of a variety of products at low cost, high quality, and short lead times. To cope with the complexity of the network design problem, the supply network has been divided into several stages in many previous researches [1]. Jang et al. [2] decompose the entire network into three sub-networks; inbound network, distribution network and outbound network.

A common objective in designing a distribution network is to determine the least cost system design such that the demands of all customers are satisfied without exceeding the capacities of the warehouses and plants. This usually involves making tradeoffs inherent among the cost components of the system that include: (1) costs of opening and operating the plants and warehouses, and (2) the inbound and outbound transportation costs.

Numerous researchers have extensively studied facility and demand allocation problems. Interested researchers may refer to detailed survey results, e.g. [3], [4], [5],

A. Gelbukh and C.A. Reyes-Garcia (Eds.): MICAI 2006, LNAI 4293, pp. 415 – 425, 2006.

[6], [7] and [8]. More recently, Jayaraman [9] studied the capacitated warehouse location problem that involves locating a given number of warehouses to satisfy customer demands for different products. Pirkul & Jayaraman [1] extended the previous problem by considering locating also a given number of plants. Tragantalerngsak et al. [10] considered a two-echelon facility location problem in which the facilities in the first echelon are uncapacitated and the facilities in the second echelon are capacitated. The goal in their model is to determine the number and locations of facilities in both echelons in order to satisfy customer demand of the product. Jang et al. [2] proposed supply network with a global bill of material. Talluri & Baker [11] presented a multi-phase mathematical programming approach for effective SC design. Their methodology develops and applies a combination of multi-criteria efficiency models, based on game theory concepts, and linear and integer programming methods. In a recent paper, Amiri [12] studied the distribution network design problem in a SC system. They use multiple levels of capacities for warehouses and plants.

In this paper, we develop a SC distribution network design model. The goal is to select the optimum numbers, locations and capacity levels of plants and warehouses to deliver the products to the retailers at the least cost while satisfying the desired service level to the retailers. Unlike most of past research, our model allows for multiple capacity levels to the plants and warehouses.

Cost or profit based optimization is the most widely used method for SC distribution network design problems. However, more customer oriented approaches are required in order to provide a sustainable competitive advantage in today's business environment. Nowadays, there is a trend to consider customer service level as more critical. Customer service level can be measured by various measures such as customer response time, consistency of order cycle time, accuracy of order fulfillment rate, delivery lead time, flexibility in order quantity.

Our current study represents an improvement over past research by presenting a SC distribution network design model that use maximal covering approach in statement of the service level. We use delivery distance in defining the coverage parameter. Maximal cover location problem (MCLP) [13] has proved to be one of the most useful facility location models from both theoretical and practical points of view. The objective of MCLP is to establish a set of facilities so as to maximize the total weight of "covered" customers/demand, where a customer is considered covered if he is located at most certain specified distance dt away from the closest facility. Maximal cover location problem has been a subject of considerable interest in the literature, and has been modified many times to meet the specific requirements of various location problems. Different from the previous models in this area, we define a coverage function which may differ among the retailers according to the service standard they request for each retailer.

In real world, SCs operate in a somehow uncertain environment. Uncertainty may be associated with target values of objectives, external supply and customer demand etc. Supply chain models developed so far, except few ones, either ignored uncertainty or consider it approximately through the use of probability concepts. However, when there is lack of evidence available or lack of certainty in evidence, the standard probabilistic reasoning methods are not appropriate. In this case, uncertain parameters can be specified based on the experience and managerial subjective judgment. Fuzzy set theory (FST) [14] provides the appropriate framework to describe and treat uncertainty [15]. In decision sciences, fuzzy sets has had a great impact in preference modeling and multi-criteria evaluation, and has helped bringing optimization techniques closer to the users needs.

The proposed model distinguishes itself from previous SC distribution network design models in the modeling approach used. To provide a more realistic model structure, decision maker's (DM) imprecise aspiration levels for the goals, and demand uncertainties are incorporated into the model through fuzzy goal programming (FGP) approach.

The paper is further organized as follows. Basic concepts and the framework of FGP are introduced in the next section. Mathematical formulation of the proposed model is presented in Section 3. In Section 4, computational experiments are given. Finally, concluding remarks and future research directions are provided in Section 5.

2 Fuzzy Goal Programming

Applying FST into goal programming (GP) has the advantage of allowing for the vague aspirations of a DM, which can then be qualified by some natural language terms. The FST in GP was first considered by Narasimhan [16]. Narasimhan and Rubin [17], Hannan [18], Ignizio [19] and Tiwari et al. [20] extended FST to the field of GP. Mohamed [21], Ohta and Yamaguchi [22], and Mohammed [23] have investigated various aspects of decision problems using FGP theoretically.

A fuzzy set A can be characterized by a membership function, usually denoted by μ, which assigns to each object of a domain its grade of membership in A. The nearer the value of membership function to unity, the higher the grade of membership of element or object in a fuzzy set A. Various types of membership functions can be used to represent the fuzzy set.

A typical FGP problem formulation can be stated as follows:

$$\text{Find } x_i \qquad i = 1, 2, \ldots n \tag{1}$$

to satisfy

$$\begin{aligned} & Z_m(x_i) \prec \overline{Z}_m && m = 1, 2, \ldots, M, \\ & Z_k(x_i) \succ \overline{Z}_k && k = M+1, M+2, \ldots, K, \\ & g_j(x_i) \le b_j && j = 1, 2, \ldots, J, \\ & x_i \ge 0 && i = 1, 2, \ldots, n. \end{aligned} \tag{2}$$

where, $Z_m(x_i)$ is the mth goal constraint, $Z_k(x_i)$ is the kth goal constraint, $\overline{Z}_m(x_i)$ is the target value of the mth goal, $\overline{Z}_k(x_i)$ is the target value of the kth goal, $g_j(x_i)$ is the jth inequality constraint and b_j is the available resource of inequality constraint j.

In formulation (1), the symbols "$\prec$ and $\succ$" denote the fuzzified versions of "$\leq$ and $\geq$" and can be read as "approximately less (greater) than or equal to". These two types of linguistic terms have different meanings. Under "approximately less than or equal to" situation, the goal m is allowed to be spread to the right-hand-side of $\overline{Z}_m$ ($\overline{Z}_m = l_m$ where l_m denote the lower bound for the mth objective) with a certain range of r_m ($\overline{Z}_m + r_m = u_m$, where u_m denote the upper bound for the mth objective). Similarly, with *approximately greater than or equal to,* p_k is the allowed left side of $\overline{Z}_k$ ($\overline{Z}_k$ - $p_k = l_k$, and $\overline{Z}_k = u_k$).

Using Belman and Zadeh's [24] approach, the feasible fuzzy solution set is obtained by the intersection of all membership functions representing the fuzzy goals. This solution set is then characterized by its membership $\mu_F(x)$ which is:

$$\mu_F(x) = \mu_{Z_1}(x) \cap \mu_{Z_2}(x) \ldots \cap \mu_{Z_k}(x) = \min[\mu_{Z_1}(x), \mu_{Z_2}(x), \ldots, \mu_{Z_k}(x)] . \tag{3}$$

Then the optimum decision can be determined to be the maximum degree of membership for the fuzzy decision:

$$\max_{x \in F} \ \mu_F(x) = \max_{x \in F} \ \min[\mu_{Z_1}(x), \mu_{Z_2}(x), \ldots, \mu_{Z_k}(x)] . \tag{4}$$

Zimmermann [25] used the max-min operator of Bellman and Zadeh [24], and by introducing the auxiliary variable λ, which is the overall satisfactory level of compromise, he transformed formulation (1-2) equivalently as follows.

$$\text{Max } \lambda \tag{5}$$

s.t.

$$\begin{aligned} &\mu_{Z_1} \geq \lambda , \\ &\mu_{Z_2} \geq \lambda , \\ &\ \vdots \quad\ \ \vdots \\ &\mu_{Z_k} \geq \lambda , \\ &g_j(x_i) \leq b_j \qquad j = 1, 2, \ldots, J , \\ &x_i \geq 0 \qquad\qquad i = 1, 2, \ldots, n , \\ &0 \leq \lambda \leq 1. \end{aligned} \tag{6}$$

3 The Proposed Model

In this section, we present the proposed distribution network design model. The network encompasses a set of retailers with known location, and possible discrete set of location zones where warehouses and plants are located. In this network, retailers have demand for a multitude of products, and the warehouses are responsible for right-time delivery of a right amount of products.

The mathematical model is developed on the basis of the following assumptions:

- The network considered encompasses a set of retailers with known locations, and possible discrete set of location zones/sites where warehouses and plants are located.
- Single warehouse and retailer take place in the potential location zones for warehouses and retailers, respectively.
- The retailers have demand for a multitude of products, and the warehouses are responsible for right-time delivery of a right amount of products.
- Decision makers of the plants, warehouses and retailers share information and collaborate with each other to design an effective distribution network.
- Decisions are made within a single period.

Formulation of the model is given in the following.

Sets:

I: set of zones where retailers are located,
J: potential warehouse locations,
K: potential plant locations,
L: set of products,
R: set of capacity levels available for warehouses,
H: set of capacity levels available for plants.

Parameters:

C_{ijl} : variable cost to transport one unit of product l from warehouse in zone j to the retailer in zone i,
T_{jkl} : variable cost to transport one unit of product l from plant in zone k to a warehouse in zone j,
f_{kh} : fixed portion of the operating cost for a plant in zone k with capacity level h,
g_{jr} : fixed portion of the annual possession and operating costs for a warehouse in zone j with capacity level r,
OP_{kh} : opening cost of a plant in zone k with capacity level h,
OW_{jr} : opening cost of a warehouse in zone j with capacity level r,
a_{il} : demand for product l by retailer in zone i,
s_l : required throughput capacity of a warehouse for product l,
W_{jr} : throughput limit of warehouse in zone j with capacity level r,
q_{kl} : required production capacity of plant in zone k for each product l,
D_{kh} : capacity of the plant in zone k with capacity level h,
dt_{ij} : distance between zone i and zone j,
m_{ij} : coverage parameter that denotes the coverage level of a retailer in zone i by a warehouse in zone j,
LB_i, UB_i : lower and upper bounds, respectively, for the service level determinant.

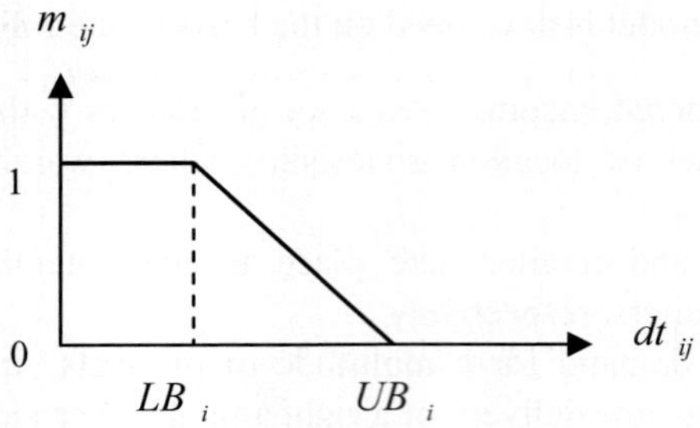

Fig. 1. Illustration of linear coverage function

Decision variables:

X_{ijl} : amount of product l transported to retailer in zone i from warehouse in zone j ,

Y_{jkl} : amount of product l transported to warehouse in zone j from plant in zone k,

Z_{jr} : binary variable that indicates whether a warehouse with capacity level r is constructed in zone j,

P_{kh} : binary variable that indicates whether a plant with capacity level h is constructed in zone k.

In terms of the above notation, the problem can be formulated as follows:

Table 1. Formulation of the objective function elements

Objective Function Element	Mathematical Formulation	
Total Cost (*TCOST*): Transportation costs of products from plants to warehouses and from warehouses to retailers + fixed costs associated with the plants and the warehouses	Min $\sum_i\sum_j\sum_l C_{ijl}X_{ijl} + \sum_j\sum_k\sum_l T_{jkl}Y_{jkl} + \sum_k\sum_h f_{kh}P_{kh} + \sum_j\sum_r g_{jr}Z_{jr}$	(7)
Investment (INV) in opening plants and warehouses	Min $\sum_k\sum_h OP_{kh}P_{kh} + \sum_j\sum_r OW_{jr}Z_{jr}$	(8)
Total Service Level (TSERVL) provided to the retailers	Max $\sum_i\sum_j\sum_l m_{ij}X_{ijl}$	(9)

s.t.

$$\sum_j X_{ijl} = a_{il} \qquad \text{for all } i \in I \text{ and } l \in L, \tag{10}$$

$$\sum_i\sum_l s_l X_{ijl} \le \sum_r W_{jr}Z_{jr} \qquad \text{for all } j \in J, \tag{11}$$

$$\sum_{r} Z_{jr} \leq 1 \qquad \text{for all } j \in J, \tag{12}$$

$$\sum_{i} X_{ijl} \leq \sum_{k} Y_{jkl} \qquad \text{for all } j \in J \textit{ and } l \in L, \tag{13}$$

$$\sum_{j} \sum_{l} q_{kl} Y_{jkl} \leq \sum_{h} D_{kh} P_{kh} \qquad \text{for all } k \in K, \tag{14}$$

$$\sum_{h} P_{kh} \leq 1 \qquad \text{for all } k \in K, \tag{15}$$

$$Z_{jr} \in \{0,1\} \qquad \text{for all } j \in J,\ r \in R, \tag{16}$$

$$P_{kh} \in \{0,1\} \qquad \text{for all } k \in K,\ h \in H, \tag{17}$$

$$X_{ijl},\ Y_{jkl} \geq 0 \qquad \text{for all } i \in I,\ j \in J,\ k \in K \text{ and } l \in L. \tag{18}$$

As can be stated in Table 1, the first objective function minimizes total cost made of: the transportation costs of products from plants to warehouses and from warehouses to retailers, and the fixed costs associated with the plants and the warehouses. While the second objective function minimizes the investment in opening plants and warehouses, the third one maximizes the total service level provided to the retailers.

Constraint set (10) ensures that all demand from retailers is satisfied by warehouses. Constraint set (11) limits the distribution quantities that are shipped from warehouses to retailers to the throughput limits of warehouses. Constraint sets (12) and (15) ensure that a warehouse and a plant, respectively, can be assigned at most one capacity level. Constraint set (13) guarantees that all demand from retailer in zone i for product l is balanced by the total units of product l available at warehouse in zone j that has been supplied from open plants. Constraints in set (14) represent the capacity restrictions of the plants in terms of their total shipments to the warehouses. Finally, constraint sets (16) and (17) enforce the binary restrictions and constraint set (18) enforces the non-negativity restrictions on the decision variables, respectively.

4 Computational Experiment

A hypothetically constructed SC distribution network design problem with 50 retailer zones, 20 potential warehouse sites and 15 potential plant sites is considered in the computational experiment. It is assumed that two different types of product are demanded by the retailers. Coordinates of the retailer zones, potential warehouses and plant sites are generated from a uniform distribution over a square with side 3000. Euclidean distances are used in defining the coverage parameters.

Before presenting the experiment, let us explain the parameter structuring of the problem we deal with. Expected demand of the retailers for the products is drawn from a uniform distribution between 100 and 1000. Five capacity levels are used for the capacities available to both the potential plants and warehouses. The opening cost of the warehouse in zone j with capacity level 3 (OW_{j3}) are drawn from a uniform distribution between 90,000 and 120,000. The opening costs of the warehouses for the other capacity levels are computed as follows: $OW_{j1} = 0.75*OW_{j3}$, $OW_{j2} = 0.85*OW_{j3}$, $OW_{j4} = 1.15*OW_{j3}$, $OW_{j5} = 1.25*OW_{j3}$. Cost coefficients of OP_{kh} are computed in terms of the warehouses costs as $OP_{kh} = 4*OW_{kh}$. Fixed portion of the annual possession and operating costs of the warehouse in zone j with capacity level 3 (g_{j3}) and the plant in zone k with capacity level 3 (f_{k3}) are drawn from a uniform distribution between 18,000 and 25,000 and 75,000 and 100,000, respectively. Fixed portion of the annual possession and operating costs of warehouses and plants for the other capacity levels are computed as follows: $g_{j1} = 0.75*g_{j3}$, $g_{j2} = 0.85*g_{j3}$, $g_{j4} = 1.15*g_{j3}$, $g_{j5} = 1.25*g_{j3}$ and $f_{k1} = 0.75*f_{k3}$, $f_{k2} = 0.85*f_{k3}$, $f_{k4} = 1.15*f_{k3}$, $f_{k5} = 1.25*f_{k3}$. Required throughput capacity of a warehouse and required production capacity of a plant for product l are given as follows: $s_1 = 1$, $s_2 = 1$ and $q_1 = 1$, $q_2 = 2$. The cost coefficients C_{ijl} and T_{jkl} are computed as being proportional to the Euclidean distances between the facilities. Specifically, C_{ijl} and T_{jkl} are drawn from a uniform distribution between $0.025*dt_{ij}$ and $0.035*dt_{ij}$ and $0.045*dt_{jk}$ and $0.055*dt_{jk}$, respectively. Lower and upper bounds for the distance (LB_i, UB_i) are assumed as (500, 650) for twelve of the retailers, (600, 750) for fifteen of the retailers and (700, 850) for the remaining retailers. Throughput limit of the warehouses and capacity of the plants are given in the following. W_{jr} = 4000; 6000; 8000; 10,000; 12,000 and D_{kh} =15,000; 20,000; 30,000; 35,000; 40,000.

To provide a more realistic model structure, DM's imprecise aspiration levels for the goals, and demand uncertainties are incorporated into the model through fuzzy modeling approach. Solutions of the problem are performed using Max-min approach and lexicographic programming (LP) approach. CPLEX 9.1 optimization software is employed in the solution stage. In the former case, upper and lower limits (u_k, l_k) for the goals are determined considering the pay-off values given in Table 2. In the latter case, *total cost* objective is assigned the first preemptive priority while *investment* and *total service level* objectives are given the second and the third priority, respectively. As it is known, lexicographic approach suffers from poor quality of solutions especially when the number of priority levels increases.

Table 2. Lower and upper limits for the goals

Goals	pay-off values		lower and upper limits	
	min	Max	l_k	u_k
TCOST	2,720,667	17,735,384	2,750,000	2,900,000
INV	1,936,093	7,708,265	2,000,000	3,000,000
TSERVL	9,185	61,532	50,000	55,000

We assume that the demand is imprecise and can be altered to some extend. Under this assumption, we state customer demand as fuzzy parameters using triangular membership functions. The lower and upper limits for the demand are assumed as 95% and 105% of the expected demand, respectively. In the first experiment, three problem instances are generated using three different α-cut levels, i.e. 0, 0.5 and 1, for the membership functions of the demand. The results are illustrated in Fig. 2 and 3.

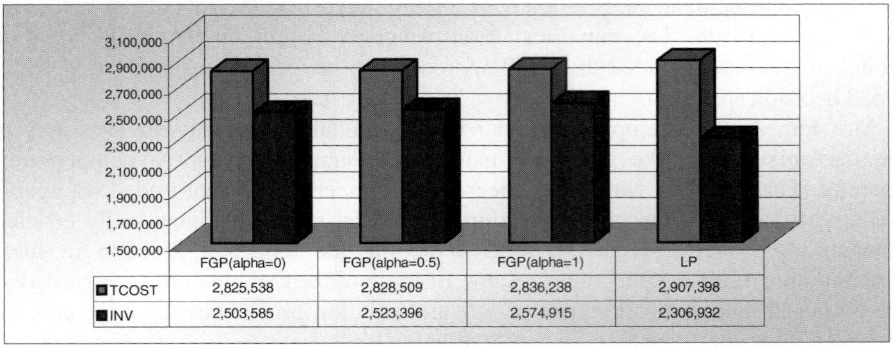

Fig. 2. Results of the problem instances in terms of TCOST and INV

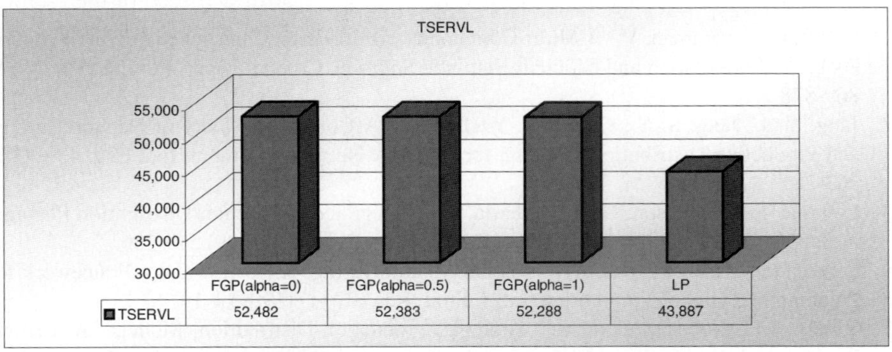

Fig. 3. Results of the problem instances in terms of TSERVL

As can be seen from the results, FGP approach provides better results in terms of *total service level* compared to the results of LP. A deterioration of 8.5% in *investment* objective corresponds to a 19.58% improvement in *total service level* objective. While the results with different α-cut levels are close to each other in terms of *total cost* and *total service level* objectives, a relatively big difference can be realized in terms of *investment* objective. It can be stated here that, the DM can obtain many number of different results using different parameter settings. Such a broad decision spectrum is crucial in today's dynamic and competitive markets.

5 Conclusion

This study represents an improvement over past research by presenting a SC distribution network design model that employs maximal covering approach in statement of the service level. Unlike most of past research, the model allows for multiple capacity levels to the plants and warehouses. The proposed model also distinguishes itself from previous research in this area in the modeling approach used. To provide a more realistic modeling structure, DM's imprecise aspiration levels for the goals, and demand uncertainties are incorporated into the model through fuzzy modeling approach. The numerical example gives insight on the viability of the model. It can be concluded that FGP approach can be used in providing DM with a broad decision spectrum.

Max-min approach employed in our computational experiments focuses only on the maximization of the minimum membership grade. It is not a compensatory operator. That is, goals with a high degree of membership are not traded off against goals with a low degree of membership. Therefore, some computationally efficient compensatory operators can be used in setting the objective function in fuzzy programming to investigate better results. Because of the combinatorial complexity of the proposed model, development of efficient solution procedures for large problem instances is an important area for future research.

References

1. Pirkul, H., Jayaraman, V.: A Multi-Commodity, Multi-Plant, Capacitated Facility Location Problem: Formulation and Efficient Heuristic Solution. Comput. Oper. Res. 25 (10) (1998) 869-878
2. Jang, Y.-J., Jang, S.-Y., Chang, B.-Y., Park, J.: A Combined Model of Network Design and Production/Distribution Planning for a Supply Network. Comput. Ind. Eng. 43 (2002) 263-281
3. Erengüc, S.S., Simpson, N.C., Vakharia, A.J.: Integrated Production/Distribution Planning in Supply Chains: An Invited Review. Eur. J. Oper. Res. 115 (1999) 219-236
4. Pontrandolfo, P., Okogbaa, O.G.: Global Manufacturing: A Review and a Framework for Planning in a Global Corporation. Int. J. Prod. Res. 37 (1) (1999) 1-19
5. Vidal, C.J., Goetschalckx, M.: Strategic Production-Distribution Models; A Critical Review With Emphasis on Global Supply Chain Models. Eur. J. Oper. Res. 98 (1) (1998) 1-18
6. Aikens, C.H.: Facility Location Models for Distribution Planning. Eur. J. Oper. Res. 22 (1985) 263-279
7. Brandeau, M.L., Chiu, S.S.: An Overview of Representative Problems in Location Research. Manage. Sci. 35 (1989) 645-674
8. Avella, P. et al.: Some Personal Views on the Current State and the Future of Locational Analysis. Eur. J. Oper. Res. 104 (1998) 269-287
9. Jayaraman, V.: An Efficient Heuristic Procedure for Practical-Sized Capacitated Warehouse Design and Management. Decision Sci. 29 (1998) 729-745
10. Tragantalerngsak, S., Holt, J., Ronnqvist, M.: An Exact Method for the Two-Echelon, Single-Source, Capacitated Facility Location Problem. Eur. J. Oper. Res. 123 (2000) 473-489

11. Talluri, S., Baker, R.C.: A Multi-Phase Mathematical Programming Approach for Effective Supply Chain Design. Eur. J. Oper. Res. 141 (2002) 544-558
12. Amiri, A.: Designing a Distribution Network in a Supply Chain: Formulation and Efficient Solution Procedure. Eur. J. Oper. Res. 171 (2006) 567-576
13. Church, R.L., Revelle, C.: The Maximal Covering Location Problem. Pap. Reg. Sci. Assoc. 32 (1974) 101-118
14. Zadeh, L.A.: Fuzzy Sets. Inform. Control. 8 (1965) 338-353
15. Petrovic, D., Roy, R., Petrovic, R.: Modeling and Simulation of a Supply Chain in an Uncertain Environment. Eur. J. Oper. Res. 109 (1999) 299-309
16. Narasimhan, R.: Goal Programming in a Fuzzy Environment. Decision Sci. 11 (1980) 325-336
17. Narasimhan, R., Rubin, P.A.: Fuzzy Goal Programming with Nested Priorities. Fuzzy Set. Syst. 14 (1984) 115-129
18. Hannan, E.L.: Some Further Comments on Fuzzy Priorities. Decision Sci. 13 (1981) 337-339
19. Ignizio, J.P.: On the Rediscovery of Fuzzy Goal Programming. Decision Sci. 13 (1982) 331-336
20. Tiwari, R.N., Dharmar, S., Rao, J.R.: Fuzzy Goal Programming - An Additive Method. Fuzzy Set. Syst. 24 (1987) 27-34
21. Mohamed, R.H: The Relationship between Goal Programming and Fuzzy Programming. Fuzzy Set. Syst. 89 (1997) 215-222
22. Ohta, H., Yamaguchi, T.: Linear Fractional Goal Programming in Consideration of Fuzzy Solution. Eur. J. Oper. Res. 92 (1996) 157-165
23. Mohammed, W.: Chance Constrained Fuzzy Goal Programming with Right-Hand Side Uniform Random Variable Coefficients. Fuzzy Set. Syst. 109 (2000) 107-110
24. Bellman, R.E., Zadeh, L.A.: Decision Making in a Fuzzy Environment. Manage. Sci. 17 (1970) 141-164
25. Zimmermann, H.-J.: Fuzzy Programming and Linear Programming with Several Objective Functions. Fuzzy Set. Syst. 1 (1978) 45-55

Route Selection and Rate Allocation Using Evolutionary Computation Algorithms in Multirate Multicast Networks

Sun-Jin Kim[1] and Mun-Kee Choi[2]

[1] Telematics & USN Future Research Team, Telematics & USN Research Division, Electronics and Telecommunications Research Institute, 161 Gajeong-dong, Yuseong-gu, Daejeon 305-700, Republic of Korea
sunjin@etri.re.kr

[2] School of IT Business, Information and Communications University, 119 Munjiro, Yuseong-gu, Daejeon, 305-732, Republic of Korea
mkchoi@icu.ac.kr

Abstract. In this paper, we simultaneously address the route selection and rate allocation problem in multirate multicast networks. We propose the evolutionary computation algorithm based on a genetic algorithm for this problem and elaborate upon many of the elements in order to improve solution quality and computational efficiency in applying the proposed methods to the problem. These include: the genetic representation, evaluation function, genetic operators and procedure. Additionally, a new method using an artificial intelligent search technique, called the coevolutionary algorithm, is proposed to achieve better solutions. The results of extensive computational simulations show that the proposed algorithms provide high quality solutions and outperform existing approach.

1 Introduction

Multicast is a kind of communication service that allows simultaneous transmission of the same message from one source to a group of destination nodes. In multirate multicasting, different users (receivers) within the same multicast group can receive service at different rates, depending on the user requirements and the network congestion level. Compared with unirate multicasting, this provides more flexibility to the users and allows more efficient usage of the network resources.

Thus far, different aspects of multicast transmission optimization have been discussed in the research [1]-[11]. These include representative selection and allocation problems which embody (group) multicast routing [1]-[3], the selection of server and path [4], Quality of Service (QoS) allocation [5], rate control or allocation [6]-[9], congestion control [10][11] and so on. Although routing and rate allocation problems mutually affect the need to use more efficient network resources, prior research has considered them separately or sequentially.

Therefore, in this paper, we simultaneously address the route selection and rate allocation problem in multirate multicast networks; that is, the problem of constructing multiple multicast trees and simultaneously allocating the rate of receivers for

A. Gelbukh and C.A. Reyes-Garcia (Eds.): MICAI 2006, LNAI 4293, pp. 426 – 438, 2006.

maximizing the sum of utilities over all receivers, subject to link capacity and delay constraints for high-bandwidth delay-sensitive applications in point-to-point communication networks. In [2], it is shown that the Delay Constrained Group Multicast Routing Problem (DCGMRP) with bandwidth requirements is NP-complete. Due to similarities between DCGMRP and our problem, this issue cannot be solved completely within a reasonable computational time, even for a moderate number of variables. Therefore, to deal with the issue, we employ the evolutionary computation algorithms, namely the genetic algorithm (GA), which has proven to be very efficient and powerful in a wide variety of combinatorial optimization problems and applications [12][13], and the coevolutionary algorithm (Co-EA)[14]-[17]. We propose methods to allocate receiver rates and to create single/multiple multicast trees, and then elaborate on the following elements: genetic representation, evaluation function, genetic operators and procedure. Additionally, the coevolutionary algorithm is proposed to more efficiently solve the problem. Extensive computational simulations are carried out on various network topologies and problem sets to evaluate the performance of our proposed algorithms. The experimental results demonstrate that the proposed methods provide high quality solutions, respond well to various situations of the network, and can be easily applied to the actual network.

2 Problem Definition

Suppose M single-source multicast trees form to serve high-bandwidth delay-sensitive applications in a point-to-point communication network, which has link capacity and transmission delay constraints, at a given moment of time, focusing on the snapshot situation. In each multicast tree transmission, the receivers can receive data at different rates.

The network is modeled as a directed graph $G = (V, E)$, where V and E represent the node set and edge (or link) set of the graph, respectively. An edge $e \in E$ from $i \in V$ to $j \in V$ is represented by $e = (i, j)$. Each edge $(i, j) \in E$ in G has capacity (or bandwidth) c_{ij} and delay d_{ij}. The network is shared by a set of M multicast groups (sessions). Each multicast group is associated with a unique source, a set of receivers, and a set of edges that the multicast group uses (the set of edges forms a tree). Thus, any multicast group $t \in M$ is specified by $\{s_t, E_t, R_t\}$, where s_t is the source node, E_t is the set of edges in the multicast tree and R_t[1] is the set of receiver nodes in multicast group t. The total rate of traffic of a multicast group over any edge on the tree must be equal to the maximum of the traffic rates of all downstream receivers of the group.

Each receiver r in multicast group t has a minimum required transmission rate $b_r \geq 0$ and a maximum required transmission rate $B_r \leq \infty$. Moreover, each receiver r in multicast group t is associated with a utility function U_r: $\Re+ \rightarrow \Re$, which is assumed to be concave, bounded and continuously differentiable in the interval $X_r = [b_r, B_r]$. Thus receiver r in multicast group t has utility $U_r\ (x_r^t)$ when it is receiving traffic at rate x_r^t, where $x_r^t \in X_r$[2]. We will refer to the variables x_r^t as the "receiver rates."

[1] Any multicast groups can have the same receivers. Therefore, the sets R_t cannot be disjoint.

[2] The sets X_r are (bounded) continuous intervals. Therefore, it is assumed that the receiver rates can be continuous.

Let R_t' be the set of all nodes without source and receivers in multicast group t. For any $k \in R_t'$, let T_k^t denote the set of receiver nodes that are included in the subtree rooted at node k in multicast group t. Now for each $k \in R_t'$, define a variable x_k^t such that it denotes the rate of traffic that the node k in multicast group t receives from its parent node. Thus, for $k \in R_t'$, x_k^t is defined as $x_k^t = \max_{k' \in T_k^t} x_{k'}^t$. For any $r \in R_t$, let P_r^t denote the unique path from source s_t to receiver r in multicast group t. As well, let z_{ij}^{rt} be equal to one when edge (i, j) is included on the unique path P_r^t, and let Δ_t denote the delay bound in multicast group t. Thus, note that the delay constraint for edge (i, j) can now be written as $\sum_{(i,j)\in E} d_{ij} z_{ij}^{rt} \le \Delta_t$.

To formulate this problem, we introduce the following notations and decision variables.

Notations

G : directed graph, $G = (V, E)$
V : node set of the graph
E : edge set of the graph
N : number of total nodes
M : number of multicast groups
s_t : source node of multicast group t
R_t : set of receiver nodes in multicast group t
i, j : index of node, $i, j \in V$, $i, j = 1, \cdots, N$
t : index of multicast group, $t = 1, \cdots, M$
r : index of receiver, $r \in R_t$, $t = 1, \cdots, M$
c_{ij} : capacity (or bandwidth) of edge (i, j)[3]
d_{ij} : delay of edge (i, j)
T_j^t : set of receiver nodes that are included in the subtree rooted at node j in multicast group t
P_r^t : unique path from source s_t to receiver r in multicast group t
X_r : rate bound of x_r^t
Δ_t : delay bound in multicast group t
$U_r(x)$: utility function in rate x

Decision variables

x_r^t : rate of the receiver r in multicast group t

$$y_{ij}^t = \begin{cases} 1 & (i,j) \in \text{multicast group } t \\ 0 & \text{otherwise} \end{cases} \qquad z_{ij}^{rt} = \begin{cases} 1 & (i,j) \in P_r^t \\ 0 & \text{otherwise} \end{cases}$$

Maximize

$$\sum_{t=1}^{M} \sum_{r \in R_t} U_r(x_r^t) \tag{1}$$

Subject to

$$\sum_{h \in V} z_{ih}^{ri} - \sum_{j \in V} z_{ji}^{rj} = \begin{cases} 1, & i = s_t \\ -1, & i = r, \quad r \in R_t, \quad t = 1,2,\cdots,M \\ 0, & i \ne s_t, r \end{cases} \tag{2}$$

[3] An edge $e \in E$ from $i \in V$ to $j \in V$ is represented by $e = (i, j)$.

$$\sum_{t=1}^{M}(\max_{k'\in T_j^t} x_{k'}^t) y_{ij}^t \le c_{ij},\quad (i,j)\in E,\ t=1,2,\cdots,M \tag{3}$$

$$\sum_{(i,j)\in E} d_{ij} z_{ij}^{rt} \le \Delta_t,\quad (i,j)\in E,\ r\in R_t,\ t=1,2,\cdots,M \tag{4}$$

$$z_{ij}^{rt} \le y_{ij}^t,\quad (i,j)\in E,\ r\in R_t,\ t=1,2,\cdots,M \tag{5}$$

$$z_{ij}^{rt}, y_{ij}^t = 0 \text{ or } 1,\quad (i,j)\in E,\ r\in R_t,\ t=1,2,\cdots,M \tag{6}$$

$$x_r^t \in X_r,\ r\in R_t,\ t=1,2,\cdots,M \tag{7}$$

The objective function defined in (1) is to ensure that the sum of utilities over all receivers is maximized. In this paper, a log function, which is usually used in the field of economics [18], is adopted, as the utility function. Constraint (2) ensures one unit flow between the source node and every destination node. Constraint (3), (4) and (7) are link capacity, delay, and maximum-minimum rate constraints, respectively. Constraint (5) and (6) ensure that y_{ij}^t and z_{ij}^{rt} are zero-one variables.

3 Methods for Receiver Rate Allocation and Multicast Tree Generation

3.1 Decision Rule for Receiver Rate Allocation

In order to decide the receiver rates, for any $r \in R_t$, let W_r^t be the bandwidth of the link directly connected with the receiver r in multicast group t and Q_r^t denote the rate allocation ratio[4] of the receiver r in multicast group t. Thus, for $r \in R_t$, the receiver rate x_r^t is calculated as $x_r^t = \min\{ x_{r-1}^t, \max\{W_r^t \cdot Q_r^t, W_r^t - \sum_{j=1, j\neq t}^{M} x_{r-1}^j \}\}$[5]. After the receiver rate x_r^t is calculated, for $k \in R_t'$, x_k^t is updated by the definition of Section 2.

3.2 Single Multicast Tree Generation

We introduced the concept of the Core-Based Tree (CBT) algorithm, which builds a bi-directional and group-shared tree rooting at a single "multicasting core" and spans to all of the multicast group member nodes with minimal cost, out of many multicast routing protocols [19][20] as the method for generating a multicast tree. In order to apply CBT algorithm to this problem, first, the maximum bandwidth available from the multicasting core to each destination is computed using a Dijkstra-like algorithm, called the *computation algorithm of maximum bandwidth*. However, this computation

[4] This reflects the extent of user satisfaction of the bandwidth (or rate) allotted to the user.

[5] This equation is a recursive function. Therefore, r-1 means the 1st previous parent node of the receiver r in the corresponding tree and W_{r-1}^t denotes the bandwidth of link directly connected with the 1st previous node of the receiver r in multicast group t. However, Q_{r-1}^t denotes the rate allocation ratio of the receiver r in multicast group t.

algorithm may be suboptimal for routing packets. That is, it may include wideband links leading to destinations that can receive only lower bandwidths.

To improve this deficiency, what we call the *computation algorithm of a multicast tree,* can be made as follows. First, the computation algorithm of maximum bandwidth begins by considering the links with maximum (or the highest level) available bandwidth, and then constructing a shortest-path spanning tree using only these links. Next, the overutilized links of the subtree are eliminated from the highest-level-bandwidth spanning tree. Then the tree must be expanded with the previously considered links that are not included in the tree and next lower level links to additional destinations using previous procedure. The algorithm continues in this manner until all the multicast destinations are reached.

3.3 Simultaneously Multiple Multicast Trees Generation with Receiver Rate Allocation

First, a method based on CBT algorithm, which we call the *CBT method*, can be achieved as follows.

(a) Each multicasting core from each group is selected randomly.
(b) According to the computation algorithm of maximum bandwidth and the computation algorithm of a multicast tree, each single multicast tree, which has the maximum bandwidth allowable and satisfies the delay constraint, is made from the source to the multicasting core[6], and from the multicasting core to destinations of the respective group.
(c) All receiver rates of each group are allocated according to the decision rule for receiver rate allocation.

The second method based on the sequence generating the multicast tree, which we call the *Sequential method*, can be executed as follows.

(a) The sequence of the group, which creates its multicast tree, is determined.
(b) (b) and (c) in the CBT method are performed by the same procedure for a multicast group selected according to (a)'s sequence[7].
(c) The bandwidths of links in the network are updated by subtracting allocated rates from former bandwidth.
(d) The (b) and (c) process repeats until all groups' multicast trees are generated and all receiver rates are allocated.

4 Proposed Evolutionary Computation Algorithms

In this problem, if each multicast tree of each group is specified, all receiver rates can be easily obtained by the decision rule for receiver rate allocation in Section 3.1.

---

[6] In this procedure, the link with maximum available bandwidth from the source to the multicasting core is connected. The bandwidth of this link becomes the upper bound of maximum available bandwidth from the multicasting core to each of the destinations.

[7] In this procedure, the maximum bandwidth available from the source to each destination is computed by the computation algorithm of maximum bandwidth and the computation algorithm of a multicast tree.

Therefore, the search procedure can be restricted to the space of variables related to constructing multicast trees.

4.1 Proposed Simple Genetic Algorithm

4.1.1 Genetic Representation and Evaluation Function

The value of the multicasting core by a binary representation is that it offers a partial individual as a potential solution in the CBT method, and that the set of multicasting cores becomes an individual. For instance, when 4 multicast groups exist in the network with 16 nodes, and the value of the multicasting core is presented at 4 bits, suppose the individual is to be represented as (0 1 0 1 1 0 1 1 0 1 1 0 1 0 0 1). This solution can be interpreted from the first to the fourth multicasting core, and should become Node 5, 11, 6 and 9[8], respectively. In the Sequential method, the sequence of the group which creates its multicast tree is an individual as a potential solution. For example, suppose an individual is to be represented as (3 4 2 1) under the same conditions as the previous case. This solution can be interpreted as requiring that the multicast tree be orderly generated by the third, fourth, second and first group. Additionally, the objective function in the formulation is used as an evaluation function.

4.1.2 Selection Scheme and Genetic Operators

A roulette wheel method based on fitness is used for the selection of parents and individuals for replacement [12][13]. It is important to make a genetic operator in order to transmit the good genetic characteristics of parents to their offsprings. Here, modification of the 2-point crossover operator, which is widely used in evolutionary algorithms [12][13], is employed in the CBT method. Instead of using a 2-point crossover to the whole individual, the 2-point crossover is applied to each group, respectively. As a mutation operator, we use random mutation in which some individuals are randomly chosen with the individual mutation rate of P_m, and the mutation operation is applied to the individuals with the gene mutation rate of P_g.

In the Sequential method, the modified order crossover (modOX) operator and inversion operator are used. The modOX proposed by Davis [21] is a modification of the order crossover, and is commonly used in sequencing problems. The modOX would create offspring that preserve the relative order in parents.

4.1.3 Procedure of Simple Genetic Algorithm

Suppose $P(t)$ is the parents in the current generation t. The neighborhood area ($N(t)$) is set, since the localized (neighborhood) interactions within populations is used to promote diversity and search efficiency. The evolutionary process in this algorithm is a type of steady-state GA [22]. The parents are selected for the reproduction process according to fitness in $N(t)$, and recombined to yield the new offspring by applying the crossover operation. The deceased parents used to form a new $N(t)'$ are selected and replaced with new offspring. In this step, the neighbors are evolved and maintained by iterations (reproduction cycles). The number of reproduction cycles is adopted here as the termination criterion. Then the mutation operation is applied to

---

[8] 0 1 0 1 : $2^2+2^0 = 5$; 1 0 1 1 : $2^3+2^1+2^0 = 11$; 0 1 1 0 : $2^2+2^1 = 6$; 1 0 0 1 : $2^3+2^0 = 9$.

the individuals in *N(t)′* according to mutation rate. When the parents are replaced with new offspring in the whole evolutionary process, the elite individual is not replaced during the reproduction process. The algorithm continues in this manner until the termination criteria are satisfied.

4.2 Proposed Coevolutionary Algorithm

Until now, to solve this problem, we proposed the simple GA, which has shown differing features from those of the coevolutionary algorithm (Co-EA). The Co-EA is a search technique simulating the evolutionary process in nature whereby one species influences and is influenced by other species. We call the species influencing the evolving species an "environment." While a species is evolving, it is interacting with and adapting to its environment. The characteristics of the Co-EA are similar to the situation where several problems are related with each other in such a manner that a change to the solution of one problem (or method) can affect those of other problems (or methods). We conceive that if the Co-EA, which combines the major features of the two (CBT and Sequential) methods in this problem, is contrived, better solutions can be obtained.

4.2.1 Procedure of Coevolutionary Algorithm

In terms of the problem considered here, the CBT and Sequential methods can be appropriately combined. In the CBT method, the multicast trees of each group are simultaneously generated and the rates of receivers are allocated at the same time; while in the Sequential method, the multicast trees of each group are sequentially generated and then the rates of receivers are allocated. In sequentially generating multicast trees, simultaneously constructing a proper bundle of multicast trees by using the CBT method can lead to some improvements. In this paper, each of the CBT and Sequential methods is considered one species. Therefore, the CBT population (Pop-C) is made up of individuals to select each multicasting core per multicast group; while the Sequential one (Pop-S) consists of individuals to represent the number of multicast groups created simultaneously and the sequence of generating multicast trees.

For the Co-EA of this problem, the localized interactions within and between populations are adopted. Each of the two populations forms a two-dimensional toroidal square lattice and the structure of the 3×3 neighborhood is used here for localized evolution. Let NC_{ij} and NS_{ij} denote the neighborhood including individual (i, j) and its eight neighbors in Pop-C and Pop-S, respectively. While one population evolves, it interacts with the other population as per the following procedure.

Step 1 (Initialization)

Generate two sets of initial populations, Pop-C and Pop-S, which contain individuals representing CBT and the Sequential method, respectively.

Step 2 (Initial fitness evaluation)

Initial fitness is evaluated for every pair of matching individuals (one from Pop-C and the other from Pop-S), and set f_{best} to the best fitness value.

Step 3 (Neighborhood setting)

An arbitrary location (i, j) is selected, which sets up NC_{ij} and NS_{ij}.

Step 4 (Evolution of NC_{ij})

Step 4.1: Two parents are selected from NC_{ij} based on fitness, and two offspring are created by applying a crossover operation.

Step 4.2: Two individuals that have a low fitness in NC_{ij} are replaced with the offspring newly created in Step 4.1.

Step 4.3: A mutation operation, if turned on, is applied to the individuals in NC_{ij}.

Step 4.4: The fitness is evaluated for the individuals newly produced, where the individual with the best fitness in NS_{ij} is selected as the environmental individual. If the fitness of the best individual is higher than f_{best}, then f_{best} is updated with the new best fitness.

Step 4.5: If the termination criteria for NC_{ij} are met, then go to Step 5. Otherwise, go to Step 4.1.

Step 5 (Evolution of NS_{ij})

Step 5.1 ~ 5.4: NS_{ij} evolves in a similar way as in Steps 4.1 ~ 4.4, where the individual with the best fitness in NC_{ij} is selected as the environmental individual.

Step 5.5: If the termination criteria for NS_{ij} are met, then go to Step 6. Otherwise, go to Step 5.1.

Step 6 (Termination criteria)

If the termination criteria are satisfied, then stop. Otherwise, go to Step 3.

Steps 4 and 5 involve the evolutionary process for NC_{ij} and NS_{ij}, respectively. Except for cooperating with the other species, the evolutionary process is based on a type of steady-state genetic algorithm and the number of reproduction cycles is used as the termination criterion for Steps 4.5 and 5.5. Step 4 and 5 alternate for the evolution of Pop-C and Pop-S, while varying the neighborhood.

In the Co-EA, the environmental individuals should be determined to assess the fitness of individuals. In this study, they are selected from the neighbors, not from all the individuals of a population. Based on fitness, a roulette wheel method is used for the selection of parents and individuals for replacement(Step 4.1-4.2 and Step 5.1-5.2).

4.2.2 Genetic Representation and Genetic Operators

As stated above, an individual in the CBT population is represented in the same way as the CBT method in the simple GA. In the Sequential population, an individual is composed of two parts. The formerly partial individual is symbolized by transforming the number of multicast groups to create simultaneously, which we call *the number of grouping*, into n bit binary numbers, and the latter one is represented by a sequential list that simply enumerates numbers generating multicast trees.

In the CBT population, the modified 2-point crossover and random mutation are used in the same way as the CBT method in the simple GA. In the Sequential population, the modified 2-point crossover operator and random mutation, and the modOX operator and inversion operator, are employed in the former and the latter part, respectively, in the same way as the CBT and Sequential methods in the simple GA.

5 Simulation Design and Results

5.1 Parameter Settings

In order to verify the performance of the proposed methods, computational experiments are carried out on various network topologies[9] and problem sets. The problem parameters for the multirate multicast networks and parameters for the proposed algorithms are set, as shown in Table 1. The proposed algorithms were coded in C++, and each experiment was repeated 10 times for every problem. Preliminary experiments were performed to determine proper parameter values, and different values were taken with respect to the problems. The total number of reproduced individuals is used for the termination of the algorithm. Since the size of solution space depends on topologies which are made using a different number of multicast groups and receiver nodes per group, the criterion is differently set for problems of each type.

Table 1. Parameter settings

Parameters for the problems	Values			
	Type A	Type B	Type C	Type D
Location of source and destination nodes	Randomly chosen			
Bandwidth among 1st layer links	Randomly chosen 5 ~ 20 MB/s		Randomly chosen 20 ~ 160 MB/s	
Bandwidth among 2nd layer links	-		Randomly chosen 5 ~ 20 MB/s	
Upper bound of link delay: the number of hops	7	10	12	
Rate allocation ration in utility function: $q \cdot \mathrm{Ln}(1+x)$	Randomly chosen 0.5 ~ 1.5 in q			
Parameters for the proposed algorithms	**simple GA**		**Co-EA**	
Population size	10×10 toroidal square lattice			
Neighborhood size	3×3 structure			
Reproduction cycles	2 or 3 times		3 or 4 times	
P_m, P_g (Mutation rate)	0.2, 0.1		0.1, 0.1	
Termination criteria of algorithm for Type A, B, C, D	3000, 8000, 15000, 20000		8000, 20000, 40000, 50000	

5.2 Evaluation of Performance

A comparison of the proposed methods using a hierarchical approach was made in terms of solution quality. Hierarchical approaches have been widely used to solve aggregated problems which combine several sub-problems that are inter-linked. For the hierarchical approach of this problem, first the route selection problem and then the

[9] The number of nodes which construct the network is 16 and 32 in Type A and Type B topologies, respectively. Type C topology consists of a two-layered network, where the number of 2nd-layer nodes connected with 1st-layer ones is 0, 12 ,15, 7, 8, 12, 18, 10, 18, 14, 2, 0 from Node 0 to Node 11 of 1st-layer, respectively. (The number of nodes in the 1st-layer: 12; the number of nodes in the 2nd-layer: 116; the number of total nodes: 128.) Type D topology exposes that the two-layered network is composed of backbone and regional networks in which the traffics are operated similar to those of Type B one. (The number of nodes in the 1st-layer: 7; the number of nodes in the 2nd-layer: 121; the number of total nodes: 128.)

rate allocation problem is solved. Therefore, each group independently creates each multicast tree according to the larger size of the sum of utilities over all receivers in each group using methods for generating single multicast trees in Section 3. Then the receiver rates of each group are sequentially allocated according to the solution of the route selection problem using the decision rule for receiver rate allocation. The representative results are shown in Table 2. The first column identifies the problems. From second to fourth columns indicate the number of total nodes (N_n), the number of multicast groups (G_n), and the number of receiver nodes per group (R_n) of each problem, respectively. From fifth to seventh and ninth columns show the sum of utilities over all receivers. In the eighth column, a comparison in solution quality between the simple GA (CBT or Sequential method) and the hierarchical approach is shown. In the last column, a comparison in solution quality between Co-EA and the hierarchical approach is shown. The Improvement Ratio (I. R.) is calculated as {(best solution-worst solution)/worst solution}×100 (%).

Table 2. Performance comparison of the hierarchical approach and the proposed methods

Problems	N_n	G_n	R_n	Hierarchical Approach	Proposed Simple GA			Proposed Co-EA	
					CBT	Sequential	I.R. (%)	Co-EA.	I.R. (%)
A-11	16	5	5	51.03	53.83	56.48	10.68	57.27	12.23
A-12			10	120.93	123.57	131.21	8.50	131.78	8. 97
A-21		8	5	97.84	101.32	108.22	10.61	110.45	12.89
A-22			10	154.17	179.24	164.07	16.26	183.39	18.95
A-31		12	5	111.38	122.51	115.74	10.00	125.56	12.73
A-32			10	238.25	273.94	263.25	14.98	280.32	17.66
B-11	32	10	8	163.39	169.89	179.24	9.70	179.36	9.77
B-12			12	244.27	256.71	273.94	12.15	276.53	13.21
B-21		18	8	357.72	393.47	370.48	9.99	395.45	10.55
B-22			12	476.04	556.29	488.16	16.86	571.05	19.96
B-31		24	8	403.07	467.37	439.36	15.95	475.74	18.03
B-32			12	760.87	852.49	776.16	12.04	862.26	13.33
B'-11	32	5	5	57.05	59.34	65.37	14.58	66.81	17.11
B'-12			10	124.68	136.39	141.63	13.59	143.07	14.75
B'-21		8	5	109.75	118.22	119.41	8.80	124.01	12.99
B'-22			10	185.42	204.43	189.45	10.25	213.55	15.17
B'-31		12	5	149.49	163.41	155.95	9.31	170.01	13.73
B'-32			10	296.74	323.85	301.83	9.14	336.64	13.45
C-11	128	10	10	280.06	298.80	311.37	11.18	331.79	18.47
C-12			20	562.12	565.51	624.97	11.18	657.06	16.89
C-13			30	828.81	872.12	908.83	9.65	954.29	15.14
C-21		20	10	561.31	583.56	611.01	8.85	646.18	15.12
C-22			20	1102.96	1117.82	1242.49	12.65	1292.01	17.14
C-23			30	1661.20	1904.69	1787.67	14.66	2007.23	20.83
C-31		30	10	781.10	804.82	926.87	18.66	958.33	22.69
C-32			20	1675.43	1867.54	1777.22	11.47	1967.12	17.41
C-33			30	2568.02	2772.75	2644.93	7.97	2879.52	12.13
C-41		40	10	997.81	1143.40	1191.01	19.36	1247.36	25.01
C-42			20	2197.30	2475.16	2374.52	12.65	2598.09	18.24
C-43			30	3117.03	3720.83	3542.67	19.37	3909.38	25.42
C-51		50	10	1291.98	1359.97	1536.88	18.96	1595.34	23.48
C-52			20	2629.28	3047.36	2687.08	15.90	3210.61	22.11
C-53			30	4107.36	4698.83	4130.07	14.40	4937.05	20.20
D-11	128	10	15	342.36	377.30	414.80	21.16	430.62	25.78
D-12			30	729.39	764.40	872.42	19.61	914.43	25.37
D-21		25	15	905.52	1003.78	1097.37	21.19	1140.59	25.96
D-22			30	1805.20	2092.94	1838.40	15.94	2203.67	22.07
D-31		50	15	1800.29	2088.98	1906.98	16.04	2241.73	24.52
D-32			30	3773.11	4331.10	4194.90	14.79	4476.42	18.64

The experimental results show that, for every problem set, all the proposed methods provide better outcomes than the hierarchical approach. We adopt the strategies of localized evolution and steady-state reproduction in the proposed methods. The new interaction arrangement results in rapid local convergence while maintaining global diversity and enhancing the performance of the optimization process. This conclusion is in good agreement with that of Davidor [23]. The superiority between the CBT and Sequential methods cannot be found due to characteristics of the method preferred according to network topologies and problem complexities (i.e., the number of nodes in the network). As the number of multicast groups in the problem set of each type becomes larger, the CBT method shows relative superiority over the Sequential method. It is thought that as the condition of the network becomes more complex, the CBT method, which considers all conditions of every multicast group at the same time, may take better effect. Among the proposed methods, the Co-EA outperforms the other two in all the problems. This makes it clear that the traditional approach to related (or aggregated) problems is less effective in exploring the solution space. It is worth noting that the improvement ratio grows larger as the problem set becomes more complex. One can conclude from the results that the proposed methods maintain their ability to achieve a good solution in more complex situations such as in actual networks.

In order to statistically compare the above results, each algorithm was run 50 times for A-12, B-11 and D-32 problems which indicated the smallest improvement ratio in A, B and D Type, and then the independent-samples t-test and one-way ANOVA were tested with SPSS tool. The results of statistical analysis show that the Hierarchical approach, CBT, Sequential and Co-EA methods have different solutions each other[10]. Although the statistical analysis is not performed about every problem, the similar results with these ones are expected to show about other problems. Finally, we could demonstrate the fact that the proposed methods improve the quality of solutions.

6 Conclusions

In this paper, we have proposed heuristic evolutionary computation algorithms that can simultaneously solve the route selection and rate allocation problem in multirate multicast networks; that is, the problem of constructing multiple multicast trees and simultaneously allocating the rate of receivers for maximizing the sum of utilities over all receivers, subject to link capacity and delay constraints for high-bandwidth delay-sensitive applications in point-to-point communication networks. In applying the proposed methods to the problem, many of the elements are elaborated in order to improve solution quality and computational efficiency. To promote population diversity and search efficiency in the algorithms, we also adopt strategies of localized evolution and steady-state reproduction. Additionally, a new coevolutionary algorithm is proposed to achieve better solutions. The results of extensive computational

[10] When the alpha value is 0.05, the null hypotheses of each problem are rejected because p value is smaller than α value (i.e., $p < 0.000$).

simulations show that the proposed algorithms provide high quality solutions and, in particular, that the Co-EA is better than the other methods. It is also implied that these algorithms perform well under varying network situations and that they are advantageously applied to actual networks.

Furthermore, the most attractive feature of the proposed algorithms is their reasonable flexibilities. These algorithms have the ability to handle various types of optimization criteria and restrictions. With a little modification, they can be applied to solve many variants of problems.

References

1. Jia, X., Wang, L.: Group multicasting routing algorithm by using multiple minimum steiner trees. Computer Comm., vol. 20. (1997) 750-758
2. Low, C.P., Song, X.: On finding feasible solutions for the delay constrained group multicast routing problem. IEEE Transactions on Computers, vol. 51, no. 5. (2002) 581-588
3. Shacham, N: Multipoint communication by hierarchical encoded data. in Proc. IEEE INFOCOM'92, vol. 3. (1992) 2107-2114
4. Fei, Z., Ammar, M., Zegura, E.W.: Multicast server selection: Problems, complexity, and solutions. IEEE Journal on Selected Areas in Communications, vol. 20, no. 7. (2002) 1399-1413
5. Lorenz, D.H., Orda, A.: Optimal partition of QoS requirements on unicast paths and multicast trees. IEEE/ACM Transactions on Networking, vol. 10, no. 1. (2002) 102-114
6. Kelly, F.P., Maulloo, A.K., Tan, D.K.H.: Rate control for communication networks: Shadow prices, proportional fairness and stability. J. Oper. Res. Society, vol. 49. (1998) 237–252
7. Low, S.H., Lapsley, D.E.: Optimization flow control-I: Basic algorithm and convergence. IEEE/ACM Trans. Networking, vol. 7, no. 6. (1999) 861–874
8. Kar, K., Sarkar, S., Tassiulas, L.: A scalable low-overhead rate control algorithm for multirate multicast sessions. IEEE Journal on Selected Areas in Communications, vol. 20, no. 8. (2002) 1541-1557
9. Kunniyur, S., Srikant, R.: End-to-end congestion control schemes: Utility functions, random losses and ECN marks. in Proc. IEEE INFOCOM 2000, Tel Aviv, Israel, vol. 3. (2000) 1323–1332
10. Matrawy, A., Lambadaris, I.: A rate adaptation algorithm for multicast sources in priority-based IP networks. IEEE Communications Letters, vol. 7, no. 2. (2003) 94-96
11. Sarkar, S., Tassiulas, L.: A framework for routing and congestion control for multicast information flows. IEEE Transactions on Information Theory, vol. 48, no. 10. (2002) 2690-2708
12. Goldberg, D.E.: Genetic Algorithm in Search Optimization & Machine Learning. Addison-Wesley, Readings (1989)
13. Michalewicz, Z.: Genetic Algorithm + Data Structures = Evolution Programs. 2nd edn. Springer-Verlag, Berlin (1994)
14. Moriarty, D.E., Miikkulainen, R.: Forming neural networks through efficient and adaptive coevolution. Evolutionary Computation, vol. 5. (1997) 373-399
15. Rosin, C.D., Belew, R.K.: New methods for competitive coevolution. Evolutionary Computation, vol. 5. (1997) 1-29
16. Maher, M.L., Poon, J: Modeling design exploration as co-evolution. Microcomputers in Civil Engineering, vol. 11. (1996) 195-210

17. Kim, Y.K., Kim, S.J., Kim, J.Y.: Balancing and sequencing mixed-model U-lines with a coevolutionary algorithm. Production Planning & Control, vol. 11, no. 8. (2000) 754-764
18. Varian, H.R.: Microeconomic Analysis. 3rd edn. Norton (2002)
19. Ballardie, T., Francis, P., Crowcroft, J.: Core Based Tress (CBT). in Proc. SIGCOMM'93 (1993) 85-95
20. Williamson, B.: Developing IP Multicasting Networks Volume I. Cisco Press (2000)
21. Davis, L.: Applying adaptive algorithms to epistatic domains. in Proc. of the Int. Joint Conf. on Artificial Intelligence (1985) 162-164
22. Syswerda, G.: A study of reproduction in generational and steady-state genetic algorithms. In G.J.E. Rawlins (ed.), Foundations of Genetic Algorithms (Morgan Kaufmann, San Marteo) (1991) 94-101
23. Davidor, Y.: A naturally occurring niche and species phenomenon: the model and first results. In R. Belew and L. Booker (ed.) Proceedings of 4th International on Conference Genetic Algorithms, San Diego (Morgan Kaufmann, San Marteo) (1991) 257-263

A Polynomial Algorithm for 2-Cyclic Robotic Scheduling

Vladimir Kats[1] and Eugene Levner[2,*]

[1] Institute for Industrial Mathematics, Beer-Sheva, Israel
vkats@iimath.com
[2] Holon Institute of Technology, Holon, Israel
levner@hit.ac.il

Abstract. We solve a single-robot m-machine cyclic scheduling problem arising in flexible manufacturing systems served by computer-controlled robots. The problem is to find the minimum cycle time for the so-called 2-cyclic (or "2-degree") schedules, in which exactly two parts enter and two parts leave the production line during each cycle. An earlier known polynomial time algorithm for this problem was applicable only to the Euclidean case, where the transportation times must satisfy the "triangle inequality". In this paper we study a general non-Euclidean case. Applying a geometrical approach, we construct a polynomial time algorithm of complexity $O(m^5 \log m)$.

1 Introduction

Fully automated production cells consisting of flexible machines and a material handling robot have become commonplace in contemporary manufacturing systems. Much research on scheduling problems arising in such cells, in particular in flowshop-like production cells, has been reported recently. A practical problem motivating this study is that encountered in an automated electroplating line for processing printed circuit boards (PCB's). Similar scheduling problems are commonly met also in food industries, steel manufacturing, plastic molding and other areas. Although there are many differences between the models, they all explicitly incorporate the interaction between the materials handling and the job processing decisions, since this interaction determines the efficiency of the cell.

This paper considers a *robotic flowshop cell* which consists of m machines $M_1, \ldots, M_m$, an input station M_0, an output station M_{m+1}, and a single robot that performs all material handling operations in the cell, i.e., the transportation of parts between the machines and the stations, as well as the loading and unloading of parts onto and from the machines and stations. To simplify the presentation, all parts are assumed to be identical; however, all results presented below are valid for the production system producing two product types. The parts are initially available at the input station M_0 and must be sequentially processed on $M_1, \ldots, M_m$ in this order, until they are finally unloaded from M_m and delivered at the output station.

There is no buffer available between the machines. Therefore, once a part is being removed from a machine, without delay it must be transported by the robot to the next station according to technological order (this condition is called *the no-wait*

A. Gelbukh and C.A. Reyes-Garcia (Eds.): MICAI 2006, LNAI 4293, pp. 439 – 449, 2006.

condition). In the practices of PCB industries, violating this condition may deteriorate the product quality and cause a defect product.

To move a part, the robot will first travel to the machine where the part is located, wait if necessary, unload the part, travel to the next machine specified by the technological sequence, and load the part. The robot repeats its moves periodically, such a production process is called *cyclic*, and the corresponding sequence of robot moves is called *a cyclic schedule*. A repeatable sequence in which each processing operation and each robot move appear *k* times during each cycle is called a *k-cyclic, or k-part, or k-degree, schedule cycle*. During each *k*-part cycle, exactly *k* parts enter the line and *k* parts are unloaded at the output station; at the end of the cycle the flowshop cell returns to its original state. An optimization problem for robotic flowshops asks to specify a *sequence of robot moves*, so as to maximize the throughput rate of the flowshop, or, equivalently, to minimize the cycle time.

Due to the importance of the robotic scheduling problems, the vast literature has appeared in recent years being devoted to both cyclic and non-cyclic formulations of these problems. Optimal schedules have been deeply studied over the past decades – we refer the interested reader to the books by Błazewicz et al., 1996, Pinedo 2002 and Sriskandarajah *et al.* 2006, as well as to the comprehensive surveys by Sethi *et al.* 1992, Hall 1999, Crama *et al.* 2000, and Dawande *et al.* 2005, and numerous references therein. In general, the multi-cyclic schedules may have a better throughput rate than the 1-cyclic ones, as have been reported by many researchers (Song *et al.* 1993, Lei and Wang 1994, Levner *et al.* 1996, Kats *et al.* 1999, Lei and Liu 2001, Che *et al.* 2002, Chu *et al.* 2003, to mention a few).

The literature on the *k*-cyclic scheduling, for $k > 1$, is not so vast, which can be explained by the increased complexity of these problems, in comparison with the 1-cyclic scheduling. To the best of our knowledge, the first works on multi-cyclic robotic scheduling have appeared in the 1960s in the former Soviet Union; Suprunenko *et al.* 1962, Aizenshtat 1963, and Blokh and Tanayev 1966 have proposed concise and elegant mathematical descriptions of the *k*-cyclic processes with transporting automatic devices and introduced the so-called *method of forbidden intervals* (MFI) for finding an optimal schedule; however, these authors did not establish its polynomiality. This method has been further developed and proved to be polynomial for the 1-cyclic case by Levner *et al.* 1997, where the upper bound of $O(m^3 \cdot \log m)$ has been obtained. However, this result is related to the 1-cyclic schedules only. Other early papers devoted to this class of scheduling problems have been limited to the development of heuristic and branch-an-bound methods (see, for example, Song *et al.* 1993, and Lei and Wang, 1994).

Special attention of the researchers has been devoted to the case of 2-cyclic scheduling. Based on the method of forbidden intervals (MFI), Levner *et al.* 1996 have proposed a geometric algorithm solving this problem fast in-practice and have conjectured that it is polynomial time. This conjecture has been proven by Chu *et al.* 2003 for the special case of the *Euclidian metrics*, in which the transportation times satisfy the "triangle inequality". These authors have proved that the complexity of the geometric algorithm is $O(m^8 \log m)$; for their proof, they have used an elaborate analysis of the MFI. Chu 2006 have presented a more sophisticated treatment of the MFI for the considered scheduling problem, which permitted him to improve the algorithm complexity for the Euclidian metrics from $O(m^8 \log m)$ to $O(m^5 \log m)$. The complexity for the general non-Euclidean case has remained an open question.

The aim of the present paper is a further study of the 2-cyclic scheduling problem. We investigate a general *non-Euclidean metrics*, where the transportation times are not required to satisfy the "triangle inequality". Here, the method of forbidden intervals is not applicable because the intervals cannot be simply merged together, as in the Euclidean case. We suggest a different geometric approach based on concepts of *feasible polygons* and *singular points* which is valid for the both cases, Euclidean as well as non-Euclidean. We enhance the geometrical scheme suggested by Levner et al. 1996 and construct an improved algorithm of complexity $O(m^5 \log m)$.

This paper is organized as follows. Section 2 gives a formal description of the problem. Section 3 present the analysis of the problem and restate it as a finite series of the linear programming problems. Section 4 introduces the singular points and estimates their total number. Section 5 presents the new polynomial algorithm and estimates its complexity. Section 6 concludes the paper.

2 Problem Formulation

For any given instance of the scheduling problem introduced in the previous section, there are two associated fixed sequences, U and S:

- a fixed and *a priori* known sequence $U = \{0, 1, 2, \ldots, m, m+1\}$ which specifies that each of identical parts is loaded at the input station M_0, processed on the machines in order $M_1, \ldots, M_m$, and then is unloaded at an output station M_{m+1};
- an *a priori* unknown sequence S of robot moves, $S = \{s(1)=0, s(2), \ldots, s(2m+2)\}$, which is to be found and specifies the ordering of $2m+2$ (material handling) operations to be performed by the robot in each cycle in the 2-cyclic schedule.

We introduce the following parameters:

p_i The processing time of a part at machine i, $i = 1, 2, \ldots, m$;
d_i The transportation time of a part from machine i to $i+1$, $i = 0, 1, 2, \ldots, m$, where "machine" $m+1$ is the unloading station; to simplify the presentation we assume that the processing time include the durations of the loading and unloading operations performed by the robot at machine i;
r_{ij} The traveling time of an unloaded robot from machine i to machine j, $i = 1, 2, \ldots, m+1$; $j=0. 1, 2, \ldots, m$;
Z_i The completion time of the ith operation performed at machine M_i, or, equivalently, the start time of robot's travel to machine M_i.

In the 2-cyclic schedules, exactly two parts enter and two parts leave the line during each cycle. It follows that the (identical) parts are loaded into the line at time

$$\ldots - kT, -kT + T_1, \ldots, -2T, -2T+T_1, -T, -T+T_1, 0, T_1, T, T+T_1, 2T, \ldots, kT+T_1, (k+1)T, ,$$

where $T_1 < T$.

Consider the part introduced into the process at time 0. Due to the no-wait condition, the part must be completed at machine i at time $Z_i = Z_{i-1} + d_{i-1} + p_i$, $i=1,\ldots,m$, $Z_0 = 0$. Correspondingly, the part introduced into the process at time T_1 must be unloaded from machine i at time T_1+Z_i. We assume that at each processing machine (i.e., the machines 1,2, …,m) no more then one part can be processed simultaneously. The ability of the robot to transport only one part at time, prohibits also values $d_{i-1}+p_i+d_i$ to be larger than T_1 and T-T_1, for any i, because in such a case the transportation of a part to machine i and from machine i will overlap in time. Thus,

$$T_1 \geq T_0 = max_{i=1,\ldots,m}\,(d_{i-1}+p_i+d_i) = max_{i=1,\ldots,m}\,(d_i+Z_i-Z_{i-1}); \tag{1a}$$

$$T-T_1 \geq T_0 = max_{i=1,\ldots,m}\,(d_{i-1}+p_i+d_i) = max_{i=1,\ldots,m}\,(d_i+Z_i-Z_{i-1}). \tag{1b}$$

Obviously, T_1 and T-T_1 are not larger than $T^0=Z_m+d_m+r_{m+1,0}$. The schedule with $T_1=T-T_1=T^0$ corresponds to a *primitive cyclic robot* route $S_0=\{0, 1, 2,\ldots,m\}$ coinciding with the technological order of machines U. Comparing T_0 and T^0, we obtain:

$$T^0 \leq m\,T_0+r_{m+1,0}. \tag{1c}$$

The periodicity of the process allows us to restrict its analysis to a single cycle confined within interval [0, T). The part which was introduced at time $-kT$, where $k=floor(Z_i/T)$ will be unloaded at time $(Z_i)mod\,T=Z_i-kT$, whereas the part which was introduced at time $-hT+T_1$, where $h=floor[(Z_i+T_1)/T]$ will be unloaded at time $(Z_i+T_1)mod\,T=Z_i+T_1-hT$. Note that station M_0 will be unloaded at time 0 and T_1.

Proposition 1. For the given time intervals T and T_1, the periodically repeated robot route is defined uniquely and can be found by ordering numbers $Y_i=(Z_i)mod\,T$ and $Y_i'=(Z_i+T_1)mod\,T$ $(i=0, 1,\ldots,m)$ in increasing order

$$0= Y_0=Y^{(*)}_{s(1)}\leq Y^{(*)}_{s(2)}\leq\ldots \leq Y^{(*)}_{s(2m+2)} < T, \tag{2}$$

where $Y^{(*)}_{s(1)}=Y_0=Z_0$. The sequence of indexes $S=\{s(1)=0, s(2),\ldots, s(2m+2)\}$ determines the robot route, which is the sequence of robot moves between the machines within time interval [0, T).

The proof is similar to the 1-cyclic case given, for instance, in Kats and Levner 1997, and is skipped here.

The sequence S is being repeated periodically, it means that after unloading machine $M_{s(2m+2)}$ the robot moves again to station $s(1) = M_0$ and at time T introduces a new part into the process. Thus, values T and T_1 fully determine the robot schedule. Similar to the 1-cyclic case (see, for instance Kats and Levner 1997), a 2-cyclic schedule is feasible iff the following inequalities are satisfied

$$Y^{(*)}_{s(k)} + R_{s(k),\,s(k+1)} \leq Y^{(*)}_{s(k+1)}, \tag{3}$$

where $R_{i,j} = d_i+r_{i+1,j}$, $k=1, 2,\ldots,(2m+2)$; $r_{s(2m+2)+1,\,s(2m+3)} = r_{s(2m+2)+1,s(1)}$, $Y^{(*)}_{s(2m+3)}=Y_0+T=T$.

Definition. The sequence of robot's moves is called a *feasible route* if it ensures a sufficient time for the robot to travel between the machines. In formal terms, the robot route is feasible iff the unloading times Y_i satisfy constraints (1a), (1b) and (3).

> Problem P_0. The 2-cyclic scheduling problem under consideration can now be formulated as follows: To find a feasible 2-cyclic robot route S minimizing the cycle time T (such a route is also called the *optimal schedule*).

3 Problem Analysis

The robot route remains unchanged as far as the set of $Y^{(*)}_{s(k)}$ values keeps the same order defined by (2); in other words, the robot route changes if and only if the order (2) is changed for some pair of $Y^{(*)}_{s(k)}$ values. To study all such changes, we will examine all possible intersections between pairs of functions Y_j and Y_j.

3.1 The Types of the Intersection Lines

The unloading times $Y_i=(Z_i) mod\ T = Z_i - kT$ are piecewise linear functions of one variable, namely, the cycle time T, whereas the times $Y_i^{'}= (Z_i+T_1) mod\ T = Z_i+T_1-hT$ are piecewise linear functions of two variables, T and T_1. At some values of T and T_1 the different functions, say, $Y^{(*)}_i$ and $Y^{(*)}_j$ intersect which means that the robot route changes at those values.

The intersections can be of four types, which are written out below; in what follows, without loss of generality, we will assume that $j > i$.

Type 1. Intersections of $Y_i = Z_i\ mod\ T$ and $Y_j = Z_j\ mod\ T$.

The intersections are determined by the equation

$$Z_i\text{-}k_iT= Z_j\text{-}k_jT$$

and take place at values

$$T=F_{ijk}=(Z_j\text{-}Z_i)/k, \tag{4}$$

where $k = k_j - k_i$, that is. $k = 1, 2,\ldots, m$.

Note that functions $Y_i = Z_i\ mod\ T$ and, respectively, $Y_j = Z_j\ mod\ T$ consist of segments of lines $Z_i\text{-}k_iT$ (k_i= 1, 2,…), and, respectively, $Z_j\text{-}k_jT$ (k_j= 1, 2,…), ranging between 0 and T: $0 \le Z_i\text{-}k_iT < T$, $0 \le Z_j\text{-}k_jT < T$. Therefore, at value $T=F_{ijk}$, only one pair of segments of lines Y_i and Y_j intersect, whereas the *infinite number* of straight lines $Z_i\text{-}k_iT$ and $Z_j\text{-}k_jT$, where $k_i = 0, 1,\ldots, k_j= k_i + k$, intersect at $T=F_{ijk}$.

As we will show below, in the considered problem P_0 the number of different k in (4) is, in fact, finite and bounded from above by the number of machines m. It is due to the fact that the cycle time T, which we are interested in, cannot be arbitrarily small but is bounded from below by T_0 (see condition (1a)).

Type 2. Intersections of $Y_i^{'}= (Z_i+T_1) mod\ T$ and $Y_j^{'}= (Z_j+T_1) mod\ T$.

This type of intersections defines the same set of points as the previous one:

$$Z_i+T_1\text{-}h_iT = Z_j+T_1\text{-}h_jT;\ \ T=F_{ijk}=(Z_j\text{-}Z_i)/k, \text{ where } k = 1, 2,\ldots, m.$$

Type 3. Intersections of $Y_i=Z_i\ mod\ T$ and $Y_j^{'}= (Z_j+T_1) mod\ T$.

For fixed T_1 the intersections take place at the points E_{ijk} similar to $T=F_{jk}$ considered above:

$$T = E_{ijk}= (Z_j+ T_1\text{-}Z_i)/k,\ k = 1,2,\ldots, m,$$

which means that those intersections are located along the lines given by equation

$$T_1= -(Z_j\text{-}Z_i)+kT,\ k =1,2,\ldots, m,$$

which (taking into account that $T_1<T$) is a composition of line segments.

Type 4. Intersections of $Y_j=Z_j \ mod \ T$ and $Y_i'= (Z_i+T_1) mod \ T$.

Similar to Case 3, those intersections are located along the lines $T_1= (Z_j-Z_i)-kT$, $k=1,2,\ldots, m$.

Consider the plane with axes T and T_1 and suppose that values T and T_1 are changed in the plane in an arbitrary way. We will say that a variable point (T, T_1) is *moving along some trajectory*. The intersection analysis considered above indicates that the robot route may change only when the trajectory crosses the following lines:

$$T = (Z_j-Z_i)/k\ , \tag{5a}$$

$$T_1= -(Z_j-Z_i)+kT, \tag{5b}$$

$$T_1= (Z_j-Z_i)-kT, \tag{5c}$$

where $k=0,1,2,\ldots, m$. We will refer to those lines as the *'route-changing lines'*.

3.2 The Number of the Route-Changing Lines

Consider now the triangular area A in the plane with coordinates (T, T_1), bounded by the inequalities $T_1 \geq T_0$, $T_1 \leq T/2$, $T_1 \geq T - T^0$.

Proposition 2. The search for an optimal solution can be restricted to the area A.

Proof is evident and is skipped

The lines (5a)-(5c) divide the area A into the regions bounded by the line segments; these regions are called *polygons*.

Proposition 3. For any fixed pair of indices (i, j), the number of different lines with different k in (5a)-(5c) crossing the area A is finite and bounded from above by the number of machines, m.

Proof is based on (1a) – (1c).

3.3 A Linear Programming Formulation of the Problem

Let us take a point $(T=x,\ T_1=y)$ inside of some polygon. This point uniquely determines the robot route. For *all* points (x,y) *inside* of the polygon the robot route *cannot change*.

Recall that in the scheduling problem P_0 under consideration, we have to find two types of interrelated variables: (1) the time values T and T_1, and (2) the corresponding robot route. Earlier, in Proposition 1, we have established that if T and T_1 are known then the robot route is defined in a unique way. Now suppose that the robot route is known while T and T_1 are unknown.

Proposition 4. For any *fixed* robot route S, the integers k and h in expressions $Y_i = Z_i \ mod \ T= Z_i - kT$ and $Y_i'= (Z_i+T_1) mod \ T =Z_i+T_1-hT$ are uniquely determined by the route.

The proof is identical to that for the 1-cyclic case in Kats and Levner 1997, 2002.

Consider now an arbitrary polygon in A and assume that the robot route in this polygon is $S =\{s(1)=0, s(2),\ldots, s(2m+2)\}$. Then the problem of finding minimal cycle time T for a *fixed robot route* S becomes the following polynomially solvable special case of the linear programming problem defined for two variables, T and T_1:

Problem P. Minimize T
subject to

$$T_1 \geq T_0 = max_{i=1,\ldots,m} (d_{i-1} + p_i + d_i),$$

$$T - T_1 \geq T_0 = max_{i=1,\ldots,m} (d_{i-1} + p_i + d_i),$$

$$Y^{(*)}_{s(k)} + R_{s(k),\, s(k+1)} \leq Y^{(*)}_{s(k+1)},$$

where $R_{ij} = d_i + r_{i+1,j}$, $k=1,2,\ldots,(2m+2)$; $r_{s(2m+2)+1,\ s(2m+3)} = r_{s(2m+2)+1,\ s(1)}$, $Y^{(*)}_{s(2m+3)} = Y_0 + T = T$, and all $Y_i^{(*)}$ are taken in their explicit form, $Y_i = Z_i - kT$ or $Y_i' = Z_i + T_1 - kT$. Here all the parameters Z_i are known input data, and k-values for each $Y_i^{(*)}$ are defined as indicated in Proposition 4.

Thus, we have arrived to the following observation: Taking into account that all points (T, T_1) in any polygon define just the same robot route, the original scheduling problem P_0 can be solved by examining all possible polygons inside the area A one after another, solving Problem P for each of them, and, finally, choosing, among all the obtained solutions, a schedule with the minimum T. As we will see in the next sub-section, the amount of polygons within the area A is at most $O(m^5)$.

3.4 The Number of Robot Routes: The Euler Formula

Let us estimate the total number of polygons in the area A, or, equivalently, the number of different feasible robot routes.

Lemma 1. The number of polygons in A is at most $O(n^5)$.

Proof. 1. First, let's estimate how many points of intersections the polygons can have. The line $T=F_{ijk}=(Z_j-Z_i)/k$ may intersect line $T_1=-(Z_g-Z_f)+hT$ or $T_1=(Z_g-Z_f)-hT$ inside area A only if $h=ceil[(Z_g-Z_f)/F_{ijk}]$ or $h=floor[(Z_g-Z_f)/F_{ijk}]$, correspondingly. It means that one line $T=F_{ijk}=(Z_j-Z_i)/k$ can cross all other lines in at most $O(m^2)$ points and then the total number of such type points, caused by all the intersections of this type, is at most $O(m^5)$.

Further, the intersection of two lines of the same type, that is, either (a) $T_1=-(Z_j-Z_i)+k'T$ and $T_1=-(Z_g-Z_f)+k''T$, or (b) $T_1=(Z_j-Z_i)-k'T$ and $T_1=(Z_g-Z_f)-k''T$, takes place at a point $T=G_{ijfgk}=[(Z_j-Z_i)-(Z_g-Z_f)]/k$, where, without loss of generality, we assume that $(Z_j-Z_i)>(Z_g-Z_f)$, $k=1,2,\ldots,m$. Note that inside the area A only one pair of lines may intersect at this point. In case (a) this pair of lines is determined by $k'=ceil[(Z_j-Z_i)/G_{ijfgk}]$ and $k''=ceil[(Z_g-Z_f)/G_{ijfgk}]$ whereas in case (b), correspondingly, by $k'=floor[(Z_j-Z_i)/G_{ijfgk}]$ and $k''=floor[(Z_g-Z_f)/G_{ijfgk}]$.

The intersection of lines of different types, that is, either (a) $T_1=-(Z_j-Z_i)+k'T$ with $T_1=(Z_g-Z_f)-k''T$ or (b) $T_1=(Z_j-Z_i)-k'T$ with $T_1=-(Z_g-Z_f)+k''T$, takes place at point $T=G'_{ijfgk}=[(Z_j-Z_i)+(Z_g-Z_f)]/k$. Inside the area A, there are only points such that $[(Z_j-Z_i) \pm (Z_g-Z_f)]/k \geq 2T_0$. Since $(Z_j-Z_i) \pm (Z_g-Z_f) \leq Z_m + Z_m \leq 2mT_0$, it immediately follows that $1 \leq k \leq 2mT_0/2T_0 \leq m$. Hence, the total number of points G_{ijfgk} and G'_{ijfgk} is $O(m^5)$. From Proposition 2 it follows that the total amount of lines (5a)-(5c) is $O(m^3)$, so the amount of intersection points of those lines with the triangular border of area A is also at most $O(m^3)$. Thus, the total number of intersection points, including those lying on the border of A, is at most $O(m^5)$.

2. Now we can estimate the total number of polygons. Denote the number of polygons in A by f, the number of intersection points in A by n, and the number of line segments connecting pairs of intersection points in A by e. Interpreting the intersection points as vertices of a planar graph, the connecting segments as edges and the polygons as faces of a planar graph (not including the outer infinitely large face), we can use the *Euler polyhedron formula* which claims:

$$f = e - n + 1.$$

For a simple, connected, planar graph with n vertices and e edges, it is well known in graph theory that, for $n \geq 3$, it holds: $e \leq 3n - 6$, and, therefore, $f \leq 2n - 5$. Thus, the total number of polygons in A is of the same order of magnitude as the number of intersection points, that is, it does not exceed $O(m^5)$. □

4 Singular Points and Their Properties

Consider any polygon p_A created by the intersection of lines (5a)-(5c) in the area A. As far as the robot route $S = \{s(1)=0, s(2),..., s(2m+2)\}$ is uniquely determined for all points (T, T_1) in p_A, we can define the polygon p_A as the set of points satisfying $2m+2$ precedence relations in inequalities (2), where each inequality in the system (2) is replaced by one of the following inequalities, using the variables Z_{sk} :

$$Z_{s(k)} - k_{s(k)}T \leq Z_{s(k+1)} - k_{s(k+1)}T, \tag{6a}$$

$$Z_{s(k)} + T_1 - k_{s(k)}T \leq Z_{s(k+1)} + T_1 - k_{s(k+1)}T, \tag{6b}$$

$$Z_{s(k)} + T_1 - k_{s(k)}T \leq Z_{s(k+1)} - k_{s(k+1)}T, \tag{6c}$$

$$Z_{s(k)} - k_{s(k)}T \leq Z_{s(k+1)} + T_1 - k_{s(k+1)}T. \tag{6d}$$

For the given robot route S, the integers $k_{s(k)}$ and $k_{s(k+1)}$ are uniquely determined by the route and do not depend on values T and T_1 in the considered polygon (see Kats and Levner 1997, 2002).

Along with p_A we consider an area of feasible schedules, denoted by p_B, it is also a polygon (which may be empty) which is located inside polygon p_A and determined by inequalities (3) in such a way that each inequality along the chain (3) is replaced by one of the following inequalities, using the variables Z_{sk} (which can be rewritten in a similar way as inequalities (2) are presented above in the form (6)):

$$Z_{s(k)} - k_{s(k)}T + R_{s(k),\, s(k+1)} \leq Z_{s(k+1)} - k_{s(k+1)}T, \tag{7a}$$

$$Z_{s(k)} + T_1 - k_{s(k)}T + R_{s(k),\, s(k+1)} \leq Z_{s(k+1)} + T_1 - k_{s(k+1)}T, \tag{7b}$$

$$Z_{s(k)} + T_1 - k_{s(k)}T + R_{s(k),\, s(k+1)} \leq Z_{s(k+1)} - k_{s(k+1)}T, \tag{7c}$$

$$Z_{s(k)} - k_{s(k)}T + R_{s(k),\, s(k+1)} \leq Z_{s(k+1)} + T_1 - k_{s(k+1)}T. \tag{7d}$$

The inequalities (7a) and (7d) can be reduced to

$$T \geq [Z_{s(k)} - Z_{s(k+1)} + R_{s(k),\, s(k+1)} + \delta T_1]/(k_{s(k)} - k_{s(k+1)}),\ \text{if } k_{s(k+1)} < k_{sk}. \tag{8}$$

or

$$T \leq [Z_{s(k+1)} - Z_{s(k)} - R_{s(k),\, s(k+1)}]/(k_{s(k+1)} - k_{s(k)}),\ \text{if } k_{s(k+1)} > k_{s(k)}, \tag{8'}$$

where $\delta = -1, 0, 1$.

Let's assume that polygon p_B is not empty; then the minimal value of the cycle time T in p_B must lie on the border of one of the inequalities (8), (8'). These borders have the following form:

$$T = (Z_j - Z_i + R_{i,j})/k \text{, or} \tag{9a}$$

$$T = (Z_j - Z_i + T_1 + R_{i,j})/k \text{, or} \tag{9b}$$

$$T = (Z_j - Z_i - T_1 + R_{i,j})/k, \tag{9c}$$

where $j > i$ and $j, i \in \{0, 1, 2, ..., m\}$; $k = 1, 2, ..., m/2$. We will call the obtained lines (9a)-(9c) *the lines of possible solutions.*

Consider the points in area A lying on lines (9a)-(9c) in which the robot route changes (we call them *singular points*). Those points are defined as the intersections of lines (9a)-(9c) with lines (5a)-(5c). The total amount of all singular points, lying on the lines of possible solutions (9a)-(9c) in area A is at most $O(m^5)$.

5 Algorithm: Description and Complexity

We present a polynomial algorithm with the worst-case complexity $O(m^5 \log m)$. The algorithm works as follows.

Step 1. Present all the intersection points and the line segments joining them for lines (5a)-(5c) in area A as, correspondingly, nodes and edges of a planar graph.
Step 2. Make the obtained planar graph Eulerian, by doubling, if needed, its edges (in order to make all the node degrees even), and build an Eulerian cycle in the obtained extended planar graph.
Step 3. Move along the Eulerian cycle and sequentially consider the polygons p_A, for instance, taking, one by one, those polygons p_A that are located on the left to each edge in the Eulerian cycle. In each polygon p_A find a robot's route determined by the system of inequalities (2).
Step 4. For the found robot route, solve the system of inequalities (3) given in form (7a) –(7d) with respect to T and T_1.
Step 5. Among all the found solutions, choose the optimal one, having the minimal T-value.

The validity of the algorithm follows from the fact that each face in the planar graph (i.e., each polygon in A) will be examined at least once.

Let us estimate its complexity. At Step 1, in order to construct the nodes-edges incidence matrix of the planar graph it is sufficient $O(n + e) = O(m^5)$ elementary operations. At Step 2, the total amount of edges, as well as the total amount of faces, in the extended Eulerian graph is increased at most twice, that is, still $O(m^5)$. The complexity of building an Eulerian cycle in the Eulerian graph is linear in the number of edges, i.e. is $O(m^5)$. At Step 3, to build a robot route in each polygon requires $O(m \cdot \log m)$ operations. At Step 4, the system of inequalities (7a)-(7d) contains only two variables, therefore, its solution can be found in $O(m \log m)$ operations (Megiddo 1983). Hence, the total complexity of this straightforward algorithm is at most $O(m^6 \log m)$.

The algorithm can be modified as follows. Instead of moving along the *route-changing lines* we can move along the *lines of possible solutions*. When moving along the latter lines in A, we can solve the LP problems separately for each of their sub-segment bounded by neighboring singular points. When any point (T, T_1) passes any singular point on the line of possible solutions (9a)-(9c), only one pair of neighboring indices in the corresponding route S changes their order, and, consequently, the corresponding systems of inequalities (7a)-(7d), in two adjacent sub-segments, differ in three inequalities only. Thus, at Step 5 there is no need to start solving the linear programming (LP) problem from scratch for each sub-segment, but rather the solution can be adjusted in $O(1)$ time; in this scheme, we only need to find an initial solution for the LP at the first sub-segment, for all lines of possible solutions (see Kats and Levner 2002 for details). Taking into account that the total amount of the lines of possible solutions is $O(m^3)$, and solving of an individual LP problem requires $O(m \log m)$, Step 5 can be done in $O(m^4 \log m)$. The total number of sub-segments is the same as the number of singular points, $O(m^5)$. Thus, the complexity of the modified algorithm will be $O(m^5 \log m + m^4 \log m) = O(m^5 \log m)$.

6 Concluding Remarks

In contrast to many previously known works which deal with 1-cyclic schedules only, this paper treats a more complicated case of 2-cyclic schedules. Many researchers have noticed and experimentally verified that the throughput in 2-cyclic schedules is usually better than in the optimal 1-part schedules. We provide a polynomial-time 2-cyclic scheduling algorithm minimizing the cycle time, or, equivalently, maximizing the throughput rate.

We have studied the general non-Euclidean case and constructed the algorithm of complexity $O(m^5 \log m)$. We believe that this worst case upper bound is not tight and can be improved. The algorithm has worked much faster in practice than the guaranteed worst-case upper bound. In our future research, we intend to improve the upper bound and to estimate the algorithm behavior on the average.

References

1. V.S. Aizenshtat, Multi-operator cyclic processes, Doklady of the Byelorussian Academy of Sciences, 1963, 7(4), 224-227 (Russian).
2. J. Blazewicz, K.H. Ecker, E. Pesch, G. Schmidt, and J. Weglarz, *Scheduling Computer and Manufacturing Processes*, Springer Verlag, Berlin, 1996
3. A.Sh. Bloch and V.S. Tanayev, Multi-operator processes, Proceedings of the Byelorussian Academy of Sciences, (physical and mathematical sciences), 1966, (2), 5-11, (Russian).
4. A. Che, C. Chu and F. Chu, Multicyclic hoist scheduling with constant processing times, *IEEE Transactions on Robotics and Automation*, February 2002, 18(1), 69-80.
5. A. Che, C. Chu, and E. Levner, A polynomial algorithm for 2-degree cyclic robotscheduling, *European Journal of Operational research*, February 2003, 145(1), 31-44.
6. C. Chu, A Faster Polynomial Algorithm for 2-cyclic robotic scheduling, *Journal of Scheduling*, 2006 (in press).
7. Y. Crama, V. Kats, J. van de Klundert, and E Levner, Cyclic scheduling in robotic flowshop, Annals of operations Research, 2000, 96(1-4), 97-123.

8. M. Dawande, H.N. Geismer, S.P. Sethi, C. Sriskandarajah, Sequencing and scheduling in robotic cells: recent developments, *Journal of Scheduling*, 2005, 8(5), 387-426.
9. M. N. Dawande, H.N. Geismer, S. P.Sethi, and C. Sriskandarajah, *Througput Optimization in Robotic Cells*, Springer, 2006.
10. V. Kats and E. Levner, Cyclic scheduling on a robotic production line, *Journal of Scheduling,* 2002, 5, 23-41
11. V. Kats and E. Levner, A strongly polynomial algorithm for no-wait cyclic robotic flowshop scheduling, *Operations Research Letters,* 1997, 21, pp. 171-179
12. V. Kats, E. Levner, and L. Meyzin, Multiple-part cyclic hoist scheduling using a sieve method, *IEEE Transactions on Robotics and Automation*, August 1999, 15(4), 704-713.
13. L. Lei and Q. Liu, Optimal cyclic scheduling of a robotic processing line with two-product and time-window constraints, *INFOR*, May 2001, 39(2), 185-199.
14. L. Lei and T.J. Wang, Determining optimal cyclic hoist schedules in a single-hoist electroplating line, *IEE Transactions*, March 1994, 26(2), 25-33.
15. E. Levner, V. Kats and C. Sriskandarajah, A geometric algorithm for finding two-unit cyclic schedules in no-wait robotic flowshop, *Proceedings of the International Workshop in Intelligent Scheduling of Robots and FMS, WISOR-96,* Holon, Israel, HAIT Press, 1996, 101-112.
16. N. Megiddo,Towards a genuinely polynomial algorithm for linear programming, *SIAM Journal on Computing*, 1983, 12, 347-353.
17. M. Pinedo, Scheduling. Theory, Algorithms and Systems, 2nd ed., Prentice Hall, 2002.
18. S.P. Sethi, C. Sriskandarajah, G. Sorger, J. Blazewicz, and W. Kubiak, Sequencing of parts and robot moves in a robotic cell, *International Journal of Flexible Manufacturing Systems*, 1992, 4, 331-358.
19. W. Song, Z.B. Zabinsky and L.Storch, An algorithm for scheduling a chemical process tank line, *Production Planning & Control*, June 1993, 4, 323-332.
20. D.A. Suprunenko, V.S. Aizenshtat, and A.S. Metel'sky, Multi-operator transformation processes, *Doklady of the Byelorussian Academy of Sciences*,1962, 6(9), 541-544 (in Russian).

A New Algorithm That Obtains an Approximation of the Critical Path in the Job Shop Scheduling Problem

Marco Antonio Cruz-Chávez[1] and Juan Frausto-Solís[2]

[1] CIICAp, Autonomous University of Morelos State
Av. Universidad 1001, Chamilpa, 62209, Cuernavaca Morelos, México
mcruz@uaem.mx
[2] Department of Computer Science, ITESM, Campus Cuernavaca
Paseo de la Reforma 182-A, Lomas de Cuernavaca, 62589, Temixco, Morelos, México
juan.frausto@itesm.mx

Abstract. This paper presents a new algorithm that obtains an approximation of the Critical Path in schedules generated using the disjunctive graph model that represents the Job Shop Scheduling Problem (JSSP). This algorithm selects a set of operations in the JSSP, where on the average ninety nine percent of the total operations that belong to the set are part of the critical path. A comparison is made of cost and performance between the proposed algorithm, CPA (Critical Path Approximation), and the classic algorithm, CPM (Critical Path Method). With the obtained results, it is demonstrated that the proposed algorithm is very efficient and effective at generating neighborhoods in the simulated annealing algorithm for the JSSP.

Keywords: Critical path, metaheuristic, schedule, slack time, neighborhood.

1 Introduction

The job shop scheduling problem (JSSP) is considered to be one of the most difficult to solve in combinatorial optimization. It is also one of the most difficult problems in the NP-hard class [1]. Due to this, the importance of finding new algorithms that help in the solution of this problem is understandable. The search for more efficient algorithms has been focused in the area of non-deterministic algorithms, given the characteristics of JSSP.

Given the good results obtained in JSSP for some non-deterministic algorithms of local search, such as simulated annealing (SA) [2, 3, 4, 5, 6, 7, 8], great interest has been taken in improving the operation of these metaheuristics. Most work has been done in searching for better neighborhood structures [2, 5, 6, 7, 9] that permit more efficient selection of neighbors.

At the moment, a very effective neighborhood structure exists, N_1 [4], that allows for the selection of neighbors in a schedule such that the search space of the JSSP decreases considerably. This allows more rapid advancement in the search for the global optimum. In order to use the structure of neighborhood N_1, it is necessary find the critical path (CP) of the schedule, which is formed by a set of operations of the JSSP. These operations are called critical operations. In this way, the only neighbors with

A. Gelbukh and C.A. Reyes-Garcia (Eds.): MICAI 2006, LNAI 4293, pp. 450 – 460, 2006.

the possibility of being chosen are those that are generated by a permutation of a pair of critical operations.

A metaheuristic has the characteristic of generating repeated local searches. Therefore, when N_1 is used, it is necessary to calculate the CP every time that a neighbor in the neighborhood [4] of the schedule is chosen. Because of this, the execution of the metaheuristic tends to be slower in large problems of job shop because of the repeated calculation of the CP. This is true even though [10] the algorithms that are used in order to calculate the CP are polynomial [11].

In JSSP, it has been proven [4] that only neighbors that are obtained through the permutation of pair of operations that belong to the CP of a schedule could have a makespan[1] less than that of the original schedule. Due to this, when working with metaheuristics in JSSP where the objective function is obtaining the minimum makespan, the structure of neighborhood N_1 or one of its derivatives [2, 3, 4, 5, 6, 7, 8] is used.

Several options exist that could improve the efficiency of the metaheuristics that use the neighborhood structure N_1. One option is to generate algorithms that calculate the critical path in a more efficient form. Another option is to generate algorithms that do not calculate the critical path. In place of this calculation, these algorithms would have a high probability of generating neighbors by a permutation of a pair of critical operations. The second option is presented in this paper. This option involves generating an algorithm that, based on certain heuristics approaches, selects a set Ω of operations from all the existent operations in the job shop. This set is selected such that it contains all of the operations that form the CP and a few others operations as well. Within the set Ω, the largest percentages of operations are critical operations, that is, Ω possesses a minimum number of non critical operations. In order to explore this second option, an algorithm was generated called CPA (Critical Path Approximation), which selects an operations set from a schedule. This operations set has the characteristic of containing all the operations belonging to the CP. These critical operations constitute 99 percent of all the operations in the set Ω.

This research contributes to the effort to find more efficient ways to use metaheuristics for JSSP with the neighborhood structure N_1 by proposing an efficient algorithm for calculating the CP.

Following this brief introduction, section two explains the disjunctive graph model of the job shop scheduling problem that is used to generate schedules where the CP and Ω are obtained. Section three presents the neighborhood structure N_1, section four introduces the algorithm proposed that generates the configuration generation mechanism for neighborhoods, called Critical Path Approximation (CPA). Section five presents the experimental results. The final section draws conclusions about the information presented in the previous sections.

2 The Disjunctive Graph Model of the JSSP

Figure 1 shows the disjunctive graph model $G = (A, E, O)$ for a JSSP of 3x3 (three machines and three jobs). This disjunctive graph is formed by three sets. The operations

[1] Maximum completion time of the jobs.

set, O, is made up of the nodes G, numbered one to nine. The processing time appears next to each operation. The beginning and ending operations (I and * respectively) are fictitious, with processing times equal to zero. The set A is composed of conjunctive arcs, each one of these arcs unites a pair of operations that belong to the same job. The operations 1, 2, and 3 are connected by one of these arcs and therefore form job one. Jobs two and three are made up of the operations 4, 5, 6 and 7, 8, 9 respectively. Each arc of A represents a precedence constraint. For example, in job one, operation two must finish before operation three begins. Set E is composed of disjunctive arcs. Each arc that belongs to E unites a pair of operations that belong to the same machine. It can be seen that operations 1, 5 and 7 are executed by machine one and united by these arcs. Likewise, machines two and three execute the operations 3, 4, 9 and 2, 6, 8 respectively. Each machine forms a clique (a subset of E completely connected). Each arc of E represents a resources capacity constraint between a pair of operations that belong to the same machine. This type of constraint indicates that the machine cannot execute more than one operation in the same interval of time.

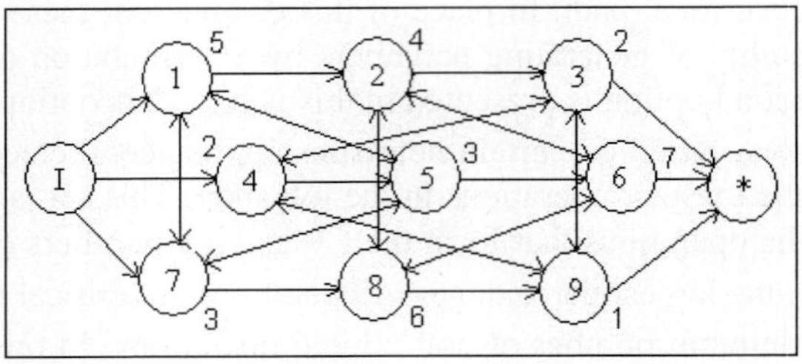

Fig. 1. Representation of a JSSP with three jobs and three machines using a disjunctive graph

3 The N_1 Neighborhood Function

The selection of the neighborhood structure strongly influences the performance of the metaheuristics [12] because the neighborhood has to be evaluated constantly. Consequently, this evaluation is the most critical one in the metaheuristics. In JSSP, the neighborhood N_1, introduced by Van Laarhoven et al. [4], has been used with great success to minimize the makespan. The evaluation of this neighborhood is made based on the set of solutions that are generated by the disjunctive graph G. Each solution (schedule) represents a digraph that does not contain cycles. In order to evaluate the neighborhood of the schedule, S, using N_1, it is necessary to find the CP of S. The neighbors in an N_1 neighborhood are generated by a permutation in a pair of adjacent operations that belong to the set of operations that form the CP of S. Figure 2 presents a schedule, S, for the JSSP shown in Figure 1, where the CP of S is demonstrated by a thicker line. The only pairs of adjacent operations that could swap in the CP are the compound pairs of operations that are executed by the same machine. For S in Figure 2, the pair of operations 1 and 7, which are executed by machine one, can be swapped. Likewise, the pair of operations 8 and 2 executed by machine two can be swapped. As one can see, in order to obtain a neighbor of S (permutation of a pair of operations of S), it is necessary to calculate the CP of S. If N_1 is used in a local search, every time that a new S is formed, it is necessary to recalculate the CP to continue evaluating N_1.

Great advantages are gained by using N_1 in local searches [4]. For example, any permutation carried out in order to find a new schedule, S', obtains a feasible schedule, as long as $S' = f(S, N_1)$. It is also possible to obtain an S' with a makespan which is less than S, although this does not happen if the swap is made with a pair of operations that do not belong to the CP.

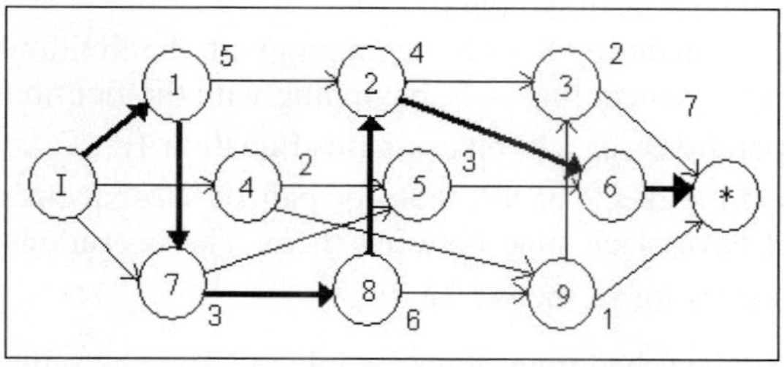

Fig. 2. A schedule of 3x3 where the operations that form the critical path are shown

An easily noted disadvantage of using N_1 is the necessity of calculating the CP constantly when N_1 is used in local searches.

The following section presents an alternate proposal to the use of N_1, which avoids repeatedly calculating the critical path of the job shop scheduling problem, consequently allowing for a reduction in the calculation time.

4 Critical Path Approximation Algorithm

The Critical Path Approximation (CPA) algorithm is based on three main lines of reasoning. The first line of reasoning is that for a defined schedule such as the one in Figure 2, the CP that is generated beginning from the fictitious operation I and ending with the fictitious operation *, is the same CP that is generated beginning with the fictitious operation * and ending with the fictitious operation I. That is, both critical paths generated in opposite directions are formed by the same operations due to being the same schedule. The second line of reasoning involves Equation 1, which indicates that upon generating the scheduling[2] starting with the fictitious operation I the start time s_i^I is obtained from the operation i that belongs to the critical path of the schedule. When this start time is added to the completion time c_i* (for the same operation), which is obtained by the scheduling beginning with the fictitious operation *, the sum is equal to the makespan (MS), where the MS is equal to the value of the CP [4] of the schedule. For $c_i^* = s_i^* + t$, s_i^* is the start time that is obtained from operation i when the scheduling starts with the fictitious operation * and t is the processing time of the operation i. The final line of reasoning that is considered for the generation of the CPA algorithm is that slack time between a pair of operations (i, j) that is part of the CP does not exist [4]. Considering the above-mentioned, it can be seen that the

[2] Start times of the operations of a schedule.

operations that fulfill both Equation 1 and the conditions of the last line of reasoning will have a high probability of belonging to the critical path of the defined schedule because they fulfill the conditions necessary for the pair (*i, j*) to belong to the CP. This means that there is neither slack between the pair (*i, j*) nor in either operation. More details are presented in CPM in [14].

$$MS = s_i^{\mathrm{I}} + c_i^{*} \tag{1}$$

The steps of the CPA algorithm are the following:

1. Take a schedule S as initial data.
2. Generate the scheduling S^{I} of S, beginning with the fictitious operation I.
3. Generate the S^{*} scheduling of S, beginning with the fictitious operation *.
4. Find the operations set Ω' that satisfies Equation 1.
5. In each machine of the JSSP, look for pair of subsequent[3] operations of Ω' that do not have slack time between them. The operations pair that satisfies this requirement forms the set Ω.

In order to obtain the scheduling of a schedule in CPA, the scheduling algorithm is used [13]. The time function of CPA is shown in Equation 2, where η is the number of operations obtained from *mxn*, *m* is the number of machines, and *n* is the number of jobs in the problem. The complexity of the algorithm is $O(\eta^{3/2})$.

$$f(\eta) = 2\eta^{3/2} + 2\eta^{1/2} \tag{2}$$

According to the three lines of reasoning, one could affirm that the set Ω includes all the operations that belong to the CP. As can be seen in the study done in [16], it is known that a permutation carried out in a pair of subsequent operations that do not have slack time between them results in a feasible schedule. Therefore, any permutation of a pair of subsequent operations that belong to the set Ω, will result in a feasible schedule.

The following is an example of how the set Ω is obtained, using the schedule of the 3x3 JSSP presented in Figure 2.

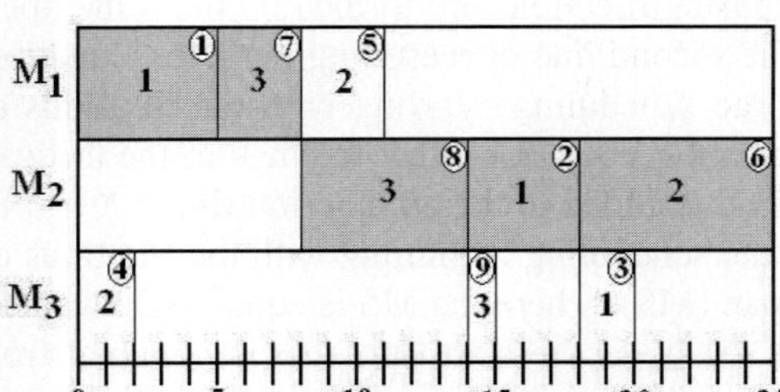

Fig. 3. Scheduling generated from Figure 2, starting with the fictitious operation I

[3] For the same machine, when operation *i* immediately precedes operation *j*, then *i*, *j* is a pair of subsequent operations.

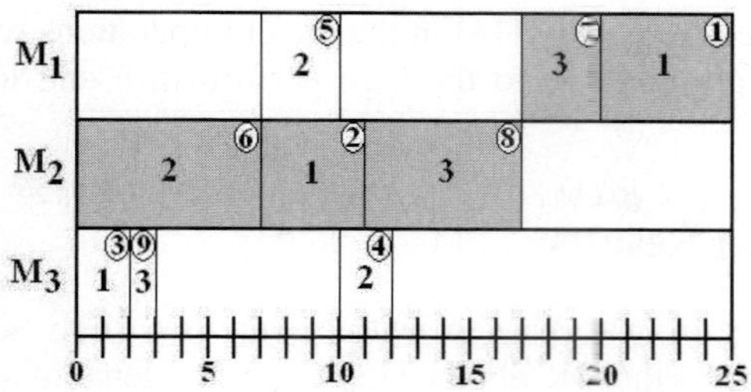

Fig. 4. Scheduling generated from Figure 2, starting with the fictitious operation*

Figure 3 presents the scheduling that is obtained starting with the fictitious operation I. Figure 4 presents the scheduling that is obtained starting with the fictitious operation*.

Table 1. Results obtained from the scheduling beginning with operation I, with operation*, and with the evaluation of the Equation 1

Operation	Scheduling		Evaluation of Equation 1
	s_i^I	s_i^*	$MS = s_i^I + c_i^*$
1	0	20	25
2	14	7	25
3	18	11	32
4	0	10	12
5	8	7	18
6	18	0	25
7	5	17	25
8	8	11	25
9	14	2	17

In Figures 3 and 4, the number of each operation is enclosed in a circle and the other number corresponds to the job where this operation is required. In these figures, the shaded gray areas correspond to the operations that fulfill Equation 1. The makespan of both schedulings is the same and equal to 25. Table 1 presents the start times of each operation obtained from Figures 3 and 4. In the table, the shaded regions represent the operations that fulfill Equation 1. As one can observe in Table 1, all the operations that form the set Ω' = {1, 2, 6, 7, 8}, belong to the CP (see Figure 2). One can see that all the operations that form the critical path are found in the set Ω'. These operations fulfill Equation 1, due to the fact that the MS obtained upon evaluating Equation 1 is the same as when evaluating for the CP (MS= 25). It can be observed in Figure 3 and 4 that the pairs of subsequent operations presented in the set Ω', do not have slack time; the pairs are (1, 7), (8, 2) and (2, 6). These pairs form the set Ω.

The following section presents a comparison of cost/performance of the CPA algorithm with a classical algorithm of polynomial time called CPM [11] (Critical Path

Method) which is used frequently [14] in the area of operations research for the planning and control of projects due to the high performance and low cost with which CPM works.

5 Computational Results

The proposed algorithm was proven with seven job shop scheduling problems benchmarks registered in the OR library [13]. Two problems of small size were used from this library, the FT06 with 6 machines, 6 jobs and 36 operations, and the FT10 with 10 machines, 10 jobs and 100 operations, both were proposed by Muth and Thompson. The problem of medium size LA40 with 15 machines, 15 jobs and 225 operations, proposed by Lawrence was used as well. Finally, four problems of larger size, proposed by Nakano and Yamada, were used which include YN1, YN2, YN3, and YN4, each one with 20 machines, 20 jobs and 400 operations.

In order to carry out the tests, a personal computer with a processor of 2.4 GHz and 640 MB in RAM was used.

The comparison of cost/performance of the CPA algorithm in the calculation of the operations pair that forms the set Ω (a set for each schedule generated randomly) was carried out with the CPM algorithm (Critical Path Method) [14].

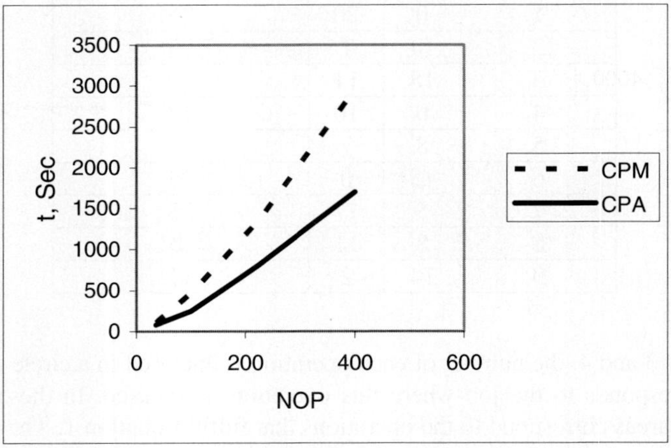

Fig. 5. Cost generated by the CPM and CPA algorithms upon calculating 800,000 critical paths (sets Ω, respectively) as the JSSP increases in size

Figure 5 presents the results obtained in the calculation of Ω and the critical path using the CPA and CPM algorithms respectively, for the problems FT06, FT10, LA40 and YN1. This figure shows the time of execution that is obtained for each algorithm when the number of operations in JSSP is increased. The time t is equal to the time that it takes the algorithm to calculate 800,000 critical paths (with CPM) or 800,000 sets Ω (with CPA). As can be observed, the cost of CPA is less than that of CPM. This figure also shows that when the number of operations (NOP) increases, the difference in times (CPM vs. CPA) needed to obtain the 800,000 critical paths (or sets Ω) is more significant. This indicates that CPA works more efficiently than CPM as the problems of job shop increase in size.

Figure 6 presents the results obtained in the calculation of critical paths using the CPM algorithms and the results obtained in the calculation of the sets Ω using the CPA algorithms for the problem YN1. This figure shows the time of execution that is obtained when the Number of Critical Paths, NCP, (Number of sets Ω, NSΩ, respectively) increases for each algorithm. The t time is equal to the time that it takes the CPM algorithm to calculate a determined number of critical paths (for CPA, number of sets Ω). As shown, the cost of CPA is less than that of CPM. Also in this figure it can be observed that when NCP or NSΩ increases, the difference in times (CPM vs. CPA) in order to obtain these critical paths (sets Ω, respectively), is made more noticeable. This indicates that CPA will work better than CPM when NCP increases. For larger problems of JSSP, the metaheuristics that use the N_1 structure need a large NCP in order to be able to execute an acceptable search within the large solution space that these problems have[4].

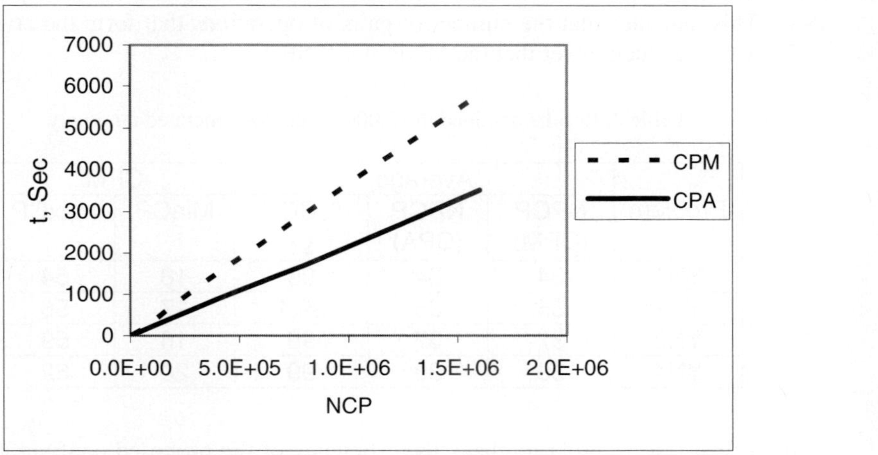

Fig. 6. Cost generated by the CPM and CPA algorithms in the problem YN1, with increasing NCP (NSΩ, respectively)

Table 2 presents a measure of the performance of the CPM and CPA algorithms. In order to evaluate this performance, the problems YN1, YN2, YN3, and YN4 were used. This table shows the average result for the calculation of 15,000 critical paths (15,000 sets Ω respectively). As can be seen upon studying the table, on the average, the NPCP (number of pairs of operations that belong to the critical path) obtained by CPM (obtained also by CPA in Ω), is between 34 and 38, depending on the problem. The MNP[5] (maximum number of pairs) that a symmetrical problem of JSSP is able to

[4] In a JSSP, the solution space is bound by $(m!)^n$.

[5] Maximum number of permutations, better known as the neighborhood size.

have is MNP= n $(n-1)$, where n is the number of jobs that the problem has; for problems YN1 to YN4, MNP= 380 pair of operations. As can be seen by studying the table, only a small part of the total pairs of operations belong to the CP (see NPCP in Table 2). In the same table, it is observed that there are a greater number of operations in the set Ω than those that exist in the critical path. These operations that are not part of the critical path make up an average of only 1% of the pairs of operations that are in Ω. The percentage of COP (Critical Operations Pairs) in the set is very high and almost constant, making up around 99% of the total number of operations pairs in Ω. It is important to clarify that in Ω, all the operations pairs that form the critical path are always present, plus a few pairs that are not part of the critical path. This means that the CPA algorithm has a very high performance in the approximation of the CP. This means that if CPA is used in metaheuristics that apply structures N_1, a probability of 99% exists that any given pair of operations chosen from Ω will pertain to the critical path. CPA allows full advantage to be taken of this neighborhood structure, but with a lower cost in generation time of the approximation of CP in order to evaluate N_1.. Table 2 also shows MinCP (Minimum number of pairs of critical operations found with CPM) generated in 15,000 tests and the MaxCP (maximum number of critical pairs found with CPM) generated in 15,000 tests for each problem of JSSP. This indicates that the number of pairs of operations that form the critical path will always be much lower that the MNP of a JSSP.

Table 2. Results obtained in 15,000 schedules generated randomly

Problem		Average		CPM	
	NPCP (CPM)	NPCP (CPA)	%COP Ω	MinCP	MaxCP
YN1	34	34	99	18	54
YN2	35	35	99.1	17	56
YN3	37	37	99	16	59
YN4	38	38	99	20	62

As a final test, in order to check the efficiency of the proposed configuration generation mechanism, the mechanism was implemented in the simulated annealing (SA) algorithm with restart presented in [8]. The cooling sequence of the simulated annealing is shown in Table 3. T_o is the initial temperature, t_f is the final temperature, C are the Metropolis cycles, and f is the cooling factor.

Table 3. Cooling sequence of the simulated annealing algorithm

Problem	T_O	T_f	C	F
FT10	64000	1	1000	0.98
LA40	200	1	750	0.99
YN1	64000	1	40000	0.98
YN2	64000	1	40000	0.98

Four problems were used to test the proposed mechanism. The results are presented in Table 4. The average and standard deviation, σ , reported in the table are the average of five executions of the SA algorithm. The SA algorithm is executed until a RE (Relative Error) of less than 2% is obtained. The longest execution time using the proposed mechanism is for the problem YN2, which was approximately 5 hours and 9 minutes. In this case, there is a RE of 1.98% when comparing the result with the best upper-bound found to this date, which is reported by Der and Steinhöfel [17]. The SA parallel algorithm of Der and Steinhöfel, which requires the calculation of the critical path by using the neighborhood N_1, took 16 hours and 30 minutes to obtain the upper-bound using a PC-cluster of 12 processors, each one of 550 MHz. In Table 4, for YN1, a RE of 1.7% was obtained in approximately 2 hours. Der and Steinhöfel [17] report a RE of 0.68% obtained in 16 hours for the same problem. In Table 4, for the FT10 problem, the optimum is obtained in less than 27 minutes. This result is obtained very quickly with respect to the time of 44 minutes, 55 seconds, reported in [8] when using the same algorithm that requires the calculation of the critical path. With the results shown in Table 4, it is proven that the configuration generation mechanism for neighborhoods proposed in this work, has a low cost, due to the short generation times needed to obtain good results for the evaluated problems with SA. It shows very good performance because it obtains results with low RE.

SA works with the neighborhood N_1 because pairs of operations that belong to the CP are permuted (99% of the time, see Table 2) using the CPA algorithm.

Table 4. Results obtained when the proposed configuration generation mechanism for neighborhoods is implemented in the SA algorithm with restart

Problem	t* sec	CS	Better MS*	Bad MS	Average MS	%RE*	σ
FT10	1585	930	930	937	931.4	0	2.8
LA40	1024	1222	1229	1234	1230.0	0.57	2.0
YN1	7659	885	900	909	904.2	1.70	2.9
YN2	18542	909	927	933	929.0	1.98	2.1

6 Conclusion

With the experimental results presented here, one can draw the conclusion that the CPA algorithm works more efficiently than the CPM algorithm with respect to cost because it obtains results more quickly. With respect to performance, CPA is competitive with CPM, because on the average, 99% of the total of pairs obtained in the set Ω belongs to the critical path. It is important to clarifying that Ω will always contain all the operation pairs that form the CP.

The use of the proposed Configuration Generation Mechanism for Neighborhoods in SA, when searching for a solution to instances of varying sizes of JSSP, enables results to be obtained efficiently with respect to cost/performance. This suggests that the proposed mechanism could work efficiently for any of the existing benchmarks of JSSP.

References

1. M.R. Garey, D.S. Johnson and R. Sethi, The complexity of Flow shop and Job shop Scheduling. Mathematics of Operations Research, Vol. I, No 2, USA, 117-129, May, 1976.
2. E.H.L. Aarts, P.J.M. Van Laarhoven, J.K. Lenstra, and N.L.J. Ulder, A computational study of local search algorithms for job shop scheduling, ORSA Journal on Computing 6, 118-125, 1994.
3. M.E. Aydin, M.E. and T. C. Fogarty, A distributed evolutionary simulated annealing algorithm for combinatorial optimisation problems, accepted for publication in Journal of Heuristics, 10 (3): 269-292, May 2004.
4. P.J.M. Van Laarhoven, E.H.L. Aarts and J.K. Lenstra. Job shop scheduling by simulated annealing. Oper. Res., 40(1):113-125, 1992.
5. T. Yamada and R. Nakano, Job-shop scheduling by simulated annealing combined with deterministic local search, Meta-heuristics: theory and applications, Kluwer academic publishers MA, USA, pp. 237-248, 1996.
6. T. Yamada, B. E. Rosen and R. Nakano, A simulated annealing approach to job shop scheduling using critical block transition operators, IEEE, 0-7803-1901-X/94, 1994.
7. K. Steinhöfel, , A. Albrecht , C.K. Wong, An Experimental Analysis of Local Minima to Improve Neighborhood Search Computers & Operations Research, 30(14):2157-2173, 2003.
8. M. A. Cruz-Chávez, J. Frausto-Solís, Simulated Annealing with Restart to Job Shop Scheduling Problem Using Upper Bounds, LNAI, ICAISC 2004, Vol. 3070, pp. 860 – 865, Springer-Verlag Pub., ISSN: 0302-9743, 2004.
9. S. Knust, Optimal conditions and exact neighborhoods for sequencing problems, Universität Osnabrück Fachbereich Mathematik/Informatik, D-49069 Osnabruck, Germany, January 1997.
10. M. A. Cruz-Chávez, J. Frausto-Solís and F. Ramos-Quintana, The Problem of Using the Calculation of the Critical Path to Solver Instances of the Job Shop Scheduling Problem, International Journal of Computational Intelligence, ENFORMATIKA, ISSN: 1304-2386, Vol. 1, No. 4, pp. 334-337, 2004.
11. S. Chanas, and P. Zielinski,., The Computational Complexity of the Critical Problems in a Network with Interval Activity Times, European Journal of Operational Research 136, 541-550, 2002.
12. H. Yildiz, Simulated Annealing & Applications to Scheduling Problems, Department of Industrial Engineering, Bilkent University, TR-06533, yildiz@ug.bcc.bilkent.edu.tr, 2000.
13. P. J. Zalzala, and Flemming: Zalsala, A.M.S. (Ali M.S.), ed., Genetic algorithms in engineering systems /Edited by A.M.S. Institution of Electrical Engineers, London, 1997.
14. F. S. Hiller, and G. J. Lieberman, Introduction to Operations Research, ISBN: 0-07-113989-3, International Editions, 1995.
15. J. E. Beasley. OR-Library: Distributing test problems by electronic mail. Journal of the Operational Research Society, Vol. 41. No. 11, 1069-1072, 1990. Last update 2003.
16. M. A. Cruz-Chávez, J. Frausto-Solís, J. R. Cora-Mora, Experimental Analysis of a Neighborhood Generation Mechanism Applied to Scheduling Problems, CERMA, vol. 2, pp. 226-229, IEEE-Comp. Soc., ISBN 0-7695-2569-5, Sep, México, 2006.
17. U. Der, K. Steinhöfel, A Parallel Implementation of Job Shop Scheduling Heuristics In Sørevik, T., Manne, F., Moe, R., Gebremedhin, A.H. (eds.), Proc. 5th International Workshop on Applied Parallel Computing, Springer-Verlag (LNCS 1947), pp. 215 - 222, 2001.

A Quay Crane Scheduling Method Considering Interference of Yard Cranes in Container Terminals

Da Hun Jung[1], Young-Man Park[2], Byung Kwon Lee[1], Kap Hwan Kim[1], and Kwang Ryel Ryu[3]

[1] Department of Industrial Engineering, Pusan National University, Busan 609-735, Korea
kapkim@pusan.ac.kr
[2] Department of Management Science, Korea Naval Academy, Jinhae 645-797, Korea
ymanpark@pusan.ac.kr
[3] Department of Computer Engineering, Pusan National University, Busan 609-735, Korea
krryu@pusan.ac.kr

Abstract. Quay cranes are the most important equipment in port container terminals, because they are directly related to the wharf productivity. This study proposes a heuristic search algorithm, called greedy randomized adaptive search procedure (GRASP), for constructing a schedule of quay cranes in a way of minimizing the makespan and considering interference among yard cranes. The performance of the heuristic algorithm was tested by a numerical experiment.

Keywords: quay cranes, port container terminals, GRASP, yard cranes.

1 Introduction

The operation at container terminal consists of discharging and loading operations, in which containers are discharged from and loaded onto a ship, and receiving and delivery operations, in which containers are transferred to and from outside road trucks. One of the most important performance measures on the terminal productivity is the turnaround time of vessels, which is the average time that a vessel stays at a terminal. Figure 1 shows various operations in container terminals.

Figure 2 shows a containership that has 28 ship-bays each of which consists of many stacks in hold and on deck. Hatch covers separates stacks on deck from those in hold. Thus, for unloading operations for each ship-bay, containers on deck must be completely discharged before the unloading operations from slots in hold can begin. On the contrary, during the loading operation, containers must be loaded into hold before containers are loaded on deck.

The planning process of the ship operation consists of the berth scheduling, the QC (quay crane) scheduling, and the discharge and load sequencing. During the process of the berth scheduling, the berthing time and position of a containership are determined. A QC schedule specifies the service sequence of ship-bays in a ship by each QC and the time schedule for the services. During the discharge and load sequencing, the discharge and load sequence of individual containers is determined.

A. Gelbukh and C.A. Reyes-Garcia (Eds.): MICAI 2006, LNAI 4293, pp. 461 – 471, 2006.

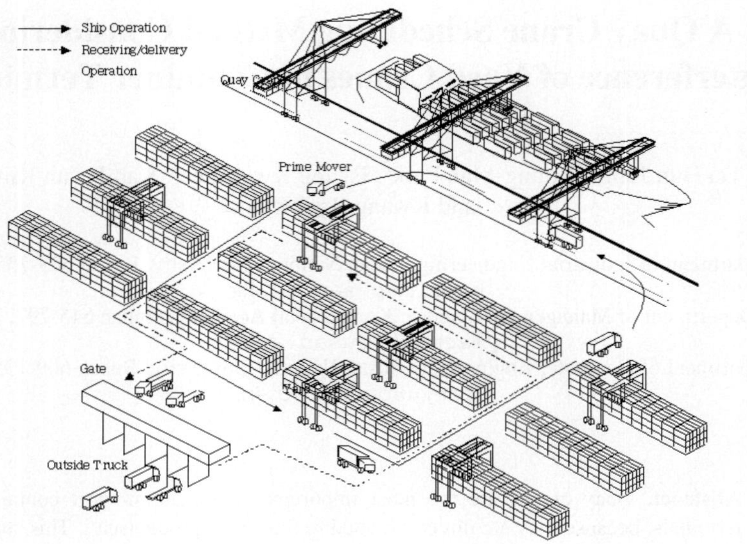

Fig. 1. Typical container flows in container terminals

Input data for the QC scheduling consists of a stowage plan of a ship and a yard map that shows the storage locations of containers in the yard. Planners are also given information on the time interval during which each QC is available, which is a result of the berth scheduling process. After constructing the QC schedule, the sequence of containers for discharging and loading operations is determined.

For constructing an efficient QC schedule, planners have to consider the sequence of TC (transfer crane) operations in the yard, interference among TCs, and rehandling of containers by TCs. Because the operations by QCs and TCs must be synchronized during the ship operation, QC operation may be delayed if the corresponding TC operation is delayed. This paper addresses the QC scheduling problem considering the progress of the operation in the yard.

Daganzo [1] was the first who discussed the QC scheduling problem. He suggested an algorithm for determining the number of cranes to assign to ship-bays of multiple vessels. Peterkofsky and Daganzo [4] also provided an algorithm for determining the departure times of multiple vessels and the number of cranes to assign to individual holds of vessels at a specific time segment. The studies by Daganzo [1] and Peterkofsky and Daganzo [4] assumed that there exists only one task in a ship-bay and did not consider the interference among QCs or precedence relationships among tasks. Park and Kim [3] addressed the QC scheduling problem using GRASP (Greedy Randomized Adaptive Search Procedures) and did not consider the interference among TCs and relocations of containers in the yard. This paper addresses the QC scheduling problem considering TC operations in yard with the objective of minimizing the turnaround time of vessels by using GRASP and greedy heuristics [2].

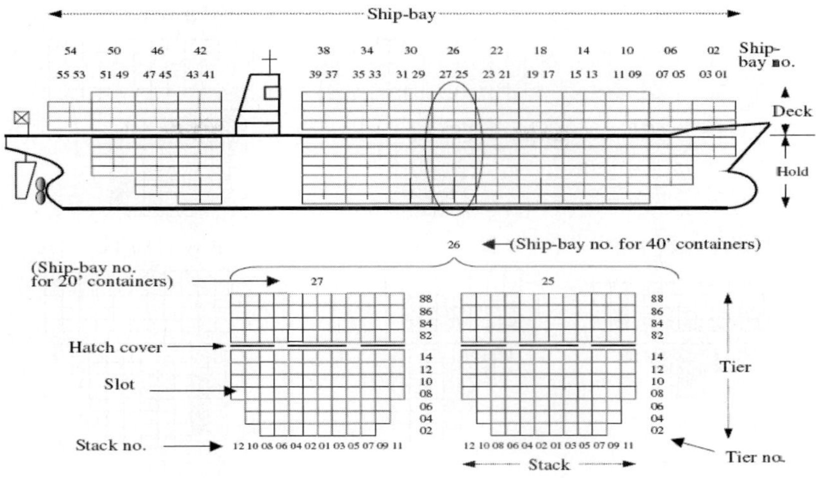

Fig. 2. Cross-sectional view of a containership

The next section describes the QC scheduling problem in more detail and the importance of considering the operation in the yard. Section 3 introduces a heuristic search algorithm, called GRASP, and applies it to the QC scheduling problem in this paper. Section 4 provides results of a computational experiment. Summary and conclusion are provided in the final section.

2 Definition of the Quay Crane Scheduling Problem

Figure 3 illustrates a stowage plan for a ship. Ship-bays with odd numbers can deliver only 20-foot containers. However, when 40-foot containers are supposed to be loaded into ship-bays 1 and 3, the combined ship-bay is numbered as ship-bay 2. Each small grid square in the stowage plan represents a slot into which a container can be stored.

Squares with a character correspond to slots which containers with specific attributes are stored at or loaded onto. The character which is written on a slot represents a specific group of containers to be loaded into or picked up from the slot. By a “group” of containers, we mean a collection of containers of the same size, the same type, and bound for the same destination port. For the sake of efficiency during the discharging and loading operations, in the stowage plan for a ship, a collection of slots that are located adjacent to each other in the ship are usually allocated to containers of the same group.

Figure 4 illustrates a yard map which shows the distribution of containers of each container group in yard-bays. A ship-cluster is defined to be a collection of containers in the same ship-bay, with the same destination port, of the same size and type, and which are located at the same hold or deck. Likewise, a yard-cluster is defined to be a collection of containers of the same vessel, with the same destination port, of the same size and type, and which are located at the same yard-bay.

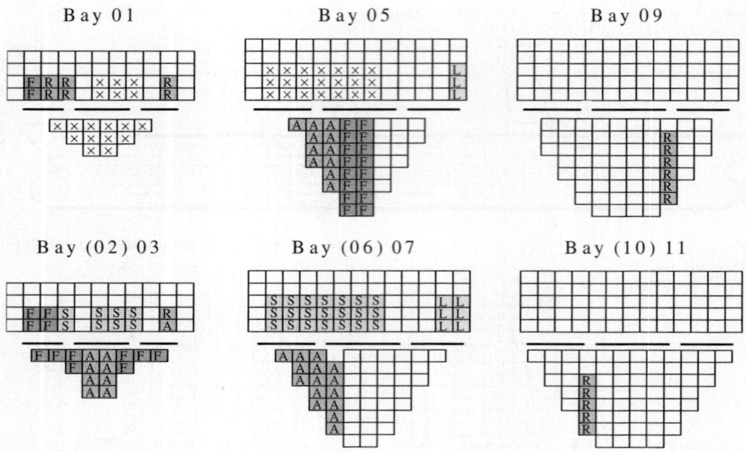

Fig. 3. An illustration of a stowage plan

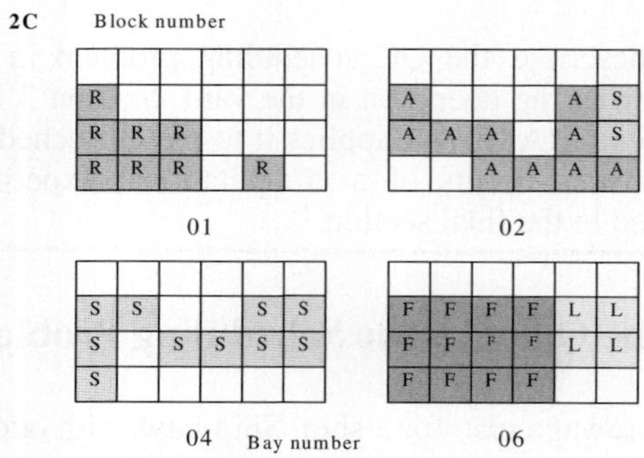

Fig. 4. An illustration of a yard map

The QC scheduling problem is similar to the m-parallel machine scheduling problem. However, the discharging and loading operation have unique characteristics. When discharging and loading operations are to be performed at the same ship-bay, the discharging operation must precede the loading operation. Also, there are precedence relationships among loading (unloading) operations in the hold and the deck of the same ship-bay. That is, in the QC scheduling problem, there are precedence relationships among ship-clusters. Also, certain pairs of ship-cluster cannot be performed simultaneously when the ship-bays of the two different ship-clusters are located too close to each other, because QCs travel on the same track and they may have interference between when they are located too close to each other. That is, two adjacent QCs must be apart from each other by at least several ship-bays.

The goal of QC scheduling is to reduce the berthing time of ship, which is equivalent to minimizing the completion time of the ship operation. The following constraints are introduced for the QC scheduling problem:

1. Each QC has a time window during which it is available.
2. There are some ship-clusters which containers cannot be loaded into or unloaded from simultaneously.
3. QCs are on the same track and thus cannot cross each other.
4. There are precedence relationships among ship clusters that must be satisfied.
5. The interference between TCs and rehandling of containers must be avoided.

Table 1 illustrates a QC schedule that shows the number of containers in each ship-cluster, the sequence of clusters to be handled, and the time schedule for each QC to handle the clusters. Because the operation of a QC must be synchronized with the operation of TCs, the delay in the operation of TCs results in the delay of the operation of QCs.

Table 1. An example of a work schedule for a QC

Quay Crane Schedule						
QC 1 (operation time: 9:00 ~ 10:25)						
Sequence	Ship cluster	No. of containers	Operation time	Yard cluster	No. of containers	Operation time
1	1	8	9:00~9:20	2	8	9:20~9:40
2	2	20	9:20~10:00	3	10	9:20~9:40
				1	10	9:40~10:00
3	3	10	10:00~10:25	7	10	10:00~10:25

3 Applying the Greedy Randomized Adaptive Search Procedure

GRASP (Greedy Randomized Adaptive Search Procedure) [2] is an iterative randomized sampling technique and it generates a solution at each iteration. The solution procedure of GRASP consists of two phases: the solution construction phase and the solution improvement phase. In the solution construction phase, one of the ship-clusters is randomly selected based on a greedy function. Then, a yard-cluster corresponding to the container group of the selected ship-cluster is selected by using a greedy heuristic rule. In the solution improvement phase, the constructed solution is locally improved by an exchange operation until no more improvement is possible. The iteration is repeated a pre-specified number of times. And then, the best solution so far is selected as the final solution. The overall procedure of GRASP is summarized in Figure 5.

The first line of pseudo-code initializes variables and input data of the problem. The statements in lines 3-6 are executed repeatedly until either of two stopping criteria becomes true. The stopping criteria are the Maximum Number of Iterations without improvement (MNI) and the Maximum Total number of Iterations (MTI). The statement in line 3 corresponds to the solution construction phase, while line 4 is for the solution improvement phase. Line 5 states that whenever an improved solution is found, the current best solution is updated. The detail procedure of the QC scheduling is described in the following.

```
Procedure Grasp( )
    InputInstance( )
    Repeat
        Phase 1: ConstructGreedyRandomizedSolution(Solution);
        Phase 2: LocalSearch(Solution);
        UpdateSolution(Solution, BestSolution );
    Until stopping criterion = true
    return(BestSolution);
end grasp;
```

Fig. 5. A pseudo-code for GRASP

3.1 Solution Construction Phase (Phase 1)

In the solution construction phase, the next ship-cluster that the QC will work on is selected randomly by using the probability which is inversely proportional to the distance between the next ship-cluster and the current ship-bay. For the selected next ship-cluster, a yard-bay with containers of the same group as that of the next ship-cluster is selected by using the greedy heuristic rule. The greedy heuristic rule selects the yard bay among yard-bays with containers of the specified group, which is located at the closest location from the current yard-bay. This paper assumes that the sweeping strategy is used to determine the number of containers to be picked up at each yard-bay. In the sweeping strategy, containers of the group requested for a corresponding ship-cluster are picked up in a visiting yard-bay as many as possible.

In the following, each step will be described in more detail.

(Step 1) Among all QCs, we select the QC which can complete all the tasks assigned to the QC in the earliest time. A tie is broken randomly.

(Step 2) A set of feasible ship-clusters for the next operation of the selected QC is constructed. Ship-clusters that violate various constraints (the precedence constraint between ship-clusters or interference among QCs) are excluded from the set of feasible ship-clusters.

(Step 3) Each ship-cluster in the set of feasible ship-clusters is assigned a probability of selection, which is inversely proportional to the distance between the ship-cluster and the current ship-cluster. The distance between ship-clusters is measured by the distance between ship-bays at which the ship-clusters are located.

(Step 4) Generate a random number between 0 and 1 and choose one of ship-clusters in the set based on the probability of selection calculated in Step 3.

(Step 5) Estimate the time for the QC to complete the transfer operation for the selected ship-cluster.

(Step 6) A yard-cluster with containers of the same group as that of the selected ship-cluster is selected by using the following greedy heuristic rule.

(Step 6-1) If the number of containers required for the selected ship-cluster is satisfied, then go to Step 7. Otherwise, go to Step 6-2.

(Step 6-2) Construct the set of feasible yard-clusters for the next ship-cluster.

(Step 6-3) Select the yard-cluster with the minimum time for the TC to start the transfer operation at the yard-cluster. To estimate the start time, the travel time of the TC, the waiting time of the TC resulting from the interference among TCs, and the time for relocating containers, must be considered. Figure 6 illustrates the space interference in which case the waiting strategy is applied.

(Step 6-4) Assign containers in the selected yard-bay to the selected ship-cluster as many as possible. Go to Step 6-1.

(Step 7) Revise the completion time of the selected QC by utilizing information on the delay of the transfer operation in the yard, which is estimated in Step 6, and the completion time of the QC obtained in Step 5

(Step 8) Check if containers are assigned to all the ship-clusters. If yes, then stop. Otherwise, go to Step 1.

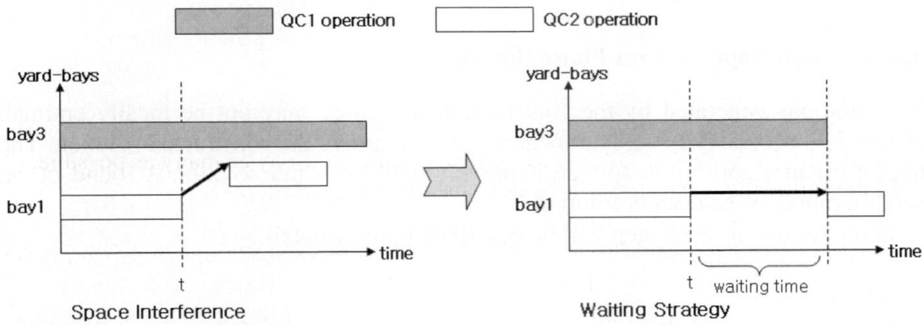

Fig. 6. An illustration of the space conflict resolution

In the following, an example is provided to illustrate Step 6 of the above algorithm. Table 2 shows the information on the selected ship-cluster in Step 4. Table 3 shows the information on yard-clusters whose container group is the same as that of the selected ship-cluster. We assume that the initial position of the TC is located at yard-bay 1 of yard-block 1. Note that the group of the selected ship-cluster in Step 4 is group A and yard-clusters with containers of group A are selected. In Step 6-2, we choose yard-cluster 8 which is located in the minimum distance from the current position of the TC. Because the number of containers in ship-cluster 1 is 15 and the number of containers in selected yard-cluster is 7, the number of containers required for ship-cluster 1 is not satisfied. Among the remaining yard-clusters, choose yard-cluster 3 which is located in the next minimum distance. Because the number of containers in the selected yard-cluster is 8, the number of containers required by ship-cluster 1 is satisfied. Table 4 illustrates the visiting sequence of TC for ship-cluster of group A.

Table 2. Data on ship cluster 1

Ship cluster	Bay	Group	Number of container
1	5	A	15

Table 3. Data on yard clusters with containers of group A

Yard cluster	Block	Bay	Group	Number of container
3	1	2	A	8
5	1	5	A	5
8	1	1	A	7
11	1	3	A	10

Table 4. Visiting sequence of the TC for ship-cluster 1

Ship cluster	Number of container	Yard cluster	Number of container
1	15	8	7
		3	8

3.2 Solution Improvement Phase (Phase 2)

The solutions generated by the construction procedure may not be locally optimal. Hence, it is necessary to apply a local search to improve the constructed solution. The improvement algorithm is applied iteratively until no better solution is found in the neighborhood of the current solution.

In the following, each step will be described in more detail.

Step 1. i=0.

Step 2. i = i + 1. If i > Total number of QCs, then stop. Otherwise, select QC i and go to step 3.

Step 3. Select a pair of ship-clusters which are assigned to QC i and for which the highest improvement in the make-span can be made by performing a pair-wise exchange (the 2-opt method). At this time, the visiting sequence of the TC which is assigned to the selected QC must be rearranged by using the greedy heuristic rule and by reevaluating the delays in the yard. If there is more than one pair of ship-clusters with the same improvement in the make-span, then select the ship-cluster with the minimum total completion time.

Step 4. If the improvement is positive, then perform the exchange. Repeat Steps 3 and 4 until no further improvement is possible. If no further improvement is possible, then go to Step 2.

4 A Numerical Experiment

In order to test the performance of the GRASP algorithm in this paper, a numerical experiment was performed by using on stowage plans and yard-maps collected from

Pusan Eastern Container Terminal (PECT) in Korea. The objective of the experiment was to search for the best set of parameters for GRASP.

The numerical experiment was conducted by using three sets of data. The sizes of the problems are listed in Table 5. Problems in Table 5 are typical real problems in PECT. As the stopping criteria, MNI and MTI were used. If MNI is set to be 10, then the solution procedure is stopped when there is no improvement in the best solution even after 10 consecutive iterations. MTI, which is the maximum total number of iterations, was set to 500 and MNI was set to 10, 20, 30, and 40.

In the GRASP algorithm, the value of r, which is the rate of adjusting probability, is used when generates the initial basic feasible solution during the solution construction procedure. Thus, if r has a large value, then the possibility for QCs to select the nearest ship-cluster is increased. The value of r set to be 0.6, 0.7, 0.8, and 0.9. For each combination of parameters (MNI, r) of stopping criteria, every problem was solved ten times. The GRASP algorithm was programmed by using C++ language under Visual C++ 6.0 compiler on Pentium 4 with 2.80GHz and 512MB RAM.

Table 5. Problems used for the experiment

Contents	Problem 1	Problem 2	Problem 3
Number of ship-cluster	32	58	81
Number of yard-cluster	42	86	132
Number of container groups	8	9	14
Number of ship-bays	71	71	71
Number of yard-blocks	10	10	10
Number of yard-bays in a block	25	25	25
Number of QCs	2	3	4
Total Number of containers	390	872	1380

Table 6. The average makespan for the example problems (seconds)

r	MNI	Problem 1	Problem 2	Problem 3
0.6	10	22,227	33,357	44,468
	20	21,924	33,092	43,240
	30	21,756	32,908	42,634
	40	21,897	32,292	42,088
0.7	10	22,192	33,050	43,138
	20	22,088	32,645	42,619
	30	21,837	32,170	41,602
	40	21,544	32,109	37,867
0.8	10	22,996	32,423	42,705
	20	22,309	32,429	42,099
	30	21,882	32,081	42,164
	40	21,987	32,006	40,814
0.9	10	22511	33,089	42,967
	20	21866	32,967	42,441
	30	22370	32,029	41,824
	40	21729	31,950	41,085

Table 6 and Table 7 show the average make-span and CPU time for different combinations of MNI and r. For all problems, the quality of the solution was improved by increasing the values of MNI and r. Especially, the make-span of problems decreased as the value of MNI increased, while the values of *r* did not affect directly the solution quality. That is, the quality of the solution was more sensitive to the value of MNI than the value of r. Also, note that the computational time tends to increase by increasing the values of MNI and r as shown in Table 7. The computational time is more sensitive to the value of MNI than to the value of r as for the solution quality.

Table 7. The average CPU time for the example problems (seconds)

r	MNI	Problem 1	Problem 2	Problem 3
0.6	10	46	267	467
	20	82	625	913
	30	160	605	1439
	40	181	1063	2091
0.7	10	46	222	491
	20	62	321	870
	30	124	661	1337
	40	231	881	6159
0.8	10	48	324	607
	20	111	515	1026
	30	166	834	1951
	40	166	1025	3252
0.9	10	54	305	528
	20	101	300	1513
	30	161	856	2588
	40	232	978	2498

5 Conclusion

This paper addressed the QC scheduling problem considering congestions in the yard, which is an important problem for the efficient operation of port terminals. GRASP algorithm was used as a basis of the algorithm in this paper. GRASP is a heuristic search algorithm with a capability to escape from a local minimum, to find near-optimal solutions to a combinatorial problem. The algorithm in this paper consists of the construction phase and the improvement phase. This study also performed a numerical experiment to find best set of parameters of the suggested algorithm.

By the numerical experiment, it was found that the computational time must be reduced for this algorithm can be used in practice. Especially, the improvement phase consumed too much time with a marginal improvement in the quality of the solution. Thus, a more efficient improvement algorithm must be developed.

Acknowledgments. This work was supported by the Regional Research Centers Program (Research Center for Logistics Information Technology), granted by the Korean Ministry of Education & Human Resources Development.

References

1. Daganzo, C. F.: The Crane Scheduling Problem. Transportation Research 23B (1989), 159-175.
2. Feo, T. A. and Resende, M. G. C.: Greedy Randomized Adaptive Search Procedures, Journal of Global Optimization, 6 (1995), 109-133
3. Kim, K. H. and Park, Y. M.: A Crane Scheduling Method for Port Container Terminals. European Journal of Operational Research, 156 (2004), 752-768
4. Peterkofsky, R. I. and Daganzo, C. F.: A Branch and Bound Solution Method for the Crane Scheduling Problem. Transportation Research 24B (1990), 159-172

Comparing Schedule Generation Schemes in Memetic Algorithms for the Job Shop Scheduling Problem with Sequence Dependent Setup Times

Miguel A. González, Camino R. Vela, María Sierra, Inés González, and Ramiro Varela

Artificial Intelligence Center. Dep. of Computer Science, University of Oviedo
Campus de Viesques, 33271 Gijón, Spain
raist@telecable.es, {mcrodriguez, sierramaria, ramiro}@uniovi.es,
ines.gonzalez@unican.es
http://www.aic.uniovi.es/Tc

Abstract. The Job Shop Scheduling Problem with Sequence Dependent Setup Times (*SDJSS*) is an extension of the Job Shop Scheduling Problem (*JSS*) that has interested to researchers during the last years. In this paper we confront the *SDJSS* problem by means of a memetic algorithm. We study two schedule generation schemas that are extensions of the well known *G&T* algorithm for the *JSS*. We report results from an experimental study showing that the proposed approaches produce similar results and that both of them are more efficient than other genetic algorithm proposed in the literature.

1 Introduction

The *SDJSS* (Job Shop Scheduling Problem with Sequence Dependent Setup Times) is a variant of the classic *JSS* (Job Shop Scheduling Problem) in which a setup operation on a machine is required when the machine switches between two jobs. This way the *SDJSS* models many real situations better than the *JSS*. The *SDJSS* has interested to a number of researchers, so we can find a number of approaches in the literature, many of which try to extend solutions that were successful to the classic *JSS* problem. This is the case, for example, of the branch and bound algorithm proposed by Brucker and Thiele in [4], which is an extension of the well-known algorithm proposed in [3][5] and [6], and the genetic algorithm proposed by Cheung and Zhou in [7], which is also an extension of a genetic algorithm for the *JSS*. Also, in [18] a neighborhood search with heuristic repairing is proposed that it is an extension of the local search methods for the *JSS*.

In this paper we apply a similar methodological approach and extend a genetic algorithm and a local search method that we have applied previously to the *JSS* problem. The genetic algorithm was designed by combining ideas taken from the literature such as for example the well-known *G&T* algorithm proposed by Giffler

A. Gelbukh and C.A. Reyes-Garcia (Eds.): MICAI 2006, LNAI 4293, pp. 472–482, 2006.

and Thomson in [9], the codification schema proposed by Bierwirth in [2] and the local search methods developed by various researchers, for example DellAmico and Trubian in [8], Nowicki and Smutnicki in [13] or Mattfeld in [12]. In [10] we reported results from an experimental study over a set of selected problems showing that the genetic algorithm is quite competitive with the most efficient methods for the JSS problem.

In order to extend the algorithm to the $SDJSS$ problem, we have firstly extended the decoding algorithm, which is based on the $G\&T$ algorithm. In this case we have considered two different extensions, the first has also considered in [11]. Furthermore, we have adapted the local search method termed N_1 in the literature to obtain a method that we have termed N_1^S.

The experimental study was conducted over the set of 45 problem instances proposed by Cheung and Zhou in [7]. We have evaluated the genetic algorithm with the two codification algorithms and then in conjunction with local search. The reported results show that the proposed genetic algorithm is more efficient than the genetic algorithm proposed in [7] and that the genetic algorithm combined with local search improves with respect to the raw genetic algorithm when both of them run for the same amount of time.

The rest of the paper is organized as it follows. In section 2 we formulate the $SDJSS$ problem. In section 3 we outline the genetic algorithm for the $SDJSS$. In section 4 we describe the extended local search method. Section 5 reports results from the experimental study. Finally, in section 6 we summarize the main conclusions.

2 Problem Formulation

We start by defining the JSS problem. The classic JSS problem requires scheduling a set of N jobs $J_1, \ldots, J_N$ on a set of M physical resources or machines $R_1, \ldots, R_M$. Each job J_i consists of a set of tasks or operations $\{\theta_{i1}, \ldots, \theta_{iM}\}$ to be sequentially scheduled. Each task θ_{il} having a single resource requirement, a fixed duration $p\theta_{il}$ and a start time $st\theta_{il}$ whose value should be determined.

The JSS has two binary constraints: precedence constraints and capacity constraints. Precedence constraints, defined by the sequential routings of the tasks within a job, translate into linear inequalities of the type: $st\theta_{il} + p\theta_{il} \leq st\theta_{i(l+1)}$ (i.e. θ_{il} before $\theta_{i(l+1)}$). Capacity constraints that restrict the use of each resource to only one task at a time translate into disjunctive constraints of the form: $st\theta_{il} + p\theta_{il} \leq st\theta_{jk} \vee st\theta_{jk} + p\theta_{jk} \leq st\theta_{il}$. The most widely used objective is to come up with a feasible schedule such that the completion time, i.e. the *makespan*, is minimized.

In the sequel a problem instance will be represented by a directed graph $G = (V, A \cup E)$. Each node in the set V represents a operation of the problem, with the exception of the dummy nodes *start* and *end*, which represent operations with processing time 0. The arcs of the set A are called *conjunctive arcs* and represent precedence constraints and the arcs of set E are called *disjunctive arcs* and represent capacity constraints. Set E is partitioned into subsets E_i with

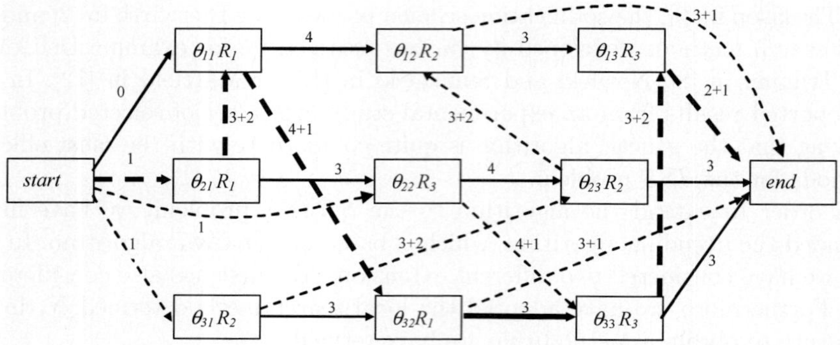

Fig. 1. A feasible schedule to a problem with 3 jobs and 3 machines. Bold face arcs show a critical path whose length, i.e. the *makespan*, is 22.

$E = \cup_{i=1,\ldots,M} E_i$. Subset E_i corresponds to resource R_i and includes an arc (v, w) for each pair of operations requiring that resource; whereas dotted arcs represent the elements of set E. The arcs are weighed with the processing time of the operation at the source node. The dummy operation *start* is connected to the first operation of each job; and the last operation of each job is connected to the node *end*.

A feasible schedule is represented by an acyclic subgraph G_s of G, $G_s = (V, A \cup H)$, where $H = \cup_{i=1..M} H_i$, H_i being a hamiltonian selection of E_i. Therefore, finding out a solution can be reduced to discovering compatible hamiltonian selections, i.e. orderings for the operations requiring the same resource or partial schedules, that translate into a solution graph G_s without cycles. The *makespan* of the schedule is the cost of a *critical path*. A *critical path* is a longest path from node start to node end. A critical block is a maximal subsequence of operations of a critical path requiring the same machine.

In the $SDJSS$, after an operation v of a job leaves machine m and before entering an operation w of another job on the same machine, a setup operation is required with duration S^m_{vw}. The setup operation can be started as soon as operation v leaves the machine m, hence possibly in parallel with the operation preceding w in its job sequence. The setup time S^m_{vw} is added to the processing time of operation v to obtain the cost of each disjunctive arc (v, w). S^m_{0v} is the setup time of machine m if v is the first operation scheduled on m and S^m_{v0} is the cleaning time of machine m if v is the last operation scheduled on m.

Figure 1 shows a feasible solution to a problem with 3 jobs and 3 machines. Dotted arcs represent the elements of set E included in the solution, while conjunctive arcs are represented by continuous arrows.

3 Genetic Algorithm for the SDJSS Problem

The JSS is a paradigm of constraint satisfaction problems and was confronted by many heuristic techniques. In particular genetic algorithms [2],[12], [16], [10] are a promising approach due to their ability to be combined with other techniques such as tabu search and simulated annealing. Moreover genetic algorithms allow for exploiting any kind of heuristic knowledge from the problem domain. In doing so, genetic algorithms are actually competitive with the most efficient methods for JSS.

As mentioned above, in this paper we consider a conventional genetic algorithm for tackling the JSS and extend it to the $SDJSS$. This requires mainly the adaptation of the decoding algorithm. Additionally we consider a local search method for the JSS and adapt it to the $SDJSS$. The key features of the genetic algorithm we have considered in this work are the following. In the selection phase all chromosomes are grouped into pairs, and then each one of these pairs is mated and mutated accordingly with the corresponding probabilities. Then, a tournament selection is done among each pair of parents and their offsprings. To codify chromosomes we have chosen permutations with repetition proposed by C. Bierwirth in [2]. In this scheme a chromosome is a permutation of the set of operations, each one being represented by its job number. This way a job number appears within a chromosome as many times as the number of operations of its job. For example, the chromosome (2 1 1 3 2 3 1 2 3) actually represents the permutation of operations $(\theta_{21}\,\theta_{11}\,\theta_{12}\,\theta_{31}\,\theta_{22}\,\theta_{32}\,\theta_{13}\,\theta_{23}\,\theta_{33})$. This permutation should be understood as expressing partial schedules for every set of operations requiring the same machine. This codification presents a number of interesting characteristics; for example, it is easy to evaluate with different algorithms and allows for efficient genetic operators. In [17] this codification is compared with other permutation based codifications and demonstrated to be the best one for the JSS problem over a set of 12 selected problem instances of common use. For chromosome mating we have considered the *Generalized Order Crossover* (GOX) that works as it is shown in the following example. Let us consider that the two following chromosomes are selected as parents for crossover

$$\text{Parent1 } (1\ 2\ 3\ \underline{3\ 2\ 1\ 1}\ 3\ 2)\quad \text{Parent2 } (3\ \underline{3}\ 2\ 3\ 1\ \underline{1\ 2}\ 2\ \underline{1})$$

Firstly, a substring is selected from Parent1 and inserted in the Offspring at the same position as in this parent. Then the remaining positions of the Offspring are completed with genes from Parent2 after having removed the genes selected from Parent1. If the selected substring from Parent1 is the one marked with underlined characters, the resulting Offspring is

$$\text{Offspring } (3\ 2\ 3\ 3\ 2\ 1\ 1\ 1\ 2).$$

By doing so, GOX preserves the order and position of the selected substring from Parent1 and the relative order of the remaining genes from Parent2. The mutation operator simply selects and swaps two genes at random. In practice the mutation would not actually be necessary due to the GOX operator has an implicit mutation effect. For example the second 3 from Parent1 is now the third one in the Offspring.

Algorithm 1. The decoding Giffler and Thomson algorithm for the JSS problem

1. A = set containing the first operation of each job;
while $A \neq \emptyset$ **do**
  2. Determine the operation $\theta' \in A$ with the earliest completion time if scheduled in the current state, that is $st\theta' + p\theta' \leq st\theta + p\theta, \forall\theta \in A$;
  3. Let R be the machine required by θ', and B the subset of A whose operations require R;
  4. Remove from B every operation that cannot start at a time earlier than $st\theta' + p\theta'$;
  5. Select $\theta* \in B$ so that it is the leftmost operation of B in the chromosome sequence;
  6. Schedule $\theta*$ as early as possible to build the partial schedule corresponding to the next state;
  7. Remove $\theta*$ from A and insert the succeeding operation of $\theta*$ in set A if $\theta*$ is not the last operation of its job;
end while
8. return the built Schedule;

3.1 Decoding Algorithm

As decoding algorithm we have chosen the well-known $G\&T$ algorithm proposed by Giffler and Thomson in [9] for the JSS and then we have made a natural extension for the $SDJSS$. The $G\&T$ algorithm is an active schedule builder. A schedule is active if one operation must be delayed when you want another one to start earlier. Active schedules are good in average and, what is most important, it can be proved that the space of active schedules contains at least an optimal one, that is, the set of active schedules is *dominant*. For these reasons it is worth to restrict the search to this space. Moreover, the $G\&T$ algorithm is complete for the JSS problem. Algorithm 1 shows the $G\&T$ algorithm for the JSS.

In order to adapt the $G\&T$ algorithm for the $SDJSS$ we have considered two possibilities. Firstly the simplest generalization that only takes into account the setup times at step 2. In Algorithm 1, $st\theta$ refers to the maximum completion time of the last scheduled operation on the machine required by θ and the preceding operation to θ in its job. Hence the algorithm can be adapted to the $SDJSS$ problem by considering $st\theta$ as the maximum completion time of the preceding operation in the job and the completion time of the last scheduled operation in the machine plus the corresponding setup time. The resulting algorithm is termed $G\&T1$, in [11] we report results from it.

The second extension termed $G\&T2$ can be derived from the algorithm $EGTA1$ developed by Ovacik and Uzsoy in [14]. In this case starting times $st\theta$ are taken as in $G\&T1$ but step 4. of the algorithm is replaced by the following

4. Remove from B every operation θ that $st\theta \geq st\theta' + p\theta' + S^R_{\theta'\theta}$ for any $\theta' \in B$;

It is easy to demonstrate that neither $G\&T1$ nor $G\&T2$ are complete. That is, there are active schedules that cannot be generated by any of the algorithms.

However, $G\&T2$ dominates to $G\&T1$, that is, the set of active schedules that can be generated by $G\&T1$ is a subset of the set of active schedules that can be generated by $G\&T2$. This way $G\&T2$ seems to be a more interesting decoding algorithm as it allows the genetic algorithm to search over a larger search space. On the other hand, $G\&T2$ allows the machines to remain idle for larger periods of time, which produces worse results in some cases as we will see in the experimental study.

4 Local Search

Conventional genetic algorithms as the one described in the previous section often produce moderate results. However meaningful improvements can be obtained by means of hybridization with other methods. One of such techniques is local search, in this case the genetic algorithm is called a memetic algorithm. Roughly speaking local search is implemented by defining a neighborhood of each point in the search space as the set of chromosomes reachable by a given transformation rule. Then a chromosome is replaced in the population by one of its neighbors, if any of them satisfies the acceptation criterion. The local search from a given point completes either after a number of iterations or when no neighbor satisfies the acceptation criterion.

In this paper we consider the neighborhood structure proposed by Nowicki and Smutnicki in [13], which is termed N_1 by D. Mattfeld in [12], for the JSS. As other strategies, N_1 relies on the concepts of critical path and critical block. It considers every critical block of a critical path and made a number of moves on the operations of the limits of each block. In [12] the transformation rules of N_1 are defined as follows.

Definition 1 (N_1). *Given a schedule H with partial schedules H_i for each machine R_i, $1 \leq i \leq M$, the neighborhood $N_1(H)$ consist of all schedules derived from H by reversing one arc (v, w) of the critical path with $v, w \in H_i$. At least one of v and w is either the first or the last member of a block. For the first block only v and w at the end of the block are considered whereas for the last block only v and w at the beginning of the block must be checked.*

The selection strategy of a neighbor and the acceptation criterion are based on a *makespan* estimation, which is done in constant time as it is also described in [8], instead of calculating the exact *makespan* of each neighbor. The estimation provides a lower bound of the *makespan*. The selected neighbor is the one with the lowest *makespan* estimation whenever this value is lower than the *makespan* of the current chromosome. Notice that this strategy is not steepest descendent because the exact *makespan* of selected neighbor is not always better than the *makespan* of the current solution. We have done this choice in the classic JSS problem due to it produces better results than a strict steepest descent gradient method. [10].

The Algorithm stops either after a number of iterations or when the estimated *makespan* of selected neighbor is larger than the *makespan* of the current chromosome.

This neighborhood relies on the fact that, for the JSS problem, reversing an arc of the critical path always maintains feasibility. Moreover, the only possibility to obtain some improvement by reversing an arc is that the reversed arc is either the first or the last of a critical block.

However, things are not the same for $SDJSS$ problem due to the differences in the setup times. As can we see in [18], feasibility is not guaranteed when reversing an arc of the critical path, and reversing an arc inside a block could lead to an improving schedule. The following results give sufficient conditions of no-improving when an arc is reversed in a solution H of the $SDJSS$ problem. In the setup times the machine is omitted for simplicity due to all of them refers to the same machine.

Theorem 1. *Let H be a schedule and (v, w) an arc that is not in a critical block. Then reversing the arc (v, w) does not produce any improvement even if the resulting schedule is feasible.*

Theorem 2. *Let H be a schedule and (v, w) an arc inside a critical block, that is there exist arcs (x, v) and (w, y) belonging to the same block. Even if the schedule H' obtained from H by reversing the arc (v, w) is feasible, H' is not better than H if the following condition holds*

$$S_{xw} + S_{wv} + S_{vy} \geq S_{xv} + S_{vw} + S_{wy} \tag{1}$$

Theorem 3. *Let H be a schedule and (v, w) an arc in a critical path so that v is the first operation of the first critical block and z is the successor of w in the critical path and $M_w = M_z$. Even if reversing the arc (v, w) leaves to a feasible schedule, there is no improvement if the following condition holds*

$$S_{0w} + S_{wv} + S_{vz} \geq S_{0v} + S_{vw} + S_{wz} \tag{2}$$

Analogous, we can formulate a similar result if w is the last operation of the last critical block.

Hence we can finally define the neighborhood strategy for the $SDJSS$ problem as follows

Definition 2. (N_1^S) *Given a schedule H, the neighborhood $N_1^S(H)$ consist of all schedules derived from H by reversing one arc (v, w) of the critical path provided that none of the conditions given in previous theorems 1, 2 and 3 hold.*

4.1 Feasibility Checking

Regarding feasibility, for the $SDJSS$ it is always required to check it after reversing an arc. As usual, we assume that the triangular inequality holds, what is quite reasonable in actual production plans, that is for any operations u,v and w requiring the same machine

$$S_{uw} \leq S_{uv} + S_{vw} \tag{3}$$

Then the following is a necessary condition for no-feasibility after reversing the arc (v, w).

Theorem 4. *Let H be a schedule and (v, w) an arc in a critical path, PJ_w the operation preceding w in its job and SJ_v the successor of v in its job. Then if reversing the arc (v, w) produces a cycle in the solution graph, the following condition holds*

$$stPJ_w > stSJ_v + duSJ_v + min\{S_{kl}/(k,l) \in E, J_k = J_v\} \tag{4}$$

where J_k is the job of operation k.

Therefore the feasibility estimation is efficient at the cost of discarding some feasible neighbor.

4.2 Makespan Estimation

For *makespan* estimation after reversing an arc, we have also extended the method proposed by Taillard in [15] for the JSS. This method was used also by Dell'Amico and Trubian in [8] and by Mattfeld in [12]. This method requires calculating *heads* and *tails*. The head r_v of an operation v is the cost of the longest path from node *start* to node v in the solution graph, i.e. is the value of stv. The tail q_v is defined so as the value $q_v + p_v$ is the cost of the longest path from v to *end*.

For every node v, the value $r_v + p_v + q_v$ is the length of the longest path from node *start* to node *end* trough node v, and hence it is a lower bound of the *makespan*. Moreover, it is the *makespan* if node v belongs to the critical path. So, we can get a lower bound of the new schedule by calculating $r_v + p_v + q_v$ after reversing (v, w).

Let us denote by PM_v and SM_v the predecessor and successor nodes of v respectively on the machine sequence in a schedule. Let nodes x and z be PM_v and SM_w respectively in schedule H. Let us note that in H' nodes x and z are PM_w and SM_v respectively. Then the new heads and tails of operations v and w after reversing the arc (v, w) can be calculated as the following

$$r'_w = max(r_x + px + S_{xw}, r_{PJ_w} + pPJ_w)$$

$$r'_v = max(r'_w + pw + S_{wv}, r_{PJ_v} + pPJ_v)$$
$$q'_v = max(q_z + pz + S_{vz}, q_{SJ_v} + pSJ_v)$$
$$q'_w = max(q'_v + pv + S_{vw}, q_{SJ_w} + pSJ_w)$$

From these new values of heads and tails the *makespan* of H' can be estimated by

$$C'_{max} = max(r'_v + pv + q'_v, r'_w + pw + q'_w)$$

which is actually a lower bound of the new *makespan*. This way, we can get an efficient *makespan* estimation of schedule H' at the risk of discarding some improving schedule.

5 Experimental Study

For experimental study we have used the set of problems proposed by Cheung and Zhou in [7]. This is a set of 45 instances with sizes 10×10, 10×20 and 20×20 and organized into 3 types. Instances of type 1 have processing times and setup times uniformly distributed in (10,50); instances of type 2 have processing times in (10,50) and setup times in (50,99); and instances of type 3 have processing times in (50,99) and setup times in (10,50). Table 1 confront the results from the genetic algorithm termed GA_SPTS reported in [7] with the results reached by the genetic algorithms proposed in this work termed $GA\_G\&T1$ and $GA\_G\&T2$. The data are grouped for sizes and types and values reported are averaged for each group.

GA_SPTS algorithm was coded in FORTRAN and run on PC 486/66. The computation time with problem sizes 10×10, 10×20 and 20×20 are about 16, 30 and 70 minutes respectively. Each algorithm was run 10 times for each instance and stopped after 2000 generations (see [7] for more details).

In $GA\_G\&T1$ and $GA\_G\&T2$ algorithms the genetic algorithm was parameterized with a population of 100 chromosomes, a number of 140 generations, crossover probability of 0.7, and mutation probability of 0.2. The genetic algorithm was run 30 times. The values reported are the best solution reached, the average of the best solutions of the 30 runs and the standard deviation. The target machine was a Pentium IV at 1.7 Ghz. and the computation time varies from about 1 sec. for the small instances to about 9 sec. for the larger ones.

As we can observe in Table 1 both algorithms improve the results obtained by the GA_SPTS. Moreover $GA\_G\&T1$ reaches better results than $GA\_G\&T2$. This is due to algorithm $G\&T1$ searches over a subspace of the space searched by $G\&T2$, and in this subspace the schedules allow the machines for a lower idle time in average, as we have commented in Section 3.1. Therefore, for a raw genetic algorithm, it seems to be better to concentrate the search over a subset of low-average schedules. For the instances that have low setup times both decoding algorithms, $G\&T1$ and $G\&T2$, are equivalent. However for problem instances with large setup times, $GA\_G\&T1$ performs much better than $GA\_G\&T2$.

For the experiments with the memetic algorithm, we have parameterized the genetic algorithms with 50 chromosomes in the population and 50 generations in order to have similar running times. The rest of the parameters remain as in previous experiments. In these cases the run time was about 1 sec. for the smaller instances and 10 sec. for the larger ones. The local search algorithm was applied to every chromosome in the initial population and also to every chromosome generated by crossover or mutation operators. The algorithm was iterated while an improving neighbor is obtained accordingly to the makespan estimation described in Section 4.2. In these case the $GA\_G\&T2\_LS$ algorithm reaches a little bit better solutions than $GA\_G\&T1\_LS$, and both of them have outperformed GA_SPTS. Table 2 confronts the results obtained by GA_SPTS with those of $GA\_G\&T1\_LS$ and $GA\_G\&T2\_LS$.

Table 1. Results from the GA_SPTS, $GA\_G\&T1$ and $GA\_G\&T2$

ZRD Inst	Size $N \times N$	Problem Type	GA_SPTS Best	Avg	StDev	$GA\_G\&T1$ Best	Avg	StDev	$GA\_G\&T2$ Best	Avg	StDev
1-5	10×10	1	835,4	864,2	21,46	785,4	800,0	6,91	785,0	803,0	8,76
6-10	10×10	2	1323,0	1349,6	21,00	1284,2	1297,0	7,53	1282,0	1300,2	9,82
11-15	10×10	3	1524,6	1556,0	35,44	1434,4	1454,8	13,18	1434,6	1455,4	12,87
16-20	10×20	1	1339,4	1377,0	25,32	1257,4	1295,6	14,58	1285,8	1323,0	15,38
21-25	10×20	2	2327,2	2375,8	46,26	2188,6	2238,4	20,49	2229,6	2278,2	22,24
26-30	10×20	3	2426,6	2526,2	75,90	2329,0	2388,0	24,57	2330,4	2385,8	23,91
31-35	20×20	1	1787,4	1849,4	57,78	1626,8	1663,0	16,62	1631,6	1680,4	17,99
36-40	20×20	2	2859,4	2982,0	93,92	2634,8	2694,8	24,83	2678,0	2727,8	23,60
41-45	20×20	3	3197,8	3309,6	121,52	3034,0	3120,2	31,01	3052,0	3119,6	29,33

Table 2. Results from the GA_SPTS, $GA\_G\&T1\_LS$ and $GA\_G\&T2\_LS$

ZRD Inst	Size $N \times N$	Problem Type	GA_SPTS Best	Avg	StDev	$GA\_G\&T1\_LS$ Best	Avg	StDev	$GA\_G\&T2\_LS$ Best	Avg	StDev
1-5	10×10	1	835,4	864,2	21,46	779,6	789,4	6,12	778,6	788,46	6,70
6-10	10×10	2	1323,0	1349,6	21,00	1272,0	1291,0	9,04	1270,0	1290,43	9,16
11-15	10×10	3	1524,6	1556,0	35,44	1433,8	1439,0	7,59	1433,8	1439,84	6,71
16-20	10×20	1	1339,4	1377,0	25,32	1232,4	1258,4	12,77	1230,2	1255,48	12,74
21-25	10×20	2	2327,2	2375,8	46,26	2175,2	2217,8	20,24	2178,4	2216,80	18,61
26-30	10×20	3	2426,6	2526,2	75,90	2222,6	2267,2	20,12	2235,2	2274,00	19,32
31-35	20×20	1	1787,4	1849,4	57,78	1588	1622,6	16,52	1590,0	1619,80	15,90
36-40	20×20	2	2859,4	2982,0	93,92	2621,8	2676,8	23,37	2610,2	2668,02	27,48
41-45	20×20	3	3197,8	3309,6	121,52	2923,2	2979,4	27,00	2926,0	2982,23	26,32

6 Conclusions

In this work we have confronted the Job Shop Scheduling Problem with Sequence Dependent Setup Times by means of a memetic algorithm. Our main contribution is to compare two decoding algorithms, $G\&T1$ and $G\&T2$, that are extensions of the $G\&T$ algorithm for the JSS problem. Neither $G\&T1$ nor $G\&T2$ are complete, but $G\&T2$ dominates to $G\&T1$. We have reported results from an experimental study on the benchmark proposed in [7] showing that $G\&T1$ is better than $G\&T2$ when the genetic algorithm is not combined with local search, and that they are very similar when used in conjunction with local search.

As future work we plan to look for new extensions of the $G\&T$ algorithm in order to obtain a complete decoding algorithm and also we will try to extend other local search algorithms that have been proved to be efficient for the JSS. Furthermore we plan to experiment with other problem instances, in particular those proposed in [4] in order to compare our genetic algorithms against the exact approaches proposed in [4] and[1].

Acknowledgements. We would like to thank Waiman Cheung and Hong Zhou for facilitating us the benchmarks problems used in the experimental study. This research has been supported by FEDER-MCYT under contract TIC2003-04153 and by FICYT under grant BP04-021.

References

1. Artigues, C., Lopez, P., and P.D., A. Schedule generation schemes for the job shop problem with sequence-dependent setup times: Dominance properties and computational analysis. Annals of Operational Research, **138**, 21-52 (2005).
2. Bierwirth, C.: A Generalized Permutation Approach to Jobshop Scheduling with Genetic Algorithms. OR Spectrum, **17**, 87-92 (1995).
3. Brucker, P., Jurisch, B., and Sievers, B. A branch and bound algorithm for the job-shop scheduling problem. Discrete Applied Mathematics, **49**, 107-127 (1994).
4. Brucker, P., Thiele, O. A branch and bound method for the general-job shop problem with sequence-dependent setup times. Operations Research Spektrum, **18**, 145-161 (1996).
5. Brucker, P. Scheduling Algorithm. Springer-Verlag, 4th edn., (2004).
6. Carlier, J. and Pinson, E. Adjustment of heads and tails for the job-shop problem. European Journal of Operational Research, **78**, 146-161 (1994).
7. Cheung, W., Zhou, H. Using Genetic Algorithms and Heuristics for Job Shop Scheduling with Sequence-Dependent Setup Times. Annals of Operational Research, **107**, 65-81 (2001).
8. Dell Amico, M., Trubian, M. Applying Tabu Search to the Job-shop Scheduling Problem. Annals of Operational Research, **41**, 231-252 (1993).
9. Giffler, B. Thomson, G. L.: Algorithms for Solving Production Scheduling Problems. Operations Reseach, **8**, 487-503 (1960).
10. González, M. A., Sierra, M. R., Vela, C. R. and Varela, R. Genetic Algorithms Hybridized with Greedy Algorithms and Local Search over the Spaces of Active and Semi-active Schedules. Springer-Verlag LNCS, To appear (2006).
11. González, M.A. and Vela, C.R. and Puente, J. and Sierra, M.R. and Varela, R. Memetic Algorithms for the Job Shop Scheduling Problem with Sequence Dependent Setup Times. Proceedings of ECAI Workshop on Evolutionary Computation, To appear (2006).
12. Mattfeld, D. C.: Evolutionary Search and the Job Shop. Investigations on Genetic Algorithms for Production Scheduling. Springer-Verlag, November (1995).
13. Nowicki, E. and Smutnicki, C. A fast taboo search algorithm for the job shop problem. Management Science, **42**, 797-813, (1996).
14. Ovacik, I. M. and Uzsoy, R. Exploiting shop floors status information to schedule complex jobs. Operations Research Letters, **14**, 251-256, (1993).
15. Taillard, E. D., Parallel Taboo Search Techniques for the Job Shop Scheduling Problem. ORSA Journal of Computing, **6**, 108-117 (1993).
16. Varela, R., Vela, C. R., Puente, J., Gmez A. A knowledge-based evolutionary strategy for scheduling problems with bottlenecks. European Journal of Operational Research, **145**, 57-71 (2003).
17. Varela, R., Serrano, D., Sierra, M. New Codification Schemas for Scheduling with Genetic Algorithms. Springer-Verlag LNCS 3562, 11-20 (2005).
18. Zoghby, J., Barnes, J. W., Hasenbein J. J. Modeling the re-entrant job shop scheduling problem with setup for metaheuristic searches. European Journal of Operational Research, **167**, 336-348 (2005).

A Fuzzy Set Approach for Evaluating the Achievability of an Output Time Forecast in a Wafer Fabrication Plant

Toly Chen

Department of Industrial Engineering and Systems Management, Feng Chia University,
100, Wenhwa Road, Seatwen, Taichung City, Taiwan
tolychen@ms37.hinet.net

Abstract. Lot output time prediction is a critical task to a wafer fab (fabrication plant). Traditional studies are focused on prediction accuracy and efficiency. Another performance measure that is as important but has been ignored in traditional studies is the achievability of an output time forecast, which is defined as the possibility that the fabrication on a wafer lot can be finished in time before the output time forecast. Theoretically, if a probability distribution can be obtained for the output time forecast, then the achievability can be evaluated with the cumulative probability of the probability distribution before the given date. However, there are many managerial actions that are more influential to the achievability. For this reason, a fuzzy set approach is proposed for evaluating the achievability of the output time forecast. The fuzzy set approach is composed of two parts: a fuzzy back propagation network (FBPN) and a set of fuzzy inference rules (FIRs). An example is used to demonstrate the applicability of the proposed methodology.

1 Introduction

Predicting the output time for every lot in a wafer fab is a critical task not only to the fab itself, but also to its customers. After the output time of each lot in a wafer fab is accurately predicted, several managerial goals can be simultaneously achieved [6]. Predicting the output time of a wafer lot is equivalent to estimating the cycle time (flow time, production lead time)of the lot, because the former can be easily derived by adding the release time (a constant) to the latter.

There are six major approaches commonly applied to predicting the output/cycle time of a wafer lot: multiple-factor linear combination (MFLC), production simulation (PS), back propagation networks (BPN), case based reasoning (CBR), fuzzy modeling methods, and hybrid approaches. Among the six approaches, MFLC is the easiest, quickest, and most prevalent in practical applications. The major disadvantage of MFLC is the lack of forecasting accuracy [6]. Conversely, huge amount of data and lengthy simulation time are two shortages of PS. Nevertheless, PS is the most accurate output time prediction approach if the related databases are continuingly updated to maintain enough validity, and often serves as a benchmark for evaluating the effectiveness of another method. PS also tends to be preferred because it allows for computational experiments and subsequent analyses without any actual execution [3]. Considering both effectiveness and efficiency, Chang et al. [4] and Chang and Hsieh [2]

A. Gelbukh and C.A. Reyes-Garcia (Eds.): MICAI 2006, LNAI 4293, pp. 483–493, 2006.

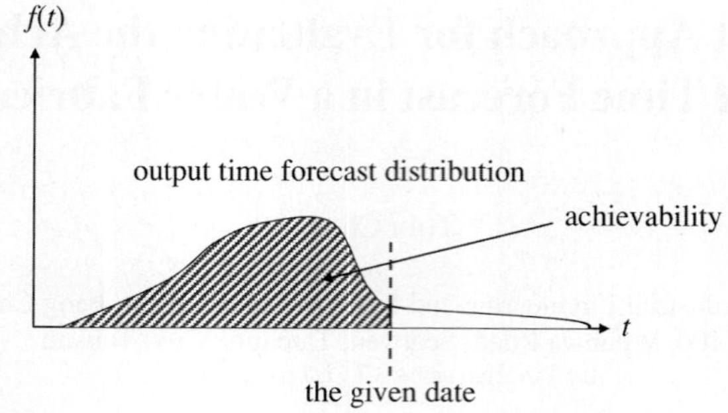

Fig. 1. The concept of "achievability"

both forecasted the output/cycle time of a wafer lot with a BPN having a single hidden layer. Compared with MFLC approaches, the average prediction accuracy measured with root mean squared error (RMSE) was considerably improved with these BPNs. For example, an improvement of about 40% in RMSE was achieved in Chang et al. [4]. On the other hand, much less time and fewer data are required to generate an output time forecast with a BPN than with PS. More recently, Chen [7] incorporated the future release plan of the factory into a BPN, and constructed a "look-ahead" BPN for the same purpose, which led to an average reduction of 12% in RMSE. Chang et al. [3] proposed a k-nearest-neighbors based case-based reasoning (CBR) approach which outperformed the BPN approach in forecasting accuracy. In one case, the advantage was up to 27%. Chang et al. [4] modified the first step (i.e. partitioning the range of each input variable into several fuzzy intervals) of the fuzzy modeling method proposed by Wang and Mendel [13], called the WM method, with a simple genetic algorithm (GA) and proposed the evolving fuzzy rule (EFR) approach to predict the cycle time of a wafer lot. Their EFR approach outperformed CBR and BPN in prediction accuracy. Chen [6] constructed a fuzzy BPN (FBPN) that incorporated expert opinions in forming inputs to the FBPN. Chen's FBPN was a hybrid approach (fuzzy modeling and BPN) and surpassed the crisp BPN especially in the efficiency respect. Another hybrid approach was proposed in Chang and Liao [5] by combining self-organization map (SOM) and WM, in which a wafer lot was classified with SOM before predicting the lot's output time with WM. Chang and Liao's approach surpassed WM, EFR, and BPN in prediction accuracy. Similarly, Chen et al. [8] combined SOM and FBPN, and the hybrid SOM-FBPN outperformed FBPN, CBR, and EFR (with only one exception in five cases).

According to these results, traditional studies are focused on prediction accuracy and efficiency. Another concept that is as important but has been ignored in traditional studies is the achievability of an output time forecast, which is defined as the possibility that the fabrication on a wafer lot can be finished in time before the output time forecast. Theoretically, if a probability distribution can be obtained for the output time forecast, then the achievability can be evaluated with the cumulative probability of the probability distribution before the given date (Fig. 1). However, there are many managerial actions (e.g. elevating the priority of the lot, lowering the priority of another lot, inserting emergency lots, adding allowance, etc.) that are more influential to the achievability. For this reason, a fuzzy set approach is proposed for evaluating the achievability of the output time forecast. The fuzzy set approach is composed of two parts: a FBPN and a set of FIRs. The FBPN is used to generate an output time forecast, and then the FIRs are applied to evaluating the achievability of the output time forecast.

2 Methodology

In this paper, a fuzzy set approach is proposed for evaluating the achievability of an output time forecast in a wafer fab. The fuzzy set approach is composed of two parts: a FBPN and a set of FIRs. The FBPN is used to generate an output time forecast, and then the FIRs are applied to evaluating the achievability of the output time forecast.

2.1 Wafer Lot Output Time Prediction with a FBPN

In the proposed methodology, a FBPN is adopted to predict the output time of a wafer lot. The configuration of the FBPN is established as follows:

1. Inputs: six parameters associated with the n-th example/lot including the average fab utilization (U_n), the total queue length on the lot's processing route (Q_n) or before bottlenecks (BQ_n) or in the whole fab (FQ_n), the fab WIP (WIP_n), and the latenesses ($D_n^{(i)}$) of the i-th recently completed lots. These parameters have to be normalized so that their values fall within [0, 1]. Then some production execution/control experts are requested to express their beliefs (in linguistic terms) about the importance of each input parameter in predicting the cycle (output) time of a wafer lot. Linguistic assessments for an input parameter are converted into several pre-specified fuzzy numbers. The subjective importance of an input parameter is then obtained by averaging the corresponding fuzzy numbers of the linguistic replies for the input parameter by all experts. The subjective importance obtained for an input parameter is multiplied to the normalized value of the input parameter. After such a treatment, all inputs to the FBPN become triangular fuzzy numbers, and the fuzzy arithmetic for triangular fuzzy numbers is applied to deal with all calculations involved in training the FBPN.
2. Single hidden layer: Generally one or two hidden layers are more beneficial for the convergence property of the network.
3. Number of neurons in the hidden layer: the same as that in the input layer. Such a treatment has been adopted by many studies (e.g. [2, 6]).
4. Output: the (normalized) cycle time forecast of the example.
5. Network learning rule: Delta rule.
6. Transformation function: Sigmoid function,

$$f(x) = 1/(1 + e^{-x}). \tag{1}$$

7. Learning rate (η): 0.01~1.0.
8. Batch learning.

The procedure for determining the parameter values is now described. A portion of the examples is fed as "training examples" into the FBPN to determine the parameter values. Two phases are involved at the training stage. At first, in the forward phase, inputs are multiplied with weights, summated, and transferred to the hidden layer. Then activated signals are outputted from the hidden layer as:

$$\tilde{h}_j = (h_{j1},\ h_{j2},\ h_{j3}) = 1/(1+e^{-\tilde{n}_j^h}), \tag{2}$$

where

$$\tilde{n}_j^h = (n_{j1}^h,\ n_{j2}^h,\ n_{j3}^h) = \tilde{I}_j^h(-)\tilde{\theta}_j^h, \tag{3}$$

$$\tilde{I}_j^h = (I_{j1}^h,\ I_{j2}^h,\ I_{j3}^h) = \sum_{all\ i} \tilde{w}_{ij}^h(\times)\tilde{x}_{(i)}, \tag{4}$$

and (–) and (×) denote fuzzy subtraction and multiplication, respectively; $\tilde{h}_j$'s are also transferred to the output layer with the same procedure. Finally, the output of the FBPN is generated as:

$$\tilde{o} = (o_1,\ o_2,\ o_3) = 1/(1+e^{-\tilde{n}^o}), \tag{5}$$

where

$$\tilde{n}^o = (n_1^o,\ n_2^o,\ n_3^o) = \tilde{I}^o(-)\tilde{\theta}^o, \tag{6}$$

$$\tilde{I}^o = (I_1^o, I_2^o, I_3^o) = \sum_{all\ j} \tilde{w}_j^o(\times)\tilde{h}_j. \tag{7}$$

To improve the practical applicability of the FBPN and to facilitate the comparisons with conventional techniques, the fuzzy-valued output $\tilde{o}$ is defuzzified according to the centroid-of-area (COA) formula:

$$o = \text{COA}(\tilde{o}) = (o_1 + 2o_2 + o_3)/4. \tag{8}$$

Then the defuzzified output o is compared with the normalized actual cycle time a, for which the RMSE is calculated:

$$RMSE = \sqrt{\sum_{\text{all examples}} (o-a)^2 / \text{number of examples}}. \tag{9}$$

Subsequently in the backward phase, the deviation between o and a is propagated backward, and the error terms of neurons in the output and hidden layers can be calculated, respectively, as

$$\delta^o = o(1-o)(a-o), \tag{10}$$

$$\tilde{\delta}_j^h = (\delta_{j1}^h,\ \delta_{j2}^h,\ \delta_{j3}^h) = \tilde{h}_j(\times)(1-\tilde{h}_j)(\times)\tilde{w}_j^o\delta^o. \tag{11}$$

Based on them, adjustments that should be made to the connection weights and thresholds can be obtained as

$$\Delta\tilde{w}_j^o = (\Delta w_{j1}^o,\ \Delta w_{j2}^o,\ \Delta w_{j3}^o) = \eta\delta^o \tilde{h}_j , \tag{12}$$

$$\Delta\tilde{w}_{ij}^h = (\Delta w_{ij1}^h,\ \Delta w_{ij2}^h,\ \Delta w_{ij3}^h) = \eta\tilde{\delta}_j^h (\times)\tilde{x}_i , \tag{13}$$

$$\Delta\theta^o = -\eta\delta^o , \tag{14}$$

$$\Delta\tilde{\theta}_j^h = (\Delta\theta_{j1}^h, \Delta\theta_{j2}^h, \Delta\theta_{j3}^h) = -\eta\tilde{\delta}_j^h . \tag{15}$$

Theoretically, network-learning stops when the RMSE falls below a pre-specified level, or the improvement in the RMSE becomes negligible with more epochs, or a large number of epochs have already been run. Then test examples are fed into the FBPN to evaluate the accuracy of the network that is also measured with the RMSE. However, the accumulation of fuzziness during the training process continuously increases the lower bound, the upper bound, and the spread of the fuzzy-valued output $\tilde{o}$ (and those of many other fuzzy parameters), and might prevent the RMSE (calculated with the defuzzified output o) from converging to its minimal value. Conversely, the centers of some fuzzy parameters are becoming smaller and smaller because of network learning. It is possible that a fuzzy parameter becomes invalid in the sense that the lower bound higher than the center. To deal with this problem, the lower and upper bounds of all fuzzy numbers in the FBPN will no longer be modified if the index proposed in Chen [6] converges to a minimal value.

Finally, the FBPN can be applied to predicting the cycle time of a new lot. When a new lot is released into the fab, the six parameters associated with the new lot are recorded and fed as inputs to the FBPN. After propagation, the network output determines the output time forecast of the new lot.

2.2 Achievability Evaluation with Fuzzy Inference Rules

The "achievability" of an output time forecast is defined as the possibility that the fabrication on the wafer lot can be finished in time before the output time forecast. Theoretically, if a probability distribution can be obtained for the output time forecast, then the achievability can be evaluated with the cumulative probability of the probability distribution before the given date. However, there are many managerial actions (e.g. elevating the priority of the lot, lowering the priority of another lot, inserting emergency lots, adding allowance, etc.) that are more influential to the achievability. Taking their effects into account, the evaluation of the achievability can be decomposed into the following two assessments: the possible forwardness of the output time forecast if the priority is elevated, and the easiness of the required priority elevation. For combining the two assessments that are uncertain or subjective in nature, the fuzzy AND operator is applied. The philosophy is that "if the output time forecast can be significantly forwarded after priority elevation, and the required priority elevation is not difficult for the lot, then the achievability of the original output time forecast is high, because the priority of the lot can be elevated before or during fabrication to quicken the progress if necessary, so as to achieve the given date." At last, a set of FIRs are established to facilitate the application.

Based on the standard fuzzy inference process, the procedure of applying the FIRs to evaluating the achievability of an output time forecast is established as:

1. Preprocess: (i) Vary the priority of the target lot (from the current level to every higher level), and then predict the output time of the target lot again with the FBPN; (ii) repeat step 1 for the other lots in the fab; (iii) calculate the forwardness (represented with *FWD*) of the output time, i.e. the reduction in the cycle time, after priority elevation for every lot in the fab; (iv) find out the maximum forwardness (represented with FWD_{max}) and the minimum forwardness (represented with FWD_{min}) across lots; (v) apply Ishibuchi's simple fuzzy partition [11] in forming the five categories of forwardness: "Insignificant (I)", "Somewhat Insignificant (SI)", "Moderate (M)", "Somewhat Significant (SS)", and "Significant (S)".
2. Fuzzify inputs: (i) Classify the forwardness of the output time forecast of the target lot into one of the five categories; (ii) request production control experts to assess the easiness of priority elevation (represented with *EAS*), and then classify the result into one of the following five categories: "Very Easy (VE)", "Easy (E)", "Moderate (M)", "Difficult (D)", and "Very Difficult (VD)". Usually the percentages of lots with various priorities in a wafer fab are controlled. The easiness of priority elevation is determined against such goals (see Fig. 2).
3. Apply fuzzy operator: The fuzzy AND operator is applied to combining the two assessments. The function used by the AND operator is *min* (minimum), which truncates the output fuzzy set.
4. Apply implication method: (i) For facilitating the application, a set of FIRs have been established in Table 1, so as to look up the achievability of the output time forecast, which is represented with linguistic terms including "Very Low (VL)", "Low (L)", "Medium (M)", "High (H)", and "Very High (VH)" (see Fig. 3). A FIR example is "If *FWD* is 'SI' AND *EAS* is 'VD' Then Achievability is 'VL'"; (ii) implication is implemented for each rule.
5. Aggregate all outputs: The outputs of all rules are combined into a single fuzzy set. The function used is *max* (maximum).
6. Defuzzify: The aggregated output can be defuzzified if necessary (e.g. comparing with that of another lot). The defuzzification method is the COA formula.

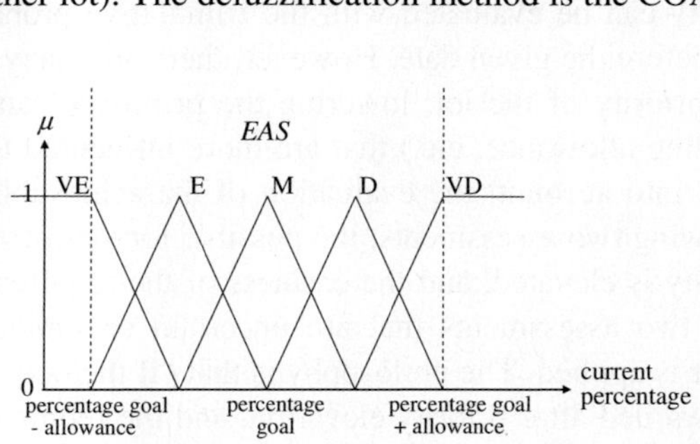

Fig. 2. Linguistic terms for *EAS*

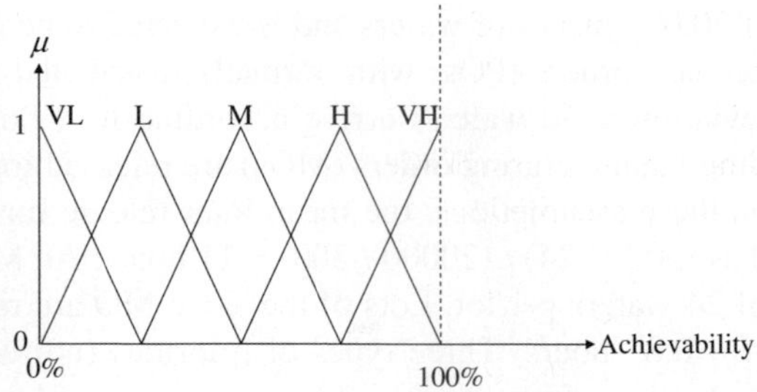

Fig. 3. Linguistic terms for achievability

Table 1. Fuzzy inference rules for determining the achievability

FWD	*EAS*	Achievability
I	-	VL
SI	VD	VL
SI	D, M, E, VE	L
M	VD	VL
M	D	L
M	M, E, VE	M
SS	VD	VL
SS	D	L
SS	M	M
SS	E, VE	H
S	VD	VL
S	D	L
S	M	M
S	E	H
S	VE	VH

3 A Demonstrative Example from a Simulated Wafer Fab

In practical situations, the history data of each lot is only partially available in the factory. Further, some information of the previous lots such as Q_n, BQ_n, and FQ_n is not easy to collect on the shop floor. Therefore, a simulation model is often built to simulate the manufacturing process of a real wafer fabrication factory [1-6, 9, 12]. Then, such information can be derived from the shop floor status collected from the simulation model [3]. To generate a demonstrative example, the simulation model constructed in Chen [6] is adopted in this study.

The basic configuration of the simulated wafer fab is the same as a real-world wafer fabrication factory which is located in the Science Park of Hsin-Chu, Taiwan, R.O.C. There are five products (labeled as A~E) in the simulated fab. A fixed product mix is assumed. The percentages of these products in the fab's product mix are assumed to be 35%, 24%, 17%, 15%, and 9%, respectively. The simulated fab has a monthly capacity of 20,000 pieces of wafers and is expected to be fully utilized (utilization = 100%). Purchase orders (POs) with normally distributed sizes (mean = 300 wafers; standard deviation = 50 wafers) arrive according to a Poisson process, and then the corresponding manufacturing orders (MOs) are released for these POs a fixed time after. Based on these assumptions, the mean inter-release time of MOs into the fab can be obtained as (30.5 * 24) / (20000 / 300) = 11 hours. An MO is split into lots of a standard size of 24 wafers per lot. Lots of the same MO are released one by one every 11 / (300/24) = 0.85 hours. Three types of priorities (normal lot, hot lot, and super hot lot) are randomly assigned to lots. The percentages of lots with these priorities released into the fab are restricted to be approximately 60%, 30%, and 10%, respectively. Each product has 150~200 steps and 6~9 reentrances to the most bottleneck machine. Totally 102 machines (including alternative machines) are provided to process single-wafer or batch operations in the fab. A horizon of twenty-four months is simulated. The maximal cycle time is less than three months. Therefore, four months and an initial WIP status (obtained from a pilot simulation run) seemed to be sufficient to drive the simulation into a steady state. The statistical data were collected starting at the end of the fourth month.

The first part of the proposed fuzzy set approach is to use the FBPN to generate an output time forecast for every lot in the simulated wafer fab. Then the FIRs are applied to evaluate the achievability of the output time forecast. Some data collected for this purpose are shown in Table 2. Take lot P001 as an example. After elevating its priority from “normal lot” to “hot lot”, the percentage of the forwardness of the output time forecast is 11.8%. The *FWD* assessment result is shown in Fig. 4. On the other hand, according to the factory configuration, the percentage goal of “hot lots” in the factory is controlled to be about 30%. We assume an allowance of 5% can be added to or subtracted from the goal. At the time lot P001 is released, the percentage of “hot lots” in the factory is recorded as 31.7%. The *EAS* assessment result is shown in Fig. 5. After applying the related FIRs and then aggregating the results, the fuzzy-valued achievability, is derived (see Fig. 6). Finally, the defuzzified value of the achievability according to the COA formula can be calculated as:

$$\frac{(\int_0^{0.17} x\cdot\frac{x}{0.25}dx+\int_{0.17}^{0.33} x\cdot 0.67dx+\int_{0.33}^{0.42} x\cdot\frac{x-0.5}{-0.25}dx+\int_{0.42}^{0.67} x\cdot 0.32dx+\int_{0.67}^{0.75} x\cdot\frac{x-0.75}{-0.25}dx)}{(\int_0^{0.17}\frac{x}{0.25}dx+\int_{0.17}^{0.33}0.67dx+\int_{0.33}^{0.42}\frac{x-0.5}{-0.25}dx+\int_{0.42}^{0.67}0.32dx+\int_{0.67}^{0.75}\frac{x-0.75}{-0.25}dx)} \tag{16}$$

=34%.

Conversely, with traditional approaches, the achievability can only be evaluated from a probabilistic viewpoint. Since traditional approaches are usually unbiased predictors, the evaluated achievability will be 50% regardless of which lot is concerned. The evaluation results by using different approaches are summarized in Table 3. The achievabilities of different lots can only be discriminated with the proposed fuzzy set approach. Then managerial actions can be taken at proper time to speed up the lots with low output time forecast achievabilities.

Table 2. Data for achievability evaluation

Lot number	Priority elevation	*FWD* %	% of new-priority lots at release time
P001	Normal → Hot	-11.8%	31.7%
P002	Normal → Super Hot	-20%	8.2%
P003	Normal → Hot	-7.2%	33.2%
P004	Super Hot	0%	10.8%
P005	Hot → Super Hot	-9.6%	11.4%

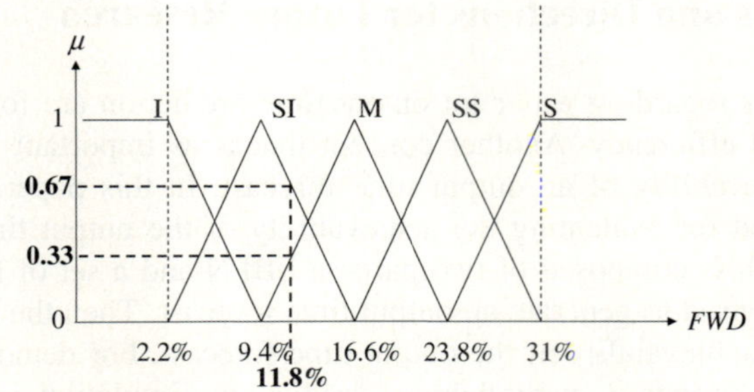

Fig. 4. The *FWD* assessment result for lot P001

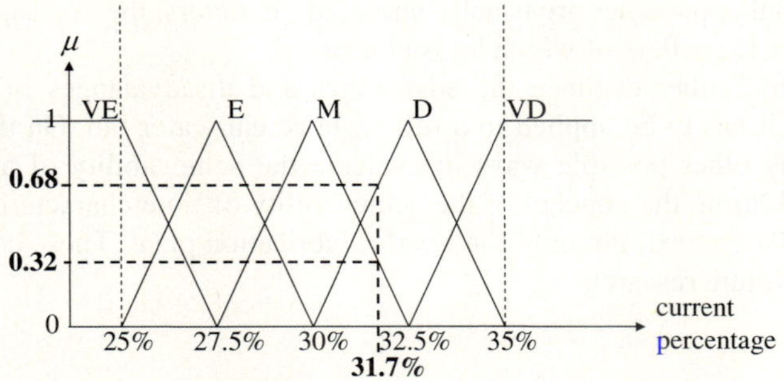

Fig. 5. The *EAS* assessment result for lot P001

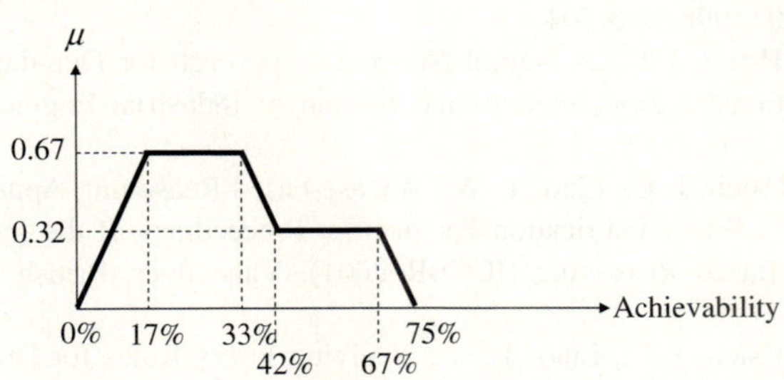

Fig. 6. The fuzzy-valued achievability for lot P001

Table 3. Achievability evaluation results with different approaches

Lot number	Achievability (traditional approach)	Achievability (the fuzzy set approach)
P001	50%	34%
P002	50%	71%
P003	50%	21%
P004	50%	13%
P005	50%	22%

4 Conclusions and Directions for Future Research

Traditional studies regarding wafer lot output time prediction are focused on prediction accuracy and efficiency. Another concept that is as important but has been ignored is the achievability of an output time forecast. In this paper, a fuzzy set approach is proposed for evaluating the achievability of the output time forecast. The fuzzy set approach is composed of two parts: a FBPN and a set of FIRs. In the first part, the FBPN is used to generate an output time forecast. Then the FIRs are applied to evaluating the achievability of the output time forecast. For demonstrating the applicability of the proposed methodology, production simulation is applied in this study to generating a demonstrative example. Conversely, with traditional approaches, the achievability can only be evaluated from a probabilistic viewpoint. Since traditional approaches are usually unbiased predictors, the evaluated achievability will be 50% regardless of which lot is concerned.

However, to further evaluate the advantages and disadvantages of the proposed methodology, it has to be applied to a full-scale actual wafer fab. On the other hand, there are many other possible ways to evaluate the achievability of an output time forecast. In addition, the concept of the achievability of time characteristics could be given in a wider context, not only for a wafer fabrication plant. These constitute some directions for future research.

References

1. Barman, S.: The Impact of Priority Rule Combinations on Lateness and Tardiness. IIE Transactions 30 (1998) 495-504
2. Chang, P.-C., Hsieh, J.-C.: A Neural Networks Approach for Due-date Assignment in a Wafer Fabrication Factory. International Journal of Industrial Engineering 10(1) (2003) 55-61
3. Chang, P.-C., Hsieh, J.-C., Liao, T. W.: A Case-based Reasoning Approach for Due Date Assignment in a Wafer Fabrication Factory. In: Proceedings of the International Conference on Case-Based Reasoning (ICCBR 2001), Vancouver, British Columbia, Canada (2001)
4. Chang, P.-C., Hsieh, J.-C., Liao, T. W.: Evolving Fuzzy Rules for Due-date Assignment Problem in Semiconductor Manufacturing Factory. Journal of Intelligent Manufacturing 16 (2005) 549-557

5. Chang, P.-C., Liao, T. W.: Combining SOM and fuzzy rule base for flow time prediction in semiconductor manufacturing factory. Applied Soft Computing 6 (2006) 198-206.
6. Chen, T.: A Fuzzy Back Propagation Network for Output Time Prediction in a Wafer Fab. Journal of Applied Soft Computing 2/3F (2003) 211-222
7. Chen, T.: A Look-ahead Back Propagation Network to Predict Wafer Lot Output Time. WSEAS Transactions on Computers 5(5) (2006) 910-915
8. Chen, T., Tsai, H. R., Wu, H. C.: Wafer Lot Output Time Prediction with a Hybrid Artificial Neural Network. WSEAS Transactions on Computers 5(5) (2006) 817-823.
9. Goldberg, D. E.: Genetic Algorithms in Search, Optimization, and Machine Learning. Addison-Wesley, Reading, MA (1989)
10. Hung, Y.-F., Chang, C.-B.: Dispatching Rules Using Flow Time Predictions for Semiconductor Wafer Fabrications. In: Proceedings of the 5th Annual International Conference on Industrial Engineering Theory, Applications and Practice, Taiwan (2001)
11. Ishibuchi, H., Nozaki, K., Tanaka, H.: Distributed Representation of Fuzzy Rules and Its Application to Pattern Classification. Fuzzy Sets and Systems 52(1) (1992) 21-32
12. Lin, C.-Y.: Shop Floor Scheduling of Semiconductor Wafer Fabrication Using Real-time Feedback Control and Prediction. Ph.D. Dissertation, Engineering-Industrial Engineering and Operations Research, University of California at Berkeley (1996)
13. Wang, L.-X., Mendel, J. M.: Generating Fuzzy Rules by Learning from Examples. IEEE Transactions on Systems, Man, and Cybernetics 22(6) (1992) 1414-1427

How Good Are the Bayesian Information Criterion and the Minimum Description Length Principle for Model Selection? A Bayesian Network Analysis

Nicandro Cruz-Ramírez[1], Héctor-Gabriel Acosta-Mesa[1],
Rocío-Erandi Barrientos-Martínez[1], and Luis-Alonso Nava-Fernández[2]

[1] Facultad de Física e Inteligencia Artificial, Universidad Veracruzana, Sebastián Camacho 5, Col. Centro, C.P. 91000, Xalapa, Veracruz, México
[2] Instituto de Investigaciones en Educación, Universidad Veracruzana, Diego Leño 8 esq. Morelos, Col. Centro, C.P. 91000, Xalapa, Veracruz, México
{ncruz, heacosta, lunava}@uv.mx,
erandi_bm@yahoo.com.mx

Abstract. The Bayesian Information Criterion (BIC) and the Minimum Description Length Principle (MDL) have been widely proposed as good metrics for model selection. Such scores basically include two terms: one for accuracy and the other for complexity. Their philosophy is to find a model that rightly balances these terms. However, it is surprising that both metrics do often not work very well in practice for they overfit the data. In this paper, we present an analysis of the BIC and MDL scores using the framework of Bayesian networks that supports such a claim. To this end, we carry out different tests that include the recovery of gold-standard network structures as well as the construction and evaluation of Bayesian network classifiers. Finally, based on these results, we discuss the disadvantages of both metrics and propose some future work to examine these limitations more deeply.

1 Introduction

One of the most important problems when trying to gain a deeper understanding of a phenomenon is how to select a good model, among different competing models, that best describes it. Such a phenomenon can be observed through the data it produces; for instance, a certain disease, say lung cancer, may be studied looking at the features the patients might exhibit: history of smoking, tuberculosis, age, etc. The idea is then to induce a model from these data so that it can reliably be used for various possible purposes: description, prognosis, diagnosis and control. The principle that has guided Science in the construction of this model is the well-known Ockham's razor: the best model to describe a phenomenon is the one which best balances accuracy and complexity. Different measures that incorporate these two components (accuracy and complexity) have been proposed: Minimum Description Length (MDL), Bayesian Information Criterion (BIC) and Akaike's Information Criterion (AIC), among others [1, 2]. The main idea of these measures is to capture the regularities present in the data in order to represent these data in a more compact way. However, it seems that some

A. Gelbukh and C.A. Reyes-Garcia (Eds.): MICAI 2006, LNAI 4293, pp. 494 – 504, 2006.

of these measures overfit the data: the accuracy term weighs more than the complexity term thus favoring complex models over simpler ones. In the context of Bayesian networks (BN), highly-dense structures (i.e., structures with a big number of arcs) reflect this overfitting of data.

In this paper, we particularly evaluate the performance of the Bayesian Information Criterion and the Minimum Description Length Principle for model selection using the framework of Bayesian networks. Specifically, we use these measures for constructing Bayesian network structures from data. It is important to notice that different authors have taken BIC to be equivalent to MDL [1, 3, 4]. Here we empirically show that if MDL is considered this way, it tends to favor complex structures; i.e., it overfits data.

The remainder of the paper is organized as follows. In section 2, we briefly review the BIC and MDL scores. In section 3, we describe the procedures for learning BN structures from data used for the tests presented here. In section 4, we evaluate the performance of BIC and MDL for model selection using all these procedures and different datasets. In section 5, we discuss the results presented in section 4 and finally, in section 6, we present some conclusions and mention some future work.

2 The Bayesian Information Criterion and the Minimum Description Length Principle

The Bayesian Information Criterion (BIC) and the Minimum Description Length Principle (MDL) [1, 2, 5-7] are based on the idea of the possibility of compressing the data using a specific model. The BIC score consists of two parts, an accuracy term and a complexity term, as definition 1 shows.

$$BIC = -\log P(D \mid \Theta) + \frac{d}{2} \log n \tag{1}$$

D represents the data, Θ represents the parameters of the model, d represents the dimension of the model and n represents the sample size. The BIC metric chooses the model with the smallest BIC value. The first term is the accuracy term and measures how well a particular model fits the data. The second term is the complexity term and punishes the complexity of the model being considered. While the first term gets better as the model gets more complex, the second term gets worse as the model gets more complex. In terms of Bayesian networks, the first term decreases when more arcs are added whereas the second term increases when more arcs are added (i.e., in theory, this second term punishes complex models more than simpler models). Hence, in combination, these two terms generally seek accurate and simple models. One thing really important to notice is that definition 1 is usually conceived as the Minimum Description Length (MDL) [1, 3, 4]. This is because Rissanen referred (in his first paper on MDL) to definition 1 as the MDL criterion [2]. Since then, such equivalence has often been considered correct. However, definition 1 only holds for large enough n. In practice, it is difficult to have a big sample size; a situation that makes this metric produce unbalanced models: the first term of definition 1 weighs more than the second term thus preferring complex models over simpler ones. In the case of the MDL Principle, a third term is added to definition 1: a constant (see definition 2) [2, 6, 7]. Throughout this paper, we refer to definition 1 as the Bayesian Information Criterion and to definition 2 as the Minimum Description Length principle.

$$MDL = -\log P(D \mid \Theta) + \frac{d}{2}\log n + C_k \tag{2}$$

C_k is a constant that does not depend on n but on k (the number of variables). For the tests carried out here, C_k is the description length of the Bayesian network structure itself and is calculated as follows (definition 3):

$$C_k = \sum_{i=1}^{k}(1 + |Pa_{x_i}|)\log k \tag{3}$$

$|Pa_{x_i}|$ denotes the cardinality of the parents of x_i in the Bayesian network being considered. Notice that C_k becomes irrelevant when $n \to \infty$. Thus, only in this case, the value of this constant is not significant and can be omitted.

3 Learning Bayesian Network Structures from Data

Roughly speaking, there are two different kinds of algorithms to induce Bayesian network structures from data: constraint-based methods and search and scoring methods [8-11]. In the first kind, conditional independence tests are used in order to decide if a pair of random variables is to be connected. The usual choices for such tests are the X^2 and the G^2 statistics, as well as entropy measures [12, 13]. In the second kind, a specific scoring metric evaluates how well a given network matches the data while a search engine is used to find the network that maximizes (or minimizes) this score [1]. The usual choice for such a score is the Cooper-Herskovits (CH) measure [9], the Minimum Description Length (MDL) [2], the Akaike's Information Criterion (AIC) [14] and the Bayesian Information Criterion (BIC) [1, 2]. According to Friedman et al. [3], definition 1 (which they call MDL) is a suitable one for this task. For the search engine, there exist various well-known AI methods: greedy-hill climbing, A*, simulated annealing, among others [1, 15], which have proved very useful for this task. In order to assess the behavior of both the BIC and MDL scores for model selection, we compare the performance of different procedures that build Bayesian network structures from data (including those that implement BIC and MDL) for two tasks: a) the recovery of gold-standard networks and b) the construction of classifiers. For the tests in a), we chose 4 different procedures: CBL2 (constraint-based), MP-Bayes (constraint-based), BICc (constraint-based and search and scoring) and MDLc (constraint-based and search and scoring). For the tests in b), we selected 8 different procedures: Naïve Bayes, CBL2, Bayes-N, MP-Bayes, BIC (search and scoring), MDL (search and scoring), BICc and MDLc [3, 12, 13, 16, 17]. All these procedures are briefly described below.

1. The Naïve Bayes classifier (NB) is one of the most effective classifiers [3] and against which state of the art classifiers have to be compared. Its main appeals are

its simplicity and accuracy: although its structure is always fixed (the class variable has an arc pointing to every attribute), it has been shown that this classifier has high classification accuracy and optimal Bayes' error [18]. In simple terms, the NB learns, from a training data sample, the conditional probability of each attribute given the class. Then, once a new case arrives, the NB uses Bayes' rule to compute the conditional probability of the class given the set of attributes selecting the value of the class with the highest posterior probability.

2. CBL2 is a constraint-based algorithm to build BN structures from data [17]. CBL2 uses mutual information and conditional mutual information tests to decide when to connect/disconnect a pair of nodes. It is a stepwise forward procedure since its initial state is an empty graph: every pair of nodes is disconnected.
3. Bayes-N belongs to a family of constraint-based algorithms [16]. It uses conditional independence tests, based on information measures, to decide if it connects or disconnects an arc between a pair of variables. It includes the use of Bonferroni's adjustment and a parameter for controlling the percentage of information gain. Bayes-N needs the explicit specification of a class variable to work properly. It is also a stepwise forward procedure.
4. MP-Bayes is a constraint-based algorithm which uses mutual information and conditional mutual information measures, combined with the statistics T, to add/delete an arc between a pair of nodes [16]. MP-Bayes is a stepwise forward procedure: it assumes, as the initial state, an empty graph. First, it starts adding arcs if the independence tests do not hold. Then, the procedure starts removing arcs if the conditional independence tests do indeed hold. It has been explicitly designed for behaving parsimoniously: it tries to build Bayesian network structures with the least number of arcs.
5. BIC is a search and scoring algorithm which uses greedy-hill climbing for the search part and the BIC metric for the scoring part. Procedure BIC takes as input an empty graph and a database of cases [16]. In every search step, it looks for a graph that minimizes the BIC score keeping the graph with that minimum score. In a nutshell, procedure BIC applies 3 different operators: the addition of an arc (in either direction), the deletion of an arc and the reversal of an arc. It finishes searching when no structure improves the BIC score of the previous network.
6. MDL is a search and scoring algorithm which uses greedy-hill climbing for the search part and the MDL metric for the scoring part. Procedure MDL takes as input an empty graph and a database of cases. In every search step, it looks for a graph that minimizes the MDL score keeping the graph with that minimum score. In a nutshell, procedure MDL applies 3 different operators: the addition of an arc (in either direction), the deletion of an arc and the reversal of an arc. It finishes searching when no structure improves the MDL score of the previous network.
7. BICc is a combined algorithm. It firstly constructs a graph using procedure MP-Bayes (constraint-based) [16]. Then, it refines this resultant graph using its greedy part (search and scoring), which uses greedy-hill climbing for the search part and the BIC metric for the scoring part.
8. MDLc is also a combined algorithm. It firstly constructs a graph using procedure MP-Bayes (constraint-based) [16]. Then, it refines this resultant graph using its greedy part (search and scoring), which uses greedy-hill climbing for the search part and the MDL metric for the scoring part.

4 Experimental Methodology and Results

For the recovery of gold-standard networks, we carried out our experiment using 5 different well-known databases for this purpose: Alarm, Child, Diagcar, Asia and Sewell & Shah. The methodology to test experimentally the performance of the procedures presented here has been mainly taken from [19] and consists of the following steps:

1. Select a specific Bayesian network structure, which will be called the gold-standard network, to represent a joint probability distribution over the set of variables taking part in the problem.
2. Using a Monte-Carlo technique, simulate a set of cases by generating a database from this joint probability distribution and the gold-standard network.
3. Give this generated database as input to the algorithms described in section 3. The resultant networks, product of running these algorithms, will be called the learned networks.
4. Obtain the accuracy of the result by comparing the difference between the gold-standard network and the learned network in terms of missing and extra arcs.

An advantageous point of using this methodology is that there exists a clear correct answer against which the learned network can be compared: the gold-standard network [8]. The use of simulated datasets is a common practice to test and evaluate the performance and accuracy of the algorithms of this and some other types. The Monte Carlo simulation technique used to generate the data to test the algorithms presented in section 3 is a technique developed by Henrion for Bayesian networks and is known as the probabilistic logic sampling method [8]. This simulation technique is an unbiased generator of cases; i.e., the probability that a specific case is generated is equal to the probability of the case according to the Bayesian network and it is also embedded in a well-known software called Tetrad [13], which has been developed to construct, among other things, Bayesian networks from data. Thus, Tetrad was used to generate databases from the description of a Bayesian network structure and a probability distribution in order to test the performance of the algorithms shown in table 1. Some of the names of the classifiers were abbreviated: CB is the CBL2 algorithm contained in the Power Constructor software and MP is the MP-Bayes procedure. Four of the databases in table 1, ALARM, CHILD, DIAGCAR and ASIA were generated using the Tetrad software. The remaining one, SEWELL & SHAH (abbreviated S&S), is a real-world database which was collected by these researchers [1] and hence was not generated using the Tetrad software. For the sake of brevity, we do not give an explanation of each database. Instead, we refer the reader to the original references [1, 8, 9, 20, 21].

For the evaluation of the algorithms with respect to the construction of classifiers, we carried out our experiment using 10 different databases from the UCI Machine Learning repository [22], which are summarized in table 2. All of them are suitable for classification purposes, as they explicitly contain a class variable. Continuous attributes were discretized using the CAIM algorithm [23]. The abbreviations of the name of the classifiers correspond to those already mentioned above (plus the NB,

Table 1. Comparison of the results given by CBL2, MP-Bayes, BICc and MDLc from running the Alarm, Child, Diagcar, Asia and Sewell and Shah (S&S) databases. "Cases" refer to the sample size while "var" refers to the number of variables involved in each database; "ma" and "ea" stand for missing arcs and extra arcs respectively. Finally, "# arcs" corresponds to the total number of arcs in the gold-standard network.

DB	**cases | var**	**CB**		**MP**		**BICc**		**MDLc**		**# arcs**
		ma	ea	ma	ea	ma	ea	ma	ea	
1. Alarm	10000|37	3	1	3	1	9	31	7	21	46
2. Child	5000|20	2	2	0	2	4	22	4	21	25
3. Diag	5000|18	6	0	4	2	6	15	6	11	20
4. Asia	1000|8	3	2	4	0	4	6	4	6	8
5. S&S	10318|5	2	0	0	0	2	2	2	2	7

Table 2. Brief descriptions of the databases used in the experiments for the construction of classifiers

DB	**# attributes**	**# classes**	**# instances**
1. car	6	4	1728
2. cmc	9	3	1473
3. flare	12	3	1066
4. german	24	2	1000
5. glass	9	7	214
6. ionos	34	2	351
7. iris	4	3	150
8. lymph	18	4	148
9. pima	8	2	768
10. wine	13	3	178

Table 3. Total number of arcs produced by each classifier

DB	**NB**	**CB**	**BayN**	**MP**
1. car	6	5	4	4
2. cmc	9	13	6	10
3. flare	12	14	10	9
4. german	24	30	11	23
5. glass	9	9	7	1
6. ionos	34	52	45	27
7. iris	4	4	5	1
8. lymph	18	21	9	10
9. pima	8	9	4	10
10. wine	13	17	15	6

Table 4. Total number of arcs produced by each classifier

DB	BIC	MDL	BICc	MDLc
1. car	5	8	5	9
2. cmc	13	14	12	21
3. flare	10	21	10	10
4. german	33	44	31	9
5. glass	4	14	4	14
6. ionos	82	64	69	46
7. iris	6	5	6	3
8. lymph	25	17	21	12
9. pima	11	12	11	9
10. wine	18	6	17	22

Table 5. Percentage of classification accuracy including the standard deviation

DB	%NB	%CB	%BayN	%MP
1. car	83.33±1.5	91.50±1.1	86.14±1.4	86.14±1.4
2. cmc	45.42%±2.2	52.55±2.2	40.12±2.2	40.12±2.2
3. flare	96.10±1.03	99.43±0.2	99.70±0.2	99.70±0.2
4. german	76.05±2.3	73.35±2.4	69.46±2.5	70.36±2.5
5. glass	70.42±5.4	64.79±5.6	47.89±5.9	60.59±5.8
6. ionos	92.31%±2.4	89.74±2.8	90.60±2.7	89.74±2.8
7. iris	96±2.7	98±1.98	98±1.98	30±6.4
8. lymph	77.55±5.6	75.51±5.8	79.59±5.4	67.35±6.3
9. pima	78.12±2.5	75.39±2.6	75.78±2.6	75.39±2.6
10. wine	98.30±1.68	96.61±2.3	89.83±3.9	89.83±3.9

Table 6. Percentage of classification accuracy including the standard deviation

DB	%BIC	%MDL	%BICc	%MDLc
1. car	84.20±1.5	68.75±1.9	83.68±1.5	80.56±1.6
2. cmc	53.77±2.2	38.70±2.2	50.92±2.2	51.53±2.2
3. flare	99.70±0.2	99.45±0.3	99.70±0.2	99.71±0.2
4. german	73.95±2.4	72.46±2.4	73.35±2.4	69.46±2.5
5. glass	59.15±5.8	52.11±5.9	59.15±5.8	60.56±5.8
6. ionos	92.30±2.4	82.91±3.4	90.60±2.7	90.60±2.7
7. iris	98±1.9	98±1.9	98±1.9	30±6.4
8. lymph	71.43±6.1	71.43±6.1	81.63±5.2	71.43±6.1
9. pima	75.39±2.6	66.80±2.9	75.39±2.6	75±2.6
10. wine	86.44±4.4	64.41±6.2	91.52±3.6	61.02±6.2

which refers to the Naïve Bayes classifier and BayN, which refers to the Bayes-N algorithm). We ran procedures Bayes-N, and MP-Bayes with their default significance (α) value of 0.05. It seems that this is the default choice for the algorithm CBL2 as well. The constraint-based part of the two combined algorithms also uses $\alpha = 0.05$.

Finally, the method used here to measure the classification accuracy of all the procedures is the one called holdout [24]. It randomly partitions the data into two groups: 2/3 of the data is for training purposes and the remaining 1/3 of these data is used for testing purposes (using a 0/1 loss function). The holdout method is the standard choice when one needs to estimate the "true" accuracies of real databases [24]. The training and test sets are the same for all the classifiers. We used Netica [21] for measuring the classification performance. Table 2 provides a brief description of each database used in these experiments. Tables 3 and 4 depict the total number of arcs of the correspondent BN classifier. Tables 5 and 6 show the classification accuracy results from running the 8 BN classifiers presented here.

5 Discussion of the Results

The tests we present here suggest an important limitation of both the BIC and the MDL scores regarding their balance between the accuracy term and the complexity term. Tables 1, 3, 4, 5 and 6 show in a condensed way this situation. But let us examine more closely the results in these tables.

Table 1 shows the performance of BIC and MDL metrics regarding the recovery of gold-standard networks. The two procedures that incorporate the BIC and MDL scores produce in ALARM, CHILD and DIAGCAR a big number of extra arcs in comparison to the other procedures. In ASIA and SEWELL & SHAH, these same procedures moderately produce more arcs. From these results, it can be inferred that there is something wrong with both scores: it seems that they give more importance to the accuracy term than to the complexity term; i.e., they tend to prefer structures with too many arcs. Moreover, it appears that the MDLc procedure produces less complex models than the BICc procedure. However, as can be seen from this table, the constant term in definition 2 is not enough to significantly improve the performance of the MDLc procedure against the BICc procedure.

Tables 3 and 4 show the total number of arcs produced by each classifier. As can be observed, the procedures that produce the highest number of arcs, for all databases, are those including the BIC or the MDL metric; a very surprising result given that such metrics were specially designed for avoiding the overfitting of data and for preferring simpler models than complex ones without incorporating prior knowledge.

Tables 5 and 6 show the performance of the BIC metric and MDL score regarding the construction of Bayesian network classifiers compared to those by the remaining procedures. Procedures containing these metrics (BIC, MDL, BICc and MDLc) do not win, as the best classifier, in databases 1, 4, 5, 9 and 10. In databases 2, 3, 6, 7 and 8, at least one of such procedures wins but with structures that have more arcs than the classifiers that do not contain either the BIC or MDL metric; i.e., these 4 procedures prefer complex structures than simpler ones (see tables 3 and 4). Thus, from the results of tables 3, 4, 5 and 6, it can again be inferred that there is something wrong with both the BIC and MDL scores: it seems that they give more importance to the accuracy term than to the complexity term; that is to say, they prefer structures with too many arcs. With this behavior, such procedures keep defying their own nature: the explicit inclusion of Ockham's razor. To explain such a situation more clearly, we need to go back to definitions 1 and 2. In short, their first term refers to how likely is that the data have been produced by a certain BN structure while their second term (and the third term in the case of MDL) refers to the punishment that both scores give to this structure (the more densely connected the network, the bigger the punishment). According to these scores, the BN structure that receives the lowest value for this score is the best. It is very important to notice that the accuracy term alone tends to favor complete BN structures (every pair of nodes is connected) [3]. As can be seen from tables 1, 3, 4, 5 and 6, although the procedures that contain the BIC and MDL metrics try to get a good classification performance, they produce too many arcs as if they had only the accuracy term. This situation has not been explicitly mentioned by any of the researchers who have proposed to use BIC or MDL for building BN classifiers from data [3, 25]. They only have shown the accuracy of classifiers using BIC and MDL without showing their complexity (total number of arcs). We strongly believe that showing the total number of arcs is important as it gives a significant clue regarding the limitation of the BIC and MDL scores that has to do with its impossibility of correctly balancing these two terms.

It is also very important to mention that the key feature of these scores is to learn useful properties of the data by only taking into account these data and the model (in our case a Bayesian network) and not making any assumption about the existence of true distributions. If this were the case, they would tend to learn simple and accurate models. However, as can be seen from the results, this is not the case. That is why we carried out two different experiments: the recovery of gold-standard networks and the construction of classifiers. In the first case, it might be argued that, because the BIC and MDL scores do not make assumptions about the existence of true distributions, they do not perform very well in the reconstruction of the gold-standard networks. But they should still be able to build simple models; a situation that is not happening. In the second case, it might be argued that, because of their ability to find regularities in data, they should produce simple and accurate classifiers. However, as can be seen from tables 3, 4, 5 and 6, this is not the case either.

Other experimental studies [26-28] show that a combined method can faithfully reconstruct a gold-standard BN structure. However, they do not show the performance of their methods as classifiers. These results seem a little bit contradictory: if the MDL score does not make any assumption about the existence of a true distribution, then this score should not necessarily produce models close to the gold-standard networks. On the other hand, as can be seen from tables 5 and 6, procedures that incorporate MDL cannot build significantly better classifiers than the other approaches in terms of both accuracy and complexity. In sum, the results suggest that the BIC and MDL's cause for overfitting is due to their impossibility of detecting local but important operator changes that may lead to better and simpler structures (see also [3]).

6 Conclusions and Future Work

We have presented a study using Bayesian networks to show the limitation of the BIC and MDL scores regarding the overfitting of data. Such a limitation has to do with the trade-off between their accuracy and complexity terms: they tend to favor densely-connected graphs over sparse ones. In a way, such a problem has been already detected by Friedman et al. [3]. They have shown that their classifiers using the BIC score perform better on some databases and worse on others and have traced the reasons to the definition of this metric: the BIC score measures the error of the learnt Bayesian networks taking into account all the variables in the problem being considered. If this global error is minimized, that does not necessarily mean that the local error that has to do with the prediction of the class given the attributes is minimized. We have detected not only this situation but also the situation in which the classifiers using BIC and MDL (BIC, MDL, BICc and MDLc) produce too many arcs. The BIC and MDL scores have been explicitly designed to avoid the overfitting of data without introducing any bias in the form of prior knowledge. As we can clearly see from the results, something wrong is happening to these measures. Thus, the parsimony principle (Ockham's razor) is not naturally followed (as it should) by these metrics. The reason of this limitation is that the definition of BIC we are taking is incomplete for we need to take into account a third term. Moreover, the third term of MDL is not enough for selecting simple models. The resultant networks chosen by procedures BIC, MDL, BICc and MDLc are the best with respect to their metrics. Nevertheless, as said before, it is really surprising that these resultant networks are, in general, very densely-connected. It is possible to formulate alternative definitions of MDL in order to balance the complexity term. So, we will be working in the future on the inclusion of other constants, such as the Fisher Information Matrix [2], to check whether these constants can improve such performance.

References

1. Heckerman, D., *A Tutorial on Learning with Bayesian Networks*, in *Learning in Graphical Models*, M.I. Jordan, Editor. 1998, MIT Press. p. 301-354.
2. Grunwald, P., *Tutorial on MDL*, in *Advances in Minimum Description Length: Theory and Applications*, P. Grunwald, I.J. Myung, and M.A. Pitt, Editors. 2005, The MIT Press.
3. Friedman, N., D. Geiger, and M. Goldszmidt, *Bayesian Network Classifiers.* Machine Learning, 1997. **29**: p. 131-163.
4. Lam, W. and Bacchus, *Learning Bayesian belief networks: An approach based on the MDL principle.* Computational Intelligence, 1994. **10**(4).
5. Grunwald, P., *Model Selection Based on Minimum Description Length.* Journal of Mathematical Psychology, 2000. **44**: p. 133-152.
6. Suzuki, J. *Learning Bayesian Belief Networks based on the MDL principle: An efficient algorithm using the branch and bound technique.* in *International Conference on Machine Learning*. 1996. Bary, Italy.
7. Suzuki, J., *Learning Bayesian Belief Networks based on the Minimum Description Length Principle: Basic Properties.* IEICE Transactions on Fundamentals, 1999. **E82-A**(10): p. 2237-2245.
8. Cooper, G.F., *An Overview of the Representation and Discovery of Causal Relationships using Bayesian Networks*, in *Computation, Causation & Discovery*, C. Glymour and G.F. Cooper, Editors. 1999, AAAI Press / MIT Press. p. 3-62.
9. Cooper, G.F. and E. Herskovits, *A Bayesian Method for the Induction of Probabilistic Networks from Data.* Machine Learning, 1992. **9**: p. 309-347.
10. Cheng, J., *Learning Bayesian Networks from data: An information theory based approach*, in *Faculty of Informatics, University of Ulster, United Kingdom.* 1998, University of Ulster: Jordanstown, United Kingdom.

11. Friedman, N. and M. Goldszmidt, *Learning Bayesian Networks from Data*. 1998, University of California, Berkeley and Stanford Research Institute. p. 117.
12. Cheng, J., Bell, D.A., Liu, W. *Learning Belief Networks from Data: An Information Theory Based Approach*. in *Sixth ACM International Conference on Information and Knowledge Management*. 1997: ACM.
13. Spirtes, P., C. Glymour, and R. Scheines, *Causation, Prediction and Search*. First ed. Lecture Notes in Statistics, ed. J. Berger, et al. Vol. 81. 1993: Springer-Verlag. 526.
14. Bozdogan, H., *Akaike's Information Criterion and Recent Developments in Information Complexity*. Journal of Mathematical Psychology, 2000. **44**: p. 62-91.
15. Heckerman, D., D. Geiger, and D.M. Chickering, *Learning Bayesian Networks: The combination of knowledge and statistical data*. Machine Learning, 1995. **20**: p. 197-243.
16. Cruz-Ramirez Nicandro, N.-F.L., Acosta-Mesa Hector Gabriel, Barrientos-Martinez Erandi, Rojas-Marcial Juan Efrain, *A Parsimonious Constraint-based Algorithm to Induce Bayesian Network Structures from Data*, in *IEEE Proceedings of the Mexican International Conference on Computer Science ENC 2005*, IEEE, Editor. 2005, IEEE: Puebla. p. 306-313.
17. Cheng, J. and R. Greiner. *Learning Bayesian Belief Network Classifiers: Algorithms and Systems*. in *Proceedings of the Canadian Conference on Artificial Intelligence (CSCSI01)*. 2001. Ottawa, Canada.
18. Duda, R.O., Hart, Peter E., Stork, David G., *Pattern Classification*. 2001: John Wiley & Sons, INC.
19. Chickering, D.M., *Learning Bayesian Networks from Data*, in *Computer Science, Cognitive Systems Laboratory*. 1996, University of California, Los Angeles: Los Angeles, California. p. 172.
20. Spiegelhalter, D.J., et al., *Bayesian Analysis in Expert Systems*. Statistical Science, 1993. **8**(3): p. 219-247.
21. Norsys, *www.norsys.com*.
22. Murphy, P.M., Aha, D.W., *UCI repository of Machine Learning Databases*. 1995.
23. Kurgan, L.A., Cios, Krzysztof J., *CAIM Discretization Algorithm*. IEEE Transactions on Knowledge and Data Engineering, 2004. **16**(2): p. 145-153.
24. Kohavi, R. *A Study of Cross-Validation and Bootstrap for Accuracy Estimation and Model Selection*. in *14th International Joint Conference on Artificial Intelligence IJCAI'95*. 1995a. Montreal, Canada: Morgan Kaufmann.
25. Cheng, J. and R. Greiner. *Comparing Bayesian Network Classifiers*. in *Fifteenth Conference on Uncertainty in Artificial Intelligence*. 1999.
26. Spirtes, P. and C. Meek. *Learning Bayesian Networks with Discrete Variables from Data*. in *First International Conference on Knowledge Discovery and Data Mining*. 1995.
27. Singh, M., Valtorta, Marco. *An Algorithm for the Construction of Bayesian Network Structures from Data*. in *9th Conference on Uncertainty in Artificial Intelligence*. 1993: Morgan Kaufmann.
28. Singh, M., Valtorta, Marco, *Construction of Bayesian Network Structures from Data: a Brief Survey and an Efficient Algorithm*. International Journal of Approximate Reasoning, 1995. **12**: p. 111-131.

Prediction of Silkworm Cocoon Yield in China Based on Grey-Markov Forecasting Model

Lingxia Huang[1], Peihua Jin[1], Yong He[2], Chengfu Lou[1], Min Huang[2], and Mingang Chen[1]

[1] College of Animal Sciences, Zhejiang University, Hangzhou 310029, China
lxhuang@zju.edu.cn

[2] College of Biosystems Engineering and Food Science, Zhejiang University, Hangzhou 310029, China
yhe@zju.edu.cn

Abstract. The method of Grey prediction and Markov Chain prediction could be used for the prediction in time order. Their combination could be extensively applied in forecasting. In this paper, we studied the precisions of Grey-Markov forecasting model based on the original data of the silkworm cocoon yield in China from 1950 to 1999. The precisions of Grey-Markov forecasting model from 2000 to 2003 are 95.56%, 95.17% and 94.40% respectively, which are higher than GM (1,1), and next to the Exponential Smoothing method and linear regression. The paper provided a scientific basis for the planned development of sericulture in China.

1 Introduction

China is the earliest and largest producer of silkworm cocoon in the world, accounting for about nearly 70 percent in the world yield during recent years [1]. Sericulture is one of the most labor-intensive sectors of the economy combining both agriculture and industry. Chinese sericulture is practiced in more than 20 million households [2]. The silkworm cocoon, raw silk and semifinished product silk have become Chinese main export commodities; earn the massive foreign exchange for China. In 2003, the silk commodity exports value amounted to 5.71 billion dollars [3]. Nowadays China is the world cocoon fiber industry center. Sericulture holds the key for generating productive employment for rural manpower and silk is also a big business in China. Therefore it is necessary to forecast the silkworm cocoon yield, which is the most basic work to be considered in developing sericulture.

In previous reports several different models for understanding, forecasting, and projecting demand for cocoon and silk yield have been used. He Yong presented a Trend-state model for forecasting the yield of silkworm cocoon in Zhejiang Province, P.R.China [4]. Giovanni Federico estimated an econometric model of world silk yield from 1870 to 1913 [5]. Gopal Naik and Santosh Kumar Singh developed a comprehensive econometric model for the Indian silk sector to generate long-term forecasts and policy simulation [6].

A. Gelbukh and C.A. Reyes-Garcia (Eds.): MICAI 2006, LNAI 4293, pp. 505 – 512, 2006.

Since the silkworm cocoon yield is affected by variant random factors, including climate, technology, price, policy etc. Some of the factors are clear, but some are incalculable or unpredictable. Therefore, the silkworm cocoon yield system is a grey system [7].

Both of the methods of Grey prediction and Markov Chain prediction could be used for the forecasting in time order. The GM (1, 1) grey forecasting model is appropriate for stationary data but random fluctuation is unsuitable. Conversely, Markov chain can predict systems, which show great randomness. Their combination could be mutually complemented and extensively applied in forecasting [8]. While the yield historical date of silkworm cocoon in China shows great randomness and the change is a nonstationary process, and there are no applicable methods for predicting, it is necessary to estimate a predictive model. In this paper, a Grey-Markov model is developed to forecast silkworm cocoon yield in China.

2 Research Methodology

The algorithm of Grey-Markov forecasting model is as follows: firstly a GM (1, 1) grey forecasting model is established to expose the trend of original date and calculate the prediction curve. Secondly a Markov transition matrix is employed to determine the state transition probability. Then, these two models could be combined to obtain the prediction range. Finally the middle point of the prediction range would be considered as the forecasting result. Generally, each step is described below:

2.1 Construction of GM (1, 1) Model

The original time series is defined as $X^{(0)}$, where $X^{(0)}$ is the system yield at time i

$$X^{(0)} = \{ X^{(0)}(1),\ X^{(0)}(2), \ldots,\ X^{(0)}(n) \}\ . \tag{1}$$

and the accumulated generating operation (AGO) of $X^{(0)}$ is given by

$$X^{(1)}(k) = \sum_{i=1}^{k} x^{(0)}(i)\ ,\ k=1,2,\ \ldots,n\ . \tag{2}$$

Where the grey generated model, based on the series $X^{(1)} = \{ X^{(1)}(1), X^{(1)}(2), \ldots, X^{(1)}(n) \}$. From $X^{(1)}$, the first-order differential equation is formed.

$$(dx^{(1)} / dt) + az = u\ . \tag{3}$$

From Eq (3), we have

$$\hat{x}^{(1)}(k+1) = (x^{(0)}(1) - \frac{u}{a})e^{-ak} + \frac{u}{a}\ . \tag{4}$$

$$\hat{x}(k+1) = \hat{x}^{(1)}(k+1) - \hat{x}^{(1)}(k) . \quad (5)$$

Where $\hat{x}(k+1)$ is the forecasting value of $x(k+1)$ at time $k+1$, and

$$\hat{a} = \begin{bmatrix} a \\ u \end{bmatrix} = (B^T B)^{-1} B^T y_N , \quad (6)$$

$$B = \begin{bmatrix} -1/2(x^1(1) + x^1(2)) & 1 \\ -1/2(x^1(2) + x^1(3)) & 1 \\ \cdots & \cdots \\ -1/2(x^1(n-1) + x^1(n) & 1 \end{bmatrix},$$

$$y_N = (x^{(0)}(2), x^{(0)}(3), \ldots, x^{(0)}(n))^T .$$

Inverse accumulated generation operation (IAGO) is made.

$$\hat{x}_0^{(0)}(k+1) = \hat{x}^{(1)}(k+1) - \hat{x}^{(1)}(k) , k=1, 2, \ldots, n-1. \quad (7)$$

A trend curve equation can be formed:

$$\hat{Y}(k) = \hat{x}^{(0)}(k+1) = ge^{-ak} . \quad (8)$$

where $g = (x^{(0)}(1) - u/a)(1 - e^{\alpha})$, k=1, 2, …,n -1. $\hat{Y}(k)$ represents the prediction value for original date series at time k.

2.2 Division of States

The values of $X^{(0)}(k+1)$ are distributed in the region of the trend curve $\hat{Y}(k)$ that may be divided into a convenient number of contiguous intervals. The trend curve $\hat{Y}(k)$ can be benchmark and divide *n* states. Each state can be represented as

$$E_i = [E_{1i}, E_{2i}] . \quad (9)$$

Where *i*=1, 2…S, S is the amount of states.

$$E_{1i} = \hat{Y}(k) + A_i . \quad (10)$$

$$E_{2i} = \hat{Y}(k) + B_i . \quad (11)$$

where E_i indicates state i , E_{1i} and E_{2i} change with time. A_i and B_i are constants, which can be determined by the original date series.

2.3 Calculation of State Transfer Probability

The transition probability of state E_i to state E_j can be expressed as:

$$P_{ij}(m) = \frac{M_{ij}(m)}{M_i} \quad (i ,j=1,2,\ldots,S) . \tag{12}$$

Where $P_{ij}(m)$ is the probability of transition from state *i* to *j* for *m* steps (in this paper, 1 step stands for 1 year), $M_{ij}(m)$ is the transition from state *i* to *j* for *m* steps, M_i is the number of original data points in state E_i .

The state transition probability matrix $R(m)$ as follows:

$$R(m) = \begin{bmatrix} p_{11}(m) & p_{12}(m) & \cdots & p_{1j}(m) \\ p_{21}(m) & p_{22}(m) & \cdots & p_{2j}(m) \\ & & \cdots & \\ p_{j1}(m) & p_{j2}(m) & \cdots & p_{ij}(m) \end{bmatrix} (i ,j=1,2,\ldots,S) . \tag{13}$$

The state transition probability $P_{ij}(m)$ reflects the transition rules of a system. The state transition probability matrix $R(m)$ describes the probability of transition from state *i* to *j*. Generally, the one-step transition matrix $R(1)$ has to be determined. Suppose the object to be forecasted is in state E_Q ($1 \le Q \le S$), row Q in matrix $R(1)$. If max $P_{Qj}(1) = P_{QL}(1)$ (j=1, 2,…, S; $1 \le Q \le S$), the state of the system may transfer from state E_Q to state E_L . If two or more transition probabilities in the row Q of matrix $R(1)$ are the same, the transition probability matrix of two-step transition matrix $R(2)$ or multi-step transition matrix $R(m)$, where $m \ge 3$, should be considered [4].

2.4 Grey-Markov Forecasting Value

After the prediction state is obtained, $\hat{Y}(k+1)$ will be the median point of the prediction state, namely

$$\hat{Y}(k+1) = 1/2(E_{1i} + E_{2i}) = \hat{Y}(k) + 1/2(A_i + B_i) . \tag{14}$$

3 The Forecast of Silkworm Cocoon Yield in China

According to the modeling steps described above, the Grey-Markov model of silkworm cocoon yield in China is investigated. The original date of silkworm cocoon yield in China from 1950 to 2003 is showed in Table 1.The first 49 data is employed for model fitting and the last 3 data is reserved for post-sample comparison [9].

Table 1. The Silkworm Cocoon Yield of China from 1950 to 2003 (unit: ton)

No.	Year	Amount	No.	Year	Amount	No.	Year	Amount
1	1950	59000	19	1968	144000	37	1986	369069
2	1951	74000	20	1969	148000	38	1987	402151
3	1952	123000	21	1970	165000	39	1988	440804
4	1953	71000	22	1971	149000	40	1989	488098
5	1954	91000	23	1972	161000	41	1990	534421
6	1955	131000	24	1973	205000	42	1991	583656
7	1956	134000	25	1974	199000	43	1992	692205
8	1957	112000	26	1975	194000	44	1993	756667
9	1958	118000	27	1976	193000	45	1994	813078
10	1959	124000	28	1977	216000	46	1995	800218
11	1960	89000	29	1978	228150	47	1996	508312
12	1961	42000	30	1979	326000	48	1997	469432
13	1962	45000	31	1980	325750	49	1998	525669
14	1963	69000	32	1981	311050	50	1999	484702
15	1964	95000	33	1982	314050	51	2000	547613
16	1965	104000	34	1983	339950	52	2001	655000
17	1966	139000	35	1984	356550	53	2002	698000
18	1967	123000	36	1985	371354	54	2003	667000

The calculation steps are as the following.

3.1 Build the GM (1, 1) Grey Forecasting Model

Using the date of silkworm cocoon yield in China from 1950 to 2000, in Table 1and Eqs (1)-(8) for model building, the GM (1, 1) model of silkworm cocoon yield is:

$$\hat{Y}(k) = \hat{X}^{(0)}(k+1) = 76105e^{0.0457k} (k=1, 2, 3\ldots, k). \tag{15}$$

where k is the series number of the year, and k=1 means that is 1950.

3.2 Partition of States

Based on the original data of silkworm cocoon yield shown in Table 1, four contiguous stats intervals are established about the curve of $X^{(0)}(k+1)$ as follows:

$$E_1 : E_{11} = \hat{Z}(k) - 1.08\overline{Y} \qquad E_{21} = \hat{Z}(k) - 0.28\overline{Y}$$

$$E_2 : E_{12} = \hat{Z}(k) - 0.28\overline{Y} \qquad E_{22} = \hat{Z}(k)$$

$$E_3 : E_{13} = \hat{Z}(k) \qquad E_{23} = \hat{Z}(k) + 0.28\overline{Y}$$

$$E_4 : E_{14} = \hat{Z}(k) + 0.28\overline{Y} \qquad E_{24} = \hat{Z}(k) + 1.08\overline{Y}$$

where $\overline{Y}$ is the average value of the original data of silkworm cocoon yield from 1950 to 2000, Fig.1 shows the original data series, the regressed curve and the states intervals.

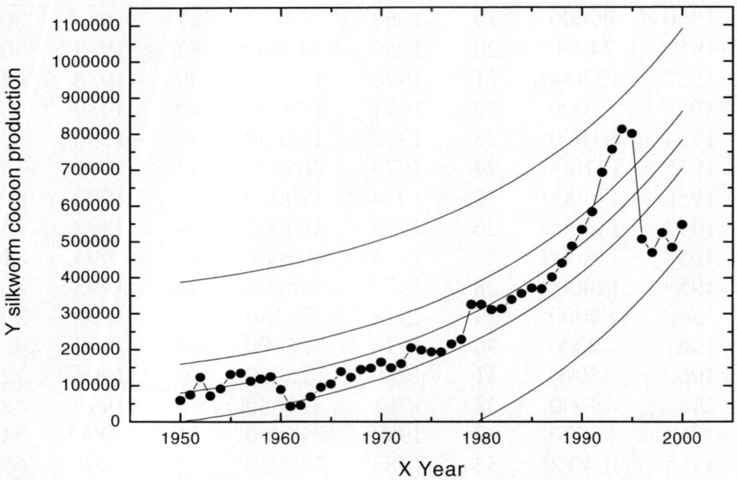

Fig. 1. The forecasting curve of the silkworm cocoon yield in China

3.3 Calculation of State Transition

The number of the original data in every interval can be obtained:

$$M_1=7,\ M_2=29,\ M_3=11,\ M_4=4$$

where M_i denotes the number of the historical data in the interval i, and i=1,2,3,4. According to Table 1 and the state of silkworm cocoon yield determined above, the one-step transfer probability matrix $R(1)$ as follows:

$$R(1) = \begin{bmatrix} \frac{5}{6} & \frac{1}{6} & \frac{0}{6} & \frac{0}{6} \\ \frac{1}{29} & \frac{24}{29} & \frac{4}{29} & \frac{0}{29} \\ \frac{0}{11} & \frac{3}{11} & \frac{7}{11} & \frac{1}{11} \\ \frac{1}{4} & \frac{0}{4} & \frac{1}{4} & \frac{3}{4} \end{bmatrix}$$

The transfer probability matrix can predict the future silkworm cocoon yield $R(1)$. The yield in 2000 year is in the E_1 state interval, so the first row should be observed. As the matrix $R(1)$ shows that the max $P_{1j} = P_{11}$ (j=1, 2, 3, 4), the silkworm cocoon yield of 2001 year is most possible in the E_1 state interval. From the way above, we can calculate the silkworm cocoon yield in 2002 and 2003 each is also most likely in the E_1 state interval.

3.4 Calculate the Forecast Value

According to Eq. (14), the date of silkworm cocoon yield in 2001is calculated, that is:

$$\hat{Y}(52) = 1/2(E_{11} + E_{21}) = 1/2(512167.3+739711.6) = 625939$$

By the same method, the silkworm cocoon yield in China in 2002 and 2003 can be calculated.

3.5 Comparison of Forecast Values with Different Forecasting Model

A comparison of forecasting value and precision between four different forecasting models is shown in Table 2.

It is showed that the precision of Grey-Markov forecasting model is much better than other three forecasting models. That means the Grey-Markov forecasting model is fit for the predication of silkworm cocoon yield in China.

Table 2. Comparison of forecast values with four different models (unit: ton)

Year		Reality amount	GM (1,1)	Secondary Exponential smoothing	Linear regression	Grey-Markov
2001	V	655000	819352	504389	599405	625940
	P		74.90%	77.01%	91.51%	95.56%
2002	V	698000	857665	491738	612004	664253
	P		77.13%	70.45%	88.68%	95.17%
2003	V	667000	897770	479087	624603	704354
	P		65.40%	71.82%	93.64%	94.40%

Note: V means value and P means precision.

4 Conclusions

Because the silkworm cocoon yield of China is influenced by lots of factors easily such as social, economical environment, technical and the natural condition, its data sequence often presents certain tendency and undulation.

The Grey-Markov forecasting model improved both of the Grey forecasting model and Markov Chain prediction model. Comparison results from four different forecasting models demonstrate the applicability and effectiveness of the proposed model. The forecasting result of this forecasting method is greatly dependent on state intervals partitioning. There is no standard rule to divide the states intervals. The number of states should be decided according to the data and the demands of the problem. There is no standard in determining the state of silkworm cocoon yield in China, so some further researches should be performed in the further, such as neural network and so on.

The Grey-Markov model used in this study also can be used in other commodity sectors for forecasting.

References

1. Gu, G.D. (ed.): Sericulture Economy and Silk Trade of the World. China Agriculture Science and Technology Press. Beijing China (2001) 204
2. Gu, G.D. (ed.): Sericulture Economy Management. Zhejiang University Press. Hangzhou China (2003)81
3. China Silk Association. (ed.): Silk Yearbook of China 2004. Silk Press. Hangzhou China (2005)102
4. He, Y.: A New Forecasting Model for Agricultural Commodities. Journal of Agricultural Engineering Research. Vol.60 (1995) 227-235
5. Federico, G.: An Econometric Model of World Silk Production, 1870-1914. Explorations in Economic History. Vol.33 (1996) 250-274
6. Gopal, N., Santosh, K. S.: Policy Simulation of the Indian Silk Industry through an Econometric Model. Journal of Policy Modeling.Vol.21 (7) (1999) 875-899
7. Deng,J.L. (ed.): Control Problems of Grey System. Huazhong University of Science and Technology Press. Wuhang China (1990) 1-2
8. He, Y., Huang,M.: A Grey-Markov Forecasting Model for the Electric Power Requirement in China. In: Alexander Gelbukh, Alvaro de Albornoz, Hugo Terashima-Marin (eds.): MICAI 2005: Advances in Artificial Intelligence. Lecture Notes in Artificial Intelligence, Vol. 3789. Springer-Verlag, Berlin Heidelberg Germany (2005)574-582
9. National Bureau of Statistic of China. (ed.): China Statistical Year Book. China Statistics Press. Beijing China (1980-2004)

A Novel Hybrid System with Neural Networks and Hidden Markov Models in Fault Diagnosis

Qiang Miao, Hong-Zhong Huang, and Xianfeng Fan

School of Mechatronics Engineering, University of Electronic Science and Technology of China, Chengdu, Sichuan, 610054, China
{mqiang, hzhuang}@uestc.edu.cn, fanxf@yahoo.com

Abstract. Condition monitoring and classification of machinery health state is of great practical significance in manufacturing industry, because it provides updated information regarding machine status on-line, thus avoiding the production loss and minimizing the chances of catastrophic machine failures. This is a pattern recognition problem and a condition monitoring system based on a hybrid of neural network and hidden Markov model (HMM) is proposed in this paper. Neural network realizes dimensionality reduction for Lipschitz exponent functions obtained from vibration data as input features and hidden Markov model is used for condition classification. The machinery condition can be identified by selecting the corresponding HMM which maximizes the probability of a given observation sequence. In the end, the proposed method is validated using gearbox vibration data.

Keywords: Feature selection, Pattern recognition, Neural networks, Hidden Markov models.

1 Introduction

Machinery condition classification can be treated as a problem of pattern recognition. In this procedure, condition classification means identifying the existence of failure by interpreting the major system variables and the operating status of machine. A failure is defined as an event when a machine proceeds to an abnormal state or a transient situation from a normal state. It is necessary to identify the occurrence of failure during its early stage for the selection of appropriate maintenance action to prevent a more severe situation. From this aspect, condition classification can usually be divided into two tasks: feature extraction and condition classification.

The purpose of feature extraction is to extract discriminative good features to be used for machinery condition classification. Here, "good feature" means objects from the same class have similar feature values and those from different classes have significantly different values. Unfortunately, in practice, features extracted from original data may have large dimensionality, which leads to the heavy computation cost. Principal Component Analysis (PCA) is one of the best known techniques in this area: the new dimensions, linear combinations of the original features, are given by the eigenvectors (ordered by decreasing eigenvalues) of the covariance matrix of input data [1]. However, in case of features with high dimension, the size of the

A. Gelbukh and C.A. Reyes-Garcia (Eds.): MICAI 2006, LNAI 4293, pp. 513 – 521, 2006.

covariance matrix is very large, as input vectors of dimension n give rise to a matrix of size $n \times n$. Dimensionality reduction with neural network is another solution to this problem. Ruck *et al.* [2] developed a feature selection method using multilayer feedfoward neural networks (MFNN). Here feature selection is a dimensionality reduction procedure by selecting a smaller subset of salient features from the original set of features. The advantage of this method is that it takes into account information about the classification problem itself when selecting features. Later, Perantonis and Virvilis [3] extended this method by considering the combination of the original features in the feature selection. In the previous research, Lipschitz exponent function has been proved to be sensitive to the health state of machinery [4, 5]. In this paper, we expand their work by utilizing it as the input feature in machinery condition monitoring, whose dimensionality is usually very large (say, around 1000). Thus, dimensionality reduction is necessary and MFNN based feature selection is employed in this paper.

Condition classification is another task in this research, which is to assign a physical object, event, or phenomenon to one of the pre-specified classes. Since most classification problems deal with observation of events that display randomness, we choose HMM which is a double stochastic approach for the classification of failure patterns. HMM can be used to solve classification problems associated with time series input data such as speech signals, and can provide an appropriate solution by means of its modeling and learning capability, even though it does not have the exact knowledge of the issues. Over the past ten years, HMM has been applied in classifying patterns in process trend analysis [6] and machine condition monitoring. Ertunc *et al.* [7] used HMM to determine wear status of drill bits in a drilling process. Atlas *et al.* [8] focused on the monitoring of milling processes with HMM at three different time scales and illustrated how HMM can give accurate wear prediction. Ocak and Loparo [9] presented the application of HMMs in bearing fault detection. These literature reviews show good capability of HMM in condition classification.

The paper is organized as follows. Section 2 introduces the procedure of feature extraction with Lipschitz exponent function and a MFNN based feature selection method. HMM based classification system is introduced in section 3. Section 4 further investigates and validates this system using gearbox vibration data. Conclusions from this research are given in section 5.

2 Feature Extraction and Selection

2.1 Wavelet and Lipschitz Exponent

Lipschitz exponent [10], also known as Holder exponent, is a term that can give quantitative description of function regularity. We say that function $f(x)$ is Lipschitz exponent α ($n< \alpha \leq n+1$) at x_0, if there exist two constants A and $h_0 > 0$ and a polynomial $P_n(x)$ of order n, such that

$$| f(x) - P_n(x-x_0) | \leq A | x-x_0|^{\alpha} \text{ for } |x-x_0| < h_0. \quad (1)$$

Here $f(x) \in L^2(R)$. The polynomial $P_n(x)$ is often associated with the Taylor's expansion of $f(x)$ at x_0 but the definition is used even if such an expansion does not exist.

Lipschitz regularity of $f(x)$ and x_0 is defined as the superior bound of all values α such that $f(x)$ is Lipschitz α at x_0. Function $f(x)$ that is continuously differentiable at a point is Lipschitz 1 at this point. If the Lipschitz regularity α of $f(x)$ at $x = x_0$, satisfies $n < \alpha < n+1$, then $f(x)$ is n times differentiable at x_0 but its nth derivative is singular at x_0 and α characterizes this singularity. Here n is a positive integer. Since the occurrence of machine failure causes the emergence of singularities in collected signal, it is a possible way to realize condition monitoring by capturing the singularities using Lipschitz exponent [11, 12]. However, Eq. (1) is not a practical way to estimate exponent α. To measure the exponent α, wavelet transform is a better choice because of its compact support [10], which generates a time-scale representation of time-domain signal and the value of wavelet coefficient $Wf(s, x)$ depends on the value of $f(x)$ in a neighborhood, of size proportional to the scale s.

When applying a wavelet transform, we consider a wavelet function $\psi(x)$ with n+1 vanishing moments, that is

$$\int_{-\infty}^{+\infty} x^k \psi(x) dx = 0, for 0 \le k < n+1 . \tag{2}$$

This condition states that the wavelet with n + 1 vanishing moments is orthogonal to the polynomials of up to order n. Then, the wavelet transform of $f(x)$ using $\psi(x)$ at the location x_0 can eliminate those polynomials up to order n. Suppose that $\psi(x)$ has n+1 vanishing moments, Mallat and Hwang [10] proved that if function $f(x)$ is Lipschitz α at x_0, $n < \alpha < n+1$, then there exists a constant A such that for all points x in a neighborhood of x_0 and any scale s,

$$| Wf(s,x) | \le A(s^{\alpha} + | x - x_0 |^{\alpha}) . \tag{3}$$

The local Lipschitz exponent of $f(x)$ at x_0 depends on the decay of $|Wf(s, x)|$ at fine scales in the neighborhood of x_0. The decay can be measured through the local maxima. Define modulus maxima as any point (s_0, x_0) such that $|Wf(s_0, x)|$ is a local maxima at $x = x_0$. Singularities can be identified by the presence of modulus maxima. If there exists a scale $s_0 > 0$, and a constant C, such that for $x \in (a, b)$ and $s < s_0$, all the modulus maxima of $Wf(s, x)$ belong to a cone defined by

$$| x - x_0 | \le Cs , \tag{4}$$

then at each modulus maxima (s, x) in the cone defined by (4),

$$| Wf(s,x) | \le Bs^{\alpha} , \tag{5}$$

which is equivalent to

$$\log_2 | Wf(s,x) | \le \log_2 B + \alpha \log_2 s . \tag{6}$$

Here, $B = A\,(1 + C^{\alpha})$.

2.2 Method for Extraction of Lipschitz Exponent Function

Inequality (6) provides an asymptotic way to estimate Lipschitz α. In this research, the wavelet transform of the collected signal generates a two-dimensional time-scale matrix. In this matrix, one dimension of the time-scale matrix (x) represents a different time point in the signal, and the other one denotes a different frequency scale (s). To simplify the method, we use linear regression method to estimate α, that is,

$$\log_2 |Wf(s,x)| = \log_2 B + \alpha \log_2 s \,, \tag{7}$$

$$\alpha = \frac{\log_2 |Wf(s,x)| - \log_2 B}{\log_2 s} \,. \tag{8}$$

The above simplification has been applied by Robertson *et al.* in [13] in structural health monitoring. In this paper, we take each column which represents the frequency spectrum of the signal at a certain time point x and calculate α using (8), then Lipschitz exponent function $Lp(x)$ can be achieved.

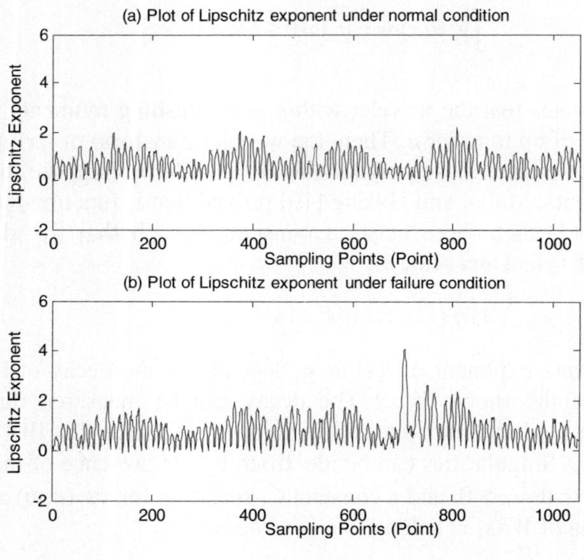

Fig. 1. Plot of Lipschitz exponent functions under two conditions in one revolution

Fig. 1 is an example of the plot of two Lipschitz exponent functions extracted from gear vibration signals in one revolution under normal and failure conditions, respectively. The details of vibration data will be given in Section 4. The failure mode is gear tooth broken. X-axis represents sampling point in one revolution and is consistent with time axis (x). Y-axis represents the Lipschitz exponent (Lp). An obvious impulse can be observed in Fig. 1(b) around the sampling point 700 on the X-axis, which is caused by the existence of gear tooth broken.

2.3 MFNN Based Feature Selection

The feature extraction procedure in the previous section generates a feature vector of 1×1052, where 1052 is related to the number of sampling points in one revolution. This conclusion is coming from the sampling rate (20kHz) of vibration signal and the corresponding gearbox mechanical specifications (rotation speed, gear ratio, etc). In addition, since the vibration signal used in this paper is collected at a period of 10 seconds with sampling rate of 20kHz, each piece of signal can be divided into a number of bins (K) with signal length = 1052. That is, K=20000×10/1052 ≈ 190. Thus, the dimension of selected feature set is high (with K=190 feature vectors) and we apply MFNN to achieve dimensionality reduction.

Consider a MFNN with one layer of input, M layers of hidden and one layer of output. The nodes in each layer receive input from all nodes in the previous layer. Inputs to the first layer of the MFNN are denoted by x_i, i=1, 2, …, N where N is the total number of features the network is to process. Output units are denoted by $o_i^{(m)}$, where the superscript (m) deontes a layer within the structure of the network (m=1, 2, …, M for hidden layers, m=M+1 for the output layer), and i labels a node within a layer. The synaptic weights are denoted by $\omega_{im-1,im}^{(m)}$, where m, i_m denote respectively the layer and the node toward which the synapse is directed and i_{m-1} denotes the node in the previous layer from which the synapse emanates. Fig. 2 shows a typical MFNN architecture consisting of three layers.

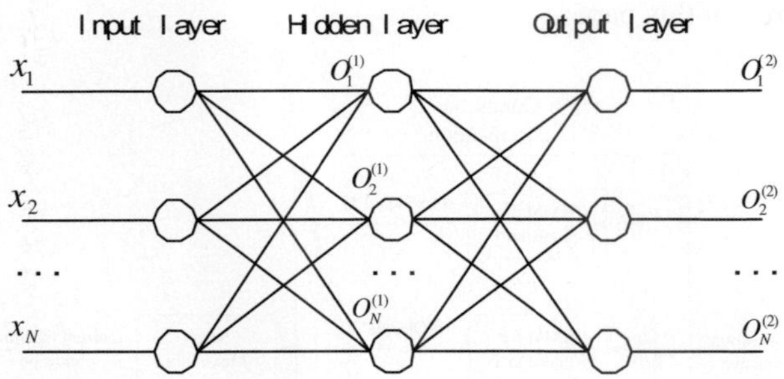

Fig. 2. Structure of a typical three-layer neural network

In this paper, a three-layer NN is used with M=1 hidden layer. Activation function $f(s)$=1/(1+exp(-s)) is chosen for nodes of hidden and output layers. More details of MFNN are given in case study.

3 Design of HMM Based Classification System

The HMM is a Markovian based model whose states cannot be observed directly. As a statistical approach to classification problem, it has been successfully applied in speech and handwriting recognition [14]. In condition classification, HMM utilizes a Markov chain to model the changing statistical characteristics that exist in machine vibration signals. In this paper, it is a discrete HMM and following items are needed to specify the model.

1. set of hidden states: $S=\{S_1, S_2,\ldots,S_N\}$, where N is the number of states in the model;
2. state transition probability distribution: $A=\{a_{ij}\}$, where $a_{ij}=P[q_{t+1}=S_j|q_t=S_i]$ for $1\leq i,j\leq N$ and q_i denotes the actual hidden state at time t;
3. set of observation symbols: $V=\{v_1, v_2,\ldots, v_M\}$, where M is the number of distinct observation symbols per hidden state;
4. observation symbol probability distribution: $B=\{b_j(k)\}$, where $b_j(k)=P[v_k$ at $t|q_t=S_j]$ for $1\leq j\leq N$, $1\leq k\leq M$;
5. initial state probability distribution: $\pi=\{\pi_i\}$, where $\pi_i=P[q_1=S_i]$ for $1\leq i\leq N$.

For convenience, we use $\lambda=(A, B, \pi)$ to describe the complete parameter set of the model. Informative features selected from Lipschitz exponent function is used as observation of HMM model. Regarding the training of HMM model $\lambda=(A, B, \pi)$, more details can be found in [5]. In this paper, it is realized by Baum-Welch algorithm, which is also called as Expectation Maximization (EM) algorithm.

An important issue in HMM modeling is the selection of hidden states. In some applications, the hidden states may have certain physical meanings; however, for most applications there is often no clear physical meanings attached to the states. We consider several HMMs corresponding to different machine conditions that we are interested in. Then, to make a decision based on an observation sequence, compute the log-likelihood for each model. If the ith model is the most likely, then declare the machine to be in the ith condition. Fig. 3 shows the structure of the classification system considered in this paper.

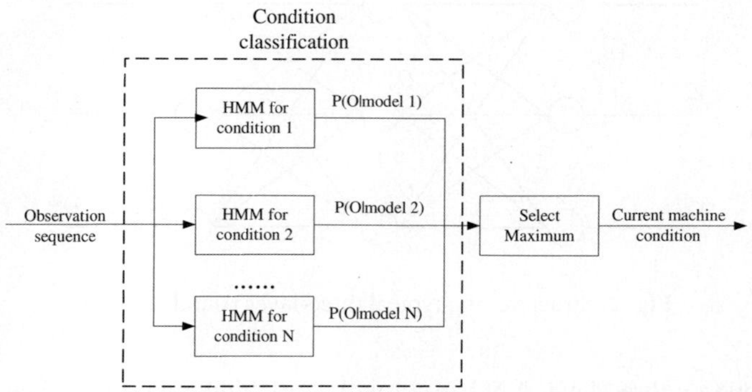

Fig. 3. The structure of the classification system

In this paper, both the state transition probability distribution A and the state-observation probability distribution B are discrete distributions. We need to specify the number of hidden states for each model since selection of hidden states will influence the performance of the model. The likelihood ratio test is a standard procedure that can be used to compare two models. However, since some models are mixtures of different Markov models, this method cannot be used directly. A more general and appealing alternative procedure is to use the Bayesian Information

Criterion (BIC) [5, 15]. The model achieving the lowest BIC value is chosen as the best one. For a model M, BIC is defined as

$$BIC(M) = -2LL(M) + p(M)\log(n) \tag{9}$$

where $LL(M)$ is the log-likelihood of the model, $p(M)$ is the total number of independent parameters in the model, and n is the number of data points in the log-likelihood.

4 Case Study

In this section, an example of gearbox vibration monitoring under laboratory environment is given to investigate the proposed condition classification system. The test rig started from brand-new state and ran until gear tooth failure. There are totally 149 data files which are collected periodically during the test. 65 of them are under normal condition and the remaining (84) under failure. Wavelet transform with the derivative of Gaussian function as wavelet function has been applied to extract Lipschitz exponent functions for each data file and dimensionality reduction based on MFNN was conducted to select the most informative features. Since the size of feature matrix is 190×1052, the number of nodes in input layer is 190. In this paper, the MFNN has three layers including one input layer, one hidden layer and one output layer. The size of feature is reduced from 190×1052 to 190×200 after dimensionality reduction.

Table 1. The result of gearbox condition classifcation with feature selection

Results of classification	Actual machinery conditions: Normal	Actual machinery conditions: Failure	Total accuracy	Total time (seconds)
Normal	56	5		
Failure	4	74	93.53%	322.18
Accuracy	93.33%	93.67%		

Table 2. The result of gearbox condition classifcation without feature selection

Results of classification	Actual machinery conditions: Normal	Actual machinery conditions: Failure	Total accuracy	Total time (seconds)
Normal	53	8		
Failure	7	71	89.21%	1092.73
Accuracy	88.33%	89.87%		

In classification step, two machinery conditions are considered, namely, normal and failure, to simplify the system. In addition, we select 5 data files from dataset of normal and failure condition, respectively, and the remaining (60 and 79, respectively) are used for testing the classification system. In order to demonstrate the performance of current research, a comparison with method in [5] is conducted in this section, which does not include feature selection step. Table 1 gives the analysis result from the experiment based on feature selection using NN. Table 2 is the analysis result without feature selection step. From the comparison, we can see that the accuracy of classification with feature selection method in this paper achieves better results and the time of computation is reduced significantly (from 1092.73 seconds to 322.18 seconds). This computation time includes training and testing of the system. The comparison demonstrates better performance with NN based feature selection applied in this paper.

5 Conclusions

In this paper, we have introduced a new machinery condition monitoring system based on the hybrid of NN and HMM techniques. This is an extension of previous work [5] in consideration of NN for feature selection and dimensionality reduction. With this step, the computation time in the next step has been greatly saved and the HMM based classification is tractable when using Lipschitz exponent function as observation. The application of Lipschitz exponent function as input of NN based classification system has been validated in [4]. In this research, condition classification was implemented by HMM based system. An example of gearbox vibration monitoring test was chosen to investigate the proposed system and analysis results show that this is an efficient scheme for machinery condition monitoring.

References

1. Pechenizkiy, M., Tsymbal, A., Puuronen, S.: PCA-based Feature Transformation for Classification Issues in Medical Diagnostics. Proceedings of the 17th IEEE Symposium on Computer-Based Medical Systems, (2004) 535-540
2. Ruck, D.W., Rogers, S.K., Kabrisky, M.: Feature selection using a multilayer perceptron. Journal of Neural Network Computing., 2 (1990) 40-48
3. Perantonis, S.J., Virvilis, V.: Dimensionality reduction using a novel neural network based feature extraction method. International Joint Conference on Neural Networks, 2 (1999) 1195-1198
4. Robertson, A.N., Farrar, C.R., Sohn, H.: Singularity detection for structural health monitoring using Holder exponents. Mechanical Systems and Signal Processing, 17(6) 2003 1163-1184
5. Miao, Q.: Application of wavelets and hidden Markov model in Condition-based Maintenance. Ph.D Thesis, University of Toronto (2005)
6. Kwon, K.C., Kim, J.H.: Accident identification in nuclear power plants using hidden Markov models. Engineering Applications of Artificial Intelligence, 12 (1999) 491-501
7. Ertunc, H.M., Loparo, K.A., Ocak, H.: Tool wear condition monitoring in drilling operations using hidden Markov models(HMM). International Journal of Machine Tools & Manufacture, 41 (2001) 1363-1384
8. Atlas, L., Ostendorf, M., Bernard, G.D.: Hidden Markov Models for Monitoring Machining Tool-Wear. IEEE ICASSP 2000, 6 (2000) 3887-3890
9. Ocak, H., Loparo, K.A.: A New Bearing Fault Detection and Diagnosis Scheme based on Hidden Markov Modeling of Vibration Signals. IEEE ICASSP 2001, 5 (2001) 3141-3144

10. Mallat, S., Hwang, W.L.: Singularity Detection and Processing with Wavelets. IEEE Transactions on Information Theory, 38(2) 1992 617-643
11. Struzik, Z.R.: Wavelet methods in (financial) time-series processing. Physica A, 296 (2001) 307-319
12. Peng, Z.K., Chu, F.L.: Application of wavelet transform in machine condition monitoring and fault diagnostics: a review with bibliography. Mechanical System and Signal Processing, 18 (2) 2004 199-221
13. Robertson, A.N., Farrar, C.R., Sohn, H.: Singularity detection for structural health monitoring using Holder exponents. Mechanical systems and Signal Processing, 17(6) 2003 1163-1184
14. Li, J., Wang, J.X., Zhao, Y.N., Yang, Z.H.: A new approach for off-line handwritten Chinese character recognition using self-adaptive HMM. Proceedings of the 5th World Congress on Intelligent Control and Automation, (2004) 4165-4168
15. User's guide, Chapter 4. March software (v. 2.10) 43-55

Power System Database Feature Selection Using a Relaxed Perceptron Paradigm

Manuel Mejía-Lavalle[1,2] and Gustavo Arroyo-Figueroa[1]

[1] Instituto de Investigaciones Eléctricas, Reforma 113, 62490 Cuernavaca, Morelos, México
[2] ITESM – Cuernavaca, Reforma 182-A, 62589 Temixco, Morelos, México
{mlavalle, garroyo}@iie.org.mx

Abstract. Feature selection has become a relevant and challenging problem for the area of knowledge discovery in database. An effective feature selection strategy can significantly reduce the data mining processing time, improve the predicted accuracy, and help to understand the induced models, as they tend to be smaller and make more sense to the user. In this paper, an effective research around the utilization of the Perceptron paradigm as a method for feature selection is carried out. The idea is training a Perceptron and then utilizing the interconnection weights as indicators of which attributes could be the most relevant. We assume that an interconnection weight close to zero indicates that the associated attribute to this weight can be eliminated because it does not contribute with relevant information in the construction of the class separator hyper-plane. The experiments were realized with 4 real and 11 synthetic databases. The results show that the proposed algorithm is a good trade-off among performance (generalization accuracy), efficiency (processing time) and feature reduction. Specifically, we apply the algorithm to a Mexican Electrical Billing database with satisfactory accuracy, efficiency and feature reduction results.

1 Introduction

Data mining is mainly applied to large amounts of stored data to look for the implicit knowledge hidden within this information. To take advantage of the enormous amount of information currently available in many databases, algorithms and tools specialized in the automatic discovery of hidden knowledge within this information have been developed. This process of non-trivial extraction of relevant information that is implicit in the data is known as Knowledge Discovery in Databases (KDD), in which the data mining phase plays a central role in this process.

It has been noted, however, that when very large databases are going to get mined, the mining algorithms get very slow, requiring too much time to process the information. Another scenario is when acquiring some attributes is expensive. One way to approach this problem is to reduce the amount of data before applying the mining process. In particular, the pre-processing method of feature selection, applied to the data before mining, has been shown to be promising because it can eliminate the irrelevant or redundant attributes that cause the mining tools to become inefficient

A. Gelbukh and C.A. Reyes-Garcia (Eds.): MICAI 2006, LNAI 4293, pp. 522 – 531, 2006.

and ineffective. At the same time, it can preserve-increase the classification quality of the mining algorithm (accuracy) [1].

Although there are many feature selection algorithms reported in the specialized literature, none of them are perfect: some of them are effective, but very costly in computational time (e.g., *wrapper* methods), and others are fast, but less effective in the feature selection task (e.g., *filter* methods).

Specifically, wrapper methods, although effective in eliminating irrelevant and redundant attributes, are very slow because they apply the mining algorithm many times, changing the number of attributes each time of execution as they follow some search and stop criteria [2]. Filter methods are more efficient; they use some form of *correlation* measure between individual attributes and the class [3][4]; however, because they measure the relevance of each isolated attribute, they cannot detect if redundant attributes exist, or if a combination of two (or more) attributes, apparently irrelevant when analyzed independently, are indeed relevant toghether [5].

In this article, we propose a feature selection method, in which the trained Perceptron interconnection weights are utilized like a measure of attribute importance. The idea is to eliminate the attributes whose associated scale factor is close to zero. Similar idea is used in the Principal Component Analysis technique (PCA) and in the Support Vector Machine (SVM) variants for Feature Selection (SVM-FS).

To cover these topics, the article is organized as follows: Section 2 surveys related work; Section 3 introduces our feature selection method; Section 4 details the experiments, emphasizing over the Mexican electric billing database; conclusions and future research directions are given in Section 5.

2 Related Work

Although there are many feature selection algorithms reported in the specialized literature, none of them are perfect: some of them are effective, but very costly in computational time (e.g., wrappers methods), and others are fast, but less effective in the feature selection task (e.g., filter methods). Wrapper methods, although effective in eliminating irrelevant and redundant attributes, are very slow because they apply the mining algorithm many times, changing the number of attributes each time of execution as they follow some search and stop criteria [2]. Filter methods are more efficient; they use some form of *information gain* measurement between individual attributes and the class [3]; however, in general they measure the relevance of each isolated attribute, so they cannot detect if redundant attributes exist, or if a combination of two (or more) attributes, apparently irrelevant when analyzed independently, indeed are relevant [4][5].

A line of research is using the scale factors produced by, for example, the Principal Component Analysis technique (PCA) the Support Vector Machine (SVM) variants for Feature Selection (SVM-FS) or the Neural Network (NN) paradigms. These approaches all eliminate the attributes whose associated scale factors are close to zero.

Specifically, in the area of NN, there exist several methods for post learning pruning interconnection weights, for example Optimal Brain Damage or Optimal

Brain Surgeon [6]. The objective of these approaches is to obtain a simplified NN, conserving good or similar classification power of the complete NN, and therefore, is not directly focused on the feature selection task. Brank et.al. [7] conducted a study to observe how several scale factor feature selection methods interact with several classification algorithms; however, in this research, no information about processing time and feature reduction is presented.

The next section presents the proposed feature selection algorithm based on a relaxed Perceptron paradigm. This method is a trade-off among performance (generalization or predicted accuracy), efficiency (processing time) and feature reduction.

3 Proposed Feature Selection Method

The method to explore is the classic Rosenblatt´s Perceptron, as strategy for relevant feature selection. We propose to use a "soft" or relaxed Perceptron (similar to [8]), in the sense that it can accept some percentage of misclassified instances, where the training stopping criterion is when no accuracy improvement is obtained. Specifically, we propose to use the generalization accuracy (Acc) and/or Balanced Error Rate (BER) as criteria to evaluate the solution quality. To obtain *Acc* ratio we apply:

$$Acc = number\ of\ instances\ predicted\ correctly\ /\ total\ instances \tag{1}$$

To obtain *BER* we use:

$$BER = 0.5\ (PIW\ /\ PI\ +\ NIW\ /\ NI\ ) \tag{2}$$

where *PIW* means "number of positive instances predicted wrong", *PI* is the "total of positive instances", *NIW* means "number of negative instances predicted wrong", and *NI* is the "total of negative instances". The neural net that we used has: a) as many inputs-interconnection weights as features, or attributes, the dataset contain, b) only one neuron with a step activation function, and c) only one output. To obtain the Perceptron output *S,* we use the equation:

$$S = U\ \{\ \Sigma_i\ W_i\ E_{ij}\ \} \tag{3}$$

where W_i are the *i* interconnection weights; E_{ij} is the input vector (with *i* elements) that form an instance *j*; and *U* is a step function that outputs *1* if $\Sigma_i W_i E_{ij} > \theta$ and *0* otherwise. θ is the Perceptron threshold.

To train the Perceptron we apply the equations:

$$W_i\ (t+1) = W_i\ (t)\ +\ \{\ \alpha(\ T - S\ )\ E_{ij}\ \} \tag{4}$$

$$\theta\ (t+1) = \theta\ (t)\ +\ \{\ -(\ T - S\ )\ \alpha\ \} \tag{5}$$

where *T* is the desired output and α is the learning rate: this user parameter can take values between 0 and 1.

Although there exist more sophisticated procedures in the area of neural network pruning [6], we choose this idea because of its simplicity (that implies efficiency) and direct application to feature selection (because of the direct relation between each feature and its Perceptron interconnection weight).

With the Feature Selection Perceptron (FS-P) we expect:

a) To use less amount of memory, because a Perceptron only requires to store as many interconnection weights as "n" attributes the database has, as opposed to PCA that builds "n^2" matrix,
b) To drop the processing time because, as opposed to SVM-FS that involves solving a quadratic optimization problem, the Perceptron converges fast to a approximate solution,
c) To avoid to carry out an exhaustive exploration (or close to exhaustive), that is to say, without having to evaluate multiple attribute subset combinations, as the wrapper methods do (they evaluate multiple subsets applying the same algorithm that will be used in the data mining phase), or some filter methods, that employ different metric to evaluate diverse attribute subsets, and that use a variety of search strategies like *Branch & Bound, Sequential Greedy, Best-First, Forward Selection, Sequential Backward Elimination, Floating, Random Search*, among others,
d) Implicitly capture the inter-dependences among attributes, as opposed to filter-ranking methods, that evaluate only the importance of one attribute against the class, like *F-score, Symmetrical Uncertainty, Correlation, Entropy, Information Gain*, etc.
e) The Perceptron can be used as a classifier too, with the possible advantage to improve accuracy because this link between the *feature selector - classifier* algorithms, that allows a implicit wrapper schema.

To execute the overall feature selection process we apply the following procedure:

FS-Perceptron (FS-P) Procedure

Given a numeric dataset with *D* attributes previously normalized [0,1], and *N* randomly chosen instances,

1. Let *AccOld* = 0 (generalization accuracy), WithoutImprove = *ni* (number of accepted epochs without accuracy improvement)
2. While *AccNew* better than *AccOld* (*ni* times)
   a. Train a (soft) Perceptron (initial weights in zero)
   b. Test after each epoch, and obtain *AccNew*
   c. If *AccNew* better than *AccOld*: save weights and do *AccOld* = *AccNew*
3. Drop attributes with small absolute interconnection weights
4. Use the *d* remain attributes ($d < D$) to create a model as the predictor with Weka´s J4.8 classifier[1] [9].

Then, the objective of this paper is to show the exploratory experimentation realized to verify/ invalidate these assumptions (hypothesis).

4 Experiments

We conducted several experiments with 11 synthetic and 4 real datasets to empirically evaluate if FS-P can do better in selecting features than other well-known

[1] We experimented using more classifiers, and we obtained similar results.

feature selection algorithms, in terms of generalized accuracy, processing time and feature reduction. We choose synthetic datasets in our experiments because the relevant features and their inter-dependencies are known beforehand.

4.1 Experimentation Details

The experimentation objective is to observe the FS-P behavior related to classification quality, feature reduction and response time.

As first experimentation phase, 10 synthetic dataset, each of them with different levels of complexity was used. To obtain the 10 datasets we use the functions described in [10]. Each of the datasets has nine attributes (1.salary, 2.commission, 3.age, 4.elevel, 5.car, 6.zipcode, 7.hvalue, 8.hyears, and 9.loan) plus the class attribute (with class label Group "A" or "B"); each dataset has 10,000 instances. The values of the features of each instance were generated randomly according to the distributions described in [10]. For each instance, a class label was determined according to the rules that define the functions. We experiment also with the corrAL synthetic dataset [11], that has four relevant attributes (A0, A1, B0, B1), one irrelevant (I) and one redundant (R); the class attribute is defined by the function Y = $(A0 \wedge A1) \vee (B0 \wedge B1)$.

Additionally, we test our proposed method with four real databases. The first one is a database with 24 attributes and 2,770 instances; this database contains information of Mexican electric billing customers, where we expect to obtain patterns of behavior of illicit customers. The second is the Ionosphere dataset taken form the UCI repository [12] with 34 attributes and 351 instances.

Finally, we experiment with two datasets taken from the NIPS 2003 feature selection challenge[2]. These datasets have very high dimensionality but relatively few instances. Specifically, Madelon database has 500 features and 2,000 instances and Gisette dataset has 5,000 features and 6,000 instances.

In order to compare the results obtained with FS-P, we use Weka´s [9] implementation of ReliefF, OneR and ChiSquared feature selection algorithms. These implementations were run using Weka´s default values, except for ReliefF, where we define 5 as the neighborhood number, for a more efficient response time. Additionally, we experiment with several Elvira´s [13] filter-ranking methods.

To select the best ranking attributes, we use a threshold defined by the largest *gap* between two consecutive ranked attributes, according to [11] (e.g., a *gap* greater than the average *gap* among all the *gaps*).

In the case of FS-P (codified with C language), we set the learning rate α to 0.6, the maximum epochs equal to 500, and the number of epochs without accuracy improve *ni* to 15, for all the experiments. All the experiments were executed in a personal computer with a Pentium 4 processor, 1.5 GHz, and 250 Mbytes in RAM. In the following sub-Section the obtained results are shown.

4.2 Experimental Results with Synthetic Databases

The results of applying FS-P to 10 synthetic datasets are shown in Table 1. We can observe that the average processing time (column 2) and epochs (column 3) is

---

[2] http://www.nipsfsc.ecs.soton.ac.uk/datasets/

Table 1. FS-P with 10 Synthetic Databases

Synthetic Database	FS-P time (secs)	FS-P Epoch	FS-P Acc (%)	FS-P+J4.8 Acc (%) 10-fCV	FS-P Attributes Selected	Oracle
1	3	40	47	100	3-7	3
2	2	24	55	100	1-2-3	1-3
3	2	18	61	68	4	3-4
4	2	17	63	84	1-3	1-3-4
5	3	34	65	82	9	1-3-9
6	4	47	66	99	1-2-3	1-2-3
7	6	59	100	98	9-1-2	1-2-9
8	4	39	100	100	1-2-4	1-2-4
9	4	48	100	97	9-1-2-4	1-2-4-9
10	3	37	99	99	4-8-7-1-2	1-2-4-7-8-9
Avg.	**3.3**	**36.3**	**75.6**	**92.7**	(2.7)	(3)

acceptable. The generalized accuracy obtained for FS-P is bad (column 4) but the resulting average accuracy of apply the selected features by FS-P to the J4.8 classifier (with 10-fold cross validation) is good (column 5). In columns 6 and 7 we can see that the features selected by FS-P are equal or near to the perfect attributes (Oracle column), in almost all cases, except for datasets 3 and 5; the average number of features selected is similar (2.7 vs. 3).

Next, we use the selected features obtained by several feature selection methods as input to the decision tree induction algorithm J4.8 included in the Weka tool. J4.8 is the last version of C4.5, which is one of the best-known induction algorithms used in data mining. We use 10-fold cross validation in order to obtain the average test accuracy for each feature subset (in all cases, we obtain similar results using *BER* as quality measure criterion). The results are shown in Table 2.

The column "Oracle/All" represents a perfect feature selection method (it selects exactly the same features that each dataset function uses to generate the class label and, in this case, is equal to the obtained accuracy if we use all the attributes). For dataset 8, only OneR cannot determine any feature subset, because ranks all attributes equally.

From Table 2 we can see that the FS-P average accuracy is better than several feature selection methods, while worse than only ReliefF.

With respect to the processing time, this is shown in Table 3. We observe that, although FS-P is computationally more expensive than ChiSquared and other filter-ranking Elvira´s methods, these algorithms cannot detect good relevant attributes or some attribute inter-dependencies; on the other hand, FS-P was faster than ReliefF, maintained good generalized accuracy. To have a better idea of the FS-P performance, we can compare the results presented previously against the results produced by an exhaustive wrapper approach. In this case, we can calculate that, if the average time required to obtain a classification tree using J4.8 is 1.1 seconds, and if we multiply this by all the possible attribute combinations, then we will obtain that 12.5 days, theoretically, would be required to conclude such a process.

Table 2. J4.8´s accuracies (%) with features selected by each method (10 Synthetic DBs)

Synthetic Database	**Method**											
	Oracle/All	ReliefF	**FS-Percep**	ChiSquar	Bhattach	Mut.Infor	KullbackLeibler-1	Matusita	OneR	KullbackLeibler-2	Euclidean	Shannon
1	100	100	**100**	100	100	100	100	100	100	67	100	67
2	100	100	**100**	73	73	73	73	73	73	73	73	100
3	100	100	**68**	100	100	100	100	100	100	100	68	59
4	100	90	**84**	84	84	84	84	84	84	84	84	84
5	100	100	**82**	74	74	82	74	74	74	82	74	60
6	99	99	**99**	99	99	99	87	87	99	68	64	69
7	98	98	**98**	98	94	86	98	86	86	86	88	94
8	100	100	**100**	100	99	99	100	99	-	99	100	98
9	97	94	**97**	97	92	85	85	92	85	85	88	85
10	99	80	**99**	99	97	97	99	97	98	97	97	80
Avg.	99.3	96.1	**92.7**	92.4	91.2	90.5	89.8	89.2	84.9	84.1	83.6	79.6

Table 3. Average processing time for each method in seconds (10 Synthetic Datasets)

Exhaustive Wrapper	ReliefF	OneR	**FS-P**	ChiSquared and Elvira
1,085,049 (12.5 days)	573 (9.55 mins.)	8	**3.3**	1

When we test with the corrAL synthetic dataset, FS-P was the only that can remove the redundant attribute (Table 4); results for FCBF and Focus methods was taken from [11]. Because the corrAL is a small dataset, processing time in all cases is near to zero seconds, and thus omitted.

Table 4. Features selected by different methods (corrAL dataset)

Method	**Features selected**
FS-Perceptron	**A0, A1,B0, B1**
ReliefF	R, A0, A1, B0, B1
OneR	R, A1, A0, B0, B1
ChiSquared	R, A1, A0, B0, B1
Symmetrical Uncertainty	R, A1, A0, B0, B1
$FCFB_{(log)}$	R, A0
$FCFB_{(0)}$	R, A0, A1, B0, B1
CFS	A0,A1,B0,B1,R
Focus	R

4.3 Experimental Results with Real Databases

Testing over the Electric Billing database, we use the selected features for each method as input to the decision tree induction algorithm J4.8 included in the Weka tool. We notice that FS-P obtains similar accuracy as Kullback-Leibler-2, but with

Table 5. J4.8´s accuracies with features selected by each method (Electric Billing database)

Method	Total features selected	Accuracy (%) 10-fold cross val	Pre-processing time
Kullback-Leibler 2	9	97.50	6 secs.
FS-Perceptron	**11**	**97.29**	**3 secs.**
All attributes	24	97.25	0 secs.
ChiSquared	20	97.18	9 secs.
OneR	9	95.95	41 secs.
ReliefF	4	93.89	14.3 mins.
Euclidean distance	4	93.89	5 secs.
Shannon entropy	18	93.71	4 secs.
Bhattacharyya	3	90.21	6 secs.
Matusita distance	3	90.21	5 secs.
Kullback-Leibler 1	4	90.10	6 secs.
Mutual Information	4	90.10	4 secs.

less processing time (Table 5). Attributes 22, 23 and 24 are random attributes and, following [14], we use this information to mark the threshold between relevant and irrelevant attributes.

Testing over the Ionosphere database, FS-P obtains similar accuracy as ReliefF, but with less processing time and good feature reduction (Table 6).

Table 6. J4.8´s accuracies with features selected by each method (Ionosphere database)

Method	Total features selected	Accuracy (%) 10-fold cross val	Pre-processing time
ReliefF	6	92.8	4 secs.
FS-Perceptron	**5**	**92.5**	**0.1 secs.**
All attributes	34	91.4	0 secs.
Mutual Information	3	86.1	1 secs.
Kullback-Leibler 1	2	86.0	1 secs.
OneR	4	85.1	1 secs.
Kullback-Leibler 2	3	83.4	1 secs.
Bhattacharyya	2	83.4	1 secs.
Matusita distance	2	83.4	2 secs.
Euclidean distance	2	82.9	1 secs.
ChiSquared	2	80.6	1 secs.
Shannon entropy	2	80.6	1 secs.

In order to compare our results with real very large databases, we experiment with Madelon and Gisette NIPS 2003 challenge datasets. In these cases we can not apply Weka or Elvira feature selection tools because they ran out of memory; so, for comparison, we use the results presented by Chen et.al [15]: they apply SVM with a radial basis function kernel as feature selection method. Table 7 show results for Madelon and Gisette datasets (N/A means information not mention in [15]).

From Table 7 we can observe that the obtained *BER* using FS-P is similar when SVM is applied; on the other hand both, accuracy and *BER,* are poor. The reason for this bad result is because Madelon is a dataset with clusters placed on the summits of a five dimensional hypercube, so, in some sense, is a variation of the XOR problem, a non-linear separable classification problem. Thus, FS-P and SVM (still with a kernel function) fails with this database.

In the case of Gisette, that contains instances of handwritten digits “4” and “9”; from Table 7 we can see that SVM obtains a superior *BER,* but FS-P achieves an acceptable BER and accuracy, using few attributes (64 against 913).

Table 7. Accuracies and *BER* with features selected by each method (Madelon- Gisette)

Database	Method	Features Total (%)	Accuracy (%) 10-fold cross val	BER	Pre-process. time
Madelon	**FS-Perceptr**	**21 (4. 2%)**	**58.35**	**0.4165**	**48 secs.**
	SVM	13 (2. 6%)	N/A	0.4017	N/A
Gisette	**FS-Perceptr**	**64 (1. 3%)**	**94. 5**	**0.0549**	**3. 3 mins.**
	SVM	913 (18. 2%)	N/A	0.0210	N/A

5 Conclusions and Future Work

We have presented an algorithm for feature selection called as FS-P that is good trade-off among generalization accuracy, processing time and feature reduction. To validate the algorithm we used 11 synthetic databases, 2 real databases, and Madelon and Gisette NIPS 2003 challenge datasets.

The results show that FS-P represent a good alternative, compared to other methods, because its acceptable processing time, accuracy and good performance in the feature selection task. For the case of the real electric billing database, FS-P obtains similar accuracy and feature reduction as Kullback-Leibler-2, but with the half of processing time.

The proposed FS-P algorithm has several advantages: (1) it requires a linear amount of memory; (2) its generalization accuracy and processing time is competitive against other methods; (3) does not realize exhaustive or combinatorial search; (4) finds some attribute inter-dependencies; and (5) obtains acceptable feature reductions. The main disadvantage is its limitation to classify only linear separable datasets.

Some future works arise with respect to FS-P improvement. For example: apply kernel functions to overcome the linear separability class limitation; try with other learning stopping criteria; realize experiments using a metric (e.g., *F-score*) to do a first attribute elimination, and then apply FS-P. Another future work will be the application of the formalism to other very large power system databases such as the national power generation performance database and the Mexican electric energy distribution database.

References

1. Guyon, I., Elisseeff, A., An introduction to variable and feature selection, Journal of machine learning research, 3, 2003, pp. 1157-1182.
2. Kohavi, R., John, G., Wrappers for feature subset selection, Artificial Intelligence Journal, Special issue on relevance, 1997, pp. 273-324.
3. Piramuthu, S., Evaluating feature selection methods for learning in data mining applications, Proc. 31st annual Hawaii Int. conf. on system sciences, 1998, pp. 294-301.
4. Molina, L., Belanche, L., Nebot, A., FS algorithms, a survey and experimental evaluation, IEEE Int.conf.data mining, Maebashi City Japan, 2002, pp. 306-313.
5. Mitra, S., et.al., Data mining in soft computing framework: a survey, IEEE Trans. on neural networks, vol. 13, no. 1, January, 2002, pp. 3-14.
6. Jutten, C., Fambon, O., Pruning methods: a review, European symposium on artificial neural networks, April 1995, pp. 129-140.
7. Brank, J., Grobelnik, M., Milic-Frayling, N. & Mladenic, D., Interaction of feature selection methods and linear classification models. Proceedings of the ICML-02 Workshop on Text Learning, Sydney, AU, 2002.
8. Gallant, S.I.: Perceptron-Based Learning Algorithms, in IEEE Transactions on Neural Networks, 1, 1990, pp. 179-191.
9. www. cs.waikato.ac.nz/ml/weka, 2004.
10. Agrawal, R., Imielinski, T, Swami, A., Database mining: a performance perspective, IEEE Trans. Knowledge data engrg. Vol. 5, no. 6, 1993, pp. 914-925.
11. Yu, L., Liu, H., Efficient feature selection via analysis of relevance and redundancy, Journal of Machine Learning Research 5, 2004, pp. 1205-1224.
12. Newman, D.J. & Hettich, S. & Blake, C.L. & Merz, C.J. UCI Repository of machine learning databases [http://www.ics.uci.edu/~mlearn/MLRepository.html]. Irvine, CA: University of California, Department of Information and Computer Science, 1998.
13. www. ia.uned.es/~elvira/ , 2004.
14. Stoppiglia, H., Dreyfus, G., et.al., Ranking a random feature for variable and feature selection, Journal of machine learning research, 3, 2003, pp. 1399-1414.
15. Chen,Y., Lin,C., Combining SVMs with various feature selection strategies. To appear in the book "Feature extraction, foundations and applications", Guyon, I. (ed), 2005.

Feature Elimination Approach Based on Random Forest for Cancer Diagnosis

Ha-Nam Nguyen[1], Trung-Nghia Vu[1], Syng-Yup Ohn[1], Young-Mee Park[2], Mi Young Han[3], and Chul Woo Kim[4]

[1] Dept. of Computer and Information Engineering, Hankuk Aviation University, Seoul, Korea
{namnhvn, nghiavtr}@gmail.com, syohn@hau.ac.kr
[2] Dept. of Cell Stress Biology, Roswell Park Cancer Institute, SUNY Buffalo, NY, USA
Young-Mee.Park@roswellpark.org
[3] Bioinfra Inc., Seoul, Korea
myhan703@hanmail.net
[4] Dept. of Pathology, Tumor Immunity Medical Research Center, Seoul National University College of Medicine, Seoul, Korea
cwkim@plaza.snu.ac.kr

Abstract. The performance of learning tasks is very sensitive to the characteristics of training data. There are several ways to increase the effect of learning performance including standardization, normalization, signal enhancement, linear or non-linear space embedding methods, etc. Among those methods, determining the relevant and informative features is one of the key steps in the data analysis process that helps to improve the performance, reduce the generation of data, and understand the characteristics of data. Researchers have developed the various methods to extract the set of relevant features but no one method prevails. Random Forest, which is an ensemble classifier based on the set of tree classifiers, turns out good classification performance. Taking advantage of Random Forest and using wrapper approach first introduced by Kohavi *et al*, we propose a new algorithm to find the optimal subset of features. The Random Forest is used to obtain the feature ranking values. And these values are applied to decide which features are eliminated in the each iteration of the algorithm. We conducted experiments with two public datasets: colon cancer and leukemia cancer. The experimental results of the real world data showed that the proposed method results in a higher prediction rate than a baseline method for certain data sets and also shows comparable and sometimes better performance than the feature selection methods widely used.

1 Introduction

Determining the relevant features is a combinatorial task in various fields of machine learning such as text mining, bioinformatics, pattern recognition, etc. Several scholars have developed various methods to extract the relevant features but none is superior in general. A good feature selection method may increase performance of the learning methods [1, 2]. The feature selection technique helps to eliminate noises or non-representative features which may impede the recognition process.

A. Gelbukh and C.A. Reyes-Garcia (Eds.): MICAI 2006, LNAI 4293, pp. 532 – 542, 2006.

Recently, Breiman proposed random forest(RF), an ensemble classifier consisting of a set of classification and regression trees(CART)[3]. This method turns out better results compared to other classifier including Adaboost, Support Vector Machine and Neural Network. Also, RF was used as a feature selection method, RF was used to rank the feature importance in [4] and applied for relevance feedback [5]. In this paper, we propose a new feature selection method based on random forest. The proposed method obtains the set of features via the feature ranking criterion. This criterion re-evaluates the importance of features according to the Gini index [6, 7] and the correlation of training and validation accuracies which are obtained from RF algorithm. Thus both feature contribution and correlation of training error are taken into account in our method. We applied this algorithm to classify several datasets such as colon cancer and leukemia cancer. The method resulted in the optimal feature set with better classification accuracy than simple ranking method and showed comparable and sometimes better results than other methods.

The rest of this paper is organized as follows. In section 2, we introduce the feature selection problem. In Section 3 we briefly review RF and its characteristics that will be used in the proposed method. Our new feature elimination method will be proposed in Section 4. Section 5 shows the experimental design of the proposed method and the analysis of the obtained results. Section 6 is our conclusion.

2 Feature Selection Problem

In this section, we briefly summarize the feature selection methodologies. The feature selection approach has been regarded as an effective way to remove redundant and irrelevant features. Thus it increases the efficiency of the learning task and improves the learning performance such as learning time, convergence rate, accuracy, etc. Much research effort has been focused on the feature selection literature [1, 2, 8-11]. In the following, we briefly introduce the feature selection problems.

There are two ways to determine the starting point in a searching space. The first strategy might start with nothing and successively adds relevance features called *forward selection*. Another one, named *backward elimination*, starts with all features and successively removes irrelevant ones. There is a heuristic strategy combining above two strategies called *bi-directional* selection [12]. In this case, the feature subset starts with null, full or randomly produced feature subset, then adds the current best feature into or removes the current worst feature from it. By that way it given the best guideline values in each iteration, until a prearranged performance requirement is met.

There are two different approaches used for feature selection method, i.e. filter approach and wrapper approach [1, 2]. The filter approach considers the feature selection process as a precursor stage of learning algorithms. One of the disadvantages of this approach is that there is no relationship between the feature selection process and the performance of learning algorithms. The second approach uses a machine learning algorithm to measure the goodness of the set of selected features. It evaluates this goodness of the set of selected features based on the performance measures of the learning algorithm such as accuracy, recall and precision values. The disadvantage of this approach is high computational cost. Some researchers proposed methods that can speed up the evaluating process to decrease this cost. Some studies used both filter and wrapper approaches in their algorithms called hybrid approaches [9, 10, 13-15]. Each feature subset is evaluated in the approaches. The filter model uses evaluation functions to evaluate the classification performances of feature subsets. There are many evaluation functions such as feature importance [1-3, 7], Gini [3, 6, 7], information gain [6], the ratio of information gain [6], etc. The wrapper model uses a learning accuracy for evaluation. In the approaches using wrapper models, all samples should be divided into two sets, i.e. training set and testing set. Then, the algorithm runs on the training set, and applies the learning result on the testing set to obtain the prediction accuracy. They usually use the cross validation technique to avoid the effect of sample division. The optimal feature set is found by searching on the feature space. In this space, each state represents a feature subset, and the size of the searching space for n features is $O(2^n)$, so it is impractical to search the whole space exhaustively, unless n is small. We should use the heuristic function to find the state with the highest evaluation. Some techniques introduced for this purpose are Hill-climbing, Best-first search, etc.

3 Random Forest

Random Forest is an ensemble classifier consisting of a set of CART classifiers using bagging mechanism [6]. By bagging, each node of trees only selects a small subset of features for a split, which enables the algorithm to create classifiers for high dimensional data very quickly. One has to specify the number of randomly selected features (*mtry*) at each split. The default value is *sqrt*(*p*) for the classification where *p* is the number of features. The Gini index [6, 7] is used as the splitting criterion. The largest possible tree is grown and not pruned. One should choose the big enough number of trees (*ntree*) to ensure that every input feature is predicted at least several times. The root node of each tree in the forest keeps a set of bootstrapped samples from the original data as the training set to build a tree. The rest of the samples, called out-of-bag(OOB) samples are used to estimate the performance of classification. The out-of-bag (OOB) estimation is based on the classification of the set of OOB samples which is roughly one third of the original samples.

The OOB estimation error can be used to calculate the generation error of the combined ensemble of trees as well as estimate for the correction and strength, which is explained as follows. We first assume a method for building a classifier H from any training set. We can construct classifiers $H(x, T_k)$ based on the bootstrap training set T_k from the given training set T. The out-of-bag classification of each sample (x, y) in training set is defined as the aggregate of the vote only over those classifiers for which T_k does not contain that sample. Thus the out-of-bag estimation of the generalization error is the error rate of the out-of-bag classifier on the training set.

The Gini index is defined as squared probabilities of membership for each target category in the node.

$$gini(N) = \frac{1}{2}\left(1 - \sum_j p(\omega_j)^2\right) \tag{1}$$

where $p(\omega_j)$ is the relative frequency of class ω_j at node N. It means if all the samples are on the same category, the impurity is zero; otherwise it is positive value. Some algorithm such as CART, SLIQ, and RF were used Gini index as splitting criterion [3, 6, 7, 16]. It tries to minimize the *impurity* of the nodes resulting from splitting based on following formula

$$gini_{split} = \sum_{i=1}^{k} \frac{n_i}{n} gini(i) \tag{2}$$

where k is the number of partitions when a node N is split into, n_i is the number of samples at child i and n be the total number of samples at node N. In Random forest the Gini decreases for each individual variable over all trees in the forest gives a fast variable important that is often very consistent with the permutation importance measure [3, 7]. In this paper we used the Gini decreases of variable as a component of the importance criteria.

4 The Proposed Algorithm

Our method uses *Random Forest* to estimate the performance consisting of the cross validation accuracy and the importance of each feature in the training data set. The irrelevant feature(s) are eliminated and only the important features are survived by means of feature ranking value. To deal with over-fitting problem, we apply n-fold cross validation technique to minimize the generalization error [6].

When computing the ranking criteria in wrapper approaches, they usually concentrate on the accuracies of the features, but not much on the correlation of the features. A feature with good ranking criteria may not turn out a good result. Also, the combination of several features with good ranking criteria may not give out a good result. To remedy the problem, we propose a procedure named Dynamic Feature Elimination based on RF (DFE-RF).

1. Train data by Random Forest with the cross validation
2. Calculate the ranking criterion for all features F_i^{rank} where i=1..n (n is the number of features).
3. Remove a feature by using *DynamicFeatureElimination* function (for computational reasons, it may be more efficient if we remove several features at a time)
4. Back to step 1 until reach the desired criteria.

In step 1, we use Random Forest with n-fold cross validation to train the classifier. In the jth cross validation, we will obtain a set of (F_j A_j^{learn} $A_j^{validation}$) that are the feature importance, the learning accuracy and the validation accuracy respectively. We will use those values to compute the ranking criterion in step 2.

The core of our algorithm is presented in step 2. In this step, we use the results from step 1 to build the ranking criterion which will be used in step 3. The ranking criterion of feature i^{th} is computed as follow

$$F_i^{rank} = \sum_{j=1}^{n} F_{i,j} \times \frac{(A_j^{learn} + A_j^{validation})}{| A_j^{learn} - A_j^{validation} | + \varepsilon} \tag{3}$$

where j=1,.., n is the number of cross validation folders; $F_{i,j}$, A_j^{learn} and $A_j^{validation}$ are the feature importance in terms of the node impurity which can be computed by Gini impurity, the learning accuracy and the validation accuracy of feature *j*-th obtained from *RandomForest* module, respectively. ε is the real number with very small value. The first factor ($F_{i,j}$) is presented the Gini decrease for each feature over all trees in the forest when we train data by RF. Obviously, the higher decrease of $F_{i,j}$ is obtained, the better rank of feature we have [3, 6] . We use the second factor to deal with the overfitting issue [6] as well as the desire of high accuracy. The numerator of the factor presents for our desire to have a high accuracy. The larger value we get, the better the rank of the feature is. We want to have a high accuracy in learning and also want not too fit the training data which so-called overfitting problem. To solve this issue, we apply the *n*-folder cross validation technique [6]. We can see that the less difference between the learning accuracy and the validation accuracy, the more stability of accuracy. In the other words, the purpose of the denominator is to reduce overfitting. In the case of the learning accuracy is equal to the validation accuracy, the difference is equal to 0, we use ε with very small value to avoid the fraction to be ∞. We also want to choose the feature with both high stability and high accuracy. To deal with this problem, the procedure chooses a feature subset only if the validation of this selected feature subset is higher than the validation of the previous selected feature set. This heuristic method ensures that the chosen feature set always has the better accuracy. As a result of step 2, we have an ordered-list of ranking criterion of features.

In step 3, we propose our feature elimination strategy based on the backward elimination approach. The proposed feature elimination strategy depends on both ranking criterion and the validation accuracy. The ranking criterion makes the order of features be eliminated and the validation accuracy is used to decide whether the chosen subset of features is permanently eliminated. In normal case, our method eliminates features having the smallest value of ranking criterion. The new subset is validated by *RandomForest* module. The obtained validation accuracy plays a role of decision making. It is used to evaluate whether the selected subset is accepted as a new candidate of features. If the obtained validation accuracy is lower than the previous selected subset accuracy, it tries to eliminate other features based on their rank values.

This iteration is stopped whenever the validation accuracy of the new subset is higher than the previous selected subset accuracy. If there is either no feature to create new subset or no better validation accuracy, the current subset of features is considered as the final result of our learning algorithm. Otherwise the procedure goes back to step 1. The set of features, which is a result of learning phase, is used as a filter to reduce the dimension of the test dataset before performing predicting those samples in classification phase.

5 Experiments

Our proposed algorithm was coded using R language (http://www.r-project.org; R Development Core Team, 2004), using *RandomForest* packages (maintained by A. Liaw and M. Wiener). We tested the proposed algorithm with several dataset include two public datasets (leukemia and colon cancer) to validate our approach. The learning and validation accuracies were determined by means of 4-fold cross validation. The data were randomly split into training sets and testing sets. In this paper, we used RF with the original dataset as the base-line method. The proposed method and the base-line method were executed with the same training and testing datasets to compare the efficiency of the two methods. Those implementations were done 50 times to test the consistency of obtained results.

5.1 Colon Cancer

The colon cancer dataset contains gene expression information extracted from DNA microarrays [1] (Availble at: http://sdmc.lit.org.sg/GEDatasets/Data/ColonTumo r.zip). The dataset consists of 62 samples in which 22 are normal samples and 40 are cancer tissue samples, each has 2000 features. The data was randomly divided into a training set of 50 samples and a testing set of 12 for 50 times.

Our final results were averaged over these 50 independent trials (Fig. 1). In our experiments, we use the default value for the *mtry* parameter (see Sec. 3) and the *ntree* parameter was tried with some different values of 500, 1000, 1500, and 2000. The average of classification results with different values of *ntree* are depicted in Fig. 2.

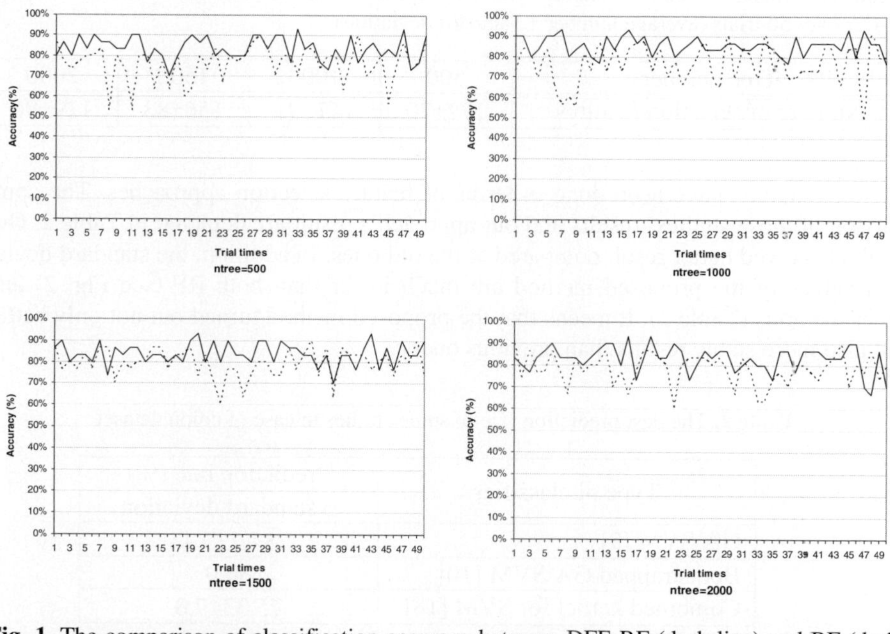

Fig. 1. The comparison of classification accuracy between DFE-RF (dash line) and RF (dash-dot line) via 50 trials with parameter *ntree* = {500, 1000, 1500, 2000} in case of colon dataset

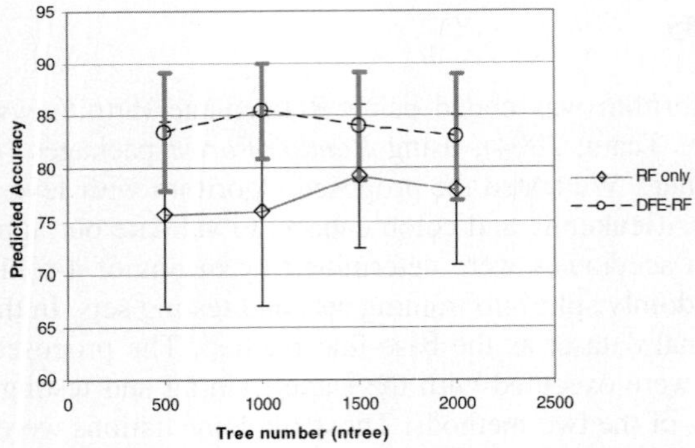

Fig. 2. The average classification rate of colon cancer over 50 trials (average % classification accuracy ±standard deviation)

The classification accuracies of the proposed algorithm are significantly better than the baseline one.

Table 1 presents the average number of selected features obtained from all experiments. The proposed method achieves the accuracy of 85.5% when performing on about 141 genes predictors retained after using the DRF-RF procedure. This number of genes only makes up about 7.1% (141/2000) of the overall genes. The method not only increases the classification accuracy but also reduces the standard deviation values (Fig. 2).

Table 1. Number of selected feature with different tree number parameters in case of colon cancer over 50 trials (average number ± standard deviation)

Tree number	500	1000	1500	2000
Number of selection features	172±70	141±91	156±83	129±96

Some studies have been done in terms of feature selection approaches. The comparison of those studies' results and our approach's result are depicted in Table 2. Our method showed better result compared to the old ones. In addition, the standard deviation values of the proposed method are much lower than both RF (see Fig. 2) and other methods (Table 2). It means that the proposed method turned out not only better but also more stable results than previous ones.

Table 2. The best prediction rate of some studies in case of colon dataset

Type of classifier	Prediction rate (%) ± standard deviation
GA\SVM [9]	84.7±9.1
Bootstrapped GA\SVM [10]	80.0
Combined kernel for SVM [18]	75.33±7.0
DFE-RF	**85.5±4.5**

5.2 Leukemia Cancer

The leukemia dataset consists of 72 samples divided into two classes ALL and AML [17] (Availble at: http://sdmc.lit.org.sg/GEDatasets/ Data/ALL-AML_Leukemia.zip). There are 47 ALL and 25 AML samples and each contains 7129 features. This dataset was divided into a training set with 38 samples (27 ALL and 11 AML) and a testing set with 34 samples (20 ALL and 14 AML). To setup the 50 independent trials, we randomly selected 4000 features among 7129 given set of features. In this experiment, the *ntree* parameter was set to 1000, 2000, 3000, and 4000. By applying DRF-RF, the classification accuracies are significantly improved in all 50 trials (Fig. 3).

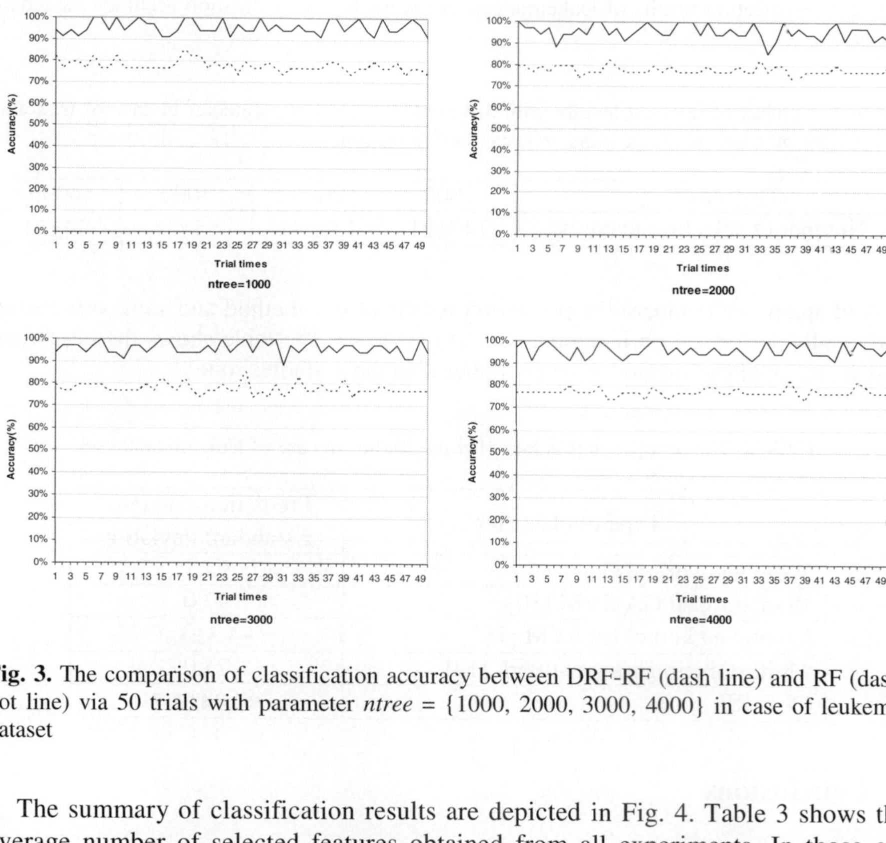

Fig. 3. The comparison of classification accuracy between DRF-RF (dash line) and RF (dash-dot line) via 50 trials with parameter *ntree* = {1000, 2000, 3000, 4000} in case of leukemia dataset

The summary of classification results are depicted in Fig. 4. Table 3 shows the average number of selected features obtained from all experiments. In those experiments, the tree number parameters do not significantly affect the classified results. We selected 50 as the number of feature elimination which is called *Step* parameter (Step=50). Our proposed method achieved the accuracy of 95.94% when performing on about 55 genes predictors retained by using DFE-RF procedure. This number of obtained genes only makes up about 0.77% (55/7129) of the whole set of genes.

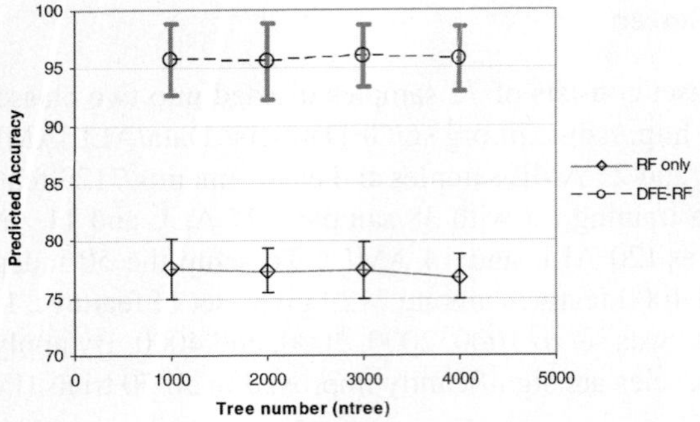

Fig. 4. Classification results of leukemia cancer (average % classification accuracy ±standard deviation)

Table 3. Number of selected feature with different tree number parameter in case of leukemia cancer over 50 trials (average number ± standard deviation)

Tree number	1000	2000	3000	4000
Number of selection features	147±21	138±41	55±21	74±51

And again, we compare the prediction results of our method and some other studies' results performed on leukemia dataset (Table 4). The table shows the classification accuracy of our method is much higher than these studies' one.

Table 4. The best prediction rate of some studies in case of leukemia data set

Type of classifier	Prediction rate (%) ± standard deviation
Weighted voting[8]	94.1
Bootstrapped GA\SVM [10]	97.0
Combined kernel for SVM [16]	85.3±3.0
Multi-domain gating network [19]	75.0
DFE-RF	**95.94±2.7**

6 Conclusions

We have presented a new feature selection method based on Random Forest. The RF algorithm itself is particularly suited for analyzing the high-dimensional dataset. It can easily deal with a large number of features as well as a small number of training samples. Our method not only employed RF by means of conventional backward elimination approach but also made it adapted to backward elimination task by using the Dynamic Feature Elimination procedure. By using the ranking criterion and the dynamic feature elimination strategy, the proposed method results in higher classification accuracy and more stable results than the original RF. The experiments with colon and leukemia datasets achieved the high recognition accuracies when compared to the original RF algorithm especially in case of leukemia cancer dataset. The proposed method also showed comparable and sometimes better performance than the widely used classification methods.

Acknowledgement

This work is supported by Korea Science & Engineering Foundation (KOSEF) through the Tumor Immunity Medical Research Center (TIMRC) at Seoul National University College of Medicine.

References

1. Kohavi, R. and John, G.H.: Wrappers for Feature Subset Selection, Artificial Intelligence (1997) pages: 273-324
2. Blum, A. L. and Langley, P.: Selection of Relevant Features and Examples in Machine Learning, Artificial Intelligence, (1997) pages: 245-271
3. Breiman, L.: Random forest, Machine Learning, vol. *45* (2001) pages: 5–32.
4. Torkkola, K., Venkatesan, S., Huan Liu: Sensor selection for maneuver classification, Proceedings. The 7th International IEEE Conference on Intelligent Transportation Systems (2004) Page(s):636 - 641
5. Yimin Wu, Aidong Zhang: Feature selection for classifying high-dimensional numerical data, Proceedings of the 2004 IEEE Computer Society Conference on Computer Vision and Pattern Recognition, vol. 2 (2004) Pages: 251-258
6. Duda, R. O., Hart, P. E., Stork, D. G.: Pattern Classification (2nd Edition), John Wiley & Sons Inc. (2001)
7. Breiman, L., Friedman, J. H., Olshen, R. A., Stone, C. J.: *Classification and Regression Trees*, Chapman and Hall, New York (1984)
8. Golub, T. R., Slonim, D. K., Tamayo, P., Huard, C., Gaasenbeek, J. P., Mesirov, J., Coller, H., Loh, M. L., Downing, J.R., Caligiuri, M. A., Bloomfield, C. D., and Lander, E.: Molecular Classification of Cancer: Class Discovery and Class Prediction by Gene Expression Monitoring," Science, vol. 286 (1999) pages: 531-537.
9. Fröhlich, H., Chapelle, O., and Schölkopf, B.: Feature Selection for Support Vector Machines by Means of Genetic Algorithms, 15th IEEE International Conference on Tools with Artificial Intelligence (2003) pages: 142
10. Chen, Xue-wen: Gene Selection for Cancer Classification Using Bootstrapped Genetic Algorithms and Support Vector Machines, IEEE Computer Society Bioinformatics Conference (2003) pages: 504
11. Zhang, H., Yu, Chang-Yung and Singer, B.: Cell and tumor classification using gene expression data: Construction of forests, Proceeding of the National Academy of Sciences of the United States of America, vol. 100 (2003) pages: 4168-4172
12. Doak. J: An evaluation of feature selection methods and their application to computer security, Technical Report CSE-92-18, Department of Computer Science and Engineering, University of Carlifornia (1992)
13. Das, S.: Filters, wrappers and a boosting-based hybrid for feature selection, Proceedings of the 18th ICML (2001)

14. Ng, A. Y.: On feature selection: learning with exponentially many irrelevant features as training examples", Proceedings of the Fifteenth International Conference on Machine Learning (1998)
15. Xing, E., Jordan, M., and Carp, R.: Feature selection for highdimensional genomic microarray data", Proc. of the 18th ICML (2001)
16. Mehta M., Agrawal R., Rissanen J.: SLIQ: A Fast Scalable Classifier for Data Mining, Proceeding of the International Conference on Extending Database Technology (1996) pages: 18-32
17. Alon, U., Barkai, N., Notterman, D., Gish, K., Ybarra, S., Mack, D., and Levine, A.: Broad Patterns of Gene Expression Revealed by Clustering Analysis of Tumor and Normal Colon Tissues Probed by Oligonucleotide Arrays, Proceedings of National Academy of Sciences of the United States of American, vol 96 (1999) Pages: 6745-6750.
18. Nguyen, H.-N, Ohn, S.-Y, Park, J., and Park, K.-S.: Combined Kernel Function Approach in SVM for Diagnosis of Cancer, Proceedings of the First International Conference on Natural Computation (2005)
19. Su, T., Basu, M., Toure, A.: Multi-Domain Gating Network for Classification of Cancer Cells using Gene Expression Data, Proceedings of the International Joint Conference on Neural Networks (2002) pages: 286-289

On Combining Fractal Dimension with GA for Feature Subset Selecting*

GuangHui Yan[1,2], ZhanHuai Li[1], and Liu Yuan[1]

[1] Dept. Computer Science & Software NorthWestern Polytechnical University, Xian 710072, P.R. China
{yangh, yuanl}@mail.nwpu.edu.cn, lizhh@nwpu.edu.cn

[2] Key Laboratory of Opto-Electronic Technology and Intelligent Control (Lanzhou Jiaotong University), Ministry of Education, 730070 Lanzhou

Abstract. Selecting a set of features which is optimal for a given task is a problem which plays an important role in a wide variety of contexts including pattern recognition, adaptive control, and machine learning. Recently, exploiting fractal dimension to reduce the features of dataset is a novel method. FDR (Fractal Dimensionality Reduction), proposed by Traina in 2000, is the most famous fractal dimension based feature selection algorithm. However, it is intractable in the high dimensional data space for multiple scanning the dataset and incapable of eliminating two or more features simultaneously. In this paper we combine GA with the Z-ordering based FDR for addressing this problem and present a new algorithm GAZBFDR(Genetic Algorithm and Z-ordering Based FDR). The algorithm proposed can directly select the fixed number features from the feature space and utilize the fractal dimension variation to evaluate the selected features within the comparative lower space. The experimental results show that GAZBFDR algorithm achieves better performance in the high dimensional dataset.

1 Introduction

Advances in data collection and storage capabilities during the past decades have led to an information increasing in most sciences. Researchers working in fields as diverse as text matching, time series analysis, Gene Expression Patterns analysis and DNA sequences analysis, face larger and larger observations and simulations on a daily basis[1][2][3][4]. Such datasets, in contrast with smaller, more traditional datasets that have been studied extensively in the past, have large number of features and enormous items simultaneously and present new challenges in data analysis. Furthermore, traditional statistical methods break down mostly because of the increase in the number of variables associated with each observation. One of the problems with these high-dimensional datasets is that,

* This work is sponsored by the National Natural Science Foundation of China (No.60573096), and the Opening Foundation of the Key Laboratory of Opto-Electronic Technology and Intelligent Control (Lanzhou Jiaotong University), Ministry of Education,China,Grant No. K04116.

A. Gelbukh and C.A. Reyes-Garcia (Eds.): MICAI 2006, LNAI 4293, pp. 543–553, 2006.

in many cases, not all the measured variables are 'important' for understanding the underlying phenomena of interest. Moreover, a dataset which appears high-dimensional, and thus complex, can actually be governed by a few simple variables/attributes(sometimes called hidden causes or latent variables). From this point of view, it is very valuable to filter out the unuseful dimensions from the high-dimensional datasets. Therefore, dimension reduction has become important techniques for automated pattern recognition, exploratory data analysis, and data mining.

In mathematical terms, the problem of dimensionality reduction can be stated as follows: given the p dimensional random variable $X = (x_1, x_2, ..., x_p)^T$, find a lower dimensional representation of it, $S = (s_1, s_2, ..., s_k)^T$ with $k \leq p$, that captures the content in the original data, according to some criterion. Generally, there are two ways of dimensionality reduction: feature selection and feature extraction. The feature extraction method generates a new low dimensional feature space from the original feature space. The new feature space is artificially generated (e.g., generated by some machine learning algorithms) and is difficult for human understanding. The feature selection method reduces the dimensions of the old feature space by carefully selecting the features subset as the new feature space. In contrast to the feature extraction, it does not do rotation or transformation of the features, thus leading to easy interpretation of the resulting features.

This paper concentrates on the combining of GA and fractal dimension based feature reduction, investigates the current method and proposes the optimized algorithm. The remainder of the paper is structured as follows. In the next section, we present a brief survey on the related techniques. Section 3 introduces the concepts needed to understand the proposed method. Section 4 presents the proposed fractal dimension algorithm. Section 5 discusses the experiments and the comparison of GAZBFDR with FDR. Section 6 gives the conclusions of this paper and indicates our future work trend.

2 Related Work

The feature selection problem has received considerable attention and numerous feature selection algorithms have been proposed in the fields of pattern recognition and machine learning, including sequential feature selection algorithms such as forwards, backwards and bidirectional sequential searches[5]; and feature weighting[6]. A recent survey on attribute selection using machine learning techniques is presented in[7] and a recent review on dimension estimation of data space can be founded in[8]. In [9], Vafaie firstly proposed the approach to features selection which uses genetic algorithms as the primary search component. Yang et al. presented an approach to feature subset selection using genetic algorithm and demonstrated its feasibility in the automated design of neural networks for pattern classification and knowledge discovery [10]. Raymer et al. proposed an approach to feature extraction using a genetic algorithm in which feature selection, feature extraction, and classifier training are performed simultaneously.

Traina firstly suggested using fractal dimension for feature selection. FDR, proposed by Traina in 2000 [11], is the first famous fractal dimension based feature selection algorithm. The main essence of FDR is to calculate the fractal dimension of the dataset, and sequentially to drop the attributes which contribute minimally to the fractal dimension until the terminal condition holds. FDR is usually intractable for the large dataset in practice for its multiple scanning of the dataset. In order to overcome the performance bottleneck of FDR in 2004 BaoYubin et al. proposed the OptFDR, which scans the dataset only once and adjusts the FD-tree dynamically to calculate the fractal dimension of the dataset[12]. But the adjust process of the FD-tree is complicated and the computational complexity is high. Furthermore, both FDR and OptFDR are suffered from the $\frac{(E-K)*(E+K+1)}{2}$ (E is the number of features in the original datasets, and K is the number of features to retain) evaluation of the fractal dimension of the dataset, and this is intolerable especially in the large dataset.

As we know there is no an approach which combine the fractal dimension with GA for feature selection. In this paper, we propose the GAZBFDR which uses GA as the search technique and the fractal dimension variation as the evaluation mechanism to obtain the sub-optimal feature subset.

3 Preliminaries and Z-Ordering Based FDR

If a dataset has self-similarity in an observation range, that is, the partial distribution of the dataset has the same structure or feature with its whole distribution, and then the dataset is said as fractal. Next, we give some related concepts.

3.1 Preliminaries

The dimensionality of the Euclid space where the data points of a dataset exist is called the embedding dimension of the dataset. In other words, it is the number of attributes of the dataset. The intrinsic dimension of a dataset is the dimension of the spatial object represented by the dataset, regardless of the space where it is embedded. Conceptually, if all features in a dataset are independent each other, then its intrinsic dimension is the embedding dimension. However, whenever there is a correlation between two or more features, the intrinsic dimensionality of the dataset is reduced accordingly. So if we know its intrinsic dimension, it is possible for us to decide how many attributes are in fact required to characterize a dataset. Due to its computational simplicity, the fractal dimension is successfully used to estimate the intrinsic dimension of the dataset in real application [13].

Generalized Fractal Dimension (GFD). Suppose a dataset that has the self-similarity property, its Generalized Fractal Dimension D_q is measured as:

$$D_q = \begin{cases} \lim\limits_{r \to 0} \frac{\sum_i p_i \log p_i^q}{\log r} & q = 1 \\ \lim\limits_{r \to 0} \frac{1}{1-q} \frac{\log \sum_i p_i^q}{\log r} & q \neq 1 \end{cases} \tag{1}$$

where r is the edge length of the *Cell* (abbr. of the hyper-rectangle) which covering the vector space, and p_i denotes the probability of finding points("bins") of the dataset in the *ith Cell*.

The measure D_q is defined for any $q \geq 0$, when q is an integer, has a physical meaning. It has been proved that: (D_0 is Hausdorff fractal dimension, D_1 is the Information Dimension, and D_2 is the Correlation Dimension). The D_1 and D_2 are particularly useful, since the value of D_1 is Shannon's entropy, and D_2 measures the probability that two points chosen within a certain distance. Changes in the Information dimension mean the changes in the entropy. Equally, changes in the Correlation Dimension mean changes in the distribution of points in the dataset. In our method we use the Correlation Dimension as the Intrinsic Dimension and the $\lceil D_2 \rceil$ as the selected features number.

Partial fractal dimension (PFD). Suppose a dataset with E features, this measurement is obtained through the calculation of the D_2 of this dataset excluding one or more attributes from the dataset[11].

For the self-similar dataset, the main idea of FDR is to eliminate the attribute which contributes minimally to the fractal dimension of the dataset and repeat that process until the terminal condition holds.

3.2 Z-Ordering Based FDR

As discussed in section 2, FDR is inefficient in practice for its multiple scanning of the dataset especially facing the large datasets. Thus, we proposed the Z-ordering Based FDR for deleting two or more features simultaneously and avoiding multiple scanning the datasets.

3.2.1 Integer Coded Z-Ordering

Z-ordering[14] technique is based on the Peano curve. However, it can not afford the high dimensional space and the overmany multilayer subdivision because of the length of its bit string. Here we adapt the variation: Integer-coded Z-ordering. Without lose of generality, suppose the features are arranged in a fixed sequence, and the integers serve as the correspondent coordinates. As in figure 1, take two dimensional space as example, the coordinate sequence is: first X axis and then Y axis, the integer sequence in each *Cell* is the coordinate sequence of this *Cell*, and the integer sequence at the cross point is the coordinate sequence of the upper level *Cell*.

3.2.2 Evaluating the Fractal Dimension Based on Integer Code Z-Ordering

The evaluation of the fractal dimension of the dataset is the foundation of ZBFDR algorithm. In figure 1, for each $Cell_i, i = 1, 2, \ldots, M$ (where M is the number of $Cells$ in the lowest level which at least contains one data point), the Z-ordering coordinate is $Coor_i = (Z_{i_1}, Z_{i_2}, \ldots, Z_{i_E}), Z_{i_j} \in 2^k | k = 0, 1, 2, \ldots,$ $Maxlevel$ (where $Maxlevel$ is the maximum level number). In order to evaluate the fractal dimension of the dataset we must count the number of points in each

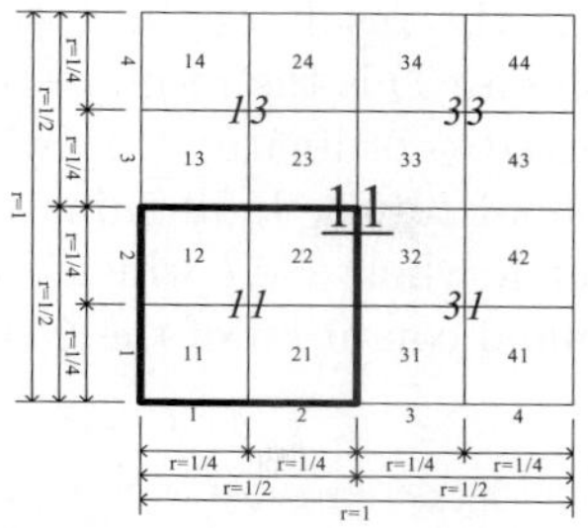

Fig. 1. Example of Integer Z-ordering Code

Cell at every level. FDR calculates the fractal dimension by constructing the FD-tree. In ZBFDR, we suggest constructing the lowest *Cell* queue, dynamically map the lower *Cell* queue into the upper *Cell* queue, and evaluate $\sum P_i^2$ of each level queue. This solution consumes lower space than FDR and has equivalent time complexity to FDR simultaneously (e.g. FDR constructs the FD-tree from the root node to the leaf node and keep the FD-tree structure in the main memory during the whole process, ZBFDR constructs the FD-tree inversely and only keep the lowest level node in the main memory for calculating the fractal dimension).

Take the two dimensional space for example as shown in figure 1, we can simply count the points contained by every minimum r *Cell*. For the bigger r *Cell* in which the count of points can be calculated with the sum of the points in the 4(2^2, the number is 2^E in E dimensional space) minimum r *Cell* contained by the upper r *Cell*. This process continued until the maximal r *Cell* is processed.

Generally, we can adjust the E dimensional coordinate of each *Cell* according to equation 2. Where $Coordinate_{old}$ is the coordinate before adjust, $Coordinate_{new}$ is the correspondent coordinate after adjust, j is the level number for merge, $j = 1$ means to map the lowest level *Cell* queue into its upper(the second lowest) level *Cell* queue, $j = 2$ means to map the second lowest level *Cell* queue into its upper(the third lowest) level *Cell* queue, and so on. Repeat this process until we get one *cell* which contains total data points.

$$\begin{cases} Coordinate_{new} = Coordinate_{old}, & (\frac{Coordinate_{old}-1}{2^{j-1}})MOD\ 2 = 0 \\ Coordinate_{new} = Coordinate_{old} - 2^{j-1}, & (\frac{Coordinate_{old}-1}{2^{j-1}})MOD\ 2 = 1 \end{cases} \quad (2)$$

We can calculate the $\sum_i P_i^2$ through merging *Cells* which has the identical coordinate and summing the point number of each *Cell*. Repeat the preceding process we can get a series of $(\log \sum_i P_i^2, \log(r))$. Thus, through plotting $\log \sum_i P_i^2$ versus $\log(r)$, and calculating the slope of the scaling range of the resulting line, we can obtain the correlation fractal dimension D_2 of the dataset.

In figure 1, the integer sequence covers the cross point is the coordinate after the mapping process, the *Cells* with italic coordinate (*1,1*) is the result of the mapping of the four smallest *Cells* locate in the bottom left corner of the square, the italic coordinate (*1,3*) is the result of the top left corner smallest four *Cells*, the italic coordinate (*3,3*) is the result of the top right corner smallest four *Cells* and the italic coordinate (*3,1*) is the result of the bottom right corner four smallest *Cells*. The underlined coordinate $\underline{(1,1)}$ which cover the center cross point of the square is the final result. It illuminates that through a series of mapping process we can get a whole *Cell* which contains all of points of the dataset and proves the terminal condition of the *Cell* merge process.

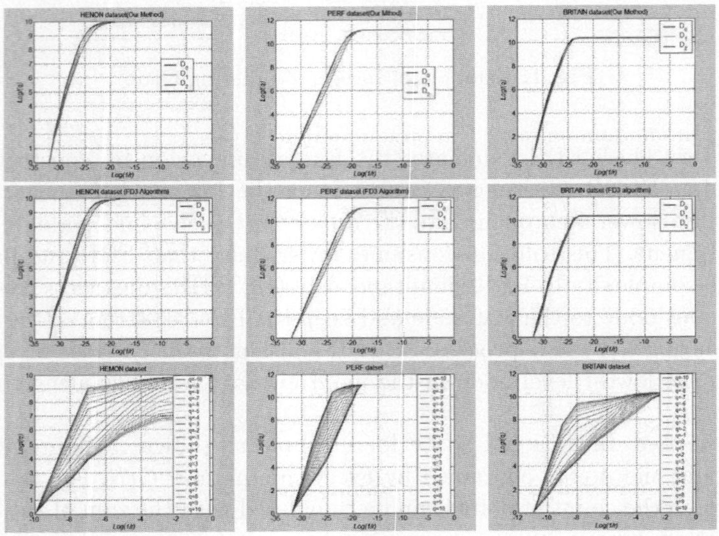

Fig. 2. Comparison Result of ZBFDR Versus FD3(The top row is the result of ZBDFR, the middle row is the result of the FD3, and the bottom row is the general dimension evaluated by ZBFDR) of the same datasets(the left column is the result of HENON dataset, the middle column is the result of PERF dataset, and the right column is the result of BRITAIN dataset))

In figure 2 the experiments are made for testing our method and the FD3 algorithm using the real dataset[15]. It is evident that the two methods get the identical fractal dimension. Considering the General Fractal Dimension we also give the results of $D_q, q = -10, -9, \ldots, -1, 0, 1, \ldots, , 9, 10$ in figure 2.

3.2.3 Simultaneously Deleting the Two or More Attributes

It is important to point out that the elimination of the selected feature does not mean deleting the data points. So we can view the elimination of the one selected dimension as the projection from E dimensional space to $E-1$ dimensional space (the elimination of the two selected dimensions as the projection from E dimensional space to $E-2$ dimensional space, and so on.). Without lose generality, we specially demonstrate the elimination of the two adjacent selected dimensions in detail. Suppose the two same level $Cell_i$ and $Cell_j$ have coordinate sequence $Coor_{i_E} = (Z_{i_1}, Z_{i_2}, \ldots, Z_{i_{i-2}}, Z_{i_{i-1}}, Z_{i_i}, Z_{i_{i+1}}, \ldots, Z_{i_E})$

and $Coor_{j_E} = (Z_{j_1}, Z_{j_2}, \ldots, Z_{j_{i-2}}, Z_{j_{i-1}}, Z_{j_i}, \ Z_{j_{i+1}}, \ldots, Z_{j_E})$ respectively. If the two $((i-1)th, ith)$ dimensions are eliminated from the E dimensional space, it is equivalent to project the E dimensional space onto the $E-2$ dimensional spaces. The coordinate sequences after projecting are listed as follows: $Coor_{i_{E-2}} = (Z_{i_1}, Z_{i_2}, \ldots, Z_{i_{i-2}}, Z_{i_{i+1}} \ldots, Z_{i_E})$ and $Coor_{j_{E-2}} = (Z_{j_1}, Z_{j_2}, \ldots, Z_{j_{i-2}}, Z_{j_{i+1}}, \ldots, Z_{j_E})$. The condition to merge the $Cell_i$ and $Cell_j$ after eliminating the two dimensions is: $Coor_{i_{E-2}}$ is identical with $Coor_{j_{E-2}}$. In fact if the $(i-1)th$ dimension and the ith dimension values of $Coor_{i_E}$ and $Coor_{j_E}$ are marked zero (that means $Coor_{i_E}$ is identical with $Coor_{j_E}$), we can merge the $Cell_i$ and $Cell_j$ directly after eliminating the two dimensions. The coordinate of the new derived $Cell$ is $Coor_{i_E}$ or $Coor_{j_E}$ with the $((i-1)th)$ and (ith) dimension coordinate values are zero. The partial fractal dimension of the $E-2$ dimensional dataset can be evaluated by the process described in the section 3.2.2.

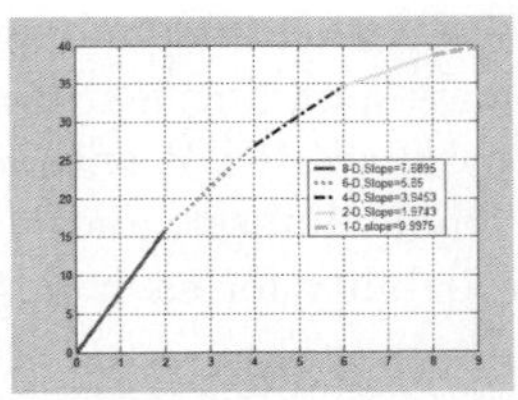

Fig. 3. Elimination of Features

Figure 3 gives the result of feature deletion of an 8 dimension synthetic stochastic dataset. It is evident that along with the feature deletion the slope of the scaling range of $\log I(q)$ versus $\log r$ becomes more and more smooth.

4 Genetic Algorithm for Feature Subset Selection

Genetic algorithm is one of the most powerful and broadly applicable stochastic search and optimization technique based on the principles from evolution theory (Holland 1976). GA exploits accumulating information about an initially unknown search space in order to bias subsequent search into promising subspaces. Since GA is basically a domain independent search technique, it is ideal for applications where domain knowledge and theory is difficult or impossible to provide [16]. The main issue of applying GA to applications is selecting an appropriate representation and an adequate evaluation function.

4.1 Chromosome Representation

Without lose generality, we fixed the features sequence. For the problem of the feature subset selection, individual solutions are simply represented with a binary string(1 if the given feature is selected, 0 otherwise) which length is E.

4.2 Main Operators

Generally, there are three basic operators in GA: Selection operator, Crossover operator and Mutation operator. Moreover, the fitness function interprets the chromosome in terms of physical representation and evaluates its fitness based on traits of desired in the solution.

4.2.1 Selection Operator

The selection (reproduction) operator is intended to improve the average quality of the population by giving the high-quality chromosomes a better chance to get copied into the next generation. The selection thereby focuses the exploration on promising regions in the solution space. Consider the definition of GFD and PFD in section 3.1 we define the fitness function as:

$$f_i = 1 - \frac{PFD_i}{GFD}, i = 1, 2, \ldots, n \tag{3}$$

Where, PFD_i is theD_2 of the dataset corresponding to the chromosome in which the gene value 1 means the corresponding feature is selected from the feature space, and can be evaluated by our ZBFDR without scanning the dataset once again, GFD is the D_2 of the whole dataset, and n is the population size. Then, we can define the selective probability for each chromosome as:

$$SP_i = \frac{f_i}{\sum_i f_i}, i = 1, 2, \ldots, n \tag{4}$$

From the equation 3 and 4, it is easy to see that the bigger PFD_i the higher value SP_i. Considering the Roulette Wheel selection technique the high value SP_i means the corresponding chromosome which has high selective probability to get into the next generation.

4.2.2 Crossover Operator

As the main genetic operator, crossover operates on both parents chromosomes and generates offspring by combining both chromosomes' features. Since the crossover technique is a key method in genetic algorithms for finding optimum solutions, it is important to implement this operation effectively for making the GA works effectively. We adapt the two-point crossover mechanism in our method. It is important to keep in mind that the fixed (e.g. K) number of features should be kept in the feature space. Since it is clear that the selected feature number needs to be kept fixed, it is desirable that the two children obtained after crossover operation also correspond to the fixed number of selected features respectively. In order to achieve this goal, we need to implement the mend mechanism which inspect the two children and force to change the illegal child chromosome into the legal one.

4.2.3 Mutation Operator

Mutation always alters one or more genes with a probability equal to the mutation rate. For improving the efficiency of the mutation operation we adapt the simple realization. Firstly, we randomly select the gene position which value is zero; then for all positions which value is 1, we randomly select one, and exchange the value of the two selected gene position.

4.2.4 Other Technique

In order to guarantee the optimal result at last we adapt the best chromosome retain mechanism during the iterative evolving process. For the best chromosome in the offspring generation we evaluate its fitness value and compare it with the best chromosome in the parent generation, if the former is less, we replace the best chromosome in the offspring population by the best chromosome in the parent population.

4.3 GAZBFDR Algorithm

Based on the above discussion, the steps of the GAZBFDR algorithm are listed as follows.

Step 0 Evaluating the GFD of the whole dataset based on our ZBFDR method, backup the lowest *Cell* queue for evaluating the PFD_i subsequent.

Step 1 Generating initial population(population *size* is 10-30 according to the dimensions of the dataset).

Step 2 Crossover operator. Select chromosomes by crossover probability P_c (0.6-0.8 in our mehod), randomly group them by pairs and use uniform two-point crossover for the crossover operation.

Step 3 Mutation operator. Select chromosomes by mutation probability P_m (0.2 in our method) and perform the mutation operation according to section 4.2.3.

Step 4 Evaluate the fitness function of chromosomes group. In this step for each chromosome we adapt our ZBFDR method evaluate its PFD_i. Then we calculate the corresponding f_i and SP_i corroding to the equation 3 and 4. At the same time, we calculate $GFD - PFD_i$ and compare it with the predefined threshold α, if $GFD - PFD_i < \alpha$ then go to step 6.

Step 5 Select *size* chromosomes as the offspring chromosomes by roulette wheel selection approach.

Step 6 Repeat Step2-Step5 until a satisfying set of solutions is obtained or the number of predetermined rounds are complete. The best solution is the optimal feasible chromosome reserved during the iteration.

5 Experiments and Evaluation

The performance experiments on the feature subset selection are made for evaluating FDR algorithm and GAZBFDR algorithm using three real datasets with fractal characteristics. The experimental results are shown in figure 4. The three datasets employed are BRITAIN dataset(A classic fractal dataset which include the datum of the coast line of England. The data item number is 1292 and the feature number varies from 2 to 62(where, two dimensions are real fractal features and the others are nonlinear dependent features with the two fractal dimension)), HENON dataset (Points in a Henon map. The data item number is 1000 and the feature number varies from 2 to 62(generated like the BRITAIN dataset)) and the PERF dataset(An "artificial" set cooked up to give a clear example of a case where the information and correlation dimension estimates differ significantly from the capacity dimension estimate. The data item number is 1000 and the feature number varies from 1 to 31(where, one dimension is real fractal feature and the others are nonlinear dependent features with the fractal dimension))[16]. In BRITAIN dataset and HENON dataset we select the two fractal features from the feature space, and for PERF dataset we select the one fractal feature. The hardware environment includes Intel Pentium IV 1.7GHz CPU, 512MB RAM, 40GB hard disk, and the software environment includes Windows 2003 and Delphi 7.

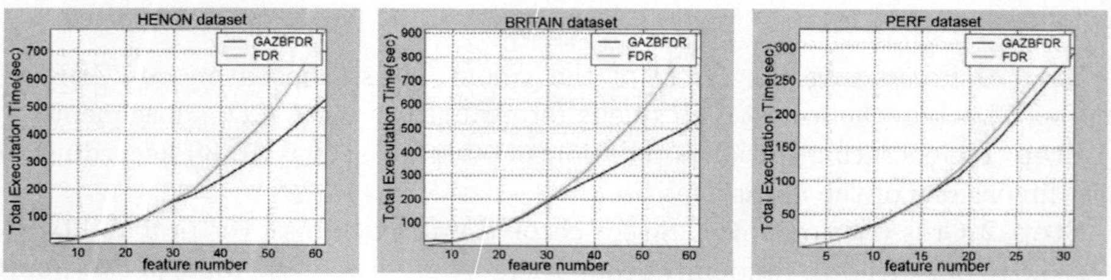

Fig. 4. Performance Comparison of GAZBFDR Versus FDR on the Real Dataset

In figure 4, it is evident that the performance of GAZBFDR is not superior than that of FDR for the small dataset (e.g., the features number is no more than 30). The reason is that for small dataset the number of calculating the PFD_i of FDR algorithm is equal or less than that of our method. For the dataset which has large amount of features (e.g., the dataset has 40 or more features) the GAZBFDR outperforms the FDR and generates the desired optimal result.

From the above discussion, we can draw the conclusions that the $\frac{(E-K)*(E+K+1)}{2}$ scans of the dataset are the key obstacles that affect the performance of FDR algorithm especially facing with the large dataset. Consequently, utilizing the GA which scans the dataset only once and reduces the number of fractal dimension evaluation can optimize the feature subset selection performance.

6 Conclusion

The GAZBFDR algorithm is proposed, which can complete the feature subset selection through scanning the dataset only once except for preprocessing. The experimental results show that GAZBFDR outperforms FDR algorithm in the large dataset. Our future work will concentrate on the high efficient algorithm for evaluating the fractal dimension, the popularization of the algorithm on non-numerical dataset, and the combination with other feature selection algorithms.

References

1. R Baeza-Yates, G Navarro. Block-addressing indices for approximate text retrieval. In: Forouzan Golshani, Kia Makki. (Eds.): Proc of the 6th Int'l Conf on Information and Knowledge Management. New York: ACM Press (1997) 1-8
2. R Agrawal, C Faloutsos, A Swami1. Efficient similarity search in sequence databases. In: David B Lomet. (Eds.): Proc of the 4th Int'l Conf Foundations of Data Organization and Algorithms. Berlin : Springer-Verlag (1993) 69-84
3. Daxin Jiang, Chun Tang, Aidong Zhang. Cluster Analysis for Gene Expression Data: A Survey. IEEE TRANSACTIONS ON KNOWLEDGE AND DATA ENGINEERING Vol. 16, No. 11. (2004) 1370-1386
4. M.D. Schena, R. Shalon, R. Davis, P. Brown. Quantitative Monitoring of Gene Expression Patterns with a Compolementatry DNA Microarray. Science, vol. 270. (1995) 467-470
5. D. W. Aha, R. L. Bankert. A Comparative Evaluation of Sequential Feature Selection Algorithms. In Artificial Intelligence and Statistics V, Springer-Verlag, New York, New York (1996) 199-206
6. M. Scherf and W. Brauer. Feature Selection by Means of a Feature Weighting Approach. Technische Universität München, Munich (1997)
7. A.Blum, P.Langley. Selection of Relevant Features and Examples in Machine Learning. AI, vol. 97. (1997) 245-271
8. Camastra Francesco. Data dimensionality estimation methods: a survey. Pattern Recognition, vol. 36. (2003) 2945-2954
9. H. Vafaie and K. A. D. Jong. Robust Feature Selection Algorithms. In Intl. Conf. on Tools with AI, Boston, MA (1993)
10. J. Yang and V. Honavar. Feature subset selection using a genetic algorithm. In J. Koza et al. (Eds.): Proceedings of the Second Annual Conference, Stanford University, CA, USA, (1997)
11. Caetano Traina Jr., Agma Traina, et al. Fast feature selection using fractal dimension. In XV Brazilian DB Symposium, João Pessoa-PA-Brazil, (2000) 158-171
12. Yubin Bao., Ge Yu., Huanliang Sun., Daling Wang. Performance Optimization of Fractal Dimension Based Feature Selection Algorithm. In:Q. Li, G. Wang, and L. Feng. (Eds.): WAIM 2004, LNCS, Vol. 3129. Springer-Verlag Berlin Heidelberg (2004) 739-744
13. Ls Liebovitch, T.Toth. A Fast Algorithm to Determine Fractal Dimensions by Box Counting[J]. Physics Letters, Vol.141A(8). (1989) 386-390
14. J.Orenstein, T.H.Merrett. A class of data structures for associative searching. In Proceedings of the Third ACM SIGACT- SIGMOD Symposium on Principles of Database Systems (1984) 181-190
15. John Sarraille and P. DiFalco. FD3. http://tori.postech.ac.kr/softwares/
16. De Jong, K. Learning with Genetic Algorithms: An overview. Machine Learning Vol. 3, Kluwer Academic publishers, (1988) 121-138

Locally Adaptive Nonlinear Dimensionality Reduction*

Yuexian Hou, Hongmin Yang, and Pilian He

Department of Computer Science and Technology,
Tianjin University, Tianjin, 300072, China
yxhou@tju.edu.cn

Abstract. Popular nonlinear dimensionality reduction algorithms, e.g., SIE and Isomap suffer a difficulty in common: global neighborhood parameters often fail in tackling data sets with high variation in local manifold. To improve the availability of nonlinear dimensionality reduction algorithms in the field of machine learning, an adaptive neighbors selection scheme based on locally principal direction reconstruction is proposed in this paper. Our method involves two main computation steps. First, it selects an appropriate neighbors set for each data points such that all neighbors in a neighbors set form a d-dimensional linear subspace approximately and computes locally principal directions for each neighbors set respectively. Secondly, it fits each neighbor by means of locally principal directions of corresponding neighbors set and deletes the neighbors whose fitting error exceeds a predefined threshold. The simulation shows that our proposal could deal with data set with high variation in local manifold effectively. Moreover, comparing with other adaptive neighbors selection strategy, our method could circumvent false connectivity induced by noise or high local curvature.

1 Introduction

Nonlinear dimensionality reduction and manifold learning are important topics in the field of machine learning, and their essence is to extract the least independent variables to describe the intrinsic dynamical characters of data. More generally, nonlinear dimensionality reduction model can model the features of abstraction process in the biological perception and mental activity of human being. In a reductive level, Barlow's hypothesis suggests that the outcome of the early processing performed in our visual cortical feature detectors might be the result of redundancy reduction process. In other words, the neural outputs are mutually as statistically independent as possible, conditioned on the received sensory messages [1]; In a high level, it is argued that meaning, as a prerequisite for thought, arises from parsimonious a re-description of perceptions [2][3].

There have been several algorithms to solve linear dimensionality reduction problem, such as PCA [4], MDS [4] and factor analysis. They are simple to implement, but failing to detect the intrinsic nonlinear structure [5]. Recently, there has been considerable interest in developing efficient algorithms for learning nonlinear manifolds. But popular

* Supported by Science-Technology Development Project of Tianjin(04310941R) and Applied Basic Research Project of Tianjin (05YFJMJC11700).

A. Gelbukh and C.A. Reyes-Garcia (Eds.): MICAI 2006, LNAI 4293, pp. 554–561, 2006.

NLDR algorithm, e.g., LLE [6], Isomap [5][7], Laplacian Eigenmaps [10] and SIE [8], suffer common weakness: the neighborhood parameters are global. And the simulation shows global parameters often fail in tackling data sets with high variation in local curvature [9].

Two strategies are commonly used for implementing adaptive NLDR. One is global method, i.e., according to some statistical criterions derived from some transcendent principia, the embedding result can be directly evaluated and selected. Global strategy is static, and does not change NLDR algorithms. The other strategy is local. It introduces adaptive neighbors selection scheme into basic NLDR algorithms. The state-of-art locally method, Locally Tangent Space Alignment (LTSA) [9], adaptively selects neighborhood parameter k according to the approximate quality between a neighbors set and its first order Taylor expansion at central point. But LTSA has a flaw: if some noisy points are involved or the local curvature is high, it is possible to select wrong neighbors which will destroy the global topology of the embedding manifold.

In this work, we present a novel adaptive neighbors selection algorithm: Locally Principal Direction Reconstruction (LPDR). It involves two steps: first, with PCA, select an appropriate k neighbors set that can be approximately embedded in an expected embedding dimensionality d, and solve its base vector set of d-dimensional principle linear subspace, i.e., the linear subspace spanned by directions with the d most variances. Secondly, according to the linear fitting error of the base vector set with respect to each neighbor point, estimate its distance to the principal linear subspace, and delete neighbors whose distance exceeds a predefined threshold. Our algorithm has a naturally geometrical sense. Simulation shows that it can effectively circumvent false connectivity induced by noisy points and high local curvature, and is simple to implement.

2 Principles

Supposed the original data set $X_D \cong \{\mathbf{x}_1, \mathbf{x}_2, \ldots, \mathbf{x}_N\}$ in R^D, NLDR problem is posed as a constrained optimization problem to solve embedding set X_d in R^d ($d<D$) under the constraints of preserving the topological and geometrical characters of X_D. The space that X_D and X_d rides on are called as original space and embedding space respectively, d is embedding dimensionality.

Isomap, SIE, LLE and Laplacian Eigenmaps share a common characteristic in that they first induce a local neighborhood structure on original space R^D, and then use this local structure to globally map the manifold to an embedding space R^d. A necessary condition making the above strategy works is that globally nonlinear embedding criterion can be approximated by the mixture of some locally linear quantities. To be specific, Isomap, SIE, LLE and Laplacian Eigenmaps approximate globally geodesic distance, globally geometrical structure and globally topological structure by the mixture of locally Euclidean distance, coefficient of locally linear combination and locally topological relation respectively. Therefore, the availability of the above algorithm implies that locally linear subspace (LLS) condition should hold, i.e., most local neighbors sets approximately reside on a d-dimensional locally linear subspace.

To verify whether LLS holds, we can apply a linear map algorithm, e.g., PCA, to map every neighbors set in a d-dimensional linear subspace and check the residual variance of embedding. If the embedding residual of a neighbors set is small, the LLS might hold in this neighbors set. Small residual variance can usually help us to determine the proper neighborhood if the curvature of local manifolds is smoothly changing. But it is not a sufficient criterion for LLS. As shown in Figure 1, the curve composed by blue points denotes a local space of the manifold, O denotes central point $\mathbf{x}_i$, the circle surrounding O denotes its neighbors region, the red line passing O denotes the tangent space of the manifold at O. In this case, although neighbors set includes few obvious outliers of locally linear manifold, the residual variance might still be small in magnitude because of relative small ratio of the outliers number to the number of points on locally linear manifold. It turns out that false connectivity is induced in graph representation due to these improper neighbors.

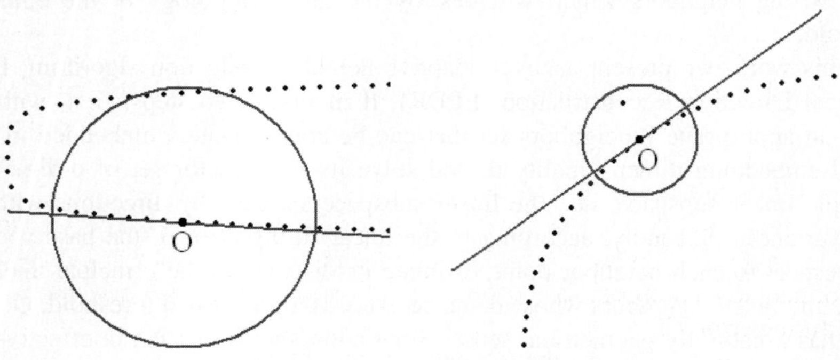

Fig. 1. Two neighbors sets with small residual variance of PCA embedding

An important distinct between LPDR and LTSA is that LPDR selects the neighbors once more according to the distance between neighbors and locally linear subspace spanned by directions with the d biggest variances, while LTSA simply deletes the neighbors whose Euclidean distance is far from the central point to guarantee a good local Taylor approximation [9]. To eliminate the influence of false connectivity due to noisy points or high local curvature, we filtrate every neighbor in a neighbors set according to its distance to locally principal direction, i.e., the linear subspace spanned by directions that are of great variances. Neighbors that are relatively far from locally principal direction will be deleted from the neighbors set even if they are near to the central point of the neighbors set. To be specific, let $L \cong \{\mathbf{v}_{i1}, \mathbf{v}_{i2}, \ldots, \mathbf{v}_{id}\}$ are the d smallest eigenvectors of the covariance matrix of $\mathbf{x}_i$'s neighbors set, then the locally principal direction centering at $\mathbf{x}_i$ is spanned by L and for every points $\mathbf{x}_{ij}$ in $\mathbf{x}_i$'s neighbors set, vector $\mathbf{y}_{ij} \cong \mathbf{x}_{ij} - \mathbf{x}_i$ can be approximately represented by the linear combination of vectors in L as long as $\mathbf{x}_{ij}$ is near to locally principal direction of $\mathbf{x}_i$. Formally,

$$\mathbf{y}_{ij} = \mathbf{V}_i \mathbf{w}_{ij} + \epsilon_{ij} \tag{1}$$

where $\mathbf{V}_i \cong [\mathbf{v}_{i1}\ \mathbf{v}_{i2}\ \ldots\ \mathbf{v}_{id}]$ is a D×d matrix, $\mathbf{w}_{ij}$ is a d×1 fitting coefficients vector of linear combination, $\boldsymbol{\epsilon}_{ij}$ is a D×1 fitting error vector. The remaining task is to solve optimal $\mathbf{w}_{ij}$ for every $\mathbf{y}_{ij}$, i=1, 2, ..., k, where k is the points number of $\mathbf{x}_i$'s neighbors set. We solve optimal $\mathbf{w}_{ij}$ in the least square error sense. Then it becomes a problem of quadratic programming and $\mathbf{w}_{ij}^*$ can be analytically attained by the formula (2) [4],

$$\mathbf{w}_{ij}^* = (\mathbf{V}_i^T \mathbf{V}_i)^{-1} \mathbf{V}_i^T \mathbf{y}_{ij} \tag{2}$$

Once optimal $\mathbf{w}_{ij}^*$ is attained, $\boldsymbol{\epsilon}_{ij}^*$ is computed by formula (1), and the norm of $\boldsymbol{\epsilon}_{ij}^*$ becomes a criterion to check whether $\mathbf{x}_{ij}$ is near to the locally principal direction centering at $\mathbf{x}_i$. Therefore we have the following algorithm.

3 Algorithm

The procedure of LPDR is summarized as follows:

Algorithm 1: adaptive neighbors selection algorithm based on locally principal direction

Input: $X_D \cong \{x_1, x_2, \ldots, x_N\}$

Output: neighbors set of every point in X_D

Parameters: the expected dimensionality d of locally linear subspaces, the maximum of neighbors number k_{max}, the minimum of neighbors number k_{min}, the increment of neighbors number Δk, the threshold of residual variance Th_{cov} and the threshold of fitting error Th_{fit}

For every $\mathbf{x}_i$ in X_D, execute the following steps

Step 1: k:= k_{max} ;

Step 2: generate $\mathbf{x}_i$'s k-nearest neighbors set $N(i) \cong \{\mathbf{x}_{i1}, \mathbf{x}_{i2}, \ldots, \mathbf{x}_{ik}\}$;

Step 3: compute its residual variance R_{cov} of d-dimensional PCA embedding;

Step 4: if $R_{cov} < Th_{cov}$ or $k = k_{min}$

then construct set $L \cong \{\mathbf{v}_{i1}, \mathbf{v}_{i2}, \ldots, \mathbf{v}_{id}\}$ that includes d eigenvector corresponding to d largest eigenvalue of covariance matrix of N(i)

else k:=max{k-Δk, k_{min}}, return 2;

Step 5: construct vectors $\mathbf{y}_{ij}$, j=1,2,...,k, where $\mathbf{y}_{ij} \cong \mathbf{x}_{ij} - \mathbf{x}_i$;

Step 6: solve optimal fitting coefficients $\mathbf{w}_{ij}^*$ of $\mathbf{y}_{ij}$, j=1,2,...,k according to formu las (2);

Step 7: compute optimal fitting error $\boldsymbol{\epsilon}_{ij}^*$ of $\mathbf{y}_{ij}$, j=1,2,...,k according to formulas (1);

Step 8: compute normalized fitting error $\boldsymbol{\epsilon}_{ij}'$ by $\boldsymbol{\epsilon}_{ij}' \cong \|\boldsymbol{\epsilon}_{ij}^*\| / \|\mathbf{y}_{ij}\|_2$, j=1,2,...,k ;

Step 9: if there are at least k_{min} normalized fitting error that is less than Th_{fit}

then $\mathbf{x}_i$'s neighbors set is composed by points whose corresponding $\boldsymbol{\epsilon}_{ij}'$ I is less than Th_{fit}

else $\mathbf{x}_i$'s neighbors set is composed by k_{min} points whose corresponding $\boldsymbol{\epsilon}_{ij}'$ are one of the k smallest.

Algorithm 1 can be used in the basic NLDR algorithm, such as Isomap, SIE, LLE and Laplacian Eigenmaps, to adaptively select the neighbors.

4 Experimental Results

Clean S-manifold data [6] and Swiss roll data with noise leading to false connectivity [5] were used in our experiments. Each data set includes 500 points. Noisy points were generated by random disturbing (Figure 2). Two data sets were respectively embedded by basis SIE [8], SIE with LTSA and SIE with LPDR. The parameters of LTSA [9] and LPDR were optimally s configured as follows:

LTSA: k_{min}=10, k_{max}=60, Δk=1, η=0.1
LPDR: k_{min}=10, k_{max}=60, Δk=1, Th_{cov}=0.005, Th_{fit}=0.1

The k parameter of basic SIE is $[(k_{max} + k_{min})/2]$, where [•] denotes the integer part. Figure 3 and Figure 4 illustrate the embedding results of the above three algorithms. As shown in Figure 3, for the clean S-manifold data, both SIE with LTSA and SIE with LPDR can gain a perfect embedding results, which is better than that of basic SIE.

As for noisy Swiss roll data, only the result attained by SIE with LPDR is qualitatively correct. It is because that the false connectivity induced by few noisy points destroys the global topology of the graphical representation of the manifold, as shown in Figure 2 (c), where the red point is a noisy point leading to false connectivity.

LTSA computes the approximate error between a neighbors set and its first order Taylor expansion at central point. If this error exceeds some threshold that is proportional to parameter η[9], LTSA simply deletes neighbors whose Euclidean distance is far from central point. The procedure is performed iteratively until approximate error is small enough or the number of neighbors reaches its low bound k_{min} [9]. In this case, except that η is small enough, it is difficult to remove noisy points near to central point. But on the other hand, small η often leads to very small neighbors sets and destroys the global connectivity of embedding manifold. Thus LTSA is limited in its ability of finding and removing noisy points near to central point. To be contrasted, based on estimating the distance between neighbors and locally principal direction, LPDR can effectively solve these problems.

Table 1. The result of 0's neighbors set by LSTA with different parameters

η =	0.02	0.04	0.06	0.08	0.1
LSTA	wrong	wrong	wrong	wrong	wrong

Table 2. The result of 0's neighbors set by LPDR with different parameters

Th =	<0.005, 0.05>	<0.005, 0.1>	<0.01, 0.005>	<0.01, 0.1>
LPDR	correct	correct	correct	wrong

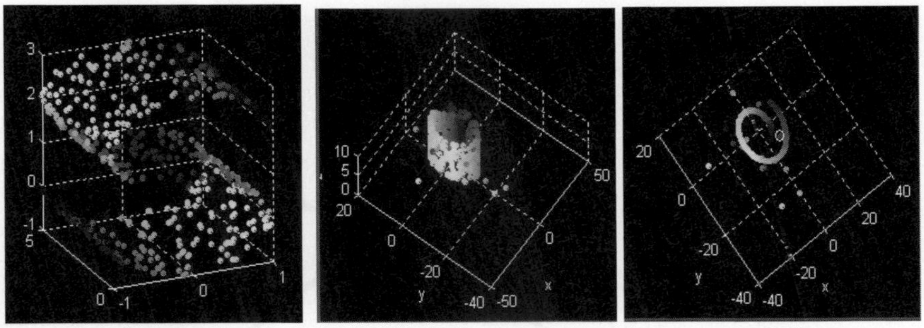

(a) (b) (c)

Fig. 2. (a)the 3-d original manifold of clean S-manifold data set (b)the 3-d original manifold of Swiss roll data set with false connectivity (c)the 2-d projection of Swiss roll data set with false connectivity

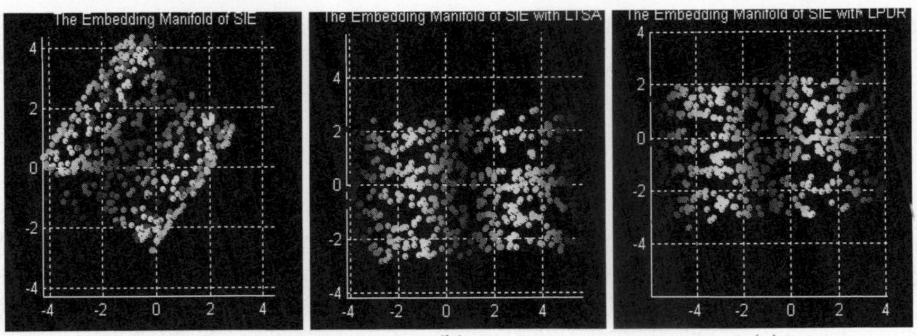

(a) (b) (c)

Fig. 3. The 2-d embedding of Clean S-manifold data set (a)the embedding manifold by basic SIE (b)the embedding manifold by SIE with LTSA (c)the embedding manifold by SIE with LPDR

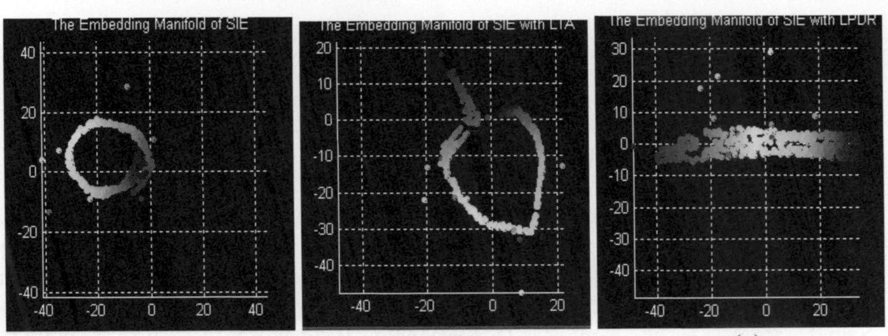

(a) (b) (c)

Fig. 4. The 2-d embedding of Swiss roll data set with false connectivity (a)the embedding result by basic SIE (b)the embedding result by SIE with LTSA (c)the embedding result by SIE with LPDR

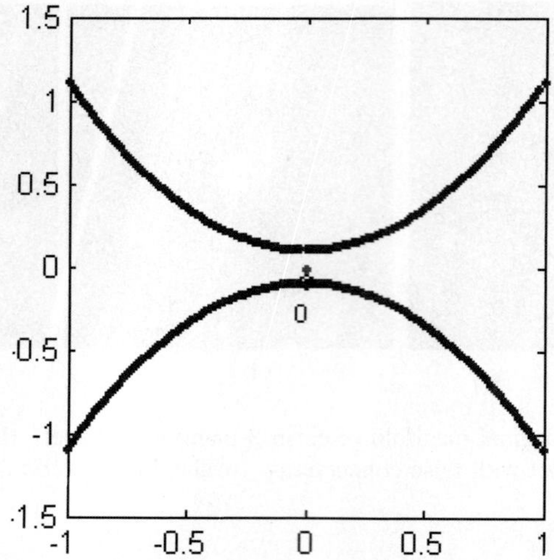

Fig. 5. A data set involved small disturbing noisy point that can induce false connectivity (the red point denotes noisy point)

5 Discussion

This paper presents an adaptive neighbors selection algorithm: based on Locally Principal Direction Reconstruction（LPDR）. Simulation shows, LPDR could adaptively select neighbors better than others. In contrast to LTSA, this algorithm could circumvent the false connectivity induced by noisy points near to reference point or high local curvature. In the further work, we will simultaneously think over the global and the local state. In addition to the adaptive neighbors selection, the locally adaptive neighbors selection scheme will introduce a threshold parameter. And the global adaptability is expected to identify the parameters by means of the statistics [11].

References

1. H. Barlow, Unsupervised learning， Neural Computation, vol. 1, pp. 295-311, 1989.
2. Gary Marcus, Programs of the Mind, Science 304: 1450-1451.
3. Eric Baum, *What Is Thought?* , MIT Press, Cambridge, MA, 2004.
4. K. V. Mardia, J. T. Kent, J. M. Bibby, Multivariate Analysis, Academic Press, London, 1979.
5. Joshua B. Tenenbaum et. al. A Global Geometric Framework for Nonlinear Dimensionality Reduction, Science, 2000, 290: 2319-2323.
6. Sam T. Roweis et. al. Nonlinear Dimensionality Reduction by Locally Linear Embedding, Science, 2000，290：2323-2326.
7. Vin De Silva and Joshua Tenenbaum, Global versus local methods in nonlinear dimensionality reduction, V. de Silva et al, NIPS'2002.

8. Yuexian Hou et. al., Robust Nonlinear Dimension Reduction: A Self-organized Approach, FSDK'05.
9. Jing Wang, Zhenyue Zhang, Hongyuan Zha, .Adaptive Manifold Learning. NIPS 2004.
10. M. Belkin, P. Niyogi, Laplacian Eigenmaps for Dimensionality Reduction and Data Representation, Neural Computation, June 2003; 15 (6):1373-1396.
11. Yuexian Hou et. al., Adaptive manifold learning Based on Statistical Criterions, Tech report of Tianjin university.

Fuzzy Pairwise Multiclass Support Vector Machines

J.M. Puche, J.M. Benítez, J.L. Castro, and C.J. Mantas

Dept. Computer Science and Artificial Intelligence,
University of Granada, 18071 Granada, Spain
{puche, j.m.benitez, castro, cmantas}@decsai.ugr.es

Abstract. At first, support vector machines (SVMs) were applied to solve binary classification problems. They can also be extended to solve multicategory problems by the combination of binary SVM classifiers. In this paper, we propose a new fuzzy model that includes the advantages of several previously published methods solving their drawbacks. For each datum, a class is rejected using information provided by every decision function related to it. Our proposal yields membership degrees in the unit interval and in some cases, it improves the performance of the former methods in the unclassified regions.

1 Introduction

At first, support vector machines (SVMs) were used to binary classification problems [6, 24]. There is more than one way to extend the model to solve *multicategory problems*. In fact, the extension of the binary SVMs to these kind of problems are an active field of research. Mostly, there are four main ways to make this extension:

- All-at-once [8, 18, 25] (AO).
- Error correcting output code [12] (ECOC).
- One-versus-all [24] (OvA).
- Pairwise classification [16] (PWC).

These methods have been reviewed in several papers [14, 21]. Although the former methods have similar generalization performance, the OvA and PWC methods are simpler and more intuitive than the AO and ECOC methods [21]. Both the AO and ECOC approaches suffer from a large computational cost: (1) The AO approaches need to compute all decision functions at once. This step requires to solve a single complex optimization problem. (2) In regard to the ECOC methods, their high computational cost is due to the length of the code and the decode strategy used. On the other hand, setting the optimum code and decode method is a research area itself. Alwein et al. [3] represent any possible decomposition into binary problems through a code matrix $M \in \{-1, 0, +1\}^{K\times l}$, where K is the number of classes and l is the number of binary problems. In this way, the OvA or PWC methods can be seen as particular coding schemes.

A. Gelbukh and C.A. Reyes-Garcia (Eds.): MICAI 2006, LNAI 4293, pp. 562–571, 2006.

When a multicategory problem is solved by means of OvA or PWC methods, unclassified regions may arise and it requires the use *tie-break rules*. To solve this issue in the OvA and PWC approaches, several solutions have been proposed:

- Vapnik [24] suggested the use of the continuous output of SVM decision function in OvA.
- Platt et al. [20] used a Directed Decision Acyclic Graph (DDAG) instead of the standard method based on vote count in PWC.
- Different researchers have developed methods to compute probability distributions for each class in PWC multiclass SVMs [26, 27]. In [9], a method for general non-probabilistic classifiers is proposed. It supposes we have a non-probabilistic classifier with an output belonging to the unit interval. The advantages of using the negative vote information are remarked in this paper.
- A fuzzy SVM model is proposed by Abe and Inoue, for both approaches OvA [15] and PWC [2].

Abe and Inoue are pioneers in hybridising multicategory SVMs models and fuzzy concepts successfully. Their models have a good generalisation performance and their validity have been shown through an exhaustive experimental analysis in several papers [22, 23].

In this paper, we focus in non-probabilistic PWC methods for multiclass SVMs.

1.1 Motivation

In the conventional SVMs, a multicategory problem with K classes is converted into K binary classification problems. In each one, class i is separated from the remaining classes. Kressel [16] converts a K multicategory problem into $K(K-1)/2$ binary classification problems, configuring the PWC.

Suppose a multiclass problem with K classes and a multicategory SVM based on one-versus-one binary SVMs to solve it. When we want to classify a datum $\mathbf{x}$, we distinguish the following two cases:

1. There exists a class with $K-1$ positive answers.
2. There is at least one negative answer for every class.

The second case is considered the problematic one. Next, we briefly describe the principal PWC methods with their advantages and drawbacks:

- *Vote count.* It is also called *Winner-Take-All* or *Max-Win*, because the final class for a datum $\mathbf{x}$ is the class i that maximizes the *sum* of positive votes. A class i obtains one positive vote when a decision boundary related with it points out that $\mathbf{x}$ belongs to the class. A negative vote for a class i happens when one decision boundary associated to the class answers that the datum to classify is not of this class.

  Using vote count can produce unclassified regions because a set of classes can have the maximum number of positive votes. It is a drawback of this method.

- *DDAG.* To solve the unclassified regions and lighten the computational cost of evaluating $K \times (K-1)/2$ binary SVMs (supposing a multiclass problem with K classes), Platt et al. proposed the use of DDAGs.

  This method classifies an example $\mathbf{x}$ in $K-1$ steps. On each one, two classes i,j are compared and one of them is rejected using the decision function that classifies i-against-j. If the decision function answers that $\mathbf{x}$ belongs to class i, DDAG method uses this information in the opposite direction: x does not belong to class j. From this point of view, DDAG method considers negative information provided by decision functions to obtain the final class for a datum $\mathbf{x}$.

  The handicap of this strategy is what happen when every class have at least one negative vote. In this case, $\mathbf{x}$ is in the problematic case described above. Class for $\mathbf{x}$ is obtained by a non-deterministic process, because it depends of the DAG structure [1].
- *Fuzzy Pairwise SVM* (FPWSVM). This method is also proposed to solve unclassified regions. The fuzzy model proposed by Abe and Inoue [2] takes into account the strength of the decision function continuous output associated to a class i to compute the membership degree for a datum $\mathbf{x}$ to this class.

  If $\mathbf{x}$ is in the problematic case, FPWSVM considers the strength of negative information provided by decision functions to obtain the class for $\mathbf{x}$. In these situations, FPWSVM considers negative information from decision boundaries to obtain the final class as DDAG. Taking into account the strength of this information overcomes DDAG method drawback for this kind of data. The class for $\mathbf{x}$ is obtained by a deterministic process.

  This fuzzy model is not standard, since the membership degrees belong to the interval $(-\infty, 1]$. In classical Fuzzy Sets Theory (FST), membership degrees fall in the unit interval.
  Class membership degree for an example is obtained by aggregating the membership degrees with the minimum (*min*) or the arithmetic average (*avg*) operator.

  The *avg* operator has an unstable behaviour [2, 22] in Fuzzy Pairwise Least Square SVMs. When using the *min* operator, this model only considers the most negative vote to classify data. This approach is not suitable in certain situations because it ignores the remaining negative vote information to reject or no a class.

1.2 Objectives

To overcome the disadvantages of the former methods, we propose a new model. It is depicted in Fig. 1. Our aim for this paper is to propose a fuzzy model for pairwise multiclass SVMs recalling the strong points of the previous methods:

- From *vote count*, the information is added by using the *sum* operator.
- In regard with *DDAG*, it considers decision functions output information to reject classes.
- Finally as *FPWSVM*, it takes into account the strength of the decision function output.

Now, the good news are that it does not share their drawbacks:

- *Vote count*: Unclassified regions may arise because a set of classes can have the maximum number of positive votes.
- *DDAG*: In the problematic case, the final class for a datum $\mathbf{x}$ is obtained by a non-deterministic process.
- *FPWSVM* using the *min* operator: An example in the problematic case is classified using only the strength of the most negative vote information for each class.

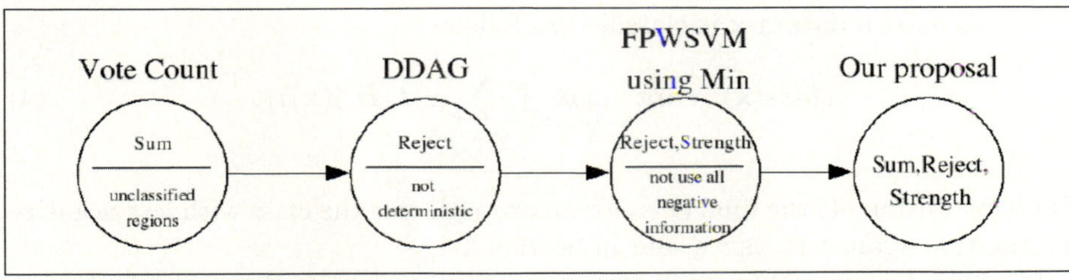

Fig. 1. Our proposal collects the advantages of the pairwise methods above and overcomes their drawbacks

1.3 Overview of Paper

This paper is divided into the following sections. We present our fuzzy proposal in Section 2. An empirical analysis including experimental results and their analysis are shown in Section 3. Finally, some conclusions are drawn.

2 Our Fuzzy Pairwise Classification Approach

Let P be a multicategory problem with K classes. In pairwise multiclass SVMs, $\frac{K(K-1)}{2}$ binary SVMs are trained (one for each pair of classes i and j).

The definition of decision function $f_{ij}(\mathbf{x})$ for the binary SVM distinguishing data between classes i and j is the following:

$$f_{ij}(\mathbf{x}) = sgn(H_{ij}(\mathbf{x})) = \begin{cases} 1 & \text{for } H_{ij}(\mathbf{x}) > 0, \\ 0 & \text{for } H_{ij}(\mathbf{x}) = 0, \\ -1 & \text{for } H_{ij}(\mathbf{x}) < 0 \end{cases} \tag{1}$$

with

$$H_{ij}(\mathbf{x}) = \sum_{k \in \mathrm{SVs}^{ij}} \alpha_k^{ij} y_k^{ij} K(\mathbf{x}_k^{ij}, \mathbf{x}) - b^{ij}. \tag{2}$$

We suppose, without loss of generality, that if $H_{ij}(\mathbf{x}) > 0$, then $\mathbf{x} \in$ class i. Moreover, we can define $H_{ji}(\mathbf{x}) = -H_{ij}(\mathbf{x})$.

As we said in Section 1.1, our fuzzy pairwise SVM model is based on the philosophy of using the information of the degree of the negative votes to reject classes. The degree of the negative votes are aggregated with the *sum* operator.

To avoid the effect of the positive votes, according to the FPWSVM philosophy with the *min* operator described above, we use the following T function on every vote:

$$T(x) = \begin{cases} 0 & x \geq 0, \\ x & \text{otherwise.} \end{cases} \tag{3}$$

This function maps the degree of positive votes to the neuter element of the *sum* operator.

In this case, a datum $\mathbf{x}$ is classified as follows:

$$class(\mathbf{x}) = \arg \max_{i=1,\ldots,K} \{ \sum_{\substack{j=1,\ldots,K \\ j \neq i}} T(H_{ij}(\mathbf{x}))\}. \tag{4}$$

Therefore, using (4) the final class for an example $\mathbf{x}$ is the class with less negative information against it, as we said in Section 1.1.

In order to improve the result interpretability, we fuzzify the strength of every vote. Next, we build a fuzzy model of a pairwise multiclass SVM as follows:

- We propose to fuzzify the output of each binary SVM with the following membership function:

$$\mu_{ij}(\mathbf{x}) = \frac{2}{1 + \exp(-2T(H_{ij}(\mathbf{x})))}. \tag{5}$$

  With our membership function $\mu_{ij}(\mathbf{x})$, we obtain membership degrees in the interval $[0, 1]$. It is the typical range of membership degrees in FST.
- The degree of membership to class i for a datum $\mathbf{x}$ is defined as follows:

$$\mu_i(\mathbf{x}) = \circledast_{\substack{j=1,\ldots,K \\ j \neq i}} \mu_{ij}(\mathbf{x}). \tag{6}$$

  Let a, b be two values belonging to the unit interval, the definition of $\circledast$ operator [19] is given by:

$$a \circledast b = \frac{ab}{1 + (1-a)(1-b)}, \tag{7}$$

  It is a t-norm of the Hamacher family [11, 13, 17].
- Finally, the resulting class for a datum $\mathbf{x}$ is the following:

$$class(\mathbf{x}) = \arg \max_{i=1,\ldots,K} \{\mu_i(\mathbf{x})\}. \tag{8}$$

  The classification results obtained through (4) are equivalent to those obtained through (8), since the used t-norm for uniting votes into the final estimates is the f-dual operator of sum operator [4].

3 Experimental Analysis

We have conducted several experiments to test the validity of our proposal and compare its generalisation performance against the previously considered methods. Four data sets compose the selected workbench.

We have considered four strategies to compare with our proposal: (A) *Vote count* without applying any *tie-break* method in the unclassified regions. (B) *DDAG*. The list used to assign the final class to a datum $\mathbf{x}$ is defined by a sorted index class list. (C) *FPWSVM* proposed by Abe and Inoue using the *min* operator.

3.1 Methodology

The selected benchmark data sets are: `segment`, `yeast`, `vehicle` and `glass` problem. The first two data sets are part of UCI repository [5] and the remaining data sets are included into Statlog collection [10].

The parameter set model selection has been conducted by following the experimental framework given in [14]:

- For the `segment`, `yeast`, `vehicle` and `glass` data sets, we have applied directly a 10-fold cross validation to evaluate the model performance. In Table 1, it is shown the best 10–CV rate.
- Input attributes for all data sets are scaled in the interval $[-1, 1]$. Detailed information about data sets can be found out in [5].
- RBF kernel $K(\mathbf{x}_i, \mathbf{x}_j) = \exp(\gamma \|\mathbf{x}_i - \mathbf{x}_j\|^2)$ are used to train every binary SVM.
- Parameter sets used to obtain the best performance are the following: $\gamma = \{2^4, 2^3, \ldots, 2^{-10}\}$ and $C = \{2^{14}, 2^{13}, \ldots, 2^{-2}\}$.
- Finally, the stopping criterion of the optimization algorithm is that the Karush-Kahn-Tucker violation is less than 10^{-3} [7].

They have been run on a Pentium IV 2.4GHz with 2GB of main memory. It runs with Fedora Core 4 operating system and software was compiled by GNU gcc 4.0.1. We used the `LIBSVM` [7] to build all multiclass methods compared in the experiments.

Table 1. Comparison using the RBF kernel (Best test rates bold-faced)

	Standard		*Fuzzy*	
Datasets	*Max-win*	*DDAG*	*Min*	$\circledast$
segment	97.48	97.61	**97.74**	**97.74**
yeast	60.78	**61.05**	**61.05**	**61.05**
vehicle	85.93	86.05	86.41	**86.52**
glass	71.50	72.89	73.83	**74.77**

3.2 Results

The four compared methods have a similar generalisation performance. Their classification results are the same when they evaluate a datum which does not belong to the unclassified regions. The behaviour of the former strategies are different when the data belong to the problematic areas. So, the differences among them will be more or less significative depending on the size of the unclassified regions.

In Table 3.2, it is displayed the best test performances of the methods in the unclassified regions. If we take into account the data in the unclassified regions, the test performance of our proposal is 70% and 71.4% for the `glass` and `vehicle` problems, respectively. The performance of the FPWSVM using the *min* is 50% and 57.1% in the unclassified regions of the previous problems considered. The results for the DDAG are poorer in these areas, its performance is the 30% and 28.6%, respectively.

Our approach obtains better results than the FPWSVM using the *min* operator in the unclassified regions because, to reject a class, we take into account all its negative information.

To explain this fact, Table 3 is presented. It shows a study case extracted from experiments with the `vehicle` data set. It is a typical case that our proposal classifies correctly, but for which FPWSVM with the *min* operator fails. The correct class for this sample is class 1. Our proposal classifies correctly every datum for which FPWSVM using the *min* operator yields right results. Besides, it provides correct answers for examples like the one shown in Table 3.

Table 2. Comparison of test performances in the unclassified regions using the RBF kernel (Best test rates bold-faced)

	Standard	*Fuzzy*	
Datasets	*DDAG*	*Min*	$\circledast$
segment	23.07	**46.15**	**46.15**
yeast	**57.14**	**57.14**	**57.14**
vehicle	28.60	57.10	**71.40**
glass	30.00	50.00	**70.00**

Table 3. A study case from the `vehicle` dataset for which FPWSVM using the *min* operator fails and our proposal hits. In bold faces real class for **x** (first column) and the obtained winner class for both compared methods (third and fourth column).

Class	μ_{ij}^{Abe}	μ_i^{Abe},*Min*	μ_{ij}	μ_i,$\circledast$
1	(−0.450, 1.000, 0.601)	−0.450	(0.578, 1.000, 1.000)	**0.578**
2	(0.443, 0.373, −1.662)	−1.662	(1.000, 1.000, 0.069)	0.069
3	(0.371, −0.373, −0.601)	−0.601	(1.000, 0.643, 0.462)	0.249
4	(−0.443, −0.371, 0.450)	**−0.443**	(0.584, 0.645, 1.000)	0.329
Final Class	$\max(\mu_i^{Abe})$	Class 4	$\max(\mu_i)$	**Class 1**

4 Conclusions

The advantages and the drawbacks of several PWC methods for multiclass SVMs have been understood. Then, a new fuzzy method has been presented. On the one hand, it includes the advantages of the previously published methods:

- It uses the *sum* operator to aggregate information provided by decision functions in the same way of vote count method.
- It takes into account negative information of decision functions to reject a class, as DDAG method.
- It considers the strength of decision functions as FPWSVM.

On the other hand, our proposal overcomes their disadvantages:

- It avoids unclassified regions.
- The final class for a datum is obtained in a deterministic way because the strength of decision function output is considered.
- It defines a coherent fuzzy model according to FST.
- It uses the $\circledast$ operator instead of the *min* operator. Thus, all negative information about a class is taken into account when a datum is classified.

We have conducted a number of experiments to test the performance of the new model applying it on several real world data sets. The empirical results show that in some cases, there is an improvement over standard methods and the fuzzy model for pairwise classification proposed by Abe and Inoue in the unclassified regions. Besides, the expressiveness is improved with fuzzy membership degrees belonging to the unit interval.

Acknowledgements

This research has been partially supported by Ministerio de Ciencia y Tecnología under projects TIC2003-04650 and TIN2004-07236.

Bibliography

[1] S. Abe. Analysis of multiclass support vector machines. In *Proceedings of International Conference on Computational Intelligence for Modelling Control and Automation (CIMCA'2003)*, pages 385–396, Viena(Austria) - February 2003.

[2] S. Abe and T. Inoue. Fuzzy support vector machines for multiclass problems. In *Proceedings of European Symposium on Artificial Neural Networks (ESANN'2002)*, pages 113–118, Bruges(Belgium) 24-26 April 2002.

[3] E. L. Allwein, R. E. Shapire, and Y. Singer. Reducing multiclass to binary: A unifying approach for margin classifiers. *Journal of Machine Learning Research*, 1:113–141, 2000.

[4] J.M. Benítez, J.L. Castro, and I. Requena. Are artificial neural networks black boxes? *IEEE Transactions on Neural Networks*, 8(5):1156–1164, September 1997.

[5] C. L. Blake and C. J. Merz. UCI Repository of machine learning databases. univ. california, dept. inform. comput. sci., irvine, ca. [*Online*] *http://www.ics.uci.edu/ mlearn/MLSummary.html.*
[6] B. E. Boser, I. M. Guyon, and V. Vapnik. A training algorithm for optimal margin classifiers. In *Fifth Annual Workshop on Computational Learning Theory.* ACM, 1992.
[7] C. C. Chang and C. J. Lin. *LIBSVM: a library for support vector machines*, 2001. Software available at `http://www.csie.` ntu.edu.tw/ cjlin/libsvm.
[8] K. Crammer and Y. Singer. On the algorithmic implementation of multiclass kernel-based vector machines. *Journal of Machine Learning Research*, 2(December):265–292, 2001.
[9] F. Cutzu. Polychotomous classification with pairwise classifiers: A new voting principle. In *Proc. 12th International Workshop on Multiple Classifier Systems*, volume LNCS 2709, 2003.
[10] D. J. Spiegelhalter D. Michie and C. C. Taylor. Machine learning, neural and statistical clasification. [*Online*] *http://www.niaad.liacc.up.pt/statlog/*.
[11] M. Detyniecki. Mathematical aggregation operator and their application to video querying. Doctoral thesis — research report 2001-2002, Laboratoire d'Informatique de Paris, 2000.
[12] T. G. Dietterich and G. Bakiri. Solving multiclass learning problems via error-correcting output codes. *Journal of Artificial Intelligence Research*, 2:263–286, 1995.
[13] H. Hamacher. *Uber logische Aggregationen nicht-binar explizierter Entscheidungskriterien.* Rita G. Fischer Verlag, Frankfurt, 1978.
[14] C. Hsu and C. Lin. A comparison of methods for multiclass support vector machines. *Neural Networks, IEEE Transactions on*, 13(2):415–425, March 2002.
[15] T. Inoue and S. Abe. Fuzzy support vector machines for pattern classification. In *Proceedings of International Joint Conference on Neural Networks (IJCNN '01)*, volume 2, pages 1449–1454, July 2001.
[16] U.H.-G. Kressel. Pairwise classification and support vector machines. In C.J.C. Burges B. Scholkopf and A.J.Smola, editors, *Advance in Kernel Methods, Chapter 15*, pages 255–268. The MIT Press, Cambridge, MA, 1999.
[17] L. I. Kuncheva. *Fuzzy classifier design.* Studies in Fuzziness and Soft Computing, Physica-Verlag, 2000.
[18] Y. Lee, Y. Lin, and G. Wahba. Multicategory support vector machines. In *Proceedings of the 33rd Symposium on the Interface*, 2001.
[19] C. J. Mantas. T-norms and t-conorms in multilayer perceptrons. In *Proceedings of the Joint 4th EUSFLAT and 11th LFA Conference (EUSFLAT-LFA'2005)*, pages 1313–1318, Barcelona(Spain) September 2005.
[20] J.C. Platt, N. Cristianini, and J. Shawe-Taylor. Large margin dags for multiclass classification. In T.K. Lee S.A. Solla and K.-R. Muller, editors, *Advances in Neural Information Processing System*, volume 12, pages 547–553. The MIT Press, 2000.
[21] R. Rifkin and A. Klautau. In defense of one-vs-all classification. *Journal of Machine Learning Research*, 5:101–104, 2004.
[22] D. Tsujinishi and S. Abe. Fuzzy least squares support vector machines for multiclass problems. *Neural Networks*, 16(5–6):785–792, 2003.
[23] D. Tsujinishi, Y. Koshiba, and S. Abe. Why pairwise is better than one-against-all or all-at-once. In *Proceedings of IEEE International Conference on Neural Networks*, volume 1, pages 693–698. IEEE Press, 2004.
[24] V. Vapnik. *Statistical Learning Theory.* John Wiley and Sons Inc. New York, 1998.

[25] J. Weston and C. Watkins. Multi-class support vector machines. Technical Report CSD-TR-98-04, Royal Holloway, University of London, Department of Computer Science, 1998.

[26] T. F. Wu, C. J. Lin, and R. C. Weng. Probability estimates for multi-class classification by pairwise coupling. *Journal of Machine Learning Research*, 5(August):975–1005, 2004.

[27] B. Zadrozny. Reducing multiclass to binary by coupling probability estimates. In *Proceedings of NIPS*, 2001.

Support Vector Machine Classification Based on Fuzzy Clustering for Large Data Sets

Jair Cervantes[1], Xiaoou Li[1], and Wen Yu[2]

[1] Sección de Computación Departamento de Ingenierá Elétrica
CINVESTAV-IPN
A.P. 14-740, Av.IPN 2508, México D.F., 07360, México
[2] Departamento de Control Automático, CINVESTAV-IPN
A.P. 14-740, Av.IPN 2508, México D.F., 07360, México
yuw@ctrl.cinvestav.mx

Abstract. Support vector machine (SVM) has been successfully applied to solve a large number of classification problems. Despite its good theoretic foundations and good capability of generalization, it is a big challenging task for the large data sets due to the training complexity, high memory requirements and slow convergence. In this paper, we present a new method, *SVM classification based on fuzzy clustering*. Before applying SVM we use fuzzy clustering, in this stage the optimal number of clusters are not needed in order to have less computational cost. We only need to partition the training data set briefly. The SVM classification is realized with the center of the groups. Then the de-clustering and SVM classification via reduced data are used. The proposed approach is scalable to large data sets with high classification accuracy and fast convergence speed. Empirical studies show that the proposed approach achieves good performance for large data sets.

1 Introduction

The digital revolution has made possible that the data capture be easy and its storage have a practically null cost. As a matter of this, enormous quantities of highly dimensional data are stored in databases continuously. Due to this, semi-automatic methods for classification from databases are necessary. Support vector machine (SVM) is a powerful technique for classification and regression. Training an SVM is usually posed as a quadratic programming (QP) problem to find a separation hyper-plane which implicates a matrix of density $n \times n$, where the n is the number of points in the data set. This needs huge quantities of computational time and memory for large data sets, so the training complexity of SVM is highly dependent on the size of a data set [1][19]. Many efforts have been made on the classification for large data sets. Sequential Minimal Optimization (SMO)[12] transforms the large QP problem into a series of small QP problems, each one involves only two variables [4][6][15]. In [11] was applied the boosting to Platt's SMO algorithm and to use resulting Boost-SMO method for speeding and scaling up the SVM training. [18] discusses large scale approximations for Bayesian inference for LS-SVM. The results of [7] demonstrate that

A. Gelbukh and C.A. Reyes-Garcia (Eds.): MICAI 2006, LNAI 4293, pp. 572–582, 2006.

a fair computational advantage can be obtained by using a recursive strategy for large data sets, such as those involved in data mining and text categorization applications. Vector quantization is applied in [8] to reduce a large data set by replacing examples by prototypes. Training time for choosing optimal parameters is greatly reduced. [9] proposes an approach based on an incremental learning technique and a multiple proximal support vector machine classifier. Random Selection [2][14][16] is to select data such that the learning be maximized. However, it could over-simplify the training data set, lose the benefits of SVM, specially if the probability distribution of the training data and the testing data are different.

On the other hand, unsupervised classification, called clustering is the classification of similar objects into different groups, or more precisely, the partitioning of a data set into subsets (clusters), so that the data in each subset (ideally) share some common trait (often proximity according to some defined distance measure). The goal of clustering is to separate a finite unlabeled data set into a finite and discrete set of "natural," hidden data structures [13]. Some results [1][5][19] show that clustering technique can help to decrease complexity of SVM training. But, they need more computations to build the hierarchical structure. In this paper we propose a new approach for classification of large data sets, named *SVM classification based on fuzzy clustering*. To the best of our knowledge, SVM classification based on fuzzy clustering has not yet been established in the literature.

In partitioning, the number of clusters is pre-defined to avoid computational cost for determining the optimal number of clusters. We only section the training data set and to exclude the set of clusters with minor probability for support vectors. Based on the obtained clusters, which are defined as mixed category and uniform category, we extract support vectors by SVM and form into reduced clusters. Then we apply de-clustering for the reduced clusters, and obtain subsets from the original sets. Finally, we use SVM again and finish the classification. An experiment is given to show the effectiveness of the new approach. The structure of the paper is organized as follows: after the introduction of the SVM and fuzzy clustering in Section II, we introduce the SVM based on fuzzy clustering classification in Section III. Section IV demonstrates experimental results on artificial and real data sets. We conclude our study in Section V.

2 Support Vector Machine for Classification and Fuzzy Clustering

Assume that a training set X is given as:

$$(\mathbf{x}_1, \mathbf{y}_1), (\mathbf{x}_2, \mathbf{y}_2), \ldots, (\mathbf{x}_n, \mathbf{y}_n) \tag{1}$$

i.e. $X = \{x_i, y_i\}_{i=1}^{n}$ where $x_i \in \mathbb{R}^d$ and $y_i \in (+1, -1)$. Training SVM yields to solve a quadratic programming problem as follows

$$\max_{\alpha_i} -\frac{1}{2}\sum_{i,j=1}^{l} \alpha_i y_i \alpha_j y_j \mathbf{K}\langle x_i \cdot x_j\rangle + \sum_{i=1}^{l}\alpha_i$$
$$\text{subject to: } \sum_{i=1}^{l}\alpha_i y_i = 0, \quad C \geq \alpha_i \geq 0, i = 1, 2, \ldots l$$

where $C > 0$, $\alpha_i = [\alpha_1, \alpha_2, \ldots, \alpha_l]^T$, $\alpha_i \geq 0, i = 1, 2, \ldots, l$, are coefficients corresponding to x_i, x_i with nonzero α_i is called Support Vector (SV). The function $\mathbf{K}$ is called the Mercel kernel, which must satisfy the Mercer condition [17].

Let S be the index set of SV, then the optimal hyperplane is

$$\sum_{i\in S}(\alpha_i y_i)K(\mathbf{x}_i, \mathbf{x}_j) + b = 0$$

and the optimal decision function is defined as

$$f(x) = sign\left(\sum_{i\in S}(\alpha_i y_i)K(\mathbf{x}_i, \mathbf{x}_j) + b\right) \tag{2}$$

where $\mathbf{x} = [x_1, x_2, \ldots, x_l]$ is the input data, α_i and y_i are Lagrange multipliers. A new object x can be classified using (2). The vector $\mathbf{x}_i$ is shown only in the way of inner product. There is a Lagrangian multiplier α for each training point. When the maximum margin of the hyperplane is found, only the closed points to the hyperplane satisfy $\alpha > 0$. These points are called support vectors SV, the other points satisfy $\alpha = 0$.

Clustering essentially deals with the task of splitting a set of patterns into a number of more-or-less homogenous classes (clusters) with respect to a suitable similarity measure, such that the patterns belonging to any one of the clusters are similar and the patterns of the different clusters are as dissimilar as possible.

Let us formulate the fuzzy clustering problem as: consider a finite set of elements $X = \{x_1, x_2, \ldots, x_n\}$ with $d-dimension$ in the Euclidian space $\mathbb{R}^d$, i.e., $x_j \in \mathbb{R}^d, j = 1, 2, \ldots, n$. The problem is to perform a partitioning of these data into k fuzzy sets with respect to a given criterion. The criterion is usually to optimize an objective function. The result of the fuzzy clustering can be expressed by a partitioning matrix U such that $U = [u_{ij}]_{i=1\ldots k,\ j=1\ldots n}$, where u_{ij} is a numeric value in $[0, 1]$. There are two constraints on the value of u_{ij}. First, total memberships of the element $x_j \in X$ in all classes is equal to 1. Second, every constructed cluster is non-empty and different from the entire set, i.e.,

$$\begin{aligned} &\sum_{i=1}^{k} u_{ij} = 1, \quad \text{for all } j = 1, 2, \ldots, n \\ &0 < \sum_{j=1}^{n} u_{ij} < n, \quad \text{for all } i = 1, 2, \ldots, k. \end{aligned} \tag{3}$$

A general form of the objective function is

$$J(u_{ij}, \mathbf{v}_k) = \sum_{i=1}^{k}\sum_{j=1}^{n}\sum_{l=1}^{k} g\left[w(x_i), u_{ij}\right]\ d\left(\mathbf{x}_j, \mathbf{v}_i\right)$$

where $w(x_i)$ is the a priori weight for each $\mathbf{x}_i$, $d(\mathbf{x}_j, \mathbf{v}_i)$ is the degree of dissimilarity between the data $\mathbf{x}_j$ and the supplemental element $\mathbf{v}_i$, which can be considered as the central vector of i-th cluster. The degree of dissimilarity is defined as a measure that satisfies two axioms: 1) $d(\mathbf{x}_j, \mathbf{v}_i) \geq 0$, 2) $d(\mathbf{x}_j, \mathbf{v}_i) = d(\mathbf{x}_i \mathbf{v}_j)$. The fuzzy clustering can be formulated into an optimization problem:

$$\begin{gathered} \text{Min} \quad J(u_{ij}, \mathbf{v}_i), \; i = 1, 2 \ldots k; \; j = 1, 2 \ldots n \\ \text{Subject to} \; : \; (3) \end{gathered}$$

This objective function is

$$J(u_{ij}, \mathbf{v}_i) = \sum_{i=1}^{k} \sum_{j=1}^{n} u_{ij}^m \left\| \mathbf{x}_j, \mathbf{v}_i \right\|^2, \qquad m > 1 \tag{4}$$

where m is call a exponential weight which influences the degree of fuzziness of the membership function. To solve the minimization problem, we differentiate the objective function in (4) with respect to $\mathbf{v}_i$ (for fixed u_{ij}, $i = 1, \ldots, k$, $j = 1, \ldots, n$) and to u_{ij} (for fixed $\mathbf{v}_i$, $i = 1, \ldots, k$) and apply the conditions of (3)

$$v_i = \frac{1}{\sum_{j=1}^{n} (u_{ij})^m} \sum_{j=1}^{n} (u_{ij})^m \mathbf{x}_j, \quad i = 1, \ldots, k \tag{5}$$

$$u_{ij} = \frac{\left(1 / \left\| \mathbf{x}_j, \mathbf{v}_i \right\|^2\right)^{1/m-1}}{\sum_{l=1}^{k} \left(1 / \left\| \mathbf{x}_j - \mathbf{v}_k \right\|^2\right)^{1/m-1}} \tag{6}$$

where $i = 1 \ldots k$; $j = 1 \ldots n$. The system described by (5) and (6) cannot be solved analytically. However, the following fuzzy clustering algorithm provides an iterative approach:

Step 1: Select a number of clusters k ($2 \leq k \leq n$) and exponential weight m ($1 < m < \infty$). Choose an initial partition matrix $U^{(0)}$ and a termination criterion ϵ.

Step 2: Calculate the fuzzy cluster centers $\left\{ \mathbf{v}_i^{(l)} \mid i = 1, 2, \ldots, k \right\}$ using $U^{(l)}$ and (5).

Step 3: Calculate the new partition matrix $U^{(l+1)}$ by using $\left\{ \mathbf{v}_i^{(l)} \mid i = 1, 2, \ldots, k \right\}$ and (6).

Step 4: Calculate $\Delta = \left\| U^{(l+1)} - U^{(l)} \right\| = \max_{i,j} \left| u_{ij}^{l+1} - u_{ij}^{(l)} \right|$. If $\Delta > \epsilon$, then $l = l + 1$ and go to Step 2. If $\Delta \leq \epsilon$, then stop.

The iterative procedure described above minimizes the objective function in (4) and leads to some of its local minimum.

3 SVM Classification Based on Fuzzy Clustering

Assuming that we have an input-output dataset. The task here is to find a set of support vectors from the input-output data, which maximize the space between classes. From the above discussion, we need to

- eliminate the input data subset which is far away from the decision hyperplane;
- find support vectors from the reduced data set.

Our approach can be formed into the following steps.

3.1 Fuzzy Clustering: *Sectioning the Input Data Space into Clusters*

According to (1), let $X = \{\mathbf{x}_1, \mathbf{x}_2, \ldots, \mathbf{x}_n\}$ be the set of n inputs data, where each data $\mathbf{x}_i$ can be considered as a point represented by a vector of dimension d as follows:

$$\mathbf{x}_i = \langle w(x_1), w(x_2), \ldots, w(x_d) \rangle$$

where $1 \leq i \leq n$. $w(x_i)$ denotes the weight of x_j in $\mathbf{x}_i$, where $0 < w_{ij} < 1$ and $1 \leq j \leq d$. Assume that we can divide the original input data set into k clusters, where $k > 2$. Note that the clusters number must be strictly > 2, because we want to reduce the original input data set, eliminating the clusters far from the decision hyperplane. If $k = 2$ the input data set would be split into the number of existent classes and the data set could not be eliminated.

The fuzzy clustering obtains k clusters center of data and also the membership function of each data in the clusters minimizing the objective function (4), where u_{ij}^m denote the membership grade of $\mathbf{x}_j$ in the cluster A_k, $\mathbf{v}_i$ denotes the center of A_k and $\|\mathbf{x}_j, \mathbf{v}_i\|$ denotes the distance of $\mathbf{x}_j$ to center $\mathbf{v}_i$.. Furthermore, $\mathbf{x}_j$ and $\mathbf{v}_i$ are vectors of dimension d. For other hand, m influences the degree of fuzziness of the membership function. Note that the total membership of the element $\mathbf{x}_j \in X$ in all classes is equal to 1.0, i.e., $\sum_{i=1}^{k} u_{ij} = 1$ where $1 \leq i \leq n$. The membership grade of $\mathbf{x}_j$ in A_k is calculated as in (6) and the cluster center v_i of A_k is calculated as in (5). The complete fuzzy clustering algorithm is developed by means of the steps 1, 2, 3 and 4 shown in the section II.

3.2 Classification of Clusters Center Using SVM

Let (X, Y) be the training patterns set where $X = \{\mathbf{x}_1, \ldots, \mathbf{x}_j, \ldots, \mathbf{x}_n\}$ and $Y = \{\mathbf{y}_1, \ldots, \mathbf{y}_j, \ldots, \mathbf{y}_n\}$ where $\mathbf{y}_j \in (-1, 1)$, and $\mathbf{x}_j = (x_{j1}, x_{j2}, \ldots, x_{jd})^T \in \mathbb{R}^d$ and each measure x_{ji} is a characteristic (attribute, dimension or variable). The process of fuzzy clustering is based on finding k partitions of X, $C = \{C_1, \ldots, C_k\}$ $(k < n)$, such that $a)$ $\cup_{i=1}^{k} C_i = X$ and $b)$ $C_i \neq \varnothing$, $i = 1, \ldots, k$, where:

$$C_i = \{\cup \mathbf{x}_j \mid \mathbf{y}_j \in (-1, 1)\}, \; i = 1, \ldots, k \tag{7}$$

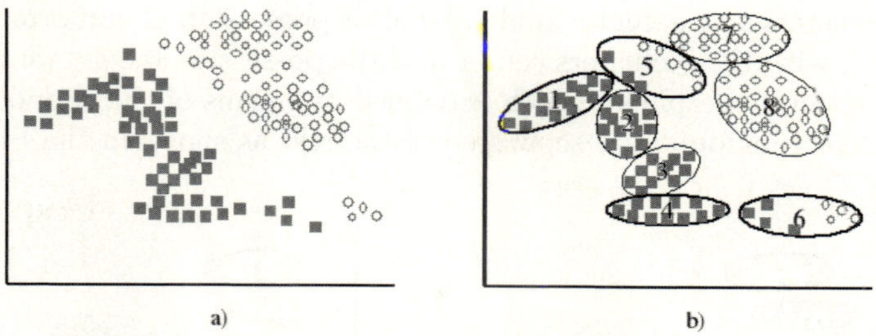

Fig. 1. Uniform clusters and mixed clusters

That is, independently that each obtained cluster contains elements with different membership grade or membership function, each element have the original possession to a class, which is shown by (7). The cluster elements obtained can have a possession of uniform class (as it is appreciated in the Figure 1(b), where the cluster elements 1, 2, 3, 4, 7 and 8 have one only possession), this type of clusters is defined as:

$$C_u = \{\cup \mathbf{x}_j \mid \mathbf{y}_j \in -1 \ \wedge \mathbf{y}_j \in 1\}$$

or in the contrary case a possession of mixed class, where each cluster has elements of one or another class (see Figure 1(b) where the clusters 5 and 6 contain elements with possession of mixed class), this type of clusters is defined as:

$$C_m = \{\cup \mathbf{x}_j \mid \mathbf{y}_j \in -1 \ \vee \mathbf{y}_j \in 1\}$$

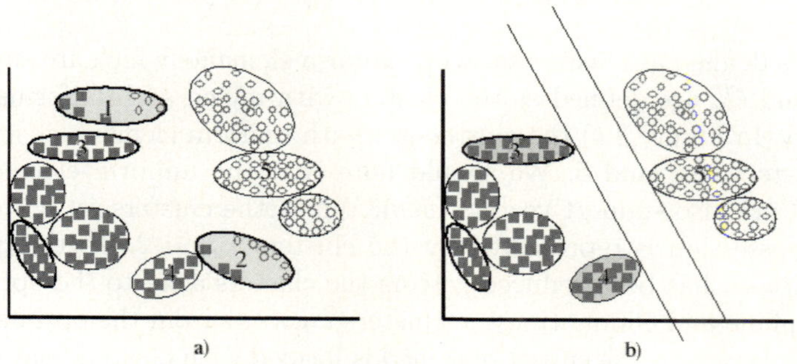

Fig. 2. Reduction of the input data set. (a) clusters with mixed elements, (b) clusters close to separation hiper-plane.

We identified the clusters with elements of mixed category and the clusters with elements of uniform category. The clusters with elements of mixed possession are separated for a later evaluation (see Figure 2 a)), because these contain elements with bigger likelihood to be support vectors. Each one of the remaining clusters has a center and a label of possession of uniform class (see Figure 2 *b*)), with these clusters center and the possession labels, we used SVM to find a decision hyperplane, which is defined by means of the support vectors, the support vectors found are separated of the rest as shows in the Figure 3 *b*).

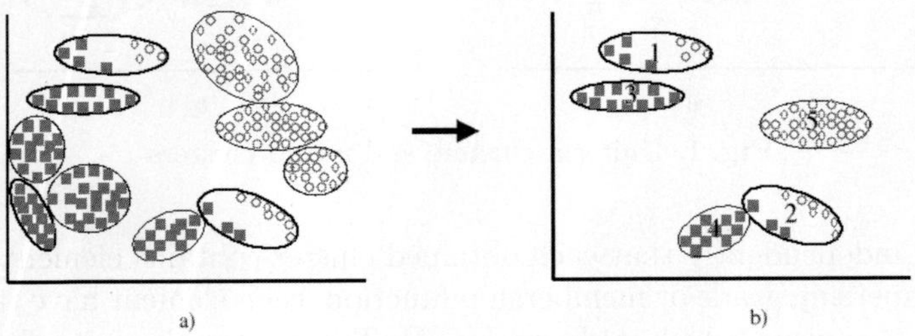

Fig. 3. Reduction of input data using partitioning clustering. *a*) Clusters of original data set. *b*) Set of reduced clusters.

3.3 De-clustering: *Getting a Data Subset*

The data subset obtained from the original data set given in (1) is formed for

$$\bigcup_{i=1}^{l} C_{m_i}, \; l \leq k \; \text{ and}$$

$$\bigcup_{i=1}^{p} C_{u_i}, \quad | \; C_u \in svc, \; p \leq k$$

where *svc* is defined as clusters set with uniform elements which are support vectors, C_m and C_u are defined as the clusters with mixed and uniforms elements respectively. In Figure 3 *b*) the clusters set with uniform elements is represented by the clusters 3, 4 and 5. We should note that the uniform elements of the clusters set are also support vectors (*svc*). While, the clusters set with elements of mixed possession is represented by the clusters 1 and 2. To this point, the original data set has been reduced getting the clusters close to the optimal decision hyperplane and eliminating the clusters far away from the optimal decision hyperplane. However, the subset obtained is formed with clusters and we needed de-clustering and to get the elements from the clusters.

The data subset obtained (X', Y') has characteristics:

$$\begin{array}{l} 1) \; X' \subset X \\ 2) \; X' \cap X = X', \; X' \cup X = X \end{array} \tag{8}$$

where this characteristics come true for X and Y. i.e., the data set obtained is a data subset from the original data set.

3.4 Classification of Reduced Data Using SVM

In this step, we used SVM on the data subset in steps 1, 2 and 3. Since the original data set is reduced significantly in the previous steps, eliminating the clusters with center far away of optimal decision hyperplane, the time of training in this stage is a lot of minor in comparison with the time of training of the original data set.

4 Experimental Results

To test and demonstrate the proposed techniques for large data sets classification, several experiments are designed and performed and the results are reported and discussed in this section.

First, let consider a simple case of classification. We generate a set of 40000 data at random, unspecified the ranges of aleatory generation. The data set has two dimensions and are labeled by X. The record r_i is labeled as "+" if $wx + b > th$ and "-" if $wx + b < th$, here th is the threshold, w is the weight associated to input data and b is the bias. In this way, the data set is linearly separable.

Figure 4 shows the input data set with 10000 (see a)), 1000 (see b)) and 100 (see c)). Now we use the fuzzy clustering to reduce the data set. After the first 3 steps of the algorithm proposed in this paper (Sections 3.1, 3.2 and 3.3), the input data sets are reduced to 337, 322 and 47 respectively, see d), e) and f) in Figure 4.

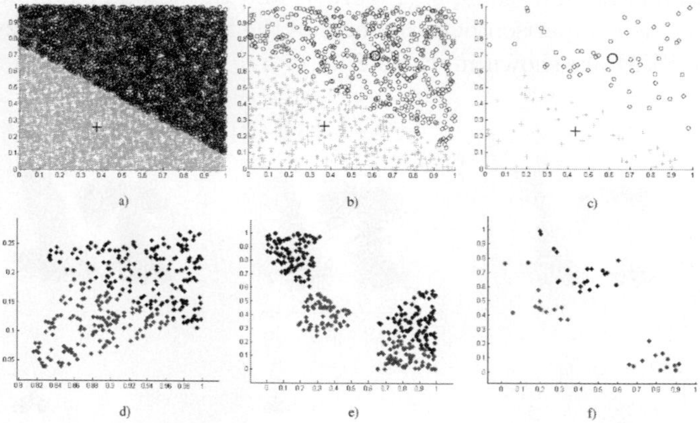

Fig. 4. Original data sets and reduced data sets with 10^4 data

We use normal SVM with linear kernel. The comparison performances of the SVM based on fuzzy clustering and normal SVM are shown in Table 1. Here "%" represents the percentage of the original data set, "#" data number, "V_s" is the number of support vectors, "t" is the total experimental time in seconds, "k" is cluster number, "Acc" is the accuracy. We can see that the data reduction is carried out with the distance between the clusters center and the optimal decision hyperplane, which provokes that some support vectors be eliminated. In spite of this, SVM based on fuzzy clustering has better performances and the training time is small compared with the normal SVM.

Table 1. Comparison between the SVM based on fuzzy clustering and normal SVM with 10^4 data

normal SVM					SVM based on fuzzy clustering			
%	#	V_S	t	Acc	V_S	t	Acc	k
0.125	500	5	96.17	99.2%	4	3.359	99.12%	10
0.25%	1000	5	1220	99.8%	4	26.657	99.72%	20
25%	10000	-	-	-	3	114.78	99.85%	50
50%	20000	-	-	-	3	235.341	99.88%	100
75%	30000	-	-	-	3	536.593	99.99%	150
100%	40000	-	-	-	3	985.735	99.99%	200

Second, we generated a set of 100,000 data at random, specified range and radio of aleatory generation as in [19]. Figure 5 shows the input data set with 1000 data (see a)), 10000 data (see b)) and 50000 data (see c)). After the fuzzy clustering , the input data sets are reduced to 257, 385 and 652 respectively, see d), e) and f) in Figure 5. For testing sets, we generated sets of 56000 and 109000 data for the first example (Figure 4) and the second example (Figure 5) respectively, the comparison performances of the SVM based on fuzzy clustering and normal SVM are shown in Table 2.

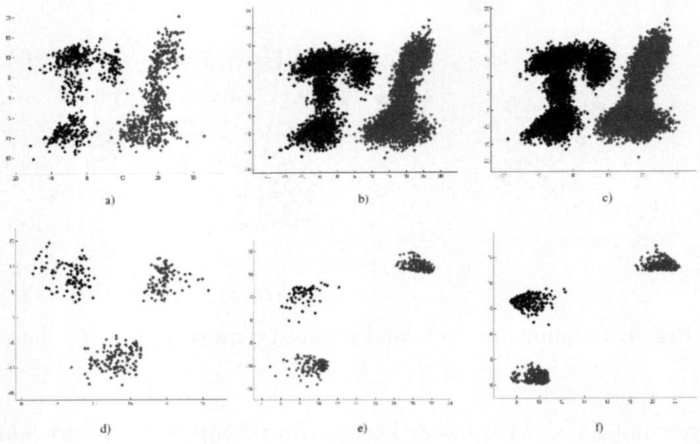

Fig. 5. Classification results with 10^5 data

Table 2. Comparison between the SVM based on fuzzy clustering and normal SVM with 10^5 data

normal SVM					SVM based on fuzzy clustering			
%	#	V_S	t	Acc	V_S	t	Acc	k
0.25%	2725	7	3554	99.80%	6	36.235	99.74%	20
25%	27250	-	-	-	4	221.297	99.88%	50
50%	54500	-	-	-	4	922.172	99.99%	100
75%	109000	-	-	-	4	2436.372	99.99%	150

Third, we use the Waveform data set [3]. The data set has 5000 waves and three classes. The classes are generated as from a combination of two or three basics waves. Each record has 22 attributes with continuous values between 0 to 6. In this example we use normal SVM with RBF kernel. Table 3 shows the training time with different data number, the performance of the SVM based on fuzzy clustering is good. The margin of optimal decision is almost the same as the normal SVM. The training time is very small with respect to normal SVM.

Table 3. Comparison between the SVM based on fuzzy clustering and normal SVM for the Wave dataset

normal SVM					SVM based on fuzzy clustering			
%	#	V_S	t	Acc	V_s	t	Acc	k
8	400	168	35.04	88.12%	162	22.68	87.3%	40
12	600	259	149.68	88.12%	244	47.96	87.6%	60
16	800	332	444.45	88.12%	329	107.26	88.12%	80
20	1000	433	1019.2	88.12%	426	194.70	88.12%	100
24	1200	537	2033.2	-	530	265.91	88.12%	120

5 Conclusion

In this paper, we developed a new classification method for large data sets. It takes the advantages of the fuzzy clustering and SVM. The algorithm proposed in this paper has a similar idea as the sequential minimal optimization (SMO), i.e., in order to work with large data sets, we partition the original data set into several clusters and reduce the size of QP problems. The experimental results show that the number of support vectors obtained using the SVM classification based on fuzzy clustering is similar to the normal SVM approach while the training time is significantly smaller.

References

1. Awad M., Khan L., Bastani F. y Yen I. L., “An Effective support vector machine (SVMs) Performance Using Hierarchical Clustering,” *Proceedings of the 16th IEEE International Conference on Tools with Artificial Intelligence (ICTAI'04)* - Volume 00, 2004 November 15 - 17, 2004 Pages: 663- 667

2. Balcazar J. L., Dai Y. y Watanabe O.,"Provably Fast Training Algorithms for support vector machine", *In Proc. of the 1st IEEE Int. Conf. on Data Mining.*, IEEE Computer Society 2001, pp. 43-50.
3. Chih-Chung Ch., and Chih-Jen L., LIBSVM: a library for support vector machines, 2001, http://www.csie.ntu.edu.tw/~cjlin/libsvm.
4. Collobert R. y Bengio S., " SVMTorch: support vector machine for large regresion problems". *Journal of Machine Learning Research*, 1:143-160, 2001.
5. Daniael B. y Cao D.,"Training support vector machine Using Adaptive Clustering", *in Proc. of SIAM Int. Conf on Data Mining 2004*, Lake Buena Vista, FL, USA
6. Joachims T.,"Making large-scale support vector machine learning practical". *In A.S.B. Scholkopf, C. Burges, editor, Advances in Kernel Methods: support vector machine* . MIT Press, Cambridge, MA 1998.
7. S.W.Kim; Oommen, B.J.; Enhancing prototype reduction schemes with recursion: a method applicable for "large" data sets, *IEEE Transactions on Systems, Man and Cybernetics, Part B*, Volume 34, Issue 3, 1384 - 1397,2004
8. Lebrun, G.; Charrier, C.; Cardot, H.; SVM training time reduction using vector quantization, *Proceedings of the 17th International Conference on pattern recognition,* Volume 1, 160 - 163,2004.
9. K.Li; H.K.Huang; Incremental learning proximal support vector machine classifiers, *Proceedings. 2002 International Conference on machine learning and cybernetics,* Volume 3, 1635 - 1637, 2002
10. Luo F., Khan L., Bastani F., Yen I., y Zhou J., "A Dynamical Growing Self Organizing Tree (DGSOT) for Hierarquical Clustering Gene Expression Profiles", *Bioinformatics*, Volume 20, Issue 16, 2605-2617, 2004.
11. Pavlov, D.; Mao, J.; Dom, B.; Scaling-up support vector machine using boosting algorithm, *Proceedings of 15th International Conference on pattern recognition,* Volume 2, 219 - 222, 2000
12. Platt J., "Fast Training of support vector machine using sequential minimal optimization. *In A.S.B. Scholkopf, C. Burges, editor, Advances in Kernel Methods: support vector machine* . MIT Press, Cambridge, MA 1998.
13. Rui Xu; Wunsch, D., II., "Survey of clustering algorithms", IEEE Transactions on Neural Networks, Volume 16, Issue 3, May 2005 Page(s): 645 - 678
14. Schohn G. y Cohn D., "Less is more : Active Learning with support vector machine", *In Proc. 17th Int. Conf. Machine Learning*, Stanford, CA, 2000.
15. Shih L., Rennie D.M., Chang Y. y Karger D.R., "Text Bundling: Statistics-based Data Reduction", *In Proc of the Twentieth Int. Conf. on Machine Learning (ICML-2003)*, Washington DC, 2003.
16. Tong S. y Koller D.,"Support vector machine active learning with applications to text clasifications", *In Proc. 17th Int. Conf. Machine Learning*, Stanford, CA, 2000
17. Vapnik V., "The Nature of Statistical Learning Theory," *Springer, N.Y.*, 1995.
18. Van Gestel, T.; Suykens, J.A.K.; De Moor, B.; Vandewalle, J.; Bayesian inference for LS-SVMs on large data sets using the Nystrom method, *Proceedings of the 2002 International Joint Conference on neural networks*, Volume 3, 2779 - 2784, 2002
19. Yu H., Yang J. y Han Jiawei, "Classifying Large Data Sets Using SVMs with Hierarchical Clusters", *in Proc. of the 9th ACM SIGKDD 2003*, August 24-27, 2003, Washington, DC, USA.
20. R.Xu, D.Wunsch, Survey of Clustering Algorithms, *IEEE Trans. Neural Networks*, vol. 16, pp.645–678, 2005.

Optimizing Weighted Kernel Function for Support Vector Machine by Genetic Algorithm

Ha-Nam Nguyen, Syng-Yup Ohn, Soo-Hoan Chae,
Dong Ho Song, and Inbok Lee

Department of Computer and Information Engineering
Hankuk Aviation University, Seoul, Korea
{nghanam, syohn, chae, dhsong, inboklee}@hau.ac.kr

Abstract. The problem of determining optimal decision model is a difficult combinatorial task in the fields of pattern classification, machine learning, and especially bioinformatics. Recently, support vector machine (SVM) has shown a better performance than conventional learning methods in many applications. This paper proposes a weighted kernel function for support vector machine and its learning method with a fast convergence and a good classification performance. We defined the weighted kernel function as the weighted sum of a set of different types of basis kernel functions such as neural, radial, and polynomial kernels, which are trained by a learning method based on genetic algorithm. The weights of basis kernel functions in proposed kernel are determined in learning phase and used as the parameters in the decision model in classification phase. The experiments on several clinical datasets such as colon cancer, leukemia cancer, and lung cancer datasets indicate that our weighted kernel function results in higher and more stable classification performance than other kernel functions. Our method also has comparable and sometimes better classification performance than other classification methods for certain applications.

1 Introduction

Support vector machine [1-6] (SVM) is a learning method that uses a hypothesis space of linear functions in a high dimensional feature space. This learning strategy, introduced by Vapnik [2], is a principled and powerful method. In the simplest and linear form, a SVM is the hyperplane that separates a set of positive samples from a set of negative samples with the largest margin. The margin is defined by the distance between the hyperplanes supporting the nearest positive and negative samples. The output formula of a linear case is

$$y = w \cdot x - b \tag{1}$$

where w is a normal vector to the hyperplane and x is an input vector. The separating hyperplane is the plane y = 0 and two supporting hyperplanes parallel to it with equal distances are

$$H_1 : y = w \cdot x - b = +1, \quad H_2 : y = w \cdot x - b = -1 \tag{2}$$

A. Gelbukh and C.A. Reyes-Garcia (Eds.): MICAI 2006, LNAI 4293, pp. 583 – 592, 2006.

Thus, the margin M is defined as

$$M = 2/\|w\| \tag{3}$$

In order to find the optimal separating hyperplane having a maximal margin, a learning machine should minimize ||w|| subject to inequality constraints. This is a classic nonlinear optimization problem with inequality constraints. An optimization problem, which can be solved by the saddle point of the Lagrange function, is following

$$L(w,b,\alpha)=\frac{1}{2}w^T w-\sum_{i=1}^{N}\alpha_i y_i([w^T x+b]-1) \tag{4}$$

where $\alpha i \geq 0$ are Lagrange multipliers.

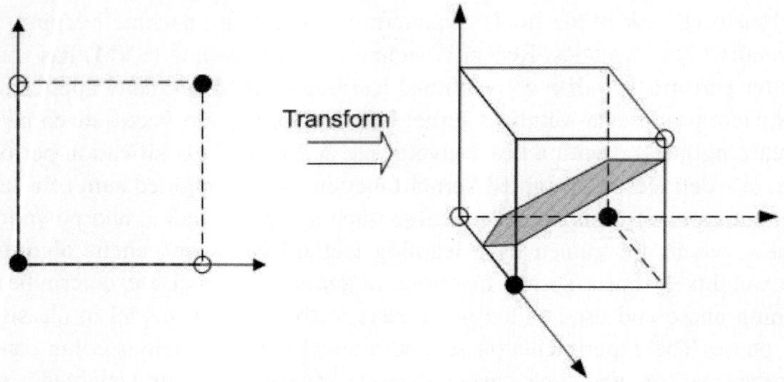

Fig. 1. An input space can be transformed into a linearly separable feature space by an appropriate kernel function

However, the limitation of computational power of linear learning machines was highlighted in the 1960s by Minsky and Papert [7]. It can be easily recognized that real-world applications require more extensive and flexible hypothesis space than linear functions. Such a limitation can be overcome by multilayer neural networks proposed by Rumelhart, Hinton and William [3]. Kernel function also offers an alternative solution by projecting the data into high dimensional feature space to increase the computational power of linear learning machines. Non-linear mapping from input space to high dimensional feature space can be implicitly performed by an appropriate kernel function (see Fig. 1). One of the advantages of the kernel method is that a learning algorithm can be exploited to obtain the specifics of application area, which simply can be encoded into the structure of an appropriate kernel function [1].

Genetic algorithm [8-10] is an optimization algorithms based on the mechanism of natural evolution procedure. Most of genetic algorithms share a common conceptual base of simulating the evolution of individual structures via the processes of selection, mutation, and reproduction. In each generation, a new population is selected based on the fitness values representing the performances of the individuals belonging to the generation, and some individuals of the population are given the chance to undergo alterations by means of crossover and mutation to form new individuals. In this way, GA performs a multi-directional search by maintaining a population of potential solutions and encourages the formation and the exchange of information among different directions. GA is generally applied to the problems with a large search space. They are different from random algorithms since they combine the elements of directed and stochastic search. Furthermore, GA is also known to be more robust than directed search methods.

Recently, SVM and GA are combined for the classification of biological data related to the diagnosis of caner diseases and achieved a good performance. GA was used to select the optimal set of features [13, 14], and the recognition accuracy of 80% was achieved in case of colon data set. In [15], they used GA to optimize the ensemble of multiple classifiers to improve the performance of classification.

In this paper, we propose weighted kernel function which is defined as the linear combination of basis kernel functions and a new learning method for the kernel function. In the proposed learning method, GA is applied to derive the optimal decision model for the classification of patterns, which consists of the set of the weights for basis kernels in our own kernel. The weighted kernel and the learning method were applied to classify three clinical data sets related to cancer diagnosis and showed better performance and more stable classification accuracy than single basis kernels.

This paper is organized as follows. In Section 2, the definition of weighted kernel and how-to constructing it from other single kernels are explained. The learning method based on our defined kernel is presented in detail in Section 3. In Section 4, the performances of weighted kernel and other kernels are compared by the experiments for the classification of clinical datasets on cancer diseases such as colon cancer, leukemia and lung cancer. Finally, conclusions are presented in section 5.

2 The Weighted Kernel Function

A kernel function provides a flexible and effective learning mechanism in SVM, and the choice of a kernel function should reflect prior knowledge about the problem at hand. However, it is often difficult for us to exploit the prior knowledge on patterns to choose a kernel function, and it is an open question how to choose the best kernel function for a given data set. According to no free lunch theorem [4] on machine learning, there is no superior kernel function in general, and the performance of a kernel function rather depends on applications.

In our case, the proposed kernel function is defined as the weighted sum of the set of different basis kernel functions. This kernel function has the form of

$$K_c = \sum_{i=1}^{m} \beta_i \times K_i \tag{5}$$

where $\beta_i \in [0,1]$ for $i = 1,...,m$, $\sum_{i=1}^{m} \beta_i = 1$, and $\{K_i \mid i = 1, \ldots, m\}$ is the set of basis kernel functions to be combined. Table 1 shows the mathematical formula of the basis kernel functions used to construct weighted kernel function. It can be proved that (5) satisfies the conditions required for kernel functions by Mercer's theorem [1].

Table 1. Kernels are chosen to experiments in our study

Kernel function	Formula
Polynomial	$(\langle x.y \rangle + 1)^2$
Radial	$e^{\left(-\gamma\|x-y\|^2\right)}$
Neural	$\tanh(s \cdot \langle x, y \rangle - c)$

The coefficients β_i play the important role of fitting the proposed kernel function to a training data set. In the learning phase, the structure of a training sample space is learned by our weighted kernel, and the knowledge of a sample space is learned and embedded in the set of coefficients β_i. In the learning phase of our approach, GA technique is applied to obtain the optimal set of coefficients β_i that minimize the generalization error of classifier. At the end of learning phase, we obtain the optimal decision model, which is used to classify new pattern samples in classification phase.

3 The Learning Method

The overall structure for classification procedure based on the proposed kernel and the learning method is depicted in Fig. 2. The procedure consists of preprocessing, learning, and classification phases.

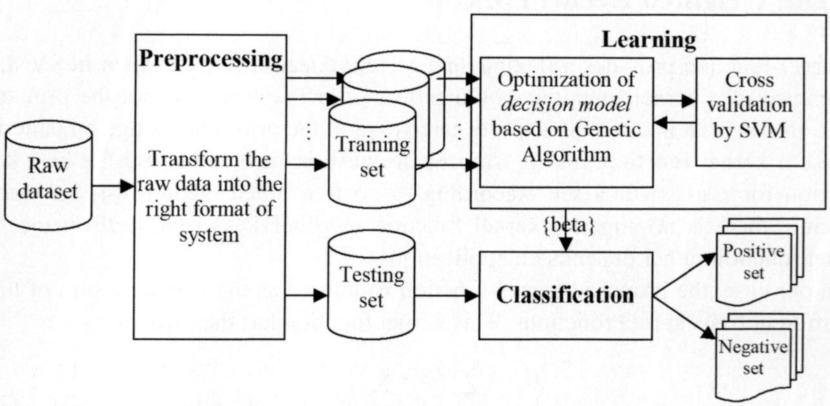

Fig. 2. Overall framework of proposed Method

Firstly, in the preprocessing stage, feature selection methods [16, 17] were used to reduce the dimensionality of the feature space of the input data. Also, the training and testing sets consisting of a number of cancer and normal patterns are selected and passed to the learning phase.

Secondly, in the learning phase, we applied a learning method based on GA and SVM techniques to obtain the optimal decision model for classification. GA generates a set of chromosomes representing decision models by evolutionary procedures. The fitness value of each chromosome is evaluated by measuring the accuracy from the classification with SVM containing the decision model associated with the chromosome. An *n*-fold validation was used to evaluate the fitness of a chromosome to reduce overfitting [4]. In the evolutionary procedure of GA, only the chromosomes with a good fitness values are selected and given the chance to survive and improve in the further generations. Roulette wheel rule [8] is used for the selection of chromosome in our learning phase. Some of the selected chromosomes are given the chance to undergo alterations by means of crossover and mutation to form new chromosomes. In our approach, one-point crossover is used, and the probabilities for crossover and mutation are 0.8 and 0.015 in turn. The procedure is repeated for a predefined number of times. At the end of GA procedure, the chromosome with the highest accuracy is chosen as the optimal decision model.

Finally, the optimal decision model obtained in the learning phase is used to in SVM for the classification of new samples in the classification phase, and the performance of the model is evaluated against test samples.

4 Experiments and Analysis

In this section, we show the results from the classification based on the model trained by the weighted kernel and the new learning method. Furthermore, the performance of the classification model with our defined kernel is compared to the performances of the models with other kernels. All the experiments are conducted on a Pentium IV 1.8GHz computer. The experiments are composed preprocessing of samples, learning by GA to obtain the optimal decision model, and classification. For GA, we have used roulette wheel rule for selection method. Our proposed method was executed with 100 chromosomes for 50 generations. Weighted kernel function and three other kernel functions in Table 1 are trained by GA in learning phase with training set. The three kernel functions are chosen since they were known to have good performances in the field of bioinformatics [4, 6, 13-15]. We used 5-fold cross validation to measure the fitness to reduce overfitting [4]. The optimal decision model obtained after 50 generations of GA is used to classify the set of test samples.

4.1 Colon Tumor Cancer

The colon cancer dataset [11] contains gene expression information extracted from DNA microarrays. The dataset consists of 22 normal and 40 cancer tissue samples and each having 2000 features.(Available at: http://sdmc.lit.org.sg/ GEDatasets/Data/ ColonTumor.zip). 42 samples were chosen randomly as training samples and the remaining samples were used as testing samples.

We chose 50 first features based on t-test statistic. The Fig. 3 showed the feature importance [16, 17, 18] of the first 15 features in decrease order. Each column represents the logarithm of p-value of all features in the data set that calculated by t-test procedure. The value above each column represents the indexes of features in the data

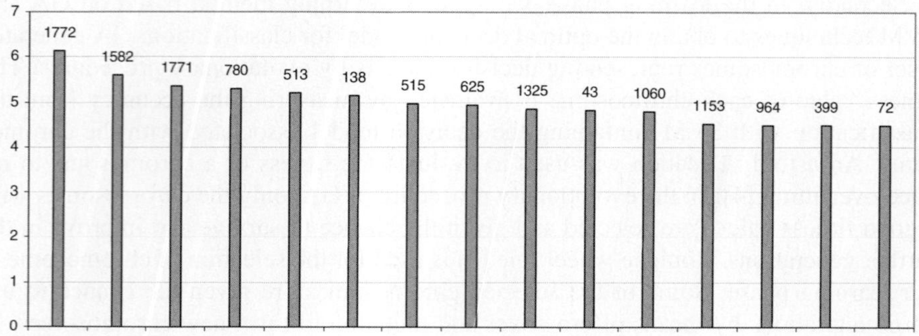

Fig. 3. The –lg(p) value of the first 15 features

set. In case of colon dataset, the proposed method with weighted kernel function also showed much higher accuracy than other kernels (see Table 2).

Table 2. The comparison of average hit rate in classification phase of weighted kernel function case with other kernel functions though 50 trials

	Polynomial	Radial	Neural	Weighted Kernel
Predicted Acc.	72.84%	82.94%	62.41%	86.23%
Standard deviation	7.07%	6.19%	5.74%	6.05%

Table 3. The best prediction rate of some studies in case of colon dataset

Type of classifier	Prediction rate ± S.D. (%)
GA\SVM [12]	84.7±9.1
Bootstrapped GA\SVM [13]	80.0
Weighted Kernel	**86.23±6.05**

The comparison of our experiments and the results of previous studies [12, 13] were depicted in Table 3. Our experiments showed the accuracies comparable to the previous ones, and the standard deviation of the prediction rate for weighted kernel is less than GA\SVM (see Table 3). It is remarked that the new kernel and the learning method result in more stable classification accuracies than previous ones.

4.2 Leukemia Cancer

The leukemia dataset [12] consists of 72 samples that have to be discriminated into two classes Acute Myeloid Leukemia (ALL) and Acute Lymphoblastic Leukemia (AML). There are 47 ALL and 25 AML samples and each sample contains 7129 features. The dataset was divided into a training set with 38 samples (27 ALL and 11 AML) and a test set with 34 samples (20 ALL and 14 AML) which are available at: http://sdmc.lit.org.sg/GEDatasets/Data/ALL-AML_Leukemia.zip).

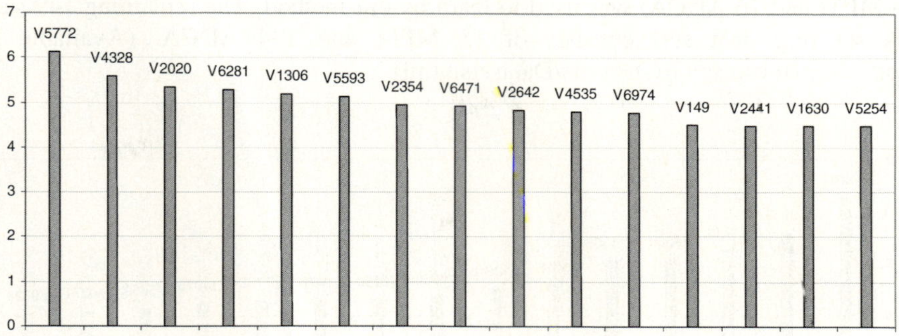

Fig. 4. The –lg(p) value of the first 15 features

Similarly for the experiment on colon cancer data set, we chose 50 features based on t-test statistic for the experiment on leukemia data set. Fig. 4 shows the feature importance of the first 15 features in decreasing order. Each column represents the logarithm of p-value of all features in the data set that calculated by t-test procedure. The value above each column represents the indexes of features in the data set. The experiments shows that our defined kernel and the proposed learning method results in more stable and higher accuracies than other kernels (see Table 4). According to Table 3, the weighted kernel shows the best average performance with 96.07% of recognition accuracy.

Table 4. The comparison of average accuracies of weighted kernel function case with single kernel functions in classification phase though 50 trials

	Polynomial	Radial	Neural	Weighted Kernel
Predicted Acc.	60.93%	95.13%	82.20%	96.07%
Standard deviation	16.11%	7.00%	12.88%	3.41%

In Table 5, we compare the prediction results from our method and other studies' performed on the same dataset [11, 13] and our result is comparable to and sometimes better than the others.

Table 5. The best prediction rate of some studies in case of leukemia dataset

Type of classifier	Prediction rate ± std (%)
Weighted voting[11]	94.1
Bootstrapped GA\SVM [13]	97.0
Weighted Kernel	**96.07±3.14**

4.3 Lung Cancer

181 tissue samples lung cancer dataset consists of 31 Malignant Pleural Mesothelioma (MPM) and 150 Adenocarcinoma (ADCA) samples. A training set of 32 samples

(16 MPM and 16 ADCA) was used to learn by our method. The remaining 149 samples set (e.g. test set) consists of 15 MPM and 134 ADCA. (Available at: http://sdmc.lit.org.sg/GEDatasets/Datasets.html)

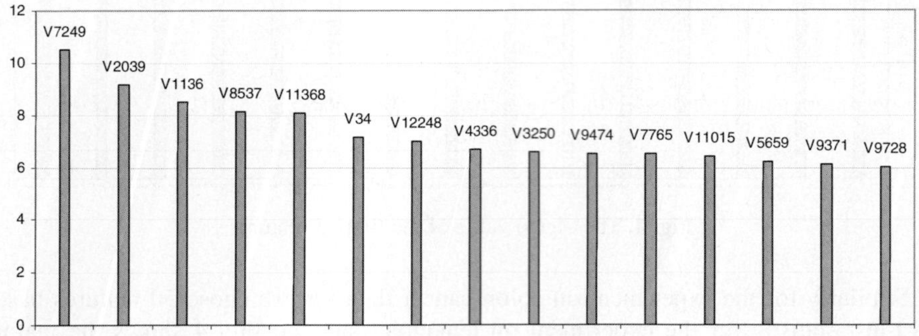

Fig. 5. The –lg(p) value of the first 15 features

Not similar to the previous experiments, we chose 10 to 50 features based on t-test statistic respectively for the experiments on lung cancer data set. Fig. 5 shows the feature importance of the first 15 features in decreasing order. Each column represents the logarithm of p-value of all features in the data set that calculated by t-test procedure. The value above each column represents the indexes of features in the data set. The experiments shows that our defined kernel and the proposed learning method results in higher accuracies than other kernels in almost cases (see Table 6 – Bold numbers). According to Table 6, the weighted kernel shows the best average performance with 100% of recognition accuracy in case of 30 and 40 features sets.

Table 6. The comparison of accuracies of weighted kernel function case with single kernel functions in classification phase though experiments on {10, 20, 30, 40, 50} feature set to figure out the best one

Number of Features	polynomial	radial	neural	Weighted Kernel
10	97.98%	97.31%	89.95%	96.64%
20	97.98%	97.98%	89.95%	**97.99%**
30	97.98%	97.98%	97.98%	**100%**
40	97.98%	98.64%	89.95%	**100%**
50	97.98%	98.64%	89.95%	**98.66%**

In Table 7, we compare the prediction results from our method and other studies' performed on the same dataset [19] and our result is comparable to and sometimes better than the others.

Table 7. The best prediction rate of some studies in case of lung cancer dataset

Type of classifier	Prediction rate(%)
Gene expression ratios [19]	96.0
Correlation network [19]	99.0
SVM [19]	99.0
The classification experiments are performed by using various g ene number per subclass, such as 10, 20, ... , 100 genes. The best accuracy among these cases was reported.	**100**
Weighted Kernel (The best case)	**100**

5 Conclusions

In this paper, we proposed a weighted kernel function by combining a set of basis kernel functions for SVM and its learning method based on GA technique to obtain the optimal decision model for classification. A kernel function plays the important role of mapping the problem feature space into a new feature space so that the performance of the SVM classifier is improved. The weighted kernel function and the proposed learning method were applied to classify the clinical datasets to test their performance. In the comparison of the classifications by our defined kernel and other three kernel functions, the weighted kernel function achieved higher and more stable accuracies in classification phase than other kernels. Thus our kernel function has greater flexibility in representing a problem space than other kernel functions.

Acknowledgement

This work was supported by the Internet Information Retrieval Research Center (IRC) in Hankuk Aviation University. IRC is a Regional Research Center of Gyeong-gi Province, designated by ITEP and Ministry of Commerce, Industry and Energy, Korea.

References

1. N. Cristianini and J. Shawe-Taylor.: An introduction to Support Vector Machines and other kernel-based learning methods, Cambridge, 2000.
2. V.N. Vapnik et. al.: Theory of Support Vector Machines, Technical Report CSD TR-96-17, Univ. of London, 1996.
3. Vojislav Kecman.: Learning and Soft Computing: Support Vector Machines, Neural Networks, and Fuzzy Logic Models (Complex Adaptive Systems), The MIT press, 2001.
4. Richard O. Duda, Peter E. Hart, David G. Stork.: Pattern Classification (2nd Edition), John Wiley & Sons Inc., 2001.
5. Joachims, Thorsten.: Making large-Scale SVM Learning Practical. In Advances in Kernel Methods - Support Vector Learning, chapter 11. MIT Press, 1999.

6. Bernhard Schökopf , Alexander J. Smola.: Learning with Kernels: Support Vector Machines, Regularization, Optimization, and Beyond (Adaptive Computation and Machine Learning), MIT press, 2002
7. M.L. Minsky and S.A. Papert: Perceptrons, MIT Press, 1969.
8. Z.Michalewicz.: Genetic Algorithms + Data structures = Evolution Programs, Springer-Verlag, 3 re rev. and extended ed., 1996.
9. D. E. Goldberg.: Genetic Algorithms in Search, Optimization & Machine Learning, Adison Wesley, 1989.
10. Melanie Mitchell.: Introduction to genetic Algorithms, MIT press, fifth printing, 1999.
11. U. Alon, N. Barkai, D. Notterman, K. Gish, S. Ybarra, D. Mack, and A. Levine.: Broad Patterns of Gene Expression Revealed by Clustering Analysis of Tumor and Normal Colon Tissues Probed by Oligonucleotide Arrays, Proceedings of National Academy of Sciences of the United States of American, vol 96, pp. 6745-6750, 1999.
12. T. R. Golub, D. K. Slonim, P. Tamayo, C. Huard, M. Gaasenbeek, J. P. Mesirov, H. Coller, M. L. Loh, J. R. Downing, M. A. Caligiuri, C. D. Bloomfield and E. S. Lander.: Molecular Classification of Cancer: Class Discovery and Class Prediction by Gene Expression Monitoring, Science, vol. 286, pp. 531–537, 1999.
13. H. Fröhlich, O. Chapelle, B. Scholkopf.: Feature selection for support vector machines by means of genetic algorithm, Tools with Artificial Intelligence, Proceedings. 15th. IEEE International Conference, pp. 142 – 148, 2003.
14. Xue-wen Chen.: Gene selection for cancer classification using bootstrapped genetic algorithms and support vector machines, The Computational Systems, Bioinformatics Conference. Proceedings IEEE International Conference, pp. 504 – 505, 2003.
15. Chanho Park and Sung-Bae Cho.: Genetic search for optimal ensemble of feature-classifier pairs in DNA gene expression profiles, Neural Networks, 2003. Proceedings of the International Joint Conference, vol.3, pp. 1702 – 1707, 2003.
16. Stefan Rüping.: mySVM-Manual, University of Dortmund, Lehrstuhl Informatik, 2000. [online] (Available:http://www-ai.cs.uni-dortmund.de/SOFTWARE/ MYSVM)
17. Kohavi, R. and John, G.H.: Wrappers for Feature Subset Selection, Artificial Intelligence (1997) pages: 273-324
18. A. L. Blum and P. Langley: Selection of Relevant Features and Examples in Machine Learning, Artificial Intelligence, (1997) pages: 245-271
19. Tom M. Michell: Machine Learning, McGraw Hill (1997)
20. C.-C. Liu, W.-S. E. Chen, C.-C. Lin, H.-C. Liu, H.-Y. Chen, P.-C. Yang, P.-C. Chang, and J. J.W. Chen: Topology-based cancer classification and related pathway mining using microarray data, Nucleic Acids Res., August 16, 2006; (2006) gkl583v1.

Decision Forests with Oblique Decision Trees

Peter J. Tan and David L. Dowe

School of Computer Science and Software Engineering, Monash University,
Clayton, Vic 3800, Australia
ptan@bruce.csse.monash.edu.au

Abstract. Ensemble learning schemes have shown impressive increases in prediction accuracy over single model schemes. We introduce a new decision forest learning scheme, whose base learners are Minimum Message Length (MML) oblique decision trees. Unlike other tree inference algorithms, MML oblique decision tree learning does not over-grow the inferred trees. The resultant trees thus tend to be shallow and do not require pruning. MML decision trees are known to be resistant to over-fitting and excellent at probabilistic predictions. A novel weighted averaging scheme is also proposed which takes advantage of high probabilistic prediction accuracy produced by MML oblique decision trees. The experimental results show that the new weighted averaging offers solid improvement over other averaging schemes, such as majority vote. Our MML decision forests scheme also returns favourable results compared to other ensemble learning algorithms on data sets with binary classes.

1 Introduction

Ensemble learning is one of the major advances in supervised learning research in recent years [10]. The outputs of an ensemble classifier are determined by a committee, in which a group of classifiers cast (possibly weighted) votes on final predictions. Generally, ensemble learning schemes are able to outperform single classifiers in predictive accuracy. The intuitive explanation for the success of ensemble learning is that mistakes made by individual classifiers are corrected by complementary results submitted by other classifiers in the committee.

The most widely adopted approaches are called Perturb and Combine (P&C) methods. P&C methods infer each classifier from a set of distinct training sets, which are generated by perturbing the unaltered original training set. An important prerequisite for the P&C methods is that the base learner must be unstable in that the inferred models are sensitive to even minor variation of the training set. Bagging (bootstrap aggregating) [4] and AdaBoost (adaptive boosting) [17] are two popular P&C methods implemented in many ensemble learning schemes. Both methods are able to generate diverse committees by feeding base learners with a set of distinct training sets drawn from the original training set.

Another way to create variations in the training sets is to alter the label of the target attribute of instances in the training set. Breiman proposed a scheme [3] which grows a set of decision trees by injecting random noise into the output

A. Gelbukh and C.A. Reyes-Garcia (Eds.): MICAI 2006, LNAI 4293, pp. 593–603, 2006.

label of the original training set. DECORATE (Diverse Ensemble Creation by Oppositional Relabeling of Artificial Training Examples) [20] is another ensemble learning scheme which has a similar motivation. But, instead of randomly altering the output labels, the algorithm inserts the artificially constructed instances (and adds to the training set) with the aim of deliberately increasing diversity among the inferred committee members.

Decision tree inducers are unstable in that resultant trees are sensitive to minor perturbations in the training data set. Largely for this reason, decision trees are widely applied as the base learners in ensemble learning schemes. Some ensemble algorithms have implemented modified decision tree inference algorithms in order to generate diverse decision forests. Ho proposed a scheme called the random subspace method [18] for constructing decision forests. When the algorithm constructs a split at each internal node of the inferred trees, candidate features are restricted to a randomly selected subset of the original input features. Dietterich introduced another ensemble learning scheme [11] that does not rely on the instability of the decision tree inducer. Instead of picking the split with the best score on the objective function, the algorithm randomly chooses a split among a pre-defined number of candidate splits with the highest score (on the objective function). Ferri et al. [16] have an interesting scheme in which the subset of the data that was deemed most difficult to classify is put aside and then delegated to another run of the classifier.

Research on combining some of the above methods to further improve the performance of ensemble learning has also shown promising results. In the random forests scheme developed in [5], bagging and random feature selection schemes were implemented to inject randomness into the decision tree growing processes.

While there are no clear winners emerging from the above ensemble schemes, all of them reported superior "right"/"wrong" predictive accuracy compared to single classifier learning schemes. In this paper, we propose a new ensemble algorithm called decision forests with oblique decision trees. The proposed ensemble learning scheme is different from other random forests in several ways. While most ensemble learning algorithms grow deep and unpruned decision trees, the base learner in our ensemble learning is Minimum Message Length (MML) oblique decision trees, which were introduced in [28]. The paper also shows how to include simple probabilistic Support Vector Machines in the internal and/or leaf nodes of decision trees. The MML coding scheme is applied to select optimal candidate trees (with overall lower MML coding) with high probabilistic prediction accuracy (low log-loss score) and smaller tree size (lower height with fewer leaf nodes). Compared to schemes with univariate trees (which cut on only one attribute at a time), using MML (multivariate) oblique trees offers potential to greatly increase the diversity of the inferred forest. A new weighted averaging scheme is also proposed. The proposed averaging scheme is based on Bayesian weighted tree averaging but uses a modified, smoothed prior on decision trees (see sec. 3.4). In order to take advantage of the above weighted averaging scheme, a new algorithm to rapidly generate a large number of distinct oblique decision trees is introduced.

2 Details of Some Related Ensemble Schemes

Bagging [4] relies on perturbing the training set. When unstable learning algorithms are applied as base inducers, a diverse ensemble can be generated by feeding the base learner with training sets re-sampled from the original training set.

Another type of P&C method is the AdaBoost algorithm, which is also referred to as an arcing (adaptive re-sampling and combining) algorithm by Breiman in [2]. The fundamental difference between bagging and AdaBoost is that while bagging is non-deterministic, AdaBoost is deterministic and iterative.

AdaBoost iteratively alters the probability over instances in the training set while performing the re-sampling. It works very well when the data is noise free and the number of training data is large. But when noise is present in the training sets, or the number of training data is limited, AdaBoost does not perform as well as Bagging and (see below) random forests.

Random forests use CART [6] as the base learner and combine several methods to generate a diverse ensemble. Each decision tree in a random forest is trained on a distinct and random data set re-sampled from the original training set, using the same procedure as bagging. While selecting a split at each internal node during the tree growing process, a random set of features is formed by either choosing a subset of input variables or constructing a small group of variables formed by linear combinations of input variables. Random forests [5] have achieved "right"/"wrong" predictive accuracy comparable to that of AdaBoost and much better results on noisy data sets. Breiman also claimed and showed that AdaBoost is a form of random forest (algorithm) [5].

3 Ensemble Learning with MML Random Forests

It has been shown that the performance of an ensemble classifier depends on the strength of individual classifiers and correlations among them [5]. MML oblique trees are shown to return excellent accuracies, especially on probabilistic predictions. The algorithm beats both C4.5 [24] and C5 on both "right"/"wrong" and especially probabilistic predictions with smaller trees (i.e., less leaf nodes) [28]. Because we would like to implement a Bayesian averaging scheme [31, sec. 8][29, sec. 4.8][13, sec. 6.1.4], performance of individual classifiers on probabilistic prediction is crucial. Therefore the MML oblique trees are chosen as the base learners in our algorithms. Due to the introduction of hyperplanes at internal nodes, the space of candidate trees is also hugely enlarged. This helps to increase diversity among the trees, especially for the data sets with fewer input attributes.

3.1 Minimum Message Length (MML)

The Minimum Message Length (MML) Principle [30,32,31,27,29] provides a guide for inferring the best model given a set of data. MML and the subsequent

Minimum Description Length (MDL) principle [25,19] are widely used for model selection in various machine learning problems, and both can be thought of as operational forms of Ockham's razor [21]. For introductions to MML, see [29,13]; and for detalis on MML, see [30,32,31,22,15,7,8]. For a comparison between MML and the subsequent MDL principle[25], see, e.g., [31] (which also gives a survey), other articles in that 1999 special issue of the *Computer Journal*, [8] and [29]. We apply the MML multivariate oblique coding scheme [28] when oblique decision trees in our new decision forests are grown.

3.2 Searching for Optimal Splits at Internal Nodes

The algorithm we propose here is tailored for searching for optimal two-dimensional hyperplanes (linear combinations of two input attributes). It works as follows:

Firstly, a random two dimensional hyperplane is generated. Then the hyperplane is rotated by 10 degrees each time, so that a set of 18 orientations is generated. For each hyperplane in the 18 orientations, a maximum of 32 cut-points were tested and the one with the minimum total code length is recorded. The process is repeated on all candidate combinations of two input attributes. The total code length is given as below. For further details of the MML coding of oblique decision trees, please see [28].

Total code length $= Part1 + Part2$, where

$Part1 = -2(D-1)\log(\frac{2}{\sqrt{D\|w\|^2+4}}) + \log\binom{N}{2}$, $Part2 = \sum_{l=1}^{L} Msg_l$,

$Msg_l = \frac{M-1}{2}(\log\frac{N_l}{12}+1) - \log(M-1)! - \sum_{m=1}^{M}(n_m+\frac{1}{2})\log(\frac{n_m+\frac{1}{2}}{N_l+\frac{M}{2}})$, where

D is the dimension of the hyperplane, N is the number of data at the internal node to be split, L is the number of child nodes resulting from the split (in this case L is 2), Msg_l is the code length for encoding leaf probability and data in each resultant lth leaf node, M is the number of classes in the data, n_m is the number of instances in class m in the particular leaf node and N_l is the number of data in leaf node l. For the remainder of this paper, $D = 2$.

3.3 An Efficient Algorithm to Generate a Larger Number of MML Oblique Trees

The idea behind our new rapid forest generation algorithms here is that, at each node, a specified number of viable splits (splits which improve the message length) are recorded. For each of these candidate splits, tentative splits are performed. The above procedure is recursively run on each resulting child node.

The forest growing process is divided into the following two parts (A and B):

A: In part A, a search tree is constructed in the following steps:
Start the tree with a single leaf node as the root node,

1. Generate a set of possible combinations of two input attributes.
2. Search for the best split by hyperplanes (i.e., those yielding the shortest two-part message length) constructed from each of the given combinations of two attributes for this node.
3. Record each of the candidate splits from step 2 that achieve better message length than the unsplit leaf node.
4. For each of the splits recorded in step 3, perform a tentative split.
5. Recursively apply this procedure on each of the child nodes generated in step 4, until the height of the search tree is H.

In this way, following a branch under an internal node in the search tree represents selecting a hyperplane split, and the subsequent subtrees under this branch are a union of candidate subtrees which would possibly be generated by such a split.

B: A random decision tree can thus be created by randomly picking a branch and one of the subsequent subtrees recursively. Create such a tree. Repeat this process until a pre-defined number of trees is generated.

In order to approximate the number of searches and the number of distinct trees that are able to be generated from a search tree, we assume that there are M viable candidate binary splits at each internal node to be searched. For a search tree with height H, it is easy to see that the number of searches is $S(H, M) = 2M \times S(H-1, M)$ and $S(2, M) = M$, thus $S(H, M) = 2^{H-2}M^{H-1}, H > 1$. The number of distinct trees, T, that can be generated from the search tree can be estimated by using the fact that $T(2, M) = M$ and $T(H, M) \approx T(H-1, M)^{2M}$, thus roughly $T(H, M) \approx M^{((2M)^{H-2})}$. To keep the computational time in rein, the algorithm puts some upper limits on M and H. In our experiments, M ranges from 25 to 50 while H ranges from 4 to 5.

3.4 Weighted Averaging of Trees

Oliver and Hand proposed a Bayesian weighted tree averaging scheme [23] in which the weights are set to be proportional to the posterior probability of each tree in the forest. Given a tree, T_i, with I internal nodes, L leaves and C classes, they give the posterior probability of the tree T_i as

$$P(T_i|D) \propto \prod_{i=1}^{I} \frac{1}{ap(i)} \prod_{i=1}^{L} (1 - \frac{1}{ap(i)}) \prod_{i=1}^{L} \frac{\prod_{j=1}^{C} M_j!}{(\sum_{j=1}^{C} M_j)!} \cdots \qquad (2)$$

where $ap(i)$ is the arity of the parent of node i, and M_j is the number of the instances belonging to class j (j$\in \{1, 2, \ldots, C\}$) in each leaf node. We initially implemented a similar scheme as one of our averaging methods. However, experimental results returned by this averaging method are worse than those by the simple arithmetic vote averaging. Investigation showed that even in forests with 1000 trees, there are always 2 to 3 trees dominating the majority (.8 to .9) of the weights. While such results may seem to be contradictory to Bayesianism, there are several possible explanations for this. One possible reason is that the prior of decision trees given by $P(T_i|D) \propto \prod_{i=1}^{I} \frac{1}{ap(i)} \prod_{i=1}^{L} (1 - \frac{1}{ap(i)})$ is not right for the oblique decision trees in the forest. Another possibility is that our uniform multinomial prior on the class probabilities is not flexible enough. Rather than fix our Beta/Dirichlet prior as having $\beta = 1$, we could more generally permit β to have a prior distribution of the rough form of $\frac{3}{2\sqrt{\beta}(1+\sqrt{\beta})^4}$ or $\frac{e^{-\frac{\beta}{\pi}}}{\pi\sqrt{\beta}}$, whose purpose is to maintain a mean equal (or ideally close) to 1 while permitting the boosting-like effect of small values of β close to 0. Another possible explanation lies in the fact that there are high correlations between the predictions submitted by the trees with the top posterior probabilities, despite their distinct tree structures. Another rather viable and simple explanation is that, like earlier studies (e.g. [23]), we have not been sampling from the posterior distribution. This could be corrected by a judicious choice of importance sampling distribution.

In this paper, we retain the uniform multinomial prior and attempt to approximate the correct weights for decision trees generated from the real posterior probabilities, proposing a new (approximate) decision tree averaging scheme for our decision forests algorithm. Because there are an indefinite number of trees in the posterior space and the real distribution of the posterior probabilities is unknown, three assumptions have been made. First, assume that the distribution of the weights of the sampled trees is like a unit Normal distribution. Secondly, we assume that the posterior $P(T_i|D)$ of the inferred trees can be sampled from the range (-R, R) (R is set to 3.5 in our tests), given that $\int_{-R}^{R} \frac{1}{\sqrt{2\pi}} e^{-\frac{x^2}{2}} dx \approx 1$. Lastly, we assume that the order of the real posterior probabilities of inferred trees is identical of that of the posterior probabilities obtained from (2). Then the weight of a decision tree, $w(T_i)$, is approximated in this scheme as follows:

1. Generate a set of weights $\{w_1, w_2, \ldots, w_S\}$, so that $w_i = \int_{x_i}^{x_i+\Delta x} \frac{1}{\sqrt{2\pi}} e^{-\frac{x^2}{2}} dx$, where $x_i = -R + (i-1)\Delta x$, $\Delta x = \frac{2R}{S}$
2. Normalize and sort $\{w_1, w_2, \ldots, w_S\}$ so that $w_1 \leq w_2 \ldots \leq w_S$ and $\sum w_i = 1$,
3. Sort the set of trees $\{T_1, T_2, \ldots, T_S\}$ so that $P(T_1|D) \leq P(T_2|D) \ldots \leq P(T_S|D)$
4. Set the weights for the trees T_i, $w(T_i) = w_i$.

In an ideal situation, doing Bayesian averaging involves integration of the posteriors over the whole model space, so $P(y|x) = \int_{\theta \in \Theta} P(y|\theta, x) P(\theta|D) d\theta$, where $P(\theta|D)$ is the posterior probability derived from the training data D. However, there are two obstacles in Bayesian averaging. The first is that when the model space is huge, such as when the models are decision trees, performing a whole integration is impractical. Another obstacle is that the posterior probabilities of inferred decision trees are difficult to calculate, due to unknown marginal probabilities of data x.

An MML decision tree inference scheme results in an optimal discretized tree space where the relative posterior probabilities of two inferred trees is given by comparing the MML two-part message lengths. The proposed weighted averaging scheme above in effect "smooths out" the weights of trees, making the weights of sampled trees vary more slowly than the rate suggested by the MML two-part message length. The motivation of such an algorithm is to compensate the bias introduced by the tree inference algorithm. As our MML tree inference algorithm prefers trees with high predictive accuracy, such a process of growing an ensemble of decision trees can be regarded as performing a form of importance sampling in the posterior space. The integration becomes $P(y|x) = \int_{\theta \in \Theta} P(y|\theta, x) \frac{P(\theta|D)}{G(\theta)} G(\theta) d\theta$, where $\frac{P(\theta|D)}{G(\theta)} \propto 2^{-msglen}$, where $msglen$ is the two-part message length of the tree model and data (although, for our predictive purposes, it might have been slightly better to use [29, sec. 3.1.7] I_0 rather than I_1 in the leaf nodes). In this paper, $G(\theta)$ is a Gaussian function which takes the two-part message length of the trees as input. Our final goal is to devise an MML inference algorithm to find a model class and inferred parameters for the optimal $G(\theta)$ (using training data). In this way, with limited number of inferred decision trees we are able to approximate the integration of the posteriors more accurately in the whole model space.

4 Experimental Results

4.1 Data Sets

We ran our experiments on 13 data sets from the UCI data repository [1], 12 of which are from Breiman's random forest paper [5]. We added BREAST-WINS as an additional two-class problem. For each data set, 10 independent 10-fold cross-validation tests were performed. A summary of the data sets is shown in table 1.

Table 1. Summary of the data sets

DATA SET	SIZE	CONTINUOUS ATB.	DISCRETE ATB.	CLASSES
BREAST	286	0	9	2
BREAST-WINS	699	0	9	2
BUPA	345	6	0	2
CLEVELAND	303	5	8	2
ECOLI	336	7	0	8
GERMAN	1000	3	21	2
GLASS	214	9	0	6
IMAGE	2310	19	0	7
IONOSPHERE	351	34	0	2
PIMA	768	8	0	2
SAT-IMAGES	6435	36	0	6
SONAR	208	60	0	2
VOWEL	990	10	0	11

4.2 Comparing and Scoring Probabilistic Predictions

In addition to the traditional right/wrong accuracy, we are also keen to compare the probabilistic performance [27, sec 5.1] [14,12,21,26] of the ensemble algorithms. In many domains, like oncological and other medical data, not only the class predictions but also the probability associated with each class is essential.

In some domains, like finance, strategies heavily rely on accurate probabilistic predictions. To compare probabilistic prediction performances, we use a metric called probabilistic costing (or log loss), defined as $P_{cost} = -\sum_{i=1}^{N} \log(p_i)$, where N is the total number of test data and p_i is the probability assigned by the model to the true (correct) class associated with test instance i. The probability p_j of an instance belonging to class j in a leaf node was estimated by $\hat{p_j} = \frac{N_j+1}{(\sum N_j)+M}$, where N_j is the number of instances belonging to the class j in the leaf node, M is the number of classes. The probabilistic costing is equivalent to the accumulated code length of the total test data encoded by an inferred model. As the optimal code length can only be achieved by encoding with the real probability distribution of the test data, it is obvious that a smaller probabilistic costing indicates a better performance on overall probabilistic prediction.

Although we don't do this here, Dowe showed (in detailed and explicit private communication after a paper at the Australian AI'2002 conference) how to modify this to include a Bayesian prior on the multinomial states by simply subtracting (a multiple of) the entropy of the prior (plus an optional but unnecessary constant).

And, rather than just numerically calculate the log-loss probabilistic bit costing on test data, if we knew the true underlying model and wished to infer a probabilistic Bayesian (or causal) network [7,8], we could quite easily calculate a Kullback-Leibler distance between the true model and such an inferred model. We would do this by looking at each combination of states (or variable values at each node, or "micro-state") in turn, looking at the Kullback-Leibler distance between the true probability and the inferred probability for each such micro-state, and then summing these Kullback-Leibler distances weighted by the true probabilities of each micro-state in turn. (These weights add up to 1.)

4.3 Comparisons with Other Ensemble Algorithms

We also compare results from our ensemble learning schemes with two other prominent ensemble learning algorithms - AdaBoost and Random Forest - for which we also run 10 independent 10-fold cross-validations tests (averaging over 10x10=100 runs) on the 13 data sets. The random forests algorithm was implemented by weka3.4.6 [33]. At each test, a random forest with 1000 decision trees, whose internal node contains a linear combination of 2 input attributes attributes, was grown. C5.0 is a commercial version of the C4.5 [24] program. To obtain the results from AdaBoost, we ran our tests by using the built-in AdaBoost function of C5.0 with a maximum of 1000 iterations or until convergence. In most cases, AdaBoost finished before 1000 runs due to diminutive or no gain in the subsequent runs. The results for MML forests are returned by forests with 1000 trees. MML oblique trees are averaged by weighted averaging of class probabilities, recalling section 3.4.

The results for the "Right"/"Wrong" classification accuracies are shown in table 2. For the 8 data sets with binary classes (asterisked, recalling Table 1), in terms of "right/wrong" accuracy, the MML forests perform best on 5 out of

Table 2. "Right"/"Wrong" classification accuracies and probabilistic costing results for forests with MML oblique trees, AdaBoost and random forests. [An asterisk (*) denotes that the target attribute of the data set is binary].

DATA SET	MML FOREST "R/W"	C5 ADABOOST "R/W"	RANDOM FOREST "R/W"	MML FOREST P_{cost}	C5 ADABOOST P_{cost}	RANDOM FOREST P_{cost}
BREAST*	73.4	72.9	71.0	23.4	23.6	N/A
BREAST-WINS*	97.4	96.3	96.7	10.2	18.0	N/A
BUPA*	67.9	68.5	73.0	30.9	30.4	N/A
CLEVELAND*	83.4	80.6	82.5	17.7	19.0	N/A
ECOLI	85.9	84.0	86.2	26.4	45.6	N/A
GERMAN*	74.1	75.4	77.1	74.7	74.5	N/A
GLASS	67.1	74.9	80.8	28.9	30.3	N/A
IMAGE	92.0	97.9	98.1	156.3	176.5	N/A
IONOSPHERE*	93.8	93.6	92.8	12.5	12.5	N/A
PIMA*	76.2	75.3	75.4	53.8	56.2	N/A
SAT-IMAGES	83.3	90.7	91.5	411.4	574.3	N/A
SONAR*	81.9	80.8	84.0	12.5	13.3	N/A
VOWEL	64.3	89.9	97.0	217.7	176.5	N/A

8 sets, second best on 1 and worst on 2; and on logarithm of probability (P_{cost}) bit costing (recall sec. 4.2), the MML forests win 5, tie on 1 and lose the other 2. The results on the 5 multiple-class data sets are interesting. In "right/wrong" scoring, random forests win 4 out of 5 and come second in 1 out of 5. But in logarithm of probability scoring, MML forests win 4 out of 5 cases. The most probable explanation is that the base learner, MML oblique decision trees [28], does not perform well in "right/wrong" scoring on data sets with multiple classes. One way to improve the performance on data sets with multiple classes might possibly be to convert a multiple class learning problem into a set of binary class learning problems, another would be to implement ideas from sec. 3.4.

As mentioned in section 4.2, we are keen to compare the performance on probabilistic predictions of ensemble learning algorithms. To obtain P_{cost} for C5.0 AdaBoost, the probabilistic prediction for each test instance is calculated by arithmetically averaging the probabilistic predictions submitted by each iteration. Unfortunately, we are unable to obtain probabilistic costing for random forests from weka [33]. Table 2 shows that MML forests have achieved better (lower) or equal probabilistic costing in 9 out of 13 data sets compared to C5.0 AdaBoost. The superior performance on probabilistic prediction of the MML forests can be attributed to the fact that both the base learner algorithm and the averaging scheme are well-suited to probabilistic predictions.

5 Conclusions

An ensemble classifier using shallow oblique decision trees, our new ensemble learning algorithm achieves favourable results on data sets with binary classes.

Our novel random decision tree generating scheme is capable of constructing a decision forest with a large number of distinct highly performing decision trees. The proposed weighted averaging scheme exploits the potential of using Bayesian weighted averaging to improve the predictive accuracy of ensemble classifiers, especially on probabilistic predictions and any predictions involving binary output classes. It is reasonable to believe that replacing the preliminary model with well developed and more elaborate models (such as mixtures of Normal distributions or other distributions) to approximate the posterior probabilities of the inferred trees can only further enhance the results from this kind of weighted averaging. The significance of the results could be improved by using advice from [9] and our own ideas from sec. 3.4 - including sampling from the posterior (via an importance sampling distribution) and generalising the prior.

References

1. C.L. Blake and C.J. Merz. UCI repository of machine learning databases, 1998. http://www.ics.uci.edu/~mlearn/MLRepository.html.
2. L. Breiman. Arcing classifiers. *The Annals of Statistics*, 26(3):801–824, Jun. 1998.
3. L. Breiman. Randomizing outputs to increase prediction accuracy. *Machine Learing*, 40:229–242, 2000.
4. Leo Breiman. Bagging predictors. *Machine Learning*, 24(2):123–140, 1996.
5. Leo Breiman. Random forests. *Machine Learning*, 45(1):5, 2001.
6. Leo Breiman, Jerome H. Friedman, Richard A. Olshen, and Charles J. Stone. *Classification And Regression Trees*. Wadsworth & Brooks, 1984.
7. Joshua W. Comley and David L. Dowe. Generalised Bayesian networks and asymmetric languages. In *Proc. Hawaii International Conference on Statistics and Related Fields*, 5-8 June 2003.
8. Joshua W. Comley and David L. Dowe. Chapter 11, Minimum Message Length and generalized Bayesian networks with asymmetric languages. In P. Grünwald, M. A. Pitt, and I. J. Myung, editors, *Advances in Minimum Description Length: Theory and Applications*, pages 265–294. M.I.T. Press, Apr 2005. Final camera-ready copy submitted Oct. 2003.
9. Janez Demšar. Statistical comparisons of classifiers over multiple data sets. *Journal of Machine Learning Research*, 7:1–30, January 2006.
10. Thomas G. Dietterich. Machine-learning research: Four current directions. *The AI Magazine*, 18(4):97–136, 1998.
11. Thomas G. Dietterich. An experimental comparison of three methods for constructing ensembles of decision trees: Bagging, boosting, and randomization. *Machine Learning*, 40(2):139–157, 2000.
12. D. L. Dowe, G.E. Farr, A.J. Hurst, and K.L. Lentin. Information-theoretic football tipping. In N. de Mestre, editor, *Third Australian Conference on Mathematics and Computers in Sport*, pages 233–241. Bond University, Qld, Australia, 1996. http://www.csse.monash.edu.au/~footy.
13. D. L. Dowe, S. Gardner, and G. R. Oppy. Bayes not Bust! Why simplicity is no problem for Bayesians. *British Journal for the Philosophy of Science*, forthcoming.
14. D. L. Dowe and N. Krusel. A decision tree model of bushfire activity. In *(Technical report 93/190) Dept. Comp. Sci., Monash Uni., Clayton, Australia*, 1993.

15. D. L. Dowe and C. S. Wallace. Kolmogorov complexity, minimum message length and inverse learning. In *14th Australian Statistical Conference (ASC-14)*, page 144, Gold Coast, Qld, Australia, 6-10 July 1998.
16. Cesar Ferri, Peter Flach, and Jose Hernandez-Orallo. Delegating classifiers. In *Proc. 21st International Conference on Machine Learning*, pages 106–110, Banff, Canada, 2004.
17. Yoav Freund and Robert E. Schapire. Experiments with a new boosting algorithm. In *International Conference on Machine Learning (ICML)*, pages 148–156, 1996.
18. Tin Kam Ho. The random subspace method for constructing decision forests. *IEEE Transactions on Pattern Analysis and Machine Intelligence*, 20(8):832–844, August 1998.
19. Manish Mehta, Jorma Rissanen, and Rakesh Agrawal. MDL-based Decision Tree Pruning. In *The First International Conference on Knowledge Discovery & Data Mining*, pages 216–221. AAAI Press, 1995.
20. Prem Melville and Raymond J. Mooney. Creating diversity in ensembles using artificial data. *Journal of Information Fusion (Special Issue on Diversity in Multiple Classifier Systems)*, 6(1):99–111, 2004.
21. S. L. Needham and D. L. Dowe. Message length as an effective Ockham's razor in decision tree induction. In *Proc. 8th International Workshop on Artificial Intelligence and Statistics*, pages 253–260, Key West, Florida, U.S.A., Jan. 2001.
22. J. J. Oliver and C. S. Wallace. Inferring Decision Graphs. In *Workshop 8 International Joint Conference on AI (IJCAI)*, Sydney, Australia, August 1991.
23. Jonathan J. Oliver and David J. Hand. On pruning and averaging decision trees. In A. Prieditis and S. Russell, editors, *Machine Learning: Proceedings of the Twelfth International Conference*, pages 430–437. Morgan Kaufmann, 1995.
24. J.R. Quinlan. *C4.5 : Programs for Machine Learning*. Morgan Kaufmann, San Mateo, CA, U.S.A., 1992. The latest version of C5 is available from http://www.rulequest.com.
25. J.J. Rissanen. Modeling by shortest data description. *Automatica*, 14:465–471, 1978.
26. P. J. Tan and D. L. Dowe. MML inference of decision graphs with multi-way joins. In *Lecture Notes in Artificial Intelligence (LNAI) 2557 (Springer), Proc. 15th Australian Joint Conf. on AI*, pages 131–142, Canberra, Australia, 2-6 Dec. 2002.
27. P. J. Tan and D. L. Dowe. MML inference of decision graphs with multi-way joins and dynamic attributes. In *Lecture Notes in Artificial Intelligence (LNAI) 2903 (Springer), Proc. 16th Australian Joint Conf. on AI*, pages 269–281, Perth, Australia, Dec. 2003.
28. P. J. Tan and D. L. Dowe. MML inference of oblique decision trees. In *Lecture Notes in Artificial Intelligence (LNAI) 3339 (Springer), Proc. 17th Australian Joint Conf. on AI*, pages 1082–1088, Cairns, Australia, Dec. 2004.
29. C. S. Wallace. *Statistical and Inductive Inference by Minimum Message Length*. Springer, 2005.
30. C. S. Wallace and D. M. Boulton. An Information Measure for Classification. *Computer Journal*, 11:185–194, 1968.
31. C. S. Wallace and D. L. Dowe. Minimum Message Length and Kolmogorov Complexity. *Computer Journal*, 42(4):270–283, 1999.
32. C. S. Wallace and P. R. Freeman. Estimation and Inference by Compact Coding. *Journal of the Royal Statistical Society. Series B*, 49(3):240–265, 1987.
33. Ian H. Witten and Eibe Frank. *Data Mining: Practical machine learning tools and techniques*. Morgan Kaufmann, San Francisco, 2nd edition, 2005.

Using Reliable Short Rules to Avoid Unnecessary Tests in Decision Trees

Hyontai Sug

Division of Computer and Information Engineering, Dongseo University, Busan, 617-716, South Korea
hyontai@yahoo.com

Abstract. It is known that in decision trees the reliability of lower branches is worse than the upper branches due to data fragmentation problem. As a result, unnecessary tests of attributes may be done, because decision trees may require tests that are not best for some part of the data objects. To supplement the weak point of decision trees of data fragmentation, using reliable short rules with decision tree is suggested, where the short rules come from limited application of association rule finding algorithms. Experiment shows the method can not only generate more reliable decisions but also save test costs by using the short rules.

1 Introduction

It is known that decision trees are one of the most important machine learning and data mining technique, and have been successful in prediction tasks. So, discovering good algorithms of decision trees with smallest error rates has been a major concern for many researchers. But despite of their wide applications as one of the most common data mining and machine learning methodologies, decision trees may not always be the best predictor, because they are built to cover all of target data set in a single tree.

When we build decision trees, the root node of each subtree is chosen among the attributes which have not yet been chosen by ancestor nodes so that the selected attribute is the best split based on their used measure in their greedy search algorithms. And moreover, as a tree is being built, each branch starts having less training data objects due to the splitting of the data set, so the reliability of each branch becomes worse than the upper branches, known as data fragmentation problem. Because of the lack of enough training data at the lower part of decision tree by the data fragmentation, as a result, a single tree may lead to unnecessary tests of attribute values and may not represent knowledge models that are best for some collection of the data objects in the target data set. In this paper, we suggest a method to supplement the weak point of decision trees of data fragmentation, utilizing reliable short rules with decision tree is suggested, where the short rules come from limited application of association rule finding algorithms. Experiment shows promising results.

A. Gelbukh and C.A. Reyes-Garcia (Eds.): MICAI 2006, LNAI 4293, pp. 604–611, 2006.

In section 2, we first briefly provide the related works to our research, and in sections 3 and 4 we present our method in detail and explain some experiments performed. Finally section 5 provides some conclusions.

2 Related Works

Decision tree algorithms are based on greedy method. So, generated decision trees are not optimum and some improvement may be possible. There have been a lot of efforts to build better decision trees with respect to error rates by focusing on splitting criteria. For example, one of standard decision tree algorithm C4.5 [1] uses entropy-based measure, and CART [2] uses purity-based measure, and CHAID [3] uses chi-square test-based measure for split.

There have been also scalability related efforts to generate decision trees for large databases such as SLIQ [4], SPRINT [5], PUBLIC [6], and RainForest [7]. SLIQ saves computing time especially for continuous attributes by using a pre-sorting technique in tree-growth phase, and SPRINT is an improved version of SLIQ to solve the scalability problem by building trees in parallel. PUBLIC tries to save some computing time by integrating pruning and generating branches. The authors of PUBLIC claimed that their algorithm is more efficient than SPRINT. RainForest saves more computing time than SPRINT when certain minimum amount of main memory is available. According to literature [6], for very large data sets computing time becomes exponential for SPRINT and polynomial for PUBLIC despite of their efforts for scalability. Moreover, these methods may generate very large decision trees for very large data sets so that there is high possibility of unnecessary tests for fringe nodes.

Generating right-sized decision trees requires a universal application of pruning [1], [2], [8], [9] so that overpruning was a natural consequence to generate smaller decision trees. In his Ph.D. dissertation [8], J. Catlett relied on overpruning to obtain comprehensible trees. As a result of this overpruning, the generated tree may not have sufficient accuracy compared to near optimal, similar sized trees.

There has been also a lot of research for feature subset selection and dimensionality reduction problem [10]. One of major problem in scientific data is that the data are often high dimensional so that it takes very long computing time for pattern recognition algorithms. To solve this problem dimensionality reduction algorithms have been invented to select the most important features so that further processing like pattern recognition algorithms can be simplified without comprising the quality of final results. On the other hand, feature subset selection algorithms try to eliminate irrelevant features from attribute set [11], [12], [13]. Irrelevant features are features that are dependent on other features so that they have bad effects on their size and error rate of generated trees.

There are also efforts to find a best rule set by applying association rule finding algorithms [14], [15], [16]. ART [17] tries to ensure good scalability by building decision list efficiently. But, because association rule finding algorithms are exhaustive algorithms so that its applicability is limited. The largest data set used for experiment to test its performance has size of only 12,960 records. There are also multidimensional association rules. Multidimensional association rules are basically an application of general association rule algorithms to table-like databases [18]. In papers like [19], [20], multidimensional association rules have better accuracy than decision trees for most of example data. The data used for the experiment are from UCI machine learning repository [21]. They also used the found association rules and other prediction methods in combination for better prediction. But large-size data were not used for comparison due to time complexity of association rule finding algorithm which is the inborn nature of the algorithm. Moreover, association rule finding algorithms can deal with interval or nominal values only, so discretization is necessary as preprocessing. Some researchers prefer decision trees to association rules because of the capability of decision trees to deal with continuous values [22].

Decision trees are one of the mostly used data mining methods, because they have many good characteristics, especially the easy-to-understand structure. But, large data sets may generate large decision trees so that understandability problem and more importantly, unnecessary tests for minority data can happen. Therefore, when there are a lot of training data, we want to appreciate the structure of decision trees, as well as to provide more economical way of prediction by providing short rules of high reliability to compensate the weak point of decision trees. The difference of our approach from other association rule algorithms is that our method tries to use the association rule algorithms in limited way to avoid the time complexity problem of the association rule algorithms so that the utility of the both algorithms can be strengthened.

3 The Proposed Method

Association rule algorithms are basic ingredients for our method. There are many research results for the algorithms; a kind of standard association algorithm, Apriori, a main memory-based algorithm for faster response time, AprioriTid [23], a hash-table based algorithm, DHP [24], random sample based algorithms [25], and parallel association algorithms [26].

In this paper a modified multidimensional association rule finding algorithm is used. The modified multidimensional association rule finding algorithm is more efficient than conventional multidimensional association rule finding algorithm, because we find association rules between so called conditional attributes and decisional attribute only. There is no need to find associations within conditional attributes as the conventional multidimensional association algorithms do. For this purpose, for example, apriori-gen( ) function of apriori[23] which makes candidate itemsets should be modified to reflect this fact and for more efficiency.

For the rule set to be of much help, we should select an appropriate minimum support number based on our knowledge of the domain and the size of the target database. Moreover, because the target database of knowledge discovery is generally very large, unlimited exhaustive rule set generation of association is almost impossible. For the rules to be reliable and significant, we need a sufficient number of supporting facts in the database. According to sampling theory, sample of size 30 or so is a reasonable size for reliable statistics [27]. Note that this sample size as minimum support number is for each individual rules and not for the entire data set. Note also that our method is independent of any specific decision tree algorithm so that any decision tree algorithm you like can be used.The following is the general procedure of the method:

1. Generate a decision tree with your favorite decision tree algorithm.
2. Run the modified multidimensional association rule finding algorithm with an appropriate minimum support and confidence to find the rules of limited length.
3. Find multidimensional association rules which have the same decisions but more confidence than the branches of the decision tree.

At the second step of the procedure, we usually supply number 2 as the rule length limit, due to time complexity of the association rule algorithm. The time complexity to find short association rules, for example, size of 2, is almost proportional to the size of databases, because most time to spend is disk access time. But, depending on the need of application domain and available resources, one may find longer association rules without any change of the procedures.

To generate a rule set, we select rules that have more than a given threshold of confidence. The confidence of a rule a1 ⇒ d1 is $|a1d1|$ / $|a1|$, where a1 is an itemset in the condition part and d1 is an itemset in the decision part and | | denotes the frequency of the itemsets. If we have fixed conditional and decisional attributes for multidimensional association rules, the confidence of a rule $Y \rightarrow Z$ is a conditional probability,

$$P(Z \mid Y) = \frac{P(Y \cap Z)}{P(Y)}.$$

So, we don't need to worry about whether they are positively or negatively correlated like conventional association rules [28]. If a rule "A" has the same decision part as another rule "B," but A's conditions are a superset of B's, where A's confidence is less or equal to B's, then "B" should be selected.

We also need to convert continuous values into symbols because association rules treats nominal values only. We use the entropy-based discretization method because it is known to be the best [21] [22].

4 Experiment

An experiment was run using the databases in UCI machine learning repository [21] called 'census-income' to confirm the effectiveness of the method. The number of instances for training is 199,523. Class probabilities for label -50000 and 50000+ are 93.8% and 6.2% respectively. The total number of attributes is 41. Among them eight attributes are continuous attributes.

We use C4.5 [1] to generate a decision tree. The eight continuous attributes are converted to nominal values based on the entropy-based discretization method

```
capital_gains = '(-inf-57]'
| dividends_from_stocks = '(-inf-0.5]'
| | weeks_worked_in_year = '(-inf-0.5]': -50000 (89427.0/200.0)
. . . . . .
| | weeks_worked_in_year = '(51.5-inf)'
| | | capital_losses = '(-inf-1881.5]'
| | | | sex = Female: -50000 (25510.0/987.0)
| | | | sex = Male
| | | | | education = Children: -50000 (0.0) *
| | | | | education = 9th grade: -50000 (579.0/9.0) *
| | | | | education = Less than 1st grade: -50000 (94.0)*
. . . . . .
| | | | | education = Masters degree (MA MS MEng MEd MSW MBA)
| | | | | | detailed_occupation_recode = 0
| | | | | | | age = '(-inf-15.5]': -50000 (0.0)*
| | | | | | | age = '(15.5-19.5]': -50000 (0.0)*
| | | | | | | age = '(19.5-24.5]': -50000 (0.0)*
. . . . . .
| | | | | | detailed_occupation_recode = 29: -50000 (5.0)*
| | | | | | detailed_occupation_recode = 2
| | | | | | | detailed_household_summary_in_household =
          Group Quarters-Secondary individual: 50000+ (0.0)*
. . . . . .
| | | | | | detailed_occupation_recode = 6
| | | | | | | detailed_household_summary_in_household =
          Child under 18 never married: -50000 (0.0)*
. . . . . .
. . . . . .
capital_gains = '(14682-inf)'
| sex = Female
| | marital_stat = Never married: 50000+ (23.0/5.0)
| | marital_stat = Married-civilian spouse present
| | |*weeks_worked_in_year = '(-inf-0.5]': -50000 (37.0/7.0)
. . . . . .
. . . . . .
```

Fig. 1. Some part of the generated decision tree from C4.5

before applying the algorithm. The generated tree has 1,821 nodes with 1,661 leaves and the error rate is 4.3%. Fig. 1 shows some part of the generated tree.

To find reliable short rules the following values are given; minimum support: 0.05%, and confidence limit: 95%, and rule length limit: 2.

Total of 182 rules are found. The average confidence of the found rules is 98% and the average number of supporting training examples in the found rules is 12,591. The following nine rules are a few examples of the found rules. The corresponding branches for the rules are indicated with a star in the generated tree of C4.5. Note that the short rules can appear many times as terminal nodes with smaller confidences than those of the short rules due to the data fragmentation. For example, rule number 8 appears ten times as a terminal node in the generated decision tree.

1. IF education = Children THEN -50000. conf:(1=47422/47422)
2. IF education = Less than 1st grade THEN -50000. conf:(1=818/819)
3. IF education = 9th grade THEN -50000. conf:(0.99=6192/6230)
4. IF age = '(-inf - 15.5]' THEN -50000. conf:(1=50348/50348)
5. IF age = '(15.5 - 19.5]' THEN -50000. conf:(1=10539/10547)
6. IF age = '(19.5 - 24.5]' THEN -50000. conf:(0.99=12816/12921)
7. IF detailed occupation record = 29 THEN -50000. conf:(0.99=5077/5105)
8. IF detailed_household_summary_in_household = Group Quarters-Secondary individual THEN 50000+. conf:(0.99=131/132)
9. IF detailed_household_summary_in_household = Children under 18 never married THEN -50000. conf:(1=50424/50426)

As you notice from the generated tree in figure 1, the test are given at the lower part of the decision tree. But, if we use these short association rules, we don't have to test the upper part of the decision tree. Instead, we can directly apply the short association rules, because they have many supporting number of objects so that they are very reliable. In other words, among the found association rules many rules are fringe nodes of the decision tree so that no additional tests are needed for reliable decisions, if we use the found association rules.

In addition, in the short rule set six attributes among 41 attributes have all possible rules with their own attributes and the lowest value of the rules' minimum confidence is 85%. Table 1 summarizes the result. Therefore, if we have some cases that have to be predicted and the cases have one of these attribute values, we can predict the class of the cases reliably without any help of decision trees.

Table 1. Attributes having rules of all possible values

attribute	number of found rules	average confidence(%)
family_members_under_18	5	94
hispanic_origin	10	93
reason_for_unemployment	6	94
region_of_previous_residence	6	94
weeks_worked_in_year	6	94

5 Conclusions

As a successful machine learning and data mining technique, decision trees are very widely used. But despite of their wide applications as one of the most common data mining and machine learning methodologies, decision trees may not always be the best predictor, because they are built to cover all of target data in a single tree. As a tree is being built, each branch starts having less training data objects, so the reliability of each branch becomes worse than the upper branches, known as data fragmentation problem. As a result, a single tree may lead to unnecessary tests of attribute values and may not represent knowledge models that are best for some collection of the data objects in the target data set.

We propose to use a modified multidimensional association rule algorithm to find short reliable rules and use them to avoid unnecessary tests in some branches of the decision tree. The modified multidimensional association rule algorithm uses the same target data set for training in a limited way, but the method dose not segment the input data set. So, we can compensate the fragmentation problem of decision trees more or so. Even if the target databases are very large, the method can be applied without difficulty, because we find very short association rules only. Moreover, the large data size may be welcome, because we may have short rules with a lot of supporting training examples, which strengthens the confidence of the rules. Therefore, the method has a good point of saving test costs and it is well suited for the task of knowledge discovery especially in very large databases that are most common in data warehouses.

If the class of a new instance can be predicted by a short rule, testing cost will be reduced, since the evaluation of other attribute values of the instance are not required, and the method provide more reliable decisions, since the short rules usually have more supporting number of examples than corresponding terminal nodes of decision trees.

References

1. Quinlan, J.R.: C4.5: Programs for Machine Learning. Morgan Kaufmann Publishers (1993)
2. Breiman, L., Friedman, J., Olshen, R., Stone, C.: Classification and Regression Trees. Wadsworth International Group, Inc.(1984)
3. StatSoft, Inc.: Electronic Statistics Textbook. Tulsa, OK, StatSoft. WEB: http://www.statsoft.com/textbook/stathome.html (2004)
4. Mehta, M., Agrawal, R., and Rissanen, J.: SLIQ : A Fast Scalable Classifier for Data Mining. (EDBT'96), Avignon, France (1996)
5. Shafer, J., Agrawal, R., and Mehta., M.: SPRINT : A Scalable Parallel Classifier for Data Mining. Proc. 1996 Int. Conf. Very Large Data Bases, Bombay, India, Sept. 1996. 544–555.
6. Rastogi, R., Shim, K.: PUBLIC : A Decision Tree Classifier that Integrates Building and Pruning. Data Mining and Knowledge Discovery, Vol. 4, no. 4. Kluwer International (2002) 315–344
7. Gehrke, J., Ramakrishnan, R., and Ganti, V.: Rainforest: A Framework for Fast Decision Tree Construction of Large Datasets. Proc. 1998 Int. Conf. Very Large Data Bases, New York, NY, August 1998. 416–427
8. Catlett, J.: Megainduction: Machine Learning on Very Large Databases. PhD thesis, University of Sydney, Australia (1991)
9. SAS: Decision Tree Modeling Course Notes. SAS Publishing (2002)
10. Jolliffe, I.T.: Principal Component Analysis. Springer Verlag, 2nd ed. (2002)

11. Almuallim, H., Dietterich, T.G.: Efficient Algorithms for Identifying Relevant Features. Proc. of the 9th Canadian Conference on Artificial Intelligence (1992) 38–45
12. Kononenko, I., et. al.: Overcoming the Myopia of Inductive Learning Algorithms with RELIEF. Applied Intelligence, Vol.7, no. 1 (1997) 39–55
13. Liu, H., Motoda, H.: Feature Extraction, Construction and Selection: A Data Mining Perspective. Kluwer International (1998)
14. Liu, B., Hsu, W., Ma, Y.: Integrating Classification and Association Rule Mining. Proc. of the 4th International Conference on Knowledge Discovery and Data Mining (KDD-98), New York, New York, (1998) 80–86
15. Liu, B., Hu, M., Hsu, W.: Multi-level Organization and Summarization of the Discovered Rule. Proc. of the 6th ACM SIGKDD International Conference on Knowledge Discovery and Data Mining, Boston, MA (2000) 208–217
16. Wang, K., Zhou, S., He, Y.: Growing Decision Trees on Support-less Association Rules. Proc. of the 6th ACM SIGKDD International Conference on Knowledge Discovery and Data Mining, Boston, MA (2000) 265–269
17. Berzal, F., Cubero, J., Sanchez, D., Serrano, J.M.: ART: A Hybrid Classification Model. Machine Learning, Vol. 54 (2004) 67–92
18. Han, J., Kamber, M.: Data Mining: Concepts and Techniques. Morgan Kaufmann Publishers (2000)
19. Li, W., Han, J., Pei, J.: CMAR: Accurate and Efficient Classification Based on Multiple Class-Association Rules. Proceedings 2001 Int. Conf. on Data Mining (ICDM'01), San Jose, CA.
20. Liu, B., Hsu, W., Ma, Y.: Integrating Classification and Association Rule Mining. Proceedings of the Fourth International Conference on Knowledge Discovery and Data Mining (KDD-98), New York, NY (1998)
21. Hettich, S., Bay, S.D.: The UCI KDD Archive [http://kdd.ics.uci.edu]. Irvine, CA: University of California, Department of Information and Computer Science (1999)
22. Witten, I.H., Frank, E.: Data Mining: Practical Machine Learning Tools and Techniques, 2nd ed. Morgan Kaufmann Publishers (2005)
23. Agrawal, R., Mannila, H., Toivonen, H., Verkamo, A.I.: Fast Discovery of Association Rules. In Advances in Knowledge Discovery and Data Mining, Fayyad, U.M., Piatetsky-Shapiro, G., Smith, P., and Uthurusamy, R. ed., AAAI Press/The MIT Press (1996) 307–328
24. Pak, J.S., Chen, M., Yu, P.S.: Using a Hash-Based Method with Transaction Trimming for Mining Association Rules. IEEE Transactions on Knowledge and Data Engineering **9(5)** (1997) 813-825
25. Toivonen, H.: Discovery of Frequent Patterns in Large Data Collections. phD thesis, Department of Computer Science, University of Helsinki, Finland (1996)
26. Savasere, A., Omiecinski, E., Navathe, S.: An Efficient Algorithm for Mining Association Rules in Large Databases. College of Computing, Georgia Institute of Technology, Technical Report No.: GIT–CC–95–04
27. Cochran, W.G.: Sampling Techniques. Willey (1977)
28. Aggarawal, C.C., Yu, P.S.: A New Frame Work for Itemset Generation. PODS98, (1998) 18–24
29. Liu, H., Hussain, F., Tan, C.L., Dash, M.: Discretization: An Enabling Techniques. Data Mining and Knowledge Discovery, Vol. 6, no. 4 (2002) 393–423

Selection of the Optimal Wavebands for the Variety Discrimination of Chinese Cabbage Seed

Di Wu, Lei Feng, and Yong He

College of Biosystems Engineering and Food Science, Zhejiang University, 310029, Hangzhou, China
yhe@zju.edu.cn

Abstract. This paper presents a method based on chemometrics analysis to select the optimal wavebands for variety discrimination of Chinese cabbage seed by using a Visible/Near-infrared spectroscopy (Vis/NIRS) system. A total of 120 seed samples were investigated using a field spectroradiometer. Chemometrics was used to build the relationship between the absorbance spectra and varieties. Principle component analysis (PCA) was not suitable for variety discrimination as the principle components (PCs) plot of three primary principle components could only intuitively distinguish the varieties well. Partial Least Squares Regression (PLS) was executed to select 6 optimal wavebands as 730nm, 420nm, 675nm, 620nm, 604nm and 609nm based on loading values. Two chemometrics, multiple linear regression (MLR) and stepwise discrimination analysis (SDA) were used to establish the recognition models. MLR model is not suitable in this study because of its unsatisfied predictive ability. The SDA model was proposed by the advantage of variable selection. The final results based on SDA model showed an excellent performance with high discrimination rate of 99.167%. It is also proved that optimal wavebands are suitable for variety discrimination.

1 Introduction

Chinese cabbage (*Brassica campestris L. Chinensis Group.*) is one of the most important vegetables consumed mainly during the winter season in Asia, especially, in China, Korea and Japan [1]. The seed of Chinese cabbage is henna and closely Ellipsoid. The surface of it is smooth and with luster while the one of aged seed is dim and lackluster. The weight of every one thousand seeds is about 1.5 to 2.2 gram. As one of the major vegetables for Chinese consumers, the planting of Chinese cabbage is significant. The variety of seed relate to many fields on Chinese cabbage, such as the output of planting, nutrition content, taste, disease resistance and time-to-market. So, the seed discrimination of Chinese cabbage is very important and necessary.

The Chinese seed markets are gradually standardizing in recent year, but some illegal merchants are still using some bad seeds which were with low output and bad disease resistance to replace choice quality seed with high price in order to sell for sudden huge profits. It is very difficult for consumers to discriminate the seed varieties of Chinese cabbage using naked eyes and the discrimination methods used by planters just are subjective, such as through color, luster, the satiety lever, weight and so on. So the precision of discrimination can not be ensured. Some novel methods were used in

A. Gelbukh and C.A. Reyes-Garcia (Eds.): MICAI 2006, LNAI 4293, pp. 612 – 621, 2006.

variety discrimination of seed, such as protein electrophoresis technique and molecular marker, but these ways need to destruct the seeds and the process of them are trivial with amount of considerable manual work and cost. In this paper, a simple, fast, non-destructive method was proposed for variety discrimination technique of Chinese cabbage seed.

Visible/Near-infrared spectroscopy (Vis/NIRS) is a technique of qualitative and quantitative analysis on organic compound using spectrum information. This technique can obtain a wide range of diverse physicochemical information as demonstrated by the diversity of applications in food and agriculture with many advantages such as fast and simple measurement, high efficient, low cost, good reproducibility, environment friendly and non-destruction based on the whole or multi-wavebands [2]. So this technique is widely applied in many fields. Nowadays, researchers have already used it in the discrimination of characteristics quality on the plant seed. Tesfaye et al. predicted the maize seed composition using single kernel NIRS [3]. Fassio et al. predicted the chemical composition in sunflower seeds by near infrared spectroscopy [4]. McCaig measured the surface color of canola, poppy, lentil [5]. Gross et al. analyzed the grain protein content, grain hardness and dough rheology [6]. The spectral technique also was used in genetic discrimination of seed [7]. However there are few methods for the variety discrimination of seed based on optics and mainly focused on the artificial vision [8]. The spectroscopy technique applied on the discrimination of seed is also only applied on the fruitage [9] and its process after harvest [10]. At present, the papers on variety discrimination of plant's seed using Vis/NIRS technique were seldom.

The principle of Vis/NIRS technique is obtaining the content and even construction of different components of samples through analyzing the spectrum information. Although the Vis/NIRS technique is widely applied in many fields, it also has several disadvantages as wide absorption band with badly overlapped, weak absorption, low sensitivity and with much noise and other no-related information. Chemometrics is commonly applied to avoid losing useful spectrum data and collinearity problem. The application of chemometrics in spectrum analysis includes these aspects: spectrum pre-process, quantity analysis model, pattern recognize and calibration transfer [11].

Principle component analysis (PCA) is a way of data mining. The spectrum bands are overlap, so the analysis of spectrum datum is very difficult. A few new variables as principle components (PCs) can be got to replace original vast variables after PCA [12], and the principle information of spectrum can be reserved, then the analysis of spectrum datum became easy. The PCs were used for distinguishing the varieties intuitively. Partial Least Squares Regression (PLS) is usually considered for a large number of applications in spectrum analysis. PLS performs the decomposition on both the spectral and concentration data simultaneously, as it takes the advantage of the correlation relationship that already exists between the spectral data and the constituent concentrations. In order to design a simple optical sensor for variety discrimination, it is important to reduce the number of selected wavebands to a minimum. Both multiple linear regression (MLR) and stepwise discrimination analysis (SDA) were executed to establish the prediction model based on several optimal wavebands and two results were compared to find out which one is better.

The aim of this study is to use Vis/NIRS spectroscopy technique coupled with chemometrics methods based on some optimal wavebands which were determined by PLS model to discriminate the varieties of Chinese cabbage seed.

2 Material and Methods

2.1 Fruit Samples and Vis-NIRS Analysis

Seed samples of Chinese cabbage, purchased at local seed company, belong to 6 varieties which are Wuyueman, Shenbao Qing No.2, Clover Pakchoi (128), Kangre 605, Huqing No1, Hongqiao Aiqingcai. Each variety has 20 samples..

Each sample with several seeds was put about half full into glass sample containers with 120 mm in diameter and 10mm in height. Then these seeds were smoothed to make sure the surface of each sample was plane. All the 120 samples were scanned at the surface by an average of 30 times in the range of 325-1075nm at 1.5cm-1 interval using a spectroradiometer (FieldSpec Pro FR A110070) Trademarks of Analytical Spectral Devices, Inc. equipped with a 150W halogen lamp as light source. Considering the field-of-view (FOV) with 25°, the horizontal distance between sample's surface and spectral probe was set as 150mm while the vertical one was 95mm. The distance between sample's surface and lamp was 230mm. Data was optimized by shorting the spectral range to 401-1000nm which means that the first 75 and the last 75 wavelength values were taken out because some noise which was caused by the system error and will affect the accuracy of data process appeared in these wavebands. Spectral data were converted into absorbance which is defined as the logarithm of the reciprocal of the reflected(R) energy (log (1/R)) and stored as ASCII datum for further data process. Thus, a total of 600 data points were collected for each sample. ASD View Spec Pro software was used to execute these processes mentioned above.

2.2 Chemometrics

Preprocessing of the Optical Data. The preprocessing of spectral data is one of the key parts to establish the model as precise as possible in the application of spectra analysis technique. Original spectral data may have some noise and other interference factors which will affect both the establishment of the model and the accuracy of the final predictive results. So it's necessary to do the preprocessing. Several chemometrics methods were applied solely and conjointly, such as moving average smoothing (MAS), multiple scatter correction (MSC) and MAS-MSC. It has been proved that the high frequency noise could be eliminated by MAS. As the fresh light will scatter in samples, it does not always travel the same distance in the samples before measured by spectroradiometer. A longer light traveling path corresponds to a lower relative reflectance value, since more light is absorbed. This causes a parallel translation of the spectra and was useless for the calibration models. MSC is applied in eliminating this kind of variation [13].

Principal Components Analysis (PCA). As absorbance data has many wavebands, these variables need to be simplified by variable reduction in order to make them more easily to interpreted. PCA [8] is a well-known reduction technique:

$$X = TP^{-1} + E \tag{1}$$

Where X is the $N\times K$ spectral data matrix, T is the $N\times A$ matrix of score vectors, P is the $K\times A$ is the matrix of loading vectors, E is the $N\times K$ residual matrix, N is the number of objects, K is the number of variables (which in our case is the number of wave numbers), and A is the number of components calculated (PCs). The first principal component describes the greatest contribution amount of spectral information. In this paper, with the first 8 PCs, it is possible to extract more than 95% of the desired variance. So, before the calibration, the spectra variation of the data was analyzed by PCA and defective spectral was eliminated.

Partial Least Squares Regression Analysis (PLS). PLS is commonly used in chemometrics analysis. With full cross validation, PLS was performed on the spectra on 401-1000nm to reduce the variable dimensions of the original independent information (X-data) and extract few but primary latent variables (LVs) which can present the characteristics (Y) of spectra belong to each sample. The extracting process is performed including both X and Y data through exchanging the score of X and Y before every new principle component is calculated and this is the different and better against PCR. So the LVs are related to dependent variables, not only to the independent variables. While in this paper, the aim of PLS is to obtain the optimal wavebands for variety discrimination thought the loading values of each LVs. The whole process was achieved in The Unscrambler V9.2 (CAMO Process AS.), a statistical software for multivariate calibration.

Multiple Linear Regression (MLR). MLR is the mostly used modeling methods. MLR yields models that are simpler and easier. Briefly, the MLR technique is

$$Y = a_0 + a_1 S(\lambda_1) + a_2 S(\lambda_2) + a_3 S(\lambda_3) + \ldots, \tag{2}$$

Where, Y is variety number set from 1 to 6 in this paper; $S(\lambda_1)$, $S(\lambda_2)$, and $S(\lambda_3)$ are the spectral data at wavelengths, λ_1, λ_2, and λ_3, respectively, and a_0, a_1, a_2, and a_3 are the regression coefficients. The selected wavelengths were added to the equation to establish model.

Stepwise Discrimination Analysis (SDA). The SDA is a linear discrimination method based on F-test for the significance of the variables. In each step one variable will be selected on the basis of its significance. Fisher [14] founded discriminate analysis (DA), and then it was ameliorated and evolved as SDA. With its satisfactory results in discriminating with different sedimentary environment, SDA was commonly applied in numerous fields such as socio-economics, medicine, psychology and geosciences. SDA evolved based on multiple discerning and the criterion is Bayesian discriminating function. The SDA is performed in four steps: first, calculate the mean value and MDE (Mean Dispersion Error) in each group and total mean value and MDE; second, filtrate the variables step by step(calculate all the discriminability of every variable, select variable, test its significance and judge which variables could be selected); third as final, identified the discrimination and classification.

3 Results and Discussion

3.1 Features of NIR Spectra and Preprocessing of Data

The average absorbance spectra from 401 to 1000 nm were showed in Fig. 1 for randomly selected samples of 6 varieties of Chinese cabbage seed. It could be observed that the spectra profiles were substantially distinguished from each other, especially at the red edge. So it indicted that it is possible to distinguish the varieties of Chinese cabbage seed. But even the spectra profiles within a class can vary due to the effects of environment and underlying difference between varying genotypes within the same class. So it will be hard to distinguish the varieties of seed quantificationally only through the spectra profile and chemometrics was executed in further analysis.

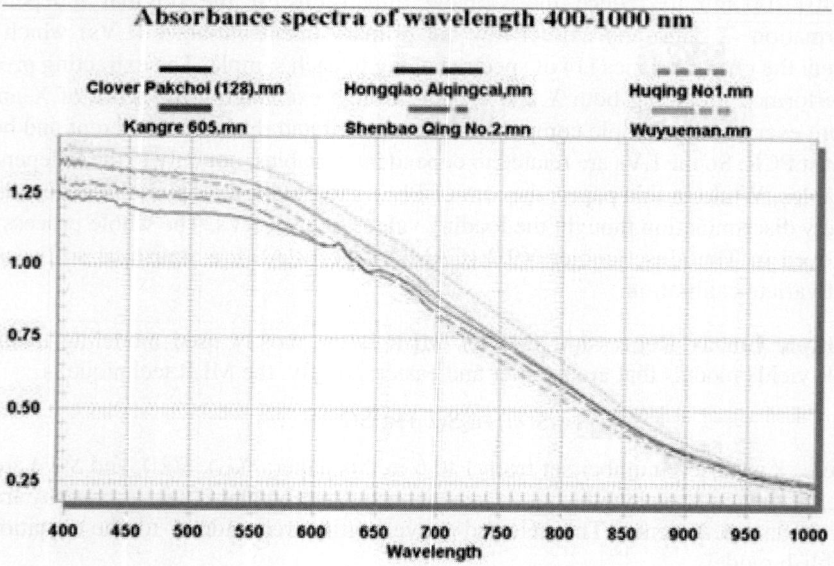

Fig. 1. Absorbance spectra of wavelength 400-1000 nm for

Before further data processing, several preprocessing were applied separately and also combined. After compared with the final predictive results, the preprocessing with 9 segments of MAS coupled MSC is the best one.

3.2 Clustering of PCA

PCA was applied to enhance the feature of variety and reduce dimensionality. Each kind of samples was numbered individually. After preprocessing, PCA was performed to obtain major PCs on the spectral data. A resultant plot of discrimination could be created with first three PCs (PC_1 as X-axis, PC_2 as Y-axis and PC_3 as Z-axis). The PCs plot could display the clustering of varieties from multiple wavebands; it can achieve discrimination. Table 1 shows the contribution and accumulative contribution of each PC individually. It could be concluded that the first three primary PCs have reached up than 99% information, so these three PCs can be used to instead of the whole 600 variables to make the variety discrimination qualitatively by using clustering plot (Fig 2). From Fig 2, all the samples which belong to six varieties (Variety 1 for Wuyueman, 2 for Shenbao Qing No.2, 3 for Kangre 605, 4 for Huqing No1, 5 for Hongqiao Aiqingcai, 6 for Clover Pakchoi (128)) are clustered well and can be distinguished clearly. So it has proved that lustering plot of the first three primary PCs can make the variety discrimination well. However, this plot only can make a qualitative discrimination and can not be used in quantitative analysis, because it could only distinguished variety from few angles when it was projected into 2-D plot, and the cluster plot only shows the calibration part and can not be used for prediction. Thus, some other chemometrics was needed to achieve the aim more quantificational.

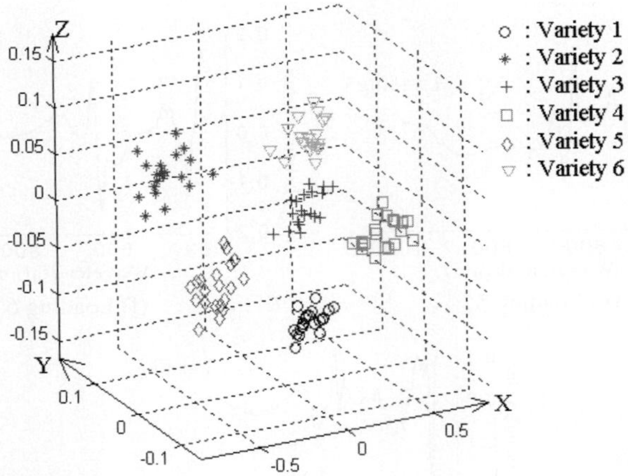

Fig. 2. Clustering plot of the PCA model with PC_1, PC_2 and PC_3 (PC_1 as X-axis, PC_2 as Y-axis and PC_3 as Z-axis)

3.3 Determination of Optimal Wavebands by PLS

After the preprocessing of spectra data, PLS process was carried out with all the 120 samples. The number of LVs in PLS analysis was determined as 7 by cross-validation. By choosing spectral wavebands with the first highest absolute loading values in each LV across the entire spectral region, 6 wavelengths were chose as the optimal ones (Fig.3.): 730nm (in LV1), 420nm (in LV2), 675nm (both in LV3 and LV4), 620nm (in LV5), 604nm (in LV6) and 609nm (in LV 7).

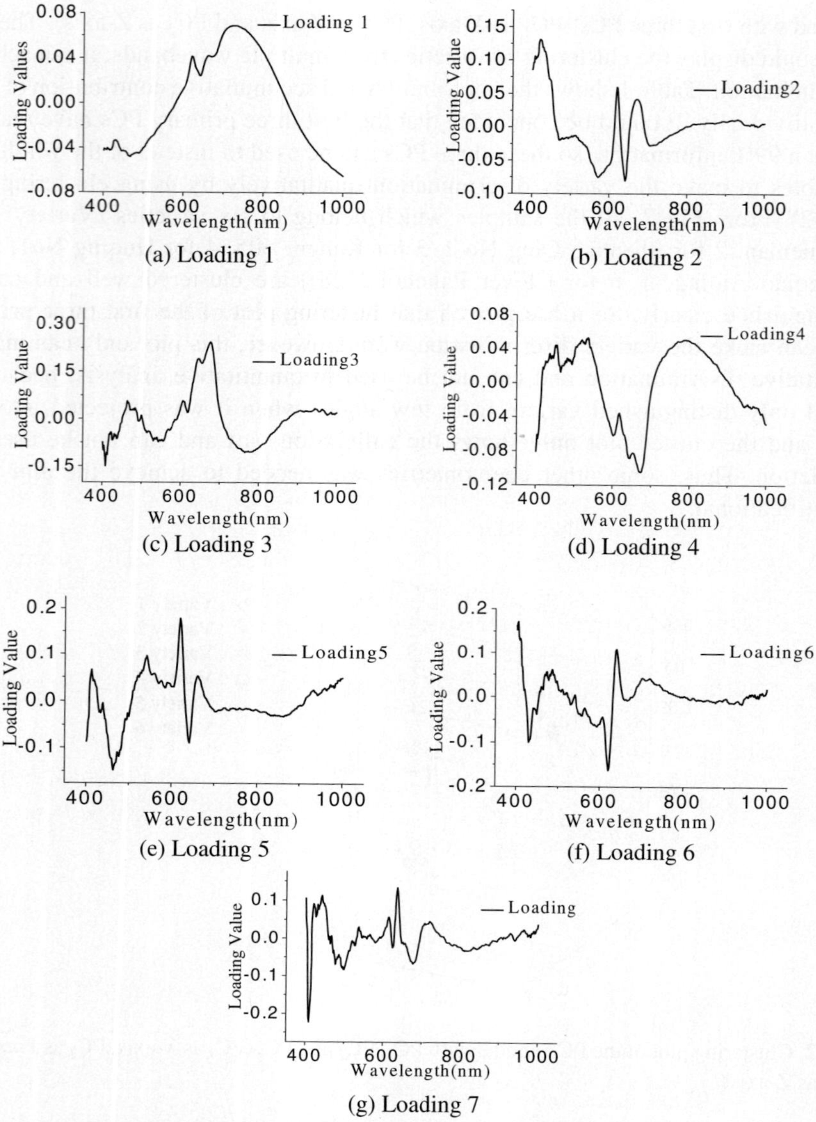

Fig. 3. Loading plots of LVs 1 to 7 (a~i) in the PLS model

Table 1. PCs and its contribution

PC	PC_1	PC_2	PC_3	PC_4	PC_5	PC_6	PC_7
Contribution (%)	90.90	5.50	2.81	0.41	0.15	0.07	0.03
Accumulative Contribution (%)	90.90	96.40	99.21	99.62	99.77	99.85	99.88

3.4 Multiple Linear Regression (MLR) Prediction Model

After the process of PLS, there was a matrix that contains 121rows (as 120 samples and one row for six variety numbers which are set as the same as chapter 3.2) and 6 columns (as the absorbance value of 6 optimal wavebands) came into being. Imported this matrix into DPS software and defined as data-block in the software. The function of MLR model was shown as follow:

$$Y=26.1 +33.8 * X_1 + 54.6 * X_2 + 73.7 * X_3 - 95.7 * X_4 - 29.8 * X_5 - 35.1 * X_6 \quad (3)$$

Where, Y is the prediction value, X_1 to X_6 are the absorbance values of each sample at 6 optima wavebands as 730nm, 420nm, 675nm, 620nm, 604nm and 609nm. The discrimination result about discrimination of varieties was presented in Table 2.

3.5 Stepwise Discrimination Analysis (SDA) Model

After the process of PLS, there was a matrix that contains 121rows (as 120 samples and one row for six variety numbers which are set as the same as chapter 3.2) and 6 columns (as the absorbance value of 6 optimal wavebands) came into being. Imported this matrix into DPS software and defined as data-block in the software. The critical value Fa=1.90. The discrimination effects are showed in Table 3.

The SDA in DPS needed to set the predicting samples as the number 0, and set other reality validation samples as the same number as chapter 3.2. The result was present in Table 1. The recognition rate is 99.167% (Table 3).

By analyzing these two results based on SDA (Table 3) and MLR (Table 2) model individually, it could be made a conclusion easily that SDA model coupled with PLS was better than the model established by MLR, and those 6 optimal wavebands are suitable for variety discrimination of Chinese cabbage seed.

4 Conclusion

This study has shown that Vis/NIRS spectroscopy coupled with SDA-PLS has demonstrated the well ability to predict 6 varieties of Chinese cabbage seeds with sufficient accuracy and non-destruction. PCA was not suitable as the PCs plot can only intuitively distinguish the varieties well. PLS was executed to select several optimal wavebands based on loading values. Two algorithm models established by MLR and SDA were used to establish the recognition model for the variety discrimination. MLR model is not suitable in this study because of its unsatisfied predictive ability. The SDA model was proposed by the advantage of variable selection. The final results based on SDA model showed an excellent performance with high discrimination rate of 99.167%. It is also proved that 6 optimal wavebands are suitable for variety discrimination. Further study includes optimizing, standardizing this technique and making it industrialization. Meanwhile the number and varieties of samples needed to be expanded.

Table 2. Prediction results of the MLR model. N-variety number, P-prediction value.

N	P	N	P	N	P	N	P	N	P	N	P
1	1.47	2	1.86	3	1.85	4	4.16	5	5.03	6	6.14
1	1.91	2	2.23	3	3.43	4	2.26	5	5.36	6	6.4
1	1.04	2	2.08	3	3.24	4	3.3	5	3.05	6	4.8
1	1.13	2	1.6	3	2.73	4	3.27	5	4.16	6	5.67
1	1.56	2	1.97	3	2.74	4	4.03	5	5.25	6	5.99
1	1.73	2	2.28	3	2.74	4	3.63	5	3.92	6	6.62
1	1.94	2	2.33	3	2.81	4	4.28	5	4.01	6	5.97
1	1.16	2	1.86	3	2.72	4	3.91	5	5.11	6	5.54
1	1.82	2	2.64	3	3.01	4	4.82	5	3.86	6	6.87
1	2.18	2	2.94	3	2.95	4	4.04	5	4.33	6	6.76
1	1.51	2	1.26	3	2.99	4	4.13	5	4.91	6	6.05
1	2.38	2	2.18	3	3.55	4	4.96	5	3.19	6	5.39
1	1.26	2	2.37	3	3.33	4	4.15	5	3.6	6	6.23
1	1.48	2	1.65	3	3.36	4	4.46	5	3.43	6	7.26
1	1.57	2	1.89	3	3.05	4	3.96	5	4.51	6	6.18
1	1.16	2	1.6	3	3.13	4	3.51	5	4.61	6	5.43
1	2.2	2	2.61	3	2.53	4	3.06	5	3.88	6	5.95
1	1.26	2	1.72	3	2.32	4	4.12	5	4.96	6	5.1
1	2.59	2	1.75	3	3.33	4	3.34	5	5.23	6	6.48
1	2.37	2	2.94	3	2.77	4	4.68	5	4.56	6	6.05

Table 3. Confusion matrix for variety discrimination of SDA model by using 6 optimal wavebands

Variety Number	Number of Predictions Classified into							Recognition Rate (%)
	1	2	3	4	5	6	Total	
1	20	0	0	0	0	0	20	100%
2	0	20	0	0	0	0	20	100%
3	0	0	20	0	0	0	20	100%
4	0	0	0	20	0	0	20	100%
5	1	0	0	0	19	0	20	95%
6	0	0	0	0	0	20	20	100%

Acknowledgements

This study was supported by the Teaching and Research Award Program for Outstanding Young Teachers in Higher Education Institutions of MOE, P. R. C., Natural Science Foundation of China (Project No: 30270773), Specialized Research Fund for the Doctoral Program of Higher Education (Project No: 20040335034), and Science and Technology Department of Zhejiang Province (Project No. 2005C21094, 2005C12029).

References

1. Park, B.J., Liu, Z.C., Kanno, A., Kameya, T.: Genetic Improvement of Chinese Cabbage for Salt and Drought Tolerance by Constitutive Expression of a B. Napus LEA Gene. Plant Sci. 169. September (2005) 553-558
2. Jacobsen, S., Søndergaard, I., Møller, B., Deslerc, T., Munck, L.: A Chemometric Evaluation of the Underlying Physical and Chemical Patterns that Support Near Infrared Spectroscopy of Barley Seeds as a Tool for Explorative Classification of Endosperm Genes and Gene Combinations. J. Cereal Sci. 42 (2005) 281-299
3. Tesfaye, M. B., Tom, C. P., Mark, S.: Development of a Calibration to Predict Maize Seed Composition Using Single Kernel Near Infrared Spectroscopy. J. Cereal Sci. 43 (2006) 236-243
4. Fassio, A., Cozzolino, D.: Non-destructive Prediction of Chemical Composition in Sunflower Seeds by Near Infrared Spectroscopy. J. Ind. Crop. Prod. 20 (2004) 321–329
5. McCaig, T.N.: Extending the Use of Visible/near-infrared Reflectance Spectrophotometers to Measure Colour of Food and Agricultural Products. Food Res. Int. 35 (2002) 731–736
6. Groos, C., Bervas, E., Charmet, G.: Genetic Analysis of Grain Protein Content, Grain Hardness and Dough Rheology in a Hard Bread Wheat Progeny. J. Cereal Sci. 40 (2004) 93-100
7. Serege´ly Z., Dea´k, T., Bisztray, G.D.: Distinguishing Melon Genotypes Using NIR Spectroscopy. Chemometr.Intell. Lab. 72 (2004) 195-203
8. Younes C., Dominique B.: Reduction of the Size of the Learning Data in a Probabilistic Neural Network by Hierarchical Clustering. Application to the Discrimination of Seeds by Artificial Vision. Chemometr. Intell. Lab. 35 (1996) 175-186
9. Kemsley, E. K., Ruault, S., Wilson, R. H.: Discrimination Between Coffea Arabica and Coffea Canephora Variant Robusta Beans Using Infrared Spectroscopy. Food Chem. 54 (1995) 321-326
10. Lankmayr, E., Mocak, J., Serdt, K., Balla, Branko., Wenzl, T., Bandoniene, D., Gfrerer, M., Siegfried, W.J.: Chemometrical Classification of Pumpkin Seed Oilsusing UV–Vis, NIR and FTIR Spectra Biochem. Biophys. Methods. 61 (2004) 95-106
11. Zhu, X.L., Yuan, H.F., Lu, W.Z. Prog. Chem. 16 (2004) 528
12. He, Y., Feng, S.J., Deng, X.F., Li, X.L.: Study on Lossless Discrimination of Varieties of Yogurt Using the Visible/NIR-spectroscopy. Food Research International, 39 (2006) 645-650
13. Go´mez, A.H., He, Y., Pereira, A.G.: Non-destructive Measurement of Acidity, Soluble Solids and Firmness of Satsuma Mandarin Using Vis/NIR-spectroscopy Techniques. J. Food Eng. 77 (2006) 313-319
14. Fisher, R.A.: The Use of Multiple Measurements in Taxonomic Problems. Ann Eugenics. 7 (1936) 179-188

Hybrid Method for Detecting Masqueraders Using Session Folding and Hidden Markov Models

Román Posadas[1], Carlos Mex-Perera[1], Raúl Monroy[2], and Juan Nolazco-Flores[3]

[1] Center for Electronics and Telecommunications, ITESM, Campus Monterrey
Av. Eugenio garza Sada 2501 Sur, Col. Tecnologico
Monterrey, N. L., CP 64849 Mexico

[2] Computer Science Department, ITESM, Campus Estado de Mexico
Carretera al lago de Guadalupe, Km. 3.5, Estado de Mexico, CP 52926, Mexico

[3] Computer Science Department, ITESM, Campus Monterrey
Av. Eugenio garza Sada 2501 Sur, Col. Tecnologico
Monterrey, N. L., CP 64849 Mexico

{A00790428, carlosmex, raulm, jnolazco}@itesm.mx

Abstract. This paper focuses on the study of a new method for detecting masqueraders in computer systems. The main feature of such masqueraders is that they have knowledge about the behavior profile of legitimate users. The dataset provided by Schonlau *et al.* [1], called SEA, has been modified for including synthetic sessions created by masqueraders using the behavior profile of the users intended to impersonate. It is proposed an hybrid method for detection of masqueraders based on the compression of the users sessions and Hidden Markov Models. The performance of the proposed method is evaluated using ROC curves and compared against other known methods. As shown by our experimental results, the proposed detection mechanism is the best of the methods here considered.

1 Introduction

A masquerader is a person that uses somebody else's computer account to gain access and impersonate a legitimate user to complete a malicious activity. Masquerade detection is usually undertaken using an anomaly detection approach, which aims at distinguishing any deviation from ordinary user behavior. A number of different methods of masquerade detection that use the Schonlau *et al.* dataset SEA [7] have been published [1,3]. The SEA dataset consists of clean and contaminated data of 50 users. This collection was obtained using the *acct* auditing mechanism, it consist of 15000 UNIX commands without arguments for each of 70 users. Then, 50 users were randomly selected as intrusion targets, so that the remaining 20 users were used as masqueraders and their data was interspersed into the data of the other 50 users. The normal behavior *profile* of each user is obtained from the first 5000 commands, which are legitimate. This

A. Gelbukh and C.A. Reyes-Garcia (Eds.): MICAI 2006, LNAI 4293, pp. 622–631, 2006.

is the *training data*. The last 10000 commands is the *testing data*, since it may contain masquerade information.

The original SEA dataset presents some problems when more realistic conditions are considered. The users who were labelled as masqueraders did not have knowledge about the behavior profiles of the users to be impersonated. Besides, they typed UNIX commands as they usually do in a normal working session. Thus, the data used as masquerade sessions is not intended to impersonate the users' activity. Moreover, it is possible to find masquerade sessions in SEA with very simple and repetitive sequences that can be easily identified even by human inspection.

To overcome these difficulties, we modified SEA using synthetic sessions as masquerade sessions. The new sessions were created using the knowledge of the behavior profile of the user to be impersonated, the modified dataset is here referred as *SEA-I* and it resembles a situation where the masquerader avoids detection mechanisms in a smarter manner.

A simple strategy was used to synthesize the masquerade sessions, we considered the knowledge of the commands frequency seen at the training phase of each legitimate user. The resultant sessions were generated following the same probability distribution of the commands of the legitimate user.

In this paper we proposed a new hybrid detection method, it is composed of two main parts, the first one is a session folding mechanism and the second is a detection mechanism based on Hidden Markov Models (HMM). The session folding is a compression stage that substitutes with labels the more relevant sequences derived from the extraction of the user grammar at the training phase. Once the test folded sessions are obtained, these are passed to the HMM based detector.

To evaluate the proposed detection method we made experiments using SEA and SEA-I datasets. The performance obtained was compared against some known methods described in the next section.

2 Overview of Methods of Masquerader Detection

In this section we describe some known methods of masquerader detection from other authors: uniqueness[2] and two others proposed by Latendresse [3].These methods have been used in this paper for comparison purposes. We evaluated the performance of such methods and the proposed one against SEA and SEA-I datasets.

A masquerade detection method is said to be *local*, if the normal behavior of a user is only based on the user's legitimate data. If the normal behavior of a user is also based on data from other users, it is said to be *global*. Since they are more informed, global detection methods are usually more accurate than local ones. However, demand more computational effort.

A given method performs *update* if, during the detection phase, the data used to classify is confirmed to be legitimate and it is added to the user profile. The update may also be local or global.

2.1 Uniqueness

Uniqueness [2] is based on the fact that commands not previously seen in the training data may indicate a masquerade session. This method extracts global statistics, that is the user profiles are based on the other users data. In this method, the fewer users that use a particular command the more indicative that a user that entered that command is a masquerader.

This method uses what is called popularity, which is an indicative of how many users use a particular command. A command has popularity i if only i users use that command. Almost half of the commands appearing in the training part of the dataset are unique with popularity one and it represents 3.0% of the data.

Uniqueness's detection model is a session score, x_u, given by:

$$x_u = \frac{1}{n_u} \sum_{k=1}^{K} W_{uk} \left(1 - \frac{U_k}{U}\right) n_{uk}$$

where

n_u is the length of the testing data sequence of user u;
n_{uk} is the number of times user u typed command k in the testing data;
K is the total number of distinct commands;
U is the total number of users;
U_k is the number of users who have used command k in the training data;

where the weights W_{uk} are

$$W_{uk} = \begin{cases} -v_{uk}/v_k, & \text{if user u's training data contains command } k, \\ 1, & \text{otherwise,} \end{cases}$$

where $v_{uk} = N_{uk}/N_u$ and, $v_k = \sum_u v_{uk}$.

N_u is the length of the training data sequence of user u;
N_{uk} is the number of times user u typed command k in the training data.

From the above formulas it is easy to see that temporal ordering of commands in a given testing sessions is ignored. The thresholds used for plotting the ROC curve can be obtained from [7]. We did not apply update for this method.

2.2 Customized Grammars

Latendresse [3] developed an intrusion detection system based on grammar extraction by the Sequitur algorithm created by Nevill-Manning and Witten [4]. By extracting hierarchical structures from a sequence of commands and generating a context-free grammar capable of building that sequence, he constructed user profiles based on the training data of SEA. Once he obtained the grammar (production rules) that represents the training data of each user, he computed the total frequency of its expansion for that user and also the frequency of that same expansion for the other users, that is the *across* frequency.

For the purpose of this paper we used the version of the experiment where no global scripts are used and the evaluation is based on the frequency of the commands of the user and across all users. As an additional variation we did not apply update.

The production evaluation function used was

$$e(p) = l_p \frac{f_p}{f_p + \frac{F_p}{k}}$$

where

p is a production of the session.
l_p is the length of the expansion of production;
f_p is the frequency of the expansion of the production;
F_p is the across frequency of the expansion of the production;
k is a tuning constant.

Finally, let F be the set of productions found in a session s, then the evaluation of s consists of the sum over all productions of s, in symbols: $\sum_{p \in F} e(p)$. This method just like Uniqueness makes use of global profiles where the normal behavior of a user is also based on data from the other users.

2.3 Command Frequencies

Another method shown by [3] where only repetitive single commands were used was also evaluated. This is a simpler version based on the frequencies of the commands without global scripts and without taking into account their temporal ordering. Because the length of the productions is equal to 1, that is, single commands, then the evaluation function shown below is obtained.

$$v(c) = \frac{f_c}{f_c + \frac{F_c}{k}}$$

where

f_c is the frequency of the command c;
F_c is the across frequency of the command c among all other 49 users;
k is a tuning constant.

The sum over all commands of a session gives the score of the session. Also it is a global profile method.

3 The Proposed Method

We propose a local hybrid method that uses compression and hidden markov models for masquerade detection. With this method we take the training

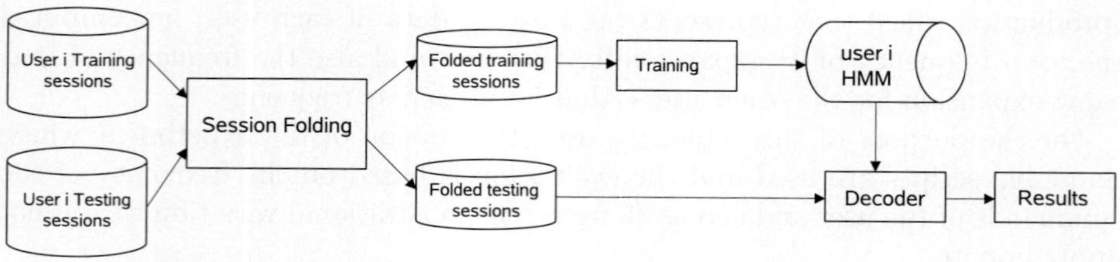

Fig. 1. Proposed detection mechanism architecture

sessions of a given user and use the Sequitur algorithm [4] to extract his grammar and make a compressed version of all the sessions. This is accomplished by substituting the sequences found by the algorithm for production rules. This process is referred to as *session folding.* These compressed sessions are what we use as training data for the HMM model. Figure 1 shows an architecture of the detection mechanism.

The session folding block works as shown in Figure 3. The Sequitur algorithm constructs a context-free grammar from the training sessions. The grammar extracts hierarchical structures that generate the sequence of training commands, see Figure 2. For testing purposes we fold the test session with the grammar obtained from the training. Once the testing session has been folded it is then evaluated by the trained HMM model to get the probability that the session was generated by the model.

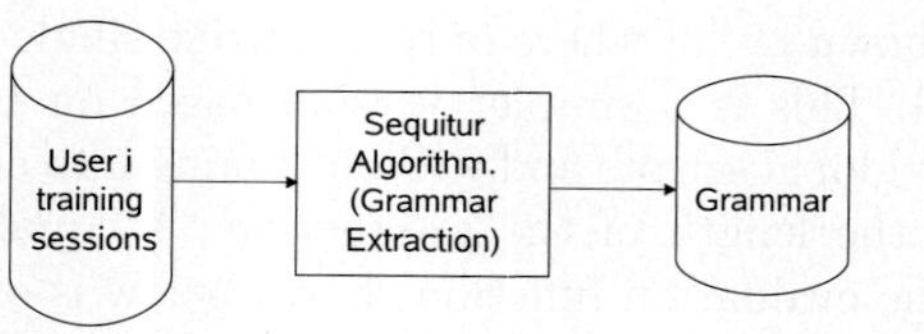

Fig. 2. Shows the grammar extraction steps

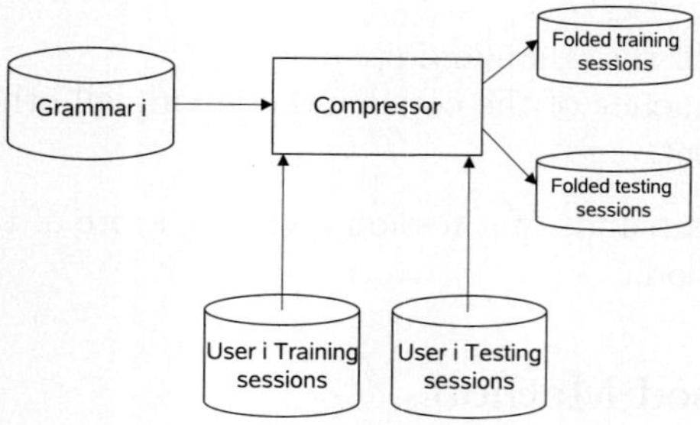

Fig. 3. Session folding architecture

The way the sessions are folded is based on the priority of the grammar symbol [6], that is the production. This priority is computed taking into account the length of the production rule, the frequency of that production in the training data and also on the total amount of data in the training sessions. The priority of the grammar symbol (rule) is obtained as follows:

$$P = \frac{l * f}{N}$$

where:

P is the priority of the grammar symbol;
l the size (length) of the grammar symbol;
N the total number of commands in the training data; and
f is the frequency of the grammar symbol.

Sequences of commands are substituted for production rules extracted from the Sequitur algorithm. Sequences with higher priority are preferred over those with a lower priority. The folded session may also contain single commands, since those may not be substituted for any production rule.

As depicted in Figure 1, the last stage of the detection mechanism is based on a HMM. As defined by [5] an HMM is a doubly stochastic process with an underlying stochastic process that is not observable (it is hidden), but can only be observed through another set of stochastic processes that produce the sequence of observed symbols.

In an HMM one or more starting and finishing states are specified. Possible transitions are made successively from a starting state to a finishing state, and the relevant transition probability and symbol output probability can be multiplied at each transition to calculate the overall likelihood of all the output symbols produced in the transition path up to that point. When all transitions are finished, the HMM generates a symbol sequence according to the likelihood of a sequence being formed along each path. In other words, when a sequence is given, there is one or more transition paths that could have formed the sequence, each path have a specific likelihood that the sequence was formed by it. The sum of all the likelihoods obtained for all such transition paths is regarded as the likelihood that the sequence was generated by the HMM. It must be mentioned that this is a local profile method.

4 Synthesis of Masquerade Sessions

In this section we present how the motivation of avoiding intrusion detection mechanisms takes the masquerader to create synthetic sessions that follow the same behavior profile of the legitimate user.

Original SEA dataset contains 15000 UNIX commands for each of 50 users, the first 5000 commands are legitimate, however in the last 10000 we may have some commands entered by a masquerader. In order to make data more tractable the user data is divided in blocks of 100 commands, each block is treated as a session. The first 50 sessions are not contaminated and thus constitute the *training dataset*. The last 100 blocks of each user may or may not be masquerade blocks. A block is either totally contaminated or legitimate from the user. Masquerading data was inserted using this rule: if no masquerader is present, then a new masquerader appears in the next session with a probability of 1%. Otherwise, the same masquerader continues to be present in the next block with a probability of 80%. SEA dataset comes with a matrix that shows where the masquerade sessions are located for each user.

SEA has been very popular to test masquerader detectors, however masquerade sessions in SEA come from working sessions of other users who had no intention to act as intruders. This is, they did not masquerade their activities.

In order to avoid detection, the intruder must act like the legitimate user, that is, he must know the victim's work profile. Here we propose a scenario where the intruder has knowledge of the legitimate user behavior and uses it to build a session with the victim's profile, this way the intrusion will not be detected, since it has the same legitimate user's customs.

Following this philosophy an intruder in order to avoid detection mechanisms may build a session with the same statistical properties than those found in the training data. Then once the command frequency properties of one user were extracted, a masquerade session can be built having the same probability distribution than the probability distribution of the training data. Masquerade sessions for all users were created with this procedure. Sequences of commands (scripts) were not taken into account when building the masquerade sessions.

Once we created the masquerade sessions for all users, they were located in exactly the same positions as the original dataset. This builds **SEA-I dataset**. In fact only the masquerade sessions were modified from SEA. All the masquerade sessions of any particular user were created taking into account only the command frequency properties of that specific user.

Now we want to know the performance of our proposed method and the other three previously mentioned methods against SEA and SEA-I datasets.

5 Experiments and Results

We need a way for comparing the performance of the methods. This can be accomplished by the usual Receiver Operating Characteristic (ROC) curves, which are parametric curves generated by varying a threshold from 0% to 100%, and computing the false alarm (false positive) and missing alarm (false negative) rate at each operating point. The false alarm rate is the rate at which the system falsely regards a legitimate user as a masquerader, while the missing alarm rate is the rate at which the system falsely regards a masquerader as a legitimate user. In general, there is a trade-off between the false alarm rate and missing alarm rate. The lower and further left a curve is, the better it is.

As we can see in Figure 4 different curves have different performance in distinct regions of the graph. We are interested in having a low false alarm rate and a

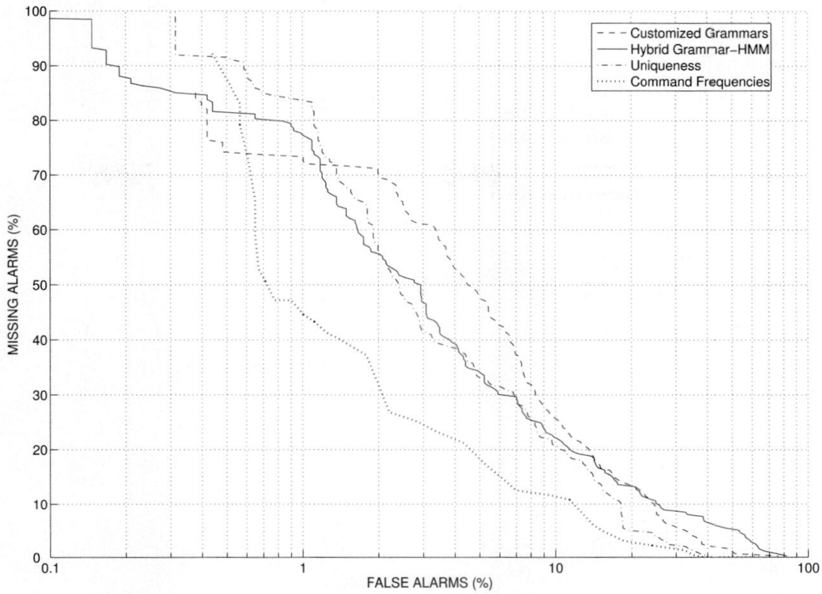

Fig. 4. Performance of detection methods with SEA dataset

low missing alarm rate. In Figure 4 we show the results of our proposed method against the other three for SEA dataset. Command Frequencies seems to be the best of all four methods. This method is global since it uses information of all other 49 users to detect masquerade sessions of a single user. The constant k has a value of 7.

In Figure 5, we show the performance of the four methods when SEA-I is used. The upper and further right the curve it is, the worse the performance the method has. Methods like Uniqueness and Command Frequencies seemed to be very good with original SEA but they are severely affected with the modified dataset no matter they have the added value of being global methods. The reason of the poor performance of Uniqueness and Command Frequency is caused by the fact that they are customized methods based on the commands frequency property of the users sessions, then they are incapable of detecting masquerade sessions created using that same frequency property. Our Hybrid Grammar-HMM method outperforms the others since it is the most further left located and always has the least false alarms variation for almost all the missing alarms range. The second better method is Customized Grammars, like ours also uses grammar extraction but its false alarm rate is bigger because the only mean to test command sequence properties is by the grammar extraction itself.

The reason for this good behavior of the proposed method is based on the fact that the initial session folding phase compresses the sessions based on grammar (scripts) properties. The less grammar symbols appear in the folded session the more indicative that the session is from a masquerader. The probability

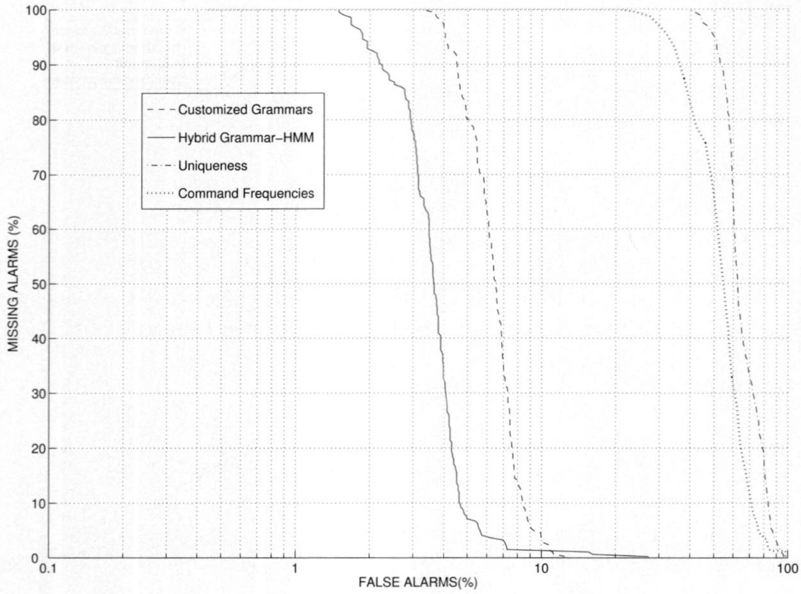

Fig. 5. Performance of detection methods with SEA-I dataset

that the sequence found in the test folded session comes from the legitimate user, is found by the previously trained HMM model.

6 Conclusions

In this paper we show the performance of an hybrid method that detects command-frequency based masquerade sessions in a UNIX-like system that outperforms best global profiles methods. This method has a good performance with original SEA dataset, even though it uses local profiles.

The incorporation of session folding based on grammar extraction and hidden markov models makes this detection method more robust and with a wider range of use. As a pending job, near future masqueraders detectors should be able to detect intruder sessions when these are based on both, frequency and sequence properties of a legitimate user profile.

Acknowledgments

The authors would like to acknowledge the Cátedra de Biométricas y Protocolos Seguros para Internet, ITESM, Campus Monterrey and Regional Fund for Digital Innovation in Latin America and the Caribbean (Grant VI), who supported this work.

M. Latendresse provided the data for the ROC curve of the Command Frequencies method.

References

1. Schonlau, M., DuMouchel, W., Ju, W., Karr, A., Theus, M., Vardi, Y.: Computer Intrusion: Detecting Masquerades. Statistical Science **16** (2001) 1-17.
2. Schonlau, M., Theus, M.: Detecting masquerades in intrusion detection based on unpopular commands. Information Processing Letters **76** (2000) 33-38
3. Latendresse, M.: Masquerade detection via customized grammars. In Julisch, K., Krügel, C., eds.: Second International Conference on Detection of Intrusions and Malware, and Vulnerability Assessment. Volume 3548 of Lecture Notes in Computer Science., Springer(2005) 141-159
4. Nevill-Manning, C.G., Witten, I.H.: Identifying hierarchical structure in sequences: a linear-time algorithm. Journal of Artificial Intelligence Research, JAIR 7 (1997) 67-82
5. Rabiner, L.R., Juang, B.H.: An introduction to Hidden Markov Models. IEEE ASSP Magazine **3** (1986) 4-16
6. Godínez, F. Hutter, D., Monroy, R.: Audit File Reduction Using N-Gram Models (Work in Progress). In patrick, A., Young, M., eds.: Proceedings of the Ninth International Conference on Finantial Cryptography and Data Security, FC'05. Volume 3570 of Lecture Notes in Computer Science., Roseau, The Commonwealth Of Dominicana, Springer-Verlag (2005) 336-340
7. Schonlau, M.: Masquerading used data. (Matthias Schonlau's home page) http://www.schonlau.net.

Toward Lightweight Detection and Visualization for Denial of Service Attacks

Dong Seong Kim, Sang Min Lee, and Jong Sou Park

Network Security Lab., Hankuk Aviation University, Seoul, Korea
{dskim, minuri33, jspark}@hau.ac.kr

Abstract. In this paper, we present a lightweight detection and visualization methodology for Denial of Service (DoS) attacks. First, we propose a new approach based on Random Forest (RF) to detect DoS attacks. The classification accuracy of RF is comparable to that of Support Vector Machines (SVM). RF is also able to produce the importance value of individual feature. We adopt RF to select intrinsic important features for detecting DoS attacks in a lightweight way. And then, with selected features, we plot both DoS attacks and normal traffics in 2 dimensional space using Multi-Dimensional Scaling (MDS). The visualization results show that simple MDS can help one to visualize DoS attacks without any expert domain knowledge. The experimental results on the KDD 1999 intrusion detection dataset validate the possibility of our approach.

1 Introduction

In this paper, we present a lightweight detection and visualization methodology for detecting Denial of Service (DoS) attacks. Firstly, we propose a new approach based on Random Forest (RF) to detect DoS attacks. The selection of important features of audit data in Intrusion Detection System (IDS) is a significant issue because all features are not essential to classify network audit data and irrelevant features not only increase computational cost, such as time and overheads but also decrease the detection rates. There are two representative methods in feature selection: wrapper [11, 13] and filter method [8, 9]. Wrapper method adopts classification algorithms and performs cross-validation to identify important features. In the other hands, filter method utilizes correlation based approaches independent of classification algorithms. Filter method is more lightweight than wrapper method in terms of computation time and overheads but it has lower detection rates than wrapper method because it is performed independent of classification algorithms [8]. In order to cope with these problems, several hybrid approaches [5, 12] which combine advantages of filter method with that of wrapper method have been studied. However, these hybrid approaches sometimes show a little degradation on detection rates with more computations rather than the naïve filter method. They even do not provide the variable importance of individual features and are complicated to implement. Therefore, we adopt Random Forest (RF) which is a stage-of-the-art data mining algorithm comparable to

A. Gelbukh and C.A. Reyes-Garcia (Eds.): MICAI 2006, LNAI 4293, pp. 632 – 640, 2006.

Support Vector Machines (SVM) [2]. The classification accuracy of RF is comparable to that of SVM. In addition, RF provides importance value of individual feature variables. We use RF to select intrinsic important features for detecting DoS attacks in a lightweight way.

We plot both DoS attacks and normal traffics in 2 dimensional space using Multi-Dimensional Scaling (MDS), with selected features. The visualization results show that simple MDS can help one to visualize DoS attacks without any expert domain knowledge.

This paper is organized as follows. In section 2, background of Random Forest is presented. In section 3, our proposed approach and its overall flow is presented. In section 4, experiments and results are presented. Finally, section 5 concludes our works.

2 Random Forest

Random Forest (RF) is a special kind of ensemble learning techniques [2] and robust concerning the noise and the number of attributes. It is also comparable and sometimes better than state-of-the-art methods in classification and regression [10]. For example, RF has lower classification (and regression) error than SVM. Moreover, RF produces additional facilities, especially individual feature importance. RF builds an ensemble of CART tree classifications using bagging mechanism [3]. By using bagging, each node of trees only selects a small subset of features for the split, which enables the algorithm to create classifiers for high dimensional data very quickly. One has to specify the number of randomly selected features (*mtry*) at each split. The default value is *sqrt(p)* for classification where *p* represents number of features. The Gini index [1] is used as the splitting criterion. The largest possible tree is grown and is not pruned. One also should choose the big enough number of trees (*ntree*) to ensure that every input feature gets predicted several times. In order to maximize classification accuracy, it is a very important to choose the optimal values of those two parameters. The root node of each tree in the forest keeps a bootstrap sample from the original data as the training set. One can arrive at an estimation of the predicting error rate, which is referred to as the out-of-bag (OOB) error rate. In summary, classification accuracy of RF is highly comparable to that of SVM, and it also produces importance values of individual features, these two properties help one to build a lightweight intrusion detection methodology with small overheads compared to previous approaches. Our proposed approach will be presented in next section.

3 Proposed Approach

An overall flow of proposed approach is depicted in Figure 1. The overall flow consists of 6 phases. In 1st phase, the experimental dataset is segmented into 3 types of dataset: learning set, validation set and testing set. The learning set is used to build

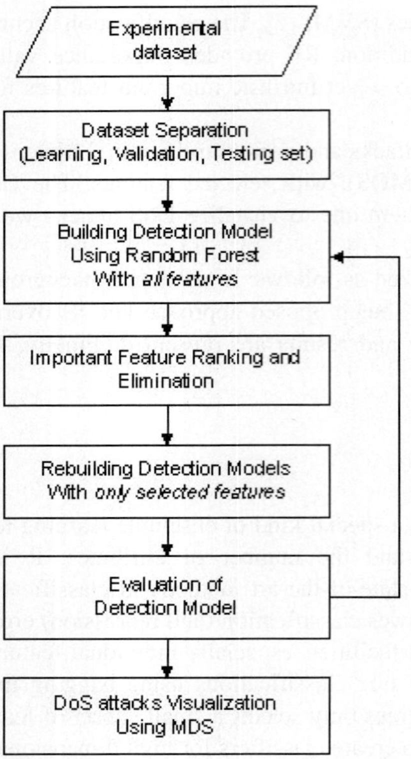

Fig. 1. An overall flow of proposed approach

intrusion detection models based on Random Forest (RF). The validation set is used to validate the built detection models. The testing set is used to evaluate the built detection models. The testing set includes 14 additional attacks so that we evaluate how the built detection models using the validation set are able to cope with unknown Denial of Service (DoS) attacks.

In 2nd phase, detection models are built using RF with all features. The RF generates individual feature importance in numerical form. In 3rd phase, we rank features according to their importance in ascending order and only select top *k* numbers of features among whole features. In 4th phase, we rebuild detection models with only *k* selected features. In 5th phase, we evaluate the detection models built in 4th phase. If the detection rates and error rates satisfy our requirements, we perform 6th phase. Otherwise, we iterate phase 2 to 5. Multi Dimensional Scaling (MDS) is used to visualize DoS attacks in 2 dimensional spaces.

To evaluate the feasibility of our approach, we carry out several experiments on KDD 1999 intrusion detection dataset [6, 7]. The following section presents the experimental results and their analysis.

4 Experiments and Discussions

4.1 Experimental Data and Environments

We have used the KDD 1999 intrusion detection dataset. The dataset contains a total of 24 attack types that fall into four main categories [7]: DoS (Denial of Service), R2L (Remote to Local, it stands for unauthorized access from a remote machine), U2R (User to Root, it stands for unauthorized access to root privileges) and probing. The data was preprocessed by extracting 41 features from the tcpdump data in the 1998 DARPA dataset and we have labeled the individual features as *f1, f2, f3, f4* and so forth. We have only used DoS type of attacks since the others have a very small number of instances so that they are not suitable for our experiments [14]. According to the overall flow presented in section 3, the dataset is divided into 3 datasets: learning set, validation set and testing set. The learning set is used to build the initial detection models based on RF. Then, the validation set is used to estimate the generalization errors of detection models. The generalization errors are represented as OOB errors in RF. In order to minimize the OOB errors, in other words, maximize detection rates, we have used 10-fold cross validation with 2000 samples. Finally, we have used the testing set to evaluate the detection models that are built by the learning set. We have used RF version (R 2.2.0) and MDS algorithm in open source R-project [17].

4.2 Experimental Results and Analysis

There are only two parameters in RF: the number of variables in the random subset at each node (*mtry*) and the number of trees in the forest (*ntree*). To get the best classification rates, that is, the best detection rates, it is essential to optimize both two parameters. We can get the optimal value of *mtry* using tuneRF() function which is provided in *randomForest* package of R-project and it turned out *mtry* = 6. In case of *ntree*, there is no specific function that figures out the optimal value as *mtry*.

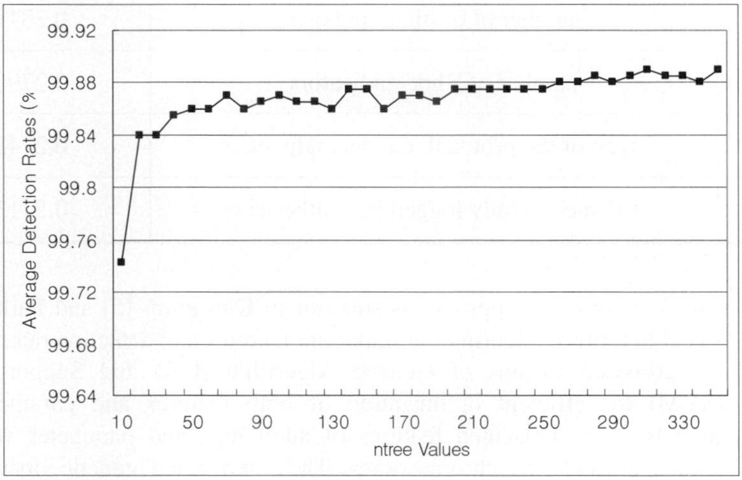

Fig. 2. Average Detection rates vs. *ntree* values of RF

Thus, we have got the optimal value of *ntree* by choosing the *ntree* value that has high and stable detection rates. We assume that 350 trees are enough to be the maximum value to evaluate our approach and detection rates are determined by equation "1 – OOB errors". The experimental results for determination of the optimal value of *ntree* are described in Figure 2. According to Figure 2, average detection rates of RF turned out the highest value when *ntree* = 310. As the results of experiments, we set two optimized parameter values: *mtry* = 6, *ntree* = 310. After the optimization of two parameters, feature selection of network audit data has carried out by employing the feature selection algorithm supported by RF. We ranked features thorough the average variable importance of each features as the results of 10-fold cross validation with 2000 samples. The top 10 important features and their properties are described in Table 1.

Table 1. Top 10 important featuresand their properties

Features	Properties	Average variable importance
*f*23	number of connections to the same host as the current connection in the past two seconds	0.4023
*f*6	number of data bytes from destination to source	0.3318
*f*24	number of connections to the same service as the current connection in the past two seconds	0.3172
*f*3	network service on the destination, e.g., http, telnet, etc.	0.3163
*f*5	number of data bytes from source to destination	0.2973
*f*13	number of ``compromised" conditions	0.2945
*f*32	number of destination hosts	0.2817
*f*10	number of ``hot" indicators	0.2796
*f*2	type of the protocol, e.g. tcp, udp, etc.	0.2742
*f*12	1 if successfully logged in; 0 otherwise	0.2713

These results showed our approach is superior to Kim *et al.* [5] and Park *et al.*'s approaches [12] in terms of figuring out important features and detection rates. Kim *et al.* [5] have proposed fusions of Genetic Algorithm (GA) and Support Vector Machine (SVM) for efficient optimization of both features and parameters for detection models. They presented features of audit data and parameter values of kernel functions of SVM as chromosomes. They performed genetic operation to figure out optimal feature set and parameter values. Their approach spent much time to perform cross-validation based on wrapper method and to execute GA operation up to 20 generations. Park *et al.* [12] have proposed Correlation-Based Hybrid Feature Selection (CBHFS) to improve Kim *et al.*'s approach [5]. They utilized filter method based on correlation based feature selection with GA and then they performed wrapper method based on SVM. Their approach is able to significantly decrease training & testing times while retaining high detection rates as well as stable feature selection results rather than Kim *et al.*'s [5]. Although both Kim *et al.* [5] and Park *et al.*'s approaches [12] have showed "optimal features", they didn't show the numeric value as the variable importance of individual features. Kim *et al.* [5] and Park *et al.*'s approaches [12] showed high detection rates comparable to our approach but they didn't give any context information enable one to use those feature in design and implementation of commercial IDS. On the other hands, our approach shows reasonable context information for each important feature. For instances, *f23* represents "number of connections to the same host as the current connection in the past two seconds" property and *f6* represents "number of data bytes from destination to source" and so on. One of principles of DoS attacks is to send a great number of packets to one single victim host within very short period of time. And the victim host is not able to process the sent packets and the receiving buffer and processor of victim host is any more available so that it is not capable of providing any further services, this is called "denial of services". These properties are very important to find DoS attacks and also used in a popular open source IDS, SNORT [15].

Then, we have carried out several times of experiments with elimination of irrelevant features. The experimental results are shown in Table 2 and Table 3. According to Table 3, our approach showed higher average detection rates comparable to Kim *et al.*'s fusion approach [5] and Park *et al.*'s hybrid feature selection approach [12].

Table 2. Detection rates (%) vs. total number of features

Total number of features	Upper	Average	Lower
21	99.95	99.89	99.8
25	100	99.925	99.85
29	99.95	99.91	99.85
33	99.95	99.905	99.85
37	99.95	99.895	99.85
41	99.95	99.89	99.85

Table. 3. The comparison results with other approaches

Approach	Average Detection rates	Pros. and Cons
Kim *et al.* [5]	99.85%	High overheads
Park *et al.* [12]	98.40%	Less overhead than Kim *et al.*'s approach
Our approach	99.87 %	Individual Feature Importance/ Less overheads than both hybrid approaches

Even our approach have less features to build intrusion detection model, our approach showed similar performance in terms of detection rates to Kim *et al.*'s [5] and Park *et al.*'s approach [12]. These results indicate that the feature selection with individual feature importance is able to be used by design and implement real commercial IDS. The previous approaches, Sung *et al.* [16] have firstly studied feature selection in IDS but their concern was to improve detection rates using wrapper approach based on artificial neural network and SVM. Kim *et al.* [5] and Park *et al.* [12] have showed meaningful results in feature selection to decrease computational overheads of IDS but their results are not such practical to be used in commercial IDS. Our approach shows the usability of feature selection because our approach guarantees very high detection rates with only selective features as well as context information of individual features. This property is able to help one to build intrusion detection methodology in a lightweight way.

As mentioned before, our approach shows comparable performance in terms of detection rates. In addition, detection method should be lightweight in terms of computational overheads. It is not easy to calculate computational overheads since other approaches adopt several fusion methods based on Genetic Algorithm (GA). But our approach based on RF uses ensemble methodology introduced in section 2. The detailed calculation of computational overheads is out of scope in this paper.

Furthermore, we visualized normal and DoS attacks patterns based on MDS [4]. An example is depicted in Figure 3. The red triangles represent normal patterns and blue circles represent DoS attacks patterns. We plotted these patterns after processing dataset using RF with only selected important features. We iteratively plot normal and DoS attacks patterns in this way and the visualization results show consistent results. This indicates that this visualization can be useful to find out intrusion status of monitoring computer and network system without expert's knowledge.

There are other visualization methodologies such as Self Organizing Maps (SOM) and Principle Component Analysis (PCA), and they also can be applied to this approach.

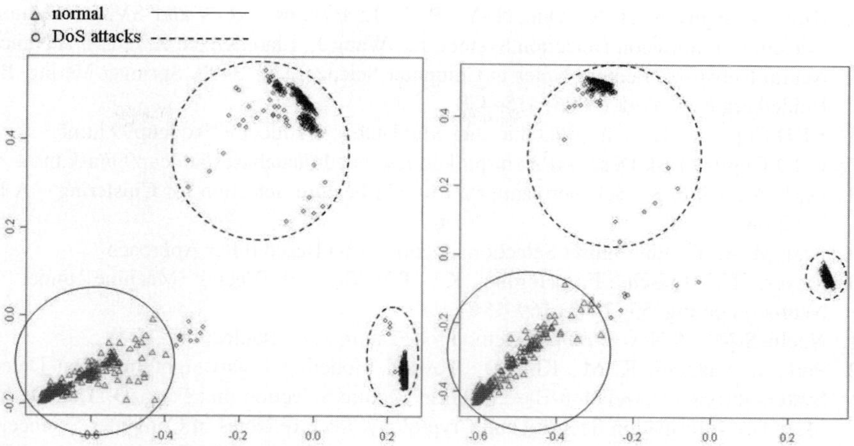

Fig. 3. MDS plots of normal and DoS attacks patterns (2 examples)

5 Conclusions

We have presented a new approach to build a lightweight Intrusion detection and Visualization methodology based on RF and MDS, respectively. Because performance of RF turns out comparable to that of SVM and it also provides variable importance of individual features. We have validated the feasibility of our approach by carrying out several experiments on KDD 1999 intrusion detection dataset. The experimental results show that our approach is able to be lightweight in detecting DoS attacks with guaranteeing high detection rates. Moreover, the visualization of normal and DoS attacks patterns using MDS is able to make one easily figure out intrusion context information.

Acknowledgement

This research was supported by the MIC (Ministry of Information and Communication), Korea, under the ITRC (Information Technology Research Center) support program supervised by the IITA (Institute of Information Technology Assessment).

References

1. Breiman, L., Friedman, J. H., Olshen, R. A., Stone, C. J.: Classification and Regression Trees. Chapman and Hall, New York (1984)
2. Breiman, L.: Random forest. Machine Learning 45(1) (2001) 5–32
3. Duda, R. O., Hart, P. E., Stork, D. G.: Pattern Classification. 2nd edn. John Wiley & Sons, Inc. (2001)
4. Young, F. W. and Hamer, R. M.: Theorv and Applications of Multidimensional Scaling, Eribaum Associates, Hillsdale, NJ, 1994

5. Kim, D., Nguyen, H.-N., Ohn, S.-Y., Park, J.: Fusions of GA and SVM for Anomaly Detection in Intrusion Detection System. In.: Wang J., Liao, X., Yi, Z. (eds.): Advances in Neural Networks. Lecture Notes in Computer Science, Vol. 3498. Springer-Verlag, Berlin Heidelberg New York (2005) 415–420
6. KDD Cup 1999 Data: http://kdd.ics.uci.edu/databases/kddcup99/kddcup99.html
7. KDD-Cup-99 Task Description: http://kdd.ics.uci.edu/databases/kddcup99/task.html
8. Dash, M., Choi, K., Scheuermann, P., Liu, H.: Feature Selection for Clustering – A Filter Soultion.
9. Hall, M. A.: Feature Subset Selection: A correlation Based Filter Approach
10. Meyer, D., Leisch, F., Hornik, K.: The Support Vector Machine under Test. Neurocomputing. 55 (2003) 169–186
11. Noelia S-M. : A New Wrapper Method for Feature Subset Selection
12. Park, J., Shazzad, K. M., Kim, D.: Toward Modeling Lightweight Intrusion Detection System through Correlation-Based Hybrid Feature Selection. In.: Feng, D., Lin, D., Yung, M. (eds.): Information Security and Cryptology. Lecture Notes in Computer Science, Vol. 3822. Springer-Verlag, Berlin Heidelberg New York (2005) 279–289
13. Kohavi, R. and John, G. H.: Wrappers for feature subset selection, Artificial Intelligence, 97(1–2):273–324, 1997
14. Sabhnani, M., Serpen, G.: On Failure of Machine Learning Algorithms for Detecting Misuse in KDD Intrusion Detection Data Set. Intelligent Analysis (2004)
15. SNORT, http://www.snort.org
16. Sung, A. H., Mukkamala, S.: Identifying Important Features for Intrusion Detection Using Support Vector Machines and Neural Networks. In Proc. of the 2003 Int. Symposium on Applications and the Internet Technology, IEEE Computer Society Press (2003) 209–216
17. The R Project for Statistical Computing, http://www.r-project.org/

Tri-training and Data Editing Based Semi-supervised Clustering Algorithm

Chao Deng and Mao Zu Guo

School of Computer Science and Technology, Harbin Institute of Technology, Postfach 15 00 01, Harbin, P.R. China
dengchao@kelab.hit.edu.cn, maozuguo@hit.edu.cn

Abstract. Seeds based semi-supervised clustering algorithms often utilize a seeds set consisting of a small amount of labeled data to initialize cluster centroids, hence improve the performance of clustering over whole data set. Researches indicate that both the scale and quality of seeds set greatly restrict the performance of semi-supervised clustering. A novel semi-supervised clustering algorithm named DE-Tri-training semi-supervised K means is proposed. In new algorithm, prior to initializing cluster centroids, the training process of a semi-supervised classification approach named Tri-training is used to label the unlabeled data and add them into initial seeds to enlarge the scale. Meanwhile, to improve the quality of enlarged seeds set, a Nearest Neighbor Rule based data editing technique named Depuration is introduced into the Tri-training process to eliminate and correct the noise and mislabeled data among the enlarged seeds. Experiments show that novel algorithm can effectively improve the initialization of cluster centroids and enhance clustering performance.

1 Introduction

In machine learning, supervised learning needs sufficient labeled data as training set to ensure generalization [1]. However, in many practical applications, such as web page classification and bioinformatics, labeling data by human is expensive and many unlabeled data are easily gathered. Therefore, semi-supervised learning that could combine labeled and unlabeled has become an attractive method. Semi-supervised learning includes semi-supervised clustering and semi-supervised classification [2].

Semi-supervised clustering (SS clustering) studies how to use little supervision to improve unsupervised clustering performance [3]. The little supervision can be class labels or pairwise constraints on some data. Existing methods fall into two approaches, i.e. constraint-based and distance-based methods [4]. Constraint-based methods using supervision to bias the search for an appropriate clustering of the data, have been the focus of recent researches [2] [4] [5], and typical methods include modifying the clustering objective function to satisfy specified constraints [6], enforcing constraints to be satisfied during cluster assignment [7], Hidden Markov Random Filed model based HMRF-Kmeans algorithm [8] and Seeded-Kmeans and Constrainted-Kmeans algorithms [5]. Both Seeded-Kmeans and Constrainted-Kmeans use labeled data as initial seeds to optimize initialization of cluster centroids, which

A. Gelbukh and C.A. Reyes-Garcia (Eds.): MICAI 2006, LNAI 4293, pp. 641 – 651, 2006.

greatly beneficial for the clustering performance. However, Basu et al. [5] showed these two seeds based SS clustering algorithms are susceptible to both the scale and the quality of seeds set—larger scale with lower noise is desirable.

From the other view, semi-supervised classification (SS classification) considers how to use supervision derived from unlabeled data to aid supervised learning when the labeled training data set is insufficient [9] Current typical approaches include using Expectation Maximum (EM) algorithm to estimate parameters of a generative model that embodies the underlying classifier[10] [11], employing transductive inference for SVM [12] and Graph-cut-based methods [13]. Blum and Mitchell [14] propose another famous SS classification paradigm named Co-training, which trains two classifiers separately on two different views and uses the predictions of each classifier on unlabeled data to augment the training set of the other. The standard Co-training algorithm [14] requires two sufficient and redundant views, but this requirement can hardly be satisfied in most applications. Therefore, Goldman et al. [15] propose an improved version, which discards the restriction of standard Co-training, but it requires two classifiers could partition the instance space into a set of equivalence classes and frequently employs time-consuming cross-validation technique during training. Tri-training, proposed by Zhou et al. [16], is another Co-training style approach. It uses three classifiers to exploit unlabeled data, and its applicability is wide since neither requires redundant views nor does it put any constraint on the three employed supervised learning classifiers. Furthermore, discarding cross-validation operation makes Tri-training more efficient for tasks with small scale of training set.

In practical clustering applications, labeled data is little, but seeds based SS clustering is susceptible to the scale and quality of seeds. To solve this problem, motivated by Tri-training process could effectively label unlabeled data from little labeled data; prior to initializing cluster centroids by seeds, we employ Tri-training process enlarging the initial labeled seeds. However, as situation indicated in [2]: when the labeled data are not sufficient to represent all the classes among unlabeled data, SS classification can not replaces SS clustering for clustering tasks, since the scale of initial seeds (training set) for Tri-training is small, the generalization on newly labeled data is poor even some class labels among enlarged seeds are missed, although the initial labeled seeds cover all labels. Therefore, Tri-training process can only be employed to aid enlarging the scale. Meanwhile, to reduce the negative influence of noise in enlarged seeds due to misclassification of Tri-training, the Nearest Neighbor Rule based data editing technique is combined into Tri-training to eliminate noise and correct misclassification to improve quality of enlarged seeds.

The rest of this paper is organized as follows. Section 2 briefly reviews two seeds based SS clustering algorithms, i.e. Seeded-Kmeans and Constrained-Kmeans. Section 3 combines Tri-training process with Depuration data editing technique, forms the DE-Tri-training process, and presents the DE-Tri-training Kmeans algorithm. Section 4 reports the experiments results on UCI datasets. Finally, Section 5 concludes and issues some future work.

2 Seeded-Kmeans and Constrained-Kmeans

Kmeans is a famous unsupervised clustering algorithm proposed by MacQueen [17]. It randomly initializes k cluster centroids, assigns data points to cluster with nearest centroid, and relocates k cluster centroids iteratively until no change on k cluster centroids. The clustering result locally minimizes the overall distortion measure between data points and means, i.e. objective function in (1)

$$J_{KMeans} = \sum_{h=1}^{k} \sum_{x_i \in X_h} \| x_i - \mu_h \|^2 \tag{1}$$

Where $\{x_i\}_{i=1}^{n}$ is set of data points, $\{X_h\}_{h=1}^{k}$ is set of k clusters and $\{\mu_h\}_{h=1}^{k}$ is set of k cluster centroids.

Unlike the random initialization of k cluster centroids in Kmeans, both Seeded-Kmeans and Constrained-Kmeans [5] employ a small amount of labeled data as initial seeds, partition these data into k clusters by their labels and calculate k clusters centroids as initialization. In addition, Constrained-Kmeans keep the grouping of labeled data in seeds unchanged throughout the clustering process.

Basu [5] showed when the fraction of labeled seeds (noise-free) increases, the performance of two algorithms significantly improves. In contrast, when the fraction of noise in labeled seeds increases, the performance significantly debases

3 Tri-training and Data Editing Based Semi-supervised Clustering Algorithm

Since Seeded-Kmeans and Constrained-Kmeans highly depend on the scale and quality of labeled seeds, if the scale of seeds could be enlarged, the quality of enlarged seeds could be improved as well as, their performance would be enhanced greatly. This idea motives us employing Tri-training to enlarge the scale, meanwhile combining Depuration to improve the quality via performing data editing over enlarged seeds.

3.1 Use Tri-training Process to Enlarge Seeds Set

In [16], the detail of Tri-training algorithm is studied. In new algorithm, we focus on employing the Co-training style process of Tri-training to enlarge the scale of seeds. Let L be the small amount of initial labeled seeds and three different classifiers, i.e. H_1, H_2 and H_3 are independently trained from L. If H_2 and H_3 agree on labeling a data point x in unlabeled data set U, then x can be labeled for H_1, and all thus x from U can be added into L forming H_1's new training set $S_1' = L \cup \{x \mid x \in U \text{ and } H_2(x) = H_3(x)\}$. Likewise, enlarged new training sets S_2' and S_3' for H_2 and H_3 can be formed. Subsequently three classifiers are re-trained by new training sets. This epoch is repeated until three classifiers don't change anymore and the training process ends. Particularly, iteratively enlarging three training sets shows the enlarging process of initial labeled seeds, as a result the union of three final training sets forms the final enlarged seeds preparing for initialization of cluster centroids.

Obviously, if H_2 and H_3 predict an incorrect label for x then H_1 would get a new training data with noise label for further training. Fortunately, Zhou et al. [16] proved that when satisfy conditions in (2), only if the amount of newly labeled data is sufficient, the increase of noise rate can not violate the PAC learnability of H_1 hypothesis.

$$|L \cup L^t|(1-2\frac{\eta_L|L|+\tilde{e}_1^t|L^t|}{|L \cup L^t|}) > |L \cup L^{t-1}|(1-2\frac{\eta_L|L|+\tilde{e}_1^{t-1}|L^{t-1}|}{|L \cup L^{t-1}|}) \tag{2}$$

Where, L^t is the new labeled data set for H_1 labeled by H_2 and H_3 in the tth iteration, $\tilde{e}_1^t$ is the error upper bound of the error rate of H_2 and H_3 in the ith iteration and η_L is the noise rate of initial labeled data set L. η_L is commonly very small, if assume $0 \le \tilde{e}_1^t, \tilde{e}_1^{t-1} < 0.5$, then condition (2) is replaced by (3)

$$0 < \frac{\tilde{e}_1^t}{\tilde{e}_1^{t-1}} < \frac{|L^{t-1}|}{|L^t|} < 1 \tag{3}$$

Where, $\tilde{e}_1^t$ could be approximated by error rate of H_2 and H_3 on initial labeled data set, In Tri-training process formula (3) acts as judge condition to determine whether new labeled L_1^t, subset of U, should be added into the initial labeled training set L.

3.2 Combine Depuration Technique to Refine Enlarged Seeds Set

Mentioned above, we could use Tri-training process label unlabeled data to enlarge the scale of initial seeds. However, the scale of initial labeled seeds is usually too small to train a classifier with good generalization, so misclassifying a certain amount of unlabeled data is unavoidable and the enlarged labeled for the classifier to train in the next iteration could contain much noise [18]. Therefore, if the mislabeled data in enlarged training set could be identified and eliminated in the Tri-training process, especially in the early iterations, the trained classifier is expected to improve the generalization that equals to improve the quality of enlarged seeds. Data editing techniques can effectively improve the quality of training set [19], Therefore, the data editing technique is combined into training iteration: Before each classifier is retrained, the enlarged training set including newly labeled data will be refined. We call this new process *Tri-training with Data Editing*, abbreviated as *DE-Tri-training*.

Since the target of Kmeans clustering, i.e. "minimizing distances between same-cluster data points" [5], agrees with the Nearest Neighbor Rule (NNR), it is reasonable to employ the NNR based data editing named *Depuration* to refine the enlarged seeds. Depuration is the first prototype selection technique , can cope with all types of imperfections (mislabeled, noisy and outliers) of the training prototypes via removing some "suspicious" data and changing the class labels of some others. Depuration identifies k nearest neighbors of specific point, then checks whether the number of neighbors with same label is not less than k' and decides eliminating this point or changing its label. According to the *generalized editing* [20] scheme, k and k' have to be defined by $(k+1)/2 \le k' \le k$, S´anchez et al. [19] reported when k and k' were set to 3 and 2 respectively, the Depuration achieved the best effect. We adopt this setting.

3.3 Tri-Training and Data Editing based Semi-supervised Kmeans Algorithm

Fig.1 shows the detail process of enlarging and editing. The scale is enlarged by iteration of Tri-training via gradually labeling unlabeled data. The editing of enlarged seeds is performed at two phases. The first phase is the Depuration over new training set following each labeling iteration along with Tri-training, mainly eliminates the noise resulting from misclassification, in addition, the outlier and misclassification in initial labeled set can be cleaned; The second phase follows relabeling over the union of final training sets by joint classifier, thus, based on better generalization of the final joint classifier, the quality of enlarged seeds is further improved by Depuration.

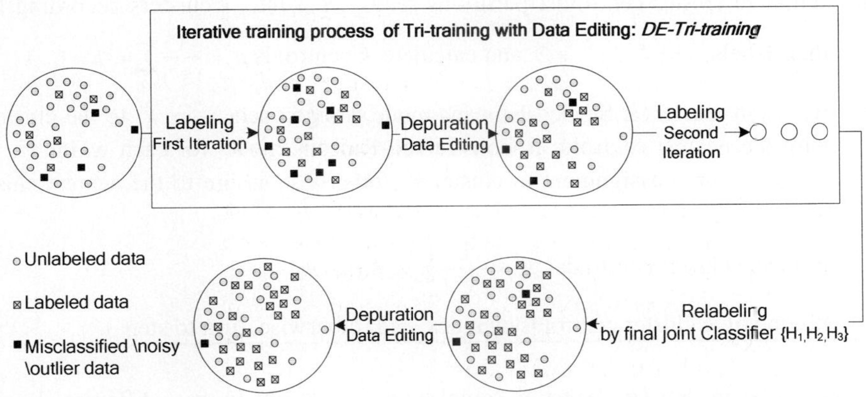

Fig. 1. Enlarging and Data Editing of seeds set from an initial small amount of labeled data set

At now, the novel algorithm can be perfectly described as follows.

Algorithm: *DE-Tri-training semi-supervised clustering*

Input: Data set $X = \{x_i\}_{i=1}^n, x_i \in \Re^d$, number of clusters k , initial labeled seeds set $S = \cup_{h=1}^k S_h, S_h \neq \varnothing$, three untrained classifiers H_1, H_2, H_3

Output: Disjoint k partitioning $\{X_h\}_{h=1}^k$ of X , locally optimizing objective function

Steps:

1. Execute *DE-Tri-training* process to enlarge and edit initial seeds set S :

1a. $L \leftarrow S, U \leftarrow X - L$; produce training sets S_1', S_2', S_3' by *Bootstrap* sampling from L and train H_1, H_2, H_3 respectively

1b. for each $H_i (i = 1, 2, 3)$:

let H_j & $H_k (j, k \neq i)$ selects and labels a subset $L_i = \{x \mid x \in U, H_j(x) = H_k(x)\}$ from U , satisfying the constraint (3), and forms new training set $S_i' = L \cup L_i$

1c. for each non-empty new labeled subset L_i in S_i' executes *Depuration*:

$S' \leftarrow S_i'$;

for each x in L_i, find three nearest neighbors in $S_i' - \{x\}$, if a class label, say c, is held by least two neighbors, set the label of x in S' to c; otherwise, remove x from S';
$S_i' \leftarrow S'$.

1d. for each $H_i (i = 1,2,3)$: if $|S_i'| > |S|$, re-train H_i with S_i'.

1e. if anyone of $H_i (i = 1,2,3)$ changes, turn to 1b.

1f. $S \leftarrow S_1' \cup S_2' \cup S_3'$; each data in $S - L$ is relabeled by final joint classifier $\{H_1, H_2, H_3\}$ via accuracy *weighted voting* principle.

1g. execute *Depuration* on newly relabeled subset $S - L$ in S (like operation in 1c).

2. Initialize cluster centroids: partitions seeds set S into k clusters according to their labels, $S = \cup_{h=1}^{k} S_h, S_h \neq \varnothing$,and calculate k centroids $\mu_h = \frac{1}{|S_h|}\sum_{x \in S_h} x,\ h = 1,..,k$
3. Reassign cluster: if Seeded-Kmeans mode, assign each x in X to the cluster with the nearest centroid; if Constrained-Kmeans mode, for each x in X, if $x \in S_h$, reserve assignment to cluster X_h, otherwise assign to the nearest cluster.
4. Relocate cluster centroids: $\mu_h = \frac{1}{|X_h|}\sum_{x \in X_h} x,\ h = 1,..,k$
5. If none of k cluster centroids changes, end; otherwise, turn to step 3.

To point out, in step *1a*, Bootstrap sampling is used to obtain three different classifiers; in [16] the final joint classifier $\{H_1, H_2, H_3\}$ classifies a new data via *majority voting* method. Since the number of clusters usually more than two, in step *lf* $\{H_1, H_2, H_3\}$ adopts *accuracy weighted voting* principle, which employs accuracies on initial seeds as weights. Meanwhile, to identify the function of Tri-training and Depuration clearly, we assume the initial labeled seeds are noise-free. Therefore, in step *1c* and step *1g* the Depuration is performed only among the newly labeled seeds.

4 Experiments

4.1 Datasets and Methodology

Experiments were conducted on six datasets from UCI repository. Information of these datasets is tabulated in Table 1. For *Letters* and *Digits* handwritten character recognition datasets, we chose two subsets of three classes: {**I, J, L**} from *Letters* and {**3, 8, 9**} from *Digits*, sampling 10% from the original datasets randomly. These classes were chosen since they represent difficult visual discrimination problems [4]. One constant attribute in *Image Segmentation* is deleted since helpless for clustering.

The program and datasets could be acquired from http://kelab.hit.edu.cn/dc.html.

Besides the new algorithm, i.e. *DE-Tri-training Seeded-Kmeans* and *DE-Tri-training Constrained-Kmeans*, in our experiments, *Random Kmeans*, *Seeded-Kmeans*,

Table 1. UCI Datasets Information used in experiments

Datasets	Scale	No. Attributes	No. Classes
Iris	150	4	3
Wine	178	13	3
Letters	227	16	3
Digits	318	16	3
Ionosphere	351	34	2
Image Segmentation	2310	18	7

Constrained-Kmeans are also tested. Moreover, to identify the function of Depuration, Tri-training without Depuration based semi-supervised Kmeans, i.e. *Tri-training Seeded-Kmeans* and *Tri-training Constrained-Kmeans*, are analyzed too.

We use the *normalized mutual information* (NMI) [2] as the evaluation criterion of clustering results. NMI determines the amount of statistical information shared by the random variables representing the cluster assignments of experimental result and the pre-labeled class assignments of the test set. In our experiments, NMI is calculated according to the definition in [21].

For each tested algorithm on each data set, the learning curve is generated by performing 10 runs of 10-fold cross-validation. For each data set, 10% are set aside as test set, and the remaining 90% are partitioned into labeled and unlabeled data set, and the results at each point of the curve are obtained by averaging over 10 runs of 10 folds. The clustering algorithm runs on the whole data set, but the NMI is calculated only on the test set.

Three classifiers in Tri-training adopt BP neural networks (BPNN). Distance metric for clustering and Depuration uses Euclidean distance, max iterations of Kmeans is 200, and threshold value of error is 1e-5. Experiments are divided into two groups: the first group is to study the function of Tri-training via setting sufficient training iterations for each BPNN, which ensures at least two final classifier's accuracy over initial labeled data greater than 0.95 when the fraction of initial labeled seeds is 0.1; the second group is mainly to identify the function of Depuration via setting insufficient training iterations resulting in at least one final classifier's accuracy less than 0.7.

4.2 Results with Sufficient Training Iterations for Each BPNN

Fig.2~Fig.7 show the clustering results of seven algorithms on six datasets. These results not only prove that both *Seeded-Kmeans* and *Constrained-Kmeans* outperform the *Random Kmeans*, basically agrees with the result of Basu [5] and Shi [2], but also clearly show that when the generalization of three BPNN classifiers are ensured by sufficient training iterations, both the scale and quality of enlarged seeds set could be improved which directly contributes to the results of *DE-Tri-training Constrained-Kmeans* and *Tri-training Constrained-Kmeans* significantly outperform the *Seeded-Kmeans* and *Constrained-Kmeans* at most cases.When training sufficient, the effectiveness of Tri-training for enlarging the scale of initial seeds is also typically showed via comparing the scale of final seeds on Iris (Fig.8) and Digits (Fig.9).

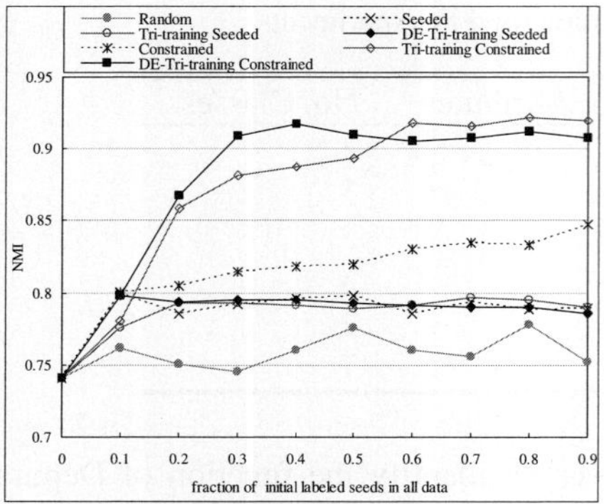

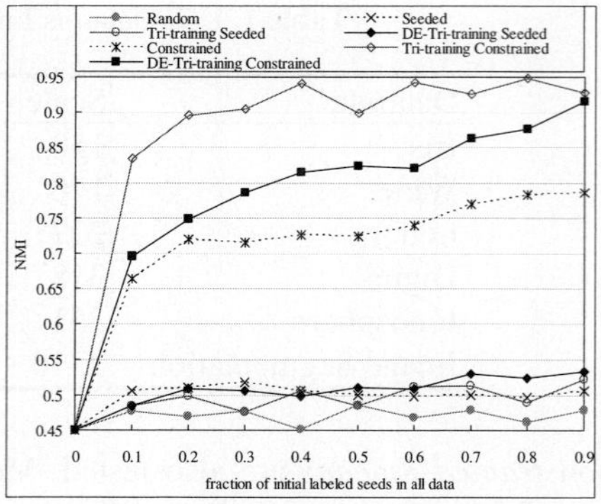

Fig. 2. NMI on Iris: 8 nodes in hidden layer, 500 iterations, learning rate=0.1

Fig. 3. NMI on Wine: 8 nodes in hidden layer, 300 iterations, learning rate=0.1

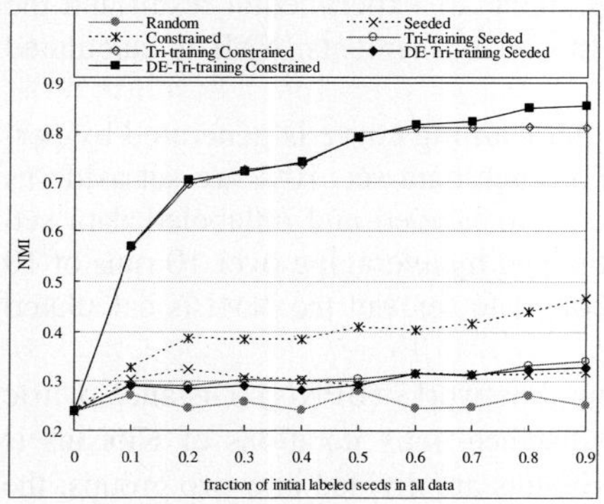

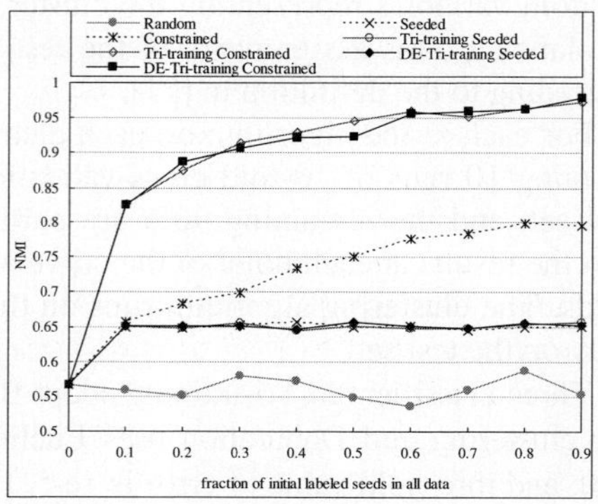

Fig. 4. NMI on Letters: 8 nodes in hidden layer, 300 iterations, learning rate=0.1

Fig. 5. NMI on Digits: 10 nodes in hidden layer, 300 iterations, learning rate=0.1

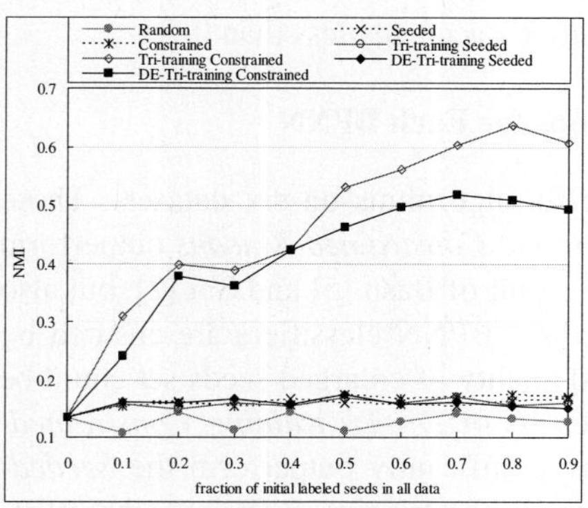

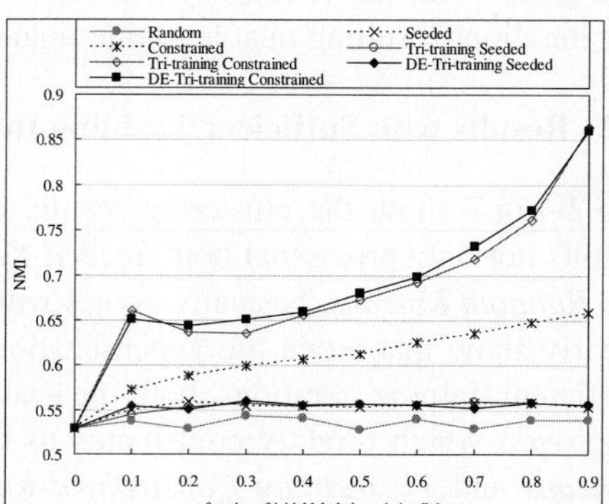

Fig. 6. NMI on Ionosphere: 12 nodes in hidden layer, 500 iterations, learning rate=0.1

Fig. 7. NMI on Image: 12 nodes in hidden layer, 1000 iterations, learning rate=0.3

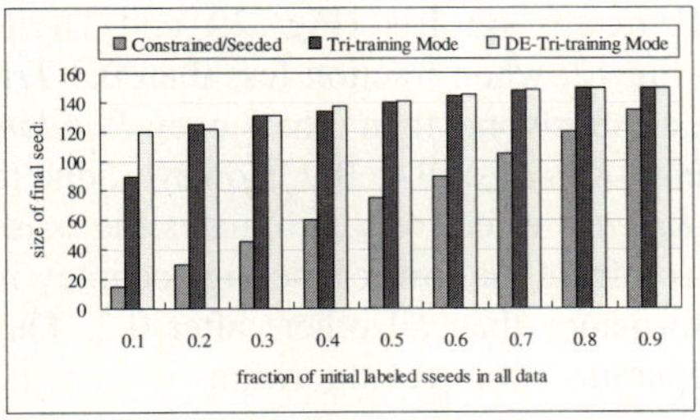

Fig. 8. Scale of final seeds set on Iris with sufficient training iterations: 8 nodes in hidden layer, 500 iterations, learning rate=0.1 (Corresponding to NMI result in **Fig. 2.**)

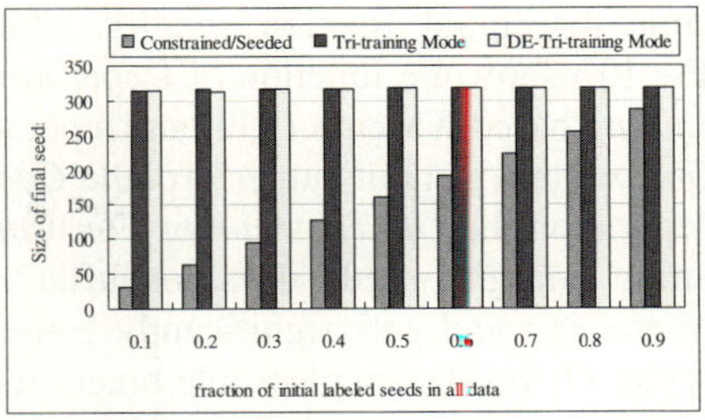

Fig. 9. Scale of final seeds set on Digits with sufficient training iterations: 10 nodes in hidden layer, 300 iterations, learning rate=0.1 (Corresponding to NMI result in **Fig. 5.**)

Moreover, we find that *Tri-training Constrained-Kmeans* outperforms the *DE-Tri-training Constrained-Kmeans* over Wine, Ionoshpere and Iris (when the fraction of initial seeds more than 0.5). This can be explained when the labeled training data enough and training iterations sufficient the labeling of Tri-training becomes more accurate, and the function of Tri-training outperforms Depuration. But we should notice that in Fig 2, when initial fraction less than 0.1 *Tri-training* based Kmeans, (without Depuration), are worse than the *DE-Tri-training* based Kmeans, and even worse than *Constrained-Kmeans* and *Seeded-Kmeans*, along with the increase of fraction, *Tri-training Constrained-Kmeans* quickly outperforms *Constrained-Kmeans* but still less than *DE-Tri-training Constrained-Kmeans* till 0.6, since the latter employs Depuration to refine the enlarged seeds. The best NMI of *Tri-training Constrained-Kmeans* in 0.9 is still equal with *DE-Tri-training Constrained-Kmeans* in 0.4 that indicates Depuration aids the latter get better performance with lower cost.

4.3 Results with Insufficient Training Iterations for each BPNN

When the generalization of BPNN classifier cannot be ensured with sufficient training, Fig.10 and Fig.11 show enlarging the seeds by Tri-training is obstructed especially

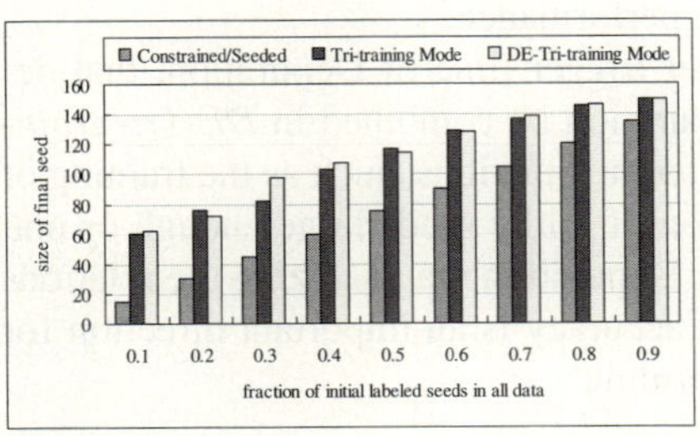

Fig. 10. Scale of final seeds set on Iris with insufficient training iterations: 8 nodes in hidden layer, 50 iterations, learning rate=0.1 (Corresponding to NMI result in **Fig. 12.**)

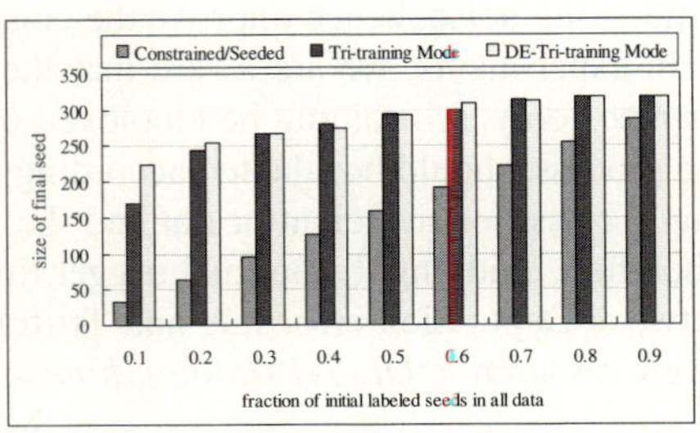

Fig. 11. Scale of final seeds set on Digits with insufficient training iterations: 10 nodes in hidden layer, 20 iterations, learning rate=0.1 (Corresponding to NMI result in **Fig. 13.**)

while the initial fraction smaller. The NMI results on Iris (Fig.12.) and Digits (Fig.13.) show the function of Depuration. In Fig.12, when fraction less than 0.3 *Tri-training* based KMenas (without Depuration), are far worse than others even *Random Kmeans*, and can not outperform the *Constrained-Kmeans* till to 0.9. However, due to Depuration the *DE-Tri-training Constrained-Kmeans* effectively eliminates the noise during enlarging seeds, does not suffer too much from the lower labeling accuracy in Tri-training and gets significantly better performance than all others after 0.2. This further proves the irreplaceable function of Depuration in novel algorithm.

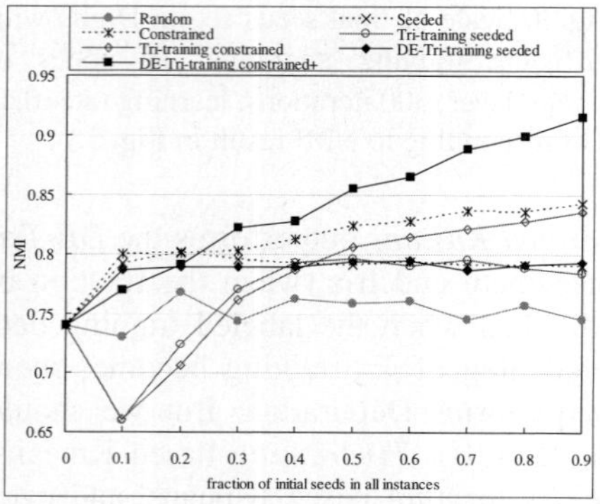

Fig. 12. NMI on Iris: 8 nodes in hidden layer, 50 iterations, learning rate=0.1

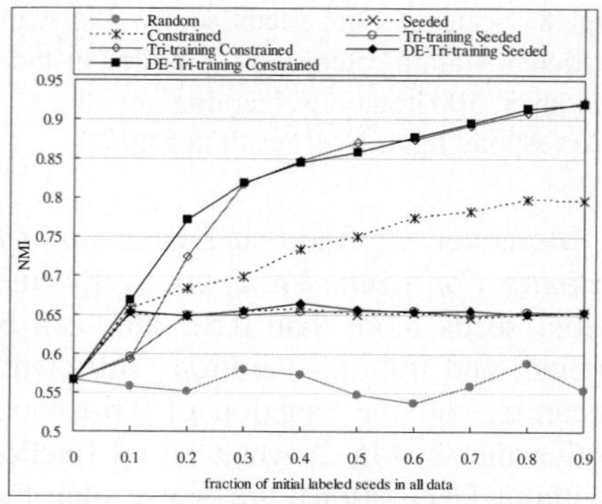

Fig. 13. NMI on Digits: 8 nodes in hidden layer, 20 iterations, learning rate=0.1

5 Conclusion

In this paper the *DE-Tri-training* semi-supervised clustering algorithm is presented. Experiments on UCI datasets indicate that prior to the initialization of cluster centroids, the novel algorithm, which employs Tri-training process combined with Depuration, can effectively enlarge the scale of initial seeds and refine the quality of enlarged seeds for semi-supervised Kmeans clustering via labeling unlabeled data and eliminating noise, hence improve the clustering performance.

In experiments, we are aware that the proper trigger time of Depuration, that determines only Tri-training be employed or Depuration be combined in *DE-Tri- training* process, should be adapted according to different situations, such as the training of single classifier sufficient or not and the fraction of initial seeds large enough or not. Therefore, studying the optimal trigger time for Depuration via analyzing the relations between Depuration error rate and Tri-training accuracy is an important direction for future research in *DE-Tri-training Kmeans* algorithm.

Acknowledgement

The work is partially supported by the Natural Science Foundation of Heilongjiang Province under Grant No.F2004-16.

References

1. Duda, R.O., Hart, P.E., Stork, D.G.: Pattern Classification. 2th edn. Wiley, New York (2001)
2. Shi Zhong.: Semi-supervised model-based document clustering: A comparative study. Machine Learning. published online, March (2006).
3. Olivier Chapelle, Bernhard Schölkopf, Alexander Zien.: Semi-Supervised Learning, MIT press. (2006). http://www.kyb.tuebingen.mpg.de/ssl-book/ssl_toc.pdf.
4. Bilenko, M., Basu, S., Mooney, R.J.: Integrating constraints and metric learning in semi-supervised clustering. In 21st International Conference on Machine Learning, Banff, Canada. (ICML-04) (2004) 81–88
5. Basu, S., Banerjee, A., Mooney, R.J.: Semi-supervised clustering by seeding. In the 19th International Conference on Machine Learning (ICML-02). (2002) 19–26.
6. Demiriz, A., Bennett, K.P., Embrechts, M.J.: Semi-supervised clustering using genetic algorithms. In Dagli C.H. et al. (eds.): Intelligent Engineering Systems Through Artificial Neural Networks(ANNIE-99), ASME Press, NewYork, NY. (1999) 809-814.
7. Wagstaff, K., Cardie, C., Rogers, S., Schroedl, S.: Constrained K-Means clustering with background knowledge. In 18th International Conference on Machine Learning. (ICML-01). (2001) 577–584.
8. Basu, S., Bilenko, M., Mooney, R.J.: A probabilistic framework for semi-supervised clustering. In the Tenth ACM SIGKDD International Conference on Knowledge Discovery and Data Mining (KDD-2004), Seattle,WA. (2004).59–68
9. Seeger M.: Learning with labelled and unlabelled data. Tech. Rep., Institute for Adaptive and Neural Computation, University of Edinburgh, UK, (2002)
10. Nigam, K., McCallum, A.K., Thrun, S., Mitchell, T.: Text classification from labeled and unlabeled documents using EM. Machine Learning, Vol. 39, (2000) 103–134.
11. Ghahramani, Z., Jordan, M.I..: Supervised learning from incomplete data via the EM approach. In Advances in Neural Information Processing Systems 6, (1994) 120–127.
12. Joachims, T.: Transductive inference for text classification using support vector machines. In the Sixteenth International Conference on Machine Learning (ICML-99), Bled, Slovenia. (1999) 200–209.
13. Blum, A., Lafferty, J., Rwebangira, M., Reddy, R.: Semi-supervised learning using randomized mincuts. In the 21st International Conference on Machine Learning (ICML-04) (2004).
14. Blum, A., Mitchell, T.: Combining labeled and unlabeled data with co-training. In the 11th Annual Conference on Computational Learning Theory (COLT-98) (1998) 92–100.
15. Goldman S., Zhou Y.: Enhancing supervised learning with unlabeled data. In the 17th International Conference on Machine Learning (ICML-00), San Francisco, CA, (2000) 327–334
16. Zhou, Z.H., Li, M.: Tri-training: Exploiting unlabeled data using three classifiers. IEEE Transactions on Knowledge and Data Engineering, Vol. 11: (2005) 1529-1541.
17. MacQueen, J.: Some methods for classification and analysis of multivariate observations. In the 5th Berkeley Symposium on Mathematical Statistics and Probability, (1967) 281–297.
18. Li, M., Zhou, Z.H.: SETRED: Self-training with editing. In the 9th Pacific-Asia Conference on Knowledge Discovery and Data Mining (PAKDD-05), Hanoi, Vietnam, LNAI 3518 (2005) 611-621.
19. Sánchez, J.S., Barandela, R., Marqués, A.I., Alejo, R., Badenas, J.: Analysis of new techniques to obtain quality training sets. Pattern Recognition Letters Vol. 24. (2003) 1015-1022.
20. Koplowitz, J., Brown, T.A. On the relation of performance to editing in nearest neighbor rules. Pattern Recognition Vol. 13, (1981)251–255.
21. Strehl, A., Ghosh, J., Mooney, R.: Impact of similarity measures on web-page clustering. In Workshop on Artificial Intelligence for Web Search (AAAI-2000), (2000) 58–64.

Automatic Construction of Bayesian Network Structures by Means of a Concurrent Search Mechanism

Mondragón-Becerra R., Cruz-Ramírez N., García-López D.A. , Gutiérrez-Fragoso K., Luna-Ramírez W.A., Ortiz-Hernández G., and Piña-García C.A.

Facultad de Física e Inteligencia Artificial, Departamento de Inteligencia Artificial, Universidad Veracruzana, Sebastián Camacho No 5, Xalapa, Ver., México, 91000
{rmondragon, ncruz}@uv.mx, {dalexgarcia, kgutierrezf, wulfranoarturo, gusorh, capiga21}@gmail.com

Abstract. The implicit knowledge in the databases can be extracted of automatic form. One of the several approaches considered for this problem is the construction of graphical models that represent the relations between the variables and regularities in the data. In this work the problem is addressed by means of an algorithm of search and scoring. These kind of algorithms use a heuristic mechanism search and a function of score to guide themselves towards the best possible solution.

The algorithm, which is implemented in the semifunctional language Lisp, is a searching mechanism of the structure of a bayesian network (BN) based on concurrent processes.

Each process is assigned to a node of the BN and effects one of three possible operations between its node and some of the rest: to put, to take away or to invert an edge. The structure is constructed using the metric MDL (made up of three terms), whose calculation is made of distributed way, in this form the search is guided by selecting those operations between the nodes that minimize the MDL of the network.

In this work are presented some results of the algorithm in terms of comparison of the structure of the obtained network with respect to its gold network.

1 Introduction

The *expert systems* are programs of computer able to produce solutions similar to which a human expert can offer without mattering what reasoning process they use to obtain them. They emulate to the human experts in an area of certain specialization [3] [6]. These systems commonly are used by the human experts like support tools to process and to represent the originating information of some field of knowledge, so that they allow them to more easily obtain the solution or solutions to a problem [6].

The construction of an expert system implies to incorporate knowledge to the computer program. By knowledge it must be understood those affirmations of

A. Gelbukh and C.A. Reyes-Garcia (Eds.): MICAI 2006, LNAI 4293, pp. 652–662, 2006.

general validity that an expert does, for example rules or probability distributions [3], whereas the data talk about the information of a certain field. The task of incorporating the knowledge is arduous and difficult, taking into account that the experts not necessarily are able to explain to detail how they reach a solution and how their knowledge is organized [6].

In order to help to solve this problem the Data Mining (DM) or Discovery of Knowledge in Databases (KDD) discipline has been developed. The main thesis of this field is that the knowledge is contained in the data in a implicit way. It makes use of techniques and originating knowledge of databases, statistic, automatic learning, artificial intelligence (AI), among others. Its objective is to extract the knowledge that, perhaps, is in form of causal relations or rules between the data [6].

In a database (DB) implicit relations between the data contained in it exist. These relations can be represented by means of different models, between which are the **graphical models** [6] [15].

A graphical model combines the **theory of graphs** and the **theory of probability**, this form, the model consists of a graph whose nodes represent variables and the edges represent dependency or conditional independence, according to be present or no [6] [15].

Within the graphical models are the **bayesian networks** (BN), also known like probability networks, causal networks or diagrams of probability influence. They are graphical structures that represent the knowledge of experts. Their purpose is to obtain conclusions from certain input data and to explain the reasoning process that is carried out to obtain a solution to a certain problem [6] [14] [21]. They are **directed acyclic graphs** (DAG), which constitute from a set of *nodes* and *edges*. Each node represents a variable and each edge a probability dependency, in which the conditional probability of each variable is specified given its parents. The variable at which it points the edge is dependent of whom it is in the origin of this one [6] [14] [21].

This work focuses in the learning of the structure of a BN following the perspective of the algorithms based on search and score. The part search is implemented through concurrent processes and the score by means of the application of the metric of length of minimum description *MDL* (*Minimum Description Length*). There are others works that learn the BN structure in a distributed way [4] [12] [20].

The developed system distributes the compute of the MDL in several machines, each one of them has access to other than it acts as server and it lodges the DB. The processes that make the search of the structure of the BN are implemented like *threads* in a single machine, this way so much is obtained a concurrent processing as one distributed to find the structure of the BN.

In the following sections is approached the concepts that serve as base the proposal mentioned here, such as learning of the structure of bayesian networks, the metric MDL, the distributed systems and the concurrence. In the part where it is described the implementation are mentioned the characteristics of Lisp, the used programming language to develop this work.

2 Learning of the Structure of a BN

As it were already said, a BN codifies the probability relations of dependency and independence between the variables of a certain problem (by means of nodes, edges and probability distributions). Two aspects exist to consider in a BN [6]:

- Its qualitative nature. It refers about the **learning of its structure**, which consists of finding the topology of the network, this is, to construct a graph that *qualitatively* shows the relations of dependency or independence between the variables involved in a certain problem. The objective is to easily know and to identify the variables that are outstanding or not for the problem at issue [6].
- Its quantitative nature. It refers about to obtain the probability distribution required by the topology of the network.

Basically, two heuristic approaches exist to construct the structure of a BN, which are: **algorithms based on restrictions** and **algorithms based on search and score** [6].

The algorithms based on restrictions make tests of conditional independence, given a DB, to look for a structure of consistent network with the dependencies or independence obtained by means of a probability model [6].

The algorithms search and score are characterized by the definition of a **metric**, that evaluates that so suitable it is the structure of the network (fitting kindness) to represent the relations between the data. In addition it incorporates a mechanism to find a structure that maximizes or minimizes this metric [6].

In the present work, it is used the approach of the search and scoring algorithms . In the following section it is exposed of what these algorithms consist.

3 Search and Scoring Algorithms

As said above, to define a searching mechanism is needed in a searching and scoring algorithm for finding BN's candidate structures, which must be evaluated by a metric for identifying the best one in order to model the relations between data. A key point is that this algorithms need to generate all the possible structures for finding the most suitable for the problem, so it is so expensive computationally because the number of possible structures increase exponentially.

A searching and scoring algorithm is constituted by two components:

- *Search algorithms*: they are used for exploring possible structures of a BN. Generally greedy algorithms has been used, some of them classic in AI, for example: Hill Climbing, Best First, Simulated Annealing and genetic algorithms.
- *Scoring Functions*: used for to guide the searching in order to find the best BN structure. A lot of metrics has been proposed, for example relative the posteriori probability with a heuristic based in the principle of the Occam's razor[1], the bayesian information criterion (BIC), the principle of minimum

[1] This principle consists of choosing models with smaller complexity but with suitable results.

description length (MDL), minimum message length (MML) and the information criterion of Akaike (AIC)[11]

The election of the suitable description of a data set constitutes the problem of selection of the model and is one of most important of the inductive and statistical inference. Principle MDL is a relatively recent method for the inductive inference that provides a generic solution to the problem of selection of the model. Since it was used in this project, a brief explanation of this metric is presented next.

3.1 MDL Score Metric

The deduction of laws and general principles of particular cases is the base for the selection of statistical models, the recognition of patterns and the automatic learning. The MDL principle is a long-range method in inductive inference, is based on the following thing: any regularity in the data can be used to compress them, whatever more regularity has, more data can be compressed, can be said then that more is learned on the data [18], *i.e.*, *the best explanation of a observed data system is the one that allows the greatest compression* (principle of the Occam's razor). On the other hand, this principle avoids the overfitting and can be used to consider the parameters and the structure of a model. MDL also is known like criterion of stochastic complexity, of this form argues their predictive capacity because it is based on that the data compression is a form of probabilistic prediction [6] [7].

As it was already indicated, the MDL principle is to learn of the data through the compression. Thus, when the search is guided by MDL is directed to select a BN of minimum length between different structures from network. The compression of the network requires a compensation between complexity and precision in the length of the data [6]. For that reason, the calculation of MDL needs to incorporate two terms basically, one to measure what so well represents the model or predicts the data and other to punish it in proportion to the complexity of the structure of the network. In addition, it is necessary to add a third term with the purpose of reducing the complexity of the network [9] [7] [22]. This balance is represented with the following equation:

$$MDL = -logP(D|\theta) + \frac{k}{2}\, log\, n + O(1) \quad (1)$$

Where: D =data
$\theta =$ bayesian network parameters
$k =$ network dimension
$n =$ number of cases or evidences

k is calculate as follow:

$$k = \sum_{1 \leq i \leq n} q_i(r_i - 1) \quad (2)$$

and $O(1)$ is obtained from the next formula:

$$O(1) = \sum_{i=1}^{n} (1 + P_{a\,i}) log\, m \tag{3}$$

Where:

m = number of variables or nodes
q_i = variable i's fathers configurations
r_i = number of states of the variable i
$P_{a\,i}$ = node i's fathers

In the application of the formula (1) to a DB it is necessary to consider the joint probabilities for the total of cases . The equation is of the following form:

$$MDL = - \sum_{1 \leq i \leq n} logP(D|\theta_i) + \frac{k}{2} log\, n + O(1) \tag{4}$$

The final result of this calculation represents the score of MDL for a network and a given DB. In order to be able to select a structure that describes the data suitably it is necessary to calculate this score for each possible structure. An alternative form of calculation exists that facilitates the score of a structure because it involves only a pair of variables, reason which the time used in this calculation is reduced considerably with respect to the necessary time for the calculation of the global MDL. The previous process is known as update of MDL [1] and is synthesized in the following equation:

$$MDL_{update} = MDL_l * (\frac{MDL_f}{MDL_i}) \tag{5}$$

Where:

MDL_{update} = score of the previous structure
MDL_f = score of the structure that involves two variables in one of the valid actions[2] (adding, deleting or reverting edges) after applying it
MDL_i = score of the structure that involves two variables before applying an action.

Until now we have commented the score function that was used in this work, in the following sections the subjects of *distributed systems* are approached and *concurrence* since this work is based on them to implement the searching mechanism and score.

4 Search and Scoring Mechanism Proposal

The proposal presented for the learning of the structure of a BN from a DB is based on the use of concurrent processes and the distribution of the calculation of the metric MDL.

Is understood by **concurrent program** the set of sequential programs that execute in *abstract parallelism*, that is do not execute in separated physical processors [2]. On the other hand, a process is an ordinary sequential program in

[2] the not valid actions are those that form cycles in the graph.

execution [2]. Whereas the group of independent machines that act altogether to make a calculation conforms what is called **distributed system** [23].

On these concepts is structured the proposal of construction of the BN structure from a DB. Next the proposal is detailed.

4.1 Concurrent Searching Mechanism and Distributed Score

The search of the BN by means of concurrent processes is made up of two parts: a coordinator process and a set of processes that make the transformations of the graph. Immediately the tasks that make these components are briefly exposed.

- The set of processes called *PAON* (**Processes of Application of Operations with respect to a Node**) transforms the structure of BN (DAG), that is to say, apply the operations *to delete*, *to put* and *to inverse* edge with respect to a reference node. They look for the operation that produces smaller MDL between their node and the rest. When they have carried out its transformation, they send its proposal (the resulting graph and its MDL) to the coordinator process.
- **Coordinator process** (from now *P*). This process takes to the control of the mechanism search and score of the structure of the DAG. It creates *PAON* necessary in agreement with the used DB. It orients the search when indicating to *PAON* on what structure must operate them(the effective DAG, or the initial or the one that until the moment it has been better, in agreement with its value of MDL) and determines when to finalize it.

The search process begins with an initial DAG, whose nodes represent the variables of the used DB. It can have three initial configurations, a DAG connectionless, a multiconnected DAG, or a DAG with edges randomly connected between the nodes [6]. This implementation uses a graph totally disconnected.

Next is the algorithm that describes the search:

1. *To initiate process P.*
   (a) *To load the DB.*
   (b) *To generate the graph initial (graph totally disconnected).*
   (c) *To calculate initial global MDL.*
   (d) *To create threads for each variable of the graph. Each thread receives the present variable on which it will work, graph and MDL:*
      1 *Each concurrent process (PAON) evaluates the valid operations (those that maintain the graph without cycles) and weights them calculating its partial MDL for its variable and all the others.*
      2 *Choose the best proposal (that diminishes the partial MDL).*
      3 *Return the selected proposal.*
   (e) *To choose the winning MDL:*
      – *If there is a tie in the proposals (that having the smaller partial MDL's).*
        Calculate the global MDL to break the deadlock and to obtain the best proposal.

  – *If there is no tie.*
    Select the best MDL.

2. *If present MDL does not improve the previous one and it has fulfilled the minimum number of iterations, it stops and shows the result.*
3. *If no, it updates the graph and the global MDL and, it goes to step 1(d) sending to PAON the new data.*

The minimum number of iterations proposed is 2, in the successive iterations verifies the condition of halt. Immediately is the algorithm of selection of the best proposal than it is implemented in P:

1. *Wait by a number of proposals and to store them in a temporary queue.*
2. *While there is propose in the queue:*
   2,1 Add the proposals to a priority queue.
3. *To take the best proposal from the collection.*
4. *To eliminate the rest of the proposals.*
5. *To continue computing and sending the best proposal to $PAON$.*

The algorithm of each $PAON$ is the following one:

1. *To receive the variable with it will work, the present graph and its MDL associated.*
2. *To obtain the set of possible actions.*
   2,1 If there are valid actions:
     Choose the action that has a smaller MDL.
     A. To send the proposal to P.
   2,2 If there are no valid actions:
     Wait until P reactivates it.

Next is showed the way in which this proposal was implemented in the Lisp language with concurrent and distributed processes.

5 Proposal Implementation

Now we describe the way the implementation of the concurrent processes and MDL distributed computation were done.

5.1 *Threads* and *Sockets* in Lisp

For developing this work it was necessary to use *LispWorks* version 4.4.5 and the tools package *GBBopen* which is included in the *portable-threads* module,with which we could be able to implement the concurrent processes.

As we said at the beginning of this paper, the PAON processes were implemented as threads. A thread is a separated task execution made in a same machine, which share the same CPU time and memory with others threads and processes. The operative system will assign the CPU time alternating the turns to one and others tasks to simulate the parallel execution. The communication between computers for carry out the MDL distributed process was implemented by using the *LispWorks' COMM* package which contains a *TCP/IP* interface. For this job we used TCP/IP *sockets* so we could get the machines communicated. A *socket* is a communication channel between two processes that are being executed in different computers (it is possible to do that on the same machine), particularly, the *TCP/IP sockets* implement a trusted bidirectional communication data flow. A connection made using *sockets* has its source into a client computer and its own destine into a server computer. The *socket* components are the IP address or client name, the port number in which the communication will be established, the address or the server name and finally the port number for receiving the clients' requests.

It will explain now, how the MDL distributed computation was obtained.

5.2 Distributed MDL Computation

In the first term of the MDL falls all the heavy computation so, is the one we have distributed. The first term is defined as the sum of the joint probability logarithms of the proved cases in a whole database. That sum is divided by assigning at each computer just a part of the whole set of cases to prove. The distributed implementation was made by means of *sockets.* As we said before, the coordinator process is who requires the MDL computation for being executed and this is as follows: The remote machines do the hardest calculation and receive as parameter a function with the followings arguments: the graph to be evaluated and an identifier of the database partition for being computed as apart of the MDL calculation.

It is necessary to wait for all the computers end its job for keep going forward with the algorithm of MDL; this way the time of latency is determined by the slowest computer. The way in which the coordinator process determines that all the computers satisfactorily concluded is by forcing them through the *socket buffers* [3] to give an output, this is because it is assumed that always we send data it will be received an answer. We will say now that it is possible to generate a dead-lock, this means to wait indefinitely for one or more computers end its job. Implementation of the MDL metric corresponds to the MDL equation (1) calculated one time at the beginning of the process and in the case of having a tie in the proposals received by P from the $PAON$.

6 Testing and Results

We illustrate our implementation using the ASIA database and its golden BN, because they are benchmark models. This database has 8 attributes and 1000 instances.

The tests consisted in the following set of methods: First we used the *k-fold Cross-validation* [5] where $1 < k \leq |DB|$ and its value is defined by the user. For

[3] *Sockets* are *steams* or data fluxes of a serial nature.

this test we set $k = 3$. To determine the precision in the BN structure classification generated with the concurrent searching, we use the **general method of probabilistic inference** which consists in calculate the conditional probability of class variable, that has value x, given the evidence[17].

6.1 Tests Description

Now we present the results obtained from the BN structure learning application proposed. In first term it is showed in Table 1 a comparison between the classification obtained with our application and the result given with the WEKA [24] tool using the same database that it was described.

Table 1. Results of the classification

DB	Number of classified instances.	% of classification
asia (weka)	842	84.20 %
asia	842	84.28 %

We obtained three BN structures with our application, which they are compared with its correspondent Golden Network that has 7 edges [6].

Table 2. Description of the resultant BN structures with respect to its Golden Network

BN	TOTAL EDGES	MISSED EDGES	INVERTED EDGES	REMAINED EDGES
G1	11	0	4	6
G2	10	2	2	3
G3	9	2	5	3

7 Conclusions and Future Work

In this paper we have presented a search and score mechanism to learn automatically a BN structure from a DB which performs the distributed computation of the MDL metric. The advantages with the distributed computation are:

- One aspect to take in count, was that the machine where the concurrent processes were executed, reducing the computed charge, taking advantage of the computed power of the rest equipments in order to do the intensive math of the MDL.
- An interesting point was that the implementation was executed in different computers and different operative systems versions. It didn't present interoperability conflicts between the different platforms.

Another point to take in count was that we added one more term to the MDL metric in order to strengthen the complexity term. This term should cause a decrease of the edges in the graph. Nevertheless, we have to check the application of the term, since it didnt seem to balance the metric in a good way: the obtained graphs had several edges and they were not quite similar to the golden networks for each DB used in the proofs.

Some aspects of our future work are detailed:

- One of the most important activities is to improve the code, since the current work does not count with a cache memory in order to make fast the calculation of the likelihoods. Furthermore it results necessary to check the functions for the detection of possible regularities of the code that it could being incorporated in other functions and avoid with this the redundancy in the compute.
- Search a mechanism that allows a dynamic performance of the distribution of the charge and not a static one. With this we will avoid computers have dead times and we will improve the performance of the whole system.
- Review the MDL metric to achieve a better heuristic in the search. It is necessary to review the complexity term (compost of two parts) in order to get compact networks that represent better the data.
- It is necessary more extensive experimental process.

Acknowledgement

We are thankful with Héctor Acosta, Angélica García, Alejandro Guerra, Guillermo Hoyos, professors of the postgrade program in Artificial Intelligence for their appreciable comments and suggestions to this paper.

References

1. Acid, S., De campos, L.M. (2003). Searching for Bayesian Network Structures in the space of restricted Acyclic Partially Directed Graphs. In Journal of Artificial Intelligence Research.
2. Ben-Ari, M. (1990). *Principles of Concurrent and Distributed Programming.* C.A.R Hoare Series Editor. Great Britain.
3. Castillo, E.M; Gutiérrez J.M. and Hadi, A.S. (1998). *Sistemas Expertos y Modelos de Redes Probabilísticas.* Academia Española de Ingeniería. http://personales.unican.es/gutierjm/BookCGH.html
4. Chen R., Sivakumar K. , and Kargupta H. (2004). *Collective mining of bayesian networks from distributed heterogeneous data.* In Knowledge and Information Systems.
5. Kohavi, R. (1995). *A Study of Cross-Validation and Bootstrap for Accuracy Estimation and Model Selection.* International Joint Conference on Artificial Intelligence (IJCAI), USA.
6. Cruz-Ramírez, N. (2001). *Building Bayesian Networks from Data: a Constraint-based Approach,*Ph.D. Thesis, Department of Psychology, Londres,The University of Sheffield.
7. Grünwald, P. D. *In Jae Myung and Mark A. Pitt,*www.mitpress.mit.edu, Consulted at November 21, 2005.

8. Fikes, R. E. and Nilsson N. J. (1971). *STRIPS: A New Approach to the Application of Theorem Proving to Problem Solving.* In Artificial Intelligence 2, United States.
9. Friedman, N., and Goldszmidt M. (1996). *Learning Bayesian networks with local structure.* In Proceedings of the Twelfth Conference on Uncertainty in Artificial Intelligence
10. Kaebling, L. P., (1993). *Learning in embedded systems*,Ed. A Bradford Book / MIT Press,Cambridge, MA.,United States.
11. Krause, P. J. *Learning probabilistic networks.*The Knowledge Engineering Review,13(4):321-351, 1998. 28
12. Lam, W. and Segre A. (2002). *A Distributed Learning Algorithm for Bayesian Inference Networks.* In IEEE Transactions on Knowledge and Data Engineering.
13. McFarland, D. (1995). *Autonomy and Self-Sufficiency in Robots.*In The Artificial Route to Artificial Intelligence, Luc Steels y Rodney Brooks editores. Ed. Lawrence Erlbaum Associates. United States.
14. Morales E. http://www.mor.itesm.mx/˜rdec/node153.html Consulted at November 23, 2005.
15. Murphy K. http://www.cs.ubc.ca/ ˜murphyk/Bayes/bnintro.html Consulted at November 23, 2005.
16. Newell A., (1991). *The Knowledge Level*, Technical report CMUCS-81-131, Carnegie Mellon University, United States.
17. Nilsson, N. J. (2001). *Inteligencia Artificial. Una nueva síntesis.* McGraw-Hill. España.
18. Rissanen J.,www.mdl-research.org, (2005, 11, 21)
19. Russell, S. J. and Norvig P. (1996). *Artificial Intelligence. A Modern Approach*, Ed. Prentice-Hall, United States.
20. K. Sivakumar, Chen R. and Kargupta H. (2003)*Learning Bayesian Network Structure from Distributed Data.* In Proceedings of the 3rd SIAM International Data Mining Conference, San Franciso.
21. Sucar, L. E.; Pérez-Brito, J.; Ruiz Suárez J. C.and Morales, E. (1997). *Learning Structure from Data and its Application to Ozone Prediction*,Applied Intelligence,Kluwer Academic Publishers, Vol. 7(4) 327-338.
22. Suzuki, J., (1999). *Learning Bayesian Belief Networks Based on the Minimum Description Length Principle: Basic Properties.* In IEICE Trans. Fundamentals.
23. Tannenbaum, A. S. and Von Steen M. (2002). *Distributed Systems. Principles and Paradigms.* Prentice Hall. USA.
24. Witten, I. H. and Frank E. (2005). *Data Mining: Practical machine learning tools and techniques*, 2nd Edition, Morgan Kaufmann, San Francisco.

Collaborative Design Optimization Based on Knowledge Discovery from Simulation

Jie Hu and Yinghong Peng

Institute of Knowledge Based Engineering, School of Mechanical Engineering, Shanghai Jiao Tong University, 1954 Hua Shan Road, Shanghai, 200030, P.R. China
{hujie, yhpeng}@sjtu.edu.cn

Abstract. This paper presents a method of collaborative design optimization based on knowledge discovery. Firstly, a knowledge discovery approach based on simulation data is presented. Rules are extracted by knowledge discovery algorithm, and each rule is divided into several intervals. Secondly, a collaborative optimization model is established. In the model, the consistency intervals are derived from intervals of knowledge discovery. The model is resolved by genetic arithmetic. Finally, The method is demonstrated by a parameter design problem of piston-connecting mechanism of automotive engine. The proposed method can improve the robustness of collaborative design optimization.

Keywords: Knowledge discovery, Simulation, Collaborative design, Optimization.

1 Introduction

The essences of collaborative design process is how to coordinate all the constraints distributed in various models and obtain the optimized solution. Various approaches have been looked into over the years for the coordinate and optimization for collaborative design. Young and O'Grady studied constraint network for modeling [1, 2] and developed several applicable constraint systems such as Spark [3], Saturn [4] and Jupiter [5]. Kong *et al.* [6] developed an internet-based collaboration system for a press-die design process for automobile manufacturers with CORBA, Java, Java3D and a relational database system. Yin *et al.* [7] presented an approach to component-based distributed cooperative design over the Internet where an extended multi-tier model (Browser/Server) is used to implement the web-based remote design system. Wang *et al.* [8] developed of a distributed multidisciplinary design optimization (MDO) environment (called WebBlow) using a number of enabling technologies including software agents, Internet/Web, and XML. Gantois and Morris [9] described a quite innovative multidisciplinary optimisation method based on robust design techniques. Giassi *et al.* [10] described a quite innovative multidisciplinary optimisation method based on robust design techniques: MORDACE (multidisciplinary optimisation and robust design approaches applied to concurrent engineering). Bai *et al.* [11] introduced the concept of the PLF (Product Layout Feature) and provided a solution to the problems of PLF modeling. As a result of the

A. Gelbukh and C.A. Reyes-Garcia (Eds.): MICAI 2006, LNAI 4293, pp. 663 – 673, 2006.

solution, collaborative design activities among multi-teams from different disciplines can be consistently carried out on PLF models in the PDM environment.

Numerical simulation has been used more and more widely in almost all of the engineering areas and has become the third mode of science complementing theory and experiment. The simulation of increasingly complex phenomena leads to the generation of vast quantities of data. The massive computing results imply much useful knowledge. In fact, much of the output computational simulations is simply stored away on disks and is never effectively used at all. Extracting the engineering knowledge implicitly contained in simulation data is very meaningful and urgent. It can help designers understand the design parameters space more clearly and then decide which one is the optimal design. Knowledge discovery in database (KDD) is the non-trivial process of identifying valid, novel, potentially useful, and ultimately understandable patterns in data. It can acquire implicit and useful knowledge in large-scale data sets, which involves an integration of multiple disciplines such as statistics, artificial intelligence, machine learning, pattern recognition and etc. KDD has made great success in commercial areas and has begun to be used in knowledge acquisition of engineering disciplines [12, 13, 14]. The overall KDD process includes data selection, data preprocessing, data transformation, data mining, interpretation and evaluation. Data Mining (DM) is an essential step where intelligent methods are applied in order to extract data patterns. An efficient and appropriative DM algorithm plays critical role in KDD process. The data source is the basis of acquiring appropriate and useful knowledge. Its selection and pre-processing are also very important for a successful knowledge discovery [15].

The problem with these researchers is that few papers have addressed the knowledge discovery and collaborative design optimization simultaneously. In this paper, a collaborative design optimization method based on knowledge discovery from simulation is introduced. First, a data-mining algorithm named fuzzy-rough algorithm is developed to deal with the data of numerical simulation. Then, a collaborative design optimization design method is presented to obtain optimized parameter. Finally, a parameter design example is presented to familiarize the reader with the application of the new method.

2 Knowledge Discovery from Simulation

As the core of the knowledge discovery, an efficient and appropriate data mining (DM) algorithm plays an important role in a successful KDD process. Recently, the rough-set theory (RST) has been used widely in knowledge reasoning and knowledge acquisition. It is proposed by Pawlak in 1982 with the concept of equivalence classes as its basic principle. Several applications have shown the success of RST. However, the basic RST algorithm can only handle nominal feature in decision table, most previous studies have just shown how binary or crisp training data may be handled. To apply the RST algorithm on real value data set, discretization must be applied as the preprocessing step to transform them into nominal feature space [16, 17]. However, for the simulation data, it is difficult to define the cuts for discretization because of the unlabeled objective attributes. Exact cut sets partitions the objects into crisp sets with sharp boundaries, which means that that an object belongs to one certain set is either affirmative or denial absolutely. This contradicts our traditional view on real world. Also, induced knowledge description with absolute real value cuts is less abstract than that with linguistic terms. In this study, an improved algorithm named fuzzy-rough sets algorithm is developed by introducing Fuzzy Set Theory to connect exact mathematical description with nature language description. Thus, it can act as the DM algorithm to deal with various types of data in knowledge discovery from the simulation data.

2.1 Fuzzy Sets Theory

The fuzzy-set theory was first proposed by Zadeh in 1965. It is concerned with quantifying and reasoning using natural language in which words can have ambiguous meanings [18].

Let U be a finite and nonempty set called *universe*. A fuzzy set X in U is a membership function $\mu_X(x)$, which to every element $x \in U$ associates a real number from the interval [0, 1], and $\mu_x(x)$ is the grade of membership of x in X. The union and intersection of fuzzy sets X and Y are defined as follows:

$$\forall x \in U: \quad \mu_{X \cup Y}(x) = Max(\mu_X(x), \mu_Y(x)) \tag{1}$$

$$\forall x \in U: \quad \mu_{X \cap Y}(x) = Min(\mu_X(x), \mu_Y(x)) \tag{2}$$

$$\forall x \in X: \quad \mu_{-X}(x) = 1 - \mu_X(x) \tag{3}$$

Fuzzy number can handle some inaccurate information with fuzzy language such as “the force is very high”, “the part is good”.

2.2 Rough Sets Theory

The rough-set theory is an extension of classic set theory for the study of intelligent systems characterized by insufficient and incomplete information. It can be treated as a tool for data table analysis. Using the concepts of lower and upper approximations, knowledge hidden in information systems can be unraveled and expressed in the form of decision rules [19].

An information system is a pair $S = (U, A)$, where U is a non-empty, finite set called the *universe* and A is a non-empty, finite set of attributes, i.e. $a: U \to V_a$ for $a \in A$, where V_a is called the value set of a. Elements of U are called objects.

Considering a special case of information system called *decision table*. A decision table is an information system of the form $S = (U, A \cup \{d\})$, where $d \notin A$ is a distinguished attribute called decision.

Assuming that the set V_d of the decision d is equal to $\{1, ..., r(d)\}$, the decision d determines the partition $\{C_1, ..., C_{r(d)}\}$ of the universe U, where $C_k = \{x \in U : d(x) = k\}$ for $1 \le k \le r(d)$. The set C_k is called the *k-th* decision class of S.

For any subset of attributes $B \subseteq A$, an equivalence relation, denoted by $IND(B)$, is called the B-indiscernibility relation, which is defined by

$$IND(B) = \{(x, y) \in U \times U : \forall_{a \in B}(a(x) = a(y))\} \tag{4}$$

Objects x, y satisfying relation $IND(B)$ are indiscernible according to attributes from B. Let $[x]_{IND(B)}$ denotes the equivalence class of $IND(B)$ corresponding to x. B-lower and B-upper approximation of X in A are defined as followed:

$$\underline{B}X = \{x \in U : [x]_{IND(B)} \subset X\} \tag{5}$$

$$\overline{B}X = \{x \in U : [x]_{IND(B)} \cap X \neq \Phi\} \tag{6}$$

Certain and possible rules can be induced from lower approximation $\underline{A}C_k$ and upper approximation $\overline{A}C_k$ respectively ($1 \le k \le r(d)$). Each object x in the two sets determines a decision rule

$$\bigwedge_{a \in A} a = a(x) \Rightarrow d(x) = r(d) \tag{7}$$

2.3 Fuzzy-Rough Sets Theory

It is very difficult that one object identified by real value attribute is exactly equal to another in decision table. So the equivalence relation in basic RST is too strict for quantitative data such as FEA simulation data. By introducing fuzzy indiscernibility relation to replace the equivalence relation in basic RST, information processing scope can be extended greatly. Then, the generated productive rules are nearer to natural language, which help understanding the mined knowledge more clearly.

For a decision table $S = (U, A \cup \{d\})$, if the value set V_a is composed of quantitative value, the value on attribute $a \in A$ can be catalogued into several fuzzy sets described by natural language such as 'low', 'normal', or 'high' etc. Assume that the set L_a of linguistic terms of attribute a is equal to $\{l_1^a, l_2^a, ..., l_{|L_a|}^a\}$. *Object* x belongs to the *l-th* fuzzy set of attribute a with fuzzy function f_{al}^x.

For any two objects x and y in U, if there exists linguistic term l of attribute a satisfying $f_{al}^x > 0$ and $f_{al}^y > 0$, it is said that there are fuzzy indiscernibility relation on single attribute a between objects x and y. The indiscernibility degree between them on the linguistic term l can be measured by $\mu_{al} = min(f_{al}^x, f_{al}^y)$. Similarly, if the same linguistic terms of an attribute subset B exist in both object x and y with membership values larger than zero, x and y are said to have a fuzzy indiscernibility relation on attribute subset B with the membership value equal to $\mu_B = min(\{min(f_{al}^x, f_{al}^y) : l \in L_a, a \in B\})$

$$IND'(B) = \{((x, y), \mu_B) : \forall_{a \in B}(f_{al}^x > 0, f_{al}^y > 0)\} \tag{8}$$

According the above fuzzy similarity relation, the universe U can be partitioned by attribute subset B. $[x]_{IND'(B)}$ denotes the fuzzy equivalence class of $IND'(B)$ defined by x. Thus fuzzy lower approximation and fuzzy upper approximation of subset X in U are defined as following.

$$\underline{B}(X)=\{([x]_{IND'(B)},\mu_B(x)):x\in U,[x]_{IND'(B)}\subseteq X\} \tag{9}$$

$$\overline{B}(X)=\{([x]_{IND'(B)},\mu_B(x)):x\in U,[x]_{IND'(B)}\cap X\neq\Phi\} \tag{10}$$

By computing $\underline{B}(C_k)$ and $\overline{B}(C_k)$ $(1\leq k\leq r(d))$, certain and possible rules can be induced respectively. Also, the member value μ_B can be viewed as the rule's efficiency measurement. This helps rule's selecting and sorting in knowledge reasoning. The generated rule set is usually redundant. Therefore, rule refinement must be made before use to ensure that the knowledge base is accurate and effective. The rule refinement criterions are listed as follows:

If the attribute description of one rule is more specific and given measure is also lower than that of another, this rule can be removed from the rule set.

If the measurement of one rule is below some given threshold value, it should be removed from the rule set.

For each rule, if one condition attribute is removed and collision occurs in rule set, then this attribute should be removed.

2.4 Detailed Steps of Knowledge Discovery

Based on the above theory, the detailed steps of knowledge discovery from the simulation data in collaborative design are summarized as following:

Step 1. According to the domain knowledge, decide the center point for fuzzy partition. Adopt a fuzzy member function to transform the quantitative value into several linguistic term descriptions.

Step 2. Compute the decision class C_k through decision attribute subset d.

Step 3. For any condition attribute subset $B\in\rho(A)$, compute the fuzzy equivalence class $IND'(B)$.

Step 4. For each decision class C_k, compute $\underline{B}(C_k)$ and $\overline{B}(C_k)$ respectively, and insert them into certain object set and uncertain object set respectively.

Step 5. Repeat step 3, 4 until all condition attribute subsets and all decision classes have been calculated.

Step 6. The certain rules are induced from certain object sets and the uncertain rules can be induced from uncertain object set. Calculate each rule's support degree, accuracy and efficiency measurement.

Step 7. Reduce the rule sets, and then add rules into fuzzy rule knowledge base.

3 Collaborative Design Optimization

After rule sets is obtained by knowledge discovery, collaborative design optimization process is implemented. In the model for collaborative design optimization, knowledge discovery-based rule sets is expressed as interval boxes, which are adopted to describe the uncertainty of design parameters quantitatively to enhance the design robustness. The model for collaborative design optimization based on knowledge discovery is formulated as:

$$\min : \boldsymbol{f}(\boldsymbol{x})$$
$$\text{s.t.}\begin{cases} \boldsymbol{g}(\boldsymbol{x}) = 0 & \boldsymbol{g} = \left[g_1, g_2, \ldots, g_p\right]^{\mathrm{T}} \\ \boldsymbol{h}(\boldsymbol{x}) \le 0 & \boldsymbol{h} = \left[h_1, h_2, \ldots, h_q\right]^{\mathrm{T}} \\ \boldsymbol{x} \in \left[\boldsymbol{x}^{\mathrm{L}}, \boldsymbol{x}^{\mathrm{U}}\right] \end{cases} \tag{11}$$

where f is design functions. $\boldsymbol{g}(\boldsymbol{x})$ and $\boldsymbol{h}(\boldsymbol{x})$ are equation and inequation constraints in the collaborative optimization model, $[x^{L}, x^{U}]$ are consistent intervals, which are derived from rule sets in the knowledge discovery process.

We regard the model as the multiobjective optimization problem, which is different from that of single-objective optimization. In single-objective optimization, the goal is to find the best solution, which corresponds to the minimum or maximum value of the objective function. In multiobjective optimization with conflicting objectives, there is no single optimal solution. The interaction among different objectives gives rise to a set of compromised solutions, largely known as the Pareto-optimal (or trade-off, nondominated, or noninferior) solutions.

Each solution of the Pareto optimal set is not dominated by any other solution. In going from one solution to another, it is not possible to improve on one objective (for example, reduction of the assembly stackup) without making at least one of the other objectives worse (for example, failure to minimize manufacturing cost).

In this paper, we solve the parameter and tolerance design problem by multiobjective genetic arithmetic, which is essentially a modification and extension of the single objective GA. The algorithm initiates in the same way as in a conventional GA, with the generation of an initial population. For the initial population, the non-inferior points or individuals are identified. If these individuals are non-inferior and feasible for the current population, then they are given the highest rank in the population. These non-inferior individuals become parents and are set to produce offspring, and then the process is repeated.

A step-by-step approach for implementing multiobjective genetic arithmetic is given below.

Step 1. Initialize population.

Each variable in the problem is represented by a binary string. All Strings are then concatenated to form an individual. An initial population of individuals is randomly generated.

Step 2. Evaluate objectives & constraints and calculate fitness.

Fitness expresses an individual's performance by taking both the objectives and constraints in account. Each individual is a binary representation of a particular design. The fitness assignment has two stages. In the first stage, only the design objectives in the optimization problem are considered and all constraints are ignored.

Dominant values of all individuals are calculated. In the second stage, the dominant value calculated from the first stage is taken as a new objective, and the constraints violation is taken as the other objective. Dominant values of all individuals are calculated in this objective-constraint space again. Each individual is ranked based on its new dominant value. Comparing with the conventional penalty based constraint-handling techniques; this Pareto ranking method gives more infeasible solutions higher chances to produce offspring. As such, there is a higher risk that the offspring generated are infeasible. Two strategies are used to bias individuals towards feasibility so that the risk of generating too many infeasible solutions can be reduced. The first strategy is that in the case where there are too few feasible solutions in a population, the rankings of some infeasible solutions with a less constraint violation may be adjusted so that solutions that are closer to the feasible domain will have higher chances to produce offspring. The second strategy is to modify rankings based on constraint violations for those individuals with the same newly found dominant value. In this case, those individuals with a smaller amount of constraint violation are preferred over those with a larger mount of constraint violation. Fitness can then be computed based on the ranks of all individuals.

Step 3. Select, crossover and mutate.

Before the parents are selected to produce offspring, the population is filtered by deleting some individuals from each niche. The number of individuals being deleted depends on how crowded or how dense the niche is. The selected parents are then tested for relative locations as part of the mating restriction. This is to prevent close parents from mating and hence to get a more even spread and uniform sampling of the Pareto set. One way to implement this would be to compute the distance (L_2 norm) between the two parents selected for reproduction by:

$$L_{ij} = \sqrt{\sum_{k=1}^{s}(f_k(x_i) - f_k(x_j))^2} \tag{12}$$

where x_i and x_j are two solutions, s is the number of objective functions. If this distance is found to be less than some limiting distance, the parents shall not be allowed to mate. The limiting distance would depend on how dense the niches are and what the range of the population is. The selection process is carried out until a sufficient number of parents have been selected to produce offspring.

Then, the selected individuals are crossed-over and mutated to produce the next generation. That is, each individual exchanges a segment of its binary string to create two new individuals. The mutation operation can occur with crossover or independent of it. This is a simple operation where the bits of an individual are randomly chosen to mutate or change. After crossover and mutation occur the next generation is formed.

Step 4. Obtain optimization solutions.

Steps 2 through 3 are repeated until the decision maker pauses the algorithm in order to impose/review constraints on the objectives or until the stopping criterion has been satisfied. The stopping criterion is illustrated as follows:

For each individual in the non-inferior set, the L_2 distance from a desired target point is computed. Hence, for each generation, one set of L_2 metrics is obtained. The mean and standard deviation of these L_2 norms are calculated. If the improvement in the mean is less than some small number, multiobjective GA is assumed to have converged and stopped.

4 Example

The following is an example to illustrate how to optimize the parameter of piston-connecting mechanism of automotive engine based on knowledge discovery. The flowchart of knowledge discovery and collaborative design optimization is shown in Fig. 1.

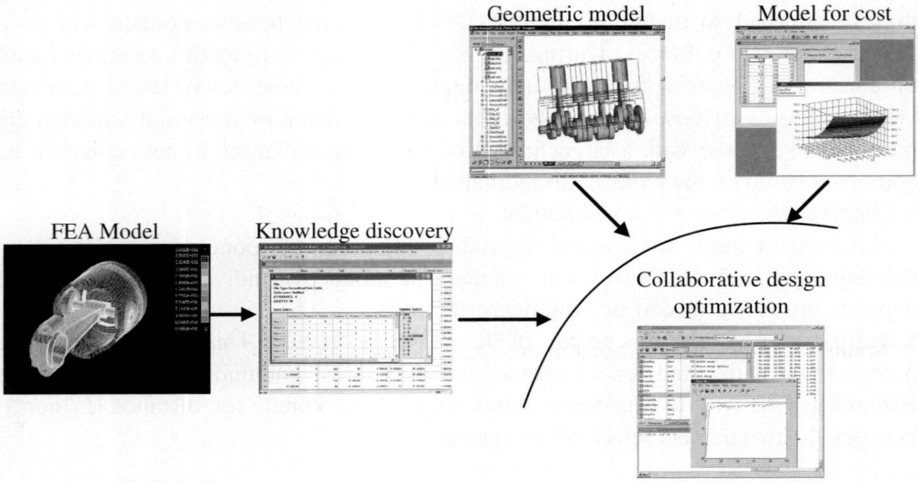

Fig. 1. The flowchart of knowledge discovery and collaborative design optimization

The step of knowledge discovery and collaborative design optimization is shown as follows.

Step 1. Knowledge discovery.

A fuzzy-rough algorithm is adopted as data mining method to meet the requirements of collaborative design optimization based on knowledge discovery, which integrates fuzzy set theory with rough set theory for acquiring explicit knowledge. It can deal with continuous data in simulation results and does not depend much on prior knowledge. Rules are extracted by fuzzy-rough set algorithm, and each rule is divided into several intervals. Finally, the consistency intervals in this example are as follows.

$x_1 \in [84,87]$, $x_2 \in [92,96]$, $x_3 \in [18,21]$, $x_4 \in [18,21]$, $x_5 \in [83,86]$, $x_6 \in [18,21]$, $x_7 \in [48,52]$, $x_8 \in [36,40]$, $x_9 \in [150,154]$, $t_1 \in [0.005,0.035]$, $t_2 \in [0.004,0.009]$, $t_3 \in [0.002,0.007]$, $t_4 \in [0.010,0.030]$, $t_5 \in [0.005,0.030]$, $t_6 \in [0.010,0.300]$.

Step 2. Collaborative design optimization.

1) Constraints and functions.

For assembly functional requirement, nominal parameters can constitute a set of equations called parameter constraints as follows.

$$\begin{cases} g_1 = x_4 - x_3 = 0.01 \\ g_2 = x_6 - x_4 = 0.03 \end{cases} \tag{13}$$

From the point of view of manufacturing process, the variations of parameter can constitute a set of equations called variation functions as follows.

$$\begin{cases} f_{S1} = \left\{[v_2 + (x_5 - x_8)\cdot\gamma_2]^2 + [v_3 + (x_5 - x_8)\cdot\gamma_3]^2\right\}^{1/2} \\ f_{S2} = \left\{[w_2 - (x_5 - x_8)\cdot\beta_2]^2 + [w_3 - (x_5 - x_8)\cdot\beta_3]^2\right\}^{1/2} \\ \ldots\ldots \end{cases} \tag{14}$$

Tolerance constraints in this example are as follows.

$$\begin{cases} h_1 = (u_1 + x_2\cdot\beta_1)^2 + (v_1 + x_2\cdot\alpha_1)^2 - (t_1/2)^2 \le 0 \\ h_2 = [v_2 + (x_5 - x_8)\cdot\gamma_2]^2 + [w_2 + (x_5 - x_8)\cdot\beta_2]^2 - (t_2/2)^2 \le 0 \\ \ldots\ldots \\ h_6 = (v_6)^2 + (w_6)^2 - (t_6/2)^2 \le 0 \end{cases} \tag{15}$$

Manufacturing cost functions in this example are as follows.

$$\begin{cases} f_{C1} = 84.708\text{-}277.022\cdot t_1 + 0.0938\cdot x_1 \text{-} 0.00396\cdot x_2 + 163.566\cdot t_1^2 \\ \quad +0.00135\cdot x_1^2 + 0.000507\cdot x_2^2 + 0.0262\cdot t_1\cdot x_1 + 0.0208\cdot t_1\cdot x_2 + 0.000245\cdot x_1\cdot x_2 \\ \quad +110.645\cdot t_1^3 \text{-} 5.874\cdot x_1^3 + 3.726\cdot x_2^3 \text{-} 0.000586\cdot t_1\cdot x_1\cdot x_2 \\ f_{C2} = 87.241\text{-}277.813\cdot t_2 + 0.0167\cdot x_3 + 0.0449\cdot(x_5\text{-}x_8) + 166.482\cdot t_2^2 + 0.0073\cdot x_3^2 \\ \quad \text{-}0.000845\cdot(x_5\text{-}x_8)^2 + 0.0498\cdot t_2\cdot x_3 + 0.0266\cdot t_2\cdot(x_5\text{-}x_8) + 0.000242\cdot x_3\cdot(x_5\text{-}x_8) \\ \quad +106.362\cdot t_2^3 \text{-} 8.238\cdot x_3^3 + 1.417\cdot(x_5\text{-}x_8)^3 \text{-} 0.00108\cdot t_2\cdot x_3\cdot(x_5\text{-}x_8) \\ \ldots\ldots \end{cases} \tag{16}$$

2) Optimization

Based on the above constraints and functions and the result of knowledge discovery, the collaborative design optimization model is established as follows.

$$\begin{cases} \min \; f_{S1}(\boldsymbol{x}), f_{S2}(\boldsymbol{x}), \ldots, f_{C1}(\boldsymbol{x}), \ldots, f_{C6}(\boldsymbol{x}) \\ s.t. \; \boldsymbol{g}(\boldsymbol{x}) = 0 \quad \boldsymbol{g}(\boldsymbol{x}) = [g_1(\boldsymbol{x}), g_2(\boldsymbol{x})]^{\mathrm{T}} \\ \quad\;\; \boldsymbol{h}(\boldsymbol{x}) \le 0 \quad \boldsymbol{h}(\boldsymbol{x}) = [h_1(\boldsymbol{x}), h_2(\boldsymbol{x}), \ldots, h_6(\boldsymbol{x})]^{\mathrm{T}} \\ \quad\;\; \boldsymbol{x} \in \left[\boldsymbol{x}^{\mathrm{L}}, \boldsymbol{x}^{\mathrm{U}}\right] \end{cases} \tag{17}$$

where $\boldsymbol{x} = (x_1, x_2, x_3, x_4, x_5, x_6, x_7, x_8, x_9, t_1, t_2, t_3, t_4, t_5, t_6)$, $f_{S1}(\boldsymbol{x})$, $f_{S2}(\boldsymbol{x})$ *et al.* are variation functions described by (14), $f_{C1}(\boldsymbol{x}),\ldots,f_{C6}(\boldsymbol{x})$ are manufacturing cost functions described by (16), g_1 and g_2 are parameter constraints described by (13), $h_1, h_1,\ldots,h_6$ are tolerance constraints described by (15), $[\boldsymbol{x}^L, \boldsymbol{x}^U]$ are consistency intervals.

Based on the method in Section 3, parameters and tolerances are optimized as follows.

x_1=85.9, x_2=95.3, x_3=19.99, x_4=20.0, x_5=84.2, x_6= 20.03, x_7=50.9, x_8=39.0, x_9=152.0, t_1=0.02, t_2=0.007, t_3=0.005, t_4=0.017, t_5=0.015, t_6=0.1.

5 Conclusions

An approach for collaborative design optimization based on knowledge discovery is presented in this paper. An algorithm, which integrates the fuzzy-set and the rough-set concepts, is proposed to adapt the simulation in the collaborative design. The knowledge discovery result is considered in the collaborative design optimization model, in which interval boxes are used to describe the uncertainties of parameters. The model is optimized by Genetic Algorithm to obtain the optimization solution. The proposed method has addressed the knowledge discovery and collaborative design optimization simultaneously to improve the robustness of collaborative design. A design example is analyzed to show the scheme to be effective.

Acknowledgments. This research is supported by the National Natural Science Foundation of China (No. 60304015 and 50575142) and the Shanghai Committee of Science and Technology (No. 055107048 and 04ZR14081).

References

1. Liau, J., Young R. E., O'Grady P.: An interactive constraint modeling system for concurrent engineering. Engineering Design and Automation, Vol.1, No.2 (1996) 105–119
2. Oh, J. S., O'Grady, P., Young, R. E.: An artificial intelligence constraint network approach to design for assembly. IIE Transactions, Vol.27, No.1 (1995) 72–80
3. Young, R. E., Greef, A., O'Grady, P.: An artificial intelligence-based constraint network system for concurrent engineering. International Journal of Production Research, Vol.30, No.7 (1992) 1715–1735
4. Fohn, S., Greef, A., Young, R. E., O'Grady, P.: A constraint-system shell to support concurrent engineering approaches to design. Artificial Intelligence in Engineering, Vol.9 (1994) 1–17
5. Liau J., Young R. E., O'Grady P.: Combining process planning and concurrent engineering to support printed circuit board assembly. Computers and Industrial Engineering, Vol.28, No.3 (1995) 615–629
6. Kong, S. H., Noh, S. D., Han, Y. G., Kim, G., Lee, K. I.: Internet-based collaboration system: Press-die design process for automobile manufacturer. International Journal of Advanced Manufacturing Technology, Vol.20, No.9 (2002) 701–708
7. Yin, G. F., Tian, G. Y., Taylor, D.: A web-based remote cooperative design for spatial cam mechanisms. International Journal of Advanced Manufacturing Technology, Vol.20, No.8, (2002) 557–563

8. Wang, Y.D., Shen, W.M., Ghenniwa, H.: A web/agent-based multidisciplinary design optimization environment. Computers in Industry, Vol.52, No.1 (2003) 17–28
9. Gantois, K., Morris, A.J.: The multi-disciplinary design of a large-scale civil aircraft wing taking account of manufacturing costs. Structural and Multidisciplinary Optimization, Vol.28, No.1 (2004) 31–46
10. .Giassi, A., Bennis, F., Maisonneuve, J.J.: Multidisciplinary design optimisation and robust design approaches applied to concurrent design. Structural and Multidisciplinary Optimization, Vol.28, No.5 (2004) 356–371
11. Bai, Y.W., Chen, Z.N., Bin, H.Z., Hu, J.: Collaborative design in product development based on product layout model. Robotics and Computer-Integrated Manufacturing, Vol.21, No.1 (2005) 55–65
12. Fayyad, U., Piatetsky-Shapiro, G., Smyth, P., Uthurusamy, R.: Advances in Knowledge Discovery in Databases, MIT Press, Cambridge, Mass. (1996)
13. Braha, D.: Data Mining for Design and Manufacturing: Methods and Applications, Kluwer academic publishers (2001)
14. Robert, L.G.: Data Mining for Scientific and Engineering Applications, Kluwer Academic Publishers (2001)
15. Jiawei, H., Micheline, K.: Data Mining: Concepts and Techniques, Morgan Kaufmann Publishers (2001)
16. Fayyad, U., Irani, K.: Multi-interval discretization of continuous-valued attributes for classification learning. Proceedings of IJCAI-93, 13th International Joint Conference on Artificial Intelligence, Sidney, AU (1993) 1022–1027
17. Nguyen, S.H., Nguyen, H.S.: Some efficient algorithms for rough set methods. Proceedings of the Sixth International Conference, Information Processing and Management of Uncertainty in Knowledge-Based Systems (IPMU-96), Granada, Spain, July 1-5 (1996) 1451–1456
18. Zadeh, L.A.: Fuzzy Sets. Information and Control, Vol.8 (1965) 338–353
19. Pawlak, Z.: Rough Set Rudiments. Bulletin of the International Rough Set Society, Vol.3, No.4 (1999) 181–186

Behavioural Proximity Approach for Alarm Correlation in Telecommunication Networks

Jacques-H. Bellec and M-Tahar Kechadi

School of Computer Science & Informatics, University College Dublin, Belfield, Dublin 4, Ireland

Jacques.Bellec@ucd.ie, Tahar.Kechadi@ucd.ie

Abstract. In telecommunication networks, alarms are usually useful for identifying faults, and therefore solving them. However, for large systems the number of alarms produced is so large that the current management systems are overloaded. One way of overcoming this problem is to filter and reduce the number of alarms before the faults can be located. In this paper, we describe a new approach for fault recognition and classification in telecommunication networks. We study and evaluate its performance using real-world data collected from 3G telecommunication networks.

1 Introduction

Telecommunication networks are growing in size and complexity, and their management is becoming more complicated. Each network element can produce a large amount of alarms when a fault is detected. The telecommunication network management system is in charge of the recording of the alarms generated by the nodes in the network. Then it displays them to the network operator. However, due to the high volume and the fragmented nature of the information, it is impossible to quickly solve the faults. Moreover, somes changes in the network such as new equipments, updated software, and network load, mean that the alarms can be very different in nature [1].

More precisely, when a fault occurs, devices can send messages to describe the problem that has been detected. But they only have a local view of the error, and then cannot describe the fault, but just its consequences. Due to the complex nature of these networks, a single fault may produce a cascade of alarms from the affected network elements. In addition, a fault can trigger other faults, for instance in the case of overloading. Even though failures in large communication networks are unavoidable, quick detection, identification of causes, and resolution of failures can make systems more robust, more reliable, and ultimately increase the level of confidence in the services that they provide [2,3].

Alarm correlation is a key functionality of a network management system that is used to determine the faults' origin, and to filter out redundant and spurious events. The alarm correlation systems generally combine causal and temporal correlation models with the network topology. The power and robustness of the models used and the algorithms developed vary from system to system. However, due to the absence of any simple, uniform, and precise presentation of the alarm-correlation problem, it is impossible to compare their relative power, or even to analyze them for their properties.

A. Gelbukh and C.A. Reyes-Garcia (Eds.): MICAI 2006, LNAI 4293, pp. 674–683, 2006.

In general, data mining techniques are adapted towards the analysis of unordered collections of data, as it finds the redundant data sequences. Generally, to analyse such a sequence, the most frequent episodes of data must be found. Unfortunately the domain of telecommunication networks is very different from the usual ones, as they have a particular behaviour compared to other data sets.

In this paper we focus on the Behavioural Proximity technique (BP). The main objective of this approach is to reduce considerably the number of alarms by clustering them according to their behaviour, to form events. Then these events are correlated to form clusters via the Event Duration Matching (EDM) algorithm. As a result, only crucial seeds of global events are presented to the network operator [4,5].

2 Background

In the past, network fault management were performed by human experts. The size and complexity of today's networks, however, have made the levels of human intervention required to perform this function prohibitively high. Currently, many systems employ event correlation engines to address this issue [6,7]. The problem of an automatic identification of events for correlation has been tackled from various perspectives. Model traversal approaches aim to represent the interrelations between the components of the network, [8] or the causal relations between the possible events in the network [9], or a combination of the two [10]. Correlations are identified as alarms that propagate through the model. Rule-based [11] and code-based [12] systems also model the relations between the events in the system, specifying the correlations according to a rule-set or codebook. Other techniques, such as neural networks [3,13] or decision trees, have also been applied to the task. These approaches vary in the level of expert knowledge required to train the system. Neural networks, for example, can require no expert input whereas model-based techniques may be fully reliant on the insights of human experts. The domain of sequential data mining addresses the specific problem of identifying relationships or correlations between events in a raw dataset, which is inherently sequential in nature, such as fault data consisting of a series of time stamped events. Mining sequential patterns can be viewed as a subset of the problem of mining associations between dataset elements in general, constrained by the temporal aspects of the data. But to deal with this, the temporal aspect is not the only one that we have to consider. In fact, the particular nature of telecommunication networks gives some strong relationships between alarms behaviour that we cannot find in other kind of data sets.

3 The Behavioural Proximity (BP) Technique

3.1 Faults, Alarms, Events and Clusters

This section presents a formal model for the BP technique. Given a set of alarms (dataset), the problem is to present to the operator only a few number of alarms that are highly considered to be the cause of root faults. Before presenting the technique, we need to define the following notions: faults, events, and clusters.

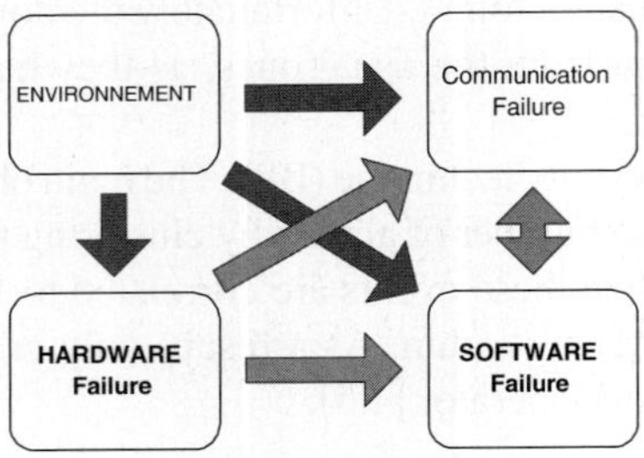

Fig. 1. Faults in telecommunication networks

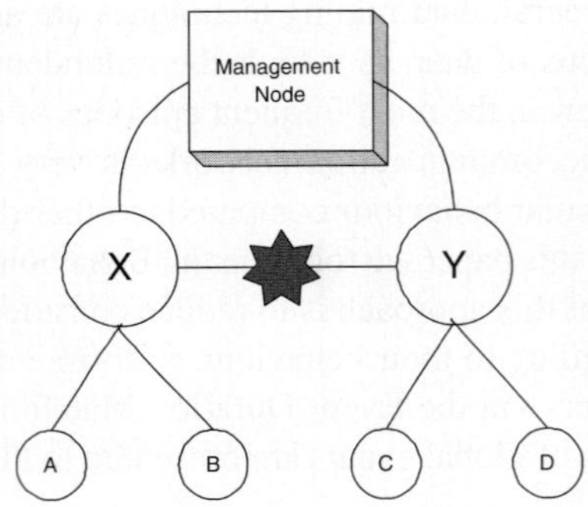

Fig. 2. A basic fault scenario

Faults. A fault is a disorder occurring in the hardware or software of the network [14]. Faults happen within the network components, and alarms are external manifestations of faults. Faults can be classified into four categories : hardware, software, telecommunication, and environment.

Figure 1 shows the four major factors of the causes of the faults. The environment cause can be a too high temperature or a wet condition in the network equipment room. The environment cause can lead to software, hardware, or communication failures, due to a cascade of failures or directly to one of these failures. We cannot take into account the alarms concerning the environment conditions, because it may not lead to a failure, but just to an indication about a possible failure.

Hardware failures are the most crucial, because they will automatically trigger other faults. Therefore, the alarms describing hardware faults are the most important because they give direct information about the fault, and are highly rated by the networks operator. Software failures can lead to some communication failures but cannot interfere with the environment or on the hardware part. They are important only if there are no hardware failures before their appearance. Finally the communication failures are important only if there is no hardware and software failure before. It is fundamental to keep in mind this ranking because our event correlation process is based on it.

We call F_S the total set of faults which can occur in a network, and F_i a particular fault.

Alarms. Alarms defined by vendors and generated by network equipment are messages observable by network operators. An alarm is the notification of a fault and may also be used in other areas to give information about a particular behaviour of the system. There may be many alarms generated for a single fault. All the alarms are logged into a centralized management system, in text format files.

For instance, In a basic scenario shown in Figure 2, there is a broken link between nodes X and Y. The alarms are generated when$A$ and C try to communicate. A knows that something is wrong since it cannot communicate with C, so it generates an alarm and sends it to the manager. In the same way, C cannot send a message to B, and it sends an alarm too; X and Y cannot pass on the messages they received from A and C respectively, and generate alarms. For example, X may send two types of alarms; one for the connection failure, and one for a dropped packet. Therefore, alarm correlation is necessary to sort out the events from the symptoms. In other words, to find the fault from the generated alarms.

According to the information architecture in telecommunication networks, an alarm can be thought of as an object. The attributes of the alarm try to describe the event that triggered it. This is a possible set of alarm attributes:

- Event timestamp: gives the time the alarm was issued
- Logged time: gives the time the alarm was recorded
- Perceived severity: gives a state ranging from critical to indeterminate
- Alarm ID: identifies the alarm by a unique serial number
- Alarm Key: it is the key composed by all alarm attributes but the ones related to the time
- Node ID: identifies the node in the subnetwork
- Event Type: gives some indications of the nature of what happened
- Probable Cause: gives some indication of why it happened
- Specific Problem: clarifies what happened

We call A the set of all possible alarms and a_k the kth alarm in the dataset corresponding to a specific period. Each alarm can be defined by a set of static parameters noted $Attr_Stat(a_i)$ and by a set of parameters related to the time noted $Attr_Time(a_i)$. In other words, $a_i = Attr_Stat(a_i) + Attr_Time(a_i)$. Each kind of alarm is identified by a key calculated by the function $Hash(Attr_Stat(a_i))$. We define identical alarms if they have the same static content with different timestamps and logged times. Namely, a_i is identical to $a_{i'}$ only if $Attr_Stat(a_i)$is equals to $Attr_Stat(a_{i'})$. From a raw data set, we can gather the alarms with the same static attributes, (i.e.; with the same key) and calculate the exact number of different kinds of alarms.

Events. An event is a set of identical correlated alarms. Let E be the set of all possible events and e_i an event of E. The event recognition is the first part of the recognition process implemented in the BP technique. The Alarm Behavioural Recognition (ABR) algorithm takes care of the event recognition as shown in Figure 4. Here is a possible set of event attributes:

- Event ID : it gives the unique ID of the event
- Start Time: gives the minimum apparition time of all embedded alarms in the event
- End Time: gives the maximum apparition time of all embedded alarms in the event
- Score: gives a score calculated according to the relevance of the attributes of the alarms
- Gravity : it is the average time of apparition of the alarms
- Event Key: the key composed by all alarm keys
- Code Type: identifies the nature of the event (Primary, secondary or tertiary)
- Nb Alarms : number of embedded alarms

Clusters. We call "cluster" a set of correlated events. In other words, it is what our technique produces and presents to the network operator. The number of clusters is not predefined, but must be significantly low compared to the number of raw input alarms.

Basically, the number of clusters returned by the BP technique represents the number of faults that should be solved by the operator.

This is a possible set of cluster attributes:

- Cluster ID : it gives the unique ID of the event
- Start Time: gives the minimum apparition time of all embedded alarms in the event
- End Time : gives the maximum apparition time of all embedded alarms in the even
- Total Score: gives a total score calculated according to the sum of all events scores which composed the cluster.
- Gravity : it is the average time of apparition of the alarms
- Event Root: the root event
- List of Events : the list of all events
- Nb Alarms : number of embedded alarms

3.2 Data Preprocessing

The data preparation phase as shown on Figure 3, consists in cleaning the data by removing the inconsistent, incomplete and non-important alarms. Indeed, noise analysis and filtering are necessary to analyse only meaningful data and get tangible results. The stamping part identifies each alarm by a unique ID and by a Hash key. The hash key is common to all the alarms with the same static attributes, so we can identify different families of alarms. So, from here an alarm a_i is defined by its ID noted ID_{a_i} and its Key $Key_{a_i} = KeyHash(Attr_{Stat}(a_i))$. The preprocessing phase gathers alarms topologically to be able to distribute the payload. The BP technique takes advantage of the distributed nature of the data to distribute the processing load among different processing nodes.

3.3 Alarm Correlation with ABR

Alarm correlation aims to pinpoint the triggering homogeneous events from the incoming alarms. It takes place after the data preparation and is the main part of the data analysis process, as shown in Figure 4. The output of this process is the creation of events which embed identical alarms.

The main idea of the Alarm Behavioural Recognition algorithm (ABR) is to correlate alarms according to their nature and their behaviour. We already defined the nature of an alarm a_i, which can be noted Key_{a_i}. We call the $Behaviour$ of an alarm the fact that there is only one occurrence or multiple occurrences of itself - in the last case only if we can determine a periodicity among them. We define the function $Occ(Key(a_i))$ which gives the number of occurrence of this key, namely the number of identical alarms which have the same attributes values. We can gather these alarms and get two kinds of events: events composed by one unique alarm and events composed by multiple alarms.

The last category can be split into three sub categories: twin, periodic and aperiodic alarms. Twins are those which are just composed by two identical alarms, so we cannot define a period among them. Periodic alarms are those which have been triggered periodically until the problem has been solved or until a maximum number of occurences has been reached. The periodic alarm behaviour interpreted in [4] is very useful for the fault recognition process because it gives some information about the fault, like its

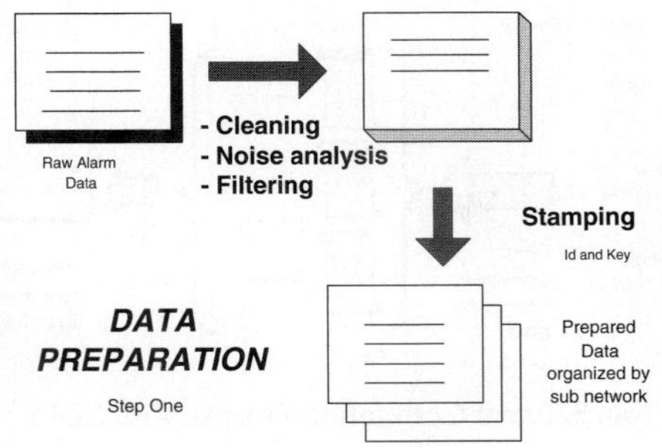

Fig. 3. Data Preparation Process

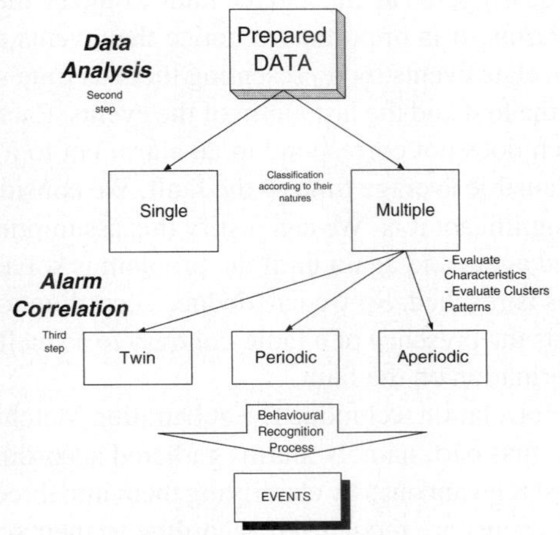

Fig. 4. Alarm Correlation Process via ABR

duration. We assume that when a fault occurs, some alarms are triggered periodically until the fault is resolved. This is the most usual policy used for triggering the alarms. The value of the period depends on the devices, components, or probes responsible for these alarms. From here, we only consider the events. In other words, we do not consider punctual elements but elements with a duration, like segments of data, even if the duration can be equal to one as for single alarms. Finally, aperiodic alarms mean that there is not a specific period among those sets of alarms. The Score-Matching (SM) algorithm introduced in [5] identifies overlapped events and determines the periodicity of those alarms. The SM output gives some periodic, twin and single sets of events.

3.4 Event Correlation

The first part of our process was data preparation and data analysis, detailed in Figure 3. After the identification of the events, we are able to define some rules to correlate them. The trade off between the amount of the available information and the fault distinguishing ability (alarm correlation ability) is made clear if we assume that two independent

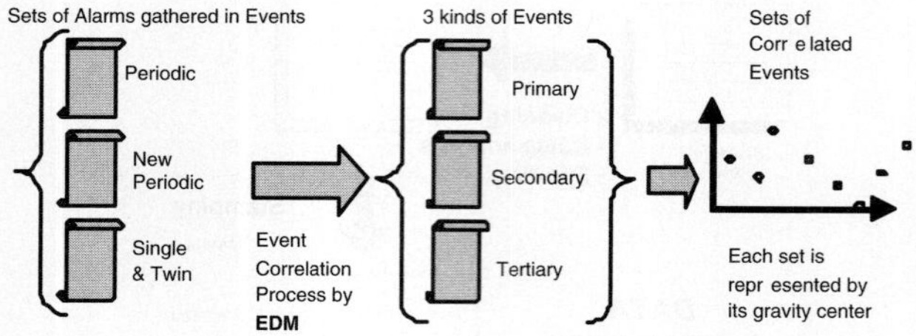

Fig. 5. Event Correlation Process with EDM

faults can not happen at the same location, and at the same time. In fact if we miss one overlapped fault in our recognition process, that does not matter because the fault would remain, alarms would be triggered again, and the fault would be identified. We deal with events and not with alarms. It is important to notice that events are composed of correlated alarms. We correlate events by representing them as time segments, namely the time elapsed between the first and the last alarm of the events. Each segment (event) has a centre of mass, which does not correspond to an alarm but to a mark making it possible to identify the plausible average time of the fault. We consider that the longer the segment is, the more significant it is. We can justify this assumption by the fact that the same alarm is triggered again and again until the problem is solved or until a specified number of occurrences is reached. So we can deduce according to the behaviour that a long segment represents the presence of a fault, contrary to a small segment which does not give sufficient information on the fault.

Figure 5 shows our correlation technique Event Duration Matching (EDM). From the events identified in the first part, namely alarms gathered according to their behaviour, EDM identifies the most relevant ones by classifying them into three categories. Primary, secondary and tertiary events are recognized according to their scores and their ranks. The scoring process uses different fields embedded in the alarms representing the events. These fields are severity, node type, notification type, alarm type code, probable cause, specific problem, event length and the number of alarms, which compose the events.

We assume that an important event would be composed of a large number of alarms triggered at a time. Meaningful events are gathered in primary sets, and less meaningful events in secondary sets, and others in tertiary sets, as shown in Figure 5.

The distinction between events is crucial because each primary event will be interpreted as a meaningful event and then used as a root for other less important events. As we can notice in Figure 6, in the EDM technique the number of clusters depends directly on the number of primary events identified by the user-defined accuracy rate. The way to evaluate the correlation between two events uses a fuzzy logic approach, with the time distance and the topographical distance. The best link between one primary and one non-primary event is selected according to the best correlation score.

4 Experimentation Results

Figure 6 and Figure 7 show experimental results of the BP technique with four subnetworks examined during 72 hours, with different classification rates. The aim of these

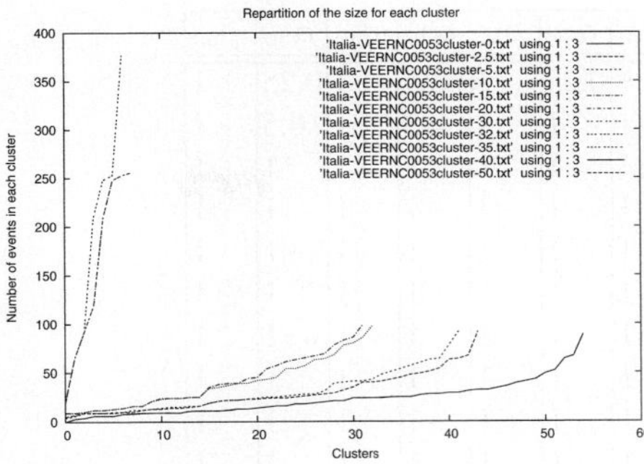

Fig. 6. Size and Number of clusters obtained by BP using different support thresholds from 0 to 50

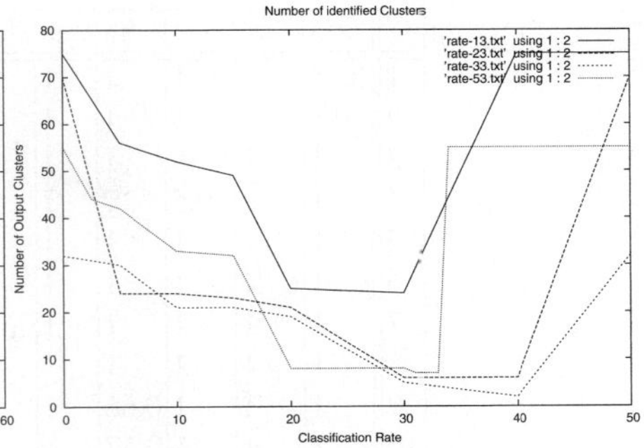

Fig. 7. Number of patterns found according to the user-defined thresholds

results is to show approximately what should be a good discrimination rate. It appears that we have a big reduction of the number of identified clusters with rates between 15% and 40%, which can be explained by the fact that there is not a huge number of highly scored events in these different data sets. This shows that the scoring function is very efficient. With a rate between 30% and 40%, we have a very small number of identified clusters for each subnetwork. Instead of having no cluster after a certain rate, namely zero primary events, we chose to upgrade secondary events to primary and tertiary to secondary. Thus, we have the same number of identified clusters with a rate equals to zero and a rate equals to the break point. Each break point depends of the data set and can be defined by the maximum discrimination rate that gets at least one identified cluster. This is shown in Figure 7 and it is between 30% and 40% for these subnetworks. The BP performance plateau is between 20% and 30%.

The data set used in this experimentation contains 6000 alarms in this particular subnetwork. With the BP technique, 1272 events were identified, and 33 clusters of events were formed with a discrimination rate equal to 10. This means that from 6000 (uncorrelated) potential events, 33 meaningful events were obtained. This represents 0.55% in this data set and around 1% in average on different subnetworks of this sample.

Table 8 shows the performance evaluation of our technique with synthetic data inserted in the raw log files. Synthetic data is composed by four types of alarms, A, B, C, D, each one having real values for its attributes provided by a network operator who identified this sequence. Each kind A, B, C, D is repeated n times periodically in m places randomly chosen (in different network nodes) for 72 hours.

$$Nb_E = Nb_D * Nb_T * Nb_P \text{ and } Nb_C = Nb_D * Nb_P * Nb_S \quad (1)$$

We defined two formulas about the number of events and alarms expected at the end of the process in 1. Inserting synthetic data is the only way to evaluate the technique without the checking of a network operator. By this way, we can predict easily what should be the good result and then compare to our technique. On table 8, we used in input $3days, 4types, 4places, 10alarmspertype$, random values for the sequence apparition time. 480 alarms were inserted among 41243 alarms. It means that we should

C	α_0	β_0	α_{10}	β_{10}	α_{20}	β_{20}	α_{30}	β_{30}	α_{40}	β_{40}	α_{50}	β_{50}
1	0.25	1	0.25	1	1	1	0.25	1	0.25	1	0.25	1
2	0.5	1	0.25	1	1	1	1	1	0.5	1	0.5	1
3	1	1	0.25	1	1	1	1	1	1	1	1	1
4	1	1	0.5	1	1	1	1	1	1	1	1	1
5	1	1	1	1	1	1	1	1	1	1	1	1
6	1	1	1	1	1	1	1	1	1	1	1	1
7	1	1	1	1	1	1	1	1	1	1	1	1
8	1	1	1	1	1	1	1	1	1	1	1	1
9	1	1	1	0.66	1	1	1	1	1	1	1	1
10	1	1	1	0.57	1	1	1	1	1	1	1	1
11	1	0.66	1	0.57	1	1	1	1	1	1	1	0.66
12	1	0.57	1	0.57	1	1	1	0.57	1	0.57	1	0.57

Fig. 8. Performance analysis of the BP technique

get 48 synthetic events, 12 clusters and 4 events per clusters corresponding to our sequence A, B, C, D. To evaluate our technique we used standard performance metrics. The performance of data mining systems is generally characterised in ters of two trade-off mesures. These are recall and precision. Recall is the percentage of relevant sequences retreived out of all those that are actually relevant; precision is the percentage of relevant sequences retrieved out of all those retreived by the algorithm. We callα_r the recall with the discrimination rate r, and β_r the precison with the discrimination rate r.

Figure 8 shows the peformance of the BP technique, with different user-defined rates from 0 to 50, and the corresponding recall and precision values. The number of identified clusters does not change from one rate to another but is not specified in input of our algorithm. The BP technique recognizes the good number of clusters indenpendently from the user-defined descrimination rate. These results show good performances in average with a recall from 25% to 100% and a precision from 57% to 100% efficiency with the rate of 20.

5 Conclusion

The main contribution of this paper is the proposition of a new fault recognition technique which satisfies the network opertor's needs. It provides the main roots of faults which appeared in the network in the form of clusters. This technique has been evaluted with real data sets and shows some valuable results. For further improvement, we are now integrating some training skills to this technique with the use of fuzzy logic reasoning.

References

1. Himberg, J., Korpiaho, K., Mannila, H., Tikanmaki, J., Toivonen, H.: Time series segmentation for context recognition in mobile devices. In: Proc. of the IEEE International Conference on Data Mining, San Jose, California, USA (2001) 203–210

2. Bouloutas, A., Galo, S., Finkel, A.: Alarm correlation and fault identification in communication networks. IEEE Trans. on Communications **4**(2/3/4) (1994) 523–533
3. Gardner, R., Harle, D.: Alarm correlation and network fault resolution using kohonen self-organising map. In: IEEE Global Telecom. Conf. Volume 3., New York, NY, USA (1997) 1398–1402
4. Bellec, J.H., Kechadi, M.T., Carthy, J.: Study of telecommunication system behavior based on network alarms. In: Workshop on Data Mining for Business, Porto, Portugal (2005)
5. Bellec, J.H., Kechadi, M.T., J.Carthy: A new efficient clustering algorithm for network alarm analysis. In: The 17th IASTED Int'l. Conference on Software Engineering and Applications (SEA'05), Phoenix, AZ, USA (2005)
6. Yamanishi, K., Maruyama, Y.: Dynamic syslog mining for network failure monitoring. In: KDD '05: Proceeding of the eleventh ACM SIGKDD international conference on Knowledge discovery in data mining, New York, NY, USA, ACM Press (2005) 499–508
7. Julisch, K.: Clustering intrusion detection alarms to support root cause analysis. ACM Trans. Inf. Syst. Secur. **6**(4) (2003) 443–471
8. Meira, D., Nogueira, J.: Modelling a telecommunication network for fault management applications. In: Proc. of NOMS'98. (1998) 723–732
9. Gopal, R.: Layered model for supporting fault isolation and recovery. In: IEEE/IFIP, Proc. of Network Operation and Management Symposium, Honolulu, Hawaii (2000)
10. Steinder, M., Sethi, A.: Non-deterministic diagnosis of end-to-end service failures in a multi-layer communication system. In: Proc. of ICCCN'01, Arizona (2001) 374–379
11. Liu, G., Mok, A., Yang, E.: Composite events for network event correlation. In: IM'99. (1999) 247–260
12. Yemini, S., Kliger, S., Mozes, E., Yemini, Y., Ohsie, D.: High speed and robust event correlation. IEEE Communications Magazine **34**(5) (1996) 82–90
13. Wietgrefe, H., Tuchs, K.D., Jobmann, K., Carls, G., Frohlich, P., Nejdl, W., Steinfeld, S.: Using neural networks for alarm correlation in cellular phone networks. Proc. of IWANNT (1997)
14. Gardner, R., Harle, D.: Methods and systems for alarm correlation. In: Proc. of Globecom'96, London, UK (1996) pp.136–140

The MineSP Operator for Mining Sequential Patterns in Inductive Databases

Edgard Benítez-Guerrero and Alma-Rosa Hernández-López

Laboratorio Nacional de Informática Avanzada, A. C.
Rebsamen No. 80, Col. Centro, CP 91000, Xalapa, México
ebenitez@lania.mx, ahl0012@lania.edu.mx

Abstract. This paper introduces MineSP, a relational-like operator to mine sequential patterns from databases. It also shows how an inductive query can be translated into a traditional query tree augmented with MineSP nodes. This query tree is then optimized, choosing the mining algorithm that best suits the constraints specified by the user and the execution environment conditions. The SPMiner prototype system supporting our approach is also presented.

1 Introduction

Data mining is the semi-automatic extraction of patterns from data. It has become an important tool in many application environments because it helps to make sense of large quantities of electronic information already stored in databases and other repositories. A number of techniques have been proposed to support complex mining of large data sets. One of these techniques is sequential pattern mining, where the objective of analyzing a database is to find sequences of events such that its statistical significance is greater than a user-specified threshold. For instance, in a bookstore database it is possible to find that 80% of the customers buy 'Digital Fortress', then 'Angels & Demons', and then 'The Da Vinci Code'. A number of algorithms to mine sequential patterns (such as Apriori [1], GSP [2], PrefixSpan [3] and others) have been proposed to date.

There exist a large number of tools developed for mining data. However they fail in supporting the data mining process adequately: analyzing data is a complicate job because there is no framework to manipulate data and patterns homogeneously. It has been recognized the need for such a framework to ease the development of data mining applications [4]. The Inductive Database approach [5] proposes to see data mining as advanced database interrogation and, in this context, query languages and associated evaluation and optimization techniques are being proposed.

In this sense, a query language for mining sequential patterns has been proposed in [6]. This language offers the user a gentle interface to GSP and provides tools to filter the resulting patterns. Some aspects of the evaluation of inductive queries written in this language have been tackled. Particularly, query optimization has been studied focusing on the materialization and reuse of results. These works are important because they introduce sequential pattern mining into the

A. Gelbukh and C.A. Reyes-Garcia (Eds.): MICAI 2006, LNAI 4293, pp. 684–694, 2006.

traditional framework for querying databases. However, two important aspects are not considered. First, evaluation of queries is done in an ad-hoc manner because formal foundations (similar to those of the relational algebra) to reason about the process are still missing. Second, while optimizing a query, it is assumed that the algorithm to be executed is GSP, while there are others that depending on the situation, are more appropriate.

In this paper we propose solutions to these problems. First, we propose to incorporate the MineSP (ψ) operator to mine sequential patterns into a modified version of the OR object-relational algebra proposed in [7]. The resulting set of operators is powerful enough to write expressions to manipulate data and sequential patterns in a same framework. Second, we contribute to the research on inductive query optimization by proposing a method to choose the algorithm to execute MineSP based on user-defined constraints and a description of the execution environment. To experiment this ideas, we have implemented the SP-Miner prototype system.

The paper is organized as follows: Section 2 discusses related work. Section 3 briefly describes the OR object-relational model and introduces the elements extending this model to represent sequential patterns. Section 4 summarizes the OR algebra and explains MineSP. Section 5 presents our solution to the problem of selecting a sequential pattern mining algorithm during query optimization. Section 6 describes the SPMiner prototype system. Section 7 finally concludes this paper.

2 Related Work

Sequential pattern mining has attracted the attention of the research community and of practitioners as well. In order to discuss relevant related work, it can be classified in algorithms, inductive query languages and evaluation techniques, optimization issues and formal foundations for inductive query processing.

An important number of algorithms to find sequential patterns from data sets has been proposed [1,2,8,9,10,3,11,12,13,14,15,16,17,18,19,20]. A usual categorization of these algorithms is based on the strategy of pattern search. One approach is to generate candidate sequences and, for each one, test its statistical significance (for instance, measuring its *support*, ie. the fraction of the sequences in the database containing a candidate sequence) in the full database. This is the approach taken by the Apriori algorithm [1] and its descendants. Another approach, adopted by PrefixSpan [3] and its family, is pattern-growth. The key idea is to avoid the generation of candidates and to focus the search in a restricted portion of the initial database, achieving this way a better performance that generate-and-test algorithms. There exists however proposals to improve the performance of Apriori by reducing the number of candidates (GSP [2]) or parallelizing its execution [8].

There is a growing interest for mining a broad class of sequential patterns. Now it is possible to find proposals (GSP [2]) exploiting the presence of a taxonomy associated to base data to mine general patterns. Time-related constraints are also being considered (GSP [2], Generalized PrefixSpan [21]). Among them we find the minimum and maximum gap constraints, that enable to specify the minimum or maximum time interval between the occurrences of two events inside a pattern, or the time window constraint, that enables to limit the maximum time between the first event and the last event of a pattern. Finally, user constraints (such that a particular event must or not appear in a pattern) are now being included in the search [12,22]. An important point to remark here is that after analyzing 15 algorithms to mine sequential patterns, we conclude that there is no 'one-size-fits-all' solution.

A number of data mining query languages and ad-hoc evaluation techniques have been proposed. These languages are usually extensions to the relational language SQL. For instance, the MINE RULE extension for mining association rules is introduced in [23]. For sequential pattern mining, the MineSQL language is presented in [6]. This SQL extension offers data types to represent sequences and patterns and functions to manipulate them. The MINE PATTERN statement has been proposed to specifically support the advanced features of GSP, such as considering the presence of a taxonomy associated to base data, slides windows, and time constraints, which can be optionally specified in a query. Our proposal for a query algebra formalizes several aspects of this work.

Optimization techniques for inductive queries have been also been proposed. [24] proposes techniques to optimize queries to mine association rules. The optimization of queries for mining sequential patterns is tackled in [25]. The authors propose a cost-based technique for optimizing MineSQL queries in presence of materialized results of previous queries. Our proposal, introduced in Sect. 5, is a complement to this work as we focus more on what an algorithm to mine sequential pattern offers than on physical aspects (disk space, for instance).

Finally, formal foundations for inductive query processing are scarce. In [23] the operational semantics of the MINE RULE expression is presented. For the case of sequential patterns, this kind of work is still missing. In Sect. 4 we explain our proposal to extend the OR algebra [7] with the MineSP operator to mine sequential patterns.

3 Data and Patterns Model

The basic components of the OR model are types [7]. An OR database schema consists of a set of row types $R_1, \ldots, R_m$, and each attribute in a row type is defined on a certain type, which can be a built-in type, an abstract data type (ADT), a collection type, a reference type or another row type. An object-relational database D on database scheme OR is a collection of row type instance sets (called OR tables) $ort_1, \ldots, ort_m$ such that for each OR table ort_i there is a corresponding row type RT_i, and each tuple of ort_i is an instance of the corresponding row type R_i.

Let us consider for instance a BOOKSTORE database (see Fig. 1). The SALES table stores the purchases of books. Its row type is composed by the identifier (C_id) of the customer who did the purchase, the date of the purchase

SALES

C_id	Date	Books
C1	10/Feb/03	{I0}
C1	01/Oct/05	{I4}
C1	02/Oct/05	{I1}
C1	15/Oct/05	{I3,I5}
C2	01/Oct/05	{I1,I4}
C2	20/Oct/05	{I2}
C2	30/Oct/05	{I5}
C3	01/Oct/05	{I8}
C3	10/Oct/05	{I6,I7}
C3	30/Oct/05	{I9}
C4	05/Oct/03	{I8}
C4	25/Oct/05	{I9}

BOOKS

B_id	Title	Author
I0	1984	Orwell
I1	Holy Blood, Holy Grail	Baigent
I2	Foundation	Asimov
I3	I, robot	Asimov
I4	Angels & Demons	Brown
I5	The Da Vinci Code	Brown
I6	Digital Fortress	Brown
I7	Harry Potter and the Sorcerer's Stone	Rowling
I8	Harry Potter and the prisoner of Azkaban	Rowling
I9	Harry Potter and the Goblet of Fire	Rowling

Fig. 1. The BOOKSTORE database

(Date) and the books that he/she bought (a set of book identifiers). The BOOKS table describes each book in detail. Its row type is composed by a book identifier (B_id), the title of the book (Title), and the author's name (Author).

Using this model, we define the ITEMSET, SEQUENCE and the PATTERN abstract data types to represent the data and pattern elements manipulated during sequential pattern mining. The definition of each ADT is as follows:

- `ITEMSET ( create: Func(boolean, set(ITEM), Timestamp), Itemset: Func(set(ITEM)), TimeStamp: Func (Timestamp))`
- `SEQUENCE ( create: Func(boolean, list(ITEMSET)), contains: Func(boolean, SEQUENCE), Sequence: Func(list(ITEMSET)), Support: Func(Float))`
- `PATTERN ( create: Func(boolean, SEQUENCE), SeqPattern: Func(list(set(ITEM))), Support:Func(FLOAT))`

An ITEMSET is a non-empty set of values called ITEMs which has a timestamp associated. The create function is a constructor that takes as input a set of ITEMs (values of any type) and a timestamp and returns a boolean value indicating the success/failure of the creation of the ITEMSET. It is possible to access its components through the Itemset() and TimeStamp() functions. An example of a value of this type is <15/Oct/05,{I3,I5}>.

A SEQUENCE is a list of itemsets ordered chronologically by their timestamps. The create function takes as input a list of ITEMSETs and returns a boolean value indicating the success or the failure of the creation of the SEQUENCE. The contains function indicates true if another sequence is contained in the current. The list [<02/Oct/05,{I1}>, <15/Oct/05,{I3,I5}>] is an example of value of this type. A frequent sequence is also called a sequential pattern. Because specific timestamps are not needed in a pattern, a PATTERN is defined as a list of set of ITEMs which has a support associated. An example of a pattern is the value <[{I1},{I5}],0.5>.

4 The MineSP Operator

Expressions in the OR algebra consist of OR operands and OR operators. An OR operand is either an OR table, a row type path expression or the result of another operation. In this section, we simply use the term "table" to refer to all the possible operands, as long as no distinction is necessary. The set of OR operators consists of the object-relational counterparts of basic relational operators – select (σ), join ($\bowtie$), Cartesian product($\times$), project (π) –, set operators – union ($\cup$), difference ($-$), intersection ($\cap$)), nest (ν), unnest (υ)–, and special operators to handle row type object identity – map(ϕ) and cap(δ) –. To the original operator set, we incorporate the operators group-by (F) and rename (ρ).

To this algebra we add the MineSP operator (ψ) to mine sequential patterns. The input of ψ is a table where one attribute is of the `SEQUENCE` datatype. The output is a table with one attribute Pattern of type `PATTERN`. It is possible to provide a set of parameters to ψ, such as minimum support, slide window, mingap, and maxgap to biased the pattern search. It is also possible to indicate if a taxonomy is available. More formally, the expression:

$$_{\mathtt{minsup,taxonomy,mingap,maxgap,window}}\psi_{\mathtt{sattr}}(\mathrm{R})$$

represents the application of operator ψ taking as input relation R with attribute *sattr* and parameters *minsup*, *taxonomy*, *mingap*, *maxgap*, *window*. The result is a relation R' such that its schema is $[Pattern]$ and each tuple t of R' is defined as $t[Pattern] = p$ for each pattern p satisfying the parameters.

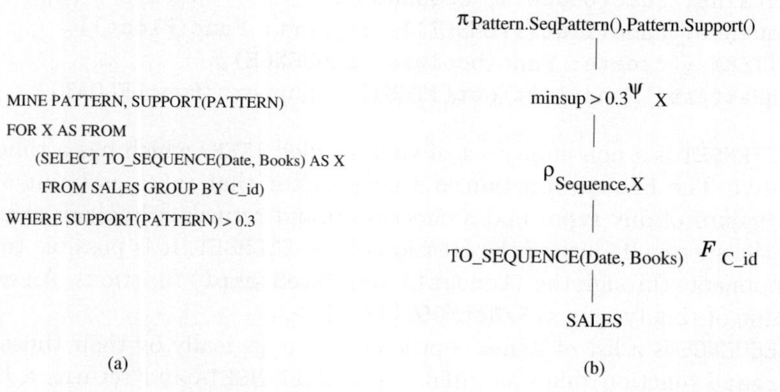

Fig. 2. Query Tree for Q

Let us consider the query *Retrieve patterns of book sales such that its support is greater than 30%* (Q). Figure 2 shows the respective MINE PATTERN expression. The corresponding query tree is shown in Fig. 2(b). First the SALES table is grouped by C_id, and for each group computed `SEQUENCE`s are created. For this, the `TO_SEQUENCE` function is called. It takes as input the attributes Date and Books of the preceding result and the result is a table with schema

$[C\_id, Sequence]$, representing the Sequence of purchases the customer with identifier C_id has done. The attribute Sequence is then renamed as X. The next step is to find the sequential patterns using the ψ operator taking as input the table computed previously, filtering the patterns that satisfy the required minimum support. Finally, patterns and their respective supports are projected.

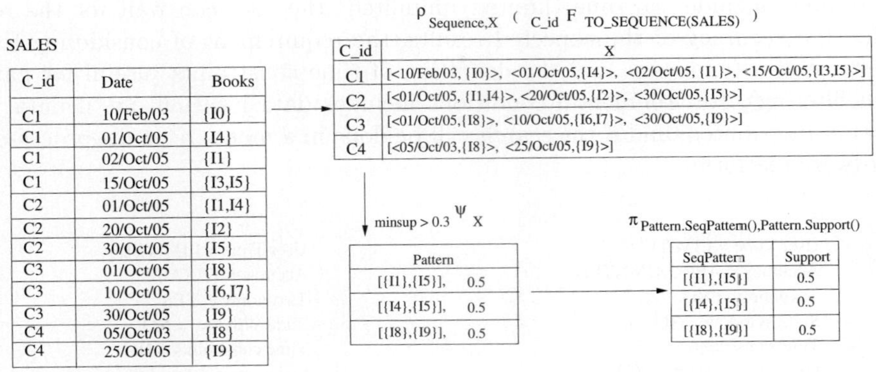

Fig. 3. Execution of the query tree for Q

Figure 3 shows a trace of the evaluation of Q over the example BOOKSTORE database. The result of grouping the individual sales by customer gives as result a table with four tuples, each one representing the sequence of sales done by a single customer. For instance, it is possible to see that customer C1 has bought books in four different times. The result of applying ψ to this table is a three-tuple table storing the patterns found. For instance, it is possible to see that customers that bought the book 'Holy Blood, Holy Grail' (I1) usually buy 'The Da Vinci Code' (I5) some time after.

5 Execution Profiles for Inductive Query Optimization

Query optimization is the process of choosing a suitable execution strategy (from several possibilities) for processing a given query tree. The result is an execution plan, i.e. a query tree in which each operator node has been annotated with the algorithm to execute it. Among the problems tackled in this stage of query processing, we find the selection of a suitable algorithm to be executed. In this section we propose a method to select an algorithm to execute the MineSP operator based on execution profiles.

5.1 Execution Profiles

As previously said, the analysis of 15 existing algorithms has lead us to conclude that no single algorithm is suitable for execution in all situations. For instance, a user might need exact patterns and he/she can wait long enough to retrieve them, while another user might need to get fast a result, sacrificing accuracy. Intuitively, in the first case we need to apply an algorithm that scans all input data in order to increase the accuracy of results, while in the second case an algorithm searching for approximate patterns is enough.

We have identified two categories of variables that affect the search for sequential patterns: user-defined constraints and environmental conditions. User constraints include the time (limited/unlimited) the user can wait for the results, the accuracy of the expected results, the requirement of considering the presence of a taxonomy, and the definition of time constraints (useful for pattern filtering). Environmental conditions includes data location, i.e. if data is local or distributed, and if the search will be done in a mono- or multi-processor hardware platform.

User Time = LIMITED
Accuracy = APROXIMATED
Taxonomy = NO
Slide Window = NO
Time constraints = NO
Location of data = LOCAL
Processor Type = MONO

(a) Profile P1

User Time = LIMITED
Accuracy = EXACT
Taxonomy = YES
Slide Window = NO
Time constraints = NO
Location of data = LOCAL
Processor Type = MONO

(b) Profile P2

Fig. 4. Sample execution profiles

An execution profile is a set of variable-value pairs, describing a particular combination of user constraints and environmental conditions. For instance, the profile P1 in Fig. 4(a) describes a situation where the user is interested in obtaining exact results, and he/she does not want to consider the existence of a taxonomy, a slide window or other time constraints. The data to be mined are local and the query will be executed in a mono-processor machine. The profile P2 in Fig. 4(b), in contrast, describes a situation where the user want to obtain exact results in a short time and considering a taxonomy.

We have modified the MINE PATTERN statement to incorporate execution profiles. The query Q can be modified as follows to integrate the profile P1:

```
MINE PATTERN, SUPPORT(PATTERN)
FOR X FROM
      (SELECT TO_SEQUENCE(Date, Books)
      FROM SALES GROUP BY C_id)
WHERE SUPPORT(PATTERN) > 0.3,
USER_TIME=LIMITED,
ACCURACY=APPROXIMATED,
DATA_LOCATION=LOCAL,
PROCESSOR_TYPE=MONO
```

Note that from the expression it is possible to infer that the user is not interested in using a taxonomy nor time constraints, and so it is not necessary to explicitly express it.

5.2 Algorithm Selection

Execution profiles are a simple way of describing user constraints and environmental conditions. In the following, we briefly explain how a profile is used to choose a suitable algorithm to execute the MineSP operator.

Table 1. Variables affecting the algorithm selection process

Algorithm	User constraints					Environmental restrictions	
	User Time	Accuracy	Taxonomy	Slide windows	Time contraints	Data location	HW platform
APRIORI	unlimited	exact	no	no	no	local	mono
MAX-MINER	unlimited	exact	no	no	no	local	mono
SPIRIT	unlimited	exact	no	no	no	local	mono
PrefixSpan	unlimited	exact	no	no	no	local	mono
GSP-F	unlimited	exact	no	yes	yes	local	mono
GSP	unlimited	exact	yes	yes	yes	local	mono
Disc-all	unlimited	exact	no	no	no	distributed	multi
ProMFS	limited	approximated	no	no	no	local	mono
Approx-MAP	limited	approximated	no	no	no	distributed	mono
SPADE	limited	exact	no	no	no	local	mono
SLPMINER	limited	exact	no	no	no	local	mono
IUS/DUS	limited	exact	no	no	no	local	mono
CATS/FELINE	limited	exact	no	no	no	local	mono
PARALELO	limited	exact	no	no	no	distributed	multi
MEMISP	limited	exact	no	no	no	distributed	multi

We have analyzed the algorithms for sequential pattern mining in terms of the variables previously presented. Figure 1 summarizes this analysis. It is possible then to use this table to select the algorithm matching a given profile. For instance, for the profile P1, the algorithm that is choose is ProMFS.

Let us note that the number of possible combinations of values for the variables is greater than those shown in Table 1. For the profile P2, for instance, there is no algorithm exactly matching the desired behavior. A naive approach to handle this situation would be to halt query processing and raise an exception. We prefer being more flexible, proposing alternatives from which the user can choose. For example, for profile P2, the MineSP operator can be executed by using GSP, which considers an existing taxonomy but requires more processing time, or other algorithms as SPADE, SLPMINER or FELINE that can execute a fast search of patterns although they do not work with a taxonomy. The user can choose the alternative closer to his original expectations.

6 The SPMINER System

We have implemented in Java the prototype system SPMINER to experiment our approach. Figure 5 shows its main components. The user issues a query Q expressed in a subset of SQL extended with object-relational features and the modified MINE PATTERN statement. The syntax of Q is then verified by the analyzer/translator. If correct, an internal representation of Q (a query tree) is generated.

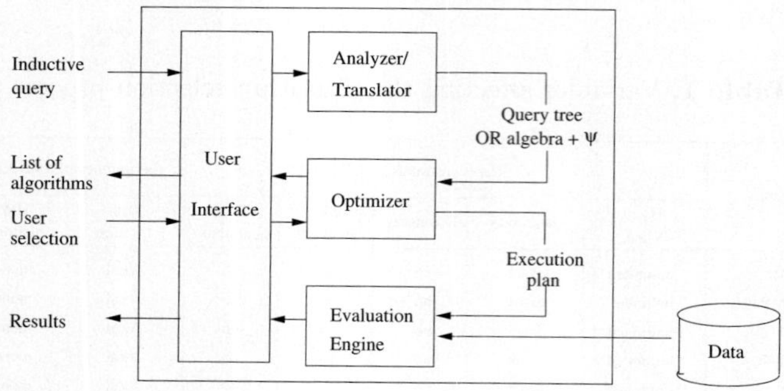

Fig. 5. The SPMINER prototype system architecture

Once the query tree has been generated, the optimizer selects an execution plan. In particular, it selects the algorithm for mining sequential patterns best suited to a given profile using the inference engine of a Prolog implementation. We represent Table 1 as a set of facts of the form $decide(name, t, a, tx, sw, tc, l, p)$, where $name$ is the name of the algorithm and t, a, tx, sw, tc, l, p represents the values for execution time, accuracy of the expected result, taxonomy, slide windows, constraints (mingap / maxgap), location of data, and processor type.

These facts are then queried. An exact match gives as result the name of the best-suited algorithm. For instance, the query `select (X, unlimited, exact, no, yes, yes, local, mono)?` returns `X = GSP-F` as answer. If there is no answer, the optimizer issues a set of slightly different queries, setting in each query a variable value as undefined, replacing it by a "don't care" value. The inference engine then searches for alternative options. If there are several alternatives, the optimizer indicates the user the features offered by each option and is prompted to choose one.

The resulting execution plan is then processed by the evaluation engine. This component executes the mining algorithm that has been chosen over the input data and returns the final result to the user.

7 Conclusions and Future Work

This paper presented some aspects of our research to integrate sequential pattern mining into the traditional framework for querying databases. We introduced

MINESP, a relational-like operator which takes as input a table with an attribute of type `SEQUENCE` and produces as output a table containing the sequential patterns found in the input table and their corresponding supports. The discovery of sequential patterns is biased depending on parameters such as mingap, maxgap, etc. This operator formalizes previous efforts done in the area (specifically SQL-like query languages to mine sequential patterns) and sets the base for our research in query processing.

Concerning this point, this paper also introduced our approach to the optimization (particularly the selection of the mining algorithm) of queries involving the MINESP operator. As the analysis of existing algorithms to mine sequential patterns has revealed, there is no single best algorithm to be applied in all situations. Execution profiles describing user expectations and environmental conditions helps on choosing the most suitable algorithm to execute a query.

Our future work includes the implementation of a real-world application to evaluate our approach. We are also interested in extending our algorithm selection framework to take into account other features inherent to data such as the presence of noise.

Acknowledgements. The authors thank the reviewers of this paper for their useful comments. The work of Ms. Hernández-López has been supported by the Mexican National Council of Science and Technology (CONACYT).

References

1. Agrawal, R., Srikant, R.: Mining Sequential Patterns. In: Eleventh International Conference on Data Engineering, Taipei, Taiwan, IEEE Computer Society Press (1995) 3–14
2. Srikant, R., Agrawal, R.: Mining Sequential Patterns: Generalizations and Performance Improvements. In: Proc. 5th Int. Conf. Extending Database Technology, EDBT. Volume 1057., Springer-Verlag (1996) 3–17
3. Pei, J., Han, J., Mortazavi-Asl, B., Pinto, H.: PrefixSpan: Mining Sequential Patterns Efficiently by Prefix Projected Pattern Growth. In: Proc. 2001 Int. Conf. Data Engineering (ICDE'01), Heidelberg, Germany (2001) 215–224
4. Imielinski, T., Mannila, H.: A Database Perspective on Knowledge Discovery. Communications Of The ACM **39** (1996) 58–64
5. De-Raedt, L.: A Perspective on Inductive Databases. SIGKDD Explorations **4**(2) (2002) 69–77
6. Wojciechowski, M.: Mining Various Patterns in Sequential Data in an SQL-like Manner. In: Advances in Databases and Information Systems, Third East European Conference, ADBIS'99, Maribor, Slovenia (1999) 131–138
7. Li, H., Liu, C., Orlowska, M.: A Query System for Object-Relational Databases. In: Proceedings of ADC'98, Perth, Australia, Springer (1998) 39–50
8. Shintani, T., Kitsuregawa, M.: Mining Algorithms for Sequential Patterns in Parallel: Hash Based Approach. In: Proceedings of PAKDD-98. Volume 1394 of LNCS., Melbourne, Australia, Springer (1998) 283–294
9. Bayardo, R.: Efficiently Mining Long Patterns from Databases. In: Proc. ACM SIGMOD Int. Conf. on Management of Data, SIGMOD 1998, Seattle, Washington, USA., ACM Press (1998) 85–93

10. Garofalakis, M.N., Rastogi, R., Shim, K.: SPIRIT: Sequential Pattern Mining with Regular Expression Constraints. The VLDB Journal (1999) 223–234
11. Zaki, M.J.: SPADE: An Efficient Algorithm for Mining Frequent Sequences. Machine Learning **42**(1/2) (2001) 31–60
12. Morzy, T., Wojciechowski, M., Zakrzewicz, M.: Efficient Constraint-Based Sequential Pattern Mining Using Dataset Filtering Techniques. In: Databases and Information Systems II, Selected Papers from the Fifth International Baltic Conference. Kluwer Academic Publishers (2002) 297–310
13. Seno, M., Karypis, G.: Slpminer: An Algorithm for Finding Frequent Sequential Patterns Using Length Decreasing Support Constraint. Technical Report 02-023, Department of Computer Science, University of Minnesota (2002)
14. Zheng, Q., Xu, K., Ma, S., Lv, W.: The Algorithms of Updating Sequential Patterns. In: Proc. of 5th Int. Workshop on High Performance Data Mining, in conjunction with 2nd SIAM Conference on Data Mining, Washington, USA (2002)
15. Cheung, W., Zaïane, O.R.: Incremental Mining of Frequent Patterns without Candidate Generation or Support Constraint. In: 7th Int. Database Engineering and Applications Symposium (IDEAS 2003), Hong Kong, China, IEEE Computer Society (2003) 111–116
16. Kum, H.C., Pei, J., Wang, W., Duncan, D.: ApproxMAP: Approximate Mining of Consensus Sequential Patterns. In: Proc. 3rd SIAM Int. Conf. on Data Mining, San Francisco, USA (2003)
17. Tumasonis, R., Dzemyda, G.: The Probabilistic Algorithm for Mining Frequent Sequences. In: ADBIS (Local Proceedings). (2004)
18. Chiu, D.Y., Wu, Y.H., Chen, A.L.P.: An Efficient Algorithm for Mining Frequent Sequences by a New Strategy without Support Counting. In: Proc. 20th Int. Conf. on Data Engineering, ICDE 2004, Boston, USA, IEEE Computer Society (2004) 375–386
19. Lin, M.Y., Lee, S.Y.: Fast Discovery of Sequential Patterns through Memory Indexing and Database Partitioning. J. Inf. Sci. Eng. **21**(1) (2005) 109–128
20. Pinto, H., Han, J., Pei, J., Wang, K., Chen, Q., Dayal, U.: Multi-Dimensional Sequential Pattern Mining. In: Proc. 10th Int. Conf. on Information and Knowledge Management, Atlanta, Georgia, USA, ACM Press (2001) 81 – 88
21. Antunes, C., Oliveira, A.L.: Generalization of Pattern-Growth Methods for Sequential Pattern Mining with Gap Constraints. In: Proceedings of the Third Int. Conf. on Machine Learning and Data Mining in Pattern Recognition (MLDM 2003). Volume 2734 of LNCS., Leipzig, Germany, Springer (2003) 239–251
22. Leleu, M., Rigotti, C., Boulicaut, J.F., Euvrard, G.: Constraint-Based Mining of Sequential Patterns over Datasets with Consecutive Repetitions. In: Proceedings of the 7th European Conf. on Principles and Practice of Knowledge Discovery in Databases (PKDD03). Volume 2838 of Lecture Notes in Computer Science., Cavtat-Dubrovnik, Croatia, Springer (2003) 303–314
23. Meo, R., Psaila, G., Ceri, S.: A New SQL-like Operator for Mining Association Rules. In Vijayaraman, T.M., Buchmann, A.P., Mohan, C., Sarda, N.L., eds.: VLDB'96, Proceedings of 22th International Conference on Very Large Data Bases, Mumbai (Bombay), India, Morgan Kaufmann (1996) 122–133
24. R. Gopalan, T. Nuruddin, Y.S.: Building a Data Mining Query Optimizer. In: Proceedings of the Australasian Data Mining Workshop. (2002)
25. Morzy, M., Wojciechowski, M., Zakrzewicz, M.: Cost-based Sequential Pattern Query Optimization in Presence of Materialized Results of Previous Queries. In: Proceedings of the Intelligent Information Systems Symposium (IIS'2002), Sopot, Poland, Physica-Verlag (2002) 435–444

Visual Exploratory Data Analysis of Traffic Volume

Weiguo Han[1], Jinfeng Wang[1], and Shih-Lung Shaw[2]

[1] Institute of Geographic Sciences & Natural Resources Research, CAS,
No. 11A Datun Road, Beijing 100101, China
[2] Department of Geography, University of Tennessee,
Knoxville, TN 37996-0925, USA
hanweiguo@263.net, wangjf@lreis.ac.cn, sshaw@utk.edu

Abstract. Beijing has deployed Intelligent Transportation System (ITS) monitoring devices along selected major roads in the core urban area in order to help relieve traffic congestion and improve traffic conditions. The huge amount of traffic data from ITS originally collected for the control of traffic signals can be a useful source to assist in transportation designing, planning, managing, and research by identifying major traffic patterns from the ITS data. The importance of data visualization as one of the useful data mining methods for reflecting the potential patterns of large sets of data has long been recognized in many disciplines. This paper will discuss several comprehensible and appropriate data visualization techniques, including line chart, bi-directional bar chart, rose diagram, and data image, as exploratory data analysis tools to explore traffic volume data intuitively and to discover the implicit and valuable traffic patterns. These methods could be applied at the same time to gain better and more comprehensive insights of traffic patterns and data relationships hidden in the massive data set. The visual exploratory analysis results could help transportation managers, engineers, and planners make more efficient and effective decisions on the design of traffic operation strategies and future transportation planning scientifically.

1 Introduction

Conventional approaches to tackling transportation congestion problems attempt to increase transportation supply by widening existing roads and building new highways. However, traffic congestion often occurs shortly after, if not before, a transportation improvement project is completed [1]. Intelligent transportation systems (ITS), which aim at improving efficiency of existing transportation systems through the use of advanced computing, real-time data sensors and communication technologies, have been suggested as an alternative approach of tackling transportation congestion problems. With the increasing deployment of ITS services, it appears that they tend to focus on using real-time data to improve traffic operations. The large amount of traffic data collected from ITS can be a useful source to assist in transportation planning and modeling by identifying major traffic patterns from the ITS data. Unfortunately, most ITS data are underutilized for planning and modeling purposes. This paper

A. Gelbukh and C.A. Reyes-Garcia (Eds.): MICAI 2006, LNAI 4293, pp. 695 – 703, 2006.

examines several visual exploratory data analysis methods for identification of traffic patterns based on ITS data collected in Beijing, China.

Due to its rapid economic growth, China has seen a fast increase of private automobiles and worsening traffic congestion problems. Beijing, the capital city of China, has experienced an annual growth of 150,000 automobiles in the past four years. According to Beijing Municipal Traffic Management Bureau, 40 percent of wage earners in Beijing spend at least one hour for one-way commute between their homes and workplaces on each workday. Beijing municipal government has realized that, if it does not address the worsening traffic congestion situation, it will become a major problem to the city's future development and the 2008 Olympic Games. Many traffic regulation approaches that have been successfully implemented in other countries have been adopted in Beijing. In addition, Beijing has deployed ITS monitoring devices along selected major roads in the core urban area of Beijing in order to help relieve the city's traffic congestion and improve the city's traffic conditions. Currently, the system collects real-time data, such as travel speed and traffic volume, and transmits the data to a database server at the traffic control center. The data are mainly used to assist in real-time control of traffic signals. It has been realized that the data should be utilized to extract hidden and valuable traffic flow patterns to support other functions such as performance monitoring, operations evaluation, transportation planning and transportation policy making.

Data mining is an approach of discovering useful information, knowledge, and rules hidden in large data sets [2]. As an important tool for data mining, data visualization displays multi-dimensional data in the forms that reflect information patterns, data relationships and trends in order to help users observe and analyze the data more intuitively. Data visualization also allows users to control and steer the data mining process based on the given visual feedback. Users therefore can take advantage of their experience and knowledge to discover implicit and valuable patterns and data relationships hidden in large data sets [3]. This paper examines several data visualization techniques, including line chart, bi-directional bar chart, rose diagram, and data image, as exploratory data analysis tools to identify hidden traffic flow patterns from the ITS data collected in Beijing. The visual exploratory analysis covers different geographic scales from street intersections to main highway arterials, which require different visualization methods to discover the hidden traffic patterns. The remaining parts of this paper are organized as follows. Section 2 is a brief review of data visualization and exploratory data analysis. Section 3 presents the visualization techniques used to explore and analyze traffic volume data. The final section offers concluding remarks and future research directions.

2 Data Visualization

Data visualization is a process of transforming information into a visual form, enabling users to observe the information. The resulting visual display enables scientists or engineers to perceive visually the features that are hidden in the data but nevertheless are needed for data exploration and analysis [5]. It is often easier to detect a pattern from a picture than from a numeric output. Graphical illustrations such as plots and graphs therefore play an essential role as tools for analysis and exploration of inherent structure in data [6]. As one of the important tools in data mining, data visualization not only assists knowledge discovery but also controls the process of data analysis. There is no single general visualization method suitable for all problems. It is important to choose appropriate visualization methods according to the task and the property of data in order to provide critical and comprehensive appreciation of the data that will benefit subsequent analysis, processing, and decision-making.

Transportation practitioners at Beijing transportation departments now use traditional online transaction processing (OLTP) of database in tabular format to evaluate, summarize, and report the current traffic status. This conventional approach makes it difficult for them to discover hidden traffic patterns in the data and to provide more specific analysis and future plans of the existing system to help relieve the worsening traffic congestion problems. The goal of this study is to provide useful visual data analysis methods for transportation managers, engineers, and planners to explore traffic volume data intuitively and to discover the hidden traffic patterns. The visual analysis results in turn could help them make more effective decisions on the design of traffic operation strategies and future transportation planning. Choosing appropriate visualization methods that are suitable for traffic volume data and can effectively convey the information to transportation managers and engineers is not a trivial task. For example, if a visualization technique such as the parallel coordinate is used to represent the traffic volume data, it may be too complex for transportation practitioners to easily interpret and compare the data.

Catarci et al. provide a set of logic rules to select effective visual representation and graphic design for visualizing the facts and data relationships [7]. Bertin also offers guidelines on how to choose the suitable visual methods to reflect data attributes [8]. Based on these guidelines reported in the literature, this study presents several visualization methods that are appropriate for representing traffic volume data and are comprehensible for transportation managers and engineers to perform effective data exploration and analysis. These methods include line chart, bi-directional bar chart, rose diagram, and data image. They could be used at the same time to gain better and more comprehensive insights of traffic patterns and data relationships hidden in the massive data set.

3 Visual Analysis of Traffic Volume Data

Traffic volume data possess several characteristics that require different visualization methods to clearly illustrate and communicate these characteristics. It is more effective for transportation managers and engineers to analyze the figures generated from these methods to convey the traffic characteristics efficiently and concisely than to read through pages or tables of data describing the traffic status. This section presents a select set of visualization methods for exploration and analysis of traffic volume data at different levels of spatial granularity (i.e., at street intersections and along main arterials) to analyze existing traffic demand, and identify ways to improve traffic flow.

3.1 Line Chart

Line chart is a simple and easy-to-understand method to show trends or changes of traffic volume over a period time or over a distance range. It is easy to identify traffic peak periods from a line chart.

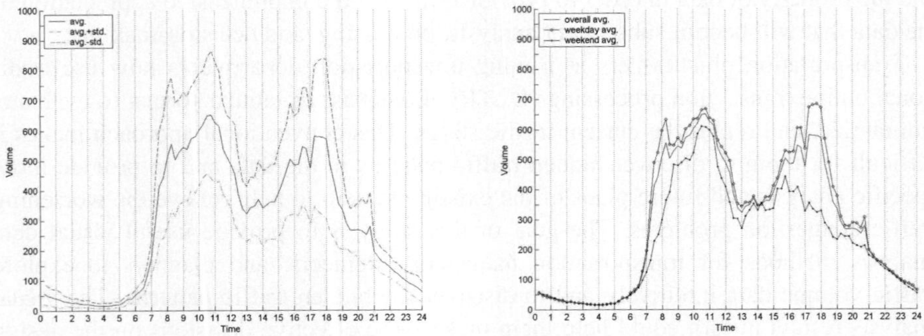

(a) (b)

Fig. 1. Line chart of the westbound average traffic volume

Using the westbound traffic volume at Xidan Intersection, which is located in the center of Xidan Culture and Shopping Area and near many central and municipal government agencies, as an example, Fig. 1(a) shows the average traffic volume curve, along with the standard deviation curves above and below average curve, and Fig. 1(b) presents the overall, weekday, weekend average traffic curve of these months respectively. These charts indicate that the location has a large daily variation of traffic volume, with two daytime peak periods occurring during working hours between 8 am and 12 am and between 2 pm and 6 pm, and one nighttime peak periods during between 8 pm and 10 pm, and the volume trend of weekends is similar to that of weekdays, but the weekend average does not demonstrate the pronounced morning peak at 8 am that is common on weekdays, the morning peak hour on weekends exists between 11 am and 12 am. Transportation engineers can use the information to assist them in evaluating the road capacity, adjusting the traffic signal timing. Transportation planners, on the other hand, can use the chart to figure out "time in a day" traffic distribution pattern for travel demand modeling.

3.2 Bi-directional Bar Chart

When traffic volumes in both directions are important to control traffic signals or to plan the number of traffic lanes, it is better to represent the data with a bi-directional bar chart. Fig. 2 shows the eastbound and the westbound average traffic volumes at Jingxi Hotel Intersection. It clearly illustrates the directional difference of traffic flows. The eastbound overall average traffic volume is much higher during the morning peak hours than the westbound overall average volume, while a reversed pattern occurs during the afternoon peak hours, so does the weekday one. The workday and

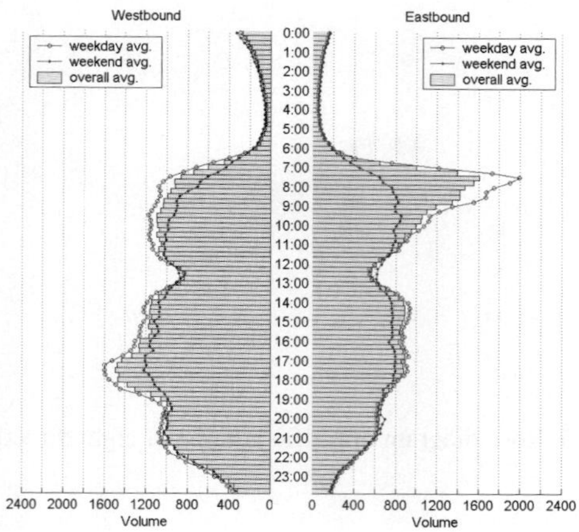

Fig. 2. Bi-directional bar chart of eastbound and westbound traffic volume

weekend average volume curves in the plot also demonstrate varying patterns of traffic, such as a significant difference of eastbound traffic volume on the morning between weekdays and weekends, and a bi-directional same trend on weekends. In addition, this chart allows an easy comparison of traffic volumes in the two opposite directions during any selected time period. These patterns reflect truly the spatial distribution patterns of workplaces and residences of citizens along the West Chang'an Street in Beijing, and more people in Beijing prefer to choose West Chang'an Street as their westbound road for business or home. Information derived from this chart can help transportation engineers to set different lengths of signal cycles at the intersection for different time periods in a day. It is also useful for the transportation department to consider the creation of reversible lanes along this street.

3.3 Rose Diagram

Transportation analysts also need to examine traffic flow data of straight flows and turning movements at each intersection. In this case, rose diagrams can be used to show percentages of each directional flow at an intersection. Transportation engineers then can use the information to adjust traffic signal phases to facilitate traffic flows. Fig. 3 shows an example of directional average traffic flows at 8 AM at the Mingguangcun Intersection (e.g., "S" for southbound straight flows and "SE" for southbound-to-eastbound turning flows, so do the remainder figures in this paper), which is a very congested intersection near the Xizhimen Subway Station. The rose diagram clearly shows that eastbound and left-turn traffic account for most traffic flows at this intersection at 8 AM. Note that right-turn traffic flow data are not included on this rose diagram since they are not currently recorded by the traffic control center in Beijing. Right-turn traffic flows at many intersections in Beijing however do cause significant interferences to other traffic flows (e.g., left-turn traffic, bicycle and pedestrian flows). Beijing transportation department should consider to record right-turn traffic volumes and include them in future traffic analysis.

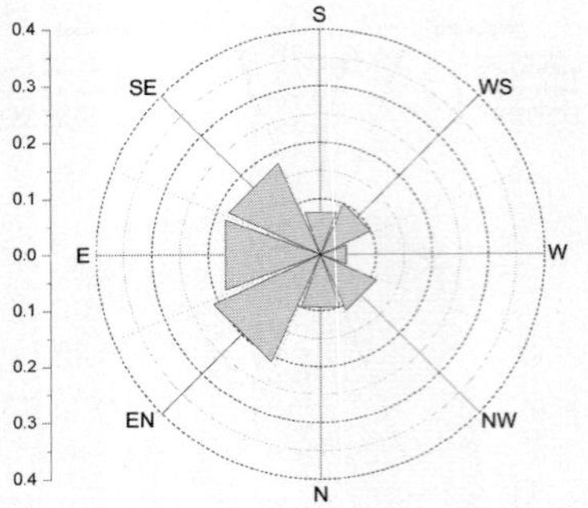

Fig. 3. Rose diagram of traffic volume of eight directions

3.4 Data Image

As traffic flows change over time, especially by time-of-day, transportation engineers need to develop multiple signal timing plans to accommodate these changes. Clearly, the rose diagram does not show the actual traffic volume value variations of each direction. Data image has been suggested as an approach of mapping data attributes to color features for visualization and exploration of higher dimensional data [9]. Marchette et al. suggest that data image method can be used to detect data outliers [10]. Healey further indicates that data image can quickly differentiate elements based on their colors for exploratory data analysis of identifying clusters or performing classification [11].

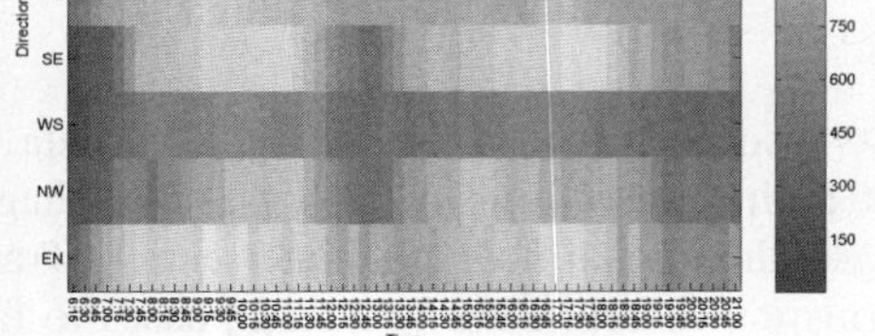

Fig. 4. Data image of average traffic volume of eight directions

Fig. 4 displays average traffic volumes from 6:00 to 21:00 for eight directional flows at the Mingguangcun Intersection in a data image. In this figure, the horizontal axis represents 15-minute time intervals and the vertical axis shows the eight directions. Again, right-turn flows are not included in this figure. Light yellow color indicates the heaviest traffic condition, and deep green color is for the lightest traffic.

In order to further help transportation engineers obtain a clear picture of the traffic flow patterns among different directions over various time period, a cluster analysis is performed to group together similar traffic patterns among different time intervals.

A hierarchical clustering algorithm based on the complete linkage clustering scheme is used to identify the clusters [9] considering its advantages over than the other clustering algorithms, such as less sensitivity to the input parameters and ease of handling of any forms of similarity (i.e. nested partitions) [12]. The leaf nodes are the directional volumes at each individual time interval, while intermediate ones indicate larger groups of homogeneous volume at several time intervals. Fig. 5 shows the hierarchical structure and the same traffic flow data with four clusters identified as bands marked on the data image. Each band suggests a particular signal timing plan that is more appropriate for specific time intervals. This enables transportation engineers to get a better idea of the time-of-day variations to help them adjust and fine-tune signal timings at each intersection. This method offers an inexpensive way to evaluate the existing operational strategies and could be used to automate the design of signal timing plans.

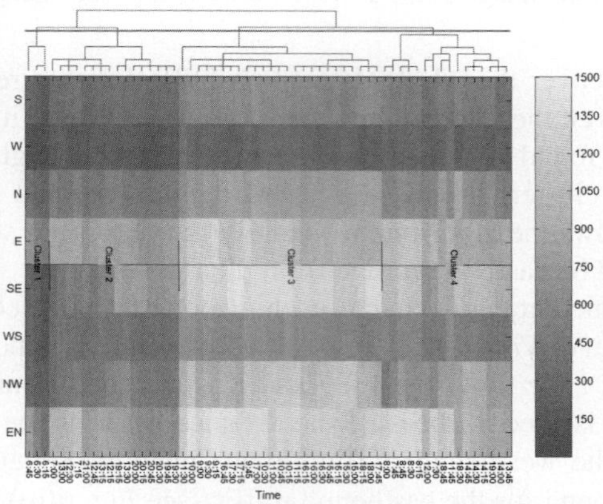

Fig. 5. Data image of average traffic volume sorted using clustering algorithm

Data images also can be used to display traffic volumes along a particular street. Fig. 6 shows examples of using data images to explore the average flow patterns for westbound and eastbound traffic along Chang'an Street, respectively. The horizontal axis again represents 15-minute time intervals. The vertical axis displays sequentially the data collected at all traffic detectors along Chang'an Street starting from Jianguomen on the east to Fuxingmen on the west. The color index is computed by

$$Colorindex(i, j) = \left[\frac{Volume(i, j)}{MaxTraffic} * Colornums \right] \quad (1)$$

where,

[…]: operator of rounding to the nearest integer

Volume(i, j): traffic volume at detector i for time interval j

MaxTraffic: maximum capacity of the road segment

Colornums: color numbers used in the color map, here is 100.

Considered that the detectors are spatially contiguous, the classical K-means partitioning clustering algorithm is used to identify the clusters in Fig. 6, it aims to divide the data set into several homogeneous clusters, which may not overlap with each

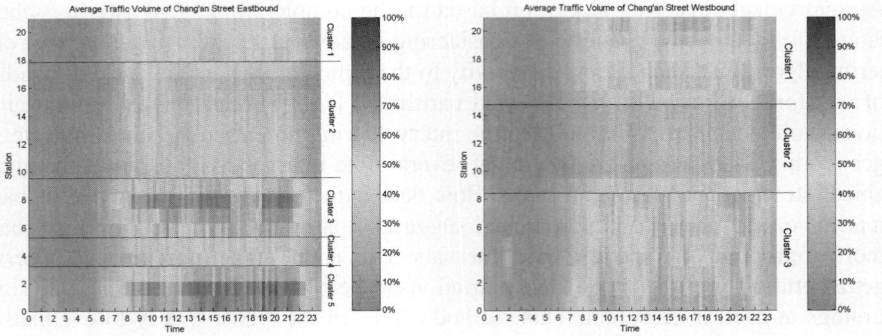

(a) (b)

Fig. 6. Data image of the average traffic volume of Chang'an Street

other but together cover the whole data space [13]. Another reason of applying this approach is that given the number *k* of partitions to be found, it is very often the case that the *k* clusters found by a partitioning method are of higher quality (i.e., more similar) than the *k* clusters produced by a hierarchical method [14]. The conceivable number, which allows the algorithm to identify the clustering structure of traffic volume datasets, could be easily discerned from the figures.

The traffic volume data collected at each detector is modeled as an *n*-dimensional vector with the form of $Vol_i = <v_1, v_2, \ldots v_j, \ldots, v_n>$, where v_j denotes the average traffic volume at detector *i* for time interval *j* and *n* is the total number of time intervals. Euclidean distance is used to measure the distance between the vectors. Five clusters are identified for the westbound traffic along Chang'an Street (see Fig. 6 (a)), and three clusters are found for the eastbound traffic (see Fig. 6(b)). Results of the cluster analysis can help transportation engineers determine better ways of synchronizing traffic signals located along a major street. The techniques of data image also could be used to evaluate traffic situation to identify the irregular patterns or locate the faulty detectors.

4 Conclusion

In this paper, several visualization methods, which are appropriate and comprehensible for visual exploratory analysis of the ITS Data, are applied to discover traffic patterns and data relationships hidden in the massive data sets. Transportation practitioners can take advantage of these techniques to extract hidden and valuable traffic flow patterns to help monitor the system performances, evaluate traffic situations, adjust the traffic signal timing, make transportation plan or policy, and so on.

Nevertheless, the functions provided by these solutions are not comprehensive in terms of the analysis and visualization of urban traffic data, and data visualization is not a substitute for data analysis, instead it complements data analysis to yield greater insights into the traffic data. The visualization tools should be utilized and developed to improve understanding of behaviors in time and space [15]. In the next future, we will program to implement an integrated framework based on data visualization, data mining, Web and GIS to provide a powerful and real-time on-line tool for transportation managers and researchers to analyze traffic situation, improve traffic condition, etc, for transportation engineers and planners to evaluate traffic capacity, design traffic signal plans, etc, and for drivers or travelers to select their routes, etc.

References

1. Miller, H.J., Shaw, S.L.. Geographic Information Systems for Transportation: Principles and Applications. Oxford University Press, New York, 2001.
2. Han, J., Kamber, M.. Data Mining: Concepts and Technologies. Morgan Kaufmann Publisher, San Francisco, 2001.
3. Miller, H.J., Han, J.. Geographic Data Mining and Knowledge Discovery. Taylor and Francis, London, 2001.
4. Gershon, N.. From perception to visualization. In: L. Rosenblum et al., (Eds.), Scientific Visualization 1994: Advances and Challenges, Academic Press, New York, 129-139, 1994.
5. Cristina, M., Oliveira, F.D., Levkowitz, H.. From visual data exploration to visual data mining: a survey. IEEE Transactions on Visualization and Computer Graphics, 9(3), 378-394 (2003).
6. Edsall, R.M.. The parallel coordinate plot in action: design and use for geographic visualization. Computational Statistics & Data Analysis, 43(4): 605-619 (2003).
7. Catarci, T., Santucci, G., Costabile, M.F., Cruz, I.. Foundations of the DARE system for drawing adequate representations. In: Proceedings of International Symposium on Database Applications in Non-Traditional Environments, IEEE Computer Society Press, 461-470, 1999.
8. Bertin, J.. Semiology of Graphics. University Wisconsin Press, Wisconsin, 1983.
9. Minnotte, M., West, W.. The data image: a tool for exploring high dimensional data sets. In: Proceedings of the ASA Section on Statistical Graphics, Dallas, Texas, 25-33, 1998.
10. Marchette, D.J., Solka J.L.. Using data images for outlier detection. Computational Statistics & Data Analysis, 43(4), 541-552 (2003).
11. Healey, C.G.. Choosing effective colors for data visualization. In: Proceedings of IEEE Visualization 1996, IEEE Computer Society Press, 263-270, 1996.
12. Kaufman, L., Rousseeuw, P.J.. Finding Groups in Data: An Introduction to Cluster Analysis. Wiley, New York, 1990.
13. Jain, A.K., Murty, M.N., Flynn, P.J.. Data clustering: a review. ACM Computing Surveys, 31(3), 264-323 (1999).
14. Raymond, T. Ng, Han, J.. CLARANS: a method for clustering objects for spatial data mining. IEEE Transactions on Knowledge and Data Engineering, 14(5), 1003-1016 (2002).
15. Dykes, J.A., Mountain D.M.. Seeking structure in records of spatio-temporal behaviour: visualization issues, efforts and applications. Computational Statistics & Data Analysis, 43(4), 581-603 (2003).

A Fast Model-Based Vision System for a Robot Soccer Team

Murilo F. Martins, Flavio Tonidandel, and Reinaldo A.C. Bianchi

Centro Universitário da FEI
Av. Humberto A. C. Branco, 3972. 09850-901 – São Bernardo do Campo – SP, Brazil
{murilofm, flaviot, rbianchi}@fei.edu.br

Abstract. Robot Soccer is a challenging research domain for Artificial Intelligence, which was proposed in order to provide a long-term problem in which researchers can investigate the construction of systems involving multiple agents working together in a dynamic, uncertain and probabilistic environment, to achieve a specific goal. This work focuses on the design and implementation of a fast and robust computer vision system for a team of small size robot soccer players. The proposed system combines artificial intelligence and computer vision techniques to locate the mobile robots and the ball, based on global vision images. To increase system performance, this work proposes a new approach to interpret the space created by a well-known computer vision technique called Hough Transform, as well as a fast object recognition method based on constraint satisfaction techniques. The system was implemented entirely in software using an off-the-shelf frame grabber. Experiments using real time image capture allows to conclude that the implemented system are efficient and robust to noises and lighting variation, being capable of locating all objects in each frame, computing their position and orientation in less than 20 milliseconds.

Keywords: Computer Vision, Artificial Intelligence, Intelligent Robotic Systems.

1 Introduction

Since it's beginning, Robot Soccer has been a platform for research and development of independent mobile robots and multi-agents systems, involving the most diverse areas of engineering and computer science. There are some problems to be solved in this domain, such as mechanical construction, electronics and control of mobile robots. But the main challenge is found in the areas related to Artificial Intelligence, as multi-agent systems, machine learning and computational vision. The problems and challenges mentioned above are not trivial, since Robot Soccer is dynamic, uncertain and probabilistic.

A computer vision system for a Robot Soccer team must be fast and robust, and it is desirable that it can handle noise and luminous intensity variations. A number of techniques can be applied for object recognition in the domain of Robot Soccer, as described by Grittani, Gallinelli and Ramírez [1] and others.

A. Gelbukh and C.A. Reyes-Garcia (Eds.): MICAI 2006, LNAI 4293, pp. 704–714, 2006.

However, all of existing systems is based on color information and, therefore, sensitive to luminous intensity variations.

This work considers the use of one well-known image segmentation technique - the Hough Transform - to locate the mobile robots and the ball on global vision images. To implement this technique – which is in most cases is implemented in robotic systems using special hardware – using only an off-the-shelf frame grabber and a personal computer, a new approach to interpret the Hough space was proposed, as well as the method used to recognize objects, which is based on constraint satisfaction methods.

This article is divided in the following way: the Hough Transform is described in Section 2. The implemented system is described in Section 3, where the implementation of Hough Transform is detailed. In Section 4, the obtained results are presented and discussed. Section 5 concludes the work and presents suggestions for future works.

2 The Hough Transform

The Hough Transform (HT) [2] is one technique of image segmentation used to detect objects through models adjustment. This technique requires that an object class is determined, and such class must be able to describe all possible instances of the referred object. The parameterization of an object class defines the form of this object, therefore, variations of color on the image, or even on the objects, do not affect the performance and the efficiency of the HT. To detect objects on an image, the HT tries to match the edges found on the image with the parameterized model of the object.

The Hough Transform has rarely been used in robotic systems operating in real time and, when used, it generally needs specific hardware due to its computational complexity. In Robot Soccer, the HT is only used to locate the ball - but not the robots - as described in Gönner, Rous, Kraiss [3] and Jonker, Caarls, Bokhove [4].

2.1 Circles Detection with Hough Transform

Circles are a very common geometric structure in Robot Soccer since all objects can be represented by one or more circles. The ball for instance is a sphere, but it becomes a circle when projected on the captured image. In FIRA MiroSot and RoboCup Small Size categories, the robots are identified through labels on their upper part. These labels can be of any form, and must contain determined a priori colored areas to allow distinction among the robots of different teams. The label used in this work has two circles at 45 degrees with respect to the front of the robot, which complies with FIRA rules (Figure 1). These circles have the same diameter of the ball used.

Circles are parameterized by the triplet (x_c, y_c, r), which defines a set of equidistant points in r from the central point represented by the Cartesian

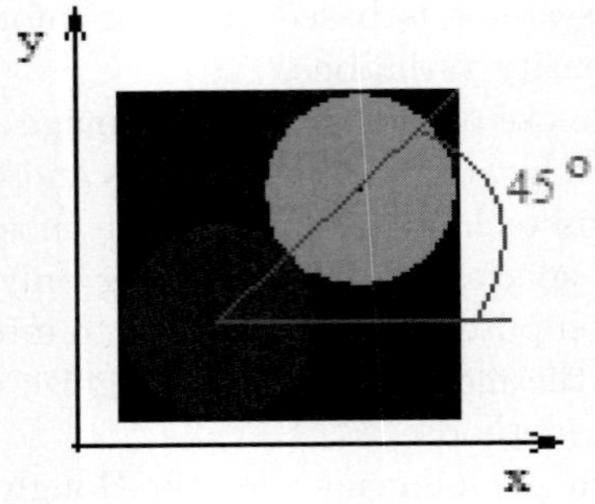

Fig. 1. Label used to identify the robots

coordinate (x_c, y_c). A circle can be parameterized using polar coordinates by the equations:

$$x = x_c + r \cdot cos\theta \text{ (1a)} \quad \text{and} \quad y = y_c + r \cdot sin\theta \text{ (1b)}.$$

In this manner, for known values of the triplet (x_c, y_c, r) and varying the angle θ in all $0 - 360$ interval, a complete circumference can be drawn. The space of parameters, also called Hough Space, is three-dimensional. In Robot Soccer, objects move in two dimensions since there is no depth variation of objects on the image, allowing a constant value for radius r to be employed. Thus, the space of parameters becomes bidimensional and it is represented by the point (x_c, y_c).

2.2 The Hough Space

To detect circles of constant radius, on an image that contains only (x, y) edge points, using the HT consists on determining which points belong to the edge of the circle centered in (x_c, y_c) and of radius r. The HT algorithm determines for each edge point of the image a set of possible centers in the Hough Space, set which will be defined iteratively by the variation of θ. Equations (1a) and (1b) become:

$$x_c = x - r \cdot cos\theta \text{ (2a)} \quad \text{and} \quad y_c = y - r \cdot sin\theta \text{ (2b)}.$$

Figure 2 demonstrates the algorithm execution for three points on a circle edge of the image on the left, and the respective Hough Space generated is shown on the right. Three circles of radius r drawn on the Hough Space, from 3 points on the edge of the circle with center (x_c, y_c) on the image, intersect themselves in only one point, which is exactly the central point of the circle on the image. Each edge point on the image generates a circle in the Hough Space. Each edge point of this circle in the Hough Space receives a vote. The greater the number of votes a point receives, the greater the probability of this point being a circle center. These points with greater probability are relative maximum of the Hough Space and they define the centers of existing objects on the image.

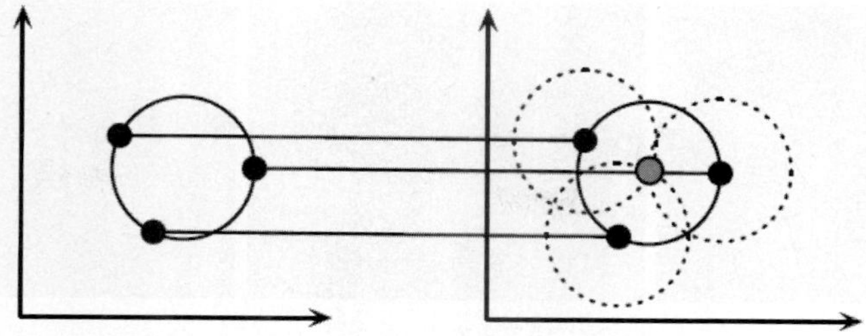

Fig. 2. Exemple of Hough Space generation

3 Description of the Implemented System

The implemented computer vision system has seven stages, as follows: image acquisition, background subtraction, application of edge filter, Hough Space generation, determination of high probability points to be centers of circles on the image and objects recognition (robots and ball).

3.1 Image Acquisition

The image acquisition system consists of an analogical camera with a composite video output and an off-the-shelf video frame grabber based on Bt-878 chipset. This equipment can acquire up to 30 frames per second. In this work, two image resolutions were used: 320x240 and 640x480 pixels, both with color depth of 24 bits. Thirty pictures were captured for each resolution. Figure 3-left presents one of the images used.

3.2 Background Subtraction

As previously mentioned, only the edges of the image are relevant to the HT. Each point of the edge is an iteration of the HT algorithm. To optimize the performance of this algorithm, a simple method of background subtraction was used. It computes the difference between the image captured and a background image, without the moving objects. The background image is updated each frame time, using a method known as Running Average [5], according the equation below:

$$B_{i+1} = \alpha \cdot F_i + (1 - \alpha) \cdot B_i$$

where the background image is represented by B, the captured image is represented by F and α is a learning rate used to determine how fast static objects become part of the background image. Although the method is simple, it is efficient for this application because the background does not suffer major modifications. The final image contains only the mobile objects, resulting in relevant edges only. The background image is presented on Figure 3-center and the result of the background subtraction can be seen on Figure 3-right.

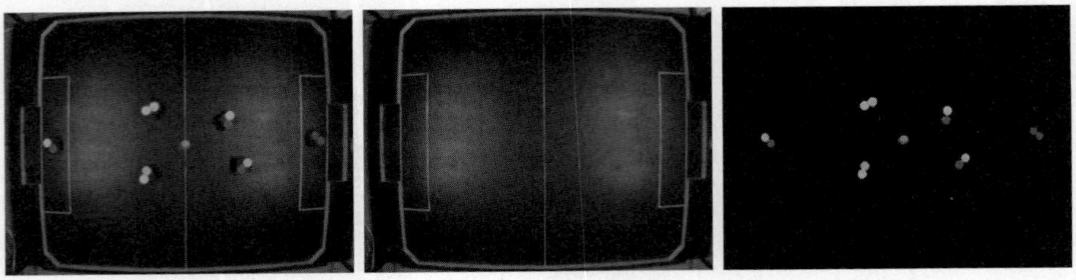

Fig. 3. (left) Captured image containing a ball and two complete teams of robots (center) background and (right) result of background subtraction

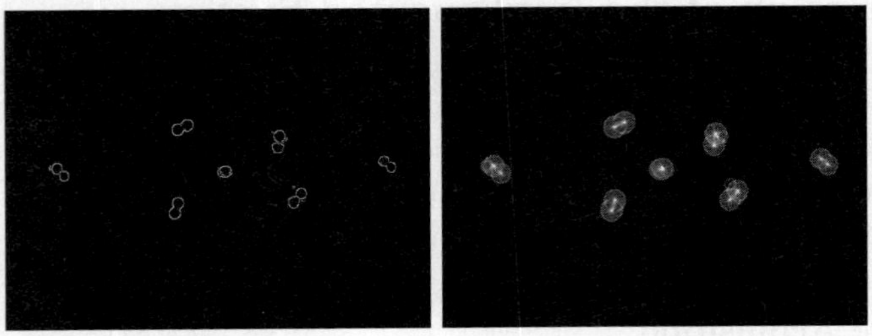

Fig. 4. (left) Result of the application of the Canny filter on Figure 3-right and (right) Hough Space generated for the edge points, where brighter points have more votes

3.3 Canny Edges Filter

There are many different techniques capable of extracting edge information on an image, as described by Forsyth and Ponce [6]. The present work uses a well-known technique for edge detection, the Canny filter [7], which produces binary images. Figure 4-left shows the result of edges detection with the Canny filter on an image that the background was subtracted (Figure 3-right) and was converted into gray scale (to lower the processing time).

3.4 Hough Space Generation

The Hough Space can be generated from the resultant binary image produced with the Canny filter. The generation of the Hough Space with the algorithm described in Section 2 is correct, but not efficient. Although this algorithm generates the Hough Space correctly, it does several redundant iterations to produce the points of possible circle centers. This redundancy happens because when varying the angle θ, it generates 360 centers points for each edge point with decimal precision. However, the digital images are composed of pixels located on a grid, where each pixel position is an integer number. Therefore, the use of decimal precision is irrelevant and redundant.

To eliminate redundancy, an algorithm for circle drawing proposed by Bresenham [8] was used. This algorithm determines points of a circle using only integers, through the addition of a value determined a priori. Moreover, the algorithm takes advantage of points symmetry in a circle: points position is computed in only one octant and by symmetry, the points of the other 7 octants are determined, without repetition of previously drawn points. In this way, the processing time for the generation of the Hough Space is minimized, allowing the use of applications in real time. The Hough Space generated for the edge points of the image in Figure 4-left can be observed in Figure 4-right.

3.5 Circles Determination from the Hough Space

After the Hough Space is generated, the following step is to find out the points that received more votes in the space in order to detect the possible circle centers (x_c, y_c), with r kept constant. It is possible to consider r constant because the distance between the camera and the field is greater than the field dimensions, and the radius variation is less than 5%. This fact also implies in no significant distortion in the images.

This stage is the one that presents greater problems in terms of circle detection. As any edge point generates a set of points (in a circle) that receives votes in the Hough Space, there might be misrepresenting votes producing false relative maximums.

The implemented algorithm verifies whether a voted point reached a minimum number of votes – determined a priori – as the Hough Space is being generated. If a point exceeds this threshold, it is stored only once in a vector of possible centers. At the end of the Hough Space generation, this vector stores the number of votes for each point that exceeded the minimum number of votes.

To guarantee that all points representing real circle centers on the image are in the vector, a low minimum number of votes is defined. But, because of this low threshold, there might be false relative maximums in this vector. Another problem is that, due to the nature of the HT and the Canny filter, a circle in the image may generate several possible centers, lying close to each other.

The first step to separate the false center from points where real circle centers are located is to order the points in the vector by the number of votes received using the Quicksort algorithm. After this ordination, the point in the first position in the vector represents the global maximum and is considered a circle center and is inserted in a new vector, the vector of centers.

As the real center of a circle can be defined as the point that was voted the most, and overlapping between two circles do not occurs, all the points that the Euclidean distance to the first center is less $2r$ can be removed from the vector of possible centers. After this, the second position will represent the second maximum and can be considered as a center, and so on.

The algorithm continues until iterations reach a maximum number of circles determined, or until the end of the vector of possible center is reached. This algorithm results in a vector with points distant enough from each other to be considered different circles.

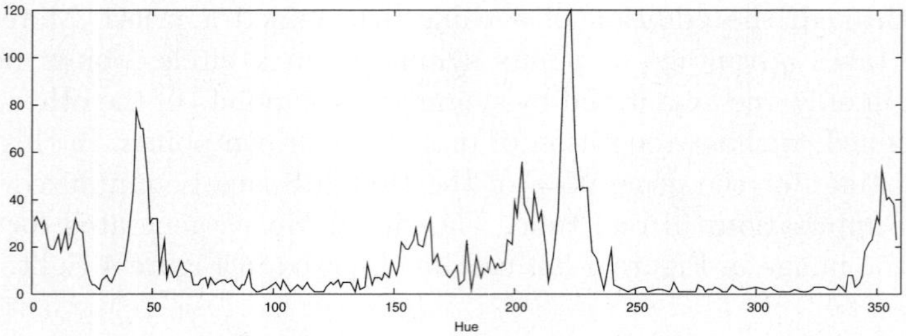

Fig. 5. Histogram for the Hue component of the pixels present in Figure 3-right

3.6 Object Recognition

This stage is the only one that considers color information and image illumination. Therefore, to successfully recognize objects it is necessary to distinguish them, what can only be done when the main colors, defined by the competition rules and different for each team, as well as the secondary colors, used in order to differentiate the robots of the same team, are known.

To define the colors in the image first the mean color of each circle is computed, using a 5 x 5 mask centered in the points found during circle detection. Then, these colors are converted from the RGB to the HSI color space [6]. In this color space, pixels are described by the triple (Hue, Saturation, Intensity). The Hue component describes the color of the pixel. It ranges from zero to 360 degrees, where zero degree is red, 60 yellow, 120 green, 240 blue and 300 degrees magenta. The Saturation component signals how white color is present, and the Intensity component represents illumination. In this color space, illumination variations do not modify the hue value of a pixel.

Using this color space, it is easy to define the colors in the image: the mean colors of the circles are ordered by the Hue component using the Quicksort algorithm. As the colors in the HSI color space are always in the same order and at least 30 degrees apart, and the number of circles of each color is known a priori, it is very easy to define the colors of the objects. For the circles in Figure 3-right, the following colors were found: one orange circle (Hue = 21), three yellow (H = 45, 48 and 50), two green (H = 154 and 160), two cyan (h = 200 and 207), three blue (all at 223) and two pink (H = 348 and 354). The histogram of the Hue component of the same image is presented in Figure 5.

Now that the color of each circle is known, deciding which circle is the ball and which ones are parts of the same robot can be done by solving a problem of constraint satisfaction. According to Russell and Norvig a constraint satisfaction problem is "a special kind of search problem that satisfies additional structural proprieties beyond the basic requirements form problems in general" [9]. In this kind problem, the states are defined by the value of a set of variables and the goals specify constraints that these values must obey. In the robot recognition problem, the constraints are that the two circles that are in the robot identification label must be at a fixed distance, $2r$. Another constraint is that each circle of a primary color must be matched with one circle of a secondary color.

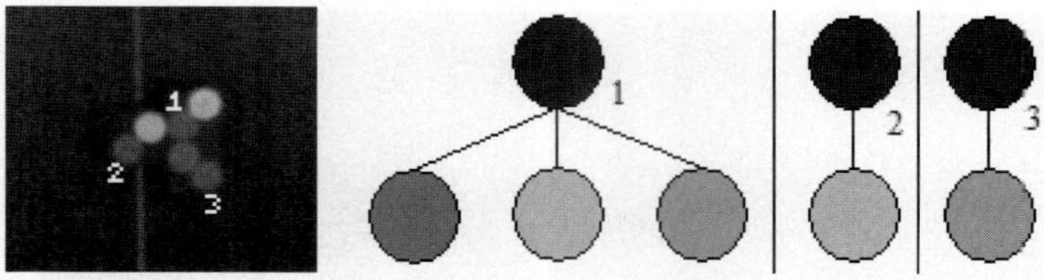

Fig. 6. (left) Image with three robots touching each other and (right) the trees build by the algorithm

To identify which circles belongs to each robot, the algorithm searches in the vector of centers which circles are of a primary color (blue or yellow): this circles are defined as roots of three trees. After defining the roots, the algorithm searches in the vector for circles that are at $2r$ from the primary color circles, and adds them as child nodes of the corresponding tree.

If all robots are located distant one from another, this procedure will result in three trees with only one root and one child, defining a robot. Having a center for each labeled circle and the position of the circles known, the algorithm determines the global position (x, y) of the robot on the image and its direction angle in relation to the axis x. As the ball is the only object that can be orange because this color cannot be used for any another object, any orange circle is considered a ball and there is no need to construct a tree to recognize balls.

However, there might be a situation where robots are close to each other, or even touching each other, as in Figure 6-left. In this case, instead of a tree for each robot, the algorithm will build one tree with three child nodes. It will also build two trees with one child node, as expected (Figure 6-right). In this case, the algorithm needs to remove child nodes from the tree with three child nodes. To do this, first nodes that are not of a secondary color are removed (it might be another robot's primary color or the ball). And second, the algorithm removes from the wrong tree the circles that are of a secondary color which are already represented in a correct tree. The algorithm will stop when all the trees are correct, representing one robot. The final output of the implemented system can be observed in Figure 7-right.

The system described in this section was developed to work in two different situations: first, when the two teams have the same kind of robot label on the top of them and second, when the opponent have a different label. In the first case, the system will recognize the opponent in the same way it recognizes its own players. In the second case, the detection of the opponent robots is done by the following method: first, from the histogram of the image resulting of background subtraction (Fig. 5), the range of the yellow color is defined; then a sparse pixel sampling is done. The result of this sampling is the position of yellow pixels that define the possible position of the opponent robots. This algorithm is very fast, as it does not sample the whole image. And as the strategy and control algorithms of the system needs only an estimate of the position of the opponents, to be able to block their attack movement or not touch them, precision is not needed.

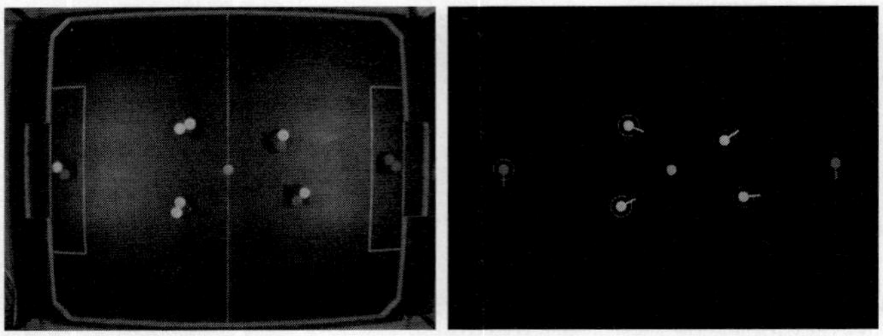

Fig. 7. (left) Captured image containing a ball and two complete teams of robots and (right) result of the execution of the system, showing the computed position of each object

4 Experiments and Results

The HT implementation was made in C++ and the computational vision library OpenCV [10] was used. The results were obtained in a computer with an Intel Pentium 4 processor running at 3.2 GHz. The program was executed under Windows XP, configured for priority in real time.

As the goal was to use the system for an application in real time, the performance evaluation considers as being an acceptable maximum time for the algorithm execution the time interval of an image acquisition. The acquisition systems commonly used in Robot Soccer, as the described in this work, are able to acquire 30 pictures per second. Therefore, the maximum time available for processing is 33 ms.

Table 1 presents the performance results for the implemented system, showing the amount of time needed for each processing stage. The values presented are the average of the execution of the system with 30 different images, in two different resolutions (320x240 pixels and 640x480 pixels, both 24 bits NTSC color images). The images used in this test contained six robots and two balls. In each image, the objects are in a different position, spread randomly over the entire field, including the corners. The difference between the sum of the stages times and the total time is small and can be considered rounding error. This results show that the implemented system is capable of recognizing objects not only in real time, but allowing 13 ms for other processes, as strategy and robots control.

As previously mentioned, all adjustable parameters of the system were kept constant for all experiments described in this work. For images with a resolution of 640x480, the radius r was set to 8 pixels, while the minimum number of votes was set to 16. For images with a resolution of 320x240, the radius r was set to 4 pixels and the minimum number to 10. The thresholds of the Canny filter were defined off-line: the low threshold used was 75 and the high threshold was 150.

To verify the robustness of the system in respect to light intensity variation, a second experience was performed: again, 6 robots and 2 balls were placed in a random position of the field and then the light intensity was slowly changed from 300 Lux to 1300 Lux. This experiment was repeated 10 times, each time placing

Table 1. Execution Times (in milliseconds)

Task	*Image size*	
	320x240	640x480
Background subtraction	0,8412 ± 0.001	5,1667 ± 0.003
Color + Canny filter	1,6163 ± 0.002	7,8435 ± 0.005
Hough Space Generation	1,4621 ± 0.006	6,3683 ± 0.02
Circle Centers Determination	0,0334 ± 0.001	0,0267 ± 0.001
Objects Recognition	0,0031 ± 0.0001	0,0023 ± 0.0001
Total time	4,0674 ± 0.009	19,4083 ± 0.03

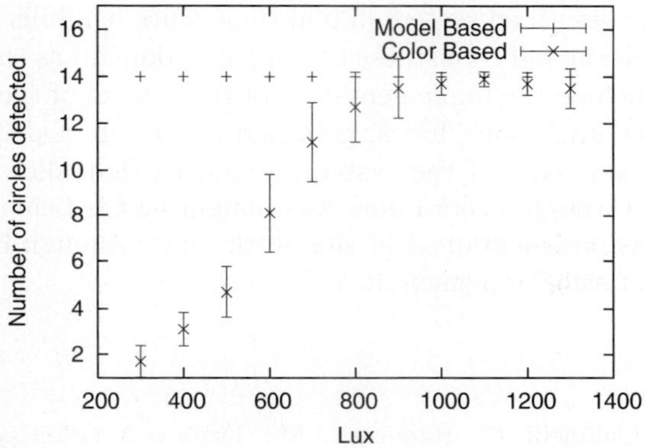

Fig. 8. Number of detected objects versus light intensity variation for the model-based system proposed in this work and the color-based system implemented by [11]

the objects in a different position, randomly chosen. To be able to compare the system described in this paper, the same experiment was performed with a color based system that uses threshold and blob coloring techniques to find the robots, calibrated at 1000 Lux [11].

The result of these experiments is presented in Figure 8. It can be seen that, while the system proposed in this work is robust to light intensity variation, detecting all objects in all the trials, the color based system only performed well when light intensity was near 1000 Lux. This experiment also indicates that color noise do not affect the system. As it is model-based, different illumination in the same image may change the color of an object, but, nevertheless, will not affect the system capability to compute the position of any object. Finally, the system was tested while controlling the robots during a real game, with the robots moving in all positions of the field, presenting the same performance as in the two experiences described above.

5 Conclusion and Future Work

This paper described the use of artificial intelligence and computer vision techniques to create a fast and robust real time vision system for a robot soccer team. To increase the system performance, this work proposes a new approach to interpret the space created by the Hough Transform, as well as a fast object recognition method based on constraint satisfaction techniques. The system was implemented entirely in software using an off-the-shelf frame grabber.

Experiments using real time image acquisition allow to conclude that the implemented system is robust and tolerant to noises and color variation since it considers just the objects form, and automatically determines the color information, needed only to distinguish the robots among themselves. Robots are well detected in every position of the field, even in the corners or inside the goal area, where light intensity is lower than in the center of the field. The measured execution performance and the tests of object recognition demonstrate that it is possible to use the described system in real time, since it fulfills the demands on performance, precision and robustness existing in a domain as the Robot Soccer.

Future works include the implementation of the control of the camera parameters, such as aperture, zoom, focus, gain and others, in real time. To be able to construct this new part of the system, a camera that allows the control of these parameters through a serial port was bought and is being tested. Finally, distortion lens was not mentioned in this work and, although being small, will be addressed in a future implementation.

References

[1] Grittani, G., Gallinelli, G., Ramírez, J.M.: Futbot: A vision system for robotic soccer. In Monard, M.C., Sichman, J.S., eds.: IBERAMIA-SBIA 2000. Volume 1952 of Lecture Notes in Artificial Intelligence., Springer (2000) 350–358
[2] Hough, P.V.C.: Machine analysis of bubble chamber pictures. In: International Conference on High Energy Accelerators and Instrumentation, CERN. (1959)
[3] Gönner, C., Rous, M., Kraiss, K.F.: Real-time adaptive colour segmentation for the robocup middle size league. In: RoboCup 2004: Robot Soccer World Cup VIII. Volume 3276 of Lecture Notes in Computer Science., Springer (2005) 402–409
[4] Jonker, P., Caarls, J., Bokhove, W.: Fast and accurate robot vision for vision based motion. In: RoboCup 2000: Robot Soccer World Cup IV. Volume 2019 of Lecture Notes in Computer Science., Springer (2000) 149–158
[5] Piccardi, M.: Background subtraction techniques: a review. In: SMC (4), IEEE (2004) 3099–3104
[6] Forsyth, D.A., Ponce, J.: Computer Vision: A Modern Approach. Pearson Higher Education (2002)
[7] Canny, F.J.: A Computational Approach to Edge Detection. IEEE Transactions on Pattern Analysis and Machine Intelligence **8**(6) (1986) 679–698
[8] Bresenham, J.: Algorithm for computer control of a digital plotter. IBM Systems Journal **4**(1) (1965) 25–30
[9] Russell, S., Norvig, P.: Artificial Intelligence: A Modern Approach. Prentice Hall, Upper Saddle River, NJ (1995)
[10] INTEL: OpenCV Reference Manual. INTEL (2005)
[11] Penharbel, E.A., Destro, R., Tonidandel, F., Bianchi, R.A.C.: Filtro de imagem baseado em matriz RGB de cores-padrão para futebol de robôs. In: XXIV Congresso da Sociedade Brasileira de Computação, Salvador, Brasil, SBC (2004)

Statistics of Visual and Partial Depth Data for Mobile Robot Environment Modeling

Luz A. Torres-Méndez[1] and Gregory Dudek[2]

[1] CINVESTAV Unidad Saltillo, Ramos Arizpe, Coahuila, C.P. 25900, Mexico
[2] Centre for Intelligent Machines, McGill University, Montreal, Quebec, H3A 2A7, CA
abril.torres@cinvestav.edu.mx, dudek@cim.mcgill.ca

Abstract. In mobile robotics, the inference of the 3D layout of large-scale indoor environments is a critical problem for achieving exploration and navigation tasks. This article presents a framework for building a 3D model of an indoor environment from partial data using a mobile robot. The modeling of a large-scale environment involves the acquisition of a huge amount of range data to extract the geometry of the scene. This task is physically demanding and time consuming for many real systems. Our approach overcomes this problem by allowing a robot to rapidly collect a set of intensity images and a small amount of range information. The method integrates and analyzes the statistical relationships between the visual data and the limited available depth on terms of small patches and is capable of recovering complete dense range maps. Experiments on real-world data are given to illustrate the suitability of our approach.

1 Introduction

One of the major goals of mobile robot research is the creation of a 3D model from local sensor data collected as the robot moves in an unknown environment. Having a mobile robot able to build a 3D map of the environment is particularly appealing as it can be used for several important applications (e.g. virtual exploration of remote locations, automatic rescue and inspection of hazardous or inhospitable environments, museums' tours, etc.). All these applications depend on the transmission of meaningful visual and geometric information. To this end, suitable sensors to densely cover the environment are required. Since all sensors are imperfect, sensor inputs must be used in a way that enables the robot to interact with its environment successfully in spite of measurement uncertainty. One way to cope with the accumulation of uncertainty is through *sensor fusion*, as different types of sensors can have their data correlated appropriately, strengthening the confidence of the resulting percepts well beyond that of any individual sensor's readings.

A typical 3D model acquisition pipeline is composed by a 3D scanner to acquire precise geometry, and a digital camera to capture appearance information. Photometric details can be acquired easily, however, to acquire dense range maps is a time and energy consuming process, unless costly and/or sophisticated hardware is used. Thus, when building 3D models or map representations of large scenes, is desirable to simplify the way range sensor data is acquired so that time

A. Gelbukh and C.A. Reyes-Garcia (Eds.): MICAI 2006, LNAI 4293, pp. 715–725, 2006.

and energy consumption can be minimized. This can be achieved by acquiring only partial, but reliable, depth information.

Surface depth recovery is essential in multiple applications involving robotics and computer vision. In particular, we investigate the autonomous integration of incomplete sensory data to build a 3D model of an unknown large-scale [1] indoor environment. Thus, the challenge becomes one of trying to extract, from the sparse sensory data, an overall concept of shape and size of the structures within the environment.

We explore and analyze the statistical relationships between intensity and range data in terms of small image patches. Our goal is to demonstrate that the surround (context) statistics on both the intensity and range image patches can provide information to infer the complete 3D layout of space. It has been shown by Lee *et al.* [6] that although there are clear differences between optical and range images, they do have similar second-order statistics and scaling properties (i.e., they both have similar structure when viewed as random variables). Our motivation is to exploit this fact and also that both video imaging and *limited* range sensing are ubiquitous readily-available technologies while complete volume scanning is prohibitive on most mobile platforms.

In summary, this research answers the question of how the statistical nature of visual context can provide information about its geometric properties. In particular, how can the statistical relationships between intensity and range data be modeled reliably such that the inference of unknown range be as accurate as possible?

2 Related Work

Most prior work focuses on the extraction of geometric relationships and calibration parameters in order to achieve realistic and accurate representations of the world. In most cases it is not easy to extract the required features, and human intervention is often required. Moreover, real world environments include a large number of characteristics and properties due to scene illumination, sensor geometry, object geometry, and object reflectance, that have to be taken into account if we want to have a realistic and robust representation.

Dense stereo vision gained popularity in the early 1990's due to the large amount of range data that it could provide [8]. In mobile robotics, a common setup is the use of one or two cameras mounted on the robot to acquire depth information as the robot moves through the environment [9]. The cameras must be precisely calibrated for reasonably accurate results. The depth maps generated by stereo under normal scene conditions (i.e., no special textures or structured lighting) suffer from problems inherent in window-based correlation. These problems manifest as imprecisely localized surfaces in 3D space and as hallucinated surfaces that in fact do not exist. Other works have attempted to model 3D objects from image sequences [2,11], with the effort of reducing the amount

[1] Large-scale space is defined as a physical space that cannot be entirely perceived from a single vantage point [5].

of calibration and avoiding restriction on the camera motion. In general, these methods derive the epipolar geometry and the trifocal tensor from point correspondences. However, they assume that it is possible to run an interest operator such as a corner detector to extract from one of the images a sufficiently large number of points that can then be reliably matched in the other images. It appears that if one uses information of only one type, the reconstruction task becomes very difficult and works well only under narrow constraints.

There is a vast body of research work using laser rangefinders for different applications, particularly, in the 3D reconstruction problem [10,12]. However, the limitations of using only one type of sensor have increased the interest in fusing two or more type of data. Specifically, the fusing of intensity and range information for 3D model building and virtual reality applications [7,12] with promising results. These methods use dense intensity images to provide photometric detail which can be registered and fused with range data to provide geometric detail. However, there is one notable difference, in our work the amount of range data acquired is *very* small compared to the intensity data.

3 Our Framework

This research work focuses on modeling man-made large-scale indoor environments. Man-made indoor environments have inherent geometric and photometric characteristics that can be exploited to help in the reconstruction. We use a robot to navigate the environment, and together with its sensors, captures the geometry and appearance of the environment in order to build a complete 3D model.

We divide the 3D environment modeling in the following stages:

- *data acquisition and registration* of the intensity and partial range data;
- *range synthesis*, which refers to the estimation of dense range maps at each robot pose;
- *data integration* of the local dense range maps to a global map; and
- *3D model representation.*

In this paper, we only cover in detail the first two stages (see [13]). Experiments were carried out into two environments of different size and type of objects they contain. The first environment is a medium-size room (9.5m × 6m × 3m. It contains the usual objects in offices and labs (e.g., chairs, tables, computers, tools, etc.) The second environment is larger (2m × 20m × 3m) and corresponds to the corridors of our building. This environment is mostly composed of walls, doors, windows. The results are shown in each of stage described next.

4 Data Acquisition and Registration

The main aspect of our data acquisition system relies on *how* the data is acquired, which provides two important benefits: *i*) it allows the robot to rapidly collect

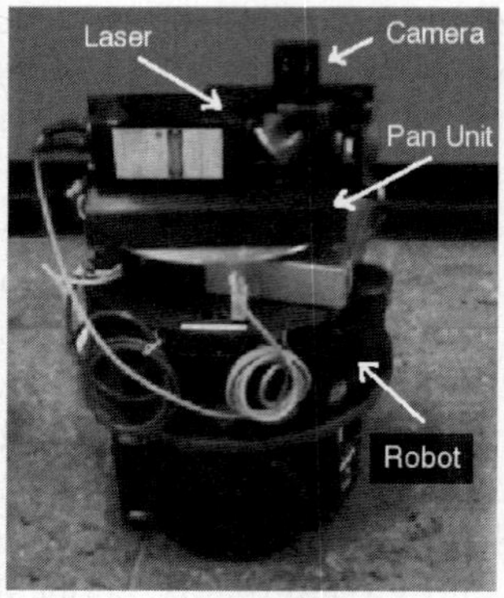

Fig. 1. Our mobile robot with the 2D laser range finder and camera mounted on it

sparse range data and intensity images while navigating the environment to be modeled, and *ii*) it facilitates the sensor-to-sensor registration. The first benefit is essential when dealing with large environments, where the acquisition of huge amount of range data is a time consuming and impractical task. The second benefit is related to the complexity of registering different types of sensor data, which have different projections, resolutions and scaling properties. To this end, an image-based technique is presented for registering the range and intensity data that takes advantage of the way data is acquired.

The mobile robot used in our experiments is a Nomad Super Scout II, manufactured by Nomadics, Inc., retrofitted and customized for this work. On top of the robot we have assembled a system consisting of a 2D laser rangefinder, from Accuity Research, Inc., and a CCD Dragonfly camera from Point Grey Research (see Figure 1) both mounted in a *pan unit*.

The camera is attached to the laser in such a way that their center of projections (optical center for the camera and mirror center for the laser) are aligned to the center of projection of the pan unit. This alignment facilitates the registration between the intensity and range data, as we only need to know their projection types in order to do image mapping.

We assume dense and uniformly sampled intensity images, and sparse but uniformly sampled range images. Since taking images from the camera is an effortless task, sampling of intensity images occurs more often than that of range images. The area covered by the sampling data is equal at each robot pose, it covers approximately a view of 90°. However, the amount of range data may vary depending essentially on the sampling strategy.

4.1 Acquiring Partial Range Data

The spinning mirror (y-axis) of the laser rangefinder and panning motor (x-axis) combine to allow the laser to sweep out a longitude-latitude sphere. Since each step taken by the pan unit can be programmed, we can have different sampling strategies to acquire sparse range data. We adopt a simple heuristic for sampling which depends on how far the robot is from the objects/walls in the scene. Thus, as the robot gets closer to objects, the subsampling can be sparser since no much details are lost, compared to when the robot is located far away.

4.2 Acquiring the Cylindrical Panorama Mosaic

A cylindrical panorama is created by projecting images taken from the same viewpoint, but with different viewing angles onto a cylindrical surface. Each scene point $\mathbf{P} = (x, y, z)^T$ is mapped to cylindrical coordinate system (ψ, v) by

$$\psi = \arctan(\frac{x}{z}), \quad v = f\frac{y}{\sqrt{x^2 + z^2}}. \tag{1}$$

where ψ is the panning angle, v is the scanline, and f is the camera's focal length. The projected images are "stitched" and correlated. The cylindrical image is built by translating each component image with respect to the previous one. Due to possible misalignments between images, both a horizontal t_x and a vertical t_y translations are estimated for each input image. We then estimate the incremental translation $\delta\mathbf{t} = (\delta t_x, \delta t_y)$ by minimizing the intensity error between two images,

$$E(\delta\mathbf{t}) = \sum_{\mathbf{i}} [\mathbf{I_1}(\mathbf{x'_i} + \delta\mathbf{t}) - \mathbf{I_0}(\mathbf{x_i})]^{\mathbf{2}}, \tag{2}$$

where $\mathbf{x}_i = (x_i, y_i)$ and $\mathbf{x}'_i = (x'_i, y'_i) = (x_i + t_x, y_i + t_y)$ are corresponding points in the two images, and $\mathbf{t} = (\mathbf{t_x}, \mathbf{t_y})$ is the global translational motion field which is the same for all pixels. After a first order Taylor series expansion, the above equation becomes

$$E(\delta\mathbf{t}) \approx \sum_{\mathbf{i}} [\mathbf{g_i^T}\delta\mathbf{t} + \mathbf{e_i}]^{\mathbf{2}}, \tag{3}$$

where $e_i = I_1(x'_i) - I_0(x_i)$ is the current intensity or color error, and $g_i^T = \nabla I_1(x'_i)$ is the image gradient of I_1 at x'_i. This minimization problem has a simple least-squares solution,

$$(\sum_i g_i g_i^T)\delta\mathbf{t} = -(\sum_{\mathbf{i}} [\mathbf{e_i g_i}]). \tag{4}$$

The complexity of the registration lies on the amount of overlap between the images to be aligned. In our experimental apparatus, as the panning angles at which images are taken is known, the overlap can be as small as 10% and still be able to align the images. To reduce discontinuities in intensity between images, we weight each pixel in every image proportionally to their distance to the edge of the image (i.e., it varies linearly from 1 at the centre of the image to 0 at the edge), so that intensities in the overlap area show a smooth transition between intensities in one image to intensities of the other image. A natural weighting function is the *hat function*,

$$\mathbf{w}(x, y) = \|\frac{h/2 - x}{h/2}\| - \|\frac{w/2 - y}{w/2}\| \tag{5}$$

Fig. 2. A cylindrical panorama

where h and w are the height and the width of the image. In our experiments, the pan unit rotates at every 18 degrees. Figure 2 presents a 180° cylindrical panorama constructed using the technique described above.

4.3 Camera-Laser Data Registration: Panorama with Depth

The panoramic image mosaic and the incomplete spherical range data must be registered for the range synthesis. An image-based technique, similar to that in [1], is used that recovers the projective model transformation by computing a direct mapping between the points in the data sets. First, we need to convert the spherical range image to a cylindrical representation similar to that of the panoramic image mosaic, to do that the radius of the cylindrical range image must be equal to the camera's focal length. This mapping is given by

$$\mathbf{P}(r, \theta, \phi) \mapsto \mathbf{P}(r, \phi, \frac{f}{\tan \theta}) \mapsto \mathbf{P}(r, \phi, h) \tag{6}$$

where r represents the distance from the center of the cylinder to the point, h is the height of the point projected on the cylinder, ϕ is the azimuth angle and f the focal length of the camera (see Fig. 3). Again, this data is sampled on a cylindrical grid (ϕ, h) and represented as a cylindrical image.

Once having the intensity and range data in similar cylindrical image representations, a global mapping between them is computed. For a point $x_l(\phi, h)$ in the cylindrical laser image, its corresponding point in the panoramic mosaic $x_c(u, v)$ is

$$\begin{aligned} u &= a\phi + \alpha, \\ v &= f\frac{Y - \Delta Y}{r} = f\frac{Y}{r} - f\frac{\Delta Y}{r} \;=\; bh - f\frac{\Delta Y}{r} \end{aligned} \tag{7}$$

where a and b are two warp parameters that will account for difference in resolution between the two images, α aligns the pan rotation, ΔY is a vertical translation between the sensors, and $Y = rh/\sqrt{f^2 + h^2}$ is the height of the 3D point $X(r, \phi, h)$. Since f, ΔY, and the r remain fixed through the experimental setup, the term $f\frac{\Delta Y}{r}$ can be approximated to a constant β. Thus, the general warp equations are:

$$u = a\phi + \alpha, \quad v = bh + \beta \tag{8}$$

The warp parameters (a, b, α, β) are computed by minimizing the sum of the squared error of two or more corresponding points in the two images. The initial

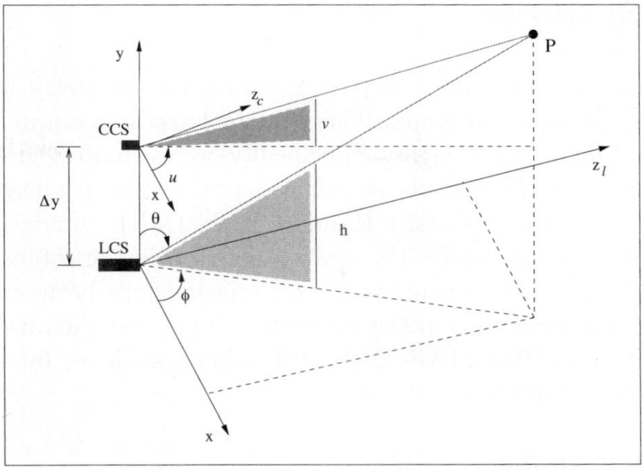

Fig. 3. Projection of the 3D point P onto cylindrical coordinates: (ϕ, h) for the range data and (u, v) for the panoramic mosaic

estimate places the panorama mosaic nearly aligned with the range data, with a moderate translation or misalignment typically of about 5 to 7 pixels. To correct this, a *local alignment* is performed using the set of corresponding control points.

For the arrangement used in these experiments, $f = 300$ pixels, $\Delta Y = 5$ cm and the range of the points is $r = 5 - 8$ m, and β is between 6 to 10 pixel units. Figure 4 shows a samples of the registered panorama mosaic (top) and range image (bottom). It is important to note that the registration was computed using only partial range data as an input, but we show the complete range map for viewing purposes.

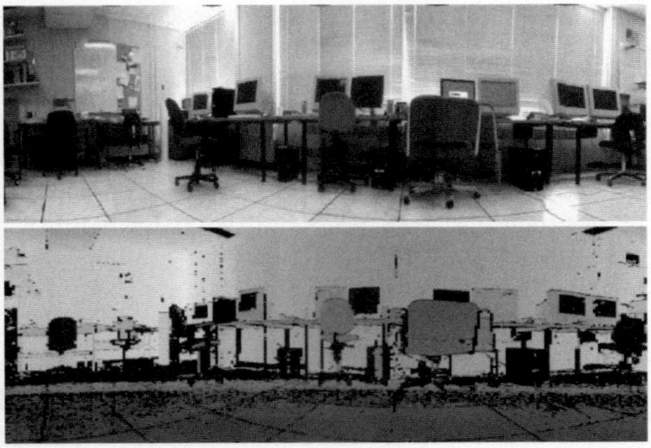

Fig. 4. A registered intensity (top) and range (bottom) data collected from our lab

5 Range Synthesis

After registering the intensity and partial range data at every robot pose, we apply our range synthesis method. The following sections detail our statistical learning method for depth recovery. Specifically, we estimate dense or high resolution range maps of indoor environments using only intensity images and sparse partial depth information. Markov Random Field (MRF) models are proposed as a viable stochastic model for the spatial distribution of intensity and range data. This model is trained using the (local) relationships between the observed range data and the variations in the intensity images and then used to compute unknown depth values. The MAP-MRF estimation is achieved by using the belief propagation (BP) algorithm.

5.1 The MRF Model

The range estimation problem can be posed as a labeling problem. A labeling is specified in terms of a set of *sites* and a set of *labels*. In our case, sites represent the pixel intensities in the matrix I and the labels represent the depth values in R. Let $\mathcal{S}$ index a discrete set of M sites $\mathcal{S} = \{s_1, s_2, ..., s_M\}$, and $\mathcal{L}$ be the set of corresponding labels $\mathrm{L} = \{l_1, l_2, ..., l_M\}$, where each l_i takes a depth value. The inter-relationship between sites and labels define the *neighborhood system* $\mathcal{N} = \{N_s \mid \forall s \in \mathcal{S}\}$, where N_s is the set of *neighbors* of s, such that (1) $s \not\in N_s$, and (2) $s \in N_r \iff r \in N_s$. Each site s_i is associated with a random variable (*r.v.*) F_i. Formally, let $\mathrm{F} = \{F_1, ..., F_M\}$ be a random field defined on $\mathcal{S}$, in which a r.v. F_i takes a value f_i in $\mathcal{L}$. A realization $f = f_1, ..., f_M$, is called a *configuration* of F, corresponding to a realization of the field. The r.v. F defined on $\mathcal{S}$ are related to one another via the neighborhood system $\mathcal{N}$. F is said to be an MRF on $\mathcal{S}$ with respect to $\mathcal{N}$ iff the following two conditions are satisfied [4]:

$$1)\ P(f) > 0 \text{ (positivity), } \quad \text{and } 2)\ P(f_i \mid f_{\mathcal{S}-\{i\}}) = P(f_i \mid f_{N_i}) \quad \text{(Markovianity).}$$

where $\mathcal{S} - \{i\}$ is the set difference, $f_{\mathcal{S}-\{i\}}$ denotes the set of labels at the sites in $\mathcal{S} - \{i\}$ and $f_{N_i} = \{f'_i \mid i' \in N_i\}$ stands for the set of labels at the sites neighboring i. The Markovianity condition describes the local characteristics of F. The depth value (label) at a site is dependent only on the augmented voxels (containing intensity and/or range) at the neighboring sites. In other words, only neighboring augmented voxels have direct interactions on each other.

The choice of N together with the conditional probability distribution of $P(f_i \mid f_{\mathcal{S}-\{i\}})$, provides a powerful mechanism for modeling spatial continuity and other scene features. On one hand, we choose to model a neighborhood N_i as a square mask of size $n \times n$ centered at pixel location i, where only those augmented voxels with already assigned intensity and range values are considered in the synthesis process. On the other hand, calculating the conditional probabilities in an explicit form to infer the exact maximum *a posteriori* (MAP) in MRF models is intractable. We cannot efficiently represent or determine all the possible combinations between pixels with its associated neighborhoods. Various techniques exist for approximating the MAP estimate, such as Markov Chain

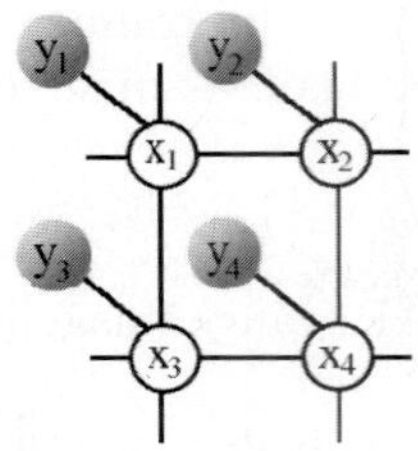

Fig. 5. Pairwise Markov network for the range estimation problem

Monte Carlo (MCMC), iterated conditional modes (ICM), etc. We avoid the computational expense of sampling from a probability distribution and use the belief propagation algorithm to compute marginal probabilities.

5.2 MAP-MRF Using Belief Propagation (BP)

In order to propagate evidence, we use a pairwise Markov network. BP efficiently estimates Bayesian beliefs in the MRF network by iteratively passing messages between neighboring nodes. The pairwise Markov network for the range estimation problem is shown in Fig. 5, where the observation node y_i is a neighborhood in intensity centered at voxel location i, and the hidden nodes x_i are the depth values to be estimated, but also hidden nodes contain the already available range data (as image patches), whose beliefs remain fixed at all times.

Learning the Compatibility Functions. A *local* subset of patches containing intensity and range are used as training pairs to learn the compatibility functions. This reflects our heuristics about how the intensity values locally provide knowledge about the type of surface that intensity value belongs to.

As in [3], we use the overlapping information from the intensity image patches themselves, to estimate the compatibilities $\Psi(x_j, x_k)$ between neighbors. Let k and j be two neighboring intensity image patches. Let d^l_{jk} be a vector of pixels of the lth possible candidate for image patch x_k which lie in the overlap region with patch j. Likewise, let d^m_{kj} be the values of the pixels (in correspondence with those of d^l_{jk}) of mth candidate for patch x_j which overlap patch k. We say that image candidates x^l_k (candidate l at node k) and x^m_j are compatible with each other if the pixels in their region of overlap agree. We assume a Gaussian noise of covariance σ_i and σ_s, respectively. Then, the compatibility matrix between range nodes k and j are defined as follows:

$$\Psi(x^l_k, x^m_j) = \exp^{-|d^l_{jk} - d^m_{kl}|^2/2\sigma^2_s}. \tag{9}$$

The rows and columns of the compatibility matrix $\Phi(x^l_k, x^m_j)$ are indexed by l and m, the range image candidates at each node, at nodes j and k.

We say that a range image patch candidate x^l_k is compatible with an observed intensity image patch y_0 if the intensity image patch y^l_k, associated with the range image patch candidate x_k^l in the training database matches y_0. Since it will not exactly match, we must again assume "noisy" training data and define the compatibility

$$\Phi(x_k^l, y_k) = \exp^{-|y_k^l - y_o|^2/2\sigma_s^2}. \quad (10)$$

The maximum a posteriori (MAP) range image patch for node i is:

$$x_{iMAP} = \arg\max_{\mathbf{x}_i} \Phi(x_i, y_i) \prod_{j \in \mathrm{N}(i)} M_{ji}(x_i). \quad (11)$$

where $N(i)$ are all node neighbors of node i, and M_{ji} is the message from node j to node i and is computed as follows (Z is the normalization constant):

$$M_{ij}(x_j) = Z \sum_{x_i} \Psi(x_i, x_j)\Phi(x_i, y_i) \prod_{k \in \mathrm{N}(i)\setminus\{j\}} M_{ki}(x_i) \quad (12)$$

An example of applying our range synthesis algorithm is shown in Fig. 6. In (a) is the input intensity, (b) the input partial range data, where 50% of the total range is unknown. The resulted synthesized range image is shown in (c), and the ground truth range image in (d), for comparison purposes. The MAR error for this example is 7.85 cm.

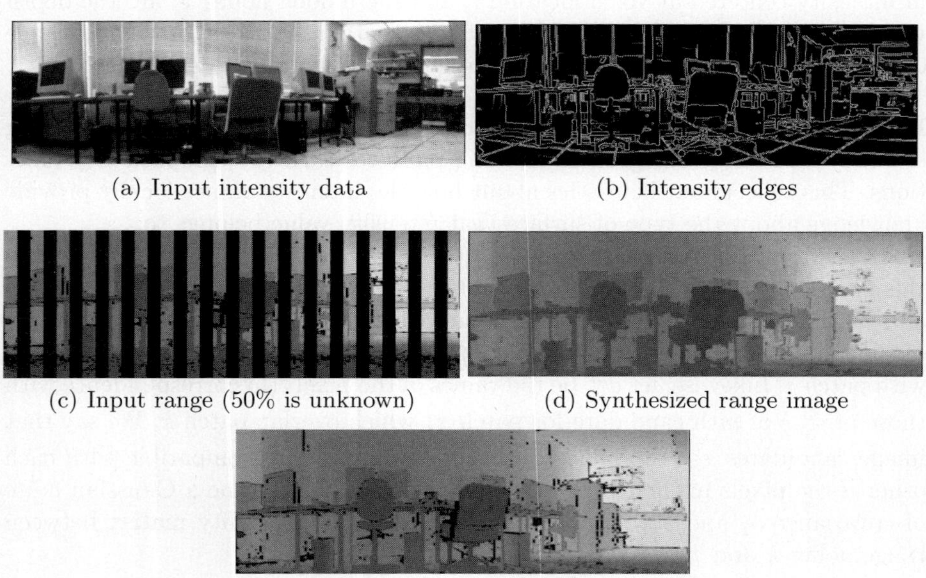

(a) Input intensity data (b) Intensity edges

(c) Input range (50% is unknown) (d) Synthesized range image

(e) Ground truth range

Fig. 6. Results on dense range map estimation. (a)-(b) Input data to our range synthesis algorithm. (c) The synthesized range image and (d) the ground truth range.

6 Conclusions

The ability to reconstruct a 3D model of an object or scene greatly depends on the type, quality and amount of information available. The data acquisition framework described here was designed to speed up the acquisition of range data by obtaining a relatively small amount of range information from the scene to be modeled. By doing so, we compromise the accuracy of our final representation. However, since we are dealing with man-made environments, the coherence of surfaces and their causal inter-relationships with the photometric information facilitate the estimation of complete range maps from the partial range data.

Acknowledgements

We would like to thank to Conacyt and NSERC for funding this research work.

References

1. D. Cobzas. *Image-Based Models with Applications in Robot Navigation.* PhD thesis, University of Alberta, Canada, 2003.
2. A.W. Fitzgibbon and A. Zisserman. Automatic 3d model acquisition and generation of new images from video sequences. In *Proceedings of European Signal Processing Conference*, pages 1261–1269, 1998.
3. W.T. Freeman, E.C. Pasztor, and O.T. Carmichael. Learning low-level vision. *International Journal of Computer Vision*, 20(1):25–47, 2000.
4. J.M. Hammersley and P. Clifford. Markov field on finite graphs and lattices. In *Unpublished*, 1971.
5. B. Kuipers. Modelling spatial knowledge. *Cognitive Science*, 2:1291–153, 1978.
6. A. Lee, K. Pedersen, and D. Mumford. The complex statistics of high-contrast patches in natural images, 2001. private correspondence.
7. M. Levoy, K. Pulli, B. Curless, S. Rusinkiewicz, D. Koller, L. Pereira, M. Ginzton, S. Anderson, J. Davis, J. Ginsberg, J. Shade, and D. Fulk. The digital michelangelo project: 3d scanning of large statues. In *SIGGRAPH*, July 2000.
8. J.J. Little and W.E. Gillett. Direct evidence for oclussion in stereo and motion. *Image and Vision Computing*, 8:328–340, November 1990.
9. D. Murray and J. J. Little. Using real-time stereo vision for mobile robot navigation. *Autonomous Robots*, 8(2):161–171, 2000.
10. L. Nyland, D. McAllister, V. Popescu, C. McCue, A. Lastra, P. Rademacher, M. Oliveira, G. Bishop, G. Meenakshisundaram, M. Cutts, and H. Fuchs. The impact of dense range data on computer graphics. In *Proceedings of Multi-View Modeling and Analysis Workshop (MVIEW part of CVPR)*, page 8, June 1999.
11. M. Pollefeys, R. Koch, M. Vergauwen, and L. Van Gool. Metric 3d surface reconstruction from uncalibrated images sequences. In *Proceedings of SMILE Workshop (post-ECCV)*, pages 138–153, 1998.
12. I. Stamos and P.K. Allen. 3d model construction using range and image data. In *CVPR*, June 2000.
13. L. Abril Torres-Méndez. *Statistics of Visual and Partial Depth Data for Mobile Robot Environment Modeling.* PhD thesis, McGill University, 2005.

Automatic Facial Expression Recognition with AAM-Based Feature Extraction and SVM Classifier

Xiaoyi Feng, Baohua Lv, Zhen Li, and Jiling Zhang

School of Electronic and Information, Northwestern Polytechnic University
710072, Xi'an, China
fengxiaoo@nwpu.edu.cn

Abstract. In this paper, an effective method is proposed for automatic facial expression recognition from static images. First, a modified Active Appearance Model (AAM) is used to locate facial feature points automatically. Then, based on this, facial feature vector is formed. Finally, SVM classifier with a sample selection method is adopted for expression classification. Experimental results on the JAFFE database demonstrate an average recognition rate of 69.9% for novel expressers, showing that the proposed method is promising.

1 Introduction

Though numerous algorithms [1]-[8] have been proposed for facial expression recognition from single images during the past years, it is still a challenge in the computer vision area.

In general, some difficulties exist for expression recognition from single images. First, it is required to locate some facial feature points accurately for feature vector extraction in most methods. Since there is still no efficient solution for this question, these feature points are usually marked manually. In [4]-[6], 34 fiducial points had to be marked manually during both training and testing procedure for feature vector extraction. In [7], facial area was cropped manually and resized. As a result, the whole expression recognition procedure is not fully automatic. Second, since there are quite limited training samples and some samples are not typical or are even inaccurate in many cases, it is hard to reach well recognition result in this situation. In [4]-[7], some samples from The Japanese Female Facial Expression (JAFFE) Database [4] are posed exactly and a few samples are marked wrongly. Besides of this, the selection of facial features is still a question since only limited information for expression actions is available from static images. Most of current works used texture information (in [4], [6], [7]) or the combination of texture and shape information (in [5]) extracted from several facial feature points to describe face, while information in several feature points is hard to reflect face's global feature exactly.

The Local Binary Pattern (LBP) technique was used to extract facial texture features in our previous work (see [8],[9]). Compared to the above methods, LBP based feature extraction needed only locate position of two pupils manually. Experimental results also show that the feature vector can describe face efficiently for expression recognition. Three questions still existed in our work: First, it is not fully automatic

A. Gelbukh and C.A. Reyes-Garcia (Eds.): MICAI 2006, LNAI 4293, pp. 726 – 733, 2006.

since pupils were needed to be located manually in our method. Second, the LBP based feature is face's global texture feature and it is effective to reflect obvious or typical expressions, but it is not good at describing small and local expression changes. Third, improper and bad training samples were still not taken into consider.

In this paper, an effective method is proposed to solve the above questions. First, AAM is modified to detect facial feature points of expressive faces automatically, then the center of eyes, mouth are calculated and faces are normalized. Second, local texture information, global texture information and shape information are combined together to form the feature vector. Third, bad samples are removed from training samples automatically and then SVM classifier is used for expression classification.

The rest of the paper is organized as follows. The database used in our experiments is first introduced in section 2. The modified AAM based feature points location and feature extraction method is proposed in section 3. In section 4, we introduce the expression classification method. Experimental results are shown in section 5. Finally in section 6 , we conclude the paper.

2 Facial Expression Database

The database we use in our study contains 213 images of Japanese Female Facial Expression (JAFFE) [4]. Ten expressers pose 3 or 4 examples of each of the seven basic expressions (happiness, sadness, surprise, anger, disgust, fear, neutral). Sample images from the database are shown in Fig.1.

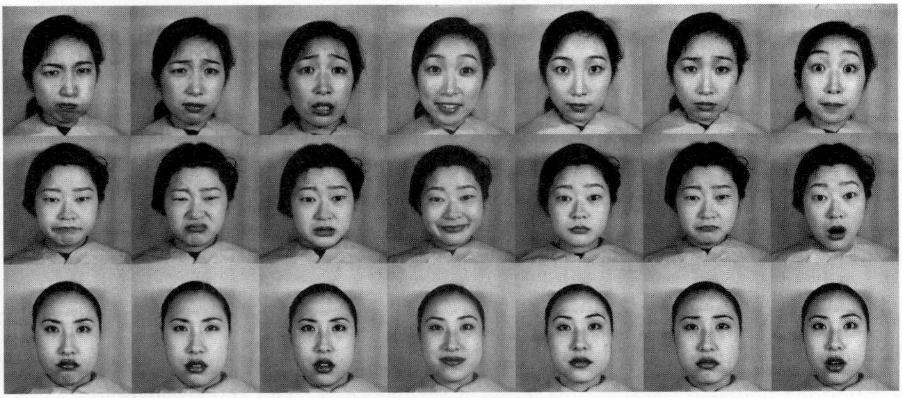

Fig. 1. Samples from the Japanese Females Facial Expression Image Database

3 Feature Extraction Based on AAM

The Active Appearance Model (AAM) is a powerful method for matching a combined model of shape and texture to unseen faces [10] and it is modified in our work for facial feature points detection.

3.1 Active Appearance Models (AAM)

The shape and texture model can be illustrated as follows:

$$s_i = \bar{s} + Q_s b_s$$
$$g_i = \bar{g} + Q_g b_g \tag{1}$$

where s_i and g_i are, respectively, the synthesized shape and shape-free texture, Q_s and Q_g are the matrices describing the modes of variation derived from the training set, b_s and b_g are the vectors controlling the synthesized shape and shape free texture.

To construct an AAM, a labeled training set is needed in which each image is accompanied with data specifying the coordinates of landmark points around the main facial features (see Fig.2). The appearance model is then obtained by constructing a shape model using the coordinate data and a texture model using both the image data and the coordinate data. The shape model is built by aligning all of the shape vectors to a common coordinate frame and performing Principal Component Analysis (PCA) on these. The shape model is then controlled by b_s and $\bar{s}$ is the mean of the aligned shape vectors. Similarly to the shape, after computing the mean shape-free texture $\bar{g}$, all the textures in the training set can be normalized with respect to it by scaling and offset of luminance values.

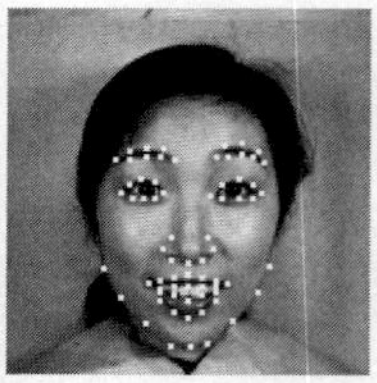

Fig. 2. Location of feature points

The unification of the presented shape and texture models into one complete appearance model is obtained by concatenating the vectors b_s and b_g and learning the correlations between them by means of a further PCA. The statistical model is then given by:

$$s_i = \bar{s} + Q_s c_i$$
$$g_i = \bar{g} + Q_g c_i \tag{2}$$

Here Q_s and Q_g are truncated matrices describing the principal modes of combined appearance variations, which are derived from the training set. $\bar{s}$ and $\bar{g}$ are the mean shape and texture of samples in the training set. c_i are the vector of appearance parameters simultaneously controlling the shape s_i and texture g_i.

In our work, 70 points (16 points in eyes, 16 points in eyebrows, 7 points in nose, 22 points in mouth, and 9 points in face contour) are selected as feature points to model face shapes (see Fig.2).

It can be seen from the experiments that the AAM based feature detection is sensitively to expressions. To assure that it can work effectively under different expressions, we produce 7 pairs of shape models and texture models from the training set, each corresponding to one kind of expressions. In the detecting procedure, the most matched one is selected as the final search result.

Another modification of basic AAM in our work is the utilization of the fact that face is symmetric during searching procedure, which will avoid some unwanted wrong searching result.

3.2 Face Normalization Based on Modified AAM

Suppose $e_l = \{(x_i, y_i) | i = 0,1,\cdots n-1\}$ describe the coordinates of searched feature points on the left eye and (x_{el}, y_{el}) denotes this eye's center. They can be calculated as follows.

$$x_{el} = \frac{1}{n}\sum_{i=0}^{n-1} x_i$$
$$y_{el} = \frac{1}{n}\sum_{i=0}^{n-1} y_i \qquad (3)$$

Center of the right eye and mouth can be obtained in the similar way.

After location of eyes and mouth, the images are registered using eyes and mouth's coordinates and cropped with an elliptical mask to exclude non-face area from the image. As a result, the size of each normalized image is 150×128(see Fig.3).

It should be noticed here that since eyes' and mouth's center are determined by several feature points, they can be calculated correctly enough for face normalization, even if several feature points are not located quite exactly. Our experiments also illustrate that the proposed center location method performs better than other methods such as valley detection method.

3.3 Feature Vector Extraction

To make the feature vector presents both local and global features of the face, the combination of local texture information, global texture information and shape information is used to form the feature vector. The Local Binary Pattern (LBP) technique is also used here for texture information extraction.

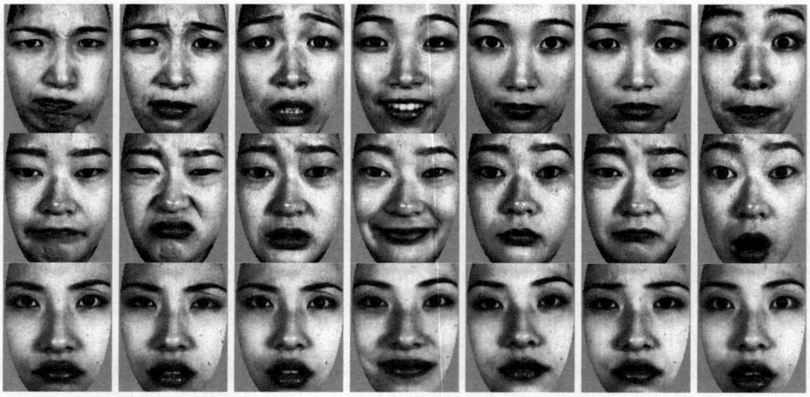

Fig. 3. Samples of the normalized images. The resolution is 150×128 pixels.

3.3.1 Texture Feature Extraction

In our previous work, global texture (suppose as v_{tg}) is extracted with the following steps: First, the normalized face area is first divided into 80 small non-overlapping regions. Then, the LBP histogram of each region is calculated. Finally, the LBP feature histograms of each region are concatenated into a single feature vector.

Here we use a similar way for global texture information extraction. While to reduce the dimension of the feature vector, we adopt its extension patterns, and also, only 36 from the 80 blocks are used for feature extraction. As a result, the dimension of this vector is 360.

The feature vector of local texture information (supposed as v_{tl}) is formed by the gray changes of each feature points detected by AAM, so the dimension of it is 70.

3.3.2 Shape Feature Extraction

In our method, the shape feature of one expressive sample is presented with the difference between its mean shape vector and that of neutrals.

Let $\overline{s}_N$ denoted the mean shape of the training neutral samples, and s_i denoted the shape of one testing sample. The shape feature of the testing sample are defined as

$$v_s = s_i - \overline{s}_N \tag{4}$$

Other shape feature of template and testing samples can be defined in the similar way with a dimension of 140.

As a result, the new feature vector v is composed as

$$v = \{v_{tg}, v_{tl}, v_s\} \tag{5}$$

4 Expression Classification with SVM

To further improve the discrimination of our method, seven expressions are decomposed to 21 expression pairs in the classification step, such as anger-fear, happiness-sadness etc, so the 7-class classification problem is decomposed into 21 two-class classification problems. A simple binary tree tournament scheme with pair-wise comparisons is used here for classifying one kind of expression. We choose SVM classifier since it is well founded in statistical learning theory and has been successfully applied to various object detection tasks in computer vision.

The SVM classifier for each expression pair (for example, anger and fear) is formed as follows: Given training samples (for example, anger and fear images) represented by their features, an SVM classifier finds the separating hyperplane that has maximum distance to the closest points of the training set. To perform a nonlinear separation, the input space is mapped onto a higher dimensional space using the second degree polynomial kernel function defined by

$$k(v,\bar{v}_i)=(1+\psi(v,\bar{v}_i))^2 \tag{6}$$

Where v and $\bar{v}_i$ are feature vectors of the testing sample and the i th training sample, ψ is defined as

$$\psi(v,\bar{v}_i)=\frac{1}{N}\sum_j\frac{\left|v^j-\bar{v}_i^j\right|}{v^j+\bar{v}_i^j} \tag{7}$$

The classifier decides on the "anger" or "fear" in an image according to the sign of the following function:

$$E(v)=\mathrm{sgn}(\sum_{i=0}^{n}\alpha_i\lambda_i k(v,\bar{v}_i)+\beta) \tag{8}$$

Where α_i is the parameter of the SVM classifier and λ_i is 1 or -1 depending on whether this training sample is an angry image or a fear image, n is the number of samples, β is a bias.

The SVM classifier is sensitive to training samples, while several samples in the JAFFE database were improper posed or even inaccurate marked. To ensure that the SVM classifier effective, the Chi square statistic (χ^2) is used to remove these bad samples from the training set, that is to say, samples whose distance is nearer the center of other kind of samples than its own is regarded as not good samples and should be removed from the training set.

5 Experimental Results

Our method is tested on the Japanese Female Facial Expression (JAFFE) Database [4], which is usually divided in three ways. The first way is to divide the whole database randomly into 10 roughly equal-sized segments, of which nine segments are used for training and the last one for testing. The second way is similar to the first one, but 193 from 213 images are divided into 9 parts. The third way is to divide the database into several segments, but each segment corresponds to one expresser.

To compare our results to other methods, we choose the third way to divide the database: 193 expression images posed by nine expressers are partitioned into nine segments, each corresponding to one expresser. Eight of the nine segments are used for both face model and expression template training and the ninth for testing. The above process is repeated so that each of the nine partitions is used once as the test set.The average of recognizing the expression of novel expressers is 69.9%.

Now we compare the recognition performance to other published methods using the same database. In [4], a result of 75% using Linear Discriminant Analysis (LDA) was reported with 193 images, but it needs to locate 34 fidual points manually. While in our method, the recognition procedure is fully automatic.

6 Conclusion

How to recognize facial expressions of a novel expresser from static images is one of the challenging tasks in facial expression recognition. The Local Binary Pattern technique was used to represent face global texture effectively in our previous work. To improve its performance, an effective feature vector is proposed in this paper, which take the local texture feature, global texture feature and shape feature into consider. To make the whole recognition procedure automatically, AAM method is modified and used for feature points' location. Finally, an effective method is proposed to remove bad sample automatically and then SVM classifier is used for expression classification. Experimental results demonstrated that our method performs well on the JAFFE database.

Acknowledgement

The author would like to thank Dr. M. Lyons for providing the facial expression database. Financial support for this work was obtained from the natural science foundation of Shaanxi province and the NWPU talent program, which are greatly acknowledged.

References

1. M. Pantic, Leon J.M. Rothkrantz: Automatic analysis of facial expressions: the state of the art, IEEE Transactions on Pattern Analysis and Machine Intelligence, Vol. 22 (2000) 1424-1445
2. B. Fasel and J. Luettin: Automatic facial expression analysis: A survey, Pattern Recognition, Vol. 36 (2003) 259-275
3. W. Fellenz, J. Taylor, N. Tsapatsoulis, S. Kollias: Comparing template-based, feature-based and supervised classification of facial expression from static images, Computational Intelligence and Applications, (1999)
4. M. Lyons, J. Budynek, S. Akamastu: Automatic classification of single facial images, IEEE Trans. Pattern Analysis and Machine Intelligence, Vol. 21(1999) 1357-1362
5. Z. Zhang: Feature-based facial expression recognition: Sensitivity analysis and experiment with a multi-layer perceptron, Pattern Recognition and Artificial Intelligence, Vol. 13(1999) 893-911

6. W. Zheng, X.Zhou, C. Zou, L. Zhao. Facial expression recognition using kernel canonical correlation analysis (KCCA), *IEEE Trans. Neural Networks*, Vol.17 (2006) 233-238
7. Y.Shinohara, N.Otsu. Facial Expression Recognition Using Fisher Weight Maps, *IEEE* Conf. on Automatic Face and Guesture Recognition (2004) 499-504
8. X.Feng, A.Hadid, M.Pietikainen. A Coarse-to-Fine Classification Scheme for Facial Expression Recognition, Image Analysis and Recognition, *ICIA 2004 Proceedings, LNCS 3212*, Springer (2004).668-675
9. X.Feng, A.Hadid, M.Pietikainen. Facial Expression Recognition with Local Binary Patterns and Linear Programming, Pattern Recognition and Image Analysis, Vol. 15 (2005) 546-549
10. T. F. Cootes, P. Kittipanya-ngam, Comparing variations on the active appearance model algorithm, *BMVC (2002)* 837-846

Principal Component Net Analysis for Face Recognition

Lianghua He[1], Die Hu[2], and Changjun Jiang[1]

[1] School of Electronics and Information Engineering, Tongji University, Shanghai, 200092, China
[2] School of Information Science and Engineering, Fudan University, Shanghai, China

Abstract. In this paper, a new feature extraction called principal component net analysis (PCNA) is developed for face recognition. It looks a face image upon as two orthogonal modes: row channel and column channel and extracts Principal Components (PCs) for each channel. Because it does not need to transform an image into a vector beforehand, much more spacial discrimination information is reserved than traditional PCA, ICA etc. At the same time, because the two channels have different physical meaning, its extracted PCs can be understood easier than 2DPCA. Series of experiments were performed to test its performance on three main face image databases: JAFFE, ORL and FERET. The recognition rate of PCNA was the highest (PCNA, PCA and 2DPCA) in all experiments.

1 Introduction

Face recognition has gone through many years and many excellent methods in feature extraction were proposed. One effective way is space transforming, i.e. transforming the original image space to another space where human faces can be easily discriminated, such as PCA[1,2], ICA[3,4], Gabor [5,6],LBP[7] and 2DPCA[8]. PCA and ICA both extend a 2-D face image to a 1D vector and extract features according to the irrelevant or independent rule. Gabor, LBP and 2DPCA have much improvement on extracting 2D dimensional discriminative information and have been paid more and more attention in recent years. But Gabor needs too much calculation because of its convolution and LBP has a too high features dimension to be accepted. For example, if we want to extract the feature in 49 sub-windows using 59 unicodes, the dimension is $49 \times 59 = 2891$ for a face image. For 2DPCA, its features do not have any physic meaning.

In this paper, a novel method called Principal Component Net Analysis (PCNA) is proposed which extracts features according to two orthogonal modes in one face image through minimizing reconstruction error without unfolding face matrix to face vector. For a face image, its texture is both the result of cubical block reflection and planar structure. Different person has different face shape, i.e. different face planar texture. Thus unfolding a face image to a vector is definitely loss some 2D spacial information. At the same time, it is also not as good as transforming it to another low 2D face space. The reason is that every row or column of one face image has its own specific physical meaning after warping and regulating. Any kind of lower dimension space transformation will break the corresponding physical structure. In this paper,

A. Gelbukh and C.A. Reyes-Garcia (Eds.): MICAI 2006, LNAI 4293, pp. 734 – 744, 2006.

different from former traditional methods, we look a face image upon as the result of two orthogonal modes projections: one mode from vertical and the other from horizontal. Then we calculate these two kinds of Principal Components (PCs) which only represent the statistical properties of row and column directions separately. The space constructed by these PCs is used to extract face features with which we can make recognition. Because these PCs are orthogonal and interweave each other and form a principal component net just like the longitudes and latitudes on earth, we call it the PCNA method.

The follow sections are organized as follows: in section 2, not only we describe the PCNA method completeness, but also study some questions when using it in face recognition. Then in section 3, a series of experiments are implemented to test our proposed PCNA method performance. Some proper conclusions are made in the last section.

2 PCNA

2.1 Introduction

In face recognition, the original data is 3D form of $h\times w\times n$ shown in Fig.1 where h,w are the height and width of regulated face images and n is the number of images.

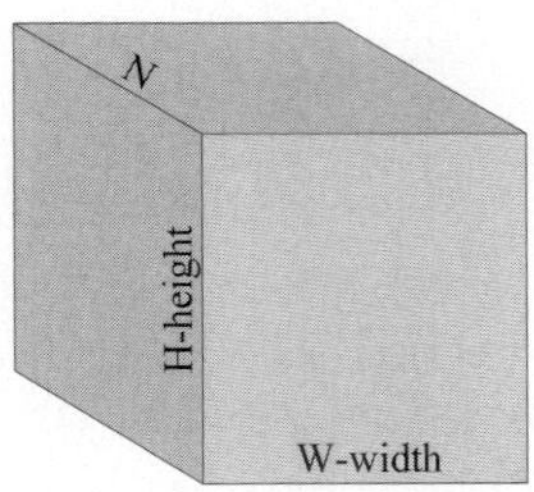

Fig. 1. The original structure of face images data

In general, most feature extraction methods unfold the original face data to a vector along row or column direction before processing which is illustrated in Fig.2. It will bring two major problems: One is that all unfolding processing will damage the spacial discriminating information definitely, on the one hand, a pixel in face image is constrained by eight pixels around it, while after been unfolded, the constraint changes to two pixels. Thus the data are more ruleless and the entropy becomes larger which makes it more difficult to extract stable features to represent the original objects. On the other hand, this can be proved by a common fact that with more 2D information in feature, 2DPCA and Gabor feature are all better than PCA and ICA[8]. The other problem is it blurs the pixels' physical meaning. In most time we do not know what the features stands for.

Thus if we want to extract more discriminable features, the processing process must on the original data. The primary question is how to extract on 3D data?

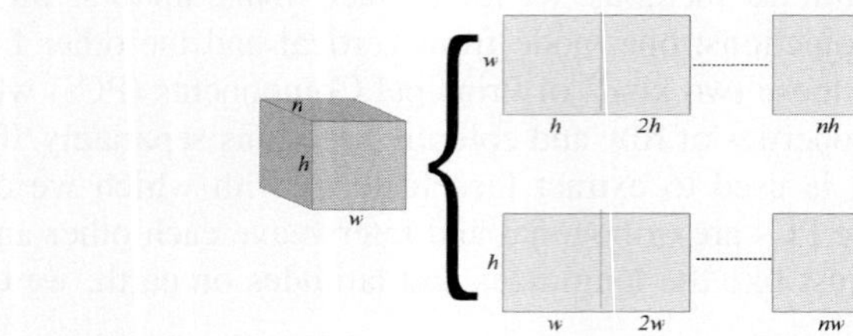

Fig. 2. The transformation form 3D face data to 2D face data

Most methods are calculated by decomposition under a given ruler with the minimal reconstruction error. The smaller the reconstruction error, the more original information it contained. If we want to decompose the original face data X in row and column way with minimal reconstruction error, its schematic representation in figure and symbol should be as in Fig.3.

$$\begin{array}{c} R_{P_r \times h} \\ \downarrow \\ X_{n\times h\times w} = Z_{n\times P_r \times P_c} \leftarrow C_{P_c \times w} + E_{n\times h\times w} \end{array}$$

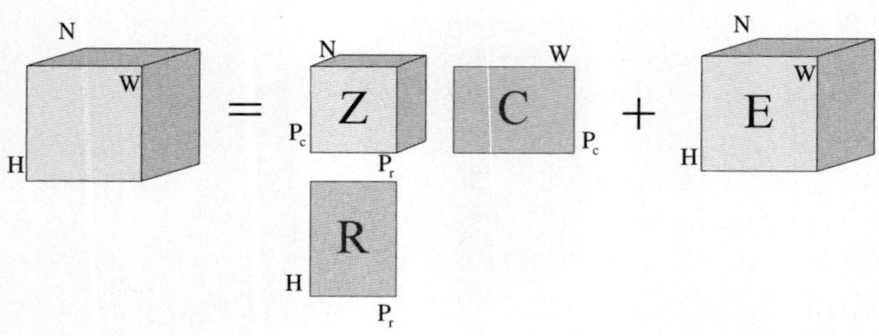

Fig. 3. The symbol schematic and figure representation of our decomposition

The mathematic expression is:

$$\tilde{X} = Z(C^T \otimes R^T) + E$$

$$f(Z,R,C) = [[X - \hat{X}]]^2 = \sum_{i=1}^{N}\sum_{j=1}^{H}\sum_{k=1}^{W}(x_{ijk} - \tilde{x}_{ijk})^2 = \sum_{i=1}^{N}\sum_{j=1}^{H}\sum_{k=1}^{W}(x_{ijk} - \sum_{p=1}^{P_r}\sum_{q=1}^{P_c} r_{jp}c_{kq}z_{ipq})^2 \quad (1)$$

Where *R* and *C* are the decomposed matrix, *X* and $\tilde{X}$ are the original and reconstruction data, *Z* is the corresponding coefficient matrix. *f* is a mean-squared loss function. At the same time, if we add some restrictions on R and C such as columnwise orthogonality, then the space they constructed could become feature extraction space. Is it possible to finish decomposition with such constraint?

After partitioning the total sum of squares, if R and C are columnwise orthonomal, the loss function *f* in (1) can be rewritten as (2):

$$f=\sum_{i=1}^{N}\sum_{j=1}^{H}\sum_{k=1}^{W}(x_{ijk}-\tilde{x}_{ijk})^{2}=\sum_{i,j,k}x_{ijk}{}^{2}+\sum_{i,j,k}\tilde{x}_{ijk}{}^{2}-2\sum_{i,j,k}x_{ijk}\tilde{x}_{ijk}=\sum_{i,j,k}x_{ijk}{}^{2}-\sum_{i,j,k}\tilde{x}_{ijk}{}^{2} \quad (2)$$

The first term is a const value, so $\min(f)$ is equivalent $\max(\sum_{i,j,k}\tilde{x}_{ijk}{}^{2})$ or $\max(\sum_{i,j,k}\tilde{x}_{ijk}x_{ijk})$ because of orthogonality.

Let $ff=\sum_{i,j,k}\tilde{x}_{ijk}x_{ijk}=\sum_{i,j,k}\sum_{i',j',k'}\sum_{pq}r_{jp}r_{j'p}c_{kq}c_{k'q}x_{ijk}\tilde{x}_{i'j'k'}$ (3)

Then we get (4)

$$\begin{aligned}ff'=\sum_{i,j,k}\sum_{i',j',k'}\sum_{pq}r_{jp}r_{j'p}c_{kq}c_{k'q}x_{ijk}\tilde{x}_{i'j'k'}-\sum_{j}\sum_{j'}\sum_{p}u_{jj'}(r_{jp}r_{j'p}-\delta^{jj'})\\-\sum_{k}\sum_{k'}\sum_{q}v_{kk'}(c_{kq}c_{k'q}-\delta^{kk'})\end{aligned} \quad (4)$$

Which express in matrix notation as (5):

$$ff'(R,C,X,U,V)=tr(X(C\otimes R)(C'\otimes R')X')-trU(R'R-I)-trV(C'C-I) \quad (5)$$

The maximum of *ff* follows from the requirement that the first order partial derivatives of ff' are simultaneously zero at the maximum of ff , and the Hessian is negative. So till now, the only question is how to solve (5) and find R, C and Z.

Fortunately, Kroonenberg and De Leeuw have done much work on this kind of mode during 1980s [9 10]. They not only gave the method of how to calculate R,C and Z through Alternating Least Squares Algorithm(ALS) after proved the nature of the solution of the maximization in (5), but also they have studied other properties such as convergence, nesting and upper bounds. In this paper, we just adopt their research result which was an alternating algorithm to solve our above mathematic problem. According to their method, if a steps have calculated, then $(a+1)-th$ step was (6):

$$(a+1)-th\ \ step\ of\ TUCKALS2$$

$$\begin{aligned}R-substep:\ p_{ii'}^{a}&=\sum_{k=1}^{N}\sum_{j'=1}^{H}\sum_{j=1}^{H}\sum_{q=1}^{P_r}c_{jq}^{a}c_{j'q}^{a}x_{ijk}x_{i'jk}\\R_{a+1}&=P_aR_a(R_a'P_a^2R_a)^{-\frac{1}{2}}\\C-substep:\ q_{jj'}^{a}&=\sum_{k=1}^{N}\sum_{i=1}^{W}\sum_{i'=1}^{W}\sum_{p=1}^{P_c}r_{ip}^{a+1}r_{i'p}^{a+1}x_{ijk}x_{ij'k}\\C_{a+1}&=Q_aC_a(C_a'Q_a^2C_a)^{-\frac{1}{2}}\\\tilde{Z}_{a+1}&=X(C_{a+1}^{T}\otimes R_{a+1}^{T})\end{aligned} \quad (6)$$

Once the reconstruction error $\|X - \tilde{X}\|$ is smaller a give value δ, then the alternation will stop and the two kinds of PCs of R and C are acquired. The next step is to calculate the coefficient matrix of Z for test set and make recognition which just likes PCA.

2.2 PCNA for Face Recognition

Unlike the traditional PCA with definitely total PCs number, PCNA can calculate designated number PCs from which we selected. In this paper, the total mean-squared error ruler is adopted (7) during selection:

$$Er = \sum_{r=1}^{H}\sum_{c=1}^{W}(I_{rc}^{r} - I_{rc}^{o})^2 \tag{7}$$

Where I^r and I^o are the image of reconstruction and original. W and H are the width and height of the face image. The relation of the total mean-squared error and PCs number is shown in left of fig.4. The right of Fig.4 shows the reconstructed images as the number of principal components varied in column and row direction. The interesting phenomenon is that the more the column direction PC, the closer in column direction to the original image, so does the row direction PC.

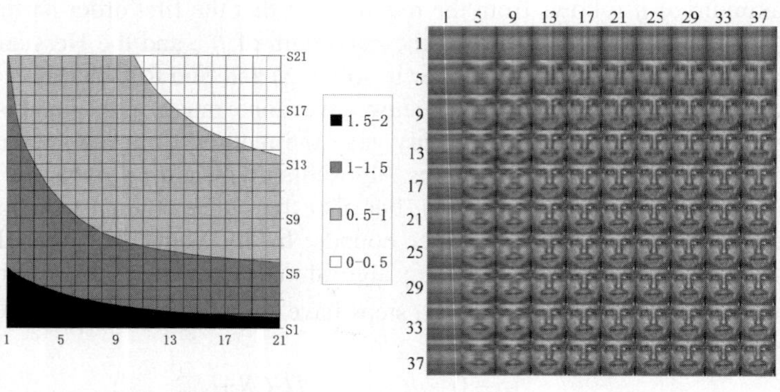

Fig. 4. Reconstruct Error vs. feature number and Reconstruct image vs. feature number

Two methods could be used to select features: one is to extract the features with designed number which all are used for recognition. The other is features are extracted as many as possible from which we make a selection. Fig.5 shows the recognition rate under the two methods of feature selection.

From the above figure, we can see that for the first method, the recognition rate increases as the feature number increasing. While in the second method, the best result, which is better than that of the first method, is not at the point of the max feature number. In order to acquire as better performance as possible, in this paper, the PCs are selected integrating both two methods. On the one hand we extract PC as much as possible to make sure the best performance in the first method. On the other hand we make a precision selection to acquire the highest recognition rate.

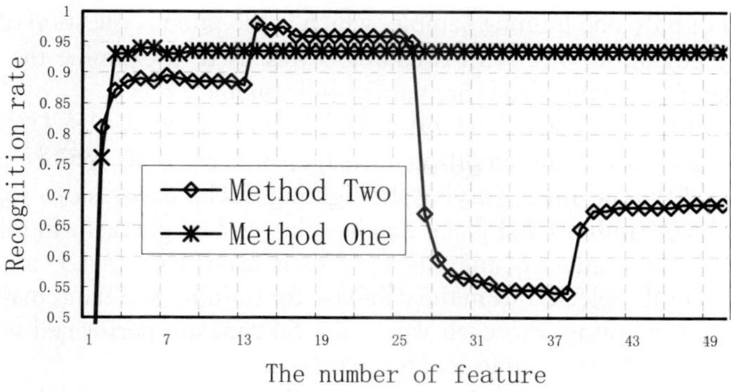

Fig. 5. The recognition result as feature number varies in method one and method two

In detail, at first, the squared core matrix is summarized on every mode respectively and two score vectors are got. Then we sort the elements of the two kinds of vectors and choose the largest ones, which is like selecting PCs in traditional PCA. Finally, the projections of these selected PCs are extracted as features of face images.

There are several novel features in our proposed method: At first, it is the first time to extract discrimination features from two orthogonal modes (column mode and row mode) without damaging face images' 2D structure and lost any 2D spacial information. Because the final used feature is feature grid, more detailed spacial information can be reserved comparing with traditional feature. Second, the whole processing is finished at one time. Although iteration calculating, there are much less than Gabor filter which needs convolution. Especially in testing stage, only few vector multiply and plus are needed. So it may be used in real time. In fact, our proposed method not only fast than Gabor, but also faster than traditional PCA. This point can be proved from rigorous mathematical formulation. For a gallery with 200, 100 $\times$ 100 images, if we use 20 PCs in PCA, then we have 20×100×100 multiplications and 20×(100×100-1) additions. But only we select all the PCs in PCNA, can we have the same calculation, which in general is impossible. Third, it can be easily understood in the view of physical essence which can be shown in Fig.4. Features from two directions have definitely corresponding physical information. Thus we can deduce which part of the face images are more important according to the selected features and this help to deeply analyzing in future. At last, the most important is our proposed method may be extended to other higher dimensional data processing, such as real 3D cubical face recognition, color face recognition etc.

3 Experiments and Results

This section evaluates the performance of our proposed algorithm PCNA compared with that of the 2DPCA and PCA algorithm based on three well-known face image databases (ORL, FERRET and JAFFE). The ORL database was used to evaluate the performance of PCNA under conditions where the pose, lighting and sample size are varied. The FERRET database was employed to test the performance of the system on the condition of only one training sample, which is the famous question of small samples in face recognition. The JAFFE database was used to examine the system performance when facial expressions are varied very much.

In the ORL database (*http://www.cl.cam.ac.uk/Research/DTG/attarchive/facedatabase.html*), there are ten different images of each of 40 distinct subjects with being taken at different times, varying the lighting, facial expressions (open / closed eyes, smiling / not smiling) and facial details (glasses / no glasses). In this paper, the strategy of different number of training samples is used. $k(k = 3,4,5)$ images of each subject are randomly selected from the database for training and the remaining images of each subject for testing. For each value of k 50 runs are performed with different random partition between training set and testing set.

The FERET face recognition database is a set of face images collected by NIST from 1993 to 1997 and now the standard for evaluating face recognition systems [13]. There are four different sets of probe images used for different testing angle. In order to make the result contain the most statistical meaning, the *fafb* probe set which contains 1,195 images of subjects taken at the same time is used. When extracting training facial features, 1192 images selected from FA gallery is used and the same subject images in FB set is used to authentication.

The JAFFE (Japanese Female Facial Expression) database is the most widely used database in facial expression recognition experiment. It contains 213 images of 7 facial expressions for 10 persons. The strategy of leave-n-out cross-validation is used, i.e. n (n = 1, 2, 3) kinds of expression images are used to train and others 7-n different kinds of expression images are used to test. Totally C_7^n groups of data are analyzed and the results are the average recognition rate.

All images are cropped to the size of 120×100 with the same gray mean and variance. Fig.6 shows sample images of three face databases after cropping and warping.

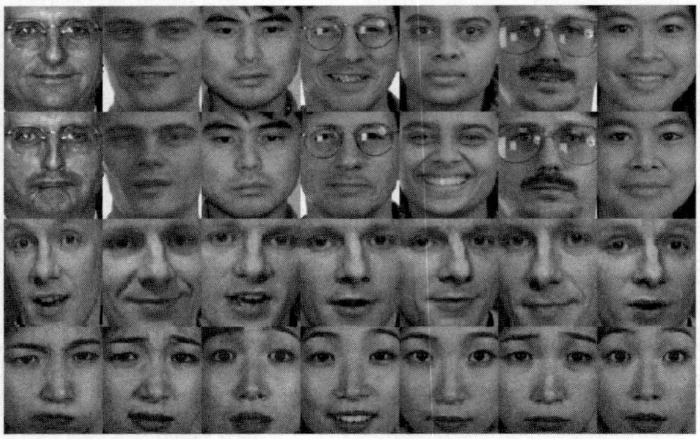

Fig. 6. Some samples in FERRET, ORL and JAFFE face database, from top to bottom, images selected from FA, FB gallery of FERRET, ORL and JAFFE face database

Three feature extraction methods of PCNA, 2DPCA and PCA are compared together and a nearest neighbor classifier was employed for classification. Note that in PCNA and 2DPCA, (8) is used to calculate the distance between two feature matrices (formed by the principal component vectors). In PCA (Eigenfaces), the common

Euclidean distance measure is adopted. Because of different feature number for three methods, in this paper reconstruction energy which represents the reconstruction ability of the selected features is used. For PCA and 2DPCA, it is calculated according to (9), where N is the number of selected features and *Ev* is the sorted eigenvalue. For PCNA, the formula is (10), where I^r is the reconstructed image and I^o is the original image. Since it is impossible to get the exactly same reconstruction energy, the ROC curves below are all fitted according to the acquired discrete data. For PCNA, the least reconstruction energy is around 90%, so there is no experimental data between 0 and 90%.

$$d(F^i,F^j)=\sum_{m=1}^{M}\sum_{n=1}^{N}(f_{mn}^i - f_{mn}^j)^2 \tag{8}$$

$$Eg = \sum_{i=1}^{PN} Ev_i \Big/ \sum_{j=1}^{EN} Ev_j \tag{9}$$

$$Eg = \sum_{r=1}^{R}\sum_{c=1}^{C} I_{rc}^r \Big/ \sum_{r=1}^{R}\sum_{c=1}^{C} I_{rc}^o \tag{10}$$

Fig.7, Fig.8, Fig.9 show the average recognition under different reconstruction energy and different training ways. In Fig.8 and Fig.9, the legend of "PCA + *i*" means the results are got with PCA method under *i* training images or *i* kinds of expression images. The same is for "2DPCA + *i*" and "PCNA + *i*".

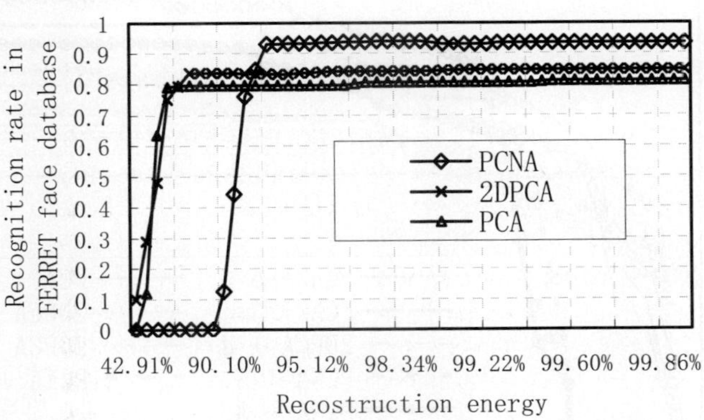

Fig. 7. Recognition results in FERET database of three methods at different reconstruction energy

From the above figures, we can see that our proposed method always outperform other two methods significantly. In the experiment on FERET database, PCNA improve the recognition rate by 14.2 percent and are 6.8 percent respectively. The main reason we think is our feature extraction method. The first step of extraction as many as PCs guarantees the completeness of information when space transforming. The second step of precision selection enhances the features effectiveness of discrimination

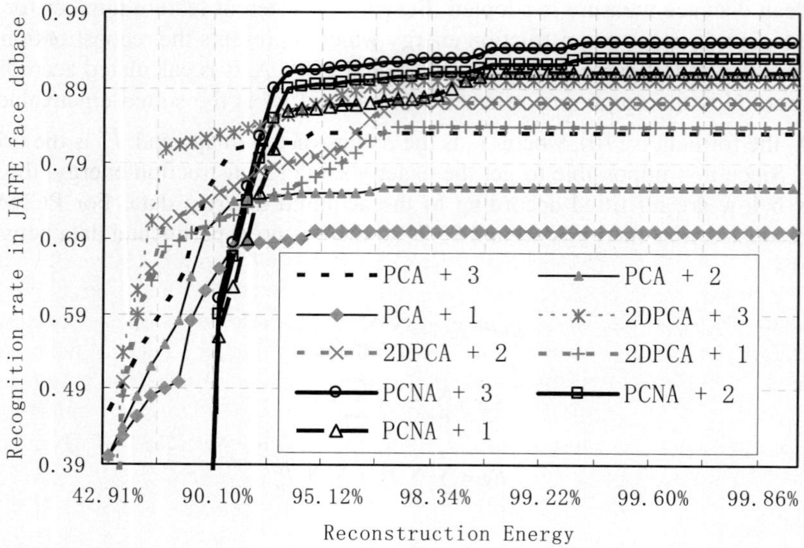

Fig. 8. Recognition results in JAFFE database of three methods with reconstruction energy and feature number variation

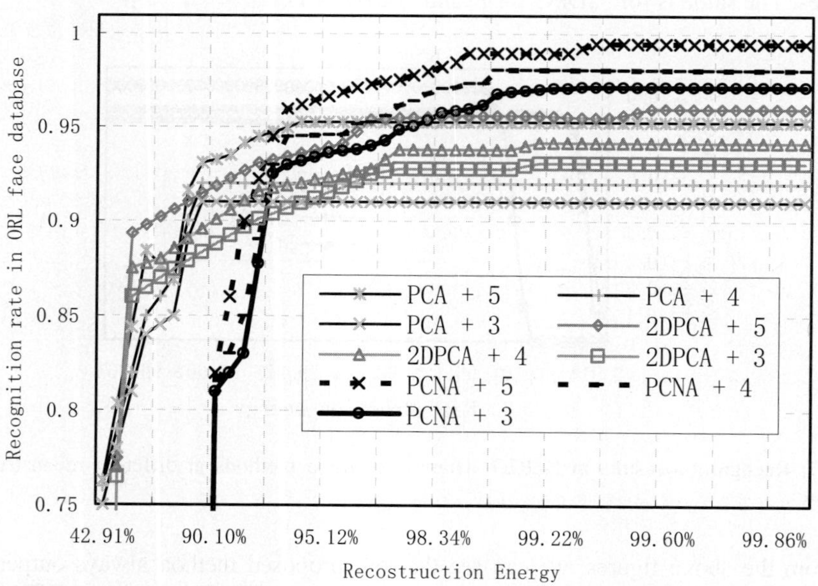

Fig. 9. Recognition results in JAFFE database of three methods with reconstruction energy and feature number variation

when discarding PCs. On the JAFFE and ORL database, except the improvement, we note that the affection of the training samples number is more greatly for PCA and 2DPCA than PCNA. The recognition rate fall faster as the training samples number decreased for PCA and 2DPCA than PCNA. The reason we considered is that PCA should need enough data to construct the high dimensional eigenspace, while to PCNA with netted structure, the dimension of row and column eigenspace is much less.

4 Conclusion

In this paper, we proposed a new feature extraction method, called Principal Component Net Analysis (PCNA), for face recognition. Different from tradition methods, the face data are analyzed directly on its original structure without any folding and unfolding. The improvement from 2DPCA is that it can be easily understood and extended to higher dimensional original data except that it has much more clarity physical meaning. All experimental results are show that PCNA overwhelm PCA and 2DPCA significantly because it uses all the face spacial discriminating information.

References

1. M. Turk, A. Pentland, Eigenfaces for Recognition, Journal of Cognitive Neurosicence, Vol. 3, No. 1, 1991, pp. 71-86
2. A. Pentland, B. Moghaddam, T. Starner, View-Based and Modular Eigenspaces for Face Recognition, Proceedings of the IEEE Conference on Computer Vision and Pattern Recognition, 21-23 June 1994, Seattle, Washington, USA, pp. 84-91
3. M.S. Bartlett, J.R. Movellan, T.J. Sejnowski, Face Recognition by Independent Component Analysis, IEEE Trans. on Neural Networks, Vol. 13, No. 6, November 2002, pp. 1450-1464
4. C. Liu, H. Wechsler, Comparative Assessment of Independent Component Analysis (ICA) for Face Recognition, Proc. of the Second International Conference on Audio- and Video-based Biometric Person Authentication, AVBPA'99, 22-24 March 1999, Washington D.C., USA, pp. 211-216
5. L. Wiskott, J.-M. Fellous, N. Krueuger, C. von der Malsburg, Face Recognition by Elastic Bunch Graph Matching, Chapter 11 in Intelligent Biometric Techniques in Fingerprint and Face Recognition, eds. L.C. Jain et al., CRC Press, 1999, pp. 355-396
6. L. Wiskott, J.-M. Fellous, N. Krueuger, C. von der Malsburg, Face Recognition by Elastic Bunch Graph Matching, IEEE Trans. on Pattern Analysis and Machine Intelligence, Vol. 19, No. 7, 1997, pp. 776-779
7. T. Ahonen, A. Hadid, and M.Pietikainen. “Face recognition with local binary patterns”.In *Proceedings of the European Conference on Computer Vision*, pages 469–481, Prague,Czech, 2004.
8. Jian Yang; Zhang, D.; Frangi, A.F.; Jing-yu Yang;Two-dimensional PCA: a new approach to appearance-based face representation and recognition Pattern Analysis and Machine Intelligence, IEEE Transactions on Volume 26, Issue 1, Jan 2004 Page(s):131 - 137
9. Pravdova, V.; Walczak, B.; Massart, D. L.; Robberecht, H.; Van Cauwenbergh, R.; Hendrix, P.; et. al. Three-way Principal Component Analysis for the Visualization of Trace Elemental Patterns in Vegetables after Different Cooking Procedures. *Journal of Food Composition and Analysis* Volume: 14, Issue: 2, April, 2001, pp. 207-225
10. L. Tucker, *Some mathematical notes on three-mode factor analysis*, Psychometrika 31, 279-311 (1966)

11. P. M. Kroonenberg, *Three-mode principal component analysis: Theory and applications*, DSWO Press, Leiden, 1983
12. S.Akamatsu, T.Sasaki, H.Fukamachi, and Y.Suenaga, Automatic extraction of target images for face identification using the sub-space classification method IEICE Trans. Inf. &Syst.,Vol.E76-D, No.10, pp.1190-1198 IEICE
13. Philips, P.J., Moon, H., Rizvi, S.A., Rauss, P.J.: The FERET evaluation methodology for face recognition algorithms. IEEE Transactions on Pattern Analysis and Machine Intelligence 22(2000) 1090-1104

Advanced Soft Remote Control System Using Hand Gesture

Jun-Hyeong Do[1], Jin-Woo Jung[2], Sung Hoon Jung[1], Hyoyoung Jang[1], and Zeungnam Bien[1]

[1] Department of Electrical Engineering and Computer Science, KAIST(Korea Advanced Institute of Science and Technology), 373-1, Guseong-Dong, Yuseong-Gu, Daejeon, 305-701, Korea
{jhdo, hoondori, hyjang}@ctrsys.kaist.ac.kr, zbien@ee.kaist.ac.kr

[2] Department of Computer Engineering, Dongguk University, 26, 3-ga, Chung-gu, Seoul, 100-715, Korea
jwjung@dongguk.edu

Abstract. In this paper, we propose an *Advanced Soft Remote Control System* so as to endow the users with the ability to control various home appliances instead of individual remote controller for each appliance and to command naturally at various places without being conscious of the view direction of the cameras. Through the developed system, the user first selects the device that he/her wants to control by pointing it with his/her hand. Then, the user can command operation of the desired functions via 10 predefined basic hand motion commands. By the experiment, we can get 97.1% recognition rate during offline test and 96.5% recognition rate during online test. The developed system complements some inconveniences of conventional remote controllers specially by giving additional freedom to persons with movement deficits and people without disabilities.

1 Introduction

We use remote controllers to control home appliances in daily life. It can be cumbersome and sometimes frustrating, however, to search for a specific remote controller where several controllers are used but randomly placed. These inconveniences are more serious for the disabled and/or the elderly by the lack of mobility [1]. Therefore, it is desired to develop a user-friendly interface system for easy and efficient operation of home-installed devices.

In order to offer an alternative for such people, recently some projects on voice control of home appliances were developed [2, 3]. However, acceptable performance of the voice-operated systems can be achieved only by sensitive microphone that is placed near the user's mouth. Additionally, the recognition of command in noisy environment becomes difficult and unstable, and it is not easy to express some spatial positions with voice command.

During the last decade, some studies on gesture recognition to control home appliances have been attempted. Among the various human-machine interfaces, the hand

A. Gelbukh and C.A. Reyes-Garcia (Eds.): MICAI 2006, LNAI 4293, pp. 745 – 755, 2006.

gesture control is considered as a promising alternative because of the natural way of communication offered by it. If the hand gesture is used as a means of controlling home appliances, no additional devices requiring physical attachment or hand-holding, such as remote controllers or microphones, are required for the control of multiple devices from various standing points at the user's house. This fact can be an important advantage of hand gesture-based HMI (Human-Machine Interface) because, from a questionnaire survey, the disabled people feel much comfortable if the human-machine interface they use does not require any physical devices on hand or any attachment of sensors to the user [1].

As for hand-gesture based systems, we find study reports on the control of a specific system [4, 5, 7, 8] or on the recognition of hand orientation and posture in restricted environments [5, 7, 9] as well as on the recognition of them assuming that there does not exist skin-colored objects except the user [6, 10]. Table 1 shows a comparison of various hand gesture-based interfaces for controlling home appliances including PC.

Table 1. Comparison of various hand gesture-based interfaces for controlling home appliances

Method	Num. of Camera	Dim. of Object Space	Environmental Modification	Hand Command	Num. of Target Objects to Control
Kahn 96 [7]	1	2D	Semi-structured (on the clean floor)	Hand pointing	1
Kohler 97 [9]	2	2D	Semi-structured (on the table)	Hand pointing + 8 hand postures	More than 6
Jojic 2000 [4]	2	2D	Unstructured	Hand pointing	1
Sato 2000 [5]	3	2D	Semi-structured (on the table)	Hand pointing	1
Do 2002 [10]	3	3D	Semi-structured (non skin-colored)	Hand pointing	More than 3
Colombo 2003 [8]	2	2D	Unstructured	Hand pointing	1
Irie 2004 [6]	2	3D	Semi-structured (non skin-colored)	Hand pointing + 5 hand postures + 2 hand motions	More than 3
(Proposed Method in this paper)	3	3D	Unstructured	Hand pointing + 10 hand motions	More than 3

Specially, the method in Irie 2004 [6] does not work well when the hand direction and the view direction of camera are not matched well because, in this paper [6], hand pointing direction is calculated only with the small hand region from cameras on the ceiling, not considering arm or face direction. Therefore, using those systems, it is hard for the user to control various appliances or to command naturally at various places without being conscious of the view direction of the cameras.

In this paper, we propose an *Advanced Soft Remote Control System* so as to endow users with the ability to control various home appliances and to command naturally at various places without being conscious of the view direction of the cameras. The *Soft Remote Control System* [10] was developed to detect pointing gestures of a user. Using the pointed information, the system can control ON/OFF operation of each electric appliances such as TV, electric lights and motor-operated curtain. I.e., when the TV is off and a user pointed TV with his/her hand, TV will be turned on by the system and when the TV is on, TV will be turned off by his/her pointing gesture. Even though *Soft Remote Control System* [10] shows the possibility to control various home appliances, it has some limitations in the sense that only "on-off" operation of the home appliances is available. For example, since TV has 3 basic functions, power on/off, channel up/down, and volume up/down, more information is required to control TV dexterously. In addition, since *Soft Remote Control System* [10] uses only skin color information to find face and hand, it does not work well where there are some skin-colored objects. An *Advanced Soft Remote Control System* is developed to solve these problems. In order to control various functions of home appliances in a natural way via hand gestures, a new face and hand detection algorithm which use a cascade classifier using multimodal cues is developed and HMM-based hand motion recognizer with pre-defined hand motion set is used. The rest of the paper is organized as follows: Section 2 introduces the configuration of the *Advanced Soft Remote Control System* in the *Intelligent Sweet Home*, and in Section 3, we deal with the hand-command recognition method in detail. In Section 4, we present our experimental results. This paper concludes in Section 5.

2 Configuration of Advanced Soft Remote Control System

Fig. 1 shows whole system configuration of the *Advanced Soft Remote Control System* in the *Intelligent Sweet Home*. Three ceiling-mounted zoom color cameras with pan/tilt modules are used to acquire the image of the room. In the vision processing system, user's commands using his/her hand gesture are analyzed and the information about them is transferred to the server via TCP/IP. Then, the server sends IR remote control signal to control the home appliances through the IR board.

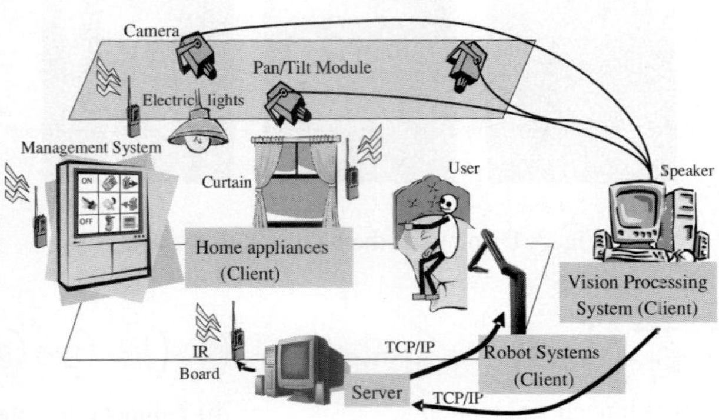

Fig. 1. Soft Remote Control System in the Intelligent Sweet Home

The command procedure of Advanced Soft Remote Control System to control various functions of the home appliances that the user wants to is shown in Fig. 2.

First, the user select a device that he/she wants to control by pointing it, and then voice and screen is used to confirm the activation of the selected device such as a voice announcement, "Curtain is selected", and display of Fig. 3, respectively. Now he/she can command operation of the desired function for the selected device via a hand gesture. The hand gestures for their operations consist of 10 basic hand motions, which are described in Fig. 4. Those gestures are selected to be easy and comfortable to take pose based on the results of a questionnaire survey [1]. If there is no command gesture in a few seconds, the activated device is released. Otherwise, the user can command the other operation for the currently activated device or select the other device by pointing it.

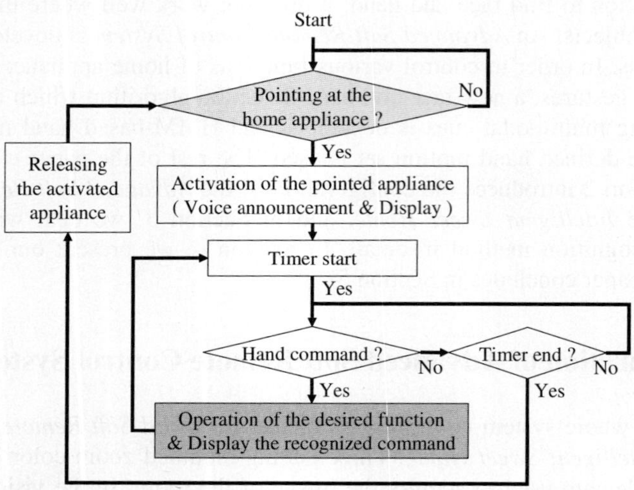

Fig. 2. The command procedure for the operation of desired function

Fig. 3. Display for the feedback to the user

(a) 1-dimentional motion (b) 2-dimentional motion

Fig. 4. Command gestures using hand motions

3 Recognition of Hand-Command

3.1 Detection/Tracking of Face and Commanding Hand

Fig. 5 shows the overall configuration of the proposed cascade classifier for the face detection.

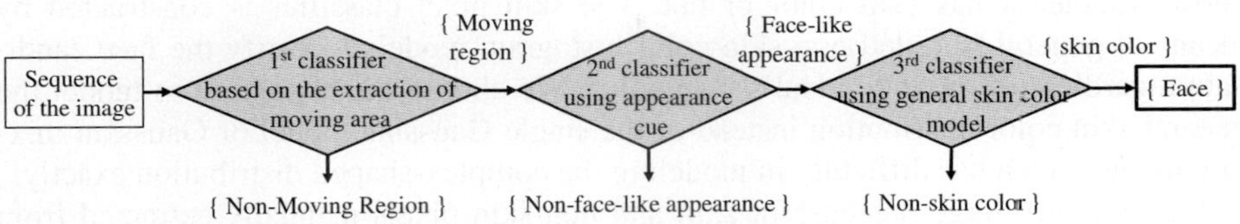

Fig. 5. Overall configuration of the cascade classifier

The cascade classifier combines all the weak classifiers to do a difficult task and makes it possible to be a fast and robust detector in such a way to filter out the regions that most likely do not contain faces immediately in each weak classifier. The proposed cascade classifier consists of three classifiers using motion, appearance, and color cue respectively. As it is a sequential system where each stage relies on the result of the previous stage, modified feature segmentation method in each stage is suggested so that the output of each classifier has enough margins in order to prevent true negative errors.

Motion cue may be a sufficient indicator for distinguishing possible human bodies from the background environment because he/her should move for doing something and does not stay motionless for a long time without special reason. It also allows decreasing of the processing time by reducing the search space for the face detection. Thus, we applied motion cue in the first stage classifier. It is well known that background suppression method is widely used to obtain the motion information [12], [13]. However, these approaches about background suppression need initial learning of background model having an empty scene with no person. And large or sudden changes in the scene may be considered as the part of foreground region though they can compensate for small or gradual changes by updating the model. In that case, they should initialize the background model again due to the failure of background modeling. As another approaches, there is a method based on change detection in intensity [14], [15]. Although it has an advantage in computational point of view, it showed that only the boundary of the objects can be checked while the interior of the objects remain unchanged if objects are not fully textured, and it is sensitive to the variation of illumination. To resolve these problems, we extract the moving region of the object without initializing the scene model by means of an adaptive filter and closing method in the first stage classifier [18].

For the second stage classifier, we adopt AdaBoost-based face detector [16] which is fast and fairly robust method and shows good empirical results in the appearance-based methods. Even though AdaBoost-based face detector itself is not fast enough to detect face in real time because of the consuming time to search over space and scale, it may show good performance for the processing time by applying it only to the extracted moving region.

Color cue is so easy to implement and insensitive to pose, expression, and rotation variation that it may be able to filter out the most of non-skin colored region. However, the filtered regions with skin color model shows noisy detection result so that it has difficulty in using the result efficiently in the next stage classifier. Therefore, we apply the color cue in the last stage classifier to verify the candidate finally. The candidate for the face which is detected in the second stage classifier may have false positive errors due to the face-like objects. Those errors can be easily detected if we know whether it has skin color or not. The skin pixel classifier is constructed by means of general skin and non-skin color histogram models to verify the face candidate regardless of the individual's skin color. We choose the histogram to model the general skin color distribution instead of the single Gaussian model or Gaussian mixture model which has difficulty in modeling the complex-shaped distribution exactly.

Using a very large database of skin and non-skin pixels manually extracted from the World Wide Web by Jones and Rehg [17], a skin and non-skin color histogram model are constructed. Each model has a size of 256 bins per color channel, and is constructed in the UV color space to consider only chrominance components.

The probability of the skin color given *uv* value is computed based on Bayes rule by following Eq. (1).

$$P(skin \mid uv) = \frac{P(uv \mid skin)P(skin)}{P(uv \mid skin)P(skin) + P(uv \mid \neg skin)P(\neg skin)} = \frac{s[uv]}{s[uv]+n[uv]} \tag{1}$$

where $s[uv]$ is the pixel count contained in bin *uv* of the skin color histogram, $n[uv]$ is the equivalent count from the non-skin color histogram.

Then, the skin pixel classifier C_s is implemented by Eq. (2).

$$C_s(u,v) = \begin{cases} 1 & if\ P(skin \mid uv) \geq \gamma \\ 0 & otherwise \end{cases} \tag{2}$$

where γ is a threshold.

After obtaining the histogram $H_i(u, v)$ of the candidate region detected in the second stage, we apply it to the skin pixel classifier for the verification of the face using Eq. (3).

$$face = \begin{cases} True & f\ \dfrac{\sum_u \sum_v H_i(u,v)C_s(u,v)}{A_i} > \theta \\ False & otherwise \end{cases} \tag{3}$$

where A_i is the size of the detected face candidate region and θ is a threshold.

The proposed face detection system is implemented in VC++ and runs on 320x240 pixels on a Pentium IV 3.2 GHz. Fig. 6 shows one of the processing results in each step. We analyze the proposed method by comparing with the combination of the second and the third stage classifier, and combination of the first and the second stage classifier with respect to detection rate, false detections, and processing time. We applied three approaches to 4 kinds of sequence (totally 1617 faces in 1835 frames). The results of the comparison with respect to false detections, missing detections, and processing time are given in Table 2.

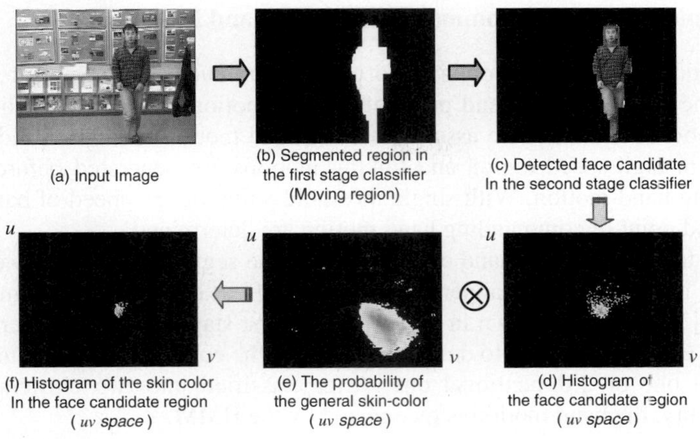

Fig. 6. Processing results during three stages of face detection

Table 2. Comparison of the proposed method and the combinations of the each two stage

Method	2nd + 3rd stage classifier	1st + 2nd stage classifier	1st+2nd+3rd stage classifier (proposed)
Detection rate	98.76%	97.90%	97.90%
False detections	117	42	11
Processing time	341 (ms/frame)	64 (ms/frame)	68 (ms/frame)

After detecting the user's face successfully, his/her commanding hand is segmented among the moving skin color blobs by considering the distance to the detected face, blob size, width/height ratio, and the detection status.

Once face or commanding hand is detected, a color based tracker with mean shift algorithm [11] is used. And if the hand does not move, it is regarded as stopping his/her gesture and it tries to detect and track other moving hand blob.

3.2 Recognition of Hand Pointing Gestures

From the segmentation results of the face and commanding hand in each two camera images, the 3D positions of them are calculated. In order to calculate the 3D position of each blob, it should be detected at least in two cameras. In case it is detected in all cameras, we average the 3D position vectors calculated from each two cameras.

We consider the pointing action as stretching out the user's hand toward the object that he/her wants to control. It is recognized by considering the changes of speed in hand motion and the distance between end point of commanding hand motion and the face position. The pointing direction is acquired by calculating the pointing vector from the 3D position of COG (Center-Of-Gravity) point of the face to that of pointing hand. Then, the *Soft Remote Control System* finds the home appliance that is nearly located on the pointing direction. Here, the hand pointing direction determined by commanding hand and face together is generally more reliable than the one only based on the elongation of the commanding hand [6].

3.3 Recognition of Hand Command Gestures (Hand Motions)

In real application, hand motion is performed in continuous manner, so it is required to determine start point and end point of desired motion from the complicated continuous motion. Therefore, we assume that the hand motion as a command gesture is performed in high speed region and linking motions are generated before and after commanding hand motion. With single threshold value on the speed of hand motion, start and end point of commanding hand motion are determined.

In order to recognize the hand command from the segmented motion, we construct a classifier in hierarchical manner to reduce the effect of ambiguity from irrelevant feature [19] in HMM as shown in Fig. 7. At the first stage of the classifier, we make use of total cumulative angle to determine whether the commanding hand motion is 1-dimentional one or 2-dimentional one. After classified into two clusters based on dimensionality, the hand motion is recognized by the HMM.

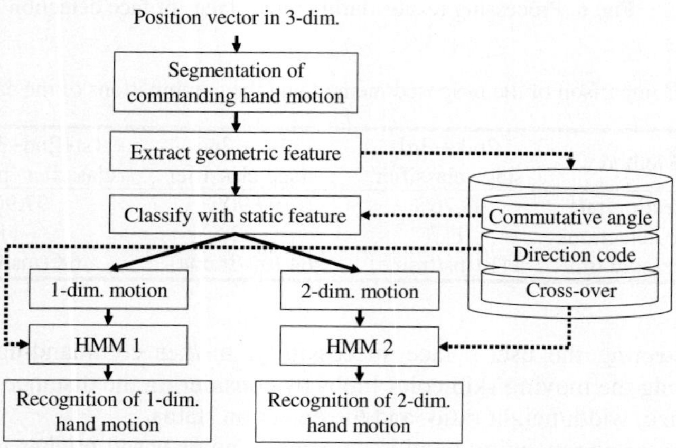

Fig. 7. Hierarchical classifier for the recognition of hand motion

To evaluate performance of classifier, dataset acquired from one random test set was constructed and tested. Firstly, test set was recognized based on single HMM classifier (See Table 3 (a)). Table 3 (b) showed that hierarchical classifier outperformed single HMM based classifier. So it is concluded that discriminability of HMM was improved by minimizing number of classes to be recognized.

When user wants to perform "UP" motion, for example, the possible sequence of the user's motion would be "UP" to command operation and "DOWN" to return to a comfortable position. Based on this consideration, we confirm that a commanding hand motion to control a home appliance in real application can be combination of hand motions, not just single hand motion. To resolve this complexity, we make the simple grammar via state automata. Additionally, we make simple rules based on several observations. If the user holds his/her hand in a certain position for the some duration, the next hand motion is considered intended one. On the other hand, if two consecutive hand motions are performed with a little pause between them, latter is regarded as an unintended one.

Table 3. Recognition results of hand command

(a) Single HMM-based classifier

Single HMM-based classifier			
Hand motion	Success rate	Hand motion	Success rate
UP	78%	BACKWARD	98%
DOWN	96%	Circle(cw*)	100%
LEFT	86%	Circle(ccw**)	90%
RIGHT	95%	Half circle(cw)	100%
FORWARD	98%	Half circle(ccw)	100%
Total		94.1%	

(*:clockwise, **:counter clockwise)

(b) Hierarchical classifier (proposed)

HMM1		HMM2	
Hand motion	Success rate	Hand motion	Success rate
UP	94%	Circle (cw*)	100%
DOWN	100%	Circle (ccw**)	98%
LEFT	98%	Half circle (cw)	100%
RIGHT	92%	Half circle (ccw)	100%
FORWARD	98%		
BACKWARD	100%		
Total		97.1%	

4 Experimental Results

The proposed *Soft Remote Control System* is implemented in VC++ and runs at the rate of about 13Hz on 320x240 pixels in each input image. The computer used is Pentium IV 3.2GHz and the cameras are auto focus color camera with a built-in type zooming function (x25) made by Honeywell Inc. For robust tracking of the user's commanding hand, we assume the user is wearing the shirts long sleeves. We conducted the *Advanced Soft Remote Control System* on TV, motor-operated curtain, and electric lights in the *Intelligent Sweet Home*. The functions of the *Advanced Soft Remote Control System* and recognition results are listed in Table 4. We did 20 times of tests per each function of each system. Totally, the success rate is 96.5%.

In addition, when the user points an appliance that he/her wants to control, the system indicates the pointed appliance with voice announcement and separate monitor screen for the feedback to the user as shown in Fig. 8. After the user's command for the selected appliance is recognized, the corresponding icon is highlighted to give the feedback to him/her.

Table 4. The appliances Controlled by Soft Remote Control System and Recognition Results

Appliance	Function	Command (moving direction of left hand)	Success rate
TV	TV On	clockwise	19/20 (95%)
	TV Off	clockwise	20/20 (100%)
	TV Channel up	up	20/20 (100%)
	TV Channel down	down	18/20 (90%)
	TV Volume up	right	20/20 (100%)
	TV Volume down	left	19/20 (95%)
Curtain	Open	left	20/20 (100%)
	Close	right	20/20 (100%)
Electric lights	On	clockwise	19/20 (95%)
	Off	counter clock wise	18/20 (90%)

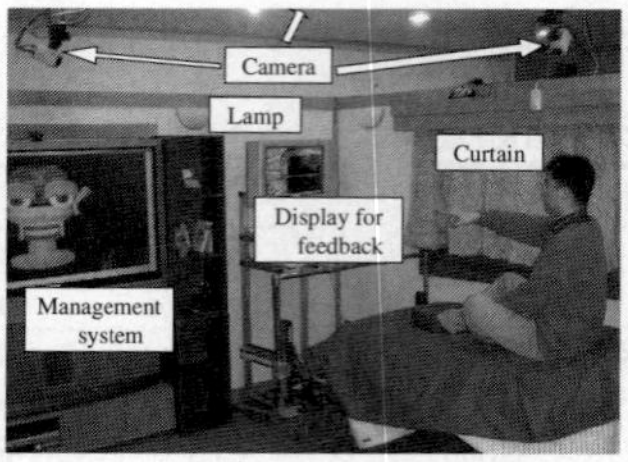

Fig. 8. Advanced Soft Remote Control System in the Intelligent Sweet Home

5 Concluding Remark

We have improved the *Soft Remote Control System* [10] using a cascade classifier using multimodal cues and HMM-based hand motion recognizer with pre-defined hand motion set to control various functions of home appliances in a natural way via hand gestures in the Intelligent Sweet Home. Since this system complements the inconvenience of conventional remote controller, it can be useful to people without disabilities as well as the aged people and persons with disabilities. Especially, even if the position of appliance changes or new appliance is installed, the user can control the appliance only after storing the position of the appliance. For the further study, we will focus on the hand motion recognition method to be able to distinguish the user's commanding hand motion from meaningless motions without constant threshold value.

Acknowledgement

This work is fully supported by the ERC program of MOST/KOSEF (Grant #R11-1999-008).

References

1. Kim, Y., Park, K.-H., Seo, K.-H., Kim, C. H., Lee W.-J., Song W.-G., Do, J.-H., Lee, J.-J., Kim, B. K., Kim, J.-O., Lim, J.-T., and Bien, Z. Z.: A report on questionnaire for developing intelligent sweet home for the disabled and the elderly in Korean living conditions. Proc. of the 8th Int. Conf. on Rehabilitation Robotics (ICORR 2003) (2003) 171–174
2. Jiang, H., Han, Z., Scuccess, P., Robidoux, S., and Sun, Y.: Voice-activated environmental control system for persons with disabilities. Proc. of the IEEE 26th Annual Northeast Bioengineering Conference (2000) 167-169
3. Lee, N. C., and Keating, D.: Controllers for use by disabled people. Computing & Control Engineering Journal, Vol. 5(3) (1994) 121-124
4. Jojic, N., Brumitt, B., et. Al.: Detection and Estimation of Pointing Gestures in Dense Disparity Maps. Proc. of 4 IEEE Int. conf. on Automatic Face and Gesture Recognition (2000) 468-475
5. Sato, S. and Sakane, S.: A Human-Robot Interface Using an Interactive Hand Pointer that Projects a Mark in the Real Work Space. Proc. of the 2000 IEEE ICRA (2000) 589-595

6. Irie, K., Wakakmura, N., and Umeda, K.: Construction of an Intelligent Room Based on Gesture Recognition. Proc. of IEEE Int. conf. on IROS (2004) 193-198
7. Kahn, R. E., Swain, M. J., Prokopowicz, P. N., Firby, R. J.: Gesture Recognition Using the Perseus Architecture. Proc. of IEEE Computer Society Conf. on Computer Vision and Pattern Recognition (1996) 734-741
8. Colombo, C., Bimbo, A. D. and Valli, A.: Visual Capture and Understanding of Hand Pointing Actions in a 3-D Environment. IEEE Tr. on systems, man, and cybernetics, Part B: Cybernetics, Vol. 33(4) 677-686
9. Kohler, M. R. J.: System Architecture and Techniques for Gesture Recognition in Unconstraint Environments. Proc. of Int. Conf. on Virtual Systems and MultiMedia (1997) 137-146
10. Do, J.-H., Kim, J. –B., Park, K. –H., Bang, W. –C. and Bien, Z. Z.: Soft Remote Control System using Hand Pointing Gesture. Int. Journal of Human-friendly Welfare Robotic Systems, Vol. 3(1) (2002) 27-30
11. Comaniciu, D., Ramesh, V., and Meer, P.: Kernel-Based Object Tracking. IEEE Trans. On Pattern Analysis and Machine Intelligence, Vol. 22(5) (2003) 564-577
12. Wren, C., Azarbayejani, A., Darrell, T., and Pentland, A.: Pfinder: Real-time tracking of the human body. IEEE Trans. Pattern Anal. Machine Intelligence, Vol. 19(7) (1997) 780-785
13. Ruiz-del-Solar, J., Shats, A., and Verschae, R.: Real-time tracking of multiple persons. In Proc. of the 12th Image Analysis and Processing (2003) 109-114
14. Neri, A., Colonneses, S., Russo, G., and Talone, P.: Automatic moving object and background separation. Signal Processing, Vol. 66(2) (1998) 219-232
15. Gavrila, D. M.: The visual analysis of human movement: A survey. Computer vision and Image Understanding, Vol. 73(1) (1999) 82-98
16. Viola, P., and Jones, M.: Rapid object detection using a boosted cascade of simple feature. Proc. of IEEE Int. Conf. on Computer Vision and Pattern Recognition (2001) 511-518
17. Jones, M., and Rehg, J.: Statistical color models with application to skin detection. Compaq Cambridge Res. Lab. Tech. Rep, CRL 98/11 (1998)
18. Do, J.-H., Bien, Z. Z.: Real-time Person Detection Method without Background Model. In Proc. of the 10th IASTED Int. Conf. Robotics and Applications (2004) 148-153
19. John, G. H., Kohavi, R., and Pfleger, K.: Irrelevant Features and the Subset Selection Problem. Proc. of the 11th Int. Conf. Machine Learning. (1994) 121-129

IMM Method Using Tracking Filter with Fuzzy Gain

Sun Young Noh[1], Jin Bae Park[1], and Young Hoon Joo[2]

[1] Yonsei University, Seodaemun-gu, Seoul, 120-749, Korea
{rkdhtm, jbpark}@control.yonsei.ac.kr
[2] Kunsan National University, Kunsan, Chunbuk, 573-701, Korea
yhjoo@kunsan.ac.kr

Abstract. In this paper, we propose an interacting multiple model (IMM) method using intelligent tracking filter with fuzzy gain to reduce tracking error for maneuvering target. In the proposed filter, the unknown acceleration input for each sub-model is determined by mismatches between the modelled target dynamics and the actual target dynamics. After an acceleration input is detected, the state estimate for each sub-model is modified. To modify the accurate estimation, we propose the fuzzy gain based on the relation between the filter residual and its variation. To optimize each fuzzy system, we utilize the genetic algorithm (GA). Finally, the tracking performance of the proposed method is compared with those of the input estimation(IE) method and AIMM method through computer simulations.

1 Introduction

The Kalman filter has been widely used in many applications. The design of a Kalman filter relies on having an exact dynamic model of the system under consideration in order to provide optimal performance [1]. However, there exist a mismatch between the modelled target dynamics and the actual target dynamics when the maneuver occurs. These problems have been studied in the field of state estimation [2,3,7]. Later, the various techniques were investigated and applied [4,6]. The recent research has been roughly divided into two main approaches. One approach is to detect the maneuver and then to cope with it effectively. Examples of this approach include input estimation (IE) techniques [2], the variable dimension (VD) filter [5], and the two-stage Kalman estimator [7], etc. In addition to basic filtering computation, these techniques require additional effort such as the estimation and detection of acceleration. The other approach is to describe the motion of a target by using multiple subfilters. The interacting multiple model (IMM) algorithm [8] and the adaptive IMM (AIMM) [15] algorithm are included in this approach. In the algorithm, a parallel bank of filters are blended in a weighted-sum form by an underlying finite-dimensional Markov chain so that a smooth transition between submodels is achieved. However, to realize a target tracker with an outstanding performance, a prior statistical knowledge on the maneuvering target should be

A. Gelbukh and C.A. Reyes-Garcia (Eds.): MICAI 2006, LNAI 4293, pp. 756–766, 2006.

supplied, i.e., the process noise variance for each sub-model in IMM should be accurately selected in advance by the domain expert who should fully understand the unknown maneuvering characteristics of the target, which is not an easy task. An approach to resolve this problem is the adaptive interacting multiple model (AIMM) algorithm [15]. However, in this method, the acceleration levels to construct the multiple models should also be predesigned in a trial and error manner, which significantly affect the tracking performance of the maneuvering target. Until now, no tractable method coping with the problem has been proposed. It remains a theoretically challenging issue in the maneuvering target tracking, and thereby should be fully tackled.

Motivated by the above observations, we propose an intelligent tracking filter with fuzzy gain to reduce the additional effort required in it is predesigned methods. The algorithm improves the tracking performance and establishes the systematic tracker design procedure for a maneuvering target. The complete solution can be divided into two stages. First, when the target maneuver occurs, the acceleration level for each sub-model is determined by using the fuzzy system based on the relation between the non-maneuvering filter residual and the maneuvering one at every sampling time. Second, to modify the accurate estimation, the target with maneuver is updated by using the fuzzy gain based on the fuzzy model. Since it is hard to approximate adaptively this time-varying variance, a fuzzy system is applied as the universal approximator to compute it. To optimize each fuzzy system, we utilize the genetic algorithm (GA). On the other hand, the GA has shown to be a flexible and robust optimization tool for many nonlinear optimization problems, where the relationship between adjustable parameters and the resulting objective functions. Finally, the tracking performance of the proposed method is compared with those of the input estimation(IE) algorithm method and the AIMM algorithm method through computer simulations.

2 Maneuvering Target Model and IMM

2.1 Dynamic Model

The dynamic equation of a target tracking is expressed as a linear discrete time model. The system model for a maneuvering target and a non-maneuvering target are described for each axis as

$$X_{k+1} = FX_k + Gu_k + w_k \tag{1}$$

$$X^*_{k+1} = FX^*_k + w_k \tag{2}$$

$$F = \begin{bmatrix} 1 & T & 0 & 0 \\ 0 & 1 & 0 & 0 \\ 0 & 0 & 1 & T \\ 0 & 0 & 0 & 1 \end{bmatrix} \qquad G = \begin{bmatrix} T^2/2 & 0 \\ 0 & T \\ T^2/2 & 0 \\ 0 & T \end{bmatrix}$$

where $X_k = \begin{bmatrix} x \; \dot{x} \; y \; \dot{y} \end{bmatrix}$ is the state vector, which is composed of the relative position and velocity of the target in the two-dimensional plane, T is the time sampling, u_k is the unknown maneuver input. The process noise w_k is zero mean white Gaussian noise with known covariance Q. The measurement equation is

$$Z_k = HX_k + v_k \tag{3}$$
$$H = \begin{bmatrix} 1\,0\,0\,0 \\ 0\,0\,1\,0 \end{bmatrix}$$

where H is the measurement matrix, and v_k is the measurement noise with zero mean white known covariance R. Both w_k and v_k are assumed to be uncorrelated. A Kalman filter consists of the hypothetical one based on the maneuvering model and the actual one based on the non-maneuvering model. From the innovation of the non-maneuvering filter based on (2), the unknown acceleration input u_k is to be estimated and detected. The estimated acceleration is then used in conjunction with a standard Kalman filter to compensate the state estimate of the target.

2.2 IMM

Traditionally, target tracking problems are solved by the linearized tracking filters, target maneuvers are often described by multiple linearized models. Here the IMM method has a limited number of sub-models for each axis, and each sub-model is represented as the estimated acceleration or the acceleration levels distributed symmetrically about the estimated one [8]. In the case of N sub-models for each axis, the set of multiple models is represented as

$$\begin{aligned} M_I &= \{m_1, m_2, \ldots, m_N\} \\ &= \{\hat{a}_k, \hat{a}_k \pm \varepsilon_1, \ldots, \hat{a}_k \pm \varepsilon_{(N-1)/2}\} \end{aligned} \tag{4}$$

where $\hat{a}_k$ is the estimated acceleration and $\pm\varepsilon_{(N-1)/2}$ is the predetermined acceleration interval.

3 Tracking Algorithm Using the Fuzzy System

3.1 Fuzzy Model of the Unknown Acceleration Input

The objective in this section is to develop an unknown acceleration input detection algorithm. Similar ideas have been explored in the literature which is the GA-based fuzzy Kalman filter algorithm [16]. When the target maneuver occurs in (1), the standard Kalman filter may not track the maneuvering target because the original process noise variance Q cannot cover the acceleration u_k. To treat u_k simply, the state prediction of the system can be determined by the Kalman filter based on the fuzzy system. The filter is based on non-maneuvering (2), which can be derived by assuming a recursive estimator of the form.

$$\hat{X}^{*m}_{k|k-1} = F\hat{X}^{*m}_{k-1|k-1} \tag{5}$$

where m is the sub-model number. The state measurement prediction of the system can be rewritten as

$$\hat{Z}^{*m}_{k|k-1} = H\hat{X}^{*m}_{k|k-1} \tag{6}$$

In the standard Kalman filter, the residual of the estimation is defined as

$$\tilde{Z}^{*m}_{k} = Z^{m}_{k} - \hat{Z}^{*m}_{k} \tag{7}$$

The acceleration input $\hat{u}_k$ for the sub-model are inferred by a double-input single-output fuzzy system, for which the jth fuzzy IF-THEN rule for each model is represented by

$$R_j : IF \quad \chi_1 \quad is \quad A_{1j} \quad and \quad \chi_2 \quad is \quad A_{2j}, \quad THEN \quad y_j \quad is \quad \hat{u}_j \tag{8}$$

where two premise variables χ_1 and χ_2 are the non-maneuvering filter residual and the difference between non-maneuvering filter residual and maneuvering filter residual, respectively, and a consequence variable y_j is the estimated acceleration input $\hat{u}_k$. The $A_{ij} \quad (i = 1, 2 \quad and \quad j = 1, 2, ..., M)$ are fuzzy sets, and it has the Gaussian membership function with the center c_{ij} and the standard deviation σ_{ij} as

$$f(x_i; \sigma_{ij}, c_{ij}) = \exp\left[\frac{(x_i - c_{ij})^2}{\sigma_{ij}^2}\right] \tag{9}$$

Using center-average defuzzification, product inference, and singleton fuzzifier, the unknown acceleration input is obtained as

$$w_j = \mu_{A_{1j}}(x_{1j}) \times \mu_{A_{2j}}(x_{2j}) \tag{10}$$

$$\hat{u}_j = \frac{\sum_{j=1}^{M} w_j y_j}{\sum_{j=1}^{M} w_j} \tag{11}$$

We will utilize the GA, in order to optimize the parameters in both the premise part and the consequence part of the fuzzy system simultaneously.

3.2 Design of IMM Algorithm with Fuzzy Gain

In the preceding section, our proposed discussion is to detect the unknown acceleration input. Once it is detected, a modification is necessary. Since the magnitude of the acceleration input is unknown, we can use the estimate $\hat{u}^m_k$ to modify the non-maneuver state when we detect the maneuver. The system equation is first modified to contain additive acceleration input.

$$\hat{X}^{m}_{k|k-1} = \hat{X}^{m}_{k|k-1} + G\hat{u}^m_k + w_k \tag{12}$$

One cycle of the proposed IMM algorithm is summarized as follows: The mixed state estimate $\widehat{X}^{0m}_{k-1|k-1}$ and its error covariance $P^{0m}_{k-1|k-1}$ are computed from the state estimates and their error covariances of sub-filters as follows:

$$\widehat{X}^{0m}_{k-1|k-1} = \sum_{n=1}^{N} \mu^{n|m}_{k-1|k-1} \widehat{X}^{n}_{k-1|k-1}$$

$$P^{0m}_{k-1|k-1} = \sum_{n=1}^{N} \mu^{n|m}_{k-1|k-1} \left[P^{n}_{k-1|k-1} + \left(\widehat{X}^{n}_{k-1|k-1} - \widehat{X}^{0m}_{k-1|k-1} \right) \cdot \left(\widehat{X}^{n}_{k-1|k-1} - \widehat{X}^{0m}_{k-1|k-1} \right)^T \right] \tag{13}$$

The mixing probability $\mu^{n|m}$ and the normalization constant α^m are

$$\mu^{n|m}_{k-1|k-1} = \frac{1}{\alpha^m} \phi^{nm} \mu^{n}_{k-1} \tag{14}$$

$$\alpha^m = \sum_{n=1}^{N} \phi^{nm} \mu^{n}_{k-1} \tag{15}$$

where ϕ^{nm} is the model transition probability from the nth sub-model to the mth one, and μ^n_{k-1} is the model probability of the nth sub-model at time $k-1$. Because of the modified maneuver state $\hat{X}^m_{k|k-1}$, the measurement residual is defined as

$$e^m_k = Z^m_k - \hat{X}^m_{k|k-1} \tag{16}$$

As soon as acceleration input is detected, the predicted states are corrected by the updated algorithm with fuzzy gain. The first step of measurement updating is to define the measurement residual, and the fuzzy gain is defined by the fuzzy system. The second step of measurement updating is the conventional Kalman gain. In the first step, consider fuzzy system with the linguistic rules

$$R_j : IF \quad x_1 \quad is \quad B_{1j} \quad and \quad x_2 \quad is \quad B_{2j}, \quad THEN \quad y_j \quad is \quad \gamma_j \tag{17}$$

where two input variables x_1 and x_1 are the filter residual and change rate of the filter residual, consequent variable y_j is the fuzzy gain with jth fuzzy rule, and B_{ij} are fuzzy set. $i \in 1, 2, ..., M$ and $j \in 1, 2, ..., M$. It has the Gaussian membership function with center $\bar{x}_{ij}$ and standard deviation $\bar{\sigma}_{ij}$ as

$$f(x_i; \bar{\sigma}_{ij}, \bar{x}_{ij}) = \exp\left(-\frac{(x_i - \bar{x}_{ij})^2}{\bar{\sigma}^2_{ij}} \right) \tag{18}$$

In this paper, the GA methods will be applied to optimize the parameters and the structure of the system. That is, the defuzzified output of the fuzzy model based on fuzzy gain, γ is given by

$$\bar{\gamma}_k = \frac{\sum_{j=1}^{M} \gamma_j B(x_{1j}) \times B(x_{2j})}{\sum_{j=1}^{M} B(x_{1j}) \times B(x_{2j})} \tag{19}$$

According to the approximation theorem by the GA, the fuzzy gain γ_j is optimized. The first measurement fuzzy gain is defined as

$$\gamma_k = \left[\bar{\gamma}_k \; \bar{\gamma}_k\right]^T \tag{20}$$

Then the state estimator under the fuzzy gain is written as

$$\hat{X}^{Fm}_{k|k-1} = \hat{X}^{m}_{k|k-1} + \gamma^m_k \tag{21}$$

And this filter can be derived by assuming a recursive estimator of the form

$$\hat{X}^{m}_{k|k} = \hat{X}^{Fm}_{k|k-1} + K^m_k e^m_k \tag{22}$$

where e_k is the measurement residual, and K^m_k is a Kalman gain whose matrices are to be determined.The update equation of the proposed filter can be modified as follows. The predicted state is replaced by (22) and the updated state $\hat{X}^m_{k|k}$ is

$$\begin{aligned} \hat{X}^{m}_{k|k} &= \hat{X}^{Fm}_{k|k-1} + K^m_k \left[Z^m_k - H\hat{X}^{Fm}_{k|k-1}\right] \\ &= (I - K^m_k H)\left[\hat{X}^{m}_{k|k-1} + \gamma^m_k\right] + K^m_k Z^m_k \end{aligned} \tag{23}$$

At the same time, the covariance matrix $P^m_{k|k}$ is also modified as

$$P^m_{k|k} = P^m_{k|k-1} - K^m_k S^m_k K^{Tm}_k \tag{24}$$

The innovation covariance S^m_k is defined as

$$S^m_k = HP^m_{k|k-1}H^T + R \tag{25}$$

Secondly, the measurement correction is the Kalman gain. We can find the optimal Kalman gain by using (24) and (25).

$$K^m_k = P^m_{k|k}H^T S^m_k \tag{26}$$

These modifications do not alter the basic computational sequence used in the standard Kalman filter. Therefore, the designed target tracking system gives satisfactory performance for diverse maneuvers.

3.3 Identification of Fuzzy Model Using the GA

To approximate the unknown acceleration input $\hat{u}_k$ and the fuzzy gain γ_k, the GA is applied to optimize the parameters in both the premise and the consequence parts. The GA represents the parameters for the given problem by the chromosome S which may contain one or more substrings. Each chromosome, therefore, contains a possible solution to the problem. The convenient way to represent the information into the chromosome is by concatenating the jth rows, which show as

$$\begin{aligned} S_j &= \{c_{1j}, \sigma_{1j}, c_{2j}, \sigma_{2j}, u_j\}, \\ S^*_j &= \{\bar{x}_{1j}, \bar{\sigma}_{1j}, \bar{c}_{2j}, \bar{\sigma}_{2j}, u_j\}, \end{aligned} \tag{27}$$

Table 1. The initial parameters of the GA

Parameters	Values
Maximum Generation (G_n)	300
Maximum Rule Number ($\mathcal{P}_r$)	50
Population Size ($\mathcal{P}_s$)	500
Crossover Rate ($\mathcal{P}_c$)	0.9
Mutation Rate ($\mathcal{P}_m$)	0.1
λ	0.75

Table 2. The fuzzy rules identified for the fuzzy gain $-0.01 < \hat{u}_1 < 0.01km/s^2$

No. of rules	Parameters				
	$\bar{x_1}$	$\bar{\sigma_1}$	$\bar{x_2}$	$\bar{\sigma_2}$	$\bar{\gamma}$
1	-0.2565	3.5869	0.4750	0.2497	0.008893
2	0.6566	1.7919	1.6407	0.5698	-0.009695
3	-1.8646	2.8599	0.0348	1.4878	0.009674
4	0.6915	0.358	0.861	0.5436	0.005906
5	1.0725	0.6909	-1.9845	0.5747	-0.003966
6	-0.9039	1.2187	0.5782	3.6104	-0.004285

where S_j and S_j^* are the real coded parameter substring for the jth fuzzy rule of the unknown acceleration input and fuzzy gain in an individual, and are the real coded parameter substring for the jth fuzzy rule in an individual. Because the objective of a target tracker is to minimize the error, the fuzzy system should be designed such that the following objective function can be minimized:

$$J = \sqrt{(sum\ of\ position\ error)^2 + (sum\ of\ velocity\ error)^2} \tag{28}$$

The premise string of each initial individual is determined randomly within the given search space. Since the GA guides the optimal solution for the purpose of maximizing the fitness function value, it is necessary to map the objective function to the fitness function form by

$$f(J) = \frac{\lambda}{J+1} + \frac{1-\lambda}{M+1} \tag{29}$$

where λ is a positive scalar which adjusts the weight between the objective function and the rule number. Each individual is evaluated by a fitness function. The performance of this approach for the target tracking is demonstrated by a simulation in Section 4.

4 Simulation Results

To evaluate the proposed filtering scheme, a maneuvering target scenario is examined. Theoretical analyses from the previous section show how to determine and update the unknown acceleration input and fuzzy gain for the maneuvering target

Table 3. The fuzzy rules identified for the fuzzy gain $0.01 \leq \hat{u}_2 \leq 0.1km/s^2$

No. of rules	Parameters				
	$\bar{x_1}$	$\bar{\sigma_1}$	$\bar{x_2}$	$\bar{\sigma_2}$	$\bar{\gamma}$
1	-1.1299	0.4812	-1.8985	3.4154	0.043957
2	0.6718	0.2726	1.416	2.096	0.011209
3	0.6718	0.9120	-1.8105	1.796	0.018979
4	-1.8985	2.3218	-0.3865	0.2721	0.040269
5	1.6011	1.7384	0.4317	0.4040	0.042398
6	1.2013	1.5141	-1.8945	4.3522	0.051333

Table 4. The fuzzy rules identified for the fuzzy gain $-0.1 \leq \hat{u}_3 \leq -0.01km/s^2$

No. of rules	Parameters				
	$\bar{x_1}$	$\bar{\sigma_1}$	$\bar{x_2}$	$\bar{\sigma_2}$	$\bar{\gamma}$
1	-1.0392	2.3006	-0.0872	1.0627	-0.04416
2	-1.0222	1.8149	-1.4291	0.159	-0.01561
3	1.7659	1.0216	-1.085	0.0841	-0.04523
4	2.3135	1.4002	1.9074	4.356	-0.04734
5	1.3201	1.0216	1.3362	0.6872	-0.05210
6	1.1125	1.8671	2.1331	0.0600	-0.04452
7	-0.2846	2.3505	-0.7628	1.3257	-0.05430
8	-0.6785	3.353	-0.4667	1.3307	-0.01395
9	1.9234	3.6593	0.7396	0.1792	-0.04718
10	2.1776	2.7179	-2.0026	0.2952	-0.02166
11	1.1157	1.1629	-2.0026	0.7687	-0.01358
12	2.0093	1.9302	-1.8028	4.088	-0.03133
13	0.3672	3.6882	-2.1529	0.7429	-0.02120

model. We assume that the target moves in a plane and its dynamics are given. For convenience, the maximum target acceleration is assumed to be $0.1km/s^2$, which is determined to sufficiently cover the target maneuver, the sampling period T is $1s$. The target is assumed to be an incoming anti-ship missile on the $x-y$ plane [14]. The initial position of the target is assumed to be $x_0 = 72.9km$, $y_0 = 3.0km$ and its velocity components are assumed to be $0.3km/s$ along the $-150°$ line to the $x-axis$. The standard deviation of the zero mean white Gaussian measurement noise is $R = 0.5^2$ and that of the random acceleration noise is $Q = 0.001^2$. The initial parameters of the GA are presented in Table 1.

After the unknown target acceleration $\hat{u}$ is determined by using the GA the modified filter is corrected by using the fuzzy gain algorithm. The fuzzy gain γ is

Table 5. The acceleration levels of the sub-models

Configurations	m_1	m_2	m_3	m_4	m_5
AIMM3	$\hat{a}(k)$	$\hat{a}(k)+0.04$	$\hat{a}(k)-0.04$	-	-
AIMM5	$\hat{a}(k)$	$\hat{a}(k)+0.02$	$\hat{a}(k)-0.02$	$\hat{a}(k)+0.04$	$\hat{a}(k)-0.04$

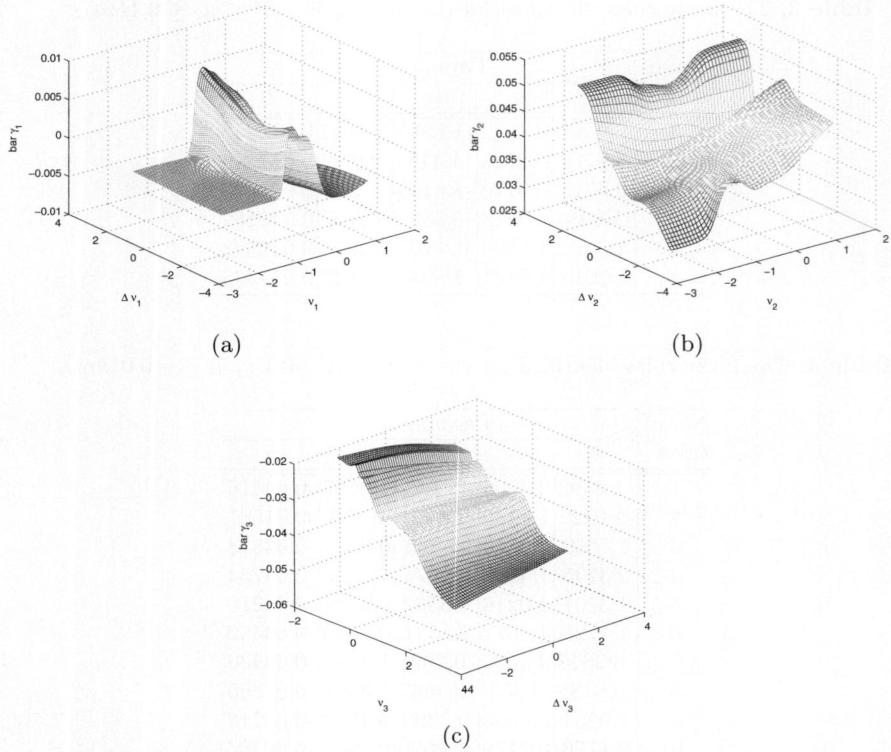

Fig. 1. The functional relationships of the fuzzy gain optimized for (a) acceleration interval, $-0.01 < \hat{a}_1 < 0.01km/s^2$, (b) acceleration interval, $0.01 \leq \hat{a}_2 \leq 0.1km/s^2$, and (c) acceleration interval, $-0.1 \leq \hat{a}_3 \leq -0.01km/s^2$

shown Table 2, 3and 4, respectively. and their functional relationships are shown in Fig 1. The performance of the proposed algorithm for the maneuvering target tracking has been compared with other algorithms. In the comparison algorithm method, the standard deviations of the bias filter and the bias-free filter for the two-stage Kalman estimator are $0.01km/s^2$ and $0.001km/s^2$, respectively, which are used only for the AIMM algorithm. The acceleration levels of submodel for the AIMM methods are shown in Table 5. The simulation results with 100 Monte-Carlo simulations shown in Fig 2. Figure 2 shows that the simulation results of the proposed method are compared with those of the IE method and AIMM method. Numerical results are shown in Table6. Table6 indicates that the normalized position and velocity errors of the proposed method are reduced by 17.44% - 31.18% and 9.60% - 31.18%, compared with the IE method and AIMM in the average sense. This implies that the proposed method provides smaller position errors and velocity errors at almost every scan time, especially during maneuvering time intervals, than the IE and the AIMM methods. This is because, although the properties of the maneuver are unknown, the unknown

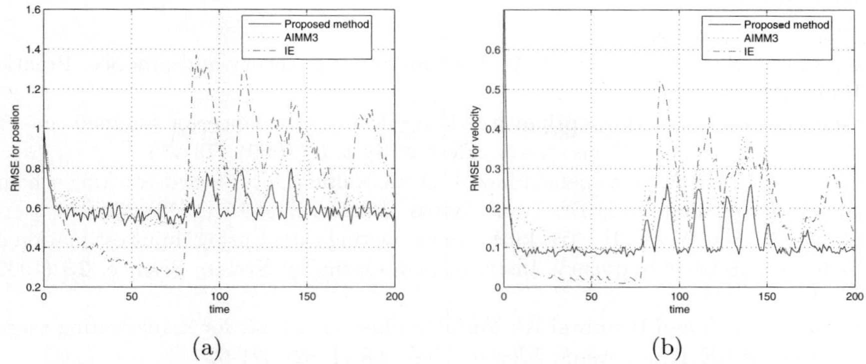

Fig. 2. The comparisons of (a) position error reduction factor and (b) velocity error reduction factor: the proposed method (dashed), IE (dash-dotted), and AIMM3 (dotted)

Table 6. The comparison of numerical results

Configurations	No. of sub-models	ζ_p	ζ_v
IE	1	0.7263	0.1777
AIMM3	3	0.6633	0.1819
Proposed method	3	0.5996	0.1223

acceleration input can be well approximated via the fuzzy system and that the once more modified filter is corrected by using fuzzy gain based on the fuzzy system, whereas the IE and AIMM methods cannot effectively deal with the complex properties of the maneuvering target.

5 Conclusion

The maneuvering target tracking via the fuzzy system has been presented. Estimate of the unknown maneuver input for each sub-model is detected by using a fuzzy system based on the mismatches between the modelled target dynamics and the actual target dynamics. Then the state estimate for each sub-model is modified by using the updated algorithm which is the fuzzy gain based on the fuzzy system. To optimize the employed fuzzy system, the GA is utilized. Finally, we have shown that the proposed filter can effectively treat a target maneuver through computer simulations for an incoming ballistic missile.

Acknowledgment

This work was supported by the Brain Korea 21 Project in 2006.

References

1. Grewal M. S., and Andrews A. P.: Kalman filtering: theory and practice. Prentice Hall. (1993)
2. Singer R.A.: Estimating optimal tracking filter performance for manned maneuvering targets. IEEE Trans. Aeros. Electro. Syst. **6** (1969) 473-483
3. Chan Y. T., Hu A. G. C., and Plant J. B.: A Kalman filter based tracking scheme with input estimation. IEEE Trans. Aeros. Electro. Syst.**15** (1979) 237-244
4. Guu J. A., and Wei C. H.: Tracking a maneuvering target using input estimation at high measurement frequency. International Journal of System Science. **23** (1992) 871-883
5. Bar-Shalom Y. and Birmiwal K.: Variable dimension filter for maneuvering target tracking. IEEE Trans. Aeros. Electro. Syst. **18** (1982) 621-629.
6. Alouani A. T., Price P., and Blair W.D.: A two-stage Kalman estimator for state estimation in the presence of random bias for tracking maneuvering targets. Proc. Of 30th IEEE Conf. Decision and Control. (1991) 2059-2002
7. Tugnait J. K.: Detection and estimation for abruptly changing systems. IEEE Trans. Autom. **18** (1982) 607-615
8. Bar-Shalom Y. and Li X.: Principles, Techniques and Software. Norwood, MA Arteck House. (1993)
9. Munir A. and Atherton. D. P.: Adaptive interacting multiple model algorithm for tracking a maneuvering target. IEE Proc. of Radar. Sonar Navig. **142** (1995) 11-17
10. Li T. H. S.: Estimation of one-dimensional radar tracking via fuzzy-Kalman filter. Proceedings of the IECON'93 International Conference. (1993) 2384-2388
11. Joo Y. H., Hwang, K. B. Kim, and Woo K. B.: Fuzzy system modeling by fuzzy partition and GA hybrid schemes. Fuzzy Sets and Systems **86** (1997) 279-288
12. Wang L.X.: A course in fuzzy systems and control. Prentice Hall, NJ, USA, (1998)
13. Carse B., Terence C., and Munro A..: Evolving fuzzy rule based controllers using genetic algorithm. Fuzzy Sets and Systems. **80** (1996) 273-293.
14. S. McGinnity and G. W. Irwin.: Fuzzy logic approach to maneuvering target tracking. IEE proc. Of Radar Sonar and Navigation. **145** (1998) 337-341
15. Munir A. and Artherton P.: Adaptive interacting multiple model algorithm for tracking a maneuvering target. IEE Proc. Radar Sonar Navig. **142** (1995) 11-17
16. Lee B. J., Park J. B., Y. Joo H., and Jin S. H..: An Intelligent Tracking Method for Maneuvering Target. International Journal of Contr. Automation and Systems **1** (2003) 93-100

Complete FPGA Implemented Evolvable Image Filters

Jin Wang and Chong Ho Lee

Department of Information Technology & Telecommunication,
Inha University, Incheon, Korea
wangjin_liips@yahoo.com.cn

Abstract. This paper describes a complete FPGA implemented intrinsic evolvable system which is employed as a novel approach to automatic design of spatial image filters for two given types of noise. The genotype-phenotype representation of the proposed evolvable system is inspired by the Cartesian Genetic Programming and the function level evolution. The innovative feature of the proposed system is that the whole evolvable system which consists of evolutionary algorithm unit, fitness value calculation unit and reconfigurable function elements array is realized in a same FPGA. A commercial and current FPGA card: Celoxica RC1000 PCI board with a Xilinx Virtex xcv2000E FPGA is employed as our hardware platform. The main motive of our research is to design a general, simple and fast virtual reconfigurable hardware platform with powerful computation ability to achieve intrinsic evolution. The experiment results show that a spatial image filter can be evolved in less than 71 seconds.

1 Introduction

Inspired by the natural evolution, evolvable hardware (EHW) is a kind of electronic device which can change its inner architecture and function dynamically and autonomously to adapt its environment by using evolutionary algorithm (EA). According to the difference in the process of fitness evaluation, EHW can be classified into two main categories: extrinsic and intrinsic EHW. Extrinsic EHW uses software simulation to evaluate the fitness value of each individual and only the elite individual is finally implemented by hardware. In recent years, with the advent of programming logic devices, it is possible to realize intrinsic evolution by evaluating a real hardware circuit within the evolutionary computation framework: the fitness evaluation of each individual is directly implemented in hardware and the hardware device will be reconfigured the same number of times as the population size in each generation. Field Programmable Gate Array (FPGA) is the most commonly used commercial reconfigurable device for digital intrinsic EHW. Due to pipelining and parallelism, the very time consuming fitness evaluation process can be accessed more quickly in FPGA based intrinsic evolution than in software simulation. A lot of work has been done in the area of FPGA implemented intrinsic evolution. Generally, these approaches can be divided into two groups:

(1) FPGA is employed for the evaluation of the candidate individuals produced by evolutionary algorithm, which is executed in a host PC or an individual embedded processor. This idea has been proposed by Zhang [1] in the image filter evolution.

A. Gelbukh and C.A. Reyes-Garcia (Eds.): MICAI 2006, LNAI 4293, pp. 767 – 777, 2006.

The author of [2] built an on-chip evolution platform implemented on a xc2VP7 Virtex-II Pro FPGA which equipped a PowerPC 405 hard-core processor to implement evolutionary algorithm. Other type of interesting approach has been reported in [3] in which the hardware reconfiguration was based on JBits API.

(2) Implementing complete FPGA based evolutions, this type of implementation integrates the evolutionary algorithm and the evaluations of the candidate circuits into a single FPGA. As an example, we can mention Tufte's and Haddow's research in which they introduced complete hardware evolution approach where the evolutionary algorithm implemented on the same FPGA as the evolving design [4]. Running complete evolution in FPGA has also been reported by Sekanina for different applications [5, 6, 7]. In his works, the full evolvable system was implemented on the top of FPGA which was named as virtual reconfigurable architecture. However, his systems were based on a specialized hardware platform-COMBO6 card which was custom-made for a special project and not achievable for most of researchers.

In this paper, we describe how to design a complete FPGA implemented evolvable system using a commercial and general FPGA card-Celoxica RC1000 PCI board [8]. Our evolvable system was designed for evolving spatial image operators. A lot of works have been done in the area of evolving spatial image filter by extrinsic evolution approach [9] and intrinsic evolution approaches [1] [6] because of their potential merit in research and industry. The objective of this paper is to exhibit the potential ability of our proposed system in the complicated application of evolving spatial image operators.

The rest of this paper is organized as follows: in the next section, we discuss the problem domain and the idea of the proposed approach. The hardware realization of the evolvable image filter is described in Section 3. The experimental results are presented in Section 4. Finally, Section 5 concludes the paper.

2 Intrinsic Evolution on FPGA

Fitness evaluation is generally computationally expensive and the most time consuming part in the evolutionary process of evolvable hardware. To speed up fitness evaluation, with the rapid development of reconfigurable devices, such as FPGA, the idea of hardware based intrinsic evolution has been proposed in the recent years. The system clock frequency of FPGA is normally slower than personal computer (PC), but it has an inherently parallel structure with flexible communication. This feature of FPGA which is similar to those in the biological neural networks offers it powerful computational ability to superior to the conventional personal computer. FPGA are widely accessible reconfigurable devices. However, in the most of applications of intrinsic evolution, there have some common problems when FPGA is considered as a hardware platform: (1) a popular idea of EHW is to regard the configuration bit string of FPGA as a chromosome for EA. This makes the chromosome length be on the order of tens of thousands of bits, rendering evolution practically impossible using current technology. (2) In today's FPGA, under the demand for 1000s or even more than 100,000s of reconfigurations to evolve a result circuit, the configuration speed of current reconfigurable device becomes an obvious bottleneck. Partial reconfiguration technology seems to be a solution to this problem for the reconfiguration process is faster than the complete reconfiguration. With the exit of Xilinx XC6200 family, JBits was introduced by Xilinx to make this work easier [3]. However, JBits is too complicated and still too slow to achieving more than 100,000s of reconfigurations in a reasonable time.

To conquer the mentioned problems, the virtual reconfigurable circuit technology [10] which is inspired by the Cartesian Genetic Programming (CGP) [11] is employed in our application as a kind of rapidly (virtual) reconfigurable platform utilizing conventional FPGA for digital EHW. For making FPGA be evolvable at a higher level and limit the size of chromosome, in virtual reconfigurable circuit, the FPGA cells are arranged into a grid of sub-blocks of cells (it is named as function elements array in the following sections). Compare with directly encoding the configuration bit string of FPGA as chromosome, the functions of each sub-block and the networks connections of the sub-blocks grid are encoded as chromosome of EA. For achieving complete hardware evolution, both of the evolutionary algorithm and the virtual reconfigurable circuit are implemented on the same FPGA to construct an intact evolvable system. In this scheme, the FPGA configuration bit string will not be changed during evolution, but rather the content of the internal registers which store the configuration information of the virtual reconfigurable circuit (which is generated by EA as chromosomes). The most obvious advantage of complete hardware evolution is that the evolvable system is complete pipelined which conquers the bottleneck introduced by slow communication between the FPGA and a personal computer and a very fast reconfiguration can be achieved (in several system clocks).

3 Implementing Evolvable System on RC1000 PCI Board

Celoxica RC1000 PCI board (as shown in Fig. 1) which has been successfully applied as a high performance, flexible and low cost FPGA based hardware platform for different computationally intensive applications [12, 13, 14] is employed as our experimental platform. Celoxica RC1000 PCI board supports traditional hardware design language: e.g. VHDL and Verilog. On the other hand, a new C like system description language called Handel-C introduced by Celoxica [8] is also supported by this board, which allows users who is not familiar with hardware design to focus more on the specification of an algorithm rather than adopting a structural approach to coding. In this paper, VHDL is employed as our design language.

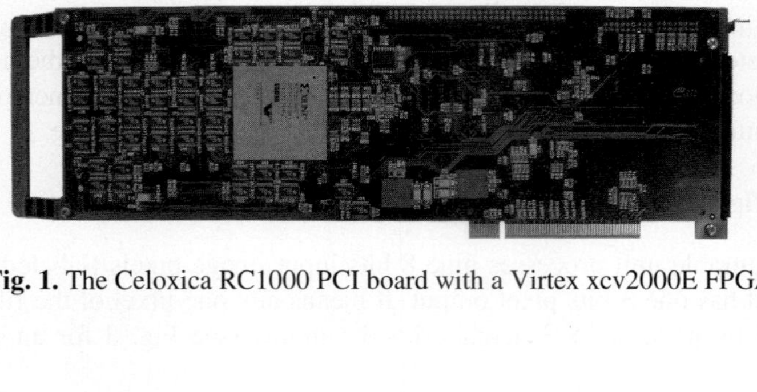

Fig. 1. The Celoxica RC1000 PCI board with a Virtex xcv2000E FPGA

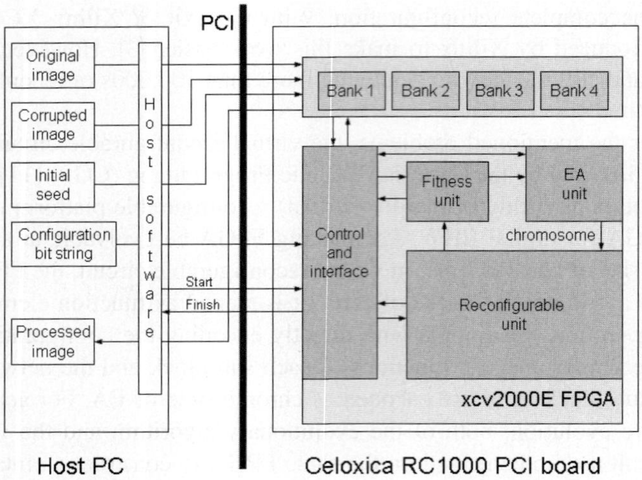

Fig. 2. Organization of the proposed evolvable system

The organization of the architecture on Celoxica RC1000 PCI board is given in Fig. 2. This architecture makes use of the on board Virtex xcv2000E FPGA chip and has 8Mbytes of SRAM which is directly connected to the FPGA in four 32-bit wide memory banks. All memory banks are accessible by the FPGA and host PC. The host software (it is a C program) that controls the flow of the data runs on the host PC. The corrupted image and original image are rearranged by the host software to support neighborhood window operations which will be detailed in section 3.1. The rearranged corrupted image, original image and the initial seed (for generating random numbers in the evolutionary process) are read and stored into the memory banks 1-3 in advance. Then the design configuration bit string is read and downloaded to the FPGA. Once this process is accomplished, the host software signals the complete FPGA implemented evolvable system to start the evolutionary operations. In Fig. 2, the proposed evolvable system is composed of four components: Reconfigurable unit, Fitness unit, EA unit and Control and interface. In the evolvable system, all operations are controlled by the control and interface which communicates with the on board SRAM and the host software. The EA unit implements the evolutionary operations and generates configuration bit string (chromosomes) to configure the reconfigurable unit. The reconfigurable unit processes the input 9×8 bits gray scale image pixels and its function is reconfigurable. Fitness unit calculates individual fitness by comparing the output image from the reconfigurable unit with the original image. Once the system evolution is finished, the evolvable system signals the host software the completion of the operation. The result image which is stored in memory bank 4 is then transmitted to the host software and saved as the result image file.

3.1 Reconfigurable Unit

The reconfigurable unit processes nine 8 bits input image pixels (labeled in Fig. 3, 4 as I0-I8) and has one 8 bits pixel output. It means any one pixel of the filtered image is generated by using a 3×3 neighborhood window (see Fig. 3 for an example, an output pixel is generated by processing its corresponding input pixel and 8 neighbors). By sliding the 3×3 neighborhood window one pixel by one pixel in the pixels array of the input corrupted image, the image can be processed.

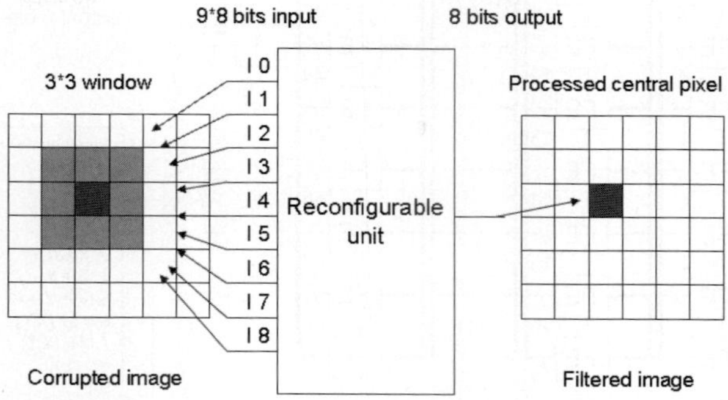

Fig. 3. Neighborhood window operation for image processing

The genotype-phenotype representation scheme in our proposed system is very similar as the Cartesian Genetic Programming [11]. The system genotype is a linear binary bit string which defines the connections and functions of a function elements (FE) array. The genotype and the mapping process of the genotype to phenotype are illustrated in Fig. 4. The main advantage of this representation of a program is that the genotype representation used is independent of the data type used in the phenotype. This feature brings us a generic and flexible platform as for a different application one would just need to change the data type, leaving the genotype unchanged. In hardware implementation, a $N \times M$ array of 2-inputs FEs has been implemented in the reconfigurable unit as system phenotype representation. In order to allow the design of evolvable image filter, the traditional CGP is expended to function level [15] and the FEs with 8 bits datapaths are employed.

In our experiment, the FEs array consists of 7 FEs layers from system input to output. Except for the last layer, 8 uniform FEs are placed in each layer. The last layer only includes one FE. The input connections of each FE are selected using 8:1 multiplexers. FE's two inputs in layer l (l=2, 3, 4, 5, 6, 7) can be connected to anyone output of FEs in layer l-1. In layer 1, the first input 8:1 multiplexer of a FE is constrained to be connected with system inputs I0-I7 and the second 8:1 multiplexer links system input I1-I8. Each FE can execute one of 16 functions which are evident from Fig. 4. Flip-flop is equipped by each FE to support the pipeline process and the reconfiguration of the FEs array is performed layer by layer, which was detailed in [10]. The active function of each FE and its two input connections are configurable and determined by the configuration bit string which is uploaded from EA unit as chromosome. By continuously altering the configuration bit string, the system can be evolved. The encoding of each FE in the chromosome is 3+3+4 bits. For the FEs array consisting of 49 units, the intact chromosome length is $(6\times 8\times 10)+10=490$ bits.

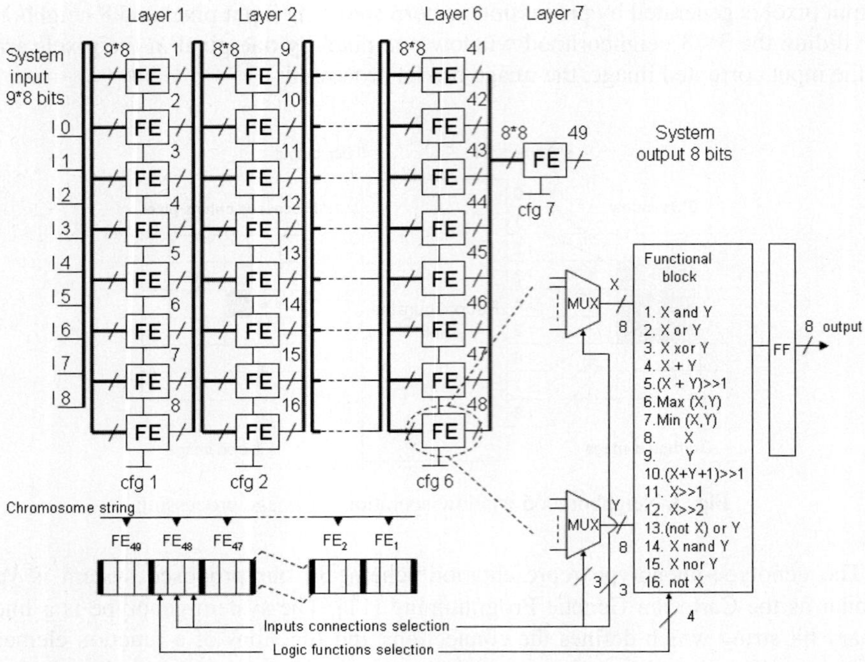

Fig. 4. Mapping chromosome string into the function elements array

3.2 Evolutionary Algorithm Unit

The evolutionary algorithm employed in EA unit is according to the 1+ λ evolutionary strategy, where λ =4. In our experiment, evolution is only based on the mutation and selection operators, crossover is not taken into account. The Flow diagram of EA operations is presented in Fig. 5.

The initial population which includes 4 individuals is generated randomly with the initial seed according to the rules 90 and 150 as described by Wolfram [16]. To get the fitness value of each individual, each of them is downloaded to the reconfigurable unit to generate a candidate circuit, respectively. By comparing the candidate circuit output image with the original image, the fitness value of each individual can be

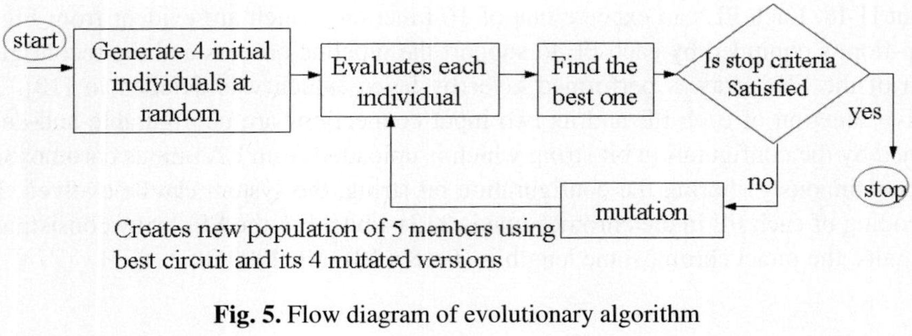

Fig. 5. Flow diagram of evolutionary algorithm

obtained. The individual with the best fitness in the initial population is selected out and the new population is generated by using the fittest individual and its 4 mutants. This process is repeated until the predefined generation number (8192) is exhausted.

3.3 Fitness Unit

The single evolutionary objective in our experiment is to minimize the difference between the filtered image and the original image which is uncorrupted by the noise. To measure the quality of the filtered image, the MDPP (mean different per pixel) based fitness function is implemented in the fitness unit. The original image size is $k \times k$ (k=256), but only a sub-area image of (k-2)$\times$ (k-2) pixels is considered, because the pixels at the image borders are untouchable for the 3×3 window and remain unfiltered. The MDPP based fitness function is described as follow:

$$fitness_{MDPP} = 255 \times (k-2)^2 - \sum_{i=1}^{k-2} \sum_{j=1}^{k-2} |v(i,j) - w(i,j)| \quad (1)$$

In the Eq. (1), v denotes the filtered image and w denotes the original image. MDPP based fitness function is calculated by comparing the diversity of each pixel in the filtered image with its corresponding pixels in the original image.

4 Results

4.1 Synthesis Report

The evolvable system was designed by using VHDL and synthesized into Virtex xcv2000E FPGA using Xilinx ISE 6.3. The synthesized result was optimized for speed and shown in Table 1. According to our synthesis report, the proposed system can be operated at 71.169MHz. However, the actual hardware experiment was run at 30MHz because of easier synchronization with PCI interface.

Table 1. Synthesis results in Virtex xcv2000E

Resource	Used	Available	Percent
Slices	8596	19200	44%
Slice Flip Flops	5479	38400	14%
4 input LUTs	14038	38400	36%
bonded IOBs:	267	408	65%

4.2 Time of Evolution

As the pipeline process is supported by the proposed evolvable system, all EA operations time as well as reconfiguration time of FEs array could be overlapped by the fitness evaluation. The total system evolution time can be determined as:

$$t = t_{init} + \frac{(k-2)^2 \times p \times ngen}{f} \quad (2)$$

Where $(k\text{-}2)^2$ is the number of processed image pixels, p is population size, $ngen$ is the number of generations and t_{init} is the time needed to generate the first output pixel of the FEs array in pipeline process (several FPGA system clocks only).

4.3 Hardware Evolution Results

Only gray scale (8 bits each pixel) image of size 256× 256 pixels was consider in this paper. Two types of additive noise which were independent of the image itself were processed: Gaussian noise (mean 0 and variance 0.008) and salt & pepper noise (the image contains 5% corrupted pixels with white or block shots). Both of the mentioned noises were generated by using Matlab functions. Two types of image filters were evolved to process the proposed noises individually. The evolved image operators were trained by using original Lena and its filtered version.

Table 2. Results for Gaussian noise (mean 0 and variance 0.008)

Mutation rate	The best MDPP	Average MDPP	Evolution time
0.8%	7.32	13.35	70.5 s
1.6%	7.13	8.95	
3.2%	6.98	8.23	
6.4%	8.39	10.00	

Table 3. Results for salt & pepper noise (5% corrupted pixels with white or block shots)

Mutation rate	The best MDPP	Average MDPP	Evolution time
0.8%	1.08	7.64	70.5 s
1.6%	1.27	3.71	
3.2%	1.13	3.23	
6.4%	2.81	4.21	

In our experiment, each evolved result was achieved after 8192 generations of EA run. To measure the quality of the filtered image, the MDPP (mean different per pixel) function was employed. Different mutation rates were tested to explore the effect of the diversity of the EA parameter. The mutation rate is defined as the percentage of the genes of the entire chromosome string, which will undergo mutation. We performed 20 runs for each experimental setting and measured the best and average MDPP by comparing the filtered images with the original image. Table 2 and Table 3 summarize the evolved filters for Gaussian and salt & pepper noises, respectively.

An example evolved circuit for processing salt & pepper noise is shown in Fig. 6. After the image filter was evolved, to test the generality of the result filter which was trained by Lena, various test images set: baboon and cameraman were employed. Fig.7 presents the processed images set by the mentioned filter in Fig.6. As a comparison, the original corrupted images are also included in Fig.7.

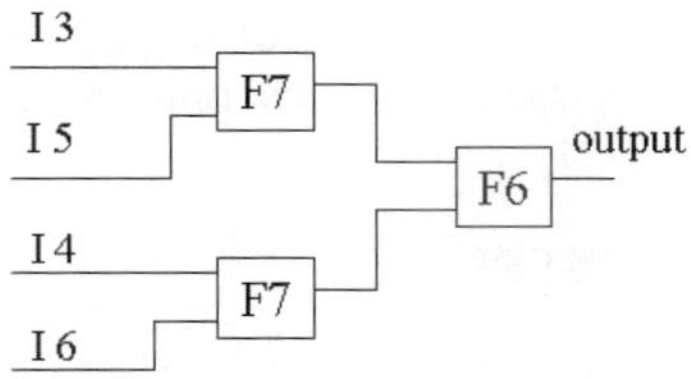

Fig. 6. An evolved circuit for processing salt & pepper noise

Fig. 7. The EHW filter trained by Lena with salt & pepper noise and tested on baboon and cameraman

Our hardware platform can run steadily under 30MHz and used only 70.5 seconds to finish 8192 generations of evolution. In reference [1], Zhang et al. have implemented a similar reconfigurable architecture in FPGA to evolve image operators which process Gaussian and salt & pepper noises. However, in their evolvable system, some evolutionary operations have been processed by host PC. Slow communication between the FPGA and the host PC becomes the bottleneck of speedup the evolution in their experiment. Considering the factors of the different population size and the generation number in their experiment, we still can announce we achieved a speedup of 20 times when compared to the report in [1]. Sekanina's group reported a very similar hardware implemented evolvable image operators in literature [6]. As shown in table 2 and 3, the image operators evolved here and in [6] present a very close performance on the quality of the processed images. A significant difference between Sekanina and our design is the hardware cost. Our design seems more compact: in the design of the evolvable image filter which employs the similar FEs array with the same size of 8×7 and includes the same number of individuals in EA unit, Sekanina used 10042 slices of Virtex II xc2v3000 FPGA and only 8596 slices in

Virtex xcv2000E FPGA was consumed in our design. According to our results reports, the mutation rate of 3.2% seems the most optimal parameter under the proposed experimental frame.

5 Conclusions

This paper has presented an approach for implementing a complete FPGA based intrinsic evolvable system in Celoxica RC1000 PCI board with a Xilinx Virtex xcv2000E FPGA. A prototype of the evolvable system was fully tested by evolving different spatial image filters to process two kinds of additional noise. This work demonstrates the generality and feasibility of the proposed hardware architecture. The powerful computation ability of the proposed evolvable system is presented in the experiments-an image operator which is expected for processing 256×256 gray scale image can be evolved in less than 71 seconds. Further work will be concentrated on developing the reported evolvable system for the automatic evolution of more complex image operators.

Acknowledgment

This work was supported by INHA University Research Grant.

References

1. Zhang, Y. et al.: Digital Circuit Design Using Intrinsic Evolvable Hardware. In: Proc. of the 2004 NASA/DoD Conference on the Evolvable Hardware, IEEE Computer Society (2004) 55-63
2. Glette, K., Torresen, J.: A Flexible On-Chip Evolution System Implemented on a Xilinx Virtex-II Pro Device. In: Proc. of the 6th Int. Conference on Evolvable Systems: From Biology to Hardware ICES 2005, LNCS 3637, Springer-Verlag (2005) 66-75
3. Hollingworth, G. et al.: The Intrinsic Evolution of Virtex Devices Through Internet Reconfigurable Logic. In: Proc. of the 3rd International Conference on Evolvable Systems: From Biology to Hardware ICES'00, LNCS 1801, Springer-Verlag (2000) 72-79
4. Tufte, G., Haddow, P.C.: Prototyping a GA Pipeline for Complete Hardware Evolution. In: Proc. of the first NASA/DoD Workshop on Evolvable Hardware, IEEE Computer Society (1999)18–25
5. Sekanina, L., Friedl, S.: On Routine Implementation of Virtual Evolvable Devices Using COMBO6. In: Proc. of the 2004 NASA/DoD Conference on Evolvable Hardware, IEEE Computer Society (2004) 63-70
6. Martínek, T., Sekanina, L.: An Evolvable Image Filter: Experimental Evaluation of a Complete Hardware Implementation in FPGA. In: Proc. of the 6th Int. Conference on Evolvable Systems: From Biology to Hardware ICES 2005, LNCS 3637, Springer-Verlag (2005) 76-85
7. Korenek, J., Sekanina, L.: Intrinsic Evolution of Sorting Networks: A Novel Complete Hardware Implementation for FPGAs. In: Proc. of the 6th Int. Conference on Evolvable Systems: From Biology to Hardware ICES 2005, LNCS 3637, Springer-Verlag (2005) 46-55
8. Celoxica Ltd. www.celoxica.com

9. Sekanina, L.: Image Filter Design with Evolvable Hardware. In: Proc. of the 4th Workshop on Evolutionary Computation in Image Analysis and Signal Processing, LNCS 2279 Springer-Verlag (2002) 255-266
10. Sekanina, L.: Virtual Reconfigurable Circuits for Real-World Applications of Evolvable Hardware. In: Proc. of the 5th Int. Conference Evolvable Systems: From Biology to Hardware ICES 2003, LNCS 2606, Springer-Verlag (2003) 186-197
11. Miller, J.F., Thomson, P.: Cartesian Genetic Programming. In: Proc. of the Third European Conference on Genetic Programming, LNCS 1802, Springer-Verlag (2000) 121-132
12. Martin, P.: A Hardware Implementation of a Genetic Programming System Using FPGAs and Handel-C. Genetic Programming and Evolvable Machines, Vol. 2, No. 4, Springer Netherlands (2001) 317–343
13. Bensaali, F. et al.: Accelerating Matrix Product on Reconfigurable Hardware for Image Processing Applications. IEE proceedings-Circuits, Devices and Systems, Vol. 152, Issue 3 (2005) 236-246
14. Muthukumar, V., Rao, D.V.: Image Processing Algorithms on Reconfigurable Architecture Using HandelC. In: Proc. of the 2004 Euromicro Symposium on Digital System Design, IEEE Computer Society (2004) 218-226
15. Murakawa, M. et al.: Hardware Evolution at Function Level. In: Proc. of Parallel Problem Solving from Nature PPSN IV, LNCS 1141, Springer-Verlag (1996) 62–71
16. Wolfram, S.: Universality and Complexity in Cellular Automata. Physica (1984)10D:1-35

Probabilistic Rules for Automatic Texture Segmentation

Justino Ramírez and Mariano Rivera

Centro de Investigación en Matemáticas A.C. (CIMAT)
A.P. 402, Guanajuato, Gto. 36240, México
{justino, mrivera}@cimat.mx

Abstract. We present an algorithm for automatic selection of features that best segment an image in texture homogeneous regions. The set of "best extractors" are automatically selected among the Gabor filters, Co-occurrence matrix, Law's energies and intensity response. Noise-features elimination is performed by taking into account the magnitude and the granularity of each feature image, i.e. the compute image when a specific feature extractor is applied. Redundant features are merged by means of probabilistic rules that measure the similarity between a pair of image feature. Then, cascade applications of general purpose image segmentation algorithms (K-Means, Graph-Cut and EC-GMMF) are used for computing the final segmented image. Additionally, we propose an evolutive gradient descent scheme for training the method parameters for a benchmark image set. We demonstrate by experimental comparisons, with stat of the art methods, a superior performance of our technique.

1 Introduction

Image segmentation consists on estimate the tessellation of the image in compact disjoint regions of pixels with similar features (for instance: gray scale, texture or color) and clearly distinguished among regions. The case of texture image segmentation problem can be defined as the detection of regions with smooth spatial variation of local statistics [1] [2]. Measures for local statistics are named features. Comparisons of segmentation using different features are reported in [3] and [4]. Therein it is concluded that there is not a feature family that would be appropriate for all the cases. For this reason there have been reported hybrid features families that combine different feature extractor families that try to take benefit of their strength and to deal with their weakness. Hybrid features have shown satisfactory results [5] [6] [7]. However, a problem with hybrid families is the facture explosion that produces noise-features (responses to unpresent features) and redundant features (a single region may have a high response to different feature extractors). These two problems affect the final segmentation because the dimensionality of the problem is artificially increased by the feature-noise and thus the segmentation algorithm may be lead by feature noise. Additionally as is normal to expect an inhomogeneous feature redundancy between regions then the segmentation is biased to detect regions with more redundant features and to miss, by effect of the noise-features, the ones without (or low) redundant features [3] [4].

A. Gelbukh and C.A. Reyes-Garcia (Eds.): MICAI 2006, LNAI 4293, pp. 778 – 788, 2006.

In this work we propose to use a huge number of feature extractors and then to eliminate noise-features and redundant features [8]. Our strategy consists of three steps:

1. Feature computation. To compute the huge number of feature images corresponding to Gabor filters (GF) [9], concurrency matrix (CM) [10], Laws' energies (LE) [11] and Intensity range (IR). We assume redundant such feature set in the sense that a single region may produce a high response in more that one image feature. Moreover, the feature set is corrupted by noise-features product of to apply feature extractors associated with no-present features in the image.
2. Feature selection. The noise reduction is preformed by eliminating feature images with granular or low response. Then the redundancy is reduced by eliminating similar image-feature by using a, herein introduced, procedure based on probabilistic rules.
3. Image Segmentation. By using the reduced set of the "best features", to segment the image in smooth and automatically detected of regions.

Additionally, we propose a training method for automatically adjusting the parameters of the three texture segmentation procedure. The training method consists of a supervised learning technique that uses as examples a set of image-segmentation pairs and an evolutive gradient descent to reduce the classification error. Experimental comparison showed a superior performance of our feature selection strategy than state of the art methods.

2 Image Texture Segmentation Method

Follows we present the details of the method for texture image segmentation that uses combined sets of features, reduces redundancy and eliminate noise with probabilistic rules. Such a feature reduction is inspired in a data mining strategy.

2.1 Feature Extraction

We select feature families widely used in the texture segmentation literature. Then subsets of such families were chosen according to their experimental range of better response [4]. For instance, according to [6], Gabor filters have a more confident response in the detection of textures with intermediate spatial frequencies: low frequencies are better distinguished by its mean gray value (in the case of low contrasted frequencies) or Laws' energies [11] (for high contrasted low frequencies). On the other hand, Gabor filters tuned to high frequencies are too sensitive to noise so that co-oncurrence matrix [6] is more suitable.

With out lost or generality, we will define the feature extractor parameters assuming an image size of 256x256 pixels

1. **Gabor Filter (GF) Bank** [9]. The bandwidth of each GF was set σ = (num of rows / 16). The GF's were center at its corresponding (u_0,v_0) and uniformly spaced at a distance equal to σ and allocated in the half Fourier spectrum corresponding to the frequencies $u\in[-\pi/2, \pi/2]$, $v\in[0,\pi/2]$. Thus 45 GF-features are computed.

2. **Co-occurrence Matrix (CM)** [10]**.** Four directions were chosen: 0, π/2, π and -π/2 and the test distances corresponded to 1 and 2 pixels. The image gray scale was quantized to 16 levels and a window of 9x9 pixels was used. As result 32 CM-features are computed.
3. **Laws' Energies (LE)** [11]**.** We compute the classical combination of convolution kernels (low-pass and high-pass) alternating in horizontal and vertical directions allowing directional diversity (the stage for rotational invariance was not performed). Therefore 25 LE-features are computed.
4. **Intensity range (IR).** For a given pixel (r) we define the similarity of its intensity value, $g(r)$, to a given intensity value (μ) by

$$HI(r) = \frac{1}{\# N_r} \sum_{s \in N_r} \exp\left(\frac{(g(s)-\mu)^2}{2\sigma^2} \right) \tag{1}$$

where σ = 4 is a parameter that controls the intensity bandwidth and N_r is a small window centered at pixel r: $N_r = \{s \in L : |r - s| < 2\}$ and L is the pixels set at the image. In our case the centers μ ∈ [0,255] are uniformly distribute in the image intensity range. 65 IR-features.

That results a feature vector with 167 entries (i.e. 167-dimension) for each pixel in the original image.

2.2 Probabilistic Rules for Feature Selection

Noise reduction. Each image-feature is normalized into the interval [0, 1] and it is smoothed by applying an inhomogeneous diffusion [12] that uses as diffusion coefficient the weights that corresponds to Huber potential [13]. Then each image is binarized (segmented into regions with high response and low response) with EC-GMMF [14] for two classes. This algorithm is implemented as the minimization of the cost function:

$$u(p,m,\sigma) = \frac{1}{2}\sum_r \left[p_r^2 \left(\frac{(g_r - m_1)^2}{2\sigma_1^2} + N \log \sigma_1 \right) + (1-p_r)^2 \left(\frac{(g_r - m_0)^2}{2\sigma_0^2} + N \log \sigma_0 \right) + \lambda \sum_{s \in N_r} (p_r - p_s)^2 \right] \tag{2}$$

where N the image size and λ is a regularization parameter (*λ=1*). As result we obtain the probability, p_r, than the pixel r has a high response and conversely *(1-p_r)*. The classes (high response and low response) are defined by the computed parameters: mean values m_1 and m_0 (with their respective standard deviations: σ_1 and σ_0). From the computed parameters we can define the following measures:

$$c = m_1 - m_0 \tag{3}$$

$$g = 1 - \frac{1}{N}\sum_r \left[p_r^2 + (1-p_r)^2 \right] \tag{4}$$

was *c* can be understood as the separability of the classes or the contrast of the feature image. On the other hand, *g* is the Gini's coefficient for entropy computation [14] and we can relate it with the granularity of the feature image: The entropy of p_r and *(1-p_r)*

is higher at the binary image borders. Thus, granular features will have larger entropy. Therefore, noise features images can be detected by its low contrast and high entropy.

Redundancy reduction. The idea is to reduce as much as possible the number of features that make possible to segment the image. Then we need to define a similarity measure between pairs of feature images. We propose one based on the association rules used in data mining [15]. First we define the association rule between a pair of images A and B as:

$$A \underset{K,Z}{\Rightarrow} B \tag{5}$$

Then, let $\hat{A}, \hat{B}$ the binaries images that result of segment the features A, B (respecttivelly) by minimizing (2). Thus we define:

$$\mathrm{K} = \frac{\sum_r \hat{A}_r \hat{B}_r}{\sum_r \hat{A}_r} \tag{6}$$

$$\mathrm{Z} = \frac{\sum_r \hat{A}_r \hat{B}_r}{N} \tag{7}$$

where K is the *confidence* (probability) that any pixel with high response in the feature A has also a high response in B. Similarly Z is the rule *support* and can be understood as the size of the intersection region of the high responses of the images A and B and N is the number of pixel in yhe image. Finally we propose to measure the similarity, $s \in [0, 1]$, between two feature images as

$$s = \max\left\{\min\left\{C_{A \Rightarrow B}, C_{B \Rightarrow A}\right\}, \min\left\{C_{A \Rightarrow \overline{B}}, C_{\overline{B} \Rightarrow A}\right\}\right\} \tag{8}$$

where $\overline{B}$ the binary image complement, $\overline{B} = 1 - \hat{B}$. Of the pair of similar feature images can be computed and the redundant ones are eliminated keeping the one with higher contrast.

2.3 Hybrid Segmentation Algorithm

Once the features are selected (we assume M features per pixel), we need to initialize the segmentation algorithm, which means that a good initial guess for number of probable homogeneus regions in the image (models) and their parameters is needed. The number of models can initially be computed with the following algorithm:

```
*Initialize: s=0.05*N, MaxRegion=s, Maxima=0.75*N.
Set NumModel=0.
*Sort by contrast the features, F, from highest to lowest.
While (MaxRegion<Maxima)
    For i=0, 1 … M,
        *Let H the set of pixels in F(i) equal to 1 that
         has not been assigned to any model.
        *Set count=Number of pixels in H.
         If MaxRegion>count>s
```

```
            *NumModel=NumModel+1
            *Compute the mean vector of the pixels in H.
            *Assign H to model NumModel.
        End If
    End For i
   *Set MaxRegion= 1.2 * MaxRegion
End While
```

In order to obtain a oversegmentation, to be posteiorly refined in posterior stages, Maxregion is initialized equal to minimum accepted support. This heuristra algorithm guaranties us that if there a region in the original image where a feature is clearly defined, such a region will be assigned an initial model.

The algorithm provides us for an initial guess for the number of models and its parameters, such values are then refines using the K-mean algorithm [16] and then alfa-beta version of the Graph Cut (GC) algorithm [17] that reduces the number of models (in all our experiments we use 15 iteration of the (GC algorithm). The final segmentation is computed using the EC-GMMF algorithm for k-classes using as initial guess the results of the GC algorithm. Contrarily to recent reported methods (see [18], for instance) the number of classes has been automatically computed, this corresponds to the number of classes with, at least, an assigned pixel. The cost function to minimize is:

$$u(p,m,\sigma)=\frac{1}{2}\sum_k\left(\sum_r\left[p_{k,r}^2\left(\frac{(g_r-m_k)^2}{2\sigma_k^2}+N\log\sigma_k\right)+\lambda\sum_{s\in N_r}(p_{k,r}-p_{k,s})^2\right]\right),$$
$$\textit{subject to} \qquad (9)$$
$$\sum_k p_{k,r}=1,\ p_{k,r}\geq 0.$$

The means μ_k are initiallized equal the result in the GC stage and the λ parameter is trained as will be explained in next section. Cost function (9) is minimized with a memory efficient Gauss-Seidel scheme by using the Lagrange's multiplier technique for the equality constraints and a projection method for the inequality ones (see [14] for more details). Given that a good initial guess is provided, the algorithm takes as much as 20 iterations to converge.

3 Parameters Training with an Evolutive Numerical Gradient Descent

A set of mosaics images, as the showed in Fig. 1, were generated by randomly choosing Brodatz texture images [19]: 30 images with 4 regions and 30 images with 5 regions. The half of each set was used for training and the other half for testing. The objective function to minimize in the training stage we the mean of the classification error for the training set (30 images). The cost function evaluation takes about 30 minutes in an Intel Pentium IV PC at 1.8 GHz and therefore the maximum number of evaluations was fixed at 1000. Acording to our experiments a simulated annealing could also converge, however the training time could be prohibitive. We expent 5 dayswith our algorithm with a limited number of evaluation of the cost function. The parameters θ= (G, C, S,λ) adjusted by the training procedure were: the threshold for the granularity (G), the contrast threshold (C), the similarity threshold (S) and the smoothness parameter (λ). The initial guess for the parameters corresponds to the trained parameters for a pair of images shown in Fig. 1. The number of models (regions) was automatically estimated by the segmentation algorithms.

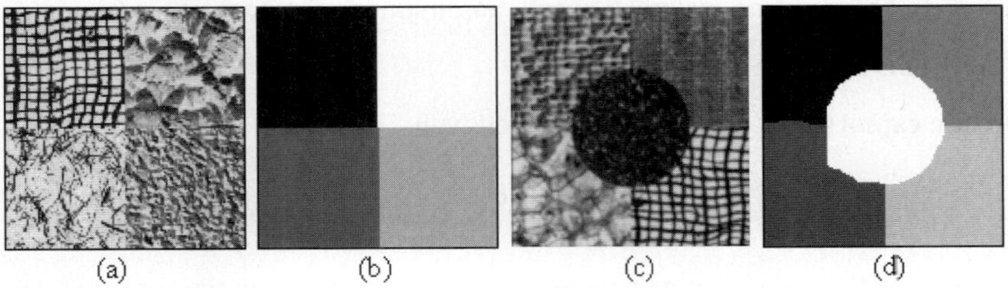

Fig. 1. A pair of the data set images and the corresponding segmentations computed with the automatically adjusted parameters (0.92, 0.25, 0.80, 3.9924). Percent of well classified pixels: (b) 99.6% and (d) 98.4%.

The training method can be summarized as follows: given an actual parameter vector θ^k, we generate λ new parameters $\tilde{\theta}^k$ in the neighborhood θ^k, we named sons the generated $\tilde{\theta}^k$. The descent step consists in choosing the new parameter vector θ^{k+1} the best among $\left\{\theta^k, \{\tilde{\theta}_i^k\}_{i=1,2,..,\lambda}\right\}$. The convergence is established if the algorithm was unable to find a son with best fitness. We use different strategies for generating the sons by depending of the stage of the training: approximation, exploration and refinement.

Approximation by stochastic gradient descent. Both forward and backward numerical gradient are computed by perturbing each parameter of θ^k. The perturbations are computed with

$$\tilde{\theta}^{j+} = \theta_j^k + \sigma_{j-1}(1+U)e_j \tag{10}$$

and

$$\tilde{\theta}^{j-} = \theta_j^k - \sigma_{j-1}(1+U)e_j \tag{11}$$

where $U \sim Uniform(0,1)$, e_j is a unitary vector with the j-th entry equal to 1 and 0 in the other entries, σ_j is a parameter that controls the exploration of the j-th parameter, we use $\sigma = (0.02, 0.02, 0.02, 0.2)$ in all our experiments. Then the sons generated by gradient steps, $\tilde{\theta}^{++}$ and $\tilde{\theta}^{--}$, are computed with

$$\tilde{\theta}^{++} = \theta^k - \alpha\sigma_j \frac{F(\tilde{\theta}^{j+}) - F(\theta^k)}{1+U} \tag{12}$$

and

$$\tilde{\theta}^{--} = \theta_j^k - \alpha\sigma_j \frac{F(\theta^k) - F(\tilde{\theta}^{j-})}{1+U} \tag{13}$$

note that the descent step was set equal to $\alpha(\sigma_j)^2$ and step size was set equal to α=h and h=0.1. The new parameters θ^{k+1} are chosen among the sons (θ^k, $\{\tilde{\theta}^{j+}\}_j$, $\{\tilde{\theta}^{j-}\}_j$, $\tilde{\theta}^{++}$, $\tilde{\theta}^{--}$) the one with minimum cost.

Stocastic exploration. Δ sons are generated with

$$\tilde{\theta}^j = \theta_j + \sigma_j \tilde{U} \tag{14}$$

where $\tilde{U} \sim Uniform(-1,1)$. The new parameters are chosen among the sons (θ^k, $\{\tilde{\theta}^j\}_j$). We use $\Delta = 10$ in all our experiments.

Refinement by stochastic gradient descent. The sons are generated a similar way than in the approximation stage but with a step size α=0.25h. The parameters upgrade is chosen as in the previous stages.

Each stage is stopped if the algorithm was unable to find a son with best fitness, for a given number of iterations (says 5). Multiple start strategy allows us to explore different local minimas.

4 Experiments

Figure 2 shows the computed segmentations of test images using the propose procedure. The initial number of features was 167 and the selected features for the images corresponding to the panels (a), (c), (e) and (g) were: 6, 6, 8, and 12, respectively.

We compare our results with two methods, a principal component analysis (PCA) method for feature selection and the recently reported method of feature fusion (FF).

The first method consists of to change the probabilistic rules proposed in subsection 2.2 for noise elimination and redundancy reduction by a data reduction using PCA [20]. Thus the parameter of the PCA based method has a two parameter: the regularization parameter (λ) of the EC-GMMF segmentation method (see subsection 2.3) and a fraction of the sum of the eigenvalues to preserve (energy preservation). Such parameters were trained with the method proposed in section 3. Segmentation results are shown in panels (b) in Figs. 3 and 4. We found that the feature selection based on PCA reduces significativelly its performance as the number of the feature space in increased. In our opinion, noise-features bias the selection because no prior knowledge about the spatial nature of the data neither the task purpose (to segment the image in a small number of relative large regions) is included.

The second method uses (instead of our large feature space) a feature vector recently reported by Clausi and Deng [6] that incorporates a mixture (**feature fusion**) of a Gabor filters (GF) bank and Co-occurrence matrix (CM). The method uses a carefully selected family of features in order to avoid, as much as possible, the problem of

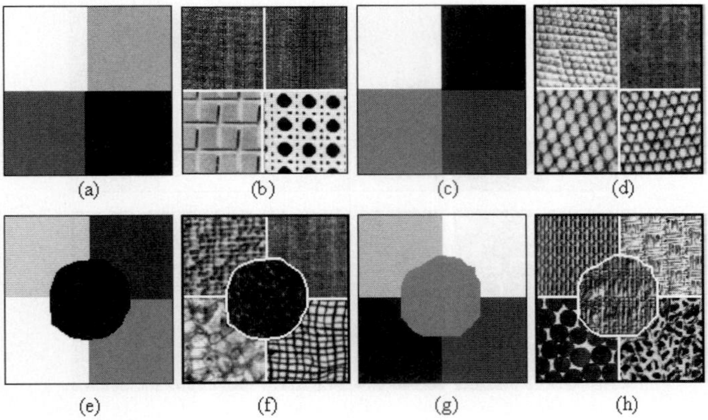

Fig. 2. Test images segmentation computed with the proposed method after the training stage: the fitted parameters were (0.92165, 0.28276, 0.83092, 4.4077). Percent of correct classified pixels: (a) 99.218%, (c) 99.609%, (e) 98.498% and (g) 97.4%.

perform PCA on a large set of features. They propose to use 24 features from the GF bank and 24 from the CM and provide a procedure for compute the GF parameters. The feature selection is computed by using PCA. The parameters for this method are the energy preservation threshold (set initially equal to 0.98, as it is recommended in [6]) and the regularization parameter (λ). This method has a better performance that PCA over a large image feature space; however the provided features may not be enough to distinguish between the regions. This disvantage is illustrated by the results panels (c) in Figs. 3 and 4.

The importance of having a large feature space is appreciated in the segmentation of Fig. 3 and 4: The confused regions in Fig. 3 were distinguished by our method by selecting intensity range features and the corresponding in Fig. 4 by selecting a Laws' energy feature.

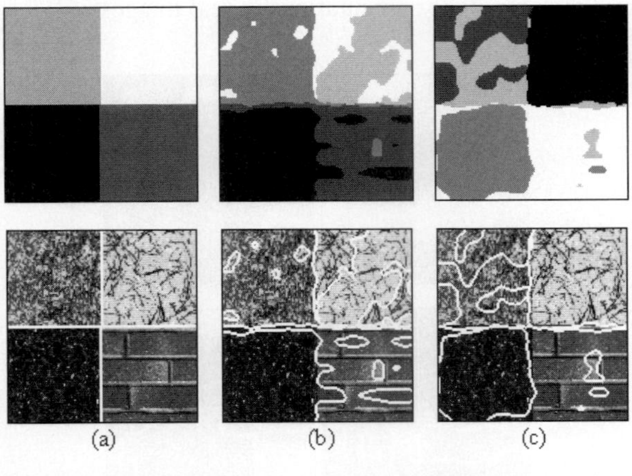

Fig. 3. Segmentation of a four regions image segmentation computed with: (a) Proposed method, (b) PCA selection and (c) Feature Fusion. The percents of correct pixels are 99.6093%, 82.0129% and 80.9509%, respectively.

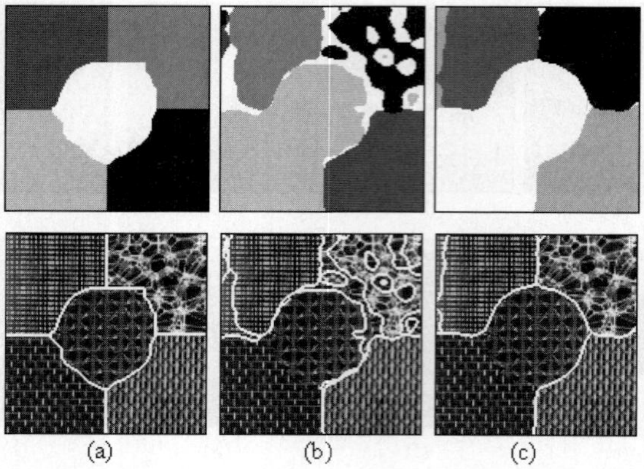

Fig. 4. Segmentation of a five regions image segmentation computed with: (a) Proposed method, (b) PCA selection and (c) Feature Fusion. The percent of correct pixels are 98.0773%, PCA 70.48339% and 77.9296% respectively.

Table 1 resumes the comparison between the segmentations computed with the proposed method and the two variants above described.

Table 1. Percents of correct segmented pixels for the propose method, proposed method but with PCA feature selection (instead of the proposed) and proposed method with fused features. The results correspond to the segmentations of the test set and are included the correctness percent for the best segmented image and for the worst one.

Algorithm	Mean	Std. Dev.	Best	Worst
Proponed	**95.3474**	**6.89**	**99.6093**	**73.3215**
PCA selection	86.6847	12.26	99.2919	54.9743
Fusion-PCA	84.1487	10.85	97.9370	52.9724

Figure 5 shows the computed segmentations in real images.

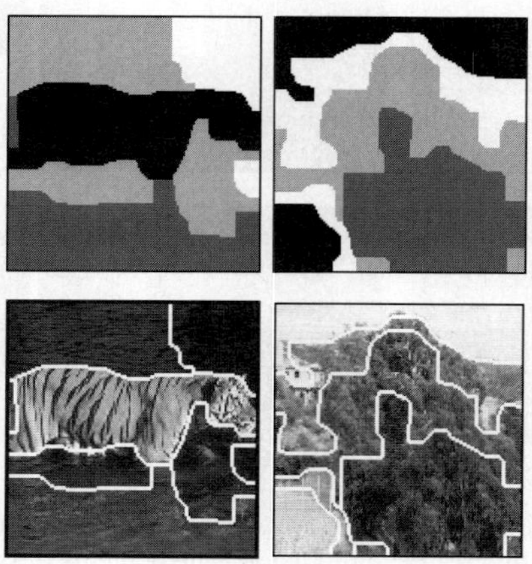

Fig. 5. Our method in real images

5 Conclusions

Feature selection is an important issue in the development of generic image segmentation algorithms because of the uncertainty in selecting the feature space. Here we presented a procedure for texture image segmentation based on selecting from a large number features a small subset that best segment the image. The feature selection process is based on probabilistic rules that codify our prior information about the granularity of the segmentation. Such a granularity is also controlled by the segmentation algorithm that introduces a spatial regularization. The performance of the proposed algorithm was demonstrated by experiments and comparisons with state of the art methods. Our methodology can easily extended to include other features by depending on the application, for instance color or multiband radar images.

We also proposed a method for adjusting the parameters. This is based on a supervised learning technique implemented as an evolutive descent strategy.

The full presented methodology is a general purpose segmentation method that could be tuned for a particular problem by learning from examples (expert segmentations).

References

1. Cogging, J. M.: A Framework for texture analysis Based on Spatial Filtering. Ph. D. Thesis, Computer Science Department, Michigan State University, East Lansing, MI, (1982).
2. Skalansky, J.: Image Segmentation and Feature Extraction. In: IEEE Trans. Syst. Man Cybern., (1978) 237-247.
3. Kam, A.H., Fitzgerald, W. J.: Unsupervised Multiscale Image Segmentation. In: Proceedings of 10th International Conference on Image Analysis and Processing (ICIAP'99) (1999) 237 – 247.
4. Chang, K.I., Bowyer, K. W., Sivagurunath, M.: Evaluation of Texture Segmentation Algorithms. IEEE Int. Conf. on Computer Vision and Pattern Recognition, Fort Collins, USA, (1999) 294-299
5. Polk, G., Liu, J. S.: Texture Analysis by a Hybrid Scheme, Store, Storage and Retrieval for Image and Video Databases VII (1998) 614- 622.
6. Clausi, D. A. and Deng, H.: Design-Based Textural Feature Fusion Using Gabor Filters and Co-Occurrence Probabilities. In: IEEE Trans. on Image Processing (2005) 925-936.
7. Liu, C., Wechsler, H.: Independent Component Analysis of Gabor Features for Face Recognition. In: IEEE Trans. on Neural Networks. (2003) 919-928
8. Guyon I., Elisseeff A.: An Introduction to Feature and Variable Selection. In Journal of Machine Learning Research (2003) 1157-1182.
9. Jain, A.K., Farrokhnia, F.: Unsupervised Texture Segmentation Using Gabor Filters. Pattern Recognition, (1991) 1167- 1186.
10. Haralick, R.M., Shanmugam, K., Dinstein, I.: Textural Features for Image Classification. In: IEEE Trans. Syst. Man. Cybern., vol 28 SMC-3, no. 6,(1973) 610-621
11. Laws, K.: Texture Image Segmentation. Ph. D. Dissertation, University of Southern California (1980)
12. Perona, P., Malik, J.: Scale-space and edge detection using anisotropic diffusion. In: IEEE Trans. Pattern Anal. Machine Intel. 12 (1990) 629-639.
13. Huber, P.J.: Robust Statistics. John Wiley and Sons, New York, NY (1981)

14. Rivera, M., Ocegeda, O., Marroquin, J.L.: Entropy Controlled Gauss-Markov Random Measure fields for early vision. In: Proc. VLSM 2005, N. Paragios et al. (Eds.), LNCS 3752, Springer- Berlin Heidelberg, Beijing China (2005) 137–148
15. Agrawal, R., Imielinski, T., Swami, A.: Mining Association Rules Between Sets of Items in Large Databases. In: Proceedings of ACM SIGMOD (1993) 207 – 216.
16. Jain, A.K., Dubes, R. C.: Algorithms for Clustering Data. Prentice Hall Advance Reference Series (1988).
17. Veksler, O.: Efficient Graph-based Energy Minimization Methods in Computer Vision, PhD. Thesis, Cornell University, (1999)
18. Min, J., Powell, M., Bowyer, K.W.: Automated Performance Evaluation of Range Image Segmentation Algorithms. In: IEEE Trans. On Systems, man, and cybernetics-Part B, vol 34 No 1, February (2004) 263-271
19. Brodatz, P.: Texture –A Photographic Album for Artists and designers, New York; Reinhold (1968).
20. Duda, R., Hart, P. Stork, D.: Pattern Classification. 2nd ed. Wiley New York (2001)

A Hybrid Segmentation Method Applied to Color Images and 3D Information

Rafael Murrieta-Cid[1] and Raúl Monroy[2]

[1] Centro de Investigación en Matemáticas
murrieta@cimat.mx
[2] Tec de Monterrey, Campus Estado de México
raulm@itesm.mx

Abstract. This paper presents a hybrid segmentation algorithm, which provides a synthetic image description in terms of regions. This method has been used to segment images of outdoor scenes. We have applied our segmentation algorithm to color images and images encoding 3D information. 5 different color spaces were tested. The segmentation results obtained with each color space are compared.

1 Introduction

Image segmentation has been considered one of the most important processes in image analysis and pattern recognition. It consists in partitioning an image into a set of different regions such that each region is homogeneous under some criteria but the union of two adjacent regions are not. A poor segmentation method may incur in two types of errors: i) over-segmentation, meaning that an object is split into several different regions; and ii) under-segmentation (which is the worst), meaning that the frontier of a class is not detected.

Existing segmentation approaches can be divided into four main categories: i) feature based segmentation (e.g. color clustering), ii) edge based segmentation (e.g. snake, edging), iii) region-based segmentation (e.g. region growing, splitting and merging) and iv) hybrid segmentation [7].

More recent methods in image segmentation are based on stochastic model approaches [1,6], watershed region growing [17] and graph partitioning [19]. Some segmentation techniques have been especially developed for natural image segmentation (see for instance [2]).

In this paper, we introduce a segmentation method, which provides a precise and concise description of an image in terms of regions. The method was designed to be a component of a vision system for an outdoor mobile robot. This vision system is capable of building a global representation of an outdoor environment.

It makes use of both an unsupervised scene segmentation (based on either color or range information) and a supervised scene interpretation (based on both color and texture). Scene interpretation is used to extract landmarks and track them using a visual target tracking algorithm. This vision system has been presented in several various papers [8,9,10,11]. However, the segmentation

A. Gelbukh and C.A. Reyes-Garcia (Eds.): MICAI 2006, LNAI 4293, pp. 789–799, 2006.

method, about its main component, has never been reported on at an appropriate level of detail.

In the design of our segmentation method, we were driven by the following assumption: unsupervised segmentation on its own without classification does not make any sense. This is because a region cannot be labelled without an interpretation mapping it to a known element or class. Thus, our segmentation method is designed to be embedded in a bigger system and satisfies the system specification.

What counts as a correct segmentation has no universally accepted answer; some researchers argue the segmentation problem is not well-defined. Following a pragmatical perspective, we take a good segmentation to be simply one in which the regions obtained correspond to the objects in the scene. Our method rarely incurs in under-segmentation and, since it yields a small number of regions, has an acceptable over-segmentation rate.

Given that our method produces regions that closely match the classes in a scene and that there tend to be a small number of regions, the computational effort required to characterize and identify a region is greatly reduced. Also, statistically speaking, the more accurate one region captures a class, the more representative the features computed out of it will be.

1.1 Related Work

Feature thresholding is one of the most powerful methods for image segmentation. It has the advantage of small storage space and ease of manipulation. Feature thresholding has been largely studied during the last 3 decades [12,14,15,18,5]. Here, we describe briefly the most relevant work in the literature (for a nice survey, the reader is referred to [18].)

In [12], Otsu introduced a segmentation method which determines the *optimal* separation of classes, using an statistical analysis that maximizes a measure of class separability. Otsu's method remains as one of the most powerful thresholding techniques [18]. It was not until recently that we have seen enhancements to this algorithm [15,5].

In [15], Liao et al. presented an algorithm for efficiently multilevel thresholding selection, that makes use of a modified variance of Otsu's method. This algorithm is recursive and uses a look-up table so reducing the number of required operations.

In [5], Huang et al. introduced a technique that combines Otsu's method and spatial analysis. So, this technique is hybrid. The spatial analysis is based on the manipulation of a pyramid data structure with a window size adaptively selected according to Lorentz's information measure.

There also are thresholding techniques that do not aim at maximizing a measure of class separability, thus departing from Otsu's approach [14,22]. In [14], the authors presented a range based segmentation method for mobile robotics. Range segmentation is carried out by calculating a bi-variable histogram coded in spherical coordinates (θ and ϕ). In [22], Virmajoki and Franki introduced a pairwise nearest neighbor based multilevel thresholding algorithm. This algorithm makes use of a vector quantization scheme, where the thresholding corresponds to minimizing the error of quantization.

We will see that our image segmentation algorithm is also hybrid, combining feature thresholding and region growing. It proposes several extensions to Otsu's feature thresholding method. Below, section 2, we give a detailed explanation of our method and argue how it extends Otsu's approach. Then, section 5, we compare our method with those above mentioned and with a previous method of ourselves, presented in [8,21].

2 The Segmentation Method

Our segmentation algorithm is a combination of two techniques: i) *feature thresholding* (also called *clustering*); and ii) *region growing.* It does the grouping in the spatial domain of square cells. Adjacent cells are merged if they have the same label; labels are defined in a feature space (e.g. color space). The advantage of our hybrid method is that the result of the process of growing regions is independent of the beginning point and the scanning order of the adjacent square cells.

Our method works as follows: First, the image is split into square cells, yielding an arbitrary image partition. Second, a feature vector is computed for each square cell, associating a class to it. Feature classes are defined using an analysis of the feature histograms, which defines a partition into the feature space. Third, adjacent cells of the same class are merged together using an adjacency graph (4-adjacency). Finally, regions that are smaller than a given threshold are merged to the most similar (in the feature space) adjacent region.

Otsu's approach determines only the thresholds corresponding to the separation between two classes. Thus, it deals only with a part of the class determination problem. We have extended Otsu's method. Our contributions are:

- We have generalized the method to find the optimal thresholds to k classes.
- We have defined the partition of the feature space which gives the optimal classes' number n^*. Where $n^* \in [2, \ldots, N]$.
- We have integrated the automatic class separation method with a region growing technique.

For each feature, λ^* is the criterion determining the optimal classes number n^*. It maximizes $\lambda_{(k)}$, the maximal criterion for exactly k classes ($k \in [2, \ldots, N]$); in symbols:

$$\lambda^* = \max\left(\lambda_{(k)}\right) \; ; \; \lambda_{(k)} = \frac{\sigma^2_{B_{(k)}}}{\sigma^2_{W_{(k)}}} \tag{1}$$

where $\sigma^2_{B_{(k)}}$ is the inter-classes variance and where $\sigma^2_{W_{(k)}}$ is the intraclass variance. $\sigma^2_{B_{(k)}}$ and $\sigma^2_{W_{(k)}}$ are respectively given by:

$$\sigma^2_{B_{(k)}} = \sum_{m=1}^{k-1} \sum_{n=m+1}^{k} \left[\omega_n \cdot \omega_m (\mu_m - \mu_n)^2\right] \tag{2}$$

$$\sigma^2_{W_{(k)}} = \sum_{m=1}^{k-1} \sum_{n=m+1}^{k} [\sum_{i \in m} (i - \mu_m)^2 \cdot p_{(i)} + \sum_{i \in n} (i - \mu_n)^2 \cdot p_{(i)}] \quad (3)$$

where μ_m denotes the mean of the level i associated with the class m, ω_m denotes the probability of class m and where $p_{(i)}$ denotes the probability of the level i in the histogram. In symbols:

$$\mu_m = \sum_{i \in m} \frac{i \cdot p_{(i)}}{\omega_m} \qquad \omega_m = \sum_{i \in m} p_{(i)} \qquad p_{(i)} = \frac{n_i}{Np}$$

The normalized histogram is considered as an estimated probability distribution. n_i is the number of samples for a given level. Np is the total number of samples. A class m is delimited by two values (the inferior and the superior limits) corresponding to two levels in the histogram. Note that this criterion is similar to Fisher's one [3], However, our criterion is pondered by the class probability and the probability of the level i.

To compute $\sigma^2_{B_{(k)}}$ and $\sigma^2_{W_{(k)}}$ (as described above) requires an exhaustive analysis of the histograms. In order to reduce the number of operations, it is possible to compute the equivalent estimators $\sigma^2_{T(k)}$ and $\mu_{T(k)}$ (respectively called *histogram total variance* and *histogram total mean*). $\sigma^2_{T(k)}$ and $\mu_{T(k)}$ are independent of the inferior and superior limits locations. For the case of k classes they can be computed as follows:

$$\mu_{T(k)} = \sum_{i=1}^{i=L} i \cdot p_{(i)} \quad ; \quad \sigma^2_{T_{(k)}} = \sum_{i=1}^{i=L} i^2 \cdot p_{(i)} - \mu^2_{T(k)} \quad (4)$$

where L is the total number of levels in the histogram.

The equivalence between $\sigma^2_{T(k)}$ and $\mu_{T(k)}$ and $\sigma^2_{B_{(k)}}$ and $\sigma^2_{W_{(k)}}$ are defined as follows:

$$\sigma^2_{B_{(k)}} = \sum_{m=1}^{k-1} \sum_{n=m+1}^{k} [\omega_n \cdot \omega_m (\mu_m - \mu_n)^2] \quad (5)$$

$$= \sum_{m=1}^{k} \omega_m \cdot (\mu_m - \mu_T)^2$$

$$\sigma^2_{T_{(k)}} = \sigma^2_{B_{(k)}} + \frac{\sigma^2_{W_{(k)}}}{k-1} \quad (6)$$

Thus, to compute $\sigma^2_{B_{(k)}}$ and $\sigma^2_{W_{(k)}}$ in terms of σ^2_T and μ_T, we proceed as follows. First, tables containing the cumulated values of $p_{(i)}, i \cdot p_{(i)}$ and $i \cdot p^2_{(i)}$ are computed for each histogram level. These values allow us to determine σ^2_T, μ_T and ω_m. Instead of computing $\sigma^2_{B_{(k)}}$ and $\sigma^2_{W_{(k)}}$, as prescribed by (2) and (3), for each class and each number of possible classes, we use the equivalences below:

$$\sigma^2_{B_{(k)}} = \sum_{m=1}^{k} \omega_m \cdot (\mu_m - \mu_T)^2 \quad (7)$$

$$\sigma^2_{W_{(k)}} = (\sigma^2_{T_{(k)}} - \sigma^2_{B_{(k)}}) \cdot (k-1) \tag{8}$$

The automatic class separation method was tested with the two histograms shown in figure 1: in both histograms the class division was tested with two and three classes. For the first histogram, the value λ^* corresponds to two classes. The threshold is placed in the valley bottom between the two peaks. In the second histogram, the optimal λ^* corresponds to three classes (also located in the valley bottom between the peaks.)

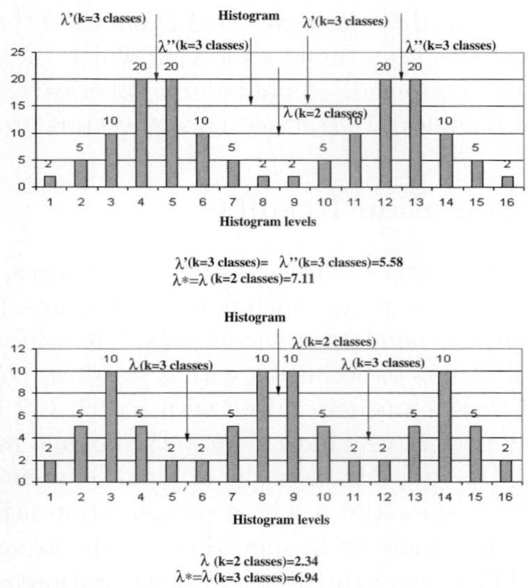

Fig. 1. Threshold Location

In the Otsu approach when the number of classes increases the selected threshold usually becomes less reliable. Since we use several features to define a class, this problem is mitigated.

2.1 The Color Image Segmentation

A color image is usually described by the distribution of the three color components R (red), G (green) and B (blue). Moreover many other features can also be calculated from these components. Two goals are generally pursued: First, the selection of uncorrelated color features [13,20], and second the selection of features which are independent of intensity changes. This last property is especially important in outdoor environments where the light conditions are not controlled [16].

We have tested our approach using several color models: R.G.B., r.g.b. (normalized components of R.G.B.), Y.E.S. defined by the SMPTE (Society of Motion Pictures and Television Engineers), H.S.I. (Hue, Saturation and Intensity) and I_1, I_2, I_3, color features derived from the Karhunen-Loève (KL) transformation of RGB. The results obtained through our experiments, for each color space, are reported and compared in section 3.

2.2 The 3D Image Segmentation

Our segmentation algorithm can be applied to images of range using 3D features as input. In our experiments we use height and normal vectors as input. We have obtained a 3D image using the stereo-vision algorithm proposed in [4].

Height and normal vectors are computed for each point in the 3D image. The height corresponds to the distance from the 3-D points of the object to the plane which best approximates the ground area from which the segmented object is emerging. The normal vectors are computed in a spherical coordinate system [14] (expressed in θ and ϕ angles). Height and normal vectors are coded in 256 levels.

3 Color Segmentation Results

We have tested our segmentation method with color images, considering 5 different color spaces. In the case of experiments with 3 features, (I_1, I_2, I_3), (R, G, B) and (r, g, b), the optimal number of classes was determined with $k \in [2, 3]$ for each feature. In the case of experiments with 2 features, (H, S) and (E, S), the optimal number of classes was determined with $k \in [2, 3, 4]$ for each feature. For these cases, we may respectively have 3^3 and 2^4 maximal number of classes.

Figures 2 I), II), III) and IV) show the original color images. Figures 2 I a), II a), III a) and IV a) show the result of segmentation using (I_1, I_2, I_3), while Figures 2 I b), II b), III b) and IV b) show these results using H and S. Figures 2 I c), II c), III c) and IV c) show the results of segmentation using (R, G, B), while Figure 2 I d), II d), III d) and IV d) show similarly but using (r, g, b). Finally, figures 2 I e), II e), III e) and IV e) show the segmentation results obtained using E and S.

Obtaining good results using only chrominance features (rgb, HS and ES) depends on the type of images. Chromimance effects are reduced in images with low saturation. For this reason, the intensity component is kept in the segmentation step. Over-segmentation errors can occur due to the presence of strong illumination variations (e.g. shadows). However, over-segmentation is preferable over under-segmentation. Over-segmentation errors can be detected and fixed during a posterior identification step.

The best color segmentation was obtained using the I_1, I_2, I_3 space, defined as [20]. Where $I_1 = \frac{R+G+B}{3}$, $I_2 = (R - B)$, $I_3 = \frac{2G-R-B}{2}$. This space components are uncorrelated. Hence, it is statistically the best way for detecting color variations. In our experiments, the number of no homogeneous regions (under-segmentation problems) is very small (2%). A good tradeoff between few regions and the absence of under-segmentation has been obtained, even in the case of complex images.

Segmented images are input to a vision system, where every region in each image is then classified, using color and texture features. Two adjacent regions are

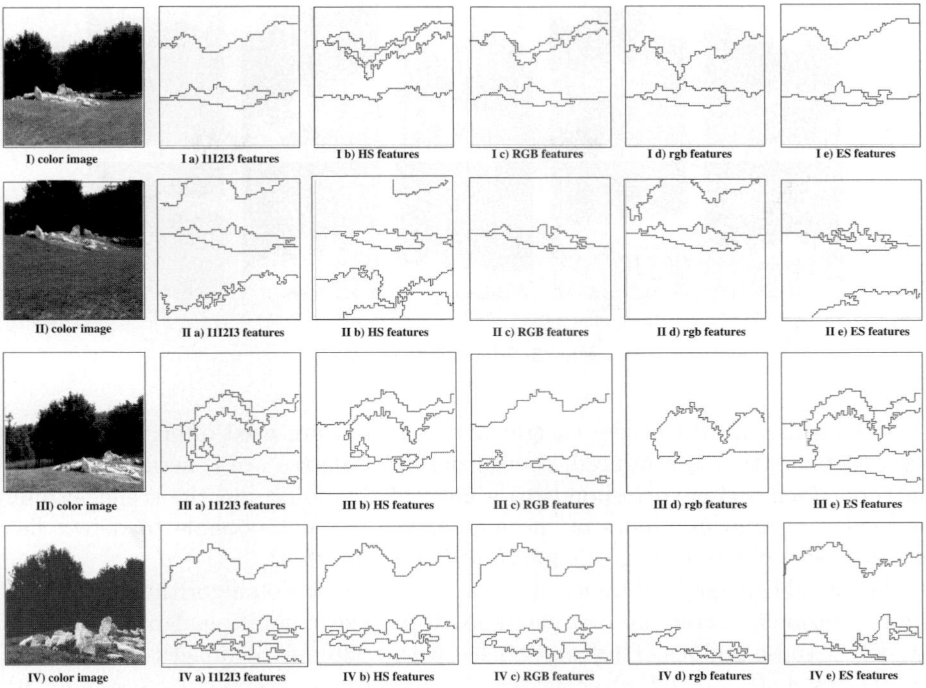

Fig. 2. Color segmentation

merged whenever they belong to the same class, thus eliminating remaining over-segmentation errors. Errors incurred in the identification process are detected and then corrected using contextual information. Example classified images are shown in figure 3. Figures 3 I a)—d) show snapshots of an image sequence. Figures 3 II a)—d) show the segmented and classified images. Different colors are used to show the various classes in the scene. Note that even though the illumination conditions have changed, the image is correctly classified. Figures 3 I e) and II e) show the effect of our method in another scene.

In this paper, we *present only our segmentation algorithm*; the whole system is described in [10]. We underline that the good performance of the whole system depends on an appropriate initial unsupervised segmentation. The segmentation algorithm presented in this paper is able to segment images without under segmentation errors and yields a small number of large representative regions.

4 3D Segmentation Results

We have also tested our segmentation method with images encoding 3D information (height and normal vectors).

We have found out that for our image database the height generally is enough to obtain the main components of the scene. Of course, if only this feature is used small objects are not detected.

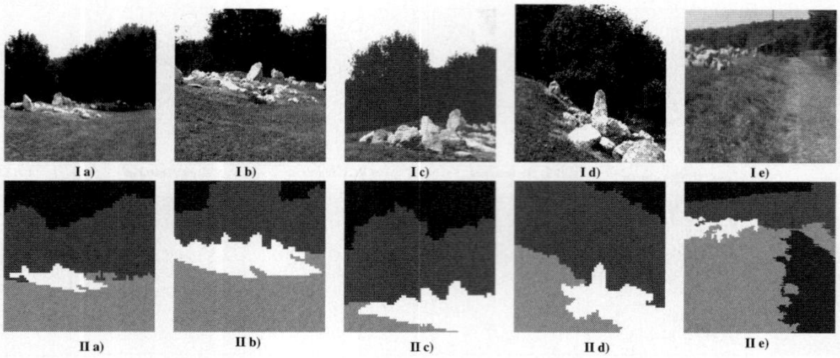

Fig. 3. Identified images

In contrast, if all features (height and normals) are used often a important over-segmentation is produced, even if only two classes are generated for each feature. Each region corresponds to a facet of the objects in the scene. If only normals are used as inputs of the algorithm, it is not possible to detect flat surfaces at a different height (e.g. a hole is not detected).

The height image is obtained using a stereo-correlation algorithms. Shadows and occlusions generate no-correlated points. Our segmentation algorithm is able to detect those regions. They are labeled with white in the images.

Figures 4 a), d) and g) show the original scenes. Figures 4 b), e) and h) show images encoding height in 256 levels. Frontiers among the regions obtained with our algorithm are shown in these images. Figures 4 c), f) and i) show the regions output by our segmentation algorithm. As mentioned above, if only the height is used small objects that do not emerge from the ground may be no detected. The small rock close to the depression (image 4 g)) is not extracted from the ground. Figure 4 l) shows an example of re-segmentation. We have applied our algorithm to the under segmented region using both height and normals. Then, the rock is successfully segmented. ϕ and θ images encoded in 256 levels are shown respectively in Figures 4 j) and k). The under segmented region was detected manually. However, we believe that it is possible to detect under segmented regions automatically, measuring some criteria such as the entropy computed over a given feature.

5 Comparing Our Method with Related Work

In [5], the image is divided into windows. The size of the windows is adaptively selected according to Lorentz's information measure and then Otsu's method is used to segment each window. Our approach follows a different scheme: the image is divided into windows, but we use our multi-thresholding technique to generate classes just once in the whole image. One class is associated to each window and then adjacent windows (cells) of the same class are merged. This reduces the number of operations by a factor of N, the number of windows. Furthermore, the approach in [5] is limited to only two classes. We have generalized our method

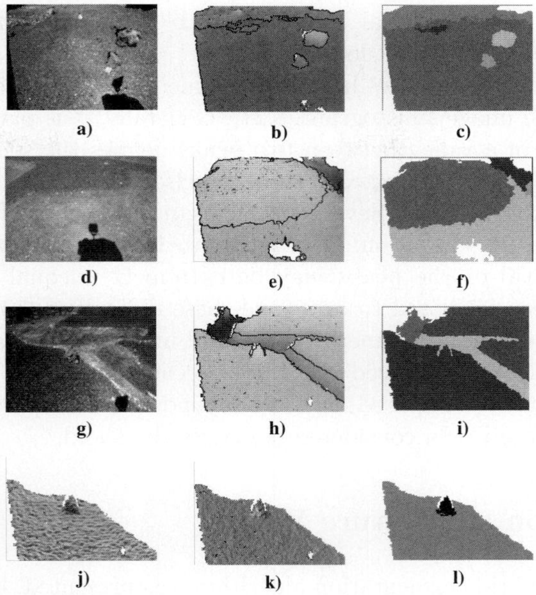

Fig. 4. 3D segmentation

to find the *optimal thresholds to k classes* and defined the partition of the feature space which gives the *optimal classes' number* n^*.

In [15], the authors introduced a method that extends Otsu's one in that it is faster at computing the optimal thresholds of an image. The key to achieve this efficiency improvement lies on a recursive form of the modified between-class variance. However, this extended method still is of the same time complexity as Otsu's one. Moreover, the introduced measure considers only variance between classes. In contrast, our proposed measure is the ratio between the inter-classes variance and the intraclass variance. Both variances are somehow equivalent [18], particularly in the case of two classes separation. However, in the case of a prioritized multi-thresholding selection problem, the combination of these two variances better selects a threshold because it looks for both: separation between classes and compactness of the classes. Hence, our method proposed a better thresholding criterion. Furthermore, the method proposed in [15] segments the images only based on feature analysis. Spatial analysis is not considered at all. Thus, there is not a control of the segmentation granularity. The segmented images may have a lot of small regions (yielding a significant over segmentation). Since our segmentation method is hybrid, it does control the segmentation granularity, thus yielding a small number of big regions.

In [22], a pairwise nearest neighbour (PNN) based multilevel thresholding algorithm is proposed. The proposed algorithm has a very low time complexity, $O(N \log N)$ (where N is the number of clusters) and obtains thresholds close to the optimal ones. However, this method just obtains sub-optimal thresholding and it does not do any spatial analysis, which implies it suffers from all the limitations that [15]'s method does.

In our previous work, classes have been defined detecting the principal peaks and valleys in the image's histogram [8,21]. Generally, it is plausible to assume that the bottom of a valley between two peaks defines the separation between two classes. However, for complex pictures, precisely detecting the bottom of the valley is often hard to achieve. Several problems may prevent us from determining the correct value of separation: The attribute histograms may be noisy, the valley flat or broad or the peaks may be extremely unequal in height. Some methods have been proposed to overcome these difficulties [13]. However, they are considerably costly and sometimes demand unstable calculations.

Compared with that proposed in [14], our technique is more generic (we may add as many features as required) and less dependent on the parameter selection. Our previous method only considered bi-classes threshold.

6 Conclusion and Future Work

In this paper a hybrid segmentation algorithm was presented. Our method provides a synthetic image description in terms of regions. We have applied our segmentation algorithm to color images and images encoding 3D information. Our method produces regions that closely match the classes in a scene and there tend to be a small number of regions. 5 different color spaces were tested. Obtaining good results with only chrominance features depends on the type of images to be segmented. Chromimance effects are reduced in images with low saturation. The best color segmentation was obtained using I_1, I_2, I_3.

As future work, we want to explore a technique to automatically detect under-segmented regions. We also want to study in detail which combination of features provides a better segmentation. We would also like to have a method that takes into account the level of detail at which the segmentation should be carried out. This way, we could extract an entire object or the object components, depending on the system requirements. Thanks to how we compute inter and intra classes variances (c.f. (7) and (8)), our method is fast enough for the applications in which we are interested. However, ongoing research considers the use of a sampling selection threshold scheme (yielding sub-optimal thresholding) to see if this improves the efficiency of our method.

References

1. Y. Delignon and A. Marzouki and P. Pieczynki. Estimation of Generalized Mixtures and its Application to Images Segmentation. *IEEE Trans. Images Processing*, Vol 6. no. 10 pp. 1364-1376, 1997.
2. Y. Deng and B.S. Manjunath. Unsupervised Segmentation of Color-Texture Regions in Images and Video. *IEEE Trans. Pattern Analysis and Machine Intelligence*, Vol 23. pp. 800-810, August 2001.
3. R.O. Duda and P.E. Hart. *Pattern Classification and Scene Analysis*, Wiley, 1973.

4. H. Haddad, M. Khatib, S. Lacroix, and R. Chatila. Reactive navigation in outdoor environments using potential fields. In *International Conference on Robotics and Automation ICRA'98*, pages 1332–1237, may 1998.
5. Q. Huang, W. Gao, and W. Cai. Thresholding Technique with Adaptive Window Selection for Uneven Lighting Image. *Pattern recognition letters*, 26, 801-808, 2005.
6. D.A.. Langan and J.W. Modestino and J. Zhang. Cluster Validation of Unsupervised Stochastic Model-Based Image Segmentation. *IEEE Trans. Images Processing*, Vol 7. no. 3 pp. 180-195, 1997.
7. J.B. Luo and E. Guo. Perceptual grouping of segmented regions in color images. *Pattern Recognition*, Vol 36. pp. 2781-2792, 2003.
8. R. Murrieta-Cid, M. Briot and N. Vandapel. Landmark Identification and Tracking in Natural Environment. *Proc IEEE/RSJ Int'l Conf. on Intelligent Robots and Systems*, pp. 179-184, 1998.
9. R. Murrieta-Cid, C. Parra, M. Devy and M. Briot. Scene Modeling from 2D and 3D sensory data acquired from natural environments. *Proc Int'l Conf. on Advanced Robotics*, pp. 221-228, 2001.
10. R. Murrieta-Cid, C. Parra, M. Devy, B. Tovar and C. Esteves. Building Multi-Level Models: From Landscapes to Landmarks. *Proc IEEE Int'l Conf. on Robotics and Automation*, pp. 4346-4353, 2002.
11. R. Murrieta-Cid, C. Parra, M. Devy. Visual Navigation in Natural Environments: From Range and Color Data to a Landmark-based Model. *Journal Autonomous Robots*,13(2), pp. 143-168, 2002
12. N. Otsu. A Threshold Selection Method from Gray-Level Histrograms. *I.E.E.E. Transaction on Systems, Man and Cybernetics*, 9(1):62–66, January 1979.
13. N.R. Pal and S.K. Pal. A review on image segmentation techniques. *Pattern Recognition*, 26(9):1277–1294, 1993.
14. C. Parra, R. Murrieta-Cid, M. Devy and M. Briot 3-D modeling and robot localization from visual and range data in natural scenes. *Lecture Notes in Computer Science 1542, Springer H. I. Christensen Ed.*, pp. 450-468, 1999.
15. Ping-Sung Liao et al, A Fast Algorithm for Multilevel Thresholding. *Journal of Information Science and Engineering*, 17, 713-727, 2001.
16. E. Saber, A.M. Tekalp, R. Eschbach, and K. Knox. Automatic Image Annotation Using Adaptative Color Classification. *Graphical Models and Image Processing*, 58(2):115–126, march 1996.
17. L. Shafarenko, M. Petrou and J. Kittler. Automatic Watershed Segmentation of Randomly Textured Color Images. *IEEE Trans. Images Processing*, Vol 6. no. 11 pp. 1530-1544, 1997.
18. M. Sezgin and B. Sankur. Survey over Image Thresholding Techniques and Quantitative Performance Evaluation. *Journal of Electronic Imaging*, 13(1), 146-165, 2004.
19. J. Shi and J. Malik. Normalized Cuts and Image Segmentation. *IEEE Trans. Pattern Analysis and Machine Intelligence*, Vol 22. No. 8 pp. 888-905, 2000.
20. T.S.C Tan and J. Kittler. Colour texture analysis using colour histogram. *I.E.E Proc.-Vis.Image Signal Process.*, 141(6):403–412, December 1994.
21. N. Vandapel, S. Moorehead, W. Whittaker, R. Chatila and R. Murrieta-Cid Preliminary results on the use of stereo, color cameras and laser sensors in Antarctica. *Lecture Notes in Control and Information Sciences 250, P. Corke et Ed.*,pp. 450-468, 1999.
22. O. Virmajoki and P. Franti. Fast Pairwise Nearest Neighbor based Algorithm for multilevel Thresholding. *Journal of Electronic Imaging*, 12(14), 648-659, 2003.

Segmentation of Medical Images by Using Wavelet Transform and Incremental Self-Organizing Map

Zümray Dokur, Zafer Iscan, and Tamer Ölmez

Istanbul Technical University, Electronics and Communication Engineering
34469 Istanbul, Turkey
{zumray, zafer, olmez}@ehb.itu.edu.tr

Abstract. This paper presents a novel method that uses incremental self-organizing map (ISOM) network and wavelet transform together for the segmentation of magnetic resonance (MR), computer tomography (CT) and ultrasound (US) images. In order to show the validity of the proposed scheme, ISOM has been compared with Kohonen's SOM. Two-dimensional continuous wavelet transform (2D-CWT) is used to form the feature vectors of medical images. According to the selected two feature extraction methods, features are formed by the intensity of the pixel of interest or mean value of intensities at one neighborhood of the pixel at each sub-band. The first feature extraction method is used for MR and CT head images. The second method is used for US prostate image.

Keywords: Segmentation of medical images, Artificial neural networks, Self-organizing map, Wavelet Transform.

1 Introduction

In this study, realization of automatic tissue segmentation was aimed and a diagnosis method which may be useful for especially inexperienced operators is presented. For this purpose, interviews with radiologists were made and their ideas and expectations were taken into account.

The constitution of the right data space is a common problem in connection with segmentation/classification. In order to construct realistic classifiers, the features that are sufficiently representative of the physical process must be searched. In the literature, it is observed that different transforms are used to extract desired information from biomedical images. Determination of features which represent the tissues best is still a serious problem which affects the results of segmentation directly. There are many types of feature extraction methods in literature. However, there is not any unique method that fits all tissue types. Frequently used feature extraction methods are auto-correlation coefficients [1], gray-level based approaches [2, 3], co-occurrence matrices [4], wavelet [5], discrete Fourier [6] and discrete cosine [7] transforms.

Segmentation of medical images is a critical subject in medical image analysis. Although the features are determined well, the segmentation algorithm must be chosen well enough to obtain good results. Up to now, various schemes have been introduced in order to accomplish this task. More recently, methods based on

A. Gelbukh and C.A. Reyes-Garcia (Eds.): MICAI 2006, LNAI 4293, pp. 800 – 809, 2006.

multi-resolution or multi-channel analyses, such as wavelet transform, have received a lot of attention for medical image analysis [8, 9].

In the literature, it is observed that incremental SOM [10, 11] have been used in pattern analysis. However, their algorithms have created some complexity in implementation. In this study, two different SOM networks were compared for the segmentation of medical images: Kohonen's SOM and ISOM network.

In the literature, different self-organizing maps were used mostly in MR image segmentation [12, 13]. Although Kohonen's SOM is a fast algorithm, it is not an incremental network. Besides, SOM's nodes are distributed in the feature space homogenously rather than concentrating on class boundaries. This structure may require an excessive number of nodes in the network. Moreover, determining the optimum neighborhood parameter still remains as a problem. In this study, a novel method which applies incremental self organizing map and wavelet transform together is presented for the segmentation of medical images. Tissues in medical images are analyzed by the wavelet transform. Incremental self-organizing map is used to determine the unknown class distribution easily.

2 Methods

2.1 Feature Extraction Methods by Wavelet Transform

In the literature, it is observed that discrete Fourier and cosine transforms have been used to form the feature vectors. In these transforms, feature extraction is performed on sub-windows within the images. Dimension of the sub-window affects the performance of the segmentation process. Hence, we drew our attention to wavelet transform to determine the features.

CWT is adequate for non-stationary signal analysis [12]. By using 2D-CWT, space-scale (time-frequency) representation of a signal can be obtained which means a higher information level. In this study, 2D-CWTs (using Gaussian wavelet) of medical images were calculated for twelve different scale parameters. Thus, twelve transformed images were obtained from the original image.

When the scale parameter of CWT is high, low frequency components of image are becoming clear and when the scale value decreases, high frequency components (details) in the image can be observed well.

Thirteen images (original image plus twelve transformed images by CWT) are used to form the feature vectors. Two feature extraction methods are used for the segmentation of medical images. In the first method, each feature vector element is formed by the intensity of one pixel of each sub-band image. Hence, the feature vector is formed by thirteen pixels' intensities. Each feature represents the information at the same spatial coordinate obtained from different sub-bands. The second method is similar to the first. However, mean value of the intensities within one neighborhood of the pixel of interest is used instead of single pixel intensity of each sub-band. This process removes noise from the features. US images contain textures with noise. The second method will only be used for the segmentation of the US image.

Since tissues in the images are represented by simple feature extraction methods, computational times of the learning and segmentation processes are quite short. Fig. 1 shows a sample representation of the pixel intensities used in both feature extraction methods.

After the feature extraction process, vectors are presented to the artificial neural networks for the training. During the training of ISOM, the number of nodes of the network is automatically determined by its unsupervised learning scheme. A label is assigned to each node and labels of all nodes are saved in an index layer. During the segmentation process, a feature vector is formed for each pixel and presented to the ISOM. The pixel under consideration is labeled by using the label of the network node,which is the nearest to the feature vector. Fig.2 depicts the segmentation process.

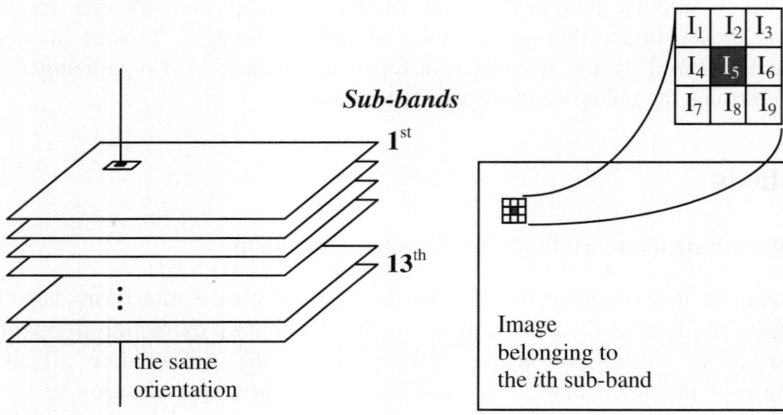

Fig. 1. Feature extraction methods: i) Black colored pixel represents the central pixel (I_5 is the pixel of interest), which is used alone for the first method, ii) The frame used for the second feature extraction method represents the nine pixels at one neighborhood of the central pixel

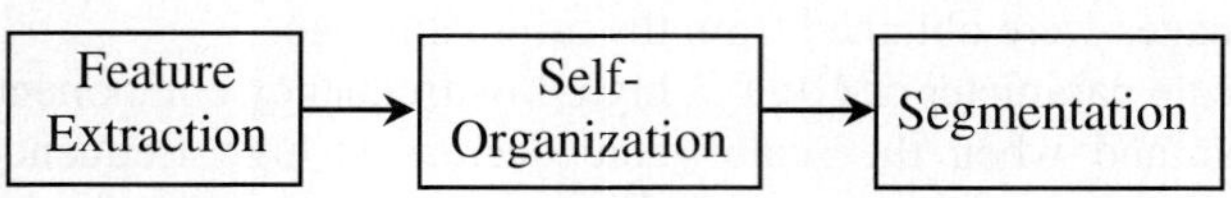

Fig. 2. Processing blocks in segmentation

3 Artificial Neural Networks

The formulation of a proper data representation is a common problem in segmentation/classification systems design. In order to construct realistic classifiers, the features that are sufficiently representative of the physical process must be found. If the right features are not chosen, classification performance will decrease. In this case, the solution of the problem is searched in the classifier structures, and artificial neural networks (ANNs) are used as classifiers.

There are four reasons to use an ANN as a classifier: (i) Weights representing the solution are found by iteratively training, (ii) ANN has a simple structure for physical implementation, (iii) ANN can easily map complex class distributions, and (iv) generalization property of the ANN produces appropriate results for the input vectors that are not present in the training set.

In unsupervised learning, network modifies its parameters by analyzing the class distributions in feature space. There is no desired output in this method or desired outputs are not used in the training algorithm. Kohonen's SOM and ISOM networks which are used in this study are both examples of unsupervised networks.

3.1 Incremental Self-Organizing Map

ISOM network used in this study is a two-layer, self-organizing incremental network. Fig. 3 shows the structure of the ISOM. The nodes in the first layer of the ISOM are formed by the feature vectors. The number of nodes in the first layer is automatically determined by the learning algorithm. The winner-takes-all guarantees that there will be only one node activated. Each output node represents different information (different portion of the feature space). The labels of the output nodes are saved in the second layer, which is called the index layer. Each output node is labeled with a different label, and represents a unique class.

Initially, a feature vector is randomly chosen from the training set, and is assigned as the first node of the network. In the study, the learning rate (η) is constant during the training, and is set to 0.02 value.

The learning algorithm steps can be summarized as follows:

Step 1: Take a feature vector from the training set.

Step 2: Compute the Euclidean distances between this input feature vector and the nodes in the network, and find the minimum distance.

Step 3: If the minimum distance is higher than the automatic threshold value, include the input vector as a new node of ISOM. Weights of this node are formed by the weights of the input vectors. Assign a counter to this new node and set the counter value to one, then go back to the first step. Otherwise, update the weights of only the nearest node (winner) according to Eq. (1). Increase the counter value of winner node by one. Decrease the learning rate.

$$w_{ji}(k+1) = w_{ji}(k) + \eta \cdot (x_i(k) - w_{ji}(k)) \tag{1}$$

where, w_{ji} is the ith weight of the jth (winner) node nearest to the input vector, x_i is the ith element of the input vector, η is the learning rate, and k is the iteration number.

Step 4: Go to *step 1* until all feature vectors are exhausted.

After the completion of training period, the nodes which have lower counter values can be removed from the network. These nodes can be determined via a node histogram in which x-axis shows the nodes' number and y-axis shows the counter values associated with these nodes. Removing process is done by assigning the labels of the nearest nodes that have greater counter values to those removed nodes. If the counter value of a node is too low, it means that this node represents a small portion of image pixels. Without the removal process, as every node of ISOM represents a class, segmentation time will become higher.

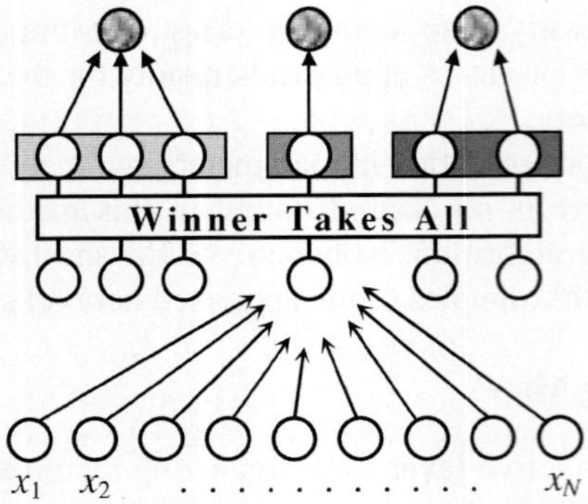

Fig. 3. Structure of ISOM. *N* is feature space dimension.

3.2 Automatic Threshold

The automatic threshold (AT) value is computed by a simple function before starting the self-organization stage. By using automatic threshold function, a standard calculation method is generated for the segmentation of medical images. Therefore, the robustness of algorithm is provided. ISOM's automatic threshold value is defined as follows:

$$AT = \sqrt{\frac{1}{M}\sum_{i=1}^{M}\sum_{j=1}^{N}\left(x_{ij} - m_j\right)^2} \quad (2)$$

In Eq. (2), *X* is the feature vector matrix of size *M*×*N*. Each row of the matrix is constituted by the elements of the feature vectors, hence, *X* holds *N*-dimensional *M* feature vectors. m_j denotes the mean value of the features on column *j*.

In fact, AT value represents the distribution of feature vectors in multi-dimensional feature space. Although AT function was simply defined, it shows high performance in generating proper threshold values depending on the number of features (dimension of vectors) and distribution in the feature space. It has been observed that the proposed function is capable of generating a reference threshold.

3.3 Node Coloring

In order to visualize the difference between tissue structures, a node-coloring scheme based on interpolation technique was used. The mathematical formulation of the method is expressed in Eq. (3).

$$C(n) = \left[\frac{C(a)}{d(n,a)} + \frac{C(b)}{d(n,b)}\right] \times \left[\frac{1}{d(n,a)} + \frac{1}{d(n,b)}\right]^{-1} \quad (3)$$

where *C*(*n*) denotes the color value of the node number *n*. *d*(*n*,*a*) and *d*(*n*,*b*) are the Euclidean distances in the feature space between node *n*, and nodes *a* and *b*, respectively. *C*(*a*) and *C*(*b*) denote the color values of the two most distant nodes (*a* and *b*) in the network. In this scheme, first of all, two most distant nodes (*a* and *b*) in the network are colored with 0 and 255 gray values. Then, the remaining nodes' colors are assigned according to their Euclidean distances to the formerly colored two nodes. Finally, segmented image colors are formed according to related nodes' colors.

4 Computer Simulations

In the study, magnetic resonance, computer tomography and ultrasound images (Figs. 4(a- c)) were segmented by using Kohonen's SOM and ISOM networks.

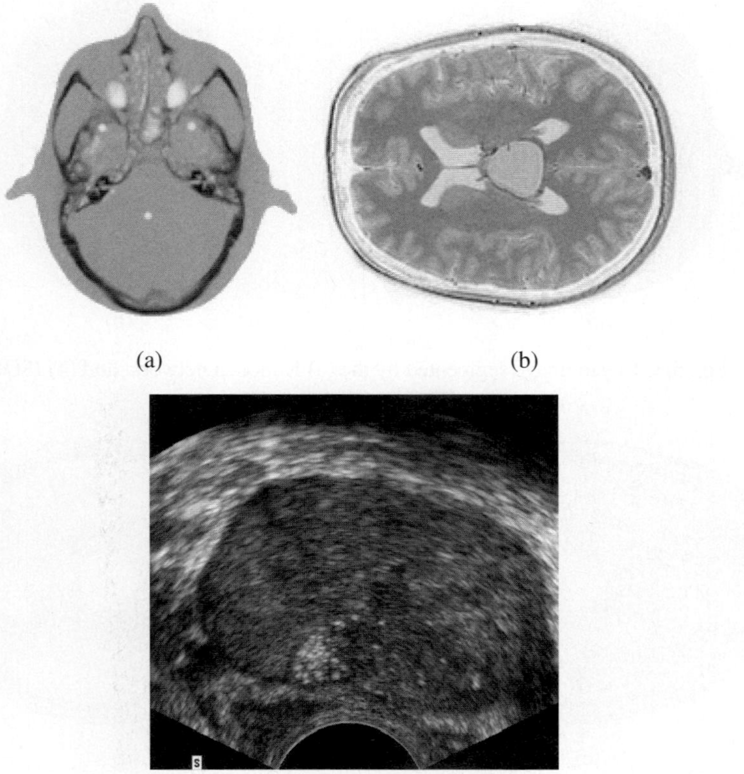

(a) (b) (c)

Fig. 4. Original (a) CT head image, (b) MR head image, (c) US prostate image

2D-CWT (using Gaussian wavelet) was used in the feature extraction processes of medical images. Simulations were performed on 2 GHz PC by using MATLAB 6.0. MR, CT and US images were segmented into five, four and five classes (labels) respectively.

The first feature extraction method is used for MR and CT head images. The second feature extraction method is used for US prostate image.

CT head image segmented by the Kohonen network and ISOM are shown in Figs. 5(a) and (b), respectively. MR head image segmented by the Kohonen network and ISOM are shown in Figs. 6(a) and (b), respectively. US prostate image segmented by the Kohonen network and ISOM are shown in Figs. 7(a) and (b), respectively. Related parameters like training time, segmentation time, number of generated nodes and the threshold values of the ISOM are shown in Table 1. In the training of Kohonen network, learning rate and neighborhood values are set to 0.02 and 1, respectively.

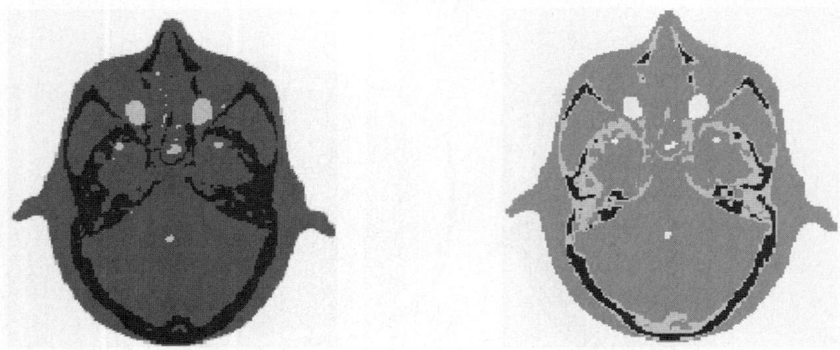

(a) (b)

Fig. 5. CT head image segmented by the (a) Kohonen network, and (b) ISOM

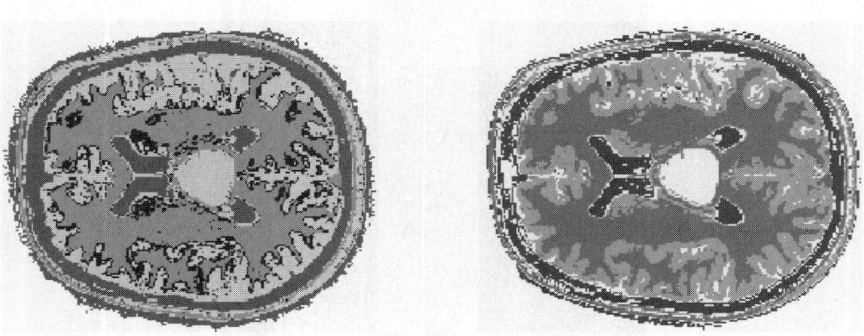

(c) (d)

Fig. 6. MR head image segmented by the (a) Kohonen network, and (b) ISOM

The training and test sets are formed visually and manually by using the computer mouse. Feature vectors in these sets contain class labels. These labels were not used during the training in unsupervised scheme. The number of classes can be determined visually for MR and CT images (not for the US image). It is observed that the numbers of classes (for MR and CT images) searched by the proposed network were the same with those of the visual judgments made by the user. Hence, the performances of both networks were compared for only MR and CT images. 100 training vectors were used during the training of networks for these images. In order to show the performances of Kohonen and ISOM networks comparatively, 100 test feature vectors (comprising of equal number of vectors for each class) were formed from the MR and CT images. Classification performances of 95% and 97% were obtained by the ISOM for MR and CT head images, respectively. 85% and 90% classification performances were obtained by the Kohonen network for MR and CT head images, respectively. Since the number of classes could not be determined visually for US image, comparative performance analysis of both networks were not realized.

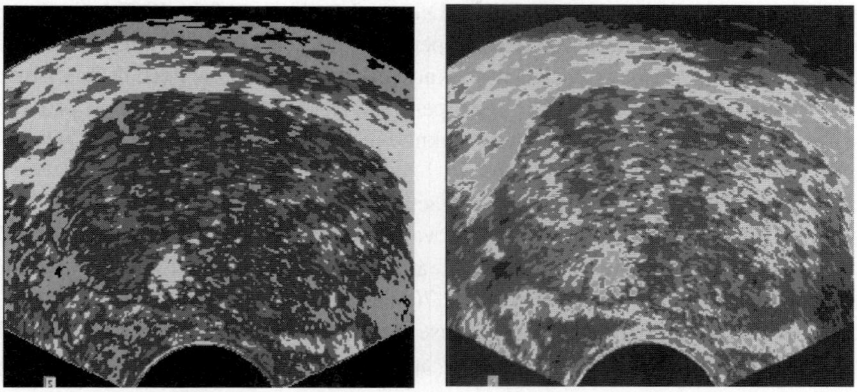

(a) (b)

Fig. 7. US prostate image segmented by the (a) Kohonen network, and (b) ISOM

Table 1. Segmentation results of ANNs

ANN	Image	Training time (sec.)	Segmentation time (sec.)	Number of nodes	Threshold values
ISOM	MR	9.21	37.25	5	600
	CT	6.41	30.65	4	1000
	US	11.12	306.82	5	1500
Kohonen Network	MR	29.30	63.76	4×4	
	CT	21.03	53.06	3×3	
	US	31.64	424.23	4×4	

5 Conclusions

Although Kohonen's SOM is a fast algorithm, it is not an incremental network. Besides, the strategy of the learning algorithm of the Kohonen network makes the output nodes locate in the feature space homogenously rather than concentrating on class boundaries. This strategy may require excessive number of nodes in the network. Moreover, the problem of determining optimum number of nodes and network topology is another disadvantage of the Kohonen network. Again, network nodes may not be capable of representing the classes well enough if network parameters such as the neighborhood and learning rate are not properly set. However, since ISOM is an incremental network, it automatically determines the proper number of nodes required for the segmentation. Furthermore, AT function significantly eliminated the threshold sensitivity of the network in the segmentation of medical images. ISOM is able to detect different clusters within a given training set by calculating a reference AT value depending on the statistics of features.

In this study, two neural networks with unsupervised learning are compared for the segmentation of medical images. With an unsupervised learning scheme, there is no need to determine the number of classes. During the training of the ISOM, the number of classes is determined automatically depending on the threshold value. The number of classes in medical images may not be known a-priori and may need to be estimated by a supervisor (clinician). The unsupervised learning scheme may provide a possibility that, for instance, some unknown tissues can be revealed after the segmentation process.

According to the selected feature extraction methods, features are formed by the intensity of the pixel of interest or mean value of intensities at one neighborhood of the pixel at each sub-band. The second feature extraction method is used to remove noise from the features. US images (Figs. 7(a) and (b)) obtained by the second feature extraction method are smoothened, because the mean of pixel intensities is used. The second feature extraction method is only applied to US images, because US images contain noise.

It is observed that cartilage tissue is represented by a different label/color in the segmented CT image (Fig. 5(b)), and tumor tissue is represented by a different label/color in the segmented MR image (Fig. 6(b)). Higher classification performances are obtained by the ISOM compared to the Kohonen network. Also, the results show that ISOM is highly a promising network for the segmentation of medical images. The proposed network was also tested on different medical images. It has been observed that ISOM generated satisfactory results for all those images. Thus, it can serve as a useful tool for inexperienced clinicians working in this area.

References

1. Chen, D.R., Chang, R.F., Huang, Y.L.: Breast Cancer Diagnosis Using Self-Organizing Map For Sonography. World Federation for Ultrasound in Med. & Biol., 26(3) (2000) 405–411
2. Loizou, C., Christodoulou, C., Pattichis, C.S., Istepanian, R., Pantziaris, M., Nicolaides, A.: Speckle Reduction in Ultrasonic Images of Atherosclerotic Carotid Plaque. 14th International IEEE Conference on Digital Signal Processing, (2002) 525-528
3. Pavlopoulos, S., Kyriacou, E., Koutsouris, D., Blekas, K., Stafylopatis, A., Zoumpoulis, P.: Fuzzy Neural Network Computer Assisted Characterization of Diffused Liver Diseases Using Image Texture Techniques on Ultrasonic Images. IEEE Eng. in Medicine and Biology Magazine, 19(1), (2000) 39-47
4. Kadyrov, A., Talepbour, A., Petrou, M.: Texture Classification with Thousands of Features. 13th British Machine Vision Conference, Cardiff-UK (2002)
5. Rajpoot, N.M.: Texture Classification Using Discriminant Wavelet Packet Subbands. 45th IEEE Midwest Symposium on Circuits and Systems, Tulsa-USA (2002)

6. Tao, Y., Muthukkumarasamy, V., Verma, B., Blumenstein, M.: A Texture Feature Extraction Technique Using 2D–DFT and Hamming Distance. 5th International Conference on Computational Intelligence and Multimedia Applications, Xi'an-China (2003)
7. Sorwar, G., Abraham, A., Dooley, L.S.: Texture Classification Based on DCT and Soft Computing. 10th IEEE International Conference on Fuzzy Systems, (2001)
8. McLeod, G., Parkin, G.: Automatic Detection of Clustered Microcalcifications Using Wavelet. The Third International Workshop on Digital Mammography, Chicago, (1996)
9. Wang, T., Karayiannis, N.: Detection of Microcalcifications in Digital Mammograms Using Wavelets. IEEE Transactions on Medical Imaging, 51(38(4)), (1998) 112–116
10. Berlich, R., Kunze, M., Steffens, J.: A Comparison Between the Performance of Feed-forward Neural Networks and the Supervised Growing Neural Gas Algorithm. In: 5th Artificial Intelligence in High Energy Physics Workshop, Lausanne, World Scientific (1996)
11. Fritzke, B.: Growing Cell Structure - A Self-Organizing Network for Unsupervised and Supervised Learning. Neural Networks, 7 (9), (1995), 1441–1460
12. Wismüller, A., Vietze, F., Behrends, J., Meyer-Baese, A., Reiser, M., Ritter, H.: Fully Automated Biomedical Image Segmentation by Self-Organized Model Adaptation. Neural Networks, 17 (2004), 1327–1344
13. Lin, K.C.R., Yang, M.S., Liu, H.C., Lirng, J.F., Wang, P.N.: Generalized Kohonen's Competitive Learning Algorithms for Ophthalmological MR Image Segmentation. Magnetic Resonance Imaging, 21 (2003), 863–870

Optimal Sampling for Feature Extraction in Iris Recognition Systems

Luis E. Garza Castañon[1], Saul Montes de Oca[2], and Rubén Morales-Menéndez[3]

Tecnológico de Monterrey, campus Monterrey
[1] Dept. of Mechatronics and Automation
[2] Automation Graduate Program Student
[3] Center for Innovation in Design and Technology Avenida Eugenio Garza Sada 2501 Sur 64, 489 Monterrey NL, México
{legarza, rmm}@itesm.mx, saul-montesdeoca@yahoo.com

Abstract. Iris recognition is a method used to identify people based on the analysis of the eye iris. A typical iris recognition system is composed of four phases: (1) image acquisition and preprocessing, (2) iris localization and extraction, (3) iris features characterization, and (4) comparison and matching. A novel contribution in the step of characterization of iris features is introduced by using a Hammersley's sampling algorithm and accumulated histograms. Histograms are computed with data coming from sampled sub-images of iris. The optimal number and dimensions of samples is obtained by the simulated annealing algorithm. For the last step, couples of accumulated histograms iris samples are compared and a decision of acceptance is taken based on an experimental threshold. We tested our ideas with UBIRIS database; for clean eye iris databases we got excellent results.

1 Introduction

Iris recognition is an important field related to the area of biometrics. Biometrics have multiple applications such as access control to restricted areas, access to personal equipments, public applications, such as banking operations [13] and relief operations as refugee management. Biometrics uses physical characteristics of individuals to provide reliable information to access secure systems. Although a wide variety of biometrics systems have been deployed, iris may provide the best solution by means of a greater discriminating power than the others biometrics [9]. Iris characteristics such as a data-rich structure, genetic independence, stability over time and physical protection, makes the use of iris as biometric well recognized.

There have been different successful implementations of iris recognition systems and even some commercial applications have been evaluated by requirement of the U.S. Department of Homeland Security [7]. For instance, the well known Daugman's system [1] used multiscale quadrature wavelets (Gabor filters) to extract texture phase structure information from the iris to generate a 2,048-bit

A. Gelbukh and C.A. Reyes-Garcia (Eds.): MICAI 2006, LNAI 4293, pp. 810–819, 2006.

iris code and to compare the difference between two iris representations by their respective Hamming distance.

In [12], iris features are extracted from a dyadic wavelet transform with null intersections. A similar method to Daugman's system is reported in [11], but using the edge detection approach to localize the iris, and techniques to deal with illumination variations, such as histogram equalization and feature characterization by average absolute deviation. In [5], iris features are extracted from an independent component analysis.

[15] uses statistical features, mean and standard deviations, from 2D wavelets transforms and Gabor filters, to make a more robust system of rotation, translation and illumination variations of images. In [6], a new method is presented to remove noise in iris images, such as eyelashes, pupil, eyelids and reflections. This approach is based on the unification of both, edge and region information. In [2] an iris recognition approach based on mutual information is developed. In that document, couples of iris samples were geometrically aligned by maximizing their mutual information and subsequently recognizing it.

Most of the previous documents use an intermediate step of filtering or transformation of iris data. This article shows an approach where direct information from selected areas of iris is applied to build a set of features. The paper is organized as follows. Section 2 describes our approach in detail. Section 3 discusses the main results and then compares them with similar approaches. Finally, section 4 concludes the paper.

2 The Approach

These ideas were tested our ideas with colored eyes images from *UBIRIS* database [14]. Images of eyes include clean samples where iris is free of any occlusion, and noisy images with moderate obstruction from eyelids and eyelashes (Fig. 1). We transform the color images representation to grey level pixels, because this format has enough information to reveal the relevant features of iris.

2.1 Iris Localization

The search of limbic and pupilar limits is achieved with the standard integrodifferential operator shown in eqn (1).

$$\overset{max}{(r, x_0, y_0)} = \left| \frac{\partial}{\partial r} G(r) * \oint_{r, x_c, y_c} \frac{I(x, y)}{2\pi r} ds \right| \tag{1}$$

where $I(x, y)$ is an image containing an eye. The operator behaves as an iterative circular edge detector that searches over the image domain (x, y) for the maximum in the partial derivative with respect to an increasing radius r, of the normalized contour integral of $I(x, y)$ along a circular arc ds of radius r and center coordinates (x_0, y_0). The symbol $*$ denotes convolution and $G_\sigma(r)$ is a smoothing function (typically a Gaussian of scale σ).

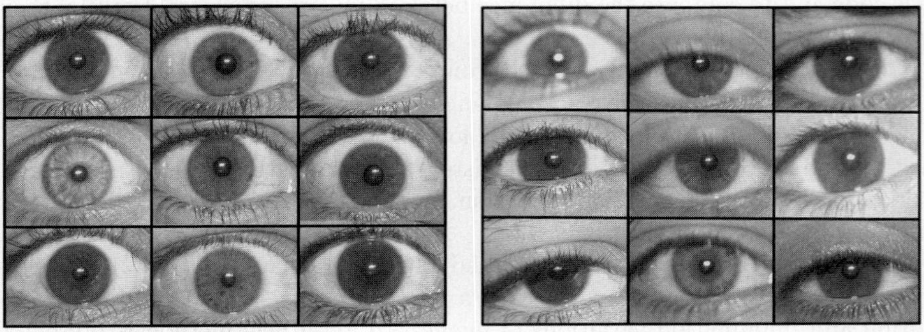

Fig. 1. Eyes samples from UBIRIS database. Left photos show clean eyes samples and right photos show noisy eyes samples.

Heavy occlusion of iris by eyelashes or eyelids needs to be handled by other methods. Eye images with heavy occlusion were discarded due to a failed localization of pupilar and limbic limits.

The extracted iris image has to be normalized to compensate the pupil dilation and contraction under illumination variations. This process is achieved by a transformation from polar to cartesian coordinates, using eqn (2). Fig. 2 shows the result of this transformation.

$$x(r,\theta) = (1-r)x_p(\theta) + rx_s(\theta) \qquad y(r,\theta) = (1-r)y_p(\theta) + ry_s(\theta) \qquad (2)$$

where $x(r,\theta)$ and $y(r,\theta)$ are defined as a linear combination of pupil limits ($x_p(\theta)$, $y_p(\theta)$) and limbic limits ($x_s(\theta)$, $y_s(\theta)$), $r \in [0,1]$, and $\theta \in [0,2\pi]$.

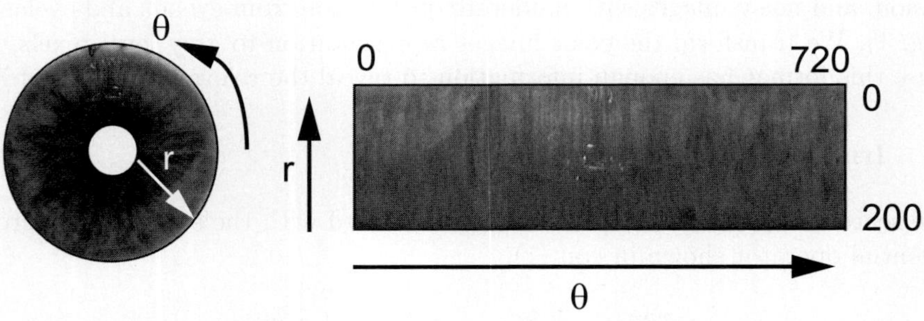

Fig. 2. Iris image transformation from polar to cartesian coordinates

2.2 Strip Processing

The iris image strip obtained in the previous step is processed by using an histogram equalization method, for compensation of differences in illumination conditions. The main objective is make all grey levels (ranging from 0 to 255) to have the same number of pixels. Histogram equalization is obtained with the cumulatived histogram, shown in eqn (3).

$$H(i) = \sum_{k=0}^{i} h(k) \tag{3}$$

where $h(k)$ is the histogram of the kth grey level, and i is the ith grey level. A flat histogram, in which every grey level has the same number of pixels, can be obtained by eqn (4):

$$G(i') = (i' + 1)\frac{N_r * M_c}{256} \tag{4}$$

where N_r and M_c are the image dimensions, i' is the i'^{th} grey level and 256 is the total number of grey levels.

2.3 Iris Sampling

Sampling strategies have been applied recently with certain degree of success in texture synthesis [3,10]. One of the main objectives of this research is to extract relevant features of iris, by sampling a set of subimages from the whole image. We introduced the Hammersley sampling algorithm. We generate a set of uniform coordinates (x, y) where the subimage is centered by using the Hammersley sequence sampling. Left pic in Fig. 3 shows a pseudo-code of the Hammersley sequence algorithm.

Hammersley sampling [4] is part of the *quasi*-Monte Carlo methods (or low-discrepancy sampling family). The *quasi*-prefix refers to a sampling approach that employs a deterministic algorithm to generate samples in a n-dimensional space. These points are as close as possible to a uniform sampling. Discrepancy refers to a quantitative measure of how much the distribution of samples deviates from an ideal uniform distribution (i.e. low-discrepancy is a desired feature).

Quasi-Monte Carlo methods as Hammersley sequences show lower error bound in multidimensional problems such as integration. Error bounds for pseudo-Monte Carlo Methods are $\mathcal{O}(N^{-1/2})$, and for classical integration is $\mathcal{O}(N^{-2/n})$. However, Hammersley sequences has a lower error bound with $\mathcal{O}(N^{-1} (log_{10}N)^{n-1})$ where N is the number of samples and n is the dimension of the design space. Usually, as n grows up Hammersley shows better results, note that a pseudo-Monte Carlo error bound is a probabilistic bound.

Fig. 4 shows the samples generated by a standard random and a Hammersley algorithms over iris strip. Properties can be appreciated in a qualitative fashion. Hammersley points have better uniformity properties because the algorithm exhibits an optimal design for placing n points on a k-dimensional hypercube.

The optimal number and dimensions of iris samples are obtained by a *SA* algorithm. The idea behind *SA* [8] is to simulate the physical annealing process of solids in order to solve optimization problems. *SA* is a generalization of

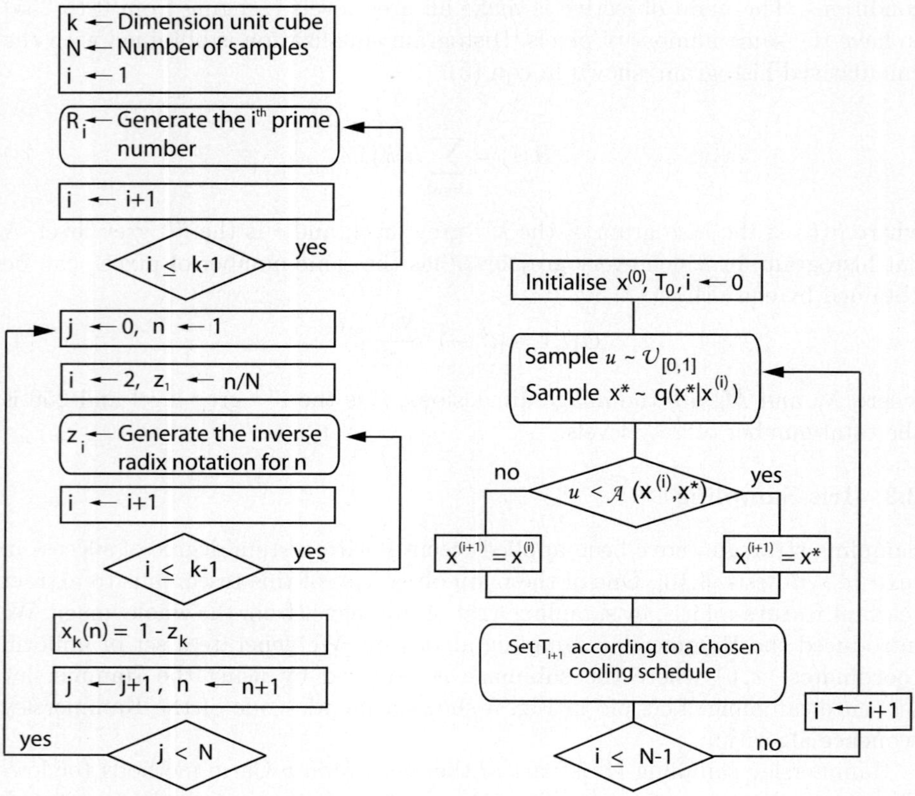

Fig. 3. Pseudocode algorithms. Left pic shows the Hammersley algorithm, while right pic shows the Simulated Annealing algorithm.

a Markov chain Monte Carlo method. A simple Monte Carlo simulation samples the possible states of a system by randomly choosing new parameters. At the end of the simulation, the collection of chosen points in the search space gives information about this space. In contrast with the simple Monte Carlo simulation, a new point in search space is sampled by making a slight change to the current point. This technique involves simulating a non-homogeneous Markov chain, whose invariant distribution at iteration i is no longer to the target function $f(x)$, but to $f^{1/T_i}(x)$ where T_i is a decreasing cooling schedule with $\lim_{i\rightarrow\infty} T_i = 0$. Under weak regularity assumptions on $f(x)$, $f^{\infty}(x)$ is a probability density which concentrates itself on the set of global maxima of $f(x)$. Right pic in Fig 3 shows a pseudo-code for the *SA* algorithm, where $A(x^{(i)}, x*) = min\{1, \frac{f^{1/T_i}(x*)q(x^{(i)}|x*)}{f^{1/T_i}(x^{(i)})q(x*|x^{(i)})}\}$ represents the acceptance probability, and the proposal distribution $q(x*|x^{(i)})$ involves sampling a candidate value $x*$ given the current value $x^{(i)}$.

We propose candidate values $x*$ for dimensions (height and width) and number of samples, to be extracted by using Hammersley algorithm. The evaluation

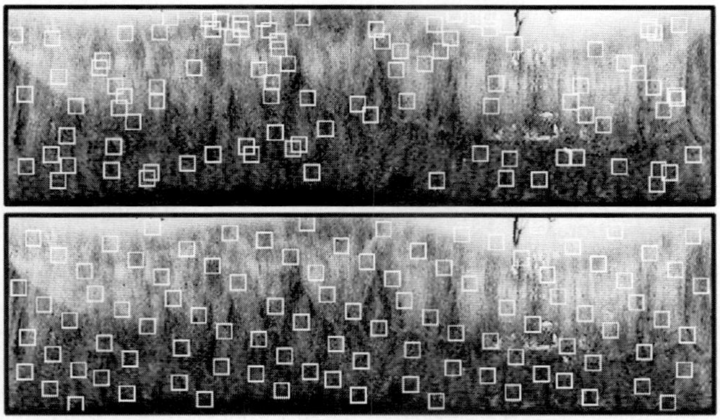

Fig. 4. Qualitative comparison of sampling schemes. Top pic shows a random sampled image. Bottom pic shows a Hammersley sampled image; Hammersley points have better uniformity properties.

of function $f(x*)$ is performed by running a full experiment of iris recognition and computing the overall efficiency.

2.4 Comparison and Matching

The iris features were represented by a set of cumulative histograms computed from sampled rectangular sub-images of iris strip. An cumulative histogram represents a feature and it is computed by using eqn (3). The complete iris is represented by a set of cumulative histograms, one of them for every sub-image. A decision of acceptance of the iris sample is taken accordingly to the minimum Euclidean distance calculated from the comparison of iris sample and irises database. A threshold is experimentally computed. Fig 5 shows the comparison and matching step.

We can formalize the method as follows. Let I be an image, representing an iris strip, let $p \in I$ be a pixel and $\omega(p) \subset I$ be a square image patch of width S_f centered at p. We built iris features by forming a set of cumulative histograms with k bins, $P_m(i)$ $i = 1 \cdots k$, $m = 1 \cdots N_f$, from a set of N_f sampled patches $\{\omega = \omega(p_1), \cdots, \omega(p_{N_f})\}$. The features of every iris in the database are represented by a set of accumulated histograms $\{P_{DB_1}(i), P_{DB_2}(i), \cdots, P_{DB_{N_f}}(i)\}$.

An iris sample features set $\{P_{SMP_1}(i), P_{SMP_2}(i), \cdots, P_{SMP_{N_f}}(i)\}$ is compared against every iris features set in a database of size ℓ, according to the norm:

$$L = \min_n \sqrt{\sum_j \sum_i (P_{DB_j}(i) - P_{SMP_j}(i))^2} \tag{5}$$

with $n = 1 \cdots \ell$, $i = 1 \cdots k$, $j = 1 \cdots N_f$. A decision to accept or reject the sample is taken based on the rule $L < \delta$, where δ is a threshold computed experimentally.

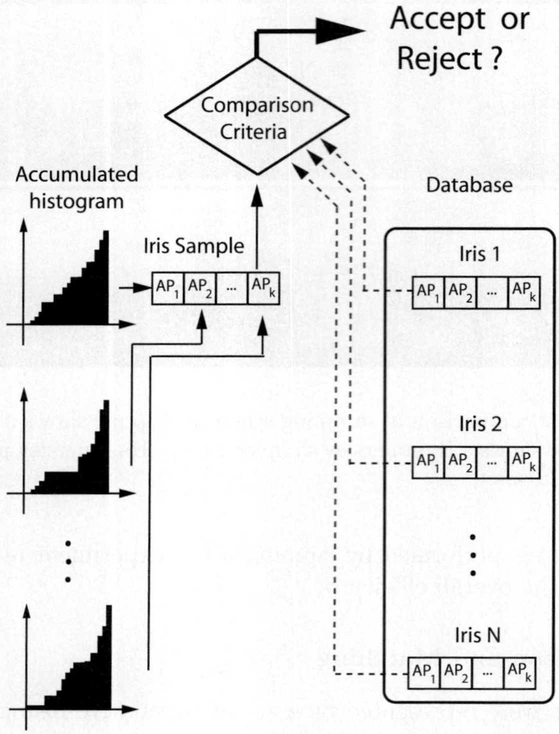

Fig. 5. The process of comparison and matching uses the histogram of every iris in database and compares them against the arriving iris. A decision is taken according to a Euclidean distance metrics and an experimental threshold.

3 Experimental Results

Experiments were run in the UBIRIS database. Images with a high percentage (i.e. more than 40 %) of occlusion and noise were discarded by visual inspection, because the difficulty to locate the iris region with integro-differential operators. Then, experimental database was built with 1013 samples coming from 173 users. With this database experiments are performed some experiments using the 100 % of samples. Table 3 shows the main results for different percentage of use of the database. First column refers to the percent of used database. For instance, 90 % means that 10 % of the worst user samples were discarded. Second column refers to the total number of iris samples, third column refers to the number of users, fourth column refers to the number of samples used for learning the decision threshold. Finally, the fifth column refers to the total number of samples used for testing.

SA algorithm was first run with a small database of 50 users and 208 iris samples in order to accelerate the optimization step. For different percentage of use of the database, we start the *SA* optimization algorithm with different dimensions and number of sub-images. The best obtained results for four different

Table 1. Experimental results

Percentage of use of the DB	Number of iris	Number of users	Number of samples for threshold computing	Number of samples for testing
100	1013	173	52	788
90	912	173	46	693
80	811	173	42	596
70	710	173	36	501
50	507	173	26	308

combinations are shown in left pic of Fig. 6. The typical performance of the *SA* algorithm is shown in right pic of Fig. 6.

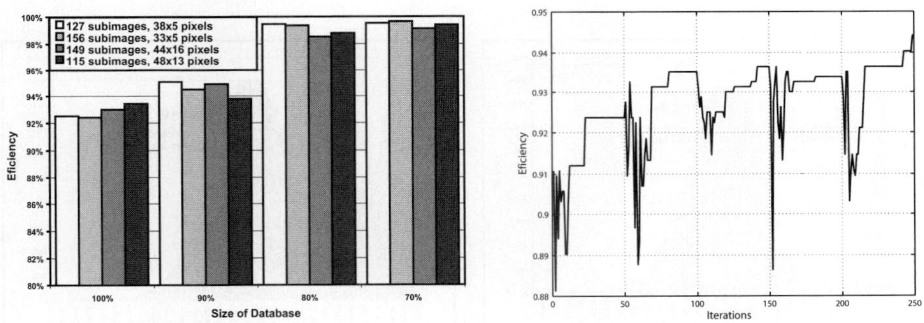

Fig. 6. *SA* optimization step. Left plot shows the best results for different percentage of use of the database for different dimensions (height, width) and number of sub-images. Right pic shows a typical run of the *SA* algorithm.

In Fig. 7, we can see the Receiving Operating Characteristic (*ROC*) curves for the different percentages of use taken from the database. Databases with cleaner iris samples (60 % and 70 %) reflects better results. In Fig. 8 we can see the distribution curves from the cumulative histograms distance of two databases used in experiments with Hammersley sampling. Distributions are more separated with lower variances when database is cleaner. The overlapping distribution curves in the right pic (Fig. 8) leads to worse results.

There are several successful results in iris recognition systems. Daugman's system [1] has been tested thoroughly with databases containing thousands of samples, and reports of 100 % of accuracy have been given. In [12], the experimental results have an efficiency of 97.9 %, working with a database of 100 samples from 10 persons. [11] reports a performance of 99.09 % in experiments with a database of 500 iris images from 25 individuals. [6] shows a performance of 98% and 99% working with the CASIA database (2,255 samples from 213 subjects). In [2], the best result is 99.05 % with a database of 384 images of 64 persons.

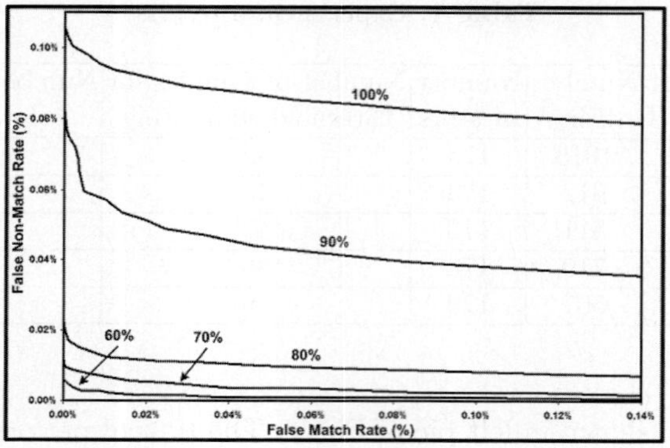

Fig. 7. Hammersley sampling ROC curve for different percentage of use of the database

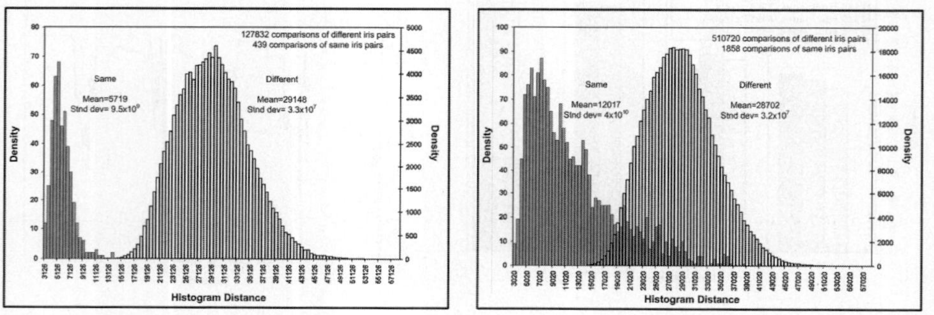

Fig. 8. Authentic-impostor distribution of accumulated histograms distance (L). Left pic shows the Hammersley sampling performance for 50 % of use of the database. Right pic shows the performance for 100 %. Left distribution corresponds to authentic person, while right distribution corresponds to impostor person in both pics.

This results are competitive with most of the mentioned works. Our best results have 100 % of efficiency working with a database of 308 samples coming from 173 persons (50 % of use of the database); also, 99 % and higher with 501 samples (70 % of use of the database) and 596 samples (80 % of use of the database).

4 Conclusions

A new approach for iris recognition has been presented. The novel contribution relies on the iris feature characterization step by using the Hammersley sampling technique and Simulated Annealing algorithms. Although experimental results show better performance for databases with cleaner eyes images, we claim that our method will conduct to an improved and faster approach, in which just a few samples of sub-images taken from irises in a database will be necessary to discard most of them in a first step, to be able to focus the effort of comparison and matching in a very reduced set of iris samples. This potential approach will lead us to test bigger databases.

References

1. J. Daugman, *How Iris Recognition Works*, IEEE Transactions on Circuits and Systems for Video Technology,14(1):21-30, 2004
2. M. Dobes, L. Machala, P. Tichasvky, and J. Pospisil, *Human Eye Iris Recognition Using The Mutual Information*, Optik, No. 9, pp. 399-404, 2004.
3. A. Efros, and T. Leung, *Texture Synthesis by Non-Parametric Sampling*, in Proceedings of the 7th IEEE International Conference on Computer Vision, Vol. 2, pp. 1033-1038, September 1999.
4. J. Hammersley, *Monte Carlo Methods for Solving Multivariate Problems*, Annals of New York Academy of Science, No. 86, pp. 844-874, 1960.
5. Y. Huang, S. Luo, and E. Chen, *An Efficient Iris Recognition System*, In Proceedings of the First International Conference on Machine Learning and Cybernetics, pp. 450-454, 2002.
6. J. Huang, Y. Wang, T. Tan, and J. Cui, *A New Iris Segmentation Method for Iris Recognition System*, In Proceedings of the 17th International Conference on Pattern Recognition, pp. 554-557, 2004
7. *Independent Testing of Iris Recognition Technology - Final Report*, International Biometric Group, May 2005.
8. S. Kirkpatrick, and C. Gelatt, and M. Vecchi, *Optimization by Simulated Annealing*, Science, 220(4598):671-680, 1983.
9. A. Jain, A. Ross, A. Prabhakar, *An Introduction to Biometric Recognition*, IEEE Transactions on Circuits and Systems for Video Technology, 14(1):4-20, 2004.
10. L. Liang, C. Liu, Y. Xu, B. Guo, and H. Shum, *Real-time Texture Synthesis by Patch-based Sampling*, ACM Transactions on Graphics, 20(3):127-150, July 2001.
11. L. Ma, Y. Wang, T. Tan, and D. Zhang, *Personal Identification Based on Iris Texture Analysis*, IEEE Transactions on Pattern Analysis and Machine Intelligence, 25(12):1519 - 1533, 2003.
12. D. de Martin-Roche, C. Sanchez-Avila, and R. Sanchez-Reillo, *Iris ecognition for Biometric Identification using dyadic wavelet transform zero-crossing*, In Proceedings of the IEEE 35th International Conference on Security Technology, pp. 272-277, 2001.
13. M. Negin, Chmielewski T., Salganicoff M., Camus T., Cahn U., Venetianer P., and Zhang G. *An Iris Biometric System for Public and Personal Use* , Computer, 33(2):70-75, 2000.
14. H. Proenca, and L. Alexandre, *UBIRIS: A Noisy Iris Image Database*, in Proceedings of the International Conference on Image Analysis and Processing, Vol. 1, pp. 970-977, 2005.
15. Y. Zhu, T. Tan, and Y. Wang, *Biometric Personal Identification Based on Iris Patterns*, In Proceedings of the 15th International Conference on Pattern Recognition, pp. 801-804, 2000.

Histograms, Wavelets and Neural Networks Applied to Image Retrieval

Alain C. Gonzalez[1,2], Juan H. Sossa[2], Edgardo Manuel Felipe Riveron[2], and Oleksiy Pogrebnyak[2]

[1] Technologic Institute of Toluca, Electronics and Electrical Engineering Department
Av. Instituto Tecnológico w/n Ex Rancho La Virgen, Metepec, México, P.O. 52140
[2] Computing Research Center, National Polytechnic Institute
Av. Juan de Dios Batiz and Miguel Othon de Mendizabal, P.O. 07738, México, D.F.
alaing@ittoluca.edu.mx, alaing@sagitario.cic.ipn.mx, hsossa@cic.ipn.mx, edgardo@cic.ipn.mx, olek@cic.ipn.mx

Abstract. We tackle the problem of retrieving images from a database. In particular we are concerned with the problem of retrieving images of airplanes belonging to one of the following six categories: 1) commercial planes on land, 2) commercial planes in the air, 3) war planes on land, 4) war planes in the air, 5) small aircrafts on land, and 6) small aircrafts in the air. During training, a wavelet-based description of each image is first obtained using Daubechies 4-wavelet transformation. The resulting coefficients are then used to train a neural network. During classification, test images are presented to the trained system. The coefficients are obtained from the Daubechies transform from histograms of a decomposition of the image into square sub-images of each channel of the original image. 120 images were used for training and 240 for independent testing. An 88% correct identification rate was obtained.

1 Introduction

Information processing often involves the recognition, storage and retrieval of visual information. An image contains visual information and what is important for information retrieval is to return an image or a group of images with similar information to a query [1]. Image retrieval deals with recovering visual information in the form of images from a collection of images as a result of a query. The query itself could be an image.

Approximately 73% of the information in cyberspace is in the form of images [2]. This information is, in general, not well organized. In cyberspace we can find photos of all kinds: people, flowers, animals, landscapes, and so on. Trying to implement a system able to differentiate among more than 10,000 classes of objects is still an open research subject. Most of the existing systems work efficiently with a few objects. When this number grows and when the objects are more complex system performance begins to deteriorate rapidly. In this paper we present a simple but effective methodology to learn and classify objects with similar characteristics. Intuitively, this problem would be much more difficult to solve than the problem of classifying completely different objects [3]. In this paper we are interested in determining if a photo of a given airplane belongs to one of the six categories show in Figure 1.

A. Gelbukh and C.A. Reyes-Garcia (Eds.): MICAI 2006, LNAI 4293, pp. 820 – 827, 2006.

The rest of the paper is organized as follows. In section 2 we give a short state of the art as it relates to the subject matter of this paper. We emphasize the main differences of our work with those reported in the literature. In section 3, we present the different steps in our approach. In section 4 we give some experimental results where we demonstrate the efficiency of the proposal. In section 5, we conclude and provide some directions for future research.

Fig. 1. Types of objects we want to differentiate. (a) Commercial plane on land, (b) commercial plane in the air, (c) war aircraft on land, (d) war aircraft in the air, (e) small aircraft on land, and (f) small aircraft in the air. All images are from http://www.aircraft-images.co.uk .

2 State of the Art

In [4], Park et al. make use of wavelets and a bank of perceptrons to retrieve images from a database of 600 images (300 for training and 300 for testing). They report an 81.7% correct recall for the training set, and 76.7% for the testing set. In [5], Zhang et al. describe how by combining wavelets and neural networks, images can be efficiently retrieved from a database in terms of the image content. They report performances near to 80%.

In [6], Manish et al. make use of wavelets to retrieve images distorted with additive noise. They report that while the added noise is under 20%, any image from the database is correctly retrieved. Above 20%, the performance of their approach decreases drastically. In [7], Puzicha et al., report a 93.38% performance by using histograms and non-supervised classification techniques. In [8], Mandal et al., report a performance of 87% by combining wavelets and histograms. Finally, in [9], Liapsis et al., present a system with a performance near 93% when combining textural and color features, 52% when only textural information is taken into account and 83% when only color information is used as the describing feature on a database composed of 210 images of the Corel Photo Gallery.

Our proposal also uses wavelets and neural networks to retrieve images from a database. It differs from other works in how the describing features are obtained. In our case, we get the image features from the histograms of a series of small windows inside each color layer (red, green and blue) of the images.

3 Methodology

We retrieve images from a database taking into account their content in terms of object shape and image color distribution. To efficiently retrieve an image, we propose to combine a multi-resolution approach, histogram computation, wavelet transformation and neural network processing. In a first step of training, our procedure computes a Daubechies 4 wavelet transform to get the desired descriptors [10], [11]. These features are represented by the wavelets coefficients of the Daubechies 4 wavelet transform. These coefficients tend to represent the semantics of the image, that is, the distribution and size of the forms in the image plus the local variation of the color of the objects and background [12], [13]. We use the three bands red, green and blue (RGB) of a color image to extract the describing features [14]. For each color band, we process each image to obtain the wavelets coefficients of the histograms of a set of sub-images partitioning the whole image (Fig. 2). In this case, an image is divided into 16 square sub-images as shown in Figure 2.

We compute the histogram of each of the 16 square gray-level sub-mages images of each image of each color channel. The histogram $h(r), r = 1, \ldots, L-1$ of an image is the function that gives the probability each gray level r can be found in the image [15]. Because a histogram does not provide information about the position of pixels in the image, we decided to combine its information with the well-known multi-resolution approach to take into account this fact. The sizes of all images to be processed were normalized to 256×256 pixels.

3.1 Wavelets Coefficients from the Histograms of a Set of Sub-images of the Original Color Image

Figure 2 shows how the wavelet coefficients that are going to be used to describe an image for its further retrieval are obtained from a set of sub-images dividing the image at each channel.

The normalized image of 256×256 pixels is first split into its three RGB channels. Refer again to Fig. 2. Each 256×256 red, green and blue image is now divided into 16 squared sub-images of 64×64 pixels each as shown in Figure 2. For each squared sub-image we then compute its corresponding gray level histogram. We

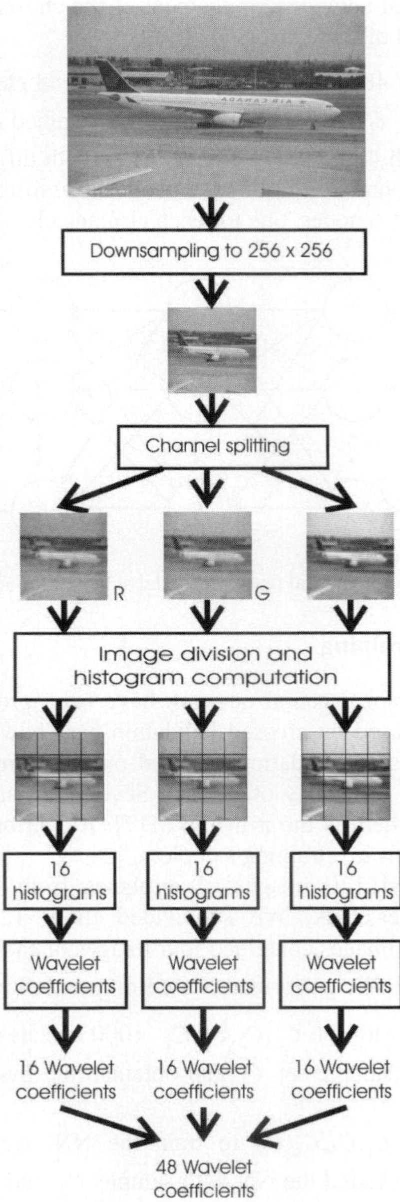

Fig. 2. Mechanism used to get the wavelet coefficients for training from the histograms of the 16 square sub-images dividing each image channel of the original color image

next apply the multi-resolution procedure to each sub-image to get 16 coefficients, one from each sub-image. Because we do this for each one of the three-color channels, we get 48 describing wavelet coefficients to be used for training.

3.2 Neural Network Architecture

Figure 3 shows the neural network arrangement of the chosen model. It is a network of perceptrons composed of three layers [16]:

1. The input layer has 48 nodes, one for each of the 48 elements of the describing wavelet vector $[x_1 \quad x_2 \quad \cdots \quad x_{48}]^T$ obtained as explained in section 3.1.
2. A hidden layer with 49 nodes. We have tested with different numbers of nodes for this layer. We found this gives gave the best classification results.
3. The output layer has 6 nodes, one for each airplane class.

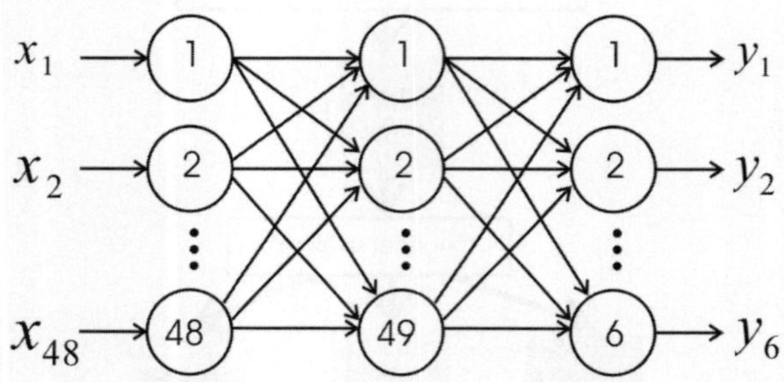

Fig. 3. Architecture of the neural network model selected for airplane classification

3.3 Neural Network Training

Several procedures to train a neural network have been proposed in the literature. Among them, the one based on crossed validation has shown to be one of the best suited for this goal. Crossed validation is based on the composition of at least two data sets to evaluate the efficiency of the net. Several variants of this method have been proposed. One of them is the π-method [17]. It distributes at random with no replacement of the patterns in a training sample.

For training we used 120 images of airplanes from the 1068 available at: http://www.aircraft-images.co.uk. We subdivided these 120 images into 5 sets $C_1,\ldots,C_5$. Each set of 24 images contained four images of each one of the six airplane classes shown in Figure 1. We performed NN training as follows:

1. We trained the NN with sets C_2,C_3,C_4,C_5. 1000 epochs were executed. We then tested the NN with sample set C_1 and obtained the first set of weights for the NN.
2. We then use sets C_1,C_3,C_4,C_5 to train the NN. Again 1000 epochs were performed. We then tested the NN with sample C_2 and obtained the second set of weights for the NN.

3. We repeated this process for training sets: C_1, C_2, C_4, C_5, C_1, C_2, C_3, C_5 and C_1, C_2, C_3, C_4, to get third, fourth and fifth weighting sets for the NN.

As a final step, we took the 120 images for training, by observing that the performance of the NN is predictable when using cross validation. We used the set of thus obtained as the weights of the neural network to be tested.

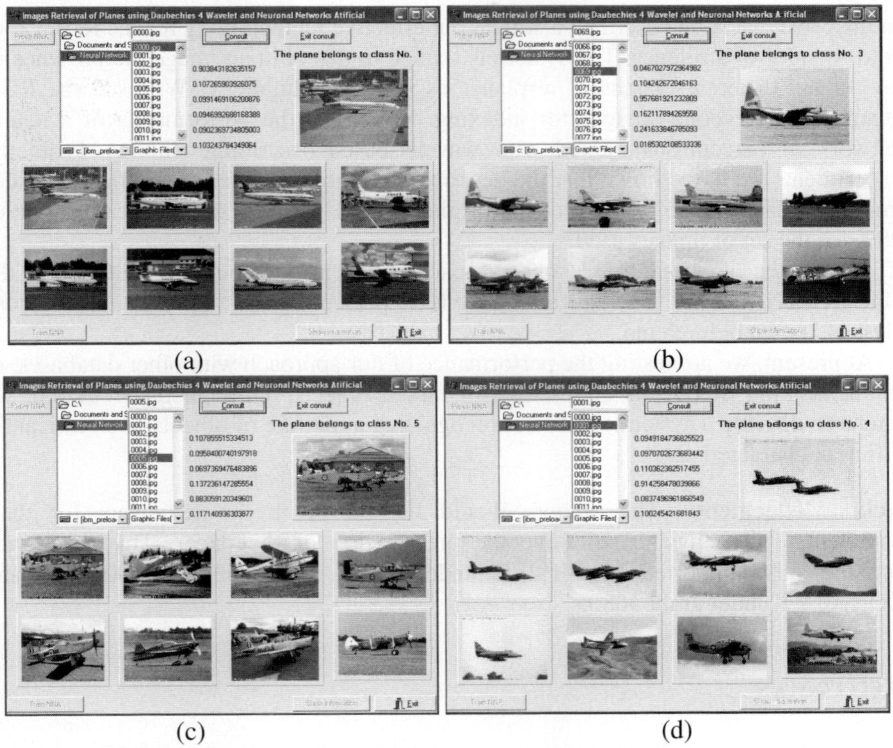

Fig. 4. Four outputs when it is presented to the system, (a) an image of a commercial airplane in land, (b) a war airplane in land, (c) a small aircraft in land, and (d) a war airplane on air

4 Experimental Results

In this section we discuss the efficiency of the proposed methodology. For this we have taken the 120 images used for training of the neural network. To these 120 images we added another 120 images taken at random from the 1068 of the database, for a total of 240 testing images. We took each of the 240 images and presented it to the trained neural network. At each step, the classification efficiency using the neural network was tested. An 88% performance was obtained for this set of images. From these experiments, we can see that proposed method achieved good classification performance for the set of images used.

Figures 4(a) through 4(d) show graphically four of the classification results. The system is configured to always show the best 8 ranked most similar images with respect to the input. Also, as the reader can appreciate, the system always responds first with the input image, obviously because this is the image best classified.

5 Conclusions and Ongoing Research

In this work we have described a simple but effective methodology for the retrieval of color images of airplanes. The system is trained to detect in an image the presence of one of six different classes of airplanes as shown in Figure 1. We used the RGB channels of the color images for indexing. We tested the performance of a neural network of perceptrons trained with wavelet-based describing features. From the experiments we have shown that the describing features obtained from 16 square sub-images of each image channel of the original image provides a classification rate of 88% for the set of images used.

Among the main features of our approach is that no previous segmentation of the object class is needed. During training we have present to the system an object whose class is known beforehand.

At present, we are testing the performance of our approach with other databases, of the same kind of objects and also with mixed objects. Through this research, we intend to develop a system capable of recognizing a mixture of objects of significantly different characteristics.

Acknowledgements. The authors would like to thank the reviewers for their comments that helped to improve the presentation of the paper. This work was economically supported by SIP-IPN under grants 20050156 and 20060517 and CONACYT under grant 46805.

References

[1] A. Del Bimbo (1999). Visual Information Retrieval, Morgan Kaufmann Publishers.

[2] S. M. Lew (2000). Next-Generation Web Searches for Visual Content, Computer, Information Retrieval, Volume 33, Number 11, Computer Society IEEE. Pp. 46-53.

[3] C. Leung (1997). Visual Information Systems, Springer.

[4] S. B. Park, J. W. Lee and S. K. Kim (2004). Content-based image classification using a neural network, Pattern Recognition Letters, 25:287-300.

[5] S. Zhang and E. Salari (2005). Image denoising using a neural network based on non-linear filter in wavelet domain, Acoustics, Speech, and Signal Processing, Proceedings IEEE International Conference ICASSP '05, 18-23 March. 2:989-992.

[6] N. S. Manish, M. Bodruzzaman and M. J. Malkani (1998). Feature Extraction using Wavelet Transform for Neural Network based Image Classification, IEEE 0-7803-4547-9.

[7] J. Puzicha, Th. Hofmann and J. M. Buhmann (1999). Histogram Clustering for Unsupervised Segmentation and Image Retrieval, Pattern Recognition Letters, 20: 899-909.

[8] M. K. Mandal and T. Aboulnasr (1999). Fast Wavelets Histogram Techniques for Image Indexing, Computer Vision and Understanding, 75(1-2):99-110.

[9] S. Liapis and G. Tziritas (2004). Color and texture image retrieval using chromaticity histograms and wavelet frames, Multimedia, IEEE Transactions on Multimedia (5):676 – 686.

[10] M. Vetterli (2000). Wavelets, Approximation, and Compression, IEEE Signal Processing Magazine. 1:59-73.

[11] I. Daubechies (1988). Orthonormal bases of compactly supported wavelets, Comm. Pure and Applied Mathematics. 41:909-996.

[12] Z. Xiong, K. Ramchandran and M. T. Orchard (1997). Space-Frequency Quantization for Wavelet Image Coding, IEEE Transactions on Image Processing, 6(5).

[13] N. Papamarcos, A. E. Atsalakis, and Ch. P. Strouthopoulos (2002). Adaptive Color Reduction, IEEE Transactions on Systems, Man and Cybernetics – Part B: Cybernetics, 32(1).

[14] R. C. Gonzalez, R. E. Woods and S. L. Eddins (2004). Digital Image Processing Using Matlab, Pearson Prentice Hall.

[15] F. D. Jou, K. Ch. Fan and Y. L. Chang (2004). Efficient matching of large-size histograms, Pattern Recognition Letters, 25:277-286.

[16] P. McGuire and G. M. T. D`Eleuterio (2001). Eigenpaxels and a Neural-Network Approach to Image Classification, IEEE Transactions on Neural Networks, 12(3).

[17] A. E. Gasca and A. R. Barandela (1999). Algoritmos de aprendizaje y técnicas estadísticas para el entrenamiento del Perceptrón Multicapa, IV Simposio Iberoamericano de Reconocimiento de Patrones, Cuba. Pp. 456-464.

Adaptive-Tangent Space Representation for Image Retrieval Based on Kansei

Myunggwon Hwang[1], Sunkyoung Baek[1], Hyunjang Kong[1], Juhyun Shin[1], Wonpil Kim[2], Soohyung Kim[2], and Pankoo Kim[1,*]

[1] Dept. of Computer Engineering, Chosun University, Gwangju 501-759, Korea
{mghwang, zamilla100, kisofire, jhshinkr, pkkim}@chosun.ac.kr
[2] Dept. of Computer Science, Chonnam National University, Gwangju 500-700, Korea
{kwpil, shkim}@iip.chonnam.ac.kr

Abstract. From the engineering aspect, the research on Kansei information is a field aimed at processing and understanding how human intelligence processes subjective information or ambiguous sensibility and how such information can be executed by a computer. Our study presents a method of image processing aimed at accurate image retrieval based on human Kansei. We created the Kansei-Vocabulary Scale by associating Kansei of high-level information with shapes among low-level features of an image and constructed the object retrieval system using Kansei-Vocabulary Scale. In the experimental process, we put forward an adaptive method of measuring similarity that is appropriate for Kansei-based image retrieval. We call it "adaptive-Tangent Space Representation (adaptive-TSR)". The method is based on the improvement of the TSR in 2-dimensional space for Kansei-based retrieval. We then it define an adaptive similarity algorithm and apply to the Kansei-based image retrieval. As a result, we could get more promising results than the existing method in terms of human Kansei.

1 Introduction

In the oncoming generation, Kansei has become an important agenda, raising a variety of issues in the computing field. As a result, many investigators have conducted trials involving the processing of Kansei information.

Kansei is a Japanese word that refers to the capability of perceiving an impression, such as "pathos," "feeling" and "sensitivity." Kansei also has meanings such as "sense," "sensibility," "sentiment," "emotion" and "intuition" [1]. Kansei is usually expressed with emotional words for example, beautiful, romantic, fantastic, comfortable, etc [2]. The concept of Kansei is strongly tied to the concept of personality and sensibility. Kansei is an ability that allows humans to solve problems and process information in a faster and more personal way. The Kansei of humans is high-level information, and the research on Kansei information is a field aimed at processing and understanding how human intelligence processes subjective information or ambiguous sensibility and how the information can be executed by a computer [3].

* Corresponding author.

A. Gelbukh and C.A. Reyes-Garcia (Eds.): MICAI 2006, LNAI 4293, pp. 828 – 837, 2006.

Particularly, Kansei information processing is studied in the multimedia retrieval field and the background of this paper is our constructed image retrieval system based on Kansei. Specifically, our study is a method of image processing aimed at accurate image retrieval based on human Kansei. In our previous study, we created the Kansei-Vocabulary Scale by associating Kansei of high-level information with shapes among low-level features of an image and constructed the object retrieval system using Kansei-Vocabulary Scale. We used the "Tangent Space Representation (TSR)" in this system for shape matching [4]. This method of measuring similarity considers the low-level features between shapes. We could find the limitation of shape matching in retrieval results. In our current system, the existing TSR is unable to deal with the Kansei information of humans. As a result, the TSR method of measuring shape similarity for retrieval of perceptually similar shapes has been limited to image retrieval based on Kansei.

The existing methods of shape matching should not depend on scale, balance, orientation, and position. However, these methods are actively used for content-based retrieval system. Human Kansei is influenced by the upper shape factors, so we propose an "adaptive-TSR" to obtain the appropriate result according to a user's Kansei and the processing of Kansei as high-level information by using TSR. One of our system's important purposes is to realize human Kansei-based retrieval. In other words, while the existing TSR does not deal with high-level information of shape our proposed method makes it possible to differentiate shapes based on Kansei.

2 Background and Related Works

A shape similarity measure useful for shape-based retrieval in image databases should be in accord with human visual perception. This basic property leads to the following requirements [5]. Firstly, shape similarity measure should permit recognition of perceptually similar objects that are not mathematically identical. Secondly, it should abstract from distortions (e.g., digitization noise and segmentation errors) and respect the significant visual parts of objects. Furthermore, it should not depend on the scale, orientation, and position of objects. Finally, shape similarity measure is universal in the sense that it allows us to identify or distinguish objects of arbitrary shapes. (i.e., no restrictions on shapes are assumed)

Longin Jan Latecki et al. proposed methods of similarity measure in which properties are analyzed with respect to retrieval of similar objects in image databases of silhouettes of 2D objects. They first established the best possible correspondence of visual parts to compute similarity measure. The similarity between corresponding parts was then computed and aggregated. They used the tangent function as the basis for the proposed similarity measure of simple polygonal arcs.

Alberto Chávez-Aragón et al., proposed a new method for content-based image retrieval, which can be divided into two main parts [6]. 1) Automatic segmentation and extraction of shapes from image sub-regions. 2) Ontological descriptions of shapes contained in images. Here the Tangent Space Representation approach is used to make a feature vector for similarity measure between shapes.

The following contents explain about Tangent Space Representation that is defined by math lab in Hamburg Univ. as it is used in the upper related works [8]. The polygonal representation is not a convenient form to calculate the similarity between two shapes, so an alternative representation such as TSR, is needed. In all subsequent steps they will not use the polygonal representation of the shape, but they will transform it into tangent space. A digital curve C is represented in the tangent space by the graph of a step function, where the x-axis represents the arc-length coordinates of points in C and the y-axis represents the direction of the line segments in the decomposition of C. Each horizontal line segment in the graph of the step function is called a step. They traverses a digital curve in a counter clockwise direction and assigns to each maximal line segment in the curve decomposition a step in the tangent space. The y-value of a step is the directional angle of the line segment and the x-extend of the step is equal to the length of the line segment normalized with respect to the length of the curve.

What they got in the former step is turned into their Tangent Space Representation because this technique is invariant, to scaling (normalizing the length of the curve), rotation and translation, and finally the shapes are ready to be indexed [7]. Then, we measure similarity between shapes using indexing values. For example, figure 1 shows a digital curve and its step function representation in the tangent space [8].

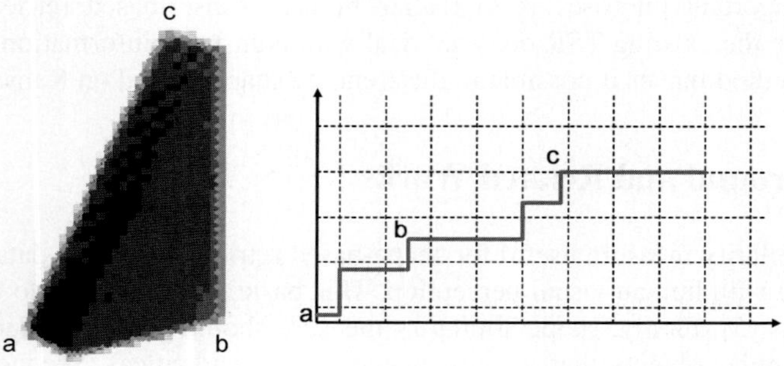

Fig. 1. Step function Representation

Recently the demand for image retrieval corresponding to Kansei has been increasing, and the studies focused on establishing those Kansei-based systems are progressing faster than ever. However, the existing image retrievals are capable of understanding the semantics of contents based on low-level features such as color, shape, and texture [9]. Retrieval of such low-level information has difficulty understanding high-level information such as the intentions or sensibilities of users. As well, there are troubles in processing and recognizing images appropriate for the users' Kansei. To solve these problems, we studied Kansei as it pertains to shape among visual information [4].

In order to cope with these limiting barriers, we attempted to associate visual information with human beings' Kansei through a relational sample scale, which is made by linking the visual information with the Kansei-vocabulary of human beings. Our primary purpose was to study retrieval based on Kansei. Specifically, how human intelligence processes subjective information and how the information can be executed by a computer.

Firstly, we collected and classified the most common shapes for the Kansei scale and defined what the most standard shapes are. Secondly, we found a relationship between the shapes and Kansei-vocabulary. As a result, we were able to produce a Kansei-Vocabulary Scale for shape and the related Kansei-vocabulary. And then we constructed the object retrieval system for evaluation based on Kansei-Vocabulary Scale by shape in [4].

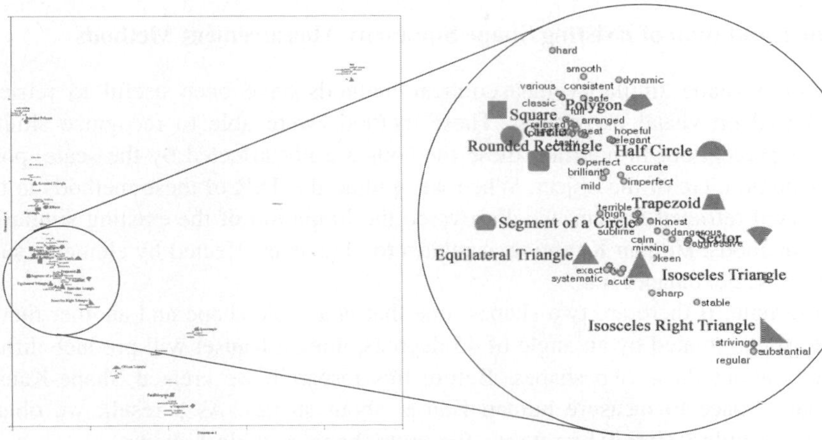

Fig. 2. Kansei-Vocabulary Scale by Shape

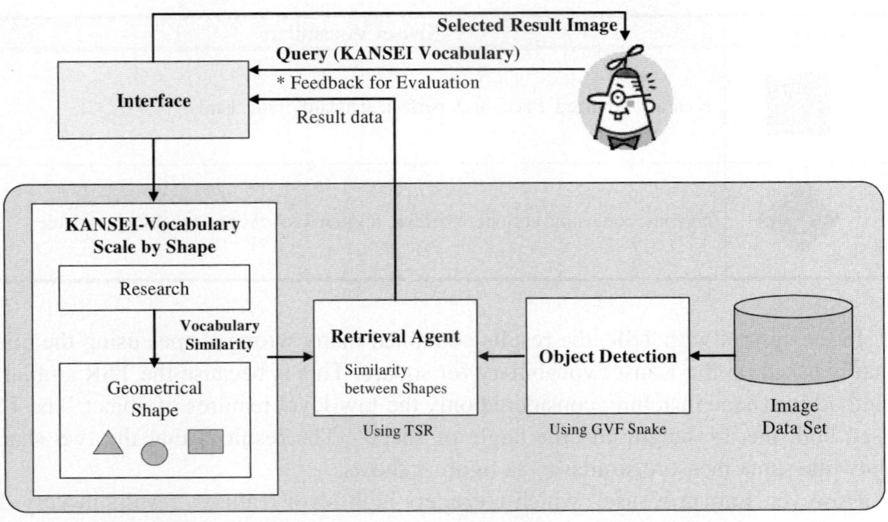

Fig. 3. Architecture of Objective Retrieval System based on Kansei

In the results of the system's evaluation, it was possible to retrieve respective object images with appropriate shapes in terms of the query's sensibility. However, we discovered an insufficiency of similarity measure produced by Tangent Space

Representation. Thus, we put forward an adaptive method of similarity measure which is appropriate to Kansei-based image retrieval. We called it "Adaptive Tangent Space Representation (adaptive-TSR)". The method was based on the improvement of the TSR in 2-dimensional space for a Kansei-based retrieval system.

3 Our Proposed Method

3.1 The Limitation of Existing Shape Similarity Measurement Methods

The existing shape similarity measurement methods have been useful to retrieve shapes based on visual perception. These methods were able to recognize similar objects of perception. In addition these methods are not affected by the scale, position, orientation, etc of the object. When we applied the TSR of these methods to the Kansei based retrieval system, we discovered the limitation of the existing similarity measure methods. Human Kansei as it relates to objects is affected by elements such as position, scale, balance, etc.

For example, if there are two shapes: one that is a basic shape and another that is the basic shape rotated by an angle of 45 degrees, human Kansei will produce different results about these two shapes. Before this research, we created Shape-Kansei Vocabulary Space to measure human Kansei about shapes. As a result, we obtain different vocabulary simply by rotating the same shape, as table 1 shows.

Table 1. Kansei Vocabulary of Shape

Shape	Kansei Vocabulary
	accurate, arranged, fixed, neat, perfect, standard, static, hard
	nervous, confusing, curious, essential, mysterious, sensible, twinkling, variable

In the system with TSR, the results contained many wrong shapes using the query that is based on the Kansei vocabulary for square. This is because the TSR similarity method for shape matching considered only the low-level features of object. The TSR used both the arc-length and the angle of shapes. The result is that the two shapes show the same measure similarity as figure 4 shows.

However, human Kansei, which considers high level features, results in very different Kansei vocabulary, as table 1 shows. Insufficient results were obtained from using the existing similarity measure method for shape retrieval based on simple perception. Therefore, we designed and proposed adaptive-TSR to complement the existing TSR to obtain suitable retrieval results based on human Kansei.

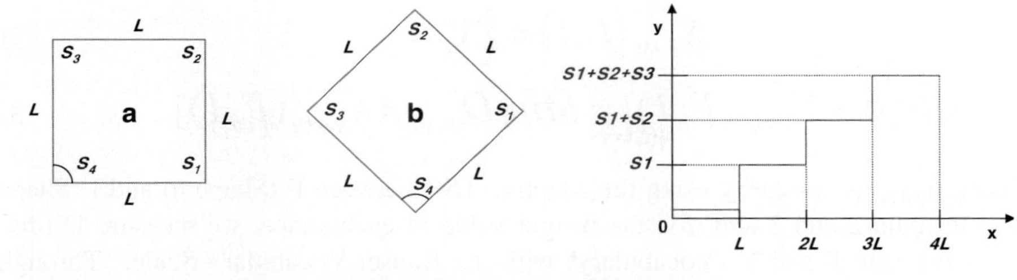

Fig. 4. Similarity Measure using TSR

3.2 Adaptive-TSR

For image retrieval using Kansei information of shape, we designed a new adaptive similarity measure method to modify the existing TSR method. This is named "adaptive-TSR." As mentioned previously, the surveyed results about Kansei information of shapes show different Kansei according to rotation despite same shape. Therefore, to apply Kansei information, we found the Kansei factor of shape then added rotation preprocess to the existing TSR. Figure 5 shows the adaptive-TSR method.

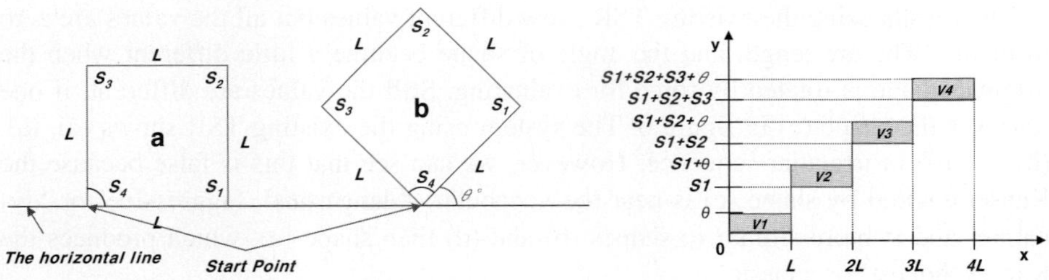

Fig. 5. Similarity Measure using Adaptive-TSR

The existing TSR method represents a step function about the value of the arc length and angle of shapes. We designed a method that is able to measure the rotation value through the inclination angle of the shape. Firstly, for this measurement, we decide the start point of shape. The start point is used to measure the similarity of the shapes. The start point is selected from the left point of the lowest points. A horizontal line passing the start point is created to measure the inclination angle. After this, a second point is decided from the first apex of the right side of the start point.

Using the start point, the second point and the horizontal line, we can calculate the rotation angle of shapes. After measuring the rotation angle, this method uses the arc length and angle of shape and represents a step function like the existing TSR. As figure 5 showed, this method can measure each different result according to the degree of rotation of the shapes. Formula 1, 2 and 3 indicate the formula of this method.

$$P_y(T(S_n)) = \begin{cases} n = 1, ang(\theta) \\ n \geq 2, ang(S_n) \end{cases} \tag{1}$$

$$S_{a-TSR}(F,I)=\sum_{i=1}^{n}V_i \tag{2}$$

$$Min[\alpha\times S_{a-TSR}(F,I)]=Min[D_{|F-V|}\times S_{a-TSR}(F,I)] \tag{3}$$

Where, $S_{a\text{-}TSR}$ is similarity using the adaptive-TSR between F (Shape a) and I (Shape b) in formula 2 and 3 and α is the weight value of each shape, we measure D (distance) between F and V (Vocabulary) with the Kansei-Vocabulary Scale. Through the above process, this method considers the difference of Kansei by the rotation angle. Using the proposed method, we developed a Kansei based image retrieval system and displayed a comparison of the existing TSR based system and our method.

4 Experimental Results and Evaluation

To evaluate the adaptive-TSR, we implemented 2 experiments. First is a simple experimentation that measures the similarity value between the existing TSR method and the adaptive-TSR method when the shapes are rotated 20, 45 and 60 degrees, as figure 6 shows. Table 2 and 3 show the results of the first experimentation.

The results using the existing TSR show different values but all the values are zero in theory. The arc length and the angle of shape become a little different when the original image is rotated by force for evaluating. Still the values are different, if one retrieves the shape (c) in figure 6. The system using the existing TSR shows (c), (a), (b) and (d) in irregular sequence. However, we can see that this is false because the Kansei elicited by shape (c) is near the vocabulary 'dangerous', 'aggressive' or 'dynamic' and is more similar to shapes (b) and (d) than shape (a), which produces the Kansei 'honest' or 'classic'.

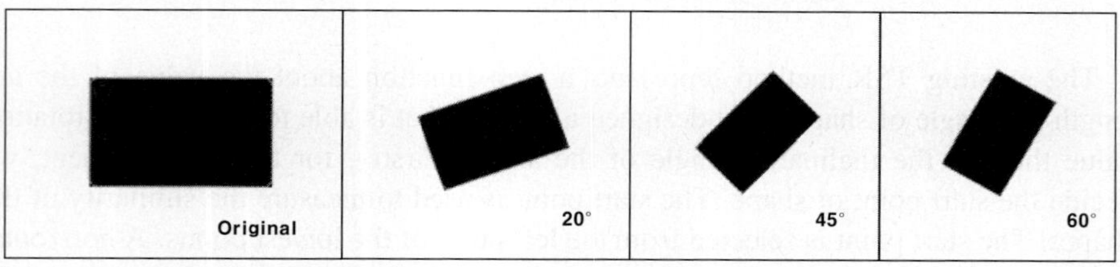

Fig. 6. Rotated Shapes

Table 2. Values using the Existing TSR

	(a) original	(b) 20°	(c) 45°	(d) 60°
(a) original		761	180	857
(b) 20°	761		763	274
(c) 45°	180	763		1037
(d) 60°	857	274	1037	

Table 3. Values using the Adaptive-TSR

	(a) original	(b) 20°	(c) 45°	(d) 60°
(a) original		17999	44190	57823
(b) 20°	17999		26191	39922
(c) 45°	44190	26191		13935
(d) 60°	57823	39922	13935	

On the other hand, the results using the adaptive-TSR display substantially different values for each shape. When someone wants to retrieve the shape (c), the result arrays (c), (d), (b) and (a) in order. This is effective in accurately applying the angle between the shape and the horizontal line despite being the same shapes. Also, through this result, the system using the adaptive-TSR can be applied to a sensitive Kansei about the inclination of the shape.

To evaluate our new method, we developed systems using the existing TSR method and the adaptive-TSR which are based on human Kansei to apply the real retrieval in the second experiment. Figures 7 and 8 are image retrieval systems and show the results using the query 'fixed' by the Shape-Kansei Vocabulary.

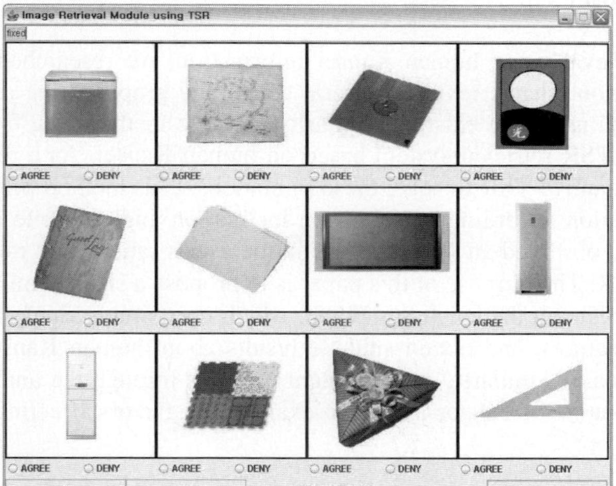

Fig. 7. Image Retrieval System using the Existing TSR Method

We tested the user's satisfaction rate through the results of the vocabulary to compare the two systems. Before providing a question to users, we asked them to exclude the Kansei elements (color, pattern, etc) excepting shape so as to not miss the aim of this system. We displayed images of each Kansei vocabulary and then record the total user's satisfaction rate. The quested result of the researched Kansei vocabulary [4] of the shape was 71% using the existing TSR system and 82% using the adaptive- TSR. This proves that the adaptive-TSR method is more efficient and accurate in the image retrieval system based on Kansei.

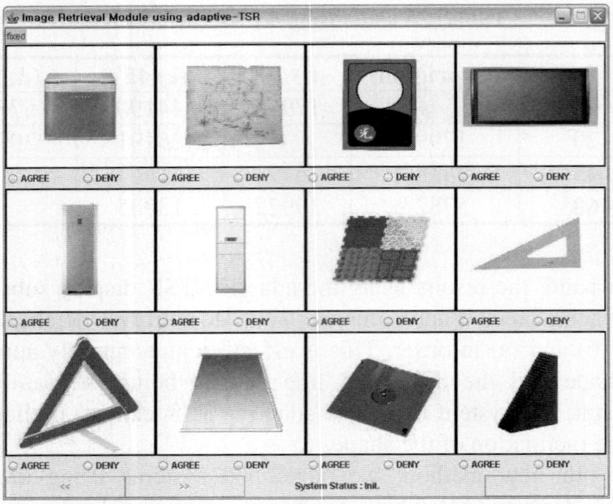

Fig. 8. Image Retrieval System using the Adaptive-TSR Method

5 Conclusions

For image retrieval using human Kansei information, we researched the shapes of visual information (shape, texture, pattern, color) and proposed the retrieval method based on Kansei using the existing similarity measure method. We found limitations in the existing TSR retrieval system based on human Kansei. As a result, this paper proposed the adaptive-TSR to solve these limitations. This method produced different Kansei information according to the shape inclination angle despite being the same object. Also we observed an 11% increase in the user's satisfaction rate above that of the existing TSR. The purpose of this paper is to propose a shape similarity method of Kansei to complement the existing method, which uses simple shape-matching based on low level features, and obtain suitable results about human Kansei. We will research Kansei based similarity measurement methods through the analysis and application of the rotation of a shape as well as examine the factors affecting Kansei.

Acknowledgments

This study was supported by Ministry of Culture & Tourism and Culture & Content Agency in Republic of Korea.

References

[1] Hideki Yamazaki, Kunio Kondo, "A Method of Changing a Color Scheme with Kansei Scales," Journal for Geometry and Graphics, vol. 3, no. 1, pp.77-84, 1999

[2] Shunji Murai, Kunihiko Ono and Naoyuki Tanaka, "Kansei-based Color Design for City Map," ARSRIN 2001, vol. 1, no. 3, 2001

[3] Nadia Bianchi-Berthouze, "An Interactive Environment for Kansei Data Mining," The Proceeding of Second International Workshop on Multimedia Data Mining, pp. 58-67, 2001

[4] Sunkyoung Baek, Myunggwon Hwang, Miyoung Cho, Chang Choi, and Pankoo Kim, "Object Retrieval by Query with Sensibility based on the Kansei-Vocabulary Scale," Computer Vision in Human-Computer Interaction, The Proceeings of the ECCV2006 Workshop on HCI, LNCS 3979, pp. 109-119, 2006

[5] Longin Jan Latecki, Rolf Lakämper, "Shape Similarity Measure Based on Correspondence of Visual Parts," IEEE Transactions on Pattern Analysis and Machine Intelligence, vol. 22, no. 10, 2000

[6] Alberto Chávez-Aragón, Oleg Starostenko, "Ontological shape-description, a new method for visual information retrieval," Proceedings of the 14th International Conference on Electronics, Communications and Computers (CONIELECOMP'04), 2004

[7] Alberto Chávez-Aragón, Oleg Starostenko, "Image Retrieval by Ontological Description of Shapes (IRONS), Early Results," Proceedings of the First Canadian Conference on Computer and Robot Vision, pp. 341-346, 2004

[8] http://www.math.uni-hamburg.de/projekte/shape/

[9] Mitsuteru KOKUBUN, "System for Visualizing Individual Kansei Information," Industrial Electronics Society, IECON 2000, pp. 1592-1597, vol. 3, 2000

[10] Sunkyoung Baek, Kwangpil Ko, Hyein Jeong, Namgeun Lee, Sicheon You, Pankoo Kim, *The Creation of KANSEI-Vocabulary Scale by Shape*, Petra Pernaer (Ed.): Proceeding of Industrial Conference on Data Mining, ibai, pp. 258-268, 2006.

Distributions of Functional and Content Words Differ Radically*

Igor A. Bolshakov and Denis M. Filatov

Center for Computing Research (CIC)
National Polytechnic Institute (IPN), Mexico City, Mexico
igor@cic.ipn.mx, denisfilatov@gmail.com

Abstract. We consider statistical properties of prepositions—the most numerous and important functional words in European languages. Usually, they syntactically link verbs and nouns to nouns. It is shown that their rank distributions in Russian differ radically from those of content words, being much more compact. The Zipf law distribution commonly used for content words fails for them, and thus approximations flatter at first ranks and steeper at higher ranks are applicable. For these purposes, the Mandelbrot family and an expo-logarithmic family of distributions are tested, and an insignificant difference between the two least-square approximations is revealed. It is proved that the first dozen of ranks cover more than 80% of all preposition occurrences in the DB of Russian collocations of Verb-Preposition-Noun and Noun-Preposition-Noun types, thus hardly leaving room for the rest two hundreds of available Russian prepositions.

1 Introduction

All words in natural language are divided to content (autonomous) and functional (auxiliary) words. Content words consist of nouns, verbs (except auxiliary and modal ones), adjectives, and adverbs, whereas functional words are prepositions, conjunctions, and particles. (We ignore pronouns in this classification.)

Prepositions are the most numerous and important functional words. They have rather abstract senses and are used to syntactically link content words. The following two types of prepositional links are topical for this paper, namely, *Verb* → *Preposition* → *Noun* (collocations of VN type) and *Noun* → *Preposition* → *Noun* (collocations of NN type), e.g. in English *differ* → *on* → (...) *issues, matter* → *for* → (...) *police*, where the ellipses are words not entering the given syntactical chains.

Content words are much more numerous than functional words. Practically all words in any machine dictionary are content words. Their rank distributions in texts usually conform to Zipf's law sloping down very slow, approximately as $1/r$, where r is the rank [2, 3]. Because of the slow slope the Zipf distribution is rarely used to determine the size of a necessary dictionary for a specific natural language processing (NLP) application. Nearly always a text under processing reveals content words that

* Work done under partial support of Mexican Government (CONACyT, SNI, SIP-IPN). Many thanks to Steve Legrand for good suggestions.

A. Gelbukh and C.A. Reyes-Garcia (Eds.): MICAI 2006, LNAI 4293, pp. 838 – 843, 2006.

are not included to the actual dictionary, and it is necessary to include new words to the dictionary or to develop a subprogram that somehow recognizes unknown words.

For functional words, no method of approximate recognition is imaginable, and NLP developers should know all the anticipated words of this class beforehand. At the same time, lists of functional words, of any kind, even short, are not closed and in principle are changeable along the time. Hence, the developers need statistical distributions for functional words much more acutely than for content words to estimate priorities that are to be given the various functional words in the systems under development.

In this paper we give empirical rank distributions of the prepositions used in two large collections of Russian collocations, namely, of VN and NN types mentioned above. The numbers of collocations with prepositions (68,533 and 31,489, respectively) seem to be statistically significant to warrant good mathematical approximations for the empirical distributions to be considered. The approximation functions are taken from the Zipf-Mandelbrot family and an expo-logarithmic family suggested in this paper. Both families gave very close least-square results and signified that distributions for functional words, as compared with content words, are much flatter for small ranks (1 to 12), and much steeper for large ranks (more than 20) sloping down approximately as $r^{-2.7}$. For such distributions, the portion of the first dozen of ranks exceeds 80%, hardly leaving room for the rest of the hundreds of prepositions known in the language. Taking the approximate distributions, one may easily determine how many prepositions are necessary to cover collocations to the level, say, 90%, 95% or 98%.

2 Relevant Rank Distributions

In linguistics and in other humanities, as well as in various other areas of the life, rank distributions of many collections approximately have the shape of the Zipf law [2, 3]:

$$P_Z(r) = H(q,R) \times r^{-q}, \quad r = 1...R. \tag{1}$$

In (1), r is the rank, $H(q,R)$ is a normalizing constant, $R >> 1$, and the constant q is close to 1. Among the most popular Zipf-governable examples, frequencies of words in English texts, frequencies of accesses to Web pages, populations of cities, and sizes of earthquakes may be mentioned.

To adapt distribution (1) to collections having a leading group with nearly the same occurrence rates, the Zipf–Mandelbrot family was proposed [4]:

$$P_M(r) = H(q,k,R) \times (k + r)^{-q}, \quad r = 1...R, \tag{2}$$

where $H(q,k,R)$ is a normalizing constant, the constant k gives the number of leaders, and q retains its proximity to 1.

This paper considers linguistic collections whose distributions can be approximated by the Zipf–Mandelbrot law with a greater value of q (more than 2.5) and k exceeding 5.

As a competitor for family (2), we propose the expo-logarithmic family

$$P_Q(r) = H(B,q,R) \times \exp(-B \times (\ln r)^q), \quad r = 1...R, \tag{3}$$

where $H(B,q,R)$ is a normalizing constant, B is a positive constant and $q > 1$.

All constants in (2) and (3) are to be estimated numerically by means of the available experimental data.

3 Preposition Distribution for VN Collocations

There are 209,105 VN collocations available in the database [1], and 68,533 of them including 243 various prepositions.

The empirical rank distribution $P(r)$ of VN prepositions proved to be very inhomogeneous. Table 1 shows the percentage of prepositions of the first twelve ranks. The

Table 1. Prepositions of 12 ranks for VN collocations

Rank	Prepos.	Gloss	Occur.	%
1	v_1	into	9094	13.3
2	v_2	in	8861	12.9
3	na_1	onto	8625	12.6
4	k	to	6484	9.5
5	na_2	on	4964	7.2
6	ot	from	3812	5.6
7	s_2	with	3570	5.2
8	po_1	on	2870	4.2
9	iz	from	2612	3.8
10	za_1	on	2202	3.2
11	o_2	about	1477	2.2
12	s_1	with	1276	1.9
		Total	55847	81.5

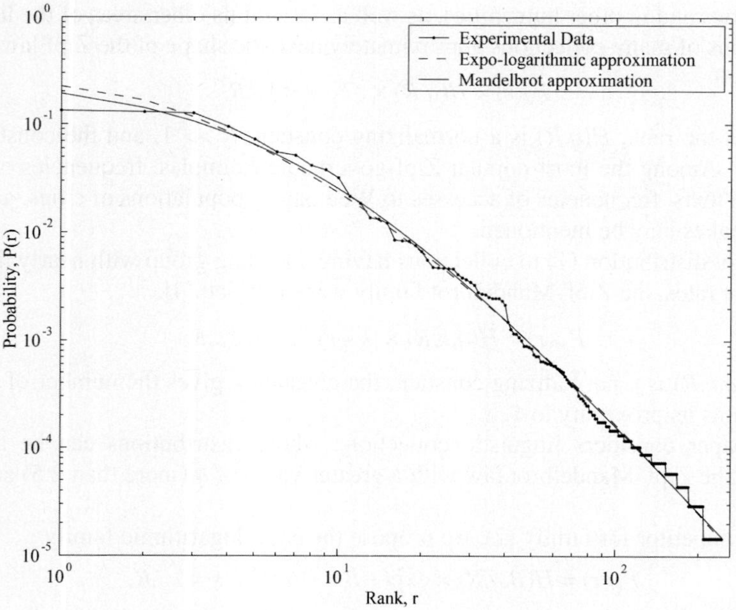

Fig. 1. Preposition distribution for VN vs. two its approximations

subindexes 1 and 2 distinguish homonymous prepositions, which are equal in letters but have different meaning and thus require different grammatical cases. For example, v_1 'into' requires accusative case, while v_2 'in' requires prepositional case.

The prepositions of the ranks r 1 to 4 (1.6% of the whole preposition set) cover 48.2% of collocations with prepositions, the ranks 1 to 12 (4.9% of the whole set) cover 81.5% of collocations, the ranks 1 to 22 (9.1% of the whole set) cover 90.4% of collocations, and the ranks 1 to 35 (14.4% of the whole set) cover 95.2 % of collocations.

The experimental data were used to construct two approximations, one of Mandelbrot and the other of expo-logarithmic families. The results are shown in Fig. 1. Both approximations are good and nearly the same for r exceeding 3. They clearly reveal a leading group and slope steeply after the rank 12. Numerically, the least-square Mandelbrot approximation is $75.1 \times (7.48 + r)^{-2.79}$, while the least-square expo-logarithmic approximation is $0.224 \times \exp(-0.562 \times (\ln r)^{1.67})$.

4 Preposition Distribution for NN Collocations

In [1], there are 133,388 collocations of the type NN, and 31,489 of them include prepositions. We considered the same 243 prepositions as for VN, but 29 of them did not occur among NN collocations. The trends of the distribution are nearly the same. Table 2 shows the percentage of prepositions of the first twelve ranks. The rightmost column shows that the ranks 1 to 10 are occupied by the same prepositions as for VN collocations, but in a slightly different order.

The prepositions of the ranks 1 to 4 (1.6% of the whole preposition set) cover 42.0% of collocations with prepositions, the ranks 1 to 12 (4.9% of the whole set) cover 82.5% of collocations, the ranks 1 to 20 (8.2% of the whole set) cover 90.2% of collocations, and the ranks 1 to 32 (13.2% of the whole set) cover 95.1% of collocations. Again, one can see a strong leading group of prepositions.

Table 2. Prepositions of 12 ranks for NN collocations

NN Rank	Prepos.	Gloss	Occur.	%	VN Rank
1	v_2	in	4271	13.6	2
2	na_1	onto	3278	10.4	3
3	k	to	2995	9.5	4
4	v_1	into	2690	8.5	1
5	s_2	with	2307	7.3	7
6	po_1	on	2143	6.8	8
7	na_2	on	1948	6.2	5
8	o_2	about	1553	4.9	11
9	*ot*	from	1395	4.4	8
10	*iz*	from	1298	4.1	9
11	*dlja*	for	1252	4.0	18
12	za_1	for	847	2.7	10
		Total	24977	82.5	

In Fig. 2 we compare the experimental data and the corresponding least-square approximations. For the Zipf-Mandelbrot approximation we obtained $30.8 \times (5.13 + r)^{-2.63}$, while for the expo-logarithmic one, $0.326\times\exp(-0.763\times(\ln r)^{1.51})$. Both approximations are good for ranks exceeding 12 and practically coincide there.

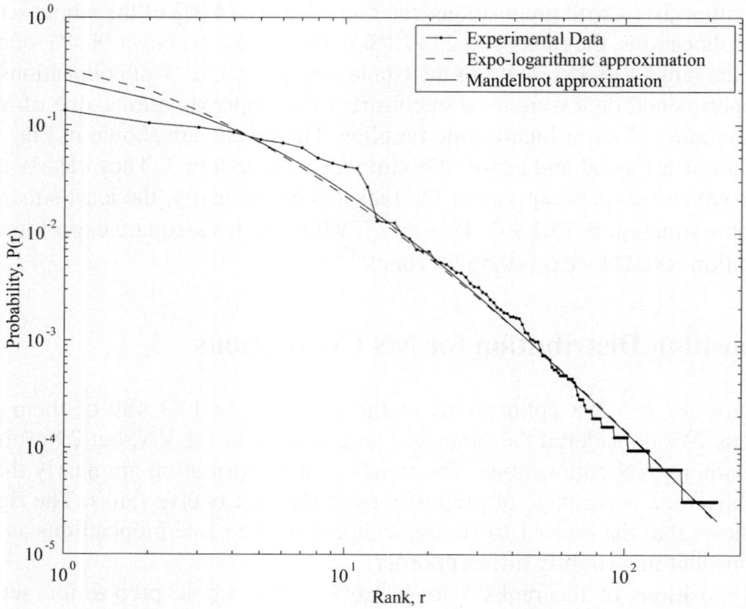

Fig. 2. Preposition distribution for NN vs. two its approximations

5 Comparison with Internet Statistics

A question may arise whether the statistics of the use of prepositions in a collocation collection, even if large, really correlate with the statistics of prepositions in texts. Hence we compared the ranks of different prepositions in our database and in the Web, e.g. in the world largest text corpus. Regrettably, a comparison is only possible when using the following simplifying assumptions.

First, any search engine delivers only document statistics, i.e. of Web pages including the given word, not of this word as such. We admit document statistics as an approximate measure of separate word usage.

Second, we cannot discriminate the page statistics of various homonymous prepositions and cannot separate the page statistics of one-word prepositions from those multiword prepositions that include these one-word units. In such a situation, we accumulated occurrence numbers in our database of 12 high rank basic prepositions, ignoring their meaning differences and whether they are standalone prepositions or proper parts of other multiword prepositions.

The results of comparison of preposition ranks for VN collocations and their ranks in Russian search engine Yandex are given in Table 3. (Web page numbers were rounded to the nearest millions.)

Table 3. Preposition ranks in VN collocations and in the Web

VN rank	Prepos.	Numbs in DB	Web page numbs. $/10^6$	Web rank
1	*v*	19168	572	1
2	*na*	13898	527	2
3	*k*	6525	303	6
4	*s*	5222	442	3
5	*ot*	3859	280	7
6	*za*	3133	266	9
7	*po*	2922	433	4
8	*iz*	2601	278	8
9	*o*	1551	370	5
10	*pod*	1124	101	12
11	*do*	932	183	11
12	*u*	853	244	10

As one can see, the 12 highest ranked prepositions in the Web are the same as in the collocation database, and the first two prepositions *v* 'in/into' and *na* 'on/onto' are merely the same. Taking into account that just the same prepositions are prevalent in the set of Russian collocations, we admit that there exist a strong rank correlation between preposition frequencies in collocation sets and in texts, and all our considerations based on collocations are to sufficient degree valid for texts.

6 Conclusions

Our statistical analysis has shown that distributions of functional words in language differ radically from those of content words. Instead of well-known Zipf-like distributions, approximations much flatter for ranks less than 10 and much steeper for ranks exceeding 20 should be applied.

The Zipf-Mandelbrot family of rank distributions fits the experimental data, sloping down approximately as $r^{-2.7}$. Alternatively, the suggested expo-logarithmic family provides very near results. Hence, any of these approximate families can be used in linguistic practice for determining how many functional words of a given class should be taken to satisfy a level of precision fitting any NL applications.

References

1. Bolshakov, I.A., Getting One's First Million…Collocations. *Lecture Notes in Computer Science* No. 2945, Springer, 2004, p. 229–242.
2. Gelbukh, A., Sidorov G,. Zipf and Heaps Laws' Coefficients Depend on Language. *Lecture Notes in Computer Science* No. 2004, Springer, 2001, p. 330–333.
3. *Wikipedia*, the WEB free encyclopedia, http://en.wikipedia.org/wiki/Zipf%27s_law
4. *Wikipedia*, the WEB free encyclopedia, http://en.wikipedia.org/wiki/Zipf-Mandelbrot_law

Speeding Up Target-Language Driven Part-of-Speech Tagger Training for Machine Translation

Felipe Sánchez-Martínez, Juan Antonio Pérez-Ortiz, and Mikel L. Forcada

Transducens Group – Departament de Llenguatges i Sistemes Informàtics
Universitat d'Alacant, E-03071 Alacant, Spain
{fsanchez, japerez, mlf}@dlsi.ua.es

Abstract. When training hidden-Markov-model-based part-of-speech (PoS) taggers involved in machine translation systems in an unsupervised manner the use of target-language information has proven to give better results than the standard Baum-Welch algorithm. The target-language-driven training algorithm proceeds by translating every possible PoS tag sequence resulting from the disambiguation of the words in each source-language text segment into the target language, and using a target-language model to estimate the likelihood of the translation of each possible disambiguation. The main disadvantage of this method is that the number of translations to perform grows exponentially with segment length, translation being the most time-consuming task. In this paper, we present a method that uses *a priori* knowledge obtained in an unsupervised manner to prune unlikely disambiguations in each text segment, so that the number of translations to be performed during training is reduced. The experimental results show that this new pruning method drastically reduces the amount of translations done during training (and, consequently, the time complexity of the algorithm) without degrading the tagging accuracy achieved.

1 Introduction

One of the classical ways to train part-of-speech (PoS) taggers based on hidden-Markov-models [1] (HMM) in an unsupervised manner is by means of the Baum-Welch algorithm [2]. However, when the resulting PoS tagger is to be embedded within a machine translation (MT) systems, the use of information not only from the source language (SL), but also from the target language (TL) has proven to give better results [3].

The TL-driven training algorithm [3] proceeds by translating every possible PoS tag sequence resulting from the disambiguation of the words in each SL text segment into the TL, and using a probabilistic TL model to estimate the likelihood of the translation corresponding to each possible disambiguation. The main disadvantage of this method is that the number of possible disambiguations to translate grows exponentially with the segment length. As a consequence of that, segment length must be constrained to keep time complexity under control,

A. Gelbukh and C.A. Reyes-Garcia (Eds.): MICAI 2006, LNAI 4293, pp. 844–854, 2006.

therefore rejecting the potential benefits of likelihoods estimated from longer segments. Moreover, translation is the most time-consuming task of the training algorithm.

This paper presents a method that uses *a priori* knowledge, obtained in an unsupervised manner, to prune or rule out unlikely disambiguations of each segment, so that the number of translations to be performed is reduced. The method proceeds as follows; first, the SL training corpus is preprocessed to compute initial HMM parameters; and then, the SL corpus is processed by the TL-driven training algorithm using the initial HMM parameters to prune, that is, to avoid translating the least likely disambiguations of each SL text segment. The experimental results show that the number of words to be translated by the TL-driven training algorithm is drastically reduced without degrading the tagging accuracy. Moreover, we have found out that the tagging accuracy is slightly better when pruning.

As seen in section 5, the open-source MT engine Opentrad Apertium [4], which uses HMM-based PoS tagging during SL analysis, has been used for the experiments. It must be pointed out that the TL-driven training method described in [3], along with the pruning method proposed in this paper, have been implemented in the package name `apertium-tagger-training-tools`, and released under the GPL license.[1]

The rest of the paper is organized as follows: Section 2 overviews the use of HMM for PoS tagging. In section 3 the TL-driven HMM-based PoS tagger training method is explained; then, in section 4 the pruning technique used in the experiments is explained in detail. Section 5 overviews the open-source MT engine used to test our new approach, the experiments conducted and the results achieved. Finally, in sections 6 and 7 the results are discussed and future work is outlined.

2 Hidden Markov Models for Part-of-Speech Tagging

This section overviews the application of HMMs in the natural language processing field as PoS taggers.

A first-order HMM [1] is defined as $\lambda = (\Gamma, \Sigma, A, B, \pi)$, where Γ is the set of states, Σ is the set of observable outputs, A is the $|\Gamma|\times|\Gamma|$ matrix of state-to-state transition probabilities, B is the $|\Gamma|\times|\Sigma|$ matrix with the probability of each observable output $\sigma \in \Sigma$ being emitted from each state $\gamma \in \Gamma$, and the vector π, with dimensionality $|\Gamma|$, defines the initial probability of each state. The system produces an output each time a state is reached after a transition.

When a first-order HMM is used to perform PoS tagging, each HMM state γ is made to correspond to a different PoS tag, and the set of observable outputs Σ are made to correspond to *word classes*. In many applications a word class is an *ambiguity class* [5], that is, the set of all possible PoS tags that a word could

[1] The MT engine and the `apertium-tagger-training-tools` package can be downloaded from `http://apertium.sourceforge.net`.

receive. Moreover, when a HMM is used to perform PoS tagging, the estimation of the initial probability of each state can be conveniently avoided by assuming that each sentence begins with the end-of-sentence mark. In this case, $\pi(\gamma)$ is 1 when γ is the end-of-sentence mark, and 0 otherwise. A deeper description of the use of this kind of statistical models for PoS tagging may be found in [5] and [6, ch. 9].

3 Target-Language-Driven Training Overview

This section overviews the TL-driven training method that constitutes the basis of the work reported in this paper. A deeper and more formal description of the TL-driven training method may be found in [3].

Typically, the training of HMM-based PoS taggers is done using the *maximum-likelihood estimate* (MLE) method [7] when tagged corpora[2] are available (supervised method), or using the Baum-Welch algorithm [2,5] with untagged corpora[3] (unsupervised method). But when the resulting PoS tagger is to be embedded as a module of a working MT system, HMM training can be done in an unsupervised manner by using information not only from the SL, but also from the TL.

The main idea behind the use of TL information is that the correct disambiguation (tag assignment) of a given SL segment will produce a more likely TL translation than any (or most) of the remaining wrong disambiguations. In order to apply this method these steps are followed: first the SL text is segmented; then, the set of all possible disambiguations for each text segment are generated and translated into the TL; next, a statistical TL model is used to compute the likelihood of the translation of each disambiguation; and, finally, these likelihoods are used to adjust the parameters of the SL HMM: the higher the likelihood, the higher the probability of the original SL tag sequence in the HMM being trained. The number of possible disambiguations of a text segment grows exponentially with its length; therefore, the number of translations to be performed by this training algorithm is very high. Indeed, the translation of segments is the most time-consuming task in this method.

Let us illustrate how this training method works with the following example. Consider the following segment in English, $s =$ *"He books the room"*, and that an indirect MT system translating between English and Spanish is available. The first step is to use a morphological analyzer to obtain the set of all possible PoS tags for each word. Suppose that the morphological analysis of the previous segment according to the lexicon is: *He* (pronoun), *books* (verb or noun), *the* (article) and *room* (verb or noun). As there are two ambiguous words (*books* and *room*) we have, for the given segment, four disambiguation *paths* or PoS combinations, that is to say:

[2] In a *tagged corpus* each occurrence of each word (ambiguous or not) has been assigned the correct PoS tag.

[3] In an *untagged corpus* all words are assigned (using, for instance, a morphological analyzer) the set of all possible PoS tags independently of context.

- $\boldsymbol{g_1}$ = (pronoun, verb, article, noun),
- $\boldsymbol{g_2}$ = (pronoun, verb, article, verb),
- $\boldsymbol{g_3}$ = (pronoun, noun, article, noun), and
- $\boldsymbol{g_4}$ = (pronoun, noun, article, verb).

Let τ be the function representing the translation task. The next step is to translate the SL segment into the TL according to each disambiguation path $\boldsymbol{g_i}$:

- $\tau(\boldsymbol{g_1}, s) =$ "*Él reserva la habitación*",
- $\tau(\boldsymbol{g_2}, s) =$"*Él reserva la aloja*",
- $\tau(\boldsymbol{g_3}, s) =$"*Él libros la habitación*", and
- $\tau(\boldsymbol{g_4}, s) =$"*Él libros la aloja*".

It is expected that a Spanish language model will assign a higher likelihood to translation $\tau(\boldsymbol{g_1}, s)$ than to the other ones, which make little sense in Spanish. So the tag sequence $\boldsymbol{g_1}$ will have a higher probability than the other ones.

To estimate the HMM parameters, the calculated probabilities are used as if fractional counts were available to a supervised training method based on the MLE method in conjunction with a smoothing technique. In the experiments reported in section 5 to estimate the HMM parameters we used the *expected likelihood estimate* (ELE) method [7] that consists of adding a fixed initial count to each event before applying the MLE method.

4 Pruning of Disambiguation Paths

Next, we focus on the main disadvantage of this training method (the large number of translations that need to be performed) and how to overcome it. The aim of the new method presented in this section is to reduce as much as possible the number of translations to perform without degrading the tagging accuracy achieved by the resulting PoS tagger.

4.1 Pruning Method

The disambiguation pruning method is based on *a priori* knowledge, that is, on an initial model M_{tag} of SL tags. The assumption here is that any reasonable model of SL tags may prove helpful to choose a set of possible disambiguation paths, so that the correct one is in that set. Therefore, there is no need to translate all possible disambiguation paths of each segment into the TL, but only the most "promising" ones.

The model M_{tag} of SL tags to be used can be either a HMM or another model whose parameters are obtained by means of a statistically sound method. Nevertheless, using a HMM as an initial model allows the method to dynamically update it with the new evidence collected during training (see section 4.2 for more details).

The pruning of disambiguation paths for a given SL text segment s is carried out as follows: First, the *a priori* likelihood $p(\boldsymbol{g_i}|s, M_{\text{tag}})$ of each possible disambiguation path $\boldsymbol{g_i}$ of segment s is calculated given the tagging model M_{tag}; then, the set of disambiguation paths to take into account is determined according to the calculated *a priori* likelihoods.

Let $T(s) = \{\boldsymbol{g_1}, \ldots, \boldsymbol{g_n}\}$ be the set of all possible disambiguation paths of SL segment s, ordered in decreasing order of their *a priori* likelihood $p(\boldsymbol{g_i}|s, M_{\text{tag}})$. To decide which disambiguation paths to take into account, the pruning algorithm is provided with a mass probability threshold ρ. Thus, the pruning method takes into account only the most likely disambiguation paths of $T(s)$ that make the probability mass threshold ρ to be reached. Therefore, for each segment s the subset $T'(s) \subseteq T(s)$ of disambiguation paths finally taken into account satisfies the property

$$\rho \leq \sum_{\forall \boldsymbol{g_i} \in T'(s)} p(\boldsymbol{g_i}|s, M_{\text{tag}}). \tag{1}$$

4.2 HMM Updating

This section explains how the model used for pruning can be updated during training so that it integrates new evidence collected from the TL. The idea is to periodically estimate a HMM using the counts collected from the TL (as explained in section 3), and to mix the resulting HMM with the initial one; the mixed HMM becomes the new model M_{tag} used for pruning.

The initial model and an improved model obtained during training are mixed so that *a priori* likelihoods are better estimated. The mixing consists, on the one hand of the mixing of the transition probabilities $a_{\gamma_i\gamma_j}$ between HMM states; and, on the other hand, of the mixing of the emission probabilities $b_{\gamma_i\sigma_k}$ of each observable output σ_k being emitted from each HMM state γ_i.

Let $\boldsymbol{\theta} = (a_{\gamma_1\gamma_1}, ..., a_{\gamma_{|\Gamma|}\gamma_{|\Gamma|}}, b_{\gamma_1\sigma_1}, ..., b_{\gamma_{|\Gamma|}\sigma_{|\Sigma|}})$ be a vector containing all the parameters of a given HMM. The mixing of the initial HMM and the new one can be done through the next equation:

$$\boldsymbol{\theta_{\text{mixed}}}(x) = \lambda(x)\, \boldsymbol{\theta_{\text{TL}}}(x) + (1 - \lambda(x))\, \boldsymbol{\theta_{\text{init}}}, \tag{2}$$

where $\boldsymbol{\theta_{\text{mixed}}}(x)$ refers to the HMM parameters after mixing the two models when x words of the training corpus have been processed; $\boldsymbol{\theta_{\text{TL}}}(x)$ refers to the HMM parameters estimated by means of the TL-driven method after processing x words of the SL training corpus; and $\boldsymbol{\theta_{\text{init}}}$ refers to the parameters of the initial HMM. Function $\lambda(x)$ assigns a weight to the model estimated using the counts collected from the TL ($\boldsymbol{\theta_{\text{TL}}}$). This weight function is made to depend on the number x of SL words processed so far. This way the weight of each model can be changed during training.

5 Experiments

In this section we overview the MT system used to train the PoS tagger by means of the TL-driven training algorithm, the experiments conducted, and the results achieved.

5.1 Machine Translation Engine

This section introduces the MT system used in the experiments, although almost any other MT architecture (which uses a HMM-based PoS tagger) may also be used in combination with the TL-driven training algorithm.

We used the open-source shallow-transfer MT engine Opentrad Apertium [4,8] together with linguistic data for the Spanish–Catalan language pair.[4] This MT engine follows a shallow transfer approach and consists of the following pipelined modules:

- A *morphological analyzer* which tokenizes the text in surface forms (SF) and delivers, for each SF, one or more lexical forms (LF) consisting of *lemma*, *lexical category* and morphological inflection information.
- A *PoS tagger* which chooses, using a first order HMM as described in section 2, one of the LFs corresponding to an ambiguous SF. This is the module whose training is considered in this paper.
- A *lexical transfer* module which reads each SL LF and delivers the corresponding TL LF.
- A *structural transfer* module (parallel to the lexical transfer) which uses a finite-state chunker to detect patterns of LFs which need to be processed for word reorderings, agreement, etc. and performs these operations.
- A *morphological generator* which delivers a TL SF for each TL LF, by suitably inflecting it, and performs other orthographical transformations such as contractions.

5.2 Results

We have tested the approach presented in section 4 to train a HMM-based PoS tagger for Spanish, being Catalan the TL, through the MT system described above.

As mentioned in section 3, the TL-driven training method needs a TL model to score the different translations $\tau(\boldsymbol{g_i}, s)$ of each SL text segment s. In this paper we have used a classical trigram language model like the one used in [3]. This language model was trained on a raw-text Catalan corpus with around 2 000 000 words.

To study the behaviour of our pruning method, experiments have been performed with 5 disjoint SL (Spanish) corpora of 500 000 words each. With all the corpora we proceeded in the same way: First the initial model was computed by means of Kupiec's method [9], a common unsupervised initialization method often used before training HMM-based PoS taggers through the Baum-Welch algorithm. After that, the HMM-based PoS tagger was trained by means of the TL-driven training method described in section 3. The HMM used for pruning was updated after every 1 000 words processed as explained in section 4.2. To

[4] Both the MT engine and the linguistic data used can be downloaded from `http://apertium.sourceforge.net`. For the experiments we have used the packages `lltoolbox-1.0.1`, `apertium-1.0.1` and `apertium-es-ca-1.0.1`.

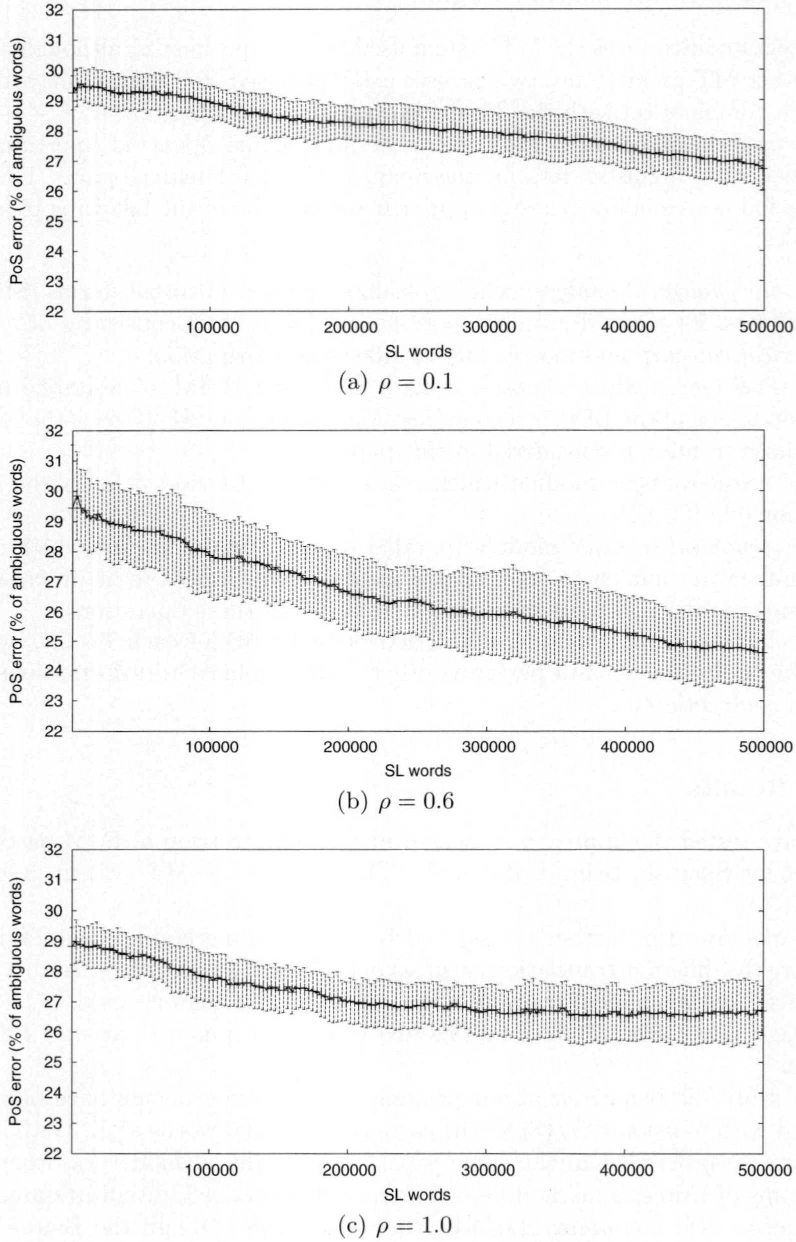

(a) $\rho = 0.1$

(b) $\rho = 0.6$

(c) $\rho = 1.0$

Fig. 1. Mean and standard deviation of the PoS tagging error rate for three different values of the probability mass threshold ρ depending on the number of words processed by the training algorithm. The error rates reported are measured using a Spanish (SL) tagged corpus with around 8 000 words, and are calculated over ambiguous and unknown words only, not over all words.

this end, the weighting function $\lambda(x)$ used in equation (2) was chosen to grow linearly from 0 to 1 with the amount x of words processed:

$$\lambda(x) = x/C, \tag{3}$$

where $C = 500\,000$ is the total number of words of the SL training corpus.

In order to determine the appropriate mass probability threshold ρ that speeds the TL-driven method up without degrading its PoS tagging accuracy we considered a set of values for ρ between 0.1 and 1.0 at increments of 0.1. Note that when $\rho = 1.0$, no pruning is done; that is, all possible disambiguation paths of each segment are translated into the TL.

Figure 1 shows, for three different values of the probability mass threshold ρ, the evolution of the mean and the standard deviation of the PoS tagging error rate; in all cases the HMM being evaluated is the one used for pruning. The error rates reported are measured on a representative Spanish (SL) tagged corpus with around 8 000 words, and are calculated over ambiguous and unknown words only, not over all words. The three different values of the probability mass threshold ρ shown are: the smallest threshold used (0.1), the threshold that provides the best PoS tagging performance (0.6, see also figure 2), and the threshold that makes no pruning at all (1.0).

As can be seen in figure 1 the results achieved by the TL-driven training method are better when $\rho = 0.6$ than when $\rho = 1.0$. Convergence is reached earlier when $\rho = 1.0$.

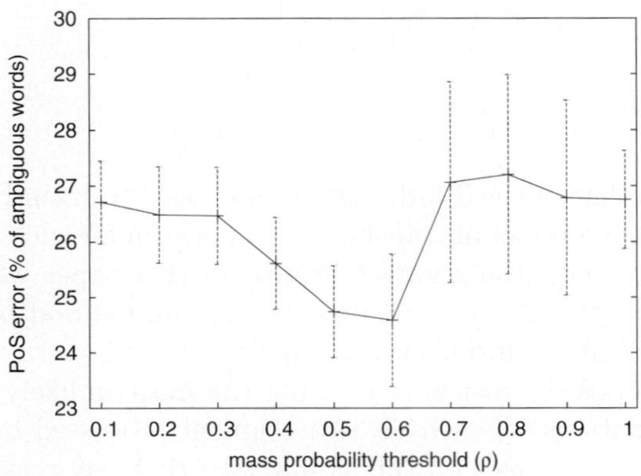

Fig. 2. Mean and standard deviation of the final PoS tagging error rate achieved after processing the whole corpus of 500 000 words for the different values of ρ used

Figure 2 shows the mean and standard deviation of the final PoS tagging error rate achieved after processing the whole training corpora for the different values of ρ. As can be seen, the best results are achieved when $\rho = 0.6$, indeed better than the result achieved when no pruning is performed. However, the standard deviation is smaller when no pruning is done ($\rho = 1.0$).

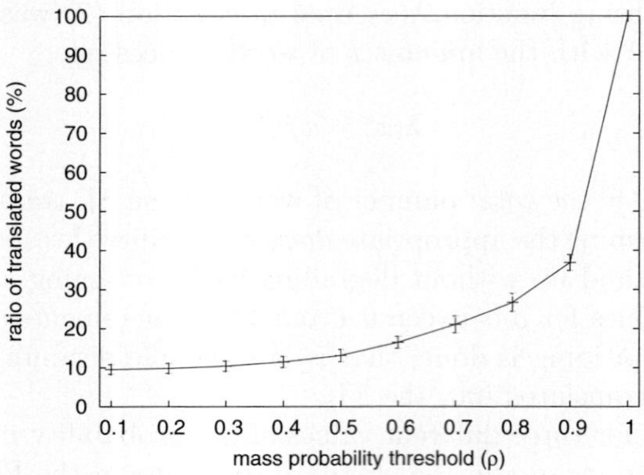

Fig. 3. Percentage of translated words for each value of the probability mass threshold ρ. The percentage of translated words is calculated over the total number of words that are translated when no pruning is done.

As to how many translations are avoided due to the proposed pruning method, figure 3 shows the average ratio, and standard deviation, of the words finally translated to the total number of words to translate when no pruning is performed. As can be seen, with $\rho = 0.6$ the percentage of words translated is around 16%. This percentage can be seen as roughly proportional to the percentage of disambiguation paths needed to reach the corresponding mass probability threshold.

6 Discussion

The main disadvantage of the TL-driven method used to train HMM-based PoS taggers [3] is that the number of translations to perform for each SL text segment grows exponentially with the segment length. In this paper we have proposed and tested a new approach to speed up this training method by using *a priori* knowledge obtained in an unsupervised way from the SL.

The method proposed consists of pruning the most unlikely disambiguation paths (PoS combinations) of each SL text segment processed by the algorithm. This pruning method is based on the assumption that any reasonable model of SL tags may prove helpful to choose a set of possible disambiguation paths, the correct one being included in that set. Moreover, the model used for pruning can be updated along the training with the new data collected while training.

The method presented has been tested on five different corpora and with different mass probability thresholds. The results reported in section 5.2 show, on the one hand, that the pruning method described avoids more than 80% of the translations to perform; and on the other hand, that the results achieved by the TL-driven training method improve if improbable disambiguation paths are not taken into account. This could be explained by the fact that HMM parameters associated to discarded disambiguation paths have a null count; however, when no pruning is done their TL-estimated fractional counts are small, but never null.

7 Future Work

The pruning method described is based on *a priori* knowledge used to calculate the *a priori* likelihood of each possible disambiguation path of a given SL text segment. It has been explained how to update the model used for pruning by mixing the initial HMM provided to the algorithm with the HMM calculated from the counts collected from the TL. In the experiments reported both HMMs have been mixed through equation (2), which needs to be provided with a weighting function λ.

For the experiments we have used the simplest possible weighting function (see equation (3)). This function makes the initial model provided to the algorithm to have a higher weight than the model being learned from the TL until one half of the SL training corpus is processed. In order to explore how fast does the TL-driven training method learns, we plan to try other weighting functions giving earlier a higher weight to the model being learned from the TL.

Finally, we want to test two additional strategies to select the set of disambiguation paths to take into account; on the one hand, a method that changes the probability mass threshold along the training; and on the other hand, a method that instead of using a probability mass threshold uses a fixed number of disambiguation paths (k-best). The last one could be implemented in such a way in which all *a priori* likelihoods do not need to be explicitly calculated before discarding many of them.

Acknowledgements

Work funded by the Spanish Ministry of Science and Technology through project TIC2003-08681-C02-01, and by the Spanish Ministry of Education and Science and the European Social Found through research grant BES-2004-4711. We thank Rafael C. Carrasco (Universitat d'Alacant, Spain) for useful comments on the target-language-driven training method.

References

1. Rabiner, L.R.: A tutorial on hidden Markov models and selected applications in speech recognition. Proceedings of the IEEE **77**(2) (1989) 257–286
2. Baum, L.E.: An inequality and associated maximization technique in statistical estimation of probabilistic functions of a Markov process. Inequalities **3** (1972) 1–8
3. Sánchez-Martínez, F., Pérez-Ortiz, J.A., Forcada, M.L.: Exploring the use of target-language information to train the part-of-speech tagger of machine translation systems. In: Advances in Natural Language Processing, Proceedings of 4th International Conference EsTAL. Volume 3230 of Lecture Notes in Computer Science. Springer-Verlag (2004) 137–148

4. Corbí-Bellot, A.M., Forcada, M.L., Ortiz-Rojas, S., Pérez-Ortiz, J.A., Ramírez-Sánchez, G., Sánchez-Martínez, F., Alegria, I., Mayor, A., Sarasola, K.: An open-source shallow-transfer machine translation engine for the Romance languages of Spain. In: Proceedings of the 10th European Associtation for Machine Translation Conference, Budapest, Hungary (2005) 79–86
5. Cutting, D., Kupiec, J., Pedersen, J., Sibun, P.: A practical part-of-speech tagger. In: Third Conference on Applied Natural Language Processing. Association for Computational Linguistics. Proceedings of the Conference., Trento, Italia (1992) 133–140
6. Manning, C.D., Schütze, H.: Foundations of Statistical Natural Language Processing. MIT press (1999)
7. Gale, W.A., Church, K.W.: Poor estimates of context are worse than none. In: Proceedings of a workshop on Speech and natural language, Morgan Kaufmann Publishers Inc. (1990) 283–287
8. Armentano-Oller, C., Carrasco, R.C., Corbí-Bellot, A.M., Forcada, M.L., Ginestí-Rosell, M., Ortiz-Rojas, S., Pérez-Ortiz, J.A., Ramírez-Sánchez, G., Sánchez-Martínez, F., Scalco, M.A.: Open-source Portuguese-Spanish machine translation. In: Computational Processing of the Portuguese Language, Proceedings of the 7th International Workshop on Computational Processing of Written and Spoken Portuguese, PROPOR 2006. Volume 3960 of Lecture Notes in Computer Science. Springer-Verlag (2006) 50–59
9. Kupiec, J.: Robust part-of-speech tagging using a hidden Markov model. Computer Speech and Language **6**(3) (1992) 225–242

Defining Classifier Regions for WSD Ensembles Using Word Space Features

Harri M.T. Saarikoski[1], Steve Legrand[2,3], and Alexander Gelbukh[3]

[1] KIT Language Technology Doctorate School, Helsinki University, Finland
Harri.Saarikoski@helsinki.fi
[2] Department of Computer Science, University of Jyväskylä, Finland
stelegra@cc.jyu.fi
[3] Instituto Politecnico Nacional, Mexico City, Mexico
gelbukh@gelbukh.com

Abstract. Based on recent evaluation of word sense disambiguation (WSD) systems [10], disambiguation methods have reached a standstill. In [10] we showed that it is possible to predict the best system for target word using word features and that using this 'optimal ensembling method' more accurate WSD ensembles can be built (3-5% over Senseval state of the art systems with the same amount of possible potential remaining). In the interest of developing if more accurate ensembles, w e here define the strong regions for three popular and effective classifiers used for WSD task (Naive Bayes - NB, Support Vector Machine - SVM, Decision Rules - D) using word features (word grain, amount of positive and negative training examples, dominant sense ratio). We also discuss the effect of remaining factors (feature-based).

1 Introduction

Numerous methods of disambiguation have been tried to solve the WSD task [1,8] but no single system or system type (e.g. classifier) has been found to perform superiorly for all target words. The first conclusion from this is that different disambiguation methods result in different performance results. System bias is the inherent and unique capability or tendency of the classifier algorithm to transform training data into a useful sense decision model. A second conclusion is that there is a 'word bias', i.e. each word poses a different set of learning problems. Word bias is the combination of factors particular to that word that cause classification systems to vary their performance considerably. Differences of up to 30% in precision at word can occur even with top systems.

Optimal ensembling method is dedicated to mutually solve these two biases, to map a particular type of system to a particular type of word. It attempts first of all to discover *n* base systems which are as strong and complementary (with regard to performance) as possible and then train itself using training words to recognize which system will be strongest for a given test word. Optimal ensembles have largely been neglected in WSD in favor of single-classifier systems trained on the same feature set?? (e.g. [7,12]) or 'conservative ensembles' (e.g. voting pool of six base systems [9]) where the same system(s) is applied for all test words. It is reasonable to assume that system (and particularly its classifier algorithm ??) strengths tend to follow

A. Gelbukh and C.A. Reyes-Garcia (Eds.): MICAI 2006, LNAI 4293, pp. 855 – 867, 2006.

changes (drops and rises) in the details of each learning task (i.e. ambiguous word). This assumption was proven correct by [13] who showed that systems differ in different regions of word grain, amount of training and most frequent (dominant) sense bias. According to [13], one base system typically excels in the lower and higher regions of a factor and another in the middle region (e.g. NB systems in grain region 12..22 while a transformation-based learner, TBL, thrived in the surrounding regions ..12 and 22.. [13]). **bridge** Effect of classifier selection on classification system performance has been reported in numerous works [2,9,12,14]. For instance, [2] studied the effect of skewing the training distribution on classifier performance. They found three classifiers (Naive Bayes or NB, SVM, Multinomial Naive Bayes) to occupy different but intact regions in word space.

In [10] we presented the method of optimal ensembling of any base systems. The method specifies how we can discover the base systems whose strengths at different learning tasks (words in WSD) complement each other. In this paper, we attempt to further generalize the effect of classifier selection on the strong region of the system using various combinations of three word factors (grain, positive vs negative examples per sense, dominant vs sub-dominant sense ratio). We present two sets of experiments using Senseval-2 and Senseval-3 English lexical sample datasets.

In section 2, we present the machine-learning tools we used for performing the system analyses and prediction tests. In section 3, we discuss the word and system factors we used for predictions. In section 4, we visualize some of the training models to be used by predictors. Final sections 5 and 6 are dedicated to discussions and conclusions.

2 Tools

Study of disambiguation systems lacks a diagnostic tool that could be used to meta-learn the effects of these factors. As a result, the following types of questions are largely unanswered: Which are the words where a system is at its strongest? What type of ensembles of systems achieve optimum performance for give target word?

We are developing a meta-classifier (MOA-SOM, 'mother-of-all-self-organizing-maps') to handle such learning tasks. The tool clusters publicly available WSD system scores [1,8] stored in database [10] based on features defining the systems (e.g. classifier algorithm, feature sets) and target words (e.g. PoS, training, word grain) by calculating the amount of correlation between systems and words. The output from MOA-SOM is the optimal classifier, feature and configuration for that target word. The feature matrix can be fed to SOM using either system names as labels and words as data points or vice versa. The SOM used is based on hierarchically clustering DGSOT [5] which was found useful in earlier WSD experiments [4]. For these tests we additionally employed the machine-learning algorithms implemented in Weka toolkit [11] for training and testing the predictors and YALE toolkit [6] for visualizing the system regions / training models.

In the next section, we define the method of optimal ensembling that was first introduced in [10].

3 Method

foundation for why factors can predict system difference

3.1 Motivation for Factors -> Predictors

The motivation behind optimal ensembles is that classifiers have inherently different solutions to deal with the different learning tasks (and processing the training data). shown in [13]...too much ped in intro already, drop some of it here. In [10] we showed how word factors (e.g. grain) can be used to build a predictor of best system for given target word. Interestingly, it seems that a good system *difference* predictor will also need to be an excellent system *performance* predictor, i.e. predictor of the accuracy of the best base system in the ensemble. Our best predictors in [10] that obtained a high of 0.85 prediction accuracy were correlated strongly or very strongly with base system performance (using Spearman's correlation coefficient we got a high of 0.88 correlation). Furthermore, we found that the very easy or very hard words exhibited little if at all difference between systems.

Based on this intimate correlation, we can draw a schematic (Figure 1) that represents the regions in word space where the biggest vs smallest differences between systems take place (see Figures 2 and 3 ?? for actual maps).

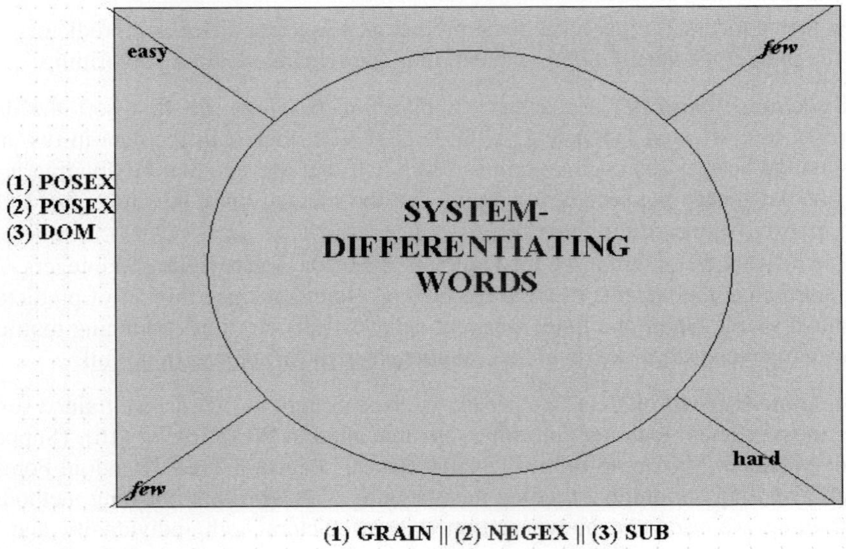

Fig. 1. System-differentiation potential in three factor pairs representing word space - (1) posex-grain, (2) posex-negex and (3) dom-sub. *Posex* is the average number of training instances per sense and *negex* the *average* number of training examples per sense-class. *Dom* and *sub* represent the training distribution between dominant (most frequent) sense and subdominant (next most frequent) sense. *Grain* is obviously the number of senses in the sense repository used in Senseval evaluations (usually WordNet).

In Figure 1, top left corner (e.g. low-grain, high-trainword) features the *easy* words that basically any system can disambiguate to highest accuracy (e.g. *graceful[a]* in Senseval-2). Bottom right corner (e.g. low-posex, high-negex) contains the *hard* words (e.g. *draw[v]* in Senseval-2) that systems find equally hard to disambiguate (typically disambiguation accuracy remains below 50%). The corners marked *few* contain very few words falling into those regions, at least in Senseval evaluations.

In our experiments [10], we largely ignored words in *easy, hard* and *few* regions from our training and testing data as well as and systems whose strength is focused in those regions. Instead we focused on the center region (*System-differentiating words*) where systems exhibit greatest differences in performance. This is simply because the feasibility of net gain by an optimal ensemble over base systems is at its greatest in that center region.

3.2 Factors More Stuff There

We introduce here the three word-based factors in explaining variations in system performance (Train, Grain, and DomSub). *Train* is average number of training instances per sense, *Grain* is the number of senses (as recorded in WordNet / WordSmyth sense repositories used in Senseval evaluations). dom? sub? dom+sub

more elsewhere, do I import test setting?

3.3 Predictors

A few factor formulas emerged as best predictors of system difference predictors. To train the predictors, we used both manual rules and machine-learning algorithms:

(1) Bisections (baseline). To achieve a bisection baseline, we first sort the data according to a selected factor (e.g. T, G, D, T+G+D), then split the data in two and calculate the net gain by each system for each half and average that by dividing it by two. The best weighting scheme we found was the square root of the unweighted sum of normalized values of the three factors: `sqrt (a*T + b*G + c*D)` where *G* stands for Grain, *T* for Train, *D* for DomSub values of target words and integers *a*, *b* and *c* normalize the weights of the three factors. Note that since this set of predictors is limited to one factor at a time, it cannot express decision rules containing multiple factors which tends to make them less reliable. keep those abbrevs or go full?

(2) Machine-learned models. T o predict the best system for words, we trained some of the most efficient learning algorithms implemented in Weka toolkit [16] (Support Vector Machine, Maximum Entropy, Naive Bayes, Decision Trees, Random Forests as well as voting committee, training data bagging and algorithm boosting methods). For training we used the abovementioned word factors both individually and in various permutations (e.g. T-G). rep method

3.4 Optimal Ensembling Method Embedded in a WSD Algorithm

In this section, we outline a method for defining and selecting maximally complementary base systems integrated inside a disambiguation algorithm:

- **Base system selection.** Run candidate base systems on training words. Investigate their performance at different types of words. Based on their performance at training words, select systems whose strong regions are as large and as distinct as possible, i.e. maximally complementary, using the following criteria:
    - biggest gross gain (defined in Evaluation below) of the constructed optimal ensemble over better of candidate base systems
    - largest number of training words won by the system
    - largest strong region define in word spaces define
    - two base systems with a large complementary nature
- **Training the predictor.** Using the training run data, train the predictors to recognize the best base system using readily available factors (e.g. word grain). Predictor can be constructed by setting decision rules manually, e.g. "use system#1 (Decision Tree -based) when number of senses (grain) < 5, system#2 (Naive Bayes -based) when grain is > 5 but not when 20 < train < 25". Alternatively, use a machine-learning algorithm to induce the rules from the training data.
    - In order to *see* maximal complementarity of selected base systems in word space, use drawing of strong regions of base systems, a visualization of the predictor training model (see Figures)
- **Testing.** Run selected base systems and the optimal ensemble according to the system-selection rules set by the best predictor on test words.
- **Evaluation.** Evaluate the performance of the optimal ensemble by comparing it to the better of the base systems. Also evaluate the predictor using *net gain* measure calculated from the following formula:

  ```
  ((PredictionAccuracy - (1.0 / NumberOfSystems)) *2)
                    * GrossGain
  ```

  PredictionAccuracy is the number of correct system-for-word predictions out of all test words and *NumberOfSystems* is the number of classes/systems to predict. *GrossGain* is a measure of the potential of the base systems when they form an ensemble, resulting from a perfect system-for-word prediction for all test words. It is calculated from all-words average net gain by either base system (e.g. in a test set of two words, if system#1 wins over system#2 by 2% at word#1 and system#2 wins over system#1 by 4% at word#2, then gross gain for all test words is (2+4) / 2 = 3%). *Net gain* is then calculated as follows: in a two-system ensemble with 0.80 prediction accuracy and 8.0% gross gain, net gain is ((0.80-0.50)*2)) * 8.0% = 4.8%.
- **Development:** Predictors and base systems should be developed together. Therefore, development of optimal ensembles can start either from good predictors or from good base systems:
    - Keep the ensemble with biggest net gain and try to find a better predictor of best system, altering learning algorithm (svm,log,nb) and/or word factors (e.g. weighting)
    - Keep the ensemble with the best predictor and alter the base systems (make one or several of them stronger) so that a bigger net gain results.

4 Tests

In this section we describe the prediction experiments of SVM/NB based systems in two WSD datasets (Senseval-2 and Senseval-3 English lexical sample).

4.1 Test Setting

We investigated the following factor pairs or word spaces (posex-negex, posex-grain and dom-sub) to define the strong regions of systems based on three classifiers (SVM/NB/D[1]) in Senseval-2 and Senseval-3 English lexical sample evaluation datasets:

Table 1. Systems based on the three classifiers in two datasets

Dataset	Classifier	System names
Senseval-2	SVM	UMCP
	NB	Duluth1, Duluth4
	D	TALP (boosted), DuluthB, Duluth5, Duluth2, Duluth3 (multi)
Senseval-3	SVM	IRST-kernel, nusels, TALP, UMCP
	NB	htsa3, CLaC1, Prob1
	D	SyntaLex3 (multi), Duluth-ELSS (multi) [2]

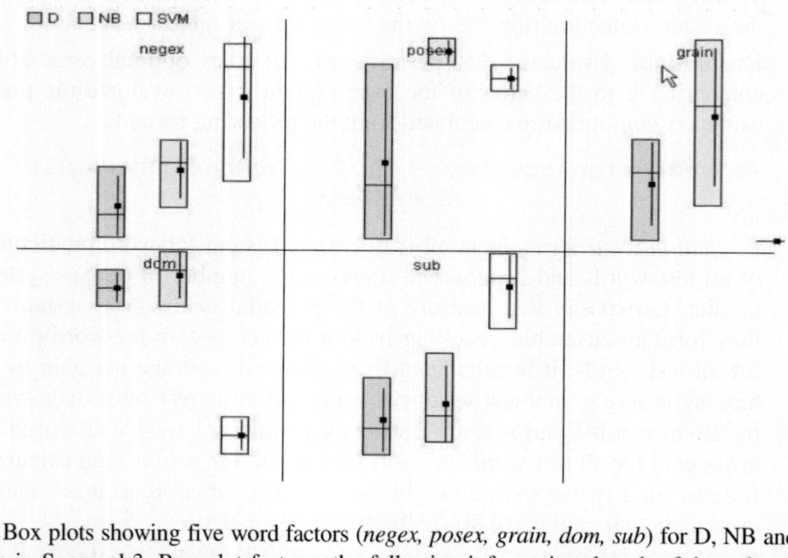

Fig. 2. Box plots showing five word factors (*negex, posex, grain, dom, sub*) for D, NB and SVM systems in Senseval-3. Box plot features the following information: length of the column is the amount of *variation* of values, and the vertical line running through that column indicates actual *maximum* and *minimum* values in the dataset. Square dot in the middle of the column is the *average* of values, horizontal line in the vicinity of that is the *median* member of the dataset.

---

[1] *D* stands for decision rule based classifiers (decision trees, decision lists, decision stumps).

[2] *Multi* signifies that several decision tree classifiers using different feature sets were bagged and a committee decision rendered. *Boosted* signifies that the classifier employed boosting technique (AdaBoost).

Two thirds of available word set was used for training the predictor model, and the remaining one third was used for testing the model. In the following box plot (Figure 2) we see the word factor values for those base systems we are investigating.

In Figure 2, we can see SVM, NB and D based systems differing in practically all factors. Specifically, the system region cores (dot inside the column) are very different and also the variation (range of the filled column) indicating the borders of its strong region.

Let us now look at the system-differentiating capability of a few factors in detail.

4.2 Strong Regions of Classifiers

Positive vs negative examples per sense. [2] used negex-posex space to illuminate the fundamental difference of SVM vs NB classifiers in a text categorization task. Let us see whether that space is equally effective discriminator for WSD systems.

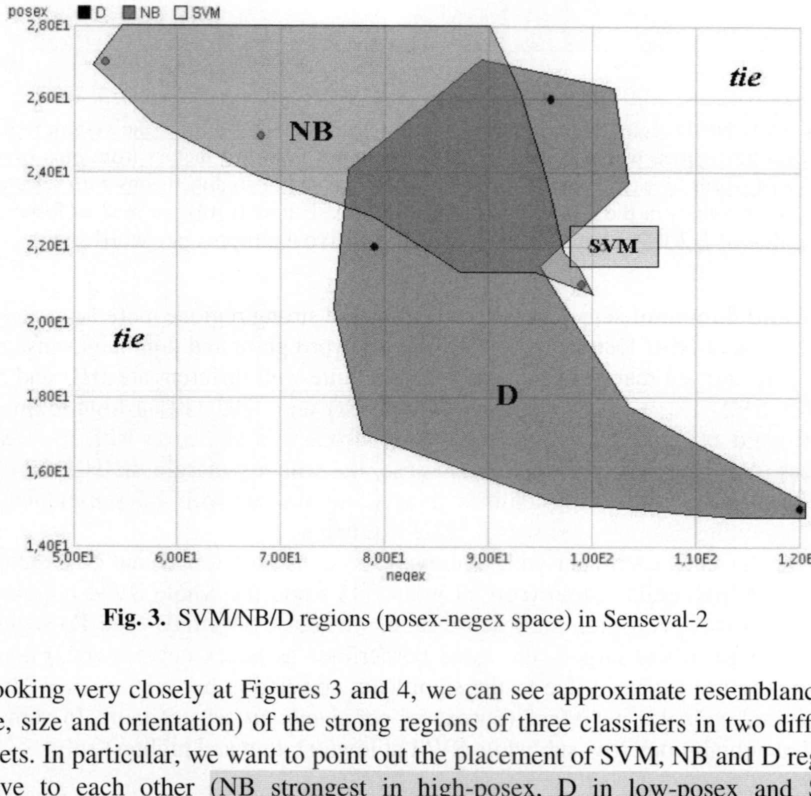

Fig. 3. SVM/NB/D regions (posex-negex space) in Senseval-2

Looking very closely at Figures 3 and 4, we can see approximate resemblance (in shape, size and orientation) of the strong regions of three classifiers in two different datasets. In particular, we want to point out the placement of SVM, NB and D regions relative to each other (NB strongest in high-posex, D in low-posex and SVM strongest in high-negex, D systems were strong in high-negex, low-posex region.) Also notice the overlapping of the regions. Those are the regions where systems are most likely to be tied, i.e. have equal performance. what about the blank regions?

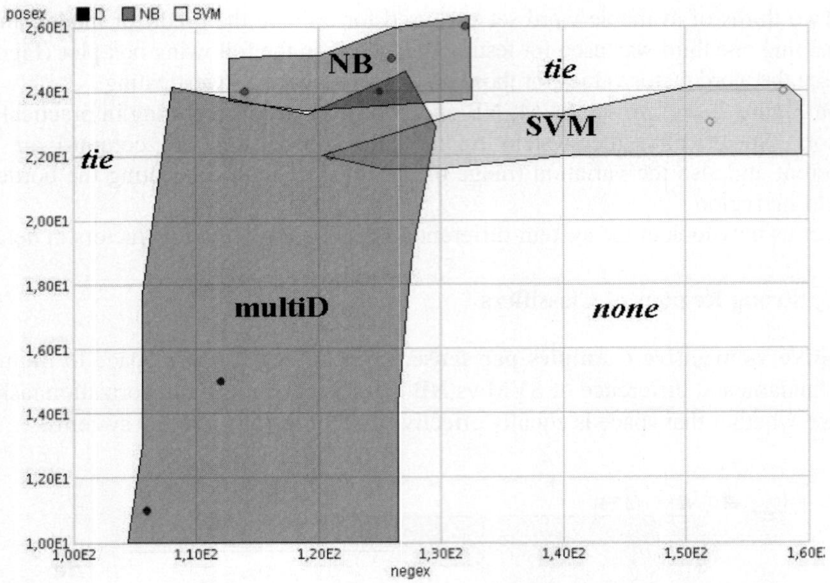

Fig. 4. SVM/NB/D regions (posex-negex space) in Senseval-3. To draw the system regions in the following figures, we calculated the *average* values for word factors from bins of 10, 20 and 30 best words by each system. i.e. this is box plot data in two dimensions with selected two factors Scale values in the figures (produced with YALE toolkit [6]) are read as follows: e.g. *posex* value of 2.20E2 means average of 220 positive examples per word sense.

Grain and dominant sense. In order to define the strong regions more accurately, we need to look at other factors as well (especially word grain and dominant sense ratio). In [10] we showed that train and grain factors quite well differentiate JHU and SMU, i.e. that SMU [7] was a low-grain (high-posex) and JHU [12] a high-grain (low-posex) word expert. For example, with verbs such as *call* and *carry* with 30-40 senses and less than 10 training examples per sense, the winning margin of JHU over SMU is at its greatest, while with nouns such as *sense* and *art* with 4-5 senses and more than 25 training examples per sense, SMU was better.

In the current experiment with Senseval-3 systems, we found that NB strength is focused on high-grain region (core at grain=11) while the whole SVM region is set around grain=7. As to dominant sense ratio, we found SVM/NB (and D) regions in Senseval-3 to follow largely the same borderlines as posex-negex map (Figure 1). This was rather expected due to the significant correlation between *average* number of training examples per sense (posex) vs per *dominant* sense (dom). In sum, NB excelled at high-dom, low-sub while SVM at low(er)-dom and high(er)-sub.

multi story: comparing single-system and multi-system decision rule systems (s2 vs s3), we can see that multi compensates at *hard* (elab hard on 3 spaces) **only if I can be sure that multiD in s3 and s2 are the same,** multi is tough on tougies (CS / JHU cannot say for s3)

5 Results

Table 2 shows nusels+IK is the maximally complementary system pair in terms of net gain but another system pair (nusels+IRST-kernel) has the higher potential (gross gain). It should also be noted that the more challenging three-system prediction task (htsa3+IRSTk+nusels) produces equally high net gain as htsa3+IRST-kernel pair.

Table 2. Results from applying the method on selected base systems from Senseval-3

base systems (gross gain)	prediction accuracy [3]	net gain (ensemble over base systems)
htsa3+IRST-kernel (4.1%)	**0.82**	**2.7%**
htsa3+nusels (3.6%)	0.70	1.4%
nusels+ IRST-kernel (**4.4%**)	0.80	2.6%
htsa3+IRSTk+nusels (6.1%)	0.55	**2.7%**
SVMall + NBall (3.8%)	0.73	1.7%

Table 3. Results from applying the method on selected base systems from Senseval-2

base systems (gross gain)	prediction accuracy	net gain (ensemble over base systems)
JHU+SMU (8.0%)	0.80	4.8%
SMU+KUN (**8.4%**)	**0.85**	**5.1%**
JHU+KUN (5.5%)	0.75	2.8%
JHU+SMU+KUN (9.5%)	0.55	4.2%
SVMall+NBall (+++)	s2 easy but few	

According to Table 3, SMU+KUN appears to have the highest gross gain, prediction accuracy and net gain, making it the maximally complementary system pair for this dataset. Furthermore, it seems that the more difficult 3-system prediction (JHU+SMU+KUN) with more gross gain loses to 2-system predictions in prediction accuracy ending up with a slightly lower net gain.

indiv systems diff: > how systems are different, that story? too complex for here, but we can say **multi/single** : smoothing of answers

Predictions. Best predictive factors (and learners) in all experiments turned out to vary according to base system pair. The most reliable learning algorithms for best-system prediction turned out to be Support Vector Machines and slightly less consistently Maximum Entropy and Naive Bayes classifiers. Machine-learning models (2) tend to work better than the corresponding bisection baseline (1). **here the story of perf->diff, refer or import?**. We eliminated each factor in turn from the

[3] *Prediction accuracy* of 0.85, for example, means that the best (better) base system was predicted right for 85 out of 100 test words.

training model to look at the contribution of the factors. The contribution of individual factors to system differentiation seems to depend heavily on the base system pair. Prediction power of the individual factors varied between 0.60 and 0.80. A combination of factors to define the strong region tended to work better than individual factors (e.g. posex+grain+domsub for SMU/JHU pair).

(*) Somewhat (un)expectedly predicting between SVM and NB clusters proved to be harder than between individual systems **or rather that the gross gain was lesser, predaccu still at par with indiv systems.** A cluster is an compound averaged from several individuals who (while sharing one factor) exhibit considerable differences. This prediction of SVM/NB was not meant for optimal ensembling, rather to define core region of those classifiers. it makes no sense to predict between clusters until clusters are adequately defined (missing feature-level factors). That was not even the idea (ensemble of 4 SVM systems, no), the idea was to discover the strong regions. > **we can say size of strong regions grows with more systems (D systems were most numerous, hence big strong region)**

6 Discussion

Systems based on various classifiers (SVM, NB and D) appear to occupy quite different regions in word space as they did for text categorization systems in [2]. The respective placements of SVM and NB in our data (Figures 2 and 3) are not the same in [2] due to different task settings but some similarity can be found: SVM is set in the middle posex region with a higher negex, NB immediately over it at lower negex. grain? D systems occupy the high-posex region.

Supporting evidence of the inherent difference of classifier on strong region can be found. First, Duluth systems in Senseval-2 [9]. We compared these 'minimal pair' define systems (NB or D based) in various word spaces (negex-posex, posex-grain, dom-sub) and ...what shall I say? that "they are placed in different regions", that adhere to Figure 3? It must adhere but test that. **this one went half-shot, I can still say it but it's not as convincing evidence.** weak they are: Duluth best 5 is 14% off best, rest 16%. Second, when looking at instance-based classifiers (SMU, GAMBL) in Senseval-2 and Senseval-3 evaluations (respectively). In both evaluations, this simple classifier is strongest at low-grain, high-train region of word space. It seems evident that systems with fairly 'simple' classifiers (Decision Stump in [9], Transformation-Based Learner in [13], SMU system in [10]) perform well with words in the *easy* region (top left corner in Figure 1). On the other hand, more complex classifiers (e.g. NB and SVM and multi-system ensembles) are more resilient to e.g. lack of training associated with high-grain words, and therefore find their core strength in the opposite corner (bottom right) of word spaces in Figure 1.

7 Conclusions and Future

We have elaborated on a method for defining the strong regions of WSD systems using a combination of known and readily available word factors. We can conclude that selection of classifier sets the approximate core of a WSD system's strong region. We found the relative strength of two most popular classifiers in WSD (Naive Bayes and Support Vector Machine) to complement each other in terms of almost all the word spaces investigated. It can now also be better understood why these two classifiers are the most popular ones experimented for WSD task: they command large but non-overlapping regions over other classifiers, i.e. disambiguate large numbers of target words to high(est) accuracy.

With a fully correct prediction of best system for all words (best prediction currently is 0.85), the method has the potential to raise state-of-the-art accuracy of WSD systems considerably more than a few percentages. We consider the remaining misclassifications (15 out of 100 test words) to be primarily due to inadequate accounting of feature-level factors: *number* of feature sets (e.g. 1-grams as opposed to 1-grams and 2-grams in sequence), or the gross number of features (e.g. 10,000 as opposed 20,000) extracted from text. Considering the sensitive nature of most classifiers with regard to changes in training data, it is more than likely that their performance differs essentially with feature factors. After all, classifiers are trained on *features*, not training examples they are extracted from, and so the number and quality of features should matter more than number of examples as such. Some system factors are also still uncharted that relate to the details of its sense decision procedure. For instance, classifier parameters were shown by [3] to have considerable effect on performance, and the specifics of the WSD method itself will obviously have an effect (e.g. [2] showed that a different feature selection scheme shifts the classifier's strong region quite considerably).

Development of highly accurate best-system predictors depends on adequate accounting of all the factors in the WSD task setting. Once such accuracy is achieved, we can directly compare other systems to each other across datasets and ultimately represent the regions of all systems (regardless of dataset and language) in one series of word spaces. Such advances are in our mind feasible in the near future and would certainly further contribute to an understanding of 'WSD equation', i.e. the exact contribution of system factors and how a system's strength shifts if we alter classifier, feature pool or any of the specifics in its decision procedure. Word spaces can be used for numerically assessing base system strength and similarity and thereby selecting maximally complementary (i.e. strong but dissimilar) systems. With that, building optimal ensembles becomes greatly facilitated, saving on computing and analysis time.

Acknowledgments

Work of the first author is supported by Department of Translation Studies of Helsinki University, Finland, and Language Technology Doctorate School of Finland (KIT). Second author is financed by COMAS Doctorate School of Jyväskylä University, Finland, and Instituto Politecnico Nacional (IPN), Mexico. Work of the third author is supported by the IPN.

References

1. Edmonds, P., and Kilgarriff, A. Introduction to the Special Issue on evaluating word sense disambiguation programs. Journal of Natural Language Engineering 8(4) (2002).
2. Forman, G., and Cohen, I. Learning from Little: Comparison of Classifiers Given Little Training. HYPERLINK "http://ecmlpkdd.isti.cnr.it/" ECML'04 . 15th European Conference on Machine Learning and the 8th European Conference on Principles and Practice of Knowledge Discovery in Databases (2004)
3. Hoste, V., Hendrickx, I., Daelemans, W. and A. van den Bosch. Parameter optimization for machine-learning of word sense disambiguation. Journal of Natural Language Engineering, 8(4) (2002) 311-327.
4. Legrand, S., Pulido JGR. A Hybrid Approach to Word Sense Disambiguation: Neural Clustering with Class Labeling. Knowledge Discovery and Ontologies workshop at 15th European Conference on Machine Learning (ECML) (2004).
5. Luo, F., Khan, L., Bastani F., Yen I-L and Zhou, J. A dynamically growing self-organizing tree (DGSOT) for hierarchical clustering gene expression profiles, Bioinformatics 2004 20(16):2605-2617, Oxford University Press. (2004)
6. Mierswa, I. and Wurst, M., Klinkenberg, R., Scholz, M. and Euler, T. YALE: Rapid Prototyping for Complex Data Mining Tasks, in Proceedings of the 12th ACM SIGKDD (KDD-06) (2006)
7. Mihalcea, R. Word sense disambiguation with pattern learning and automatic feature selection. Journal of Natural Language Engineering, 8(4) (2002) 343-359.
8. Mihalcea, R., Kilgarriff, A. and Chklovski, T. The SENSEVAL-3 English lexical sample task. Proceedings of SENSEVAL-3 Workshop at ACL (2004).
9. Pedersen, T. Machine Learning with Lexical Features: The Duluth Approach to Senseval-2. Proceedings of SENSEVAL-2: Second International Workshop on Evaluating Word Sense Disambiguation Systems (2002).
10. Saarikoski, H. and Legrand, S. Building an Optimal WSD Ensemble Using Per-Word Selection of Best System. In CIARP-05, 11th Iberoamerican Congress on Pattern Recognition, Cancun, Mexico, to appear in Lecture Notes in Computer Science, Springer (2006).
11. Witten, I., Frank, E. Data Mining: Practical Machine Learning Tools and Techniques (Second Edition). Morgan Kaufmann (2005).
12. Yarowsky, D., S. Cucerzan, R. Florian, C. Schafer and R. Wicentowski. The Johns Hopkins SENSEVAL2 System Descriptions. Proceedings of SENSEVAL-2 workshop (2002).
13. Yarowsky, D. and Florian, R. Evaluating sense disambiguation across diverse parameter spaces. Journal of Natural Language Engineering, 8(4) (2002) 293-311.
14. Zavrel, J., S. Degroeve, A. Kool, W. Daelemans, K. Jokinen. Diverse Classifiers for NLP Disambiguation Tasks. Comparisons, Optimization, Combination, and Evolution. TWLT 18. Learning to Behave. CEvoLE 2 (2000) 201–221.

senseval-2 and -3 systems

15. Seo, H-C., Rim, H-C. and Kim, S-H. KUNLP system in Senseval-2. Proceedings of SENSEVAL-2 Workshop (2001) 222-225.
16. Strapparava, C., Gliozzo, A., and Giuliano, C. Pattern abstraction and term similarity for Word Sense Disambiguation: IRST at Senseval-3. In Proceedings of SENSEVAL-3 workshop (2004).

17. Manning, C., Tolga Ilhan, H., Kamvar, S., Klein, D. and Toutanova, K. Combining Heterogeneous Classifiers for Word-Sense Disambiguation. Proceedings of SENSEVAL-2, Second International Workshop on Evaluating WSD Systems (2001) 87-90.
18. Lee, Y-K., Ng, H-T., and Chia, T-K. Supervised Word Sense Disambiguation with Support Vector Machines and Multiple Knowledge Sources. In Proceedings of SENSEVAL-3 workshop (2004).
19. Grozea, C. Finding optimal parameter settings for high performance word sense disambiguation. In SENSEVAL-3: Third International Workshop on the Evaluation of Systems for the Semantic Analysis of Text, Barcelona, Spain (2004).

<u>AdaBoost, TALP</u>

Impact of Feature Selection for Corpus-Based WSD in Turkish

Zeynep Orhan[1] and Zeynep Altan[2]

[1] Department of Computer Engineering, Fatih University 34500, Büyükçekmece, Istanbul, Turkey
zorhan@fatih.edu.tr
[2] Department of Computer Engineering, Maltepe University 34857, Maltepe, Istanbul, Turkey
zaltan@maltepe.edu.tr

Abstract. Word sense disambiguation (WSD) is an important intermediate stage for many natural language processing applications. The senses of an ambiguous word are the classification of usages for that word. WSD is basically a mapping function from a context to a set of applicable senses depending on various parameters. Resource selection, determination of senses for ambiguous words, decision of effective features, algorithms, and evaluation criteria are the major issues in a WSD system. This paper deals with the feature selection strategies for word sense disambiguation task in Turkish language. There are many different features that can contribute to the meaning of a word. These features can vary according to the metaphorical usages, POS of the word, pragmatics, etc. The observations indicated that detecting the critical features can contribute much than the learning methodologies.

1 Introduction

The human being acquire the incredible ability of understanding or interpreting the given text or discourse at the very early ages. This task can be thought to be a very simple one that can be simulated by machines; however, natural languages are inherently ambiguous and difficult to be processed by computers. Having a better communication with the computers is, of course, not the major reason behind the researches about natural language processing (NLP), there are many other application areas such as text summarization, translation, information extraction, speech analysis and synthesis and so on where we need to understand text and discourse.

Miller [6] expresses the complexity of languages and emphasizes that the machines' inability to understand the information they hold restricts their usefulness. Therefore, this becomes a bottleneck for the increasing amount of information kept in e-format. The real source of the problem is the complex structure of the natural languages. When we are dealing with the complexity of languages, one of the difficulties we have to consider is the lexical ambiguity. This type of ambiguity which is an important problem at the bottom level of NLP applications does not have a perfect solution yet. Syntactic or semantic lexical ambiguity is the fundamental problem of NLP systems and disambiguation is necessary, or at least helpful, for

A. Gelbukh and C.A. Reyes-Garcia (Eds.): MICAI 2006, LNAI 4293, pp. 868 – 878, 2006.

many applications in one way or another [5]. The ultimate goal of the word sense disambiguation (WSD) researches is determining the most suitable sense of an ambiguous word among the possible set of senses for that specific word in a given text or discourse.

It has been stated that WSD is necessary in machine translation and additionally a word can be disambiguated whenever one can see *N* words on either side [14]. This view formed the basic ideas of the WSD approaches. In fact, his point of view is only concerning one part of the fact; however the decision function does not solely depends on those N words in human language processing system. Additionally, there is even no consensus on the definition of a sense. The debates on this issue lead to various perspectives in the history. Aristotle claims that words correspond to objects, thus meaning is independent of context. An interesting view emphasizes the usage rather than the meaning of the word and assumes that there are no predefined word senses, but usage of a word in a context determines meaning [16]. Some others believe that meaning is based on frequencies of words [2] or meaning of a word stems from its syntagmatic use in discourse [1].

In recent years, WSD is one of the unsolved problems for Turkish as in many other languages. It is obvious that, the concepts and the meaning of words will definitely play a vital role for the increasing number of studies on Turkish search engines and in many other fields in the very near future. Thus, the requirement of the corpus based studies linguistically analyzing annotated texts will increase in parallel.

Turkish includes many ambiguous words and generally grammatical features are not sufficient to disambiguate them. As an example, Turkish Language Society (TDK) dictionary contains 38 different senses for the word "gel (come)[1]" excluding proverbs. The following sentences are chosen from TDK dictionary and demonstrate 4 different senses of "gel" [14]:

(a) Dün akşam amcam bize geldi (3rd sense: Yesterday my uncle visited us)
(b) Ondan kimseye kötülük gelmez (11th sense: He never harms anybody)
(c) Buranın havası iyi geldi (21st sense: The environment made him feel better)
(d) Burnundan kan geldi (25th sense: His nose was bleeding or blood came out of his nose).

In WSD, the first step must be determination of the set of applicable senses of a word for a particular context. This set can be formed by using sources like dictionaries. However, labeling word senses via dictionary definitions may not result in the expected set of senses, since this works best for skewed distributions where one sense is predominant. Also, definitions can often be vague. It is very difficult to decide the number of senses and the distinctions between these senses for a given word. Senses are determined by their usages, cultures, time and domain of discourse etc. The next step will be the selection of features that can be helpful for resolving the

[1] The verbs in Turkish has "mek/mak" suffix for the infinitive forms. "gelmek" in Turkish corresponds to "to come" in English. The root words are given in the text, since root words can have different senses by using suffixes.

ambiguity. Then the last step will be assignment of the correct sense in the given context.

Machine learning techniques are used to automatically acquire disambiguation knowledge in NLP and in many other fields as well. Supervised machine learning methods are successfully applied by utilizing sense-tagged corpora and large-scale linguistic resources for WSD.

In this study, the general facts mentioned above and special cases for Turkish have been exhaustively scrutinized. In Section 2 some issues in Turkish WSD has been explained along with the experimental setup and the results obtained from all phases of the study. In the last section, a general evaluation and conclusion have been provided for commenting on the results and future work.

2 Issues in Turkish WSD

Sense classification and granularity is one of the main problems in WSD. This set can be formed by using sources like dictionaries, thesauri, translation dictionaries etc. The next step will be the selection of features that can be helpful for resolving the ambiguity. Then the last step will be the determination of the most appropriate sense in the given context.

The available language processing resources are the critical factors for the success of testing. Electronic dictionaries, thesauri, bilingual corpora, parsers, morphological analyzers, ontologies like WordNet are the typical electronic resources that can be considered. Other than these, the structures of the specific languages must be taken into account, since the senses of a word and the factors that are affecting sense distinctions vary dramatically for different languages.

The disambiguation process is a mapping function from a set of given features plus our general knowledge to the senses of the given word. The mapping function is very sensitive to the selected features and therefore precision and recall can be increased/ decreased depending on the features that are going to be used. One possible feature can be collocation words (e.g. "hoş" in "hoş geldiniz (welcome)" or "karşı" in "karşı geldi (he opposed)"). Other types of features can be the affixes, syntactic categories or POS of the words preceding and succeeding the target word, ontological information, etc. In this study, we are trying to determine these effective features in WSD for Turkish.

The last item that must be thought is the evaluation process of the systems. There is no standard method for evaluating the successes of WSD applications, although there are some projects like SENSEVAL in the world [12].

2.1 Corpora for Turkish WSD

English and very few other languages have been widely studied in NLP researches. Lesser studied languages, such as Turkish suffer from the lack of wide coverage electronic resources or other language processing tools like ontologies, dictionaries, morphological analyzers, parsers etc. There are some projects for providing data for NLP applications in Turkish like METU Corpus Project [10]. It has two parts, the main corpus and the Treebank that consists of parsed, morphologically analyzed and disambiguated sentences selected from the main corpus, respectively. The sentences are given in XML format and provide many syntactic features that can be helpful for WSD and sense tags are added manually.

The texts in main corpus have been taken from different types of Turkish written texts published in 1990 and afterwards. It has about two million words. It includes 999 written texts taken from 201 books, 87 papers and news from 3 different Turkish daily newspapers. XML and TEI (Text Encoding Initiative) style annotation have been used [10]. The distribution of the texts in the Treebank is similar to the main corpus. There are 6930 sentences in this Treebank. These sentences have been parsed, morphologically analyzed and disambiguated. In Turkish, a word can have many analyses, so having disambiguated texts is very important. Frequencies of the words have been found as it is necessary to select appropriate ambiguous words for WSD. There are 5356 different root words and 627 of these words have 15 or more occurrences, and the rest have less [11].

2.2 Sense Classification

The words can be thought as the tools for referring to objects, relations and events in the world. If we think about the meaning of a word as the entity it refers to, there may be some problems such as the words co-referring to an entity that have completely different meaning from the words themselves have. For example "üç" means "three" and "kağıt" means "paper" in Turkish. However, when they are used together "üç kağıt" means "trick" which eventually becomes a new entity.

Another candidate for the meaning of a word can be the dictionary definition given for that word. There may be a list of definitions that is applicable for a given word in a given dictionary, but this may not be the sense classification. For example in one of the Turkish dictionaries the verb "gelmek (to come)" has 38 senses [14] and the same verb has 35 senses in another one [13]. Although the dictionaries are the first source for learning the meaning of a word they have many inconsistencies. It can be claimed that they are more accurate than any individual's knowledge of the meaning, but they are written depending on the usages and this is a contradiction. The dictionary definitions are also given by using some other words which causes circularity.

In Turkish there are many idioms, proverbs and compound words other than the normal usages and these types of usages make the sense classification task more complex. The number of senses that are applicable for many words may become intractable. Furthermore, some of the word senses have no or very rare occurrences in the corpus.

It is very difficult to decide the number of senses and the distinctions between these senses for a given word. Senses are determined by their usages, cultures, time and domain of discourse etc. For example the word "gök" has senses like "sky, heavens, blue, azure, not matured" but the usages of "blue, azure, not matured" are very rare in contemporary Turkish, and the first two senses are used more frequently. The language has a dynamic structure and sometimes some new words/senses are being added or some old ones are forgotten.

Table 1. Translations of three senses of Turkish word "gelmek" in English and French

Language	Sense 1	Sense 2	Sense 3
Turkish	Varmak, geriye dönmek, gitmek	Çıkmak, getirilmiş olmak	Peyda olmak
English	to come	To originate, to come from	To appear, to happen
French	Venir, arriver	Venir de, sortir, provenir, être originaire, être apporté de	Venir, Se présenter á le'esprit

Table 2. Selected words, their number of senses for FG and CG sets along with the number of instances in the corpus. The senses listed in the second column are the basic ones and does not cover all possible senses.

Words	Meaning	FG # senses	CG # senses	#instances
al	take, get, red	30	6	265
çalış	work, study, start	6	2	101
çık	climb, leave, increase	28	7	238
geç	pass,happen, late	19	8	146
gir	enter, fit, begin, penetrate	15	4	134
ara	distance,break,interval, look for	10	7	136
baş	head, leader, beginning, top, main, principal	9	5	102
el	hand, stranger, country	6	5	157
göz	eye, glance, division, drawer	8	6	111
kız	girl,virgin, daughter, get hot, get angry	4	2	89
ön	front, foreground, face, breast, prior, preliminary anterior	10	3	68
sıra	queue, order, sequence, turn, regularity, occasion desk	5	2	54
yan	side, direction, auxiliary, askew, burn, be on fire be alight	8	4	96
yol	way, road, path, method, manner, means	10	5	88
yüz	face, obverse, surface, cheek, hundred, swim,skin	6	6	61
böyle	so, such, thus, like this, in this way	5	3	57
büyük	big, extensive, important, chief, great, elder	6	2	95
doğru	straight, true, accurate, proper, fair, honest, line towards, around	8	3	55
küçük	little, small, young, insignificant, kid	7	2	40
öyle	such, so, that	4	2	38

These limitations enforced us to find some other ways for determining the senses of Turkish words. Our first attempt was obtaining the set of senses by grouping the senses given in the dictionaries and usages in the Treebank. In this process we put the similar or related senses under the same sense class and ignored some of the rarely used ones. Unfortunately, the resulting set of senses, especially for some of the words were still intractable. As a second attempt, we thought that translations of the given words in other languages could be the candidates of the senses. But this approach had its own limitations and problems. Translations are one of the application areas of WSD, but it is not limited to this only, so this approach may not be suitable for some other applications. Moreover, one word may have different set of translations in different target languages as shown in Table 1. Another problem is the usages that may not be translated reflecting the senses exactly to another language such as "el koymak" in Turkish means "to confiscate", although "el" means "hand" and "koymak" means "to put". The final decision about the sense tagging has been achieved by using two sets, fine-granular (FG) and coarse-granular (CG) respectively as in Senseval project [12].

Ambiguous Turkish words have been selected and examined for various aspects considering the frequencies and the number of senses. The FG and CG sets have been used for observing the effect of granularity. The words and their number of senses for fine and CG sets are provided in Table 2. The verbs (al, çalış, çık, geç, gir), nouns (ara, baş, el, göz, kız, ön, sıra, yan, yol, yüz) and other words (böyle, büyük, doğru, küçük, öyle) were chosen from the corpus among the ones that have 30-40 or more frequencies. Sense tags are marked from TDK dictionary by adding some extra senses that are not listed in the dictionary but occur in the corpus. FG senses are the unions of TDK senses and these added senses. CG senses are obtained from FG senses by grouping related or similar senses and have definitely less elements.

2.3 Machine Learning Algorithms

Machine learning techniques have been widely applied to NLP tasks and WSD as well. Bayesian probabilistic algorithms [8], neural networks [8], decision trees [18], instance based learning (alternatively memory based or exemplar based learning) [9] etc. are the most frequently used methods in this domain. There is a system so called WEKA developed at the University of Waikato in New Zealand. It includes famous machine learning algorithms [17]. In the evaluation k-fold cross validation has been used where k=10. Many different applications report contradictory results about the performances of various algorithms in the literature [1] and this complicates the task of evaluation.

All features were applied to three different algorithms. These algorithms, AODE (Aggregating one-dependence estimators) which is an improved version of famous Naive Bayes statistical method, IBk (Instance-based learning) and J48 decision tree method were tested by using Weka. The average performance results for FG and CG sets by using AODE, IBk and J48 algorithms are provided in Table 3. After analyzing the first test results, we decided to continue the tests practicing only IBk, since the differences among the methods could be neglected.

Table 3. Average performance results (rounded % accuracy) for FG and CG senses by using AODE, IBK and J48 algorithms for different POS

	FG			CG		
POS	**AODE**	**IBK**	**J48**	**AODE**	**IBK**	**J48**
Verbs	43	46	45	61	63	60
Nouns	70	73	66	81	82	75
Other	57	65	61	85	88	74
All	57	61	57	75	77	69

2.4 Feature Selection

The appropriate sense of an ambiguous word can be successfully selected whenever a window size of N words in the neighborhood has been considered. Surrounding words and their part of speech (POS), keywords or bigrams in the context and various syntactic properties etc are some possible candidates for WSD. The ones that are included in [9] are surrounding words, local collocations, syntactic relations, POS and morphological forms.

Table 4. Selected features and feature combinations in the experiments

Features	Abbr.	Features	Abbr.
All feature combinations	all	Target word possessor	Hİ
Previous word root	ÖK	Target-subsequent word relation	HŞ
Previous word POS	ÖT	Subsequent word root	SK
Previous word case marker	ÖHE	Subsequent word POS	ST
Previous word possessor	Öİ	Subsequent word case marker	SHE
Previous-target word relation	ÖŞ	Subsequent word possessor	Sİ
Previous word root + POS	ÖKT	Subsequent-target word relation	SŞ
Previous word root and case marker	ÖKHE	Subsequent word root + POS	SKT
Previous word root and possessor	ÖKİ	Subsequent word root and case marker	SKHE
Previous word root + POS + case marker	ÖKTHE	Subsequent word root and possessor	SKİ
Previous word root + POS+ possessor	ÖKTİ	Subsequent word root + POS+ case marker	SKTHE
Previous word root + POS + case marker + possessor	ÖKTHEİ	Subsequent word root + POS + possessor	SKTİ
Target word POS	HT	Subsequent word root + POS + case marker + possessor	SKTHEİ
Target word case marker	HHE		

Effective features for WSD may also vary for different languages and word types. Although, some features are common in many languages some others may be language specific. Turkish is an agglutinative language and is based upon suffixation; therefore, grammatical functions are indicated by adding various suffixes to stems. This is a major distinction of Turkish compared to many European languages. Turkish has a SOV (Subject-Object-Verb) sentence structure but other orders are possible as well and so the effective features must be searched in the previous context for the verbs. However, nouns or other words can be effected both from the previous and subsequent contexts. Additionally, pragmatic and semantic relations that are generally language specific and difficult to acquire may be necessary.

The features are selected by considering three basic word groups: The previous and subsequent words that are related with the target word and the ambiguous word itself. Same set of features for all groups have been used. These features include root, POS, case marker, possessor and word's relation with the next word. All these features and their combinations that are thought to be effective in Turkish have been tested by the algorithms mentioned above. Table 4 summarizes these features and their combinations along with the abbreviations. The feature "all" includes all the features from all three groups in the sentence. The previous or subsequent words do not have to be the consecutive words around target word and variable number of words can be extracted for different contexts. The relational structure in the corpus allows obtaining all related words in any part of the sentence; therefore one can obtain the whole words in context of Turkish free word order structure providing high degree of flexibility.

2.5 Results

We can't assert that each argument of a feature set would differ in their performance to disambiguate the words individually. A group of the features should probably give similar results. The results of the sensitivity analysis, with all arguments of feature set, will facilitate to distinguish the effective characteristics, and to decide the parameter choices for each POS. Table 5 and Table 6 provide the sensitivity analysis of IBk algorithm for various features on fine and CG senses. The columns shown as baseline are the percentages of the most frequently used senses (MFS) among the rest.

Table 5. Sensitivity analysis of FG senses vs. various features

Words(FG)	Features	Accuracy(%)	Avg.(%)	Baseline (MFS) (%)
al	ÖK,ÖKTHE	34,38	36,0	14
çalış	ÖKHE,ÖHE,ÖKT,HDŞ,ÖK	54,52,51,51,45	50,6	31
çık	ÖKHE,ÖK,HDŞ,ÖŞ	29,28,23,21	25,3	15
geç	ÖK,HDHE,Öİ	40,29,29	32,7	24
gir	HDHE,ÖKHE,ÖK,ÖŞ,HDİ,ÖHE,ÖT	55,53,52,51,51,49,48	51,3	46
ara	ALL,ÖKHDTSK,ÖKSK,ÖK,SK,HDT	57,53,47,46,36,36	45,8	20
baş	ALL,ÖKTSK,ÖKT,ÖK,HDŞ,SK	71,64,59,59,52,40	57,5	27
el	HDHE,ST,SK,Öİ	82,77,75,75	77,3	67
göz	ÖKSK,SK,HDHE	85,81,72	79,3	64
kız	ÖKHDTSK,SKİ,SKHE,SK,HDT	84,81,80,77,74	79,2	60
ön	ÖKSK,ÖK,HDT,HDŞ,HDİ,Sİ	69,61,53,51,51,51	56,0	45
sıra	ALL, ÖKHDT,ÖKSK,ÖK,SK	57,53,47,46,36	47,8	57
yan	ÖKHDTSK,ALL,ÖKHESK,SK,HDHE,HDT,ÖK	62,62,58,53,50,48,42	53,6	35
yüz	HDHE,ÖKTHEİ,ALL,SK,ÖT	94,91,86,83	88,5	63
böyle	ÖKHDTSK,ALL,ÖKTSKT,HDT,HDŞ,SK	90,90,70,70,65,60	74,2	36
büyük	ÖKTSKT,ÖKTSK,ÖKSK,ÖT	51,40,40,37	42,0	24
doğru	ÖHE,HDT,HDİ	74,72,67	71,0	45
küçük	SŞ,ÖT,ÖŞ,ÖKT,ÖKHESKHE	75,62,62,62,62	64,6	33
öyle	ÖŞ,ALL,ST,SK,HDT	91,83,75,75,75	79,8	63

In FG task the net gains are more significant but the overall performance is lower than the CG task. The performance also effected from the baselines and the number of senses of the ambiguous words. The results are more sensitive to the features than the algorithms. The results of verbs for FG senses demonstrate that the previous word root and case marker have considerable impact on the disambiguation. The baseline for verb "çık" is 15% and only by using the ÖK the accuracy increases by 13%. When case marker is added to this (ÖKHE) the increase in the accuracy is only 1%. On the other hand, the accuracy increase of verb "çalış" by ÖK is 14% and together with case marker we can have a further increase of 9%. The same results can far or less be inferred for CG senses. It can be claimed that the features ÖK and ÖKHE are seemed to be significant in verb senses; however, there may be contradictory examples. For example, the best feature for the disambiguation of verb "gir" is HDHE by giving an increase of 9%.

The results yield that for nouns and other POS words ÖK, SK, ST, HDT and HDHE become important and this is somehow different from the verbs. While "al" obtains its best result using ÖK, ÖKTHE (see Table 3) for fine-coarse granular senses, the same word gets best result according to baseline with ÖK and ÖŞ features. We can realize from Table 4 and Table 5 that these feature selections differ for all words. Therefore, highly reduced senses of verbs for coarse-granular changes the feature sets. For example, the word "kız" as a noun gives %100 accuracy result for coarse-granular analysis with HDT feature; but the fine-granular experiments with 5 best different features gives % 84 accuracy at most(for ÖKHDTSK feature). It can be seen that similar result is obtained for the word "küçük" in others words classification.

Table 6. Sensitivity analysis of CG senses vs. various features

Words(CG)	Features	Accuracy(%)	Avg.(%)	Baseline (MFS) (%)
al	ÖK,ÖŞ	61,49	55,0	47
çalış	ÖHE,ÖKTHE,ÖŞ,ÖKHE	76,76,75,73	75,0	66
çık	ÖKHE,ÖKTİ,ÖKT,ÖKİ,ÖŞ,ÖK	57,56,55,54,54,53,53	54,6	47
geç	ÖK,ÖŞ,Öİ	50,40,39	43,0	35
gir	ÖKİ,ÖKHE,ÖK,HDHE	66,65,64,63	64,5	58
ara	ÖKHDTSK,ALL,ÖKSK,ÖK,SK	67,70,57,52,47	58,6	30
baş	ÖKHE,ÖK,ÖHE,HDŞ	83,78,61,64	71,5	57
el	HDHE,ÖŞ,ÖHE,ST,HDŞ	87,82,82,77,77	81,0	69
göz	ÖKSK,SK,ST	86,85,85	85,3	76
kız	HDT	100	100,0	86
ön	HDŞ,HDİ,ÖKSK,Sİ,SHE,ÖK,HDT	92,92,89,87,87,87,87	88,7	83
sıra	ALL,ÖKSK,SK,ÖK	93,91,85,77	86,5	60
yan	ALL,ÖKHDTSK,SK,HDT,HDHE,ÖK	77,72,62,61,58,54	64,0	49
yüz	HDHE,ÖKTHEİ,ALL,SK,ÖT	94,91,86,83	88,5	63
böyle	ALL,ÖKTSKT,ÖKHESKHE,ÖKHDTSK	100,90,85,85	90,0	61
büyük	ÖKTSK,ÖKT,ÖK,ÖT	74,71,71,65	70,3	59
doğru	ÖKHE,HDT,SKHE,ÖKSK	94,94,88,88	91,0	58
küçük	ST	100	100,0	70
öyle	ÖŞ,ALL,ST	100,91,83	91,3	79

Finally, we compared the results for FG and CG senses of verbs, nouns and others according to all features and best feature selections in Table 7. The results indicate that the best feature set can compete with the fixed feature set that includes all the features. Best feature set is even better for the words other than the verbs. It can be inferred that the optimal set of features is more helpful than using many features that may include irrelevant ones.

Table 7. Average performance results for FG and CG sets by using IBk algorithm for all POS by a fixed feature set and average of maximum best feature set

	FG		CG	
POS	**FixFeature**	**BestFeature**	**FixFeature**	**BestFeature**
Verbs	46	41	63	62
Nouns	73	73	82	87
Other	65	76	88	94
All	61	63	77	81

3 Conclusion and Future Work

WSD is an important problem in NLP systems. It has been investigated for many years, however there are stil too many problems that have to be solved. First of all we need a to find a model for the human language processing system. In order to do this we must have a coherent and plausible representation model for the entities in the world analogous to the humans. Sense classification and its representation in the human brain have to be explored.

The study on Turkish verbs demonstrates that there are many different factors on sense disambiguation process. Despite examining a small set of words, the results point out some important clues about the ambiguity problem. Considering the accuracy or average values may be misleading and the number of senses, baselines and net gains has to be considered. The impact of selected features is more significant than the algorithms. The size of the feature set is not proportionally increasing the performance due to the irrelevant features. Finding optimal set of features will be crucial.

We are planning to increase our test data for the future studies. We also intend to develop a basic ontological classification of the words in the corpus. This ontological structure will be added to our algorithm as one or two extra features. Thus, our corpus based approximation presented in this study will be combined with a new estimation, which is a knowledge-based taxonomy deriving a hybrid approach.

References

1. Barwise, J., and Perry., J: Situations and Attitudes. Cambridge, MA: MIT Press (1983).
2. Bloomfield, L.: Language. New York: Henry Holt (1933).
3. Daeleman, W.: Machine Learning Of Language: A Model And A Problem, ESSLLI'2002 Workshop On ML Approaches In CL, August 5-9, Trento, Italy, (2002) 134-145
4. Edmonds, P.: SENSEVAL: The evaluation of word sense disambiguation systems, *ELRA Newsletter*, Vol. 7 No. 3, (2002) 5-14

5. Ide, N., Veronis, J.: Introduction To The Special Issue On Word Sense Disambiguation: The State Of The Art, Computational Linguistics, 24(1), (1998) 1-40
6. Miller, G., Ambiguous Words, iMP Magazine: http://www.cisp.org/imp/march_2001/miller/ 03_01miller.htm , March 22, (2001).
7. Montoyo, A., Su´arez, A., Rigau, G., Palomar, M.: Combining Knowledge and Corpus-based Word Sense Disambiguation Methods, JAIR 23 (2005) 299-330.
8. Mooney, R. J.: Comparative Experiments On Disambiguating Word Senses: An Illustration Of The Role Of Bias In Machine Learning, In Eric Brill, Kenneth Church, Editors, Proceedings Of The Conference EMNLP, ACL, Somerset, NJ (1996) 82–91
9. Ng, H.T., Lee, H.B.: Integrating Multiple Knowledge Sources to Disambiguate Word Sense: An Exemplar-Based Approach. In Proceedings Of The 34th Annual Meeting Of ACL, Santa Cruz, Morgan Kaufmann Publishers (1996) 40–47
10. Oflazer, K., Say, B., Tur, D. Z. H., Tur, G.: Building A Turkish Treebank, Invited Chapter In Building And Exploiting Syntactically-Annotated Corpora, Anne Abeille Editor, Kluwer Academic Publishers (2003)
11. Orhan, Z., Altan, Z.: Determining Effective Features for Word Sense Disambiguation in Turkish, IU - JEEE, Vol. 5, No. 2 (2005) 1341-1352
12. Preiss, J., Yarowsky, D.: The Proceedings of SENSEVAL-2: Second International Workshop on Evaluating Word Sense Disambiguation Systems, (2001)
13. Tuğlacı, P.: Okyanus Ansiklopedik Türkçe Sözlük, ABC Kitabevi, İstanbul (1995)
14. Türkçe Sözlük(Turkish Dictionary): TDK (2005) http://tdk.org.tr/sozluk.html
15. Weaver, W.: Translation. Mimeographed, 12 pp., Reprinted in Locke, William N. and Booth, A. Donald (1955) (Eds.), Machine translation of languages.John Wiley & Sons, New York,(1949)15-23.
16. Wittgenstein L.: Philosophical Investigations translated by G E M Anscombe, Oxford: Basil Blackwell, (1953).
17. Witten, I.H., and Frank E.: DataMining: Practical Machine Learning Toolsand Techniques with Java Implementations, Morgan Kaufmann, San Francisco (1999)
18. Yarowsky, D.: Hierarchical Decision Lists For Word Sense Disambiguation, Computers And The Humanities, 34(2) (2000) 179-186

Spanish All-Words Semantic Class Disambiguation Using Cast3LB Corpus*

Rubén Izquierdo-Beviá, Lorenza Moreno-Monteagudo,
Borja Navarro, and Armando Suárez

Departamento de Lenguajes y Sistemas Informáticos.
Universidad de Alicante. Spain
{ruben, loren, borja, armando}@dlsi.ua.es

Abstract. In this paper, an approach to semantic disambiguation based on machine learning and semantic classes for Spanish is presented. A critical issue in a corpus-based approach for Word Sense Disambiguation (WSD) is the lack of wide-coverage resources to automatically learn the linguistic information. In particular, all-words sense annotated corpora such as SemCor do not have enough examples for many senses when used in a machine learning method. Using semantic classes instead of senses allows to collect a larger number of examples for each class while polysemy is reduced, improving the accuracy of semantic disambiguation. Cast3LB, a SemCor-like corpus, manually annotated with Spanish WordNet 1.5 senses, has been used in this paper to perform semantic disambiguation based on several sets of classes: lexicographer files of WordNet, WordNet Domains, and SUMO ontology.

1 Introduction

One of the main problems in a corpus-based approach to Word Sense Disambiguation (WSD) is the lack of wide-coverage resources in order to automatically learn the linguistic information used to disambiguate word senses. This problem is more important when dealing with languages different from English, such as Spanish.

Current approaches to disambiguation using WordNet senses suffer from the low number of available examples for many senses. Developing new hand-tagged corpora to avoid this problem is a hard task that research community tries to solve with semi-supervised methods. An additional difficulty is that more than one sense is often correct for a specific word in a specific context. In this cases, it is hard (or even impossible) to choose just one sense per word.

Using semantic classes instead of WordNet senses provides solutions to both problems [3] [15] [9] [11] [16]. A WSD system learns one classifier per word using the available examples in the training corpus whereas semantic class classifiers can use examples of several words because a semantic class groups a set of senses,

* This paper has been supported by the Spanish Government under projects CESS-ECE (HUM2004-21127-E) and R2D2 (TIC2003-07158-C04-01).

A. Gelbukh and C.A. Reyes-Garcia (Eds.): MICAI 2006, LNAI 4293, pp. 879–888, 2006.

which are related from a semantic point of view. Therefore, semantic classes allow more examples per class, reduce the polysemy, and allow less ambiguity. Different collections of semantic classes have been proposed. Three of them are used in this paper: lexicographer files (LexNames) of WordNet [5], WordNet Domains (WND) [4] and SUMO ontology [8].

The main goal of this paper is to perform semantic class disambiguation in Spanish, similarly to [15] where several experiments were done with semantic classes for English using SemCor. We used the Cast3LB corpus, a manually annotated corpus in Spanish, for training and testing our system.

The rest of this paper is organized as follows: we first present some previous work related with semantic classes. Section 3 describes the three set of classes used and the Cast3LB corpus. In the next section, section 4, experiments and features are explained. Section 5 shows the results obtained and, finally, some conclusions and futur work are discussed in section 6.

2 Related Work

The semantic disambiguation based on coarse classes rather than synsets is not a new idea. In [9] a method to obtain sets of conceptual classes and its application to WSD is presented. This method is based on the selectional preferences of the verb: several verbs specify the semantic class of its arguments. For example, the selectional preferences of the direct object of a verb like "to drink" is "something liquid".

Other paper that tries to develop semantic disambiguation based on semantic classes is [16]. He uses the Roget's Thesaurus categories as semantic classes.

In [11] LexNames are used in order to automatically learn semantic classes. Its approach is based on Hidden Markov Model.

[15] focuses on the general idea of getting more examples for each class based on a coarse granularity of WordNet. They use LexNames and SUMO ontology in order to translate SemCor senses to semantic classes. They obtain the best results with a reduced features set of the target word: only lemma, PoS and the most frequent semantic class calculated over the training folders of the corpus are used. By using these features they obtain an accuracy of 82.5% with LexNames, and an accuracy of 71.9% with SUMO. According to their results, they conclude that it is very difficult to make generalization between the senses of a semantic class in the form of features.

The aim of [3] is to overcome the problem of knowledge acquisition bottleneck in WSD. They propose a training process based on coarse semantic classes. Specifically, they use LexNames. Once a coarse disambiguation is obtained, they apply some heuristics in order to obtain the specific sense of the ambiguous word (for example, the most frequent sense of the word in its semantic class). They use some semantic features. However, due to the difficulty of making generalization in each semantic class, they do not apply the features as a concatenated set of information. Instead of this, they apply a voting system with the features.

3 Semantic Classes and Cast3LB

In this section, the three sets of classes and the Cast3LB corpus used are described briefly.

3.1 Sets of Semantic Classes

WordNet synsets are organized in forty five lexicographer files, or **LexNames**, based on syntactic categories (nouns, verbs, adjectives and adverbs) and logical groupings, such as person, phenomenon, feeling, location, etc. WordNet 1.5 has been used in the experiments since our corpus is annotated using this WordNet version.

SUMO (Suggested Upper Merge Ontology) provides definitions for general-purpose terms and gathers several specific domains ontologies (such as communication, countries and regions, economy and finance, among others). It is limited to concepts that are general enough to address (at a high level) a broad range of domain areas. SUMO has been mapped to all of WordNet lexicon. Its current version is mapped to WordNet 1.6. and it contents 20,000 terms and 60,000 axioms. It has 687 different classes.

WordNet Domains are organized into families, such as sport, medicine, anatomy, etc. Each family is a group of semantically close SFCs (subject field codes) among which there is no inclusion relation. SFCs are sets of relevant words for a specific domain. Currently, there are 164 different SFCs, organized in a four level hierarchy, that have been used to annotate WordNet 1.6 with the corresponding domains (including some verbs and adjectives).

3.2 The Cast3LB Corpus

In Cast3LB all nouns, verbs and adjectives have been manually annotated with their proper sense of Spanish WordNet, following an all-words approach[1] [6]. Cast3LB examples have been extracted from the Lexesp corpus[10] and the Hermes Corpus[2]. The corpus is made up of samples of different kinds of texts: news, essays, sport news, science papers, editorials, magazine texts and narrative literary texts. In Table 1 statistical data about the corpus is shown. Cast3LB has approximately 8,598 annotated words (36,411 out of 82,795 occurrences): 4,705 nouns, 1,498 verbs, and 2,395 adjectives.

Table 1. Amount of words in the Cast3LB corpus

	Nouns	Verbs	Adjectives
Occurrences	17506	11696	7209
Words	4705	1498	2395

[1] In an all-words approach, all words with semantic meaning are labelled.

[2] `nlp.uned.es/hermes/`

Comparing Cast3LB to other corpora annotated with senses, it has a medium size (although Cast3LB is being currently extended up to 300,000 words under the project CESS-ECE). It is smaller than SemCor (250,000 words) [5] and MultiSemCor (92,820 annotated words for Italian) [1]. However, it has more annotated words than the all-words corpora used at SENSEVAL-3 for Italian (5,189 words: 2,583 nouns, 1,858 verbs, 748 adjectives) [13] or English (5000 words approximately) [12].

The corpus has 4,972 ambiguous words out of 8,598, which means that 57.82% of them has two or more senses in Spanish WordNet. The corpus polysemy degree according to each set of classes (WN senses, LexNames, WND and SUMO) is shown in table 2.

Table 2. Polysemy in the Cast3LB corpus

	Senses	LexNames	WND	SUMO
Adjectives	5.69	1.14	2.32	1.27
Nouns	3.84	2.42	2.28	2.95
Verbs	6.66	3.17	2.04	4.35
All	4.91	2.65	2.23	2.96

More information about the annotation process of Cast3LB can be found in[7].

4 Experiments

The experiments have been designed in order to analyze the behaviour of a WSD method based on semantic classes when different sets of classes are used. 10-fold cross-validation has been used and the accuracy for each experiment is averaged over the results of the 10 folds.

4.1 Features

Using information contained in Cast3LB, we want to know how different information affect the disambiguation task based on semantic classes. In this section, we present different kinds of information that have been used in the experiments.

Word Information

This information refers to word form, lemma and PoS. PoS feature allows a coarse semantic disambiguation. Since many words have senses as nouns, verbs or adjectives at the same time, previous knowledge about their PoS tags in some context helps to discard some of such senses. Moreover, Spanish language has a richer morphology than English. So, PoS tags include morphological information as gender and number. In the experiments, we have used this kind of information from target word and words surrounding it.

Bigrams
Words and lemmas within the target word context have been selected to build up the bigrams. Target word is not included in bigrams. With this information we want to find patterns or word co-occurrences that reveal some evidence about the proper class of the target word.

Syntactic Information
Each verb has been marked with their arguments and its syntactic function (subject, object, indirect object, etc.), that is, the subcategorization frame of the verb. So, for each ambiguous word, its syntactic constituents and the syntactic function of the phrase in which it occurs are known, allowing us to use all this information to enrich the set of features.

Topic Information
As topic information, the kind of text in which the target word occurs is used. Cast3LB texts are organized in several folders according to the kind of text: news, sports, etc. The name of such folders is used as an additional feature for the examples extracted from their texts.

In addition, we have used the name of the file as a feature because, in general, different occurrences of a word in the same text tend to have the same sense [18]. This topic information refers only to the target word.

4.2 Description of the Experiments

As said before, we have studied how a WSD system based on semantic classes behaves when different sets of classes are used. Support Vector Machines (SVM) [14] have been selected because their good performance when dealing with high dimensional input space and irrelevant features, as proven in SENSEVAL-3.

The experiments consist of using different kinds of information for each set of classes. The purpose, besides of comparing the performance of the three set of classes, is to reveal which types of features supply relevant information to the learning process by means of excluding them in a particular experiment[3]. Therefore, the experiments are divided into two sets: one set considering only one kind of information for each experiment, and the other set using more than one kind of information. The list of experiments with one type of information is:

- **Word Information (*W*):** word, lema and PoS at -3,-2,-1,0,+1,+2,+3
- **Bigrams (*B*):** word and lemma bigrams at (-3,-2),(-2,-1),(-1,+1),(+1,+2) and (+2,+3)
- **Syntactic Information (*S*):** syntactic function and phrase type of the ambiguous word
- **Topic Information (*T*):** topic information of the target word

[3] We have used a context of 3 words to the left and right of the target word, although Gale, Church and Yarowsky showed that a bigger window is better for class classification. The reason to do so is that we are not interested in reaching the best results, but comparing different semantic classes and kinds of information.

And the list of experiments combining different types of information is:

- **All information** ($WBST$)**:** all the available information is used to train the classifiers. That is: *Word inf.+Bigrams inf.+Syntactic inf.+Topic inf.*
- **Excluding bigrams inf.** (WST)**:** it is the same experiment as the *All information* experiment excluding bigrams information. That is: *Word inf.+ Syntactic inf.+Topic inf.*
- **Excluding syntactic inf.** (WBT)**):** not taking into account syntactic information. That is: *Word inf.+Bigrams inf.+Topic inf.*
- **Excluding topic inf.** (WBS)**:** we do not use topic information of the target word in this case. That is: *Word inf.+Bigrams inf.+Syntactic inf.*
- **Context** (WB_{cont})**:** word information at -3,-2,-1,+1,+2,+3 and bigram information of surrounding words.

Notice that no automatic tagging of Cast3LB has been performed but all this information is already available in the corpus. Our main goal is to test the advantages of using semantic classes instead of senses.

5 Evaluation and Results

In this section, the results for each category set (LexNames, WND and SUMO) are shown. The results are separated by PoS and by kind of experiment. Although all semantic annotated words (nouns, verbs and adjectives) have been used to create the classifiers, only nouns and verbs have been selected to test them: in the LexNames set, there are only three possible classes for adjectives; adjective polisemy in SUMO is 1.27, that is nearly monosemic.

As explained before, a SVM learning algorithm has been used, specifically an implementation due to Thorsten Joachims: *SVMLight*[4]. The configuration for the SVM module is simple for a first test: a linear kernel with a 0.01 value for the c regularization parameter.

To verify the significance of the results, one-tailed paired t-test with a confidence value of $t_{9,0.975} = 2.262$ has been used, selecting the results of the $WBST$ experiment as baseline to compare with other experiments. Significant experiments, according to t-test, are highlighted in next tables.

The upper part of Table 3 shows the ordered accuracy[5] values for one kind of information experiments using the three sets of classes and considering only nouns. The ranking for the experiments in the three cases is the same and the bests results are reached by the W experiment using the features: words, lemmas and PoS. The reason is that, while the target word is not usually used for WSD, it plays an important role in semantic class disambiguation. This is so because examples of different words are used to train a semantic class classifier. T and

[4] `svmlight.joachims.org`

[5] All experiments have resulted in 100% of coverage((correct+wrong)/total). In this case, precision(correct/(correct+wrong)) and recall(correct/total) are the same, and are referred as accuracy in this paper.

S experiments have the worst results, because such information is excessively general for certain contexts.

Additionally, results for WND are slightly different than for LexNames and SUMO, mainly because LexNames is a very small set of classes, and the mapping of SUMO and WordNet is done between concepts and concrete senses. WND is more like a sense clustering where each cluster groups a semantically related senses but not necessarily hyperonyms or hyponyms. This results into a different distribution of examples depending on the set of classes.

Table 3. Accuracy for nouns

experiment	LEX	experiment	WND	experiment	SUMO
W	84.09	W	**79.62**	W	81.43
B	**67.72**	B	**69.83**	B	**61.84**
T	**61.86**	T	**67.72**	T	**53.49**
S	**60.47**	S	**63.29**	S	**52.07**
WST	84.7	WST	**83.3**	WST	81.9
WBT	84.4	WBS	82.6	WBT	81.7
$WBST$	84.3	$WBST$	82.5	$WBST$	81.5
WBS	83.8	WBT	**79.8**	WBS	**80.6**
WB_{cont}	**69.4**	WB_{cont}	**71.5**	WB_{cont}	**64.3**

In the bottom part of the same Table 3 results for the experiments with several kinds of information are shown. In order to find out to which extent one kind of information influences the disambiguation results, we compare the results obtained by experiments excluding one kind of information to those obtained by the experiment $WBST$ (using all available information). SUMO and LexNames seem to have the same behaviour while WND is different.

As expected, the worst results are obtained by the **Context** experiments, since they do not contain information about the target word, which is very important in semantic class disambiguation, as we mentioned before.

Syntactic information does not seem to have much influence on semantic disambiguation when using SUMO or LexNames. However, this information seems to play a rol in semantic disambiguation using WND.

Topic information is apparently more relevant for the disambiguation process, for SUMO and LexNames at least. Topic information is useful when combined with other kind of features. Likely, topic information needs to be based on a more sophisticated source than few categories in which the texts are classified. Moreover, text classification tools or even a topic search based on broad context windows will probably provide a more accurate set of features.

Results for verbs are shown in Table 4. As in the previous experiments for nouns, LexNames and SUMO behave in a similar way while WND does not. As we expected, the results for verbs are worse than for nouns, due to the greater polysemy of verbs. An exception is WND where results for verbs are similar to

Table 4. Accuracy for verbs

experiment	LEX	experiment	WND	experiment	SUMO
W	**76.12**	W	87.13	W	68.57
B	**53.14**	B	**86.38**	B	**45.19**
T	**47.67**	T	**86.12**	T	**40.75**
S	**46.23**	S	**85.29**	S	**38.72**
WST	**76.1**	WBT	87.2	WST	**69.0**
WBT	75.4	WST	87.0	WBT	68.7
$WBST$	74.9	WBS	87.0	$WBST$	68.1
WBS	74.6	$WBST$	86.9	WBS	**67.3**
WB_{cont}	**55.7**	WB_{cont}	**86.6**	WB_{cont}	**47.4**

results for nouns because the polysemy for nouns (2.28) and verbs (2.04) in this class set is similar.

Finally, table 5 shows overall results for the disambiguation process taking into account both, nouns and verbs. As expected, the results reflect the same behaviour than considering verbs and nouns separately. Nouns have a bigger impact on SUMO and LexNames, while verbs do on WND. The reason is that verb polysemy is bigger than noun polysemy for SUMO and LexNames. However, noun polysemy is bigger than verb polysemy in the case of WND.

Table 5. Accuracy for nouns and verbs

experiment	LEX	experiment	WND	experiment	SUMO
W	**81.61**	W	**81.96**	W	**77.43**
B	**63.17**	B	**74.99**	B	**56.66**
T	**57.44**	T	**73.45**	T	**49.53**
S	**56.03**	S	**70.14**	S	**47.91**
WST	**82.0**	WST	**84.5**	WST	**77.9**
WBT	81.6	WBS	83.9	WBT	**77.7**
$WBST$	81.5	$WBST$	83.9	$WBST$	77.4
WBS	**81.0**	WBT	**82.1**	WBS	**76.5**
WB_{cont}	**65.2**	WB_{cont}	**76.2**	WB_{cont}	**59.0**

6 Conclusions and Future Work

In this paper, an approach to WSD for Spanish based on semantic classes has been presented. Spanish, as other languages has not many resources for training WSD systems. We have used the Cast3LB corpus, a manually annotated Spanish corpus with WordNet senses.

Some experiments have been carried out in order to study the performance of semantic class disambiguation using three sets of classes: LexNames, SUMO and WordNet Domains. The results are quite similar for each one. Only the results obtained for WND are different.

As the experiments show, the most important information for semantic class disambiguation has to do with the target word. As we have said, examples of different words are used to train a semantic class classifier, and that is why the specific word is so important. On the contrary, others kinds of information and context information are not useful for semantic class disambiguation. Therefore, a more appropriate feature definition must be done for semantic class.

The experiments show that LexNames and SUMO have similar results, while WND behaves in a different way. As stated before, the reason is that LexNames and SUMO are based on WordNet hierarchy. SUMO has been mapped to WordNet 1.6. However, we can conclude that this mapping does not provide any improvement compared to LexNames, since the results for both are quite similar. WND seems to be a more proper resource for semantic class disambiguation in open-domain texts.

At present we are focused on a deeper study of the influence of topic information in WSD based on semantic classes. Although we think that topic information could be useful for semantic class disambiguation, the number of topics we have used does not seem to be large enough. Moreover, we think than topic information can be more useful for the disambiguation of some words than for others. We want to develop a technique to identify those words that are specially affected by topic information. In order to do so, we are testing some threshold techniques to increase precision, labelling only those contexts which are high confidently classified.

Additionally, we are now working on a richer feature definition as well as applying semantic class classification on WSD, Information Retrieval and Question Answering. We are also studying the feasibility of this approach to extract new annotated examples from the Web in order to enlarge Cast3LB.

References

1. L. Bentivogli and E. Pianta. 2005 Exploiting Parallel Texts in the Creation of Multilingual Semantically Annotated Resources: The MultiSemCor Corpus. *Natural Language Engineering. Special Issue on Parallel Text.*11(3). Pp. 247-261.
2. Montserrat Civit, MA Martí, Borja Navarro, Núria Bufí, Belén Fernández and Raquel Marcos. 2003. Issues in the Syntactic Annotation of Cast3LB. *4th International on Workshop on Linguistically Interpreted Corpora (LINC-03), EACL 2003 workshop.* Budapest, Hungary.
3. Upali S. Kohomban and Wee Sun Lee. 2005. Learning Semantic Classes for Word Sense Disambiguation. *Proceeding of the 43th Annual Meeting of the Association for Computational Linguistics*, Michigan, USA.
4. Bernardo Magnini and Gabriela Cavaglia. 2000. Integrating Subject Field Codes into WordNet. *Proceedings of LREC-2000, Second International Conference on Language Resources and Evaluation.* Athens, Greece.
5. G. A. Miller, C. Leacock, T. Randee and R. Bunker. 1993. A Semantic Concordance *Proceedings of the 3rd ARPA Workshop on Human Language Technology* San Francisco.
6. Borja Navarro, Montserrat Civit, MA Antonia Martí, Raquel Marcos, Belén Fernández. 2003 Syntactic, Semantic and Pragmatic Annotation in Cast3LB. *Corpus Linguistics 2003 Workshop on Shallow Procesing of Large Corpora.*, Lancaster, UK.

7. Borja Navarro, Raquel Marcos and Patricia Abad. 2005 Semantic Annotation and Inter-Annotators Agreement in Cast3LB Corpus. *Fourth Workshop on Treebanks and Linguistic Theories (TLT 2005)* Barcelona, Spain.
8. Ian Niles and Adam Pease. 2001 Towards a Standard Upper Ontology *Proceedings of 2nd International Conference on Formal Ontology in Information Systems (FOIS'01)*", Ogunquit, USA
9. Philip Resnik. 1997. Selectional preference and sense disambiguation. *ACL SIGLEX Workshop on Tagging Text with Lexical Semantics: Why, What, and How?*, Washington D.C., USA.
10. N. Sebastián, M.A. Martí, M. F. Carreiras and F. Cuetos 2000. *LEXESP: Léxico Informatizado del Español* Edicions de la Universitat de Barcelona Barcelona
11. Frederique Segond, Anne Schiller, Gregory Grefenstette and Jean-Pierre Chanod. 1997. An Experiment in Semantic Tagging using Hidden Markov Model Tagging. *Automatic Information Extraction and Building of Lexical Semantic Resources for NLP Applications, Proceedings of ACL 97*, pp. 78-81, Madrid, Spain.
12. Benjamin Snyder and Martha Palmer. 2004 The English All-Word Task. *Porceedings of SENSEVAL-3: Third International Workshop on the Evaluation of Systems for the Semantic Analysis of Text* Barcelona, Spain
13. Marisa Uliveri, Elisabetta Guazzini, Francesca Bertagna and Nicoletta Calzolari. 2004 Senseval-3: The Italian All-words Task, *Proceeding of Senseval-3: Third International Workshop on the Evaluation of Systems for the Semantic Anlysis of Texts*, Barcelona, Spain
14. Vladimir Vapnik. 1995. *The Nature of Statistical Learning Theory.* Springer.
15. Luis Villarejo, Lluis Márquez and German Rigau. 2005. Exploring the construction of semantic class classifiers for WSD. *Revista de Procesamiento del Lenguaje Natural*, 35:195-202.
16. David Yarowsky. 1992. Word-Sense Disambiguation Using Statistical Models of Roget's Categories Trained on Large Corpora.. *Proceedings, COLING-92*, pp. 454-460, Nantes, France.
17. Piek Vossen. 1998. EuroWordNet: a multilingual database with lexical semantic networks for European Languages.
18. W. Gale, K. Church and D. Yarowsky. 1992. One Sense per Discourse.. *Proceedings of the 4th. DARPA Speech and Natural Language Workshop*, pp. 233-237.

An Approach for Textual Entailment Recognition Based on Stacking and Voting

Zornitsa Kozareva and Andrés Montoyo

Departamento de Lenguajes y Sistemas Informáticos
Universidad de Alicante, Spain
{zkozareva, montoyo}@dlsi.ua.es

Abstract. This paper presents a machine-learning approach for the recognition of textual entailment. For our approach we model lexical and semantic features. We study the effect of stacking and voting joint classifier combination techniques which boost the final performance of the system. In an exhaustive experimental evaluation, the performance of the developed approach is measured. The obtained results demonstrate that an ensemble of classifiers achieves higher accuracy than an individual classifier and comparable results to already existing textual entailment systems.

1 Introduction and Motivation

Textual Entailment Recognition (RTE) task captures a broad range of semantic-oriented inferences needed across many Natural Language Processing applications. This task consists in recognizing whether the meaning of one text can be inferred from another text [3]. The assertions made in an entailed sentence must be obtained from the text passage directly, or be logically derivable from it. For example the meaning of "Post International receives papers by Austin" is inferred from "Austin sells papers to Post International", so the two sentences entail each other.

In the first textual entailment challenge, a wide variety of techniques are proposed. From simple n-gram coincidence approaches [15] to probabilistic approaches that mine the web [8]. However, the majority of the systems [7], [10], [18] experiment with different threshold and parameter settings to estimate the best performance. This parameter adjustment process is related to the carrying out of numerous experiments and from another side the selected settings are dependent on the development data which can lead to incorrect reasoning for the entailment system as can be seen in [9].

For this reason, we decide to present a machine learning entailment approach that determines the result of the entailment relation in an automatic way. Machine learning techniques for named entity recognition [16], part-of-speech tagging [13] and parsing [2] among others are known to perform better than rule-based systems.

The motivations for the proposal of a textual entailment (TE) machine learning approach consists in the advantages of avoiding threshold determination, the

A. Gelbukh and C.A. Reyes-Garcia (Eds.): MICAI 2006, LNAI 4293, pp. 889–899, 2006.

ability to work with large number of features, the allowance to integrate information from multiple levels of representation such as morphologic, syntactic, semantic or combination among them.

Our contribution consists in the design of lexical and semantic features that measure the similarity of two texts to determine whether the texts entail each other or not, and the creation of complementary classifiers that are combined through stacking and voting. Previous TE research did not take advantage of such approach.

In the experimental evaluation, the contribution and the limitation of the modelled attributes for the text entailment recognition are shown. We demonstrate that the classifiers' ensemble boosts the individual performance of the lexical and semantic classifiers. Additionally, a comparative study with already existing TE approaches is performed. The obtained results showed that the recognition of text entailment with machine learning based approach is possible, and yields comparable results to the already existing systems.

This paper is organized as follows: Section 2 is related to the description of the lexical and semantic attributes, Section 3 explains the combination methodology, Section 4 and 5 describe the experimental evaluation of the proposed approach and comparison with already existing systems. Finally, we conclude in Section 6 and discuss some future work directions.

2 Feature Representation

Text entailment can be due to lexical, syntactic, semantic, pragmatic variabilities, or to a combination among them. Therefore, various attributes are needed for its resolution. For our approach, we modelled lexical and semantic information by the help of text summarization [11] and similarity [12] measures.

In an exhaustive research study, we tested three machine learning algorithms (k-Nearest Neighbours, Maximum Entropy and Support Vector Machines (SVM)) together with a backward feature selection algorithm. According to the obtained results, the best performing algorithm is SVM, and the best features are the one described below:

f_1: $n-gram = \frac{c}{m}$, obtains the ratio of the consecutive word overlaps c in the entailing text T and the entailed hypothesis H, and later this ratio is normalized by the number of words m in H. According to the $n-gram$ attribute, the more common consecutive words two sentences have, the more similar they are. Therefore, the textual entailment example T: *Mount Olympus* towers up from *the center of the earth* and H: *Mount Olympus* is in *the center of the earth.* is determined correctly. First the ratio of common $n-grams$ is high both for T and H, and second most of the constituents in H are mapped into T, which shows that the hypothesis can be inferred from the text.

f_2: $LCS = \frac{LCS(T,H)}{n}$, estimates the similarity between T with length m and H with length n, by searching in-sequence matches that reflect sentence level word order. The longest common subsequence (LCS) captures sentence level structures in a natural way. In the example, T: A male rabbit is called a buck and *a female rabbit is called a* doe, just like deer. and H: *A female rabbit is called a* buck., most of the constituents of H are mapped into T. However, the entailment relation between the two texts does not hold, because according to T, the female rabbit is called "doe" not "buck". Therefore, we incorporated a more sensitive measure – the skip-gram.

$f_{3,4}$: $skip\_gram = \frac{skip\_gram(T,H)}{C(n, skip\_gram(T,H))}$, where $skip\_gram(T,H)$ refers to the number of common skip grams (e.g. pair of words in sentence order that allow arbitrary gaps) found in T and H, $C(n, skip\_gram(T,H))$ is a combinatorial function, where n is the number of words in H. Note that in contrast to LCS, skip-grams need determinate length. Only bi and tri-skip grams are calculated, because skip-grams higher than three do not occur so often. For the texts, T: *Elizabeth Dowdeswell is* the Under Secretary General at the United Nations Offices at Nairobi and *Executive Director of the United Nations Environment Programme.* and H: *Elizabeth Dowdeswell is Executive Director of the United Nations Environment Programme.*, both skip-gram measures identify correctly that H is inferred by T, as all skip-grams of H are mapped into T.

To obtain the following attributes, we used the TreeTager part-of-speech tagger [17]. For the similarity measures, we used the WordNet::Similarity package [14].

f_5, f_6: nT, nH is 1 if there is a negation in T/H, 0 otherwise. These attributes treat only explicit negations such as "no, not, n't".

f_7: *number* identifies that "four-thousand" is the same as 4000, "more than 5" indicates "6 or more", "less than 5" indicates "4 or less". For perfect matches *number* is 1. When T and H do not have numeric expression, the attribute is 0, while partial matches have values between 0 and 1.

f_8: *Np* identifies the proper names in T and H, and then lexically matches them. Consecutive proper names that are not separated by special symbols as coma or dash are merged and treated as a single proper name for example "Mexico City" is transformed into one Np "Mexico_City". The value of *Np* is 1 for a perfect match between the proper name of T and the proper name of H, such as "London" and "London". *Np* is 0 when there are no proper names or the existing proper names are completely different. Partial matches as "Mexico_City" and "Mexico" have value 0.5, because from two words only one is completely matched.

f_9, f_{10}: *adv, adj* is 1 for perfect match of adverbs/adjectives between T and H, 0 when there is no adverb/adjective in one or both of the sentences, and between 0 and 1 for partial matches.

The next attributes estimate the noun/verb similarity between T and H. We did not use a word sense disambiguation (WSD) module, through which we will know the adequate word senses, however we use two different similarity measures the one of lin and the path. These measures associate different word senses to the noun/verb pairs and then estimate the WordNet similarity related to these senses. Although we did not use WSD, we obtain similarity evidence from two different similarity measures and different word senses. That allows us to capture the semantic variability in a broader way.

f_{11}, f_{12}: $n\_lin/path = \frac{\sum_{i=1}^{n} sim(T,H)_{lin/path}}{n}$, estimates the similarity $sim(T,H)_{lin/path}$ for the noun pairs in T and H according to the measure of lin/path, against the maximum noun similarity n for T and H.

f_{13}, f_{14}: $v\_lin/path = \frac{\sum_{j=1}^{v} sim(T,H)_{lin/path}}{v}$, determines the similarity $sim(T,H)_{lin/path}$ of the verbs in T and H according lin/path measure, compared to the maximum verb similarity v for T and H.

f_{15}, f_{16}: $nv\_lin/path = \frac{\sum_{i=1}^{n} sim(T,H)_{lin/path} * \sum_{j=1}^{v} sim(T,H)_{lin/path}}{n*v}$ measures the similarity of the nouns and the verbs in T and H. With this inter-syntactic information, the system is able to capture the similarity between patterns such as "X works for Y" and "Y's worker is X".

f_{17}: $units = \prod_{unit=1}^{k} \left(\frac{\sum_{i=1}^{l} sim(T,H)}{l} \right)$ represent the text similarity between T and H. Units correspond to the different constituents in a sentence, for which the noun/verb similarity is determined with attributes f_{11} and f_{12}, and the rest of the units are lexically matched.

In a ten-fold cross validation, the described attributes are divided in two complementary sets: $Lex=\{f_1,f_2,f_3,f_4,f_5,f_6,f_7\}$ and $Sim=\{f_8,f_9,f_{10},f_{11},f_{12},f_{13},f_{14},f_{15},f_{16},f_{17}\}$. These sets obtain similar results in accuracy, but they resolve different text entailment examples. The *Lex* set recognizes the false TE examples, while the *Sim* determines correctly the positive TEs. The most informative attributes for set *Lex* are f_2 and f_4, while for set *Sim* f_8 and f_{11} are determined. We denote these subsets as *bLex* and *bSim*.

3 Combining Methodology

[6] states that an ensemble of classifiers is potentially more accurate than an individual classifier. This is one of the reasons for which we decided to study how to combine the generated classifiers. The other reason is the design of the complementary feature sets.

With the objective to combine several classifiers, the fist condition to be examined is feature set complementarity. This is needed to establish complementary classifiers that are able to resolve different examples. Their combination is beneficial, because together the classifiers will resolve more cases. To evaluate the complementarity of our feature sets, the kappa measure [1] is used. According to kappa, set *Lex* and *Sim* are complementary, and so are their subsets.

A problem that arises is how to identify which classifier gives the more precise class prediction for a given example. In our approach, this is resolved by the calculation of a confidence score that measures the distance between the predicted value of the example and the training prototypes.

3.1 Stacking

Combining classifiers with stacking can be considered as meta-learning e.g. learning about learning. For our approach stacking is applied in the following way. In the first phase, multiple classifiers generated by the four different feature sets are produced. They represent the set of base-level classifiers. In the second phase, a meta-level classifier that combines the features of the best performing classifier together with the outputs of the base-level classifiers is learned. Thus the new meta-classifier is generated. The output of the meta-classifier is considered as the final result of the stacking method.

3.2 Majority Voting

Many techniques that aim to combine multiple evidences into a singular prediction are based on voting. Our approach uses majority voting that consists in using the generated output of the several classifiers and compares them. The final decision about the class assignment is taken regarding the class with the majority votes. Examples for which the classifiers disagree, acquire the class of the classifier with the highest performance.

4 Experimental Evaluation

After the description of the designed attributes and the combination methods, this section describes the experimental evaluation.

4.1 Data Set

There are not many textual entailment data sets, therefore for the performed experiments we use the development and test data sets provided by the Second Recognising Textual Entailment Challenge (RTE 2)[1]. The examples in these data sets have been extracted from real Information Extraction (IE), Information Retrieval (IR), Question Answering (QA) and Text Summarization (SUM) applications.

The distribution of the entailment examples is balances e.g. 50% of the examples entail each other and 50% do not. The development set consists of 800 text-hypothesis pairs, which we use as training examples. The other set of 800 text-hypothesis pairs is used for testing. The provided data sets are for the English language. Performances are evaluated with the RTE2 evaluation script[2]. According to the script, systems are ranked and compared by their accuracy scores.

4.2 Experiment 1: Single Classifier

The first carried out experiment, examines the performances of the individual feature sets. The obtained results for the development and the test data are shown in Table 1. All classifiers outperform a baseline that counts the common unigrams between T and H.

[1] http://www.pascal-network.org/Challenges/RTE2/

[2] http://www.pascal-network.org/Challenges/RTE2/Evaluation/

Table 1. Results for the individual feature sets with RTE2 data

sets	Acc.	IE	IR	QA	SUM
devLex	56.87	49.50	55.50	51.00	71.50
devbLex	57.75	49.50	57.00	51.50	73.00
devSim	60.12	54.00	61.00	59.00	66.50
devbSim	57.13	54.50	61.00	49.50	63.50
testLex	54.25	52.00	53.50	55.50	56.00
testbLex	**56.75**	**46.00**	**55.50**	**56.50**	**69.00**
testSim	54.25	50.00	55.50	47.50	64.00
testbSim	52.38	49.00	51.50	52.00	57.00
baseline	50.50	51.00	50.00	48.50	52.50

As we previously described in Section 2, set *Lex* and *bLex* rely on word overlap information captured by text summarization measures therefore, the majority of the correctly resolved examples both for the development and the test data are obtained for the summarization task.

These features identify faultlessly that T: "*For the year, the Dow rose 3 percent, while the S'P 500 index added 9 percent.*" and H: "*For the year, the Dow gained 3 percent, the S'P rose 9 percent.*" infer the same meaning, because there is a high number of overlapping words in the both texts. The attributes of set *Lex* are good for entailment, because by mapping the majority of the words from the hypothesis into the text indicates that both texts have similar context and infer the same meaning. However, the attributes in *Lex* and *bLex* are sensitive to the length of the sentence, that is why they penalize texts composed of many words. Normally the hypothesis has less words than the text, and according to the attributes, the entailment relation for such sentences is most likely not to hold.

The other feature sets *Sim* and *bSim* rely on semantic information and for them textual entailment holds when T and H have many similar words. For these attributes, the entailment problem converts to a similarity problem, e.g. the more similar words two text share, the more similar meaning they reveal. The majority of the correctly resolved TE examples are for summarization. In contrast to the previous feature sets, the majority of the obtained mistakes for *Sim* and *bSim* are false positive pairs. In other words the classifiers predicted examples as true, which in reality were false. The favor of the positive class is due to the modelled similarity attributes.

Our similarity attributes reflect the similarity of the nouns/verbs according to the measure of lin/path, in respect to the maximum noun/verb similarity for a text-hypothesis pair. When all nouns/verbs have high (or low) similarity according to the measure of lin/path, the final similarity function identifies correctly the entailment relation between the two sentences. The measures fail, when the ratio of the strongly similar and dissimilar noun/verb pairs is the same, then the entailment relation is considered as positive, which is not always correct. For the pairs *"Scientists have discovered that drinking tea protects against heart disease by improving the function of the artery walls."* and *"Tea protects from some diseases.*", the noun pairs "tea–tea" and "disease-disease" have the value of 1 due to the perfect match, the same happens to the verb "protect-protect". As all words of the hypothesis are match with those of the text and their similarity score is high, this indicates that the texts entail each other. Although other noun/verb pairs are present, the similarity measures determine the entailment relation for the sentences as correct. A disadvantage of the similarity measures comes from the WordNet[3] repository. When a word is not present in WordNet, then the similarity cannot be determined correctly. One way to overcome such obstacle is the usage of corpus statistics, the web or Latent Semantic Analysis.

The four feature sets *Lex*, *Sim*, *bLex* and *bSim*, obtained the lowest resolution for the IE task. This is acceptable for the lexical overlap sets, because they consider only continuous or insequence word coincidences. Although set *Sim* and *bSim* have an attribute that matches proper names, the experiments demonstrate that this attribute is not sensitive enough. To identify correctly that *"Former Uttar Pradesh minister Amar Mani Tripathi, his wife Madhu Mani and three others are currently in jail in connection with the killing of the poetess."* and *"Madhu Mani is married to Amar Mani Tripathi."* infer the same meaning, a named entity recognizer and entity relation extraction are needed. The named entity recognizer will identify that "Amar Mani Tripathi" and "Madhu Mani" are persons and the relations "X is the wife of Y" and "X is married to Y" describe the same event. Thus, the proper names can be weighted and the performance of the IE task can be improved.

4.3 Experiment 2: Stacking

The performance of the individual classifiers obtained similar accuracy scores, but they covered different entailment examples. Therefore, studying the way to combine the generated classifiers was a reasonable intention. The stacking experiment started with the creation of a meta-learner from a single classifier. Considering the accuracy score of the development data, the best performance of a single classifier is achieved with *Sim* feature set. This classifier is taken and selected as a base-classifier. The obtained outputs together with the predicted classes of *devSim* are used as two additional features to the initial feature set of *Sim*. In this way the meta-classifier is created. The obtained results are shown in Table 2.

The creation of a meta-classifier from the output of a single classifier does not improve the performance. After this observation is made, staging from one to two classifiers, then considering the outputs of the three and finally the outputs of the four classifiers is done. The results show that the more classifiers are incorporated, the better the performance of the meta-learner is becoming.

For the development data, stacking improved the performance of the ensemble of classifiers. In Table 1 can be seen that for QA, the individual classifiers have accuracy ranging from 49% to 59%. When stacking is applied, the QA performance is boosted to 70%. This indicates that separately the four feature sets

[3] wordnet.princeton.edu/

Table 2. Results for stacking with RTE2 data

sets	Acc.	IE	IR	QA	SUM
dev1Classif	62.12	54.50	61.50	62.00	70.50
dev4Classif	68.63	58.50	68.00	70.50	77.50
test4Classif	54.87	54.00	56.00	50.00	59.50

resolve different QA examples e.g. one set identifies correctly the true TE examples while the other the negative and when they are ensembled, the performance increases.

The performance of the test data is quite different compared to the development data. This performance is influenced and related to the low coverage of the individual feature sets for the test data as can be seen in Table 1. Although for three of the four feature sets, the stacking method improved the overall accuracy of the test data, surprisingly set *bSim* only with its two attributes achieves the best result. Another reason for the performance concerns the accumulated errors by the individual classifiers, which are transmitted to stacking.

4.4 Experiment 3: Majority Voting

This experiment concerns the combination of the classifiers by majority voting. The combined classifiers are *Lex* with *Sim* and *bLex* with *bSim*. The obtained results are shown in Table 3.

Table 3. Results for voting with RTE2 data

sets	Acc.	IE	IR	QA	SUM
devLexSim	61.12	52.00	64.50	57.00	71.00
testLexSim	54.37	53.00	54.50	50.50	59.50
devbLexSim	62.12	54.50	61.50	62.00	70.50
testbLexSim	55.00	49.50	54.00	54.50	62.00

For the development set, majority voting performed better than each one of the individual feature sets, but among all development runs, the stacking method achieved the best score. For the test data, stacking performed around 54.87%, due to the introduced noise of the other classifiers. Compared to it, voting reached 55.00% accuracy, but this result is not significant[4] and does not improve the final performance.

When the presence of the correct classes for the test examples is used, the voting combination of classifiers *Lex* and *Sim* (or *bLex* and *bSim* respectively) reaches 75% accuracy. In a real application, the presence of the real class is not existing, therefore for our experiment this information is not used. The 75% accuracy score

[4] z' with 0.975% of confidence.

demonstrates the cooperation and the performance that can be reached by the different feature sets. An improvement for the classifier combination methods is the usage of another confidence score, such as the entropy distribution.

5 Comparative Study

The formulation and the evaluation of the proposed textual entailment approach with a single data set is insufficient to demonstrate and confirm the behavior of the approach. Therefore, we decided to present a comparative study with systems that participated in the First Recognising Textual Entailment Challenge (RTE1) [4].

For this study the attributes described in Section 2 are used and the three experiments carried out in Section 4 are performed. The new development and test data sets come from the RTE1 challenge[5]. In this data sets, textual entailment for seven NLP tasks (Comparable Documents (CD), Reading Comprehension (RC), Machine Translation (MT), Paraphrase Acquisition (PP), IR, QA, IE) has to be resolved.

Table 4. Comparative evaluation with RTE1 data

sets	Acc.	CD	IE	MT	QA	RC	PP	IR
tL	51.25	74.67	50.83	48.33	39.23	48.57	56.00	35.56
tS	57.50	66.00	55.83	48.33	56.92	57.14	56.00	60.00
tbL	52.50	77.33	49.17	51.67	36.92	47.14	58.00	44.44
tbS	54.13	66.00	45.00	56.67	47.92	47.14	54.00	62.22
tS	**58.13**	**62.67**	**55.83**	**52.50**	**59.23**	**58.57**	**54.00**	**61.11**
tV	**57.70**	**74.67**	**50.83**	**48.33**	**56.92**	**57.14**	**56.00**	**60.00**
S_1	59.25	68.67	58.33	46.67	58.46	52.14	80.00	62.22
S_2	58.60	83.33	55.83	56.67	49.23	52.86	52.00	50.00
S_3	56.60	78.00	48.00	50.00	52.00	52.00	52.00	47.00
S_4	49.50	70.00	50.00	37.50	42.31	45.71	46.00	48.89

The obtained results of the four feature sets, together with the stacking and voting combination are shown in Table 4. In the same table are shown the performances of some system from the RTE1 challenge. With S_1 and S_2 are denoted the two best performing systems [5] and [8] for the RTE1 challenge. System S_3 [10] is an intermediate performing one, while S_4 [15] obtained the lowest accuracy score. We placed these systems, so that a general overview for the ability of the systems to recognize textual entailment can be obtained. As can be seen in Table 4, the accuracy performance varies from 49.50% to 59.25%.

Set *Lex* and *bLex* resolve the majority of the comparable document examples, while set *Sim* and *bSim* influenced the information retrieval performance. Stacking and voting boosted the performance of the classifiers with around 2% compared to the best individual set and from 1% to 5% compared to the individual *Lex*, *bLex* and *bSim* sets. Considering the achieved results from Subsections 4.3 and 4.4, and those of the new data set, it can be concluded that the combination methods can improve the performance of the individual classifiers, but are strongly related to the data sets and the outcomes of the individual classifiers.

5 http://www.pascal-network.org/Challenges/RTE/

Table 4 shows that the machine learning results are comparable with those of the other systems. Although the other approaches used more ample information, our machine learning approach outperformed thirteen from the sixteen participants and reached 58.13% accuracy. The developed feature sets confirmed that are applicable to the resolution of SUM, IR and PP.

6 Conclusions and Future Work

The main contributions of this paper consist in the proposal of lexical and semantic attributes through which textual entailment can be recognized. Additionally, we explore how stacking and voting techniques affect the performance of a TE machine-learning based approach. The experiments show that for the development set, stacking and voting outperform all single classifiers. This indicated that several distinct classifiers can be combined efficiently and boost the final performance. However, for the test data stacking and voting are outperformed by a single classifier *bSim*. This is due to the combination techniques which require a reasonable level of performance of the individual classifiers. As the performance of the individual *Lex* and *Sim* sets were particularly weak in the test, the combination scheme did not benefit.

The designed lexical features are brittle as they rely on literal matches, while the semantic features rely on conceptual matching, hence they are limited in coverage. These limitations lead to low individual performance and later the classifier combination effect was hampered. The performance of the best lexical feature set (e.g. skip-grams and LCS), achieves the best performance which suggests that H and T are quite similar with respect to their surface word choices, and that a lexical matching is sufficient for TE recognition.

To confirm the robustness of the proposed approach, we evaluate it on two textual entailment data sets and compare it to already existing TE systems. The obtained results demonstrate that the recognition of textual entailment with the proposed attributes and the combination of several classifiers yields comparable results to a probabilistic, first logic order and other approaches.

In the future we will focus on more specific TE features, as similarity does not always infer entailment. We are interested in creating back-off strategies that use lexical features at first and then lean upon the semantic ones. We want to explore more classifiers in stacking. To overcome the limitations of the presented similarity attributes, WordNet will be compared to LSA. Other attributes that handle implicit negations, named entity recognition and syntactic variabilities will be modelled.

Acknowledgements

This research is funded by the projects CICyT number TIC2003-07158-C04-01, PROFIT number FIT-340100-2004-14, and GV04B-276.

References

1. J. Cohen. A coefficient of agreement for nominal scales. *Educ. Psychol.*, 1960.
2. M. Collins and B. Roark. Incremental parsing with the perceptron algorithm. In *Proceedings of the ACL*, 2004.
3. I. Dagan and O. Glickman. Probabilistic textual entailment: Generic applied modeling of language variability. In *PASCAL Workshop on Learning Methods for Text Understanding and Mining*, 2004.
4. I. Dagan, O. Glickman, and B. Magnini. The pascal recognising textual entailment challenge. In *Proceedings of the PASCAL Workshop on RTE*, 2005.
5. R. Delmonte, S. Tonelli, A. P. Boniforti, A. Bristot, and E. Pianta. Venses – a linguistically-based system for semantic evaluation. In *Proceedings of the PASCAL Workshop on Recognising Textual Entailment*, 2005.
6. T. Dietterich. Machine-learning research: Four current directions. *AI Magazine*, pages 97–136, Winter 1997.
7. A. Fowler, B. Hauser, D. Hodges, ian Niles, A. Novischi, and J. Stephan. Applying cogex to recognize textual entailment. In *Proceedings of the PASCAL Workshop on Recognising Textual Entailment*, 2005.
8. O. Glickman, I. Dagan, and M. Koppel. Web based probabilistic textual entailment. In *Proceedings of the PASCAL Workshop on Recognising Textual Entailment*, 2005.
9. V. Jijkoun and M. de Rijke. Recognizing textual entailment using lexical similarity. In *Proceedings of the PASCAL Workshop on Recognising Textual Entailment*, 2005.
10. M. Kouylekov and B. Magnini. Recognizing textual entailment with edit distance algorithms. In *Proceedings of the PASCAL Workshop on Recognising Textual Entailment*, 2005.
11. C. Lin and F. J. Och. Automatic evaluation of machine translation quality using longest common subsequence and skip-birgam statistics. In *Proceedings of ACL*, 2004.
12. D. Lin. An information-theoretic definition of similarity. In *Proceedings of the 15th International Conference on Machine Learning*, 1998.
13. L. Màrquez, L. Padró, and H. Rodríguez. A machine learning approach to pos tagging. 1998.
14. S. Patwardhan, S. Banerjee, and T. Pedersen. Using measures of semantic relatedness for word sense disambiguation. In *Proceedings of the Fourth International Conference on Intelligent Text Processing and Computational Linguistics*, 2003.
15. D. Pérez and E. Alfonseca. Application of the bleu algorithm for recognising textual entailments. In *Proceedings of the PASCAL Workshop on Recognising Textual Entailment*, 2005.
16. T. K. Sang and Erik F. Introduction to the conll-2002 shared task: Language-independent named entity recognition. In *Proceedings of CoNLL-2002*, 2002.
17. H. Schmid. Probabilistic part-of-speech tagging using decision trees. In *Proceedings of International Conference on New Methods in Language Processing*, 2004.
18. M. Montes y Gomez, A. Gelbukh, and A. Lopez-Lopez. Comparison of conceptual graphs. In *Proceedings of MICAI*, pages 548–556, 2000.

Textual Entailment Beyond Semantic Similarity Information

Sonia Vázquez[1], Zornitsa Kozareva[1], and Andrés Montoyo[1]

Department of Software and Computing Systems
University of Alicante
{svazquez, zkozareva, montoyo}@dlsi.ua.es

Abstract. The variability of semantic expression is a special characteristic of natural language. This variability is challenging for many natural language processing applications that try to infer the same meaning from different text variants. In order to treat this problem a generic task has been proposed: Textual Entailment Recognition. In this paper, we present a new Textual Entailment approach based on Latent Semantic Indexing (LSI) and the cosine measure. This proposed approach extracts semantic knowledge from different corpora and resources. Our main purpose is to study how the acquired information can be combined with an already developed and tested Machine Learning Entailment system (MLEnt). The experiments show that the combination of MLEnt, LSI and cosine measure improves the results of the initial approach.

1 Introduction

In our daily life, we use different expressions to transmit the same meaning. Therefore, Natural Language Processing (NLP) applications, such as Question Answering, Information Extraction, Information Retrieval, Document Summarization, Machine Translation among others, need to identify correctly the sentences that have different surface forms, but express the same meaning. This semantic variability task is very important and its resolution leads to improvement in system's performance [1].

The task of Textual Entailment (TE)[2][3] consists in given two text fragments, set whether the meaning of one text (the hypothesis) can be inferred from the meaning of the other text. For example: Text(He died of blood loss) and Hypothesis(He died bleeding), in this case, the hypothesis infer the same meaning than test. For the resolution of the TE task, different approaches have been developed [4] [5] [6] [7].

In this paper, we describe a novel approach for the modelling and extraction of semantic information with Latent Semantic Indexing (LSI)[8] and the cosine measure. In LSI, the traditional approaches use large corpora to represent a term-document matrix through which the semantic information is obtained. However, we propose an approach where the corpora consist of the TE text/hypothesis sentences and the vector space is a text-hypothesis/hypothesis-text matrix. In addition, LSI is applied with the WordNet Domains resource [9]. Instead of measuring the similarity of a term-document matrix, we construct a term-domain matrix. To our knowledge, current researchers did not take advantage of such information. Moreover, we have used the cosine measure with two types of information: from corpus and from Relevant Domains (RD) resource [10].

A. Gelbukh and C.A. Reyes-Garcia (Eds.): MICAI 2006, LNAI 4293, pp. 900–910, 2006.

In order to show the contribution of our approach, we conduct an exhaustive evaluation. In the experiments, we study and compare the traditional corpus-based approach to the ones we propose. Then, we examine the effect of the incorporation of the new semantic similarity information to our previous TE system [11].

2 Semantic Knowledge Representation with LSI

LSI is a computational model that takes advantage of a property of natural language: words of the same semantic field usually appear in the same context. This model establishes word's relations from a large linguistic corpus using a vectorial-semantic space where all terms are represented (term-document matrix). In order to obtain appropriate information, terms have to be distributed in documents, paragraphs or sentences. This distribution will determine which is the co-occurrence among different terms and the threshold of using other terms in the same context. In other words, LSI extracts relations among terms and documents and tries to reduce the current noise in these relations. For this purpose, and once the term-document matrix is obtained, LSI uses a variant of factorial analysis: the Singular Value Decomposition (SVD). This technique uses a recursive algorithm to decompose the term-document matrix into three other matrices, that contain singular vectors and singular values. These matrices show a breakdown of the original data into linearly independent factors. Moreover, a great number of these factors are very small and can be ignored in order to obtain an approximated model with less factors. The final result is a reduced model of the initial term-document matrix that will be used in order to establish word similarities.

This section presents how we extract information from different linguistic resources and how we apply LSI method in order to extract word similarity information from a semantic space. We are interested in how LSI contributes to resolve TE because it has been not applied before in such task.

For our purpose, we have done different experiments using three types of corpus. The first one is British National Corpus (BNC)[12] and we build the LSI semantic space using the documents in BNC. The obtained term-document matrix will be used by the LSI method. The second corpus is obtained from sentences of Text and Hypothesis of RTE2. In this case, we build two type of matrices: text-hypothesis matrix (rows are the text sentences and columns are the hypothesis sentences) and hypothesis-text matrix (rows are hypothesis sentences and columns are the text sentences). The main purpose of using these different type of matrices is to measure how important the words are in the semantic space in order to extract relevant information. And the last type of corpus is obtained from WordNet Domains resource. In this case we build a term-domain matrix using the information provided by WordNet Domains [9].

All these matrices representation types are described in subsections below.

2.1 Semantic Space from Corpus

British National Corpus has a collection of about 4000 documents obtained from national newspapers, specialist periodicals and journals for all ages and interests... This corpus provides useful information in order to establish word relations from their frequency in documents.

For our purpose, we build a term-document matrix where rows represent all the possible terms in the corpus and columns represent all the documents. In our first approximation, we extract all words previously stemmed and compute how many times each word appears in each document. This information is provided to the LSI module in order to obtain a new conceptual space.

Once we have our conceptual space based on the information provided by the BNC corpus we can establish how similar each pair of sentences are. In our case, we want to infer if each T_i-H_i pair (where $i = 1..n$ is the number of pairs in RTE2) infer the same meaning. For this purpose and using LSI method, we have done two types of experiments: one extracting the 20 more relevant documents to each sentence and other extracting the 800 more relevant words of each sentence. The final result for each type of experiment is a normalized value between 0-1 to illustrate how similar are each pair of sentences (the more closer to 1 the more similar they are).

2.2 Semantic Space from Text-Hypothesis

In this section we present another kind of experiments using as source of information the words of Text and Hypothesis sentences. In this case, we want to establish how similar are each T-H pair by using as semantic space: Text sentences or Hypothesis sentences. In other words, we build two different types of matrices: one using Text sentences as corpus and other using Hypothesis sentences as corpus.

The Hypothesis-Text matrix has one column for each Text sentence. So, in order to establish how similar H-T are, we compute for each Hypothesis sentence which are the most relevant Text sentences according our conceptual space. The result is a list of the 20 most relevant Text sentences with a similarity value associated. If the Text couple of the Hypothesis we are searching is among the 20 Text sentences extracted, we extract the similarity value given by the LSI method (between 0-1) in other case, H-T has a value of 0 similarity.

The same procedure is used to build the Text-Hypothesis matrix and compute how similar T-H pairs are.

2.3 Semantic Space from WordNet Domains

In this section we show how to create a term-domain matrix from the information of WordNet Domains in order to obtain a new semantic space. So, the first step is obtaining the set of domain labels because we will have one column for each domain label in our term-domain matrix. In this case we have a hierarchy with about 200 labels.

Once we know how many domain labels are, we need to extract which words are related to each domain label. In other words, we must obtain a list of words for each domain label using the information of WordNet Domains. In this step we extract the information of WordNet glosses and assign to each word its associated domain. That is to say, we have grouped all word senses (with their gloss and examples) in domain labels in order to do pairs of word-domain. An example of how domain labels are assigned to each word sense is showed in Table 1.

In this case, the word brass has associated for each sense different domain labels and in WordNet Domains all word senses in are tagged in the same way as brass in

Table 1. Labelling brass senses with domains

Synset	Domain	Word Sense	Gloss
02330776	music	Brass#1	a wind instrument that consists of a brass tube (usually of variable length) blown by means of a cup-shaped or funnel-shaped mouthpiece
06071657	administration politics	Brass#2	the persons (or committees or departments etc.) who make up a governing body and who administer something; "he claims that the present administration is corrupt";
03792240	factotum	Brass#3	impudent aggressiveness; "I couldn't believe her boldness"; "he had the the effrontery to question my honesty"
02331254	factotum	Brass#4	an ornament or utensil made of brass
02331144	tourism	Brass#5	a memorial tablet made of brass

Table 1. To obtain a list of word-domain pairs, we assume that words of glosses are semantically closer to the word sense defined. So, we assign for each word of the gloss the same domains assigned for the word sense defined. For example, brass#1 has the gloss *"a wind instrument that consists of a brass tube (usually of variable length) blown by means of a cup-shaped or funnel-shaped mouthpiece"*, and the domain *"music"*, therefore, each word in its gloss is related to domain *"music"*[1].

Once we obtain all word-domain pairs, we build a word-domain matrix in order to obtain a new semantic space with LSI, based on information from domain classification.

3 Application of the Cosine Measure

In order to identify different similarities among words we need to establish one way to measure the degree of similarity. In this work we choose a vector based approach, the cosine measure. This approach measures the distance between two words using co-occurrence vectors. Each word is represented with one co-occurrence vector and the degree of similarity between two words is obtained by measuring the distance between its associated co-occurrence vectors. So, in order to obtain co-occurrence vectors there are different types of lexical relationships that can be used. The traditional corpus-based approach is based on building a type of vectors named word co-occurrence vectors. This type of vectors represent a word by their patterns with other words in a corpus. In other words, we can measure the similarity between two words using grammatical relations (co-occurrence of words in specific syntactic relations) or non grammatical relations (co-occurrence of words in a n-words window). However, we can consider other type of co-occurrence vectors using an alternative representation: document co-occurrence vectors. In this case, relations among words are extracted from a set of documents and the similarity between each pair of words is computed by measuring their overlap in the set of documents.

[1] In order to obtain word-domain pairs we only consider nouns, verbs, adjectives and adverbs.

Next subsections present a description of how we obtain co-occurrence vectors to measure the similarity between both sentences Text and Hypothesis. We introduce two different types of co-occurrence vectors, one based on corpus information and the other based on a lexical resource (Relevant Domains) obtained from a lexical database.

3.1 Document Frequency

In our first approach we study the effect of using the cosine measure with the information provided by the BNC. This corpus provides a set of about 4000 documents and we establish the similarity between two words using document co-occurrence vectors. Our purpose is to establish how similar are the Text (T) and Hypothesis (H) sentences by their semantic distance.

The first step is representing T and H with vectors. Each vector has around 4000 attributes, one for each document in BNC. In our case, each vector represents one sentence (T or H). So, in order to give value to each attribute of the vector we need to compute which is the frequency of all words in the sentence in each documents in the corpus. Notice that the number of words in T and H is different, so, we need to normalize the results obtained according to the number of words of each sentence.

In addition, once obtained the information provided by frequencies of words we calculate the Inverse Document Frequency (*idf*). This measure is commonly used in Information Retrieval and provides high values for rare words and low values for common words. The Equation 1, gives the *idf* formula where N is the total number of documents and n_w is the number of documents that contains the word w. The *idf* is the final value used for representing each attribute of the co-occurrence vectors. This value is referred as Document Frequency (DF).

$$idf_w = \log\left(\frac{N}{n_w}\right) \tag{1}$$

Once obtained the document co-occurrence vectors, we can measure the similarity between two sentences (T and H) by the value of the cosine (Equation 2).

$$\cos(T,H) = \frac{T \cdot H}{|T|\,|H|} = \frac{\sum_{i=1}^{n} T_i \cdot H_i}{\sqrt{\sum_{i=1}^{n} {T_i}^2} \cdot \sqrt{\sum_{i=1}^{n} {H_i}^2}} \tag{2}$$

In our study, we use different cosine boundaries in order to establish which are the most appropriate values to extract correct inferences between T and H. The results of applying this measure are showed in Table 3.

3.2 Relevant Domains

This section presents a second approach to infer semantic relations between T and H. In this approach, we obtain the cosine measure using Relevant Domains (RD) [10] information in order to represent domain co-occurrence vectors. The RD resource is obtained from WordNet Domains (WND) [9] that is an extension of WordNet. The characteristics and structure of this resource has been explained in section 2.3.

In order to extract the RD we use the words of WordNet glosses. In Table 1 we have an example of how the glosses are related to domains. We label the words of glosses with their appropriate domain. This information is used to compute how relevant is one word to each domain. So, once we know how many times one word appears with one domain in the whole lexical database, we can establish with the Association Ratio (AR) [13] (Equation 3), which are the most relevant domains to this word.

$$AR(w, D) = Pr(w|D)\, log_2 \frac{Pr(w|D)}{Pr(w)} \quad (3)$$

Therefore, the RD contains all words of WordNet Domains with their most relevant domains sorted by the AR. For example, here we have an extraction of how AR is calculated for the word *"organ"*: *Organ{Surgery-0.189502, Radiology-0.109413, Sexuality-0.048288, Optics-0.048277, Anatomy-0.047832, Physiology-0.029388, ...- ...}*.

In our work, we use this resource in order to build domain co-occurrence vectors. This kind of vectors have as many attributes as many domains. To measure the distance between T and H sentences we extract all words of each sentence, obtain which are their RD and build the domain co-occurrence vectors. Therefore, once we have each pair of domain co-occurrence vectors we calculate their semantic distance with the cosine measure.

One of the reasons of using this type of resource is because we want to establish how corpus dependent is the cosine measure. In other words, we can extract word frequencies from different corpora and obtain different results when we calculate the distance between the same pair of sentences. So, with the RD resource we try to avoid the corpus dependence because word-domain pairs are extracted from a lexical database and relations are obtained according their meanings and not according a specific field or document classification.

4 Experimental Results

This section presents a set of experiments using our different approaches. In one hand, we have done experiments with LSI using as corpus the BNC, WordNet Domains, Text sentences and Hypothesis sentences. And in the other hand, we have done experiments with the cosine measure using a document frequency approach and a new approach using Relevant Domains resource. Moreover, we have combined these different approaches with our machine-learning system in order to study the effect of adding this new information. As a result, we find that the combination of LSI and cosine with the machine-learning system improves the textual entailment results.

4.1 The *RTE2* Data

For our experimental setup, we use the development and test data sets provided by the Second Recognizing Textual Entailment Challenge (RTE2)[2]. The examples in these

[2] http://www.pascal-network.org/Challenges/RTE2/

data sets have been extracted from real Information Extraction (IE), Information Retrieval (IR), Question Answering (QA) and Text Summarization (SUM) applications. The corpus includes 1600 English text-hypothesis entailment examples, of which 800 are used as a development data and the remaining 800 pairs as a test data. In RTE2 the corpus is balanced, 50% are true examples and the other 50% are false examples.

The performances of our experiments are determined with the RTE2 evaluation script[3]. According to the script, systems are ranked and compared by their accuracy scores.

4.2 LSI

The LSI experiments show the influence of the usage of different corpora through which the sense of two sentences can be inferred.

As we describe in Section 2 we build the LSI initial matrix from different types of corpora. Therefore, for each kind of corpus we have obtained different results for the TE task. The information used in each experiment is explained here [4]:

- **BNC corpus** *(LSI_BNC_NoTag)*. Results using lemmatized words from BNC.
- **H sentences** *(LSI_LemaH, LSI_NoLemaH)*. Results using as corpus H sentences and building two different matrices: one with lemmatized words and another with no lemmatized words.
- **T sentences***(LSI_LemaT, LSI_NoLemaT)*. Results using as corpus T sentences and building two different matrices: one with lemmatized words and another with no lemmatized words.
- **Relevant Domains** *(LSI_RD)*. Results using the relevant domains of each T_sentence and each H_sentence.

Table 2 shows the results obtained from different experiments with LSI.

As we can see, the best results are obtained using the Text sentences (LSI _LemaT) and the Relevant Domains (LSI_RD). The first approach uses as corpus all Text sentences, and the Hypothesis sentences are used as input to the LSI module. In this case, the results are 56.87% for the development data set and 54.25% for the test data set. This results are better than the (LSI_LemaH) because Text sentences provide more lexical information that can be used. So, in order to infer whether 2 sentences have the same meaning we need an appropriate base context. The second approach uses as corpus the RD resource. In this case, the initial matrix is obtained from the information of WordNet Domains. We use this semantic space in order to extract how similar are T-H sentences. As a result, we obtain a percentage of 56.98% for the development data set and 54.51% to the test data set. In this case, the results are good because words are semantically related according to their associated domains and this information improves the results of QA and SUM.

The other experiments reveal that we have not enough information to establish a correct TE detection, so we can use this information as a random baseline.

---

[3] http://www.pascal-network.org/Challenges/RTE2/Evaluation/

[4] Each experiment is preceded by *dev* (development dataset) or by *test* (test dataset).

Table 2. Results for the LSI

Sets	Acc.	IE	IR	QA	SUM
devLSI_BNC_NoTag	49.90	49.87	49.15.	50.15	50.43
devLSI_LemaH	53.25	52.00	48.00	54.00	59.00
devLSI_NoLemaH	50.17	50.15	50.03	50.22	50.28
devLSI_LemaT	**56.87**	**51.50**	**58.00**	**56.50**	**61.50**
devLSI_NoLemaT	52.88	50.50	53.00	48.00	60.00
devLSI_RD	**56.98**	**52.25**	**58.60**	**56.83**	**60.25**
testLSI_BNC_NoTag	49.67	49.43	49.00	50.02	50.24
testLSI_LemaH	49.38	52.50	48.50	49.00	47.50
testLSI_NoLemaH	53.37	50.50	54.00	49.00	60.00
testLSI_LemaT	**54.25**	**50.50**	**48.00**	**57.00**	**61.50**
testLSI_NoLemaT	53.63	52.50	50.00	50.00	62.00
testLSI_RD	**54.51**	**50.55**	**48.53**	**56.73**	**62.25**

4.3 Cosine

This experimental section shows the result of the measurements of the similarity of the sentences with the cosine measure. In Table 3, we present the results of the traditional document frequency cosine approach and those of the RD approach. The document frequency reaches 52% accuracy and can be used as a TE baseline. Both the development and test data sets reached 54% with the RD experiment. This similarity of performance is due to the fact that the context information given by the sentences is not very representative and does not provide enough knowledge. Therefore, on its own the cosine measure cannot establish the TE relation between the sentences, but still can be useful when combined with other information sources.

Table 3. Results for the cosine measure

Sets	Acc.	IE	IR	QA	SUM
devCosine_DF	52.60	48.63	47.32	55.13	59.32
devCosine_RD	54.25	50.50	48.00	57.00	61.50
testCosine_DF	52.18	46.13	49.43	55.34	57.83
testCosine_RD	54.00	46.50	56.50	56.00	57.00

4.4 Combination of MLEnt with LSI and the Cosine Measure

The experiments revealed that LSI and the cosine are not powerful enough to establish the correct TE relation of two sentences. However, they still contribute and provide useful information. We believe that when these techniques are combined with other knowledge sources, the TE inference can be improved. We used a previous Machine learning TE system (MLEnt) and added the information provided for both LSI and cosine measure. Our purpose is studying whether the combination of MLEnt with semantic information improves the previous results.

In Table 4 there are several experiments combining the MLEnt system with both LSI and cosine measures. We can distinguish two types of experiments: one with the previous MLEnt system and other with the combination of LSI and cosine measure. Each experiment is detailed next:

- **MLEnt with previous features** *(MLEnt_Lex, MLEnt_Sem)*. Results of the previous MLEnt system with Lexical or Semantical features.
- **MLEnt with LSI** *(MLEnt_Lex_LSI_LemaT, MLEnt_Sem_LSI_LemaT)*. Results of the previous MLEnt system with LSI. In this case, we use as corpus for LSI the Text sentences with lemmatized words.
- **MLEnt with cosine** *(MLEnt_Lex_cosine,MLEnt_Sem_cosine)*. Results of the previous MLEnt system with the cosine measure. In this case, cosine is obtained from Relevant Domains.
- **MLEnt with LSI and cosine** *(MLEnt_Lex_LSI_LemaT_cosine, MLEnt_Sem_LSI _LemaT_cosine)*. Results of the previous MLEnt system with LSI and cosine measure. In this case, we use LSI with T-sentences and cosine with Relevant Domains.

In order to measure the effect of adding semantic information in the MLEnt system we have selected the best results obtained in the experiments with LSI and cosine.

Table 4. Results for the combination of MLEnt with LSI and the cosine measure

Sets	Acc.	IE	IR	QA	SUM
devMLEnt_Lex	56.87	49.50	55.50	51.00	71.50
devMLEnt_Sem	60.12	54.00	61.00	59.00	66.50
devMLEnt_Lex_LSI_LemaT	**62.03**	**56.13**	**62.53**	**60.32**	**69.15**
devMLEnt_Lex_cosine	56.91	49.45	55.62	52.13	70.43
devMLEnt_Lex_LSI_LemaT_cosine	57.13	49.50	55.50	52.50	71.00
devMLEnt_Sem_LSI_LemaT	**62.56**	**57.13**	**62.83**	**60.54**	**69.75**
devMLEnt_Sem_cosine	60.21	54.13	61.06	59.14	66.54
devMLEnt_Sem_LSI_LemaT_cosine	**61.75**	**56.00**	**59.50**	**62.50**	**69.00**
testMLEnt_Lex	51.75	52.00	53.50	55.50	46.00
testMLEnt_Sem	54.25	50.00	55.50	47.50	64.00
testMLEnt_Lex_LSI_LemaT	**55.01**	**51.23**	**55.83**	**47.96**	**65.03**
testMLEnt_Lex_cosine	52.57	49.50	44.95	53.73	62.13
testMLEnt_Lex_LSI_LemaT_cosine	54.87	46.50	53.00	56.00	64.00
testMLEnt_Sem_LSI_LemaT	**56.18**	**52.03**	**56.53**	**50.14**	**66.03**
testMLEnt_Sem_cosine	54.42	50.22	55.62	47.61	64.25
testMLEnt_Sem_LSI_LemaT_cosine	**56.50**	**53.00**	**58.00**	**57.50**	**57.50**

As Table 4 shows, the experiments carried out combining LSI and cosine information improve the previous results of the MLEnt system. We noticed that adding this information as a new feature to our MLEnt system obtain better results. So, the addition of semantic information is a good way to improve the results in a MLEnt system. In fact, the best score is about 62% for the development data set and about 57% for the test data set. This score was obtained in an experiment that combined the results of LSI, cosine and MLEnt system.

In conclusion, we can assume that LSI and cosine measure provide useful information that can improve a previous a machine-learning entailment system.

5 Conclusions

This paper presents a TE approach based on semantic similarity information obtained by the LSI and the cosine measure. Initially, we compare the influence of different corpora such as the BNC and the text-hypothesis sentence space. The experiments show that the results of a big corpus do not influence so much the one produced by the text-hypothesis space. The information in a corpus depends on the domain or the topic and can influence the relevance of a word or a whole sentence. In order to avoid such dependencies, we propose two approaches: LSI and cosine measure based on Relevant domains resource. These approaches consider information from a static resource, WordNet Domains lexical data base, that is more relevant than a dynamic corpus where the frequency ratio or presence of words changes. Therefore, we noticed that the results using the development and test data are similar reaching 54% for the cosine and 54.5% for the LSI methods.

Once we studied the contribution of LSI and the cosine, we noticed that the provided information by these techniques is not sufficient for the correct and ample recognition of TE. For this reason, we conducted another experiment, where the combination of LSI, the cosine and an already existing machine-learning based TE system were studied. The exhaustive experiments show how this combination improves results with 61.75% for the development data set and 56.50% for the test data set.

In conclusion, we noticed that LSI is a powerful NLP tool which serves for the extraction of semantic information and can improve the results of an existing machine-learning system. We explored different functions of this technique, however in the future, we want to use its properties in order to extract synonym, antonym and other type of word relations. Moreover, in this work the semantic similarity is evaluated considering the whole sentence, which introduces lots of noise. Therefore, we plan to study the influence of using syntagmatic information instead of using the whole sentence.

Acknowledgements

This research has been partially funded by the Spanish Government under project CICyT number TIC2003-07158-C04-01 and PROFIT number FIT-340100-2004-14 and by the Valencia Government under project numbers GV04B-276.

References

1. Kozareva, Z., Montoyo, A.: The role and the resolution of textual entailment for natural language processing applications. In: 11th International Conference on Applications of Natural Language to Information Systems (NLDB). (2006)
2. Dagan, I., Glickman, O., Magnini, B.: The pascal recognising textual entailment challenge. In: Proceedings of the PASCAL Challenges Workshop on Recognising Textual Entailment. (2005)

3. Dagan, I., Glickman., O.: Probabilistic textual entailment: Generic applied modeling of language variability. In: PASCAL Workshop on Learning Methods for Text Understanding and Mining. (2004)
4. Akhmatova, E.: Textual entailment resolution via atomic propositions. (In: Proceedings of the PASCAL Challenges Workshop on Recognising Textual Entailment, 2005.) 61–64
5. Herrera, J., Peñas, A., Verdejo., F.: Textual entailment recognition based on dependency analysis and wordnet. (In: Proceedings of the PASCAL Challenges Workshop on Recognising Textual Entailment,2005.)
6. Jijkoun, V., de Rijke, M.: Recognizing textual entailment using lexical similarity. (In: Proceedings of the PASCAL Challenges Workshop on Recognising Textual Entailment,2005.)
7. Montes, M., Gelbukh, A., López, A., Baeza-Yates, R.: Flexible comparison of conceptual graphs. In: DEXA. Lecture Notes in Computer Science, Springer-Verlag (2001) 102–111
8. Deerwester, S., Dumais, S.T., Furnas, G.W., Landauer, T.K., Harshman, R.: Indexing by latent semantic indexing. In: Journal of the American Society for Information Science. Volume 41. (1990) 321–407
9. Magnini, B., Cavaglia, G.: Integrating Subject Field Codes into WordNet. In Gavrilidou, M., Crayannis, G., Markantonatu, S., Piperidis, S., Stainhaouer, G., eds.: Proceedings of LREC-2000, Second International Conference on Language Resources and Evaluation, Athens, Greece (2000) 1413–1418
10. Vázquez, S., Montoyo, A., Rigau, G.: Using relevant domains resource for word sense disambiguation. In: IC-AI. (2004) 784–789
11. Kozareva, Z., Montoyo, A.: Mlent: The machine learning entailment system of the university of alicante. In: Proceedings of the PASCAL Challenges Workshop on Recognising Textual Entailment. (2006)
12. Aston, G.: The british national corpus as a language learner resource. (In: TALC 96)
13. Church, K., Hanks, P.: Word association norms, mutual information and lexicograhy. Computational Lingüistics **16** (1990) 22–29

On the Identification of Temporal Clauses

Georgiana Puşcaşu*, Patricio Martínez Barco, and Estela Saquete Boró

Department of Software and Computing Systems
University of Alicante, Spain
{georgie, patricio, stela}@dlsi.ua.es

Abstract. This paper describes a machine learning approach to the identification of temporal clauses by disambiguating the subordinating conjunctions used to introduce them. Temporal clauses are regularly marked by subordinators, many of which are ambiguous, being able to introduce clauses of different semantic roles. The paper also describes our work on generating an annotated corpus of sentences embedding clauses introduced by ambiguous subordinators that might have temporal value. Each such clause is annotated as temporal or non-temporal by testing whether it answers the questions *when*, *how often* or *how long* with respect to the action of its superordinate clause. Using this corpus, we then train and evaluate personalised classifiers for each ambiguous subordinator, in order to set apart temporal usages. Several classifiers are evaluated, and the best performing ones achieve an average accuracy of 89.23% across the set of ambiguous connectives.

1 Introduction

Temporality is a key dimension of natural language. Access to temporal information conveyed in text can lead to improvement in the performance of many Natural Language Processing (NLP) applications, such as Question Answering (QA), Automatic Summarisation, Topic Detection and Tracking, as well as any other NLP application involving information about temporally located events.

Natural language conveys temporal information in a wide variety of ways, including tense, aspect, narrative sequence, or expressions carrying it explicitly or implicitly. Any framework that models time and what happens or is obtained in time consists of four fundamental entities: *events*, *states*, *time expressions* and *temporal relations*. An *event* is intuitively something that happens, with a defined beginning and end [22]. *States* pertain in reality and describe conditions that are constant throughout their duration. *Temporal expressions* (TEs) are natural language phrases carrying temporal information on their own. *Temporal relations* hold between two events, between an event and a TE or between two TEs. Temporal relations can be expressed by means of verb tense, aspect, modality, as well as temporal adverbials such as: prepositional phrases (*on Monday*), adverbs of time (*then*, *weekly*) and temporal clauses (*when the war ended*). Temporal clauses, or more specifically the subordinating conjunctions that introduce them, represent an explicit way of expressing temporal relations holding between two events.

The present paper addresses the identification of temporal clauses by disambiguating the cue phrases that may introduce them. Temporal clauses are subordinate clauses

* Currently on research leave from University of Wolverhampton, United Kingdom.

A. Gelbukh and C.A. Reyes-Garcia (Eds.): MICAI 2006, LNAI 4293, pp. 911–921, 2006.

defining the temporal context of the clause they are dependent on. As in the case of other dependent clauses, temporal clauses are regularly marked by cue phrases which indicate the relation between the dependent and main clauses. For the purpose of identifying temporal clauses, a set of cue phrases that normally introduce this type of clauses has been put together. In the following, we will call it the set of temporal subordinators (**STS** ={*after*, *as*, *as/so long as*, *as soon as*, *before*, *once*, *since*, *until/till*, *when*, *whenever*, *while/whilst*}). The large majority of these cue phrases are ambiguous, being able to introduce clauses showing different semantic roles. Therefore, one can not conclude, by only considering the cue phrase, that the introduced clause is temporal or not. For example, a *since*-clause can either be temporal or causal. The set of ambiguous subordinators (**SAS**) includes *as*, *as/so long as*, *since*, *when*, *while/whilst*.

This paper will therefore report on an empirical investigation of all temporal connectives, as well as on the design and evaluation of statistical models associated to each ambiguous connective, aiming to set apart the cases when the introduced clauses are temporal. The paper is structured as follows: Section 2 motivates our intentions to recognise temporal clauses and surveys related work, Section 3 explores the grammatical characteristics of temporal clauses and illustrates the ambiguity of the connectives involved in the present study. A machine learning approach to the identification of temporal clauses, as well as the development of a corpus used for training and evaluation are presented in Section 4. Section 5 describes the experiments and the results obtained by implementing and testing this approach on the developed corpus. Finally, in Section 6, conclusions are drawn and future directions of research considered.

2 Motivation and Previous Work

Temporal clauses are an explicit way to express temporal relations between events. But, presently, events are not automatically identifiable according to the existing intuitive definition. Current domain-independent approaches consider as event a text unit, at a coarser-grained scale the sentence, and at a finer-grained scale the clause ([11]). An eventuality is seen as corresponding with an elementary discourse unit (EDU), that is a state of affairs in some spatio-temporal location, involving a set of participants ([2]). Researchers in discourse parsing have proposed different competing hypotheses about what constitutes an EDU. While some take the EDUs to be clauses [5], others see them as sentences [14], prosodic units [6], or intentionally defined discourse segments [4]. Considering the state-of-the-art of current NLP tools, clause splitting is feasible and good performance can be achieved ([11],[16]). We have therefore chosen the clause as elementary unit of discourse and, consequently, as the expression of one event.

Recently, the automatic recognition of temporal and event expressions in natural language has become an active area of research in computational linguistics and semantics. Therefore, a specification language for the representation of events, temporal expressions and temporal links connecting them, TimeML [17], has been developed.

Many research efforts have focused on temporal expression recognition and normalisation ([12], [22], [3], [21], [15]). The importance of the proper treatment of TEs is reflected by the relatively large number of NLP evaluation efforts centered on their identification and normalisation, such as the MUC 6 and 7 Named Entity Recognition tasks, the ACE-2004 Event Recognition task, the Temporal Expression Recognition and Normalisation (TERN) task.

In what events are concerned, a wealth of previous work ([13], [25], [10]) has explored different knowledge sources to be used in inferring the temporal order of events. Mani and Shiffman ([11]) consider clauses as the surface realisation of events, employ clause splitting to automatically identify events, time-stamp the clauses containing temporal expressions, and finally order them using a machine learning approach. Filatova and Hovy ([3]) obtained 82% accuracy on time-stamping 172 clauses for a single event type. Other efforts in the area of event ordering include determining intra-sentence temporal relations ([9]), as well as inter-sentence temporal relations ([23]). One may therefore conclude that the identification of clauses, and especially of clauses with a temporal value, can play an important role in capturing the temporal dimension of text.

As we have seen so far, many researchers in the field of temporal information extraction start by identifying and normalising TEs, continue with time-stamping the clauses embedding TEs, and then order the events using mainly verb phrase characteristics and the appearance of certain temporal connectives (like *before*, *after*, *since*). Still, there is little in the literature on automatically detecting when a clause introduced by such connectives is temporal or not. Although the treatment of time expressions is an important first step towards the automatic handling of temporal phenomena, much temporal information is not absolute but relative. Temporal clauses, just as temporal expressions, offer an anchoring in time for the events described in the clauses they are subordinate to. Unlike TEs, they require a deeper analysis in order to be able to anchor those events on a timeline, and sometimes, when the temporal clauses serve only to temporally relate an event to another, finding an anchor is not even possible.

Temporal clauses can be used in the task of event ordering. A study of temporal connectives for the purpose of event ordering was presented by Lapata and Lascarides ([9]). The authors collected sentences containing temporal cue phrases, removed the cue phrases, and then trained a model that guessed the removed marker. Some of these cue phrases are temporally ambiguous, but since the authors were only interested in recovering the cue phrase itself, they do not address the disambiguation task. Another related study ([7]) aimed at classifying 61 different discourse connectives into five different classes. One of the classes employed in this study was *temporal* and the statistical model was based on each connective's pattern of cooccurrence with other connectives.

The present effort to identify temporal clauses can aid in marking up text according to TimeML. Among other elements to be used in the annotation of temporal information, TimeML defines *signals* as textual elements that make explicit either the relation holding between two entities, or the modality of an event, or the fact that one verb refers to two or more separate events. Temporal subordinators are included among the signals defined by TimeML. Within the task of automatically annotating *signals*, the classifiers presented in this paper can decide whether or not a certain occurrence of a subordinator is used to temporally relate two events (meaning that it should be annotated with the TimeML SIGNAL tag) or has another usage within the discourse (no SIGNAL tag).

The present study on temporal clauses is part of an on-going investigation for a methodology to provide better treatment to temporal-sensitive questions in the context of QA. It will serve to order events with respect to each other in order to be able to answer questions like *Did event X happen before event Y?*. We envisage it will also prove useful in the retrieval of non-frequent answers that take the form of temporal clauses within the retrieved passages and that require deeper processing in order to extract the answer expected by the user. Let's suppose that the user asks *When was DaimlerChrysler formed?* and a retrieved paragraph is *DaimlerChrysler was formed when Daimler-Benz and the Chrysler Corporation merged.* If no precise date is associated to the merge of the two companies, then the question *When did Daimler-Benz and the Chrysler Corporation merge?* should be generated and answered to. As it can be noticed, the QA process will become a cyclic one, in order to provide better answers to temporally sensitive questions.

3 Grammatical Overview of Temporal Clauses

An adverbial clause of time relates the time of the situation denoted by the clause to the time of the situation expressed by the determined main clause ([18]). Semantically, temporal clauses may express time position, duration or frequency. Temporal adverbial clauses generally require a subordinator. Most common temporal adverbial clause subordinators are (according to [18]): *after*, *as*, *as/so long as*, *as soon as*, *before*, *once*, *since*, *until/till*, *when*, *whenever*, *while/whilst*.

Semantic analysis of adverbial clauses is in general complicated by the fact that many subordinators introduce clauses with different meanings, as illustrated below in the case of temporal subordinators:

* *when* used for time and concession

(1) ***When** I awoke one morning, I found the house in an uproar.* (temporal *when*-clause)

(2) *She paid **when** she could have entered free.* (concessive *when*-clause)

* *as* used for manner, reason and time

(3) *The policeman stopped them **as** they were about to enter.* (temporal *as*-clause)

(4) *I went to the bank, **as** I had run out of cash.* (reason *as*-clause)

(5) *She cooks a turkey **as** her mother used to do.* (similarity/comparison *as*-clause)

(6) ***As** he grew older, he was wiser.* (proportion *as*-clause)

* *while/whilst* used for time, concession and contrast

(7) *He looked after my dog **while** I was on vacation.* (temporal *while*-clause)

(8) ***While** I don't want to make a fuss, I feel I must protest at your interference.* (concessive *while*-clause)

(9) ***While** five minutes ago the place had presented a scene of easy revelry, it was now as somnolent and dull as the day before payday.* (contrast *while*-clause)

* *since* used for reason and time

(10) *I've been relaxing **since** the children went away on vacation.* (temporal *since*-clause)

(11) *He took his coat, **since** it was raining.* (reason *since*-clause)

* *as long as/so long as* used for conditional and temporal clauses

(12) ***As long as** Japan has problems with non-performing loans, the economy will not recover robustly.* (temporal *as/so long as*-clause)

(13) *I don't mind which of them wins it **so long as** Ferrari wins.* (conditional *as/so long as*-clause)

The subordinators listed above are the ones we will disambiguate using the methodology described in Section 4 and evaluated in Section 5. The remaining temporal subordinators are not disambiguated, as the clauses they introduce always have a temporal value, even if those clauses may also convey other meanings:

* *after*, apart from time, may indicate cause
 (14) ***After** Norma spoke, she received a standing ovation.*
* *before* may combine time with purpose, result or condition
 (15) *Go **before** I call the police!*
* *until/till*, apart from their main temporal meaning, may imply result
 (16) *She massaged her leg **until** it stopped hurting.*
* *whenever* may combine time with condition, or time with cause and condition, or time with contingency, but it is primarily used to introduce a frequency adverbial or habitual conditions
 (17) ***Whenever** I read I like to be alone.*
* *once* may imply, apart from time, contingency, condition and reason
 (18) *My family, **once** they saw the mood I was in, left me completely alone.*
* *as soon as* illustrates the proximity in time of the two situations
 (19) ***As soon as** I left, I burst out laughing.*

4 Methodology

4.1 Creating an Annotated Corpus

For the purpose of identifying temporal clauses, we have used the Susanne Corpus ([20]), a freely available corpus developed at Oxford University consisting of 14,299 clauses. Figure 1 illustrates the distribution of all temporal subordinators in Susanne Corpus, derived by counting all the clauses introduced by each subordinator **t**∈**STS** (for the ambiguous subordinators no distinction was made between temporal/non-temporal usages). All **STS** subordinators account for 859 clauses in the Susanne Corpus.

For each subordinator **s**∈**SAS**, we have extracted all the sentences including subordinate clauses initiated by **s** (either **s** was the first word in a clause, or it was preceded only by coordinating conjunctions or modifying adverbs such as *just*, *even*, *especially*). This extraction methodology automatically excludes the cases when subordinators like *since* or *as* occupy the first position in a sentence and play the role of a preposition (***As** a detective, I always pay close attention to details.*).

Out of all the levels of annotation embedded in the Susanne Corpus, we have preserved only clause and sentence boundaries. Afterwards, each clause introduced by **s** was annotated with an extra attribute (TEMPORAL="YES"/"NO") showing its temporal nature, at the same time indicating which clause it is subordinate to. The annotation was made by simply testing whether or not the subordinate clause can answer any of the questions *when*, *how often* or *how long* with respect to the action of its superordinate clause.

Due to the fact that there were only 9 occurrences of *as/so long as* in the Susanne Corpus, we have extracted from the Reuters Corpus [19] 50 more sentences including clauses introduced by any of the two connectives. We have then split the selected sentences into clauses and annotated each occurrence of the connective as temporal or non-temporal.

The extracted sentences were then parsed using Conexor's FDG Parser ([24]), with the aim of a realistic evaluation, independent of the manually attached POS-labels present in Susanne Corpus. The Conexor parser gives information on a word's POS, morphological lemma and it's functional dependency on surrounding words.

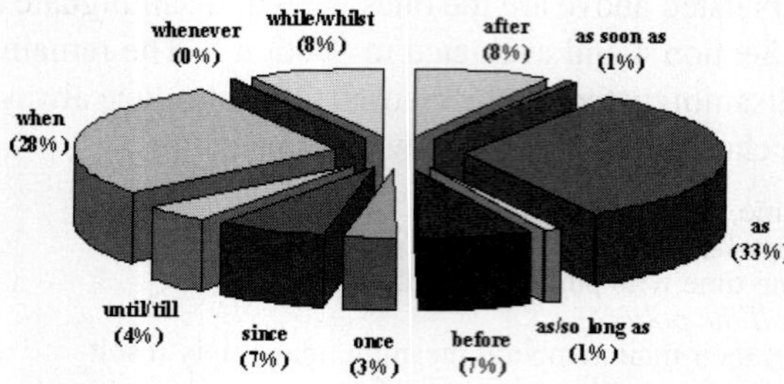

Fig. 1. Distribution of temporal subordinators in Susanne Corpus

4.2 A Machine Learning Approach

Machine learning has been successfully employed in solving many NLP tasks. There has been much recent interest in machine learning approaches to discourse parsing. One example of employing machine learning in the disambiguation of discourse markers is provided by Hutchinson ([8]). The author aims at acquiring the meaning of a wide set of discourse markers (140) and classifying them along three dimensions: polarity, veridicality and type (i.e. causal, temporal or additive). Though, the temporal class of discourse markers used for training purposes included most subordinators able to introduce temporal clauses, with no attempt being made to set apart their non-temporal usages. Also, the author has excluded from his experiments discourse markers which showed a high degree of ambiguity across classes.

The machine learning method we selected to apply to the problem discussed in this paper is *memory based learning* (MBL). MBL is a supervised inductive learning algorithm for solving classification tasks. It is founded on the hypothesis that the extrapolation of behaviour from stored representations of earlier experience to new situations, based on the similarity of the old and the new situation, is of key importance. The MBL algorithm we used for learning, and then classifying, is k-nearest neighbours. For the purposes of the work described in this paper, the default learning algorithm of the software package called TiMBL [1] was employed (k-nearest neighbours, information gain weighting; k = 1 - due to the reduced quantity of training data available). The evaluation was performed with the *leave-one-out* approach (similar to 10-fold cross-validation), a reliable way of testing the real error of a classifier. The underlying idea is that every instance in turn is selected once as a test item, and the classifier is trained on all remaining instances.

Each training/test instance has been characterized by features pertaining to the classes described in the following section.

4.3 Feature Description

For the purpose of identifying temporal clauses, several classes of features have been designed:

[I] ***Collocation features*** encode information (the word and its part of speech) about the words situated within a window of two preceding and two following words with respect to the investigated subordinator. The motivation behind including the surrounding words as features lies in the fact that, many times, a word's meaning can be inferred from its nearby context. The morphological information of the context words is also useful in predicting the usage of a subordinator.

[II] ***Verb features*** The verb phrase of the subordinate clause (SubVP) and the verb phrase of the main clause (MainVP) are identified using a set of grammatical rules, and then classified along the following dimensions:

* MODALITY: ***future*** (*will, shall, be going to*), ***obligation/necessity*** (*must, should, have (got) to, ought to, need to, be supposed to*), ***permission/possibility/ability*** (*can, could, may, might*);
* ASPECT: simple, progressive, perfective, perfective progressive;
* TENSE: ***present, past***;
* VOICE: ***active, passive***;
* POSITIVENESS: ***affirmative, negative***
* TENSE SIGNATURE: this feature conveys the representation normally used with verb phrases, that combines tense, modality and aspect (for example, it has the value ***Future Simple*** in the case of future modality and simple aspect, ***Present Progressive*** in the case of present tense and progressive aspect). It has been introduced to verify if it produces better results than the combination of simple features characterising the verb phrases.

[III] ***Verb connection features*** This class includes:

* MainVP-SubVP: a feature that encodes the tense signatures of the two verb phrases and was included because there are many regularities manifested by the main-subordinate clause pairs corresponding to certain semantic roles (for example in the case of *when*-clauses, the correspondence ***Past Tense Simple - Past Tense Simple*** signals a temporal use)
* SAME LEMMA: a feature indicating whether the two VPs lemmas are identical (this may indicate contrastive, therefore non-temporal, clauses, as in *During school, Sue liked Chemistry* ***while*** *John liked Maths.*)

[IV] ***Cooccurrence features*** are used to indicate whether or not, within the span covered by each feature, certain subordinator-specific phrases appear, thus pointing to a certain semantic role. The possible spans covered by these features are the same clause and the main clause span. In the case of *as*, the same clause span feature indicates whether *if* or *though* or *to whether* follow *as*, pointing to a non-temporal usage. The feature corresponding to the main clause span illustrates the presence within this span of:

* *so*, *same*, *as*, *such*, in the case of *as* (indicating non-temporal usage)
* *then*, *in that case*, for *as/so long as* (indicating non-temporal usage)
* *rather*, *however*, *therefore*, *how*, in the case of *since* (indicating non-temporal usage)
* *then*, *always*, *never*, *often*, *usually*, *every*, in the case of *when* (indicating temporal usage)
* *yet*, *besides*, *on the other hand*, *instead*, *nevertheless*, *moreover*, in the case of *while/whilst* (indicating non-temporal usage)

[V] ***Structural feature*** denotes the position of the subordinate clause with respect to the matrix (before, after or embedded), also indicating the presence/absence of punctuation signs between the two clauses.

[VI] ***FDG-based feature*** contains information provided by the Conexor FDG-parser that predicts the type of relation holding between the subordinate and matrix clauses. This information is normally attached by the parser to the verb phrase of the subordinate clause.

The classes of features described so far were defined so that their values can be automatically extracted from any text analysed with Conexor.

5 Experiments

In order to assess the impact of the feature classes defined above, we have evaluated several feature combinations using the ML method and settings described in Section 4.2. As baseline for each connective we have considered a classifier that assigns to all instances the class most commonly observed among the annotated examples. Twelve different models have been evaluated in order to compare the relevance of various feature classes to the classification of each temporal connective. The evaluated models are described in detail in the following:

* **MainVP (Tense Signature only).** This model is trained using only the tense signature of the main clause's verb phrase.
* **MainVP (All features).** For the main clause's VP, the five characteristics included in the verb features class (modality, aspect, tense, voice, positiveness) have been selected.
* **SubVP (Tense Signature only).** The model is trained using only the tense signature of the subordinate clause's VP.
* **SubVP (All features).** The five simple features of the VP corresponding to the subordinate clause are used for training.
* **BothVP (MainVP + SubVP).** All features characterising the two verb phrases are included in this model.
* **BestVP.** This model designates the best performing VP model observed so far.
* **VPCombi (BestVP + VPConnection).** The best performing verb phrase model, together with the verb connection features are employed at this stage.
* **VPCombi + Collocation features.** This model comprises the combination of VP features, as well as the features characterising the context of the connective.
* **VPCombi + Cooccurrence features.** This model is trained with the VPCombi model features combined with the cooccurrence features of the corresponding connective.
* **VPCombi + Structural feature.** The VPCombi model together with the structural feature form the present model.
* **VPCombi + FDG-based feature.** This model comprises the VPCombi model features and the FDG-based feature denoting the functional dependency holding between the two clauses.
* **VPCombi + Best combination.** The present model embeds the features of the VPCombi model, as well as the best combination of features chosen from the four feature classes: collocation, cooccurrence, structural and FDG-based.
* **All.** This model is trained with all feature classes described in Section 4.3.

All models' accuracy when classifying each connective use as temporal or not is revealed by Table 1. Figures in bold indicate the best performing model per connective.

The best model for *as* (88.17%) includes the grammatical features of the two verb phrases, the verb phrase connection features, the collocation and functional dependency

Table 1. Accuracy of various classifiers in discovering temporal usages of ambiguous connectives

CONNECTIVE / **CLASSIFIER**	AS	AS LONG AS SO LONG AS	SINCE	WHEN	WHILE WHILST
Baseline	*67.38%*	*73.21%*	*85.00%*	*86.86%*	*52.77%*
MainVP (Tense Signature only)	74.19%	64.28%	96.66%	84.74%	58.33%
MainVP (All features)	76.70%	64.28%	96.66%	84.32%	47.22%
SubVP (Tense Signature only)	70.25%	78.57%	90.00%	90.67%	75.00%
SubVP (All features)	74.55%	80.35%	96.66%	87.28%	75.00%
BothVP = MainVP + SubVP	81.72%	75.00%	95.00%	91.94%	72.22%
BestVP = MAX(MainVP, SubVP, BothVP)	81.72%	80.35%	96.66%	91.94%	75.00%
VPCombi = BestVP + VPConnection	81.72%	**82.14%**	95.00%	92.37%	76.38%
VPCombi + Collocation features	86.02%	67.85%	95.00%	89.40%	65.27%
VPCombi + Cooccurrence features	81.72%	82.14%	96.66%	**92.79%**	81.94%
VPCombi + Structural feature	81.00%	69.64%	96.66%	90.25%	83.33%
VPCombi + FDG-based feature	83.87%	76.78%	95.00%	90.67%	79.16%
VPCombi + Best combination	**88.17%**	82.14%	**98.33%**	92.79%	**84.72%**
All features	86.37%	71.42%	98.33%	91.10%	73.61%

features. The collocation features proved to be useful only in the case of *as*, due to many cases where the connective was preceded by another *as* followed by an adjective or an adverb, signalling non-temporal usage.

In the case of *as/so long as*, the best model (82.14%) comprises the features characterising the subordinate clause VP and the VPConnection.

Since is best dealt with by the VP features of the main clause, combined with VP-Connection, structural and cooccurrence features (98.33%). The verb phrase of the main clause proves to be very important in the classification of *since*, because a temporal *since*-clause generally requires the Present or Past Perfective in the matrix clause.

The best classifier for *when* (92.79%) combines the features corresponding to both verb phrases, VPConnection and cooccurrence.

In the case of *while/whilst*, the best performing model (84.72%) includes the subordinate clause's VP, the VPConnection, the structural and the FDG-based features.

An examination of errors revealed two main causes. On the one hand, there are cases when the syntactic parser fails in identifying verbs, thus leading to erroneous values being attached to the features attached to the verb phrases of the two clauses.

On the other hand, due to the fact that the classifiers do not rely on a semantic analysis of the clauses connected by a certain connective, two syntactically similar pairs of main-subordinate clauses will lead to the same class being assigned to the connective lying between them. This lack of semantic information leads to many classification errors, as exemplified below:

(20) ***As** she held her speech, he thought about what they had spoken before.*
(temporal *as*-clause, correctly classified as temporal)

(21) ***As** we expected, my uncle recovered fast.*
(non-temporal *as*-clause, but incorrectly classified as temporal)

Bearing in mind that this research is mainly aimed to be included in a temporal-sensitive Question Answering system, and that a previous investigation of temporal questions has revealed the need to identify what questions should be decomposed in order to have more chances of being correctly answered, we have also performed an experiment to distinguish temporal clauses that serve as time anchor (22) from temporal clauses that, apart from referring to time, carry the meaning of habitual condition (23).

(22) *Who was the ruler of Egypt* ***when*** *the World War II started?*
(first submit to a QA system *When did World War II start?*, then substitute in the original question the temporal clause with the answer, *1939*, and finally resubmit the question *Who was the ruler of Egypt in 1939?*)

(23) *Where can I find a keychain that beeps or chirps* ***when*** *I clap my hands?*
(in this case no decomposition is necessary, *when* being synonym to *whenever* or *at any time that*)

The experiment we have performed employed the data annotated for *when*, more precisely the temporal usages of *when*. Each temporal usage was labelled with one of the classes: TIME_ANCHOR or HABITUAL. Afterwards, using the same features as in our previous experiments, we have evaluated several classifiers for distinguishing between the two temporal usages of *when*. The best performing classifier was found to be a combination of VPConnection and cooccurrence features, with an accuracy of 95.12%, the baseline being 91.21% (evaluated on a set of 205 annotated examples).

This classifier can be employed in setting apart habitual conditions, irrespective of the temporal connective used to connect the habitual sequence of events.

6 Conclusion

NLP applications place increasing demand on the processing of temporal information under any form it may appear in text. Temporal clauses are used to establish temporal relations between events, but also to bring into focus a novel temporal referent whose unique identifiability in the reader's memory is presupposed, thus updating the current reference time.

The present paper proposes a machine learning approach to the identification of temporal clauses, by training a classifier for each temporal connective manifesting semantic ambiguity. There is a variation in performance between different subordinators, with the classifiers for *as* and *while/whilst* at 21%, respectively 32%, above the baseline. The average accuracy across all investigated connectives is 89.23%, significantly above the average baseline of 73.04%. We believe that an increased size of the training set could lead to an improved performance. In the case of all connectives, the most informative features have proved to be those derived from the verb phrases of the main and subordinate clauses.

The approach presented in this paper is robust, domain-independent and highly relevant to future work involving temporally ordering events, producing TimeML compliant data, and finally improving temporal-sensitive QA. Future work will also investigate other machine learning algorithms that might prove more suited to the present task, as well as the correlation between the semantic classes of the verbs occurring in the main and subordinate clauses, and the temporal value of the subordinate clause.

References

1. W. Daelemans, J. Zavrel, K. Sloot, and A. Bosch. TiMBL Tilburg Memory Based Learner, version 51. Ilk technical report 04–02, 2004.
2. D. Davidson. *The Logical Form of Action Sentences*. University of Pittsburgh Press, 1967.
3. E. Filatova and E. Hovy. Assigning Time-Stamps to Event-Clauses. In *Proceedings of the 2001 ACL Workshop on Temporal and Spatial Information Processing*, 2001.
4. B. Grosz and C. Sidner. Attentions, Intentions, and the Structure of Discourse. In *Computational Linguistics*. 1986.
5. J. Haiman and S. Thompson. *Clause Combining in Grammar and Discourse*. John Benjamins, 1988.
6. J. Hirschberg and D. Litman. Empirical Studies on the Disambiguation of Cue Phrases. In *Computational Linguistics*. 1993.
7. B. Hutchinson. Automatic Classification of Discourse Markers by their Cooccurrences. In *Proceedings of ESSLLI'03 Workshop on The Meaning and Implementation of Discourse Particles*, 2003.
8. B. Hutchinson. Acquiring the Meaning of Discourse Markers. In *Proceedings of ACL 2004*, 2004.
9. M. Lapata and A. Lascarides. Inferring Sentence-Internal Temporal Relations. In *Proceedings of HLT-NAACL 2004*, 2004.
10. A. Lascarides and J. Oberlander. Temporal Connectives in a Discourse Context. In *Proceedings of the European Chapter of the Association for Computational Linguistics*, 1993.
11. I. Mani and B. Shiffman. Temporally Anchoring and Ordering Events in News. In J. Pustejovsky and R. Gaizauskas, editors, *Time and Event Recognition in Natural Language*. John Benjamins, 2004.
12. I. Mani and G. Wilson. Robust temporal processing of news. In *Proceedings of ACL 2000*, 2000.
13. M. Moens and M. Steedman. Temporal Ontology and Temporal Reference. In *Computational Linguistics*. 1988.
14. Livia Polanyi. *A Formal Model of the Structure of Discourse*. Journal of Pragmatics, 1988.
15. G. Puscasu. A Framework for Temporal Resolution. In *Proceedings of the LREC2004*, 2004.
16. G. Puscasu. A Multilingual Method for Clause Splitting. In *Proceedings of the 7th Annual Colloquium for the UK Special Interest Group for Computational Linguistics*, 2004.
17. J. Pustejovsky, R. Sauri, A. Setzer, R. Gaizauskas, and R. Ingria. TimeML Annotation Guidelines Version 1.0. http://www.cs.brandeis.edu/ jamesp/arda/time/, 2002.
18. R. Quirk, S. Greenbaum, G. Leech, and J. Svartvik. *A Comprehensive Grammar of the English Language*. Longman, 1985.
19. Reuters Corpus. Volume 1, English language. http://about.reuters.com/, 2000.
20. Geoffrey Sampson. *English for the computer: the SUSANNE corpus and analytic scheme*. Oxford University Press, 1995.
21. F. Schilder and C. Habel. From Temporal Expressions to Temporal Information: Semantic Tagging of News Messages. In *Proceedings of the 2001 ACL Workshop on Temporal and Spatial Information Processing*, 2001.
22. A. Setzer. *Temporal Information in Newswire Articles: An Annotation Scheme and Corpus Study*. PhD thesis, University of Sheffield, 2001.
23. A. Setzer and R. Gaizauskas. On the Importance of Annotating Event-Event Temporal Relations in Text. In *Proceedings of the LREC Workshop on Temporal Annotation Standards*, 2002.
24. P. Tapanainen and T. Jaervinen. A non–projective dependency parser. In *Proceedings of the 5th Conference of Applied Natural Language Processing, ACL*, 1997.
25. B. Webber. Tense as Discourse Anaphor. *Computational Linguistics*, 14(2):61 – 73, 1988.

Issues in Translating from Natural Language to SQL in a Domain-Independent Natural Language Interface to Databases

Juan J. González B.[2], Rodolfo A. Pazos Rangel[1], I. Cristina Cruz C.[2], Héctor J. Fraire H.[2], Santos Aguilar de L.[2], and Joaquín Pérez O.[1]

[1] Centro Nacional de Investigación y Desarrollo Tecnológico (CENIDET)
{pazos, jperez}@cenidet.edu.mx
[2] Instituto Tecnológico de Cd. Madero, Mexico
{jjgonzalezbarbosa, ircriscc}@hotmail.com, hfraire@prodigy.net.mx, Santosaguilar13@itcm.edu.mx

Abstract. This paper deals with a domain-independent natural language interface to databases (NLIDB) for the Spanish language. This NLIDB had been previously tested for the Northwind and Pubs domains and had attained good performance (86% success rate). However, domain independence complicates the task of achieving high translation success, and to this end the ATIS (Air Travel Information System) database, which has been used by several natural language interfaces, was selected to conduct a new evaluation. The purpose of this evaluation was to asses the efficiency of the interface after the reconfiguration for another domain and to detect the problems that affect translation success. For the tests a corpus of queries was gathered and the results obtained showed that the interface can easily be reconfigured and that attained a 50% success rate. When the found problems concerning query translation were analyzed, wording deficiencies of some user queries and several errors in the synonym dictionary were discovered. After correcting these problems a second test was conducted, in which the interface attained a 61.4% success rate. These experiments showed that user training is necessary as well as a dialogue system that permits to clarify a query when it is deficiently formulated.

1 Introduction

Different types of interfaces have been developed in order to find more useful computer solutions for users, especially for those that depend on information. Among those stand out Natural Language Interfaces to Databases (NLIDBs). An NLIDB is a system that allows users to access information stored in a database by typing queries expressed in some natural language (e.g., English or Spanish)[1].

One of the main characteristics that researchers are proposing in the development of NLIDBs is domain independence, which means that the interface can be used with different databases. Another characteristic that NLIDBs should posses is the ease configuration, which means that expert people are not needed to define/change the NLIDB configuration for the database that will be accessed, i.e.,

A. Gelbukh and C.A. Reyes-Garcia (Eds.): MICAI 2006, LNAI 4293, pp. 922–931, 2006.

it should not be necessary that information systems or database administrators devote a great amount of time and effort to configure or reconfigure NLIDBs.

The NLIDB that we developed translates Spanish natural language queries to the formal language SQL. It is a domain independent interface that can be automatically configured and uses database metadata to analyze nouns, prepositions and conjunctions present in the queries issued to the database. This interface was tested using the Northwind and Pubs databases of SQL Server 7.0 [2].

Although the experiments with those databases yielded good results (86% success rate), the goal of achieving domain independence complicates the semantic analysis of users' queries and therefore the task of delivering a high translation success ratio. Therefore, we consider important to perform a new evaluation of the interface using a different domain rather than those used for testing in order to asses the efficiency of the interface after reconfiguration for the new domain and to detect the problems that affect translation success.

Upon detecting these problems we can identify aspects of the Spanish language that must be considered in the NLIDB development, since this language has many variations in several aspects such as the morphological system, which is treated by several investigators for devising techniques useful for processing it [3].

For this evaluation the ATIS domain (Air Travel Information System) was selected. This database has been used for the evaluation of other natural language processing systems. A corpus was created using queries in Spanish and the results obtained in the translation process (in the ATIS domain) were analyzed.

2 Characteristics of the NLIDB

The NLIDB [2] translates Spanish queries into formal language SQL. The main characteristics of the interface are the following:

- It is domain independent and the configuration process is automatic. To this end it relies on several dictionaries: the dictionary of synonyms, the metadata dictionary and the domain dictionary.
- During the translation process it does not require any user intervention.
- An analysis of nouns, dates and numeric values is performed in order to determine the columns and tables involved in the query, and a treatment of preposition *de* and conjunction *y* using set theory is carried out.
- The translation technique uses an algorithm that constructs the relational graph of the database to find the implicit relationships involved in the query.

The solution of the problem of obtaining an exact understanding of a user's query can benefit from information regarding invariant parts of the sentence, like prepositions and conjunctions, which can be exploited for facilitating the query translation process.

In this project will be utilized the preposition "de" and the conjunction "y", by having a very high frequency of use in the Spanish language [4].

The purpose of the proposed approach is designing a technique that permits better translation of a natural language query into Structured Query Language (SQL) and that requires minimum configuration effort for operating with different domains. The proposed general architecture of the system is shown in Figure 1, and a short description of the constituent modules and their contribution to the translation module is given below.

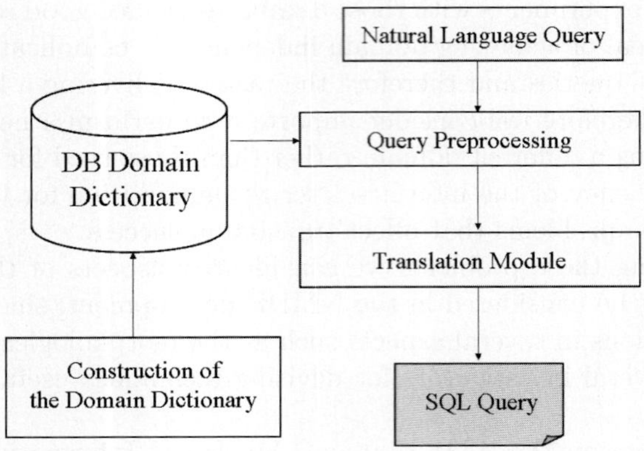

Fig. 1. General architecture of the system

Query Preprocessing: The preprocessor analyzes each word of the sentence in order to obtain its lexical, syntactic, and semantic information. The built-in parser extracts the lexical and syntactic information, whereas the semantic information can be extracted only by interacting with the domain dictionary.

The output of this module consists of the query labeled. The query is divided into words that are the minimal meaningful units of the sentence, and for each word information of the following types is included: lexical (word stems, synonyms and antonyms), morphosyntactic (grammatical category according to its function in the sentence) and semantic (meaning of the word with respect to the database).

Translation Module: This module receives the labeled sentence and processes it in three phases which are described in the following paragraphs. After carrying out the three phases, an equivalent SQL expression is generated.

Phase 1: Identification of the select and where phrases. The query phrases that define the SQL select and where clauses are identified in order to pinpoint the columns (and tables) referred to by these phrases that include at least one noun (and possibly prepositions, conjunctions, articles, adjectives, etc.). We assume that the phrase that defines the select clause always precedes the phrase that defines the where clause. In Spanish, the words that separate these phrases are: verbs, *cuyo* (whose), *que* (that), *con* (with) *de* (from, with), *donde* (where), *en* (in, on, at), *dentro de* (inside), *tal que* (such that), etc.

Phase 2: Identification of tables and columns. In order to pinpoint the columns and tables referred by the nouns in the select/where phrases, preposition *de* (of) and conjunction *y* (and) that relates nouns, are represented by operations using set theory, because of the role they play in queries.

If there exists a select/where phrase that includes two nouns p and q related by preposition *de* (of), then the phrase refers to the common elements (columns or tables) referred to by p and q. Formally, $S(p\ prep\_de\ q) = S(p) \cap S(q)$, where $S(x)$ is the set of columns or tables referred to by phrase x. Conjunction y (and) expresses the notion of addition or accumulation, such that if there is a select phrase that involves two nouns p and q related by conjunction y (and), then the phrase refers to all the elements referred to by p and q. Formally, $S(p\ conj\_y\ q) = S(p) \cup S(q)$.

Consider the query: *cuáles son los nombres y direcciones de los empleados* (which are the names and addresses of the employees). It is necessary to apply two set operations: a union, corresponding to the conjunction y (and), and an intersection, corresponding to the preposition *de* (of). A heuristics is applied to determine the order of the two operations.

The output of Phase 2 is the semantic interpretation of the select and where phrases (i.e. the columns and tables referred to by these phrases), which will be used in Phase 3 to translate them into the select and where clauses of the SQL statement.

Phase 3: Construction of the relational graph. The translation module has a graph structure that represents the database schema, where the relationships (table links) among tables are included. The columns, tables, and search conditions obtained in previous phases are marked on the graph, and from this structure a subgraph is constructed that represents the user's query.

A classification of the queries was done defining six types according to the kind of information contained in the query: (1) explicit table and column information, (2) explicit table information and implicit column information, (3) implicit table information and explicit column information, (4) implicit table and column information, (5) special functions required, and (6) impossible or difficult to answer.

3 The ATIS Database Used for Evaluation

The ATIS database contains information about flights, flight fares, cities, airports and services organized into a relational database schema, which comprises 28 tables. ATIS has been used to test different natural language processing systems, including natural language interfaces such as CMU Phoenix [5], MIT [6], BBN Byblos [7], Chronus [8], and Precise [9]. The last paper describes an evaluation of Precise and shows the results obtained after several improvement phases performed on the interface. Additionally, ATIS is representative of the databases that can be usually found in real-world applications.

4 Obtaining the Corpus

In order to conduct the evaluation, it was necessary to obtain a corpus of Spanish queries for the ATIS domain. A group of 40 students was asked to formulate queries in Spanish for the database. For formulating their queries the users were given the database schema (including the descriptions of table and column information) and information contained in the database. Additionally, the students were given a brief explanation about the kind of queries they could formulate and a few examples. The resulting corpus consists of 70 queries which where classified into the 6 types defined (Table 1).

Table 1. Classification of queries

	Query Type	Number of queries
I	Explicit tables and columns	30
II	Explicit tables and implicit columns	19
III	Implicit tables and explicit columns	10
IV	Implicit tables and columns	8
V	Special functions required	1
VI	Impossible or difficult to answer	2

5 First Experiment

The 70 queries were introduced into the interface to obtain the percentage of queries correctly answered, queries answered with additional information and queries with incorrect answer. Table 2 shows the results obtained from the experiment.

Table 2. Results from the first experiment

<table>
<tr><th>Queries</th><th>Ocurrences</th><th>Combined</th><th>%</th></tr>
<tr><td>Correct</td><td>18</td><td rowspan="2">35</td><td rowspan="2">50%</td></tr>
<tr><td>Correct with Additional Information</td><td>17</td></tr>
<tr><td>Incorrect</td><td>35</td><td>35</td><td>50%</td></tr>
<tr><td>Total</td><td>70</td><td>70</td><td>100%</td></tr>
</table>

6 Problems and Solutions

The queries answered incorrectly were carefully analyzed, which revealed a series of problems in which a satisfactory translation of the queries could not be obtained, and an action was devised as a solution in order to observe its influence on the results.

Several important problems were found related to the wording of queries. Three of the most important cases are:

- The use of prepositions in this case was dealt with from the semantic point of view. Recently, investigations have been carried out about prepositions such as the *syntactic prepositional phrase (PP) attachment disambiguation problem* [10,11]; however, in this case we detect an error regarding what preposition has to be used, as illustrated by the following example:
  In the query *"Dame el número de vuelo* **del** *código de vuelo 144576" (Give me the flight number* **of** *flight code 144576)*, the interface interprets that the *flight code* (código de vuelo) has a *flight number* (número de vuelo) which is not true, because the one that has a *flight code* and a *flight number* is the flight; therefore, the query must be written as follows: *"Dame el número de vuelo* **con** *código de vuelo 144576" (Give me the flight number* **with** *flight code 144576)*, since the preposition *with* (con) can be used to express a condition.
- In a query the nouns refer to columns or tables. Preposition *of* (de) is used to connect two nouns, as long as they refer to a single column (through one or more nouns) that belongs to a table (referred to by one or more nouns). For example, when two nouns are connected by preposition *of* (de) the usual interpretation is that both nouns describe a column, or the first refers to a column and the second refers to a table.
  Consider the query:

  Dame la ubicación del código del aeropuerto ATL
  (Give me the location of the airport code ATL)

  In this case the noun *location* (ubicación) refers to a column and the nouns *code* (código) and *airport* (aeropuerto) refer to another column. The two columns referred to by the nouns become associated by preposition *of* (del). The relationship of ownership that this preposition establishes does not allow an appropriate interpretation of the query, since the *location* of *airport code* does not exist in the domain.
  Analyzing the query we can find out that *airport code* identifies an airport, and this is a noun that refers to a table which contains the column *location.*
  Therefore, replacing the nouns by one referring just to the name of the table is needed, in this case *airport*; thus the query has to be rewritten as follows:

  Dame la ubicación del aeropuerto ATL
  (Give me the location of airport ATL)

- Other problems are exemplified by the next query:

  Dame la hora de salida y hora de llegada del aeropuerto de Boston con destino a Atlanta
  (Give me the departure time and the arrival time of airport Boston with destination Atlanta)

This query has the explicit columns *departure time* (hora de salida) and *arrival time* (hora de llegada) but the tables are implicit. Although the interface can deal with this kind of queries, in this case it is not clear because the noun *airport* is related to the columns through preposition *of* (del), which complicates its interpretation since it establishes a relationship of ownership between the columns and the table; i.e., the interface interprets that the airport has arrival and departure times, but the flight table is the one that has arrival and departure times. Therefore, if the noun flight (vuelo) that refers to the tables where the columns are found is added to the query, it will be rewritten as follows:

Dame la hora de salida y hora de llegada de los vuelos del aeropuerto de Boston con destino a Atlanta
(Give me the departure time and the arrival time of flights from airport Boston with destination Atlanta)

Our translation technique uses a relational graph to find automatically the implicit relationships between tables of the database and requires the absence of cycles in the database schema. In this case, Figure 2 shows a cycle in the ATIS database, specifically constituted by tables *Flight class*, *Compound class*, *Flight fare* and *Fare*.

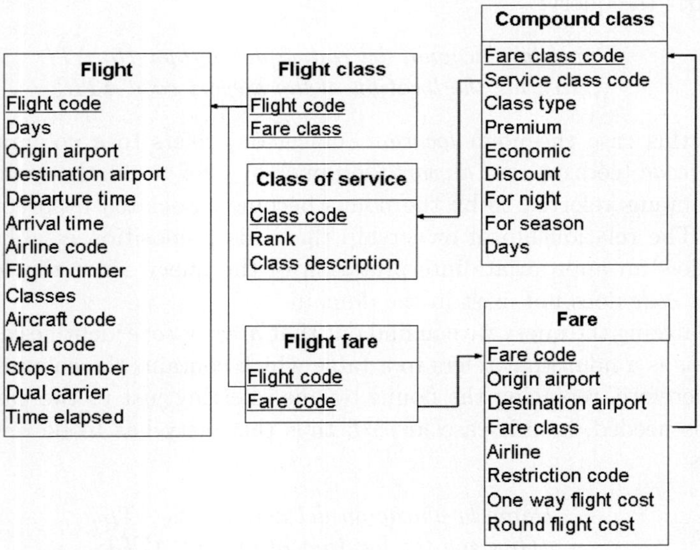

Fig. 2. General architecture of the system

When cycles are found, the correct translation of natural language queries is difficult, because this causes the interface not to be able to identify appropriately the relationships implicit in the user query [12]. For example, the result of translating the query *"Dame el número de vuelo con clase FIRST"* (*Give me the flight number with class FIRST)* is:

SELECT flight.flight_number FROM class_of_service, compound_class, flight,flight_class, flight_fare WHERE (class_of_service.class_description LIKE '%FIRST%' OR compound _class.class_type LIKE 'FIRST' AND flight_fare.flight_code = flight.flight_code AND flight_class.flight_code = flight.flight_code AND compound_class.fare_class = flight_class. fare_class AND compound_class.base_class = class_of_service.class_code

Due to the existence of the cycle, the existing relationship between table *Compound class* and table *Flight class* is included in the answer when there is not an implicit relationship in the query. Some authors propose the use of views to solve this problem [13].

Finally, one of the problems found was in the synonym dictionary of the interface, due to an incorrect association of some synonyms; specifically the nouns *days* (días), *schedule* (horario) and *time* (tiempo) were considered synonyms of the noun *hour (hora)* In theses circumstances, the query *"Dame las horas de salida de los vuelos con destino a Atlanta" (Give me the departure times of the flights with destination Atlanta)* generated the following translation to SQL:

SELECT flight.arrival_time, flight.departure_time, flight.flight_days, flight.time_elapsed FROM day_name, flight, flight_day, time_interval WHERE flight.to_airport LIKE '%Atlanta%'

in which the tables *Day name*, *Flight day* and *Time interval* in the FROM clause and the columns *Arrival time*, *Flight days* and *Time elapsed* in the SELECT clause are unnecessary. In order to eliminate this kind of problems in the translation, the dictionary of synonyms was revised.

7 Second Experiment

Table 3 shows the success rate obtained by the interface using the ATIS domain, once the problems explained above were identified and the solutions were implemented.

A fundamental part of the interface evaluated is the use of the descriptions of columns through nouns. At present, the interface lacks a mechanism to work with databases whose columns have adjectives in their descriptions, for this reason an improvement in this respect is considered necessary. The ATIS database contains some columns whose description requires an adjective, and therefore a correct answer for the queries involving such descriptions could not be obtained. For example, in the query *"Dame el costo de vuelo redondo del aeropuerto de origen DEL y el aeropuerto de destino ATL" (Give me the round flight cost from the origin airport DEL to the destination airport ATL)*, an adjective is used in order to describe a column (*round* flight cost).

Table 3. Results from the second experiment

<table>
<tr><th>Queries</th><th>Ocurrences</th><th>Combined</th><th>%</th></tr>
<tr><td>Correct</td><td>26</td><td rowspan="2">43</td><td rowspan="2">61.4%</td></tr>
<tr><td>Correct with Additional Information</td><td>17</td></tr>
<tr><td>Incorrect</td><td>27</td><td>27</td><td>38.6%</td></tr>
<tr><td>Total</td><td>70</td><td>70</td><td>100%</td></tr>
</table>

8 Conclusions

The evaluation carried out shows that our NLIDB could be configured easily for the ATIS database. This domain presents important characteristics for choosing it for this evaluation, mainly, it is representative of the databases can be usually found in real-world applications, and the number of tables and relationships of the database. The experiments conducted permitted to identify some important problems: the inadequate wording of queries, the presence of cycles in the database schema, and the incorrect synonymy relationship among some nouns in the dictionary. After solving these problems an 11.4% improvement was achieved in the results obtained by the interface.

One of the areas that can be improved in the interface is the analysis of adjectives because at present only the nouns in the descriptions of the database are taken into account. Another of the improvements that can be developed for the interface is the treatment of verbs in the query. In some cases users formulate sentences where verbs (instead of nouns) are used for referring to columns or tables. For these cases it is necessary to have a technique that analyzes the verbs and interprets the user's query.

Training users for eliminating the problem of an inadequate wording of queries is considered necessary. If users are trained in the interface operation and the adequate wording of queries, they can possibly take more advantage of the translation process.

The implementation of a user-NLIDB dialogue system for obtaining additional information to clarify deficiently formulated queries is proposed, so that a translation that meets the real requirements of the user can be attained. A better answer precision is also expected to be attained with this system; i.e., reduce the percentage of queries for which excess information is retrieved.

References

1. Androutsopoulos, I., Ritchie, G. D. and Thanisch, P.: Natural Language Interfaces to DataBases - An Introduction. Department of Artificial Intelligence, University of Edinburgh, 1995.
2. Pazos, R., Pérez O. J., González, B. J., Gelbukh, A. F., Sidorov, G. and Rodríguez, M. M.: A Domain Independent Natural Language Interface to Databases Capable of Processing Complex Queries. Lecture Notes in Artificial Intelligence, Vol. 3789,2005, pp. 833-842.

3. Gelbukh, A. and Sidorov, G., Approach to construction of automatic morphological analysis systems for inflective languages with little effort. Lecture Notes in Computer Science, N 2588, Springer-Verlag, 2003, pp. 215-22.
4. Montero,J.M. Sistemas de conversión texto voz. B.S.thesis. Universidad Politécnica de Madrid. http://lorien.die.upm.es/ juancho
5. Ward, W.: Evaluation of the CMU ATIS System. Proc. DARPA Speech and Natural Language Workshop, 1991, pp. 101-105.
6. Zue, V., Glass, J., Goodine, D., Leung, H., Philips, M., Polifroni, J. and Seneff, S.: Preliminary ATIS Development MIT. Proc. DARPA Speech and Natural Language Workshop, 1990, pp. 130-135.
7. Kubala, F., Austin, S., Barry, C., Makhoul, J., Placeway, P. and Schwartz, R.: BYBLOS Speech Recognition Benchmark Results. Proc. Workshop on Speech and Natural Language, 1991 pp. 77-82.
8. Pieraccini, R., Tzoukermann, E., Gorelov, Z., Levin, E., Lee, C. and Gauvain, J.: Progress Report on the Chronus System: ATIS Benchmark Results, 1992.
9. Popescu, A. M., Armanasu, A., Etzioni, O., Ko, D. and Yates, A.: Modern Natural Language Interfaces to Databases: Composing Statical Parsing with Semantic Tractability. University of Washington, 2004.
10. Calvo, H. and Gelbukh, A., Improving Prepositional Phrase Attachment Disambiguation Using the Web as Corpus. Lecture Notes in Computer Science, N 2905, Springer, 2003, pp. 604-610.
11. Calvo, H. and Gelbukh, A. Acquiring Selectional Preferences from Untagged Text for Prepositional Phrase Attachment Disambiguation. Lecture Notes in Computer Science, N 3136, Springer, 2004, pp. 207-216.
12. Fagin, R.: Degrees of Acyclicity for Hypergraphs and Relational Database Schemes. Journal of the ACM, Vol. 30 No. 3, 1983, pp.514-550
13. Microsoft English Query Tutorials available with standard installation in SQL SERVER 7.0.

Interlinguas: A Classical Approach for the Semantic Web. A Practical Case*

Jesús Cardeñosa, Carolina Gallardo, and Luis Iraola

Validation and Business Applications Research Group
Facultad de Informática. Universidad Politécnica de Madrid
28660 Madrid, Spain
{carde, carolina, luis}@opera.dia.fi.upm.es

Abstract. An efficient use of the web will imply the ability to find not only documents but also specific pieces of information according to user's query. Right now, this last possibility is not tackled by current information extraction or question answering systems, since it requires both a deeper semantic understanding of queries and contents along with deductive capabilities. In this paper, the authors propose the use of Interlinguas as a plausible approach to search and extract specific pieces of information from a document, given the semantic nature of Interlinguas and their support for deduction. More concretely, the authors describe the UNL Interlinguas from the representational point of view and illustrate its deductive capabilities by means of an example.

1 Introduction

Many activities that revolve around an advantageous use of the web are based on the efficiency to find not only documents but also on the capability to find a specific piece of information concerning a specific question from the user. The generation of a precise answer to a query requires, on the one hand, a process of semantic understanding of the query and, on the other, deductive capabilities to generate the answer.

Most recent approaches are based on the representation of contents according to the XML standard [1], where the structure of a document is explicit. XML is particularly adequate to find explicitly marked data. If those data are not explicitly marked and they are "only" deducible, current models can only be assisted by Natural Language Processing (NLP) techniques in order to find a solution to a given query. However, current NLP models generally lack of any sort of deductive capability.

In this paper, a new approach based on a classical concept in Artificial Intelligence is described. This approach is based on the use of interlinguas to represent contents, thus rescuing these representational systems from oblivion after their failure in the early nineties, when they did not meet their expectations in the Interlingua-based Machine Translation systems. The use of a concrete interlingua, Universal Networking Language, will be justified, and the utility of its deductive capabilities for question answering systems will be explained by means of a short example.

* This paper has been sponsored by the Spanish Research Council under project HUM-2005-07260 and the UPM project EXCOM-R05/11070.

A. Gelbukh and C.A. Reyes-Garcia (Eds.): MICAI 2006, LNAI 4293, pp. 932 – 942, 2006.

2 Interlinguas

Interlinguas are mainly defined by the following characteristics:

1. The interlingual approach attempts to find a meaning representation common to many (ideally to all) natural languages, a representation that leaves aside 'surface' details and unveils a common structure.
2. An interlingua is just another language in the sense that it is autonomous and thus its components need to be defined: vocabulary and semantic relations mainly.
3. Senses and not words are usually the semantic atoms of interlinguas.
4. Thematic and functional relations are established among the semantic atoms of the interlingua. These relations, being semantic in nature, allow for universality and depth of abstraction and analysis.

However, although interlinguas may very well provide the knowledge representation mechanisms required both for machine translation (MT) and multilingual text generation as well as for large scale knowledge representation tasks, there are some obstacles in the design and further use of an interlingua:

- For multilingual generation and MT purposes, interlinguas are so close to the knowledge level that text generation is hindered by the lack of surface information.
- The design of an interlingua is a highly complex task; it has been proved almost unfeasible to find a suitable way to represent word meanings that is at the same time a) able to accommodate a wide variety of natural languages, b) easy to grasp and use, c) precise and unambiguous and d) expressive enough to capture the subtleties of word meanings expressed in natural languages.

The issue of representing the knowledge contained in texts written in a natural language is not new. It dates back to pioneering work in knowledge representation in the AI field [2], [3]. Interlinguas appeared after the creation of knowledge representation languages based on natural language. Developed within the MT field, classical interlinguas include ATLAS [4] or PIVOT [5]. These interlinguas are paradigmatic of the dominant approach towards interlinguas; they are designed as a general domain representational system for a large number of natural languages.

Interlingua-based MT systems did not meet the expectations they created, mainly due to the linguistic problems posed by their insufficiency to express surface phenomena and to an incomplete and unsatisfactory account of lexical meaning. However, the development of interlinguas continued and classical interlinguas evolved into the so-called Knowledge Based Machine Translation Systems. Under this label are included the KANT interlingua [6] and the Text Meaning Representations of the Mikrokosmos system [7]. These developments highlight the knowledge representation dimension of the interlingua as well as the linguistic aspects, adopting an ontological and frame-based approach for the definition of the concepts. However, the burden of such an intense and detailed knowledge based conceptual modelling can only be afforded in specific domains and for a limited number of language pairs.

Other interlingual devices such as Lexical Conceptual Structures (LCS) [8] are based on sophisticate lexical semantics analysis oriented by linguistic theories [9]. LCS representations are based on a limited number of primitive concepts that serve as building blocks for the definition of all remaining concepts. This approach is well suited for semantic inference, but at the expense of limiting the capabilities of representing the lexical richness present in natural languages.

These interlinguas are hindered by the fact that they are restricted to specific domains. Besides, they require substantial work for building up a conceptual base. The use of semantic primitives may be justified for inferential purposes but their actual design and application in a multilingual (or simply in a NLP environment) is difficult and they pose more problems than they solve. However, the use of classical interlinguas, together with similar deep semantic representations, has been reconsidered in recent years, due to the necessity of designing advanced search engines to support the Semantic Web. The use of Conceptual Graphs is an example, with some interesting results, as shown in [10], [11].

In the next section, it will be presented a new approach based on the use of an Interlingua that produces a content representation that removes away the details of the source language, so qualifying as a language independent representation.

3 The Universal Networking Language (UNL)

During the nineties, the University of the United Nations developed the Universal Networking Language (UNL), a language for the representation of contents in a language independent way, with the purpose of overcoming the linguistic barrier in Internet. It was only after years of intensive research and great efforts when the set of concepts and relations allowing the representation of any text written in any natural language was defined. This language has been proven tractable by computer systems, since it can be automatically transformed into any natural language by means of linguistic generation processes, just following its specifications [12].

The UNL is composed of three main elements: universal words, relations and attributes. Formally, a UNL expression can be view as a semantic net, whose nodes are the Universal words, linked by arcs labelled with the UNL relations. Universal Words are modified by the so-called attributes. The specifications of the language formally define the set of relations, concepts and attributes.

3.1 Universal Words

They constitute the vocabulary of the language, i.e., they can be considered the lexical items of UNL. To be able to express any concept occurring in a natural language, the UNL proposes the use of English words modified by a series of semantic restrictions that eliminate the lexical ambiguity present in natural languages. When there is no English word suitable for expressing a particular concept, the UNL allows the use of words coming from other languages. Whatever the source, universal words usually require semantic restrictions for describing precisely the sense or meaning of the base word. In this way, UNL gets an expressive richness from the natural languages but without their ambiguity. For example, the verb "land" in English has several senses and different predicate frames. Corresponding UWs for two different senses of this verb in UNL would be:

1. The plane landed at the Geneva airport.

land(icl>do, plt>surface, agt>thing, plc>thing)

This UW corresponds to the definition "To alight upon or strike a surface". The proposed semantic restrictions stand for:

- **icl>do**: (where *icl* stands for *included*) establishes the type of action that "lands" belongs to, that is, actions initiated by an agent.
- **plt>surface**: (where *plt* stands for *place to*) expresses an inherent part of the verb meaning, namely that the final direction of the motion expressed by "land" is onto a surface.
- **agt>thing, plc>thing**: (where *agt* stands for *agent* and *plc* stands for *place*) establish the obligatory semantic participants of the predicate "land".

2 .We (agt) landed on a lonely island (plc):

land(icl>do, src>water, agt>thing, plc>thing)

This UW corresponds to the definition "To come to land or shore". This UW differs from the previous one in the restriction *src>water* (*src* standing for *source*) that expresses an inherent part of the verb meaning, namely that the motion expressed by "land" is initiated from water. Although this method is far from perfect, it shows some advantages. Firstly, there is a consensual and "normalized" way to define UWs and how they should be interpreted. Thus, the meaning of stand-alone UWs can be easily grasped. Secondly, it is devoid of the ambiguity inherent to natural language vocabularies.

A first reproach that could be made to this interlingual vocabulary is its anglo-centred vision, which may aggravate the problem of lexical mismatches among languages. However, this system permits and guarantees expressivity and domain independency. For a more comprehensive view of the UW system, the reader is referred to [13].

The complete set of UWs composes the **UNL dictionary**. The UNL dictionary is complemented with local bilingual dictionaries, connecting UWs with headword (or lemmas) from natural languages. Local dictionaries are formed by pairs of the form:

<Headword, UW>

Where Headword is any word from a given natural language and UW the corresponding representation of one of its senses in UNL. The following are pairs linking Spanish headwords with their UWs:

1. <aterrizar, land(icl>do, plt>surface, agt>thing, plc>thing)>
2. <desembarcar, land(icl>do, src>water, agt>thing, plc>thing)>

The UNL dictionary constitutes a common lexical resource to all natural languages currently represented in the project, so that word senses of different natural languages become linked via their common UWs.

3.2 Relations

The second element of UNL is a set of conceptual relations. Relations form a closed set defined in the specifications of the interlingua that characterise a set of semantic notions applicable to most of the existing natural languages. For instance, the notion of initiator or cause of an event (its agent) is considered one of such notions since it is found in most natural languages. The current specification of UNL includes 41 conceptual relations. They are best presented grouping them into conceptually related families:

- **Causal relations**: including *condition*, *purpose*, or *reason*.
- **Temporal relations**: including instant, period, sequence, co-occurrence, initial time or final time.
- **Locative relations**: including physical place, origin, destination, virtual place, intermediate place and affected place.
- **Logical relations**: these are conjunction, disjunction, attribution, equivalence and name.
- **Numeric relations**: these are quantity, basis, proportion and range.
- **Circumstantial relations**: *method, instrument* and *manner.*
- **Argument relations**: agent, object, goal and source.
- **Secondary argument relations**: co-agent, co-object, co-attribution, beneficiary, and partner.
- **Nominal relations**: *possession, modification, destination, origin* and *meronymy (part of).*

These relations are complemented with three additional ones, which are only used for constructing semantic restrictions for UWs, they are:

- **icl**: meaning *included in,* a hypernym of a UW.
- **equ**: meaning *equal to*, a synonym of a UW.
- **iof**: meaning *instance of*, an instance of a class denoted by an UW.

Selecting the appropriate conceptual relation plus adequate universal words allows UNL to express the propositional content of any sentence. For example, in a sentence like "The boy eats potatoes in the kitchen", there is a main predicate ("eats") and three arguments, two of them are instances of argumentative relations ("boy" is the *agent* of the predicate "*eats",* whereas "potatoes" is the *object*) and one circumstantial relation ("kitchen" is the *physical place* where the action described in the sentence takes place).

The UNL specifications provide a definition in natural language of the intended meaning of these semantic relations and establish the contexts where relations may apply, such as the nature of the origin and final concept of the relation. For example, an agent relation can link an action (as opposed to an event or process) and a volitional agent (as opposed to a property or a substance).

3.3 Attributes

Contextual information is expressed in UNL by means of *attributes labels*. These attributes include notions such as:

- Information depending on the speaker, such as the time of the described event with respect to the moment of the utterance, the communicative goal of the utterance, epistemic or deontic modality.
- Contextual information affecting both to the participants and to the predicate of the sentence, such as aspect, number (and gender) of participants and negation defined as the "complement set" denoted by an entity.

- Pragmatic notions that affect the presentation of the information (what is considered to be the *theme* and *topic* of the sentence), reference of the entities contained in a UNL graph (UNL distinguishes between *definite*, *indefinite* and *generic* reference) and discourse structuring.
- Typographical and orthographical conventions. These include formatting attributes such as *double quotations, parenthesis, square brackets*, etc.

Attribute labels are attached to UWs and have the following syntax:

.@<attribute_label>

4 Knowledge Representation with UNL

The UNL code takes the form of a directed hyper-graph. *Universal Words* constitute the nodes of the graph, while arcs are labelled with *conceptual relations*. The graphical representation of the UNL graph corresponding to the sentence "The boy eats potatoes in the kitchen" is graphically shown in figure 1. In the graph, @def means an entity or concept with definite and known reference; @pl means plurality and @entry designate the head of the sentence.

Any UNL graph is canonically presented in textual form as a set of arcs. The syntax of each arc is as follows:

<name of the relation> (<source UW> , <target UW>)

Figure 2 displays the textual form of the UNL graph. By means of these three components UNL clearly differentiates between propositional meaning and contextual meaning of linguistic expressions: the part of the graph consisting of the universal words plus the conceptual relations represents the propositional part of a given text. The addition of UNL attributes to that graph conveys the pragmatic and contextual information of the linguistic act..

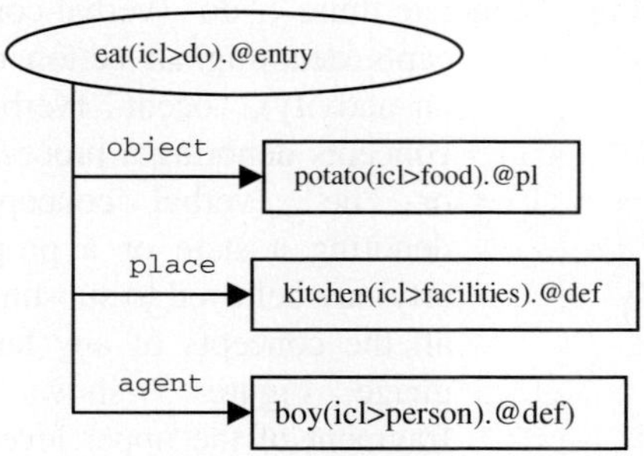

Fig. 1. Graphical representation of a UNL expression

```
[S:1]
{source_sentence}
The boy eats potatoes in the
kitchen
{/ source_sentence}
{unl}
agt(eat(icl>do).@entry,
    boy(icl>person).@def)
plc(eat(icl>do).@entry,
 kitchen(icl>facilities).@def)
obj(eat(icl>do).@entry,
    potato(icl>food).@pl)
{/unl}
[/S]
```

Fig. 2. Textual representation of UNL

4.1 UNL for Knowledge Inference

When there is a need of representing knowledge in a domain-independent way, researches turn back to natural language (e.g. Wordnet, the Generalized Upper Model [13] or even CyC[1]) to explore the "semantic atoms" that knowledge expressed in natural languages is composed of. UNL follows this philosophy, since it provides an interlingual analysis of natural language semantics. The reasons why UNL could be backed as a firm knowledge representation language can be summarised in the following points:

1. The set of necessary relations existing between concepts is already standardized. Although some of these *conceptual relations* have a strong linguistic basis (such some uses of the "obj" or "aoj" relation) other relation groups such as the logical (conjunction, disjunction), temporal, spatial and causative (condition, instrument, method) relations have been widely employed in semantic analysis as well as in knowledge representation.
2. Similarly, the set of necessary attributes that modify concepts and relations is fixed and well-defined, guaranteeing a precise definition of contextual information. Thus, UNL provides mechanisms to clear-cut propositional from contextual meaning.
3. The *semantic atoms* (UWs) are not concepts but word senses, mainly extracted from the English lexicon for convenience reasons and (implicitly) organized according to hierarchical relations, like those present in Wordnet.
4. UNL syntax and semantics are formally defined.

But to really serve as a language for knowledge representation and extraction, UNL must support deduction mechanisms. These deduction mechanisms are based on a set of semantic restrictions that implicitly make up a knowledge base (KB). This KB is endowed with classical relations, such as the *is-a* relation (represented in UNL by "icl"), synonymy ("equ" relation) and *part-of* relation ("pof" relation).

The upper levels of the KB are fixed and language neutral. Terms such as "thing" (standing for any nominal entity), "abstract thing", "concrete thing", "do" (verbal concepts denoting an action or an activity), "occur" (verbal concepts denoting a process) or "be" (verbal concepts denoting a state or a property) are believed to subsume all the concepts of any language. Figure 3 shows a fragment of the upper levels of the KB, where all arrows stands for the "*included in*" (icl) relation.

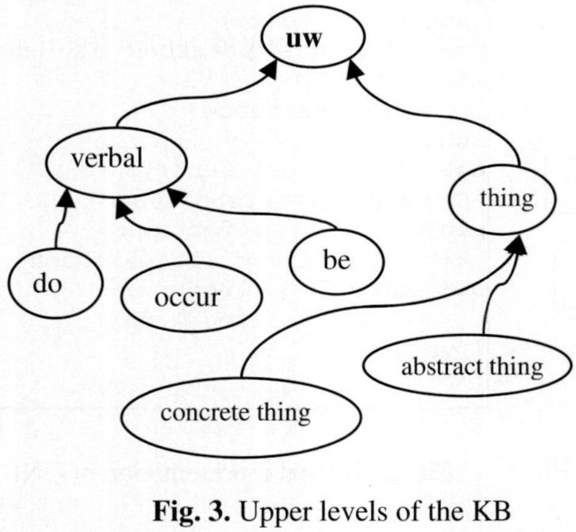

Fig. 3. Upper levels of the KB

However, as far as the terminal leaves of the hierarchy

[1] http://www.cyc.com

are concerned, the UNL KB adopts a maximal position, to the extent that any word sense present in any natural language is a candidate to be inserted in the KB, without any further decomposition into semantic primitives.

Non-taxonomic relations become of paramount importance in the KB, since they constitute the main mechanism for establishing the combinatory possibilities of UWs, and thus constraint the creation of coherent knowledge bases. For example, the verbal concept "do" is linked to "thing" by means of the "agent" relation (figure 4), thus imposing the obligatory presence of an agent for the verbal concept "do" and all its descendents. On the other hand, verbal concepts under "occur" are characterized by the absence of an agent; therefore an arc like the one in figure 5 would be rejected by the knowledge base.

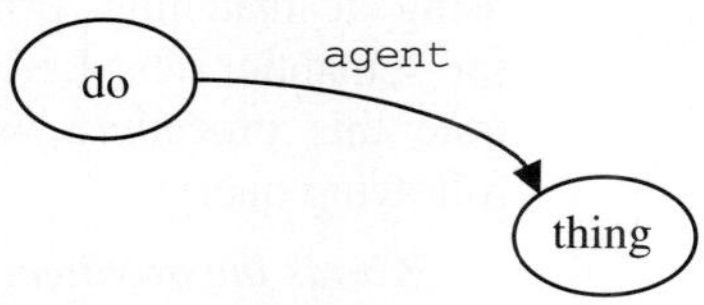

Fig. 4. A non taxonomic relation

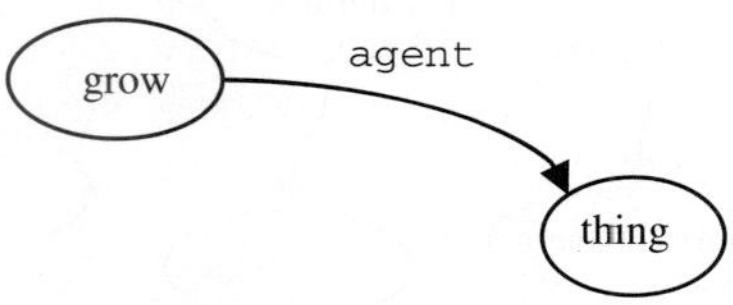

Fig. 5. An incorrect relation

From an *extensional* point of view, UNL relations can be viewed as a finite set of tuples of the form <semantic relation, uw_1, uw_2>. Given the huge amount of tuples that it may contain, the UNL KB is best viewed from an *intensional* point of view as a first order logical theory composed of a finite set of axioms and inference rules. Most of the axioms state plain semantic relations among UWs, now viewed as atomic formulas of the form relation (uw_1, uw_2). See some examples of the "evolution" from tuples into formulas, being "icl" and "agt" abbreviations for "included" and "agent" respectively:

<icl, helicopter, concrete thing> → icl(helicopter, concrete thing)
<icl, ameliorate, do> → icl(ameliorate, do)
<agt, do, thing> → agt(do, thing)

Besides atomic formulas, the theory contains complex formulas, like the one stating the transitivity of the "icl" relation:

$$\forall w_1 \forall w_2 \forall w_3 (\mathrm{icl}(w_1, w_2) \wedge \mathrm{icl}(w_2, w_3) \rightarrow \mathrm{icl}(w_1, w_3))$$

As for the inference rules, a subset of the standard rules present in first order theories may suffice for defining the relation of syntactic consequence among formulas. The UNL KB is then formally defined as the closure of the set of axioms under the consequence relation.

For any two UWs w_1, w_2 and any conceptual relation r, the UNL KB should be able to determine whether linking w_1, w_2 with r is allowed (makes sense in principle) or if it is against the intended use of w_1, w_2 and r. If the KB is viewed as a theory, the question is then if the formula $r(w_1, w_2)$ is a consequence (a theorem) of the set of axioms that form the KB or it is not. The axioms needed for answering such questions are mostly derived from the intended usage of the UNL conceptual relations and the broader semantic classes each UW belongs to.

4.2 An Example of Deduction for Question Answering Systems

This section describes an example of representation that supports a question answering system. The following text deals with quite a representative building of Spain:

```
  The edifice housing the Town Museum was designed by the architect
Pedro de Ribera with the purpose of establishing an orphanage on it.
```

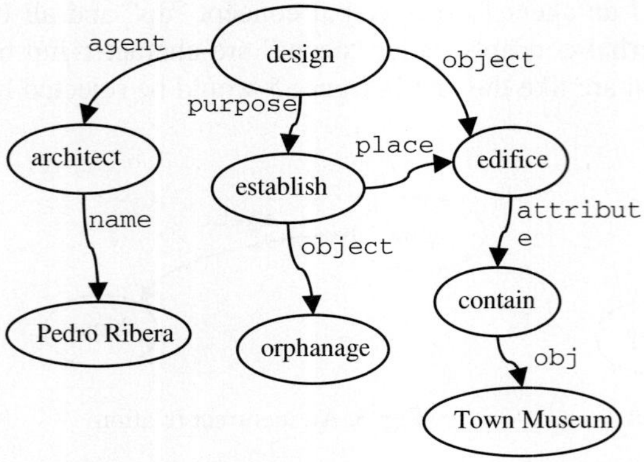

Fig. 6. UNL graphical representation of text

Its UNL graphical representation is that of figure 6. If a direct query is posed to the system, the deduction process is straightforward, simply using a matching procedure for semantic nets. Let's illustrate this procedure with the following query:

Who is the architect of the Town Museum?

This question is converted into its UNL form by means of natural language analyzing modules. Wh- questions typically request specific pieces of information. When this query is transformed into UNL, "who" turns into the target node to be searched (that is, the unknown node), and the noun phrase "architect of the Town Museum" turns into the binary relation:

mod(architect, "Town Museum")

Where "mod" simply establishes a general relation between two concepts. The next step is to link the unknown node "who" with either "architect" or "Town Museum". The query's linguistic structure implies that the speaker is asking for the name of a person (the entity described as architect in the question), therefore the missing relation in the query is *nam,* and the UNL representation of the query is:

nam(architect, ?)
mod(architect, "Town Museum")

In the UNL representation of the complete text, "architect" is not directly linked to "Town Museum" and in between these two nodes there is a subgraph composed of the nodes "design", "edifice", "contain" and finally "Town Museum" (as shown in figure 7).

By means of this subgraph, it can be seen that between "architect" and "Town Museum", there exists at least one path that guarantees the connectivity between both nodes. That is, it makes sense to talk about an "architect that is related in someway to the Town Museum"[2]. Later, it will be searched whether there is any node pending from node "architect" by means of the *nam* relation, which is the case. Therefore, the

[2] A note of caution has to be made, we are not claiming that the "mod" relation is equivalent to the combination of relations present between "architect" and "Town Museum" in the subgraph of figure 7.

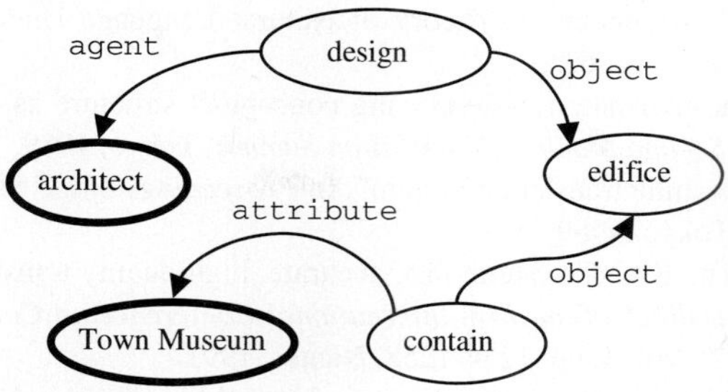

Fig. 7. Subgraph

unknown node (the target of the query) should be "Pedro Ribera", which is the (correct) answer to the posed query. Naturally, not always inference will be so straightforward and accurate. Many different situations may arise. But diversion does not mean here impossibility to solve problems. A model of knowledge representation based on UNL is valid for answering queries provided that the information is complete (since imprecision will not blur the inference process. That is to say, UNL can be efficiently used in closed domains where information is coherent.

5 Conclusions

Apart from multilingual text generation applications, UNL is currently being employed as text representation formalism in tasks such as information extraction, and integration with other linguistic ontologies. UNL should not be seen either as just another interlingua neither as just another knowledge representation formalism. Its goal is to serve as an intermediate *knowledge* representation that can exploited by different knowledge intensive tasks. UNL is a formalism worth to be considered particularly in those scenarios where:

1. Multilingual acquisition and dissemination of textual information is required,
2. Deep text understanding is required for providing advanced services such as question answering, summarization, knowledge management, knowledge-based decision support, language independent document repositories, etc. For all these tasks, a domain and task dependent knowledge base is needed and building it from UNL representations presents distinct advantages over other approaches.
3. Finally, several issues describe the UNL novelty in order to become a "de facto" standard because it is supported by a worldwide organization. On the other hand, it is necessary to remark that the representation of word senses instead of concepts increases significantly the power of UNL in comparison with other approaches. This is due to the approach to produce content representations that are closer to the linguistic surface than other representations are, thus making easier the understanding user queries.

References

[1] http://www.w3.org/XML/

[2] Quillian M.R. 1968 Semantic Memory. Semantic Information Processing. M.Minsky (Ed.), MIT press

[3] Schank, R.C (1972). Conceptual Dependency: A Theory of Natural Language Understanding, Cognitive Psychology, Vol 3, 532-631
[4] H. Uchida, "ATLAS-II: A machine translation system using conceptual structure as an Interlingua", in *Proceedings of the Second Machine Translation Summit*, Tokyo, 1989.
[5] K. Muraki, "PIVOT: Two-phase machine translation system". In *Proceedings of the Second Machine Translation Summit*, Tokyo, 1989.
[6] E. H. Nyberg, and T. Mitamura, "The KANT system: fast, accurate, high-quality translation in practical domains", in *Proceedings of the 14th International Conference on Computational Linguistics* (COLING '92), vol. 4, pp. 1254-1258, Nantes, 1992.
[7] S. Beale, S. Nirenburg S. and G. Mahesh, "Semantic Analysis in the Mikrokosmos Machine Translation Project", in *Proceedings of the Second Symposium on Natural Language Processing* (SNLP-95). Bangkok, Thailand. 1995.
[8] B. Dorr, "Machine Translation Divergences: A Formal Description and Proposed Solution", *Computational Linguistics*, vol 20(4), pp 597-633, 1994.
[9] Jackendoff, R., *Semantic Structures*. Current Studies in Linguistics series. Cambridge, Massachusetts: The MIT Press, 1990
[10] M. Montes, A.Gómez, A. López, A.Gelbukh. "Information retrieval with Conceptual Graph Matching". *Lecture Notes in Computer Science*, N 1873, Springer Verlag, 2000, pp 312-321
[11] M. Montes, A..Gómez, A..Gelbukh, A. López. "Text mining at Detail Level Using Conceptual Graphs". *Lecture Notes in Computer Science* N 2393, Springer, 2002 pp 122-136
[12] H. Uchida, *The Universal Networking Language Specifications, v3.3*, 2004. Available at http://www.undl.org.
[13] I. Boguslavsky, J. Cardeñosa, C. Gallardo, L. Iraola. "The UNL Initiative: An Overview", *Lecture Notes in Computer Science*, vol 3406, pp 377 – 387, 2005
[14] Bateman, J.A; Henschel, R. and Rinaldi, F. (1995) The Generalized Upper Model 2.0. http:// www.darmstadt.gmd.de/publish/komet/gen-um/newUM.html.

A Fuzzy Embedded GA for Information Retrieving from Related Data Set

Yang Yi, JinFeng Mei, and ZhiJiao Xiao

Computer Science Department, ZhongShan University, GuangZhou 510275, China
issyy@mail.sysu.edu.cn

Abstract. The arm of this work is to provide a formal model and an effective way for information retrieving from a big related data set. Based upon fuzzy logic operation, a fuzzy mathematical model of 0-1 mixture programming is addressed. Meanwhile, a density function indicating the overall possessive status of the effective mined out data is introduced. Then, a soft computing (SC) approach which is a genetic algorithm (GA) embedded fuzzy deduction is presented. During the SC process, fuzzy logic decision is taken into the uses of determining the genes' length, calculating fitness function and choosing feasible solution. Stimulated experiments and comparison tests show that the methods can match the user's most desired information from magnanimity data exactly and efficiently. The approaches can be extended in practical application in solving general web mining problem.

1 Introduction

By collecting vast completely uncontrolled, heterogeneous documents, the web has become the largest easy available repository of data. However, the exponential growth and the fast pace of change of the web makes really hard to retrieve all relevant information exactly [2,3], more complex vehicles for the information retrieving from huge amount of information are in dire needs. Etzioni et al [3] had listed the key requirements of document clustering. Information retrieving can be considered as mapping, clustering or association, which denotes that mining out information belonging to the set according to some query condition with probability.

Human beings are much more efficiently than computers in solving real world ill-defined, imprecisely formulated problems by fuzzy method. Soft computing, which is a kind of fuzzy intelligent algorithm can be viewed as a consortium of various computing tools to exploit the tolerance for imprecision and uncertainty to achieve tractability, robustness and low cost [1,5,6,7]. As a new way to represent vagueness in every day life, fuzzy sets attempt to model human reasoning and thinking process, so, lots of the application of fuzzy logic falls under information Retrieving. Some algorithms for mining association attributes by using fuzzy logic techniques have been suggested in Choi[2].

Yager[6] presented a framework for formulating linguistic and hierarchical queries. The information Retrieving language is described which enables users to specify the interrelationships between desired attributes of documents. Pasi and Villa [5] proposed a methodology for semi-structured document Retrieving.

A. Gelbukh and C.A. Reyes-Garcia (Eds.): MICAI 2006, LNAI 4293, pp. 943 – 951, 2006.

To find out more accurate and exact tied up information from a huge amount of related data is always a big challenge. This problem can also be considered as a kind of feature selection. There are known two general approaches to solve feature selection, which is filter and wrapper, the method used in this paper can be considered a hybrid algorithm.

In this paper, firstly, some important and efficient fuzzy rules for retrieving more accurate information from huge related data are analyzed; secondly, the fuzzy programming model which is to describe the problem as a whole is designed; then, a soft computing algorithm which is a genetic algorithm embedded the above fuzzy rules is discussed; lastly, experiments and tests evaluate the soft computing's calculation efficient.

2 Problem Description

We would like to stress that the class/style files and the template should not be manipulated and that the guidelines regarding font sizes and format should be adhered to. This is to ensure that the end product is as homogeneous as possible.

Suppose that there are magnanimity, distributed, multi-media and unstructured information, and the formats of the information may be text, HTML, UML, multi-media or some other types. All of the information can be queried and made of use. A denotes the input information set of querying, $A=\{a_i \in A, i=1,2,...,m\}$. A can be divided into m attributes according the semantic meaning, which is expressed by $a_i \in A$. B is the decision set, which is mapped from A and its dimension is n. $b_j \in B$ corresponding to every information will make up of the subset of B. w_j is the weight of b_j, $0 < w_j \leq 1$. The possibility for every item in A to be mined out or not lies on a fuzzy number, which is the degree of the fuzzy membership function, denoted by μ. $\mu_{\tilde{b}_j \tilde{a}_i}$ is the degree of fuzzy membership function which indicates the relationship of b_j to attribute $a_i \in A$.The objective of the problem is: according to the query requirements, to match and mine out the most related information from huge amount of data with efficiency, veracity and without interfering of irrespective information.

3 Fuzzy Rules and Decision

We set up the fuzzy logic decision methodology for solving the problem as follows.

1□Draw out the fuzzy attributes and constraint by studying, investigating, tracking, analyzing and indexing on the problems. 2□Conclude the fuzzy rules and factors. 3□Make fuzzy decisions.

It can be noticed that within set A, there are two kinds of relationship between the attributes, which are "AND" and "OR" with regard to the query condition. If the relationship between attributes is "consistent", the situation is called "AND". Otherwise, if the relationship between attributes is "repellent", it will be "OR". The algorithm designed has the ability to recognize these symbols automatically by identify the semantic meaning. The essence of this problem is to try to find out the closest relationship between b_j and a_i, the fuzzy methods used to resolve it are concluded as follows.

Fuzzy Rule 1. Those information and data which are irrespective with the query condition will be ignored and will not be located.

Fuzzy Rule 2. If there is some information or data which has some relationship with the query condition in the decision space, meanwhile, there exist some consistent attributes within the information or data, then, all these information and data will be find out and listed with some sequence strategy.

Fuzzy Rule 3. If there is some information or data which has some relationship with the query condition in the decision space, meanwhile, there exists some repellent attributes within these information or data, then, the intersection of the information and data will be listed with some sequence strategy.

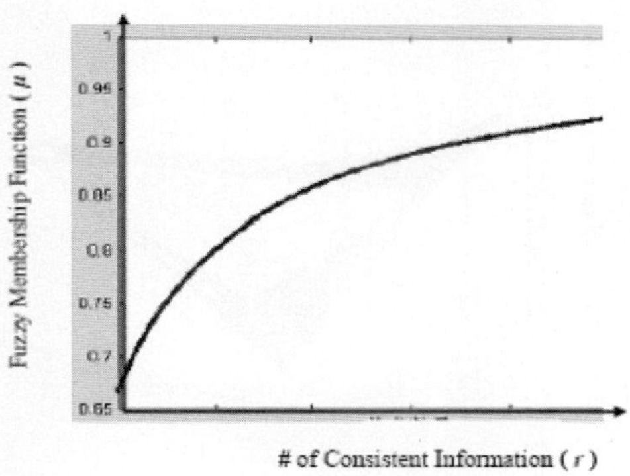

Fig. 1. Fuzzy membership function under consistent information

The fuzzy factor and fuzzy decision are summed up by adopting all above Fuzzy Rules, those are introduced as follows.

Factor 1. For $b_j \in B$, if b_j hasn't any consistency neither repellant relationship with a_i, then, the fuzzy membership function $\mu_{\tilde{b}_j A}$ is defined as: $\mu_{\tilde{b}_j A}$ □0.

Factor 2. For $b_j \in B$, if it fits r items of consistent attributes to $a_i \in A$, then the fuzzy membership function indicating the relationship of b_j with A is presented by formula (1), shown in Fig. 1.

$$\mu_{1\tilde{b}_j A} = r/(r+1) \,. \qquad (1)$$

Factor 3. For $b_j \in B$, if it fits r items of consistent attributes and s items of repellent attributes to $a_i \in A$, then the fuzzy membership function indicating the relationship of b_j with A is presented by formula (2), shown in Fig. 2.

$$\mu_{2\tilde{b}_j A} = | r - s | / (r + s) . \tag{2}$$

Factor 4. Then the overall fuzzy membership function indicating the relationship of b_j with A is designed as formula (3).

$$\mu_{3\tilde{b}_j A} = \begin{cases} r/(r+1), & \text{consistent} \\ | r - s | / (r + s), & \text{repellent} \end{cases} . \tag{3}$$

Traditionally, the number of n in B is usually rather big, since it is the number of mined out or to be mined out information, and generally, there may exist lots of information and data related with the query conditions. Whereas, r and s are the embodiments of attributes in A, they are query condition, usually $1 \le r < 10$ and $1 \le s < 10$.

The following fuzzy decisions are gained according to above Fuzzy Factors.

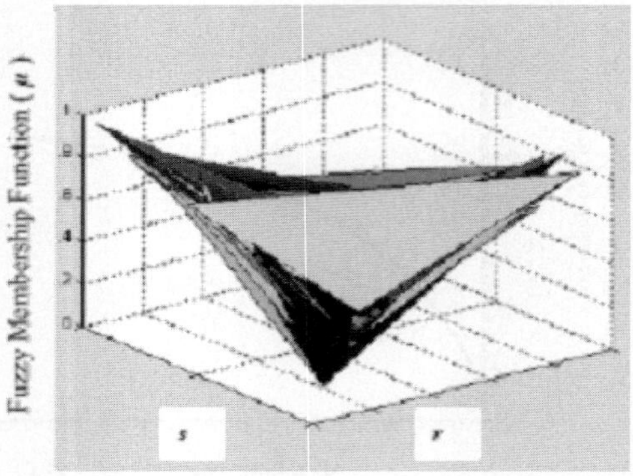

Fig. 2. Fuzzy membership function under repellent information

Decision 1. $\tilde{D}_1$, $\mu_{\tilde{b}_j}$ represents the degree of fuzzy membership for the feasibility of b_j will be mined out, and it is described by following expression.

$$\mu_{\tilde{b}_j} = \mu_{1\tilde{b}_j A} \otimes \mu_{2\tilde{b}_j A} \otimes \mu_{3\tilde{b}_j A} . \tag{4}$$

$$\mu_1 \otimes \mu_2 = \frac{\mu_1 \mu_2}{\varphi + (1-\varphi)(\mu_1 + \mu_2 - \mu_1 \mu_2)}, . \varphi \in (0,1)$$

Decision 2. $\tilde{D}_2$, $\mu_{\tilde{B}}$ represents the degree of fuzzy membership of mined out data set B, it is described by following expression.

$$\mu_{\tilde{B}} = \sum_{j=1}^{n} \otimes w_j \tilde{\mu}_{b_j} . \tag{5}$$

In order to guarantee the veracity character of the output information, besides consider B 's fuzzy membership function degree, its distribution and consistency has also been taken into account. Figure 3 shows an example of trapezia, which indicates how the value of distributing of the consistency is calculated. a is the value of information by most optimistic estimating, d is the value of information by most pessimistic estimating, and b is middle.

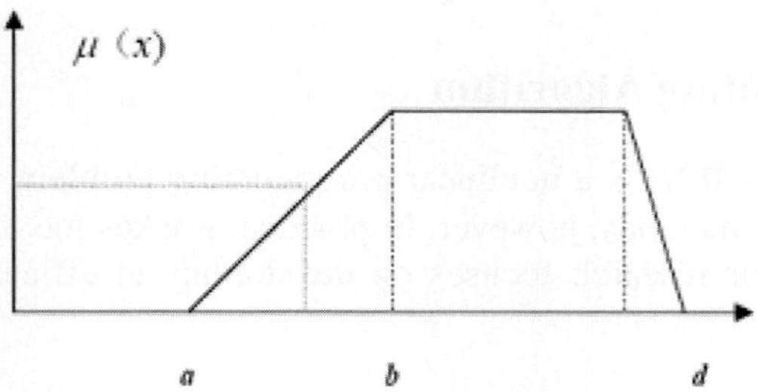

Fig. 3. Distribution of fuzzy member ship function

The ratio of the effective information occupancy in B can be reflected by formula (6).

$$density(\alpha \le x \le \beta) = \int_{\alpha}^{\beta} \mu(x)dx \Big/ \int_{a}^{d} \mu(x)dx \quad (6)$$

Formula (6) can indicate the overall possessive status of valuable and effective data in the expected mined out information. Keeping this value big enough can assure the finding out information is just what needed and avoid redundant results.

4 Fuzzy Logic Based Mathematical Model

The fuzzy mathematical programming model is proposed and expressed by $F-WM$.

$$\text{Define } x_j,\ x_j = \begin{cases} 1, & \text{if } b_j \text{ will be mined out} \\ 0, & \text{otherwise} \end{cases} \quad (7)$$

$$F-WM \quad : \quad \max \sum_{j=1}^{p} \otimes w_j \mu_{\tilde{b}_j} x_j \ . \quad (8)$$

$$\text{s.t.} \qquad p \ge 1.\backslash \quad (9)$$

$$p \le n \quad (10)$$

$$density(j \le p) = \sum_{j=1}^{p} w_j \mu_{\tilde{b}_j} x_j \Big/ \sum_{j=1}^{n} w_j \mu_{\tilde{b}_j} \ge \theta, \in (0,1) \quad (11)$$

$$w_j \mu_{\bar{b}_j} x_j \geq \delta, \quad j \in \{p\}, \delta > 0 \ , \ x_j \in \{0,1\} \tag{12}$$

p is the numbers of the information to be mined out; constraint (9) ensures the results. Constraint (10) ensures the set of solution is feasible, which is a part of the general data set. The object of the problem is not only to find out the useful information, but also to ignore the redundant information, by using δ and θ, constraint (11) and (12) will filter out the information which is not close enough to the requirements.

5 Soft Computing Algorithm

It is clear that $F-WM$ is a nonlinear programming problem. In theory, it may be solved by various methods, however, in practice, it takes too long in computational time to solve. Our research focuses on developing an efficient and easy way to solve it.

5.1 Encoding

A string of natural numbers is adopted in the encoding. For example, if the data set of (1st , 3rd, 217th , 5th, 4th, 7th, 9th, 100th, 251st) is to be mined out, then, after comparing the value of the fuzzy membership degree, and according to the Longest-First-Sequence (LFS) principle, the gene may be illustrated as: (1, 3, 217, 5, 4, 7, 9, 100, 251). Since the relationship between the target and the source is different for different querying situation, the length of the gene is not a constant. We use fuzzy deductive technique to determine the length of the genes. The mainly process is recommended as follows, named by Deciding the gene-length in GA :

Begin // Deciding the gene-length in GA

Randomly select q information $b_i \in B, i = 1,2,...q$ □

let $q \approx 7$;

fuzzy membership function degree□ l : $l = \sum_{j=1}^{q} \mu_{\bar{b}_j} \Big/ q$

gene-length fuzzy membership function □ $\mu_{\bar{l}} = l/(1+l)$

gene's length is: $gen\_length = n * \mu_{\bar{l}}$

End

It can be predicted that if there is more related information in the source data, the gen_length will be bigger, otherwise, it will be shorter. This lead to a more efficient algorithm and the results will be more accurate.

5.2 Procedure of Soft Computing Algorithm for F-WM

The methodology of GA participating in the SC calculation is illustrated as follows.

Fitness function. $F-WM$'s objective, illustrated in formula (8) is the fitness function, which is to maximum the overall fuzzy membership function on useful information.

Genetic operators. To maintain the feasibility of reproduced chromosome, some special crossover operators such as PMX, OX, CX and UN have been proposed [6,7], The one-point crossover is operated on the individuals with probability p_c. The mutation operation adopted is to randomly select a bit in all bits with probability p_m.

GA Selecting strategy. Roulette wheel proportional selection and quintessence selecting strategy that is to replace the random one solution in one generation by the best solution of the pre-generation is the selecting strategy

Stopping criterion. A large integer NG denoting the maximum number of generation, based on the size of the problem to be solved, it is pre-selected.

The step by step procedure of SC for $F-WM$ is designed as following.

```
Begin  // Soft Computing algorithm
  Initialization
        Specifying NG , p_c , p_m , A , a_i , m , b_i , n and B ;
        k_1 = k_2 = 0 .
  Do Deciding the gene-length in GA
        k_1 = k_1 + 1 , if k_1 > NG ,;
        go to  Scheduling the Genes in z*
        else, continue.
  Produce an initial population by traditional GA
  Do crossover and mutation operation
        new generation is born.
  Calculate fitness function
        according to formula (1)-(6) and (8).
  Selection
        select the feasible solution by formula (11) and (12);
        choose the genes from feasible data set by  strategy.
  Save current best result
        z* ,□
        k_2 = k_2 + 1 ;   if k_2 > NG ,
        go to "Deciding the gene-length in GA";
        else go to  Do crossover and mutation operation.
  Scheduling the genes in z*
        schedule the gens in z* with the rule of LFS,
        and according to their fuzzy membership degrees,
        those are the final results to be listed.
End
```

6 Numerical Results

The algorithm was programmed in VC++6.0 and run on PIII 1.9MHZ/256M PC. p_c =0.7 and p_m =0.07. We used different size data sets to test the SC, some of the results are presented in Table 1 and Table 2. The calculation speed and the average percentage of errors are addressed.

Several practical data sets tests are carried out to evaluate the algorithm's correctness feature, as shown in Table 1. We compare the experiment results with the real optimal solution. It indicates that, no mater the data size is big or is small, the SC's optimal solution percentage is mostly larger than 90%, which means that the SC can locate most part of the useful information from the source with small amount of redundant data.

Table 1. Performance of SC

Data Set (point * dimensions)	CPU (sec.)	Ave. Error
100 * 7	1.11	1.67%
500 * 7	2.21	3.74%
2500 * 7	2.31	4.53%
2500 * 10	6.11	5.91%
4000 * 7	5.99	8.29%
5000 * 10	6.89	10.29%

A SVM is used for comparing with SC as shown in Table 2. It can be noticed that the speed for SVM and SC is almost same, but the percentage of optimal solution is quite different. The correctness of SC is much better than SVM, and the SC has a higher ability in handling overlapping data since fuzzy operation is embedded in the calculation process.

Table 2. Comparison of SC and SVM

Data Set (point * dimensions)	Methods	CPU (sec.)	Ave. Error
100 * 7	*SC*	1.11	1.67%
	SVM	1.11	23.12%
500 * 7	*SC*	2.21	4.74%
	SVM	2.31	19.53%
2500 * 7	*SC*	5.11	3.91%
	SVM	6.32	27.32%
4000 * 7	*SC*	5.99	8.99%
	SVM	6.89	29.29%

7 Analysis and Conclusions

A fuzzy logic decision based information retrieving approach is discussed. The fuzzy mathematical model to maximum the closest relationship information data set is designed, and an improved genetic algorithm with fuzzy rules, factors and decision combined is illustrated. The advantages of the method presented can be concluded from following things.

By using the querying data set, complex querying is supported, which make it possible to describe the desired information more comprehensively, in full-scale and in all-sided.

By introducing the density function on expected mined out data set, the valuable information percentage can be evaluated and guaranteed. Then, the overall possessive status of effective data can be assured.

By embedded fuzzy calculation in the encoding, the gene's length becomes changeable according to the situation of information correlation, which means, if there is more information related with the query condition, the gene's length will be longer, otherwise, the gene's length will be shorter. So, the algorithm will only achieve the most valuable information, at the same time, useless and redundant information will not be mined out.

The approach described can reduce the complex degree of decision space; let the huge amount of uncontrolled information index-able and manage-able. Our further work will focus on optimization in the calculation process, especially in the fuzzy logic decision period, and will also try to extend the algorithm in large scale practical environment usage.

Acknowledgment

This paper is supported by the National Natural Science Foundation of China under Grant No. 60573159.

References

1. Baldonado, M., Chang, C.-C.K., Gravano, L., Paepcke, A.: The Stanford Digital Library Metadata Architecture. Int. J. Digit. Libr. 1 (1997) 108–121
2. Choi, D.Y.: Enhancing the Power of Web Search Engines by Means of Fuzzy Query. Decision Support Systems, 35 (2003) 31-44.
3. Etzioni, S., Hanks, T., Jiang, R.M., Karp, O. and Waarts, O.: Efficient Information Gathering on The Internet. 37th Annual Symposium on Foundations of Computer Science (FOCS '96).
4. Montesi, D., Trombetta, A. and Dearnley, P.A.: A Similarity Based Relational Algebra for Web and Multimedia Data. Information Process and Management, 39 (2003) 307-322.
5. Pasi, G. and Villa, R.: Personalized News Content Programming (PENG): A System Architecture. 16th International Workshop on Database and Expert Systems Applications (DEXA'05)1008-1012.
6. Yager, R.: Misrepresentations and Challenges. IEEE Expert: Intelligent Systems and Their Application, Aug (1994) 41-42.
7. Yi, Y. and Wang, D.W.: Soft Computing for Scheduling with Batch Setup Times and Earliness-tardiness Penalties on Parallel Machines. J. Int. Manuf., 14 (2003) 311-322.

On Musical Performances Identification, Entropy and String Matching

Antonio Camarena-Ibarrola and Edgar Chávez

Universidad Michoacana de Sán Nicolás de Hidalgo
Edif "B" Ciudad Universitaria CP 58000
Morelia, Mich., México
{camarena, elchavez}@umich.mx

Abstract. In this paper we address the problem of matching musical renditions of the same piece of music also known as *performances*. We use an entropy based Audio-Fingerprint delivering a framed, small footprint AFP which reduces the problem to a string matching problem. The Entropy AFP has very low resolution (750 ms per symbol), making it suitable for flexible string matching.

We show experimental results using dynamic time warping (DTW), Levenshtein or *edit* distance and the Longest Common Subsequence (LCS) distance. We are able to correctly (100%) identify different renditions of masterpieces as well as pop music in less than a second per comparison.

The three approaches are 100% effective, but LCS and Levenshtein can be computed online, making them suitable for monitoring applications (unlike DTW), and since they are distances a metric index could be use to speed up the recognition process.

1 Introduction

The alignment of musical performances has been a subject of interest in several *Music Information Retrieval* disciplines such as *Polyphonic Audio Matching* [1], *querying by melody* [2] and *score-performance matching* [3], or its on line version called *score-performance following* [4]. The last discipline has the goal of qualifying where a performance is in respect to a score, thus enabling automatic accompaniment and automatic adding of special effects based on the position of the performance in time, according to meta-data included in the score.

In this paper we propose a method for comparing performances allowing online detection of occurrences in an audio channel, for this purpose, we make use of efficient and versatile aligning techniques developed for matching DNA sequences [5] and for finding strings occurrences in texts allowing errors [6]. Tests using the classical DTW technique were also included as a reference. Hidden Markov Models (HMM) were not considered in the experiments due to the fact that they need training to compute their optimal parameters and topology which has to be done at designing time, if the collection of songs changed, the topology would not be optimal any more, redesigning the HMM every time a song is added to the

A. Gelbukh and C.A. Reyes-Garcia (Eds.): MICAI 2006, LNAI 4293, pp. 952–962, 2006.

collection is impractical especially if the HMM has already been implemented in hardware (i.e Field Programmable Gate Arrays), therefore, using HMM as an aligning technique was discarded.

For the feature extraction level, a string AFP based on an Information Content Analysis was preferred since it has probed to be very robust to signal degradations although never tried in matching musical performances [7], also because it is a string AFP of short length being the outcome of a low resolution analysis.

AFPs are compact content based representations of audio files which must be robust to common signal degradations like noise contamination, equalization, lossy compression and re-recording (Loudspeakers to microphone transmission). Existing AFPs are basically of four kinds: (I) *Sequences of Feature Vectors* also known as *trajectories* or *traces* since they are extracted at equally spaced periods of time, an example of this is the spectral flatness based AFP used by MPEG-7 [8]. (II) *Single vectors* are the smallest AFPs, they usually include the means and variances of features extracted from the whole song, (i.e Beats per Minute) this AFPs do not require any aligning technique but are not very robust to signal degradations. (III) *Strings* resulting from codification of feature vectors. Haitsma-Kalker "Hash string" [9] or the entropy-based AFP used in this work [7] are good examples of this kind of AFPs. (IV) HMMs are also used as AFPs, normally a HMM is built for each one of the songs from the collection [10].

For the purpose of matching performances, *trajectories* AFPs are suitable for DTW, however, to compare them using flexible string matching techniques, they would have to be subject to some vector quantization technique in order to turn them into strings, this implies some precision loss. *String* AFPs are suitable for matching performances using flexible string matching distances. Haitsma-Kalker's AFPs are extremely long strings since they were designed to identify songs with only 3 seconds of audio and therefore result from a very high resolution analysis, however they are impractical in matching performances for the high computational cost needed for aligning them. For example, a 5 minute song would be represented by a string whose length would be of 25 862 characters each one from an alphabet of 2^{32}. Finally, since the spectral entropy based AFP is obtained from a low resolution analysis a 5 minute song will produce a string of only 400 characters from an alphabet of 2^{24}, quite suitable for our problem.

1.1 The Spectral Entropy Based Audio Fingerprint

Claude Shannon stated that the level of *information* in a signal could be measured with Boltzman's formula (1) for computing entropy in gases which as we know is a measure of chaos or disorder [11].

$$H(x) = E[I(p)] = \sum_{i=1}^{n} p_i I(p) = -\sum_{i=1}^{n} p_i ln(p_i) \qquad (1)$$

Entropy has been used in speech signals as a segmentation criterium in noisy environments [12] and in deciding the desirable frame rate in the analysis of Speech signals [13], but it had never been used as the main feature used for matching audio files. Recently, a first Entropy-based AFP was proposed in [14] which estimates the *information content* in audio signals every second directly in time domain using histograms, later the same authors proposed an espectral entropy based AFP [7] which is more robust to noise, equalization and loudspeaker to microphone transmission than the spectral flatness based AFP adopted by MPEG-7 [15]. The espectral entropy based AFP results from the codification of the sign of the derivative in time of the entropy for critical bands 1 to 24 according to Bark scale. The signal is first segmented in frames of 1.5 seconds with 50 percent overlapping so that one vector of 24 ceros and ones is obtained every 750 milliseconds, to every frame, a Hanning window is applied, then taken to the frequency domain via the fast fourier transform (FFT). For every critical band, the result is considered to be a two dimensional (i.e. real and imaginary part), random variable with gaussian distribution and mean zero, according to [16]. The spectral entropy for band p is determined using equation (2)

$$H = ln(2\pi e) + \frac{1}{2} ln(\sigma_{xx}\sigma_{yy} - \sigma_{xy}^2) \tag{2}$$

where σ_{xx} and σ_{yy} also known as σ_x^2 and σ_y^2 are the variances of the real and the imaginary part respectively and $\sigma_{xy} = \sigma_{yx}$ is the covariance between the real and the imaginary part of the spectrum in its rectangular form and so $\sigma_{xy}\sigma_{yx} = \sigma_{xy}^2$

Just as a spectrogram indicates the amount of energy a signal has both on time and frequency, a *entropygram* show the information level for every critical band and frame position in time. Figure 1 shows the entropygram of two performances of Mozart's *Serenade Number 13 Allegro* and figure 2 shows the entropygrams of two performances of Tchaikovsky's *Nutcracker waltz of the Flower.*

The sign of the Entropygram's time derivative is coded to built the string AFP as indicated in equation (3) where the bit corresponding to band b and frame n (i.e. $b(n, b)$) is determined with the sign of the difference of the entropygram's

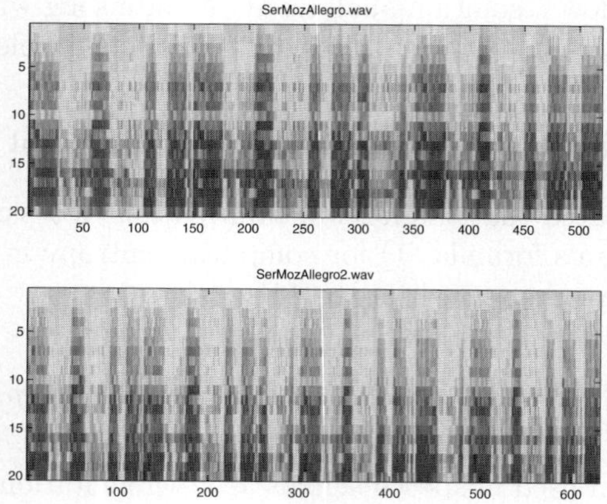

Fig. 1. Entropygrams of the two performances of Mozart's *Serenade Number 13 Allegro*

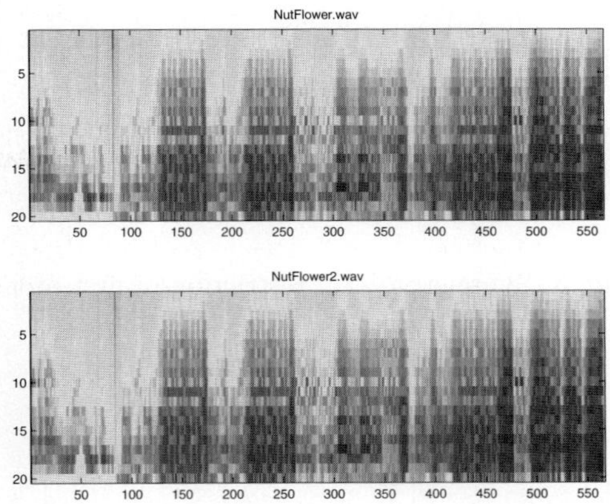

Fig. 2. Entropygrams of the two performances of Tchaikovsky's *Nutcracker waltz of the flower*

entries $H(n, b)$ and $H(n-1, b)$. This is the same as coding the information of wether the entropy for each band is increasing or not.

$$\begin{aligned} b(n,b) &= 1 \qquad \forall \quad H(n,b) - H(n-1,b) > 0 \\ &= 0 \qquad \forall \quad H(n,b) - H(n-1,b) \leq 0 \end{aligned}$$

The spectral entropy based AFP can be seen as a string formed with symbols of 24 bits so that the alphabet size is 2^{24} and the number of symbols equals the duration of the musical performance in seconds multiplied by 4/3.

1.2 DTW

Aligning two performances $R(n)$, $0 \leq n \leq N$ and $T(m)$, $0 \leq m \leq M$ is equivalent to finding a warping function $m = w(n)$ that maps indices n and m so that a time registration between the time series is obtained. Function w is subject to the boundary conditions $w(0) = 0$ and $w(N) = M$ and might be subject to local restrictions, an example of such restriction is that if the optimal warping function goes through point (n, m) it must go through either $(n-1, m-1)$, $(n, m-1)$ or $(n-1, m)$ as depicted in figure 3, a penalization of 2 is charged when choosing $(n-1, m-1)$ and of 1 if $(n, m-1)$ or $(n-1, m)$ are chosen, this way the three possible paths from $(n-1, m-1)$ to (n, m) (i.e. first to $(n, m-1)$ and then (n, m)) will all have the same cost of 2. Other local restrictions defined by Sakoe and Chiba [17] can be used.

Let $d_{n,m}$ be the distance between frame n of performance R and frame m of performance T, then the optimal warping function between R and T is defined by the minimum accumulated distance $D_{n,m}$ as in (3).

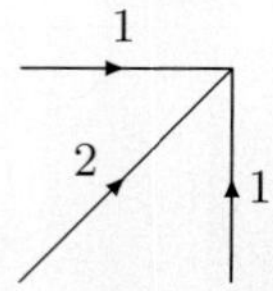

Fig. 3. Symmetric local restriction of first order

$$D_{n,m} = \sum_{p=1}^{n} d_{R(p),T(w(p))} \tag{3}$$

Once a local restriction is selected, $D_{N,M}$ can be computed using the recurrence defined in equations (4),(5) and (6), which correspond to local restriction shown in figure 3. Based on this recurrence $D_{N,M}$ can be efficiently obtained using dynamic programming.

$$D_{i,0} = \sum_{k=0}^{i} d_{i,0} \tag{4}$$

$$D_{0,j} = \sum_{k=0}^{j} d_{0,j} \tag{5}$$

$$D_{i,j} = min \begin{cases} D_{i-1,j-1} + 2d_{i,j} \\ D_{i-1,j} + d_{i,j} \\ D_{i,j-1} + d_{i,j} \end{cases} \tag{6}$$

1.3 String Distances

The Levenshtein distance between two strings is defined as the number of operations needed to convert one of them into the other, the considered operations are *inserts*, *deletes* and *substitutions* and sometimes *transpositions*, a different cost to each operation may be considered depending on the specific problem. If only substitutions are allowed with the cost of 1, the distance is the same as the Hamming distance, if only insertions and deletions are allowed both with the cost of 1 the distance is known as the *Longest common subsequence* (LCS) distance, finally if only insertions are allowed at the cost of 1, the asymmetric *Episode distance* is obtained [6].

To compute the Levenshtein distance between the string t of length N and the string p of length M the equations (7),(8) and (9) are used assuming all edit operations (insert,delete and sustitutions) have the same cost of 1.

$$C_{i,0} = i \quad \forall \quad 0 \leq i \leq N \tag{7}$$

$$C_{0,j} = j \qquad \forall \;\; 0 \leq j \leq M \tag{8}$$

$$C_{i,j} = \begin{cases} C_{i-1,j-1} & t_i = p_j \\ min[C_{i-1,j-1}, C_{i,j-1}, C_{i-1,j}] + 1 & t_i \neq p_j \end{cases} \tag{9}$$

The classical approach for computing the Levenshtein distance relies in Dynamic Programming, for instance, the Levenshtein distance between the string "hello" and the string "yellow" is 2 as can be seen on location $(5, 6)$ of matrix (10) corresponding to two operations (i.e substitute "h" by a "y" and add a "w" at the end)

		y	e	l	l	o	w
	0	1	2	3	4	5	6
h	1	**1**	2	3	4	5	6
e	2	2	**1**	2	3	4	5
l	3	3	2	**1**	2	3	4
l	4	4	3	2	**1**	2	3
o	5	5	4	3	2	**1**	**2**

(10)

There is no need for keeping the whole dynamic programming table in memory. The Levenshtein distance can be computed maintaining only one column. To do so, initialize this only column with $C_i = i$ and then use equation (11) to update it while reading the text.

$$C_i^{'} = \begin{cases} C_{i-1} & t_i = p_j \\ min[C_{i-1}, C_{i-1}^{'}, C_i] + 1 & t_i \neq p_j \end{cases} \tag{11}$$

Where $C^{'}$ is the column being computed and C is the previous one

For the purpose of finding occurrences of a pattern on a text we must allow a match to occur at any time, this is achieved by setting $C_0^{'} = 0$ and monitoring if the last element on every column is less or equal to the predefined maximum distance. In matrix (12) the string *att* is found at positions 2, 3 and 5 with one error (i.e. substrings *at*, *atc*) and position 6 without errors inside the text *atcatt*.

		a	t	c	a	t	t
	0	0	0	0	0	0	0
a	1	0	1	1	0	1	1
t	2	1	0	2	1	0	1
t	3	2	**1**	**1**	2	**1**	**0**

(12)

2 Experiments

The original goal for this work was to test the spectral entropy based AFP described in section 1.1 in the problem of matching musical performances and see how well this features could be aligned with a traditional techniques like DTW. However, using efficient and versatile aligning techniques commonly used in matching DNA sequences allows finding occurrences of music by any of its performances in an audio channel, which could not be done with DTW since it would require having both whole songs prior to the aligning. However DTW was included in the experiments as a reference to mesure the aligning capabilities of the Levenshtein and the LCS distances.

2.1 Using the Longest Common Subsequence Distance

To use the spectral entropy based AFP as a string, the symbols are considered to belong to an alphabet that is too large (2^{24}), it would be naive to consider two symbols as completely different just because they differ in one bit, remember that the symbols are made of bits that result from an information content analysis on unrepeatable audio segments, therefore, we considered two symbols as different only if the Hamming distance was grater than 7.

Once defined the rule to decide wether two symbols are different or not, the LCS distance will be used hopping that the same sequence of acoustic events will be present in both performances, only shorter subsequences in one of them with respect to the other, in this context a symbol represents an acoustic event.

The recurrence defined in (13),(14) and (15) is used with dynamic programming to compute the LCS distance.

$$C_{i,0} = i \qquad \forall \quad 0 \leq i \leq N \tag{13}$$

$$C_{0,j} = j \qquad \forall \quad 0 \leq j \leq M \tag{14}$$

$$C_{i,j} = \begin{cases} C_{i-1,j-1} & t_i = p_j \\ min[C_{i,j-1}, C_{i-1,j}] + 1 & t_i \neq p_j \end{cases} \tag{15}$$

2.2 Using the Levenshtein Distance

Using a threshold to decide wether an acoustic event equals another may seem dangerous, so instead of throwing away the differences between the symbols, they may be used as the substitution cost in the Levenshtein distance while keeping the insertion and deletion cost to 1.

$$C_{i,j} = min \begin{cases} C_{i-1,j-1} + d(t_i, p_j) \\ C_{i,j-1} + 1 \\ C_{i-1,j} + 1 \end{cases} \tag{16}$$

Where $d(t_i, p_j) = Hamming(t_i, p_j)/24$ since t_i and p_j are made from 24 bits and we want $d(t_i, p_j)$ to be a value between 0 and 1.

2.3 Using DTW

Using local restriction depicted in figure 3, DTW was implemented with dynamic programming based on the recurrences defined with equations (4),(5) and (6) with $d_{i,j}$ being the Hamming distance between row i of one performance's AFP and row j of the other performance's AFP.

2.4 Normalizing the Distances

The Levenshtein distance between performances of length N and M can not be greater than the length of the longest one of them, so in order to normalize the Levenshtein distance it was divided by $max(N, M)$, once normalized, it was posible to set a threshold to decided wether two performances match or not. The LCS distance can not be grater than $N + M$, so in order to normalize the LCS distance it was divided by $N + M$. The DTW distance was also divided by $N + M$.

2.5 The Test Set

Pairs of Master pieces from Mozart and Tchaikovsky played by different orchestras as well as pairs of beatles's songs played at two different events formed the

Table 1. Pairs of Performances for the experiments. Performers: (i) *The Beatles.* (ii) *London Festival Orchestra, Cond.: Henry Adolph.* (iii) *London Festival Orchestra, Cond.: Alberto Lizzio.* (iv) *Camerata Academica, Cond.: Alfred Scholz.* (v) *Slovak Philharmonic Orchestra, Cond.: Libor Pesek.* (vi) *London Philharmonic Orchestra, Cond.: Alfred Scholz.*

Name	dur1	dur2
All my loving	2:09 (i)	2:08 (i)
All you need is love	3:49 (i)	3:46 (i)
Come together	4:18 (i)	4:16 (i)
Eleanor Rigby	2:04 (i)	2:08 (i)
Here comes the sun	3:07 (i)	3:04 (i)
Lucy in the sky with diamonds	3:27 (i)	3:27 (i)
Nowhere man	2:40 (i)	2:44 (i)
The Nutcracker Waltz of the flowers	7:09 (ii)	7:06 (iii)
The Nutcracker Dance of the Reeds	2:39 (ii)	2:41 (iii)
Octopus's garden	2:52 (i)	2:48 (i)
Mozart's Serenade 13 Menuetto	2:19 (iv)	2:10 (v)
Mozart's Serenade 13 Allegro	6:30 (iv)	7:52 (v)
Mozart's Serenade 13 Romance	6:45 (iv)	5:47 (v)
Mozart's Serenade 13 Rondo	3:24 (iv)	2:55 (v)
Sgt Pepper's Lonely hearts	2:01 (i)	2:01 (i)
Something	3:02 (i)	2:59 (i)
Swan Lake theme	3:14 (ii)	3:13 (iii)
Symphony 41 Molto Allegro	8:50 (vi)	8:55 (vi)
With a little help from my friends	2:44 (i)	2:43 (i)
Yellow submarine	2:37 (i)	2:35 (i)

test set of 40 audio files, the set of pairs is listed on table 1 where for each pair the duration of both performances is shown.

2.6 Results

The 40 audio files of the test set were put into comparison against each other, the 1 600 resulting distances were stored in a confusion matrix and represented as gray tones in figures 4, 5 and 6. A low distance is represented as a dark gray tone and a high distance as a light gray tone, the first raw have the distances between the first audio file and the rest of them, the second raw are the distances between the second audio file and every other one, and so on. Since the audio files share a unique prefix if they correspond to the same song, the ideal resulting graphical confusion matrix would be all white with 20 black squares along the main diagonal, each square's wide would have to be of exactly of two columns. Figure 4 corresponds to the experiment using DTW, figure 5 is the graphical confusion matrix when using LCS distance and figure 6 corresponds to the use of the Levenshtein distance.

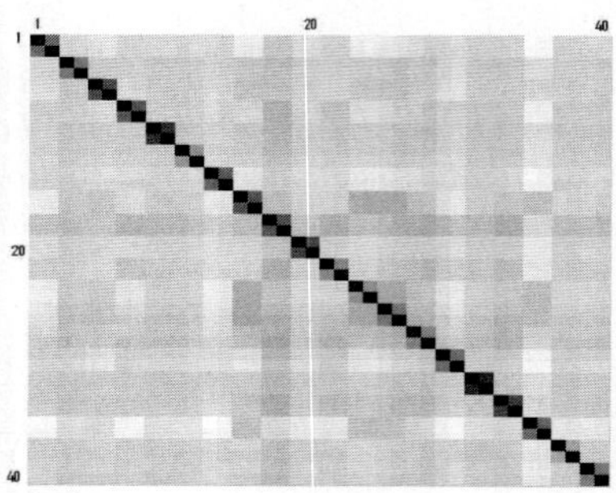

Fig. 4. Confusion Matrix result from using DTW

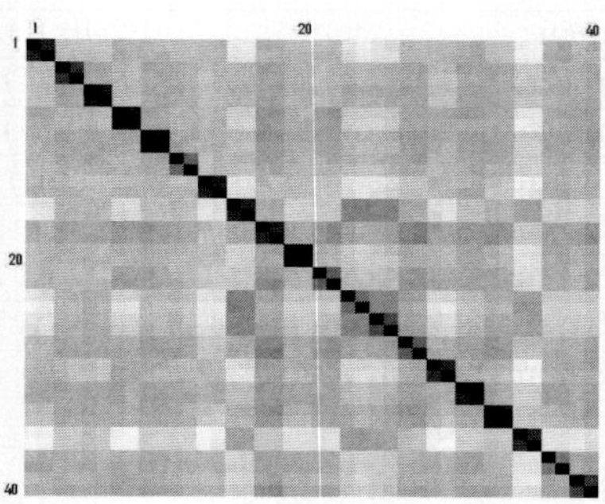

Fig. 5. Confusion Matrix result from using the Longest Common Subsequence distance

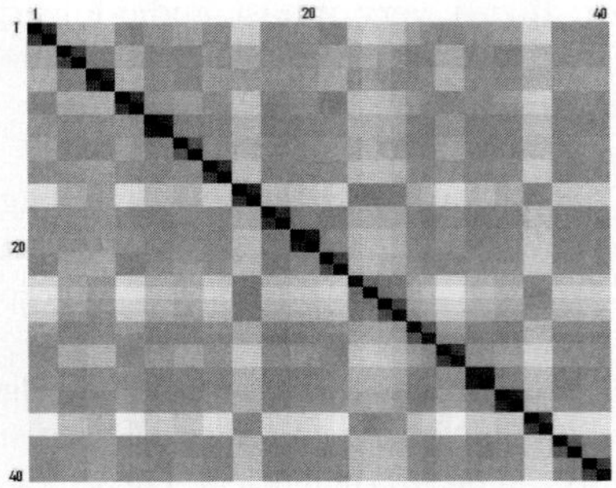

Fig. 6. Confusion Matrix result from using The Levenshtein distance

3 Conclusions

The espectral entropy based string AFP was successfully used in the problem of matching audio performances, the other string AFP of Haitsma-Kalker produces so long strings that for a four minute song a string of 20 690 symbols is obtained while a string of only 320 symbols is obtained with the entropy based AFP, aligning such long strings is impractical and so no tests were included for the Hash string AFP. The three aligning techniques tried, DTW, LCS and Levenshtein distance worked very well, either using the nearest neighbor criterium or simply selecting a threshold every performance matched the other performance of the same song. The flexible string based aligning techniques are more adequate in the issue of monitoring occurrences of performances in audio signals as described in subsection 1.3. We believe that more algorithms developed in the field of matching DNA sequences [5] can be adjusted to their use in Music Information Retrieval using the spectral entropy based string AFP.

References

1. Hu, N., Dannenberg, R.B., Tzanetakis, G.: Polyphonic audio matching and alignment for music retrieval. IEEE Workshop on Applications of Signal Processing to Audio and Acoustics (2003)
2. Shalev-Shwartz, S., Dubnov, S., Friedman, N., Singer, Y.: Robust temporal and spectral modeling for query by melody. Proc of ACM SIGIR'02 (2002)
3. Cano, P., Loscos, A., Bonada, J.: Score-performance matching using hmms. Proceedings ICMC99 (1999)
4. Dixon, S.: Live tracking of musical performances using on-line time warping. Proc of the 8th Int Conf on Digital Audio Effects (DAFx'05) (2005)
5. Gusfield, D.: Algorithms on Strings, Trees, and Sequences. Computer Science and Computational Biology. Cambridge University Press (1997)
6. Navarro, G., Raffinot, M.: Flexible Pattern Matching in Strings. Practical On-Line Search for Texts and Biological Sequences. Volume 17. Cambridge University Press (2002)

7. Ibarrola, A.C., Chavez, E.: A very robust audio-fingerprint based on the information content analysis. IEEE transactions on Multimedia (submitted) available: http://lc.fie.umich,mx/~camarena.
8. Hellmuth, O., Allamanche, E., Cremer, M., Kastner, T., NeuBauer, C., Schmidt, S., Siebenhaar, F.: Content-based broadcast monitoring using mpeg-7 audio fingerprints. International Symposium on Music Information Retrieval ISMIR (2001)
9. Haitsma, J., Kalker, T.: A highly robust audio fingerprinting system. IRCAM (2002)
10. P. Cano, E.B., Kalker, T., Haitsma, J.: A review of algorithms for audio fingerprinting. IEEE Workshop on Multimedia Signal Processing (2002) 169–167
11. Shannon, C., Weaver, W.: The Mathematical Theory of Communication. University of Illinois Press (1949)
12. Shen, J.L., Hung, J.w., Lee, L.s.: Robust entropy-based endpoint detection for speech recognition in noisy environments. In: Proc. International Conference on Spoken Language Processing. (1998)
13. You, H., Zhu, Q., Alwan, A.: Entropy-based variable frame rate analysis of speech signal and its applications to asr. In: Proc. IEEE International Conference on Acoustics, Speech and Signal Processing (ICASSP). (2004)
14. Ibarrola, A.C., Chavez, E.: A robust, entropy-based audio-fingerprint. IEEE International Conference on Multimedia and Expo 2006 (ICME2006) To appear (2006)
15. Group, M.A.: Text of ISO/IEC Final Draft International Standar 15938-4 Information Technology - Multimedia Content Description Interface - Part 4: Audio. MPEG-7 (2001)
16. Martin, R.: Noise power spectral density estimation based on optimal smoothing and minimum statistics. IEEE Transactions on Speech and Audio Processing **9** (2001) 504–512
17. Sakoe, H., Chiba, S.: Dynamic programming algortihm optimization for spoken word recognition. IEEE transactions on Acoustics and Speech Signal Processing (ASSP) (1978) 43–49

Adaptive Topical Web Crawling for Domain-Specific Resource Discovery Guided by Link-Context

Tao Peng, Fengling He, Wanli Zuo, and Changli Zhang

College of Computer Science and Technology, Jilin University, Key Laboratory of Symbol Computation and Knowledge Engineering of the Ministry of Education, Changchun 130012, China
taopengpt@yahoo.com.cn

Abstract. Topical web crawling technology is important for domain-specific resource discovery. Topical crawlers yield good recall as well as good precision by restricting themselves to a specific domain from web pages. There is an intuition that the text surrounding a link or the link-context on the HMTL page is a good summary of the target page. Motivated by that, This paper investigates some alternative methods and advocates that the link-context derived from reference page's HTML tag tree can provide a wealth of illumination for steering crawler to stay on domain-specific topic. In order that crawler can acquire enough illumination from link-context, we initially look for some referring pages by traversing backward from seed URLs, and then build initial term-based feature set by parsing the link-contexts extracted from those reference web pages. Used to measure the similarity between the crawled pages' link-context, the feature set can be adaptively trained by some link-contexts to relevant pages during crawling. This paper also presents some important metrics and an evaluation function for ranking URLs about pages relevance. A comprehensive experiment has been conducted, the result shows obviously that this approach outperforms Best-First and Breath-First algorithm both in harvest rate and efficiency.

1 Introduction

With the rapid growth of information and the explosion of web pages from the World Wide Web, it gets harder for search engines to retrieve the information relevant to a user. Then topical crawlers are becoming important tools to support applications such as specialized Web portals, online searching, and competitive intelligence. A crawler is the program that retrieves web pages for a search engine, which is widely used today. A topic driven (also called focused crawler) crawler is designed to gather pages on a specific topic. Topical crawlers carefully decide which URLs to scan and in what order to pursue based on previously downloaded pages information. Early, there are Breadth-First crawler [1], Depth-First crawlers such as Fish Search [2] and other focused crawlers include [3,5,6]. And there are some crawling algorithms, such as Shark Search [3], a more aggressive variant of De Bra's Fish Search and some evaluation methods for choosing URLs [4].

A. Gelbukh and C.A. Reyes-Garcia (Eds.): MICAI 2006, LNAI 4293, pp. 963 – 973, 2006.

To design an efficient focused crawler that only collecting relevant pages from the WWW, the choice of strategy for prioritizing unvisited URLs is crucial [8]. In this paper, we present a method to utilize link-context for determining the priorities. The link-context is a kind of extended anchor text. Anchor text is the "highlighted clickable text" [12] in source code, which appears within the bounds of an <A> tag. Since the anchor text tends to summarize information about the target page, we pursue the intuition that it is a good provider of the context of the unvisited URLs. By applying it in prioritizing the unvisited URLs and guiding the crawling, the crawler's performance will be maximized.

The availability of link structure between documents in web search has been used to effectively rank hypertext documents [9, 10], and it was known already in 1994 that anchor text is useful for web search [11]. Nadav Eiron and Kevin S. McCurley in [12] presented a statistical study of the nature of anchor text and real user queries on a large corpus of corporate intranet documents. Kenji Tateishi et al. in [13] evaluated Web Retrieval Methods Using Anchor Text. Iwazume et. al. [14] guided a crawler using anchor text along with ontology. Jun Li in [8] proposed a focused crawler guided by anchor texts using a decision tree. Soumen chakrabarti in [15] suggested the idea of using DOM offset, based on the distance of text tokens from an anchor on a tag tree, to score links for crawling. Gautam Pant in [16] introduced a framework to study link-context derivation methods. The framework included a number of metrics to understand the utility of a given link-context. The paper described link-context derivation methods that make explicit use of the tag tree hierarchy and compared them against some of the traditional techniques.

Anchor text is too short, not enough informative, so we expand it to link-context, and employ dictionary built by the link-context from in-link pages of the seed URLs. As traditional dictionary is also too large to prioritize the unvisited URLs efficiently, our new kind of small size dictionary is more suitable for ranking the link-context of out-links from the visited page. We use DOM offset and HTML tag tree to expand the anchor text to make it more useful, and apply it in two aspects in the process of focused crawling, the measurement and prediction.

2 Our Methods

Generally, anchor text, like user's query of a search engine, is typically very short and consist of very few terms on average. Furthermore, many web page designers don't give their summarization as anchor text, instead they tend to write the anchor text as "next", "click here" or "more", with descriptive text above or below the link. In these cases, the anchor text is useless to us. We should also use the information around the anchor text. The short anchor text causes another problem. The human users, with intelligence and experience, can quickly and skillfully determine whether the context of the target document is relevant to the topic they are interested. But its concision makes it a very hard for a program to judge just on so few words. Our approach expands the anchor text to link-context, and makes use of link-context to guide crawling to reduce the effect of the two problems above.

Another problem we need to pay attention to is the dictionary used to compute the similarity of anchor text with given topic. Every focused crawler has at least one classifier with a high dimension dictionary consisting of lots of words related to the topic. Obviously, this kind of dictionary does not suit to rank link-context. The link-context, which is shorter containing fewer words than web page document, will only matches very few words in this dictionary. Then the difference of every two link-contexts is so small that to prioritize them based on the result is ineffective, undistinguishable. We need a new method to build a small-size dictionary to compute the similarity of anchor text with given topic. In our study, we compiled a dictionary by utilizing seed URLs' in-link pages' link-context. And the dictionary can be updated by some "good" link-contexts to relevant pages. Fig. 1 illustrates the architecture of our topical crawler.

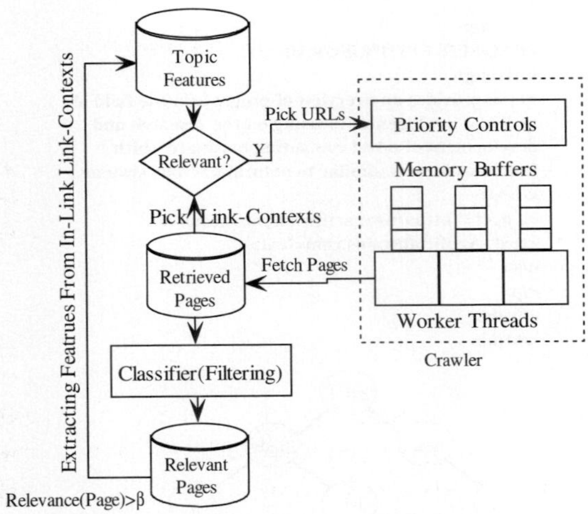

Fig. 1. Architecture of our topical crawler

2.1 Deriving Link-Context from HTML Tag Tree

Today, in a web page, texts and links about the same topic are usually grouped into one content block. The size of the content block is varied. The big one may cover the whole web page, while the small one only takes 1/8 or 1/16 of the web page's total space. Including information provided by the same content block where the link appears is an effective way to enrich the context of the anchor text. Gautam Pant in [16] presented two link-context derivation techniques. We use the method of deriving link-context from Aggregation Nodes, with some modifications. We tidy the HTML page into a well-formed one web page beforehand[1] because many web pages are badly written. We insert missing tags and reorder tags in the "dirty" page to make sure that we can map the context onto a tree structure with each node having a single parent and all text tokens that are enclosed between <text>…</text> tags appear at leave nodes on the tag tree. This preprocessing simplifies the analysis.

[1] http://www.w3.org/People/Raggett/tidy/

First, we locate the anchor. Next, we treat each node on the path from the root of the tree to the anchor as a potential aggregation node (shaded in Fig. 2.). From these candidate nodes, we choose the parent node of anchor, which is the grandparent node of the anchor text as the aggregation node. Then, all of the text in the sub-tree rooted at the node is retrieved as the context of the anchor (showed in rectangle of Fig. 2.). If one anchor appears in many different blocks, combine the link-context in every block as its full link-context.

```
<html>
<head>
<title>Illustration</title>
</head>
<body>
<h4>Artificial Intelligence</h4>
<p>
<strong>
<text>SITE LISTINGS</text>
</strong>
<text>provides an overview of progress in the field of
artificial intelligence, focusing on the research and
development of novel computing hardware which
functions in ways similar to natural nervous systems.
</text>
<a href="http://www.artificialbrains.com/">
<text>ArtificialBrains.com<text>
</a>
</p>
</body>
</html>
```

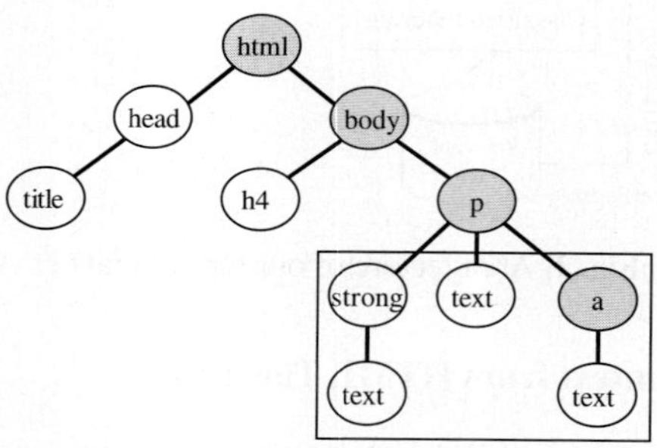

Fig. 2. An HTML page and the corresponding tag tree

Compared with [16], we fixed the aggregation node. In fact, for each page we have an optimal aggregation node that provides the highest context similarity for the corresponding anchor with different aggregation node. It is very laborsome to tidy up web pages every time we analyze the web pages. Large size contexts may be too "noisy" and burdensome for some systems. Too small contexts, like single anchor texts, provide limited information about the topic. We set a tradeoff on quantity and quality.

2.2 Extracting Features from In-Link's Link-Context

Conventional search engines and focused crawlers tend to underestimate in-link pages, emphasizing only on the anchor text of out-link. The link-context of seed

URLs' in-link pages, to our knowledge, provides basic and very useful description of the topic focused by seed URLs.

There are two types of anchor text for information retrieval mentioned in [13].

(1) An anchor text that summarizes content of a web page (hereafter, page anchor)
(2) An anchor text that summarizes content of a web site (hereafter, site anchor)

Site anchor is a coarse description, using the expressions shared on the entire web site. For instance, suppose a web site where furniture information on an entire company is treated. There, "furniture" and "furnishings" are often shown as anchor texts of the main page. Page anchor is a detailed description, not included terms in site anchor. In the above instance, the anchor texts of the internal pages are such as "bed", "desk" and "sofa".

We build a small-size initial dictionary, which on average contains more than 500 words, based on seed URLs. To collect not only page anchors but also the site anchors for fully summarizing the entire content of the seed URL pages, we apply Google API[2]. The seed URLs are submitted to Google and many pages (10-30 per seed URL) linked to seed URLs are received. We then use the method of deriving link-context of these pages to get a set of words related to the topic of the seed URLs. After eliminating stopwords and stemming, we build the dictionary and term-based features. To get in-link pages' link-context and make sure these contexts is related to the topic, the seed URL should focus on one given topic or one topic dominating the whole page, instead of containing many different topics. The seed URLs should also link to authority pages, with many in-links. Then the dictionary built will be big enough and topic oriented.

In the experiment in section 3, we also manually compiled a low dimension dictionary to summarize the topic focused by the seed URLs, which outperformed the dictionary generated automatically. After all, link-contexts are influenced by page designers' opinion, and when expanding anchor text, we may introduce some noise. But that kind of expert dictionary requires us to generate it manually once we change the seed URLs, which is time consuming. Taking this into consideration, it is more flexible and convenient to build the dictionary automatically.

2.3 Estimation Metrics of Relevance

Not all pages which crawler observed are relevant during crawling. So pages referring to that topic are more important, and should be visited as early as possible. Similarly, if a page points to lots of authority pages, then the page is a high *hub* score page [7]. For retrieved some more relevant pages, unvisited URLs must be prioritized by some evaluation metrics. While manual evaluations of link-context derivation method are ideal, such evaluation techniques well not scale up with thousands of unvisited URLs. Hence, we depend on automated techniques. After removing stopwords and stemming to normalize the words, the cleaned link-context of links in the page crawled is processed to compute similarity. In our focused crawler, we compute the weight of each term in the link-context based on TF-IDF weighting scheme and generate a set of topic keywords based on the top n highest weight keywords in the seed pages' link-contexts. TF-IDF assigns the weight to word i in link-context k in proportion to the

[2] http://www.google.com/apis/

number of occurrences of the word in the link-context, and in inverse proportion to the number of link-contexts in the collection for which the word occurs at least once. In the TF-IDF weighting scheme, the weight for word *i* in link-context *k* is given by:

$$a_{ik} = f_{ik} * \log(\frac{N}{n_i}). \tag{1}$$

Where a_{ik} is the weight of word *i* in link-context *k*. Let f_{ik} be the frequency of word *i* in link-context *k*, *N* the number of link-contexts in the collection after stopword removal and word stemming, n_i the total number of times word *i* occurs in the whole collection.

We define the evaluation function *I*(*u*) to prioritize the unvisited URL *u* that the crawler will be pursued, *p* is the parent page of *u*.

$$I(u) = \omega_1 \times sim(c,q) + \omega_2 \times hub(p) \tag{2}$$

Where $\sum_{i=1}^{2} \omega_i = 1$. A high *I*(*u*) value indicates *u* links more relevant page to the topic.

The evaluation function is a weighted combination of followed metrics:

1. *sim*(*c, q*) (similarity of link-context *c* to topic *q*): The similarity of link-context *c* of unvisited url *u* to the vector of term-based features *q* is measured based one the following formula, which is called context similarity.

$$sim(c,q) = \frac{v_c \cdot v_q}{\|v_c\| \cdot \|v_q\|}. \tag{3}$$

Where $v_c \cdot v_q$ is the dot (inner) product of the two vectors. And $\|v\|$ is the Euclidean norm of the vector v.

2. *hub*(*p*) (the evaluation of hubs property): Hub pages are defined to be Web pages which point to lots of "important" pages relevant a topic.

$$hub(p) = \frac{|L_p|}{\frac{\sum_{i=1}^{N} |L_i|}{N}}. \tag{4}$$

Where $|L_p|$: the number of out links of page p ;

$\frac{\sum_{i=1}^{N} |L_i|}{N}$: the average number of out-links of the pages that are already downloaded.

2.4 Adaptive Crawling Procedure

In the process of crawling, whenever a web page is downloaded, we pick up all anchors. If the page linked by the anchor has been crawled or the anchor is in the queue of crawling, the anchor is omitted. Then we parse the page's DOM tree to get link-context of the anchor, compute the similarity with the term-based features. Then the similarity is treated as priority. The unvisited URL that has highest priority will be first fetched to crawl. Whenever a new batch of anchors is inserted into the waiting queue, the queue will be readjusted to create its new frontier. After parsing, the pages will be classified by conventional classifier with a high dimension dictionary. Some "good" relevant pages' in-link contexts will be preprocessed (eliminating stopwords and stemming) and introduced to dictionary. Algorithm 1 shows our adaptive crawling procedure.

Algorithm 1. Adaptive Crawling Algorithm
Input: starting_url, seed URLs
Procedure:

```
for each u in seed URLs
    DB = fetch_context(u)
dictionary = extract_features(DB )
enqueue(url_queue, starting_url)
while (not empty(url_queue))
    url = dequeue(url_queue)
    page = crawl_page(url)
    enqueue(crawled_queue, url)
    if relevance(page) ≥ β
        relevant_pageDB = page
        goodlinkcontextDB = extract_linkcontext(url)
        if |goodlinkcontextDB| ≥ λ
            dictionary = extract_features(goodlinkcontextDB)
    link_contexts = extract_contexts(page)
    evaluate(link_contexts)
    url_list = extract_urls(page)
    for each u in url_list
        if (u ∉ url_queue and u ∉ crawled_queue )
        enqueue(url_queue, u)
        reorder_queue(url_queue)
```

Key function description:

enqueue(queue,element)	:append element at the end of queue
dequeue(queue)	:remove the element at the beginning of queue and return it
extract_linkcontext(url)	:derive link_context of url
extract_contexts(page)	:derive link_contexts of page's out-links
reorder_queue(queue)	:reorder queue by link's priority
extract_features(Database)	:extract topic features from Database

3 The Experiments and Results

In the experiment, we built focused crawlers that use different techniques for obtaining link contexts, and tested our method using multiple crawls over 37 topics covering hundreds of thousands of pages. Under the guide of each method, crawler downloaded the page judged as relevant. We used a conventional classifier to decide whether the page is relevant. *Harvest ratio* and *Target recall* is used to evaluate the result. Our focused crawler is multi-threaded and implemented in java. Multithreading provides for reasonable speed-up when compared with a sequential crawler. We use 70 threads of execution starting from 100 relevant URLs (Seed URLs) picked from Open Directory Project (ODP, http://dmoz.org/) while running a crawler and only the first 10 KB of each Web page is downloaded. In the evaluation function $I(u)$, every weight ω_i is variable. Fig 3 shows the dynamic plot of harvest-ratio versus weight ω_1. We assign ω_1 =0.8, which the performance of the crawler is best after crawling 5000 pages.

$$harvest - ratio = \frac{relevant\_pages}{pages\_downloaded} . \tag{5}$$

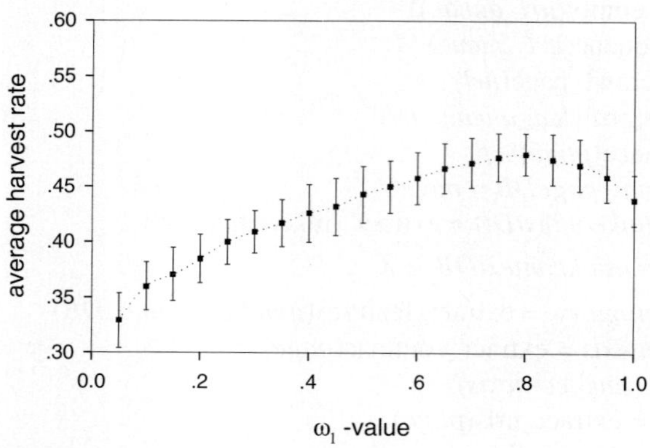

Fig. 3. Dynamic plot of harvest-ratio versus weight ω_1. Performance is averaged across topics and standard errors are also shown.

We also implement Breadth-First and Best-First crawler. Breadth-First without judging on the context of the unvisited URLs, performed not well. It depends heavily on the localization of the relevant pages and web sites. Best-First predicts the relevance of the potential URLs by referring to the whole context of the visited web page. All out-links in one page have same priority. It only grouped the unvisited URLs based on the page picked up from, and there is no difference within each group. So it has low accuracy when there is a lot of noise in the page or the page has multiple topics, as showed in Fig. 4. (a). This weakness can be just overcome by link-context crawler. However, it sometimes outperformed link-context, showed in Fig. 4. (b), since a web page provides enough information and words to judge with a higher dimension dictionary than link-context when the web page is about a single topic.

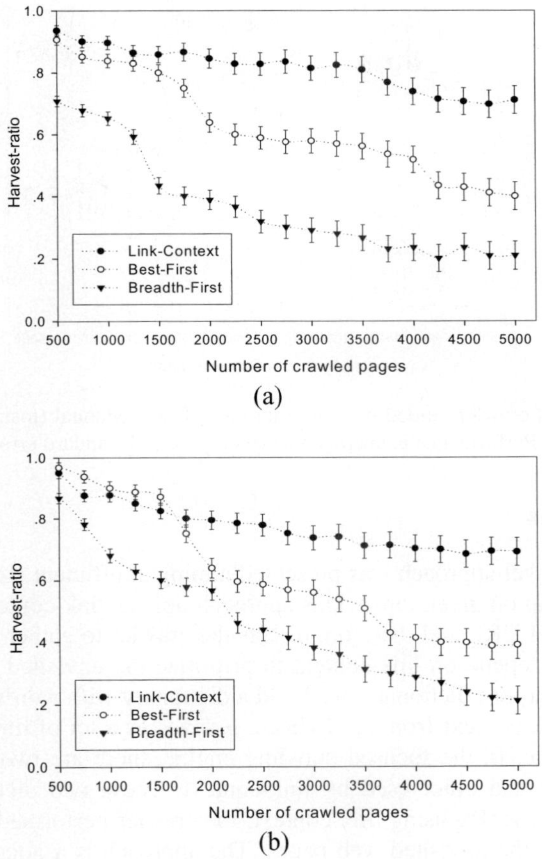

Fig. 4. Dynamic plot of harvest-ratio versus number of crawled pages. Performance is averaged across topics and standard errors are also shown.

In Fig. 4, we notice that crawler guided by link-context is not stable at the beginning of crawling, for its dictionary is changed with the seed URLs, influenced by the quality of the seed URLs' in-link link-contexts. But it always outperformed Breadth-first. When many of the pages crawled consist of different topic blocks, Link-context outperformed Best-First, since its judgments is based on web page block and the noise from other blocks has little effect on it. This characteristic of link-context crawler is appreciated for web pages where multitopics dominate in WWW.

It is common that crawler guided by dictionary build manually outperforms automatically generated dictionary. Fig. 5 shows the case where the performance of the two approaches is quite different. Building a dictionary manually is an optimal strategy but difficult in practice. However it still proved that with a small-size dictionary, the link-context crawler effectively retrieves relevant pages and stays on the given topic. Like the case displayed, most of the link-context crawlers performed well in early crawling process and that guarantees a good initiation.

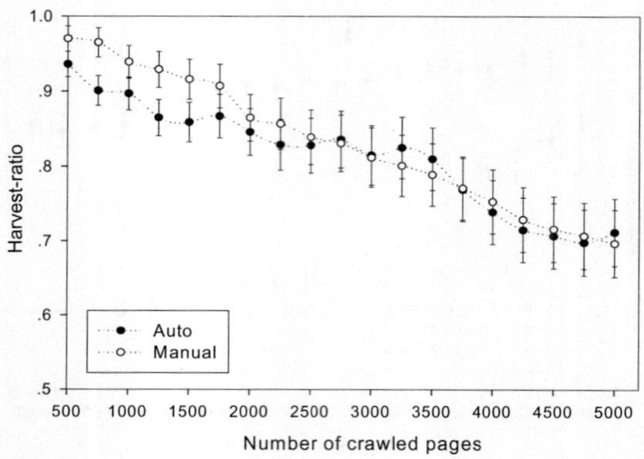

Fig. 5. Link-context crawler guided by Auto (automated) and Manual (manually) built dictionary on a set of data. Performance is averaged across topics and standard errors are also shown.

4 Conclusions

In this paper, a novel approach was presented aiming at efficient steering the focused crawler to maintain on given topic. This approach utilizes link-context illumination to prioritize unvisited URL and therefore directs the crawler to gather the more relevant pages. When we depend on link-context to prioritize the unvisited URLs, instead of using a general-purpose dictionary, we build a dictionary with words weighted by just getting in-link link-context from seed URLs. It saves us a lot of time to select words to summarize topic. In the focused crawling engine, there are two dictionaries, one used by classifier and other used by link-context. These two dictionaries can't be incorporated into one. By using link-context, the crawler performed well in forecasting the context of the unvisited web pages. The approach is a good assistant for focused crawler. It prioritizes the links picked up from the pages classified by the classifiers and improved the performance of crawler, making it more efficient to crawl only relevant pages. A comprehensive experiment proves that this approach is superior to some existing algorithms. By combining link-context crawler with existing methods such as Best-First, more promising results may be expected by overcoming each other's weakness and performing perfectly on prioritizing unvisited URLs.

Acknowledgment

This work is sponsored by the National Natural Science Foundation of China under grant number 60373099.

References

1. Pinkerton, B.: Finding What People Want: Experiences with the WebCrawler. In: Proc. 1st international World Wide Web Conference (1994)
2. De Bra, R. D. J. Post.: Information Retrieval in the World-Wide Web: Making Client-based Searching Feasible. Proceedings of the First International World-Wide Web conference, Geneva (1994)

3. Hersovici, M., M. Jacovi, Y. S. Maarek, D. Pelleg, M. Shtalhaim, and S. Ur: The shark-search algorithm-An application:Tailored Web site mapping. Proc. 7th Intl. World-Wide Web Conference (1998)
4. J. Cho, H. Garcia-Molina, L. Page: Efficient Crawling Through URL Ordering. In Proceedings of 7th World Wide Web Conference (1998)
5. F. Menczer, R. Belew.: Adaptive retrieval agents: internalizing local context and scaling up to the web. Machine Learning 39 (2–3) (2000) 203–242
6. G. Pant and F. Menczer.: Topical Crawling for Business Intelligence. Proc. 7th European Conference on Research and Advanced Technology for Digital Libraries (ECDL) (2003)
7. J. Johnson, K. Tsioutsiouliklis, C. L. Giles.: Evolving strategies for focused Web crawling . Proceedings of the Twentieth International Conference on Machine Learning (ICML-2003), Washington DC (2003)
8. Jun Li, Kazutaka Furuse, and Kazunori Yamaguchi. Focused Crawling by Exploiting Anchor Text Using Decision Tree. WWW2005, May 10-14, 2005, Chiba, Japan. ACM 1-59593-051-5/05/0005
9. Jon Kleinberg, Authoritative sources in a hyperlinked environment, in: Proc. of the 9th ACM-SIAM Symposium on Discrete Algorithms, 1998
10. S. Brin and L. Page. The PageRank Citation Ranking: Bringing Order to the Web. In Technical Report available at http://www-db.stanford.edu/~backrub/pageranksub.ps, January 1998
11. Oliver A. McBryan. GENVL and WWWW: Tools for taming the Web. In Proceedings of the First International Conference on the World Wide Web, Geneva, Switzerland, May 1994. CERN
12. Nadav Eiron, Kevin S. McCurley: Analysis of anchor text for web search. SIGIR 2003: 459-460
13. Kenji tateishi,Hideki Kawai,susumu Akamine,Katsushi Matsuda and Toshikazu Fukushima, Evaluation of Web Retrieval Method Using Anchor Text. In Proceedings of the 3rd NTCIR Workshop, pp25-29, 2002
14. M. Iwazume, K. Shirakami, K. Hatadani, H. Takeda, and T. Nishida. Iica: An ontology-based internet navigation system. In AAAI-96 Workshop on Internet Based Information Systems, 1996
15. Chakrabarti, K. Punera, M. Subramanyam, "Accelerated focused crawling through online relevance feedback", WWW 2002, pp. 148-159
16. G. Pant. Deriving Link-context from HTML Tag Tree. In 8th ACM SIGMOD Workshop on Research Issues in Data Mining and Knowledge Discovery, 2003

Evaluating Subjective Compositions by the Cooperation Between Human and Adaptive Agents

Chung-Yuan Huang[1], Ji-Lung Hsieh[2], Chuen-Tsai Sun[2], and Chia-Ying Cheng[2]

[1] Department of Computer Science and Information Engineering
Chang Gung University
259 Wen Hwa 1st Road, Taoyuan 333, Taiwan, Republic of China
gis89802@csie.cgu.edu.tw
[2] Department of Computer Science
National Chiao Tung University
1001 Ta Hsueh Road, Hsinchu 300, Taiwan, Republic of China
{gis91572, ctsun, gis92566}@cis.nctu.edu.tw

Abstract. We describe a music recommender model that uses intermediate agents to evaluate music composition according to their own rules respectively, and make recommendations to user. After user scoring recommended items, agents can adapt their selection rules to fit user tastes, even when user preferences undergo a rapid change. Depending on the number of users, the model can also be applied to such tasks as critiquing large numbers of music, image, or written compositions in a competitive contest with other judges. Several experiments are reported to test the model's ability to adapt to rapidly changing conditions yet still make appropriate decisions and recommendations.

Keywords: Music recommender system, interactive evolutionary computing, adaptive agent, critiquing subjective data, content-based filtering.

1 Introduction

Since the birth of the Netscape web browser in 1994, millions of Internet surfers have spent countless hours searching for current news, research data, and entertainment—especially music. Users of Apple's Musicstore can choose from 2,000,000 songs for downloading. Having to deal with so many choices can feel like a daunting task to Internet users, who could benefit from efficient recommender systems that filter out low-interest items [1-3].

Some of the most popular Internet services present statistical data to point users to items that they might be interested in. News websites place stories that attract the broadest interest on their main pages (like news on www.cnn.com), and commercial product stores such as amazon.com use billboards to list current book sales figures and to make recommendations that match collected data on user behaviors (like bestseller, Hot 100 on www.amazon.com). However, these statistical methods are less useful for making music, image, or other artistic product recommendations to users whose subjective preferences can cross many genres. Music selections are often made based on mood or time of day [4, 5].

A. Gelbukh and C.A. Reyes-Garcia (Eds.): MICAI 2006, LNAI 4293, pp. 974 – 984, 2006.

Two classical approaches to personalized recommender systems are content-based filtering and collaborative filtering. Content-based filtering methods focus on item content analyses and recommend items similar to interested items given by user in the past [1, 6], while the experts use collaborate filtering method to make the group of users with common interests share their accessed information [7-9]. Common design challenges of previous approaches include:

1. When the recommended item is far different from the user's preferences, the user still can only access or select these system-recommended items, and cannot access the potential good items which never appear in the set of recommended items. This problem can be solved possibly with an appropriate feedback mechanism [7].
2. In a collaborative filtering approach, new items may not be selected due to sparse rating histories [7].
3. User preferences may change over time or according to the moment, situation, or mood [4, 5].
4. Because of the large body of subjective compositions, the required large amount of time for forming suitable recommendations needs to should be reduced [4, 5].

In light of these challenges, we have created a music recommender system model which was designed to reduce agent training time through user feedback. Model design consists of three steps: a) content-based filtering methods are used to extract item features, b) a group of agents make item recommendations, and c) an evolution mechanism is used to make adjustments according to the subjective emotions and changing tastes of users.

2 Related Research

2.1 Recommender Systems

The two major components of recommender systems are items and users. Many current systems use algorithms to make recommendations regarding music [3, 9, 10], images, books [11], movies [12, 13], news, and homepages [7, 14, 15]. Depending on the system, the algorithm uses a pre-defined profile or user rating history to make its choices. Most user-based recommender systems focus on grouping users with similar interests [7-9], although some do try to match the preferences of single users according to their rating histories [1, 6].

Recommender systems play a role to use multiple mapping techniques to connect item and user layers, requiring accurate and appropriate pre-processing and presentation of items for comparison and matching. Item representations can consist of keyword-based profiles provided by content providers or formatted feature descriptions extracted by information retrieval techniques. Accordingly, item feature descriptions in recommender systems can be keyword- or content-based (Fig. 1). Features for items, such as movies or books, are hard to extract because movies are composed of various kinds of media [6] and content analysis of books encounters the problem of natural language processing. Their keyword-based profiles are often determined by content providers. However, current image and audio processing techniques now allow for programmed extraction of content-based features represented by factors that include tempo and pitch distribution for music and chroma and luminance distribution for images.

Previous recommender systems can be classified in terms of content-based filtering versus collaborative filtering. Standard content-based filtering focuses on classifying and comparing item content without sharing recommendations with others identified as having the same preferences. Collaborative filtering method focuses on how users are clustered into several groups according to their preference. To avoid drawbacks associated with keyword-based searching (commonly used for online movie or book store databases), other designers emphasize content-based filtering focusing on such features as energy level, volume, tempo, rhythm, chords, average pitch differences, etc. Many music recommender system designers acknowledge drawbacks in standard collaborative filtering approaches—for instance, they can't recommend two similar items if one of them is unrated. To address the shortcomings of both approaches, some systems use content features for user classification and other systems find out group users with similar tastes [7, 16].

To address challenges tied to human emotion or mood and solve the sparsity problem of collaborative filtering method, some music and image retrieval system designers use IEC to evaluate item fitness according to user parameters [4, 5]. We adopted IEC for our proposed model, which uses agent evolutionary training for item recommendations. The results of our system tests indicate that trained agents are capable of choosing songs that match both user taste and emotion.

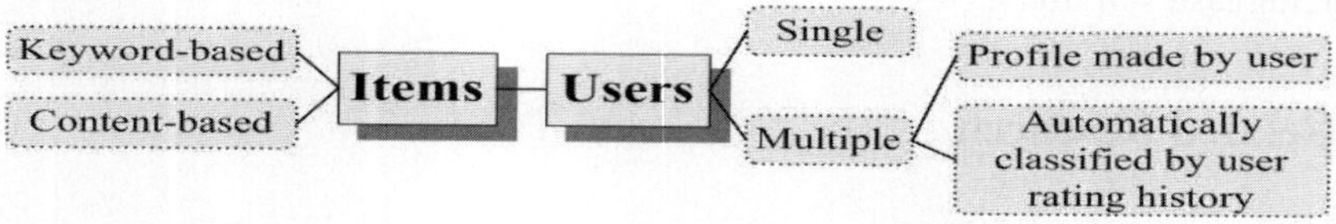

Fig. 1. Recommender system classifications

2.2 Interactive Evolutionary Computing

Genetic algorithm (GA) is an artificial intelligence system that allows for searches of solutions to optimization problems [17]. According to GA construction rules, the structure of an individual's chromosome is designed according to the specific problem and genes are randomly generated once the system is initialized. Following GA procedures include 1) using a fitness function to evaluate the performance of various problem solutions, 2) selecting multiple individuals from current population, 3) modifying the selected individuals by mutation and crossover operators, and 4) deciding which individuals should be preserved or discarded for the next run; discarded solutions are replaced by new ones whose genes are preserved). A GA repeats this evolutionary procedure until an optimal solution emerges. The challenge of music recommendation was defining a fitness function that accurately represents subjective human judgment. Only then can such a system be used to make judgments in art, engineering, and education [4, 5].

Interactive Evolutionary Computing (IEC) which is an optimization method can meet the need of defining a fitness function by involving the human preferences. IEC is a GA technique whose fitness of chromosome is measured by a human user [18]. The main factor affecting IEC evaluation is human emotion and fatigue. Since users cannot make fair judgments when processing run evaluations, results will change for different occasions according to the user's emotional state at any particular moment. Furthermore, since users may fail to adequately process large populations due to fatigue, searching for goals with smaller population sizes within fewer generations is an important factor. Finally, the potential for fluctuating human evaluations can result in inconsistencies across different generations [19].

3 Using Evolutionary Agents for a Music Recommender System

3.1 Model Description

In our model, intermediate agents play the roles which select music compositions according to their chromosome and recommend to user. The system's six function blocks (track selector, feature extractor, recommendation agent module, evolution manager, user interface, and database) are shown in Figure 2.

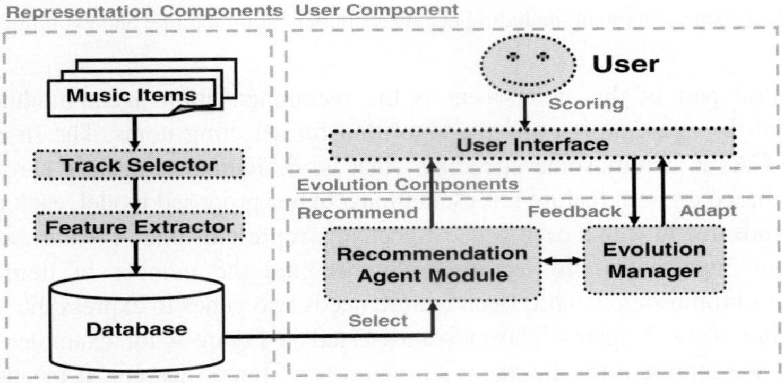

Fig. 2. Six model components including track selector, feature extractor, database, recommendation agent module, evolution manager, and user interface

A representation component consists of the track selector, feature extractor, and database function blocks, all of which are responsible for forming item feature profiles. This component translates the conceptual properties of music items into useful information with specific values and stores it in a database for later use. In other words, this is a pre-processing component. Previous recommender systems established direct connections between user tastes and item features. In contrast, we use trainable agents to automatically make this connection based on a detailed item analysis. The track selector is responsible for translating each music composition into textual file, while feature extractor is responsible for calculating several statistical feature measurements (such as pitch entropy, pitch density, and mean pitch value for all tracks mentioned in Section 4). Finally, database function block stores these statistical features for further uses.

An evolution component includes a recommendation agent module and evolution manager. The former is responsible for building agent selection rules according to music features extracted by the representation component, while the latter constructs an evolution model based on IEC and applies a GA model to train the evolutionary agent. In our proposed model, user evaluations serve as the engine for agent adaptation (Fig. 3).

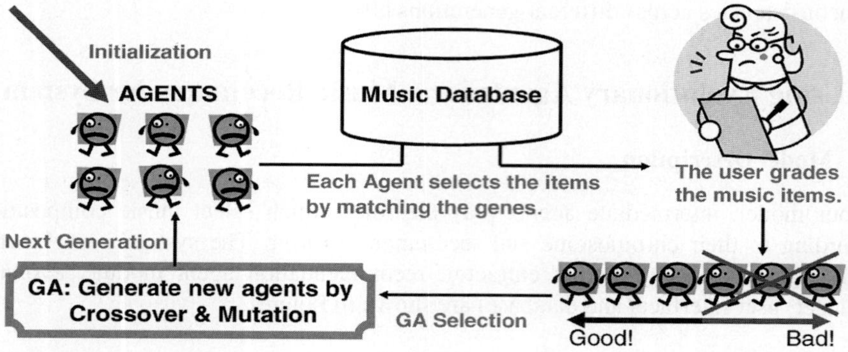

Fig. 3. Evolution component, including agent recommendation module and evolution manager

A central part of this component is the recommendation agent module, which consists of the agent design and the algorithm for selecting items. The first step for standard GAs is chromosome encoding—that is, designing an agent's chromosomal structure based on item feature representations. In our proposed model, each agent has one chromosome in which each gene respectively represents one of feature value. The gene value represents item feature preference and the number of item features represents chromosome length. Each feature needs two genes to express the mean and range value. Take 3 agents' chromosomes listed in Figure 4 for example, f1_mean and f1_range represent the 1st agent's preference of tempo feature. It means that 1st agent prefers the tempo between 30 and 40 beats per minute. The 1st agent will select the songs which have the tempo 35 ± 5 bests per minute and velocities 60 ± 10. The value of gene also can be "*Don't care*". We also perform the real number mutation for each mean and range value, and one-point crossover for selected pair of agents' chromosomes.

The evolution manager in our model is responsible for the selection mechanism that preserves valuable genes for generating more effective offspring. The common procedure is selecting good agents to serve as the parent population, creating new individuals by mixing parental genes, and replacing eliminated agents. However, when dealing with subjective evaluations, human's preference changing can result in lack of stability across runs. Accordingly, the best agents in previous rounds may get low grades because of change of human's preference, and therefore be discarded prematurely. As a solution, we propose the idea of agent fame values that are established according to previous behaviors. The higher the value is, the greater the possibility that an agent will survive. The system's selection method determines which agents are discarded or recombined according to weighted fame values and local grades in each round, with total scores being summed with an agent's fame value in subsequent rounds.

CHROMOSOME

AgentID	f1_mean	f1_range	f2_mean	f2_range	...
1	35	5	60	10	...
2	60	3	95	4	...
3	83	5	120	10	...

Fig. 4. Agent chromosome. Each gene represents a mean or range value of music feature. Whole chromosomes represent selection rules for agents to follow when choosing favorite items. The chromosome in this figure encodes two music features.

Another important GA design issue is deciding when to stop agent evolution. System convergence is generally determined via learning curves, but in a subjective system this task (or deciding when an agent's training is complete) is especially difficult in light of potential change of user preference and emotion. Our solution is based on the observation that the stature of judges in a music or art competition increases or decreases according to decisions they make in previous competitions. In our system, agent fame value varies in each round. The system monitors agent values to determine which ones exceed a pre-defined threshold; those agents are placed in a "V.I.P pool." Pool agents cannot be replaced, but they can share their genes with other agents. Once a sufficient number of stable V.I.P. agents are established, the system terminates the evolution process. For example, if one of agent got six points fame value and the system pre-define threshold is six points high, the agent will be placed in a V.I.P pool. This mechanism just sets for preserving the possible good agents.

A user component consists of an interface for evaluating agent recommendations based on standards such as technicality, melody, style, and originality. The user interface is also responsible for arranging agents according to specific application purposes. For example, for finding joint preference between two different users, the user interface component will initialize and arrange two set agents for these two users respectively.

An agent selects items of interest from the database according to selection rules and makes appropriate recommendations to the user, who evaluates items via the interface. Evaluations are immediately dispatched to the agent, whose evolution is controlled according to performance and GA operations (e.g., crossover, mutation, and selection). The evolution manager is responsible for a convergence test whose results are used to halt evolution according to agent performance.

3.2 Applications

We designed our model so that the chromosomes of surviving agents contain selection rules that be able to represent user profiles. Concurrently, user profiles formed by agent chromosomes can be compared among multiple users. Combined, distributing agents can be utilized for three kinds of applications:

1. Users can train sample groups of agents. The agent evaluation function can be altered to reflect a sum of several user profiles, thus representing the tastes of multiple users. However, true system convergence will be difficult to achieve due to disagreements among user opinions. As in the case of scoring entries in art or music competitions, extremely high and low scores can result in total scoring bias.
2. Users can train their own agents and share profiles. According to this method (which is similar to collaborative filtering), the system compares user profiles formed by the agents' chromosomes and identifies those that are most similar. Collaborative recommendations can be implemented via partial exchanges among agents.
3. Users can train their own agents while verifying the items selected by other users' agents. In the art or music competition scenario, users can train their own agents before verifying the agents of other users to achieve partial agreement. Pools of agents from all users will therefore represent a consensus. If one user's choice is rejected by the majority of other users following verification, that user will be encouraged to perform some agent re-training or face the possibility that the agent in question will be eliminated from the pool. For this usage, the user interface is responsible for arranging and exchanging the agents between different users.

4 Experiments

Our experimental procedures can be divided into two phases:

- Training phase. Each user was allotted six agents for the purpose of selecting music items—two songs per agent per generation (12 songs per generation). Since subjective distinctions such as "good or bad music" are hard to distinguish according to a single grading standard, user give multiple scores to each songs according to difference standard. Each agent received two sets of scores from user, with three scores in each set representing melody, style, and originality. The chromosome of any agent receiving high grades from a user six times in a row was placed in the system's V.I.P pool; the chromosome was used to produce a new chromosome in the next generation. This procedure was repeated until the system determined that evolutionary convergence had occurred. The system stopped at the user's request or when the V.I.P pool contained four agents, whichever came first.
- Validation phase. This phase consisted of a demonstration test for verifying that system-recommend songs matched the user's tastes. Experimental groups consisted of 20 songs chosen by 6 trained agents; control groups consisted of 20 songs chosen by 6 random agents. User evaluations confirmed or refuted agent capabilities. Users were not told which selections belonged to the respective groups.

4.1 Model Implementations

Musical items were stored and played in polyphonic MIDI format in our system, because the node data in MIDI files can be extracted easily compared with data in audio wave format [1]. The track selector translates each MIDI file into a textual format respectively; we list the beginning part of textual feature file in Table 1 for example. Polyphonic items consist of one track for melody and additional tracks for accompanying instruments or vocals. The melody track (considered the representative track) contains the most semantics. Since the main melody track contains more distinct notes with different pitches than the other tracks, it was used for feature extraction based on pitch density analysis. According to previous research [3], this method is capable of achieving an 83 percent correctness rate. Track pitch density is defined as *Pitch density = NP / AP*, where *NP* is the number of distinct pitches on the track and *AP* is the number of all possible distinct pitches in the MIDI standard. After computing the pitch densities of all targeted music object tracks, the track with the highest density was identified as the representative polyphonic track.

Table 1. Part of textual MID feature file

Unit	Length	At	Time	Track	Channel	Note	Velocity
314	53	1162ms	197ms	T4	C4	d2	68
319	50	1181ms	185ms	T3	C3	d4	71
321	48	1188ms	178ms	T3	C3	b3	74
...	...	...	...	...	...	...	...

Purpose of feature extractor is to extract features from the perceptual properties of musical items and transform them into distinct data. We focused on seven features for our proposed system; new item features should be also added when possible.

1. Tempo, defined as the average note length value derived from MIDI files.
2. Volume, defined as the average value of note velocities derived from MIDI files.
3. Pitch entropy, defined as: $PitchEntropy = -\sum_{j=1}^{NP} P_j \log P_j, where Pj = \frac{N_j}{T}$, where N_j is the total number of notes with a corresponding pitch on the main track and T is the total number of main track notes.
4. Pitch density, as defined earlier in this section.
5. Mean pitch value for all tracks.
6. Pitch value standard deviation. Large standard deviations indicate a user preference for musical complexity.
7. Number of channels, reflecting a preference for solo performers, small ensembles, or large bands/orchestras.

Genes in standard GA systems are initialized randomly. However, in our proposed system the random agents will probably fail to find items that match their genetic information because the distribution of extracted features is unbalanced. We therefore suggest pre-analyzing feature value distribution and using the data to initialize agent chromosomes. By doing so, it is possible to avoid initial agent preferences that are so unusual that they cannot possibly locate preferred items. Furthermore, this procedure prevents noise and speeds up agent evolution. Here we will use tempo as an example of music feature pre-analysis. Since the average tempo for all songs in our database was approximately 80 beats per minute (Fig. 5), a random choice of tempo between 35 and 40 beats per minute resulted in eventual agent replacement or elimination and a longer convergence time before convergence for the entire system. For this reason,

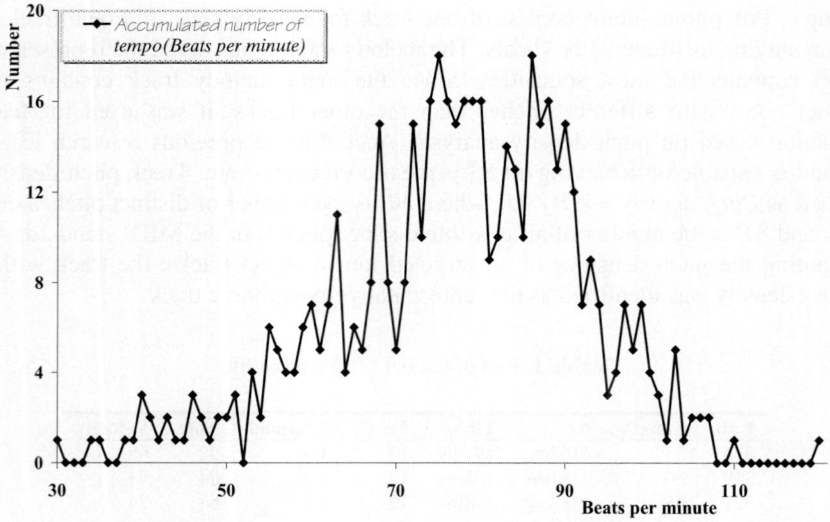

Fig. 5. Statistical curve for tempo distribution in our sample of 1,036 MIDI files

average values in our system were limited: 60 percent of all initial tempo ranges deviated between 1 and –1 and 80 percent between 2 and –2. This led to a speeding up of the agent evolution process.

4.2 Recommendation Quality

Recommendation quality is measured in terms of precision rate and weighted grade. Precision rate is defined as *Precision_rate* = N_S / N, where N_S is the number of successful samples and N the total number of music items. Weighted grades equals to summation of M_i divided by N, where M_i represents music item grades and N the total number of music items. Users were given six levels to choose from for evaluating chosen items.

Users were asked to evaluate experimental and control group selections. Experimental group agents evaluated songs recommended by agents that they had trained and control group agents evaluated songs at random. After users completed their tests, the system calculates precision rates and weighted grades. Finally, the songs recommended by the trained agents had an average precision rate of 84 percent and average weighted grade of 7.38, compared to 58.33 percent and 5.54 for songs recommended by the random agents.

4.3 Convergence Test

GA-based models commonly perform large numbers of iterations before arriving at convergence. In order to trace learning progress, we let users perform one demonstration (validation) test after every round; results are shown in Figure 6a. Curve A reflects a steady increase in effectiveness and convergence after eight rounds. Curve B reflects a lack of progress for agents that make random selections without training.

In addition to recommendation quality and convergence tests, we made an attempt to identify clear differences between experimental and control group music selections by extracting their respective features. As shown in Figure 6b, obvious differences were noted in terms of tempo and entropy, indicating that the trained agents converged unique preferences and did not blindly select items. Take one user's experimental result as an example, the user's preferences of feature tempo is quite different from the average tempo in control group.

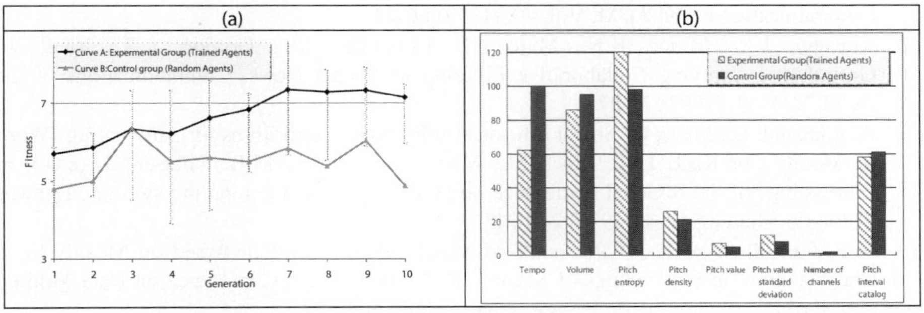

Fig. 6. (a) Convergence test and evolution generation of 10 users. Curve A represents an average of fitness values of 60 agents belong to 10 users. (b) One user results example.

5 Conclusion

Our proposed recommendation model can evaluate a large body of subjective data via a cooperative process involving both system agents and human users. Those users train groups of agents to find items that match their preferences, and then provide ongoing feedback on agent selections for purposes of further training. Agent training entails IEC methods and agent fame values to address the issue of change in human emotions. The agent fame value concept is also used as a convergence condition to promote agent population diversity and to propagate useful genes. Model flexibility was expressed in terms of replacing or altering functional blocks such as user interface which allows for usages of multiple users. We suggest that with refinement and modifications, our model has potential for use by referees to critique large numbers of subjective compositions (in such areas as art, music and engineering) and to make recommendations for images by extracting features (e.g., brightness, contrast, or RGB value) and encoding the information into agent chromosomes.

References

1. Kazuhiro, I., Yoshinori, H., Shogo, N.: Content-Based Filtering System for Music Data. 2004 Symposium on Applications and the Internet-Workshops. Tokyo Japan. (2004) 480
2. Ben Schafer, J., Konstan, J.A., Riedl, J.: E-Commerce Recommendation Applications. Data Mining and Knowledge Discovery, Vol. 5. (2001) 115-153
3. Chen, H.C., Chen, A.L.P.: A Music Recommendation System Based on Music and User Grouping. Journal of Intelligent Information Systems, Vol. 24. (2005) 113-132

4. Cho, S.B.: Emotional Image and Musical Information Retrieval with Interactive Genetic Algorithm, Proceedings of the IEEE, Vol. 92. (2004) 702-711
5. Cho, S.B., Lee, J.Y.: A Human-Oriented Image Retrieval System using Interactive Genetic Algorithm, IEEE Transactions on Systems, Man and Cybernetics, Part A, Vol. 32. (2002) 452-458
6. Li, Q, Myaeng, S.H., Guan, D.H., Kim, B.M.: A Probabilistic Model for Music Recommendation Considering Audio Features, in Information Retrieval Technology, Vol. 3689. (2005) 72-83
7. Balabanovic, M., Shoham, Y.: Fabs: Content-based, Collaborative Recommendation, Communication of the ACM, Vol. 40. (1997) 66-72
8. Konstan, J.A., Miller, B.N., Maltz, D., Herlocker, J.L., Gordon, L.R., Riedl, J.: GroupLens: Applying Collaborative Filtering to Usenet News, Communications of the ACM, Vol. 40. (1997) 77-87
9. Shardanand, U., Maes, P.: Social Information Filtering: Algorithms for Automating "Word of Mouth", In Katz, L.R., Mack, R., Marks, L., Rosson, M.B., Nielsen, J. (eds.), in Proceedings of the SIGCHI conference on Human factors in computing systems, Denver, Colorado, United States. (1995) 210-217
10. Kuo, F.F., Shan, M.K.: A Personalized Music Filtering System Based on Melody Style Classification, in Proceedings of Second IEEE International Conference on Data Mining, (Maebashi City, Gumma Prefecture, Japan. (2002) 649-652
11. Mooney, R.J., Roy, L.: Content-Based Book Recommending using Learning for Text Categorization, In Nurnberg, P.J., Hicks, D.L., Furuta, R. (eds.), in Proceedings of the fifth ACM conference on Digital libraries, (San Antonio, Texas, United States. (2000) 195-204
12. Fisk, D.: An Application of Social Filtering to Movie Recommendation, Bt Technology Journal, Vol. 14. (1996) 124-132
13. Mukherjee, R., Sajja, E., Sen, S.: A Movie Recommendation System - An Application of Voting Theory in User Modeling, User Modeling and User-Adapted Interaction, Vol. 13. (2003) 5-33
14. Chaffee, J., Gauch, S.: Personal Ontologies for Web Navigation, in Proceedings of the ninth international conference on Information and knowledge management. McLean, Virginia, United States. (2000) 227-234
15. Chiang, J.H., Chen, Y.C.: An Intelligent News Recommender Agent for Filtering and Categorizing Large Volumes of Text Corpus, International Journal of Intelligent Systems, Vol. 19. (2004) 201-216
16. Pazzani, M.J.: A Framework for Collaborative, Content-Based and Demographic Filtering, Artificial Intelligence Review, Vol. 13. (1999) 393-408
17. Holland, J.H.: Adaptation in Natural and Artificial Systems, Ann Arbor: University of Michigan Press. (1975)
18. Takagi, H.: Interactive Evolutionary Computation: Fusion of the Capabilities of EC Optimization and Human Evaluation, in Proceedings of the IEEE, Vol. 89. (2001) 1275-1296
19. Maes, P.: Agents that Reduce Work and Information Overload, Communications of the ACM, Vol. 37. (1994) 31-40

Using Syntactic Distributional Patterns for Data-Driven Answer Extraction from the Web

Alejandro Figueroa[1] and John Atkinson[2,⋆]

[1] Deutsches Forschungszentrum für Künstliche Intelligenz - DFKI, Stuhlsatzenhausweg 3, D - 66123, Saarbrücken, Germany
[2] Department of Computer Sciences, Universidad de Concepción, Concepción, Chile
alejandro@coli.uni-sb.de, atkinson@inf.udec.cl

Abstract. In this work, a data-driven approach for extracting answers from web-snippets is presented. Answers are identified by matching contextual distributional patterns of the expected answer type(EAT) and answer candidates. These distributional patterns are directly learnt from previously annotated tuples {*question, sentence, answer*}, and the learning mechanism is based on the principles language acquisition. Results shows that this linguistic motivated data-driven approach is encouraging.

Keywords: Natural Language Processing, Question Answering.

1 Introduction

The increase of the amount of information on the Web has led search engines to deal with a huge amount of data as users have become retrievers of all sorts. Nowadays, search engines are not only focusing on retrieving relevant documents for a user's particular request. They also provide other services (i.e., Group Search, News Search, Glossary), hence the complexity of the request of the users has addressed the research to Question Answering (QA) systems. These aim to answer natural language (NL) questions prompted by users, by searching the answer in a set of available documents on the Web. QA is a challenging task due to the ambiguity of language and the complexity of the linguistic phenomena that can be found in NL documents.

Typical questions to answer are those that look for name entities as answers (i.e., *locations*, *persons*, *dates*, *organizations*). Nevertheless, QA systems are not restricted to these kinds of questions. They also try to deal with more complex ones that may require demanding reasoning tasks while the system is looking for the answer [11].

Usually, QA systems start by analyzing the query [4,7] in order to determine the EAT. The EAT allows the QA system to narrow the search space [8], while it is ranking documents, sentences or sequences of words in which the answer is

⋆ This research is sponsored by FONDECYT, Chile under grant number 1040469 "*Un Modelo Evolucionario de Descubrimiento de Conocimiento Explicativo desde Textos con Base Semantica con Implicaciones para el Analisis de Inteligencia.*"

A. Gelbukh and C.A. Reyes-Garcia (Eds.): MICAI 2006, LNAI 4293, pp. 985–995, 2006.

supposed to be. This set of likely answers is called *answer candidates*. In this last step of the zooming process, the QA system must decide which are the most suitable answers for the triggering query. This extraction and ranking of answer candidates is traditionally based on [6,7,8] frequency counting, pattern matching and detecting different orderings of query words, called *paraphrases*. Answer extraction modules attempt to take advantage of the redundancy provided by different information sources. This redundancy increases significantly the probability of finding a *paraphrase*, in which the answer can be readily identified. Normally, QA systems extract these paraphrases at the sentence level [10]. The rules for identifying paraphrases can manually be written or automatically learnt [6,10], and they can consist of pre-parsed trees [10], or simple string based manipulations [6]. In general, *paraphrases* are learnt by retrieving sentences that contain preciously annotated question-answer pairs. For example in [10], anchor terms (i.e., "Lennon 1980") are sent to the web, in order to retrieve sentences that contain query and answer terms. Then, patterns are extracted from this set of sentences with their likelihood being proportional to their redundancy on the Web[7]. In most cases, the new set of retrieved sentences is matched with paraphrases in order to extract new answers. At the same time, a huge set of paraphrases [6] decreases considerably the need of deep linguistic processing like: anaphora or synonym resolution. In some cases, it reduces the extraction to a pattern matching by means of regular expressions[10]. As a result, strategies based on paraphrases tend to perform better when questions aim for a name entity as an answer: *Locations*, *Names*, *Organizations*. But, they perform poorly when they aim for *Noun Phrases*[10].

Due to the huge amount of paraphrases, statistical methods are also used for extracting answers. In [5], a strategy for answering questions is learnt directly from data. This strategy conceives the answer extraction problem as a binary classification problem in which text snippets are labelled as correct or incorrect. The classifier is based on a set of features from lexical n-grams to parse trees. The major problem of statistical-based approaches is that, frequently, they get inexact answers, which usually consist of substrings of the answer, the answer surrounded by some context words, or strings highly closed to answers.

Nevertheless, it is still unclear how each different technique contributes to deal with the linguistic phenomena that QA systems face while searching for the answer. One solution for this may involve a trade-off between the implementation of rule-based and easy re-trainable data-driven systems. In [10], a strategy for combining the output of different kinds of answer extractors is introduced. This re-ranker is based on a *Maximum Entropy Linear Classifier*, which was trained on a set of 48 different types of features such as ranking in the answer extraction modules, redundancy, negative feedback, etc. Results show that a good strategy for combing answer extractors, based mainly on different strategies, can significantly improve the overall performance of QA systems [11].

Strategies based on paraphrases aim to find a re-writing of the query within the text where the answer is easily identified. Their main drawback is that whenever the answer is in an context, which do not match any re-writing rule, it will not be identified. In this work, we take advantage of the redundancy of the Web in a different way. We claim that some answers can be readily identified by comparing their syntactic behaviour on snippets with the syntactic behavior of the EAT. The likelihood of answers to the EAT is supported by syntactical distributional patterns presented on their occurrences. In this data-driven strategy, the syntactic behavior of the EAT is directly learnt from previously annotated tuples {*question, sentence, answer*}. In contrast to another approaches, we do not use general-purpose classifiers, we base our learning process on Pinker's language acquisition theory [3]. This states that innate knowledge and a learning strategy along with negative evidence are required for a child to successfully acquire many linguistics properties including syntactic categories. In our approach, the innate knowledge includes previously annotated tuples and the negative evidence is a set of words with an ambiguous syntactic behavior. Learning is carried out into two phases: a likelihood metric to identify how likely the syntactic behavior of the EAT is, and a mechanism to have new evidence added to the innate knowledge.

Instead of combining the output of many answer extractors, the output is used for annotating pairs {*sentence, answer*} which are used for inferring the syntactic behavior of the EAT afterwards. Thus, any manual annotation or dependence on the context of the query is removed. The model takes advantage of the redundancy of the web so as to obtain words that behave best compared to the EAT, in contrast to other approaches, in which some metric according to their frequency is used for measuring the likelihood of strings as answers.

The answer extraction strategy was assessed with 781 questions regarding locations. The model interprets this kind of question as one of the most complex and ambiguous scenarios for our strategy, because locations have an ambiguous syntactic behaviour in English. The annotator makes usage of a lexical database of locations for ranking answers to location-related questions and annotating pairs {sentence,answer}, the returned rank is only used as a baseline. Overall results suggest that our method is robust and can efficiently find right answers and even uncover more accurate answers in presence of ambiguity. This also manage to even find answers to questions that could not be distinguished in our baseline.

This paper is organized as follows: section 2 describes the strategy for acquiring syntactic behavior patterns for the EAT, section 3 discusses our answer extraction strategy, in section 4 the experiments and main results are highlighted.

2 Automatic Acquisition of Syntactic Categories

The most commonly used document representation is known as the *Vector Space Model*. Here, a document D is represented as a vector in a space in which each dimension is associated with the frequency of one word w_i in the dictionary W.

$$D = (freq(w_1), freq(w_2), \ldots, freq(w_\omega)) \in \Re^\omega$$

In this representation, some grammatical information is lost as the order of words and punctuation is ignored leading to broken phrases. For example,

"*Albert Einstein*" is split into "*Albert*" and "*Einstein*" without representing their syntactic relation. This model also does not take into account the role of words as modifiers in their local context, and/or as suppliers of the predicate or argument of the main proposition being expressed.

The role of a word in a text is given by its *syntactic category* (i.e., *noun*, *verb*, *adjective*). From the statistical viewpoint, *syntactic rules* involve distributional patterns, whereas in linguistics, *distributional analysis* is referred to as the study of syntactic properties that are in essence distributional.

Many efforts have been put in modelling the syntactic behavior of words using unsupervised mechanisms [1,2]. In these two approaches[1,2], each word $w_i \in W$ is represented by two vectors, called *syntactic context vectors*. The dimensions of the first vector $\phi^l(w_i)$ represent how often the other words in W appear immediately to the left of w_i, whereas the second vector $\phi^r(w_i)$ follows a similar strategy for words that appear immediately to the right. To illustrate this, consider the next two sentences: "*Galway is in Ireland*" and "*Dublin is located in Ireland*". The *syntactic context vectors* of these sentences are sketched in matrices of tables 1 and 2.

Table 1. Left Syntactic Context Vectors

	Dublin	Galway	in	Ireland	is	located
Dublin	0	0	0	0	0	0
Galway	0	0	0	0	0	0
in	0	0	0	0	1	1
Ireland	0	0	**2**	0	0	0
is	1	1	0	0	0	0
located	0	0	0	0	1	0

Table 2. Right Syntactic Context Vectors

	Dublin	Galway	in	Ireland	is	located
Dublin	0	0	0	0	1	0
Galway	0	0	0	0	1	0
in	0	0	0	2	0	0
Ireland	0	0	0	0	0	0
is	0	0	1	0	0	1
located	0	0	1	0	0	0

In table 1, we read that "*in*" appears two times to the left of "*Ireland*", and in table 2, "*Ireland*" appears two times to the right of "*in*". The main problem of the *syntactic context vectors* is that the degree of overlap can not be computed in the original vector space due to its sparseness. A simple cosine-based similarity measure may draw misleading classifications, even though the frequency of words is high. For example: "*a*" and "*an*" do not share any neighbors as "*an*" appears whenever the sound of the next word starts with a vowel so consequently, the similarity is zero, although they have the same syntactic category [1].

The first approach is due to Goldsmith and Belkin [2], who constructed a nearest-neighbor graph (i.e., matrix) in which vertices represented words and edges were pairs of words whose distribution in the corpus was similar. For this graph, they used the top 500 and 1000 frequent words. For each pair of words, the cosine of the angle of its *syntax context vector* was computed, and the 5, 10, 20 and 50 closest neighbors were selected. From the constructed matrix, a canonical representation C is built, in which a value of zero was assigned to every element in the diagonal and wherever was a zero was in the original matrix, a value of one was assigned whenever a value was greater than zero in the original matrix. A diagonal matrix E is defined to contain the degree values for each vertex. Then, the normalized *laplacian* of $E - C$ is computed to contain non-negative eigenvalues. The first and the second eigenvectors -corresponding to the lowest eigenvalues- derived from each *syntax context vector* were used to build a graphic representation of the syntactic behavior of the words in the corpus. These vectors have a coordinate for each of the K most frequent words in the corpus. Using these lowest-valued eigenvectors was suggested to provide a good graphical representation of words, in the sense that words with similar left-hand neighbors will be close together in the graph.

Even though this strategy does not lead to a sharp distinction of syntactic categories, it can distinguish syntactically heterogeneous set of words [2]. The strategy was evaluated for two languages French and English. For English, the syntax category of many constituents (i.e., *non-infinitive verbs*, *infinite verbs*, *nouns*, *etc*) were correctly inferred. For French, other categories such as *female nouns*, *plural nouns*, *finite verbs*, *etc.* were clustered.

A similar model for the acquisition of syntactic categories from raw text in presence of ambiguity is also introduced by [1]. In this model (TAG SPACE), two matrices are built from the *syntactic context vectors* of the 250 most frequent words. The *Singular Value Decomposition* (SVD) was used for reducing the dimension of both matrices and so dealing with data sparseness. The dimension of the matrices in the reduced space was 50 and a *group average agglomeration algorithm* was applied for clustering.

In both approaches, *syntactic context vectors* are represented in a specially designed space, in which different syntactical categories show distinctions. Consequently, *syntactic context vectors* of words were found to contain information about their syntactic behavior.

3 The Answer Extractor System

Once a Natural-Language query triggers our QA system (`QA-SYSTEM`), this is sent out to Google so to retrieve a small number of snippets (i.e., usually 30), which are then normalized and cleaned up of math symbols and html tags. Next, the system performs the query analysis in order to determine the EAT by a simple

Wh-keyword matching. If the EAT is a location, it triggers our answer extraction module based on the acquisition of distributional syntactic patterns (`SCV-AE`).

3.1 Answer Extraction by Acquiring Syntactic Patterns

First, the answer extractor (`SCV-AE`) extracts `WEB ENTITIES` from the retrieved snippets. A `WEB ENTITY` is a stream of words in which every word of the sequence starts with a capital letter, for instance: "*Robbie Williams*", "*London*", etc. Then, the negative evidence is used for filtering the `WEB ENTITIES` according to a list of banned `WEB ENTITIES`, we see as banned words, query terms and words that usually start with a capital letter on web snippets (i.e., page, home, link, etc). This rule for distinguishing `WEB ENTITIES` is considered as part of the innate knowledge.

From here, the set of sentences (determined by punctuation signs) and `WEB ENTITIES` are passed on to our **Automatic Annotator** (AA) which returns at most three ranked answers and the sentences where they occur. The annotated sentences are used by `SCV-AE` for updating the *syntactic context vectors*, and for computing the value of the likelihood L for every `WEB ENTITY`. The learning strategy is seen as the synergy between the annotator and the answer extractor. The rank of answers returned by `AA` is only used as a baseline.

`AA` is based on a strategy for extracting answers to questions which aim at a location as answer. This measures the similarity between the query and each sentence by aligning characters of the query in each sentence. In addition, `AA` validates each `WEB ENTITY` using a lexical database of locations (WordNet). This strategy can identify answers if and only if they are on the lexical database.

Let Q be the set of all questions that triggered the `QA-SYSTEM` which aimed to the same EAT. A is the set of answers to the questions in Q. Each component ϕ_i of the *syntactic context vectors* of the EAT of Q is given by:

$$\phi_i^l(EAT) = sum_{\forall A_j \in A} freq(w_i, A_j)$$

$$\phi_i^r(EAT) = sum_{\forall A_j \in A} freq(A_j, w_i)$$

Where $freq(w_i, A_j)$ is the frequency in which w_i occurs immediately to the left of A_j, the sum over all $A_j \in A$ gives the frequency of w_i to the left of the EAT, and $freq(A_j, w_i)$ is the homologous to the right. Next, $\phi^l(EAT)$ and $\phi^r(EAT)$ provide the information of the role of the EAT in the local context. For the simplicity's sake, ϕ^l and ϕ^r refer to *syntactic context vectors* $\phi^l(EAT)$ and $\phi^r(EAT)$ respectively. If we consider our illustrative example, $\phi^l(LOCATION)$ and $\phi^r(LOCATION)$ are shown in table 3.

Note that ϕ^r represents the null vector as there is no word occuring to the right of the EAT LOCATION. Then, the **Syntactic Likelihood of an answer** A' is computed as follows:

$$L(A') = \phi^l \phi^l(A') + \phi^r \phi^r(A') \tag{1}$$

Table 3. Syntactic Context Vectors for EAT LOCATION

	Dublin	Galway	in	Ireland	is	located
ϕ^l	0	0	**2**	0	0	0
ϕ^r	0	0	0	0	0	0

Where $\phi^l \phi^l(A^{'})$ is the sum of the product of each component of the *left syntactic context vector* of the EAT, whereas the *left syntactic context vector* of the answer $A^{'}$, $\phi^r \phi^r(A^{'})$ is the homologous to the right. Every answer is measured according to the amount of its context words in the snippets that match the context words of the EAT and the strength of this matching is according to their frequencies. At this point, the redundancy of the web is taken into account. The context words are assumed to occur more often in the context of the EAT have a stronger relationship with the EAT, and therefore, are stronger indicators for scoring a new answer. Consider a document consisting of the following sentence: "*Saar is in Saarbrücken.*". Tables 4 and 5 illustrate the obtained *syntactic context vectors.*

Table 4. Left Syntactic Context Vectors of the Document

	Saar	in	is	Saarbrücken
Saar	0	0	0	0
in	1	0	0	0
is	0	1	0	0
Saarbrücken	0	0	1	0

Table 5. Right Ssyntactic Context Vectors of the Document

	Saar	in	is	Saarbrücken
Saar	0	0	0	0
in	1	0	0	0
is	0	1	0	0
Saarbrücken	0	0	1	0

Computation of the likelihood of each word to the EAT can be seen in table 6. Note that the only word that contributes to the likelihood is "*in*"-when it is to the left to EAT-, then the only match occurs with the occurrence of "*in*" to the left of "*Saarbrücken*". As a result, this is the only word with likelihood greater than zero.

Experiments suggest that this likelihood is strongly affected by the data sparseness. However, the aim of the approach is not to cluster words to uncover their syntactic categories. The model assumes that every $A_j \in A$ has the same syntactic behavior in the local context of the answer. Thus the main interest is in the likelihood of $A^{'}$.

Table 6. Syntactic Context Vectors for EAT LOCATION

	Saar	in	is	Saarbrücken
$\phi^l\phi^l(A')$	0	0	0	2
$\phi^r\phi^r(A')$	0	0	0	0
Total	0	0	0	**2**

4 Experiments and Results

`SCV-AE` was assessed with three kinds of questions: miscellaneous where-typed questions from the CLEF and TREC corpus, an example question is as follows:

Where did the 1992 Olympic Games take place?

Next, a set of questions concerning capitals and cities around the world were tested. These have the following template:

where is < city >?

Where < *city* > is replaced with other cities (i.e., *Berlin*). We consider as a correct answer the name of the country, for example, *Germany*.

For the third kind of questions, a list of monuments around the world was tested with a template similar to that of the cities:

where is Fontana della Barcaccia?

We accepted either a city or a country as a correct answer (i.e., Rome or Italy). An **alternative answer** is another city or country that has also a monument or a city with the same name as the requested place. For example, for "*where is Santo Domingo?*", the system answered "*Venezuela*" instead of "*Dominican Republic*" (there is a place named "*Santo domingo*" in Venezuela). We considered three set of questions, due to the fact that the CLEF/TREC questions are oriented to their respectively corpus, that is, the provided answer patterns correspond their corpus. Our system answers questions using the web as a target. Accordingly, it is unknown in advance whether one of occurrences of the answer will match the provided answer patterns[7]. Considering that there is no much variations on names of countries and cities, the `SCV-AE` was assessed with an additional set of questions.

Table 7 and 8 show the results for a set of 781 questions. The MRR (*Mean Reciprocal Rank*) values are 0.833 and 0.830 for `AA` and `SCV-AE` respectively considering all the correct answers. Our strategy can also be compared with the approach by [9] which scored MRR values below 0.55 for a given set of locations. Note that this system also uses WordNet and other linguistic resources such as gazetteers. The performance of both the annotator and `SCV-AE` is worst for the CLEF/TREC dataset. Here, `SCV-AE` could not answer 60 (out of 229) questions (20.20%), whereas `AA` did it with 58 out of 229 (25.33%). If we consider the set of monuments/capitals, `AA` could not find an answer for 40 out of 552 (7.25%) questions, `SCV-AE` (6.16%). Our `SCV-AE` could not answer either because

Table 7. AA Results for Location Questions (Baseline)

Settings				Exact Answers			Alt. Answers		
Set	Total	MRR	No Answer	1st	2nd	3rd	1st	2nd	3rd
Capitals	186	0.88	14	155	11	2	4	-	-
World Heritage Monuments	209	0.91	7	177	14	5	6	-	-
Biggest monuments	51	0.84	6	40	3	-	1	1	-
Greece	58	0.78	10	43	5	-	-	-	-
Stotland/Ireland/Wales	58	0.94	3	54	-	-	-	1	-
TREC-2002	39	0.64	13	21	2	-	3	-	-
TREC-2001	27	0.73	6	18	-	2	1	-	-
TREC-2000	70	0.66	20	41	6	1	2	-	-
TREC-1999	22	0.57	9	12	1	-	-	-	-
CLEF-2004	61	0.78	12	42	3	-	4	-	-
Total	781	0.833	100	603	45	10	21	2	-
%	-	-	12.8	77.21	5.76	1.28	2.69	0.26	-

the answer was a term on the query (10 questions) or because there was no answer at all. Note that the difference can also be due to some questions `SCV-AE` was able to answer but `AA` did not annotate, which may be due to certain dependency on the lexical database. There are a few cases where `AA` was able to annotate pairs {answer,sentence} with the right answer, whereas `SCV-AE` did not find enough evidence to identify the answer as a location (i.e., answering the query "*Where is Sanna?*"). On the other hand, `SCV-AE` was capable of providing answers even when it was not possible to find them on the lexical database (i.e., capitals of Kyrgyzstan (Bishkek) and East Timor (Dili)). In addition, `SVC-AE` succeeds to identify answers when they were spelt in their original language and surrounded by text in English. However, this could not detect answers while they were surrounded by text written in another language.

Note that there are some questions in this dataset that the strategy could not identify as locations (i.e., *Where did 'N Sync get their name?* - the initial letter of their member names) and so the strategy was unable to answer. On the other hand, the `SCV-AE` module assisted us to identify answers to questions such as *Where is bile produced?* (liver), *Where is the Sea of Tranquility?* (moon), *Where is the volcano Olympus Mons located?*(mars), *Where does chocolate come from?* (Cacao). `SCV-AE` was able to determine more precise locations (i.e., *where is Gateway Arch?* Jefferson National Expansion Memorial).

Some examples of questions that could not be answered or annotated: *Where did Bill Gates go to college?*, *Where did bocci originate?*, *Where do lobsters like to live?*. In most cases, the right answer was ranked at the first position in almost 80% of the questions and at the second place at about 7% of the times. It is also important to highlight that the influence of the answers passed on from the `AA` module to the `SCV-AE` module biased the answers obtained by the `SCV-AE` module in the first answered questions.

Table 8. SCV-AE Results for Location Questions

Settings				Exact Answers			Alt. Answers		
Set	Total	MRR	No Answer	1st	2nd	3rd	1st	2nd	3rd
Capitals	186	0.88	11	154	11	6	4	-	-
World Heritage Monuments	209	0.91	4	154	20	3	25	2	1
Biggest monuments	51	0.84	7	37	-	1	6	-	-
Greece	58	0.82	8	39	5	-	6	-	-
Stotland/Ireland/Wales	58	0.92	4	53	1	-	-	-	-
TREC-2002	39	0.67	11	24	1	1	1	1	-
TREC-2001	27	0.75	6	18	-	1	2	-	-
TREC-2000	70	0.65	20	41	4	3	2	-	-
TREC-1999	22	0.59	8	12	2	-	-	-	-
CLEF-2004	61	0.69	13	36	3	5	2	2	-
Total	781	0.830	92	568	47	20	48	5	1
%	-	-	11.78	72.73	6.02	2.56	6.15	0.64	0.13

5 Conclusions

This paper discussed a new data-driven approach which takes advantage of the large volume of documents on the web. Unlike related approaches using general-purpose classifiers or intensive linguistics tasks or knowledge sources (i.e. parses, stemmers, lexical databases, formalisms), our model exploits a purpose-built learning approach based on Pinker's theory of learning distributional syntactic categories. In our approach, distributional patterns are seen as syntactic context vectors, the innate knowledge is represented as previously annotated tuples {*question, sentence, answer*} and negative evidence is interpreted as ambiguous words. In contrast with statistically motivated approaches, our strategy was still capable of distinguishing precise answers strings.

The model takes advantage of the redundancy of the web as a source of multiple paraphrases and answer occurrences. Hence it can learn the syntactic behavior of the EAT from annotated tuples {*question, sentence, answer*}, and compare it with the syntactic behaviour of occurrences of words on snippets. The designed strategy sharply identifies answers on the web due to the localized context of web snippets. Here, occurrences of the answer have a similar syntactical behavior so that they can readily be identified. Accordingly, for some kind of questions, parsing or tagging is not necessary for detecting which words match the syntactic category of the EAT. Moreover, the strategy does not need to match the context of the query for identifying answers and so using query re-writing rules for some kinds of questions is not mandatory.

For the actual experiments, location questions were only considered as they involve fewer candidate answers. Thus, the assessment becomes less ambiguous and allows ambiguous syntactical patterns to easily be identified by our learning mechanism. Note that dates and locations as well as some prepositional phrases syntactically behave similarly in English. Assessing the strategy by using different kinds of questions (i.e., persons, organizations) is also being planned in a future research.

References

1. Schütze, H. *Ambiguity Resolution in Language Learning*, Computational and Cognitive Models. CSLI Lecture Notes, number 71, 1997.
2. Belkin, M., Goldsmith, J. *Using eigenvectors of the bi-gram graph to infer grammatical features and categories*, Proceedings of the Morphology/Phonology Learning Workshop of ACL-02, 2002.
3. Pinker, S. *Language Learnability and Language Development*, Cambridge MA: Hardvard University Press, 1984.
4. Rijke, M., Monz, C. *Tequesta: The University of Amsterdam's Textual Question Answering System*, NIST Special Publication SP, 2002.
5. Lita, L., V., Carbonell, J. *Instance-based question answering: a data driven approach*, Proceedings of EMNLP, 2004.
6. Dumais, S., Banko, M., Brill, E., Lin, J., Ng, A. *Web question answering: is more always better?*, Proceedings of SIGIR-2002, 2002.
7. Dumais, S., Banko, M., Brill, E., Lin, J., Ng, A. *Data-Intensive question answering*, In proceedings of the tenth Text REtrieval Conference (TREC 2001), November 2001, Gaithersburg, Maryland.
8. De Chalendar, G., Dalmas, T., Elkateb-Gara, F., Ferret, O., Grau, B., Hurault-Planet, M., Illouz, G., Monceaux, L., Robba I., Vilnat A. *The question answering system QALC at LIMSI: experiments in using Web and WordNet*, NIST Special Publication SP, 2003.
9. Monz, C. *From Document Retrieval to Question Answering*, IILC Dissertation Series DS-2003-4, *Institute for Logic, Language and Computation*, University of Amsterdam, 2003.
10. Echihabi, A., Hermjakob, U., Hovy, E., Marcu, D., Melz, E., Ravichadran, D. *How to select an answer String?*, Advances in Textual Question Answering, Kluwer, 2004
11. Moldovan, D., Harabagui, S., Clark, C., Bowden, M., Lehmann, J., Williams, J. *Experiments and Analysis of LCC's two QA Systems over TREC 2004*, TREC 2004, 2004.

Applying NLP Techniques and Biomedical Resources to Medical Questions in QA Performance

Rafael M. Terol, Patricio Martinez-Barco, and Manuel Palomar

Departamento de Lenguajes y Sistemas Informáticos
Universidad de Alicante
Carretera de San Vicente del Raspeig - Alicante - Spain
Tel.: +34965903772; Fax.:+34965909326
{rafamt, patricio, mpalomar}@dlsi.ua.es

Abstract. Nowadays, there is an increasing interest in research on QA over restricted domains. Concretely, in this paper we will show the process of question analysis in a medical QA system. This system is able to obtain answers to different natural language questions according to a question taxonomy. In this system we combine the use of NLP techniques and biomedical resources. The main NLP technique is the use of logic forms and the pattern matching technique in this question analysis performance.

1 Introduction

Open-domain textual Question-Answering (QA), as defined by the TREC competitions [1], is the task of extracting the right answer from text snippets identified in large collections of documents where the answer to a natural language question lies.

Open-domain textual QA systems are defined as capable tools to extract concrete answers to very precise needs of information in document collections. The main components of a QA system could be summarized in the following steps: Question Analysis, Document Retrieval, Relevant Passages Selection and Answer Extraction. These components are related to each other and process the textual information available on different levels until the QA process has been completed.

The natural language questions formulated to the system are processed initially by the question analysis component. This process is very important since the quantity and quality of the information extracted in this analysis will condition the performance of the remaining components and therefore, the final result of the system.

Examples of these kinds of QA systems in open domains can be located in authors such as Moldovan [11], Sasaki [17] and Zukerman [18].

[1] The Text REtrieval Conference(TREC) is a series of workshops organized by the National Institute of Standards and Technology (NIST), designed to advance the background in Information Retrieval (IR) and QA.

A. Gelbukh and C.A. Reyes-Garcia (Eds.): MICAI 2006, LNAI 4293, pp. 996–1006, 2006.

Our research experience in QA and Information Retrieval (IR) research areas motivated our development of these kinds of systems (excluded auto-references) and their evaluation in international evaluation forums such as Text REtrieval Conference (TREC) [15] [16] and Cross Language Evaluation Forum (CLEF) [2] [3]. These tracks evaluate the systems in open domains. For instance, in open domains, a system can respond to society questions such as *where was Marilyn Monroe born?*, *what is the name of Elizabeth Taylor's fourth husband?*; geography questions such as *where is Halifax located?* and so on.

Nowadays, textual QA is also exhibited in specific domains such as clinical [5], tourism [1], medical [14] and so on.

According to official results of the QA track at the last TREC conference, QA systems in open domains are between 30% and 40% of precision. In a restricted domain such as medical domain, it is necessary to highly improve this score due to the critical information that is handled in these medical areas where erroneous information can originate serious risks to people's health (no answer is better that incorrect answers).

Moreover, the use of these open-domain textual QA systems in concrete domains such as medical domain do not produce good results because these systems use natural language processing generic resources such as WordNet [9] which is not specialized in medical terms. For instance, in Niu et al. previous work [13] showed that current technologies for factoid QA in open domains were not adequate for clinical questions, whose answers must often be obtained by synthesizing relevant context. To adapt to this new characteristic of QA in the medical domain, they exploited semantic classes and relations between them in medical text. This is the reason why our research effort is directed towards the textual QA on medical domain. This paper focuses on describing the design features of the module that classify and analyze the natural language questions in our textual QA system on medical domain (excluded auto-reference). The following sections show in detail the design features of this module.

2 Motivation

There exist several agents that can interact in the clinical domains such as doctors, patients, laboratories and so on. All of them need quick and easy ways to access electronic information. Access to the latest medical information helps doctors to select better diagnoses, helps patients to know about their conditions, and allows to establish the most effective treatment. These facts produce a lot of information and different types of information between these agents that must be electronically processed. For example, people want to obtain competent medical answers to medical questions: when they have some unknown symptoms and want to know what they could be related to, or when they want to know another medical opinion about the best way to treat their disease, or when they can ask experienced doctors any medical questions related to any unknown symptoms or their state. All these features conclude that the number and the type of medical questions that a medical QA system can respond to is very great.

These facts motivated us to design and develop our own QA system in the medical domain. This QA system is capable of answering medical questions according to a medical question taxonomy. This question taxonomy is based on the study developed by Ely *et al* [6] whose main objective is to develop a taxonomy of doctor's questions about patient care that could be used to help answer such questions. In this study, the participants were 103 Iowa family doctors and 49 Oregon primary care doctors. The authors concluded that clinical questions in primary care can be categorized into a limited number of generic types. A moderate degree of interrater reliability was achieved with the the taxonomy developed in this study. The taxonomy may enhance the understanding of doctors' information needs and improve the ability to meet those needs. According to this question taxonomy, the ten most frequent questions formulated by doctors are ranked in the following enumeration:

1. What is the drug of choice for condition x?
2. What is the cause of symptom x?
3. What test is indicated in situation x?
4. What is the dose of drug x?
5. How should I treat condition x (not limited to drug treatment)?
6. How should I manage condition x (not specifying diagnostic or therapeutic)?
7. What is the cause of physical finding x?
8. What is the cause of test finding x?
9. Can drug x cause (adverse) finding y?
10. Could this patient have condition x?

Thus, our medical QA system is capable of answering natural language questions according to this set of ten generic medical questions, discarding other questions (medical and from other domains). The fact that our QA system is only able to answer questions in this question taxonomy produces on one hand a lower recall but on the other hand a higher precision with the aim that our system will be very useful in the medical domain according to this question taxonomy. The next section shows in detail the module of our medical QA system that builds the patterns of the questions treated by the system according to the question taxonomy presented.

3 Question Taxonomy Processing

This section details how our medical QA system builds a generic pattern for each one of the ten generic questions treated by our medical QA system. Two approaches are managed by the system in this pattern building off-line task: manual pattern generation and supervised automatic pattern generation. These two approaches are described in the following subsections but previously the next subsection shows the presents all the NLP resources (in open domains and in medical domains) used in this computational process.

3.1 NLP Resources

To accomplish their goals, the following NLP resources are used: Logic Forms, Medical Named Entities Recognition and Semantic Knowledge. We show how the system uses these three NLP resources as follows:

Logic Forms. The logic form of a sentence is calculated through an analysis of dependency relationships between the words of the sentence. Our approach employs a set of rules that infer several aspects such as the assert, the type of assert, the identifier of the assert and the relationships between the different asserts in the logic form. Our NLP technique used to infer the logic is different to other techniques that accomplish the same goal such as Moldovan's [10] that takes as input the parse-tree of a sentence, or Mollá's [12] that introduces the flat form as an intermediate step between the sentence and the logic form. Our logic form, similar to Moldovan's logic form, is based on the format of logic form defined by eXtended WordNet [7]. For example, the logic form "*nerve:NN(x3) NNC(x4, x3, x5) cell:NN(x5) consist_of:VB(e1, x4, x10) large:JJ(x1) cell:NN(x2) NNC(x1, x2, x9) body:NN(x9) and:CC(x10, x1, x7) nerve:NN(x6) NNC(x7, x6, x8) fiber:NN(x8)*" is automatically inferred from the analysis of dependency relationships between the words of the sentence "*Nerve cells consist of a large cell body and nerve fibers*". In this format of logic form each assert has at least one argument. The first argument is usually instantiated with the identifier of the assert and the rest of the arguments are identifiers of other asserts related to this assert. For instance, in the assert "*nerve:NN(x3)*", its type is noun *(NN)* and its identifier is instantiated to *x3*; in the assert "*NNC(x4, x3, x5)*", its type is complex nominal *(NNC)*, its identifier is instantiated to *x4*, and the other two arguments indicate the relationships to other asserts: *x5* and *x3*.
Medical Named Entities Recognition. This NLP resource is used to identify the different entities in the medical domain. Moreover, this resource must be able to classify them into: name of drugs, name of symptoms, name of diseases, name of dysfunction and so on. This resource is based on the knowledge base Unified Medical Language System (UMLS) [8], concretely the UMLS Metathesaurus knowledge source.
Semantic Knowledge. In order to extract semantic knowledge two different resources are used. On the one hand, WordNet [9] to extract semantic relationships between general-purpose terms. On the other hand, UMLS Metathesaurus to obtain medical semantic relationships between medical terms.

Once these three NLP resources have been presented the following subsections show how the system applies them in its two approaches of the pattern building task. This off-line task consists of the definition of the patterns that identify each generic question. These patterns are composed by a combination of types of medical entities and verbs. These patterns can be generated according to two different ways: the first one consists of the easy process of definition of patterns by an advanced user of the system, and the second one consists of the automatic generation of the patterns through the processing of questions according to the question taxonomy. We are going to describe these two different ways of generating patterns.

3.2 Manual Pattern Generation

The manual definition of these patterns can be performed easily as follows:

- Identification of types of medical entities that must match in the generic question.
- Identification of verbs that must match in the generic question.
- Automatic expansion of these verbs according to their similarity relationships with other ones in the WordNet lexical database.
- Setting the medical entities lower threshold (MELT) of each pattern. MELT can be defined as the minimum number of medical entities that must match between the pattern and the question formulated by the user.
- Setting the medical entities upper threshold (MEUT) of each pattern. MEUT can be defined as the maximum number of medical entities that can match between the pattern and the question formulated by the user.
- Setting the possible expected answer types.

As an example of this manual pattern generation for the first generic question "What is the drug of choice for condition x?", Table 1 shows the medical entities associated to this generic question and Table 2 shows the combination of these entities by way of patterns.

Table 1. Medical Entities associated to the first generic question

Word	Medical Entities
drug	Pharmacologic Substance Clinical Drug
x	Disease or Syndrome Quantitative concept Sign or Symptom

Table 2. Patterns associated to the first generic question

Pattern Id.	Pattern	MELT	MEUT
P_{11}	Pharmacologic Substance + Disease or Syndrome	2	3
P_{12}	Pharmacologic Substance + Quantitative concept	2	3
P_{13}	Pharmacologic Substance + Sign or Symptom	2	3
P_{14}	Clinical Drug + Disease or Syndrome	2	3
P_{15}	Clinical Drug + Quantitative concept	2	3
P_{16}	Clinical Drug + Sign or Symptom	2	3

Continuing with this example, the main verb of a question formulated by the user according to this first generic question must correspond to one of the following verbs in the list (*treat, control, take, associate with, help, prevent, manage, indicate, relieve, evaluate, help, fight and solve*). This list of verbs is automatically completed with the verbs in the WordNet lexical database that have similarity relations to the first ones. Finally the expected answer types of this generic question are manually corresponded to the "Pharmacologic Substance" and "Clinical Drug" UMLS semantic types.

3.3 Supervised Automatic Pattern Generation

The automatic generation of these patterns by the system is performed through the processing of questions matched to the question taxonomy according to the following steps:

- Derivation of the logic form associated to each question.
- Medical Named Entities Recognition in the logic form of those asserts whose type is noun (NN) or complex nominal (NNC) including their possible adjective modifiers (JJ).
- Recognition of the main verb in the logic form.
- Automatic expansion of this main verb in the logic form through the similarity relations with other verbs in the WordNet lexical database.
- Automatic setting of the MELT whose score is set to the number of medical entities in the logic form minus one.
- Automatic setting of the MEUT of which the score is set to the number of medical entities in the logic form.
- Manual setting of the possible expected answer types.

This process is supervised by an advanced user of the system that can modify the results obtained by the system in each step.

Table 3 shows an example of this supervised automatic pattern generation for the first generic question "What is the drug of choice for condition x?".

Table 3. Supervised Automatic Generation of a pattern associated to the first generic question

Question:	What drugs are administered for the treatment of hypertension?
LF:	drug:NN(x2) administer:VB(e1, x4, x2) for:IN(e1, x3) treatment:NN(x3) of:IN(x3, x1) hypertension:NN(x1)
ME of drug:	Pharmacologic Substance (PS)
ME of treatment:	Funcional Concept (FC)
ME of hypertension:	Disease or Syndrome (DS)
Automatic Pattern:	PS + FC + DS. MELT=2 and MEUT=3
Supervised Pattern:	PS + DS. MELT=2 and MEUT=2

Continuing with this example, the main verb of the question (administer) is automatically extended with the verbs in the WordNet lexical database that have similarity relations to it. Also, the expected answer types are manually set to at least one of the UMLS semantic types.

Once the patterns of the questions treated by the system according to the question taxonomy have been built, the next section shows in detail the module of our medical QA system that classifies and analyzes the natural language questions that users can ask to the system.

4 Classification and Analysis of Questions

This section presents the design features of the module from our medical QA system that classifies and analyzes the natural language questions that users can ask. This computational process is based on two different tasks:

- **Question Classification:** assigning one of the generic patterns to each one of the questions that the user asks our system.
- **Question Analysis** performing a complex process on the question according to the matched generic question and its respective matched pattern.

The next subsections describe the two different tasks in detail.

4.1 Question Classification

This Question Classification task starts after the user enters the question into the system. In the QA system, ten classes of questions are managed according to the ten generic questions treated by the system. Then, this task has to decide if the question formulated to the system belongs to one class (matches with one of the generic questions) or not. To accomplish this goal, this task focuses on the treatment of patterns derived from the questions asked by users to the QA system and it performs according to the following steps:

- Entering the question to the system.
- Inferring the logic form of the question.
- Extraction of the main verb in the logic form.
- Recognition of the medical entities of those asserts whose type is noun (NN) or complex nominal (NNC) including their possible adjective modifiers (JJ).
- Construction of the question pattern and setting the medical entities score in question (MESQ). MESQ can be defined as the number of medical entities in the logic form of the question.
- Getting those patterns of questions of which the list of verbs contains the main verb of the logic form and $MELT \leq MESQ \leq MEUT$.
- Setting the entities matching measure (EMM) which is defined as the number of medical entities that match between the question and the pattern.
- Selection of the pattern whose difference between EMM and MELT is the lowest one.

Table 4 shows an example of this question classification task using the following question “What drug treats temperature?” formulated to our QA system.

Table 4. Example of the Question Classification Task

Question:	What drug manages temperature?
LF:	drug:NN(x2) manage:VB(e1, x2, x1) temperature:NN(x1)
Main verb:	manage
ME of drug:	Pharmacologic Substance
ME of temperature:	Quantitative Concept
Q Pattern:	Pharmacologic Substance + Quantitative Concept. MESQ=2
Comparable Patterns:	P_{11}, P_{12}, P_{13}, P_{14}, P_{15} and P_{16}
EMM:	$P^Q_{11}=1$, $P^Q_{12}=2$, $P^Q_{13}=1$, $P^Q_{14}=0$, $P^Q_{15}=1$ and $P^Q_{16}=0$
Selected Pattern:	P_{12}
Matched Question Class:	*GE*1 (first generic question)

4.2 Question Analysis

Once the question is matched to a generic pattern from one of the ten generic questions treated by the system, this Question Analysis task firstly captures the semantics of the Natural Language question asked to the system. As mentioned before, WordNet and UMLS Metathesaurus are used in this performance. The following step consists of the recognition of the expected answer type. These medical answer types can be diseases, symptoms, dose of drugs, and so on, according to the possible answers to the ten generic questions treated by the system. After that, the keywords are identified. These question keywords are directly recognized by applying a set of heuristics to the asserts and the relationships between asserts in the logic form. Like question keywords our QA system identifies complex nominals and nouns recognized as medical expressions (using Medical Named Entities Recognition) including their possible adjective modifiers, the rest of the complex nominals and nouns including their possible adjective modifiers and the main verb in the logic form. For instance, in the part of the logic form "... high:JJ(x3) blood:NN(x1) NNC(x3, x1, x2) pressure:NN(x2) ...", the assert *x3* is recognized as a *Disease or Syndrome* and then "high blood pressure" is treated as a keyword. These question keywords can be expanded by applying a set of heuristics. As example, medical expressions can be expanded using similarity relations given by ULMS Metathesaurus. Thus, according to UMLS Metathesaurus, "high blood pressure" can be expanded to "hypertension".

This set of question keywords is sorted by priority, so if too many keywords are extracted from the question, only a maximum number of keywords are searched in the information retrieval process.

5 Evaluation

Even though open-domain QA systems can be evaluated according to TREC and CLEF evaluation tracks, when a QA system is directed to any restricted domain do not exist these kinds of evaluation tracks. This is the main motivation why the evaluation of the question classification task is based on the evaluation presented by Chung *et al.* in their previous research work [4]. Thus, to evaluate the goodness of the question classifier task, a set of different questions has been developed. These questions have been designed as follows:

- GQ_1: Five questions that are matched to the first generic question; GQ_2: Five questions that are related to the second generic question;...; GQ_{10}: Five questions that are adjusted to the tenth generic question. Several instructions about the manual construction of these types of questions were given to a group of people that did not work on the design and development phases of the QA system. After that, five questions for each generic pattern were selected.
- OQ: The set of 200 questions of the last QA English Track at CLEF 2005 conference were also included to evaluate the robustness of the system in a noisy environment. Examples of these questions could be the following ones: "What is BMW?", "What is the FARC?", "Who is Silvio Berlusconi?", and so on.

Figure 1 shows how the question classifier task is able to classify each one of the given questions in one of the following classes of questions:

- **GE**: These classes of questions include each one of the ten generic questions. Thus, the GE_1 class is corresponded with the generic question "What is the drug of choice for condition x?"; the GE_2 class is matched with the generic question "What is the cause of symptom x?",..., and the GE_{10} class is arranged with the generic question "Could this patient have condition x?".
- **OE**: This class includes the rest of the questions from other domains.

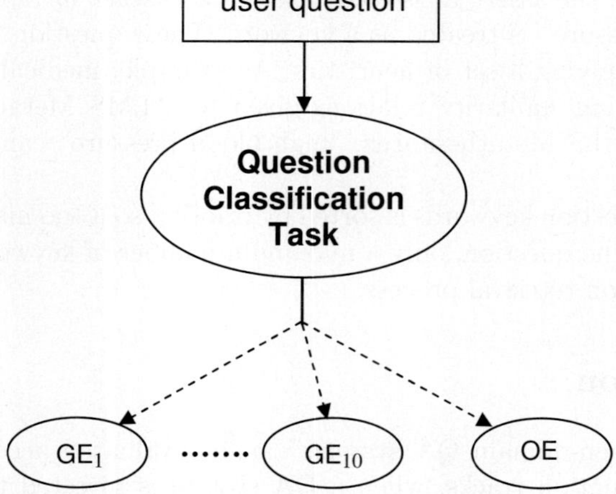

Fig. 1. Question Classification Task

Then the evaluation task consist of checking if each one of the 250 evaluation questions (GQ_1, ..., GQ_{10} and OQ) have been correctly classified in the appropriate class of questions (GE_1, ..., GE_{10} or OE). As an evaluation measure, we apply the precision measure (P) defined as the ratio between the number of correctly classified questions over the number of classified questions. Table 5 shows the results obtained in this question classification task. The Classified Class column expresses the class of questions that we are evaluating. The Related Class column shows the correct related class associated to each classified class. The Questions column present the number of classified questions. The Correct column indicates the number of questions that have been correctly classified according to the related class. The Precision column shows the precision of this classification task that agrees with the presented evaluation measure.

Table 5. Evaluation of the Question Classification Task

Classified Class	Related Class	Questions	Correct	Precision
GQ	GE	50	42	0.84
OQ	OE	200	194	0.97
Overall	-	250	231	0.944

According to the overall row in Table 5, the precision score of the question classifier task is 94,4%. This good score will positively condition the right performance of the following parts of this QA process in the medical domain.

6 Conclusions and Future Works

In this paper, the necessity to improve the precision of QA systems in restricted domains such as the medical domain has been justified. In this medical domain, our research effort has focused on the design and development of a QA system capable of answering a set of questions based on a medical question taxonomy formulated towards studies of doctor's questions about patient care. The method for question processing when doing QA in the medical domain has been presented. It uses the extended WordNet and also the Unified Medical Language System Methatesaurus. This computational process consists of three steps: (1) pattern generation, (2) question classification, and (3) question analysis.

We will aim to develop a global framework for QA systems in any restricted domain.

References

1. Farah Benamara. Cooperative Question Answering in Restricted Domains: the WEBCOOP Experiment. In *ACL 2004 Workshop on Question Answering in Restricted Domains*, Barcelona, Spain, July 2004.
2. *4th Workshop of the Cross-Language Evaluation Forum, CLEF 2003*, Trondheim, August 2003.

3. *5th Workshop of the Cross-Language Evaluation Forum, CLEF 2004*, Bath, UK, 2004.
4. Hoojung Chung, Young-In Song, Kyoung-Soo Han, Do-Sang Yoon, Joo-Young Lee, Hae-Chang Rim and Soo-Hong Kim A Practical QA System in Restricted Domains. In *Proceedings of 42nd Annual Meeting of the Association for Computational Linguistics, Workshop on Question Answering in Restricted Domains*, Barcelona, Spain, July 2004.
5. Dina Demner-Fushman and Jimmy Lin. Knowledge Extraction for Clinical Question Answering: Preliminary Results. In *Proceedings of the AAAI-05 Workshop on Question Answering in Restricted Domains*, Pittsburgh, Pennsylvania, July 2005.
6. John W Ely, Jerome A Osheroff, Paul N Gorman, Mark H Ebell, M Lee Chambliss, Eric A Pifer and P Zoe Stavri. A taxnomy of generic clinical questions: classification study. *BMJ 2000*, 321:429–432, 2000.
7. S. Harabagiu, G.A. Miller, and D.I. Moldovan. WordNet 2 - A Morphologically and Semantically Enhanced Resource. In *Proceedings of ACL-SIGLEX99: Standardizing Lexical Resources*, Maryland, June 1999, pp.1-8.
8. Donald A. B. Lindberg, Betsy L. Humphreys, and Alexa. T. McCray. The Unified Medical Language System. In *Methods of Information in Medicine, 32(4)*, pages 281-291, August 1993.
9. G.A. Miller WordNet: An on-line lexical database. *International Journal of Lexicography 3, 4* (Winter 1990), pp.235-312.
10. Dan Moldovan and Vasile Rus. Logic Form Transformation of WordNet and its Applicability to Question-Answering. In *Proceedings of 39th Annual Meeting of the Association for Computational Linguistics*, Toulouse, France, July 2001.
11. Dan Moldovan, Christine Clark, Sanda Harabagiu, and Steve Maiorano. COGEX: A Logic Prover for Question Answering. In *Proceedings of HLT-NAACL 2003. Human Language Technology Conference*, pages 87–93, Edmonton, Canada, 2003.
12. Diego Mollá, Rolf Schwitter, Michael Hess and Rachel Fournier. ExtrAns, an answer exraction system. *T.A.L. special issue on Information Retrieval oriented Natural Language Processing*, pages 495–522, 2002.
13. Yun Niu, Graeme Hirst, Gregory McArthur and Patricia Rodriguez-Gianolli. Answering clincal questions with role identification. In *Proceedings of 41st annual meeting of the Association for Computational Linguistics, Workshop on Natural Language Processing in Biomedicine*, Sapporo, Japan, July 2003.
14. Yun Niu and Graeme Hirst. Analysis of Semantic Classes in Medical Text for Question Answering. In *Proceedings of 42nd Annual Meeting of the Association for Computational Linguistics, Workshop on Question Answering in Restricted Domains*, Barcelona, Spain, July 2004.
15. *The Ninth Text Retrieval Conference (TREC 9)*, Gaithersburg, Maryland, 2000.
16. *The Eleventh Text Retrieval Conference(TREC 2002)*, Gaithersburg, Maryland, 2002.
17. Yutaka Sasaki. Question Answering as Question-Biased Term Extraction: A New Approach toward Multilingual QA. In *Proceedings of 43th Annual Meeting of the Association for Computational Linguistics*, Michigan, USA, June 2005.
18. Ingrid Zukerman and Bhavani Raskutti. Lexical Query Paraphrasing for Document Retrieval. In Hsin-Hsi Chen and Chin-Yew Lin, editors, *Proceedings of the 19th International Conference on Computational Linguistics, COLING 2002*, Taipei, Taiwan, August 2002.

Fast Text Categorization Based on a Novel Class Space Model

Yingfan Gao[1], Runbo Ma[2], and Yushu Liu[1]

[1] School of Computer Science & Technology, Beijing Institute of Technology, Beijing, P.R. China
gaoyingf@126.com, Liuyushu@bit.edu.cn
[2] College of Physics and Electronics,Shanxi University,Taiyuan, P.R. China
Marunbo_haha@126.com

Abstract. Automatic categorization has been shown to be an accurate alternative to manual categorization in which documents are processed and automatically assigned to pre-defined categories. The accuracy of different methods for categorization has been studied largely, but their efficiency has seldom been mentioned. Aiming to maintain effectiveness while improving efficiency, we proposed a fast algorithm for text categorization and a compressed document vector representation method based on a novel class space model. The experiments proved our methods have better efficiency and tolerable effectiveness.

1 Introduction

Text classification (TC) is a supervised learning task, which is defined as automatically identifying of the topics or class labels (predefined) for new documents based on the likelihood suggested by a training corpus of labeled documents[1]. There are a lot of machine learning approaches and statistics method used in Text Classification, including Support Vector Machines(SVM) introduced by Vapnik[16], Rocchio by Rocchio[2], K-nearest Neighbor Classification (kNN)[3], Linear Least Square Fit(LLSF) developed by Yang[17], decision trees with boosting by Aote[18], Neural network and Naïve Bayes[19] et al.

Most of the above-mentioned approaches adopt the classical Vector Space Model(VSM)[4] in which the content of a document is formalized as a dot of multi-dimension space and all the classes and unclassified documents can be represented by vectors. Naturally, the methods based on the distance between vectors can be used for TC. Rocchio and kNN are typical representative. To measure the similarity of document to each category, the representation of document and category vector is very essential. The above-mentioned VSM is very popular in the representation of document vector. But to the representation of category, no model are widely accepted and used. Rocchio established the central category vector using positive and negative instances in training corpus[2] and its special case called centroid[6] vector algorithm. Huang ran, Guo Songshan[7] proposed using class space model to represent category vector. In this model, the frequency which a term occurs in a category would be the element of the term-category matrix. But no absolute good results show us the

A. Gelbukh and C.A. Reyes-Garcia (Eds.): MICAI 2006, LNAI 4293, pp. 1007 – 1016, 2006.

above-mentioned representation of category to be propagable. We consider it is because the existing representation methods of category vector could not describe the class space wholly. Due to the importance of representation of category, we propose a novel Class Space Model which is based on a powerful database model called Global Extendable Database (GEDB) .

kNN is the simplest strategy that searches the k-nearest training documents to the test document and use the categories assigned to those training documents to decide the category of the test document. kNN is easy to be implemented for it need not the training stage that most other classification methods must have and many experimental researches show that kNN method offers promising performance in text classification. The main drawbacks of kNN method are its space and time requirement which makes this method unsuitable for some applications where classification efficiency is stressed. To keep the advantages of kNN such as no training and easy to implement and overcome its disadvantages such as complexity of space and time, we propose a novel fast algorithm for TC which use GEDB to save and extract information from text corpus before training and testing stages, a novel class space model to represent category vectors, and a compressed document vector representation method to reduce calculation of the similarity between a test document and each category vector .

The accuracy of different methods for categorization has been compared in a great deal of literatures, but few of them did the comparison in term of efficiency. Our aim is to propose techniques to maintain effectiveness while improving efficiency. This paper is organized as follows. Section 2 describes the GEDB, class space model and compressed document vector representation method. Section 3 describes the fast algorithm for TC. Section 4 presents the experiments and the results. Section 5 summarizes the conclusions and future work.

2 Establishment of Class Space Model

2.1 Classical Vector Space Model

In classical Vector Space Model (VSM), Each document is mapped as a dot of the multi-dimension space in VSM. All the classes and unclassified documents can be represented by vectors such as $((T_1,W_1; T_2,W_2;\ldots\ldots;T_m,W_m)$ where T_i is the i-th term, W_i is the corresponding weight used to reflect the term's importance in the document. To calculate term weight, the classical TF.IDF approach consider two factors: 1) TF(term frequency):the frequency of the occurrence of the term in the document; 2)IDF(inverse document frequency): it varies inversely with the number of documents n_k to which T_k is assigned in a collection of N documents.

Though VSM exerts well in information retrieval, we don't think VSM is a good model for TC. Terms in VSM could not reflect enough information for category. So we seek answers to the following questions with empirical evidence: how to get enough term information for category and how to establish a better class space model.

2.2 Global Extendable DataBase

To assure the terms in our model of having enough information for categories, a database should be pre-established which include a great deal information for categorization and is independent of feature space model and categorization algorithm. There are three fundamental characteristics about the database above.

Firstly, it is global. The information included should be all-around and as much as possible. One main part of the database is called *term-class space* which involves information about terms in categories. Fig.1 shows the primary form of it. The other part of the database is called *term-document space* which is informative complement for term-class space. It adds the relationship between term and document such as term frequency,term position in documents of categories to the database and makes it more rounded.

– Number of Categories Number of Keywords
– Name of Class$_1$ Number of documents in Class$_1$
Name of Class$_2$ Number of documents in Class$_2$
… … … …
Name of Class$_n$ Number of documents in Class$_n$

– Keyword$_1$
{term frequency ; document frequency }in Class$_1$
{term frequency ; document frequency }in Class$_2$
… … … …
{term frequency ; document frequency }in Class$_n$

– Keyword$_2$
{term frequency ; document frequency }in Class$_1$
{term frequency ; document frequency }in Class$_2$
… … … …
{term frequency ; document frequency }in Class$_n$
… … … … …
Keyword $_m$
{term frequency ; document frequency }in Class$_1$
{term frequency ; document frequency }in Class$_2$
… … … …
{term frequency ; document frequency }in Class$_n$

Fig. 1. Term-class space with *n* categories and *m* keywords (or terms)

Secondly, it is expandable. The database should be set aside enough space and interface for future work to add more useful information for categorization at any moment,so we call this database Global Expendable database (GEDB).

Thirdly, it is independent. Our purpose is that GSDB can embody the full property of data collections and it is only related to the data sets and independent of categorization algorithm and feature space model. This kind of independency makes expandability above more easy to implement.

2.3 Class Space Model

The powerful GEDB gives us opportunity to establish class space model with some information in it. We would establish class space model according to term-class space of GEDB (see Fig.1), not taking information of term-document space into account for a while.

Training set D with document set $\{d_1,d_2,\ldots\ldots,d_p\}$;

Classified results by experts: $\{Class_1, Class_2,\ldots,Class_n\}$;

All meta-items (viz., full terms in training set): $\{term_1,term_2,\ldots\ldots, term_z\}$.

Def.1: Define f_{ij} as the frequency of the occurrence of $term_i$ in the documents that belongs to $Class_j$.

Def.2: Define df_{ij} as the number of documents to which $term_i$ is assigned in a collection of documents that belongs to $Class_j$.

Def.3: Define cd_j as the number of documents in $Class_j$.
(i=1,2,…,z; j=1,2,…,n)

1. Establish a matrix A with $Class_j$ as columns, $term_i$ as rows, and df_{ij} as the elements.

$$A=\begin{vmatrix} df_{11} & df_{12} & \cdots & df_{1n} \\ df_{21} & df_{22} & \cdots & df_{2n} \\ \cdots & \cdots & \cdots & \cdots \\ df_{z1} & df_{z2} & \cdots & df_{zn} \end{vmatrix} \quad (i=1,2,\ldots,z;\ j=1,2,\ldots,n) \tag{1}$$

2. Establish a matrix B with $Class_j$ as columns, $term_i$ as rows, and f_{ij} as the elements.

$$B=\begin{vmatrix} f_{11} & f_{12} & \cdots & f_{1n} \\ f_{21} & f_{22} & \cdots & f_{2n} \\ \cdots & \cdots & \cdots & \cdots \\ f_{z1} & f_{z2} & \cdots & f_{zn} \end{vmatrix} \quad (i=1,2,\ldots,z;\ j=1,2,\ldots,n) \tag{2}$$

3. According to GSDB, we can establish a vector $CD=\{cd_1, cd_2,\ldots\ \ldots, cd_n\}$, which cd_j as the elements.
4. Combining matrix A, B and vector CD, we could establish a new matrix CT with $Class_j$ as columns, $term_i$ as rows, and W_{ij} as the elements. The process of building CT is very flexible. We could select the useful factors for categorization from GSDB and establish different matrix CT.

$$CT=\begin{vmatrix} w_{11} & w_{12} & \cdots & w_{1n} \\ w_{21} & w_{22} & \cdots & w_{2n} \\ \cdots & \cdots & \cdots & \cdots \\ w_{z1} & w_{z2} & \cdots & w_{zn} \end{vmatrix} \quad (i=1,2,\ldots,z;\ j=1,2,\ldots,n) \tag{3}$$

In our experiments, we choose two different methods to establish CT.

$$1.\ w_{ij}=\frac{f_{ij}\times df_{ij}}{cd_j^2} \qquad 2.\ w_{ij}=\frac{df_{ij}}{cd_j} \tag{4}$$

Matrix CT is the class space model we want. The columns of CT represent categories and the rows of CT represent term items. W_{ij} means the weight of $term_i$ in $Class_j$ (i=1,2,…,z; j =1,2,…,n) and is used to measure the discrimination ability of terms between categories.

2.4 Document Vector Representation

Generally, the unclassified document vector is a super sparse vector including all terms in class space. The traditional vector representation such as VSM would have to spend a lot of expenses dealing with the sparse problem of vectors. We propose using the {term, weight} pairs to represent the unclassified document instead of using classical VSM, where terms are those who appear in the unclassified document and the weight of the terms has been described in section 2.3. For example, the weight of $term_i$ in $Class_x$ is calculated using the formula $w_{ix} = \frac{f_{ix} \times df_{ix}}{cd_x^2}$ (see Eq.4(1)). According to the definition of f_{ix} , df_{ix}, and cd_x, df_{ix} is equal to 1 and cd_x is equal to 1 too, so W_{ix} is equal to f_{ix}. If using the formula $w_{ix} = \frac{df_{ix}}{cd_x}$ (see Eq.4(2)), df_{ix} is equal to 1 and cd_x is equal to 1,so W_{ix} is equal to 1.

In this method, we use the {term, weight} pairs to represent the unclassified document where only terms appearing in unclassified documents are concerned, not including all features in class model. That makes feature space seem to be compressed, so the method is also called compressed document vector representation.

3 Fast Algorithm for Text Categorization

It's hard to turn a whole world, but it's easy to turn myself. Search the most suitable and similar peer with the individual's characteristics instead of making the whole groups do the same things, then the complex behavior caused by the latter is avoided. What's the groups should do is describing themselves fully and clearly so as to make the light individual easily decide which group is the most suitable for it. The groups' description has a space complexity of O(N) where N is the number of the characteristics of the group. Moving group may bring the complexity of $O(N^2)$. But when we make the individual do the same thing, the price would be O(lgN).

Take the idea to TC. When a new document comes, it would be active to choose an existing text category, not be passive to be classified. Category sets $\{Class_j\}$(j=1,2,…,n) are equivalent to the groups above and each unclassified document is equivalent to the individual above. We have established class space model to describe category sets in section 2.3 and represented the unclassified document using compressed document vector representation method in section 2.4. Our algorithm for TC is based on distance between vectors. One of approaches is to calculate the cosine similarity[5] between the unclassified document vector and each category vector.

The algorithm includes searching $\{term_i\}$ in GEDB and limited times calculation of $\sum_i w_{ix} \cdot w_{ij}$. It's very simple to search $term_i$ in a z dimensionality space of full terms where z is the number of keywords(terms) in GEDB. The worst situation of searching times is equal to $\log_2 z$. If terms are organized by Hash table, the search speed would be improved greatly. The algorithm is as follows:

Input : Unclassified document $Class_x$; Class space model CT.
Output: Classified $Class_x$

1. $Class_x$ could be represented as compressed document vector, viz.,{$term_i$, $weight_i$} pairs. Calculating W_{ix} has been described in Section 2.4 where $term_i$ is the i-th term among terms which appears in unclassified document $Class_x$
2. Search $term_i$ in the GEDB. Find out all W_{ij} which is located at the intersection of the row $term_i$ and the column $Class_j$ of the matrix CT where j is the j-th category .
3. According to the existing matrix CT, calculate similarity of each category and unclassified document. $SimCT_{jx} = \sum_i w_{ix} \cdot w_{ij}$ (i,j are described in 1,2)
5. Select the largest one from {$SimCT_{1x}$, $SimCT_{2x}$,… …,$SimCT_{nx}$ } where n is the total number of categories in Class Space.
6. $Class_x$ is attributed to the $Class_j$ where $SimCT_{jx}$ is the maximal among { $\overset{n}{\underset{j=1}{sim CT_{jx}}}$ }.

Fig. 2. Fast Algorithm for Text Categorization

4 Experiments and Results

4.1 Experiment Preparation

We evaluate the proposed approach by using Reuters version 3, remove the training and test documents that belong to two or more categories from the corpus, and select the top 10 categories to form our compiled Apte corpus. We implemented algorithm with VC++ 6.0 under Windows XP. Experiments were carried out on a PC with P4 1.6GHz CPU and 512MHz memory. The goal of experiments is to evaluate the performance (effectiveness and efficiency) of our approach.

– Precision and recall[10], micro-averaging and macro-averaging[11] are used for effectiveness measurements.
– Speedup are used for efficiency measurements. Speedup is defined as: Speedup = T_{before} / T_{after} where T_{before} are the time cost for classifying a test document based on Reuters-Apte before using a new method and T_{after} are the time cost after using a new method.

kNN is the simplest categorization algorithm which is also based on the distance measure between vectors and we have described its advantages and disadvantages in section1. Based on the reasons above, we use kNN to compare with our experiments.

4.2 Experiments for Establishing Class Space Model

In Section 2.3, we use two methods to establish matrix CT. (see Eq.3 and Eq.4).

Exp.1: Use $w_{ij} = \frac{f_{ij} \times df_{ij}}{cd_j^2}$ to form CT.

That means the matrix A,B and vector CD are all used to form CT. The information used includes f_{ij}, df_{ij}, and cd_j (see Def..1,2,and 3). According to algorithm in section3 on compiled Ape corpus , we could see the results in Table.1.

Table 1. Precision and Recall of Exp. 1

Categories	Training sets	Testing sets	Precision	Recall
Acq	1597	750	0.7987	0.8307
Coffee	93	25	0.7692	0.8
Crude	255	124	0.7557	0.7983
Earn	2840	1170	0.8705	0.8102
Interest	191	90	0.6822	0.811
Money-fx	215	100	0.7314	0.79
Moneysupply	123	30	0.7575	0.8333
Ship	111	38	0.756	0.8157
Sugar	97	32	0.75	0.8437
Trade	251	88	0.7395	0.8068

From results of Table1, we could get the micro-averaging and macro-averaging of 10 categories.
micro-precision=0.8157, micro-recall=0.8157;
macro-precision=0.7611, macro-recall=0.814.

Exp.2: Use $w_{ij} = \frac{df_{ij}}{cd_j}$ to form CT.

That means only the matrix A and vector CD are used to form CT . The information used includes df_{ij}, and cd_j (see Definition 1,2,and 3). The same experimental condition as Exp.1 and we could see the results in Table.2.

Table 2. Precision and Recall of Exp.2

Categories	Training sets	Testing sets	Precision	Recall
Acq	1597	750	0.8778	0.8626
Coffee	93	25	0.8148	0.88
Crude	255	124	0.8538	0.8952
Earn	2840	1170	0.9141	0.9009
Interest	191	90	0.7778	0.8556
Money-fx	215	100	0.8416	0.85
Moneysupply	123	30	0.8667	0.8667
Ship	111	38	0.8421	0.8421
Sugar	97	32	0.8235	0.875
Trade	251	88	0.80612	0.8977

From results of Table2, we could get the micro-averaging and macro-averaging of 10 categories.
micro-p =0.8831, micro-r =0.8831 macro-p =0.8419, macro-r =0.8726.

4.3 Efficiency Compared with an Improved kNN Algorithm

Literature[12] proposed a fast kNN TC approach based on pruning the training corpus to improve the inefficiency of existing kNN. By pruning, the size of training corpus can be condensed sharply so that time-consuming on kNN searching can be cut off significantly. The experiments of literature[12] uses identical compiled Ape corpus with us and it's experimental results are in Table.3.

Our experimental results(Exp.1,2) are shown in Table.4.

Combining Table 3 and 4, we could see the following Table.5.

Table 3. Results of Literature[12]

		No pruning	Pruning
Classification efficiency	Time-cost/ per document(sec)	582	107
	Speedup	-	5.44
Performance	Micro-p	0.940	0.911
Training Corpus	Size	5773	993
	Pruning ratio	-	82.8%
Platform	P4 1.4GHz, 256MHz RAM , Windows 2000 , VC++6.0		

Table 4. Results of Exp. 1,2

		Exp. 1	Exp 2
Classification efficiency	Time-cost/ per document(sec)	0.0812403	0.071886
	Total Running Time (sec.)	198.79491	175.9059
Performance	Micro-p	0.8157	0.8831
Training Corpus	Size	5773	5773
Platform	P4 1.6GHz, 512MHz RAM , Windows XP , VC++6.0		

Table 5. Contrast of Efficiency between algorithm of ours and literature[12]

	No pruning	Pruning	Exp.1	Exp.2
Time-cost/ per document(sec)	582	107	0.0812403	0.071886
Speedup	-	5.44	7164	8096

The contrast results above can be seen more clearly in Fig3.

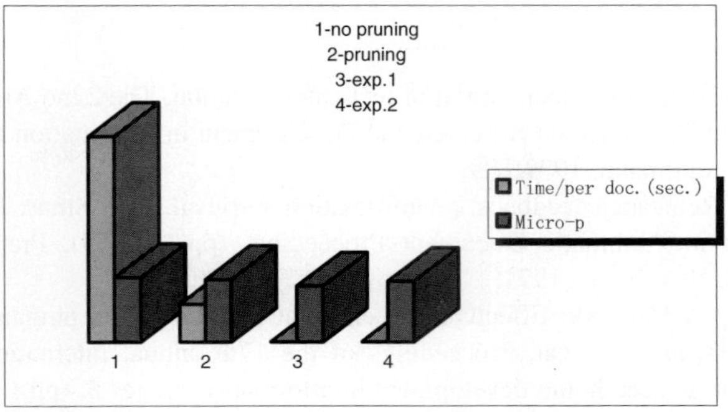

Fig. 3. Contrast of 4 Experiments

5 Conclusions and Future Works

From section 4.2, we found whether or not adding the element f_{ij} to matrix CT is a different point between exp.1 and 2. The experimental results show that exp2 in which matrix CT is established only by df_{ij} and cd_j has better precision and recall than exp 1. It's disappointing that f_{ij} didn't make the precision and recall higher but made them fall. We consider that it is because the noise influence brought by f_{ij} exceeds the benefit brought by it by providing information for categorization. Moreover,we found the all existing methods of feature selection methods could get information from matrix A(Eq. 1). IG, MI, Chi[10,13,14] employ the theory of information entropy to measure the feature's ability for categorization. These facts provide more idea for our W_{ij}. Making full use of the information in GEDB to establish the class space model is a challenging task. It could not be done well only by simple addition or multiplication. More theories such as the Information Theory and Artificial Intelligence theory should be employed into it. The results in section4.3 show that compared with the literature[12], our fast algorithm for TC has absolute advantage of speed without sacrificing effectiveness much. Similar comparision has also been done with the literature[15], and the same conclusion has been drawn. Because of length of this paper, we would not give the actual experimental contrast.

Experimental results above proved the advantages of efficiency and effectiveness of our novel algorithm. Compared with the many complicated algorithm for TC, our algorithm is simple and efficient. It introduces reverse thinking to the field of TC. That is, it is not let categories identify unclassified document, but let the unclassified document to select categories to which it should be attributed. The advantage of GEDB and full feature class space gives us more thinking and implementing space. Compressed document representation and fast algorithm make the efficiency assured.

In the future, we are to add more semantic information to GEDB and solve the problems that cannot be done well only by statistical methods. Our future work includes also using better feature dimension reduction technologies to reduce the influence of noise and establishing more effective class space model. It's profitable to establish a platform for experiments to test all ideas freely and quickly. The project is ongoing.

References

1. Yang,Y. & Liu,X. A re-examination of text categorization. The 22nd Annual International ACM SIGIR Conference on Research and Development in Information Retrieval ,(pp. 42-49).Morgan Kaufmann, 1999.
2. Rocchio, J. Relevance feedback in information retrieval. The Smart Retrieval System-Experiments in Automatic Document Proceeding, (pp.313-323). Prentice-Hall, Englewood, Cliffs, New Jersy . 1971.
3. Yang,Y. Expert Network: Effective and efficient Learning from human decisions in text categorization and retrieval. Proceedings of the 17th annual international ACM SIGIR conference on Research and development in information retrieval, (pp.13-22). Dublin, Ireland, July, 1994.
4. Salton,G. & Mcgill, M. J. An Introduction to Modern Information Retrieval. McGraw-Hill, New York,1983.
5. Salton,G. Automatic text processing: the transformation. Addison Wesley, 1989.
6. Aas, K. & Eikvil,L. Text categorisation: A survey. Technical report, Norwegian Computing Center. http://citeseer.nj.nec.com/aas99text.html, 1999.
7. Huang,R. & Guo,S.H. Research and Implementation of Text Categorization System Based on Class Space Model (in Chinese). Application Research of Computers,22(8),60-64, 2005 .
8. Arango, G. , Williams, G. & Iscoe,N. Domain Modeling for Software. The International Conference on. Software Engineering. ACM Press, Austin, Texas,1991.
9. Lewis,D.D. Reuters-21578 Text Categorization Test Collection. http://www.daviddlewis.com/ resources/ testcollections/reuters21578, 2004 .
10. Yang,Y & Pedersen,J.O.. A comparative study on feature selection in text categorization . Proceedings of ICML 297, 14th International Conference on Machine Learning,(pp.412-420). San Francisco: Morgan Kaufmann Publishers Inc.,1997.
11. Sebastiani,F. Machine learning in automated text categorization. ACM Computing Surveys,34(1), 1-47,2002 .
12. Zhou,S.G.,Ling, T.W.,Guan,J.H.,Hu,J.T.& Zhou,A.Y. Fast text classification: a training-corpus pruning based approach.. Database Systems for Advanced Applications, 2003. (DASFAA 2003). Proceedings. Eighth International Conference on 26- 28 March 2003,(pp.127 – 136).
13. Lewi, D.D. & Ringuette,M. A comparison of two learning algorithms for text classification. In Proc.of the Third Annual Symposium on Document Analysis and Information Retrieval(SDAIR'94), (pp. 81-93),1994 .
14. Wiener,E., Pedersen,J.O.,& Weigend, A.S. A neural network approach to topic spotting. The Fourth Annual Symposium on Document Analysis and Information Retrieval(SDAIR'95) , (pp.317-332). Las Vegas, NV,1995.
15. Shanks,V.& Williams,H.E. Fast categorisation of large document collections. String Processing and Information Retrieval (SPIRE 2001),(pp.194-204),2001.
16. Vapnik,V. The Nature of Statistical Learning Theory. New York. Springer-Verlag,1995.
17. Yang,Y., Chute,C.G. An example-based mapping method for text categorization and retrieval. ACM Transaction on Information Systmes(TOIS), 12(3), (pp.252~277),1994 .
18. Aote C., Damerau, F.& Weiss, S. Text mining with decision rules and decision trees. Workshop on Learning from text and the Web, Conference on Automated Learning and Discovery,1998 .
19. Mitchell ,T. Machine Learning. McGraw:Hill, 1996.

A High Performance Prototype System for Chinese Text Categorization

Xinghua Fan

College of Computer Science and Technology,
Chongqing University of Posts and Telecommunications, Chongqing 400065, P.R. China
fanxh@cqupt.edu.cn

Abstract. How to improve the accuracy of categorization is a big challenge in text categorization. This paper proposes a high performance prototype system for Chinese text categorization, which mainly includes feature extraction subsystem, feature selection subsystem, and reliability evaluation subsystem for classification results. The proposed prototype system employs a two-step classifying strategy. First, the features that are effective for all testing texts are used to classify texts. Then, the reliability evaluation subsystem evaluates the classification results directly according to the outputs of the classifier, and divides them into two parts: texts classified reliable or not. Only for the texts classified unreliable at the first step, go to the second step. Second, a classifier uses the features that are more subtle and powerful for those texts classified unreliable to classify the texts. The proposed prototype system is successfully implemented in a case that exploits a Naive Bayesian classifier as the classifier in the first and second steps. Experiments show that the proposed prototype system achieves a high performance.

1 Introduction

Text categorization (TC) is a task of assigning one or multiple predefined category labels to natural language texts. To deal with this sophisticated task, a variety of statistical classification methods and machine learning techniques have been exploited intensively [1], including the Naïve Bayesian (NB) classifier [2], the Vector Space Model (VSM)-based classifier [3], the example-based classifier [4], and the Support Vector Machine [5].

Text filtering is a basic type of text categorization (two-class TC). There are many real-life applications [6], a typical one of which is the ill information filtering, such as erotic information and garbage information filtering on the web, in e-mails and in short messages of mobile phones. It is obvious that this sort of information should be carefully controlled. On the other hand, the filtering performance using the existing methodologies is still not satisfactory in general. The reason lies in that there exist a number of documents with high degree of ambiguity, from the TC point of view, in a document collection, that is, there is a fuzzy area across the border of two classes (for the sake of expression, we call the class consisting of the ill information-related texts, or, the negative samples, the category of TARGET, and, the class consisting of the ill

A. Gelbukh and C.A. Reyes-Garcia (Eds.): MICAI 2006, LNAI 4293, pp. 1017 – 1026, 2006.

information-not-related texts, or, the positive samples, the category of Non-TARGET). Some documents in one category may have great similarities with some other documents in the other category, for example, a lot of words concerning love story and sex are likely appear in both negative samples and positive samples if the filtering target is erotic information.

Fan et al observed that most of the classification errors result from the documents falling into the fuzzy area between two categories, and present a two-step TC method based on Naive Bayesian classifier [6][7][8], in which the idea is inspired by the fuzzy area between categories: in the first step, a Naive Bayesian classifier is used to fix the fuzzy area between categories; in the second step, a Naive Bayesian classifier same as that in the first step with more subtle and powerful features is used to deal with documents in the fuzzy area, which are considered as unreliable in the first step.

How to improve the accuracy of categorization is a big challenge in TC. To tackle this problem, this paper presents a high performance prototype system for Chinese text categorization including a general two-step TC framework, in which the two-step TC method in [6][7][8] is regarded as an instance of the general framework, and then presents the experiments that are used to validate the assumption as the foundation of two-step TC method.

The rest of this paper is organized as follows. Section 2 describes the prototype system. Section 3 describes an instance of the prototype system and its experiments. Section 4 presents the assumption validation experiments. Section 5 summaries the whole paper.

2 The Proposed Architecture for Chinese Text Categorization

General two-step TC framework

In the first step, the features, which are regarded as effective for all texts, are extracted and selected. Next, a classifier uses these features to classify texts. Then, the classification results are evaluated directly according to the outputs of the classifier, and divided two parts: texts classified reliable or not. Only for the texts classified unreliable in the first step, go to the second step. In the second step, the features, which are regarded as more subtle and powerful for those texts classified unreliable, are extracted and selected. Then, a classifier uses those features to classify the texts classified unreliable in the first step.

Two-step TC method depends on such an **Assumption**: for a given classifier, there exists a space, in which the texts classified unreliable gather in a fuzzy area, and the total documents in the fuzzy area are smaller than all texts in the collection. Only on the assumption is true, the two-step TC method is effective.

The key of the general two-step TC framework is as fellows. (1) Two types of feature (one is used at the first step, and the other is used at the second step) must be found for a give text data set; and (2) for a given classifier, there must exist a method, which can be used to evaluate the classification results directly according to the outputs of the classifier.

For the first problem, generally a possible solution can be obtained by observing the given text data set. For the second problem, normally a possible solution is to build a two-dimension or multi-space space using the outputs of the classifier directly, in which most of texts classified unreliable fall into a fuzzy area. Thus the classification results can be evaluated by observing whether they fall into the fuzzy area.

Architecture of the prototype system

The architecture of prototype system corresponding to the general two-step TC framework is illustrated as Figs. 1 and 2, which correspond the training process and the testing process respectively. The prototype system consists of six components as follows.

(1) **Texts-preprocessing module** transforms the input free text into the formatted text that can be used by the system directly. For example, in the realized instance of prototype system described at Section 3, text-preprocessing module is a Chinese word segment system, and its output is Chinese texts that have segmented.

(2) **Feature extraction subsystem** extracts the features, which types are defined by a user, from the formatted texts outputted by text-preprocessing module. At the

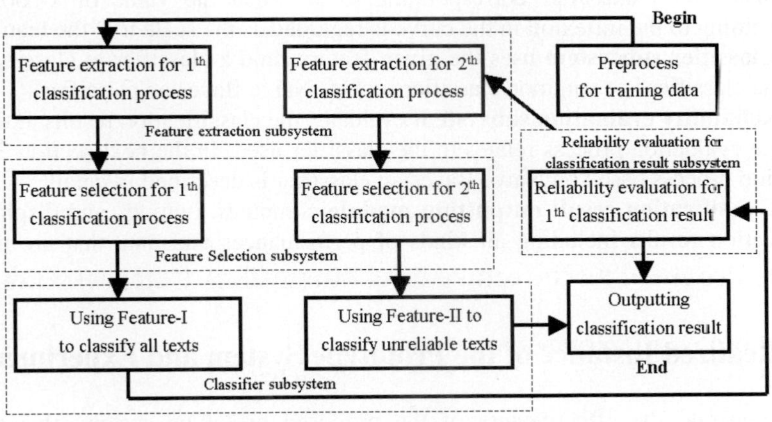

Fig. 1. Training process of the prototype system

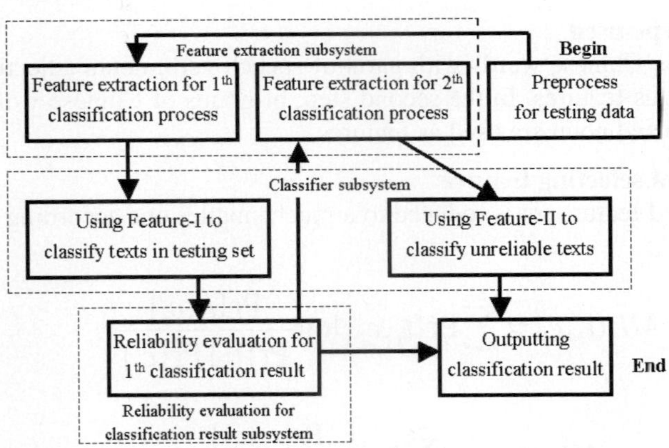

Fig. 2. Testing process of the prototype system

training stage, its input is all texts in the training set, and its output is a feature list, in which each record includes a feature and its corresponding frequency appeared. At the testing stage, its input is all texts in the testing set and a feature list that is determined by feature selection subsystem at the training stage. And its output is a feature vector list, in which each record represents a testing text.

(3) **Feature selection subsystem** selects those features that are effective for all texts. The input is the feature list outputted by the feature extraction subsystem, and the output is a feature list, in which each record only consists of a feature. Feature selection comprises the following processes: 1) Feature compression, i.e., filtering directly those features that have no class-distinguish-ability, according to their frequency appeared in different class texts. 2) Computing the measure such as mutual information (MI) [9] for every feature, and sorting the feature list simplified at the previous step. The top n features consist of the feature set used by a classifier; here n is the scale of feature set. 3) Determine the scale n of the feature set. The process is to draw a curve, in which x-coordinate is the feature number N, and y-coordinate is the performance of a classifier corresponding to N. Then the value of x-coordinate corresponding to the inflexion in the curve is regarded as the scale n of the feature set.

(4) **Classifier subsystem** uses the given features and a classifier to classify texts. Here, the classifier is a common classifier such as Naive Bayesian classifier.

(5) **Reliability evaluation subsystem** evaluates the classification results at the first step. The evaluation process relates to the classifier used. In the next section 3.1, the evaluation process based on Naive Bayesian classifier is described in detail.

(6) **Classification result outputting module** computes, outputs, and displays the classification results including all kinds of performances and data that are used to analyze.

3 A Realized Instance of the Prototype System and Experiments

To demonstrate the effectiveness of the proposed prototype system, this section presents a case that exploits a Naive Bayesian classifier as the classifier, and applies it to classify Chinese texts with high degree of ambiguity.

The feature type used

In the first step, Chinese words with parts-of-speech verb, noun, adjective and adverb are considered as features. In the second step, bi-grams of Chinese words with parts-of-speech verb and noun are used as features.

The formula of selecting feature

The compressed feature set is reduced to a much smaller one according to formula (1) or formula (2).

$$MI_1(t_k,c) = \sum_{i=1}^{n} \Pr\{t_k,c_i\} \log \frac{\Pr\{t_k,c_i\}}{\Pr\{t_k\}\Pr\{c_i\}}, \quad (1)$$

$$MI_2(t_k,c) = \sum_{i=1}^{n} \log \frac{\Pr\{t_k,c_i\}}{\Pr\{t_k\}\Pr\{c_i\}}, \quad (2)$$

where t_k stands for the kth feature, which may be a Chinese word or a word bi-gram, and c_i is the ith predefined category.

3.1 Reliability Evaluation Based on Naive Bayesian Classifier

Reliability evaluation based on two-class naive Bayesian classifier

We use the Naïve Bayesian classifier to fix the fuzzy area in the first step. For a document represented by a binary-valued vector $d = (W_1, W_2, \ldots, W_{|D|})$, the two-class Naïve Bayesian classifier is given as

$$\begin{aligned} f(d) &= \log \frac{\Pr\{c_1|d\}}{\Pr\{c_2|d\}} \\ &= \log \frac{\Pr\{c_1\}}{\Pr\{c_2\}} + \sum_{k=1}^{|D|} \log \frac{1\text{-}p_{k1}}{1\text{-}p_{k2}} + \sum_{k=1}^{|D|} W_k \log \frac{p_{k1}}{1\text{-}p_{k1}} - \sum_{k=1}^{|D|} W_k \log \frac{p_{k2}}{1\text{-}p_{k2}} \end{aligned} \quad (3)$$

where $\Pr\{\bullet\}$ is the probability that event $\{\bullet\}$ occurs, c_i is category i, and $p_{ki}=\Pr\{W_k=1|c_i\}$ $(i=1,2)$. If $f(\mathrm{d}) \geqslant 0$, the document d will be assigned the category label c_1, otherwise, c_2. Let

$$Con = \log \frac{\Pr\{c_1\}}{\Pr\{c_2\}} + \sum_{k=1}^{|D|} \log \frac{1\text{-}p_{k1}}{1\text{-}p_{k2}} , \quad (4)$$

$$X = \sum_{k=1}^{|D|} W_k \log \frac{p_{k1}}{1\text{-}p_{k1}} , \quad (5)$$

$$Y = \sum_{k=1}^{|D|} W_k \log \frac{p_{k2}}{1\text{-}p_{k2}} , \quad (6)$$

where Con is a constant relevant only to the training set, X and Y are the measures that the document d belongs to categories c_1 and c_2 respectively.

We rewrite (3) as

$$f(d) = X - Y + Con \quad (7)$$

Apparently, $f(d)=0$ is the separate line in a two-dimensional space with X and Y being X-coordinate and Y-coordinate. In this space, a given document d can be viewed as a point (x, y), in which the values of x and y are calculated according to (5) and (6). The distance from the point (x, y) to the separate line will be

$$Dist = \frac{1}{\sqrt{2}}(x - y + Con) . \quad (8)$$

Thus, the space can be partitioned into reliable area and unreliable area as

$$\begin{cases} Dist_2 \le Dist \le Dist_1, & \text{Decision for } d \text{ is unreliable} \\ Dist > Dist_1, & \text{Assigning the label } c_1 \text{ to } d \text{ is reliable} \\ Dist < Dist_2, & \text{Assigning the label } c_2 \text{ to } d \text{ is reliable} \end{cases} \quad (9)$$

where $Dist_1$ and $Dist_2$ are constants determined by experiments, $Dist_1$ is positive real number and $Dist_2$ is negative real number.

Reliability evaluation based on multi-class naive Bayesian classifier
For a document represented by a binary-valued vector $d = (W_1, W_2, \ldots, W_{|D|})$, the multi-class Naïve Bayesian Classifier can be re-written as

$$c^* = \arg\max_{c_i \in C}(\log \Pr\{c_i\} + \sum_{k=1}^{|D|} \log\ (1\text{-}p_{ki}) + \sum_{k=1}^{|D|} W_k \log \frac{p_{ki}}{1\text{-}p_{ki}}) \ , \tag{10}$$

where Pr{ • } is the probability that event { • } occurs, $p_{ki}=\Pr\{W_k=1|c_i\}$, (i=1,2, …, |C|), C is the number of predefined categories. Let

$$MV_i = \log \Pr\{c_i\} + \sum_{k=1}^{|D|} \log\ (1\text{-}p_{ki}) + \sum_{k=1}^{|D|} W_k \log \frac{p_{ki}}{1\text{-}p_{ki}} \ , \tag{11}$$

$$MV_{\max\_F} = \underset{c_i \in C}{\text{maximum}}(MV_i) \ , \tag{12}$$

$$MV_{\max\_S} = \underset{c_i \in C}{\text{second\_maximum}}(MV_i) \ , \tag{13}$$

where MV_i stands for the likelihood of assigning a label $c_i \in C$ to the document d, and MV_{max_F} and MV_{max_S} are the maximum and the second maximum over all MV_i ($i \in |C|$) respectively. We approximately rewrite (10) as

$$f(d) = MV_{\max\_F} - MV_{\max\_S} \ . \tag{14}$$

We try to transfer the multi-class TC described by (10) into a two-class TC described by (14). Formula (14) means that the binary-valued multi-class Naïve Bayesian classifier can be approximately regarded as searching a separate line in a two-dimensional space with MV_{max_F} being the X-coordinate and MV_{max_S} being the Y-coordinate. The distance from a given document, represented as a point (x, y) with the values of x and y calculated according to (12) and (13) respectively, to the separate line in this two-dimensional space will be:

$$Dist = \frac{1}{\sqrt{2}}(x - y) \ . \tag{15}$$

The value of *Dist* directly reflects the degree of confidence of assigning the label c^* to the document d.

3.2 Experiments Based on Naive Bayesian Classifier

Experiments based on two-class naive Bayesian classifier
The dataset used here is composed of 12,600 documents with 1,800 negative samples of TARGET and 10,800 positive samples of Non-TARGET. It is split into 4 parts randomly, with three parts as training set and one part as test set. All experiments in this section are performed in 4-fold cross validation.

Five methods are tried as follows.

Method-1: Use Chinese words as features, reduce features with (2), and classify documents directly without exploring the two-step strategy.

Method-2: Same as Method-1 except feature reduction with (1).

Method-3: Same as Method-2 except Chinese word bi-grams as features.

Method-4: Use the mixture of Chinese words and Chinese word bi-grams as features, reduce features with (1), and classify documents directly.

Method-5: Use Chinese words as features in the first step and then use word bi-grams as features in the second step, reduce features with (1), and classify the documents in two steps.

Table 1. Performance comparisons of the five methods in two-class TC

Method	Precision	Recall	F_1
Method-1	78.04%	88.72%	82.67%
Method-2	93.35%	88.78%	91.00%
Method-3	93.15%	94.17%	93.65%
Method-4	95.86%	91.11%	93.42%
Method-5	97.19%	93.94%	95.54%

Note that the proportion of negative samples and positive samples is 1:6. Thus if all the documents in the test set is arbitrarily set to positive, the precision will reach 85.7%. For this reason, only the experimental results for negative samples are considered in evaluation, as given in Table 1. For each method, the number of features is set by the highest point in the curve of the classifier performance with respect to the number of features (For the limitation of space, we omit all the curves here). The numbers of features set in five methods are 4000, 500, 15000, 800 and 500+3000 (the first step + the second step) respectively.

Comparing Method-1 and Method-2, it shows that feature reduction formula (1) is superior to (2). Moreover, the number of features determined in the former is less than that in the latter (500 vs. 4000). Comparing Method-5 with Method-2, Method-3 and Method-4, it shows that the two-step approach is superior to either using only one kind of features (word or word bi-gram) in the classifier, or using the mixture of two kinds of features in one step. Table 1 shows that the proposed prototype system, which corresponds Method-5, achieves a high performance (95.54% F_1).

Experiments based on multi-class naive Bayesian classifier

A dataset is constructed, including 5 categories and the total of 17756 Chinese documents. The document numbers of five categories are 4192, 6968, 2080, 3175 and 1800 respectively, among which the last three categories have the high degree of ambiguity each other. The dataset is split into four parts randomly, one as the test set and the other three as the training set. We again run the five methods described above. The experimentally determined numbers of features regarding the five methods are 8000, 400, 5000, 800 and 400 + 9000 (the first step + the second step) respectively.

The average precision, average recall and average F_1 over the five categories are used to evaluate the experimental results, as shown in Table 2. Table 2 shows very similar conclusions as that in the two-class TC.

Table 2. Performance comparisons of the five methods in multi-class TC

Method	Average Precision	Average Recall	Average F_1
Method-1	92.14%	91.13%	91.48%
Method-2	97.03%	97.38%	97.20%
Method-3	98.36%	98.17%	98.26%
Method-4	97.99%	98.03%	98.01%
Method-5	98.58%	98.55%	98.56%

4 The Experiments to Validate the Assumption

To validate the assumption, the two measures, error rate (**ER**) and region percentage (**RP**), are introduced, which definitions are as follows.

$$\text{ER} = \frac{\text{the number of texts misclassed in a given region}}{\text{the number of all texts misclassed in a test set}} \times 100\%$$

$$\text{RP} = \frac{\text{the number of texts falling into a give region}}{\text{the number of all texts in a test set}} \times 100\%$$

Using a naive Bayesian classifier as the classifier, seven cases are tried as follows:

Case-1: Use Chinese word as feature, and reduce features with (1).
Case-2: Use bi-gram of Chinese characters as feature, and reduce features with (1).
Case-3: Use bi-gram of Chinese words as feature, and reduce features with (1).
Case-4: Use the mixture of Chinese word and bi-gram of Chinese word as feature, and reduce features with (1).
Case-5: Use the mixture of bi-gram of Chinese Character and bi-gram of Chinese word as feature, and reduce features with (1).
Case-6: Use Chinese word as feature, and reduce features with (2).
Case-7: Use bi-gram of Chinese characters as feature, and reduce features with (2).

Suppose that the two-class dataset and multi-class dataset in the previous section are Dataset-I and Dataset-II respectively. For Dataset-I, Case-1 and case-2 are tried, and the corresponding experimental results are illustrated as Table 3.

Table 3. Assumption validation results on Dataset-1

Case	Error Rate	Region Percentage
Case-1	95.21%	36.87%
Case-2	97.48%	40.23%

To obtain the **ER** and **RP** in every case, first the curves that the performance (including **ER** and **RP**) of a classifier changes with the distance *Dist* are drawn, and then the constant $Dist_1$ and $Dist_2$ in (9) are determined according to the inflexion on the curves, finally acquire the corresponding **ER** and **RP**. For example, for the Case-2 in Table 3, the curves are illustrated as Fig.3. From Fig.3, the constant $Dist_1$ and $Dist_2$ are determined as 32 and –52 respectively, and the corresponding performances of the classifier are given in Fig.3.

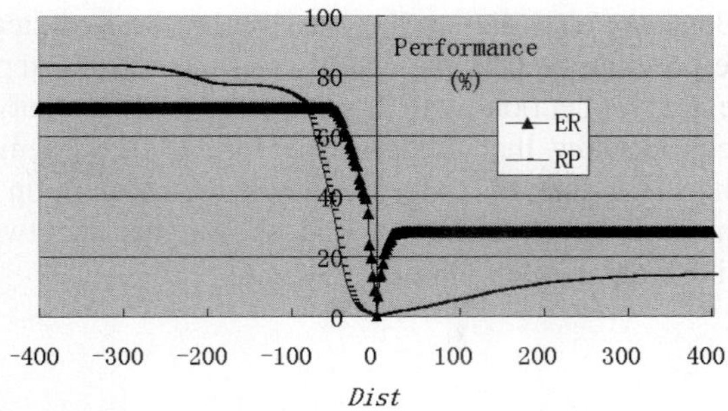

Fig. 3. The curves that error rate and region percentage change with the distance *Dist*

Table 3 shows that exploiting different feature reduction formula, the **Assumption** is true because most of classifying error occurs in a region, but all texts in the region is a fraction of all texts in a test set (97.48% vs.40.23%, and 95.21% vs. 36.87%).

For Dataset-2, seven cases are tried, and the corresponding experimental results are illustrated as Table 4. Comparing the results in Case-1, Case-2, Case-3, Case-4 and case 5, it shows that exploiting different type of features (Chinese word, bi-gram of Chinese character and bi-gram of Chinese word) and different mixture of features (the mixture of Chinese word and bi-gram of Chinese word, the mixture of bi-gram of Chinese Character and bi-gram of Chinese word), the **Assumption** is true. Comparing Case-1 vs. Case-6 and Case-2 vs. Case-7, it shows that exploiting the same feature and different feature reduction formula (Chinese word + (1) or (2), Chinese character bi-gram +(1) or (2)), the **Assumption** is true.

Table 4. Assumption validation results on Dataset-2

Case	Case-1	Case-2	Case-3	Case-4	Case-5	Case-6	Case-7
Error Rate	95.53%	93.0%	85.31%	88.89%	93.51%	82.59%	72.63%
Region Percentage	13.09%	9.8%	11.8%	7.89%	8.81%	20.31%	4.08%

Based on the above analysis, the **Assumption** is true. Thus, the two-step TC method that uses the **Assumption** as foundation is effective. As a result, the proposed prototype system that exploits the two-step method should achieve a high performance. The conclusion is consistent with experimental result in section 3.

5 Conclusions

This paper presents a high performance prototype system that exploits a two-step strategy for Chinese text categorization. The characteristic of the proposed system lies in that it has a reliability evaluation subsystem for classification results, which can evaluate the classification results directly according to the outputs of the classifier used at the first stage. The system is successfully implemented in an instance that exploits a Naive Bayesian classifier as the classifier at the first step, and a classifier same as that in the previous step as the classifier at the second step. Experiments on two-class Chinese text collection with high degree of ambiguity and multi-class Chinese text collection show that the proposed prototype system achieves a high performance. At the same time, this paper validates the assumption as the foundation of two-step TC method by experiments, and shows that the two-step method is feasible and effective from another view.

References

1. Sebastiani, F. Machine Learning in Automated Text Categorization. ACM Computing Surveys, 34(1):1-47, 2002.
2. Lewis, D. Naive Bayes at Forty: The Independence Assumption in Information Retrieval. In Proceedings of ECML-98, 4-15, 1998.
3. Salton, G. Automatic Text Processing: The Transformation, Analysis, and Retrieval of Information by Computer. Addison-Wesley, Reading, MA, 1989.
4. Mitchell, T.M. Machine Learning. McCraw Hill, New York, NY, 1996.
5. Yang, Y., and Liu, X. A Re-examination of Text Categorization Methods. In Proceedings of SIGIR-99, 42-49,1999.
6. Xinghua Fan. Causality Reasoning and Text Categorization, Postdoctoral Research Report of Tsinghua University, P.R. China, April 2004.
7. Xinghua Fan, Maosong Sun, Key-sun Choi, and Qin Zhang. Classifying Chinese texts in two steps. IJCNLP2005, LNAI3651, pp.302-313, 2005.
8. Xinghua Fan, Maosong Sun. A high performance two-class Chinese text categorization method. Chinese Journal of Computers, 29(1), 124-131, 2006.
9. Dumais, S.T., Platt, J., Hecherman, D., and Sahami, M. Inductive Learning Algorithms and Representation for Text Categorization. In Proceedings of CIKM-98, Bethesda, MD, 148-155, 1998.
10. Sahami, M., Dumais, S., Hecherman, D., and Horvitz, E. A. Bayesian Approach to Filtering Junk E-Mail. In Learning for Text Categorization: Papers from the AAAI Workshop, 55-62, Madison Wisconsin. AAAI Technical Report WS-98-05, 1998.

A Bayesian Approach to Classify Conference Papers

Kok-Chin Khor and Choo-Yee Ting

Faculty of Information Technology
Multimedia University
63100 Cyberjaya, Malaysia
{kckhor, cyting}@mmu.edu.my

Abstract. This article aims at presenting a methodological approach for classifying educational conference papers by employing a Bayesian Network (BN). A total of 400 conference papers were collected and categorized into 4 major topics (*Intelligent Tutoring System*, *Cognition*, *e-Learning*, and *Teacher Education*). In this study, we have implemented a 80-20 split of collected papers. 80% of the papers were meant for keywords extraction and BN parameter learning whereas the other 20% were aimed for predictive accuracy performance. A feature selection algorithm was applied to automatically extract keywords for each topic. The extracted keywords were then used for constructing BN. The prior probabilities were subsequently learned using the Expectation Maximization (EM) algorithm. The network has gone through a series of validation by human experts and experimental evaluation to analyze its predictive accuracy. The result has demonstrated that the proposed BN has outperformed Naïve Bayesian Classifier, and BN learned from the training data.

1 Introduction

Conference organizers often prepare guidelines and scopes so that contribution of research papers can be made according to the predefined categories. To enhance the classification process, whether or not to be done by human experts, keywords are often a prerequisite. Keywords are means of classification as they often reflect the center of discussion of a particular paper. In this study, we treat the conference paper classification as an instance of documentation classification problem. To date, various approaches have been proposed for documentation classification such as K-Nearest Neighbors and Support Vector Machines (SVM) [1, 2]. Bayesian approach is one of the approaches that receive considerably attention [3, 4, 5, 6, 7].

The physical and logical aspects of a document are considered in extracting the keywords from conference papers. The physical aspect of a document refers to layout structure of physical components like characters, words, lines and paragraphs. On the other hand, the logical aspect of a document refers to a set of logical functions or labels that need to be assigned to the physical component [3]. Documents such as web documents are lacking of physical and logical organization and it will usually cause difficulties in retrieving information. However, conference papers are well-structured documents. Authors are required to follow the guideline provided by the conference organizers in preparing their papers. Keywords are often required by the conference

A. Gelbukh and C.A. Reyes-Garcia (Eds.): MICAI 2006, LNAI 4293, pp. 1027 – 1036, 2006.

organizer to be included in the papers. The keywords are normally located in a single paragraph and the paragraph itself is always started with word "Keywords". By making use of the organizations of the conference papers, keywords of a conference paper can be extracted for classification purposes.

Keywords provided by authors are not necessary in the form of single keywords. Most of the time *compound keywords* are used instead. For example, authors might use keywords "Bayesian Artificial Intelligence" rather than separating it into two parts, "Bayesian" and "Artificial Intelligence". Research work has been conducted to include the compound terms in classification of documents and the result is promising [7]. However, considering *compound keywords* for classifying conference papers is expected to bring less significant effect to the classification process as the number of keywords involved in a conference paper is not many. Moreover, different *compound keywords* can be used by different authors to reflect the same topic of discussion. The same *compound keywords* are unlikely to occur in all other conference papers. Examples of *compound keyword* such as "Bayesian Network", "Bayesian Approach", and "Naïve Bayesian Classifier" belong to the same topic which is "Bayesian Artificial Intelligence". All these keywords share one same word "Bayesian" which suggest the topic of the papers. Therefore, considering *single keywords* by separating *compound keywords* would be sufficient for the purpose of classifying the conference papers. Apart from that, variations of a keyword are common in conference papers, for instance, "Classify", "Classifying", and "Classification". To ease the classification process, variation of a keyword need to be mapped into a common representation. Various stemming algorithms have been proposed by researchers to achieve the mapping purpose [8, 9, 10].

Seeing the importance of using keywords as an indicator for classification, in this study, we shall firstly present our methodology for extracting appropriate keywords from a set of papers, and secondly, constructing a BN [11] from the extracted keywords. The novel approach of this project is combining human expert and machine learning technique to correctly classify the conference papers. In this study, we scoped our study to educational conference papers and taking into consideration of four topics only. The topics we have selected are the *e-Learning*, *Teacher Education*, *Intelligent Tutoring System,* and C*ognition Issues*. In the rest of this article, the discussions will be centered on the proposed approach for (1) automatic keywords extraction and data preparation, and (2) construction of BN from the keywords.

2 Keywords Extraction and Data Preparation

In this study, the keyword selection process was performed prior to the construction of BN. Fig. 1 depicts the algorithm for extracting keywords from a set of documents $\mathcal{D}$. Let $\mathcal{C}$ denotes the *compound keywords* that the author has defined in a particular document $\mathcal{D}_a$. The *compound keywords* $\mathcal{C}$ are commonly found between the "*Keywords*", and "*Introduction*" sections in $\mathcal{D}_a$. Referring to the algorithm, the extraction of phrases must be performed first before subsequent refinement of keywords extraction process can be carried out. The refinement process resulting in $\mathcal{K}$ where

$\mathcal{K}$ denotes the *single keywords* extracted from $\mathcal{C}$. From $\mathcal{K}$, the extraction process proceeds with the function *RemoveNonKeywords* to eliminate symbols "---", ":", ",", and ";" as these are non useful keywords. Besides, numbers and common function words such as the "a", "on", and "of" will also be removed since they are trivial for classifying conference papers. The extracted keywords are stemmed by the Porter Stemmer [8] that aims at removing the commoner morphological and inflexional endings from *single keywords*. Finally, the function *Stemmer* will stem the refined single keywords $\mathcal{K}$ before being appended to the array $\mathcal{K}_S$.

Algorithm **Keyword Extraction** ( )
Input: Training documents $\mathcal{D}$
$\mathcal{D}_a \leftarrow$ each document in $\mathcal{D}$,
$\mathcal{C} \leftarrow$ array of compound keywords $\{\mathcal{C}_1,\ldots, \mathcal{C}_n\}$ in $\mathcal{D}_a$
$\mathcal{K} \leftarrow$ array of single keywords $\{\mathcal{K}_1,\ldots, \mathcal{K}_n\}$
$\mathcal{K}_S \leftarrow$ array of stemmed keywords $\mathcal{K}$
For each $\mathcal{D}_a$ in $\mathcal{D}$
    Locate "keywords" or "keyword" section in $\mathcal{D}_a$
    If found then
        $\mathcal{C} \leftarrow$ extract $\{\mathcal{C}_1,\ldots, \mathcal{C}_n\}$
        $\mathcal{K} \leftarrow$ extract $\{\mathcal{K}_1,\ldots, \mathcal{K}_n\}$
        RemoveNonKeywords($\mathcal{K}$)
        $\mathcal{K}_S \leftarrow$ *Stemmer* ($\mathcal{K}$)
    End if
Next
Count_KeywordFrequency ($\mathcal{K}_S$)
Output: Top 7 stemmed keywords $\mathcal{K}_S$ that are ranked based on frequencies

Fig. 1. Algorithm for extracting single keywords $\mathcal{K}_S$ from training documents $\mathcal{D}$. This algorithm aims at extracting top 7 keywords that are ranked based on collection frequencies from a set of documents. Examples of keywords extracted from 80 papers for the topic *Intelligent Tutoring Systems* are depicted in Table. 1.

In the extraction process, 80% of the collected conference papers are used to determine the *collection frequency* of all the stemmed keywords for each topic (Table. 1). We refer *collection frequency* to the number of documents in which a particular keyword occurs. As depicted in Table 1, the stemmed keywords are ranked in descending order accordingly. The top seven stemmed keywords $\mathcal{K}_S$ of each topic will be extracted for constructing the BN. Since the topics are related to education issues, some of the topics are expected to share the same *single keywords*.

Table 1. The stemmed keywords of the topic Intelligent Tutoring Systems

Topic	Keywords	Frequency
Intelligent Tutoring Systems	Intellig*	77
	System*	61
	Tutor*	58
	Learn*	32
	Educ*	29
	Agent*	21
	Environ*	21
	Decision	10
	Fuzzy	9
	Database	9
	Neural	8

* *keywords that are selected for BN construction after multiple 80% random selection of 100 documents for the topic Intelligent Tutoring System*

After running the keywords selection algorithm for each of the topics, the keywords are as shown in the following table. We categorized them into *main* and *shared* keywords. The 80% of the collected conference papers are again used to prepare training dataset. The keywords of each paper will be compared with the set of keywords that are selected based on c*ollection frequency*. If there is a match, "y" will be assigned. "n" will be assigned if otherwise (Table. 2). The other 20% of the conference papers will also undergo the same comparison process but they will be used for preparing testing dataset.

Table 2. Sample table for storing the keywords of each topic

teacher	educ	develop	profession	…	metadata	Topic
y	n	y	n	…	n	Teacher Education
y	y	n	n	…	n	Teacher Education
:	:	:	:		:	:
n	n	n	n	…	n	Cognition
n	n	n	n	…	y	Cognition

3 Bayesian Networks Construction

3.1 Bayesian Network

The Bayesian network (BN) a.k.a the Belief Network (Fig. 2) is a graphical model for probabilistic reasoning. It is now widely accepted for reasoning under uncertainty. A BN is a representation of a joint probability distribution over a set of statistical variables:

$$P(x_1,...,x_n) = \prod_{i=1}^{n} P(x_i \mid parents(x_i)) \qquad (1)$$

The wide acceptance of BN is mainly due to its capability to explicitly represent of both qualitative and quantitative aspect. The qualitative aspect is presented by its graph structure while as for quantitative aspect, through its marginal and conditional probabilities. BN graph structure is a Directed Acyclic Graph (DAG) and formally represents the structural representation of variables in the domain. The causal interpretation, however, is often being described through the direct probabilistic dependencies among the variables.

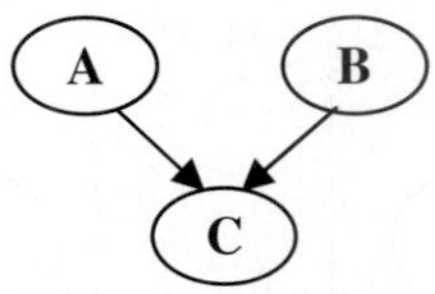

Fig. 2. A simple BN with 3 nodes

The quantitative aspect is presented through the *Conditional Probability Table* (CPT), which describes the probability of each value of the child node, conditioned on every possible combination of values of its parents. In Fig. 1, assuming that all the nodes have 2 states, thus the CPT for node C is a $2^3 = 8$ probability values entry. By having both the qualitative and quantitative representation of BN, posterior probabilities of query variables can be calculated in light of any evidence. By applying Bayes' rule and a variety of inference algorithms, BN can be used to perform *diagnostic*, *predictive* and *inter-causal* reasoning, as well as any combination of these.

3.2 Classification and Dependencies of Nodes in Bayesian Network

Fig. 3 depicts the proposed BN for classifying educational conference papers. The network is categorized into 5 sub-networks, namely the *Teacher Education* sub-network, *Intelligent Tutoring System* sub-network, *Cognition* sub-network, and *e-Learning* sub-network. These sub-networks consist of combinations of *Main Topic* node ($\mathcal{T}$), *Sub-topic* node ($\mathcal{S}$), *Keyword* node ($\mathcal{E}$), and S*hared-keyword* nodes ($\mathcal{Y}$). The *Main Topic* node $\mathcal{T}$ (node *Topic*) is a node with 4 states δ with $\delta \in$ {*ITS*, *Cognition*, *e-Learning*, and *TeacherEduc*}. The second type of nodes is the S*ub-topic node* ($\mathcal{S}$). This node is introduced aiming at grouping the *keyword* nodes together and can take the values {*yes*, *no*}. The arcs drawing from the *Topic* node to S*ub-topic* nodes indicate dependencies between these nodes. Increasing the probability of a *sub-network* node will in turn increases the probabilities of other *sub-network* nodes and *Main Topic* node. In this study, the *keyword* nodes are keywords that are extracted from the *Keyword Extraction* algorithm (Fig. 1) and can take the values {yes, no}. They are *evidential* nodes as in light of receiving evidences, the posterior probability of the corresponding *Sub-topic* node is retrieved upon updating the network. For instance, instantiating the nodes *develop*, *scienc*, *knowledg*, *teacher*, and *profession* to "*y*" will increase the probability of the node *subTeacher*. Since there is an immediate dependency between the node *subTeacher* and Topic, increasing the probability of *subTeacher* will subsequently increase the certainty of the state *Teacher* in the node *Topic*. Thus, the paper is categorized into the *Teacher Education* topic.

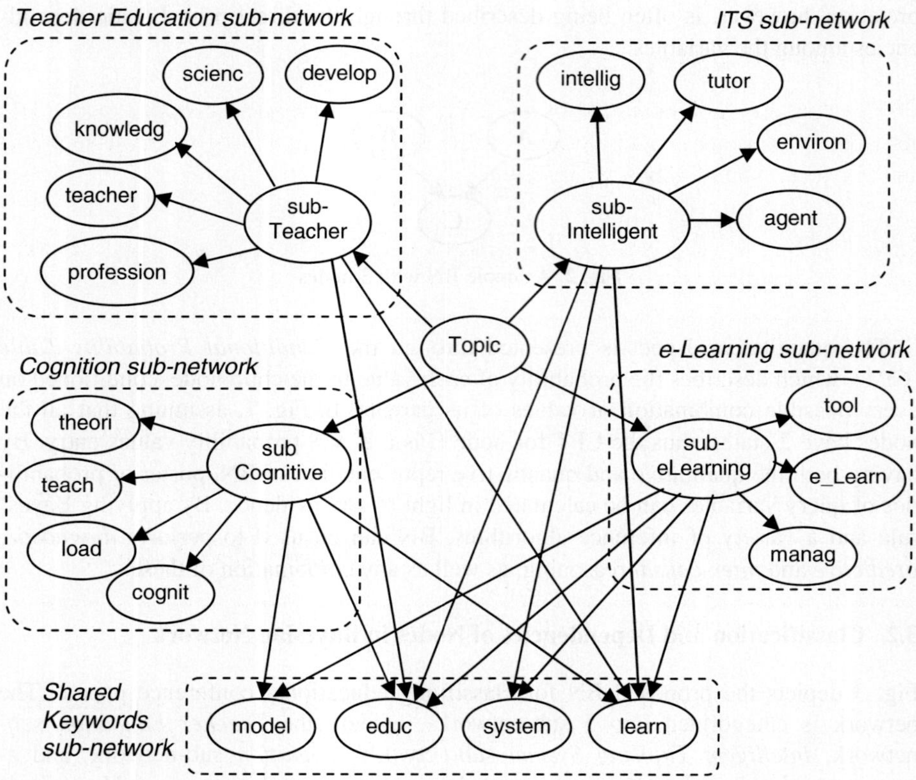

Fig. 3. BN for classifying educational conference papers. The nodes are keywords that are extracted through the *Keyword Extraction* algorithm (Fig.1).

As discussed in section 2, there are overlapping keywords during the keywords selection process. In this study, we have selected the 4 mostly shared keywords to be included in our proposed model. These keywords are transformed into the *Shared-keyword* node $\mathcal{Y}$ (nodes *model*, *educ*, *system*, and *learn*) in the network (Fig. 3). To model the dependencies of these overlapping keywords with the topics, arcs are drawn from the *Sub-topic* nodes to these four nodes.

The proposed network was subsequently applied the Expectation Maximization (EM) algorithm to learn the parameters of nodes. The experts verify the parameters learned through the EM algorithm before evaluating the network.

4 Evaluation

In this study, we have performed a two-phase evaluation process on the proposed BN. The first phase is *case-based evaluation*. The *case-based evaluation* involved human experts in evaluating the appropriateness of the selected keywords and "playing" with the network. The second phase is the *predictive evaluation* where the accuracy of proposed BN is compared with Naïve Bayesian Classifier (NBC) and BN learned from training data.

4.1 Case-Based Evaluation

This evaluation phase consisted of three activities that involved human experts. The activities are (1) verifying of keywords selected, (2) "manipulating" with the network, and (3) refinement of network parameters.

Table 3. The finalized stemmed *main* and *shared* keywords for each topic. These keywords were verified by human experts.

Topic	Keywords
e-Learning	Tool, e-Learn, Manag, Model*, Educ*, System*, Learn*
Intelligent Tutoring Systems	Intellig, Tutor, Environ, Agent, Educ*, System*, Learn*
Teacher Education	Develop, Scienc, Knowledge, Teacher, Profession, Educ*, Learn*
Cognition	Theori, Teach, Load, Cognit, Model*, Educ*, Learn*

* *keywords that are shared with other Topics*

The experts were firstly presented with the keywords extracted through the keywords selection algorithm depicted in Fig. 1. They were given the all the keywords with the corresponding frequencies sorted descending for each topic. After finalizing the extracted keywords, the keywords are then being verified for its suitability to be categorized into *main* and *shared* keywords (Table 3). Having the all keywords finalized, the subsequent task is to allow the experts "played" around with the network. The experts are given a set of keywords (Table 4) to be entered into the network as evidences (example of evidence tuple *<y, n, n, y, y...>)* and observed the classification outputs of the network. The experts randomly selected 5 out of 20 documents from each topic as sample for classification measurement. Table 4 shows that both experts demonstrated a very high accuracy of classification given by the network.

In the next section, we shall describe how we evaluated the proposed BN by comparing its predictive accuracy against the Naïve Bayesian Classifier (NBC) and Bayesian network learned from the training documents.

Table 4. The classification accuracy (%) with respect to human expert classification. It is noticed that the topic *Intelligent Tutoring System* has the highest classification accuracy.

Expert	**Accuracy of Classification (%)**			
	Teacher Education	**Cognition**	**Intelligent Tutoring System**	**e-Learning**
1	100	100	100	100
2	80	80	100	80
3	80	80	80	100
Average %	86.67	86.67	93.34	93.34
Overall %	**90.0**			

4.2 Predictive Evaluation

We conducted experiments to investigate the predictive accuracy of the proposed network against BN learned from training documents (Fig. 4(a)) and NBC (Fig. 4(b)). In this study, 80% of the documents were meant for learning the structures and parameters of networks while 20% were used for predictive accuracy measurement. To prevent any *memorizing* effect of networks, the testing documents (20%) were totally different from those meant for training (80%).

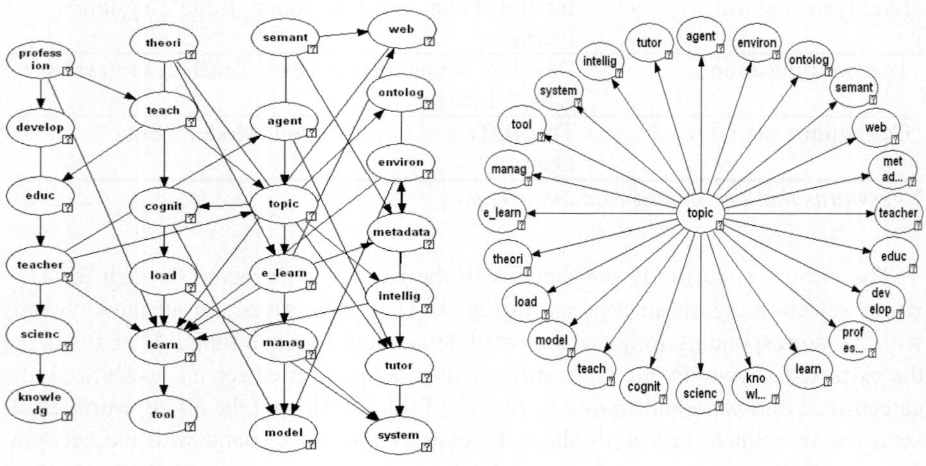

(a) (b)

Fig. 4. (a) BN learned from training documents, (b) Naïve Bayesian Network

Table 5 shows the results of experiments on predictive accuracy of the three networks. Compare to learned BN, the proposed network has performed better for the topics *Teacher Education*(85%), *e-Learning*(95%), and *Intelligent Tutoring Systems*(75%). However, there is a moderately drop of predictive accuracy for the topic *Cognition*(80%). Thus, in general, the proposed BN is having a higher predictive accuracy (83.75%) compare to the learned BN (76.25%). The comparison between proposed BN and NBC shows that the predictive accuracy of topic *e-Learning* has increased significantly (95%). However, there are a moderately drop of predictive accuracy in the other 2 topics (*Teacher Education*=85%, *Cognition*=80%). Averagely, the proposed BN has a slightly better performance as its average predictive accuracy is slightly higher than NBC (82.5%).

Table 5. Predictive accuracy in percentage for proposed BN, NBC and BN learned from training dataset

Topic	Proposed BN	BN Learned from Data	NBC
Teacher Education	85	75	90
e-Learning	95	60	75
Cognition	80	95	90
Intelligent Tutoring System	75	75	75
Average (%)	**83.75**	**76.25**	**82.5**

In short, the proposed BN performed better compared to NBC and BN learned from training data although there are topics where the performance of proposed network performed slightly lower. Our investigation reviewed that the dropping of predictive accuracy is mainly due to the nature of NBC and learned BN structures that are more adapted to the certain topics. Apart from that, there are papers that are unable to be classified correctly mainly because authors used the combination of keywords with very low collective frequencies but yet able to reflect the center discussion or topic of the papers.

5 Conclusion and Future Work

We proposed a BN to classify educational conference papers. In this study, we scoped our educational conference papers to the topics *e-Learning*, *Teacher Education*, *Intelligent Tutoring System,* and C*ognition Issues*. The proposed network has integrated both machine learning technique and human expert parameters elicitation. The efficiency of the network was measured by comparing its predictive accuracy against human experts' classification, BN learning from training documents, and Naïve Bayesian network. The experimental results suggested that the proposed network has achieved 90% rated by human expert while obtaining an average of 83.75% that is higher than BN learning from training documents (76.25%), and Naïve Bayesian network(82.5%).

We shall extend this work to classifying educational conference papers to other topics which include *Metacognition*, *Pedagogical Agent*, and *Ontology*. Since there are conference papers without "keywords" section, thus, automatically identifying keywords is a crucial part. We shall look into information theory as our base to solve the challenge.

Acknowledgement. The Bayesian Networks models mentioned in this paper were created using the GeNIe and SMILE modeling application developed by the Decision Systems Laboratory of the University of Pittsburgh (http://www.sis.pitt.edu/~dsl).

References

1. Eui-Hong (Sam) Han., George Karypis., Vipin Kumar.: Text Categorization Using Weight Adjusted K-Nearest Neighbor Classification. Lecture Notes in Computer Science, Vol. 2035. Springer-Verlag Berlin Heidelberg (2001) p.53
2. Atakan Kurt., Engin Tozal.:Classification of XSLT-Generated Web Documents with Support Vector Machines. Lecture Notes in Computer Science, Vol. 3915. Springer-Verlag Berlin Heidelberg (2006) 33-42.
3. Souad Souafi-Bensafi., Marc Parizeau., Frank Lebourgeois., Hubert Emptoz.: Bayesian Networks Classifiers Applied to Documents. Proceeding of the 16th International Conference on Pattern Recognition, Vol 1. IEEE (2002) 483-486
4. Luis M. de Campos., Juan M. Fernandez-Luna., Juan F. Huete.: A Layered Bayesian Network Model for Document Retrieval. Lecture Notes in Computer Science, Vol. 2291. Springer-Verlag Berlin Heidelberg (2002) 169-182
5. Yong Wang., Julia Hodges., Bo Tang.: Classification of Web Document using a Naïve Bayes Method. Proceedings of the 15th IEEE International Conference on Tools with Artificial Intelligence, IEEE (2003) 560–564
6. Wai Lam., Kon-Fan Low.: Automatic Document Classification Based on Probabilistic Reasoning: Model and Performance Analysis. International Conference on Systems, Man, and Cybernatics, Vol 3. IEEE (1997) 2719-2723
7. Jing Bai., Jian Yun Nie., Guihong Cao.: Integrating Compound Terms in Bayesian Text Classification. Proceedings of the 2005 IEEE/WIC/ACM International Conference on Web Intelligence. IEEE (2005) 598-601
8. The Porter Stemming Algorithm. http://www.tartarus.org/martin/PorterStemmer/
9. The Lancaster Stemming Algorithm. http://www.comp.lancs.ac.uk/computing/research/stemming/index.htm
10. The UEA-Lite Stemmer. http://www.cmp.uea.ac.uk/Research/stemmer/
11. Pearl, J.: Probabilistic Reasoning in Intelligent Systems: Networks of Plausible Inference. Morgan Kaufmann, San Mateo, CA (1988)

An Ontology Based for Drilling Report Classification

Ivan Rizzo Guilherme[1], Adriane Beatriz de Souza Serapião[1], Clarice Rabelo[2], and José Ricardo Pelaquim Mendes[2]

[1] São Paulo State University, IGCE, DEMAC, Av. 24A 1511, 13506700 Rio Claro, Brazil
{ivan, adriane}@rc.unesp.br
[2] The State University of Campinas, FEM, DEP, Campinas, Brazil
{clarice, jricardo}@dep.fem.unicamp.br

Abstract. This paper presents an application of an ontology based system for automated text analysis using a sample of a drilling report to demonstrate how the methodology works. The methodology used here consists basically of organizing the knowledge related to the drilling process by elaborating the ontology of some typical problems. The whole process was carried out with the assistance of a drilling expert, and by also using software to collect the knowledge from the texts. Finally, a sample of drilling reports was used to test the system, evaluating its performance on automated text classification.

1 Introduction

In different areas of specialization, many documents generated relate the problems which occurred during the analysis carried out, the diagnosis procedure taken and the solutions provided. These documents represent an important source of knowledge.

Well-Engineering is one of these specialized areas dealt with in this work. Petroleum well-drilling activity is complex and extremely dependent on technical skills and engineering competence. During the drilling process, a great amount of information is generated, representing a relevant source of knowledge, as mentioned before [1,2].

Part of this information is automatically obtained from equipment, while another part is generally reported in text format. Such information is analyzed by engineers involved in well-design projects, as they evaluate operation executions and identify problems to provide solutions. In this way, technology evolution in the information system area provides greater capability of generating and storing data in text format, which is a significant source of institutional knowledge for oil companies.

The ontology herewith has been proposed so as to provide solutions for the problems generated from either the use of different terminologies related to equivalent concepts or the use of a same term related to different concepts. In this way, the ontology is used to explore information associated to a specific domain as it represents the meaning of the domain terms. This meaning representation is used to organize, share and facilitate knowledge exploration.

Ontology acquisition from texts has been under great investigation. However, many of the tools applied to ontology acquisition are still developed towards texts written in English, not Portuguese.

A. Gelbukh and C.A. Reyes-Garcia (Eds.): MICAI 2006, LNAI 4293, pp. 1037 – 1046, 2006.

This paper presents an ontology based system for drilling report classification. A semi-automatic methodology is used to learn the ontology from technical reports. The whole process was assisted by a drilling expert, using a tool to extract the ontology from the texts. The ontology generated contains terms and knowledge related to problems in drilling processes. Finally, a sample of drilling reports was used to test the system, evaluating its performance on automated text classification.

2 Ontology Building Methodology

The methodology proposed for semi-automated text analysis is an interactive process between the expert and the software tool based on intelligent text processing. Its application allows a specialist (a domain user) to improve his/her expertise and to learn more about the domain analyzed.

Text analysis is usually a very hard task due to the necessity of having a complete dictionary with a large number of terms available and the semantic ambiguity of the language used [3]. However, this analysis can be easier in more specialized texts, when the number of words and the semantic used in their internal communications are sharply defined in the domain of the specific community.

The ontology proposed in this work was created by using a semi-automatic text analysis tool (Figure 1). A sample of texts from the analyzed domain is required to generate a list of words with specific meaning for the study context. Expert knowledge is necessary to appropriately define the syntax, which has symbols associated to labels of the ontology meta-structure.

The ontology labels are related to each word from the list, generating the word dictionary. All instances of ontology are created by selecting a set of words combinations according to the syntax to represent the knowledge in the considered domain. Summarizing the applied methodology:

1. *(Expert)* Selection of a sample of texts from the analyzed domain;
2. *(Text Analysis Tool)* Search for words in the sample of selected texts. A list of words with their corresponding frequencies of occurrences is generated;
3. *(Expert)* Selection of words with strong meaning for the context considered and syntax (grammar) definition. The word dictionary is generated;
4. *(Text Analysis Tool)* Text analysis tool is used to create a list of word combinations based on the syntax definition and ontology structuring;
5. *(Expert)* Selection of phrases from the list of word combinations with strong meaning for the considered domain, generating the ontology phrase dictionary. It is also possible to refine the grammar or manually adjust word combinations, for example, by adding restriction terms in some of them. In this case, if the dictionary is used to analyze a text that contains the phrase and also a restriction term in the same event description, the system will not be able to identify it;
6. *(Text Analysis Tool)* Using the ontology phrase dictionary generated, the text analysis tool is used to process all new desired sets of texts to analyze or to classify them according to the ontology defined.

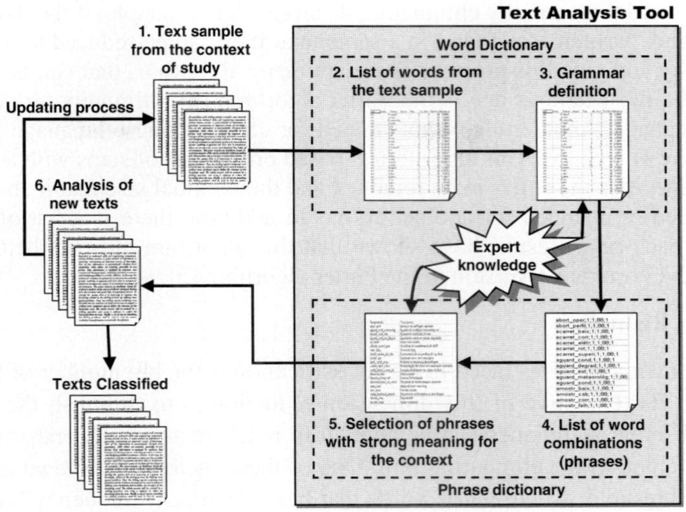

Fig. 1. Methodology for automated text processing

3 Word Dictionary

The text sample is used to generate a list of existing terms. A term may be either a single word or made up of multiple ones. Some relevant aspects to validate this model are the methods applied to extract these terms from the documents and to determinate the weight of each one of them (index process). This weighting process must reflect the importance of each term in both document and set of document context. A description of the sequence of steps used to generate the list of words is presented below.

Separation in Tokens

In this initial step, the text of entry is separated in a series of tokens. In this work, a token is represented by a set of words separated by the space character. The objective is to separate the text into words in the Portuguese language, which requires that some special characters be also considered, such as words with accents.

Meaningless Word Removal

The process is characterized by the removal of those words that have no relevant meaning to the context. Among these words to be eliminated are articles and pronouns. This process is usually based on a list of removable words (stop-words), which can be edited by the user if necessary. This procedure is executed in a simple way: for each token extracted, its presence on the list of removable words is checked. If it is confirmed, the process finishes and a new token is analyzed. If not, the process of analyzing that token continues to the next level.

Word Rooting

In all the Portuguese words, there is an invariable element that is responsible for their essential meaning, which is named radical (4). The rooting process objective is to reduce the word to its root by eliminating its affixes. For example, if the words "write", "writing" and "written" are found in a same text, they can be reduced to a single radical "writ" by applying this process. There are many algorithms that can be used in this process. The most famous one is the Porter algorithm [6], originally proposed for the English language. Another algorithm created for the Portuguese language is described by Orengo & Huyck [5]. This algorithm is based on a series of steps with a set of rules. Each rule specifies the suffix to be removed and the minimal size that it should have to be eliminated or changed for another suffix. In addition, there is a list of exceptions applied to each rule. Results have shown that this algorithm presents better performance than the Portuguese version of the Porter algorithm [5].

Dimension Reduction

One of the main problems faced in text classification is the big number of terms in the dictionary. The objective of this dimension reduction is to diminish the Word Dictionary. Different techniques can be applied to reach such a goal, and some of them are implemented in the computing tool. One of these methods is known as document frequency threshold, where those words that have document frequency below the cut value are eliminated.

Another algorithm was also developed to select the words which have the highest entropy, since both very frequent and rare words are, in general, meaningless for any purpose of analysis. The relevance of a word for any analysis is, then, related to its entropy in the data base. The entropy **h(w)** of the words **w** is then calculated as:

$$h(w) = -p \log p,$$

where word probability **p** is calculated as the quotient of the number of its instances (**Np**) by the total number of instances of all terms (**Nt**). The relevant words **w** are those exhibiting entropy greater than a defined threshold.

The software also allows the manual addition of new words. Figure 2 shows a screen copy of the software used.

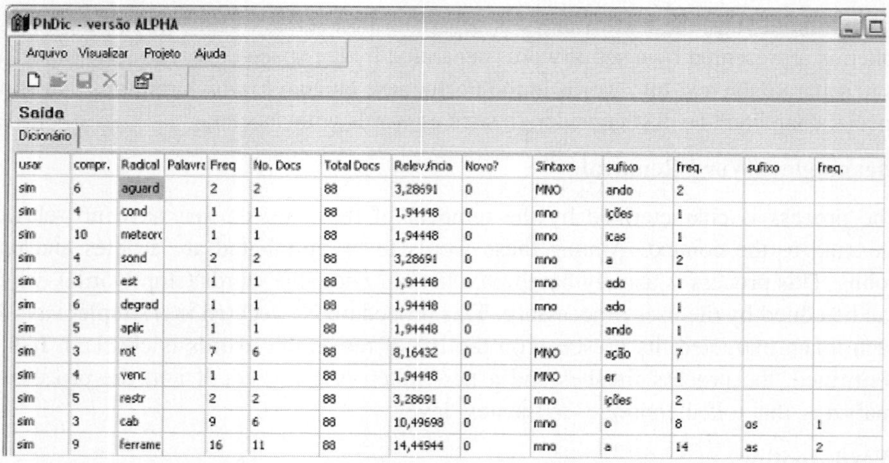

Fig. 2. Tool used to generate the list of terms for the word dictionary

4 Ontology Phrase Dictionary

The knowledge structure is generated in a way so as to allow its application in technical report classification. In this way, syntax that allows the identification of the concept associations and the ontology structure is specified.

Concept Structure

The words in the dictionaries created by the expert are related to primitive concepts relevant to the intended analysis of context. The possible theories the user may be interested to disclose are specified by means of syntax (or grammar), where the primitive concepts are listed. This grammar represents the specialist's knowledge and encodes either ontology as in the case of the natural grammars, or some kind of specific knowledge. The concepts defined in the ontology; are described by the well formed formula (wff) of the language obeying the syntax. Syntax associates concepts taken as key words (start symbols or triggers) and complementary words (non-terminal symbols or slots), with complex concepts described by phrases (terminal symbols).

Let the derivation chain:

$$\mathbf{VVV} \Rightarrow \mathbf{vvvPLA} \Rightarrow \mathbf{vvvplaTIM} \Rightarrow \mathbf{vvvplatim}$$

define a wff, requiring information about a place to be incorporated into the phrase associated with a given verb **VVV**, before information about time is checked so that it can be part of the sentence.

Tokens are, therefore, used to assign dictionary words to concepts or to syntactical classes of a language or symbolic classes. In the above examples, the tokens **VVV/vvv; PLA/pla and TIM/tim** are associated to the (key) words assigned as verbs and (complementary) words speaking about time, objects and place.

The complexity of the syntax (grammar) to be implemented to support the analysis is, therefore, dependent both on the complexity of the tokens, which correlates, in turn, to the complexity of the set of primitive concepts of a given area of expertise; as well as to the complexity of the concatenation properties assigned to these tokens, which are related to the complexity of the possible relations shared by those primitive concepts.

The syntactic tokens are presumed to be tuples of letters, whose length is specified by the user according to the complexity of the set of concepts to be worked out. Initial symbols (verbs, triggers and other key words) are composed of capital letters; terminal symbols are described by means of small letters, and non terminal symbols are composed of substrings of both types of letters. The concatenation rule used is that of complementation between capital and small letters, that is to say, the capital letters match their corresponding small letters, allowing for token concatenation.

In the above examples, the token **VVV** concatenates with the token **vvvPLA** because the substrings **VVV** and **vvv** are complementary strings. The syntax used encoded into a set of tokens associated with its syntactical classes, and token concatenation guides the analysis of word associations and the ontology structure.

These words are related to the primitive concepts of the area of expertise. The syntax used in the analysis of data base must, therefore, encode the basic relations between the primitive concepts supported by the knowledge defining the area of expertise. By using the initial text sample, the concepts generated are evaluated. In this process, some adjustments can be made such as the addition of new words or syntax changes. At the end of this process, the word dictionary and the ontology phrase dictionary are created.

Ontology Structure

In some cases, the texts that describe the problem are complex. The construction of complex concepts may be obtained from the composition of simpler ones. The concept structuring process is based on the ontology definition in the specialization area. The concepts defined in the ontology phrase dictionary are integrated into the ontology structure in a way that describes the concept defined. Figure 3 shows the system interface of the Ontology Phrase Dictionary.

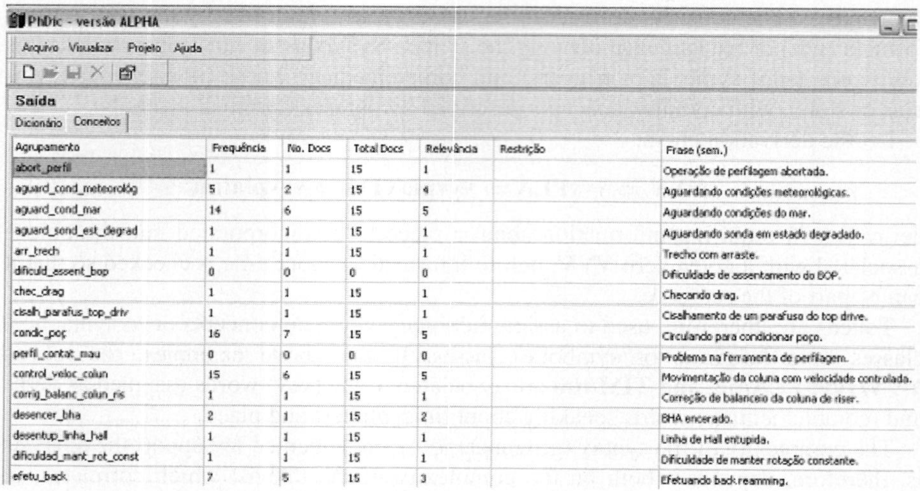

Agrupamento	Frequência	No. Docs	Total Docs	Relevância	Restrição	Frase (sem.)
abort_perfil	1	1	15	1		Operação de perfilagem abortada.
aguard_cond_meteorológ	5	2	15	4		Aguardando condições meteorológicas.
aguard_cond_mar	14	6	15	5		Aguardando condições do mar.
aguard_sond_est_degrad	1	1	15	1		Aguardando sonda em estado degradado.
arr_trech	1	1	15	1		Trecho com arraste.
dificuld_assent_bop	0	0	0	0		Dificuldade de assentamento do BOP.
chec_drag	1	1	15	1		Checando drag.
cisalh_parafus_top_driv	1	1	15	1		Cisalhamento de um parafuso do top drive.
condic_poç	16	7	15	5		Circulando para condicionar poço.
perfil_contat_mau	0	0	0	0		Problema na ferramenta de perfilagem.
control_veloc_colun	15	6	15	5		Movimentação da coluna com velocidade controlada.
corrig_balanc_colun_ris	1	1	15	1		Correção de balanceio da coluna de riser.
desencer_bha	2	1	15	2		BHA encerado.
desentup_linha_hall	1	1	15	1		Linha de Hall entupida.
dificuldad_mant_rot_const	1	1	15	1		Dificuldade de manter rotação constante.
efetu_back	7	5	15	3		Efetuando back reamming.

Fig. 3. Process of generating the ontology drilling problems (interface of the Ontology Phrase Dictionary)

5 An Application of Automated Text Processing of Drilling Problems

The methodology presented in this paper is applied to a community involving personnel in well-construction activities in petroleum upstream industry and they refer to drilling and completion operations.

Petroleum companies generate daily operational reports containing descriptions of all occurrences detected, at least, on a half-hour time basis. These records represent a great source of knowledge since they contain all events, classified by operations, in a time sequence, including abnormal occurrences detected while drilling. The importance of such knowledge it is related to the learning process that might help the companies to manage the risks involved in the activity.

Based on these reports, the methodology presented in this paper is used to create a knowledge representation (ontology phrase dictionary) of drilling problems and uses this knowledge to build an intelligent system to analyze and classify a sample of reports that are in text format (Figure 4).

The text processing was completed by running two different analyses: a manual classification and using the semi-automatic tools. The automated text processing was initiated based on the same sample of drilling records used for the manual analysis. First, the automated text analysis tool was used to generate a word dictionary based on the sample of texts given. Some examples are shown in Tab. 1. The tool used also allows the manual addition of new words.

Table 1. Word dictionary created using a text analysis tool

Radical	Suffix	Suffix Freq
Drill	ing	4
Fluid		
Loss	es	9
Mud		

At this point, it is important to define the syntax correctly. The reason is that the syntax drives the process of associating the words, creating a sentence that represents the problem description. For the same example given previously, by properly defining the grammar, different word combinations were created (see Tab. 2).

Table 2. Example of the Ontology Phrase Dictionary associated to the problem of "Loss of drilling fluid"

Word combination	Restriction	Phrase (Problem Description)
fluid_loss	without	Loss of drilling fluid
mud_loss	without	Loss of drilling fluid
format_loss	without	Loss of drilling fluid

Processing all records available, also considering the combinations added manually, generated a large number of associations to define different abnormal occurrences. However, some of them had no real meaning for the context treated here and only a few of them were used to generate a dictionary of drilling problems.

Another important adjustment that can be made is the addition of some negation terms that are used to create new combinations with opposite meanings. Some words can be also used as a restriction during the problem identification process. In this paper, for example, the word "without" was used as a restriction to the phrases in Tab. 2. Therefore, when the system was used to analyze a new sample of texts, event descriptions that contained those phrases and the word "without" were not identified.

It is also important to remember that this is an interactive process, with the possibility of modifying and adjusting the system according to the convenience. More associations can be created later, updating the system depending on the necessity.

The final step consisted of analyzing a new sample of reports using the ontology phrase dictionary elaborated. The results obtained with the system application are shown in the next section.

6 Results and Conclusion

In order to evaluate the performance of the result obtained and the quality of the ontology created, the text processing was completed by running two different analyses: a manual classification and another one using the semi-automatic tools. A sample of fifteen drilling reports was used, each text related to different wells drilled and operations. Considering all records together, there were more than four thousand sentences or activity descriptions to be analyzed.

The manual analysis consisted basically of reading the reports; identifying abnormal occurrences and actions taken to mitigate the potential injuries; and mapping them. The manual processing provided a better comprehension of the natural language used in the reports to describe the problems. Although this manual analysis seems to be a simple procedure, it required expert knowledge as the process of reading all texts is very time consuming and also exhausting. In addition, the large number of different events described makes the analysis more susceptible to errors.

<table>
<tr><th>Original Text File</th><th>Concept (from Ontology Phrase Dictionary)</th><th>System Classification</th><th>Manual Classification</th></tr>
<tr><td>Repair of hydraulic leak in a pipe handler.</td><td>hydr_leak</td><td>Hydraulic Leak.</td><td>Equipment repair.</td></tr>
<tr><td rowspan="2">Circulation due to poor hole cleaning. Mud loss detected at 2650m.</td><td>loss_form</td><td>Loss of drilling fluid.</td><td rowspan="2">Mud loss.</td></tr>
<tr><td>clean_poor</td><td>Poor hole cleaning.</td></tr>
<tr><td>Stuck pipe without rotation. Working to free the column under 2833 m.</td><td>drillstr_stick</td><td>Drillstring sticking.</td><td>Drillstring sticking.</td></tr>
<tr><td rowspan="2">Connecting top drive and taking drillstring out of the hole with rotation and traction due to excessive torque and drag.</td><td>excess_torqu</td><td>Excessive torque.</td><td>Not identified.</td></tr>
<tr><td>excess_drag</td><td>Excessive drag.</td><td>Not identified.</td></tr>
</table>

Fig. 4. Results obtained from both analysis: the manual classification and the one applying the system developed

The automated text processing was initiated based on the same sample of drilling records used for the manual analysis. Using the text analysis tool and the defined ontology, the sample of texts was classified. As a result, a report similar to the one obtained from manual text processing was generated, containing all problems identified. Figure 4 presents a comparison between the results of both analyses for a small sample of texts contained in the drilling reports.

As it is possible to observe from the example presented in Figure 4, both analysis presented similar results related to the identification of drilling problems. The main difference between both methods was the period of time required to conclude the process. The manual analysis was concluded in two weeks, including time spent to generate the final report, while the intelligent system applied was almost fifty per cent less time consuming.

It is important to say that most of the time spent with the automated processing was related to the ontology phrase dictionary elaboration and some adjustments made, which means that, once this step was concluded, the real time required to classify new samples of texts is only a few minutes.

It is also relevant to remember that manual processing is more susceptible to errors when dealing with a large amount of information. In this case, a well defined ontology might present better performance, requiring only regular updates in order to guarantee its efficiency with the text classification.

A second difference between the manual and the automated analysis is related to a few occurrences that are identified in one method, but not in the other one. This observation shows that both methods have failures, but the automated system can be pointed out as being more trustworthy since a manual analysis of very extensive texts, for example drilling reports, is much more susceptible to human failure.

However, the system's semi-automatic report classification requires a regular procedure of updating. This is necessary because there is always the possibility of new problems or different descriptions to be used in drilling reports. In this way, this updating process is recommended to guarantee a greater efficiency for the identification of abnormal occurrences.

7 Conclusion

The ontology generated is an important source of knowledge and it can be used for training purposes and qualification of new professionals in the area. Furthermore, the knowledge extracted can be also very useful to plan new operation activities in petroleum engineering.

The automation of text classification is also a great tool to facilitate these professional activities. The results obtained with the automated process can provide information about the frequencies of abnormal occurrences, which can be used by oil companies to identify the major problems and treat and prevent the most common ones.

Acknowledgement

This work was partially supported by CNPq (research projects CT-Petro/MCT/CNPq 504863/2004-5 and CT-Petro/MCT/CNPq 504528/2004-1).

References

1. Miura, K., Guilherme, I.R., Morooka, C.K. and Mendes, J.R.P, 2003, "Processing Technical Daily Reports in Offshore Petroleum Engineering – An Experience", Journal of Advanced Computational Intelligence and Intelligent Informatics, Vol. 7, No. 2, 223-228p.
2. Morooka, C.K., Rocha, A.F., Miura, K. and Alegre, L., 1993, "Offshore Well Completion Operational Knowledge Acquisition and Structuring", Eleventh International Offshore Mechanics and Arctic Engineering Conference (OMAE), ASME, Glasgow, Scotland.
3. Rocha, A. F., Guilherme, I. R., Theoto, M., Miyadahira, A. M. K. and Koizumi, M. S., 1992, "A neural Network for extracting Knowledge from Natural Language Data Bases", IEEE Transactions on Neural Network, Vol. 3, No. 5.
4. Faraco, C.E. & Moura, F.M. Língua e Literatura, Editora Ática, 1996
5. Orengo, V.M. & Huyck, C. A Stemming Algorithm for the Portuguese Language, Proceeding SPIRE 2001:186-193.
6. Porter, M. F.,An algorithm for suffix stripping, *Program*, **14**(3):130-137, July 1980.

Topic Selection of Web Documents Using Specific Domain Ontology

Hyunjang Kong[1], Myunggwon Hwang[1], Gwangsu Hwang[1], Jaehong Shim[1], and Pankoo Kim [2]

[1] Dept. of Computer Engineering, Chosun University, 375 Seosuk-dong Dong-Ku Gwangju 501-759 South Korea
{kisofire, hmk2958, hwangs00, jhshim}@chosun.ac.kr
[2] Corresponding Author, Dept. of Computer Engineering, Chosun University
pkkim@chosun.ac.kr

Abstract. This paper proposes a topic selection method for web documents using ontology hierarchy. The idea of this approach is to utilize the ontology structure in order to determine a topic in a web document. In this paper, we propose an approach for improving the performance of document clustering as we select the topic efficiently based on domain ontology. We preprocess the web documents for keywords extraction using *Term Frequency* formula and we build domain ontology as we branch off the partial hierarchy from WordNet using an automatic domain ontology building tool in preprocessing step. And we select a topic for the web documents based on domain ontology structure. Finally we realized that our approach contributes the efficient document clustering.

1 Introduction

Nowadays, there are many documents on the Web, and it is impossible to classify them by human. As the growing of Internet, many researchers focus on classifying and processing the web documents. One of the core approaches is to find a topic of web documents. Our approach for selecting a topic for a web document is exploiting the domain ontology. In order to find a topic efficiently, we firstly analyze the web document to extract the keywords using *Term Frequency* formula. Second, we build the domain ontology for the specific subject by taking away a specific part from WordNet. Third, we map the keywords onto the domain ontology concepts. Finally we determine a topic using the domain concept definition formula. Based on the selected topic, we could expect to improve the performance of documents clustering. This paper suggests the topic selection method for improving the performance of document classification. Ontology-based topic selection involves determining a topic, which represents the subject of web documents most accurately, and distributing web documents into the appropriate node in ontology based on the determined topic.

This paper is organized as follows: Section 2 presents related works. In Section 3, we present the preprocessing tasks for supporting our approach. In Section 4, we present our approach, which consists of the mapping module, topic selection module,

A. Gelbukh and C.A. Reyes-Garcia (Eds.): MICAI 2006, LNAI 4293, pp. 1047 – 1056, 2006.

and ontology extension module. Section 5 presents the experimental results and evaluation. Finally, we conclude our study in Section 6.

2 Related Works

Most of existing approaches for topic identification exploit ontology structure to classify huge data [1][2][5][6][7][10]. In these methods, several features of documents such as Keywords, Title of documents, Term Frequency Values are used for topic selection as they map the features onto the ontology concepts. In here, the topic of the new document will be identified by computing the document features. And then, the document belongs to a node in ontology based on topic. Other methods represent a document using WordNet hierarchy [9][12]. These approaches use WordNet to collect the keywords and generalize the concepts to identify the topic. Our approach for topic selection of web documents also is based on WordNet hierarchy. The most comparable methods to our approach are the simple Term Frequency Value-based topic selection and HTML Tag(especially, Title Tag) based topic selection. In evaluation part of this paper, we compare the experimental results between these three approaches(Term Frequency based method, Title Tag-based method, and our approach) about the accuracy rate of topic selection.

3 Preprocessing for Selecting Topic of Web Documents

Current documents clustering approaches tend to disregard several major aspects. First, document clustering is an objective method. It does not consider that people may view the same documents from completely different perspectives [3][4]. Thus, document clustering methods need to provide multiple subjective perspectives on the same document set. Second, document clustering highly depends on the space of word vectors. In this case, document clustering is very difficult because every data point tends to have the same distance [8]. Third, document clustering is often useless because it does not explain why the document was categorized into a particular cluster. In our study, we consider the problem mentioned above for the efficient documents clustering. In our method, preprocessing involves the keyword extraction, and domain ontology construction.

3.1 Keyword Extraction

Web documents are written by huge terms. In this case, it is very hard to determine the topic of the documents. Until now, two kinds of ways have been suggested for topic selection. One way is to rely on *Term Frequency* value. A *Term Frequency* calculates how often each term occurs in documents. The other way is based on the HTML tag because some of the HTML tags indicate the location represented the topic of documents. In the preprocessing step, we utilize the *Term Frequency* for analyzing a topic for web documents.

Term frequency is usually combined with inverse document frequency. But we just consider the *Term Frequency* in this study to extract the keywords for web documents. *Term frequency* in the web documents gives a measure of the importance of the term within the particular document. And the formula calculating term frequency is as following:

$$tf = \frac{n_i}{\sum_k n_k}$$

In above formula, $\sum_k n_k$ means the total of all terms, which the document contains, n_i is the number of occurrence of the specific term. *Term Frequency* support the fact how important a term is in a document. And values gained through above formula are the indispensable data in our approach for finding a topic for web documents.

For example, we measure *Term Frequency* of web documents using above formula. Figure 1 shows the results measuring *Term Frequency*.

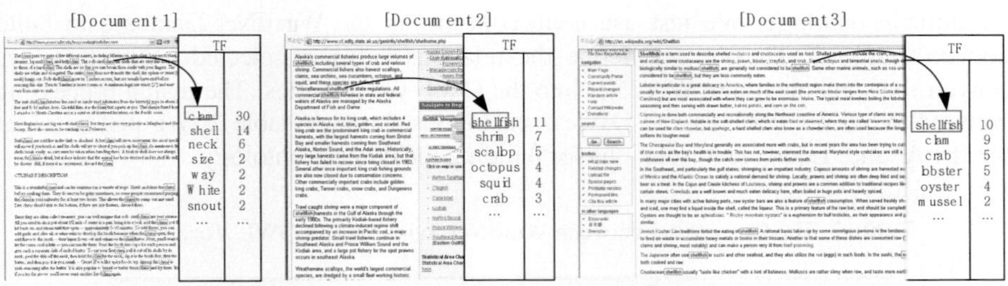

Fig. 1. Measuring Term Frequency about Three Web Documents

Based on *Term Frequency*, we extract the keywords among all terms in the document. For the keyword extraction, we propose the fomula as follows:

$$\{T_i\} \subset \sum_{i=0}^{n} \frac{TF_i}{W} = 1$$

In this formula, TF_i is the values of *Term Frequency* and W is the weight value. Through this formula, we extract the set of terms$\{T_i\}$ until the calculated value become a value 1.

As we apply this formula to the results of *Term Frequency* in Figure 1, we extract the keywords in the documents. Table 1 shows the extracted keywords.

Table 1. The Extracted Keywords when the W is 30 above Formula

Document 1	Document 2	Document 3
clam	Shellfish, shrimp, scallop, octoups, squid	Shellfish, clam, crab, lobster

The extracted keywords will use in the mapping module described in Section 4.1.

3.2 Domain Ontology Construction

The domain ontology in our approach is defined the background knowledge used for topic selection of documents. The domain ontology that we have used here roughly corresponds to the structure of WordNet, but the ontology is domain-specific rather than original WordNet. Because WordNet is extremely huge, it is very hard to control. Thus, we use the specific part of WordNet for increasing the efficiency of ontology in the document clustering.

For building the domain ontology, we develop the automatic domain ontology building tool based on WordNet. This tool has two features. First feature is to extract the domain part from WordNet automatically. And second feature is to record the extracted part using Web Ontology Language(OWL). For example, we want to build the domain ontology about seafood. In this preprocessing, we build the domain ontology based on WordNet. The constructed domain ontology is a simple structured data that consists of the classes and 'IS-A' and 'Equivalent' relations. For building domain ontology, we select the domain concept(seafood) in our tool. Then, the system accesses the WordNet Database and analyzes it. Secondly, we use the Pointers, Synsets and Words tables in the WordNet Database because these tables contain the data that we need for building the domain ontology. We just use noun concepts in the WordNet Database to build domain ontology. Thirdly, we define the relations between selected concepts as we convert the symbols of the WordNet into the OWL vocabularies. The match processing between WordNet symbols and OWL vocabularies shows in table 2. We just consider the 'IS-A' and 'Equivalent' relations for building the domain ontology.

Table 2. The Converting between WordNet Symbols and OWL Vocabularies

The WordNet Symbols	OWL Vocabularies
@, ~	owl:superClassOf, owl:subClassOf
Same Synset ID	owl:equivalentClass

Figure 2 illustrates the screen shot of our automatic ontology building tool.

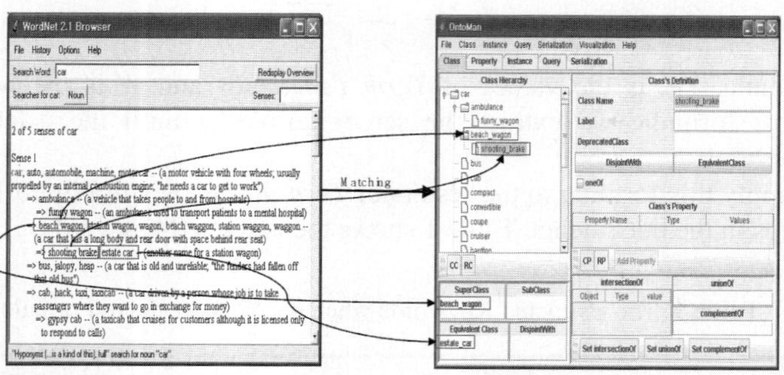

Fig. 2. Converting WordNet to Domain Ontology using the Automatic Ontology Building Tool

In domain ontology building process, the nouns in the Words table change into class names of ontology. And symbols(@,~) and same Synset_ID in WordNet convert into the OWL vocabularies(owl:subClassOf and owl:equivalentClass) each. Based on above transformation, we build the domain ontology automatically using our tool. Finally, our tool records the domain ontology using OWL language. Table 3 shows the part of domain ontology written by OWL.

Table 3. The Part of Domain Ontology Written by OWL

```
<owl:Class rdf:ID="Food" />

<owl:Class rdf:ID="Seafood" />
   <rdfs:subClassOf rdf:resource="#Food" />
</owl:Class>
. . . . .
<owl:Class rdf:ID="Shellfish" />
   <rdfs:subClassOf rdf:resource="#Seafood" />
   <owl:equivalentClass rdf:resource="#mollusk
" />
   <owl:equivalentClass rdf:resource="#mollusc
" />
</owl:Class>
. . . . .
<owl:Class rdf:ID="Clam" />
   <rdfs:subClassOf rdf:resource="#Shellfish" />
</owl:Class>
```

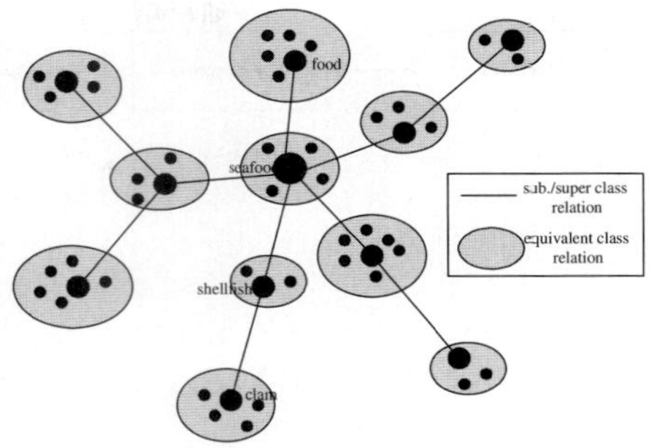

The domain ontology will use in the domain concept definition module described in Section 4.2.

4 Topic Selection of Web Documents

Our approach has three main modules: The mapping module, domain concept definition module and ontology extension module. The input of our approach is extracted keywords in the web documents through preprocessing(Section 3.1). And then, we try to determine a topic of web documents using the domain ontology. Figure 3 shows the overview of our approach.

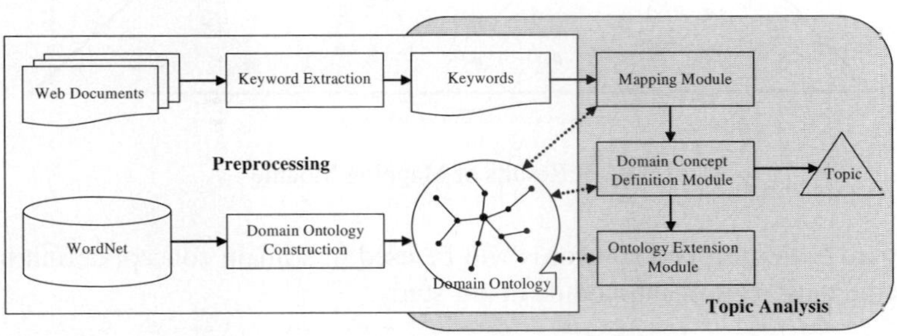

Fig. 3. The Overview of the Topic Selection of Web Documents

4.1 Mapping Module

In mapping module, the keywords will be mapped onto the ontology concepts. However, there are several keywords, which may not be mapped onto domain ontology concepts. In this case, we process an alternative way. It is to throw away keywords, which are not mapped onto domain ontology concepts and take the mapped keywords as the input data of the domain concept definition module. Figure 4 shows the flow of mapping module.

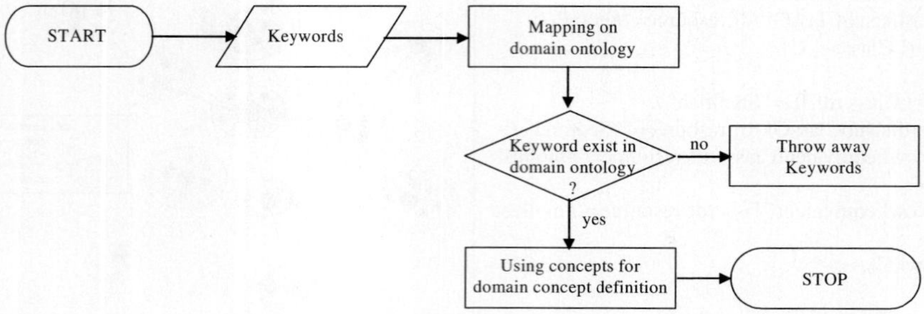

Fig. 4. Mapping Module

In mapping module, we input the keywords in sequence of the Term Frequency values. And then, we check keywords, which are mapped onto domain ontology concepts. Figure 5 shows the results after processing mapping module.

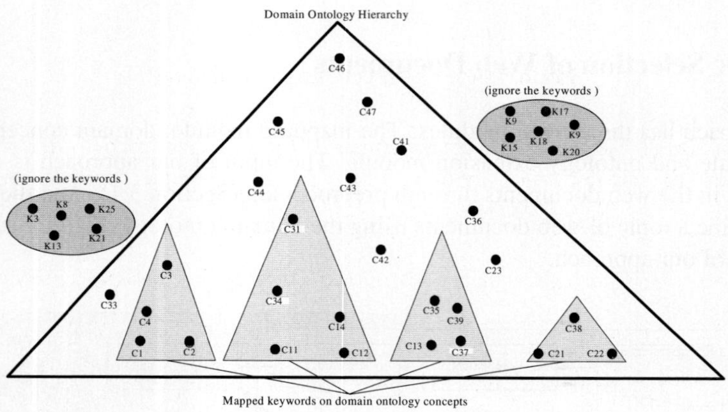

Fig. 5. Results of Mapping Module

In Figure 5, the mapped keywords will be used in domain concept definition module. It is the most significant module in our study.

4.2 Domain Concept Definition Module

As mentioned in Section 4.1 briefly, this module is the core of our approach. In domain concept definition module, we find a domain concept that will be determined as a topic in our study for web documents using the mapped keywords through mapping module. The domain concept is defined based on the ontology hierarchy. For selecting the topic, we use the formula as follows:

$$DomainConcept = \max_{c \in S(c_1, c_2)} \left[-\log P(c) \right]$$

Where, $S(c_1, c_2)$ is the set of concepts that subsume both c_1 and c_2. To maximize the representative, the similarity value is set to the content value of the node, whose *P(c)* value is the largest among these super classes.

For example, we use the keywords in Table 1. And we mapped the keywords onto the pre-constructed domain ontology in Section 3.2. Finally we apply the domain concept definition formula to select the topics of each document. Figure 6 illustrates the processing of the domain concept definition module based on the sample example.

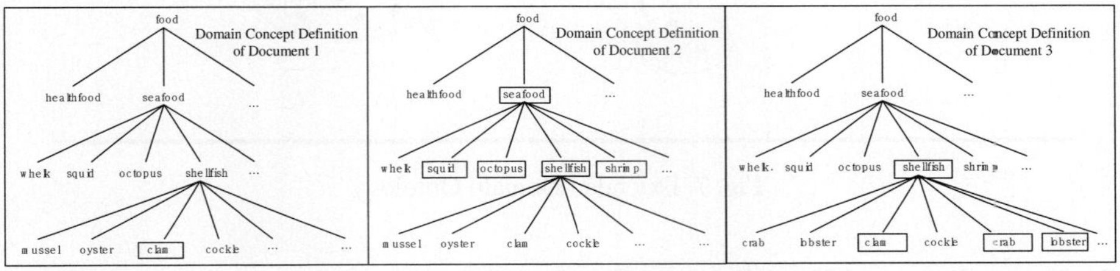

Fig. 6. Domain Concept Definition Module

Table 4 shows the selected domain concepts for web documents after processing the domain concept definition module. These concepts are the topics of the sample documents.

Table 4. Selected Topics of Documents after Processing Domain Concept Definition Module

	Document 1	Document 2	Document 3
Topic	clam	seafood	shellfish

4.3 Ontology Extension Module

For the efficient documents clustering, we need a method for managing the domain ontology. Therefore, we propose this module. In this module, we make relations (*hasURI, hasKeywords*) between nodes in domain ontology and web documents based on topics. Through our study, we select the topics of documents and we add the documents related to the domain ontology using the *hasURI and hasKeywords* relations. Figure 7 shows the structure of the extended domain ontology through ontology extension module.

As illustrated in Figure 7, domain ontology is very flexible and it is able to reconstruct automatically every time the document is analyzed.

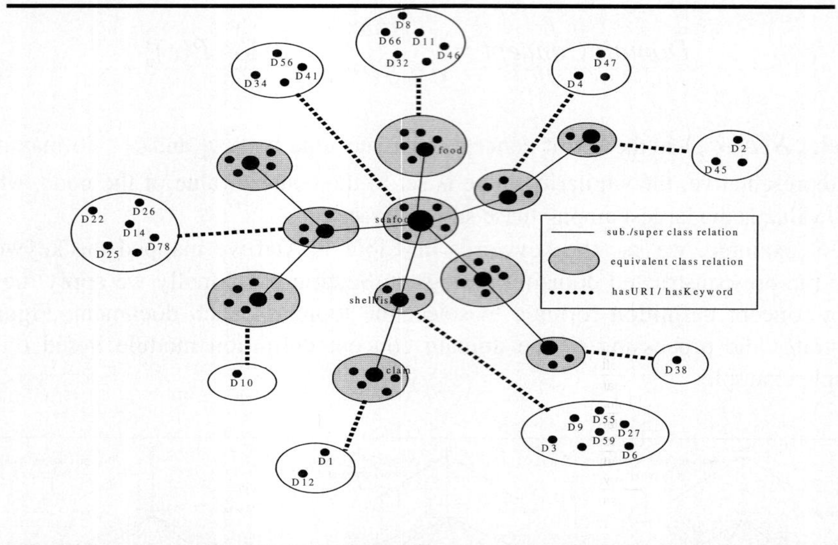

Fig. 7. Extended Domain Ontology

5 Experimental Results and Evaluation

This section describes the evaluation of our approach comparing with other two existing methods for topic selection. We tested our approach with 100 web documents searched from the *Yahoo!* about query 'clam'. These 100 web documents are the results gained through the query 'clam' in order of hit sequence. We measured the accuracy of the topic selection using a precision and recall formula as below: *Precision = hits / (hits + mistakes) and Recall = hits / total documents*. Table 5 shows the result of accuracy rate on the three approaches: TF values-based method, Title tag-based method and our proposed approach.

Table 5. Precision and Recall of Testing

Topic Selection	Our Approach	Title Tag-based	TF value-based
Precision	76.62 %	73.25 %	67.39 %
Recall	59 %	63 %	62 %

Table 6 shows the parts of the processing that we select the topics for the 100 web documents using the three methods.

Each approach's precisions are 76.62%, 73.25%, and 67.39%. Through the testing results, we realized that our approach obtained the highest accuracy rate for the topic selection of web documents. In testing, our approach extracted 476 keywords from the 100 web documents through the keyword extraction module. And 64.4%

Table 6. Topic selection of Web Documents using Three Approaches

Searched Web Documents(Yahoo!)	Term Frequency-based	Title Tag-based	Our Approach
beardedclamsociety.com	clam(11),society(4),man(2), founders(2),almighty(2)	Welcome to the BeardedClamSociety	Domain : clam
clam.it		idee che sprigionano calore	Domain : not defined
clamav.elektrapro.com	site(2),virusesdb(2),page(1), link(1),webmaster(1)	ClamAV website has Moved!	Domain : web
clamav.net	clamav(8),gmt(5),antivirus(5), story(5)	ClamAV: Project News	Domain : network
clamav.net/binary.html	clamav(24),packages(20), port(8),debian(7)	ClamAV: Binary packages	Domain : not defined
clamcorp.com	fish(5),trap(5),clam(5),yukon(1), site(1)	Portable Ice Fishing Shelters Clam and Fish Trap	Domain : seafood
clamwin.com	antivirus(11),clamwin(9), software(7),virus(7)	ClamWin Free Antivirus. GNU GPL Free Software Open Source Virus Scanner	Domain : computer
en.wikipedia.org/wiki/Clam	clam(20),wikipedia(69),razor(5), shell(3),article(3)	Clam - Wikipedia, the free encyclopedia	Domain : clam
enchantedlearning.com/subjects/invertebrates/bivalve/Clamprintout.shtml	clam(11),site(7),shells(4),year(3), click(3)	Clam-Enchanted Learning Software	Domain : shellfish
fatfree.com/recipes/soups/happy-clam-chowder	water(6),liquid(5),gluten(4), soy(4),milk(4)	happy-clam-chowder recipe from FatFree	Domain : liquid_food
iua.upf.es/mtg/clam	clam(12),framework(5),binary(4), major(4)	CLAM:: C++ Library for Audio and Music	Domain : clam
mimix.com	overview(14),partner(8), business(7),mimix(7)	MIMIX.com ~ High Availability, Data Protection, Disaster Recovery, Replication	Domain : business

keywords were mapped onto domain ontology concepts through mapping module. Finally, we had the highest precision and lowest recall rate. Thus, we expect the efficient topic selection for web documents using our approach.

6 Conclusion and Future Works

In this paper, we have shown how to use domain ontology in order to fine the topic of the web documents. We have compared our approach with other existing approaches, which are Term Frequency-based method and Title Tag-based method. Through the testing, we realized that our approach support more efficient topic selection than other methods. In the preprocessing of our approach, we propose the keyword extraction module and domain ontology building module. And we apply the extracted keywords and domain ontology for the topic selection of web documents. However, for future work, our topic selection prototype system intends to depend on the domain ontology so a large ontology should be implemented. The topic selection method will be designed to find important several topics per document.

References

1. Chekuri, C., Goldwasser, M.H, Raghavan, P., Upfal, E.: Web Search Using Automated Classification. Poster at the Sixth International World Wide Web Conference (WWW6) (1997)
2. Gelbukh, A., Sidorov, G., Guzman, A.: Use of a Weighted Topic Hierarchy for Document Classification. In Václav Matoušek et al (eds.): Text, Speech and Dialogue in Poc. 2nd International Workshop. Lecture Notes in Artificial Intelligence, No.92, ISBN 3-540-66494-7, Springer-Verlag., Czech Republic (1999) 130-135

3. Gövert, N., Lalmas, M., Fuhr, N.: A Probabilistic Description-Oriented Approach for Categorizing Web Document. Proceeding of the Eighth International Conference on Information Knowledge Management, Kansas City, MO USA (1999) 475-482
4. Greiner, R., Grove, A, Schuurmans, D.: On learning hierarchical Classifications (1997)
5. Grobelnik, M., Mladenic, D.: Fast Categorization. In Proceedings of Third International Conference on Knowledge Discovery Data Mining (1998)
6. Koller, D., Sahami, M.: Hierarchically Classifying Documents Using Very Few Words. In the Proceeding of Machine Learning (ICML-97) (1997) 170-176
7. Lee, J. Shin, D.: Multilevel Automatic Categorization for Webpages. The INET Proceeding '98 (1998)
8. Lin, C.Y, Hovy, E.: Identifying Topics by Position. In the Proceeding of The Workshop of Intelligent Scalable Text Summarization '97 (1997)
9. Lin, C.Y: Knowledge-based Automatic Topic Identification. In the Proceeding of The 33rd Annual Meeting of the Association for Computational Linguistics '95 (1995)
10. McCallum, A., Rosenfeld, R., Mitchell, T., Ng, Y.A.: Improving Text Classification by Shrinkage in a Hierarchy of Classes. Proceeding of the 15th Conference on Machine Learning (ICML-98) (1998)
11. Quek, C.Y, Mitchell, T: Classification of World Wide Web Documents. Seniors Honors Thesis, School of Computer Science, Carnegie Melon University (1998)
12. Scott, S., Matwin, S.: Text Classification using WordNet Hypernyms. In the Proceeding of Workshop – Usage of WordNet in Natural Language Processing Systems, Montreal, Canada (1998)

Speech Recognition Using Energy, MFCCs and Rho Parameters to Classify Syllables in the Spanish Language

Sergio Suárez Guerra, José Luis Oropeza Rodríguez, Edgardo Manuel Felipe Riveron, and Jesús Figueroa Nazuno

Computing Research Center, National Polytechnic Institute,
Juan de Dios Batiz s/n, P.O. 07038, Mexico
ssuarez@cic.ipn.mx, j_orope@yahoo.com.mx, edgardo@cic.ipn.mx, jfn@cic.ipn.mx

Abstract. This paper presents an approach for the automatic speech recognition using syllabic units. Its segmentation is based on using the Short-Term Total Energy Function (STTEF) and the Energy Function of the High Frequency (ERO parameter) higher than 3,5 KHz of the speech signal. Training for the classification of the syllables is based on ten related Spanish language rules for syllable splitting. Recognition is based on a Continuous Density Hidden Markov Models and the bigram model language. The approach was tested using two voice corpus of natural speech, one constructed for researching in our laboratory (experimental) and the other one, the corpus Latino40 commonly used in speech researches. The use of ERO and MFCCs parameter increases speech recognition by 5.5% when compared with recognition using STTEF in discontinuous speech and improved more than 2% in continuous speech with three states. When the number of states is incremented to five, the recognition rate is improved proportionally to 98% for the discontinuous speech and to 81% for the continuous one.

1 Introduction

Using the syllable as the information unit for automatic segmentation applied to Portuguese improved the error rate in word recognition, as reported by [1]. It provides the framework for incorporating the syllable in Spanish language recognition because both languages, Spanish and Portuguese, have as a common characteristic well structured syllable content [2].

The dynamic nature of the speech signal is generally analyzed by means of characteristic models. Segmentation-based systems offer the potential for integrating the dynamics of speech at the phoneme boundaries. This capability of the phonemes is reflected in the syllables, like it has been demonstrated in [3].

As in many other languages, the syllabic units in Spanish are defined by rules (10 in total), which establish 17 distinct syllabic structures. In this paper the following acronyms are used: Consonant – C, Vocal – V; thus, the syllabic structures are formed as CV, VV, CCVCC, etc.

A. Gelbukh and C.A. Reyes-Garcia (Eds.): MICAI 2006, LNAI 4293, pp. 1057 – 1066, 2006.

The use of syllabic units is motivated by:

- A more perceptual model and better meaning of the speech signal.
- A better framework when dynamic modeling techniques are incorporated into a speech recognition system [4].
- Advantages of using sub words (i.e. phonemes, syllables, triphones, etc) into speech recognition tasks [5]. Phonemes are linguistically well defined; the number of them is little (27 in the Spanish language) [6]. However, syllables serve as naturally motivated minimal units of prosodic organization and for the manipulation of utterances [7]. Furthermore, the syllable has been defined as "a sequence of speech sounds having a maximum or peak of inherent sonority (that is apart from factors such as stress and voice pitched) between two minima of sonority" [8]. The triphones treat the co-articulation problem to segment words structure as a more useful method not only in Spanish language. The triphones, like the syllables, are going to be nowadays as a good alternative for the speech recognition [5].

Table 1. Frequency of occurrence of ten monosyllables used in corpus Latino40

Word	Syllable configuration	Number of times	% in the vocabulary
De	Deaf Occlusive + Vocal	1760	11.15
La	Liquid + Vocal	1481	9.38
El	Vocal + Liquid	1396	8.85
En	Vocal + Nasal	1061	6.72
No	Nasal + Vocal	1000	6.33
Se	Fricative + Vocal	915	5.80
Que	Deaf Occlusive + Vocal	891	5.64
A	Vocal	784	4.97
Los	Liquid + Vocal + Fricative	580	3.67
Es	Vocal + Fricative	498	3.15

Table 2. Percentage of several syllabic structures in corpus Latino40

Syllable structure	Vocabulary Rate (%)	Accumulated in the vocabulary (%)
CV	50.72	50.72
CVC	23.67	74.39
V	5.81	80.2
CCV	5.13	85.33
VC	4.81	90.14
CVV	4.57	94.71
CVVC	1.09	95.8

The use of syllables has several potential benefits. First, syllabic boundaries are more precisely defined than phonetic segment boundaries in both speech waveforms and in spectrographic displays. Second, the syllable may serve as a natural organizational unit useful for reducing redundant computation and storage [4]. In [11] some works about corpus speech creation are discussed. There are not antecedents of speech recognition systems using the syllables rules in the training system for the Spanish language. Table 1 lists the frequencies of occurrence of ten monosyllables used in corpus Latino40 and its percentage in the vocabulary. Table 2 shows the percentage of several syllabic structures in corpus Latino40.

2 Continuous Speech Recognition Using Syllables

In automatic speech recognition research (ASR) the characteristics of each basic phonetic unit in a large extent are modified by co-articulation. As a result, the phonetic features found in articulated continuous speech, and the phonetic features found in isolated speech, have different characteristics. Using the syllables the problem is the same, but in our approach the syllables were directly extracted from the speech waveform, whose grammatical solution were found later using a dedicated expert system. Figure 1 shows the result of the segmentation using STTEF [3].

It can be noted that the energy is more significant when the syllable is present and it is a minimum when it is not. The resulting relative minimum and maximum energy are used as the potential syllabic boundaries. The term syllabic unit is introduced to differentiate between the syllables defined generally on the phonological level and the syllabic segments.

Thus, each syllable can be independently stored in a file. Our database uses 10 phrases with 51 different syllables. For each phrase 20 utterances were used, 50% for training and the remainder for recognition, and there were produced by a single female speaker at a moderate speaking rate.

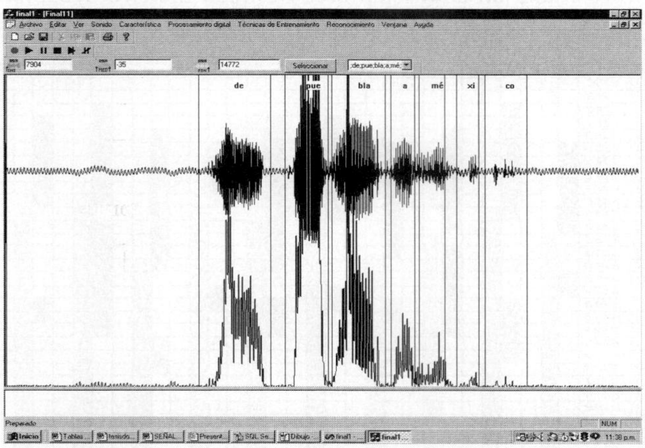

Fig. 1. Syllables speech segmentation labeling

3 Training Speech Model Using Data Segments

The Energy Function of the High Frequency (ERO parameter) is the energy level of the speech signal at high frequencies. The fricative letter, s, is the most significant example. When we use a high-pass filter, we obtain the speech signal above a given cut-off frequency f_c, the RO signal. In our approach, a cut-off frequency $f_c = 3500$ Hz is used as the threshold frequency for obtaining the RO signal. The speech signal at a lower frequency is attenuated. Afterwards, the energy is calculated from the Equation (1) for the ERO parameter in each segment of the resultant RO signal. Figure 2 shows graphically the results of this procedure for Short-Term Total Energy Function (STTEF) and ERO parameter in the case of the word 'cero'.

$$ERO = \sum_{i=0}^{N-1} ROi^2 \tag{1}$$

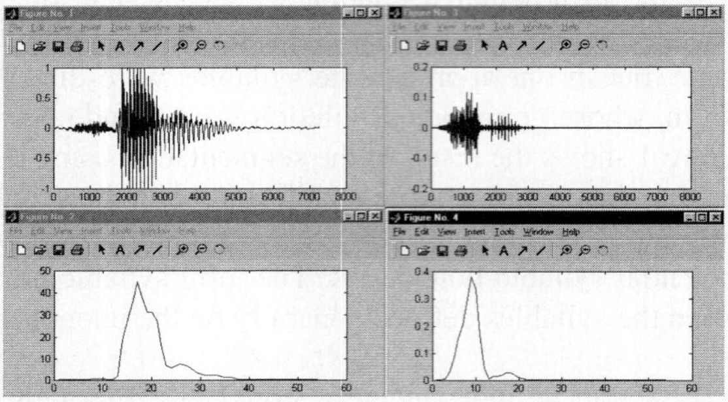

Fig. 2. STTEF (*left*) and ERO (*right*) parameters in the Spanish word 'cero'

Figure 3 shows the energy distribution for ten different words 'cero' spoken by the same speaker. We found an additional area between the two syllables (ce-ro) using

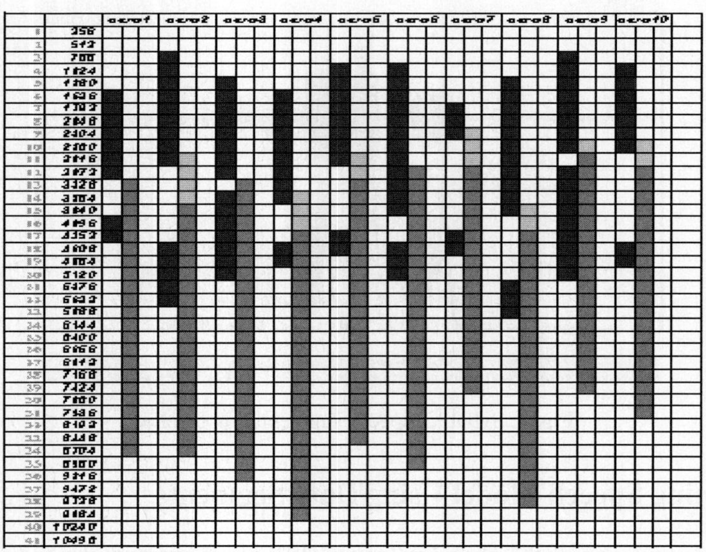

Fig. 3. Energy distribution for ten different words 'cero'

our analysis. In the figure, the dark gray rectangle represents the energy before using the filter, ERO; a medium gray rectangle the energy of the signal after using the filter, STTEF; and a light gray rectangle represents the transition region between both parameters. We call this region the Transition Energy Region -RO.

Figure 4 shows the functional block diagram representing the algorithm used in our approach to extract the signal characteristics.

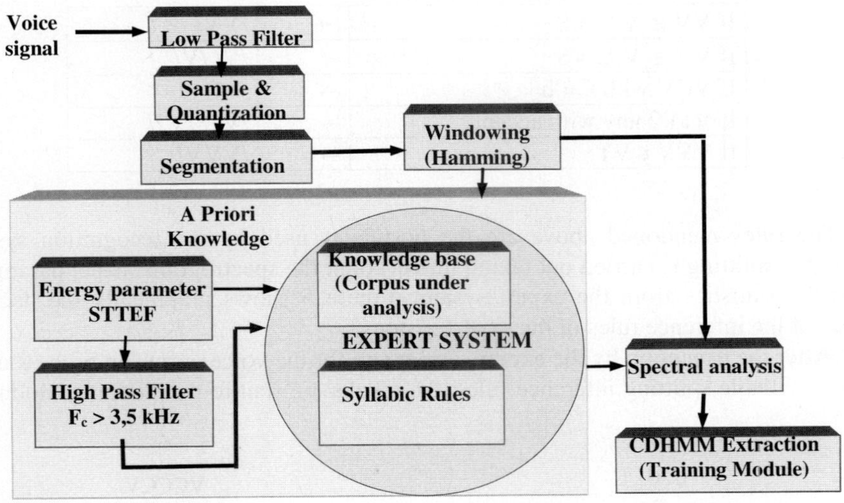

Fig. 4. Functional block diagram for syllable splitting

In the training phase an expert system uses the ten rules for syllable splitting in Spanish. It receives the energy components STTEF and the ERO parameter extracted from the speech signal. Table 3 shows the basic sets in Spanish used by the expert system for the syllable splitting. Table 4 shows the inference rules created in the expert system, associated with the rules for splitting words in syllables.

Table 3. Basic sets in Spanish used during the syllable splitting

CI = {br,bl,cr,cl,dr,fr,fl,gr,gl,kr,ll,pr,pl,tr,rr,ch,tl}	Non-separable Consonant
VD={ai,au,ei,eu,io,ou,ia,ua,ie,ue,oi,uo,ui,iu,ay,ey,oy}	Vocal Diphthong and hiatus
VA={a}	Open Vocal
VS={e,o}	Half-open Vocal
VC={i,u}	Close Vocal
CC={ll.rr,ch}	Compound Consonant
CS={b,c,d,f,g,h,j,k,l,m,n,ñ,p,q,r,s,t,v,w,x,y,z}	Simple Consonant
VT={iai, iei, uai, uei, uau, iau, uay, uey}	Vocal Triphthong and hiatus

Table 4. Inference rules of the expert system

Inference rules		
If CC ^ CC ∈ CI	→	/CC/
If VCV	→	/V/ /CV/
If VCCV	→	/VC/ /CV/
If VCCCV	→	/VCC/ /CV/
If C1C2 ^ C1='h' or C2='h'	→	/C1/ /C2/
If VV ∉ VA, VS	→	/VV/
If VV ∈ VA, VS	→	/V/ /V/
If VCV with C='h'	→	/VCV/
If V1V2 any with accent	→	/V1/ /V2/
If VVV ϵ VT	→	/VVV/

The rules mentioned above are the postulates used by the recognition system. Syllable splitting is carried out taking into account the spectrogram shape, parameters and the statistics from the expert system. Figure 5 shows graphically the decision trees of the inference rules of the expert system.

After the execution by the expert system and for the voice corpus in process of the entire syllable splitting inference rules, the results are sent to the Training Module as

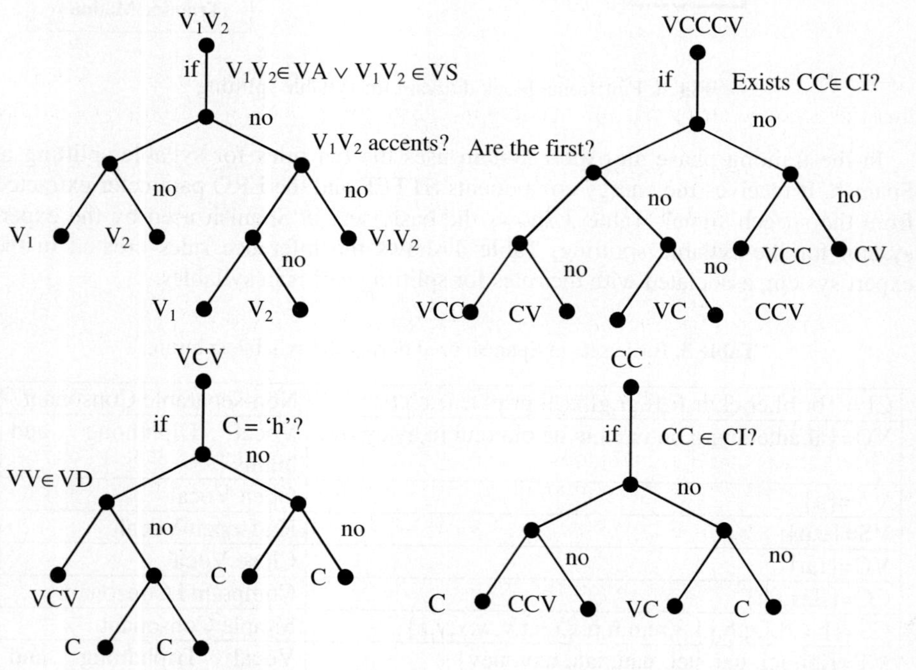

Fig. 5. Decision trees for the inference rules created in the expert system

the initial parameters. Then, the necessary models are created for each syllable during the process of recognition.

During the recognition phase, the Recognition Module receives the Cepstral Linear Prediction Coefficients from the signal in processes. They are used to calculate the probabilities of each element in the corpus. The recognized element is that with a higher probability. The final result of this process is the entire speech recognition.

4 Model for Continuous Speech Recognition

In our approach, speech recognition is based on a Hidden Markov Model (HMM) with Continuous Density and the bigram [5] like a language model described by Equation (2).

$$P(W) = P(w_1)\prod_{i=2}^{N} P(w_i|w_{i-1}) \tag{2}$$

Where W represents the words in the phrase under analysis w_1 on the corpus; w_i represents a word in the corpus; P (W) is the probability of the language model; $P(w_i)$ is the probability of a given word in the corpus. In automatic speech recognition it is common to use expression (3) to achieve better performance:

$$\overset{*}{W} = \arg\max\left[P(O|W)P(W)\right] \tag{3}$$

Here, $\overset{*}{W}$ represents the word string, based on the acoustic observation sequence, so that the decoded string has the maximum a posteriori probability *P (O|W)*, called the acoustic model.

Language models require the estimation of a priori probability *P(W)* of the word sequence $w = w_1 + w_2 + \cdots + w_N$. *P(W)* can be factorized as the following conditional probability:

$$P(W) = P(w_1 + w_2 + \cdots + w_N) = P(w_1)\sum_{i=1}^{N} P(w_i \mid w_{i-1}) \tag{4}$$

The estimation of such a large set of probabilities from a finite set of training data is not feasible.

The bigram model is based on the approximation based on the fact that a word only depends statistically on the temporally previous word. In the bigram model shown by the equation (2), the probability of the word $w^{(m)}$ at the generic time index *i* when the previous word is $w^{(m^1)}$ is given by:

$$\hat{P}(w_i = w^{(m)} \mid w_{i-1} = w^{m^1}) = \frac{N(w_i = w^{(m)} \mid w_{i-1} = w^{(m^1)})}{N(w^{m^1})} \tag{5}$$

where the numerator is the number of occurrences of the sequence $\left\langle w_i = w^{(m)}, w_{i-1} = w^{(m^1)} \right\rangle$ in the training set.

5 Experiments and Results

Taking into account the small redundancy of syllables in the corpus Latino40, we have designed a new experimental corpus with more redundant syllables units, prepared by two women and three men, repeating ten phrases twenty times each to give one thousand phrases in total.

Table 5 shows the syllables and the number of times each one appear in phrases of our experimental corpus.

Three Gaussian mixtures were used for each state in the HMM with three and five states, using twelve Mel Frequency Cepstral Coefficients (MFCCs). Tables 6 and 7 show the results of recognition for the discontinuous and continuous cases, respectively, referred to the experimental corpus. The accentuation of Spanish words was not considered in the analysis.

Table 5. Syllables and the number of each type into our experimental corpus

Syllable	#Items	Syllable	#Items	Syllable	#Items
de	2	es	3	zo	1
Pue	1	pa	2	rios	1
bla	1	cio	1	bio	1
a	5	e	2	lo	1
Me	1	o	1	gi	1
xi	1	ahu	1	cos	1
co	1	ma	2	el	1
cuauh	1	do	1	true	1
te	1	cro	1	que	1
moc	1	cia	1	ri	2
y	1	ta	1	ti	1
cuau	2	en	1	lla	1
tla	2	eu	1	se	2
mo	2	ro	1	ria	1
re	2	pro	1	po	1
los	1	to	1	si	1
ble	1	sis	1	tir	1

Table 6. Percentage of discontinuous recognition

Segmentation	Hidden Markov (%) with 3 states	Models states (%) with 5 states
STTEF	90	96
STTEF + ERO	95.5	98

Table 7. Percentage of continuous recognition

Segmentation	Hidden Markov(%) with 3 states	Models states (%) With 5 states
STTEF	78	79
STTEF + ERO	79.5	81

6 Conclusion

The results shown in this paper demonstrate that we can use the syllables as an alternative to the phonemes in an automatic speech recognition system (ASRS) for the Spanish language. The use of syllables for speech recognition avoids the contextual dependency found when phonemes are used.

In our approach we used a new parameter: the Energy Function of the Cepstral High Frequency parameter, ERO. The incorporation of a training module as an expert system using the STTEF and the ERO parameter, taking into account the ten rules for syllable splitting in Spanish, improved considerably the percent of success in speech recognition. The use of the ERO parameter increased by 5.5% the speech recognition with respect to the use of STTEF in discontinuous speech and by more than 2% in continuous speech with three states. When the number of states was incremented to five, the improvement in the recognition was increased to 98% for discontinuous speech and to 81% for continuous speech.

MFCCs and CDHMMs were used for training and recognition, respectively.

It was also demonstrated that comparing our results with [9], for English, we obtained a better percent in the number of syllables recognized when our new alternative for modeling the ASRS was used for the Spanish language.

The improvement of the results shows that the use of expert systems or conceptual dependency [10] is relevant in speech recognition of the Spanish language when syllables are used as the basic features for recognition.

References

1. Meneido H., Neto J. Combination of Acoustic Models in Continuous Speech Recognition Hybrid Systems, INESC, Rua Alves Redol, 9, 1000- 029 Lisbon, Portugal. 2000.
2. Meneido, H. Joâo P. Neto, J., and Luis B. Almeida, L., INESC-IST. Syllable Onset Detection Applied to the Portuguese Language. 6th European Conference on Speech Communication and Technology (EUROSPEECH'99) Budapest, Hungary, September 5-9. 1999.
3. Suárez, S., Oropeza, J.L., Suso, K., del Villar, M., Pruebas y validación de un sistema de reconocimiento del habla basado en sílabas con un vocabulario pequeño. Congreso Internacional de Computación CIC2003. México, D.F. 2003.
4. Su-Lin Wu, Michael L. Shire, Steven Greenberg, Nelson Morgan., Integrating Syllable Boundary Information into Speech Recognition. Proc. ICASSP, 1998.
5. Rabiner, L. and Juang, B-H., Fundamentals of Speech Recognition, Prentice Hall
6. Serridge, B., 1998. Análisis del Español Mexicano, para la construcción de un sistema de reconocimiento de dicho lenguaje. Grupo TLATOA, UDLA, Puebla, México. 1993.

7. Fujimura, O., UCI Working Papers in Linguistics, Volume 2, Proceedings of the South Western Optimality Theory Workshop (SWOT II), Syllable Structure Constraints, a C/D Model Perspective. 1996.
8. Wu, S., Incorporating information from syllable-length time scales into automatic speech recognition. PhD Thesis, Berkeley University, California. 1998.
9. Bilmes, J.A. A Gentle Tutorial of the EM Algorithm and its Application to Parameter Estimation for Gaussian Mixture and Hidden Markov Models, International Computer Science Institute, Berkeley, CA. 1998.
10. Savage Carmona Jesus, A Hybrid System with Symbolic AI and Statistical Methods for Speech Recognition, Doctoral Thesis, University of Washington. 1995.
11. Uraga, E. (1999), Modelado Fonético para un Sistema de Reconocimiento de Voz Contínua en Español, Tesis Maestría, ITESM Campus Cuernavaca, Maestría en Ciencias Computacionales.

Robust Text-Independent Speaker Identification Using Hybrid PCA&LDA

Min-Seok Kim[1], Ha-Jin Yu[1], Keun-Chang Kwak[2], and Su-Young Chi[2]

[1] School of Computer Science, University of Seoul,
Dongdaemungu Seoul, 130-743, Korea
{Ms, hjyu}@uos.ac.kr
[2] Human-Robot Interaction Research Team
Intelligent Robot Research Division
Electronics and Telecommunication Research Institute (ETRI), 305-700, Korea
{kwak, chisy}@etri.re.kr

Abstract. We have been building a text-independent speaker recognition system in noisy conditions. In this paper, we propose a novel feature using hybrid PCA/LDA. The feature is created from the convectional MFCC(mel-frequency cepstral coefficients) by transforming them using a matrix. The matrix consists of some components from the PCA and LDA transformation matrices. We tested the new feature using Aurora project Database 2 which is intended for the evaluation of algorithms for front-end feature extraction algorithms in background noise. The proposed method outperformed in all noise types and noise levels. It reduced the relative recognition error by 63.6% than using the baseline feature when the SNR is 15dB.

1 Introduction

As the need of security grows, speaker recognition which recognize who told some speech have a great potential to be excellent and convenient keys. However, the performance of the current speaker recognition technology has not reached the level of human expectation. The major difficulty in speaker recognition is the background noise which is not easily avoidable. In noisy environment, the performance of the system can be severely degraded. A lot of researches have been done for such environment, and numerous useful solutions have been found[2][3] such as cepstral subtraction and SNR-dependent cepstral normalization algorithm, but many of them need some prior knowledge of the condition, such as signal-to-noise ratio and characteristics of the noise. However, in real situations, we may not have enough time to acquire such information. In this research, we do not use any prior knowledge of the new environment for speaker identification. We use clean speech for speaker enrollment and test the system with speech data in various noise conditions without any additional adaptation session.

In this research, we propose a new feature using hybrid PCA/LDA approach. Principle component analysis (PCA) has been used successfully by many researchers to reduce the dimension of original feature vectors and reduce the computational cost [4-6]. Linear Discriminant Analysis (LDA) also has been used as a feature extraction

A. Gelbukh and C.A. Reyes-Garcia (Eds.): MICAI 2006, LNAI 4293, pp. 1067 – 1074, 2006.

method that provides a linear transformation of n-dimensional feature vectors into m-dimensional space ($m < n$), so that samples belonging to the same class are close together but samples from different classes are far apart from each other [7]. Openshaw and et. al. [8] showed that the linear discriminant analysis combination of MFCC and PLP-RASTA gives the best performance.

In this research, we propose a feature extracted by using hybrid PCA/LDA. PCA seeks a projection that best represents the data, and LDA seeks a projection that best separates the data [11]. If we combine the two results, we can expect the noise robustness from PCA which finds the uncorrelated directions of maximum variances in the data space that are invariant to noisy condition, and also expect discriminant capability from LDA.

The idea of hybrid PCA/LDA is introduced for face recognition. Su and et. al. [9] proposed a face recognition algorithm using hybrid feature. In their process, principal component analysis and linear discriminant analysis features of frequency spectrum are extracted, which are taken as the input of the RBFN (radius base function network). Zhao and et. al. [10] described a face recognition method which consists of two steps: first they project the face image from the original vector space to a face subspace via PCA, and then they use LDA to obtain a best linear classifier.

In this paper, we use the similar approach as in [9], but we select some components of the PCA/LDA transformation vectors and used Gaussian mixture models as the speaker identifier.

The rest of the paper is organized as follows. In the next session, we introduce the baseline speaker recognition system using Gaussian Mixture model which is very well known to many researchers in speaker recognition. This is followed by the description of the PCA and LDA. In section 3 we describe the feature transformation methods using hybrid PCA/LDA that we propose to improve the performance. Section 4 then presents some description of the experiment condition we use to define our goal and the experimental results. Finally, Section 5 gives the summary and conclusions.

2 The Baseline Speaker Identification System Using GMM

To build speaker models, we use Gaussian mixture models which are the most prevalent approach.

2.1 Gaussian Mixture Model (GMM) [12]

Gaussian mixture models (GMMs) are the most prominent approach for modeling in text-independent speaker recognition applications. In GMM, each speaker's acoustic parameter distribution is represented by a speaker dependent mixture of Gaussian distributions,

$$p(\mathbf{x} \mid \lambda) = \sum_{i=1}^{M} w_i g_i(\mathbf{x}), \qquad \sum_{i=1}^{M} w_i = 1 \tag{1}$$

where M is the number of mixtures, w_i mixture weights and Gaussian densities g_i are,

$$g_i(\mathbf{x}) = \frac{1}{(2\pi)^{D/2} |\Sigma_i|^{1/2}} \exp\left\{-\frac{1}{2}(\mathbf{x}-\boldsymbol{\mu}_i)^T \Sigma_i^{-1} (\mathbf{x}-\boldsymbol{\mu}_i)\right\}. \quad (1)$$

Maximum likelihood parameters are estimated using the EM algorithm. For speaker identification, the log-likelihood of a model given an utterance $X = \{\boldsymbol{x}_1, ..., \boldsymbol{x}_T\}$ is computed and the speaker associated with the most likely model for the input utterance is chosen as the recognized speaker $\hat{S}$.

$$\hat{S} = \arg\max_{1\le k\le S} \sum_{t=1}^{T} \log p(\mathbf{x}_t | \lambda_k) \quad (2)$$

2.2 Principal Component Analysis (PCA)

Principal component analysis is a linear orthogonal transform that can remove the correlation among the vector components. It is used to reduce the dimension of the feature vector so that the processing time and space can be reduced. It processes the training feature vectors by the following steps.

Step 1. Subtract the mean from each of the data dimensions.
Step 2. Calculate the covariance matrix.
Step 3. Calculate the eigenvectors and eigenvalues of the covariance matrix. We use unit eigenvectors, that is, their lengths are all one. The eigenvectors are perpendicular to each other.
Step 4. Choose components and form a transformation matrix $\boldsymbol{w}$. The eigenvector with the highest eigenvalues is the direction with the greatest variance. We order them by eigenvalue and take the k eigenvectors with the highest eigenvalues, and form a matrix $\boldsymbol{w}$ with these eigenvectors in the columns.
Step 5. Transform the feature vectors using the transformation matrix formed in step 4.

$$TransformedData = \boldsymbol{w} \times RowData \quad (3)$$

2.3 Linear Discriminant Analysis (LDA)[11]

While PCA seeks directions that are efficient for representation, discriminant analysis seeks directions that are efficient for discrimination. For LDA, we first define within-class scatter and between-class scatter. Then we seek a transformation matrix **W** that maximizes the ratio of the between-class scatter to the with-class scatter.

3 The Proposed Hybrid PCA/LDA Feature

Our feature is based on the 63 dimensional feature vectors which consist of 20th order mel-frequency cepstral coefficients (MFCC) [3] with energy and their first and second derivatives. The proposed features are transformed via the matrix consists of the mixture of components from PCA and LDA transformation matrices as follows:

Select n components with the highest eigenvalues from the PCA transformation matrix and m components with highest eigenvalues from the LDA transformation matrix, where $n + m = 63$.

Figure 1 depicts this process. The hybrid features are labeled as:

$$\mathrm{P}n\mathrm{L}m$$

where n is the number of components from PCA transformation matrix and m is the number of the components from LDA transformation matrix.

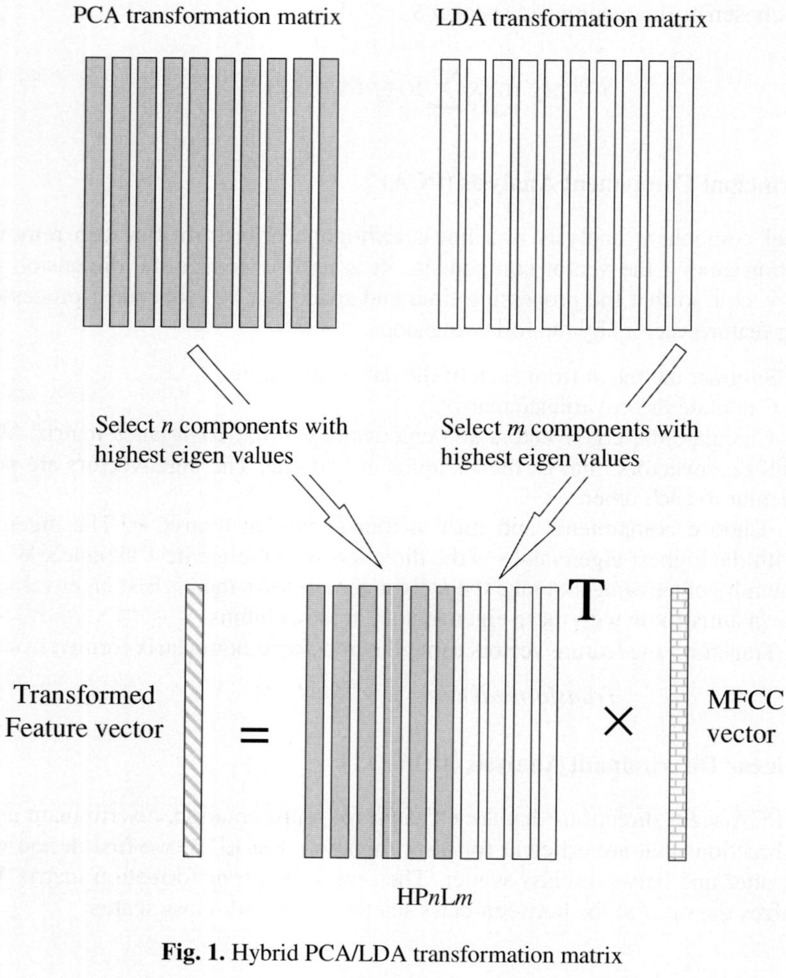

Fig. 1. Hybrid PCA/LDA transformation matrix

4 Experimental Evaluation of the Proposed System

We used the Aurora project Database 2.0 which is a revised version of the Noisy TI digits database distributed by ELDA. ELDA (Evaluations and Language resources Distribution Agency) is set up to identify, classify, collect, validate and produce the language resources which may be needed by the HLT (Human Language Technology) community. The database is intended for the evaluation of algorithms for front-end feature extraction algorithms in background noise. The TI digits database contains speech which was originally designed and collected at Texas Instruments, Inc. (TI) for the purpose of designing and evaluating algorithms for speaker-independent recognition of connected digit sequences. There are 326 speakers (111 men, 114 women, 50 boys and 51 girls) each pronouncing 77 digit sequences. The corpus was collected at TI in 1982 in a quiet acoustic enclosure using an Electro-Voice RE-16 Dynamic Cardiod microphone, digitized at 20kHz. In Aurora project Database 2.0, "Clean" corresponds to TIdigits training data downsampled to 8 kHz and filtered with a G712 characteristic. "Noisy" data corresponds to TIdigits training data downsampled to 8 kHz, filtered with a G712 characteristic and noise artificially added at several SNRs (20dB, 15dB, 10 dB, 5dB).

Four noises are used:

- recording inside a subway
- babble
- car noise
- recording in an exhibition hall

In all 326 speakers, we used 110 speakers who are designated as the training set by ELDA. From the files in “TRAIN” folders in the data CDs, we selected the sentences consist of more than four digits in “CLEAN” folders as training data, and used the sentences consist of more than five digits in the rest of the folders as test data. The folders used as test data are the folders of noisy data (N1_SNR5 ~ N4_SNR20). The length of the training data is about 90 msec per a speaker. The total number of test utterances is 450. We used 20th order mel-frequency cepstral coefficients (MFCC) [3] with energy and their first and second derivatives as the basis feature.

Table 1 through 4 show the recognition rates using different feature transformation methods in different noise levels. The result is obtained using Gaussian mixture models with 128 mixtures. Figure 2 shows the speaker recognition rate of each method

Table 1. Recognition rate of baseline feature

	BaseLine				
	Subway	Babble	Car	Exhibition	Average
20 dB	100.00	100.00	100.00	100.00	100.00
15 dB	95.45	100.00	96.61	96.92	97.25
10 dB	63.01	80.33	62.16	60.95	66.61
5 dB	25.64	33.33	19.18	26.85	26.25
Average	71.03	78.42	69.49	71.18	72.53

averaged for all kinds of noises. They show that our proposed hybrid PCA/LDA transformation gives the best performance than using PCA or LDA in all noise levels and all kinds of noises. It reduced the relative recognition error by 63.6% than using the baseline feature when the SNR is 15dB.

In these experiments, the transformation matrix with 62 components from the PCA transformation matrix and one component with the highest eigen value from the LDA transformation matrix (P62L1) gives the best result among all the hybrid combinations (P62L1, P61L2, P60L3, … , P3L60, P2L61, P1L62).

Table 2. Recognition rate of PCA derived feature

	PCA				
	Subway	Babble	Car	Exhibition	Average
20 dB	100.00	100.00	100.00	100.00	100.00
15 dB	99.09	99.17	99.15	98.46	98.97
10 dB	68.79	85.79	70.27	57.40	70.56
5 dB	19.66	36.59	18.49	17.59	23.08
Average	71.89	80.39	71.98	68.36	73.15

Table 3. Recognition rate of LDA derived feature

	LDA				
	Subway	Babble	Car	Exhibition	Average
20 dB	94.12	100.00	99.19	92.19	96.38
15 dB	70.91	95.04	88.14	74.62	82.18
10 dB	35.84	62.30	70.27	30.77	49.80
5 dB	9.40	17.07	6.16	7.41	10.01
Average	52.57	68.6	65.94	51.25	59.59

Table 4. Recognition rate of hybrid PCA/LDA derived feature

	Hybrid PCA/LDA (P62L1)				
	Subway	Babble	Car	Exhibition	Average
20 dB	100.00	100.00	100.00	100.00	100.00
15 dB	99.09	100.00	100.00	96.92	99.00
10 dB	67.63	84.70	75.68	60.95	72.24
5 dB	29.91	43.90	22.60	25.93	30.59
Average	74.16	82.15	74.57	70.95	75.46

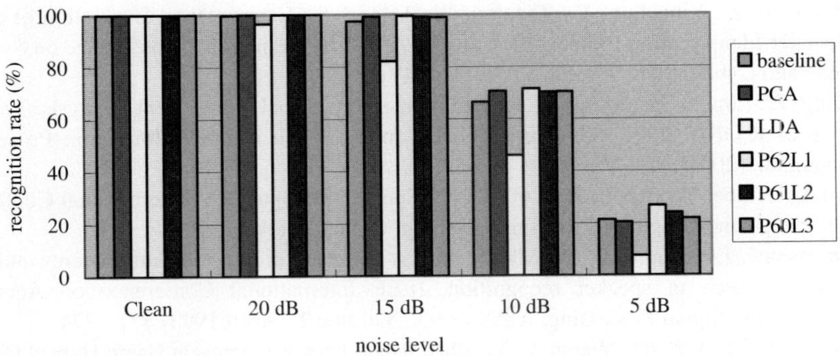

Fig. 2. Speaker recognition rate of each method averaged for all kinds of noises

5 Conclusions

This paper has presented a speaker recognition system in noisy conditions. The goal of our research is to build a system that can perform moderately well in noisy conditions without any prior knowledge about the new situation or adaptation process. In this paper we proposed a new feature transformation method via hybrid PCA/LDA. The feature is created from the convectional MFCC(mel-frequency cepstral coefficients) by transforming them using a matrix. The matrix consists of some components from the PCA and LDA transformation matrices. We tested the new feature using Aurora project Database 2 which is intended for the evaluation of algorithms for front-end feature extraction algorithms in background noise. The proposed method is very simple but gives a relative error reduction of 63.6% than using the baseline feature when the SNR is 15dB. We are planning to apply this method to speaker verification.

Acknowledgement

This work was supported by the robot project of Intelligent Robot Research Division in Electronics and Telecommunication Research Institute (ETRI).

References

1. Campbell, J.P.: Speaker Recognition: A Tutorial, Proceedings of the IEEE, Vol 85, No 9, (1997) 1437-1462.
2. Acero, A.: Acoustical and Environmental Robustness in Automatic Speech Recognition, Kluwer Academic Publishers, Boston, (1993)
3. Huang, X., Acero, A., Hon, H.: Spoken Language Processing, A Guide to Theory, Algorithm, and System Development, Prentice Hall, (2001)
4. Tsai, S.-N., Lee, L.-S.: Improved Robust Features for Speech Recognition by Integrating Time-Frequency Principal Components (TFPC) and Histogram Equalization (HEQ), 2003 IEEE Workshop on Automatic Speech Recognition and Understanding, (2003) 297 – 302.

5. Wanfeng, Z., Yingchun, Y., Zhaohui, W., Lifeng, S,: Experimental Evaluation of a New Speaker Identification Framework using PCA, IEEE International Conference on Systems, Man and Cybernetics, Volume 5, (2003) 4147 – 4152.
6. Ding, P., Liming, Z.: Speaker Recognition using Principal Component Analysis, Proceedings of ICONIP 2001, 8th International Conference on Neural Information Processing, Shanghai, (2001)
7. Jin, Q, Waibel, A.: Application of LDA to Speaker Recognition," International Conference on Speech and Language Processing, Beijing, China, October. 2000.
8. Openshaw, J.P., Sun, Z.P. and Mason, J.S.; A comparison of composite features under degraded speech in speaker recognition, IEEE International Conference on Acoustics, Speech, and Signal Processing, ICASSP-93., Volume 2, (April 1993) 371 - 374
9. Su, H.-T., Feng, D.-D., Wang, X.-Y., Zhao R.-C.: Face Recognition Using Hybrid Feature, Proceedings of the Second International Conference on Machine Learning and Cybernetics, Xi'an, (November 2003) 3045-3049
10. Zhao, W., Chellappa, R., Krishnaswamy, A.: Discriminant analysis of principal components for face recognition, Proceedings of the Third IEEE International Conference on Automatic Face and Gesture Recognition, (April 1998) 336 - 341
11. Duda, R. O., Hart, P. E., Stork, D. G.: *Pattern Classification (2nd Edition)*, Wiley-Interscience, 2000
12. Reynolds, D.A., Rose, R.C.: Robust Text-Independent Speaker Identification Using Gaussian Mixture Speaker Models, IEEE Transactions on Speech Audio Processing, vol. 3, no. 1, (1995) 72-83.

Hybrid Algorithm Applied to Feature Selection for Speaker Authentication

Rocío Quixtiano-Xicohténcatl[1], Orion Fausto Reyes-Galaviz[1], Leticia Flores-Pulido[1], and Carlos Alberto Reyes-García[2]

[1] Universidad Autónoma de Tlaxcala, Facultad de Ciencias Básicas, Ingeniería y Tecnología, México
ic20012063@alumnos.ingenieria.uatx.mx, {orionfrg, aicitel}@ingenieria.uatx.mx

[2] Instituto Nacional de Astrofísica, Óptica y Electrónica, México
kargaxxi@inaoep.mx

Abstract. One of the speaker authentication problems consists on identifying a person only by means of his/her voice. To obtain the best authentication results, it is very important to select the most relevant features from the speech samples, this because we think that not all of the characteristics are relevant for the authentication process and also that many of these data might be redundant. This work presents the design and implementation of a Genetic-Neural algorithm for feature selection used on a speaker authentication task. We extract acoustic features such as Mel Frequency Cepstral Coefficients, on a database composed by 150 recorded voice samples, and a genetic feature selection system combined with a time delay feed-forward neural network trained by scaled conjugate gradient back propagation, to classify/authenticate the speaker. We also show that after the hybrid system finds the best solution, it almost never looses it, even when the search space changes. The design and implementation process, the performed experiments, as well as some results are shown.

Keywords: Speaker Authentication, Search Space, Feed-Forward, Hybrid System, Genetic Algorithms.

1 Introduction

Speaker authentication is the process of verifying the claimed identity of a speaker based on his/her voice characteristics or the informational content of his/her voice. For example, if a person is trying to be another and gives a sample of his voice; the process will know if there's a match, accepting or denying that person.

In the speaker recognition and authentication fields, most of the techniques used deal with feature extraction, feature selection, and reduction of dimensionality. These tasks generally analyze the signal in terms of time and frequency domains. Researches of these fields deal generally with problems where the number of features to be processed is quite large. They also try to eliminate environmental noise conditions or noise produced by recording devices, redundant information, and other undesirable conditions which may decrease the recognition accuracy.

A. Gelbukh and C.A. Reyes-Garcia (Eds.): MICAI 2006, LNAI 4293, pp. 1075–1084, 2006.

This work proposes a method to select and extract the best features to represent a speech sample, which uses genetic algorithms combined with feed forward neural networks, to accomplish this purpose. The genetic algorithm uses elitist methods, crossover and mutation operations to generate new populations of individuals, and combines neural networks to obtain the individuals' fitness value at each generation. The proposed algorithm has the particularity that in each generation, the search space is changed in order to adapt the genetic algorithm, not only to a specific search area, but to a more global search area. This work proves, that when the best individual is found, the algorithm almost never looses it, even when the search space is changed at every generation.

Several results were obtained by making different kinds of experiments; they consist on changing the crossover rate, mutation rate, number of generations, and number of individuals. From them a recognition percentage of up to 93.48% has been reached on the authentication of fifteen different speakers. On the other hand, a vector reduction of almost 50% was achieved when applying the complete algorithm.

On the next section we will present a review of prior comparative studies on the speaker authentication field. Section 3 details the fundamental basis in speaker authentication process and describes our proposed system. Section 4 deals with acoustic processing and our feature extraction method which uses the Mel Frequency Cepstral Coefficients (MFCCs) method [1]. A fundamental theory on speaker pattern classification, time delay feed forward neural networks, genetic algorithms, and our proposed hybrid system is given in Section 5. The complete system description is on Section 6. Our experimental results and comments are presented in Sections 7 and 8.

2 State of the Art

Recently, some research efforts have been made in the speaker recognition and authentication fields, showing promising results. Miramontes de León used the Vector Quantization method in text-independent speaker recognition tasks, applied to phone threats; he reduced the search space and obtained a recognition percentage between 80 and 100% [2]. Pelecanos, used the Gaussian Mixture Model combined with a Vector Quantization method, for relatively well-clustered data, obtaining a training time equivalent to 20% less of the time taken with the standard method, composed by Gaussian Mixture Models, and achieving an accuracy percentage of 90% [3]. Hsieh used the Wavelet Transform combined with Gaussian Mixture Models to process Chinese language, using voice samples from phone calls, and reached an accuracy of 96.81% [4]. Oh obtained a dimensionality reduction, applied on voice, text, numbers, and images patterns, by using a simple genetic algorithm; a Hybrid Genetic Algorithm combined with a one-layer Neural Network, and sequential search algorithms, he obtained a recognition result of 96.72% [5]. Ha-Jin used MFCCs for feature extraction of voice samples, Principal Component Analysis for dimensionality reduction, and Gaussian Mixture Models for classification, obtaining an accuracy of 100%; this

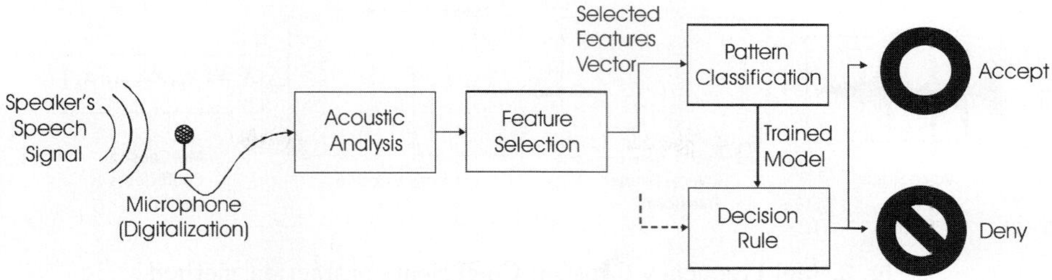

Fig. 1. Speaker Authentication System

method classifies the voice samples but doesn't discriminate an intruder [6]. The results reported on these works highlight the advances done in the exploration of this field.

3 Speaker Authentication Process

The speaker authentication process is basically a pattern recognition problem, and it is similar to speech recognition. The goal is to take the speaker's sound wave as an input, and at the end authenticate the speaker's name. Generally, the Speaker authentication process is done in two steps; the first step is the acoustic processing, or features extraction, while the second is known as pattern processing or classification. In the proposed system, we have added an extra step between both of them, called feature selection (Fig. 1). For our case, in the acoustic analysis, the speaker's signal is processed to extract relevant features in function of time. The feature set obtained from each speech sample is represented by a vector, and each vector is taken as a pattern. Next, all vectors go to an acoustic features selection module, which will help us select the best features for the training process, and at the same time to efficiently reduce the input vectors. The selection is done through the use of genetic algorithms. As for the pattern recognition methods, four main approaches have been traditionally used: pattern comparison, statistical models, knowledge based systems, and connectionist models. We focus in the use of the last one.

4 Acoustic Processing

The acoustic analysis implies the application and selection of filter techniques, feature extraction, signal segmentation, and normalization. With the application of these techniques the signal is described in terms of its fundamental components. One speech signal is complex and codifies more information than the one needed to be analyzed and processed in real time applications. For this reason, in our speaker authentication system we use a feature extraction function as a first plane processor. Its input is a speech signal, and its output is a vector of features that characterizes key elements of the speech sound wave. In this

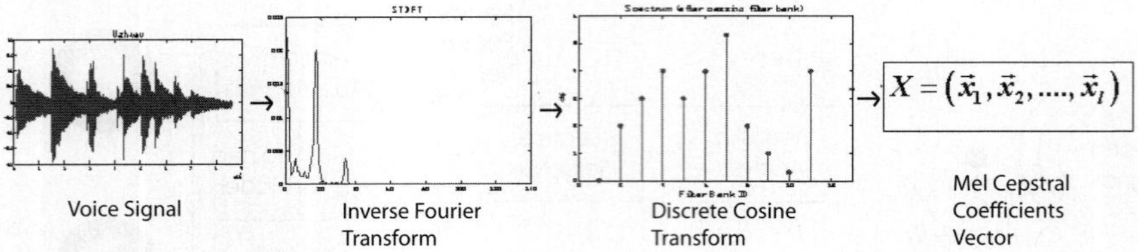

Fig. 2. Mel Frequency Cepstral Coefficients extraction method

work we used Mel Frequency Cepstral Coefficients (MFCC) [1] as our feature extraction method.

4.1 Mel Frequency Cepstral Coefficients

The first step of speech processing, once we have the voice samples, is to obtain (from these samples) the spectral characteristics. This step is necessary because the important information of the sample is codified in the frequency domain, and the speech samples are recorded by means of electronic devices in the time domain. When the time domain is converted to the frequency domain we obtain the parameters which indicate the occurrence of each frequency.

There is a wide variety of ways to represent the speech samples in their parametric form. One of the most commonly used on speaker authentication tasks are MFCCs. The human ear decomposes the received sound signals in its fundamental frequencies. Located in the inner ear we find the cochlea which has a conic spiral form. This is one of the three cavities that form the physical structure of the ear [7]. This cochlea filters the frequencies in a natural way. The sound waves are introduced inside this structure bouncing on its walls and getting inside the spiral with low or high frequency, taking into account each wave length of the frequency [8].

MFCCs are based on the frequency response the human ear perceives. This method behaves as a filter bank linearly distributed in low frequencies and with logarithmic spacing on the higher frequencies. This is called the Mel Frequency Scale, which is linear below 1000 Hz, and logarithmic above 1000 Hz (Fig. 2) [2].

5 Speaker Pattern Classification

After extracting the acoustic features of each speech sample, feature vectors are obtained; each one of these vectors represents a pattern. These vectors are later used for the feature selection and the classification processes. For the present work, we focused on connectionist models, also known as neural networks, to classify these vectors (patterns). They are reinforced with genetic algorithms to select the best features of the vector in order to improve the training/testing process, obtaining with this, a more efficient Genetic-Neural hybrid classification system.

5.1 Genetic Algorithms

During the last years, there has been a growing interest on problem solving systems based on the evolution and hereditary principles. Such systems maintain a population of potential solutions, they use selection processes based on fitness of individuals which compose that population, and genetic operators. The evolutionary program is a probabilistic algorithm which maintains a population of individuals, $P(t) = x_1^t, ..., x_n^t$ for an iteration t. Each individual represents a potential solution to the problem. Each solution x_i^t is evaluated to give a measure of its fitness. Then, a new population (iteration $t+1$) is formed by selecting the fitter individuals (select step). Some members of the new population undergo transformations (alter step) by means of genetic operators to generate new solutions. There are unitary transformations m_i (mutation type), which create new individuals by performing small changes in a single individual ($m_i : S \rightarrow S$), and higher order transformations c_j (crossover type), which create new individuals by combining genetic information of several (two or more) individuals ($cj : S_{x \ldots S \rightarrow S}$). After a number of generations, the program converges. It is hoped that the best individual represents a near optimum (reasonable) solution [9].

5.2 Neural Networks

Artificial neural networks (ANN) are widely used on pattern classification tasks, showing good performance and high accuracy results. In general, an artificial neural network is represented by a set of nodes and connections (weights). The nodes are a simple representation of a natural neural network while the connections represent the data flow between the neurons. These connections or weights are dynamically updated during the network's training. In this work, we will use the Feed Forward Time Delay Neural Network model, selected because this model has shown good results in the voice recognition field [10].

5.3 Feed-Forward Time Delay Neural Network

Input Delay refers to a delay in time, in other words, if we delay the input signal by one time unit and let the neural network receive both the original and the delayed signals, we have a simple time delay neural network. This neural network was developed to classify phonemes in 1987 by Weibel and Hanazawa [11].

The Feed-Forward Time Delay neural network doesn't fluctuate with changes; the features inside the sound signal can be detected no matter in which position they are in. The time delays let the neural network find a temporal relation directly in the input signal and in a more abstract representation of the hidden layer. It does this by using the same weights for each step in time [10].

5.4 Scaled Conjugate Gradient Back-Propagation

The neural network's training can be done through a technique known as back-propagation. The scaled conjugate methods are based on the general optimization strategy. We use scaled conjugate gradient back-propagation (SCGBP) to train the neural networks because this algorithm shows a lineal convergence on most of the problems. It uses a mechanism to decide how far it will go on a specific direction, and avoids the time consumption on the linear search by a learning iteration, making it one of the fastest second order algorithms [12].

5.5 Hybrid System

We designed a genetic algorithm, an evolutionary program to reduce the number of input features by selecting the most relevant characteristics of the vectors, used on the classification process. The whole feature selection process is described in the following paragraphs.

As we mentioned before, we obtain an original matrix by putting together every vector obtained by each speech sample. Then, to work with our hybrid system, we firstly unite together a speaker's samples. Each speaker has ten speech samples, and there are 15 different speakers, this means that we have 150 samples belonging to 15 different classes. After each class is united, we first shuffle its columns randomly and separate 70% of that class for training and 30% for testing, each piece, altogether with the other classes, builds a training matrix and a testing matrix, providing a different training data set on each experiment. After building the training matrix, and before training the neural network, we shuffle it again, to assure that all the labels are not in sequential order.

Having done this, we obtain a training matrix of size $p \times q$, where p is the number of acoustic features of each speech sample, and q is the number of samples. We want to reduce this matrix to a size $m \times q$, where m is the number of randomly selected characteristics. In order to do this, we first need to generate randomly an initial population of n individuals, each having a length of p. These individuals are represented by a randomly generated binary code. We then use these individuals to generate n different matrices, simply by comparing each row of every individual with each row of the training matrix. If number "1" appears in any row of any given individual, then we must take the whole row of the training matrix that corresponds to that individual's row, if there's a "0", we do not take that particular row. In this sense, that's the way an individual reduces the training matrix to n smaller matrices. The row dimension of the matrix can be calculated simply by adding all the "1s" of each individual. The column dimension never changes.

After doing this, we generate n different neural networks, which will be trained by the n generated matrices. Obtaining with these n different results, this will be later used, as the fitness function, to select the best individuals that achieved the best accuracy, from that generation. To choose which individuals are going to pass to the next generation, we simply sort them from the best result to the worst. Next we eliminate the individuals that gave the worst results by using elitism on the bottom half of the individuals in a given generation. Having the best half of individuals chosen, we create a new generation using the roulette algorithm. Then we perform crossover and mutation operations on the new generation of individuals. At this point we considered that the best individual of each generation passes to the next generation unchanged.

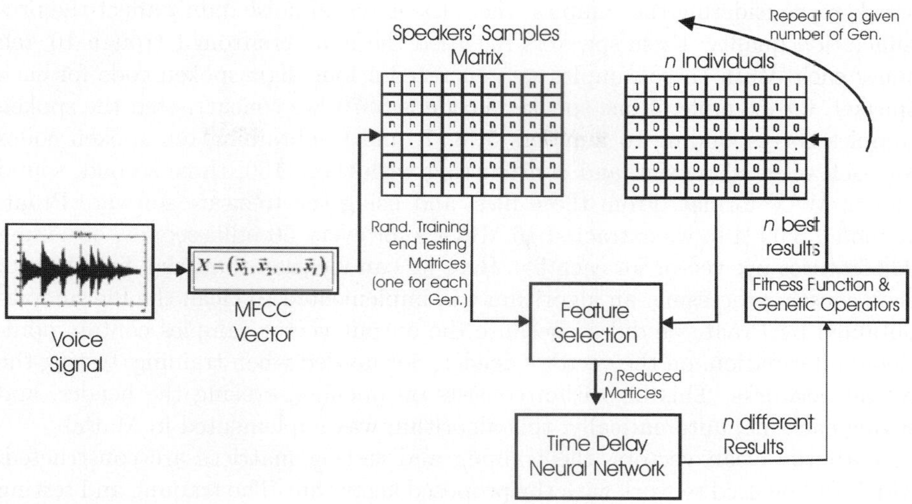

Fig. 3. Schematic design of the Hybrid System

For every two newly generated parents, we generate a random number that goes from 0 to 1, we then compare this number to our crossover rate, if the number is smaller that the crossover rate, those parents will suffer a crossover operation. This means that we combine the information contained in both individuals to generate two offspring with information of the original parents. If the randomly generated number is bigger than our crossover rate, we let those individuals pass to the next generation unchanged.

After doing so, for every offspring, we generate a random number that goes from 0 to 1, we compare this number to our mutation rate, if the number is smaller than this rate, the individual is mutated. To do this, we generate a random number that goes from 1 to p, that number represents a row of the individual, if there's a number "1" in that row, we change it to "0" and vice versa. If the number is bigger than our mutation rate, we let this individual pass to the next generation unchanged.

When we have the new generation of individuals, we eliminate the training and testing data set and randomly generate a new one, in order to change the search space. We do this step to avoid an over fitting of the hybrid system on a particular search space (Fig. 3).

We repeat these steps for a given number of generations stated by the user. At the end we obtain an individual that represents the selected features to be kept to obtain good accuracy results.

6 System Implementation

The database is composed of 47,304 speech samples containing the digits and other set of isolated words [13]. For our experiments, we selected 15 different speakers, considering the samples where the external noise didn't affect the pronunciation quality; these speakers recorded the numbers from 1 trough 10, ten times each. With these samples we generated a four digit spoken code for each speaker, for example, if one speaker's code is 5879, we concatenated the spoken samples corresponding to numbers 5, 8, 7, and 9, obtaining ten spoken codes for each selected person, and constructing with these 150, three second, sound files in WAV format. From these files, and using the freeware software Praat, version 4.3.09 [14], we extracted 16 MFCCs for every 50 milliseconds, obtaining 944 features per vector for each file. Here we can mention that, as a final part of the acoustic processing, an algorithm was implemented to clean the file samples obtained by Praat, we did so because the output vector samples contain additional information, on the vector's header, not needed when training/testing the neural networks. This algorithm consists on opening, erasing the header, and saving each file, automatically; this algorithm was implemented in Matlab.

With the clean vectors, the training and testing matrices are constructed, which will be used to work with the proposed algorithm. The training and testing matrices are reduced by using the genetic algorithm, at the end; with the help of the fitness function (described on the previous section), we obtain an individual which will tell us which features we have to use in order to obtain higher accuracy on the speaker authentication stage.

The particularity of our proposed algorithm is that, in each generation, we create a new training and testing matrices, changing the whole search space and sometimes resulting in an accuracy loss. In other words, we keep a record of the best individual in each generation, nonetheless we have observed that when a particular individual obtains high accuracy in one generation, on the next one, the accuracy sometimes decreases, being still the best individual with the best overall accuracy in the population. The overall time the hybrid system took to complete one experiment was calculated by equation 1, which considers the processor used on the experiments:

$$t = (3\,\text{min} \times N_{gen} \times N_{ind}) + (N_{gen} \times 0.5\,\text{min}) \tag{1}$$

7 Experimental Results

In order to obtain several results, and assure the reliability of our proposed algorithm, we experimented with different parameters to observe its behavior, by changing the mutation and crossover rates, the number of individuals, and the number of generations. In Table 1, we show the results obtained, by changing the mentioned parameters, and with the help of the testing matrix. These are the best average results obtained by making three tests of each experiment.

On Table 2, we show on the 1st and 2nd columns the number of generations and individuals used to perform the experiments, the 3rd column shows the final size of the reduced matrix, given by the best genetically selected individual. We can see how the individual never changes, as showed on the 4th column, where we show the range of generations in which the individual stays the same. The 5th

Table 1. Best overall results on different experiments, using different number of generations and individuals, also using different crossover/mutation rate

Generations	Individuals	0.25/0.01	0.25/0.09	0.15/0.01	0.15/0.09	0.05/0.09
5	10	90.63%	93.48%	93.41%	92.48%	88.70%
10	5	91.07%	91.68%	89.50%	91.15%	90.22%
10	10	90.26%	90.95 %	91.88%	90.44%	86.59%
25	10	91.05%	91.22 %	91.46%	91.06%	89.97%

Table 2. Experimental results where the number of features was preserved during several generations

Gen.	Ind.	Num. of Sel. Feat.	Num. of Gen.	Crossover rate	Mutation rate
10	10	[456]	**[3-10]**	0.25	0.01
5	10	[456]	[3-5]	0.15	0.01
10	5	[454]	[5-10]	0.15	0.01
10	10	[456]	[3-10]	0.15	0.01
25	10	[456]	**[9-25]**	0.15	0.01
10	10	[476]	**[4-10]**	0.15	0.09
25	10	[467]	[21-25]	0.15	0.09

ad 6th columns show the crossover and mutation rates used on the experiments. It's highlighted (in bold letters), which experiments kept the same individual during a longer period.

8 Conclusions and Future Work

The time that each neural network took to be trained and tested was of around three minutes, depending on the number of features in the reduced training matrix, and the time spent to read the corpus, to build the new training/testing matrices, in each generation was of 30 seconds. Concluding that the time spent for each experiment was always longer than two hours, considering that the shorter experiments were of 5 generations with 10 individuals. At the end, we obtained higher accuracy that when using a simple neural network system, although, of course, the time spent to train and test the simple system, was much lower. Once the training of the system is completed, the time it takes for the trained neural network, and the hybrid system, to recognize a new feature vector, is done in real time.

Using the hybrid system, we were able to reduce the vector up to 50% of the original size. And the hybrid algorithm adapted to the whole database, instead of only adapting to a particular one. We consider that a global adaptation is better than a local one, and the results are considerably good. On other experiments, we introduced four intruders, males and females, "saying" the same four digits code of four authorized speakers, males and females, (authenticated by the TDNN). 3 out of 4 tests gave good results when denying the access to those intruders.

We are working on new experiments where we make each speaker say the same four digits code in order to test the system robustness. We also want to experiment with other combinations of mutation and crossover rates, also to implement an uniform crossover and mutation algorithm. We need to compare the actual results with results given in experiments where the search space never changes. And, experiment with user defined individual's size, where we control the number of '1s' in an individual's vector from the beginning, and also use the vector's dimensionality as a part of the fitness function.

References

1. Lawrence Rabiner, Biing-Hwang Juang. Fundamentals of Speech Recognition. Prentice Hall Signal Processing Series. ISBN: 0-13-015157-2.(1993)
2. Miramontes de León G., De la Rosa Vargas J. I. and García E. Application of an Annular/Sphere Search Algorithm for Speaker Recognition. Proceedings of the 15th International Conference on Electronics, Communications and Computers, 0-7695-2283-1/05 IEEE. CONIELECOMP, (2005).
3. Pelecanos J., Myers S., Sridharan S. and Chandran V. Vector Quantization based Gaussian Modeling for Speaker Verification. Proceedings of the International conference on Pattern Recognition (ICPR'00). IEEE Computer Society Press, ISBN: 0-7695-0750-6. (2000).
4. Hsieh C., Lai E., Wang Y. Robust Speaker Identification System based on Wavelet Transform and Gaussian Mixture Model. Journal of Information Science and Engineering Vol. 19 No. 2, 267-282, March, (2003).
5. Oh I. S., Lee J. S. and Moon B. R. Hybrid Genetic Algorithms for Feature Selection. IEEE Transactions on Pattern Analysis and Machine Intelligence, VOL. 26, NO. 11. (2004)
6. Ha-Jin Yu. Speaker Recognition in Unknown Mismatched Conditions Using Augmented Principal Component Analysis. LNCS-3733, Springer Verlag, ISBN: 3-540-29414-7. (2005).
7. Balagué A. J. Diccionario Enciclopédico Baber. Editorial Baber, 1119 E. Broadway Street Glendale, California 91205. (1991).
8. Bernal J., Bobadilla J., Gómez P. Reconocimiento de voz y fonética acústica. Ed. Alfaomega Ra-Ma , Madrid, España. (2000).
9. Michalewicz Z., Genetic Algorithms + Data Structures = Evolution Programs. 3rd. Edition, November 26. Springer, ISBN: 3540606769. (1998).
10. Hilera J., Martínez V. Redes Neuronales Artificiales Fundamentos, modelos y aplicaciones. Alfaomega, Madrid, España. (2000).
11. A. Weibel, T. Hanazawa, G. Hinton, K. Shikano, and K.J. Lang, "Phoneme Recognition Using Time Delay Neural Networks," IEEE Trans. Acoustics, Speech, Signal Proc., ASSP-37: 32'339, (1989).
12. Orozco Garca, J., Reyes-García, C.A., Clasificación de Llanto del Bebé Utilizando una Red Neural de Gradiente Conjugado Escalado. Memorias de MICAI/TAIA 2002, Mérida, Yuc., México, April, pp 203-213, ISBN 970-18-7825-6. (2002)
13. PhD Reyes Carlos A. Sistema Inteligente de Comandos Hablados para Control de Dispositivos Caseros, Mxico. Project Supported by COSNET, (2005).
14. Paul Boersma and David Weenink. Praat, doing phonetics by computer version 4.3.09 www.praat.org. Copyright 1992-2005 by. Institute of Phonetic Sciences. University of Amsterdam Herengracht 3381016CG Amsterdam. (2005).

Using PCA to Improve the Generation of Speech Keys

Juan A. Nolazco-Flores, J. Carlos Mex-Perera,
L. Paola Garcia-Perera, and Brenda Sanchez-Torres

Computer Science Department
ITESM, Campus Monterrey.
Av. Eugenio Garza Sada 2501 Sur, Col. Tecnológico,
Monterrey, N.L., México, C.P. 6484
jnolazco@itesm.mx, carlosmex@itesm.mx, paola.garcia@itesm.mx,
a00771543@itesm.mx

Abstract. This research shows the improvement obtained by including the principal component analysis as part of the feature production in the generation of a speech key. The main architecture includes an automatic segmentation of speech and a classifier. The first one, by using a forced alignment configuration, computes a set of primary features, obtains a phonetic acoustic model, and finds the beginnings and ends of the phones in each utterance. The primary features are then transformed according to both the phone model parameters and the phones segments per utterance. Before feeding these processed features to the classifier, the principal component analysis algorithm is applied to the data and a new set of secondary features is built. Then a support vector machine classifier generates an hyperplane that is capable to produce a phone key. Finally, by performing a phone spotting technique, the key is hardened. In this research the results for 10, 20 and 30 users are given using the YOHO database. 90% accuracy.

1 Introduction

Nowadays, the security theme is acquiring more and more attention. People from all over the world are very close related to the use of computers and systems that depend on information technology. New algorithms and improvements to the old ones are making the field more competitive and having efficient cryptosystems is a necessity for any organisation. Trying to solve this problem, the biometric field is of growing interest. A biometric data (intrinsic information of some specific user characteristic) has several advantages among other cryptosystems employed in the past [14]. For instance, it can be used for user identification and verification, and lately as generator of keys for cryptosystems. For verification, biometrics can be employed in access control tasks, such as: access to restricted areas or restricted computer systems. On the other hand, when used for identification they can be employed for forensic tasks. In some cases, the simple access control is not enough and the authentication protocols that relay

A. Gelbukh and C.A. Reyes-Garcia (Eds.): MICAI 2006, LNAI 4293, pp. 1085–1094, 2006.

on cryptography are needed. Then, in order to transform plain messages to encrypted messages (as cryptography declares) a key is needed, but also it is an imprescindible requirement to recover (decipher) the message. For the purpose of this research, a speech biometric is used to generate such a key.

Among other biometrics, the speech was chosen because it has the property of flexibility. This means that the key is changeable according to the speaker demand or system needs. Furthermore, if for each different spoken phrase a key is assigned, then an automatic random number generator can be employed to construct such a system. For the purpose of this research, it is convenient to make the key phone-dependent by using a forced aligned speech segmentation and afterwards make a suitable classification that can distinguish among users. Since, the text and the word-to-phone dictionary are known information, then we can relate each phone segment to its corresponding acoustic model. Using this information, a classifier is fed with features which are function of both the phone model and the parametrised signal of the phone's segment.

In this work, we use a *speech segmentation technique* known as forced alignment (widely used in the automatic speech recognisers field), and a SVM (Support Vector Machine) classifier with spherically normalized data as the core to implement the architecture in Figure 1. The outputs of the speech segmentation step include the Mel-Frequency Cepstral Coefficients (MFCC), the phonetic acoustic model and the segmentation of each utterance in phones. By combining this information a set of primary features is constructed. Next, for increasing the accuracy of the key a normalisation and the principal Component Analysis (PCA) are performed to the data to finally produce a secondary set of features. The SVM is fed with these secondary features and a key is generated. Figure 1 is divided in two parts, the upper part refers to the test stage (online and user interface), the lower part refers to the training stage where all the models are computed.

In the literature, we found a work developed by Monrose *et. al* [9]. His method deals with a partition plane in a feature vector space for cryptographic speech key generation. The drawback of his approach is the difficulty to find a suitable partition plane due to the high number of possible planes. Therefore, a more flexible way to produce a key - in which the exact control of the assignation of the key values is available- is needed.

The main objective of this proposal is to improve the bit accuracy results in a cryptographic speech key generation task. In this paper, we focus on the PCA and on the use of the spherical normalisation [16] to scatter the data in order to make a suitable separation of users' features. Furthermore, since, the text and the word-to-phone dictionary are known information, then we can make a selection of the highest phone accuracies computed by the SVM classifier, this is what we call phone spotting.

In section II, the HMM concepts are reviewed. In section III, SVM theory is reviewed. In section IV, experimental results are discussed. Finally, in section V, comments and conclusions are given.

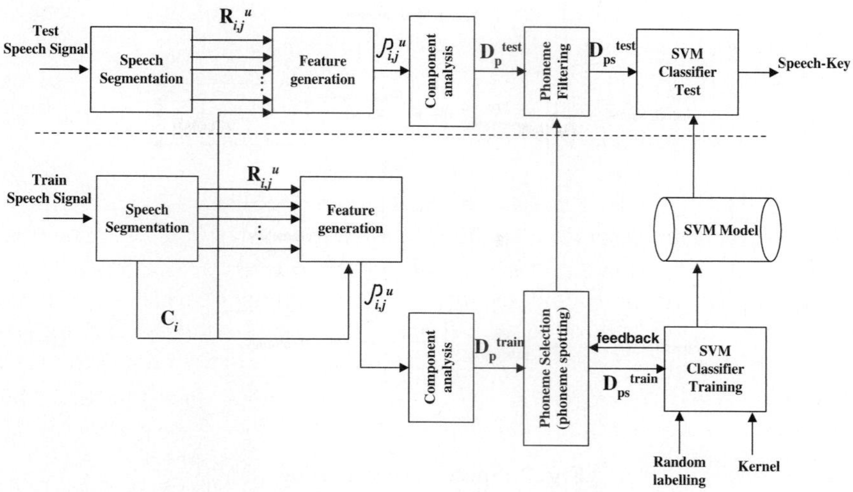

Fig. 1. Speech Key Architecture

2 Speech Segmentation and HMM

In a general scheme of a speech segmentation method using forced-alignmet, the first step is known as pre-processing, as shown in Figure 2. The speech signal is divided into short overlapped windows and transformed in *Mel frequency cepstral coefficients* (MFCC). As a result an n-dimension vector, $(n-1)$-dimension MFCCs followed by one energy coefficient is formed. To emphasize the dynamic features of the speech in time, the time-derivative (Δ) and the time-acceleration (Δ^2) of each parameter are calculated [13,5].

Then the Hidden Markov Models (HMM) are used to model the acustic unites. HMM are the leading technique to develop this task and often for any speech modelling [12,6]. The HMM architecture is a graph with nodes and arcs. The nodes can be emitting or nor emitting states. Non-emiting states are usually the initial and final states. The arcs has a transition probability between states. Associated to each state there is a probability density function, which allows to obtain the visited sequence of states. The compact notation of the HMM is denoted as $\lambda = (A, B, \pi)$ [6]. The parameter set N, M, A, B, and π is calculated using the training data and it defines a probability measure $Prob(O|\lambda)$.

Afterwards, in order to find the segmentation in phones of each utterance, the text-dependent Viterbi aligment is used (this method is based on automatic top-down speech recognition [2,3]). This technique determines an approximation of the actual pronunciation of each phone in a utterance; *i.e.* the beginnings and ends of each phone in time.

The last resulting model has the inherent characteristics of real speech. The output probability density function of the HMM are commonly represented by Gaussian Mixture Densities with means, means weights and covariances as important parameters. To determine the parameters of the model and reach con-

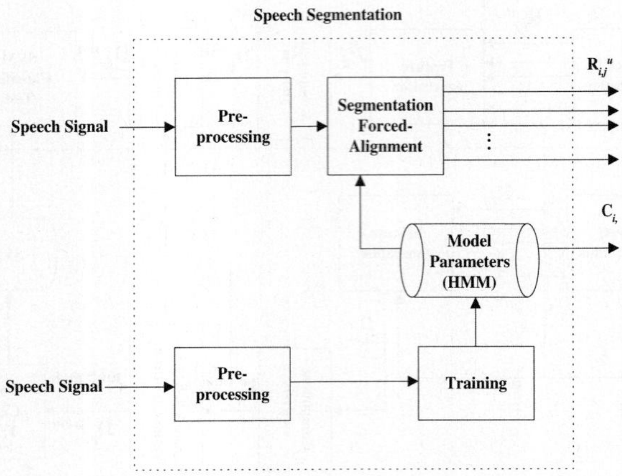

Fig. 2. Speech Segmentation

vergence it is necessary to first make a guess of their value. Then, more accurate results can be found by optimising the likelihood function and using Baum-Welch re-estimation algorithm.

3 Feature Generation

In this section, we describe the procedure to combine the phone model parameters and the MFCCs vectors of the phone's segment to generate secondary features used as input of the SVM .

Lets assume that the phones are modelled with a three-state left-to-right HMM, and that the middle state is the most stable part of the phone representation, let,

$$C_i = \frac{1}{K}\sum_{l=1}^{K} W_l G_l, \tag{1}$$

where G is the mean of a Gaussian, K is the total number of Gaussians available in that state, W_l is the weight of the Gaussian and $i \in P$ is the index associated to each phone (P is the universe of all the possible phones).

Let, $g(1)...g(n)$, be the sequence of the MFCCs in an utterance, and $R_1...R_s$ be the disjoint nonempty ranges such that $\bigcup_{u=1}^{S} R_u = [1, n]$, where S is the total number of phones in an utterance. Then, for simplicity, we can define $G(R_1)...G(R_s)$ as the phone segments in an utterance.

The utterances can be arranged forming the sets $G(R_{i,j}^u)$, where i is the index associated to each phone, j is the j-th user, and u is an index that beginnings in zero and increments every time the user utters the phone i.

Then, the feature vector is defined as $\psi_{i,j}^u = \mu(R_{i,j}^u) - C_i$ where $\mu(R_{i,j}^u)$ is the mean vector of the data in the MFCC set $R_{i,j}^u$, and $C_i \in \mathcal{C}_P$ is known as the matching phone mean vector of the model.

Let us denote the set of vectors, $D_p = \{\psi_{p,j}^u \mid \forall\, u, j\}$ where $p \in$ is a specific phone.

Then, $D_p^{train} = \{[\psi_{p,j}^u, b_{p,j}] \mid \forall\, u, j\}$ where $b_{p,j} \in \{-1, 1\}$ is the ramdom key bit or class assigned to the phone p of the j-th user.

After this part, a normalisation is needed that can scatter the data and facilitate the classification. One approach is given by [16]. Considering the SVM characteristics, it has been observed that the best way to perform the trainning is by mapping the data to a higher space, in order to stablish a hyperplane classifier. The spherical normalisation is an effective solution to map each feature vector into the surface of a unit hypersphere embedded in a space that has one dimension more than the original vector itself. This makes possible to improve the performance of SVM using high order polynomial kernels. To map the feature hyperplane to the hypersphere it is necessary to consider the distance d from the origin of the hemisphere to the input hyperplane and make a data projection. By denoting an expression in a kernel form,

$$K(\psi_i, \psi_m) = \frac{\psi_i \cdot \psi_m}{\sqrt{(\psi_i^2 + d^2)(\psi_m^2 + d^2)}} \tag{2}$$

After performing the normalisation, the data is not known to be orthogonal. To increase the key accuracy, it is a common procedure to increment the dimensions of the MFCCs vectors, however, it makes it difficult to the system to perform a fast computation. PCA is a statistical technique that allows the reduction of dimensions and extraction of characteristics of correlated data of high dimensions to data uncorrelated. By identifying the principal components it is possible to order them in decreasing order so if dimensions with lowest correlated are eliminated the lost of information is minimum.

3.1 Principal Components Analisys

We assume $\mathbf{x}_p = \left[\psi_{p,1}^1 ... \psi_{p,j}^u ... \psi_{p,J}^U\right]$ where ψ are the M- dimensional normalised feature vectors per phone, U is the total number of repetitions of each phone and J is the total number of users. From this matrix, the covariance matrix $\mathbf{x}_p$: is calculated as follows, $\boldsymbol{Cov} = \boldsymbol{E}(\boldsymbol{x}_p \boldsymbol{x}_p^T)$.

PCA does the extraction of characteristics calculating from covariance matrix, their eigenvectors and eigenvalues. Λ is the diagonal matrix of eigenvalues, $\Lambda = diag(\lambda_1, ..., \lambda_M)$ and V is the orthogonal eigenvectors of $\boldsymbol{Cov}$.

The principal components can be calcultated following Equation 3.

$$\rho = \boldsymbol{V} \boldsymbol{x}_p^T \tag{3}$$

Lastly, knowing that each vector ρ is associated to a j user, a p phone and a u repetition. Let,

$$D_p^{train} = \{[\rho_{p,j}^u, b_{p,j}] \mid \forall\, u, j\}.$$

On the other hand, the set D_p^{test} is defined as

$$D_p^{test} = \{[\psi_{p,j}^u{}^*, y_{p,j}{}^*] \mid \forall\, u, j\}$$

where $y_{p,j}{}^* \in \{-1, 1\}$ is the *key bit*, with unknow value.

Using the SVM as a classifier, a set of hyperplanes per phone are obtained from the SVM training. According to D_p^{train} assignations it is possible to model a key for a specific user, and a specific utterance that can obtain $y_{p,j}{}^*$ with a certain accuracy probability.

Once the random labels are related to their principal components constructing a secondary feature set, the classification can be made.

4 Support Vector Machine

The *Support Vector Machine* (SVM) is a common algorithm used for pattern recognition. In this research it is employed as a classifier that can transform feature data into a binary key. SVM was first developed by Vapnik and Chervonenkis [4]. Although it has been used for several applications, it has also been employed in biometrics [11,10].

Given the observation inputs and a function-based model, the goal of the basic SVM is to classify these inputs into one of two classes. Afterwards, the following set of pairs are defined $\{\rho_i, y_i\}$; where $\rho_i \in R^n$ are the training vectors and $y_i = \{-1, 1\}$ are the labels.

The method relies on a linear separation of the data previously mapped in a higher dimension space $\mathbb{H}$, by using $\phi : \mathbb{R}^n \to \mathbb{H}; \phi \to \phi(\rho)$. For the generalisation purpose, let the margin between the separator hiperplane be,

$$\{\mathbf{h} \in \mathbb{H} | \langle \mathbf{w}, \mathbf{h} \rangle_{\mathbb{H}} + \varpi_0 = 0\} \tag{4}$$

and the data $\phi(\rho)$ is maximed. Moreover, the SVM learning algorithm finds an hyperplane (w, b) such that,

$$\min_{\rho_i, b, \xi} \frac{1}{2} w^T w + C \sum_{i=1}^{l} \xi_i \tag{5}$$

$$\text{subject to } y_i(w^T \phi(\rho_i) + b) \geq 1 - \rho_i \tag{6}$$

$$\xi_i \geq 0$$

where ξ_i is a slack variable and C is a positive real constant known as a tradeoff parameter between error and margin. Equations 4, 5 and 6 can be transformed into a dual problem represented by the Lagrange multipliers α_i. Thus,

$$\sum_{i=1}^{l} \alpha_i - \frac{1}{2} \sum_{i=1, m=1}^{l} \alpha_i \alpha_m y_i y_m \langle \phi(\rho_i), \phi(\rho_m) \rangle \tag{7}$$

$$\sum_{i=1}^{l} \alpha_i y_i = 0, C \geq \alpha_i \geq 0. \tag{8}$$

α_i can be solved as a quadratic programming (QP) problem. The resulting values $\alpha_i \in \mathbb{R}$ have a close relation with the training points ρ_i.

To extend the linear method to a nonlinear technique, the input data is mapped into a higher dimensional space by function ϕ. However, exact specification of ϕ is not needed; instead, the expression known as kernel $K(\rho_i, \rho_j) \equiv \phi(\rho_i)^T \phi(\rho_m)$ is defined. There are different types of kernels as the linear, polynomial, radial basis function (RBF) and sigmoid.

For the purpose of this research, the RBF and the spherical normalised kernel were used:

- The RBF kernel is denoted as: $K(\rho_i, \rho_m) = e^{(-\gamma||\rho_i - \rho_m||^2)}$, where $\gamma > 0$.
- The spherically normalised polynomial kernel based on Equation 2 is denoted as

$$K_{SN}(\rho_i, \rho_m) = \frac{1}{2^n}\left(\frac{\rho_i \cdot \rho_m + d}{\sqrt{(\rho_i \cdot \rho_i + d^2)(\rho_m \cdot \rho_m + d^2)}}\right)^n$$

The spherical normalisation and the PCA are applied to both the D_p^{test}, and D_p^{train} sets. Afterwards, the phone feature filtering (phone spotting) is performed using the best accuracy results obtained in D_p^{train} selecting D_{ps}^{train}. The sets D_{ps}^{test} are computed according to the phone-dependent models chosen in this training phase. This research considers just binary classes and the final key is obtained by concatenating the bits produced by each selected phone. For instance, if a user utters three phones: /F/, /AO/, and /R/, and just /F/ and /R/ are selected the final final key is $K = \{f(D_{/F/}), f(D_{/R/})\}$. Thus, the output is formed by two bits.

In order to decide which phones to use, the SVM average classification accuracy ratio is defined

$$\eta = \frac{\alpha}{\beta}. \tag{9}$$

where α is the number of times that the classification output matches the correct phone class on the test data and β is the total number of phones to be classified.

By performing the statistics and choosing an appropiate group of phones that compute the highest results in the trainning stage, with output D_{ps}^{train}, a key with high performance can be obtained. Just this selection of phones will be able to generate the key in the test stage.

5 Experimental Methodology and Results

In this research the YOHO database was used to perform the experiments [1,7]. The Hidden Markov Models Toolkit (HTK) by Cambridge University Engineering Department [8] configured as a forced-alignment viterbi (automatic speech segmentation) was used to perform the experiments. The important results of the speech processing phase are the twenty sets of C_i given by the HMM and the $G(R_{i,j}^u)$ segmentation. The phones used are: /AH/, /AO/, /AX/, /AY/, /EH/, /ER/, /EY/, /F/, /IH/, /IY/,/K/, /N/, /R/, /S/, /T/, /TH/, /UW/, /V/, /W/.

The methodology used to implement the SVM training is as follows. Firstly, the training set for each phone (D_p^{train}) is transformed using the spherical normalisation and the PCA algorithm. Afterwards, a one-bit random label ($b_{p,j}$) is assigned to each user per phone. Since a random generator of the values (-1 or 1) is used, the assignation is different for each user. The advantage of this random assignation is that the key entropy grows significantly, if the key bits are given in a random fashion with a uniform probability distribution. The classification of all vectors was performed using SVMlight [15]. The behaviour of the SVM is given in terms of Equation 9, and by performing the phone spotting obtaining D_{ps}^{train} and D_{ps}^{test} are computed (the phones with the highest accuracy and its SVM model are selected and the models that developed the lowest accuracy values are removed).

The SVM employs an RBF and a polynomial kernel to perform the experiments. The accuracy results η are computed for the selected phones. The statistics were obtained as follows: 500 trials were performed for 10 and 20 and 30 users. The results for 10, 20, 30 users are depicted in Figure.

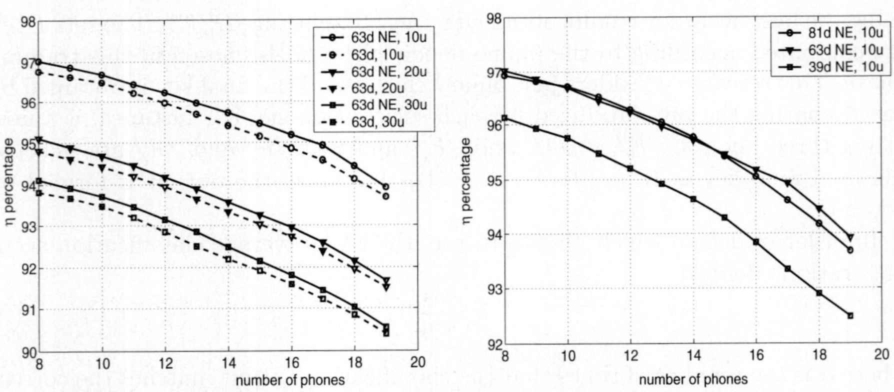

(a) Results of η for different number of users

(b) Results of η by increasing the MFCC's dimensions

Fig. 3. Basic results of η

As shown in Figures 3 and Figure 4, by using the spherically normalisation kernel the results become better for all the cases. For instance, for 10 users the key accuracy goes from 96.65% to 97.01%. Figure 3.a shows the behaviour for 10, 20, and 30 users with normalization. Figure 3.b shows the effect of incrementing the dimensions of the MFCCs. If the dimensions are increased, better results are obtained, but the computing time increases. Then, Figures 4.a and 4.b show that if a combination of PCA and spherical normalisation are included the results can be mantained. This is also the behaviour for the different number of users. The most complex experiment was performed using 30 users, but the result shows that higher than 90% accuracy can be achieved. As in phone spotting, if less phones

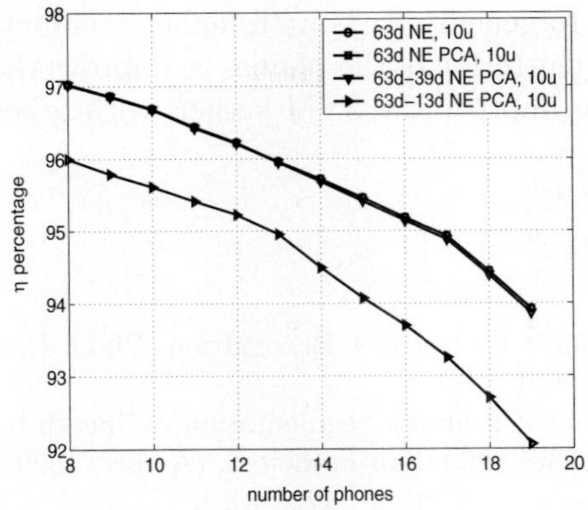

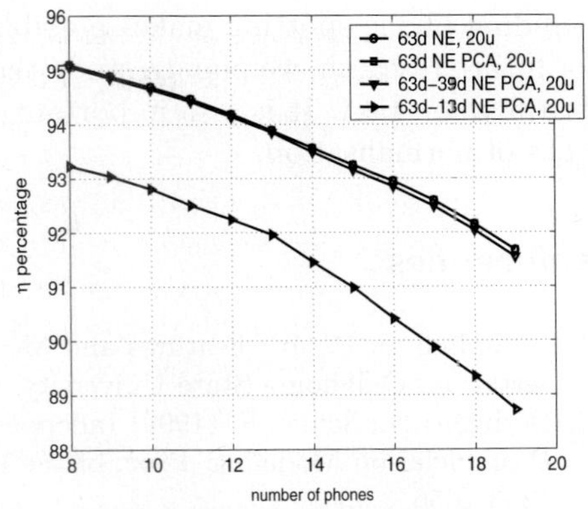

(a) Results of η by including PC analysis, 10 users

(b) Results of η by including PC analysis, 20 users

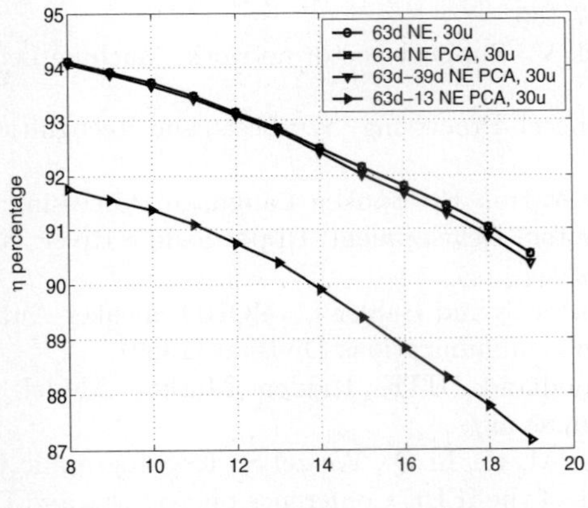

(c) Results of η by including PC analysis, 30 users

Fig. 4. Results of η including the spherical normalisation and the PC analysis

are taken in account it is possible to compute keys with higher accuracies. Furthermore, the use of the PCA algorithm can reach almost the same results for all cases with less coefficients. To have realiable combinations of phones to create the key, at least eight phones are considered in each key construction.

6 Conclusion

An architecture improvement was described for the generation of a cryptographic key from speech signal. The method showed that if a combination of spherically normalised kernel and a PCA is included the accuracy results can improve. The results based on the YOHO database were shown. An advantage of the normalisation is that it spreads the data causing a better classification. Moreover, by exploring the PCA, there is a reduction in time and processing. Furthermore, including phone spotting makes possible to generate keys with higher accuracy. For future research, we plan to study the clustering of the phones to improve the classification task. It is also important to improve the SVM kernels with other types of normalisation.

References

1. Campbell, J. P., Jr.: Features and Measures for Speaker Recognition. Ph.D. Dissertation, Oklahoma State University, (1992)
2. Beringer, N.; Schiel, F. (1999) Independent Automatic Segmentation of Speech by Pronunciation Modeling. Proc. of the ICPhS 1999. San Francisco. (August 1999). 1653-1656.
3. Binnenpoorte, D., S. Goddijn and C. Cucchiarini. How to Improve Human and Machine Transcriptions of Spontaneous Speech. In Proceedings ISCA and IEEE Workshop on Spontaneous Speech Processing and Recognition (SSPR). (April 2003). Tokyo, Japan. 147-150
4. Cortes, C., Vapnik V.: Support-vector network. Machine Learning 20, (1995) 273-297
5. Furui S. Digital Speech Processing, Synthesis, and Recognition. Mercel Dekker,inc. New York, 2001.
6. Huang X., Acero A.,Hon H.: Spoken Language Processing: A Guide to Theory, Algorithm and System Development. Upper Saddle River, NJ: Prentice Hall PTR (2001).
7. Higgins, A., J. Porter J. and Bahler L.: YOHO Speaker Authentication Final Report. ITT Defense Communications Division (1989)
8. Young,S., P. Woodland: HTK Hidden Markov Model Toolkit home page. http://htk.eng.cam.ac.uk/
9. Monrose F., Reiter M. K., Li Q., Wetzel S.: Cryptographic Key Generation From Voice. Proceedings of the IEEE Conference on Security and Privacy, Oakland, CA. (2001)
10. E. Osuna, Freund R., and Girosi F.: Support vector machines: Training and applications. Technical Report AIM-1602, MIT A.I. Lab. (1996)
11. E. Osuna, Freund R., and Girosi F.: Training Support Vector Machines: An Application to Face Recognition, in IEEE Conference on Computer Vision and Pattern Recognition, (1997) 130-136
12. Rabiner L. R. A tutorial on hidden Markov models and selected applications in speech recognition. Proceedings of the IEEE, 77(2):257–286, February 1989.
13. Rabiner L. R. and Juang B.-H.: Fundamentals of speech recognition. Prentice-Hall, New-Jersey (1993)
14. Uludag U., Pankanti S., Prabhakar S. and Jain A.K.: Biometric cryptosystems: issues and challenges, Proceedings of the IEEE , Volume: 92 , Issue: 6 (2004)
15. Joachims T., SVMLight: Support Vector Machine, SVM-Light Support Vector Machine http://svmlight.joachims.org/, University of Dortmund, (1999).
16. Wan, V. Renals S.: Speaker Verification Using Sequence Discriminant Support Vector Machines IEEE Transactions on speech and audio processing, VOL. 13, NO. 2, March 2005.

Verifying Real-Time Temporal, Cooperation and Epistemic Properties for Uncertain Agents*

Zining Cao

Department of Computer Science and Engineering
Nanjing University of Aero. & Astro., Nanjing 210016, China
caozn@nuaa.edu.cn

Abstract. In this paper, we introduce a real-time temporal probabilistic knowledge logic, called *RATPK*, which can express not only real-time temporal and probabilistic epistemic properties but also cooperation properties. It is showed that temporal modalities such as "always in an interval", "until in an interval", and knowledge modalities such as "knowledge in an interval", "common knowledge in an interval" and "probabilistic common knowledge" can be expressed in such a logic. The model checking algorithm is given and a case is studied.

1 Introduction

Verification of reaction systems by means of model checking techniques is now a well-established area of research [6]. In this paradigm one typically models a system S in terms of automata (or by a similar transition-based formalism), builds an implementation P_S of the system by means of a model-checker friendly language such as the input for *SMV* or *PROMELA*, and finally uses a model-checker such as *SMV* or *SPIN* to verify certain temporal property φ the system: $M_P \models \varphi$, where M_P is a temporal model representing the executions of P_S. As it is well known, there are intrinsic difficulties with the naive approach of performing this operation on an explicit representation of the states, and refinements of symbolic techniques (based on *OBDD*'s, and *SAT* translations) are being investigated to overcome these hurdles. Formal results and corresponding applications now allow for the verification of complex systems that generate more than 10^{20} states.

The field of multi-agent systems has also recently become interested in the problem of verifying complex systems. In *MAS*, modal logics representing concepts such as knowledge, belief, and intention. Since these modalities are given interpretations that are different from the ones of the standard temporal operators, it is not straightforward to apply existing model checking tools developed for $LTL \backslash CTL$ temporal logic to the specification of *MAS*. The recent developments of model checking *MAS* can broadly be divided into streams: in the first category standard predicates are used to interpret the various intensional notions and these are paired with standard model checking techniques based on

* This work was supported by the National Science Foundation of China under Grant 60473036.

A. Gelbukh and C.A. Reyes-Garcia (Eds.): MICAI 2006, LNAI 4293, pp. 1095–1104, 2006.

temporal logic. Following this line is [24] and related papers. In the other category we can place techniques that make a genuine attempt at extending the model checking techniques by adding other operators. Works along these lines include [4,17] and so on.

Real-time is sometimes an important feature of software system. To describe the property of real-time *MASs,* one should express not only real-time temporal temporal but also epistemic property. Furthermore, given that agents work in unknown environments, and interact with other agents that may, in turn, be unpredictable, then it is essential for any formal agent description to incorporate some mechanism for capturing this aspect. Within the framework of executable specifications, formal descriptions involving uncertainty must also be executable. To express the probabilistic epistemic property in *MAS*, Ferreira, Fisher and Hoek introduced probabilistic epistemic temporal logic *PROTEM* in [10,11], which is a combination of temporal logic and probabilistic belief logic $P_F KD45$ [10]. For example, one can express statements such as "if it is probabilistic common knowledge in group of agents Γ that φ, then Γ can achieve a state satisfying ψ". Kooi's work [21] combined the probabilistic epistemic logic with the dynamic logic yielding a new logic, *PDEL*, that deals with changing probabilities and takes higher-order information into account. The syntax of *PDEL* is an expansion of probabilistic epistemic logic by introducing dynamic logic formulas. The semantics of *PDEL* is based on a combination of Kripke structure and probability functions.

In this paper, we present a real-time temporal probabilistic knowledge logic *RATPK*, which is an extension of knowledge by adding real-time temporal modalities, probability modality and cooperation modality. Although its syntax is simple, we can express the property such as "always in an interval", "until in an interval", "knowledge in an interval", "common knowledge in an interval", "everyone knows with probability", "probabilistic common knowledge" and etc. We also studied the model checking algorithm for *RATPK*.

The rest of the paper is organized as follows: In Section 2, we present a real-time temporal probabilistic knowledge logic *RATPK*, give its syntax and semantics. Furthermore, in Section 3, we give a model checking algorithm. In Section 4, we study a case. The paper is concluded in Section 5.

2 A Logic *RATPK*

To express the cooperation property in open systems, Alur and Henzinger introduced alternating-time temporal logic *ATL* in [2], which is a generalisation of *CTL*. The main difference between *ATL* and *CTL* is that in *ATL*, path quantifies are replaced by cooperation modalities. For example, the *ATL* formula $\langle\langle\Gamma\rangle\rangle \bigcirc \varphi$, where Γ is a group of agents, expresses that the group Γ can cooperate to achieve a next state that φ holds. Thus, we can express some properties such as "agents 1 and 2 can ensure that the system never enters a fail state". An ATL model checking systems called $MOCHA$ was developed [1]. In MAS, agents are intelligent, so it is not only necessary to represent the temporal properties but also necessary to express the mental properties. For example, one may need to express statements such as "if it is common knowledge in group of agents Γ that φ, then Γ can cooperate to ensure ψ". To represent and verify such properties, a temporal epistemic logic $ATEL$ was presented in [17]. This logic extended ATL with knowledge modalities such as "every knows" and common knowledge. In this section, we propose a logic *RATPK,* which can express real-time temporal, cooperation and probabilistic knowledge properties. Furthermore, a model checking algorithm for *RATPK* was given.

2.1 Syntax of *RATPK*

The well form formulas of *RATPK* are defined as follows.

Definition 4. [17] The set of formulas in *RATPK*, called L^{RATPK}, is given by the following rules:

(1) If $\varphi \in$atomic formulas set Π, then $\varphi \in L^{RATPK}$.

(2) If $\varphi \in$proposition variables set V, then $\varphi \in L^{RATPK}$.

(3) If $\varphi \in L^{RATPK}$, then $\neg\varphi \in L^{RATPK}$.

(4) If $\varphi, \psi \in L^{RATPK}$, then $\varphi \wedge \psi \in L^{RATPK}$.

(5) If φ, $\psi \in L^{RATPK}$, $\Gamma \subseteq \Sigma$, then $\langle\langle\Gamma\rangle\rangle \bigcirc \varphi$, $\langle\langle\Gamma\rangle\rangle[]\varphi$, $\langle\langle\Gamma\rangle\rangle\varphi U\psi \in L^{RATPK}$.

(6) If $\varphi, \psi \in L^{RATPK}$, $\Gamma \subseteq \Sigma$, then $\langle\langle\Gamma\rangle\rangle[]_{[i,j]}\varphi$, $\langle\langle\Gamma\rangle\rangle\varphi U_{[i,j]}\psi \in L^{RATPK}$.

(7) If $\varphi \in L^{RATPK}$, then $K_a\varphi$, $E_\Gamma\varphi$, $C_\Gamma\varphi \in L^{RATPK}$, where $\Gamma \subseteq \Sigma$.

(8) If $\varphi \in L^{RATPK}$, then $K_a^p\varphi$, $E_\Gamma^p\varphi$, $C_\Gamma^p\varphi \in L^{RATPK}$, where $a \in Agent$, $\Gamma \subseteq \Sigma$, $p \in [0,1]$. Intuitively, $K_a^p\varphi$ means that agent a knows the probability of φ is no less than p. $E_\Gamma^p\varphi$ means that every agent in Γ knows the probability of φ is no less than p. $C_\Gamma^p\varphi$ means that "the probability of φ is no less than p" is a common knowledge by every agent in Γ.

The following abbreviations are used:

$K_a^{>p}\varphi \overset{def}{=} \neg K_a^{1-p}\neg\varphi$, here $K_a^{>p}\varphi$ means that agent a knows the probability of φ is greater than p.

$K_a^{<p}\varphi \overset{def}{=} \neg K_a^p\varphi$, here $K_a^{<p}\varphi$ means that agent a knows the probability of φ is less than p.

$K_a^{\leq p}\varphi \overset{def}{=} K_a^{1-p}\neg\varphi$, here $K_a^{\leq p}\varphi$ means that agent a knows the probability of φ is no more than p.

$K_a^{=p}\varphi \overset{def}{=} K_a^p\varphi \wedge K_a^{1-p}\neg\varphi$, here $K_a^{=p}\varphi$ means that agent a knows the probability of φ is equal to p.

Similarly, we can define $E_\Gamma^{>p}\varphi$, $C_\Gamma^{=p}\varphi$, and etc. Thus using $K_a^p\varphi$, $E_\Gamma^p\varphi$ and $C_\Gamma^p\varphi$, we can express various of probabilistic knowledge properties.

2.2 Semantics of *RATPK*

We will describe the semantics of *RATPK*.

Definition 5. A model S of *RATPK* is a concurrent game structure [2] $S = (\Sigma, Q, \Pi, \pi, e, d, \delta, \sim_a, P_a$, here $a \in \Sigma)$, where

(1) Σ is a finite set of agents, in the following, without loss of generality, we usually assume $\Sigma = \{1, ..., k\}$.

(2) Q is a finite, nonempty set, whose elements are called possible worlds or states.

(3) Π is a finite set of propositions.

(4) π is a map: $Q \to 2^{\Pi}$, where Π is a set of atomic formulas.

(5) e is an environment: $V \to 2^{Q}$, where V is a set of proposition variables.

(6) For each player $a \in \Sigma = \{1, ..., k\}$ and each state $q \in Q$, a natural number $d_a(q) \geq 1$ of moves available at state q to player a. We identify the moves of player a at state q with the numbers $1, ..., d_a(q)$. For each state $q \in Q$, a move vector at q is a tuple $\langle j_1, ..., j_k \rangle$ such that $1 \leq j_a \leq d_a(q)$ for each player a. Given a state $q \in Q$, we write $D(q)$ for the set $\{1, ..., d_1(q)\} \times ... \times \{1, ..., d_k(q)\}$ of move vectors. The function D is called move function.

(7) For each state $q \in Q$ and each move vector $\langle j_1, ..., j_k \rangle \in D(q)$, a state $\delta(q, j_1, ..., j_k)$ that results from state q if every player $a \in \Sigma = \{1, ..., k\}$ choose move j_a. The function is called transition function.

(8) $\sim_a$ is an accessible relation on Q, which is an equivalence relation.

(9) P_a is a probability function: $Q \times \wp(Q) \to [0, 1]$, such that for every a, $P_a(s, \{s' | l_a(s) = l_a(s')\}) = 1$.

The definition of computation of a concurrent game structure is similar to the case of Kripke structure. In order to give the semantics of *RATPK*, we need to define strategies of a concurrent game structure.

Strategies and their outcomes. Intuitively, a strategy is an abstract model of an agent's decision-making process; a strategy may be thought of as a kind of plan for an agent. By following a strategy, an agent can bring about certain states of affairs. Formally, a strategy f_a for an agent $a \in \Sigma$ is a total function f_a that maps every nonempty finite state sequence $\lambda \in Q^+$ to a natural number such that if the last state of λ is q, then $f_a(\lambda) \leq d_a(q)$. Thus, the strategy f_a determines for every finite prefix λ of a computation a move $f_a(\lambda)$ for player a. Given a set $\Gamma \subseteq \Sigma$ of agents, and an indexed set of strategies $F_\Gamma = \{f_a \mid a \in \Gamma\}$, one for each agent $a \in \Gamma$, we define $out(q, F_\Gamma)$ to be the set of possible outcomes that may occur if every agent $a \in \Gamma$ follows the corresponding strategy f_a, starting when the system is in state $q \in Q$. That is, the set $out(q, F_\Gamma)$ will contain all possible q-computations that the agents Γ can "enforce" by cooperating and following the strategies in F_Γ. Note that the "grand coalition" of all agents in the system can cooperate to uniquely determine the future state of the system, and so $out(q, F_\Sigma)$ is a singleton. Similarly, the set $out(q, F_\emptyset)$ is the set of all possible q-computations of the system.

We can now turn to the definition of semantics of *RATPK*.

Definition 6. Semantics of *RATPK*

$[[\langle\langle \Gamma \rangle\rangle \bigcirc \varphi]]_S = \{q \mid$ there exists a set F_Γ of strategies, one for each player in Γ, such that for all computations $\lambda \in out(q, F_\Gamma)$, we have $\lambda[1] \in [[\varphi]]_S$.$\}$

$[[\langle\langle\Gamma\rangle\rangle[]\varphi]]_S = \{q \mid$ there exists a set F_Γ of strategies, one for each player in Γ, such that for all computations $\lambda \in out(q, F_\Gamma)$ and all positions $i \geq 0$, we have $\lambda[i] \in [[\varphi]]_S.\}$

$[[\langle\langle\Gamma\rangle\rangle\varphi U\psi]]_S = \{q \mid$ there exists a set F_Γ of strategies, one for each player in Γ, such that for all computations $\lambda \in out(q, F_\Gamma)$, there exists a position $i \geq 0$, such that $\lambda[i] \in [[\psi]]_S$ and for all positions $0 \leq j < i$, we have $\lambda[j] \in [[\varphi]]_S.\}$

$[[\langle\langle\Gamma\rangle\rangle[]_{[i,j]}\varphi]]_S = \{q \mid$ there exists a set F_Γ of strategies, one for each player in Γ, such that for all computations $\lambda \in out(q, F_\Gamma)$ and all positions $i \leq m \leq j$, we have $\lambda[m] \in [[\varphi]]_S.\}$

$[[\langle\langle\Gamma\rangle\rangle\varphi U_{[i,j]}\psi]]_S = \{q \mid$ there exists a set F_Γ of strategies, one for each player in Γ, such that for all computations $\lambda \in out(q, F_\Gamma)$, there exists a position $i \leq m \leq j$, such that $\lambda[m] \in [[\psi]]_S$ and for all positions $0 \leq k < m$, we have $\lambda[k] \in [[\varphi]]_S.\}$

$[[K_a\varphi]]_S = \{q \mid \text{for all } r \in [[\varphi]]_S \text{ and } r \in \sim_a (q) \text{ with } \sim_a (q) = \{q' \mid (q, q') \in \sim_a\}\}$

$[[E_\Gamma\varphi]]_S = \{q \mid \text{for all } r \in [[\varphi]]_S \text{ and } r \in \sim_\Gamma^E (q) \text{ with } \sim_\Gamma^E (q) = \{q' \mid (q, q') \in \sim_\Gamma^E\}\}$, here $\sim_\Gamma^E = (\cup_{a\in\Gamma} \sim_a)$.

$[[C_\Gamma\varphi]]_S = \{q \mid \text{for all } r \in [[\varphi]]_S \text{ and } r \in \sim_\Gamma^C (q) \text{ with } \sim_\Gamma^C (q) = \{q' \mid (q, q') \in \sim_\Gamma^C\}\}$, here $\sim_\Gamma^C$ denotes the transitive closure of $\sim_\Gamma^E$.

$[[K_a^p\varphi]]_S = \{q \mid P_a(q, \sim_a (q) \cap [[\varphi]]_S) \geq p\}$, here $\sim_a (q) = \{r \mid (q, r) \in \sim_a\}$;

$[[E_\Gamma^p\varphi]]_S = \cap_{a\in\Gamma}[[K_a^p\varphi]]_S$;

$[[C_\Gamma^p\varphi]]_S = \cap_{k\geq 1}[[(F_\Gamma^p)^k\varphi]]_S$, here $[[(F_\Gamma^p)^0\varphi]]_S = Q$, $[[(F_\Gamma^p)^{k+1}\varphi]]_S = [[E_\Gamma^p(\varphi \wedge (F_\Gamma^p)^k\varphi)]]_S$.

Intuitively, $\langle\langle\Gamma\rangle\rangle \bigcirc \varphi$ means that group Γ can cooperate to ensure φ at next step; $\langle\langle\Gamma\rangle\rangle[]\varphi$ means that group Γ can cooperate to ensure φ always holds; $\langle\langle\Gamma\rangle\rangle\varphi U\psi$ means that group Γ can cooperate to ensure φ until ψ holds; $\langle\langle\Gamma\rangle\rangle[]_{[i,j]}\varphi$ means that group Γ can cooperate to ensure φ always holds in the interval of $[i, j]$; $\langle\langle\Gamma\rangle\rangle\varphi U_{[i,j]}\psi$ means that group Γ can cooperate to ensure φ until ψ holds in the interval of $[i, j]$. For example, a *RATPK* formula $\langle\langle\Gamma_1\rangle\rangle \bigcirc \varphi \wedge \langle\langle\Gamma_2\rangle\rangle[]_{[i,j]}\psi$ holds at a state exactly when the coalition Γ_1 has a strategy to ensure that proposition φ holds at the immediate successor state, and coalition Γ_2 has a strategy to ensure that proposition ψ holds at the current and all future states between time i and j.

3 Model Checking for *RATPK*

In this section we give a symbolic model checking algorithm for *RATPK*. The model checking problem for *RATPK* asks, given a model S and a *RATPK* formula φ, for the set of states in Q that satisfy φ. In the following, we denote the desired set of states by $Eval(\varphi)$.

For each φ' in $Sub(\varphi)$ do
    case $\varphi' = \langle\langle\Gamma\rangle\rangle \bigcirc \theta : Eval(\varphi') := CoPre(\Gamma, Eval(\theta))$
    case $\varphi' = \langle\langle\Gamma\rangle\rangle[]\theta :$
        $Eval(\varphi') := Eval(true)$
        $\rho_1 := Eval(\theta)$
        repeat

```
            Eval(φ') := Eval(φ') ∩ ρ1
            ρ1 := CoPre(Γ, Eval(φ')) ∩ Eval(θ)
        until ρ1 = Eval(φ')
    case φ' = ⟨⟨Γ⟩⟩θ1Uθ2 :
        Eval(φ') := Eval(false)
        ρ1 := Eval(θ1)
        ρ2 := Eval(θ2)
        repeat
            Eval(φ') := Eval(φ') ∪ ρ2
            ρ2 := CoPre(Γ, Eval(φ')) ∩ ρ1
        until ρ1 = Eval(φ')
    case φ' = ⟨⟨Γ⟩⟩[]_[i,j] θ :
        k := j
        Eval(φ') := Eval(true)
        while k ≠ 0 do
            k := k − 1
            if k ≥ i then Eval(φ') := CoPre(Γ, Eval(φ')) ∩ Eval(θ)
            else Eval(φ') := CoPre(Γ, Eval(φ'))
        end while
    case φ' = ⟨⟨Γ⟩⟩θ1U_[p,q]θ2 :
        k := j
        Eval(φ') := Eval(false)
        while k ≠ 0 do
            k := k − 1
            Eval(φ') := CoPre(Γ, Eval(φ') ∪ Eval(θ2)) ∩ Eval(θ1)
        end while
    case φ' = K_a θ : Eval(φ') := {q | Img(q, ∼a) ⊆ Eval(θ)}
    case φ' = E_Γ θ : Eval(φ') := ∩_{a∈Γ} Eval(K_a θ)
    case φ' = C_Γ θ :
        Eval(φ') := Eval(true)
        repeat
            ρ := Eval(φ')
            Eval(φ') := ∩_{a∈Γ}({q|Img(q, ∼a) ⊆ Eval(θ)} ∩ ρ)
        until ρ = Eval(φ')
    case φ' = K^p_a θ : Eval(φ') := {q | P_a(Img(q, ∼a) ∩ Eval(θ)) ≥ p}
    case φ' = E^p_Γ θ : Eval(φ') := ∩_{a∈Γ} Eval(K^p_a θ)
    case φ' = C^p_Γ θ :
        Eval(φ') := Eval(true)
        repeat
            ρ := Eval(φ')
            Eval(φ') := ∩_{a∈Γ}({q|P_a(Img(q, ∼a) ∩ Eval(θ) ∩ ρ) ≥ p})
        until ρ = Eval(φ')
end case
return Eval(φ, e)
```

The algorithm uses the following primitive operations:

(1) The function Sub, when given a formula φ, returns a queue of syntactic subformulas of φ such that if φ_1 is a subformula of φ and φ_2 is a subformula of φ_1, then φ_2 precedes φ_1 in the queue $Sub(\varphi)$.

(2) The function Reg, when given a proposition $p \in \Pi$, returns the set of states in Q that satisfy p.

(3) The function $CoPre$. When given a set $\Gamma \subseteq \Sigma$ of players and a set $\rho \subseteq Q$ of states, the function $CoPre$ returns the set of states q such that from q, the players in Γ can cooperate and enforce the next state to lie in ρ. Formally, $CoPre(\Gamma, \rho)$ contains state $q \in Q$ if for every player $a \in \Gamma$, there exists a move $j_a \in \{1, ..., d_a(q)\}$ such that for all players $b \in \Sigma - \Gamma$ and moves $j_b \in \{1, ..., d_b(q)\}$, we have $\delta(q, j_1, ..., j_k) \in \rho$.

(4) The function $Img : Q \times 2^{Q\times Q} \to Q$, which takes as input a state q and a binary relation $R \subseteq Q \times Q$, and returns the set of states that are accessible from q via R. That is, $Img(q, R) = \{q' \mid qRq'\}$.

(5) Union, intersection, difference, and inclusion test for state sets. Note also that we write $Eval(true, e)$ for the set Q of all states, and write $Eval(false, e)$ for the empty set of states.

Partial correctness of the algorithm can be proved induction on the structure of the input formula φ. Termination is guaranteed since the state space Q is finite.

Proposition 1. The algorithm given in the above terminates and is correct, i.e., it returns the set of states in which the input formula is satisfied.

The cases where $\varphi' = K_a\theta$, $\varphi' = E_\Gamma\theta$, $\varphi' = C_\Gamma\theta$, $\varphi' = K_a^p\theta$, $\varphi' = E_\Gamma^p\theta$ and $\varphi' = C_\Gamma^p\theta$ simply involve the computation of the Img function at most polynomial times, each computation requiring time at most $O(|Q|^2)$. Furthermore, real-time CTL model checking algorithm can be done in polynomial time. Hence the above algorithm for $RATPK$ requires at most polynomial time.

Proposition 2. The algorithm given in the above costs at most polynomial time on $|Q|$.

A famous efficient model checking technique is symbolic model checking [22], which uses ordered binary-decision diagrams (*OBDDs*) to represent Kripke structures. Roughly speaking, if each state is a valuation for a set X of Boolean variables, then a state set ρ can be encoded by a Boolean expression $\rho(X)$ over the variables in X. For Kripke structures that arise from descriptions of closed systems with Boolean state variables, the symbolic operations necessary for CTL model checking have standard implementations. In this case, a transition relation R on states can be encoded by a Boolean expression $\underline{R}(X, X')$ over X and X',where X' is a copy of X that represents the values of the state variables after a transition. Then, the *pre-image* of ρ under R, i.e., the set of states that have R-successors in ρ, can be computed as $\exists X'(\underline{R}(X, X') \wedge \underline{\rho}(X'))$. Based on this observation, symbolic model checkers for CTL, such as $\widetilde{SMV}$ [6], typically use *OBDDs* to represent Boolean expressions, and implement the Boolean and pre-image operations on state sets by manipulating *OBDDs*.

To apply symbolic techniques to our model checking algorithm, we should mainly give symbolic implementation of the computation of $Eval(K_a\theta)$, $Eval(E_\Gamma\theta)$, $Eval(C_\Gamma\theta)$, $Eval(K_a^p\theta)$, $Eval(E_\Gamma^p\theta)$ and $Eval(C_\Gamma^p\theta)$. The computation of $Eval(K_a\theta)$ can also be done using standard symbolic techniques. When given an equivalence relation $\sim_a$ and a set ρ of states, suppose that $\underline{\sim_a}(X', X)$ is a Boolean expression that encodes the equivalence relation $\sim_a$ and $\underline{\rho}(X')$ is a Boolean expression that encodes the set ρ of states, then $\{q \mid Img(q, \sim_a) \subseteq \rho\}$ can be computed as $\exists X'(\underline{\sim_a}(X', X) \wedge (X \rightarrow \underline{\rho}(X')))$. The computation of $Eval(E_\Gamma\theta)$, $Eval(C_\Gamma\theta)$, $Eval(K_a^p\theta)$, $Eval(E_\Gamma^p\theta)$ and $Eval(C_\Gamma^p\theta)$ can be done similarly.

4 A Case Study

In this section we study an example of how *RATPK* can be used to represent and verify the properties in multi-agent systems. The system we consider is a train controller (adapted from [1]). The system consists of three agents: two trains and a controller–see Figure 1. The trains, one Eastbound, the other Westbound, occupy a circular track. The trains cost one hour to pass through the circular track. At one point, both tracks need to pass through a narrow tunnel. There is no room for both trains to be in the tunnel at the same time, therefore the trains must avoid this to happen. Traffic lights are placed on both sides of the tunnel, which can be either red or green. Both trains are equipped with a signaller, that they use to send a signal when they approach the tunnel. The train will enter the tunnel between 300 and 500 seconds from this event. The controller can receive signals from both trains, and controls the colour of the traffic lights within 50 seconds. The task of the controller is to ensure that trains are never both in the tunnel at the same time. The trains follow the traffic lights signals diligently, i.e., they stop on red.

In the following, we use in_tunnel_a to represent that agent a is in the tunnel.

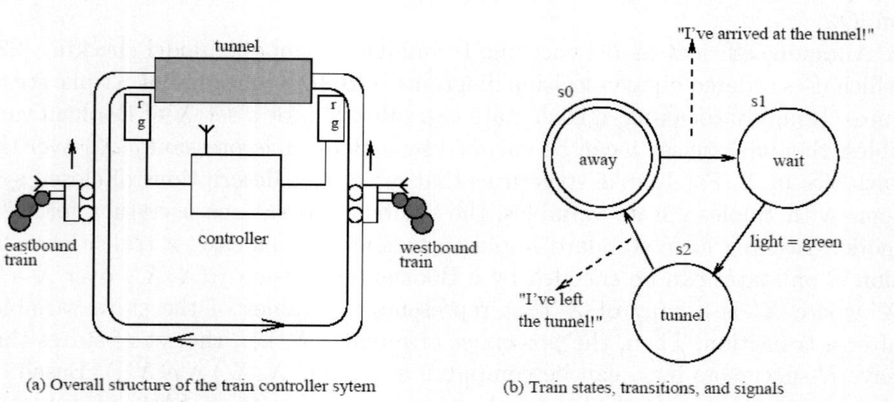

Fig. 1. The local transition structures for the two trains and the controller

Firstly, consider the property that "when one train is in the tunnel, it knows the other train is not the tunnel":

$\langle\langle\emptyset\rangle\rangle[](in\_tunnel_a \rightarrow K_a \neg in\_tunnel_b)$ $(a \neq b \in \{TrainE, TrainW\})$

We now consider the formula that express the fact that "it is always common knowledge that the grand coalition of all agents can cooperate to get train a in the tunnel within one hour":

$\langle\langle\emptyset\rangle\rangle[]C_\Sigma\langle\langle\Sigma\rangle\rangle <>_{[0,1hour]}$ in_tunnel_a $(a \in \{TrainE, TrainW\})$, where we abbreviate $\langle\langle\Gamma\rangle\rangle <>_{[i,j]} \varphi$ as $\neg\langle\langle\Gamma\rangle\rangle[]_{[i,j]}\neg\varphi$.

We can verify these formulas by using our model checking algorithm for *RATPK*, and results show that the above propertiesy hold in the system. In some cases, the communication is not unreliable, and the signal send by trains may be not received by the train controller. Therefore the train controller may have probabilistic knowledge such as "the probability of '*TrainE* has send a signal' is no less than 0.6." Such properties can also be expressed in *RATPK* and verified by our model checking algorithm.

5 Conclusions

Recently, there has been growing interest in the logics for representing and reasoning temporal and epistemic properties in multi-agent systems [4,11,16,17,20,21,24]. In this paper, we present a real-time temporal probabilistic knowledge logic *RATPK*, which is a succinct and powerful language for expressing complex properties. In [14], Halpern and Moses also presented and study some real-time knowledge modalities such as ϵ-common knowledge C_G^ϵ, $\langle\rangle$-common knowledge $C_G^{\langle\rangle}$ and timestamped common knowledge C_G^T. It is easy to see that all these modalities can be expressed in *RATPK,* for example, $C_G^{\langle\rangle} \Leftrightarrow \langle\rangle C_G$ and $C_G^T \Leftrightarrow []_{[T,T]} C_G$. Moreover, the approach to model checking *RATPK* is studied. It is also hopeful to apply such *RATPK* logic and this model checking algorithm to verify the correctness of real-time protocol systems.

References

1. R. Alur, L. de Alfaro, T. A. Henzinger, S. C. Krishnan, F. Y. C. Mang, S. Qadeer, S. K. Rajamni, and S. Tasiran, MOCHA user manual, University of Berkeley Report, 2000.
2. R. Alur and T. A. Henzinger. Alternating-time temporal logic. In Journal of the ACM, 49(5): 672-713.
3. A. Arnold and D. Niwinski. Rudiments of μ-calculus. Studies in Logic, Vol 146, North-Holland, 2001.
4. M. Bourahla and M. Benmohamed. Model Checking Multi-Agent Systems. In Informatica 29: 189-197, 2005.
5. J. Bradfield and C. Stirling. Modal Logics and mu-Calculi: An Introduction. In Handbook of Process Algebra, Chapter 4. Elsevier Science B.V. 2001.
6. E. M. Clarke, J. O. Grumberg, and D. A. Peled. Model checking. The MIT Press, 1999.

7. Zining Cao, Chunyi Shi. Probabilistic Belief Logic and Its Probabilistic Aumann Semantics. J. Comput. Sci. Technol. 18(5): 571-579, 2003.
8. H. van Ditmarsch, W van der Hoek, and B. P. Kooi. Dynamic Epistemic Logic with Assignment, in AAMAS05, ACM Inc, New York, vol. 1, 141-148, 2005.
9. E. A. Emerson, C. S. Jutla, and A. P. Sistla. On model checking for fragments of the μ-calculus. In CAV93, LNCS 697, 385-396, 1993.
10. N. de C. Ferreira, M. Fisher, W. van der Hoek: Practical Reasoning for Uncertain Agents. Proc. JELIA-04, LNAI 3229, pp82-94.
11. N. de C. Ferreira, M. Fisher, W. van der Hoek: Logical Implementation of Uncertain Agents. Proc. EPIA-05, LNAI 3808, pp536-547.
12. R. Fagin, J. Y. Halpern, Y. Moses and M. Y.Vardi. Reasoning about knowledge. Cambridge, Massachusetts: The MIT Press, 1995.
13. R. Fagin, J. Y. Halpern, Y. Moses, and M. Y. Vardi. Common knowledge revisited, Annals of Pure and Applied Logic 96: 89-105, 1999.
14. J. Y. Halpern and Y. Moses. Knowledge and common knowledge in a distributed environment. J ACM, 1990, 37(3): 549-587.
15. W. van der Hoek. Some considerations on the logic PFD: A logic combining modality and probability. J. Applied Non-Classical Logics, 7(3):287-307, 1997.
16. W. van der Hoek and M. Wooldridge. Model Checking Knowledge, and Time. In Proceedings of SPIN 2002, LNCS 2318, 95-111, 2002.
17. W. van der Hoek and M. Wooldridge. Cooperation, Knowledge, and Time: Alternating-time Temporal Epistemic Logic and its Applications. Studia Logica, 75: 125-157, 2003.
18. M. Jurdzinski. Deciding the winner in parity games is in UP∩co-UP. Information Processing Letters, 68: 119-134, 1998.
19. M. Jurdzinski, M. Paterson and U. Zwick. A Deterministic Subexponential Algorithm for Solving Parity Games. In Proceedings of ACM-SIAM Symposium on Discrete Algorithms, SODA 2006, January 2006.
20. M. Kacprzak, A. Lomuscio and W. Penczek. Verification of multiagent systems via unbounded model checking. In Proceedings of the 3rd International Conference on Autonomous Agents and Multiagent Systems (AAMAS-04), 2004.
21. B. P. Kooi. Probabilistic Dynamic Epistemic Logic. Journal of Logic, Language and Information 2003, 12: 381-408.
22. K. L. McMillan. Symbolic model checking: An Approach to the State Explosion Problem. Kluwer Academic, 1993.
23. I. Walukiewicz. Completeness of Kozen's axiomatisation of the propositional μ-calculus. Information and Computation 157, 142-182, 2000.
24. M. Wooldridge, M. Fisher, M. Huget, and S. Parsons. Model checking multiagent systems with mable. In Proceedings of the First International Conference on Autonomous Agents and Multiagent Systems (AAMAS-02), 2002.

Regulating Social Exchanges Between Personality-Based Non-transparent Agents*

G.P. Dimuro, A.C.R. Costa, L.V. Gonçalves, and A. Hübner

Escola de Informática, PPGINF, Universidade Católica de Pelotas
96010-000 Pelotas, Brazil
{liz, rocha, llvarga, hubner}@ucpel.tche.br

Abstract. This paper extends the scope of the model of regulation of social exchanges based on the concept of a supervisor of social equilibrium. We allow the supervisor to interact with personality-based agents that control the supervisor access to their internal states, behaving either as transparent agents (agents that allow full external access to their internal states) or as non-transparent agents (agents that restrict such external access). The agents may have different personality traits, which induce different attitudes towards both the regulation mechanism and the possible profits of social exchanges. Also, these personality traits influence the agents' evaluation of their current status. To be able to reason about the social exchanges among personality-based non-transparent agents, the equilibrium supervisor models the system as a Hidden Markov Model.

1 Introduction

Social control is a powerful notion for explaining the self-regulation of a society, and the various possibilities for its realization have been considered, both in natural and artificial societies [1,2]. Social rules may be enforced by *authorities* that have the capacity to force the agents of the society to follow such rules, or they may be *internalized* by the agents, so that agents follow such rules because they were incorporated into the agents' behaviors.

The centralized social exchange control mechanism presented in [3,4] is based on the Piaget's theory of *social exchange values* [5].[1] It is performed by an *equilibrium supervisor*, whose duty is: (i) to determine, at each time, the target equilibrium point for the system; (ii) to decide on which actions it should recommend agents to perform in order to lead the system towards that equilibrium point; (iii) to maintain the system equilibrated until another equilibrium point is required. For that, the supervisor builds on *Qualitative Interval Markov Decision Processes* (QI-MDP) [3,4], MDP's [11] based on Interval Mathematics [12].

In this paper, trying to advance the development of a future model of *decentralized* social control, we extend the centralized model presented in [3,4], to

* This work has been partially supported by CNPq and FAPERGS.

[1] A discussion about related work on value-based approaches was presented in [6]. Values have been used in the MAS area, through value and market-oriented decision, and value-based social theory [7,8,9]. However, other work based on social exchange values appeared only in the application to the modeling of partners selection [10].

A. Gelbukh and C.A. Reyes-Garcia (Eds.): MICAI 2006, LNAI 4293, pp. 1105–1115, 2006.

consider a *personality-based* agent society. We allow the agents to have different personality traits, which induce different attitudes towards the regulation mechanism (blind obedience, eventual obedience etc.) and the possible profits of social exchanges (egoism, altruism etc.). Also, these personality traits influence the agents' evaluation of their current status (realism, over- or under-evaluation). So, the agents may or may not follow the given recommendations, thus creating a probabilistic social environment, from the point of view of social control.

We observe that the study of personality-based multiagent interactions can be traced back to at least [13,14,15], where the advantages and possible applications of the approach were extensively discussed. In both works, personality traits were mapped into goals and practical reasoning rules (internal point of view). Modeling personality traits from an external (the supervisor's) point of view, through state transition matrices as we do here, seems to be new.

The agents are able to control the supervisor access to their internal states, behaving either as *transparent agents* (that allow full external access to their internal states) or as *non-transparent agents* (that restrict such external access). When the agents are transparent, the supervisor has full knowledge of their personality traits and has access to all current balances of values, and so it is able to choose, at each step, the adequate recommendation for each agent [6].

In the paper, we focus on the supervisor dealing only with non-transparent agents. The supervisor has no direct access to their balances of *material* exchange values, and must thus rely on observations of what the agents report each other about their balances of *virtual* exchange values, considering also that the agents are influenced by their personalities in their subjective evaluation of their current status. We also assume that, due to the non-transparency, the supervisor has no direct knowledge of the agents' personality traits.

To solve the problems of determining the most probable current state of the system, recognizing agent's personalities and learning new personalities traits, the supervisor uses a mechanism based on Hidden Markov Models (HMM) [16].

The paper is structured as follows. In Sect. 2, we review the modelling of social exchanges. Section 3 presents the proposed regulation mechanism. Section 4 introduces the exchanges between personality-based agents. The HMM is introduced in Sect. 5, and simulation results in Sect. 6. Section 7 is the Conclusion.

2 The Modelling of Social Exchanges

The evaluation of an exchange by an agent is done on the basis of a *scale* of *exchange values* [5], which are of a qualitative nature – subjective values like those everyone uses to judge the daily exchanges it has (*good*, *bad* etc.). In order to capture the qualitative nature of Piaget's concept of scale of exchange values [5], techniques from Interval Mathematics [12] are used, representing any value as an interval $X = [x_1, x_2]$, with $-L \leq x_1 \leq x \leq x_2 \leq L$, $x_1, x_2, L \in \mathbb{R}$.[2]

[2] According to Piaget [5], the subjective nature of social exchange values prevents approaching social exchanges with methods normally obtained in Economy, since there the affective personality traits of the social agents are often abstracted away to allow economic behaviors to be captured in their rational constitution.

A *social exchange* between two agents, α and β, is performed involving two types of stages. In stages of type $\mathrm{I}_{\alpha\beta}$, the agent α realizes a service for the agent β. The exchange values involved in this stage are the following: $r_{\mathrm{I}_{\alpha\beta}}$ (the value of the *investment* done by α for the realization of a service for β, which is always *negative*); $s_{\mathrm{I}_{\beta\alpha}}$ (the value of β's *satisfaction* due to the receiving of the service done by α); $t_{\mathrm{I}_{\beta\alpha}}$ (the value of β's *debt*, the debt it acquired to α for its satisfaction with the service done by α); and $v_{\mathrm{I}_{\alpha\beta}}$ (the value of the *credit* that α acquires from β for having realized the service). In stages of the type $\mathrm{II}_{\alpha\beta}$, the agent α asks the payment for the service previously done for β, and the values related with this exchange have similar meaning. $r_{\mathrm{I}_{\alpha\beta}}$, $s_{\mathrm{I}_{\beta\alpha}}$, $r_{\mathrm{II}_{\beta\alpha}}$ and $s_{\mathrm{II}_{\alpha\beta}}$ are called *material values*. $t_{\mathrm{I}_{\beta\alpha}}$, $v_{\mathrm{I}_{\alpha\beta}}$, $t_{\mathrm{II}_{\beta\alpha}}$ and $v_{\mathrm{II}_{\alpha\beta}}$ are the *virtual values*. The order in which the exchange stages may occur is not necessarily $\mathrm{I}_{\alpha\beta} - \mathrm{II}_{\alpha\beta}$. We observe that the values are undefined if either no service is done in a stage of type I, or no credit is charged in a stage of type II. Also, it is not possible for α to realize a service for β and, at the same, to charge him a credit.

A *social exchange process* is a sequence of stages of type $\mathrm{I}_{\alpha\beta}$ and/or $\mathrm{II}_{\alpha\beta}$. The *material results*, according to the points of view of α and β, are given by the sum of the well defined material values involved in the process, and are denoted, respectively, by $\mathbf{m}_{\alpha\beta}$ and $\mathbf{m}_{\beta\alpha}$. The *virtual results* $\mathbf{v}_{\alpha\beta}$ and $\mathbf{v}_{\beta\alpha}$ are defined analogously. A social exchange process is said to be in *material equilibrium* if $\mathbf{m}_{\alpha\beta}$ and $\mathbf{m}_{\beta\alpha}$ are around a reference value $s \in \mathbb{R}$. Observe that, in any exchange stage, either α or β has to perform a service, so decreasing its material results.

3 The Social Exchange Regulation Mechanism

Figure 1 shows the architecture of our social exchange regulation mechanism, which extends the one proposed in [4] with a learning module based on HMM [16]. The *equilibrium supervisor*, at each time, uses an *Evaluation Module* to analyze the conditions and constraints imposed by the system's external and internal environments (not shown in the figure), determining the target equilibrium point. To regulate *transparent* agents, the supervisor uses a Balance Module (Σ) to calculate their *balances* of material results of the performed exchanges. To regulate *non-transparent* agents, the supervisor uses an observation module (*Obs.*) to access the virtual values (debts and credits) that they report, and the HMM module to recognize and maintain an adequate model of the personality traits of such agents, generating *plausible balances* of their material exchange values.

Taking both the directly observed and the indirectly calculated material results, together with the currently target equilibrium point, the supervisor uses the module that implements a personality-based QI–MDP to decide on recommendations of exchanges for the two agents, in order to keep the material results of exchanges in equilibrium. It also takes into account the virtual results of the exchanges in order to decide which type of exchange stage it should suggest.

The *states* of a QI–MDP [4] are pairs $(E_{\alpha,\beta}, E_{\beta,\alpha})$ of classes of material results (investments and satisfactions) of exchanges between agents α and β, from the

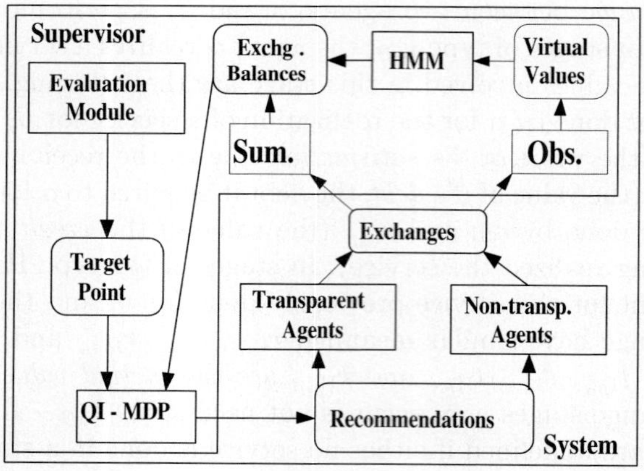

Fig. 1. The regulation mechanism for personality-based social exchanges

point of view of α and β, respectively.[3] $\mathbf{E}_s = \{E_s^-, E_s^0, E_s^+\}$ is the set of the supervisor representation of the classes of *unfavorable* (E_s^-), *equilibrated* (E_s^0) and *favorable* (E_s^+) material results of exchanges, related to a target equilibrium point s. $(E^0_{\alpha,\beta}, E^0_{\beta,\alpha})$ is the *terminal* state, when the system is in equilibrium.

The *actions* of the QI–MDP model are state transitions that have the form $(E^i_{\alpha,\beta}, E^j_{\beta,\alpha}) \mapsto (E^{i'}_{\alpha,\beta}, E^{j'}_{\beta,\alpha})$, with $i, i', j, j' \in \{-, 0, +\}$, which may be of the following types: a *compensation action*, which directs the agents' exchanges to the equilibrium point; a *go-forward action*, which directs them to increasing material results; a *go-backward action*, which directs them to decreasing material results.

The supervisor has to find, for the current state $(E^i_{\alpha,\beta}, E^j_{\beta,\alpha})$, the action that may achieve the terminal state $(E^0_{\alpha,\beta}, E^0_{\beta,\alpha})$. The choice of actions is constrained by the rules of the social exchanges and some transitions are *forbidden* (e.g., both agents increasing results simultaneously), so in some cases the supervisor has to find alternative paths in order to lead the system to the equilibrium.

An action generates an *optimal exchange recommendation*, consisting of a partially defined exchange stage that the agents are suggested to perform. Also, by the analysis of the agent's virtual results (debts and credits), the supervisor recommends a specific type of exchange stage (I or II).

4 Social Exchanges Between Personality-Based Agents

We define different levels of obedience to the supervisor that the agents may present: (i) *Blind Obedience* (the agent always follows the recommendations), (ii) *Eventual Obedience* (the agents may not follow the recommendations, according to a certain probability) and (iii) *Full Disregard of Recommendations* (the agent always decides on its own, disregarding what was recommended).

[3] In this paper, we considered just a sample of classes of material results. See [3,4] for the whole family of classes of a QI-MDP, and the procedure for determining them.

The agents may have different social attitudes that give rise to a state-transition function, which specify, for each obedience level, and given the current state and recommendation, a probability distribution $\Pi(\mathbf{E}_s)$ over the set of states $\mathbf{E}_s$ that the interacting agents will try to achieve next, depending on the their personality traits. In the following, we illustrate some of those personality traits (Table 1): (i) *Egoism* (the agent is mostly seeking his own benefit, with a high probability to accept exchanges that represent transitions toward states where it has favorable results); (ii) *Altruism* (the agent is mostly seeking the benefit of the other, with a high probability to accept exchanges that represent transitions toward states where the other agent has favorable results). (iii) *Fanaticism* (the agent has a very high probability to enforce exchanges that lead it to the equilibrium, avoiding other kinds of transitions); (iv) *Tolerance* (the agent has a high probability to enforce exchanges that lead it to the equilibrium if his material results are far from that state, but it accepts other kinds of transitions).

Table 1. A pattern of probability distribution $\Pi(\mathbf{E}_s)$ for individual agent transitions

	Egoist agents			Altruist agents		
$\Pi(\mathbf{E}_s)$	E^0	E^+	E^-	E^0	E^+	E^-
E^0	low	very high	very low	low	very low	very high
E^+	low	very high	very low	low	very low	very high
E^-	low	very high	very low	low	very low	very high
	Fanatic agents			**Tolerant agents**		
$\Pi(\mathbf{E}_s)$	E^0	E^+	E^-	E^0	E^+	E^-
E^0	very high	very low	very low	high	low	low
E^+	very high	very low	very low	high	low	low
E^-	very high	very low	very low	high	low	low

Table 2 shows parts of sample state-transition functions $\mathbf{F}$ for systems composed by (a) two tolerant agents and (b) two egoist agents that always disregard the supervisor's recommendations. The mark **X** indicates that the transition is forbidden according to the social exchange rules (both agents cannot increase their material results simultaneously, as explained in Sect. 3). The system (b) presents an absorbent state, (E^-, E^-), meaning that the system is not able to leave that state if it reaches it[4], and so may never achieve the target equilibrium point. We remark that even if the agents present a certain level of obedience, there may be a great deal of uncertainty about the effects of the supervisor's recommendations. For example, considering an obedience level of 50%, the state-transition functions shown in Table 2 becomes the ones shown in Table 3.

Since the supervisor has no access to the current state (material results of exchanges), it has to rely on observations of the agents' evaluations of their virtual results (*debts* (D), *credits* (C) or null results (N)). Due to their personality traits, they may present different attitudes concerning such evaluations (Table 4): (i) *Realism* (the agent has a very high probability to proceed to realistic evaluations); (ii) *Over-evaluation* (the agent has a very high probability to report that

[4] The probability 100% in the last line of Table 2(b) just means that the agents refuse to exchange, remaining in the same state (E^-, E^-).

Table 2. Parts of state-transition functions **F** for pairs of agents that always disregard recommendations

(a) (tolerant, tolerant) agents

F (%)	(E^0,E^0)	(E^0,E^+)	(E^0,E^-)	(E^+,E^0)	(E^+,E^+)	(E^+,E^-)	(E^-,E^0)	(E^-,E^+)	(E^-,E^-)
(E^0,E^0)	63.90	**X**	13.70	**X**	**X**	2.90	13.70	2.90	2.90
(E^+,E^-)	49.20	10.50	10.50	10.50	2.20	2.20	10.50	2.20	2.20
(E^-,E^-)	**X**	**X**	37.85	**X**	**X**	8.10	37.85	8.10	8.10

(b) (egoist, egoist) agents

F (%)	(E^0,E^0)	(E^0,E^+)	(E^0,E^-)	(E^+,E^0)	(E^+,E^+)	(E^+,E^-)	(E^-,E^0)	(E^-,E^+)	(E^-,E^-)
(E^0,E^-)	**X**	**X**	0.00	**X**	**X**	0.00	15.00	85.00	0.00
(E^+,E^+)	2.20	12.00	0.70	12.00	64.10	4.00	0.70	4.00	0.30
(E^+,E^-)	2.20	12.80	0.00	12.00	68.00	0.00	0.70	4.30	0.00
(E^-,E^-)	**X**	**X**	0.00	**X**	**X**	0.00	0.00	0.00	100.00

Table 3. Parts of state-transition functions **F** for pair of agents with 50% of obedience

(a) (tolerant, tolerant) agents

F (%)	(E^0,E^0)	(E^0,E^+)	(E^0,E^-)	(E^+,E^0)	(E^+,E^+)	(E^+,E^-)	(E^-,E^0)	(E^-,E^+)	(E^-,E^-)
(E^0,E^0)	81.95	**X**	6.85	**X**	**X**	1.45	6.85	1.45	1.45
(E^+,E^-)	74.6	5.25	5.25	5.25	1.10	1.10	5.25	1.10	1.10
(E^-,E^-)	**X**	**X**	18.92	**X**	**X**	29.05	18.92	29.05	4.06

(b) (egoist, egoist) agents

F (%)	(E^0,E^0)	(E^0,E^+)	(E^0,E^-)	(E^+,E^0)	(E^+,E^+)	(E^+,E^-)	(E^-,E^0)	(E^-,E^+)	(E^-,E^-)
(E^0,E^-)	**X**	**X**	0.0%	**X**	**X**	25.00	7.50	67.50	0.00
(E^+,E^+)	51.10	6.00	0.35	6.00	32.05	2.00	0.35	2.00	0.15
(E^+,E^-)	51.10	6.40	0.00	6.00	34.00	0.00	0.35	2.15	0.00
(E^-,E^-)	**X**	**X**	0.00	**X**	**X**	25.00	0.00	25.00	50.00

Table 4. A pattern of probability distribution $\Pi(\mathbf{O})$ over the set of observations $\mathbf{O} = \{N, D, C\}$ of agents' evaluations of their virtual results, in each state

	Realistic agents			Over-evaluator agents			Under-evaluator agents		
$\Pi(\mathbf{O})$	D	N	C	D	N	C	D	N	C
E^0	very low	very high	very low	very low	low	very high	very high	low	very low
E^+	very high	very low	very low	low	medium	high	very high	very low	very low
E^-	very low	very low	very high	very low	very low	very high	high	medium	low

Table 5. Part of an observation function **G** for (under-eval.,over-eval.) agents

G (%)	(N,N)	(N,D)	(N,C)	(D,N)	(D,D)	(D,C)	(C,N)	(C,D)	(C,C)
(E^0,E^0)	4	0	16	16	0	64	0	0	0
(E^0,E^-)	0	0	20	0	0	80	0	0	0
(E^+,E^-)	0	0	0	0	0	100	0	0	0
(E^-,E^-)	0	0	30	0	0	50	0	0	20

it has credits); (iii) *Under-evaluation* (the agent has a very high probability to report that it has debts). Table 5 shows part of a sample observation function **G** that gives a probability distribution of observations of evaluations of virtual results for a pair of (under-evaluator,over-evaluator) agents, in each state.

5 Reasoning About Exchanges

To be able to reason about exchanges between pairs of non-transparent personality-based agents, the supervisor models the system as Hidden Markov Model [16].

Definition 1. *A Hidden Markov Model (HMM) for exchanges between non-transparent personality-based agents is a tuple* $\langle \mathbf{E}_s, \mathbf{O}, \pi, \mathbf{F}, \mathbf{G} \rangle$*, where: (i) the set* $\mathbf{E}_s$ *of states is given by the pairs of classes of material results, where s is the equilibrium point:* $\mathbf{E}_s = \{(E^0, E^0), (E^0, E^+), (E^0, E^-), (E^+, E^0), (E^+, E^+), (E^+, E^-), (E^-, E^0), (E^-, E^+), (E^-, E^-)\}$*; (ii) the set* $\mathbf{O}$ *of observations is given by the possible pairs of agents' evaluations of virtual results:* $\mathbf{O} = \{(N, N), (N, D), (N, C), (D, N), (D, D), (D, C), (C, N), (C, D), (C, C)\}$*; (iii)* π *is the initial probability distribution over the set of states* $\mathbf{E}_s$*; (iv)* $\mathbf{F} : \mathbf{E}_s \rightarrow \Pi(\mathbf{E}_s)$ *is the state-transition function, which gives for each state, a probability distribution over the set of states* $\mathbf{E}_s$*; (v)* $\mathbf{G} : \mathbf{E}_s \rightarrow \Pi(\mathbf{O})$ *is the observation function that gives, for each state, a probability distribution over the set of observations* $\mathbf{O}$*.*

This model allows the supervisor to perform the following tasks:

Task 1: to find the probability of a sequence of agents' evaluations of virtual results, using a *backward-forward* algorithm [16];
Task 2: to find the most probable sequence of states associated to a sequence of agents' evaluations of virtual results, using the *Viterbi* algorithm [16];
Task 3: to maintain an adequate model of the personality traits of the agents, given their observable behaviors: the supervisor adjusts the parameters of its current model to the probability of occurrence of a frequent sequence of observations (via the *Baum-Welch* algorithm [16]), in order to compare the resulting model with the known models and to classify it.

Notice that, whenever a new non-transparent agent join the society, the supervisor assumes the position of an observer, building HHMs in order to obtain an adequate model of the personality traits of such agent and to find the most probable state of the system at a given instant. After that, it is able to start making recommendations. We assume that obtaining the model of an agent's personality traits is independent of the agent's degree of obedience. Of course, to discover the degree of obedience of an agent is a trivial task.

6 Simulation Results

Some simulation results were chosen for the discussion, considering the supervisor's tasks detailed in Sect. 5. For that, adaptations of the well-known algorithms *backward-forward* (for task 1), *Viterbi* (for task 2) and *Baum-Welch* (for task 3) (see [16]), were incorporated in the supervisor behaviour (Fig. 1, HHM module).

6.1 Simulation of Tasks 1 and 2

The methodology used for the analysis of the performance of the supervisor in the tasks **1** and **2** considered: (i) test-situations with two agents, combining all different personality traits; (ii) a uniform initial probability distribution π over the set of states; (iii) the computation of the probabilities of occurrence of all sequences of two consecutive observations (agents' evaluations); (iv) the computation of the most probable sequence of states that generates each observation.

Table 6(a) presents some peculiar results obtained for a pair of *tolerant/realist* agents. As expected, the simulations showed that the observations reflected the actual state transitions. The most probable sequences of observations were those ending in null virtual results, associated to transitions toward the equilibrium (e.g., obs. 1, 2, 3). The state transitions that did not faithfully reflect the observations were those that took the place of transitions that are forbidden, according to the social rules of the modelling. For example, the transition found for observation 4 (which presented the lowest occurrence probability, for sequences ending in null results) was found in place of $(E^0, E^-) \rightarrow (E^0, E^0)$, since the latter is a forbidden transition. Observations with very low probability were associated, in general, to transitions that went away from the equilibrium (e.g., obs. 5).

Table 6(b) shows some selected results for a pair of (*tolerant/under-evaluator*, *tolerant/over-evaluator*) agents. As expected, the transitions did not always reflect the observations (e.g., obs. 1, 2). Nonetheless, the overall set of simulations showed that almost 70% of the observations ending in null results coincided with transitions ending in the equilibrium. However, those observations presented very low probability (e.g., obs. 1 and 3, the latter having the lowest occurrence probability, since it reflected an adequate transition, which was not expected for non realist agents). Observation 4 presented the highest occurrence probability, and its associated transition towards to the equilibrium point was the most expected one for a pair of tolerant agents. There was always a high probability that the agents evaluated their virtual results as (D, C) whenever they were in the equilibrium state, as expected. In general, sequences of observations containing the results (D, C) were the most probable; on the contrary, sequences of observation presenting (C, D) had almost no probability of occurrence (e.g., obs. 5).

Table 6(c) shows some results for a pair of (*egoist/realist*, *altruist/realist*) agents. The observations ending in null virtual results presented very low probabilities, although, in general, they reflected the actual transitions. Observation 2 was the most probable sequence ending in null virtual results. Observation 3 represents that particular case discussed before, in which the corresponding faithful transition was not allowed, and, therefore, the actual transition did not reflect the observation. The most probable observations were those associated to transitions that made the agents depart away from the equilibrium (e.g., obs. 4), or those associated to transitions that maintained benefits for the egoist agent and loss for the altruist agent (e.g., obs. 5).

Table 6(d) shows some results for a pair of (*egoist/under-evaluator*, *altruist/over-evaluator*) agents. The sequences of observations ending in null virtual results presented very low probability (e.g., obs. 1, 2 and 3), but they are still significant because they coincided with transitions ending in the equilibrium. The other sequences of observations that did not end in null results, but corresponded to transitions that led to the equilibrium (e.g., obs. 4), presented no probability of occurrence. Notice the very high probability of observation 5, that reflected exactly the combination of those extreme personalities.

Table 6. Simulation results for pair of agents

(a) (tolerant/realist,tolerant/realist)				(b) (tolerant/under-eval., tolerant/over-eval.)			
N	Observation	Probab.	State Transition	N	Observation	Probab.	State Transition
1	(N,N)-(N,N)	3.6%	$(E^0, E^0) \rightarrow (E^0, E^0)$	1	(N,N)-(N,N)	0.084%	$(E^-, E^+) \rightarrow (E^0, E^0)$
2	(D,D)-(N,N)	3.4%	$(E^+, E^+) \rightarrow (E^0, E^0)$	2	(D,C)-(N,N)	1.902%	$(E^-, E^-) \rightarrow (E^-, E^0)$
3	(D,N)-(N,N)	3.3%	$(E^+, E^0) \rightarrow (E^0, E^0)$	3	(C,D)-(N,N)	0.014%	$(E^-, E^+) \rightarrow (E^0, E^0)$
4	(N,C)-(N,N)	1.5%	$(E^0, E^0) \rightarrow (E^0, E^0)$	4	(D,C)-(D,C)	35.28%	$(E^+, E^-) \rightarrow (E^0, E^0)$
5	(D,N)-(D,D)	0.3%	$(E^+, E^0) \rightarrow (E^+, E^+)$	5	(C,D)-(C,D)	0.0004%	$(E^-, E^+) \rightarrow (E^-, E^+)$

(c) (egoist/realist, altruist/realist)				(d) (egoist/under-eval., altruist/over-eval.)			
N	Observation	Probab.	State Transition	N	Observation	Probab.	State Transition
1	(N,N)-(N,N)	0.36%	$(E^0, E^0) \rightarrow (E^0, E^0)$	1	(N,N)-(N,N)	0.002%	$(E^-, E^+) \rightarrow (E^0, E^0)$
2	(D,D)-(N,N)	0.42%	$(E^+, E^+) \rightarrow (E^0, E^0)$	2	(D,C)-(N,N)	0.070%	$(E^+, E^-) \rightarrow (E^0, E^0)$
3	(C,N)-(N,N)	0.27%	$(E^-, E^0) \rightarrow (E^0, E^-)$	3	(D,N)-(N,N)	0.016%	$(E^+, E^+) \rightarrow (E^0, E^0)$
4	(N,N)-(D,C)	5.07%	$(E^0, E^0) \rightarrow (E^+, E^-)$	4	(C,D)-(C,D)	0.000%	$(E^-, E^+) \rightarrow (E^0, E^0)$
5	(C,D)-(D,C)	5.35%	$(E^-, E^+) \rightarrow (E^+, E^-)$	5	(D,C)-(D,C)	53.71%	$(E^+, E^-) \rightarrow (E^+, E^-)$

6.2 Simulation of Task 3

The methodology used for the analysis of the performance of the equilibrium supervisor in the task **3** considered the following steps: (i) given a frequently noticed sequence of observations of evaluations of virtual results, the HMM is adjusted by generating new parameters (initial distribution, transition and emission matrices) for the probability of such observations; (ii) the new HMM is compared with the models known by the supervisor, stored in a library: the difference between the new HMM and each of such models is evaluated by using the infinite norm, $\|X - Y\|_\infty$, where X is any parameter of a reference HHM, Y is the respective parameter of the new HHM, and $\|A\|_\infty = max_i \sum_{j=1}^{n} \mid A_{ij} \mid$ is the maximum absolute row sum norm of a matrix A; (iii) the new HMM is then classified as either describing a new model of personality traits or being of one of the kinds of models maintained in the library, according to a given error.

To adjust the parameters of a given model, we used the Baum Welch algorithm [16] (which we noticed happened to preserve the compliance of the transition matrices to the exchange rules). Table 7 shows the analysis done by the supervisor when observing the interactions between five non-transparent agents and the others personality-based agents. The results were obtained by comparing adjusted HMM´s (for probabilities of observations) with the other models of pairs of agents, considering the maximum error of 0.7. For simplicity, only realist agents were considered.

For the observation in line 1 (probability of 80%, in interactions with tolerant agents), the least error between the new model and all other models resulted in

Table 7. Recognition of new personality traits (T = tolerance, E = egoism, A = altruism)

N	Observation	Prob. (%)	Least Error (model)	Personality Trait
1	(D,D)-(N,N)-(N,N)	80	0.6 (T,T)	tolerance
2	(D,D)-(N,N)-(N,N)	100	1.0 (T,T)	new classification
3	(D,N)-(D,D)-(D,D)	60	0.6 (E,E)	egoism
4	(N,N)-(C,C)-(C,C)	40	0.6 (A,A)	altruism
5	(D,C)-(C,N)-(D,C)-(C,N)	50	1.2 (T,T)	new classification

its compatibility with a model of *tolerant* agents. So, the supervisor classified the non-transparent agent as *tolerant.* For the observation in line 5 (probability of 50%, in interactions with tolerant agents), the least error found was larger than the admissible error, and then the supervisor concluded that the agent had a new personality trait. Line 2 shows the dependence of the results on the probability of the observation: if in line 1 it was 100%, the supervisor would conclude that the agent presented a new personality trait.

7 Conclusion

The paper leads toward the idea of modelling agents' personality traits in social exchange regulation mechanisms. It extends the centralized regulation mechanism based on the concept of equilibrium supervisor by introducing the possibility that personality-based agents control the supervisor access to their internal states, behaving either as transparent agents (agents that allow full external access to their internal states) or as non-transparent agents (agents that restrict such external access). We studied three sample sets of personality traits: (i) blind obedience, eventual obedience and full disregard of recommendations (related to the levels of adherence to the regulation mechanism), (ii) fanaticism, tolerance, egoism and altruism (in connection to preferences about balances of material results), and (iii) realism, over- and under-evaluation (in connection to the agents' tendencies in the evaluation of their own status).

The main focus was on dealing with non-transparent agents, when the supervisor has to make use of an observation module, implemented as a HHM, to be able to recognize and maintain an adequate model of the personality traits of such agents. This may be important for open agent societies as, for example, in applications for Internet. Also, it seems that the consideration of the agent (non)transparency feature is new to the issue of social control systems.

To analyze the efficiency of the supervisor observation module, we performed simulations which results showed that the approach is viable and applicable. Also, the simulations hinted on the possibility of establishing sociological properties of the proposed HMM, like the property that the adjustment of a given model by the Baum-Welch procedure preserves the constraints imposed by the rules that regulate the value-exchange processes.

Future work is concerned with the internalization of the supervisor into the agents themselves, going toward the idea of self-regulation of exchange processes, not only distributing the decision process [17], but also considering incomplete information about the balances of material results of the exchanges between non-transparent agents, in the form of a *personality-based qualitative interval* Partially Observable Markov Decision Process (POMDP) [18,19].

References

1. Castelfranchi, C.: Engineering social order. In Omicini, A., Tolksdorf, R., Zambonelli, F., eds.: Engineer. Societ. in Agents World. Springer, Berlin (2000) 1–18
2. Homans, G.C.: The Human Group. Harcourt, Brace & World, New York (1950)

3. Dimuro, G.P., Costa, A.C.R., Palazzo, L.A.M.: Systems of exchange values as tools for multi-agent organizations. Journal of the Brazilian Computer Society **11** (2005) 31–50 (Special Issue on Agents' Organizations).
4. Dimuro, G.P., Costa, A.C.R.: Exchange values and self-regulation of exchanges in multi-agent systems: the provisory, centralized model. In Brueckner, S., Serugendo, G.M., Hales, D., Zambonelli, F., eds.: Proc. Work. on Engineering Self-Organizing Applic., Utrecht, 2005. Number 3910 in LNAI, Berlin, Springer (2006) 75–89
5. Piaget, J.: Sociological Studies. Routlege, London (1995)
6. Dimuro, G.P., Costa, A.C.R., Gonçalves, L.V., Hübner, A.: Centralized regulation of social exchanges between personality-based agents. (In: Proc. of the Work. on Coordination, Organization, Institutions and Norms in Agent Systems, COIN@ECAI'06, Riva del Garda, 2006)
7. Antunes, L., Coelho, H.: Decisions based upon multiple values: the BVG agent architecture. In Barahona, P., Alferes, J.J., eds.: Proc. of IX Portug. Conf. on Artificial Intelligence, Évora. Number 1695 in LNCS, Berlin (1999) 297–311
8. Miceli, M., Castelfranchi, C.: The role of evaluation in cognition and social interaction. In Dautenhahn, K., ed.: Human cognition and agent technology. John Benjamins, Amsterdam (2000) 225–262
9. Walsh, W.E., Wellman, M.P.: A market protocol for distributed task allocation. In: Proc. III Intl. Conf. on Multiagent Systems, Paris (1998) 325–332
10. Rodrigues, M.R., Luck, M.: Analysing partner selection through exchange values. In Antunes, L., Sichman, J., eds.: Proc. of VI Work. on Agent Based Simulations, MABS'05, Utrecht, 2005. Number 3891 in LNAI, Berlin, Springer (2006) 24–40
11. Puterman, M.L.: Markov Decision Processes. Wiley, New York (1994)
12. Moore, R.E.: Methods and Applic. of Interval Analysis. SIAM, Philadelphia (1979)
13. Carbonell, J.G.: Towards a process model of human personality traits. Artificial Intelligence **15** (1980) 49–74
14. Castelfranchi, C., Rosis, F., Falcone, R., Pizzutilo, S.: A testbed for investigating personality-based multiagent cooperation. In: Proc. of the Symp. on Logical Approaches to Agent Modeling and Design, Aix-en-Provence (1997)
15. Castelfranchi, C., Rosis, F., Falcone, R., Pizzutilo, S.: Personality traits and social attitudes in multiagent cooperation. Applied Artif. Intelligence **12** (1998) 649–675
16. Rabiner, L.R.: A tutorial on Hidden Markov Models and selected applications in speech recognition. Proc. of the IEEE **77** (1989) 257–286
17. Boutilier, C.: Multiagent systems: challenges and oportunities for decision theoretic planning. Artificial Intelligence Magazine **20** (1999) 35–43
18. Kaelbling, L.P., Littman, M.L., Cassandra, A.R.: Planning and acting in partially observable stochastic domains. Artificial Intelligence **101** (1998) 99–134
19. Nair, R., Tambe, M., Yokoo, M., Pynadath, D., Marsella, S.: Taming decentralized POMDPs: Towards efficient policy computation for multiagent settings. In: Proc. 18th Intl. Joint Conf. on Artificial Intelligence, IJCAI'03, Acapulco (2003) 705–711

Using MAS Technologies for Intelligent Organizations: A Report of Bottom-Up Results

Armando Robles[1,2], Pablo Noriega[1], Michael Luck[2], and Francisco J. Cantú[3]

[1] IIIA - Artificial Intelligence Research Institute
Bellaterra, Barcelona, Spain
[2] University of Southampton, Electronics and Computer Science
Southampton, United Kingdom
[3] ITESM Campus Monterrey
Research and Graduate Studies Office, Monterrey, N.L. México
{arobles, pablo}@iiia.csic.es, mml@ecs.soton.ac.uk,
fcantu@itesm.mx

Abstract. This paper is a proof of concept report for a bottom-up approach to a conceptual and engineering framework to enable Intelligent Organizations using MAS Technology. We discuss our experience of implementing different types of server agents and a rudimentary *organization engine* for two industrial-scale information systems now in operation. These server agents govern knowledge repositories and user interactions according to workflow scripts that are interpreted by the organization engine. These results show how we have implemented the bottom layer of the proposed framework architecture. They also allow us to discuss how we intend to extend the current organization engine to deal with institutional aspects of an organization other than workflows.

1 Introduction

This paper reports results on two particular aspects of our progress towards a framework to support knowledge intensive organizations: the design of server domain agents and the implementation of an organization engine.

We are proposing a framework for the design of systems enabled by electronic institutions that *drive* the operation of actual corporate information systems. This is an innovative approach to information systems design since we propose ways of stating how an organization is supposed to operate: *its institutional prescription*, and having that prescription control the information system that handles the day to day operation of the organization: *the enactment of the organization*. We are not restricting our proposal to any particular domain of application but we do have in mind organizations that are self-contained (i.e. with a boundary that separates the organization from its environment) and have a stable character (i. e., whose mode of operation does not change very rapidly). We should also make clear that our proposal is not intended for organizational design, what we are proposing is a framework for the design and deployment of agent-based systems that support already designed organizations. Finally, we should point out that we are designing a framework to be applied to new information systems but as this paper demonstrates we find it is also applicable, with some reservations, to the conversion of traditional legacy information systems.

A. Gelbukh and C.A. Reyes-Garcia (Eds.): MICAI 2006, LNAI 4293, pp. 1116–1127, 2006.

In our framework we propose a conceptual architecture and the tools to build corporate information systems. The framework we propose is built around the notion of electronic institution (EI) [2] and uses agent-based technologies intensively. Instead of using the notion of electronic institutions to represent and harness only static procedural features —as is currently the case— we propose to extend the notion of electronic institution to capture conveniently more flexible procedural features. In order to capture other non-procedural institutional features of an organization as well, we use the extended notion of electronic institution and develop different sorts of agents and agent architectures —server agents, organization agents and user agents. In addition to those accretions we are also involved in the consequent extension of available tools in order to handle the added expressiveness and functionality.

In previous papers we have outlined the framework [10] and discussed its components from a top-down perspective [11] and reported the first implementation experiences [13]. In this paper we recount our experience with the *agentification* of two existing corporate information systems of the type we want to be able to capture with our framework and discuss how we plan to extend that experience for the intended framework. The experience of agentifying these industrial scale systems had two main outcomes: a family of actual server agents that deal with the knowledge repositories and user interfaces of the two application domains and a rough version of the organization engine that we propose for the full-blown framework.

The paper is organized as follows: after a quick review of relevant background, we present our basic proposal, in Section 3, and in Section 4 what we have accomplished in the bottom-up agentification process. We then discuss why and how we intend to evolve a workflow engine into an organizational engine in Section 5. Finally, in Section 6 we present ongoing work and conclusions.

2 Background

2.1 Organizations

We think of an organization, a firm, as a self-contained entity where a group of individuals pursue their collective or shared goals by interacting in accordance with some shared conventions and using their available resources as best they can [9,7,1]. This characterization focuses on the social processes and purpose that give substance and personality to a real entity and naturally allows to consider people, processes, information and other resources as part of the organization. We choose to use this particular notion in our discourse because at least for the moment we do not want to commit to other organization-defining criteria like sustainability, fitness in its environment or status and substitutability of personnel. We want to focus further in what have been called *k*nowledge-intensive or *intelligent* organizations whose distinguishing feature is the explicit recognition of their corporate-knowledge and know-how as an asset [6].

The everyday operation of an organization consists of many activities that are somewhat structured and that involve personnel, clients and resources of different sorts. It is usual for organizations to manage and keep track of those activities through on-line information systems that are usually called corporate information systems (*CIS*). We will assume that intelligent organizations have *CIS* and we will further assume that corporate knowledge and know-how may be contained in the *CIS*.

Hotels, hospitals and other types of organizations, have conventions that structure or *institutionalize* their activity in consistent ways so that employees and clients have some certainty about what is expected of them or what to expect from each other. These conventions are usually also a convenient way of establishing procedures that save coordination and learning efforts and pinpoint issues where decision-making is regularly needed. These institutional conventions usually take the form of organizational roles, social structures, canonical documents, standard procedures, rules of conduct, guidelines, policies and records; that is, habits and objects, that participants adhere to in a more or less strict way (cf. e.g. [14]).

Our aim is to design a framework that is fit to capture such institutional aspects of an intelligent organization and make them operational as part of its *CIS*.

2.2 Electronic Institutions

We adopt the concept of electronic institution, EI, as defined in the IIIA and specified through the following components: a *dialogical* framework —that defines ontology, social structure and language conventions— and a *deontological component* that establishes the pragmatics of admissible illocutory actions and manages the obligations established within the institution [8].

EI is currently operationalized as EI_0 [2]. In particular, its deontological component is specified with two constructs that we will refer to in the rest of the paper: First, a *performative structure* that includes a network of scenes linked by transitions. Scenes are role-based interaction protocols specified as finite state machines, arcs labelled by illocutions and nodes corresponding to an institutional state. Transitions describe the role–flow policies between scenes. Second, a set of *rules of behavior* that establish role-based conventions regulating commitments. These are expressed as pre and post-conditions of the illocutions admissible by the performative structure.

There is a set of tools (EIDE)[2] that implements EI_0 electronic institutions. It includes a specification language (ISLANDER) generating an executable EI and middleware (AMELI) that activates a run-time EI to be enacted by actual agents.

We want to take advantage of these developments to capture the institutional aspects of an organization and be able to incorporate these aspects as part of a *CIS*. More precisely, we will use EI notions to represent stable institutional activities, roles, procedures and standard documents. We will also take advantage of EI as coordination artifacts to organize corporate interactions according to the (institutional) conventions of the organization. Finally, we will use an extended version of EI_0 in order to specify and implement an organization engine that enacts the institutional conventions of an organization by driving the operation of the components of its CIS.

3 A Proposal for EI-Enabled Organizations

Our aim is to design a conceptual framework to deal with the design and construction of corporate information systems. Since we intend to make such framework applicable for knowledge-intensive *CIS* and we find that the notion of electronic institution is well adapted to this purpose, we are calling it a framework for EI-enabled organizations. We are proceeding in the following manner:

Agentify the components of standard *CIS* with three types of agents owned and controlled by the organization: *server agents*, *user agents*, and *staff agents*.

Encapsulate institutional knowledge as (a) agentified knowledge repositories of different types (business rules, workflow scripts), (b) decision-making capabilities, guidelines or policies that are modelled as staff agents, and (c) the choice of functions that are delegated in staff agents.

Extend the notion of electronic institution to describe and implement properly the significant institutional aspects of an organization.

Build an operative environment where a prescriptive description of an organization governs and reacts with the *CIS* that handles the day-to-day operation of the organization.

Figure 1 (left) outlines the functional architecture of the framework. That functional architecture has been motivated and described elsewhere ([10], [11]), however, for the purpose of this paper we may say that the top layer is a prescriptive definition of the organization that the bottom layer eventually grounds on the components (users, transactions, programs, data) of the business domain. The core is an *organization engine* built around an *EI* that implements and enforces the institutional conventions through a middleware that maps them into the agentified *CIS* in the bottom layer.

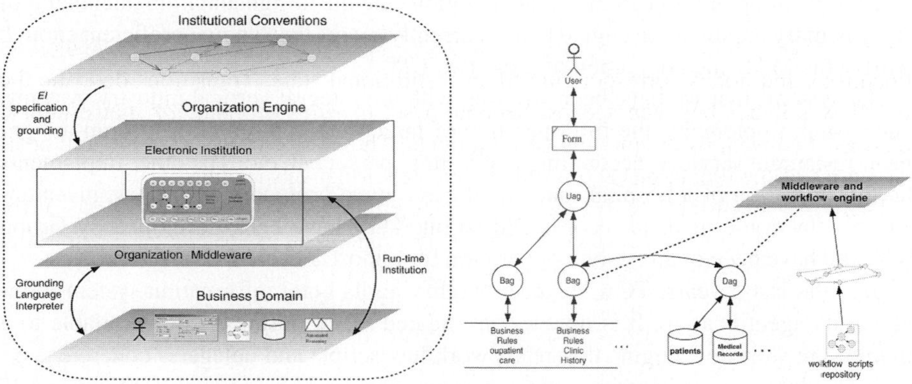

Fig. 1. Architectural diagram of the proposed framework (left) and the implemented workflow engine for the outpatient care system involving *U*ser, *B*usiness rule and *D*atabase server agents(right)

- *The electronic institution layer* implements the normative specification using as input the *performative scripts* produced by the *EI* specification language. The run-time functionalities of this layer are similar to those of AMELI [3,2] since it runs in close interaction with the organization middleware and it guarantees that all interactions comply with the institutional conventions.
- *The organization middleware layer* contains a *grounding language interpreter* and uses it to pass *grounding language commands* from the run-time EI to the CIS components and map actions in the CIS with state transitions in the run-time EI.

Thus, the grounding language is used to specify the sequencing of instantiation of *performative scripts* as well as agent behaviour in order to manage interactions with the actual *CIS* elements: users, interfaces and knowledge repositories. The basic functions of this middleware layer are:

- to log users into the organization, controlling user roles, agent resources and security issues.
- to monitor user interaction,
- to execute the *grounding language* interpreter,
- to implement interaction devices[1], and
- to control the actual mappings between the *grounding language* interpreter and domain entities.

4 A Bottom-Up Approach

4.1 The Agentified *CIS*

We have approached the design of our framework from both ends. The top-down approach is centered in the theoretical and computational extensions of the EI_0 developments (c.f. [11]). The bottom-up approach that we explore in this paper has consisted in the agentification of two *CIS* in actual operation, and the design and implementation of a rudimentary organization engine that is currently a workflow engine proficient enough to drive the MAS-ified operation of those two *CIS*.

The systems that we have been working with are integral vertical industry systems. One system implements the full operation of large hotels: reservations, room assignment, restaurant services, accounting and billing, personnel, etc. The other implements the full operation of a hospital: outpatient care, nurse protocols, pharmacy, inventory control, electronic medical records and so on. They have been developed by Grupo TCA and have been in an evolving operation for almost 20 years.[2]

Over the last 5 years, TCA has been modifying its hotel information system to facilitate its agentification. It is now a consolidated set of business rules available to a middleware workflow engine that reads workflow scripts and delegates concrete tasks and procedures to participating user and server agents. This modestly *MAS-ified CIS* whose architecture is reported in [13] is already operational in 15 hotels. In the health care domain, TCA has *MAS-ified* the outpatient care subsystem [12] as a first step for the agentification of their integral hospital information system. These two *MAS-ified CIS*, show how we intend to put our proposal to work and, as we report below, the experience brought to light many issues that should be taken into account for the development of our framework.

---

[1] For those domain entities that need to be in contact with external agents we have developed a special type of server agent that we call *interaction device*. These devices implement interfacing capabilities between external users and other domain elements, e.g. form handling, data base calls, business rule triggering.

[2] TCA is a medium-size privately owned information systems company that has been active in the design and development of integral information systems since 1982 for the Latin American market.

4.2 The Workflow Engine

The workflow engine (WF-engine) is currently operational and implements a restricted version of the main component of the organization middleware: the organization engine. Once initiated, WF-engine reads a workflow script from a repository and interprets the commands contained in it. The commands are executed in the sequence dictated by the workflow conditional directives, and each command triggers the inter-operation of server agents that control domain components —data bases, business rules, forms— and their interaction with human users.

Figure 1 (right) illustrates how the workflow engine supervises the agents that handle specialized domain components, such as databases or business rule repositories — a specialized *business rule* server agent (Bag) fetches, from a central repository, business rules that use data provided by another specialized *database* server agent (Dag), to provide input to a *user agent* (Uag) that displays it in a user form.

Each workflow specification is stored in a repository as a workflow script. Since each domain component is represented in the environment by a specialized *server agent*, we have implemented commands for sending requests to the corresponding *server agents* for their execution of business rules, data base accesses, reports definitions, and for end-user interactions.

Each task specified in a protocol is implemented as one of the following domain actions:

– a business rule, that could be as simple as a single computation or as complex as a complete computer program;
– a data base access to add, delete, modify or retrieve information from a data base;
– a user interaction through a specialized form; or
– a reference to another workflow script.

We have built an interpreter that takes a workflow script and produces a set of actions. This implementation involves activation of server and user agents of different types, the sequencing of their actions and the parameter loading and passing during those actions. The interpreter uses the following commands:

– read workflow specification script,
– initialize variables,
– load defaults for variables and data, and
– execute workflow commands.

Initially, the workflow interpreter reads the main workflow script and starts executing the specified commands, controlling and sequencing the interaction between the intervening agents as well as loading and executing other possible workflow scripts specified in the main workflow.

Here is a workflow script segment used in the Back Office module of the Hotel Information System to implement the task of adding a supplier.[3] The script specifies the coordination of interactions between database, business-rule and user agents (who use specialized forms).

[3] Script and business rules are taken from TCA's `hot500.wf` and `hot500.br` repositories.

Procedure `AddSupplier`

```
begin
    InitializeVariables;
    Interact(UserAgent(DefineGrid(grid01)));
    Interact(UserAgent(InputFields(grid01,Supplier)));
    Interact(BRServerAgent(ConsistencyCheck));
    Interact(DBServerAgent(Suppliers,New));
end
```

WF-Engine Functional Features. *Agent mediated interactions* The WF-engine acts as a link between the user interface and the data base and business rule repositories, but all interactions are mediated by ad-hoc server agents.

Specialized server agents for domain components. The main function of the specialized server agents is to act as a business domain components (including business rule repositories and data bases) facilitators for all user agents that may be logged-in at several client sessions.

The user interface is mediated by a user agent that is regarded as a client for the business rule and data base server agents.

Persistent communication. Once the interaction between a *user agent* and a *server agent* is established, the infrastructure makes sure that the communication between both agents is persistent until one of the agents decides to terminate it.

Business rule triggering. As shown in the previous examples, workflow scripts are currently not much more than sequences of conditional clauses that invoke, through specialized agents, the activation of specific business rules. Business rules are special-purpose programs, stored in a repository that may be accessed by a business rule agent who is able to trigger rules and use the results of such triggerings. Business rule agents (BRagents) react to workflow transitions by requesting business rule inputs either from database server agents who query a data base or from user agents that read input from a user form. With those inputs, the BRagent triggers a rule whose result is passed to a data base server agent or a user agent or, more frequently, is used by the BRagent to change the workflow state.

WF-Engine Programming Functionalities. *Context of interaction.* The system programmer is responsible for maintaining the context of all agent interactions because as agent interactions evolve, they modify the context of the world, updating data and status variables as required.

Precedence of execution. During workflow execution, event value verification takes precedence over sequential process execution; that is, in the middle of a conditional execution, it is possible to break the sequential flow and skip directly to the first command of another conditional clause.

Workflow scope of execution. Regarding the scope of workflow execution, once a flat form or grid is addressed, all subsequent workflow commands will be made in the scope of that specific flat form or grid, until another one is addressed.

Scope of variables. Global variables are available in the scope of the workflow definition, that is, in the workflow specification the programmer can test for the value of variables defined as global by any *server agent*. It is the programmer's responsibility to define and maintain the proper scope for the required variables.

WF-Engine Limitations. The WF-engine has no control over *what is said between agents*. Because of the way workflow scripts are currently implemented, it deals only with specific conditional commands that test for contextual changes represented by changes in data and status variables. This is an important limitation whenever we want to deal with complex interactions, because we are forced to "hardwire" the control code for the execution of alternative procedures in the workflow script or in the business rules it involves.

In the WF-engine we implemented in this experiment we designed specific commands that deal with the transfer of data between the workflow engine and user or server agents. While it is natural to transfer information as data, the transfer of *control* data that may alter or modify agent behavior is undesirable but due to the limited expressiveness of workflow scripts we had to implement it in the WF-engine. We have used working memory to pass control data, but this use entails the messy problem of dealing with global variables and thus imposing severe restrictions on agent autonomy.

In the implementations described here we only use *reactive* agents. Such a primitive implementation is enough for the current needs but we may readily change their specification to involve more sophisticated behavior to take advantage of more sophisticated organization engines.

5 From WF-Engine to O-Engine

Lessons Learned. Our experience of *MAS-ifing* two *CIS*, has brought to light many pertinent issues for an organizational engine. The main lessons are:

Complexity trade-off. Considering the agentification of systems with equivalent functionalities, our experience with the MAS-ification shows that when business rules capture much of the discretional (rational) behaviour of agents, it is enough to use simple procedural rules to implement those procedures where the business rules are involved. Conversely, as business rules become simpler, the procedural requirements become more involved, the need for agent discretional behaviour is increased, and the need for handling agent commitments arises. The more "atomic" the business rules are, the more complexity is needed to handle them, both in the flow of control and in the agent behavior.

Agent commitments. These two experiments have also shown that if we do not have a structural mechanism to control the commitments generated through agent interactions, we need to hard-wire the required program logic to keep track of pending commitments inside each agent, as part of the workflow or inside some business rules. Assume that agent a performs an action x at time t and establishes a commitment to do action y at time, say $t + 3$. If action x is implemented as a business rule, then we must have a mechanism to send a return value to the $BRagent$, or some way to set a variable in some kind of working memory.

Viable approach. We have described how we *MAS-ified* two *CIS*. In the process, we have outlined the construction of the required server and user agents, have developed the required business rules, and specified the workflow needed for the appropriate sequence of execution between the intervening agents. In this sense we have been able to implement two CIS that correspond roughly to the type of EI-enabled CIS we want to build with our framework.

Even though the WF-engine is an embryonic version of an organizational engine and workflow scripts are clumsy parodies of EI-performative scripts, we have shown that specialized server agents, knowledge repositories and display devices may be driven by a prescriptive specification and some intended benefits are already available even in this rudimentary examples:

- We found considerable savings in software-development time and effort avoiding duplicate code by building business rule server agents and business rule repositories, since the same agent scheme can exploit similar repositories.
- We ensured *problem separation* at system design time, allowing domain experts to define the appropriate workflow and leaving to the engineer the task of engineering server agent behaviour. By having business rules managed by server agents, the problem is reduced to implementing some control over these agents.
- Separating workflow and business rule definitions from business rule and workflow control begets a considerable simplification of the system upgrading process. This simplification allows us a glimpse at the possibility of having dynamic behavior in the CIS prescription.

Additional Functionality for the O-Engine. In our framework, we want to be able to prescribe what the valid interactions among agents are. We have decided that the only valid mechanism for agent interaction —to communicate requests, assertions, results— should be illocutions. Hence, instead of using working memory, we need a proper grounding language and a mechanism to control agent illocutions and the ensuing commitments over time. This suggests us the use of production rules and an inference mechanism that will be used to define and operate the institutional conventions of performative scripts and also to load knowledge bases of staff agents.

We need to design a proper *grounding language* to map the sequencing and instantiation of *performative scripts* and server agents illocutions in order to manage interactions with the domain components.

How to Define and Implement the O-Engine. In order to address the issues mentioned in this section, we need to change the definition of a workflow engine into a more sophisticated organization engine that handles performative scripts —that capture more information than workflows— illocutory interactions and dynamic agent commitments.

We will implement this required functionality by extending the concept of Electronic Institution. In fact each *performative script* is built as an electronic institution and an extension of the current machinery for transitions is used to intertwine the scripts. We will also need to extend the expressiveness of ISLANDER by having sets of modal formulae (norms) as a way of specifying performative scripts [4,5]. The grounding language will be a gradual extension —as we increase the functionality and autonomy of server agents— of the primitive commands that we use to load WF scripts and sequence the interaction of intervening agents and their calls to business rule and databases that we now hide in the WF interpreter. Once the *performative script* is modelled and specified (using an extension of IIIA's ISLANDER tool), it is saved in a *performative scripts* repository. The organizational engine reads and instantiates each *performative script* as needed.

The current EI_0 operationalization of EI [2] will be taken as the starting point for these purposes but we are extending it to have a better representation of organizational activities, the extended functionality and a leaner execution.

6 Final Remarks

Recapitulation. In [10] we took a top–down approach for the definition of a framework for enacting intelligent organizations. We proposed having a prescriptive specification that drives the organization's information system day to day operation with an organizational engine based on electronic institutions. In this paper we report our experiences with a bottom-up approach where we tested and proved adequate a rudimentary version of the proposed framework. In this paper we also discussed how we expect to attain the convergence of the top–down and bottom–up approaches by, on one hand, transforming the WF-engine that is now functional in two industrial-scale *CIS*s into an *organization engine* that may deal with more elaborate organizational issues and, on the other hand, implementing the extensions of EI_0 that the organizational engine entails.

Programme. Our intention is to be able to build and support large information systems that are effective and flexible. What we are doing is to device ways of stating how an organization should work and, in fact, making sure that the prescribed interactions are isomorphic with the actions that happen in the information system. We realize that there is a tension between the detailed specification of procedures and the need to a continuous updating of the system and since we know that the ideal functioning will be changing, we want that the actual operation changes as well. In order to achieve this flexibility we are following three paths:

- Making the information system *agent-pervasive*. This way we make sure that all interactions in the CIS become, in fact, illocutions in the organizational engine, and then we may profit from all the advantages that electronic institutions bring about to express complex interaction protocols and enforce them.
- Simultaneously we are going for *plug-able components* —performative scripts, business rule and knowledge repositories, server agents, user agents— that are easy to specify, assemble, tune and update so that we can use them to deploy interaction protocols that are stable, quickly, and thus allowing us to update these protocols parsimoniously.
- We count on *staff agents* that are reliable and disciplined (since they are part of the organization) and, because they may have better decision-making capabilities and because we can localize their knowledge, we can build into them the flexibility needed to accommodate less frequent interactions or atypical situations (and thus simplify interaction protocols) and also to accommodate more volatile conventions (and thus save us from more frequent updates).

We entertain the expectation that we will be able to incorporate autonomic features into our systems.

Next steps. An outline. In the top-down strategy we are (a) looking into the formal and conceptual extensions of the EI_0 so that we may handle complex performative structures and assemble them from simpler performative scripts. (b) Devising ways of expressing deontological conventions declaratively, so that we may specify performative scripts declaratively and logically enforce them. (c) Defining the guidelines for a grounding language that translates EI manageable illocutions into CIS components actions.

In the bottom-up approach we will (a) start enriching server agents so they can interact with EI_0 performative structures, with "more atomic" business rules and with the other application domain entities. (b) We will also develop user agents and interaction devices further, so that we have better access and control for external users of the system. (c) We will also start implementing actual performative scripts, staff agents and appropriate business rules, on one side, and a grounding language to handle their interactions on the other. (d) We will extend the current WF-engine to handle (c).

In the implementational front we foresee (a) a prototype organization engine, built on top of EIDE, to handle the bottom-up developments. (b) An extension to the ISLANDER (ISLAplus) tool to handle the new expressiveness of the organizational engine. (c) A leaner version of EIDE that instantiates an ISLAplus specification into an organization engine and enacts it on a CIS.

Acknowledgments

This research is partially funded by the Spanish Ministry of Education and Science (MEC) through the Web-i-2 project (TIC-2003-08763-C02-00) and by private funds of the TCA Research Group.

References

1. Howard E. Aldrich, editor. *Organizaions and Environments*. Prentice Hall, 1979.
2. Josep Lluis Arcos, Marc Esteva, Pablo Noriega, Juan A. Rodríguez-Aguilar, and Carles Sierra. Environment engineering for multiagent systems. *Engineering Applications of Artificial Intelligence*, (submitted), October 2004.
3. Marc Esteva, Juan A. Rodriguez-Aguilar, Bruno Rosell, and Josep Lluis Arcos. AMELI: An agent-based middleware for electronic institutions. In *Third International Joint Conference on Autonomous Agents and Multi-agent Systems (AAMAS'04)*, pages 236–243, New York, USA, July 19-23 2004.
4. Andres Garcia-Camino, Pablo Noriega, and Juan Antonio Rodriguez-Aguilar. Implementing norms in electronic institutions. In *Fourth International Joint Conference on Autonomous Agents and Multiagent Systems*, 2005.
5. Andres Garcia-Camino, Juan Antonio Rodriguez-Aguilar, Carles Sierra, and Wamberto Vasconcelos. A Distributed Architecture for Norm-Aware Agent Societies. In *Fourth International Joint Conference on Autonomous Agents and Multiagent Systems. Declarative Agent Languages and Technologies workshop (DALT'05)*, 2005. (forthcoming).

6. Jay Liebowitz and Tom Beckman. *Knowledge Organizations*. Saint Lucie Press, Washington, DC, 1998.
7. James G. March and Herbert A. Simon. *Organizations*. John Wiley and sons, New York, USA., 1958.
8. Pablo Noriega. *Agent Mediated Auctions: the Fishmarket Metaphor*. PhD thesis, Universitat Autònoma de Barcelona (UAB), Bellaterra, Catalonia, Spain, 1997. Published by the Institut d'Investigaci en Intelligncia Artificial. Monografies de l'IIIA Vol. 8, 1999.
9. Douglas C. North. *Institutions, Institutional change and economic performance*. Cambridge Universisy press, 40 west 20th Street, New York, NY 10011-4211, USA, 1990.
10. Armando Robles and Pablo Noriega. A Framework for building EI–enabled Intelligent Organizations using MAS technology. In M.P. Gleizes, G. Kaminka, A. Nowé, S. Ossowski, K. Tuyls, and K. Verbeeck, editors, *Proceedings of the Third European Conference in Multi Agent Systems (EUMAS05)*, pages 344–354., Brussel, Belgium, December 2005. Koninklijke Vlaamse Academie Van Belgie Voor Wetenschappen en Kunsten.
11. Armando Robles, Pablo Noriega, Francisco Cantú, and Rubén Morales. Enabling Intelligent Organizations: An Electronic Institutions Approach for Controlling and Executing Problem Solving Methods. In Alexander Gelbukh, Álvaro Albornoz, and Hugo Terashima-Marín, editors, *Advances in Artificial Intelligence: 4th Mexican International Conference on Artificial Intelligence, Proceedings ISBN: 3-540-29896-7*, pages 275 – 286, Monterrey, NL, MEX, November 2005. Springer-Verlag GmbH. ISSN: 0302-9743.
12. Armando Robles, Pablo Noriega, Michael Luck, and Francisco Cantú. Multi Agent approach for the representation and execution of Medical Protocols . In *Fourth Workshop on Agents Applied in Healthcare (ECAI 2006)*, Riva del Garda, Italy, Aug 2006.
13. Armando Robles, Pablo Noriega, Marco Robles, Hector Hernandez, Victor Soto, and Edgar Gutierrez. A Hotel Information System implementation using MAS technology. In *Industry Track – Proceedings Fifth International Joint Conference on AUTONOMOUS AGENTS AND MULTIAGENT SYSTEMS (AAMAS 2006)*, pages 1542–1548, Hakodate, Hokkaido, Japan, May 2006.
14. Pamela Tolbert and Lynn Zucker. chapter The Institutionalization of Institutional Theory, pages 175–190.

Modeling and Simulation of Mobile Agents Systems Using a Multi-level Net Formalism

Marina Flores-Badillo, Mayra Padilla-Duarte, and Ernesto López-Mellado

CINVESTAV Unidad Guadalajara
Av. Científica 1145 Col. El Bajío, 45010 Zapopan, Jal. México

Abstract. The paper proposes a modeling methodology allowing the specification of multi mobile agent systems using nLNS, a multi level Petri net based formalism. The prey-predator problem is addressed and a modular and hierarchical model for this case study is developed. An overview of a nLNS simulator is presented through the prey predator problem.

1 Introduction

Nowadays Multi Agent Systems (MAS) is a distributed computing paradigm that is attracting the attention of many researchers in AI applications. Petri Nets and their extensions have been widely used for modeling, validating and implementing large and complex software systems.

In the field of MAS, high level Petri Nets have been well adopted for modeling agents of parts of them, because these formalisms allow representing in a clear and compact manner complex behavior. In [5] and [6] the Valk's Elementary Object System [8] has been extended in a less restrictive definition of a three-level net formalism for the modeling of mobile physical agents; later in [7] that definition is extended to a multilevel Petri Net System, the nLNS formalism.

In this paper the nLNS formalism is used to show that it is possible to model the well-know Prey-Predator problem in a modular and hierarchical way.

This paper is organized as follows. Section 2 presents a version of the Prey-Predator problem and describes the nLNS formalism. Section 3 presents a methodology for building modular and hierarchical models. Finally, section 4 gives an overview of a software tool for simulating nLNS models.

2 Background

In this section we describe the held version of the prey predator problem and present an overview of the nLNS formalism.

2.1 The Prey Predator Problem

The original version of the Prey-Predator pursuit problem was introduced by Benda, et al [1] and consisted of four agents (predators) trying to capture an agent (prey) by surrounding it from four directions on a grid-world (fig. 1). This problem (and several

A. Gelbukh and C.A. Reyes-Garcia (Eds.): MICAI 2006, LNAI 4293, pp. 1128 – 1138, 2006.

variations) has been studied by several researchers. Kam-Chuen, et al [2] used a genetic algorithm to evolve multi-agent languages for agents; they show that the resulting behavior of the communicating multi-agent system is equivalent to that of a Mealy finite state machine whose states are determined by the concatenation of the strings in the agents' communication language. Haynes and Sen [3] used genetic programming to evolve predator strategies and showed that a linear prey (pick a random direction and continue in that direction for the rest of the trial) was impossible to capture. In [4] Chainbi, et al. used CoOperative Objets to show how this language may be used for the design and model of the problem.

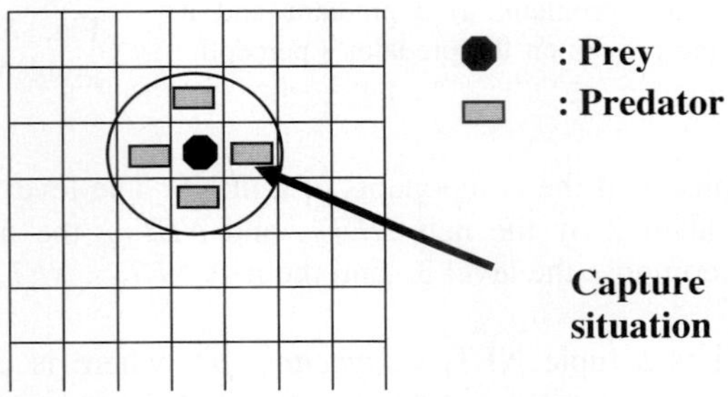

Fig. 1. The prey-predator problem: the prey is captured by predators

The held version of the Prey-Predator problem is specified below:

1. There is only one prey and one predator.
2. The world is a n×n grid.
3. Both prey and predator agents are allowed to move in only four orthogonal directions: Up, Right, Left, Down.
4. Prey and predator are allowed to choose when to move.
5. The predator can perceive the prey only if it is in its perception scope (Fig. 2), prey and predator perceive each other at the same time.
6. When a prey has perceived a predator, it chooses a direction in a random way except to the predator position.
7. When a predator has perceived a prey, it moves on the direction of the prey.
8. Attack condition, a prey is attacked when its position is occupied by a predator (Fig. 3).
9. The prey dies once that it has received three attacks (the prey is allowed to recover its strengths).

2.2 A Multi-level Net Formalism

This section includes only an overview of nLNS; a more accurate definition is detailed in [7].

An nLNS model consists mainly of an arbitrary number of nets organized in *n* levels according to a hierarchy; *n* depends on the degree of abstraction that is desired in the model. A net may handle as tokens, nets of deeper levels and symbols; the nets of level *n* permits only symbols as tokens, similarly to CPN. Interactions among nets are declared through symbolic labeling of transitions.

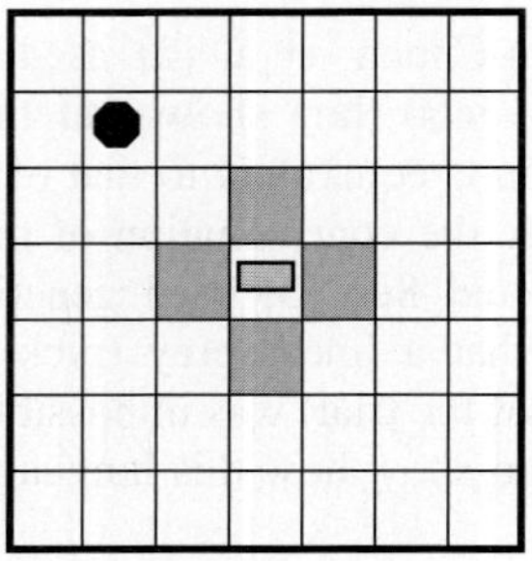

Fig. 2. The prey-predator problem: a) a predator and its perception scope, b) the prey is on the predator's perception scope

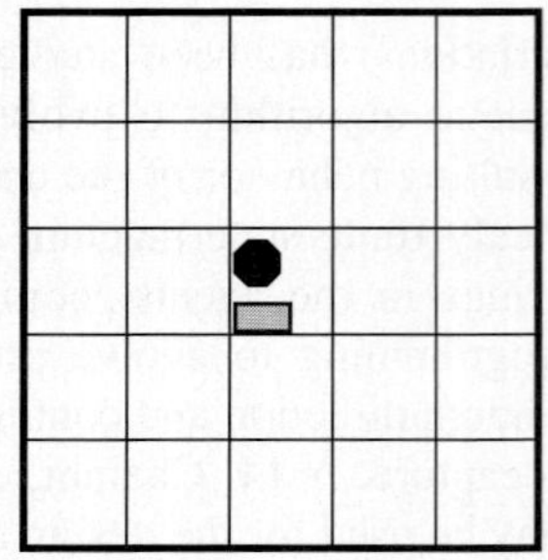

Fig. 3. The prey-predator problem: attack condition

Figure 4 sketches pieces of the components of a nLNS. The level 1 is represented by the net NET_1, the level 2 by the nets $NET_{2,1}$ and $NET_{2,2}$, the nets $NET_{3,1}$, $NET_{3,2}$, $NET_{3,3}$, and $NET_{3,4}$ compose the level 3, and the nets $NET_{4,1}$, $NET_{4,2}$, $NET_{4,3}$ form the level 4.

A net of level i is a tuple $NET_i = (typenet_i, \mu_i)$, where is composed by a PN structure, the arcs weight (π ((*p*, *t*), *lab*) or π ((*t*, p), *lab*)) expressed as multi sets of variables, and a transition labeling declaring the net interaction. μ_i is the marking function.

A nLNS model, called net system, is a n-tuple NS= (NET_1, NET_2, … NET_n) where NET_1 is the highest level net, and $NET_i = \{NET_{i,1}, NET_{i,2}, \ldots, NET_{i,r}\}$ is a set of r nets of level i.

The components of a model may interact among them through synchronization of transitions. The synchronization mechanism is included in the enabling and firing rules of the transitions; it establishes that two or more transitions labeled with the same symbol must be synchronized. A label may have the attributes ≡, ↓, ↑, which express local, inner, and external synchronization.

A transition *t* of a net of level i NET_i is enabled with respect to a label lab if:

1. There exists a binding b_t that associates the set of variables appearing in all π((*p*, *t*), *lab*).
2. It must fulfill that $\forall p \in \bullet t$, $\pi((p, t), lab)_{<bt>} \subseteq \mu_i(p)$. ($<b_t>$ is not necessary when the level net is *n*).
3. The conditions of one of the following cases are fulfilled:

   Case 1. If there is not attributes then the firing of *t* is autonomously performed.

   Case 2. If *lab* has attributes one must consider the combination of the following situations:

{≡} It is required the simultaneous enabling of the transitions labeled with $lab^{\equiv}$ belonging to other nets into the same place *p'* of the next upper level net. The firing of these transitions is simultaneous and all the (locally) synchronized nets remain into *p'*.

{↓}) It is required the enabling of the transitions labeled with $lab^{\uparrow}$ belonging to other lower level nets into •*t*. These transitions fire simultaneously and the lower level nets and symbols declared by $\pi((p, t), lab)_{<bt>}$ are removed.

{↑}) It is required the enabling of at least one of the $t' \in p'$•, labeled with $lab^{\downarrow}$, of the upper level net where the *NETi* is contained. The firing of *t* provokes the transfer of *NETi* and symbols declared into $\pi((p', t'), lab)_{<bt>}$.

The firing of transitions in all level nets modifies the marking by removing $\pi((p, t), lab)_{<bt>}$ in all the input places and adding $\pi((t, p), lab)_{<bt>}$ to the output places.

In fig. 4, NET_1 is synchronized through the transition labeled with $a^{\downarrow}$ with $NET_{2,2}$, $NET_{3,2}$, $NET_{3,4}$ and $NET_{4,2}$ by mean the transitions (locally synchronized) labeled with $a^{\uparrow}$; all these transitions must be enabled to fire. The simultaneous firing of the transitions removes these nets from the input places.

$NET_{2,1}$, $NET_{3,1}$ and $NET_{4,1}$ are synchronized through the transitions labeled with $b^{\downarrow}$, $b^{\equiv}$, $b^{\uparrow}$ respectively; the firing of the transitions changes the marking of $NET_{2,1}$ and $NET_{3,1}$; $NET_{4,1}$ is removed from the place of $NET_{2,1}$.

$NET_{3,3}$ is removed from the input place of $NET_{2,2}$ and $NET_{4,3}$ is removed from $NET_{3,3}$; this interaction is established by $c^{\downarrow}$, $c^{\downarrow\uparrow}$, $c^{\uparrow}$, respectively.

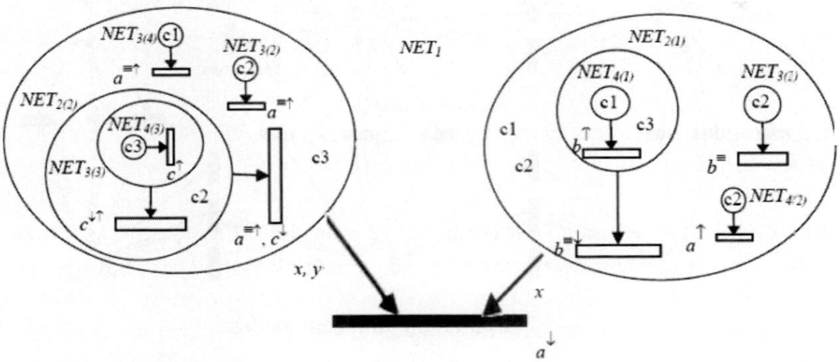

Fig. 4. Piece of 4-LNS

3 Modeling the Prey Predator Problem

3.1 General Strategy

The use of nLNS induces a modular and hierarchical modeling methodology allowing describing separately the behavior of all the involved components and then to integrate such models into a global one through the transition synchronization. For our version of the Prey-Predator problem we consider that 3 levels are enough for the modeling.

The first level structures the environment where the agent prey and predator move through, the second level represents the behavior of the agent prey and predator, and the third level describes a specific item of the agent prey.

3.2 Model of the Environment

For simplifying the model we consider a 3×3 grid-world; however this structure can be generalized by adding more nodes to the net. The Figure 5 shows the structure of the environment, a Net of level 1 where places represent each region of the grid which are connected to each other through transitions. The arcs represent the directions in which, each agent is allowed to move (right, left, up, down). The initial marking of the system has a net of level 2 which represents the agent prey, and other net of level 2 which represents the agent predator.

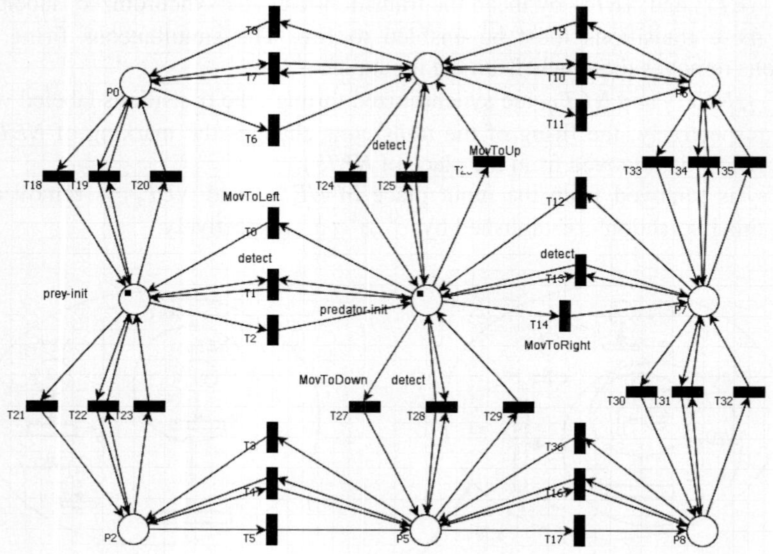

Fig. 5. Environment model

Since the predator and prey has the same detection scope, both of them use the transitions marked with the word ***detect***. There is one of these transitions for each place that belongs to the detection scope. We use the transitions marked with ***MovTo*** for representing the possible allowed directions that both Prey and Predator may move. For example, Predator is allowed to move, from de original position, to the right, left, up and down direction. The prey is allowed to move, from the original position, to the left, down, and up direction.

In the second level nets we can observe that once that detection has happened, the prey will move to one of the allowed directions except on the direction of the predator. The predator will move to the prey direction if the transition marked ***hungry*** occurred, otherwise it will ignore the prey position. If the both Predator and Prey are in the same place, the predator will attack (***attack***) the prey until the prey run away or die.

3.3 Model of the Predator

The agent predator is modeled as a Level 2 Net (Fig. 6). This net describes the general behavior of a predator. The initial marking states that the predator is in a satiety state, thus if it detects a prey with the ***detect*** transition, it will ignore the prey position and it can move to the four allowed directions. The labels on the transition marked with ***detect*** has external synchronization with the environment. The transition marked with ***hungry*** is used for change the behavior of the predator; when a ***detect*** transition is fired it will ignore the allowed directions and then it will move to the position occupied by Prey (***MoveDirect*** which its label has external synchronization with the environment). Also the Predator can move freely (***MovFree***) on search of a prey (if it did not detect a prey yet). When a Predator is in the same position that a prey, he will attack the prey (transition marked with ***attack,*** which has external synchronization with the environment). If the prey runs away, the predator will return to the search. If the prey dies (it received 3 attacks), the predator will try to find another prey. If we want modify the problem for including more than one predator, we will need more levels for modeling agent cooperation and communication protocols.

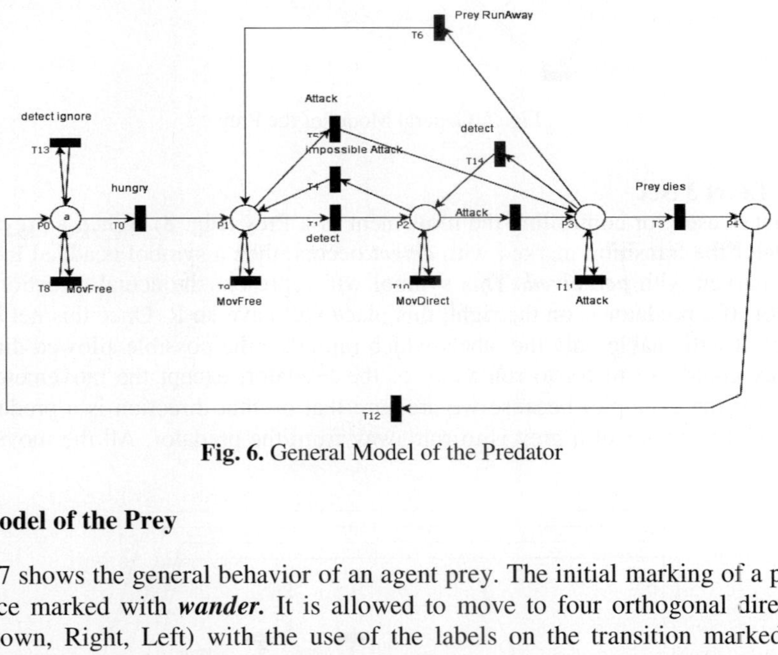

Fig. 6. General Model of the Predator

3.4 Model of the Prey

Figure 7 shows the general behavior of an agent prey. The initial marking of a prey is the place marked with ***wander.*** It is allowed to move to four orthogonal directions (Up, Down, Right, Left) with the use of the labels on the transition marked with ***MoveTo*** which are synchronized with the level 1 net describing the environment. If a Prey detects a Predator (***detect),*** it will try to escape from Predator and move to the allowed directions but the predator direction. The Prey only moves if it has strengths, for that we used a place marked with ***strengths*** which represents the maximal number of times that a predator can attack him before kill him. When this place loses all his tokens, the prey will die (***die***); however the Prey has the opportunity to recover his strengths when it is in the state represented by the place marked ***wander***. If the Prey still has strengths, it will be able to run away from a predator attack. A net of level 3 will help to the prey to "remember" the last visited position for avoiding going back to that direction.

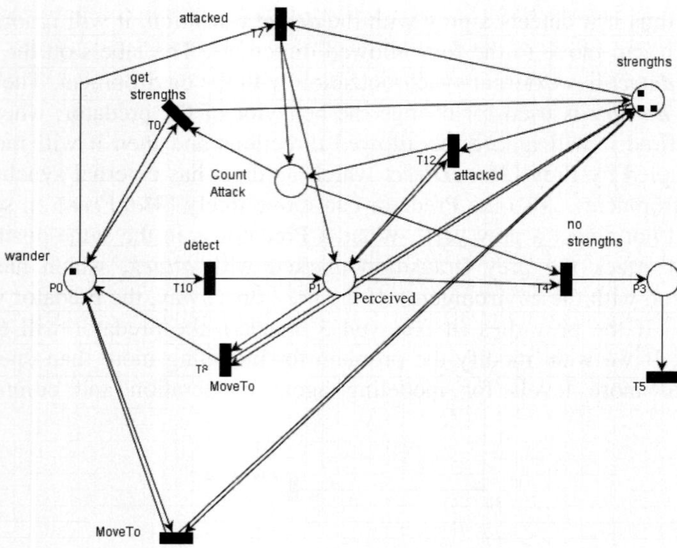

Fig. 7. General Model of the Prey

3.4.1 Level 3 Net

This net is used for controlling the movement of a Prey (Fig. 8). When a prey detects a predator the transition marked with ***detect*** occurs; then a symbol is added inside the place marked with ***perceived.*** This symbol will represent the actual direction of the predator. If a predator is on the right, this place will have an R. Once this net has that symbol, it will enable only the labels which represent the possible allowed directions the Prey could use to try to run away of the Predator, except the movement to the ***Right*** (for the example) because we are sure that on that direction is a predator and the normal behavior of a prey is to run away from the predator. All the movements'

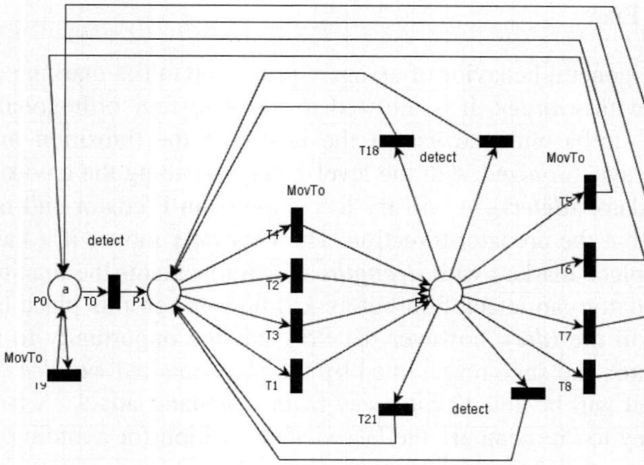

Fig. 8. Level 3 Net. Prey's Internal Net

labels have external synchronization with the prey net. When the prey has chosen a direction, the place marked with *run* will have a symbol which represents the last direction. If the Prey came from the left, this place will have an L and the enabling rules will do the same as the previous place.

4 Model Simulation

The simulation of Prey Predator problem has been performed through the execution of the 3-level net model described above. This task has been possible with the help of a software tool that allows the visual edition and the interactive execution of n-level net models expressed in nLNS.

The tool provides facilities for the interactive execution of the model: for a current marking the system indicates which transitions are enabled and with respect to which label are they enabled; then the user selects what transition to fire.

Below we are including several views of the edited model. Every net is built in a single window and it can be saved and updated for model adjustments.

In figure 9 we can see that the allowed directions for the prey and predator are enabled with the initial marking; also the perception label is enabled too (*PreyLeft_PredRight, MovPredUp, MovPredDown, MovPredLeft, MovPredRight, MovPreyUp, MovPreyDown)*

In Fig. 10 we can observe the transitions enabled with the initial marking (*PreyLeft_PredRight, MovPreyUp, MovPreyDown)*

In figure 11 we can see the transitions enabled with the initial marking (PreyLeft_PredRight, MovPredUp, MovPredDown, MovPredLeft, MovPredRight, hungry). And in the fig. 12 we have fired the transitions with the labels *hungry,* next *PreyLeft_PredRight,* then *MovPreyUp,* and finally *MovePredLeft*. The agents can perceive each other again *PreyUp_PredDown*.

As we show in fig. 13, we have fired the transition with the label *PreyUp_PredDow*. On the second place of the Net we have the color D which represents the predator's direction; so the prey only can move to the right *MovPreyRigh*. In fig. 14 we have

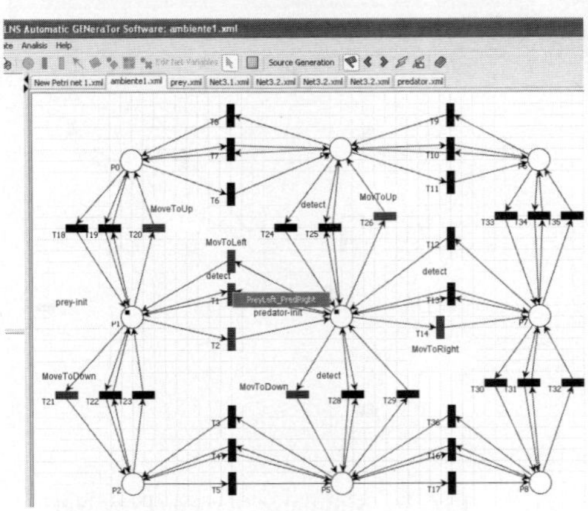

Fig. 9. Simulator screen (environment net)

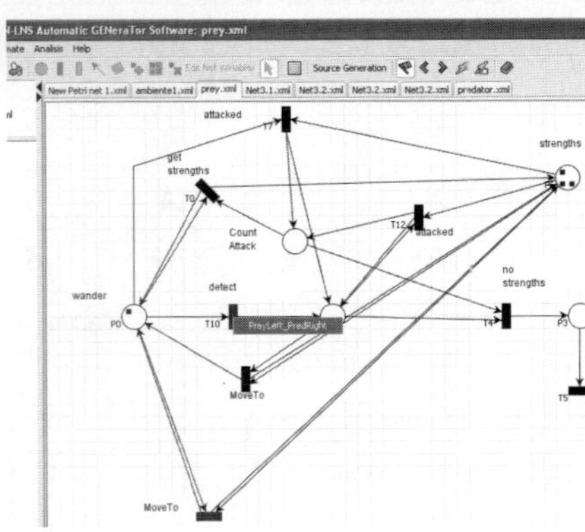

Fig. 10. Simulator screen (prey net)

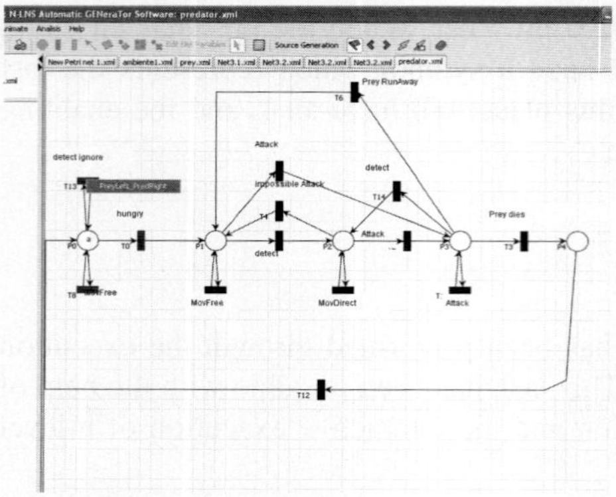

Fig. 11. Simulator screen (predator net)

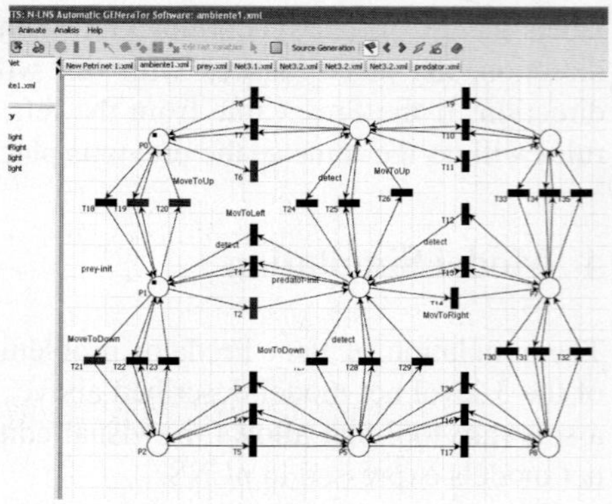

Fig. 12. Simulator Screen (environment net 2)

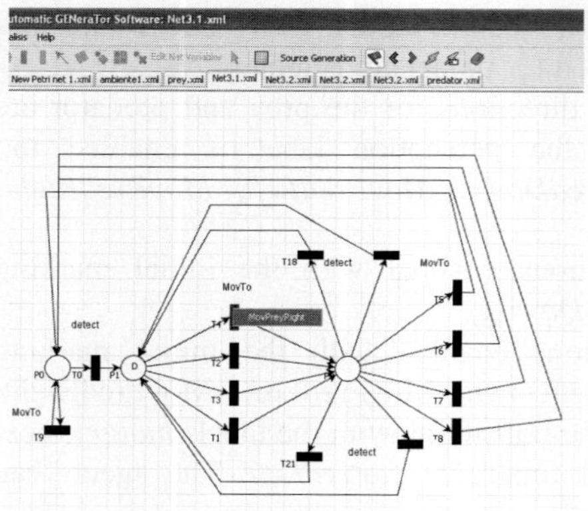

Fig. 13. Simulator Screen (Level 3 Net)

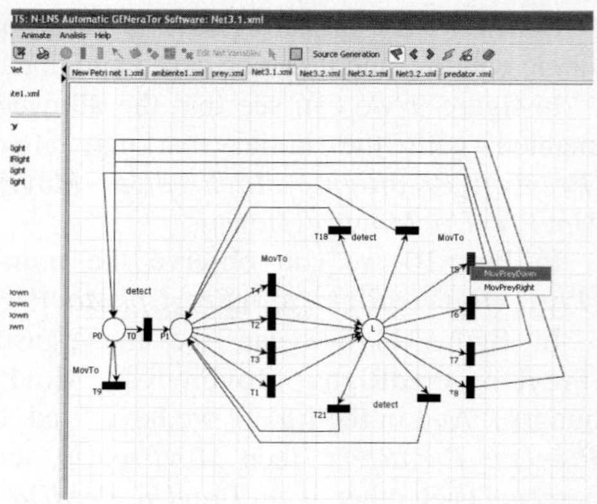

Fig. 14. Simulator Screen (Level 3 Net 2)

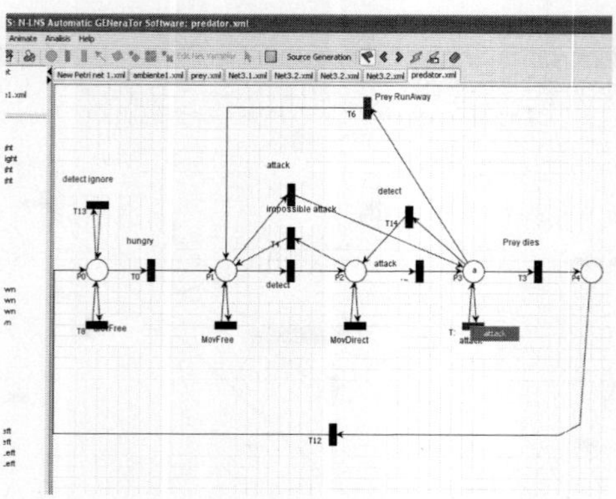

Fig. 15. Simulator Screen (predator net)

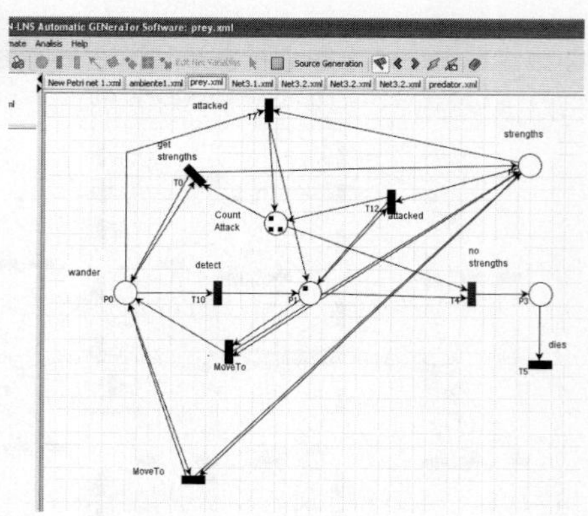

Fig. 16. Simulator Screen (Prey Net)

fired the transition with the label *MovPreyRigh.* On the third place we have the color L which means that the prey came from the left direction. The prey is not going to go back to that direction. Only the labels *MovPreyDown* and *MovPreyRight* are enabled.

In figure 15 the Prey and predator are in the same place so, the predator attacked the prey and it can attack again. In fig. 16 the predator attacked the prey for 3 times; the prey does not have strengths anymore, so it dies.

In figure 17 we the prey has died the predator restart the search of another prey. It cannot perceive the dead prey.

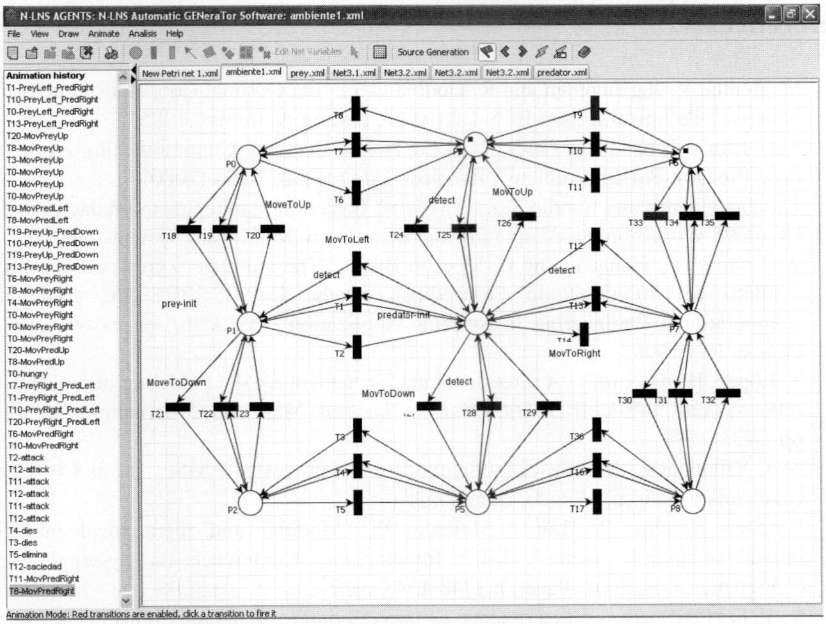

Fig. 17. Simulator Screen (Environment net)

5 Implementation Issues

Prototypes of multi mobile agent systems have been developed from nLNS specifications; they have been coded in Java using the facilities of JADE, according to a methodology presented in [7]. The software has been distributed and tested into several networked (LAN) personal computers.

6 Conclusions

Modeling and simulation can be used in the earliest stages of developing life cycle of multi mobile agent systems. This allows validating the functioning requirements avoiding backtracking in software design and implementation.

The use of nLNS allows obtaining modular and hierarchical models whose components are nets which have a simple structure, in the most cases. Thus the nets are first conceived separately and then they are integrated within the pertinent models and interrelated through the transition synchronization.

The Prey Predator problem herein presented illustrates several key issues inherent to interactive mobile agent systems.

Current research addresses the automated generation of Java code from specifications in nLNS using the tool herein described.

References

[1] M. Benda, V. Jagannathan and R. Dodhiawalla, "On Optimal Cooperation of Knowledge Sources," Technical Report BCS-G2010-28, Boeing AI Center, 1985.

[2] Kam-Chuen Jim, C. Lee Giles, ”Talking Helps: Evolving Communicating Agents for the Prey-Predator Pursuit Problem”. Artificial Life 6(3): 237-254 (2000)

[3] Thomas Haynes and Sandip Sen. “Evolving behavioral strategies in predators and prey”. IJCAI-95 Workshop on Adaptation and Learning in Multiagent Systems,1995

[4] W. Chainbi, C. Hanachi, and C. Sibertin-Blanc. “The multiagent prey-predator problem : A Petri net solution”. In Proceedings of the IMACS-IEEESMC conference on Computational Engineering in Systems Application (CESA'96), pages 692--697, Lille, France, July 1996.

[5] E. López, H. Almeyda. “A three-level net Formalism for the modeling of multiple mobile robot systems”. Proc. IEEE Int. Conf. on Systems, Man, and Cybernetics, Oct. 5-8, 2003 pp. 2733-2738.

[6] N. I. Villanueva. “Multilevel modeling of batch processes”. MSc. Thesis Cinvestav-IPN Guadalajara, Jalisco, México, Dec. 2003.

[7] Sánchez Herrera, R., López Mellado, E. “Modular and hierarchical modeling of interactive mobile agents”, IEEE Internacional Conference on Systems, Man and Cybernetics, Oct. 2004. Page(s): 1740-1745 vol.2

[8] R. Valk “Petri nets as token objects: an introduction to elementary object nets”. Int. Conf. on application and theory of Petri nets, 1998, pp1-25, Springer-Verlag

Using AI Techniques for Fault Localization in Component-Oriented Software Systems*

Jörg Weber and Franz Wotawa

Institute for Software Technology, Technische Universität Graz, Austria
{jweber, wotawa}@ist.tugraz.at

Abstract. In this paper we introduce a technique for runtime fault detection and localization in component-oriented software systems. Our approach allows for the definition of arbitrary properties at the component level. By monitoring the software system at runtime we can detect violations of these properties and, most notably, also locate possible causes for specific property violation(s). Relying on the model-based diagnosis paradigm, our fault localization technique is able to deal with intermittent fault symptoms and it allows for measurement selection. Finally, we discuss results obtained from our most recent case studies.

1 Introduction

Several research areas are engaged in the improvement of software reliability during the development phase, for example research on testing, debugging, or formal verification techniques like model checking. Unfortunately, although substantial progress has been made in these fields, we have to accept the fact that it is not possible to eliminate all faults in complex systems at development time.

Thus, it is highly desirable to augment complex software systems with autonomous runtime fault detection and localization capabilities, especially in systems which require high reliability. The goal of our work is to detect and, in particular, to locate faults at runtime without any human intervention. Though there are numerous techniques like runtime verification which aim at the detection of faults, there is only litte work which deals with fault localization at runtime. However, it is necessary to locate faults in order to be able to automatically perform repair actions. Possible repair actions are, for example, the restart of software components or switching to redundant components.

In this paper we propose a technique for runtime diagnosis in component-oriented software systems. We define components as independent computational modules which have no shared memory and which communicate among each other by the use of events, which can contain arbitrary attributes. We suppose that the interactions are asynchronous.

We assume that, as often the case in practice, no formalized knowledge about the application domain exists. Moreover, we require the runtime diagnosis to

* This research has been funded in part by the Austrian Science Fund (FWF) under grant P17963-N04. Authors are listed in alphabetical order.

A. Gelbukh and C.A. Reyes-Garcia (Eds.): MICAI 2006, LNAI 4293, pp. 1139–1149, 2006.

impose low runtime overhead in terms of computational power and memory consumption. Ideally, augmenting the software with fault detection and localization functionality necessitates no change to the software. Moreover, to avoid damage which could be caused by a faulty system, we have to achieve quick detection, localization, and repair. Another difficulty is the fact that the fault symptoms are often intermittent.

Our approach allows one to assign user-defined properties to components and connections. The target system is continuously monitored by rules, i.e., pieces of software which detect property violations. The fact that the modeler can implement and integrate arbitrary rules provides sufficient flexibility to cope with today's software complexity. In practice, properties and rules will often embody elementary insights into the software behavior rather than complete specifications. The reason is that, due to the complexity of software systems, often no formalized knowledge of the behavior exists and the informal specifications are coarse and incomplete.

Our model is similar to that proposed in [1] and which was previously used for the diagnosis of hardware designs [2], but we argue that the approach in [1] is too abstract to capture the complex behavior of large software components.

In order to enable fault localization, complex dependencies between properties can be defined. When a violation occurs, we locate the fault by employing the model-based diagnosis (MBD) paradigm [3,4]. In terms of the classification introduced in [5], we propose a state-based diagnosis approach with temporal behavior abstraction.

We provide a formalization of the architecture of a component-based software system and of the property dependencies, and we outline an algorithm for computing the logical model. Moreover, we present a runtime fault detection and localization algorithm which allows for measurement selection. Furthermore, we give examples related to the control software of autonomous robots and discuss the results of case studies. The concrete models which we created for this system mainly aim at the diagnosis of severe faults like software crashes and deadlocks.

2 Introduction to the Model Framework

Figure 1 illustrates a fragment of a control system for an autonomous soccer robot as our running example. This architectural view comprises basically independent components which communicate by asynchronous events. The connections between the components depict the data flows.

The Vision component periodically produces events containing position measurements of perceived objects. The Odometry periodically sends odometry data to the WorldModel (WM). The WM uses probability-based methods for tracking object positions. For each event arriving at one of its inputs, it creates an updated world model containing estimated object positions. The Kicker component periodically creates events indicating whether or not the robot owns the ball. The Planner maintains a knowledge base (KB), which includes a qualitative representation of the world model, and chooses abstract actions based on this knowledge. The content of the KB is periodically sent to a monitoring application.

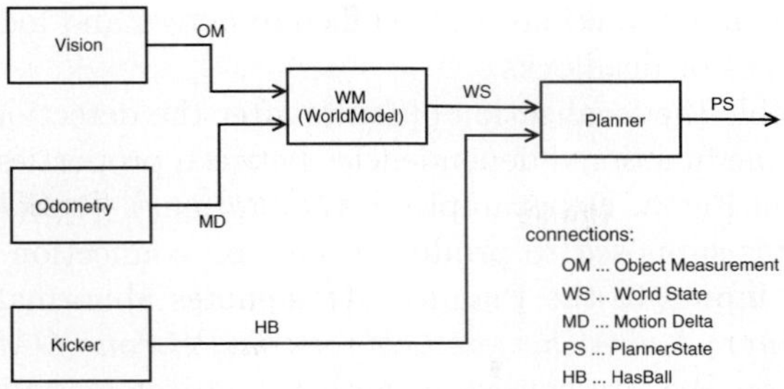

Fig. 1. Architectural view on the software system of our example

We propose a behavior model of software components which abstracts from both the values (content) of events and the temporal behavior. Our model assigns sets of *properties*, i.e. constraints, to all components and connections. Properties may capture temporal constraints, constraints on the values of events, or a combination of both. At runtime, the system is continuously monitored by *observers*. Observers comprise *rules*, i.e., pieces of software which monitor the system and detect property violations.

In the logical model the properties are represented by *property constants*. We use the proposition $ok(x, pr, s)$ which states that the property pr holds for the component or connection x during a certain period of time, namely the time between two discrete observation snapshots s_{i-1} and s_i. While the system is continuously monitored by the rules, the diagnosis itself is based on multiple snapshots which are obtained by polling the states of the rules (violated or not violated) at discrete time points. Each observation belongs to a certain snapshot, and we use the variable s as a placeholder for a specific snapshot. The diagnosis accounts for the observations of all snapshots. This approach to MBD is called multiple-snapshot diagnosis or state-based diagnosis [5]. For the sake of brevity we will often use the notation $ok(x, pr)$ instead of $ok(x, pr, s)$.

An example for a component-related property is np, expressing that the number of processes (threads) of a correctly working component c must exceed a certain threshold. In our running example, pe denotes that events must occur periodically on a connection, and $cons\_e$ is used to denote that the value of events on a certain connection must not contradict the events on connection e.

Figure 2 depicts the properties which we assign to the connections. For example, the rules for $ok(WS, cons\_OM)$ check if the computed world models on connection WS correspond to the object position measurements on connection OM. Ideally, an observer would embody a complete specification of the tracking algorithm used in the WM component. In practice, however, often only incomplete and coarse specifications of the complex software behavior are available. Therefore, the observers rely on simple insights which require little expert knowledge. The rules of the observer for $ok(WS, cons\_OM)$ could check if all environment objects which are perceived by the Vision are also part of the computed world models, disregarding the actual positions of the objects. Our experience has shown that such abstractions often suffice to detect and locate severe faults like software crashes or deadlocks.

In order to enable the localization of faults after the detection of property violation(s), we define functional dependencies between properties on outputs and inputs as shown in Fig. 3. For example, $\neg AB(Planner) \rightarrow ok(PS, pe)$ indicates that the Planner is supposed to produce events on connection PS periodically, regardless of the inputs to the Planner. AB denotes abnormality of a component. $\neg AB(Planner) \wedge ok(WS, cons\_OM) \rightarrow ok(PS, cons\_OM)$ states that, if the world states on WS are consistent with the object measurements on OM, then the same must hold for the planner states on PS; i.e., $ok(PS, cons\_OM)$ depends on $ok(WS, cons\_OM)$. Note that a property on an output connection may also depend on multiple input properties. This is the case for the property $ok(WS, pe)$.

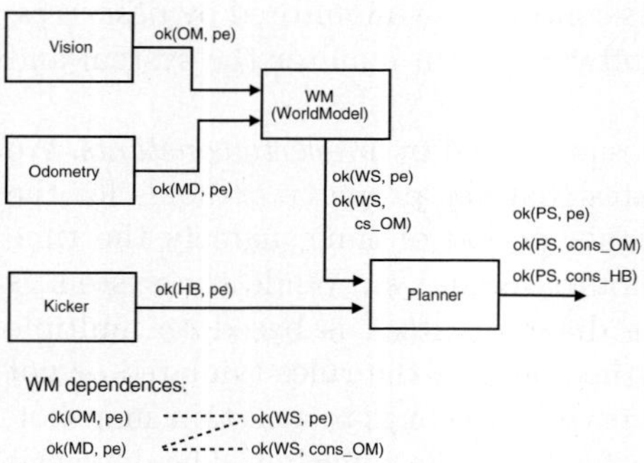

Fig. 2. The model assigns properties to connections

$$\begin{aligned}
&\neg AB(Vision) \rightarrow ok(OM, pe)\\
&\neg AB(Odometry) \rightarrow ok(MD, pe)\\
&\neg AB(WM) \wedge ok(OM, pe) \wedge ok(MD, pe)\\
&\quad \rightarrow ok(WS, pe)\\
&\neg AB(WM) \wedge ok(OM, pe)\\
&\quad \rightarrow ok(WS, cons_OM)\\
&\neg AB(Kicker) \rightarrow ok(HB, pe)\\
&\neg AB(Planner) \rightarrow ok(PS, pe)\\
&\neg AB(Planner) \wedge ok(WS, cons_OM)\\
&\quad \rightarrow ok(PS, cons_OM)\\
&\neg AB(Planner) \rightarrow ok(PS, cons_HB)\\
&\text{for each comp. } c: \neg AB(c) \rightarrow ok(c, np)
\end{aligned}$$

Fig. 3. The dependencies between properties in our example

To illustrate our basic approach we outline a simple scenario by locating the cause for observed malfunctioning. We assume a fault in the WM causing the world state WS and, as a consequence, the planner state PS to become inconsistent with the object position measurements OM. As a result, the observer for $ok(PS, cons\_OM, s)$ detects a violation, i.e. $\neg ok(PS, cons\_OM, s_0)$ is an observation for snapshot 0. All other observers are initially disabled, i.e. they do not provide any observations.

Based on this observation, we can compute diagnosis candidates by employing the MBD [3,4] approach for this observation snapshot. By computing all (subset minimal) diagnoses, we obtain three single-fault diagnosis candidates, namely $\{AB(Vision)\}$, $\{AB(WM)\}$, and $\{AB(Planner)\}$.

After activating observers for the output connections of these candidates, we obtain the second observation snapshot $ok(OM, pe, s_1)$, $ok(WS, pe, s_1)$, $\neg ok(WS,\ cons\_OM, s_1)$, $ok(PS, pe, s_1)$, $\neg ok(PS, cons\_OM, s_1)$, and $ok(PS,$ $cons\_HB, s_1)$. This leads to the single diagnosis $\{AB(WM)\}$.

3 Formalizing the Model Framework

In Definition 1 we introduce a model which captures the architecture of a component-oriented software system and the dependencies between properties.

Definition 1 (SAM). *A software architecture model (SAM) is a tuple* $(COMP, CONN, \Phi, \varphi, out, in)$ *with:*

- *a set of components* $COMP$
- *a set of connections* $CONN$
- *a (finite) set of properties* Φ
- *a function* $\varphi : COMP \cup CONN \mapsto 2^{\Phi}$*, assigning properties to a given component or connection.*
- *a function* $out : COMP \mapsto 2^{CONN}$*, returning the output connections for a given component.*
- *the (partial) function* $in : COMP \times CONN \times \Phi \rightarrow 2^{CONN \times \Phi}$*, which expresses the functional dependencies between the inputs and outputs of a given component* c*. For all output connections* $e \in out(c)$ *and for each property* $pr \in \varphi(e)$*, it returns a set of tuples* (e', pr')*, where* e' *is an input connection of* c *and* $pr' \in \varphi(e')$ *a property assigned to* e'*.*

This definition allows for the specification of a set of properties Φ for a specific software system. We introduce a function φ in order to assign properties to components and connections. The function in returns for each property pr of an output connection a set of input properties PR' on which pr depends.

For example, those part of the SAM which relates to the WM component and its output connection WS are defined as follows (Fig. 3):

$$\begin{aligned}
&\varphi(WM) = \{np\},\ \varphi(WS) = \{pe, cons_OM, eo\}\\
&out(WM) = \{WS\}\\
&in(WM, WS, pe) = \{(OM, \{pe\}), (MD, \{pe\})\},\\
&in(WM, WS, cons_OM) = \{(OM, \{pe\})\}
\end{aligned}$$

The logical model is computed by Alg. 1. Based on a SAM, it generates the logical system description SD.

Algorithm 1. The algorithm for computing the logical model
Input: The SAM.
Output: The system description SD.
COMPUTEMODEL($COMP, CONN, \Phi, \varphi, out, in$)
(1) $SD := \{\}$.
(2) For all $c \in COMP$:
(3) For all $pr \in \varphi(c)$: add $\neg AB(c) \rightarrow ok(c, pr, s)$ to SD.
(4) For all $e \in out(c)$, for all $pr \in \varphi(e)$: add

$$\neg AB(c) \wedge \bigwedge_{(e', pr') \in in(c, e, pr)} ok(e', pr', s) \rightarrow ok(e, pr, s) \quad \text{to } SD.$$

Note that the universal quantification implicitly applies to variable s. It denotes a discrete snapshot of the system behavior. Each observation $(\neg)ok(x, pr, s_i)$ relates to a certain snapshot s_i, where i is the snapshot index. A diagnosis is a solution for all snapshots. The temporal ordering of the different snapshots is not taken into account.

It is also important that, supposed that the number of snapshots is finite, the logical model which is computed by this algorithm can be easily transformed to propositional Horn clauses and thus the model is amenable to efficient logical reasoning. The size of the model in terms of number of literals depends on the number of components, the max. fan-in and fan-out of components (i.e., the max. number of input and output connections, resp.), the max. number of properties assigned to each component and connection, and the number of snapshots which compose the observations of the final diagnosis.

Theorem 1. *The number of literals in SD after the transformation to Horn clauses is* $O(n_s \cdot n_c \cdot (m \cdot f)^2)$, *where* n_s *is the (max.) number of snapshots,* $n_c = |COMP|$, *m is the maximum fan-in and fan-out, and f the max. number of properties for each component and connection (i.e.,* $|\varphi(x)| \leq f$ *for all* $x \in COMP \cup CONN$*).*

Note that the set PR' which is returned by the function *in* has the size $m \cdot f$ in the worst case. Assuming that n_s is very small, which is the case in practice, the number of literals is of order $O(n_c \cdot (m \cdot f)^2)$.

4 Runtime Monitoring and Fault Localization

The runtime diagnosis system consists of two modules, the *diagnosis module (DM)* and the *observation module (OM)*. These modules are executed concurrently. While the DM performs runtime fault detection and localization at the logical level, the OM continuously monitors the software system and provides the abstract observations which are used by the DM.

Let us consider the OM first. It basically consists of observers. Each observer comprises a set of rules which specify the desired behavior of a certain part of the software system. A rule is a piece of software which continuously monitors that part. The execution of the rules is concurrent and unsynchronized. When a rule detects a violation of its specification, it switches from state *not violated* to the state *violated*. To each observer a set of atomic sentences is assigned which represent the logical observations.

Furthermore, an observer may be enabled or disabled. A disabled observer does not provide any observations, but it may be enabled in the course of the fault localization. Note that it is often desired to initially disable those observers which otherwise would cause unnecessary runtime overhead.

Definition 2 (Observation Module OM). *The OM is a tuple* (OS, OS_e), *where OS is the set of all available observers and* $OS_e \subseteq OS$ *the set of those observers which are currently enabled.*

Definition 3 (Observer). *An observer $os \in OS$ is a tuple (R, Ω) with:*

1. *a set of rules R. For a rule $r \in R$, the boolean function violated(r) returns true if a violation of its specification has been detected.*
2. *A set of atomic sentences Ω. Each atom $\omega \in \Omega$ has the form $ok(x, pr, s)$, where $x \in COMP \cup CONN$, $pr \in \varphi(x)$, and s is a variable denoting an observation snapshot (see Definition 1).*

An observer detects a misbehavior if one or more of its rules are violated. Let $v(OS_e)$ denote the set of observers which have detected a misbehavior, i.e. $v(OS_e) = \{(R, \Omega) \in OS_e \mid violated(r) = true, r \in R\}$. Then the total set of observations of a certain snapshot s_i is computed as shown in Alg. 2.

Algorithm 2. The algorithm for computing the set of observations
Input: The set of enabled observers and a constant denoting the current snapshot.
Output: The set OBS which comprises ground literals.
COMPUTEOBS(OS_e, s_i)
(1) $OBS := \{\}$.
(2) For all $os \in OS_e$, $os = (R, \Omega)$:
(3) If $os \in v(OS_e)$: add $\bigwedge_{\omega \in \Omega} \neg\omega$ to OBS
(4) else: add $\bigwedge_{\omega \in \Omega} \omega$ to OBS.
(5) For all atoms $\alpha \in OBS$: substitute s_i for variable s.

Algorithm 3 presents the algorithm which is executed by the diagnosis module DM. The inputs to the algorithm are the logical system description SD, which is returned by the *computeModel* algorithm (Alg. 1), and an observation module $OM = (OS, OS_e)$.

Algorithm 3. The runtime diagnosis algorithm
Input: The logical system description and the observation module.
PERFORMRUNTIMEDIAGNOSIS(SD, OM)
(1) Do forever:
(2) Query the observers, i.e. compute the set $v(OS_e)$.
(3) If $v(OS_e) \neq \{\}$:
(4) Set $i := 0$, $OBS := \{\}$, $finished := false$; i is the snapshot index
(5) While *not finished*:
(6) Wait for the symptom collection period δ_c.
(7) Recompute $v(OS_e)$.
(8) $OBS := OBS \cup OBS_i$, where $OBS_i := computeOBS(OS_e, s_i)$
(9) Reset all rules to *not violated*.
(10) Compute D: $D := \{\Delta | \Delta$ is a min. diagnosis of $(SD, COMP, OBS)\}$.
(11) If $|D| = 1$ or the set $OS_s := ms(SD, OBS, OS, OS_e)$ is empty: start repair, set $finished := true$.
(12) Otherwise: set $i := i{+}1$, enable observers in OS_s, and set $OS_e := OS_e \cup OS_s$.

The algorithm periodically determines whether a misbehavior is detected by an observer. In this case, it waits for a certain period of time (line 6). This gives the observers the opportunity to detect additional symptoms, as it may take some time after faults manifest themselves in the observed system behavior. Thereafter, the diagnoses are computed (line 10) using Reiter's Hitting Set algorithm [3].

Note that the violated rules are reset to *not violated* after computing the logical observations (line 9). Therefore, an observer which detects a misbehavior in snapshot s_j may report a correct behavior in s_{j+1}. This is necessary for the localization of multiple faults in the presence of intermittent symptoms.

When we find several diagnoses (lines 11 and 12), it is desirable to enable additional observers in $OS \setminus OS_e$. We assume the function $ms(SD, OBS, OS, OS_e)$ to perform a measurement selection, i.e. it returns a set of observers OS_s ($OS_s \subseteq OS \setminus OS_e$) whose observations could lead to a refinement of the diagnoses. We do not describe the function ms in this paper. In [4] a strategy based on Shannon entropy to determine the optimal next measurement is discussed.

The fault localization is finished when either a unique diagnosis is found or the diagnoses cannot be further refined by enabling more observers (line 11).

We finally discuss the computational complexity of the diagnosis computation. For most practical purposes it will be sufficient to search only for subset-minimal diagnoses which can be obtained by using Reiter's algorithm. Furthermore, by transforming the model to Horn clauses, we can perform consistency checks in the same order as the number of literals (see Theorem 1) [6]. The number of required calls to the theorem prover (TP) is of order $O(2^{n_c})$ with $n_c = |COMP|$. However, if the max. cardinality k of the diagnoses is much smaller than the number of components, which is usually the case in practice, then the number of required TP calls is approximately $O(n_c^k)$. For example, $k = 2$ if there are only single and dual-fault diagnoses.

Theorem 2. *Assuming that $k \ll n_c$ and that n_s is very small, the overall complexity of the diagnoses computation is approximately $O(n_c^{k+1} \cdot (m \cdot f)^2)$ (see Theorem 1).*

5 Case Studies and Discussion

We implemented the proposed diagnosis system and conducted a series of experiments using the control software of a mobile autonomous soccer robot. The implemented measurement selection process may enable multiple observers at the same time in order to reduce the time required for fault localization.

The components of the control system are executed in separate applications which interact among each other using CORBA communication mechanisms. The software runs on a Pentium 4 CPU with a clock rate of 2 GHz. The model of the software system comprises 13 components and 14 connections. We introduced 13 different properties. 7 different types of rules were implemented, and the observation module used 21 instances of these rule types.

For the specification of the system behavior we used simple rules which embody elementary insights into the software behavior. For example, we specified the minimum number of processes spawned by certain applications. Furthermore, we identified patterns in the communication among components. A simple insight is the fact that components of a robot control system often produce new events either periodically or as a response to a received event. Other examples are rules which express that the output of a component must change when the input changes, or specifications capturing the observation that the values of certain events must vary continuously.

We simulated software failures by killing single processes in 10 different applications and by injecting deadlocks in these applications. We investigated if the faults can be detected and located in case the outputs of these components are observed. In 19 out of 20 experiments, the fault was detected and located within less than 3 seconds; in only one case it was not possible to detect the fault. Note that we set the symptom collection period δ_c to 1 second (see Alg. 3, line 6), and the fault localization incorporated no more than 2 observation snapshots.

Due to the small number of components and connections, the computation of the diagnoses required only a few milliseconds. Furthermore, the overhead (in terms of CPU load and memory usage) caused by the runtime monitoring was negligible, in particular because calls to the diagnosis engine are only necessary after an observer has detected a misbehavior.

Furthermore, we conducted 6 non-trivial case studies in order to investigate more complex scenarios. We injected deadlocks in different applications. We assumed that significant connections are either unobservable or should be observed only on demand, i.e. in course of the fault localization, because otherwise the runtime overhead would be unacceptable. In 4 scenarios we injected single faults, while in the other cases 2 faults occurred in different components almost at the same time. Moreover, in 2 scenarios the symptoms were intermittent and disappeared during the fault localization.

In all of the 6 case studies, the faults could be correctly detected and located. In two cases, the fault was immediately detected and then located within 2 seconds. In one case the fault was detected after about 5 seconds, and the localization took 2 more seconds. However, in three case studies the simple rules detected the faults only in certain situations, e.g. when the physical environment was in a certain state.

We gained several insights from our experiments. In general, state-based diagnosis appears to be an appropriate approach for fault localization in a robot control system as a particular example for component-oriented software. We were able to identify simple patterns in the interaction among the components, and by using rules which embody such patterns it was possible to create appropriate models which abstract from the dynamic software behavior. Furthermore, the approach proved to be feasible in practice since the overhead caused by the runtime monitoring is low.

The main problem is the fact that simple rules are often too coarse to express the software behavior. Such rules may detect faults only in certain situations. Therefore, it may happen that faults are either not detected or that they are detected too late, which could cause damage due to the misbehavior of the software system. Hence, it is desirable to use more complex rules. However, appropriate rules are hard to find since, in practice, often no detailed specification of the software exists. Furthermore, the runtime overhead would increase significantly.

The usage of simple rules also has the effect that more connections must be permanently observed than it would be the case if more complex rules were used. For example, in the control system we used in our experiments we had to observe more than half of the connections permanently in order to be able to detect severe faults like deadlocks in most of the components.

6 Related Research and Conclusion

There is little work which deals with model-based runtime diagnosis of software systems. In [7] an approach for model-based monitoring of component-based software systems is described. The external behavior of components is expressed by Petri nets. In contrast to our work, the fault detection relies on the alarm-raising capabilities of the components themselves and on temporal constraints.

In the area of fault localization in Web Services, the author of [8] proposes a modelling approach which is similar to ours. Both approaches use grey-box models of components, i.e. the dependencies between the inputs and outputs of components are modelled. However, their work assumes that each message (event) on a component output can be directly related to a certain input event, i.e. each output is a response which can be related to a specific incoming request. As we cannot make this assumption, we abstract over a series of events within a certain period of time.

Another approach to model the behavior of software is presented in [9]. In order to deal with the complexity of software, the authors propose to use probabilistic, hierarchical, constraint-based automata (PHCA). However, they model the software in order to detect faults in hardware. Software bugs are not considered in this work.

In the field of autonomic computing, there are model-based approaches which aim at the creation of self-healing and self-adaptive systems. The authors of [10] propose to maintain architecture models at runtime for problem diagnosis and repair. Similar to our work, they assign properties to components and connectors. However, this work does not employ fault localization mechanisms.

Rapide [11] is an architecture description language (ADL) which allows for the definition of formal constraints at the architecture level. The constraints define legal and illegal patterns of event-based communication. Rapide's ability for formalizing properties could be utilized for runtime fault detection. However, Rapide does not provide any means for fault localization.

This paper presents a MBD approach for fault detection and, in particular, fault localization in component-oriented software systems at runtime. Our model allows one to introduce arbitrary properties and to assign them to components and connections. The fault detection is performed by rules, i.e. pieces of software which continuously monitor the software system. The fault localization utilizes dependencies between properties. We provide algorithms for the generation of the logical model and for the runtime diagnosis. Finally, we discuss case studies which demonstrate that our approach is frequently able to quickly detect and locate faults. The main problem is the fact that simple rules may often be insufficient in practice.

We intend to evaluate our approach in other application domains as well. Moreover, our future research will deal with autonomous repair of software systems at runtime.

References

1. Steinbauer, G., Wotawa, F.: Detecting and locating faults in the control software of autonomous mobile robots. In: Proceedings of the 19th International Joint Conference on AI (IJCAI-05), Edinburgh, UK (2005) 1742–1743
2. Friedrich, G., Stumptner, M., Wotawa, F.: Model-based diagnosis of hardware designs. Artificial Intelligence **111** (1999) 3–39
3. Reiter, R.: A theory of diagnosis from first principles. Artificial Intelligence **32** (1987) 57–95
4. de Kleer, J., Williams, B.C.: Diagnosing multiple faults. Artificial Intelligence **32** (1987) 97–130
5. Brusoni, V., Console, L., Terenziani, P., Dupré, D.T.: A spectrum of definitions for temporal model-based diagnosis. Artificial Intelligence **102** (1998) 39–79
6. Minoux, M.: LTUR: A Simplified Linear-time Unit Resolution Algorithm for Horn Formulae and Computer Implementation. Information Processing Letters **29** (1988) 1–12
7. Grosclaude, I.: Model-based monitoring of software components. In: Proceedings of the 16th Eureopean Conference on Artificial Intelligence, IOS Press (2004) 1025–1026 Poster.
8. Ardissono, L., Console, L., Goy, A., Petrone, G., Picardi, C., Segnan, M., Dupré, D.T.: Cooperative Model-Based Diagnosis of Web Services. In: Proceedings of the 16th International Workshop on Principles of Diagnosis. DX Workshop Series (2005) 125–132
9. Mikaelian, T., Williams, B.C.: Diagnosing complex systems with software-extended behavior using constraint optimization. In: Proceedings of the 16th International Workshop on Principles of Diagnosis. DX Workshop Series (2005) 125–132
10. Garlan, D., Schmerl, B.: Model-based adaptation for self-healing systems. In: WOSS '02: Proceedings of the first workshop on Self-healing systems, New York, NY, USA, ACM Press (2002) 27–32
11. Luckham, D., et al.: Specification and analysis of system architecture using RAPIDE. IEEE Transactions on Software Engineering **21** (1995) 336–355

Exploring Unknown Environments with Randomized Strategies

Judith Espinoza, Abraham Sánchez, and Maria Osorio

Computer Science Department
University of Puebla
14 Sur and San Claudio, CP 72570
Puebla, Pue., México
chuzamuciel@yahoo.com.mx, {asanchez, aosorio}@cs.buap.mx

Abstract. We present a method for sensor-based exploration of unknown environments by mobile robots. This method proceeds by building a data structure called SRT (Sensor-based Random Tree). The SRT represents a roadmap of the explored area with an associated safe region, and estimates the free space as perceived by the robot during the exploration. The original work proposed in [1] presents two techniques: SRT-Ball and SRT-Star. In this paper, we propose an alternative strategy called SRT-Radial that deals with non-holonomic constraints using two alternative planners named SRT_Extensive and SRT_Goal. We present experimental results to show the performance of the SRT-Radial and both planners.

Keywords: Sensor-based nonholonomic motion planning, SRT method, randomized strategies.

1 Introduction

Building maps of unknown environments is one of the fundamental problems in mobile robotics. As a robot explores an unknown environment, it incrementally builds a map consisting of the locations of objects or landmarks. Many practical robot applications require navigation in structured but unknown environments. Search and rescue missions, surveillance and monitoring tasks, and urban warfare scenarios, are all examples of domains where autonomous robot applications would be highly desirable. Exploration is the task of guiding a vehicle in such a way that it covers the environment with its sensors. We define *exploration* to be the act of moving through an unknown environment while building a map that can be used for subsequent navigation. A good exploration strategy can be one that generates a complete or nearly complete map in a reasonable amount of time.

Considerable work has been done in the simulation of explorations, but these simulations often view the world as a set of floor plans. The blueprint view of a typical office building presents a structure that seems simple and straightforward -rectangular offices, square conference rooms, straight hallways, and right angles

A. Gelbukh and C.A. Reyes-Garcia (Eds.): MICAI 2006, LNAI 4293, pp. 1150–1159, 2006.

everywhere- but the reality is often quite different. A real mobile robot may have to navigate through rooms cluttered with furniture, where the walls may be hidden behind desks and bookshelves. The central question in exploration is: *Given what one knows about the world, where should one move to get as much new information as possible?* Originally, one only knows the information that can get from its original position, but wants to build a map that describes the world as much as possible, and wants to do it as quick as possible. Trying to introduces a solution to this open problem, we present a method for sensor-based exploration of unknown environments by non-holonomic mobile robots.

The paper is organized as follows. Section II presents briefly the RRT approach. Section III gives an overview of the SRT method. Section IV explains the details of the proposed perception strategy, SRT-Radial. Section V analyzes the performance of the two proposed planners, SRT_Extensive and SRT_Goal. Finally, the conclusions and future work are presented in Section VI.

2 RRT Planning

While not as popular as heuristic methods, non-reactive planning methods for interleaved planning and execution have been developed, with some promising results. Among these are agent-centered A^* search methods [2] and the D^* variant of A^* search [3]. Nevertheless, using these planer requires discretization or tiling of the world in order to operate in continuous domains. This leads to a tradeoff between a higher resolution, with is higher memory and time requirements, and a low resolution with non-optimality due to discretization. On the other hand, RRT (Rapidly-Exploring Random Trees) approach should provide a good compliment for very simple control heuristics, and take much of the complexity out of composing them to form navigation systems. Specifically local minima can be reduced substantially through lookahead, and rare cases need not be enumerated since the planner has a nonzero probability of finding a solution or its own through search. Furthermore, and RRT system can be fast enough to satisfy the tight timing requirements needed for fast navigation.

The RRT approach, introduced in [4], has become the most popular single-query motion planner in the last years. RRT-based algorithms where first developed for non-holonomic and kinodynamic planning problems [7] where the space to be explored is the state-space (i.e. a generalization of configuration space ($\mathcal{CS}$) involving time). However, tailored algorithms for problems without differential constraints (i.e. which can be formulated in $\mathcal{CS}$) have also been developed based on the RRT approach [5], [6]. RRT-based algorithms combine a construction and a connection phase. For building a tree, a configuration q is randomly sampled and the nearest node in the tree (given a distance metric in $\mathcal{CS}$) is expanded toward q. In the basic RRT algorithm (which we refer to as RRT-Extend), a single expansion step of fixed distance is performed. In a more greedy variant, RRT-Connect [5], the expansion step is iterated while keeping feasibility constraints (e.g. no collision exists). As explained in the referred articles, the probability that a node is selected for expansion is proportional to the area of its Voronoï region. This biases the exploration toward unexplored portions of the space. The approach can be used for unidirectional or bidirectional exploration. The basic construction algorithm is given in Figure 1.

A simple iteration is performed in which each step attempts to extend the RRT by adding a new vertex that is biased by a randomly-selected configuration. The EXTEND function selects the nearest vertex already in the RRT to the given sample configuration, x. The function NEW_STATE makes a motion toward x with some fixed incremental distance ϵ, and tests for collision. This can be performed quickly ("almost constant time") using incremental distance computation algorithms. Three situations can occur: Reached, in which x is directly added to the RRT because it already contains a vertex within ϵ of x; Advanced, in which a new vertex $x_{new} \neq x$ is added to the RRT; Trapped, in which the proposed new vertex is rejected because it does not lie in X_{free}. We can obtain different alternatives for the RRT-based planners [6]. The recommended choice depends on several factors, such as whether differential constraint exist, the type of collision detection algorithm, or the efficiency of nearest neighbor computations.

BUILD_RRT(x_{init})
$\mathcal{T}$.init(x_{init});
for *k=1* **to** K
$x_{rand} \leftarrow$ RANDOM_STATE();
EXTEND($\mathcal{T}, x_{rand}$);
Return $\mathcal{T}$

EXTEND($\mathcal{T}, x$)
$x_{near} \leftarrow$ NEAREST_NEIGHBOR($x, \mathcal{T}$);
if NEW_STATE($x, x_{near}, x_{new}, u_{new}$) **then**
$\mathcal{T}.add.vertex(x_{new})$;
$\mathcal{T}.add.edge(x_{near}, x_{new}, u_{new})$;
if $x_{new} = x$ **then**
Return *Reached;*
else
Return *Advanced;*
Return *Trapped;*

Fig. 1. The basic RRT construction algorithm

3 The SRT Method

Oriolo et al. described in [1] an exploration method based on the random generation of robot configurations within the local safe area detected by the sensors. A data structure called Sensor-based Random Tree (SRT) is created, which represents a roadmap of the explored area with an associated Safe Region (SR). Each node of the SRT consists of a free configuration with the associated Local Safe Region (LSR) as reconstructed by the perception system; the SR is the union of all the LSRs. The LSR is an estimate of the free space surrounding the robot at a given configuration; in general, its shape will depend on the sensor characteristics but may also reflect different attitudes towards perception. We will present two exploration strategies obtained by instantiating the general method with different perception techniques.

The authors presented two techniques in their work. The first, where the LSR is a ball, realizes a conservative attitude particularly suited to noisy or low-resolution sensors, and results in an exploration strategy called SRT-Ball. The second technique is confident, and the corresponding strategy is called STR-Star; in this case, the LSR shape reminds of a star. The two strategies were compared by simulations as well as by experiments. The method was presented under the assumption of perfect localization provided by some other module. The algorithm implementing the SRT method can be described as follows.

```
BUILD_SRT(q_init, K_max, I_max, α, d_min)
q_act = q_init;
for k=1 to K_max
  S ← PERCEPTION(q_act);
  ADD(T, (q_act, S));
  i ← 0;
  loop
    θ_rand ← RANDOM_DIR;
    r ← RAY(S, θ_rand);
    q_cand ← DISPLACE(q_act, θ_rand, α · r);
    i ← i + 1;
  until (VALID(q_cand, d_min, T) o i = I_max)
  if VALID(q_cand, d_min, T) then
    MOVE_TO(q_cand);
    q_act ← q_cand;
  else
    MOVE_TO(q_act.parent);
    q_act ← q_act.parent;
Return T;
```

This method is general for sensor-based exploration of unknown environments by a mobile robot. The method proceeds by building a data structure called SRT through random generation of configurations. The SRT represents a roadmap of the explored area with an associated Safe Region, an estimate of the free space as perceived by the robot during the exploration.

4 Exploration with SRT-Radial

As mentioned before, the form of the safe local region S reflects the sensors characteristics, and the perception technique adopted. Besides, the exploration strategy will be strongly affected by the form of S. The authors in [1] presented a method called SRT-Star, which involves a perception strategy that completely takes the information reported by the sensor system and exploits the information provided by the sensors in all directions. In SRT-Star, S is a region with star form because of the union of several 'cones' with different radii each one, as in Figure 2. The radius of the cone i can be the minimum range between the distance of the robot to the closest obstacle or the measurable maximum rank of the sensors. Therefore, to be able to calculate r, the function RAY must identify first, the correspondent cone of θ_{rand}.

While the conservative perception of SRT-Ball ignores the directional information provided by most sensory systems, SRT-Star can exploit it. On the opposite, under the variant implemented in this work and in absence of obstacles, S has the ideal form of a circumference, a reason that makes unnecessary the identification of the cone. This variant is denominated "SRT-Radial" [8], because once generated the direction of exploration θ_{rand}, the function RAY draws up a ray from the current location towards the edge of S, and the portion included within S, corresponds to the radius in the direction of θ_{rand}, as can be seen in Figure 2. Therefore, in the presence of obstacles, the form of S is deformed, and for different exploration directions, the radii lengths vary. To allow a performance comparison among the three exploration strategies, we have run the same simulations under the assumption that a ring of range finder is available. The same parameter values have been used.

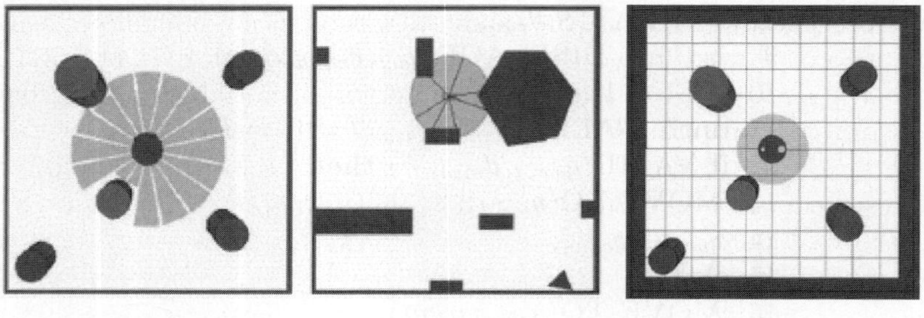

Fig. 2. Left, Safe local region S obtained with the strategy of SRT-Star perception. Notice that the extension of S in some cones is reduced by the sensors rank of reach. In the middle, different radii obtained in the safe local region S with the SRT-Radial perception's strategy. Right, Safe local region S obtained with the strategy of SRT-Ball.

5 Experimental Results

In order to illustrate the behavior of the SRT-Radial exploration strategy, we present two planners, the SRT_Extensive and the SRT_Goal. The planners were implemented in Visual C++ V. 6.0, taking advantage of the MSL[1] library's structure and its graphical interface that facilitates to select the algorithms, to visualize the working environment and to animate the obtained path. The library

[1] http://msl.cs.uiuc.edu/msl/

GPC[2] developed by Alan Murta was used to simulate the sensor's perception systems. The modifications done to the SRT method are mainly in the final phase of the algorithm and the type of mobile robot considered. To perform the simulations, a perfect localization and the availability of sonar rings (or a rotating laser range finder) located on the robot are supposed. In general, the system can easily be extended to support any type and number of sensors.

In the first planner, the SRT_Extensive, a mobile robot that can be moved in any direction (a holonomic robot), as in the originally SRT method, is considered. The SRT_Extensive planner finishes successfully, when the automatic backward process goes back to the initial configuration, i.e., to the robot's departure point. In this case, the algorithm exhausted all the available options according to the random selection in the exploration direction. The planner obtained the corresponding roadmap after exploring a great percentage of the possible directions in the environment. The algorithm finishes with "failure" after a maximum number of iterations.

In the second planner, a hybrid motion planning problem is solved, i.e., we combined the exploration task with the search of an objective from the starting position, the Start-Goal problem. The SRT_Goal planner explores the environment and finishes successfully when it is positioned in the associated local safe region at the current configuration, where the sensor is scanning. In the case of not finding the goal configuration, it makes the backward movement process until it reaches the initial configuration. Therefore, in SRT_Goal, the main task is to find the objective fixed, being left in second term the exhaustive exploration of the environment. In SRT_Goal, the exploratory robot is not omnidirectional, and it presents a constraint in the steering angle, $|\phi| \leq \phi_{max} < \pi/2$. The SRT_Goal planner was also applied to a motion planning problem, taking into account all the considerations mentioned before. The objective is the following: we suppose that we have two robots; the first robot can be omnidirectional or to have a simple no-holonomic constraint, as mentioned in the previous paragraph. This robot has the task of exploring the environment and obtaining a safe region that contains the starting and the goal positions. The second robot is non-holonomic, specifically a car-like robot, and will move by a collision-free path within the safe region. A local planner will calculate the path between the start and the goal configurations, with an adapted RRTExtExt method that can be executed in the safe region in order to avoid the process of collisions detection with the obstacles. The RRTExtExt planner was chosen because it can easily handle the non-holonomic constraints of the car-like robots and it is experimentally faster than the basic RRTs [6].

In the simulation process, the robot along with the sensor's system move in a 2D world, where the obstacles are static; the only movable object is the robot. The robot's geometric description, the workspace and the obstacles are described with polygons. In the same way, the sensor's perception zone and the safe region are modeled with polygons. This representation facilitates the use of the GPC library for the perception algorithm's simulation. If S is the zone that the sensor

[2] http://www.cs.man.ac.uk/~toby/alan/software/

can perceive in absence of obstacles and SR the perceived zone, the SR area is obtained using the difference operation of GPC between S and the polygons that represent the obstacles.

The SRT_Extensive algorithm was tested in environments with different values for K_{max}, I_{max}, α, d_{min}. A series of experiments revealed that the algorithm works efficiently exploring environments almost in its totality. Table 1 summarizes the results obtained with respect to the number of nodes of the SRT and the running time. The running time provided by the experiments corresponds to the total time of exploration including the time of perception of the sensor. Figures 3 and 4 show the SRT obtained in two environments. The CPU times and the number of nodes change, according to the chosen algorithm, to the random selection in the exploration direction and the start and goal positions of the robot in the environment, marked in the figures with a small triangle.

Table 1. Results of SRT_Extensive method

	Environment 1	Environment 2
Nodes (min)	92	98
Nodes (max)	111	154
Time (min)	132.59 sec	133.76 sec
Time (min)	200.40 sec	193.86 sec

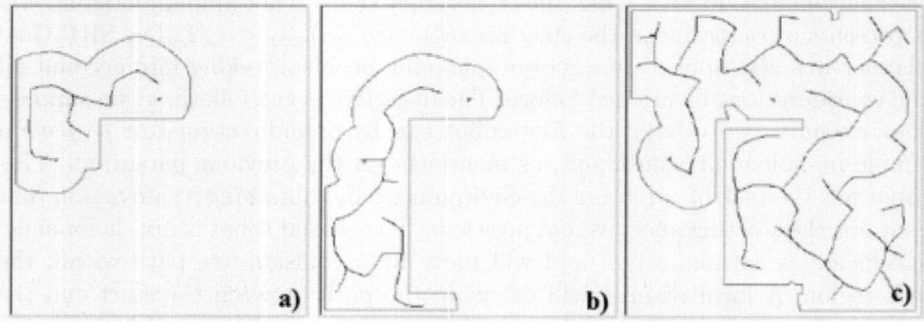

Fig. 3. SRT and explored region for the environment 1. a) Time = 13.16 sec, nodes = 13. b) Time = 30.53 sec, nodes = 24. c) Time = 138.81 sec, nodes = 83.

One can observe how the robot completely explores the environment as much, fulfilling the entrusted task, for a full complex environment covered of obstacles or for a simple environment that it contains narrow passages. The advantage of the SRT-Radial perception strategy can be seen in these simulations, because it takes advantage of the information reported by the sensors in all directions, to generate and validate configurations candidates through reduced spaces. Because of the random nature of the algorithm, when it selects the exploration direction, it can leave small zones of the environment without exploring.

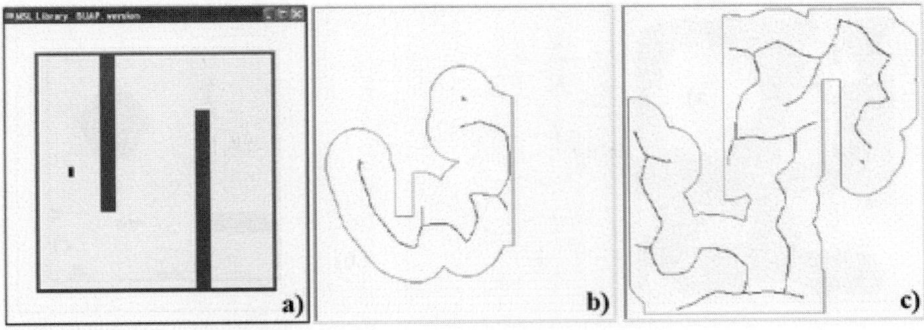

Fig. 4. SRT and explored region for the environment 2. a) Another interesting environment. b) Time = 25.34 sec, nodes = 19. c) Time = 79.71 sec, nodes = 41.

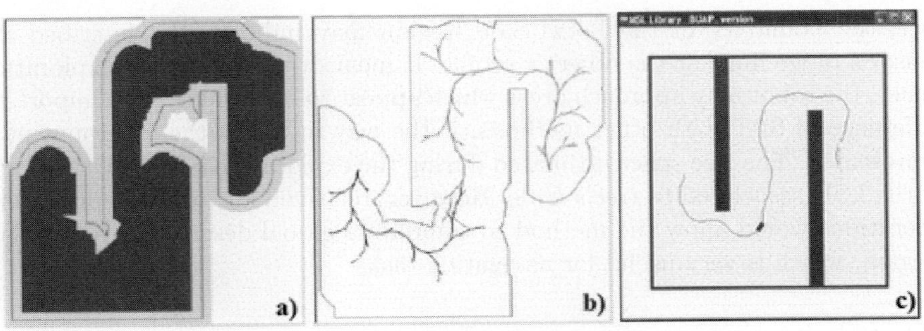

Fig. 5. a) Safe region and the security band. b) The RRT obtained with the RRTExtExt planner in 5.20 sec and 593 nodes. c) The path found for a forward car-like robot.

The SRT_Goal algorithm finishes when the goal configuration is within the safe region of the current configuration or finishes when it returns to the initial configuration. When the SRT_Goal algorithm has calculated the safe region that contains the starting and the final position, a second robot of type car-like has the option of executing locally new tasks of motion planning with other RRT planners. The safe region guarantees that the robot will be able to move freely inside that area since it is free of obstacles and it is unnecessary a collision checking by the RRT planners. But, we do not have to forget the geometry of the robot when it executes movements near the border between the safe region and the unknown space, because there is always the possibility of finding an obstacle that can collide with the robot. Therefore, it is necessary to build a security band in the contour of the safe region to protect the robot of possible collisions and to assure its mobility. Figures 5 and 6 show the security band, the calculated RRT and the path found for some mobile robots with different constraints.

After many experiments made with both planners, we note that the SRT method does not make a distinction between obstacles an unexplored areas. In

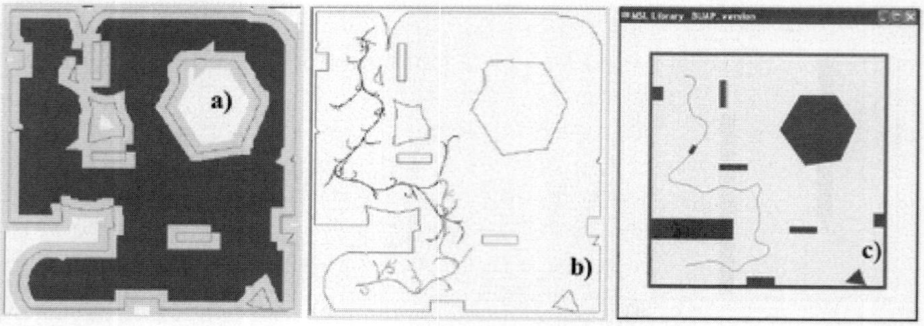

Fig. 6. a) Safe region and the security band. b) The RRT obtained with the RRTExtExt planner in 13.49 sec and 840 nodes. c) The path found for a smoothing car-like robot.

fact, the boundary of the Local Safe Region may indifferently described the sensor's range limit or the object's profile. It means that during the exploration phase, the robot may approach areas which appear to be occluded. An important difference of SRT with other methods, is the way in which the environment is represented. The free space estimated during the exploration is simply the union of the LSR associated to tree's node. However, relatively simple post-processing operations would allow the method to compute a global description of the Safe Region, which is very useful for navigation tasks.

6 Conclusions and Future Work

We have presented an interesting extension of the SRT method for sensor-based exploration of unknown environments by a mobile robot. The method builds a data structure through random generation of configurations. The SRT represents a roadmap of the explored area with an associated Safe Region, an estimate of the free space as perceived by the robot during the exploration. By instantiating the general method with different perception techniques, we can obtain different strategies. In particular, the SRT-Radial strategy proposed in this paper, takes advantage of the information reported by the sensors in all directions, to generate and validate configurations candidates through reduced spaces. SRT is a significant step forward with the potential for making motion planning common on real robots, since RRT is relatively easy to extend to environments with moving obstacles, higher dimensional state spaces, and kinematic constraints.

If we compare SRT with the RRT approach, the SRT is a tree with edges of variable length, depending on the radius r of the local safe region in the random direction θ_{rand}. During the exploration, the robot will take longer steps in regions scarcely populated by obstacles and smaller steps in cluttered regions. Since, the tree in the SRT method is expanded along directions originating from q_{act}, the method is inherently depth-first. The SRT approach retains some of the most important features of RRT, it is particularly suited for high-dimensional configuration spaces.

In the past, several strategies for exploration have been developed. One group of approaches deals with the problem of simultaneous localization and mapping, an aspect that we do not address in this paper. A mobile robot using the SRT exploration has two advantages over other systems developed. First, it can explore environments containing both open and cluttered spaces. Second, it can explore environments where walls and obstacles are in arbitrary orientations.

In a later work, we will approach the problem of exploring an unknown environment with a car-like robot with sensors, i.e., to explore the environment and to plan a path in a single stage with the same robot. The integration of a localization module into the exploration process based on SLAM techniques is currently under way.

References

1. Oriolo G., Vendittelli M., Freda L. and Troso G. "The SRT method: Randomized strategies for exploration", *IEEE Int. Conf. on Robotics and Automation*, (2004) 4688-4694
2. Koenig S. "Agent-centered search: Situated search with small look-ahead", *Proc. of the Thirteenth National Conference on Artificial Intelligence*, AAAI Press (1996)
3. Stentz A. "The D* algorithm for real-time planning of optimal traverses", *Technical Report CMU-RI-TR-94-37*, Carnegie Mellon University Robotics Institute, (1994)
4. LaValle S. M. "Rapidly-exploring random trees: A new tool for path planning", *TR 98-11, Computer Science Dept.*, Iowa State University, (1998)
5. Kuffner J. J. and LaValle S. M. "RRT-connect: An efficient approach to single-query path planning" *IEEE Int. Conf. on Robotics and Automation*, (2000) 995-1001
6. LaValle S. M. and Kuffner J. J. "Rapidly-exploring random trees: Progress and prospects", *Workshop on Algorithmic Foundations of Robotics*, (2000)
7. LaValle S. M. and Kuffner J. J. "Randomized kinodynamic planning", *International Journal of Robotics Research*, Vol. 20, No. 5, (2001) 378-400
8. Espinoza León Judith. "Estrategias para la exploración de ambientes desconocidos en robótica móvil", *Master Thesis*, FCC-BUAP (in spanish) (2006)

Integration of Evolution with a Robot Action Selection Model

Fernando Montes-González[1], José Santos Reyes[2], and Homero Ríos Figueroa[1]

[1] Facultad de Física e Inteligencia Artificial, Universidad Veracruzana, Sebastián Camacho No. 5, Xalapa, Ver., México
{fmontes, hrios}@uv.mx

[2] Departamento de Computación, Facultad de Informática, Universidade da Coruña, Campus de Elviña, 15071 A Coruña
santos@udc.es

Abstract. The development of an effective central model of action selection has already been reviewed in previous work. The central model has been set to resolve a foraging task with the use of heterogeneous behavioral modules. In contrast to collecting/depositing modules that have been hand-coded, modules related to exploring follow an evolutionary approach. However, in this paper we focus on the use of genetic algorithms for evolving the weights related to calculating the urgency for a behavior to be selected. Therefore, we aim to reduce the number of decisions made by a human designer when developing the neural substratum of a central selection mechanism.

1 Introduction

The problem of action selection is related to how to make the right decision at the right time [1]. Entities that make the right decisions at the right time have more opportunity to survive than others not making a good guess of what a right decision implies. However, it is not evident for a human designer to know exactly what a right decision implies, or to have an idea of what a right decision should look like. In that sense ethologists have observed animals *in situ* to study their social habits and foraging behaviors in order to build models that capture changes in behavior and which add together to make complex behaviors. As a consequence, some researchers in robotics have taken a deep look at how ethologists have come to terms with the problem of developing models for explaining the decision process in animals. One common approach in robotics consists of modeling a complex behavior pattern as a single behavior that has to cope with the mishaps of the task to be solved. On the other hand, another approach foresees the various situations that the robot has to solve and models simple behaviors that when assembled together show complex patterns (process fusion). It should be noticed that both approaches have been successfully used to model foraging behavior in robots.

For instance the work of Nolfi proposes the evolution of can-collection behavior as a complete solution [2]. However, as the author points out [3], in order to know whether the use of a genetic algorithm is feasible, we should answer the questions: What are we evolving? And How to evolve it? Furthermore, Seth [4] remarks on the

A. Gelbukh and C.A. Reyes-Garcia (Eds.): MICAI 2006, LNAI 4293, pp. 1160 – 1170, 2006.

potential problems of the artificial separation in the design of behavioral modules and the process fusion of these behaviors. Some of these problems are related to the concurrence of behaviors in the process fusion and the artificial separation between behavioral description and the mechanistic implementation level. On the other hand the work of Kim & Cho incrementally evolved complex behaviors [5]. These authors discuss the difficulty of evolving complex behaviors in a holistic way, and offer a solution of combining several basic behaviors with action selection. In addition, the work of Yamauchi & Randall Beer [6] also points out the use of a modular and incremental network architecture instead of a single network for solving an entire task. As a result, we conclude that building animal robots (*animats*) meets specific needs that roboticists have to fulfill if the resolution of a task is to exhibit a complex behavior pattern. Nevertheless, the rationale for preferring one approach to another sometimes follows the developmental background of the solution we are proposing. Because we are looking at biologically plausible models of central selection that have incrementally been built; we are looking at the integration of perception and -possibly redundant reactive module behaviors for the right selection at the behavioral process fusion. Even more, we are interested in further developing the model of central selection; as a consequence, in our architecture, we have to incrementally include from simpler to complex behavioral modules and from engineered to biologically plausible selection mechanisms.

In this paper, we are trying to focus on both the design and the evolution of the action selection mechanism, and behaviors to be selected, as a hybrid solution to the problem of action selection. Hence, we employ an evolutionary approach to optimize, at incremental stages, both behavior and the selection mechanism. The use of evolution is ruled out from the design of those sequential behaviors that are composed of a series of motor commands always executed in the same order. In order to facilitate the integration of evolution with action selection, a modular and extensible model of action selection is required. For our experiments we use a model of central action selection with sensor fusion (CASSF), the evolution of its internal parameters for selection, and the use of evolution in the development of the behavior patterns related to the exploration of the surrounding area. Nevertheless, a brief background on Genetic Algorithms is first required and is explained in section 2. Later on, in section 3 we explain the use of evolution in the design of neural behaviors: *cylinder-seek*, *wall-seek* and *wall-follow*; additionally, we introduce the following behaviors: *cylinder-pickup* and *cylinder-deposit*. In turn, these five behaviors will be used in conjunction to solve the foraging task set for a Khepera robot. The selection of a behavior is done by a central selection model namely CASSF that is presented in section 4. Next, in section 5 we present the results of the integration of genetic algorithms with the selection mechanism and neural behaviors. Finally, in section 6 we provide a general discussion highlighting the importance of these experiments.

2 Predominance in Robot Behavior

Several evolutionary methods have been considered by the robotics community for producing either the controllers or the behaviors required for robots to accomplish a task and survive in real environments. These methods include Genetic Algorithms

(GAs), Evolutionary Strategies, Genetic and Evolutionary Programming and Co-evolution, although in this study we have used GAs [7]. Examples of the use of evolutionary methods in the modeling of elementary behavior controllers for individuals can be found in existing literature [4, 6, 8]. A common approach relies on the use of neural networks with genetic algorithms (GAs) [9]. In this approach, once the topology of the neural network has been decided, a right choice of the neural weights has to be made in order to control the robot.

Different selection of the weights of the neural controller will produce different individuals for which their resulting performance will range from clumsy to clever behavior. If we were to generate all possible performances of individuals according to their selection of weights, a convoluted landscape will be obtained. As a consequence, a gradient ascent has to be followed in order to find the optimal performance amongst all individuals. Therefore, at every step of the artificial evolution, the selection of more adapted individuals for solving a particular task predominates over the less adapted and eventually the fittest will emerge. However, a complete understanding has to be provided regarding whom the best individuals are, in order to let fitness and evolutionary operators come to terms.

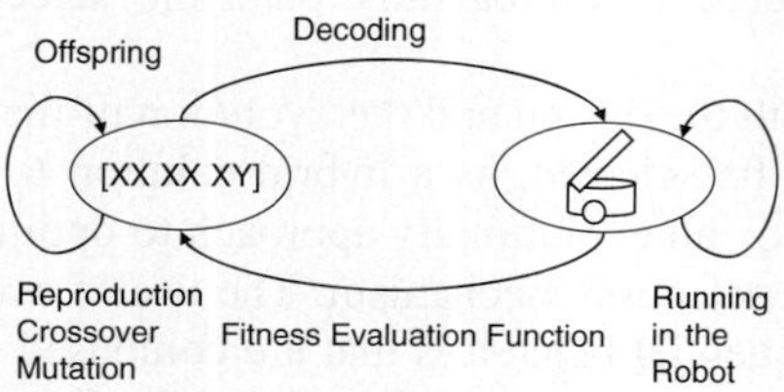

Fig. 1. The new offspring is generated from the genotype of previous robot controllers

Fig. 2. The Khepera robot set in the middle of a squared arena with simulated food (wooden-cylinders)

At the beginning of the evolutionary process the initial population of neural controllers is made of random neural controllers, next their fitness is evaluated, and then GAs' operators are applied. *Selection* chooses to breed the fittest individuals into the next offspring using crossover and mutation. *Tournament selection* is an instance of selection that chooses to breed new individuals from the winners of local competitions. Often selection occurs by means of agamic reproduction that inserts intact the fittest individuals into the next generation, which guarantees that the best solution so far found is not lost (*elitism*). *Crossover* is an operator that takes two individual encodings and swaps their contents around one or several random points along the chromosome. *Mutation* occurs with a probabilistic flip of some of the chromosome bits of the new individuals (in general, with a random change of the alleles of the genes). The latter operator explores new genetic material, so better individuals may be spawned. Whether neural controllers of basic behaviors, or modules in the selection mechanism, the individual genotypes directly encode the weights (real coding) of a particular neural module. Direct encoding is the one most used in evolutionary robotic experiments [9].

The performance of a neural controller depends on its resolution of the proposed task in a limited period of time in the test environment. The production of new offspring (Figure 1) is halted when a satisfactory fitness level is obtained. Evaluating robot fitness is very time-consuming, therefore, in the majority of the cases a robot simulator is preferred to evaluate candidate controllers that can finally be transferred to the real robot. The use of an hybrid approach combining both simulation and real robots [3, 10], and the use of noisy sensors and actuators in simulations, minimizes the "reality gap" between behaviors in simulation and real robots [9]. For an example of a behavior entirely evolved in a physical robot refer to the work of Floreano & Mondana [8].

Fig. 3. The behaviors for the selection mechanism were developed using the Webots Simulator

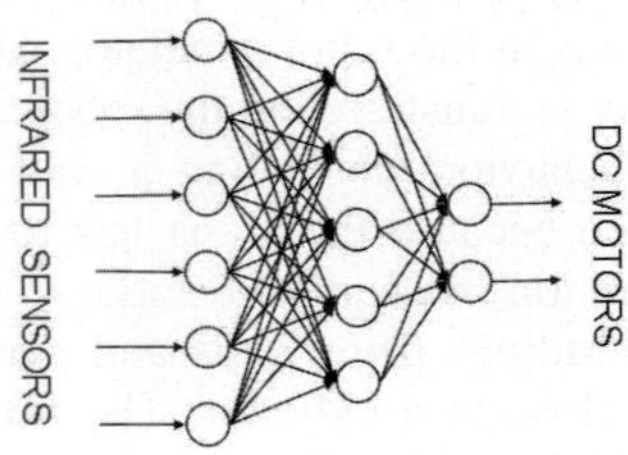

Fig. 4. The behaviors *wall-seek*, *wall-follow* and *cylinder-seek* share the same Neural Network substrate

3 The Development of Behavioral Modules

The use of commercial robots, and simulators, has become a common practice nowadays among researchers focusing in the development of control algorithms for these particular robots. The Khepera robot (Figure 2) is a small robot [11], which has been commonly used in evolutionary robotics. The detection of objects in the robot is possible with the use of eight infrared sensors all around its body. Despite many simulators for the Khepera being offered as freeware, the use of a commercial simulator may be preferred over freeware in evolutionary experiments. The development of foraging experiments in simulation often requires the control of a functional gripper. For instance Webots is a 3D robot simulator [12] that fully supports the control of both the simulated and the real gripper turret attachment (Figure 3).

In this work we use a global foraging behavioral type, which requires the robot to take cylinders from the center to the corners of an arena. Different basic behaviors are used, three of these for traveling around the arena, which share the same neural topology; and two behaviors for handling a cylinder, which were programmed as algorithmic routines. For behaviors sharing the same neural substrate we have employed the next simple neural network architecture, a fully connected feedforward multilayer-perceptron neural network with no recurrent connections (Figure 4). Afferents are sent from the 6 neurons in the input layer to the 5 neurons in the middle layer; in turn, these middle neurons send projections to the 2 neurons at the output layer. The infrared sensors values of the Khepera range from 0 to 1023, the higher the value the closer the object, the readings of the six frontal sensors are made binary with a collision threshold $th_c = 750$. The use of binary inputs for the neural network facilitates the transference of the controller to the robot by adapting the threshold to the readings of the real sensors.

The output of the neural network is scaled to ± 20 values for the DC motors. The genetic algorithm employs a direct encoding for the genotype as a vector **c** of 40 weights. Random initial values are generated for this vector $\mathbf{c}_i$, $-1 < \mathbf{c}_i < 1$, and $n=100$ neural controllers form the initial population G_0. The two best individuals of a generation are copied as a form of *elitism*. *Tournament selection*, for each of the $(n/2)-1$ local competitions, produces two parents for breeding a new individual using a single random *crossover* point with a probability of 0.5. The new offspring is affected with a *mutation* probability of 0.01. Individuals in the new offspring are evaluated for about 25 seconds in the robot simulator. Once the behavior has been properly evolved, the controller is transferred to the robot for a final adjustment of the collision threshold.

The behavior for finding a wall (*wall-seek*) can be seen as a form of obstacle avoidance because the arena has to be explored without bumping into an obstacle. The selection mechanism decides to stop this behavior when a wall has been reached. Sensor readings from walls and corners are different from the readings of infrared sensors close to a cylinder. The fitness formula for the obstacle behavior (adapted from [13]) in *wall-seek* was

$$f_{c1} = \sum_{i=0}^{3000} abs(ls_i)(1-\sqrt{ds_i})(1-\max\_ir_i) \tag{1}$$

Where for iteration i: *ls* is the linear speed in both wheels (the absolute value of the sum of the left and right speeds), *ds* is the differential speed on both wheels (a measurement of the angular speed), and *max_ir* is the highest infrared sensor value. The use of a fitness formula like this rewards those fastest individuals who travel on a straight line while avoiding obstacles.

On the other hand, behavior representing running parallel to a wall resembles some kind of obstacle avoidance because if possible the robot has to avoid obstacles while running in a straight line close to a wall until a corner is found. The selection mechanism chooses to stop this behavior when a corner has been found. Next, the fitness formula (adapted from [14]) employed for the behavior *wall-follow* was as follows

$$f_{c2} = f_{c1} * (tgh)^2 \tag{2}$$

In this formula the tendency to remain close to walls (*tgh*), or thigmotaxis, is calculated as the fraction of the total time an individual is close to a wall. Therefore, a fitness formula such as this selects the individuals that travel near the wall with an avoidance behavioral type.

A *cylinder-seek* behavior is a form of obstacle avoidance with a cylinder sniffer-detector. The robot body has to be positioned right in front of the cylinder if the collection of the can is to occur. The locating cylinder behavior shares the same architecture as the behavior previously described, and its fitness formula was as follows

$$f_{c3} = f_{c1} + K_1 \cdot cnear + K_2 \cdot cfront \tag{3}$$

A formula such as this select individuals, which avoid obstacles and reach cylinders at different orientations (*cnear*), capable of orienting the robot body in a position where the gripper can be lowered and the cylinder collected (*cfront*). The constants K_1 and K_2, $K_1 < K_2$, are used to reward the right positioning of the robot in front of a cylinder.

Due to the sequential nature of the *cylinder-pickup* and the *cylinder-deposit* behaviors a more pragmatic approach was employed. These behaviors were programmed as algorithmic routines with a fixed number of repetitions for clearing the space for lowering the arm, opening the claw, and moving the arm upwards and downwards. Once all the mentioned behaviors were evolved and designed, they were transferred to the Khepera robot.

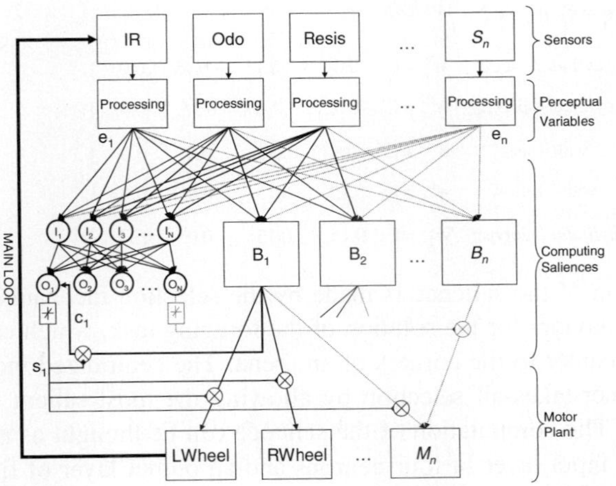

Fig. 5. In the CASFF model, perceptual variables (e_i) form the input to the decision neural network. The output selection of the highest salience (s_i) is gated to the motors of the Khepera. Notice the busy-status signal (c_1) from behavior B1 to the output neuron.

4 Central Action Selection and Genetic Algorithms

In previous work an effective model of central action selection was used for the integration of the perceptions from the robot body sensors and the motor expression of the most bidding behavior [15]. The centralized model of action selection with sensor fusion (CASSF) builds a unified perception of the world at every step of the main control loop (Figure 5). Therefore, the use of sensor fusion facilitates the integration of multiple non-homogenous sensors into a single perception of the environment. The perceptual variables are used to calculate the urgency (salience) of a behavioral module to be executed. Furthermore, behavioral modules contribute to the calculation of the salience with a busy-status signal indicating a critical stage where interruption should not occur. Therefore, the salience of a behavioral module is calculated by weighting the relevance of the information from the environment (in the form of perceptual variables) and its busy status. In turn, the behavior with the highest salience wins the competition and is expressed as motor commands sent directly to the motor wheels and the gripper. Next, we explain how the salience is computed using hand-coded weights. Firstly, the perceptual variables wall_detector(e_w), gripper_sensor(e_g), cylinder_detector(e_c), and corner_detector(e_r) are coded from the various typical readings of the different sensors. These perceptual variables form the context vector, which is constructed as follows ($\mathbf{e} = [e_w, e_g, e_c, e_r]$, $e_w, e_g, e_c, e_r \in \{1,0\}$). Secondly, five different behaviors return a current busy-status (c_i) indicating that ongoing activities should not be interrupted. Thirdly, the current busy-status vector is formed as next described, $\mathbf{c} = [\, c_s, c_p, c_w, c_f, c_d \,]$, $c_s, c_p, c_w, c_f, c_d \in \{1,0\}$, for *cylinder-seek*, *cylinder-pickup*, *wall-seek*, *wall-follow*, and *cylinder-deposit* respectively. Finally, the salience (s_i) or urgency is calculated by adding the weighted busy-status ($c_i \cdot w_b$) to the weighted context vector ($\mathbf{e} \cdot [\mathbf{w}_j^e]^T$). Then with $w_b = 0.7$ we have:

$$
\begin{array}{lllllll}
\mathbf{s}_i = \mathbf{c}_i \cdot w_b + \mathbf{e} \cdot \left(\mathbf{w}_j^e\right)^T & for & & & & & \\
\text{cylinder-seek} & \mathbf{w}_s^e = [& 0.0, & -0.15 & -0.15, & 0.0 &], \\
\text{cylinder-pickup} & \mathbf{w}_p^e = [& 0.0, & -0.15, & 0.15, & 0.0 &], \\
\text{wall-seek} & \mathbf{w}_w^e = [& -0.15, & 0.15, & 0.0, & 0.0 &], \\
\text{wall-follow} & \mathbf{w}_f^e = [& 0.15, & 0.15, & 0.0, & 0.0 &], \\
\textit{cylinder}\text{-deposit} & \mathbf{w}_d^e = [& 0.15, & 0.15, & 0.0, & 0.15 &]
\end{array}
\tag{4}
$$

The calculation of the salience is made by the selection mechanism to choose the most relevant behaviors for the solution of the foraging task, which consists of taking cylinders in the center to the corners of an arena. The centralized model of selection implements winner-takes-all selection by allowing the most salient behavior to win the competition. The computation of the salience can be thought as a decision neural network with an input layer of four neurons and an output layer of five neurons with the identity transfer function. The Khepera raw sensory information is fed, into the neural network, in the form of perceptual variables. Next, the input neurons distribute the variables to the output neurons. The behavior that is selected sends a busy signal to the output neurons when its salience is above the salience of the other behaviors. A selected behavior sends a copy of this busy signal to the five output neurons, and the five behavioral modules may all be selected, thus each of the five behaviors add five more inputs to the output neurons. However, the definition of the behavioral modules is yet to be explained. *Cylinder-seek* travels around the arena searching for food while avoiding obstacles, *cylinder-pickup* clears the space for grasping the cylinder, *wall-seek* locates a wall whilst avoiding obstacles, *follow-wall* travels next to a proximate wall, and *cylinder-deposit* lowers and opens an occupied gripper.

In this paper we have used GAs to tune the weights of the decision network for these behaviors. Each of the five output neurons of the decision network weighs four perceptual variables plus five different busy signals. Then, the evolution of the decision network employs a direct encoding for the chromosome **c** of 45 weights. Random initial values are generated for the initial population G_0 of $n=80$ neural controllers. Elitism and tournament selection were used for the evolution of a behavior. A new individual was spawned using a single random crossover point with a probability of 0.5. Individuals of the new offspring mutate with a probability of 0.01, and their fitness is evaluated for about 48 seconds.

The fitness formula for the weights of the decision network was

$$f_{c4} = K_1(f_{c2} + fwf + fcf) + (K_2 \cdot pkfactor) + (K_3 \cdot dpfactor) \quad (5)$$

The evolution of the weights of the neural network were evolved using in the fitness formula (f_{c4}) the constants K_1, K_2 and K_3 with $K_1<K_2<K_3$ for the selection of those individuals that avoid obstacles (f_{c2}), follow walls (*fwf*), and find the arena walls and corners (*fcf*). Nevertheless, the fitness formula prominently rewards the collection of cylinders inside the arena (*pkfactor*), and their release close the outside walls (*dpfactor*). The average fitness of a population, for over 25 generations, and its maximum individual fitness is next shown in Figure 6.

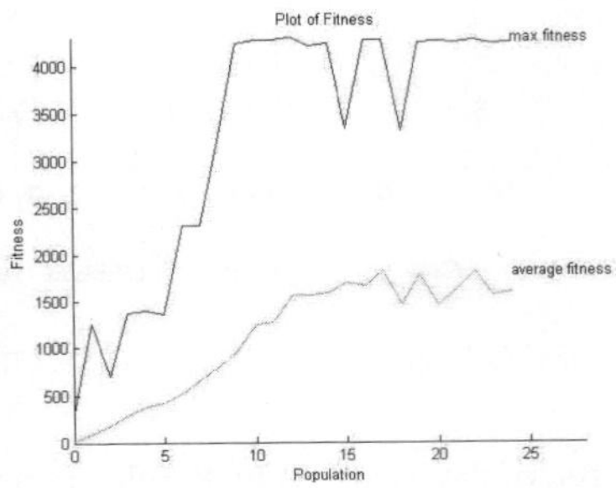

Fig. 6. Fitness is plot across 25 generations. For each generation the highest fitness of one individual was obtained from its maximum fitness over three trials in the same conditions, and the maximum fitness of all the individuals was averaged as a measure of the population fitness. Individuals are more rewarded if they avoid obstacles, collect cylinders, and deposit cylinders close to the corners. The evolution is stopped when the maximum fitness stabilizes over a fitness value of 4000.

5 Experiments and Results

The foraging task was set in an arena with cylinders as simulated food. Communication from a computer host to the robot was provided from a RS232 serial interface. In order to facilitate the use of the resistivity sensor in the gripper claw, the cylinders that simulated food were covered with foil paper. It should be noticed that in this paper a behavior is considered as the joint product of an agent, environment, and observer. Therefore, a regular grasping-depositing pattern in the foraging task is the result of the selection of the behavioral types: cylinder-seek, cylinder-pickup, wall-seek, wall-follow and cylinder-deposit in that order. Commonly, this task is formed by four grasping-depositing patterns of foiled cylinders; the ethogram in Figure 7 resumes this task [with a time resolution in seconds]. Collection patterns can be disrupted if for example the cylinder slips from the gripper or a corner is immediately found. Additionally, long search periods may occur if a cylinder is not located. Infrared are noisy sensors that present similar readings for different objects with different orientations. Similar sensor readings can be obtained when the robot is barely hitting a corner or the robot is too close to a wall with a 45 degree angle. The latter explains the brief selection of the wall-seek behavior in the ethogram in Figure 7.

On the other hand, in Figure 8 we observe that the ethogram for the evolved decision network is formed by the following behaviors cylinder-seek, cylinder-pickup, wall-seek and cylinder-deposit with the wall-follow behavior not being selected. The use of a fitness function for shaping selection as a single pattern is optimizing the selection of the behavior in time and in the physical environment. Therefore, the execution of wall-follow behavior is a feature that does not survive during the process of evolution even though the fitness function rewards those individuals that follow walls.

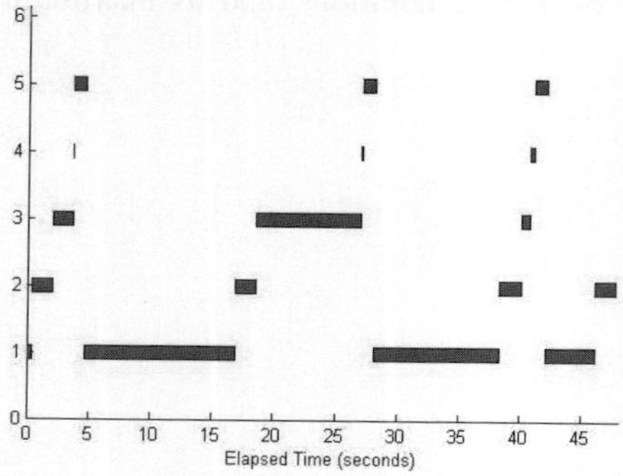

Fig. 7. Ethogram for a typical run of the hand-coded decision network. The behaviors are numbered as 1-cylinder-seek, 2-cylinder-pickup, 3-wall-seek, 4-wall-follow, 5-cylinder-deposit and 6-no action selected. Notice the regular patterns obtained for a collection of 4 cylinders with 3 cylinder deposits. The individual in this ethogram shows a 76 % of the highest evolved fitness.

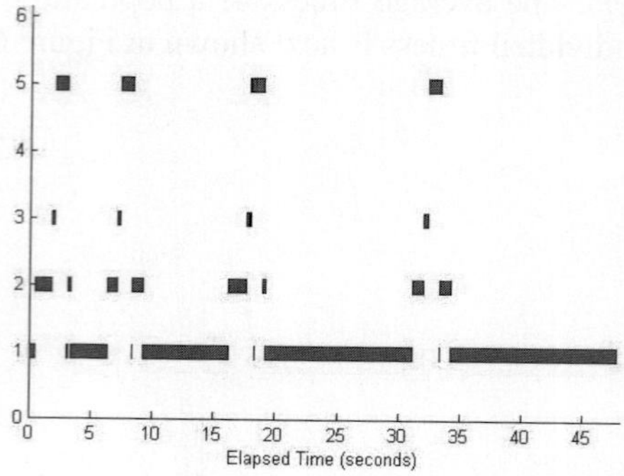

Fig. 8. Ethogram for a run of the evolved decision network. Behaviors are coded as the previous ethogram. Here we observe that behavior patterns regularly occur, however, the behavior *follow-walls* is never selected. The number of collected cylinders is the same as the cylinders deposited (a total of 4). This individual presents a 99 % of the highest evolved fitness.

Previously, we mentioned that a behavior should be considered as the joint product of an agent, environment, and observer. However, there is an additional factor that should be taken into account, which is the fitness of the agent that is solving the foraging task, who finally alters the order in the selection of the behaviors. In Figure 9, we observe that network-evolved individuals have the highest fitness (collecting 4 cylinders); although, these individuals also have the worst fitness (collecting none of the cylinders). The evolved individuals excluded the selection of the *follow-wall* behavior. In contrast, hand-coded-network individuals have a similar collecting performance mostly between 3 and 2 cylinders, all executing the five behaviors in the right order; however, these individuals fail to collect all 4 cylinders because of long searching-cylinders and wall-finding periods. The diverse selection of the five basic behaviors to hand and evolved designs can be explained in terms of what Nolfi [16] establishes as the difference between the "distal" and "proximal" description of behavioral types. The first one comes from the observer's point of view, which inspires hand designs. On the other hand, a proximal description is best described as the agent's point of view from its sensory-motor systems, which utterly defines the different reactions of the agent to particular sensory perceptions. An important consideration of Nolfi´s work is that there is no correspondence between the distal and proximal descriptions of behaviors. This should account for our explanation of why evolution finds different combinations for selection and the use of basic behaviors in order to obtain an improved overall foraging behavior.

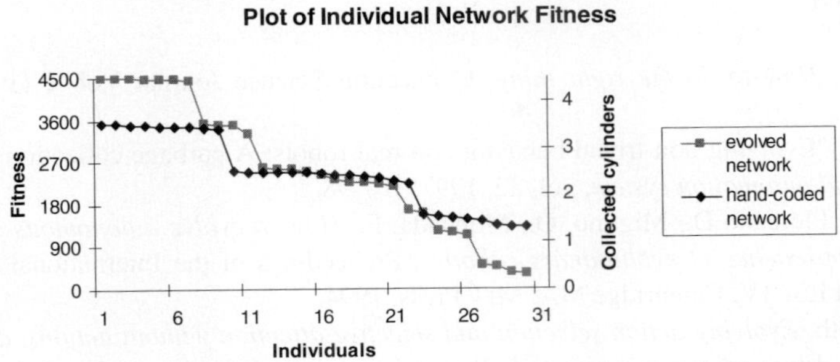

Fig. 9. Plot of the decision fitness of 30 individuals. The secondary Y-axis shows the number of collected cylinders. We observe that although the evolved decision network presents the highest fitness, this network also produces the worst individuals. In contrast, the hand-coded decision network holds a similar fitness for all their individuals.

6 Conclusions

The integration of evolution with a central action selection mechanism using non-homogenous behavior was carried out in this study. Additionally, behaviors related to exploring the arena were also evolved. However, sequential behavior for handling the cylinders was programmed as algorithmic procedure. Exploration behavior was modeled as the first step, and the decision network as the second step, in the evolution of our model. Next, we compared the fitness of the evolved decision network with that of the hand-coded network using the same evolved and sequential behaviors. The evolved decision and the hand-coded networks present differences in their fitness and selection of behavior.

The reason behind these differences is the result of the distal and the proximal descriptions of behavioral selection in our model. The use of a proximal fitness function for the evolved decision network evaluates a complex behavioral pattern as a single behavior ruling out the selection of one of the behavioral types (*wall-follow*) modeled in the distal definition of the hand-coded decision network. As a result of our experiments, we conclude that for any kind of behavioral modules, it is the strength of their salience which finally determines its own selection, and ultimately its own fitness value.

Finally, we are proposing that the integration of evolution and action selection somehow fixes the artificial separation of the distal description of behaviors. Furthermore, we believe that the use of redundant neural components sharing the same neural substratum, which may incrementally be built, should shed some light in the fabrication of biologically-plausible models of action selection. However, the co-evolution of the behaviors and the selection network has first to be explored.

Acknowledgment

This work has been sponsored by CONACyT-MEXICO grant SEP-2004-C01-45726.

References

1. P. Maes, *How to do the right thing*, Connection Science Journal **Vol. 1** (1989), no. 3, 291-323.
2. S. Nolfi, "Evolving non-trivial behaviors on real robots: A garbage collection robot", *Robotics and automation system*, vol. 22, 1997, 187-98.
3. S. Nolfi, Floreano D., Miglino, O., Mondada, F., *How to evolve autonomous robots: Different approaches in evolutionary robotics*, Proceedings of the International Conference Artificial Life IV, Cambridge MA: MIT Press, 1994.
4. A. K. Seth, *Evolving action selection and selective attention without actions, attention, or selection*, From animals to animats 5: Proceedings of the Fifth International Conference on the Simulation of Adaptive Behavior, Cambridge, MA. MIT Press, 1998, 139-47.
5. S.-B. C. Kyong-Joong Kim, *Robot action selection for higher behaviors with cam-brain modules*, Proceedings of the 32nd ISR(International Symposium in Robotics), 2001.
6. B. R. Yamauchi B., *Integrating reactive, sequential, and learning behavior using dynamical neural networks*, From Animals to Animats 3, Proceedings of the 3rd International Conference on Simulation of Adaptive Behavior, MIT Press/Bradford Books, 1994.
7. J. H. Holland, *Adaptation in natural and artificial systems*, MIT Press, 1992.
8. D. Floreano, Mondana F., *Evolution of homing navigation in a real mobile robot*, IEEE Transactions on Systems, Man and Cybernetics **26** (1996), no. 3, 396-407.
9. S. Nolfi and D. Floreano, *Evolutionary robotics*, The MIT Press, 2000.
10. J. Santos and R. Duro, *Artificial evolution and autonomus robotics (in spanish)*, Ra-Ma Editorial, 2005.
11. F. Mondana, E. Franzi and I. P., *Mobile robot miniaturisation: A tool for investigating in control algorithms*, Proceedings of the 3rd International Symposium on Experimental Robotics, Springer Verlag, 1993, 501-13.
12. Webots, "http://www.cyberbotics.com", Commercial Mobile Robot Simulation Software, 2006.
13. D. Floreano and F. Mondana, *Automatic creation of an autonomous agent: Genetic evolution of a neural-network driven robot*, From Animals to Animats III: Proceedings of the Third International Conference on Simulation of Adaptive Behavior, MIT Press-Bradford Books, Cambridge MA, 1994.
14. D. Bajaj and M. H. Ang Jr., *An incremental approach in evolving robot behavior*, The Sixth International Conference on Control, Automation, Robotics and Vision (ICARCV'2000), 2000.
15. F. M. Montes González, Marín Hernández A. & Ríos Figueroa H., *An effective robotic model of action selection*, R. Marin et al. (Eds.): CAEPIA 2005, LNAI 4177 (2006), 123-32.
16. S. Nolfi, *Using emergent modularity to develop control systems for mobile robots*, Adaptive Behavior **Vol. 5** (1997), no. 3/4, 343-63.

A Hardware Architecture Designed to Implement the GFM Paradigm

Jérôme Leboeuf Pasquier and José Juan González Pérez

Departamento de Ingeniería de Proyectos
Centro Universitario de Ciencias Exactas e Ingenierías
Universidad de Guadalajara
Apdo. Postal 307, CP 45101, Zapopan, Jalisco, México
jleboeuf@dip.cucei.udg.mx,
joseph13jj@dip.cucei.udg.mx

Abstract. Growing Functional Modules (GFM) is a recently introduced paradigm conceived to automatically generate an adaptive controller which consists of an architecture based on interconnected growing modules. When running, the controller is able to build its own representation of the environment through acting and sensing. Due to this deep-rooted interaction with the environment, robotics is, by excellence, the field of application. This paper describes a hardware architecture designed to satisfy the requirements of the GFM controller and presents the implementation of a simple mushroom shaped robot.

1 Introduction

Growing Functional Modules (GFM) introduced in a previous paper [1], is a prospective paradigm founded on the epigenetic approach, first introduced in Developmental Psychology [2] and presently applied to autonomous robotics. This paradigm allows the design of an adaptive controller and its automatic generation as described in the following section.

An architecture based on interconnected modules is compiled to produce an executable file that constitutes the controller. Each module corresponds to an autonomous entity able to generate a specific and suitable list of commands to satisfy a set of input requests. Triggering the effective commands results from learning which is obtained by comparing the input request with their corresponding feedback. As a consequence, at each instant, the internal structure of the module, commonly built as a dynamic network of cells, is adapted to fit the correlation corresponding to the generated commands and the obtained feedback [3]. The adaptation of the internal structure determines the type of module: each type integrates a particular set of growing mechanisms according to the category of tasks it should solve. For example, firstly the RTR-Module and then its improved version, the RTR2-Module are specialized in performing basic automatic control; their growing internal structures are described respectively in [4] and [5]. The graphic representation of the RTR2-Module presented in figure 1, shows the input-output values along with the internal dynamic structure.

A. Gelbukh and C.A. Reyes-Garcia (Eds.): MICAI 2006, LNAI 4293, pp. 1171 – 1178, 2006.

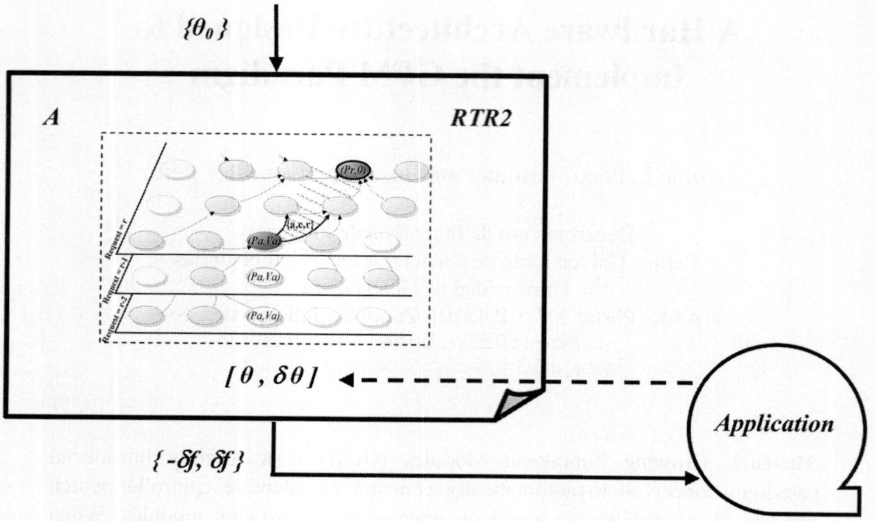

Fig. 1. Illustration of the RTR2-Module: the feedback [θ ,δ θ] provided in response to a command ±δf focused on satisfying a request θ_0 leads the growing of the dynamic internal structure

According to the previous description, the consistency of the feedback is a key element to produce a consistent learning. In particular, considering virtual applications like 3D simulation, only those offering a high quality rendering could be connected to a GFM controller. Evidently, the kind of feedback desired for a GFM controller may only be obtained by sensing the real world; therefore, robotics is an ideal field of application for the current paradigm. Concerning software, portability and "genericity" have been matter of a particular emphasis. For example some potential improvements to the previously mentioned RTR-Module have been ignored to allow this module to attend a wider range of applications. Similarly, a common protocol has been established to connect every GFM systems to its application. In particular, the choice of using an external system and its associated communication link rather than an embedded one is justified by the necessity of studying the behavior of the GFM controller. Thus, the main task of the embedded control card is restricted to a cycle that includes the following steps:

- waiting for a command from the GFM controller,
- executing it, which commonly consists of applying the corresponding shift to the designated actuator,
- reading all sensors and computing their values,
- sending back a formatted list of values to the controller.

Despite of its apparent simplicity, implementing in hardware the requirements of the embedded controller presents several difficulties; they are described in the next sections along with their potential solutions.

2 General Specifications

First of all, the choice of a control card to be embedded in several simple robots must satisfy some obvious specifications including: a low energy consumption, a reduced size and an affordable cost. Besides, flexibility, reliability and universality are other significant criteria as most users will be students. These prior considerations restrict the investigation to a low number of well proven and accessible products. On the other hand, due to the fact that the GFM controller must not be embedded for convenience, and considering the simplicity of the processing cycle described in the previous section, the power of the processor could be considered as not critical; nevertheless, the GFM applications involve many communications with actuators and sensors and ultimately might include audio or video signal pre-processing. Of the two, the audio processing would by far use the most CPU cycles as it will include at least one Fourier Transform. An alternative consists of implementing this pre-processing on an extra card and thus, reduce the main control card requirements. Next, some control applications like the inverted pendulum presented in [4] and [5], involve real time processing. In such circumstances, timing is determined by the application and not by the controller: i.e. after applying to the corresponding actuator an input command, the application waits for a predefined period of time before reading the sensors and sending their values back to the controller. Consequently, an additional criterion is the ability of the control card to manage real time processing. Until recently, the only solution to manage all these constraints jointly was using a Xilinx card [6] but, its codification results very difficult due to its dynamically reconfigurable architecture programmed with the VHSIC Hardware Description Language (VHDL). Furthermore and in accordance with the protocols requirements described in the next section, the Xilinx card does not include pulse width modulation, I^{2}C or even RS-232 hardware communication ports; finally, the Xilinx card does not incorporate analog-digital (A/D) converters. Recently, MicroChips proposed a new control card called PicDem HPC and built around the PIC18F8722 microcontroller [7]; a potentially satisfactory solution in consideration of our requirements. Additionally, the availability of a C compiler [8] reduces development time and effort.

In the following sections, the study and development of a solution, based on the PicDem HPC control card, is presented.

3 Handling Actuators

Despite a wide offering of actuators on the market, the electrical actuators commonly employed in GFM robotic applications may be classified into two categories: servomotor and direct current (DC) motor.

The servomotors are traditionally controlled by pulse width modulation (PWM) that consists in sending a pulse with a predefined frequency to the actuator, the length of the pulse width indicates the desired position. The PIC microcontroller offers two possible implementations of the PWM.

The first one is resolved though hardware using the embedded PWM module which implies configuring two specific registers: the period of the signal is set in PR2 while the pulse width is given by the T2CON value. Then, the instruction CCPxCON allows the selection of the desired DIO pin. Nonetheless, this microcontroller only allows configuring five digital ports. Furthermore, the GFM paradigm requires moving all servomotors step-by-step which implies a very expensive operation to compute the T2CON value each time, due to the potential number of servomotors involved. Furthermore, the GFM paradigm requires moving all servomotors step by step that implies to compute each time the T2CON value, a too expensive operation due to the potential number of involved servomotors.

Consequently, a better solution is to implement the servomotors' control in software. A simple driver (see code listing figure 2) is programmed to emulate the PWM: this driver computes the next position adding or resting a step, taking into account that, moves produced by a GFM controller, are always generated step by step. Thus, the pulse is generated with the BSF instruction that actives a specific pin for a duration corresponding to the high pulse length. Controlling all servos at the same time requires multiplexing this process; such a task is possible because the refresh frequency of the servo is much lower than the frequency of these pulses. As the applications use different kind of servomotors, a library containing a specific driver for each one, has been developed.

```
INIT     BSF    SERVO,0        ;Pin servo On
         CALL   MINIM_ON       ;Call minimum On
         CALL   DELAY_ON       ;Call function delay
         BCF    SERVO,0        ;Pin servo Off
         CALL   MINIM_OFF      ;Call minimum Off
         CALL   DELAY_OFF      ;Call function delay
         GOTO   INIT           ;End of cycle
```

Fig. 2. Code listing of the driver in charge of controlling the PWM port

The second category, the DC motors, cannot be directly controlled by the card due to the high intensity they require in input. Thus, two digital control pins are connected to an H-bridge that amplifies the voltage and intensity to satisfy the motor's requirements and also protects the microcontroller from peaks of current. The H-bridge is a classical electronic circuit consisting of four transistors placed in diamond. The two digital pins indicate the desired direction of the motor; optionally, a third pin could be used to specify the velocity. This third pin acts as a potentiometer controlling the voltage and current by means of a pulse width modulation sent to a fixed output pin.

4 Handling Sensors

Compared with traditional robots, epigenetic ones require more sensors since feedback is essential to expand the growing internal structure of each modules; this means higher requirements in terms of communication ports, either analog or digital.

To connect basic digital sensors, digital input-output (DIO) pins are required; the proposed card offered seventy digital input/output pins. Digital sensors, including mainly contact and infrared switches, are directly connected to the DIO pins; while the signal of analog sensors including, for example photocells, rotation sensors, pressure or distance sensors must be first digitalized through an analog-digital (A/D) converter. The traditional solution, consisting of using an external A/D converter, offers a good resolution but extends the hardware and uses many pins from the control card. A better and obvious solution consists of using one of the sixteen embedded A/D converters that uses the three registers ADCONx and offers a sufficient precision of ten bits. The first register ADCON0 is used to indicate the input pin for the analog signal and also acts as a switch, the second register ADCON1 specifies which pin is configured as analog and finally, the third register ADCON2 selects the conversion clock.

5 Communication Requirements

Handling actuators and basic sensors do not fulfill all the requirements; in practice, faster and more sophisticated communication protocols must be considered.

First, a high speed port is necessary to communicate with the controller considering that feedback may include video and audio signals. The control card offers two embedded RS232 ports with a maximum speed of 115,200 bits per second. In consideration of video signal, this implies using a low resolution or a slow frame rate. Moreover, during the tests, the maximum communication speed appears to be 57,600 bits per second. Consequently, the use of a single control card must be discarded when implementing complex robots include higher signals requirements.

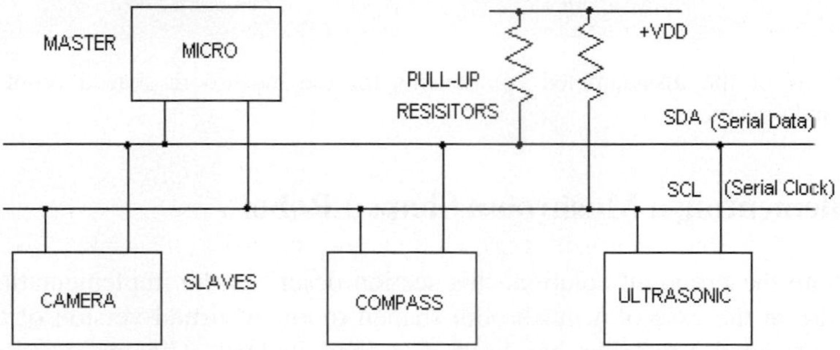

Fig. 3. I²C connection diagram to communicate with the mentioned peripherals

Nevertheless, there is still the need of connecting a compass, an ultrasonic sensor and, more recently, a camera by means of an I²C communication port which is a standard designed by Philips Corporation® in 1980 [9]. I²C's protocol only uses two lines: the first one transmits the clock signal (SCL) while the other is used for full-duplex communication (SDA); it allows connecting several masters with several slaves; the only restriction is that all masters must share the same clock signal. Three transmission speed are available: standard mode (100 KBits per second), fast mode (400 KBits per second) and high speed (3.4 MBits per second). Opportunely, the control card includes an I²C port that allows connecting the previously mentioned peripherals; the resulting diagram is given figure 3.

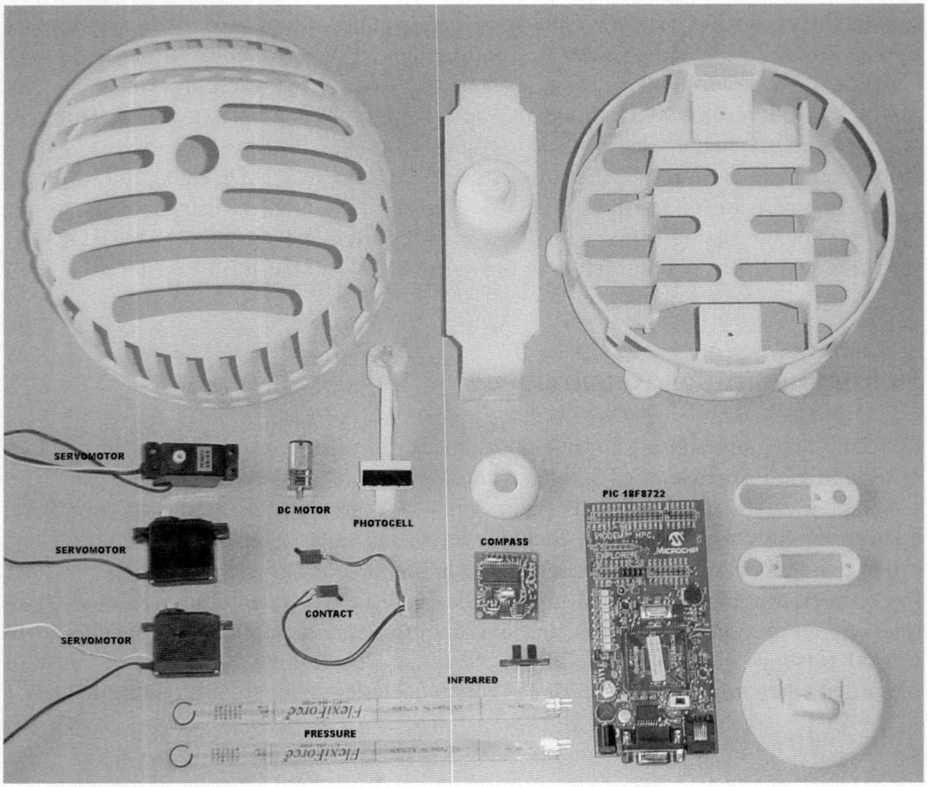

Fig. 4. View of the disassembled components for the mushroom shaped robot including actuators and sensors

6 Implementing a Mushroom Shaped Robot

To illustrate the proposed solution, this section describes the implementation of this architecture in the case of a mushroom shaped robot. A virtual version of this robot and its associated controller has been described in [10]. The real version differs mainly in the presence of an extra actuator on the foot of the robot and some extra sensors situated on the leg that should detect potential causes of damage. Figure 4 shows a view of all the components of the robot, including three servomotors, a DC motor and the following list of sensors: two pressure sensors, three rotation sensors, a photocell, two contact sensors, an infrared switch and a compass.

The block diagram of the embedded control board is given figure 5. First, a serial communication allows the card to communicate via the standard protocol with the personal computer that hosts the GFM controller. Secondly, four actuators including three servomotors and one DC motor communicate through respectively, the PWM ports and two DIO pins. Then, the photocell, the rotation sensors and the pressure sensors are connected through six A/D converters. The contact and infrared switches

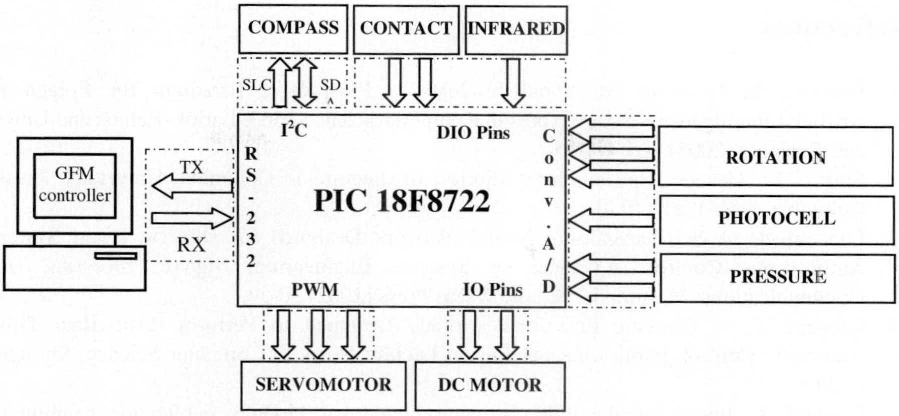

Fig. 5. Block diagram of the embedded control board corresponding to the mushroom shaped robot

are directly sensed through three DIO pins. Finally, the compass uses an I^2C communication port.

Therefore, the complete architecture may be tested by means of a remote control application executed on the external computer, before using the GFM controller.

7 Conclusions

The purpose of this paper is to describe a novel architecture developed to implement the embedded control board connected to an autonomous controller based on the Growing Functional Module paradigm. The main challenge induced by this paradigm consists in involving a higher number of communications ports because of a more elevated feedback required from the environment.

The proposed solution using a PicDem HPC satisfies the initial requirements of a simple application; i.e. an application without audio-video signals, but with a high number of digital inputs-outputs and analog inputs. As an illustration, this architecture is applied to handle the actuators and sensors of robots, like the mushroom shaped one described in the previous section which has been successfully implemented.

When facing robotic applications with a large number of actuators and sensors, a more complex architecture involves the same card and drivers; nevertheless, several subsets of sensors and actuators are handled by subsystems hosted on more rudimentary cards but powered by the same microcontroller. This solution and its application to a four-legged robot will be described in a forthcoming paper.

In the case of robots requiring high level signals processing like voice and video, none of the previous architectures offers sufficiently capacity; mainly because of the high communication rate with the controller, but additionally, for the elevated processing requirements. Such high processing requirements could be satisfied by using a small single board computer which we are presently investigating.

References

1. Leboeuf, J.: Growing Functional Modules, a Prospective Paradigm for Epigenetic Artificial Intelligence. Lecture Notes in Computer Science 3563. Larios, Ramos and Unger eds. Springer (2005) 465-471
2. Piaget, J.: Genetic Epistemology (Series of Lectures). Columbia University Press, Columbia, New York (1970)
3. Leboeuf, J.: A Self-Developing Neural Network Designed for Discrete Event System Autonomous Control. Advances in Systems Engineering, Signal Processing and Communications, Mastorakis, N. eds. Wseas Press (2002) 30-34.
4. Leboeuf, J.: A Growing Functional Module Designed to Perform Basic Real Time Automatic Control, publication pending in Lecture Notes in Computer Science, Springer (2006)
5. Leboeuf, J.: Improving the RTR Growing Functional Module, publication pending in proceedings of IECON, Paris (2006)
6. CoolRunner II CPLD Family, Xilinx internal documentation (2006)
7. Microchip, PIC18F8722 Family Data Sheet, 64/80-Pin, 1 Mbit, Enhanced Flash Microcontroller with 10-but A/D and NanoWatt Technology (2004)
8. MPLAB C18 C Compiler User's Guide, Microchip Technology Inc's internal documentation (2005)
9. Phillips Corporation, I^2C bus specification vers.2.1, internal documentation (2000)
10. Leboeuf, J., Applying the GFM Prospective Paradigm to the Autonomous and Adaptive Control of a Virtual Robot, Lecture Notes in Artificial Intelligence, Springer 3789 (2005) 959-969

Fast Protein Structure Alignment Algorithm Based on Local Geometric Similarity

Chan-Yong Park[1], Sung-Hee Park[1], Dae-Hee Kim[1], Soo-Jun Park[1], Man-Kyu Sung[1], Hong-Ro Lee[2], Jung-Sub Shin[2], and Chi-Jung Hwang[2]

[1] Electronics and Telecommunications Research Institute, 161 Gajung, Yusung, Daejeon, Korea
{cypark, sunghee, dhkim98, psj, mksung}@etri.re.kr
[2] Dept. of Computer Science, Chung Nam University (CNU), Daejon, Korea
{hrlee, iplsub, cjhwang}@ipl.cnu.ac.kr

Abstract. This paper proposes a novel fast protein structure alignment algorithm and its application. Because it is known that the functions of protein are derived from its structure, the method of measuring the structural similarities between two proteins can be used to infer their functional closeness. In this paper, we propose a 3D chain code representation for fast measuring the local geometric similarity of protein and introduce a backtracking algorithm for joining a similar local substructure efficiently. A 3D chain code, which is a sequence of the directional vectors between the atoms in a protein, represents a local similarity of protein. After constructing a pair of similar substructures by referencing local similarity, we perform the protein alignment by joining the similar substructure pair through a backtracking algorithm. This method has particular advantages over all previous approaches; our 3D chain code representation is more intuitive and our experiments prove that the backtracking algorithm is faster than dynamic programming in general case. We have designed and implemented a protein structure alignment system based on our protein visualization software (MoleView). These experiments show rapid alignment with precise results.

1 Introduction

Since it is known that functions of protein might be derived from its structure, functional closeness can be inferred from the method of measuring the structural similarity between two proteins [1]. Therefore, fast structural comparison methods are crucial in dealing with the increasing number of protein structural data. This paper proposes a fast and efficient method of protein structure alignment.

Many structural alignment methods for proteins have been proposed [2, 3, 4, 5, 6] in recent years, where distance matrices, and vector representation are the most commonly used. Distance matrices, also known as distance plots or distance maps, contain all the pair-wise distances between alpha-carbon atoms, i.e. the Cα atoms of each residue [3]. This method has critical weak points in terms of its computational complexity and sensitivity to errors in the global optimization of alignment. Another research approach represents a protein structure as vectors of the protein's secondary

A. Gelbukh and C.A. Reyes-Garcia (Eds.): MICAI 2006, LNAI 4293, pp. 1179 – 1189, 2006.

structural elements (SSEs; namely α-helices and β-strands). In this method, a protein structures are simplified as a vector for efficient searching and substructure matching [5]. But, this approach suffers from the relatively low accuracy of SSE alignments, and in some cases, it causes a failure in producing an SSE alignment due to the lack of SSEs in the input structures.

A major drawback of these approaches is that it needs to perform an exhaustive sequential scan of a structure database to find similar structures to a target protein, which makes all previous methods not be feasible to be used for the large structure databases, such as the PDB [4].

This paper is organized as follows. In Section 2 a new alignment algorithm is proposed. We propose the 3D chain code and apply the backtracking algorithm for protein alignment. In Section 3 we show alignment result as RMSD and computation time.

2 The Proposed Protein Structure Alignment Algorithm

The algorithm comprises four steps. (Figure 1) Step 1: We make a 3D chain code for 3-dimensional information of the protein. Since the protein chain is similar to thread, we regard a protein chain as a thread. Then, we convert the thread into a progressive direction vector and use the angles of the direction vector as local features. This method basically exploits the local similarity of the two proteins. Step 2: For local alignment of the two proteins, we compare each of the 3D chain code pairs. If two 3D

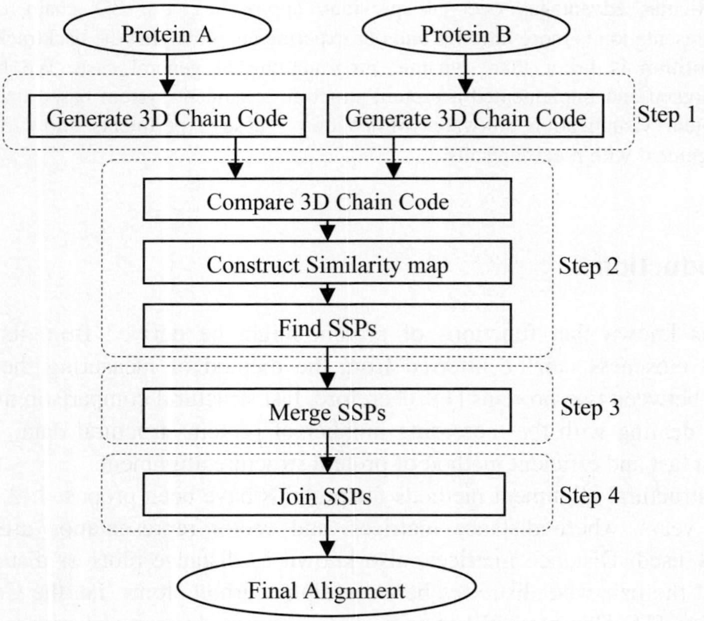

Fig. 1. Overall algorithm steps

chain code pairs are similar, we plot a dot on the similarity map. After finishing the comparison of the two 3D chain code pairs, we make a similar substructure pair(*SSP*)set. Step 3: For fast calculation, we merge *SSP*s with secondary structure information of the proteins. Step 4: We apply a backtracking algorithm to join *SSP* by combing the gaps between two consecutive *SSP*s, each with its own score.

In this section, we provide a detailed description of the new algorithm and its implementation.

2.1 3D Chain Code

The protein structure data are obtained from the Protein Data Bank [4]. For each residue of the protein we obtain the 3D coordinates of its Cα atoms from the PDB file. As a result, each protein is represented by approximately equidistant sampling points in 3D space. To make a 3D chain code, we regard four *C*α atoms as a set (Fig 2)[18]. We calculate a homogeneous coordinate transform to create a new coordinate (u,v,n) composed of a Up Vector $(C\alpha_i, C\alpha_{i+1})$ and a directional vector $(C\alpha_{i+1}, C\alpha_{i+2})$ as the new axis coordinate.

This method uses the following equation:

$$\textit{Homogeneous Coordinate Transform} \quad T = \begin{Bmatrix} R_{11} & R_{12} & R_{13} & 0 \\ R_{21} & R_{22} & R_{23} & 0 \\ R_{31} & R_{32} & R_{33} & 0 \\ T_1 & T_2 & T_3 & 1 \end{Bmatrix} \tag{1}$$

The directional vector *Dir* (R_{31}, R_{32}, R_{33}) is:

$$R_{31} = \frac{x_3 - x_2}{\|v\|},\quad R_{32} = \frac{y_3 - y_2}{\|v\|},\quad R_{33} = \frac{z_3 - z_2}{\|v\|},$$
$$\|v\| = \sqrt{(x_3 - x_2)^2 + (y_3 - y_2)^2 + (z_3 - z_2)^2} \tag{2}$$

Up vector Up (R_{21}, R_{22}, R_{23}) is:

$$Up = Up_w - (Up_w \cdot Dir) * Dir,$$
$$Up_w = (x_1 - x_2,\ y_1 - y_2,\ z_1 - z_2) \tag{3}$$

Right vector *R* (R_{11}, R_{12}, R_{13}) is:

$$R = Up \times Dir \tag{4}$$

Translation vector $T(T_1, T_2, T_3)$ is:

$$T = (-x3, -y3, -z3) \tag{5}$$

The transform *T* is applied to $C\alpha_{i+3}$ to calculate a transformed $C\alpha'_{i+3}$ (x_t, y_t, z_t). Then, we convert $C\alpha'_{i+3}$ to a spherical coordinate. The conversion from cartesian coordinate to spherical coordinate is as follows:

$$r = \sqrt{x_t^2 + y_t^2 + z_t^2}$$
$$\theta = \tan^{-1}\left(\frac{y_t}{x_t}\right), \qquad (-\pi < \theta < \pi) \tag{6}$$
$$\phi = \cos^{-1}\left(\frac{z_t}{r}\right) = \cos^{-1}(z_t) \quad (-\pi < \phi < \pi)$$

For protein structure matching, the C_a atoms along the backbone can be considered as equally spaced because of the consistency in chemical bond formation. Since we can use the same polygonal length between the C_a atoms, we regard r as 1 in the spherical coordinate.

By following this step, the 3D chain code (CC_A) of protein A is created for a protein chain:

$$CC_A = \{\{\emptyset_1,\theta_1\}, \{\emptyset_2,\theta_2\}, \ldots \{\emptyset_n,\theta_n\}\} \tag{7}$$

Where n is the total number of amino acid of protein A minus 3.

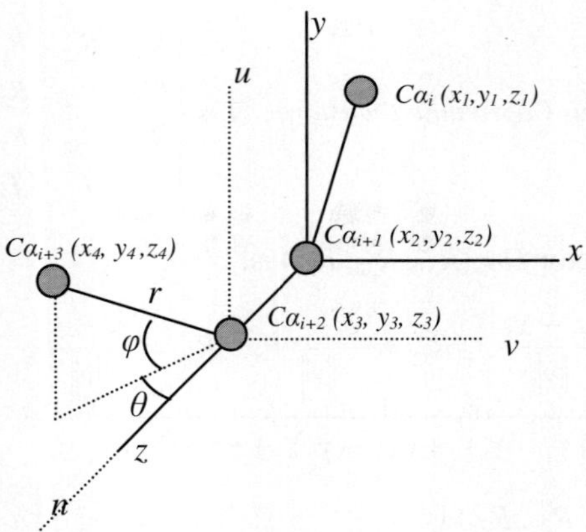

Fig. 2. The 3D chain code

2.2 Finding Similar Substructure Pair Set

Because the 3D chain code represents a relative direction in the 4 atoms of a protein, we can compare local similarity of two proteins by means of comparing 3D chain code of the two proteins.

Given two proteins, we construct a similarity map. The similarity map represents how much two proteins are aligned together. The entry $D(i,j)$ of the similarity map denotes the similarity between the 3D chain code values of the i_{th} residue of protein A($\{\emptyset_i,\theta_i\}$) and the j_{th} residue of protein B($\{\emptyset_j,\theta_j\}$), and is defined by the following equation.

$$D(i,j) = \sqrt{(\phi_i - \phi_j)^2 + (\theta_i - \theta_j)^2} \tag{8}$$

This measure is basically the Euclidian distance. After calculating each *D(i,j)* for for *i* and *j*, we obtain the entry value below than degree angles of threshold (T_d) in similarity map. We use 10 as T_d in our experiments. Figure 3 shows an example of a similarity map for the 3D chain code between two particular proteins called 1HCL and 1JSU:A.

By using this similarity map, our goal is to find all *SSP*s in the map. A *SSP* is represented as a diagonal line in the map. For finding a *SSP*, we find first element *D(i,j)* with the value below T_d and then, find the next element at *D(i+1, j+1)* and *D(i-1, j-1)* with the value below T_d and the same procedure is repeated until the next elements is below T_d. This process can be viewed as finding diagonal lines in the similarity map. After finding a *SSP*, we define it as a $SSP_l^k(i,j)$(Fig.4).

$$SSP_l^k(i,j) = \{ \{\{\varnothing_{i+0},\theta_{i+0}\}, \{\varnothing_{i+1},\theta_{i+1}\}, \ldots \{\varnothing_{i+l},\theta_{i+l}\}\}, \\ \{\{\varnothing_{j+0},\theta_{j+0}\}, \{\varnothing_{j+1},\theta_{j+1}\}, \ldots \{\varnothing_{j+l},\theta_{j+l}\}\} \} \quad (9)$$

(*k* is the index of *SSP*, *l* is the length of the *SSP*, *i* is the index of protein A, *j* is the index of protein B).

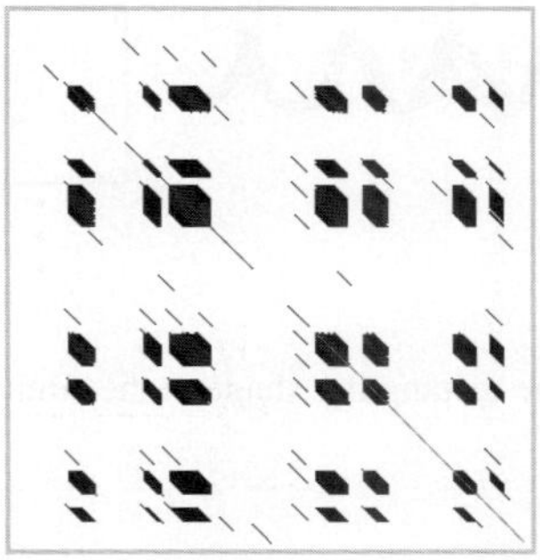

Fig. 3. The similarity map of 1HCL and 1JSU:A

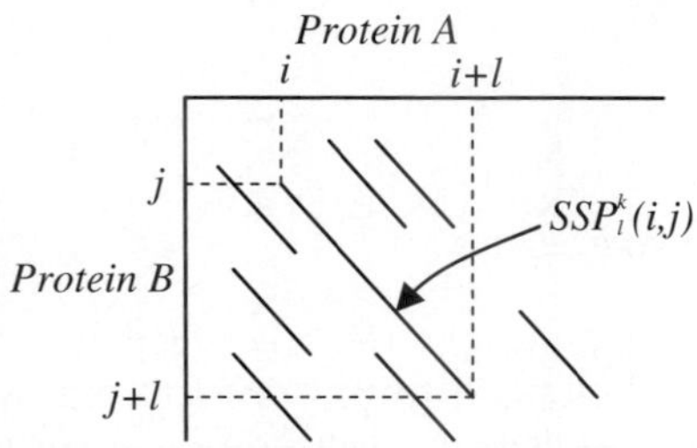

Fig. 4. The *k*-th $SSP_l^k(i,j)$ in similarity map

2.3 Merging Similar Substructure Pairs

In the previous section, we have found many *SSP*s. Because the computation time of the protein alignment depends on the number of *SSP*s, we merge specific *SSP*s into a *SSP*.

In the similarity map, we find rectangular shape which is composed of many *SSPs*. The *SSP*s which has same secondary structure cause the rectangular shape.(Figure 5) For example, if protein A and protein B has same *α-helix* structure, they have a similar geometric structure each 1 rotation turn. The *β-strands* are same. In this case, we merge *SSP*s with same secondary structure into a single *SSP*. After merging *SSP*s, the similarity map is shown in Figure 6.

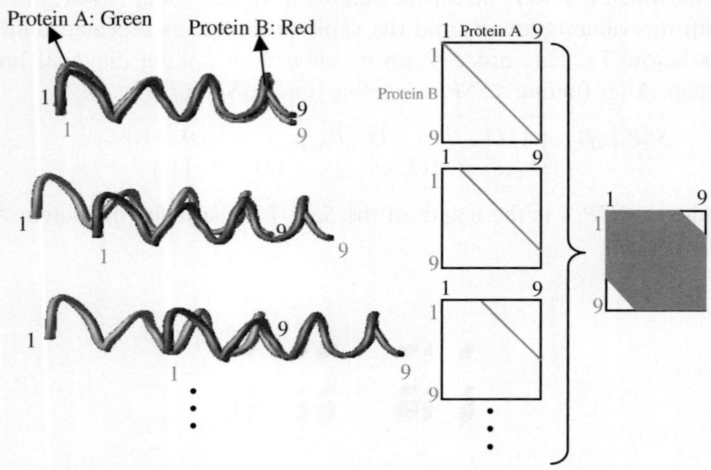

Fig. 5. The rectangular shape in the similarity map

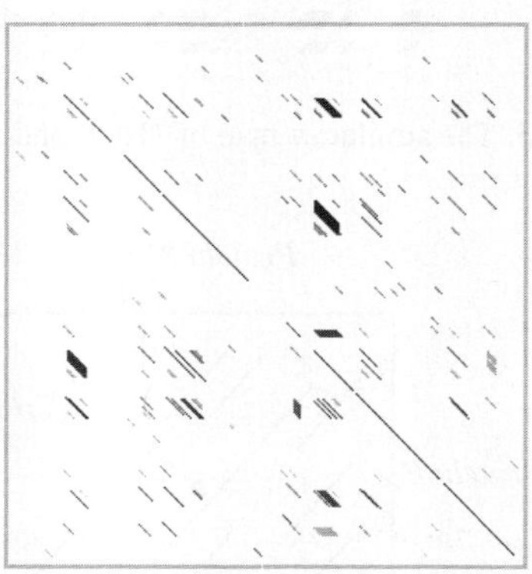

Fig. 6. After merging *SSP*s, the similarity map of 1HCL and 1JSU:A

2.4 Joining Similar Substructure Pairs

In this section, we should find optimal *SSP*s, which describe a possible alignment of protein A with protein B.

We apply the modified backtracking algorithm [15] for joining *SSP*s. The backtracking algorithm is a refinement of the brute force approach, which systematically searches for a solution of a problem from among all the available options. It does so by assuming that the solutions are represented by the vectors (s_1, ..., s_m) of values and by traversing, in a depth-first manner, the domains of the vectors until the solutions are found. When invoked, the algorithm starts with an empty vector. At each stage it extends the partial vector with a new value. On reaching a partial vector (s_1, ..., s_i) which cannot represent a partial solution by promising function, the algorithm backtracks by removing the trailing value from the vector, and then proceeds by trying to extend the vector with alternative values.

The traversal of the solution space can be represented by a depth-first traversal of a tree. We represent the *SSP*s as nodes (v_i) of the state space tree. The simple pseudo code is shown in figure 7.

```
void backtrack(node v) // A SSP is represented as a node
{
    if ( promising(node v) )
        if (there is a solution at node v)
            Write solution
        else
            for ( each child node u of node v )
                backtrack(u);
}
```

Fig. 7. The backtracking algorithm

We use a connectivity value for each *SSP* as a promising function. If two *SSP*s (SSP_k and SSP_{k+1}) have a similar 3D rotation and translation below the threshold, the promising function returns the value true. The pseudo code is shown in figure 8.

```
bool promising (node v)
{
    Transform T = parentNode().SSP1.GetTransform();
    v.SSP2.apply(T);
    double f = RMSD(v.SSP1, v.SSP2);
    return (f>threshold)? FALSE: TRUE;
}
```

Fig. 8. The promising function in the backtracking algorithm

The root node in the tree is the first *SSP*. After running this algorithm, many solutions are established. We calculate the RMSD value from the solutions offered. Then, we select a solution with the minimum RMSD value.

3 Implementation and Results

We have testes our algorithm on a MoleView visualization tool(Figure 9). MoleView is a Win2000/XP-based protein structure visualization tool. MoleView was designed to display and analyze the structural information contained in the Protein Data Bank (PDB), and can be run as a stand-alone application. MoleView is similar to programs such as VMD , MolMol , weblab, Swiss-Pdb Viewer, MolScript, RasMol, qmol[16], and raster3d[17], but it is optimized for a fast, high-quality rendering of the current PC-installed video card with an easy-to-use user interface.

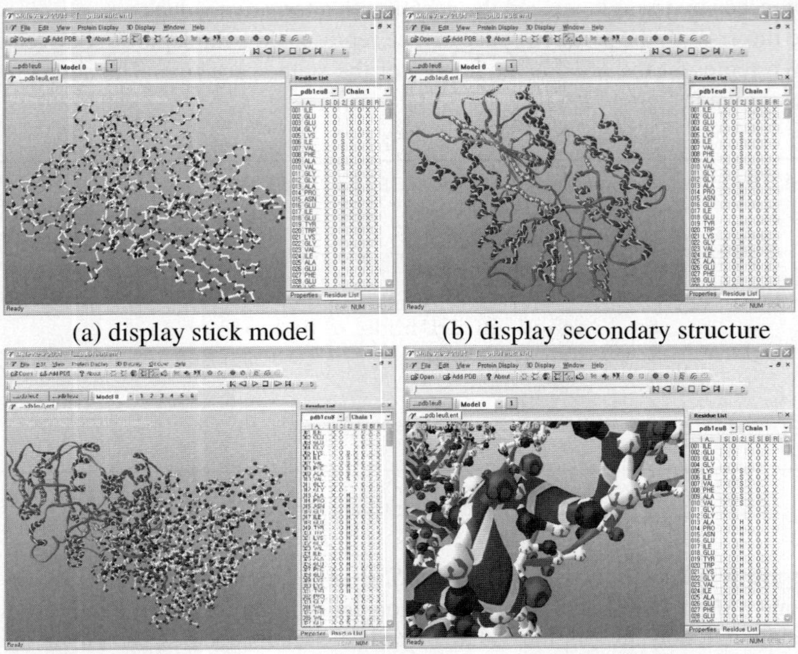

(a) display stick model (b) display secondary structure

(c) display ball and stick model and secondary structure (d) Close look at (c)

Fig. 9. The screenshot of MoleView

Our empirical study of the protein structure alignment system using the 3D chain code could lead to very encouraging results. Figure 10 shows the alignment result of protein 1HCL_ and 1JSU_A. These protein are cyclin-dependent protein kinases, the uncomplexed monomer (1HCL:_) in the open state and the complex with cyclin and P27 (1JSU:A) in the closed state. While the sequences of the uncomplexed and complexed state are almost identical with 96.2% homology, there are significant conformational differences. Differences are found in both active site. The RMSD of the two proteins is 1.70 and the alignment time is 0.41 sec.

Figure 11 shows the alignment result for protein 1WAJ_ and 1NOY_A. These proteins are the DNA Polymerase. The residues that matched are [7,31]-[63,78]-[87,102]-[104,119]-[128,253]-[260,297]-[310,372] of the protein 1WAJ and [6,30]-[60,75]-[84,99]-[101,116]-[124,249]-[256,293]-[306,368] of 1NOY_A. The number of alignment is 261 and the RMSD is 2.67. The processing time for alignment is 13.18 sec. The processing time is very short. In CE [7], this time is 298 seconds.

A further result is our use as a test of the protein kinases, for which over 30 structures are available in the PDB. The results of a search against the complete PDB using the quaternary complex of the cAMP-dependent protein kinase in a closed conformation (1ATP:E) as a probe structure is presented in Table 1. The average RMSD is 2.45 and the average alignment time is 0.54 sec.

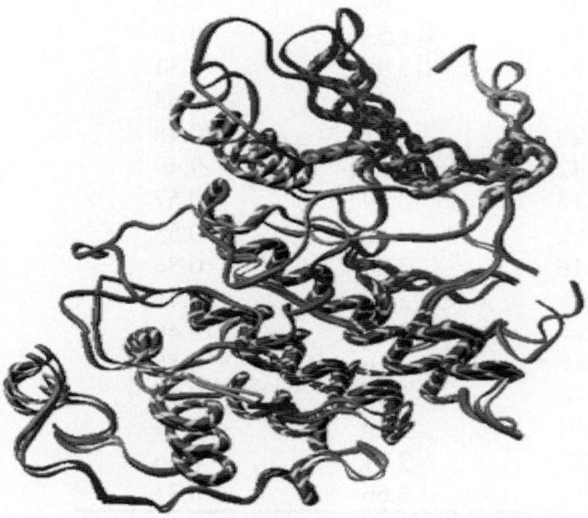

The number of aligned AA: 202

RMSD is 1.70

Alignment time is 0.41 sec

Matched SSP

[18,23]-[31,58]-[64,133]-[153,162]-[168, 279]
[29,34]-[39,66]-[72,141]-[162,171]-[177, 288]

Fig. 10. The alignment between 1HCL_ and 1JSU_A(Image captured by MoleView)

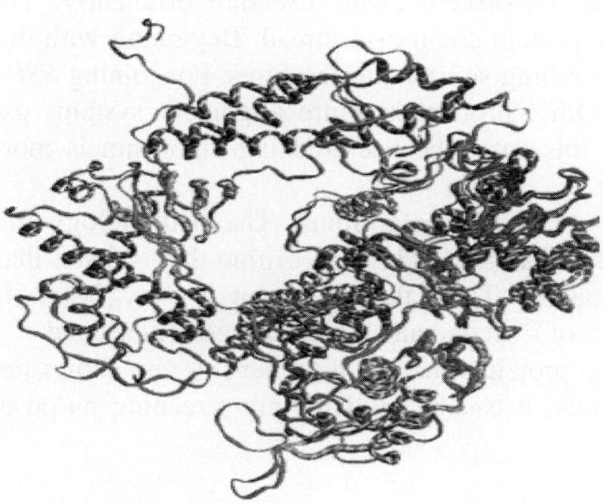

The number of aligned AA: 261

RMSD is 2.67

Alignment time is 13.18 sec

Matched SSP

[6,30]-[60,75]-[84,99]-[101,116]-[124,249]-[256,293]-[306,368]
[7,31]-[63,78]-[87,102]-[104,119]-[128,253]-[260,297]-[310,372]

Fig. 11. The alignment between 1WAJ_ and 1NOY_A (Image captured by MoleView)

Table 1. Experimental results of protein alignment

No.	Chain 2	#Alignment	RMSD	***Time(seconds)***
1	1APM_E	336	0.54	0.91
2	1CDK_A	336	0.80	0.51
3	1YDR_E	324	0.66	0.48
4	1CTP_E	304	2.63	0.49
5	1PHK_	233	1.68	0.43
6	1KOA_	118	1.53	0.70
7	1KOB_A	166	2.95	0.54
8	1AD5_A	111	3.43	0.68
9	1CKI_A	120	2.61	0.48
10	1CSN_	142	2.77	0.46
11	1ERK_	116	2.99	0.57
12	1FIN_A	73	2.46	0.55
13	1GOL_	116	3.07	0.56
14	1JST_A	88	2.60	0.45
15	1IRK_	64	3.25	0.46
16	1FGK_A	44	3.16	0.55
17	1FMK_	97	2.37	0.67
18	1WFC_	101	3.44	0.54
19	1KNY_A	27	2.41	0.46
20	1TIG_	25	3.66	0.31

4 Discussion and Conclusion

This paper proposed a noble protein structure alignment method through the 3D chain code of a protein chain direction vector and a backtracking algorithm for joining *SSP*s. The 3D chain code represents the protein chain structure efficiently. The essential concept here is the idea of a protein chain as a thread. Beginning with this idea, we made a 3D chain code for searching similar substructures. For joining *SSP*s, we use the backtracking algorithm. Other protein structure alignment systems use dynamic programming. However, in this case, the backtracking algorithm is more intuitive and operates more efficiently.

This algorithm has particular merit, unlike other algorithms. The methodology uses a 3D chain code that is more intuitive and a backtracking algorithm that is faster than dynamic programming generally speaking. Thus, the alignment is very faster. In general cases, the alignment time is 0.5 of a second and rarely exceeds 1.0 second.

Consequently, because the proposed protein structure alignment system shows fast alignment with relatively precise results, it can be used for pre-screening purposes using the huge protein database.

References

[1] Philip E. Bourne and Helge Weissig: Structural Bioinformatics, Wiley-Liss, 2003.

[2] Taylor, W. and Orengo, C., “Protein structure alignment,” Journal of Molecular Biology, Vol. 208(1989), pp. 1-22.

[3] L.Holm and C.Sander, "Protein Structure Comparison by alignment of distance matrices", Journal of Molecular Biology, Vol. 233(1993), pp. 123-138.

[4] Rabian Schwarzer and Itay Lotan, "Approximation of Protein Structure for Fast Similarity Measures", Proc. 7th Annual International Conference on Research in Computational Molecular Biology(RECOMB) (2003), pp. 267-276.

[5] Amit P. Singh and Douglas L. Brutlag, "Hierarchical Protein Structure Superposition using both Secondary Structure and Atomic Representation", Proc. Intelligent Systems for Molecular Biology(1993).

[6] Won, C.S., Park, D.K. and Park, S.J., "Efficient use of MPEG-7 Edge Histogram Descriptor", ETRI Journal, Vol.24, No. 1, Feb. 2002, pp.22-30.

[7] Shindyalov, I.N. and Bourne, P.E., "Protein structure alignment by incremental combinatorial extension (CE) of the optimal path", Protein Eng., 11(1993), pp. 739-747.

[8] Databases and Tools for 3-D protein Structure Comparison and Alignment Using the Combinatorial Extension (CE) Method (http://cl.sdsc.edu/ce.html).

[9] Chanyong Park, et al, MoleView: A program for molecular visualization, Genome Informatics 2004, p167-1

[10] Lamdan, Y. and Wolfson, H.J., "Geometric hashing: a general and efficient model-based recognition scheme", In Proc. of the 2nd International Conference on ComputerVision (ICCV), 238-249, 1988.

[11] Leibowitz, N., Fligelman, Z.Y., Nussinov, R., and Wolfson, H.J., "Multiple Structural Alignment and Core Detection by Geometric Hashing", In Proc. of the 7th International Conference on Intelligent Systems for Molecular Biology (ISMB), 169-177, 1999

[12] Nussinov, R. and Wolfson, H.J., "Efficient detection of three-dimensional structural motifs in biological macromolecules by computer vision techniques", Biophysics, 88: 10495-10499, 1991.

[13] Pennec, X. and Ayache, N., "A geometric algorithm to find small but highly similar 3D substructures in proteins", Bioinformatics, 14(6): 516-522, 1998.

[14] Holm, L. and Sander, C., "Protein Structure Comparison by Alignment of Distance Matrices", Journal of Molecular Biology, 233(1): 123-138, 1993.

[15] S. Golomb and L. Baumert. Backtrack programming. *J. ACM*, 12:516-524, 1965.

[16] Gans J, Shalloway D Qmol: A program for molecular visualization on Windows based PCs Journal of Molecular Graphics and Modelling 19 557-559, 2001

[17] http://www.bmsc.washington.edu/raster3d/

[18] Bribiesca E. A chain code for representing 3D curves. Pattern Recognition 2000;33: 755–65.

Robust EMG Pattern Recognition to Muscular Fatigue Effect for Human-Machine Interaction

Jae-Hoon Song[1], Jin-Woo Jung[2], and Zeungnam Bien[3]

[1] Air Navigation and Traffic System Department,
Korea Aerospace Research Institute,
45 Eoeun-dong, Yuseong-gu, Daejeon 305-333, Korea
jhsong@kari.re.kr

[2] Department of Computer Engineering, Dongguk University,
26 Pil-dong 3-ga, Jung-gu, Seoul 100-715, Korea
jwjung@dongguk.edu

[3] Department of Electrical Engineering and Computer Science,
Korea Advanced Institute of Science and Technology,
373-1 Guseong-dong, Yuseong-gu, Daejeon 305-701, Korea
bien@kaist.edu

Abstract. The main goal of this paper is to design an electromyogram (EMG) pattern classifier which is robust to muscular fatigue effects for human-machine interaction. When a user operates some machines such as a PC or a powered wheelchair using EMG-based interface, muscular fatigue is generated by sustained duration time of muscle contraction. Therefore, recognition rates are degraded by the muscular fatigue. In this paper, an important observation is addressed: the variations of feature values due to muscular fatigue effects are consistent for sustained duration time. From this observation, a robust pattern classifier was designed through the adaptation process of hyperboxes of Fuzzy Min-Max Neural Network. As a result, significantly improved performance is confirmed.

1 Introduction

As the number of the elderly is rapidly increasing along with the number of the handicapped caused by a variety of accidents, the social demand for welfare and support of state-of-the-art technology are also increasing to lead more safe and comfortable lives. In particular, the elderly or the handicapped have serious problems in doing a certain work with their own effort in daily life so that some assistive devices or systems will be very helpful to assist such people or to do the work instead of human beings endowing as much independence as possible so as to improve their quality of life. There are a variety of devices to assist their ordinary activities. One of useful methods is the electromyogram (EMG)-based interface. EMG can be acquired from any available muscle regardless of disability levels. Therefore, a design of EMG-based interface can follow the concept of universal design scheme. Another advantage of EMG is the ease-of-use. EMG-based interface is very intuitive since it reflects human intention on movement.

A. Gelbukh and C.A. Reyes-Garcia (Eds.): MICAI 2006, LNAI 4293, pp. 1190 – 1199, 2006.

Besides, there is a significant weakness in EMG-based interface, time-varying characteristics of EMG signals mainly from muscular fatigue effect. For example, when a user operates a powered wheelchair by his/her EMG, the user has to sustain a muscle contraction to control both direction and speed of the powered wheelchair. If the muscle contraction is sustained, muscular fatigue is generated by the contraction time and system performance is degraded by this fatigue effect.

The main goal of this paper is to design an EMG pattern classifier which is robust to muscular fatigue effects for human-machine interaction. For this objective, the previous works about muscular fatigue effects are introduced with problems in section 2. Our approach to solve muscular fatigue effects are addressed in section 3. Finally, experimental results are shown in section 4.

2 Muscular Fatigue Effect in EMG Pattern Recognition

According to a dictionary, fatigue is defined by the feeling of extreme physical or mental tiredness [1]. Muscular fatigue is, therefore, a fatigue due to sustained muscular contraction. Since a muscle movement accompanies with a variety of neural transmissions, muscular fatigue is expressed by complicated procedures. Muscular fatigue is known to be divided by central fatigue and peripheral fatigue according to sustained time of muscle contraction [2]. Central fatigue is defined as a fatigue of neural transmission, such as a decrease of the motor unit (MU) firing rate [2]. Peripheral fatigue is defined as a fatigue related to biochemical metabolism, such as an accumulation of metabolic by-products in the active muscles and a deficiency of energy sources [2]. Central fatigue is appeared through a couple of hours and a few days. Besides, peripheral fatigue is appeared through a few second and a few minute [3]. Therefore, peripheral fatigue is more important factor for HMI. We mainly considered peripheral fatigue in this paper.

A muscular fatigue including peripheral fatigue can be expressed by the relations of characteristic frequencies such as median frequency (MDF) and mean frequency (MNF) [4]. Both MDF and MNF are defined by the following mathematical Eq. (1) and (2), respectively. Here, $P(\omega)$ represents the power spectrum at the specific frequency.

$$\int_0^{MDF} P(\omega)d\omega = \int_{MDF}^{\infty} P(\omega)d\omega = \frac{1}{2}\int_0^{\infty} P(\omega)d\omega \tag{1}$$

$$MNF = \frac{\int_0^{\infty} \omega P(\omega)d\omega}{\int_0^{\infty} P(\omega)d\omega} \tag{2}$$

A representatively previous work regarding muscular fatigue compensation of EMG-based interface is a research about a prosthetic hand, named by 'Utah arm' [5]. Here, muscular fatigues generated by repetitive muscle movements (radial flexion motion) are improved by the fatigue compensating preprocessor. And, Winslow et al. [6] proposed a fatigue compensation method using artificial neural networks for functional electrical stimulation (FES) to generate stimulations with suitable intensity at a proper time. But, these all results of previous works are based on a specific single muscle movement, not considering various muscle movements together.

Besides, it is generally desired that more than two wrist movements are dealt with together for EMG-based human-machine interaction. For example, the required degree-of-freedom in the PC mouse control or powered wheelchair control is more than five; up, down, left, right, and click or stop (See Fig. 1). Therefore, fatigue levels are also different motion-by-motion even in a same muscle [7]. After all, a new fatigue compensation method is desired to meet together with fatigue effects of various motions from human intention.

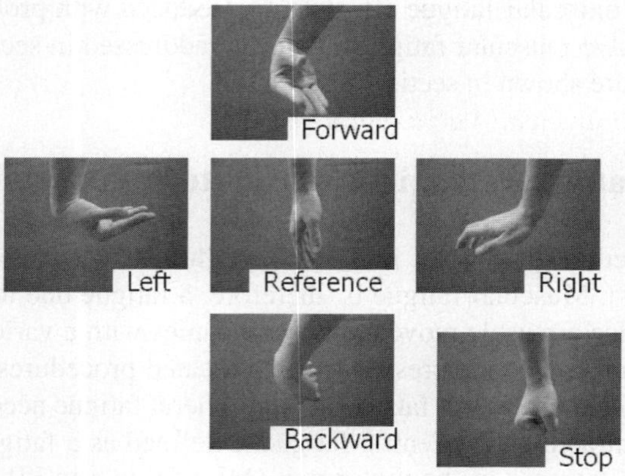

Fig. 1. 6 Basic Motions for Human-Machine Interaction

3 Robust EMG Pattern Recognition to Muscular Fatigue Effect

3.1 Adaptation Method to Muscular Fatigue Effect

There are several assumptions to be used for implementing the adaptation process of EMG pattern recognizer to muscular fatigue effects. The first assumption is that there is only one user for one recognizer. It considers excluding the effect of individual difference. The second assumption is that the locations of EMG electrodes are always same with 4 channels like Fig. 2. The third assumption is about a method of the

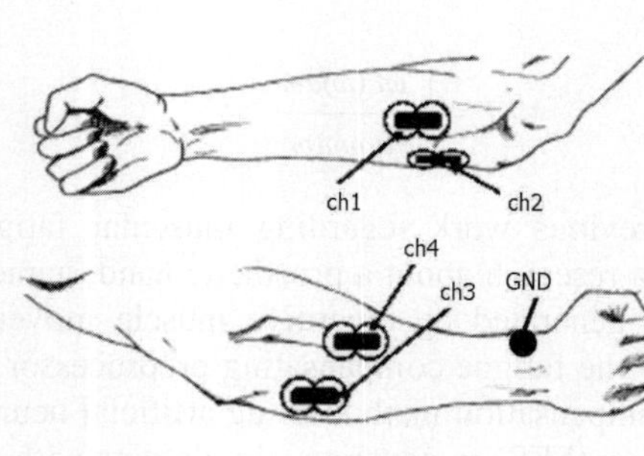

Fig. 2. Placement of surface electrodes for EMG acquisition

muscle contraction. Sustained motions are considered instead of repetitive muscle movements. And recovery process is accompanied simultaneously with the ends of his/her motion.

And the forth assumption is that EMG signal can be quasi-stationary when EMG signal is segmented by short periods [8]. This assumption may be verified with Fig. 3. Fig. 3 shows the variations of a feature value, Difference Absolute Mean Value (DAMV, See Eq. (3)), during 60 sec with one of the six basic motions including the reference motion. Each signal acquisition is repeatedly performed as many as ten times through sustained contractions for each defined basic motion. Here, fatigue effects between adjacent trials are excluded by assigning three minutes rest.

Difference Absolute Mean Value (DAMV) [9]

DAMV is the mean absolute value of the difference between adjacent samples and expressed by Eq. (3). Here, N is the size of time-window for computing.

$$DAMV = \frac{1}{N-1}\sum_{i=1}^{N} | x_{i+1} - x_i | \tag{3}$$

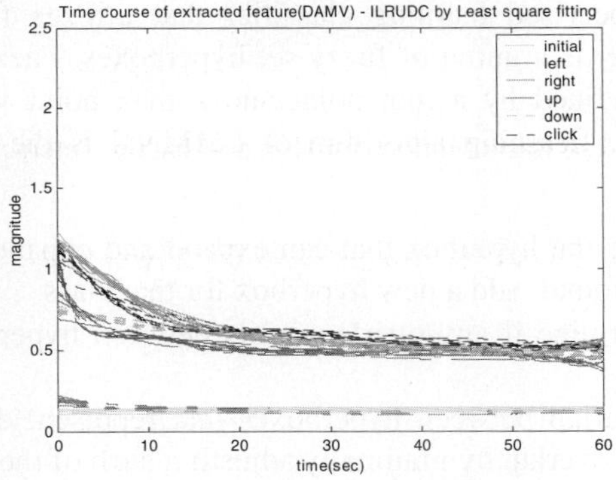

(a) DAMV at channel #3

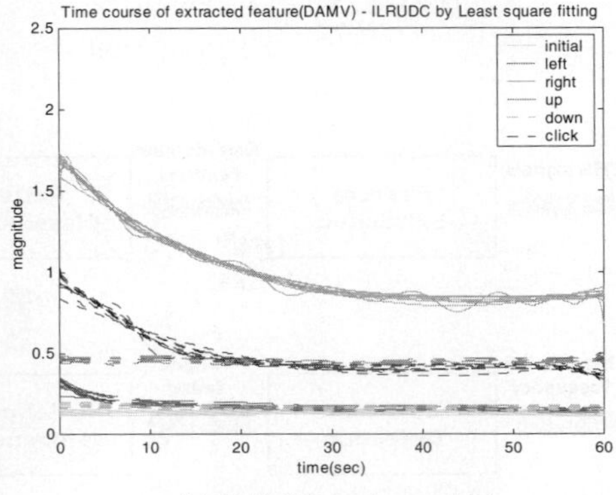

(b) DAMV at channel #4

Fig. 3. Time-dependent feature variations

Fig. 3 shows that the trends of feature variations are consistent. This observation is still same in four other volunteers' tests. After all, the amount of feature variation from initial value may be estimated using the contraction time. And, the muscle contraction time may be estimated as the lasting time of human motion based on the third assumption on the continuous muscle contraction. As a result, the degradation in system performance by the muscular fatigue effect can be compensated with differential feature value, DAMV in Fig. 3, by estimating the muscle contraction time via the lasting time of human motion.

3.2 Robust EMG Pattern Recognizer

The suggested block diagram of robust EMG pattern recognizer is shown in Fig. 4. In Fig. 4, the above part is a general pattern recognition scheme and the below one is additional adaptation process for robust EMG pattern recognition to the muscular fatigue effect. Here, Except DAMV, three additional features [9], Integral Absolute Value (IAV), Zero-Crossing (ZC), and Variance (VAR), are used for the pattern classification (See Eq.(4),(5),(6)). And Fuzzy Min-Max Neural Network [10] is adopted as a pattern classification method by its conspicuous on-line learning ability.

FMMNN is a supervised learning classifier that utilizes fuzzy sets as pattern classes. Each fuzzy set is a union of fuzzy set hyperboxes. Fuzzy set hyperbox is an n-dimensional box defined by a min point and a max point with a corresponding membership function. Learning algorithm of FMMNN is the following three-step process [10]:

- *Expansion*: Identify the hyperbox that can expand and expand it. If an expandable hyperbox can't be found, add a new hyperbox for that class.
- *Overlap test*: Determine if any overlap exists between hyperboxes from different classes.
- *Contraction*: If overlap between hyperboxes that represent different classes does exist, eliminate the overlap by minimally adjusting each of the hyperboxes.

$$IAV = \frac{1}{N}\sum_{i=1}^{N} |x_i| \tag{4}$$

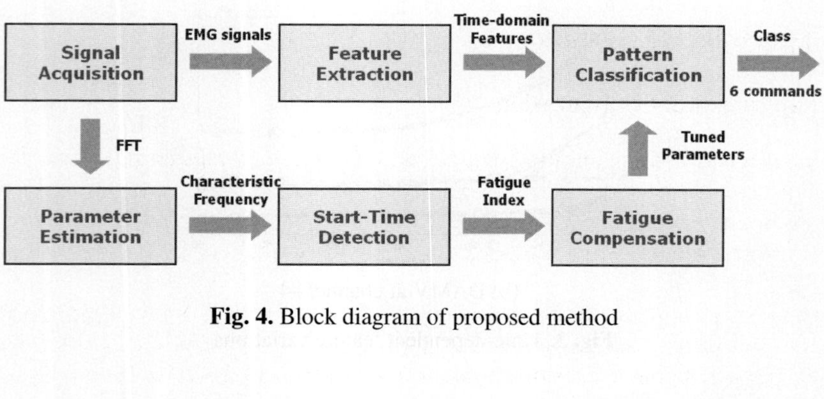

Fig. 4. Block diagram of proposed method

$$ZC = \sum_{i=1}^{N} \mathrm{sgn}(-x_i x_{i+1}),\ \mathrm{sgn}(x) = \begin{cases} 1, & if\ x > 0 \\ 0, & otherwise \end{cases} \tag{5}$$

$$VAR = \frac{1}{N-1} \sum_{i=1}^{N} (x_i - E\{x\})^2 \tag{6}$$

$E\{x\}$ is a mean value for a given segment. And, N is the size of time-window for computing.

In Fig. 4, adaptation process consists of three sub-parts: parameter estimation, start-time detection, and fatigue compensation.

Parameter Estimation: Two characteristic frequencies, MDF and MNF in Eq. (1) and (2) are calculated with the given signal.

Start-Time Detection: A transition between any two basic motions defined in Fig. 1 naturally goes by reference posture since reference posture is defined as relaxation posture. Thus, the start-time of muscle contraction for another motion can be found by detecting reference posture. By several experiments on the values of both MDF and MNF for various human motions, a rule described in Eq. (7) has been found and used for detecting the start-time and initializing the time instant of a motion.

If $MDF\ at\ channel\ \#3 < 40Hz$ and $MDF\ at\ channel\ \#4 < 40Hz$ and $MNF\ at\ channel\ \#3 < 60Hz$ and $MNF\ at\ channel\ \#4 < 60Hz$, then start-time is detected. (7)

Fatigue Compensation: The fatigue compensation is performed simply using the graph in Fig. 3 because the graph in Fig. 3 can be used as a look-up-table to find the amount of compensation at the detected time. Specifically, the proposed fatigue compensation method is to adjust min-max values of hyperboxes in FMMNN according to the consistent feature variation in Fig. 3 for every 2 seconds. After these adjusting, min-max values of hyperboxes are re-adjusted through the learning algorithm of FMMNN, such as expansion, overlap test and contraction. This re-adjustment process is also done for every 2 seconds with the first step. Here, the meaning of 2 seconds is the minimum time period to be able to observe the muscular fatigue effect in EMG signal.

4 Experimental Results

4.1 Experimental Configuration

Proposed robust EMG pattern recognizer was applied to controlling a mouse for human-computer interaction environment. Five non-handicapped men who have no prior knowledge about experiments were volunteered for this experiment. The objective of experiment was to follow six motions: reference, up, down, left, right, and click.

EMG signals were acquired with a 4-ch EMG signal acquisition module like Fig. 5 which was specially designed for low noise, high gain, ease-to-use and small size. Sample rate for signal acquisition was used as 1 kHz and a size of time-window for analysis was 128 ms. The same experiments were performed for five subjects but measured EMG signals were different from each subject due to their own physiological characteristics and slightly different locations of electrodes.

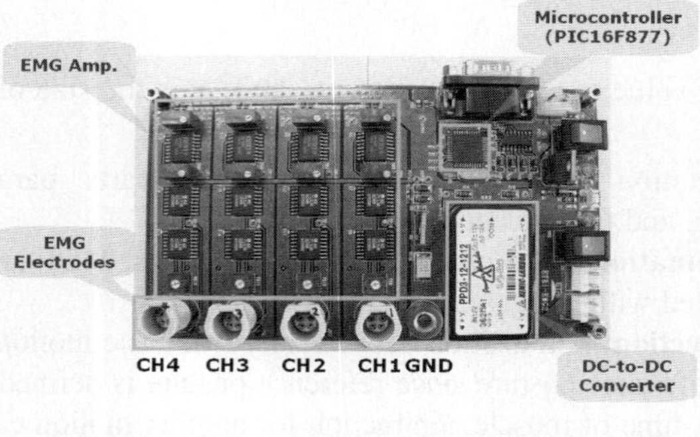

Fig. 5. Developed EMG signal acquisition module

4.2 Experimental Results

IAV, ZC, VAR and DAMV are extracted from four channel EMG signals. Fig. 6 shows a distribution of DAMV (ch. #3 and ch. #4) in two-dimensional feature space.

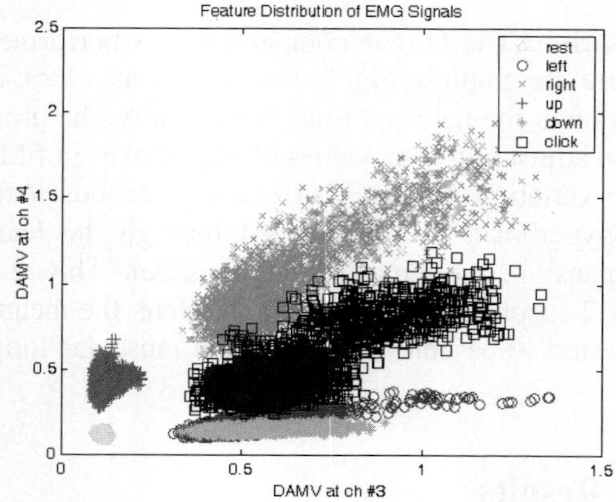

Fig. 6. Feature distribution of EMG signal in two-dimensional space

As mentioned above, the trends of feature variations are consistent. Even though feature distributions are varied by sustained time of muscle contractions, class boundaries of FMMNN are correspondingly adjusted by proposed fatigue compensation method. Fig. 7 represents that hyperboxes of proposed method well reflect time-varying feature distributions due to muscular fatigue effects.

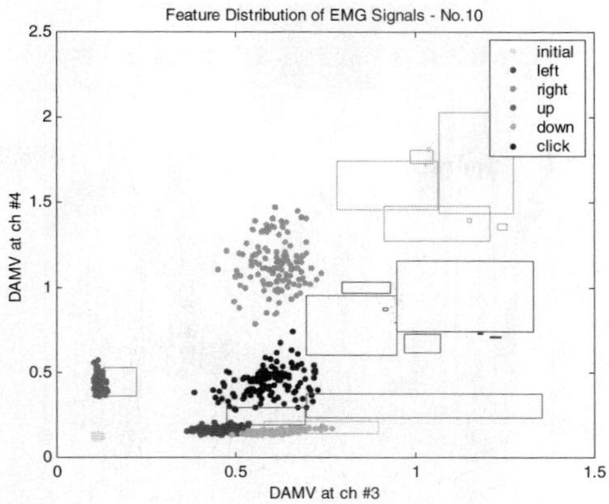

(a) Before application

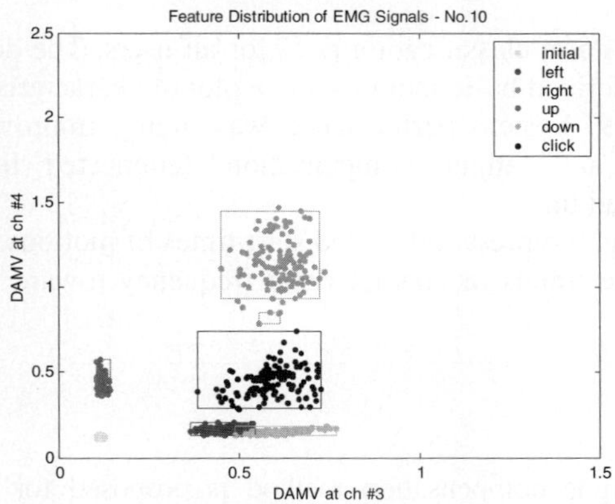

(b) After application

Fig. 7. Comparison of class boundaries

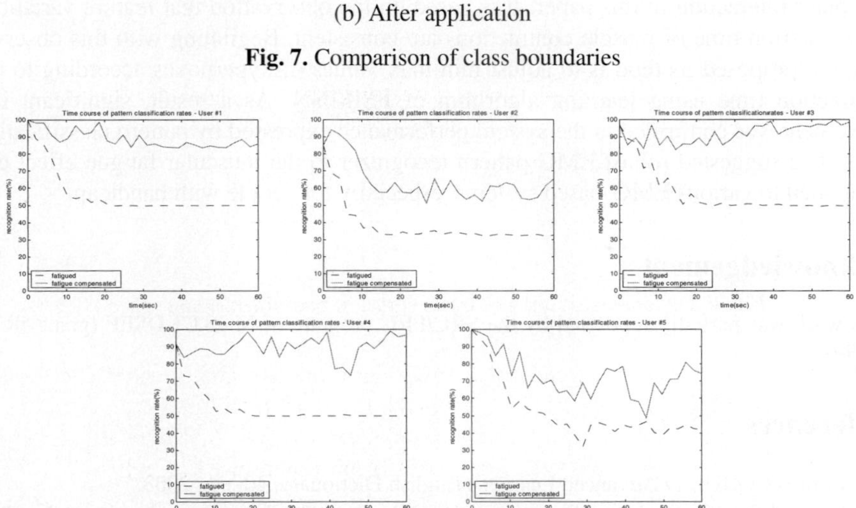

(a) user #1 (b) user #2 (c) user #3 (d) user #4 (e) user #5

Fig. 8. Fatigue compensated pattern classification rates for multiple users

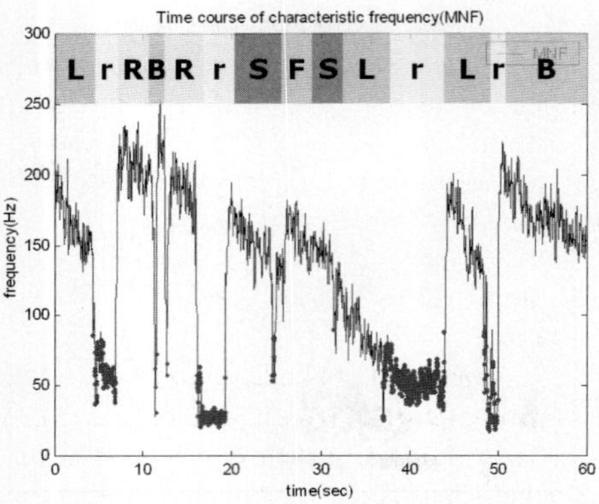

Fig. 9. Designed input pattern and the variation of characteristic frequency (MNF at CH #3)

Fig. 8 refers to pattern classification rates for all users. The designed input pattern including all of predefined basic motions and a plot of characteristic frequency, MNF, are shown in Fig. 9. System performance was highly improved by the proposed method, FMMNN and fatigue compensation, (connected line) compared with FMMNN only (dotted line).

Bold points in Fig. 9 represent detected start-times of motions. If a muscle contraction is sustained, the trends of characteristic frequency toward lower frequency are obviously observed.

5 Conclusion

Novel muscular fatigue compensation method is proposed for EMG-based human-computer interaction in this paper. It is based on the observation that feature variations for a duration time of muscle contractions are consistent. Beginning with this observation, the proposed method is to adjust min-max values of hyperboxes according to the contraction time using learning algorithm of FMMNN. As a result, significant improvement was confirmed in the system performance expressed by pattern classification rates. The suggested robust EMG pattern recognizer to the muscular fatigue effect can be applied to various EMG-based systems, especially for people with handicap.

Acknowledgement

This work was partially supported by the SRC/ERC program of MOST/KOSEF (grant #R11-1999-008).

References

1. Collins COBUILD Advanced Learner's English Dictionary, 4th ed., 2003.
2. Bigland-Ritchie, B., Jones, D.A., Hosking, G.P., Edwards, R.H.: Central and peripheral fatigue in sustained maximum voluntary contractions of human quadriceps muscle. Journal of Clinical Science and Molecular Medicine, Vol. 54 (6):609-14, June 1978.

3. Kiryu, T., Morishiata, M., Yamada, H., Okada, M.: A muscular fatigue index based on the relationships between superimposed M wave and preceding background activity. IEEE Transactions on Biomedical Engineering, Vol. 45 (10):1194-1204, Oct. 1998.
4. Bonato, P., Roy, S.H., Knaflitz, M., de Luca, C.J.: Time-frequency parameters of the surface myoelectric signal for assessing muscle fatigue during cyclic dynamic contractions. IEEE Transactions on Biomedical Engineering, Vol. 48 (7):745 - 753, July 2001.
5. Park, E., Meek, S.G.: Fatigue compensation of the electromyographic signal for prosthetic control and force estimation. IEEE Transactions on Biomedical Engineering, Vol. 40 (10):1019-1023, Oct. 1993.
6. Winslow, J., Jacobs, P.L., Tepavac, D.: Fatigue compensation during FES using surface EMG. Journal of Electromyography and Kinesilogy, Vol. 13 (6):555-568, Mar. 2003.
7. Chen, J.-J.J., Yu, N.-Y.: The validity of stimulus-evoked EMG for studying muscle fatigue characteristics of paraplegic subjects during dynamic cycling movement. IEEE Transactions on Rehabilitation Engineering, Vol. 5 (2): 170-178, Jun. 1997.
8. Knox, R.R., Brooks, D.H., Manolakos, E., Markogiannakis, S.: Time-series based features for EMG pattern recognition: Preliminary results. Bioengineering Conference, Proceedings of the IEEE Nineteenth Annual Northeast, March 18-19 1993.
9. Boostani, R., Moradi, M.H.: Evaluation of the forearm EMG signal features for the control of a prosthetic hand. Journal of Physiological Measurement, Vol. 24:309-319, May 2003.
10. Simpson, P.: Fuzzy min-max neural networks - Part 1: Classification. IEEE Transactions on Neural Networks, Vol. 3:776-786, Sep. 1992.

Classification of Individual and Clustered Microcalcifications in Digital Mammograms Using Evolutionary Neural Networks

Rolando R. Hernández-Cisneros and Hugo Terashima-Marín

Center for Intelligent Systems, Tecnológico de Monterrey, Campus Monterrey
Ave. Eugenio Garza Sada 2501 Sur, Monterrey, Nuevo León 64849 Mexico
a00766380@itesm.mx, terashima@itesm.mx

Abstract. Breast cancer is one of the main causes of death in women and early diagnosis is an important means to reduce the mortality rate. The presence of microcalcification clusters are primary indicators of early stages of malignant types of breast cancer and its detection is important to prevent the disease. This paper proposes a procedure for the classification of microcalcification clusters in mammograms using sequential difference of gaussian filters (DoG) and three evolutionary artificial neural networks (EANNs) compared against a feedforward artificial neural network (ANN) trained with backpropagation. We found that the use of genetic algorithms (GAs) for finding the optimal weight set for an ANN, finding an adequate initial weight set before starting a backpropagation training algorithm and designing its architecture and tuning its parameters, results mainly in improvements in overall accuracy, sensitivity and specificity of an ANN, compared with other networks trained with simple backpropagation.

1 Introduction

Worldwide, breast cancer is the most common form of cancer in females and is, after lung cancer, the second most fatal cancer in women. Survival rates are higher when breast cancer is detected in its early stages. Mammography is one of the most common techniques for breast cancer diagnosis, and microcalcifications are one among several types of objects that can be detected in a mammogram. Microcalcifications are calcium accumulations typically 100 microns to several mm in diameter, and they sometimes are early indicators of the presence of breast cancer. Microcalcification clusters are groups of three or more microcalcifications that usually appear in areas smaller than 1 cm^2, and they have a high probability of becoming a malignant lesion.

However, the predictive value of mammograms is relatively low, compared to biopsy. The sensitivity may be improved having each mammogram checked by two or more radiologists, making the process inefficient. A viable alternative is replacing one of the radiologists by a computer system, giving a second opinion [1].

A computer system intended for microcalcification detection in mammograms may be based on several methods, like wavelets, fractal models, support vector

A. Gelbukh and C.A. Reyes-Garcia (Eds.): MICAI 2006, LNAI 4293, pp. 1200–1210, 2006.

machines, mathematical morphology, bayesian image analysis models, high order statistic, fuzzy logic, etc.

The method selected for this work was the difference of gaussian filters (DoG). DoG filters are adequate for the noise-invariant and size-specific detection of spots, resulting in a DoG image. This DoG image represents the microcalcifications if a thresholding operation is applied to it. We developed a procedure that applies a sequence of Difference of Gaussian Filters, in order to maximize the amount of detected probable microcalcifications (signals) in the mammogram, which are later classified in order to detect if they are real microcalcifications or not. Finally, microcalcification clusters are identified and also classified into malignant and benign.

Artificial neural networks (ANNs) have been successfully used for classification purposes in medical applications, including the classification of microcalcifications in digital mammograms. Unfortunately, for an ANN to be successful in a particular domain, its architecture, training algorithm and the domain variables selected as inputs must be adequately chosen. Designing an ANN architecture is a trial-and-error process; several parameters must be tuned according to the training data when a training algorithm is chosen and, finally, a classification problem could involve too many variables (features), most of them not relevant at all for the classification process itself. Genetic algorithms (GAs) may be used to address the problems mentioned above, helping to obtain more accurate ANNs with better generalization abilities. GAs have been used for searching the optimal weight set of an ANN, for designing its architecture, for finding its most adequate parameter set (number of neurons in the hidden layer(s), learning rate, etc.) among others tasks. Exhaustive reviews about evolutionary artificial neural networks (EANNs) have been presented by Yao [2] and Balakrishnan and Honavar [3].

In this paper, we propose an automated procedure for feature extraction and training data set construction for training an ANN. We also describe the use of GAs for 1) finding the optimal weight set for an ANN, 2) finding an adequate initial weight set for an ANN before starting a backpropagation training algorithm and 3) designing the architecture and tuning some parameters of an ANN. All of these methods are applied to the classification of microcalcifications and microcalcification clusters in digital mammograms, expecting to improve the accuracy of an ordinary feedforward ANN performing this task.

The rest of this document is organized as follows. In the second section, the proposed procedure along with its theoretical framework is discussed. The third section deals with the experiments and the main results of this work. Finally, in the fourth section, the conclusions are presented.

2 Methodology

The mammograms used in this project were provided by the Mammographic Image Analysis Society (MIAS) [4]. The MIAS database contains 322 images, with resolutions of 50 microns/pixel and 200 microns/pixel. In this work, the images with a resolution of 200 microns/pixel were used. The data has been reviewed by a consultant radiologist and all the abnormalities have been identified and marked. The truth data consists of the location of the abnormality and the radius of a circle which encloses it. From the totality of the database, only 25 images contain microcalcifications. Among these 25 images, 13 cases are diagnosed as malignant and 12 as benign. Some related works have used this same database [5], [6], [7]. The general procedure receives a digital mammogram as an input, and it is conformed by five stages: pre-processing, detection of potential microcalcifications (signals), classification of signals into real microcalcifications, detection of microcalcification clusters and classification of microcalcification clusters into benign and malignant. The diagram of the proposed procedure is shown in Figure 1. As end-products of this process, we obtain two ANNs for classifying microcalcifications and microcalcifications clusters respectively, which in this case, are products of the evolutionary approaches that are proposed.

2.1 Pre-processing

This stage has the aim of eliminating those elements in the images that could interfere in the process of identifying microcalcifications. A secondary goal is to reduce the work area only to the relevant region that exactly contains the breast.

The procedure receives the original images as input. First, a median filter is applied in order to eliminate the background noise, keeping the significant features of the images. Next, binary images are created from each filtered image, intended solely for helping the automatic cropping procedure to delete the background marks and the isolated regions, so the image will contain only the region of interest. The result of this stage is a smaller image, with less noise.

2.2 Detection of Potential Microcalcification (Signals)

The main objective of this stage is to detect the mass centers of the potential microcalcifications in the image (signals). The optimized difference of two gaussian filters (DoG) is used for enhancing those regions containing bright points. The resultant image after applying a DoG filter is globally binarized, using an empirically determined threshold. A region-labeling algorithm allows the identification of each one of the points (defined as high-contrast regions detected after the application of the DoG filters, which cannot be considered microcalcifications yet). Then, a segmentation algorithm extracts small 9x9 windows, containing the region of interest whose centroid corresponds to the centroid of each point. In order to detect the greater possible amount of points, six gaussian filters of sizes 5x5, 7x7, 9x9, 11x11, 13x13 and 15x15 are combined, two at a time, to construct 15 DoG filters that are applied sequentially. Each one of the 15 DoG filters was applied 51 times, varying the binarization threshold in the interval [0, 5] by increments of 0.1. The points obtained by applying each filter are added to the points obtained by the previous one, deleting the repeated points. The same procedure is repeated with the points obtained by the remaining DoG filters. All of these points are passed later to three selection procedures.

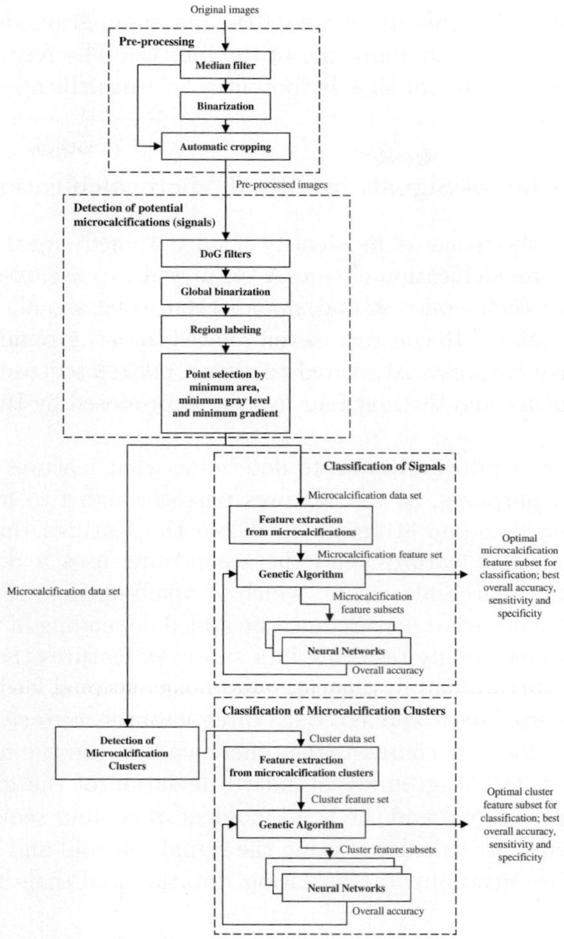

Fig. 1. Diagram of the proposed procedure

These three selection methods are applied in order to transform a point into a signal (potential microcalcification). The first method performs selection according to the object area, choosing only the points with an area between a predefined minimum and a maximum. For this work, a minimum area of 1 pixel (0.0314 mm^2) and a maximum of 77 pixels (3.08 mm^2) were considered. The second methods performs selection according to the gray level of the points. Studying the mean gray levels of pixels surrounding real identified microcalcifications, it was found they have values in the interval [102, 237] with a mean of 164. For this study, we set the minimum gray level for points to be selected to 100. Finally, the third selection method uses the gray gradient (or absolute contrast, the difference between the mean gray level of the point and the mean gray level of the background). Again, studying the mean gray gradient of point surrounding real identified microcalcifications, it was found they have values in the interval [3, 56] with a mean of 9.66. For this study, we set the minimum gray gradient for points to be selected to 3, the minimum vale of the interval. The result of these three selection processes is a list of signals (potential microcalcifications) represented by their centroids.

2.3 Classification of Signals into Real Microcalcifications

The objective of this stage is to identify if an obtained signal corresponds to an individual microcalcification or not. A set of features are extracted from the signal, related to their contrast and shape. From each signal, 47 features are extracted: seven related to contrast, seven related to background contrast, three related to relative contrast, 20 related to shape, six related to the moments of the contour sequence and the first four invariants proposed by Hu in a landmark paper [8].

There is not an a priori criterion to determine what features should be used for classification purposes, so the features pass through two feature selection processes [9]: the first one attempts to delete the features that present high correlation with other features, and the second one uses a derivation of the forward sequential search algorithm, which is a sub-optimal search algorithm. The algorithm decides what feature must be added depending of the information gain that it provides, finally resulting in a subset of features that minimize the error of the classifier (which in this case was a conventional feedforward ANN). After these processes were applied, only three features were selected and used for classification: absolute contrast (the difference between the mean gray levels of the signal and its background), standard deviation of the gray level of the pixels that form the signal and the third moment of contour sequence. Moments of contour sequence are calculated using the signal centroid and the pixels in its perimeter, and are invariant to translation, rotation and scale transformations [10].

In order to process signals and accurately classify the real microcalcifications, we decided to use ANNs as classifiers. Because of the problems with ANNs already mentioned, we decided also to use GAs for evolving populations of ANNs, in three different ways, some of them suggested by Cantú-Paz and Kamath [11]. The first approach uses GAs for searching the optimal set of weights of the ANN. In this approach, the GA is used only for searching the weights, the architecture is fixed prior to the experiment. The second approach is very similar to the previous one, but instead of evaluating the network immediately after the initial weight set which is represented in each chromosome of the GA, is assigned, a backpropagation training starts from this initial weight set, hoping to reach an optimum quickly [12]. The last approach is not concerned with evolving weights. Instead, a GA is used to evolve a part of the architecture and other features of the ANN. The number of nodes in the hidden layer is very important parameter, because too few or to many nodes can affect the learning and generalization capabilities of the ANN. In this case, each chromosome encodes the learning rate, a lower and upper limits for the weights before starting the backpropagation training, and the number of nodes of the hidden layer.

At the end of this stage, we obtain three ready-to-use ANNs, each one taken from the last generation of the GAs used in each one of the approaches. These ANNs have the best performances in terms of overall accuracy (fraction of well classified objects, including microcalcifications and other elements in the image that are not microcalcifications).

2.4 Detection of Microcalcification Clusters

During this stage, the microcalcification clusters are identified. The detection and posterior consideration of every microcalcification cluster in the images may produce better results in a subsequent classification process, as we showed in [13]. Because of this, an algorithm for locating microcalcification cluster regions where the quantity of microcalcifications per cm^2 (density) is higher, was developed. This algorithm keeps adding microcalcifications to their closest clusters at a reasonable distance until there are no more microcalcifications left or if the remaining ones are too distant for being considered as part of a cluster. Every detected cluster is then labeled.

2.5 Classification of Microcalcification Clusters into Benign and Malignant

This stage has the objective of classifying each cluster in one of two classes: benign or malignant. This information is provided by the MIAS database.

From every microcalcification cluster detected in the mammograms in the previous stage, a cluster feature set is extracted. The feature set is constituted by 30 features: 14 related to the shape of the cluster, six related to the area of the microcalcifications included in the cluster and ten related to the contrast of the microcalcifications in the cluster. The same two feature selection procedures mentioned earlier are also performed in this stage. Only three cluster features were selected for the classification process: minimum diameter, minimum radius and mean radius of the clusters. The minimum diameter is the maximum distance that can exist between two microcalcifications within a cluster in such a way that the line connecting them is perpendicular to the maximum diameter, defined as the maximum distance between two microcalcifications in a cluster. The minimum radius is the shortest of the radii connecting each microcalcification to the centroid of the cluster and the mean radius is the mean of these radii.

In order to process microcalcification clusters and accurately classify them into benign or malignant, we decided again to use ANNs as classifiers. We use GAs for evolving populations of ANNs, in the same three different approaches we used before for classifying signals. The first approach uses GAs for searching the optimal set of weights of the ANN. The second approach uses a GA for defining initial weight sets, from which a backpropagation training algorithm is started, hoping to reach an optimum quickly. The third approach uses a GA for evolving the architecture and other features of the ANN as it was shown in a previous stage, when signals were classified. Again, each chromosome encodes the learning rate, a lower and upper limits for the weights before starting the backpropagation training, and the number of nodes of the hidden layer. For comparison, a conventional feedforward ANN is used also.

At the end of this stage, we obtain three ready-to-use ANNs, each one taken from the last generation of the GAs used in each of the approaches. These ANNs have the best performances in terms of overall accuracy (fraction of well classified clusters).

3 Experiments and Results

3.1 From Pre-processing to Feature Extraction

Only 22 images were finally used for this study. In the second phase, six gaussian filters of sizes 5x5, 7x7, 9x9, 11x11, 13x13 and 15x15 were combined, two at a time, to construct 15 DoG filters that were applied sequentially. Each one of the 15 DoG filters was applied 51 times, varying the binarization threshold in the interval [0, 5] by increments of 0.1. The points obtained by applying each filter were added to the points obtained by the previous one, deleting the repeated points. The same procedure was repeated with the points obtained by the remaining DoG filters. These points passed through the three selection methods for selecting signals (potential microcalcifications), according to region area, gray level and the gray gradient. The result was a list of 1,242,179 signals (potential microcalcifications) represented by their centroids.

The additional data included with the MIAS database define, with centroids and radii, the areas in the mammograms where microcalcifications are located. With these data and the support of expert radiologists, all the signals located in these 22 mammograms were preclassified into microcalcifications, and not-microcalcifications. From the 1,242,179 signals, only 4,612 (0.37%) were microcalcifications, and the remaining 1,237,567 (99.63%) were not. Because of this imbalanced distribution of elements in each class, an exploratory sampling was made. Several sampling with different proportions of each class were tested and finally we decided to use a sample of 10,000 signals, including 2,500 real microcalcifications in it (25%).

After the 47 microcalcification features were extracted from each signal, the feature selection processes reduced the relevant features to only three: absolute contrast, standard deviation of the gray level and the third moment of contour sequence. Finally, a transactional database was obtained, containing 10,000 signals (2500 of them being real microcalcifications randomly distributed) and three features describing each signal.

3.2 Classification of Signals into Microcalcifications

In the third stage, a conventional feedforward ANN and three evolutionary ANNs were developed for the classification of signals into real microcalcifications.

The feedforward ANN had an architecture of three inputs, seven neurons in the hidden layer and one output. All the units had the sigmoid hyperbolic tangent function as the transfer function. The data (input and targets) were scaled in the range [-1, 1] and divided into ten non-overlapping splits, each one with 90% of the data for training and the remaining 10% for testing. A ten-fold crossvalidation trial was performed; that is, the ANN was trained ten times, each time using a different split on the data and the means and standard deviations of the overall performance, sensitivity and specificity were reported. These results are shown in Table 1 on the row "BP".

Table 1. Mean (%) and standard deviation of the sensitivity, specificity and overall accuracy of simple backpropagation and different evolutionary methods for the classification of signals into real microcalcifications

	Sensitivity		**Specificity**		**Overall**	
Method	Mean	Std. Dev.	Mean	Std. Dev.	Mean	Std. Dev.
BP	75.68	0.044	81.36	0.010	80.51	0.013
WEIGHTS	72.44	0.027	84.32	0.013	82.37	0.011
WEIGHTS+BP	75.81	0.021	86.76	0.025	84.68	0.006
PARAMETERS	73.19	0.177	84.67	0.035	83.12	0.028

For the three EANNs used to evolve signal classifiers, all of their GAs used a population of 50 individuals. We used simple GAs, with gray encoding, stochastic universal sampling selection, double-point crossover, fitness based reinsertion and a generational gap of 0.9. For all the GAs, the probability of crossover was 0.7 and the probability of mutation was $1/l$, where l is the length of the chromosome. The initial population of each GA was always initialized uniformly at random. All the ANNs involved in the EANNs are feedforward networks with one hidden layer. All neurons have biases with a constant input of 1.0. The ANNs are fully connected, and the transfer functions of every unit is the sigmoid hyperbolic tangent function. The data (input and targets) were normalized to the interval [-1, 1]. For the targets, a value of "-1" means "not-microcalcification" and a value of "1" means "microcalcification". When backpropagation was used, the training stopped after reaching a termination criteria of 20 epochs, trying also to find individual with fast convergence.

For the first approach, where a GA was used to find the ANNs weights, the population consisted of 50 individuals, each one with a length of $l = 720$ bits and representing 36 weights (including biases) with a precision of 20 bits. There were two crossover points, and the mutation rate was 0.00139. The GA ran for 50 generations. The results of this approach are shown in Table 1 on the row "WEIGHTS". In the second approach, where a backpropagation training algorithm is run using the weights represented by the individuals in the GA to initialize the ANN, the population consisted of 50 individual also, each one with a length of $l = 720$ bits and representing 36 weights (including biases) with a precision of 20 bits. There were two crossover points, and the mutation rate was 0.00139 ($1/l$). In this case, each ANN was briefly trained using 20 epochs of backpropagation, with a learning rate of 0.1. The GA ran for 50 generations. The results of this approach are shown in Table 1 on the row "WEIGHTS+BP".

Finally, in the third approach, where a GA was used to find the size of the hidden layer, the learning rate for the backpropagation algorithm and the range of initial weights before training, the population consisted of 50 individuals, each one with a length of $l = 18$ bits. The first four bits of the chromosome coded the learning rate in the range [0,1], the next five bits coded the lower value for the initial weights in the range [-10,0], the next five bits coded the upper value for the initial weights in the range [0,10] and the last four bits coded the number of neurons in the hidden layer, in the range [1,15] (if the value was 0, it was changed to 1). There was only one crossover point, and the mutation rate was 0.055555 ($1/l$). In this case, each ANN was built according to the parameters coded in the chromosome, and trained briefly with 20 epochs of backpropagation, in order to favor the ANNs that learned quickly. The results of this approach are shown also in Table 1, on the row "PARAMETERS".

We performed several two-tailed Students t-tests at a level of significance of 5% in order to compare the mean of each method with the means of the other ones in terms of sensitivity, specificity and overall accuracy. We found that for specificity and overall accuracy, evolutionary methods are significantly better than the simple backpropagation method for the classification of individual microcalcifications. No difference was found in terms of sensitivity, except that simple backpropagation was significantly better than the method that evolves weights.

We can notice too that, among the studied EANNs, the one that evolves a set of initial weights and is complemented with backpropagation training is the one that gives better results. We found that in fact, again in terms of specificity and overall accuracy, the method of weight evolution complemented with backpropagation is significantly the best of the methods we studied. Nevertheless, in terms of sensitivity, this method is only significantly better than the method that evolves weights.

3.3 Microcalcification Clusters Detection and Classification

The process of cluster detection and the subsequent feature extraction phase generates another transactional database, this time containing the information of every microcalcification cluster detected in the images. A total of 40 clusters were detected in the 22 mammograms from the MIAS database that were used in this study. According to MIAS additional data and the advice of expert radiologists, 10 clusters are benign and 30 are malignant. The number of features extracted from them is 30, but after the two feature selection processes already discussed in previous sections, the number of relevant features we considered relevant was three: minimum diameter, minimum radius and mean radius of the clusters.

As in the stage of signal classification, a conventional feedforward ANN and three evolutionary ANNs were developed for the classification of clusters into benign and malignant. The four algorithms we use in this step are basically the same ones we used before, except that they receive as input the transactional database containing features about microcalcifications clusters instead of features about signals. Again, the means of the overall performance, sensitivity

Table 2. Mean (%) and standard deviation of the sensitivity, specificity and overall accuracy of simple backpropagation and different evolutionary methods for the classification of microcalcification clusters

	Sensitivity		Specificity		Overall	
Method	Mean	Std. Dev.	Mean	Std. Dev.	Mean	Std. Dev.
BP	55.97	0.072	86.80	0.032	76.75	0.032
WEIGHTS	72.00	0.059	92.09	0.038	86.35	0.031
WEIGHTS+BP	89.34	0.035	95.86	0.025	93.88	0.027
PARAMETERS	63.90	0.163	85.74	0.067	80.50	0.043

and specificity for each one of these four approaches are reported and shown in Table 2.

We also performed several two-tailed Students t-tests at a level of significance of 5% in order to compare the mean of each method for cluster classification with the means of the other ones in terms of sensitivity, specificity and overall accuracy. We found that the performance of evolutionary methods is significantly different and better than the performance of the simple backpropagation method, except in one case. Again, the method that evolves initial weights, complemented with backpropagation, is the one that gives the best results.

4 Conclusions

Our experimentation suggests that evolutionary methods are significantly better than the simple backpropagation method for the classification of individual microcalcifications, in terms of specificity and overall accuracy. No difference was found in terms of sensitivity, except that simple backpropagation was significantly better than the method that only evolves weights. In the case of the classification of microcalcification clusters, we observed that the performance of evolutionary methods is significantly better than the performance of the simple backpropagation method, except in one case. Again, the method that evolves initial weights, complemented with backpropagation, is the one that gives the best results.

Acknowledgments

This research was supported by the Instituto Tecnológico y de Estudios Superiores de Monterrey (ITESM) under the Research Chair CAT-010 and the National Council of Science and Technology of Mexico (CONACYT) under grant 41515.

References

1. Thurfjell, E. L., Lernevall, K. A., Taube, A. A. S.: Benefit of independent double reading in a population-based mammography screening program. Radiology, **191** (1994) 241-244.

2. Yao, X.: Evolving artificial neural networks. in Proceedings of the IEEE, **87**(9) (1999) 1423-1447.
3. Balakrishnan, K., Honavar, V.: Evolutionary design of neural architectures. A preliminary taxonomy and guide to literature. Technical Report CS TR 95-01, Department of Computer Sciences, Iowa State University (1995).
4. Suckling, J., Parker, J., Dance, D., Astley, S., Hutt, I., Boggis, C., Ricketts, I., Stamatakis, E., Cerneaz, N., Kok, S., Taylor, P., Betal, D., Savage, J.: The Mammographic Images Analysis Society digital mammogram database. Exerpta Medica International Congress Series, **1069** (1994) 375-378. http://www.wiau.man.ac.uk/services/MIAS/MIASweb.html
5. Gulsrud, T. O.: Analysis of mammographic microcalcifications using a computationally efficient filter bank. Technical Report, Department of Electrical and Computer Engineering, Stavanger University College (2001).
6. Hong, B.-W., Brady, M.: Segmentation of mammograms in topographic approach. In IEE International Conference on Visual Information Engineering, Guildford, UK (2003).
7. Li, S., Hara, T., Hatanaka, Y., Fujita, H., Endo, T., Iwase, T.: Performance evaluation of a CAD system for detecting masses on mammograms by using the MIAS database. Medical Imaging and Information Science, **18**(3) (2001) 144-153.
8. Hu, M.-K.: Visual pattern recognition by moment invariants. IRE Trans. Information Theory, Vol. **IT-8** (1962) 179-187.
9. Kozlov, A., Koller, D.: Nonuniform dynamic discretization in hybrid networks. In Proceedings of the 13th Annual Conference of Uncertainty in AI (UAI), Providence, Rhode Island, USA (2003) 314-325.
10. Gupta, L., Srinath, M. D.: Contour sequence moments for the classification of closed planar shapes. Pattern Recognition, **20**(3) (1987) 267-272.
11. Cantú-Paz, E., Kamath, C.: Evolving neural networks for the classification of galaxies. In Proceedings of the Genetic and Evolutionary Computation Conference, GECCO 2002, San Francisco, CA, USA (2002) 1019–1026.
12. Skinner, A., Broughton, J. Q.: Neural networks in computational material science: traning algorithms. Modeling and Simulation in Material Science and Engineering, **3** (1995) 371-390.
13. Oporto-Díaz, S., Hernández-Cisneros, R. R., and Terashima-Marín H.: Detection of microcalcification clusters in mammograms using a difference of optimized gaussian filters. In Proceedings of the International Conference in Image Analysis and Recognition (ICIAR 2005), Toronto, Canada (2005) 998–1005.

Heart Cavity Detection in Ultrasound Images with SOM

Mary Carmen Jarur[1] and Marco Mora[1,2]

[1] Department of Computer Science, Catholic University of Maule
Casilla 617, Talca, Chile
mjarur@spock.ucm.cl
[2] IRIT-ENSEEIHT
2 Rue Camichel, 31200 Toulouse, France
marco.mora@enseeiht.fr

Abstract. Ultrasound images are characterized by high level of speckle noise causing undefined contours and difficulties during the segmentation process. This paper presents a novel method to detect heart cavities in ultrasound images. The method is based on a Self Organizing Map and the use of the variance of images. Successful application of our approach to detect heart cavities on real images is presented[1].

1 Introduction

Ultrasound heart images are characterized by high level of speckle noise and low contrast causing erroneous detection of cavities. Speckle is a multiplicative locally correlated noise. The speckle reducing filters have origin mainly in the synthetic aperture radar community. The most widely used filters in this category, such as the filters of Lee [7], Frost [2], Kuan [6], and Gamma Map [10], are based on the coefficient of variation (CV).

Currently the detection of heart cavities considers two steps. The first one corresponds to the filtering of the noise using anisotropic diffusion and the CV [15,12]. The second one is the detection of the contours based on active contours [13,8]. In spite of the good results of this approach, both stages have a high complexity.

For images segmentation, several schemes based on neuronal networks have been proposed. Supervised methods are reported in [9], and unsupervised segmentation techniques by using Self-Organizing Map (SOM) have been presented in [4,1,11].

In order to reduce the computation cost of the current techniques, this paper presents the first results of a novel approach to detect heart cavities by using neural networks. Our method combines elements of the filtering in images affected by speckle such as the variance, and the advantages shown by SOM in segmentation of images.

[1] The authors of this paper acknowledge the valuable contributions of Dr. Clovis Tauber and Dr. Hadj Batatia from the Polytechnical National Institute of Toulouse, France, during the development of this research.

A. Gelbukh and C.A. Reyes-Garcia (Eds.): MICAI 2006, LNAI 4293, pp. 1211–1219, 2006.

Matlab, the Image Processing Toolbox and the Neural Networks Toolbox were used as platform to carry out most of the data processing work. The paper is organized as follows. The next section will review the self organizing map. Section 3 details our approach to heart cavity detection. The experimental results are shown in section 4. The paper is concluded in section 5.

2 The Self Organizing Map

The Self-Organizing Map (SOM), proposed by Kohonen, also called Kohonen network has had a great deal of success in many applications such as reduction of dimensions, data processing and analysis, monitoring of processes, vectorial quantification, modeling of density functions, clusters analysis, and with relevance for our work in image segmentation [5]. The SOM neural networks can learn to detect regularities and correlations in their input and adapt their future responses to that input accordingly. The SOM network typically has two layers of nodes and does a no lineal projection of multidimensional space about output discrete space represented by a surface of neurons. The training process is composed by the following procedures:

1. Initialize the weights randomly.
2. Input data is fed to the network through the processing elements (nodes) in the input layer.
3. Calculate the similitude between the input data and the neurons weight.
4. Determinate the winning neuron, that is, the node with the minimum distance respect to the input data is the winner.
5. Actualization of the weights of the winning neuron and its neighborhood, adjusting its weights to be closer to the value of the input pattern.
6. If it has got the maximum number of iterations, the learning process stops, in other case it returns to the step 2.

For each input data x_i, the Euclidean distance between the input data and the weights of each neuron $w_{i,j}$ in the one-dimensional grid is computed (step 3) by:

$$d_j = \sum_{i=0}^{n-1} [x_i(t) - w_{i,j}(t)]^2 \tag{1}$$

The neuron having the least distance is designated the winner neuron (step 4). Finally the weights of the winner neuron are updated (step 5) using the following expression:

$$w_{i,j}(t+1) = w_{i,j}(t) + h_{ci} \cdot [x_i(t) - w_{i,j}(t)] \tag{2}$$

The term h_{ci} refers to a neighborhood set, N_c, of array points around the winner node c . Where $h_{ci} = \alpha(t)$ if $i \in N_c$ and $h_{ci} = 0$ if $i \notin N_c$, where $\alpha(t)$ is some monotonically decreasing function of time $(0 < \alpha(t) < 1)$.

With respect to the number of iterations, this must be big enough due to the statistics requirements as well as proportional to the number of neurons. It is suggested to be 500 times per map neuron [5].

3 Proposed Approach to Heart Cavity Detection Using SOM

To detect the contours of the heart cavities in ultrasound images is a complex task. The boundaries of the cavities are not very well defined due to speckle and the low contrast of the images. In order to detect the cavities our approach supposes the existence of three classes of zones in the image: the exterior of the cavity, the interior of the cavity, and the border between both zones. This supposition allows to simplify the problem, and it can be visually verified in the figures presented in this paper.

Our proposal to detect heart cavities has three stages. The first one calculates the variance of the pixels of the image. The second one considers the training of a SOM neural network using the variance-based image. The third one is the classification of the image with the weights of the training stage. The final stage allows to detect the three types of zones previously mentioned.

3.1 Variance Processing

The image is characterized by intensity at position (i, j) as $I_{i,j}$. The first step for processing the image is to calculate $I_{var}(I)$. Each component of $I_{var}(I)$ contains the variance of each pixel with a neighborhood of 3 by 3 pixels as shown in figure 1. The local variance is calculated as:

$$I_{var}(I_{i,j}) = var(Nh_{i,j}) \tag{3}$$

where $Nh_{i,j}$ is the set of pixels that forms the region centered in i, j of 3 by 3 pixels composed by:

$$Nh_{i,j} = \{I_{i-1,j-1}, I_{i-1,j}, \ldots, I_{i+1,j}, I_{i+1,j+1}\} \tag{4}$$

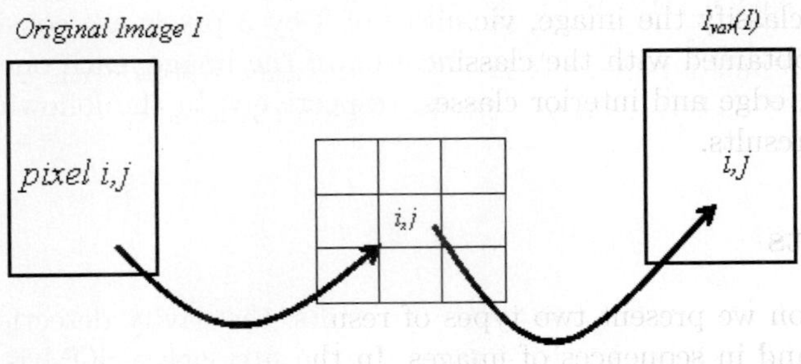

Fig. 1. The neighborhood of pixel i, j

In the case of pixels on the image limits the neighborhood is composed only by the existing pixels. The local variance is mapped between $[0 - 1]$ range by expression:

$$I^*_{var}(I_{i,j}) = \frac{1}{1 + I_{var(I_{i,j})}} \tag{5}$$

The $I^*_{var}(I)$ matrix is the output of this stage and the input of SOM.

3.2 Training of SOM and Classification of Images

The elements of the $I^*_{var}(I)$ matrix are the input data for the training of SOM. The network has nine inputs which correspond to a neighborhood of 3 by 3 of each pixel of $I^*_{var}(I_{i,j})$. The inputs are fully connected to the neurons onto a one-dimensional (1-D) array of outputs nodes. The network has three outputs to classify the image in: exterior, interior and edge. Figure 2 shows the network structure.

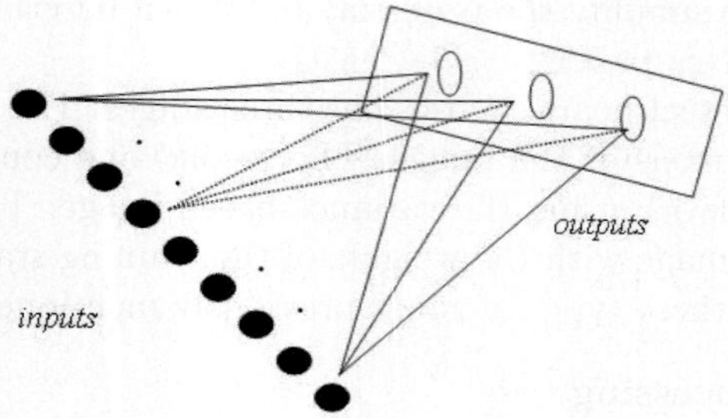

Fig. 2. Structure of SOM used for cavity detection

The learning of the network was done using all the pixels in the image. After training the network, it will be able to characterize the initial image in three zones.

The learning algorithm considered the following characteristics: topology type is one-dimensional of 3 nodes, Euclidean distance function (1), and learning rate $\alpha = 0.8$.

The classification is made with the obtained weights from the training process. In order to classify the image, vicinities of 3 by 3 pixels are considered. Three images are obtained with the classification of the image, each one representing the exterior, edge and interior classes, respectively. In the following section we present the results.

4 Results

In this section we present two types of results: the cavity detection in individual images and in sequences of images. In the first one a SOM is trained with the image to classify. The second one presents a sequence of images of a heart movement video. A single image of the sequence is used to train the network, and weights obtained in this training are used to segment all the images of the video.

4.1 Cavity Detection in Individual Images

The first result corresponds to an ultrasound intra cavity image. Figure 3(a) shows the original image (I) and figure 3(b) presents the $I^*_{var}(I)$ which corresponds to variance-based image.

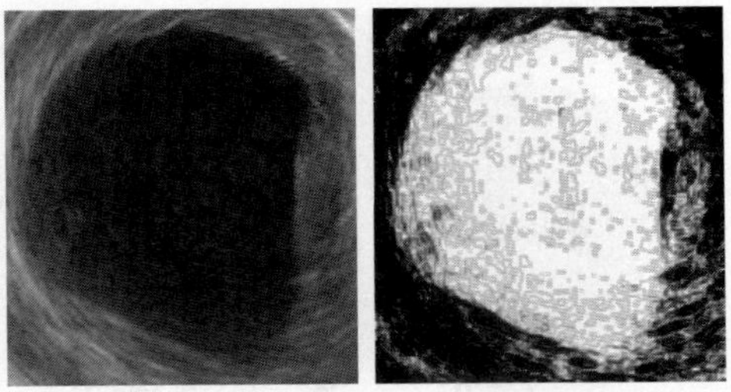

(a) Original image (b) Variance-based image

Fig. 3. Heart intra cavity image and its variance-based image

For the second phase the $I^*_{var}(I)$ is presented to SOM for training. Figure 4 shows the output of SOM after training. Figure 4(a) represents the interior class, figure 4(b) the edge class, and figure 4(c) the exterior class. We use the interior class image in order to find the edges of the cavities. Figure 4(d) shows the edge detection using gradient operator with a Sobel mask [3].

To improve the results, traditional techniques of image processing such as erosion, smoothing by median filter, and dilatation are applied [3]. The erosion by eliminating the small bodies of the image is shown in figure 5(a), the smoothing by median filter is shown in figure 5(b), and the dilatation to recover the size of the objects is shown in figure 5(c). The final edge is visualized in figure 5(d).

Another result of our approach is shown in figure 6. Figure 6(a) shows the ultrasound image with two cavities, and the process previously described is applied. Figure 6(b) shows the interior class given by SOM, figure 6(c) shows the edge of interior class by using the Sobel method, and figure 6(d) shows the edge of interior class after improvements.

The results of cavity detection show that the network is able to identify the cavities efficiently.

4.2 Cavity Detection in Sequences of Images

The images shown in this section correspond to a sequence that represents the movement of the heart. The training process is made with a single image of the sequence. With the weights of this training all the images of the sequence are classified.

Figures 7(a-d) correspond to the original images of the heart movement sequence, figures 7(e-h) are the variance-based images, figures 7(i-l) show the interior class of SOM, figures 7(m-p) correspond to the improvements of the previous images, and finally figures 7(q-t) show the final contour on the original images.

The results show that with the parameters obtained in the training using a single image, the neuronal network allows to suitably classify the rest of the images of the sequence. The characteristic of generalization of the neuronal networks increases the degree of autonomy of our approach by classifying patterns that do not belong to the training set.

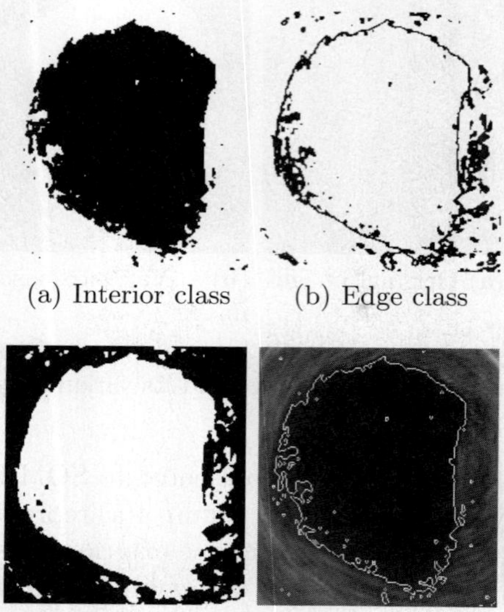

(a) Interior class (b) Edge class (c) Exterior class (d) Edges of interior class

Fig. 4. Decomposition of variance image in three classes by SOM

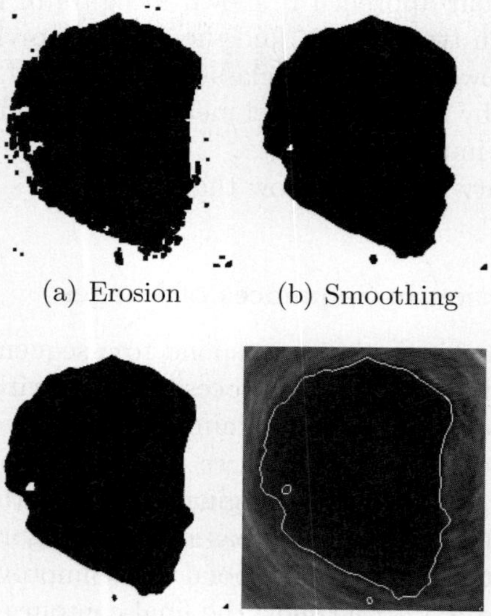

(a) Erosion (b) Smoothing (c) Dilation (d) Final edge

Fig. 5. Improvements in the cavity detection of the interior class image

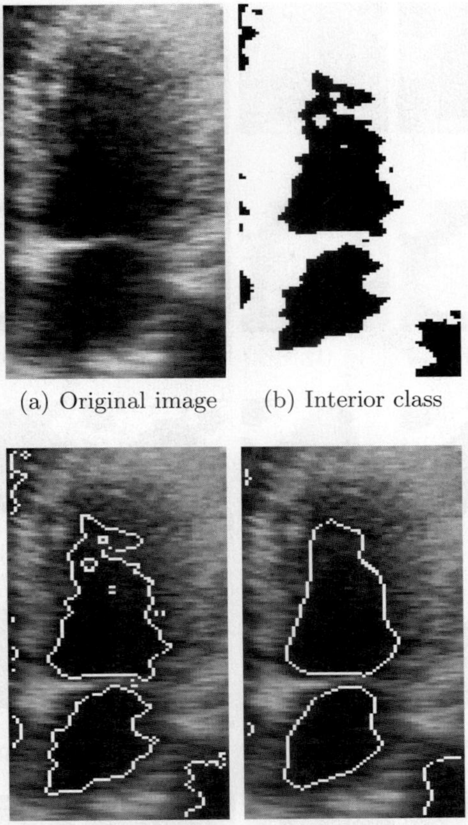

(a) Original image (b) Interior class

(c) Edges of interior class (d) Edges after improvements

Fig. 6. Cavity detection with SOM for an image with two cavities

5 Conclusion

This paper has presented a novel approach for heart cavity detection in ultrasound images based on SOM.

Our approach presents several advantages. The computational cost is low regarding techniques based on anisotropic diffusion and active contours. It is important to observe that the results in many cases show cavity edges completely closed nevertheless the high level of speckle contamination and low contrast of the ultrasonic images. Moreover, due to the unsupervised learning of SOM, our solution presents more autonomy than when supervised neuronal networks are used. Finally due to the generalization capacity of the neuronal network, we can suitably classify a images sequence of similar characteristics, training the network with a single image of the sequence.

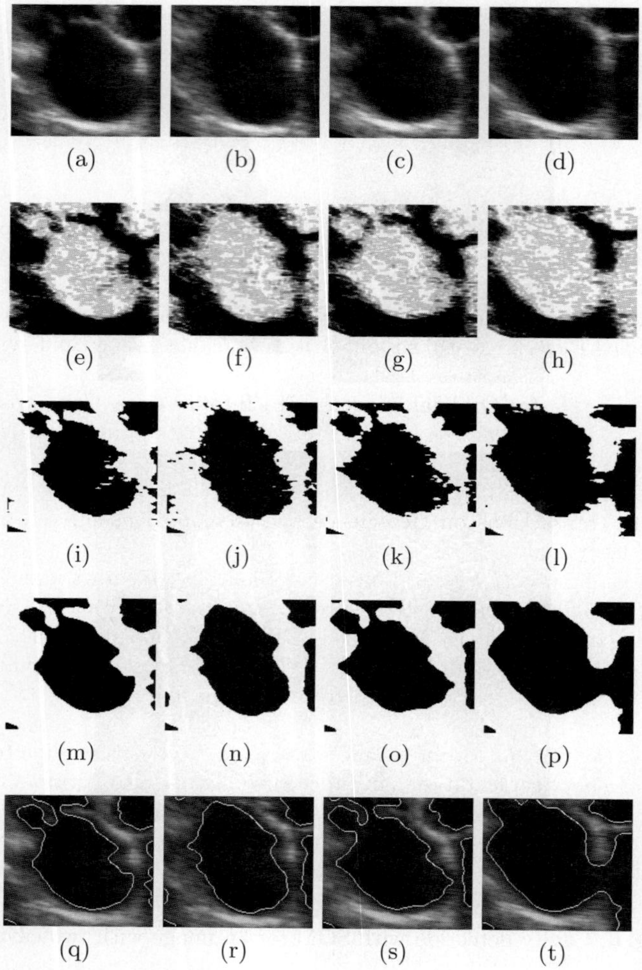

Fig. 7. Sequence of four images

The use of SOM provides a good tradeoff between the optimal segmentation and computational cost. Finally, our work shows that the use of SOM is a promising tool for heart cavity detection in ultrasound images.

References

1. Dong G. and Xie M., "Color Clustering and Learning form Image Segmentation Based on Neural Networks" , IEEE Transactions on Neural Networks, vol. 16, no. 4, pp. 925-936, 2005.
2. Frost V., Stiles J., Shanmugan K. and Holtzman J., "A model for radar images and its application to adaptive digital filtering of multiplicative noise", IEEE Transactions on Pattern Analysis and Machine Intelligence, vol. PAMI-4, pp. 157-166, 1982.

3. Gonzalez R., Woods R.,"Digital Images Processing" , Addison-Wesley, 1992.
4. Jiang Y. ,Chen K. and Zhou Z., "SOM Based Image Segmentation", Lecture Notes in Artificial Intelligence no. 2639, pp. 640-643, 2003.
5. Kohonen T.,"Self-Organizing Maps", Berlin, Germany: Springer-Verlag. 2001.
6. Kuan D., Sawchuk A., Strand T. and Chavel P., "Adaptive restoration of images with speckle", IEEE Transaction on Acoustics, Speech and Signal Processing, vol. 35, pp. 373-383, 1987.
7. Lee J., "Digital image enhancement and noise filtering by using local statistic", IEEE Transactions on Pattern Analysis and Machine Intelligence, vol. PAMI-2, pp. 165-168, 1980.
8. Levienaise-Obadia B. and Gee A., "Adaptive Segmentation of Ultrasound Images", in Electronic Proceedings of the Eight British Machine Vision Conference (BMVC), 1997.
9. Littmann E., Ritter H., "Adaptive Color Segmentation: A Comparison of Neural Networks and Statistical Methods", IEEE Transactions on Neural Networks, vol. 8, No 1, pp. 175-185, 1997.
10. Lopes A., Touzi R. and Nezry E., "Adaptive speckle filters and scene heterogeneity", IEEE Transactions on Geoscience and Remote Sensing, vol. 28, no. 6, pp. 992-1000, 1990.
11. Moreira J. and Costa L., "Neural-based color image segmentation and classification using self-organizing maps", in Proceedings of the IX Brazilian Symposium of Computer Vision and Image Processing (SIBGRAPI'96), pp. 47-54, 1996.
12. Tauber C., Batatia H. and Ayache A., "A Robust Speckle Reducing Anisotropic Diffusion", IEEE International Conference on Image Processing (ICIP), pp. 247-250, 2004.
13. Tauber C., Batatia H., Morin G. and Ayache A.,"Robust B-Spline Snakes for Ultrasound Images Segmentation", in Proceedings of IEEE Computers in Cardiology, 2004.
14. Yu Y. and Acton S., "Edge detection in ultrasound imagery using the instantaneous coefficient of variation", IEEE Transaction on Image Processing, vol. 13, no. 12, pp. 1640-1655, 2004.
15. Yu Y. and Acton S., "Speckle Reducing Anisotropic Diffusion", IEEE Transaction on Image Processing, vol.11, no. 11, 2002.

An Effective Method of Gait Stability Analysis Using Inertial Sensors

Sung Kyung Hong, Jinhyung Bae, Sug-Chon Lee, Jung-Yup Kim, and Kwon-Yong Lee

School of Mechanical and Aerospace Engineering, Sejong University
Seoul, 143-747, Korea
skhong@sejong.ac.kr

Abstract. This study aims to develop an effective measurement instrument and analysis method of gait stability, particularly focused on the motion of lower spine and pelvis during gait. Silicon micromechanical inertial instruments have been developed and body-attitude (pitch and roll) angles were estimated via closed-loop strapdown estimation filters, which results in improved accuracy of estimated attitude. Also, it is shown that the spectral analysis utilizing the Fast Fourier Transform (FFT) provides an efficient analysis method, which provides quantitative diagnoses for the gait stability. The results of experiments on various subjects suggest that the proposed system provides a simplified but an efficient tool for the evaluation of both gait stabilities and rehabilitation treatments effects.

1 Introduction

Abnormal walking due to accident or disease limits the physical activity. Assessment of abnormal gait has been evaluated by gait analysis technique as a function of time, distance, kinematical motion, joint loads, and muscle forces, etc [1]. This gait analysis provides useful information in several clinical applications such as functional assessment after hip and knee arthroplasty, rehabilitation treatments by using prosthesis, or assistive devices, and risk evaluation of falls in elderly persons suffering from arthritis. However, for the systematic gait analysis, specially designed facilities such as CCD camera, force plate, electromyography, and data handling station as well as laboratory space including specific pathway and well-trained technician are essential. In addition, it takes a long time for analyzing the data, and data from only a few steps are representative of the gait performance instead of long time walking. For these requirements gait analysis has not been widely used but used for research purposes within a laboratory.

Recent advances in the size and performance of micromechanical inertial instruments enable the development of a device to provide information about body motion to individuals who have gait problems. The usefulness of micromechanical inertial sensors has been shown in several applications [2-6]. However, in most of these researches, just the efficiency of the inertial sensors for clinical usage has been

A. Gelbukh and C.A. Reyes-Garcia (Eds.): MICAI 2006, LNAI 4293, pp. 1220 – 1228, 2006.

emphasized, and the defects of inertial sensors (such as integration drift in the estimated orientation due to nondeterministic errors [7]) and the methods of effective data analysis [8] have been overlooked.

In this research, a low-cost and accurate micromechanical inertial instrument and a simplified but effective method for analyzing gait stability are provided. Particularly, focusing our tentative interests on lower spine and pelvis motion during gait, the propose instrument is placed on the spur of S1 spine as described in Ref. [6]. As shown in Figure 1, the proposed system consists of two parts: one is the micromechanical inertial instrument incorporating inertial sensors and closed-loop strap-down attitude estimation filters, and another is the digital analysis unit incorporating data acquisition and signal analysis functions in both time and frequency domain, which provides quantitative diagnoses for the gait stability. We performed on 30 rheumatism patients, 3 patients with prosthetic limb, and 10 healthy subjects to show the practical aspect of the proposed system. The results suggest that the proposed system can be a simplified and efficient tool for the evaluation of both gait stabilities and rehabilitation treatments effects.

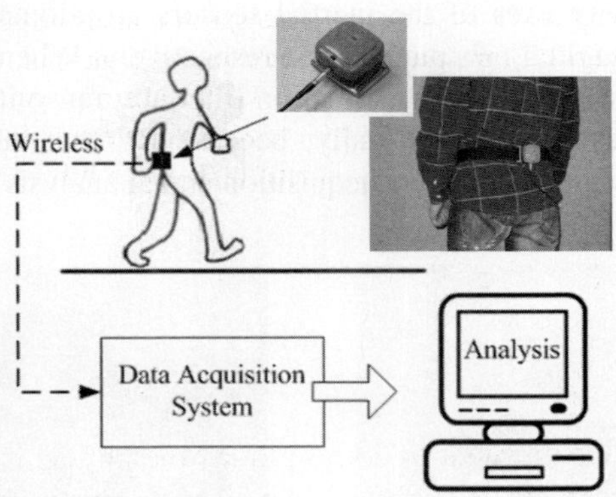

Fig. 1. Proposed system configurations

2 Methods

2.1 Micromechanical Inertial Instrument

The micromechanical inertial instrument includes an inertial sensor unit (ADXRS300, KXM52), a micro-processor (ATMEA8), a RF transmitter (Bluetooth), and a battery (Ni-MH) power module. The micromechanical sensors, which are described in Refs [9], consist of a so-called "chip" or "die" that is constructed from treated silicon. The sensing element is a proof mass (inertial element) that is deflected from its equilibrium position by an angular velocity in the case of gyroscope (gyro), and by a linear acceleration in the case of accelerometer.

Requirements for motion sensor performance can be estimated from the performance needed to control postural stability. Further requirements involve sensor size (small enough for body mounting) and power consumption (small enough to be battery powered for at least 12 hours). The single and double inverted pendulum models for human standing yields estimated natural frequencies of 0.4 Hz and 0.5 Hz, respectively, while the natural frequency during running is about 5 Hz [10]. Thus, the required bandwidth for motion sensors to provide estimates of body attitude would be approximately 10 Hz, which is twice the natural frequency during running. From human psychophysical experiments, the detection thresholds for linear acceleration and angular rate [11] are 0.05g and 1 deg/s, respectively. The performance of inertial sensors selected for this study is summarized in Table 1. To achieve better performance, temperature dependent characteristics such as scale factor (sensitivity) and noise (bias) of inertial sensors should be compensated as described in Ref. [12]. The performance of the sensors after software temperature compensation is depicted in bracket in Table 1.

The micromechanical inertial instruments are housed in a 58 x 58 x 30 cm^3 package (Figure 2) fastened to the spur of S1 spine, which is the segment of our tentative interests. The sensitivity axes of the inertial sensors are aligned with the subject's frontal (ϕ, roll) and sagittal (θ, pitch) axes, respectively. When the switch is turned on, the attitude (ϕ and θ) from the estimation filter are transmitted into PC at 50Hz. A person can walk everywhere naturally, because RF transmitter eliminates long cords from inertial instruments to data acquisition/signal analysis computer.

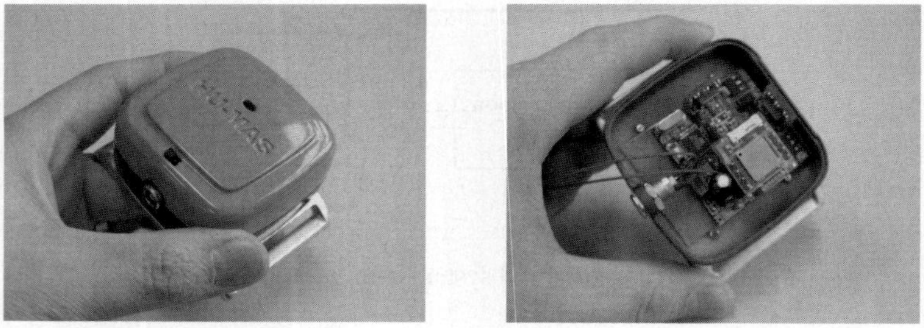

Fig. 2. Prototype of Micromechanical Inertial Instrument

Table 1. Inertial sensors specification

Parameters	Gyroscope (ADXRS 300)	Accelerometer (KXM 52)
Resolution	0.1 deg/sec	1 mg
Bandwidth	40 Hz	100 Hz
Bias Drift	50 deg/hr (20 deg/hr)	2 mg
Scale Factor Error	0.1% of FS (0.01% FS)	0.1% of FS

2.2 Closed-Loop Strapdown Attitude Estimation Filter

Both the gyro and accelerometer signals contain information about the orientation of the sensor. The sensor orientation can be obtained by integration of the rate signal (*p*, *q*, and *r*) obtained form gyros (Eq. 1). The rate signal from the gyro contains undesirable low-frequency drift or noise, which will cause an error in the attitude estimation when it is integrated. To observe and compensate for gyro drift, a process called augmentation is used, whereby utilizing other system states compensates gyro errors. One of the approaches which we used is so called the accelerometer aided mixing algorithm of SARS [7]. This scheme is derived from the knowledge that accelerometers (*f*) do not only measure the linear acceleration, but also gravitational vector (*g*). This knowledge can be used to make estimation of the attitude (Eq. 2) that is not very precise but does not suffer from integration drift from accelerometers. A 0.03 Hz low-pass filter, which must roll off at 1/frequency squared, is used to remove the part of the signal due to linear and angular acceleration while keeping the part due to gravity vector.

$$\begin{bmatrix} \dot{\phi} \\ \dot{\theta} \\ \dot{\psi} \end{bmatrix} = \begin{bmatrix} 1 & \sin\phi\tan\theta & \cos\phi\tan\theta \\ 0 & \cos\phi & -\sin\phi \\ 0 & \dfrac{\sin\phi}{\cos\theta} & \dfrac{\cos\phi}{\cos\theta} \end{bmatrix} \begin{bmatrix} p \\ q \\ r \end{bmatrix} \tag{1}$$

$$\theta = \sin^{-1}\left(\frac{f_x}{g}\right), \qquad \phi = \sin^{-1}\left(\frac{-f_y}{g\cos\theta}\right) \tag{2}$$

This scheme involves a set of 3-axis rate gyro (*p, q,* and *r*) that provides the required attitude information as results of integration in combination with a 2-axis accelerometer (f_x and f_y). The main idea of this scheme is that proper combining (PI-filtering) gyro and accelerometer measurements could make precise attitude information available. The block diagram of the processing scheme used for the prototype device is shown in Figure 3. This combination of rate gyros with accelerometers can give a considerably improved accuracy of the estimated attitude. These measurements showed that the estimated attitude angle has an rms error of ~1 deg over a 0- to 10-Hz bandwidth without limits of operating time.

2.3 Spectral Analysis Utilizing the FFT

Usually it is difficult and ambiguous to analyze the characteristics of motion and stability directly from the raw signals measured in a time domain because of their complex fluctuations and some zero-mean random noise. So we tried to extract the quantitative features for identifying gait motion. The technique is tc identify the frequency components and their magnitude of a signal buried in a noisy time domain signal. The discrete Fourier transforms of the signal is found by taking the Fast Fourier transform (FFT) algorithm [13]. The Fourier transform of a time domain signal *x(t)* is denoted by *x(ω)* and is defined by

$$X(\omega) = \int_{-\infty}^{\infty} x(t)e^{-jwt}\,dt \tag{3}$$

which transforms the signal *x(t)* from a function of time into a function of frequency *ω*. Also the power spectrum, a measurement of the power at various frequencies, is calculated. This power spectrum may be used as an important data for medical diagnosis of gait stability and degree of gait training. These algorithms are processed running Matlab/Simulink on the digital analysis computer.

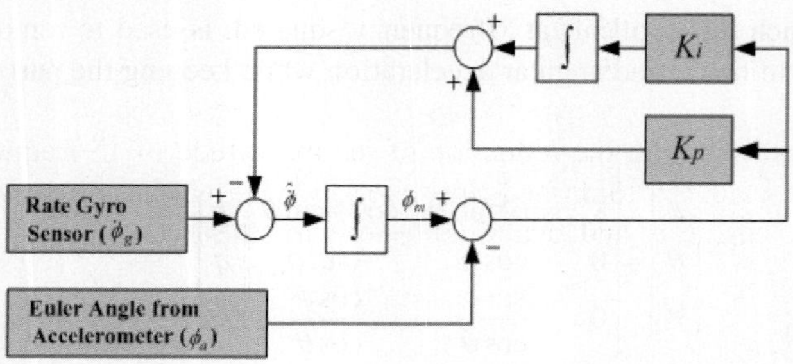

Fig. 3. Block diagram of attitude estimation procedure

3 Experimental Results

In this study, 30 patients with rheumatism, age 50-70 years, and 3 patients with prosthetic limb, age 30-40 years, were selected as subjects. The micromechanical inertial instrument was fixed on near the spur of S1 spine of patients to check pelvis fluctuation when they walk (Figure. 1). Subjects walked down a 10 m runway, at a self-determined pace repetitively. Also, the gait motions of 10 young healthy subjects, age 20-30 years, were measured for comparison with the patient's.

It was observed qualitative features of gait motion in both roll and pitch axes from the data of time domain (Figure 4) that healthy subjects showed little fluctuations with rhythmic, while patients with rheumatism and prosthetic limb showed relatively big fluctuations and less rhythmic.

On the other hand, it was observed quantitative features of gait motion in both axes from the data of frequency domain (Figure 5) that healthy subjects showed single dominant frequency (1~2Hz) with small magnitude (<10 dB), while patients with rheumatism and prosthetic limb showed multiple dominant frequencies (1~5 Hz, 1~3 Hz) with big amplitude (>200dB). The experimental results for roll axis were summarized in Table 2.

Table 2. Experimental results for roll axis

Subjects	Time Domain		Frequency Domain	
	Fluctuation	Rhythmic	Dominant Freq.	Magnitude
Healthy	Small(<2 deg)	Quite	1 Hz	< 10dB
Rheumatism	Med.(<7 deg)	Less	1, 3, 5 Hz	< 500dB
Prosthetic limb	Big (<12 deg)	Less	1, 1.8, 2.5 Hz	< 15000dB

From Figure 6, it is shown that the quantitative features of frequency-magnitude data of each subject can be categorized clearly. It should be also noted that these features show the repeatability and consistency among each categorized subjects. This explains the practical aspects of the proposed system which provides quantitative and reliable diagnoses for the gait stability.

To evaluate the rehabilitation treatment effects, rheumatism subjects were re-tested after 2 months' physical fitness. Figure 7 shows the effectiveness of the physical fitness by noting the reduction of the magnitude of 1st frequency (moving from solid line category to dashed line category). Hence, the proposed system can be used as an objective and quantitative tool for the evaluation of rehabilitation treatment effects.

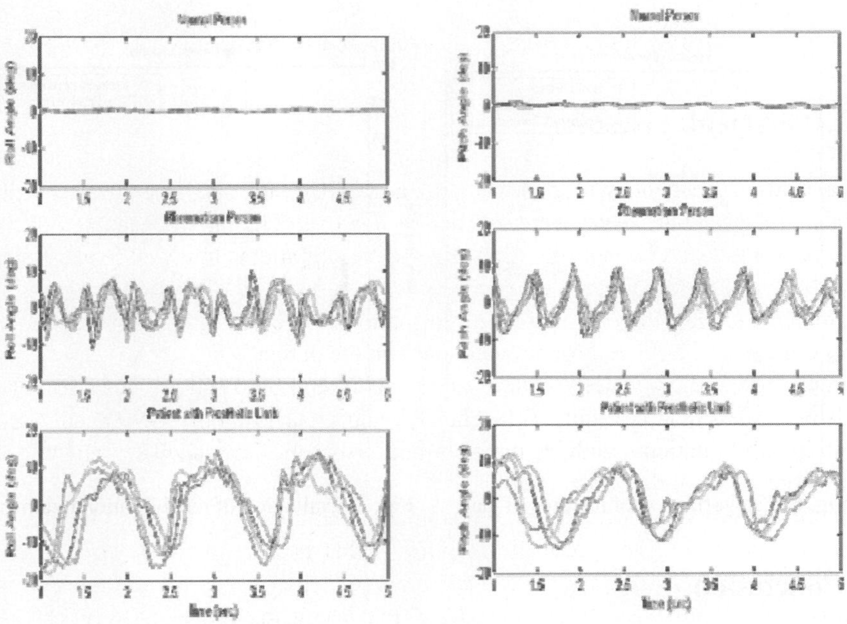

Fig. 4. Gait motion and stability in time domain

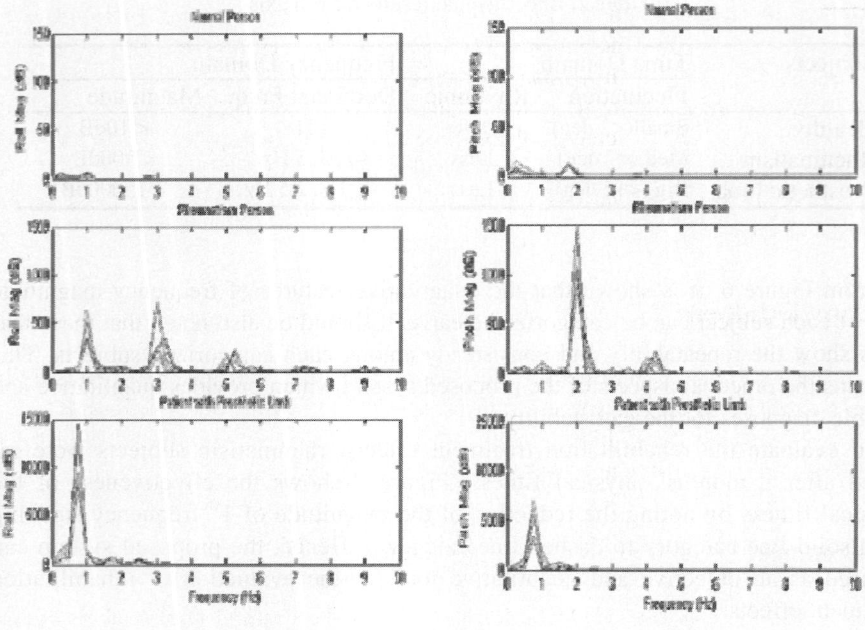

Fig. 5. Gait motion and stability in frequency domain

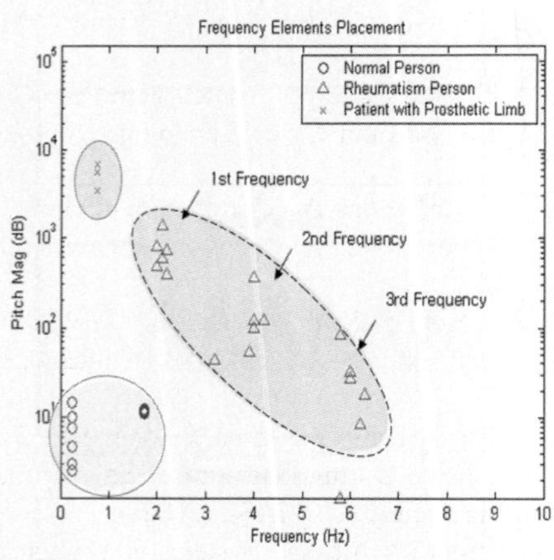

Fig. 6. Categorization of features of gait

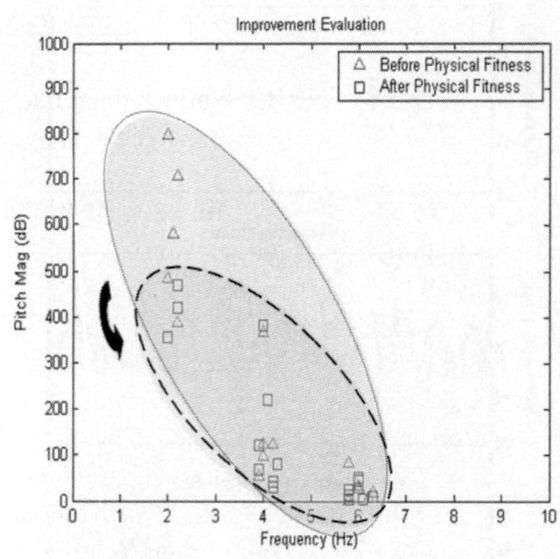

Fig. 7. Evaluation of rehabilitation treatments

5 Conclusion

A new, low-cost and accurate micromechanical inertial instrument and a simplified but effective method for analyzing gait stability have been proposed. By utilizing of the low cost inertial sensors and closed-loop strapdown attitude estimation filter, we can measure the attitude fluctuations characterizing gait motion accurately. Also, it is shown that the frequency analysis utilizing the Fast Fourier transform (FFT) provides quantitative diagnoses for the gait stability. We performed experiments on 30 rheumatism patients, 3 patients with prosthetic limb, and 10 healthy subjects to show the practical aspect of the proposed system. The results suggest that the proposed system can be a simplified and efficient tool for the evaluation of both gait stabilities and rehabilitation treatments effects. Another benefit of the proposed system is cordless, small and light, thus it has various applications of clinical practice by placing it on the segments of interest.

Acknowledgment

Authors gratefully acknowledge the help of Dr. H.-Y. Lee, Department of Nursing in Seoul National University, for assistance in subjects testing and preliminary data processing. We also would like to thank S-J Yoon, CEO of Motionspace Inc., for the support in hardware design and manufacturing.

References

1. Tsuruoka, M., Shibasaki, R., Murai S., Wada, T.: Bio-Feedback Control Analysis of Postural Stability using CCD Video Cameras and a Force-Plate Sensor Synchronized System. IEEE International Conference on System, Man, and Cybernetics (1998) 3200-3205
2. Conard, W., Marc, S., *et al.*: Balance Prosthesis Based on Micromechanical Sensors Using Vibrotactile Feedback of Tilt. IEEE Trans. On Biomedical Eng. Vol 48 No.10 (2001) 1153-61
3. Griffin, B., Huber, B., Wallner, F., Fink, T.: A 'Sense of Balance' AHRS with Low-Cost Vibrating Gyroscopes for Medical Diagnostics. Symposium Gyro Technology, Stuttgart (1997)
4. Lee, C.-Y. Lee, J.-J.: Estimation of Walking Behavior Using Accelerometers in Gait Rehabilitation. International Journal of Human-Friendly Welfare Robotic Systems Vol.3, No.2. (2002) 32-36
5. Ochi, F., Abe, K., Ishigami, S., Otsu, K., Tomita, H.: Trunk Motion Analysis in Walking using Gyro Sensors. Proceedings 19th International Conference IEEE/EMBS. Chicago, IL. USA (1997)
6. Stanford, C. F., Francis, P. R., Chambers, H. G: The Effects of Backpack Loads on Pelvis and Upper Body Kinematics of the Adolescent Female During Gait. Proceedings 7th annual meeting Gait and Clinical Movement Analysis Society (GCMAS). (2002)
7. Hong, S.K.: Fuzzy Logic based Closed-Loop Strapdown Attitude System for Unmanned Aerial Vehicle. Sensors and Actuators A-Physical (2002)
8. Kitagawa, M., Gersch, W.: Smoothness Priors Analysis of Time Series. Lecture Notes in Statistics 116 (1996)
9. Kourepenis, A., Borenstein J, *et al.*: Performance of MEMS Inertial Sensors. AIAA GNC Conference (1998)
10. Jones, G.M., Milsum, J.H.: Spatial and Dynamic Aspects of Visual Fixation. IEEE Trans. Bio-Med Eng. Vol. BME-12 (1966) 54-62
11. Benson A.J.: Effect of Spaceflight on Thresholds of Perception of Angular and Linear Motion. Arch Otorhinolaryngol Vol. 244(3) (1987) 147-154

12. Hong, S.K.: Compensation of Nonlinear Thermal Bias Drift of Resonant Rate Sensor (RRS) using Fuzzy Logic. Sensors and Actuators Vol. 78 (1999) 143-148
13. Duhamel, P., and Vetteril, M.: Fast Fourier Transforms. A Tutorial Review and a state of the art. Vol. 19. Signal Processing. (1990).259-299

Author Index

Printing: Mercedes-Druck, Berlin
Binding: Stein+Lehmann, Berlin

Lecture Notes in Artificial Intelligence (LNAI)

Vol. 4293: A. Gelbukh, C.A. Reyes-Garcia (Eds.), MICAI 2006: Advances in Artificial Intelligence. XXVIII, 1232 pages. 2006.

Vol. 4265: L. Todorovski, N. Lavrač, K.P. Jantke (Eds.), Discovery Science. XIV, 384 pages. 2006.

Vol. 4264: J.L. Balcázar, P.M. Long, F. Stephan (Eds.), Algorithmic Learning Theory. XIII, 393 pages. 2006.

Vol. 4259: S. Greco, Y. Hata, S. Hirano, M. Inuiguchi, S. Miyamoto, H.S. Nguyen, R. Słowiński (Eds.), Rough Sets and Current Trends in Computing. XXII, 951 pages. 2006.

Vol. 4253: B. Gabrys, R.J. Howlett, L.C. Jain (Eds.), Knowledge-Based Intelligent Information and Engineering Systems, Part III. XXXII, 1301 pages. 2006.

Vol. 4252: B. Gabrys, R.J. Howlett, L.C. Jain (Eds.), Knowledge-Based Intelligent Information and Engineering Systems, Part II. XXXIII, 1335 pages. 2006.

Vol. 4251: B. Gabrys, R.J. Howlett, L.C. Jain (Eds.), Knowledge-Based Intelligent Information and Engineering Systems, Part I. LXVI, 1297 pages. 2006.

Vol. 4248: S. Staab, V. Svátek (Eds.), Managing Knowledge in a World of Networks. XIV, 400 pages. 2006.

Vol. 4246: M. Hermann, A. Voronkov (Eds.), Logic for Programming, Artificial Intelligence, and Reasoning. XIII, 588 pages. 2006.

Vol. 4223: L. Wang, L. Jiao, G. Shi, X. Li, J. Liu (Eds.), Fuzzy Systems and Knowledge Discovery. XXVIII, 1335 pages. 2006.

Vol. 4213: J. Fürnkranz, T. Scheffer, M. Spiliopoulou (Eds.), Knowledge Discovery in Databases: PKDD 2006. XXII, 660 pages. 2006.

Vol. 4212: J. Fürnkranz, T. Scheffer, M. Spiliopoulou (Eds.), Machine Learning: ECML 2006. XXIII, 851 pages. 2006.

Vol. 4211: P. Vogt, Y. Sugita, E. Tuci, C. Nehaniv (Eds.), Symbol Grounding and Beyond. VIII, 237 pages. 2006.

Vol. 4203: F. Esposito, Z.W. Raś, D. Malerba, G. Semeraro (Eds.), Foundations of Intelligent Systems. XVIII, 767 pages. 2006.

Vol. 4201: Y. Sakakibara, S. Kobayashi, K. Sato, T. Nishino, E. Tomita (Eds.), Grammatical Inference: Algorithms and Applications. XII, 359 pages. 2006.

Vol. 4200: I.F.C. Smith (Ed.), Intelligent Computing in Engineering and Architecture. XIII, 692 pages. 2006.

Vol. 4198: O. Nasraoui, O. Zaiane, M. Spiliopoulou, B. Mobasher, B. Masand, P. Yu (Eds.), Advances in Web Minding and Web Usage Analysis. IX, 177 pages. 2006.

Vol. 4196: K. Fischer, I.J. Timm, E. André, N. Zhong (Eds.), Multiagent System Technologies. X, 185 pages. 2006.

Vol. 4188: P. Sojka, I. Kopeček, K. Pala (Eds.), Text, Speech and Dialogue. XV, 721 pages. 2006.

Vol. 4183: J. Euzenat, J. Domingue (Eds.), Artificial Intelligence: Methodology, Systems, and Applications. XIII, 291 pages. 2006.

Vol. 4180: M. Kohlhase, OMDoc – An Open Markup Format for Mathematical Documents [version 1.2]. XIX, 428 pages. 2006.

Vol. 4177: R. Marín, E. Onaindía, A. Bugarín, J. Santos (Eds.), Current Topics in Artificial Intelligence. XV, 482 pages. 2006.

Vol. 4160: M. Fisher, W. van der Hoek, B. Konev, A. Lisitsa (Eds.), Logics in Artificial Intelligence. XII, 516 pages. 2006.

Vol. 4155: O. Stock, M. Schaerf (Eds.). Reasoning, Action and Interaction in AI Theories and Systems. XVIII, 343 pages. 2006.

Vol. 4149: M. Klusch, M. Rovatsos, T.R. Payne (Eds.), Cooperative Information Agents X. XII, 477 pages. 2006.

Vol. 4140: J.S. Sichman, H. Coelho, S.O. Rezende (Eds.), Advances in Artificial Intelligence - IBERAMIA-SBIA 2006. XXIII, 635 pages. 2006.

Vol. 4139: T. Salakoski, F. Ginter, S. Pyysalo, T. Pahikkala (Eds.), Advances in Natural Language Processing. XVI, 771 pages. 2006.

Vol. 4133: J. Gratch, M. Young, R. Aylett, D. Ballin, P. Olivier (Eds.), Intelligent Virtual Agents. XIV, 472 pages. 2006.

Vol. 4130: U. Furbach, N. Shankar (Eds.), Automated Reasoning. XV, 680 pages. 2006.

Vol. 4120: J. Calmet, T. Ida, D. Wang (Eds.), Artificial Intelligence and Symbolic Computation. XIII, 269 pages. 2006.

Vol. 4114: D.-S. Huang, K. Li, G.W. Irwin (Eds.), Computational Intelligence, Part II. XXVII, 1337 pages. 2006.

Vol. 4108: J.M. Borwein, W.M. Farmer (Eds.), Mathematical Knowledge Management. VIII, 295 pages. 2006.

Vol. 4106: T.R. Roth-Berghofer, M.H. Göker, H.A. Güvenir (Eds.), Advances in Case-Based Reasoning. XIV, 566 pages. 2006.

Vol. 4099: Q. Yang, G. Webb (Eds.), PRICAI 2006: Trends in Artificial Intelligence. XXVIII, 1263 pages. 2006.

Vol. 4095: S. Nolfi, G. Baldassarre, R. Calabretta, J.C.T. Hallam, D. Marocco, J.-A. Meyer, O. Miglino, D. Parisi (Eds.), From Animals to Animats 9. XV, 869 pages. 2006.

Vol. 4093: X. Li, O.R. Zaïane, Z. Li (Eds.), Advanced Data Mining and Applications. XXI, 1110 pages. 2006.

Vol. 4092: J. Lang, F. Lin, J. Wang (Eds.), Knowledge Science, Engineering and Management. XV, 664 pages. 2006.

Vol. 4088: Z.-Z. Shi, R. Sadananda (Eds.), Agent Computing and Multi-Agent Systems. XVII, 827 pages. 2006.

Vol. 4087: F. Schwenker, S. Marinai (Eds.), Artificial Neural Networks in Pattern Recognition. IX, 299 pages. 2006.

Vol. 4068: H. Schärfe, P. Hitzler, P. Øhrstrøm (Eds.), Conceptual Structures: Inspiration and Application. XI, 455 pages. 2006.

Vol. 4065: P. Perner (Ed.), Advances in Data Mining. XI, 592 pages. 2006.

Vol. 4062: G. Wang, J.F. Peters, A. Skowron, Y. Yao (Eds.), Rough Sets and Knowledge Technology. XX, 810 pages. 2006.

Vol. 4049: S. Parsons, N. Maudet, P. Moraitis, I. Rahwan (Eds.), Argumentation in Multi-Agent Systems. XIV, 313 pages. 2006.

Vol. 4048: L. Goble, J.-J.C.. Meyer (Eds.), Deontic Logic and Artificial Normative Systems. X, 273 pages. 2006.

Vol. 4045: D. Barker-Plummer, R. Cox, N. Swoboda (Eds.), Diagrammatic Representation and Inference. XII, 301 pages. 2006.

Vol. 4031: M. Ali, R. Dapoigny (Eds.), Advances in Applied Artificial Intelligence. XXIII, 1353 pages. 2006.

Vol. 4029: L. Rutkowski, R. Tadeusiewicz, L.A. Zadeh, J.M. Zurada (Eds.), Artificial Intelligence and Soft Computing – ICAISC 2006. XXI, 1235 pages. 2006.

Vol. 4027: H.L. Larsen, G. Pasi, D. Ortiz-Arroyo, T. Andreasen, H. Christiansen (Eds.), Flexible Query Answering Systems. XVIII, 714 pages. 2006.

Vol. 4021: E. André, L. Dybkjær, W. Minker, H. Neumann, M. Weber (Eds.), Perception and Interactive Technologies. XI, 217 pages. 2006.

Vol. 4020: A. Bredenfeld, A. Jacoff, I. Noda, Y. Takahashi (Eds.), RoboCup 2005: Robot Soccer World Cup IX. XVII, 727 pages. 2006.

Vol. 4013: L. Lamontagne, M. Marchand (Eds.), Advances in Artificial Intelligence. XIII, 564 pages. 2006.

Vol. 4012: T. Washio, A. Sakurai, K. Nakajima, H. Takeda, S. Tojo, M. Yokoo (Eds.), New Frontiers in Artificial Intelligence. XIII, 484 pages. 2006.

Vol. 4008: J.C. Augusto, C.D. Nugent (Eds.), Designing Smart Homes. XI, 183 pages. 2006.

Vol. 4005: G. Lugosi, H.U. Simon (Eds.), Learning Theory. XI, 656 pages. 2006.

Vol. 3978: B. Hnich, M. Carlsson, F. Fages, F. Rossi (Eds.), Recent Advances in Constraints. VIII, 179 pages. 2006.

Vol. 3963: O. Dikenelli, M.-P. Gleizes, A. Ricci (Eds.), Engineering Societies in the Agents World VI. XII, 303 pages. 2006.

Vol. 3960: R. Vieira, P. Quaresma, M.d.G.V. Nunes, N.J. Mamede, C. Oliveira, M.C. Dias (Eds.), Computational Processing of the Portuguese Language. XII, 274 pages. 2006.

Vol. 3955: G. Antoniou, G. Potamias, C. Spyropoulos, D. Plexousakis (Eds.), Advances in Artificial Intelligence. XVII, 611 pages. 2006.

Vol. 3949: F.A. Savacı (Ed.), Artificial Intelligence and Neural Networks. IX, 227 pages. 2006.

Vol. 3946: T.R. Roth-Berghofer, S. Schulz, D.B. Leake (Eds.), Modeling and Retrieval of Context. XI, 149 pages. 2006.

Vol. 3944: J. Quiñonero-Candela, I. Dagan, B. Magnini, F. d'Alché-Buc (Eds.), Machine Learning Challenges. XIII, 462 pages. 2006.

Vol. 3937: H. La Poutré, N.M. Sadeh, S. Janson (Eds.), Agent-Mediated Electronic Commerce. X, 227 pages. 2006.

Vol. 3932: B. Mobasher, O. Nasraoui, B. Liu, B. Masand (Eds.), Advances in Web Mining and Web Usage Analysis. X, 189 pages. 2006.

Vol. 3930: D.S. Yeung, Z.-Q. Liu, X.-Z. Wang, H. Yan (Eds.), Advances in Machine Learning and Cybernetics. XXI, 1110 pages. 2006.

Vol. 3918: W.-K. Ng, M. Kitsuregawa, J. Li, K. Chang (Eds.), Advances in Knowledge Discovery and Data Mining. XXIV, 879 pages. 2006.

Vol. 3913: O. Boissier, J. Padget, V. Dignum, G. Lindemann, E. Matson, S. Ossowski, J.S. Sichman, J. Vázquez-Salceda (Eds.), Coordination, Organizations, Institutions, and Norms in Multi-Agent Systems. XII, 259 pages. 2006.

Vol. 3910: S.A. Brueckner, G.D.M. Serugendo, D. Hales, F. Zambonelli (Eds.), Engineering Self-Organising Systems. XII, 245 pages. 2006.

Vol. 3904: M. Baldoni, U. Endriss, A. Omicini, P. Torroni (Eds.), Declarative Agent Languages and Technologies III. XII, 245 pages. 2006.

Vol. 3900: F. Toni, P. Torroni (Eds.), Computational Logic in Multi-Agent Systems. XVII, 427 pages. 2006.

Vol. 3899: S. Frintrop, VOCUS: A Visual Attention System for Object Detection and Goal-Directed Search. XIV, 216 pages. 2006.

Vol. 3898: K. Tuyls, P.J. 't Hoen, K. Verbeeck, S. Sen (Eds.), Learning and Adaption in Multi-Agent Systems. X, 217 pages. 2006.

Vol. 3891: J.S. Sichman, L. Antunes (Eds.), Multi-Agent-Based Simulation VI. X, 191 pages. 2006.

Vol. 3890: S.G. Thompson, R. Ghanea-Hercock (Eds.), Defence Applications of Multi-Agent Systems. XII, 141 pages. 2006.

Vol. 3885: V. Torra, Y. Narukawa, A. Valls, J. Domingo-Ferrer (Eds.), Modeling Decisions for Artificial Intelligence. XII, 374 pages. 2006.

Vol. 3881: S. Gibet, N. Courty, J.-F. Kamp (Eds.), Gesture in Human-Computer Interaction and Simulation. XIII, 344 pages. 2006.

Vol. 3874: R. Missaoui, J. Schmidt (Eds.), Formal Concept Analysis. X, 309 pages. 2006.